D0331124

Management Policy and Strategy

Text, Readings, and Cases

Management Policy and Strategy
Text, Readings, and Cases

George A. Steiner
University of California, Los Angeles

John B. Miner
Georgia State University

Macmillan Publishing Co., Inc.
NEW YORK

Collier Macmillan Publishers
LONDON

Printed in the United States of America

The text portion of this book has been published separately, with minor alterations, under the complete title *Management Policy and Strategy,* copyright © 1977 by Macmillan Publishing Co., Inc.

Macmillan Publishing Co., Inc.
866 Third Avenue, New York, New York 10022

Collier Macmillan Canada, Ltd.

Library of Congress Cataloging in Publication Data

Steiner, George Albert, (date)
Management policy and strategy.

Includes index.
1. Management. 2. Management—Addresses, essays, lectures. 3. Management—Case studies. I. Miner, John B., joint author. II. Title.
HD31.S6888 658.4 76-16800
ISBN 0-02-416750-9

Printing: 4 5 6 7 8 Year: 8 9 0 1 2 3

Preface

Schools of business typically offer a capstone course concerned with "business policy." Our book is for use in such a course, but its content and structure are somewhat different from those of traditional texts.

The rationale for this volume is that a sufficient body of knowledge has now been developed directly in the field of organizational policy and strategy to justify compiling it and providing it to students as background for their study of actual business situations. In years past the tendency has been to review either the management process literature or the functional areas of business, such as marketing and finance, as a preliminary to the analysis of cases, business games, experiences in real organizations, and the like. We believe it is much more important to focus directly on policy and strategy formation and implementation. Furthermore, we believe enough now is known from theory, research, and practical experience to justify such a focus. This is not to say that a knowledge of management process and business functions is unimportant but only that these topics are covered elsewhere in the business curriculum. The subject matter of this book is seldom covered—and never in the depth provided here.

The book supports several developments that we detect in the teaching of policy courses. Discussions with many instructors of policy courses, together with an examination of books used, reveal some significant new trends and needs: a focus on top management and the total organization rather than upon functional areas; stress on strategic management in contrast with operational management; the use of top management strategy as a new integrating concept of analysis; introduction into classroom discussion of basic research on the identification, evaluation, and implementation of strategy; expansion of analysis beyond the business sector to include the not-for-profit sector; the addition of materials concerning business ethics, morality, and social responsibility; and the use of descriptive materials to complement cases.

We believe that these requirements in policy courses can be achieved best by a study of real life cases amplified by selected readings and knowledge of the best research and description of organizational policy and strategy. The structure of our presentation is based on the identification, evaluation, and implementation of top management policy and strategy. Other aspects of the policy and strategy area are also covered, such as the role of the chief executive officer in policy and strategy decision making, the place of strategic planning in this process, the ways in which environment affects policy and strategy, and major theories and practices associated with formulating and implementing strategy.

In Chapter 1 we explain in detail the parts of the book. We also present what we consider the principal objectives of a policy course. The book is designed for both graduate and undergraduate courses, although we anticipate more rapid coverage and the use of more supplementary materials at the graduate level. The book should also have appeal to practicing managers. Although management's deciding on operationally successful policy and strategy is more a matter of art and wisdom than of skill in using decision-making tools and specific pieces of knowledge, we believe that research findings in this field have powerful pragmatic applications. Many of these are included in this book, and we hope, therefore, that line managers and staff specialists in all organizations will find valuable uses for the volume.

The study of organizational policy and strategy in universities is receiving a new emphasis. We predict that in the future policy/strategy studies will be increasingly emphasized and that there will emerge a new discipline for the field. Our initial purpose in writing this book was to stimulate and strengthen such a development.

The authors' collaboration on this volume has been a rewarding and enriching experience. The first author has spent much of his life working in the fields of top management planning and business and society; his early preparation was in economics. The second author has been involved in personnel management and organizational behavior and was originally trained in psychology. We have divided our task so that each of us might focus on those aspects of the total policy/strategy formation and implementation process he knows best. At an early point in our writing we made a strategic decision of our own—not to sacrifice the unique contributions that each of us might make to the coverage of particular topics to the demands of fully unified presentation and integrated style. We believe that the book is, in fact, richer and broader in its treatment because of this decision to utilize fully our diverse backgrounds.

We are deeply indebted to the many scholars and practitioners who have written about policy and strategy. Many of them and their written works are recognized in this book and to them this book is dedicated.

We wish also to thank Betty Delbridge, secretary to George Steiner, and Barbara Williams, administrative assistant to John Miner, who were most helpful in preparing the manuscript.

G. A. S.
J. B. M.

Contents

PART I

The Nature and Importance of Business Policy/Strategy

Chapter 1
INTRODUCTION 3
Chapter 2
THE NATURE OF POLICY/STRATEGY 17
Chapter 3
THE CENTRAL ROLE OF POLICY/STRATEGY IN ORGANIZATIONS 29

PART II

Key Overall Forces in Policy/Strategy Formulation and Implementation

Chapter 4
THE CHANGING ORGANIZATIONAL ENVIRONMENT 41
Chapter 5
THE CHANGING SOCIAL ROLE OF BUSINESS 57
Chapter 6
MANAGERIAL AND ORGANIZATIONAL STYLES 71

READINGS

1 *Profiles of Chief Executive Officers* 89
A. The Chief Executive Officer: Personal Management Styles Business Week 89
B. Young Top Management: The New Goals, Rewards, Life Styles Business Week 97

CASES

1 Aerosol Techniques, Inc. CHARLES W. HOFER 105
2 Polaroid Corporation H. DEANE WONG 131

3 Metropolis City Museum of Art PATRICK H. ELA 143

PART III

Formulating Business Policy/Strategy

Chapter 7
SYSTEMATIC PLANNING IN STRATEGIC MANAGEMENT 149
Chapter 8
IDENTIFYING STRATEGIES AND POLICIES TO EVALUATE 181
Chapter 9
EVALUATING AND CHOOSING AMONG POLICY/STRATEGY ALTERNATIVES 207
Chapter 10
INDIVIDUALS IN POLICY/STRATEGY FORMATION 225
Chapter 11
GROUP ASPECTS OF POLICY FORMATION 241
Chapter 12
ALTERNATIVE APPROACHES TO DECISION MAKING 257
Chapter 13
THE ROLES OF CONSULTANTS AND ADVOCATES 271

READINGS

2 *Myth of the Well-educated Manager* J. STERLING LIVINGSTON 287
3 *Reforming the Strategic Planning Process: Integration of Social Responsibility and Business Needs* IAN H. WILSON 304
4 *What Program Budgeting Is and Is Not* DAVID NOVICK 314
5 *Shaping the Master Strategy of Your Firm* WILLIAM H. NEWMAN 326
6 *Impact of Social Sanctions on Product Strategy* GEORGE FISK 344
7 *Computers: Snow White and the Seven Dwarfs (RCA, GE, Univac, Control Data, NCR, Burroughs, Xerox)* JOEL E. ROSS and MICHAEL J. KAMI 362

CASES

4 Illini GEORGE A. STEINER 373
5 The Ecological Monitoring Corporation (EMC) H. SCOTT WATSON 381
6 Stouffer Foods Services Group JOHN DOUTT and JOSEPH LATONA 400
7 Ski-Kit, Inc. ROBERT WILLIAMS 413
8 Kramer Carton Company RICHARD HILL 444
9 Two Contrasting Strategies 467
A. The Mattel Debacle: How It Took Shape ROBERT A. ROSENBLATT 467

B. Hewlett-Packard: Where Slower Growth Is Smarter Management *Business Week* 473
10 American Motors Corporation 1972–1975 KAREN BOULTON and STEVEN M. GREEN 478
11 A. H. Robins Company VICTOR F. ZONANA 500
12 Tasty Foods, Inc. 506
13 White Motor Corporation WILLIAM SCHLENDER and ELEANOR BRANTLEY SCHWARTZ 507
14 Durard Plastics Company THOMAS S. DUDICK 521
15 Drexler Technology Corporation PAUL L. GOODMAN and CARLTON A. PEDERSON 525
16 Heublein, Inc. CHARLES W. HOFER 540
17 Amtrak J. RUSSELL ROY, ROBERT HICKCOX, and DAVID A. BROCK 570
18 Mississippi Test Facility EDMUND R. GRAY and RAYMOND V. LEISKOR 594

PART IV

Implementing Policy/Strategy

Chapter 14
ORGANIZATIONAL STRUCTURES AND PROCESSES FOR IMPLEMENTING POLICIES AND STRATEGIES 607
Chapter 15
FORMAL SYSTEMS FOR IMPLEMENTING POLICIES AND STRATEGIES 625
Chapter 16
THE ROLE OF PEOPLE IN IMPLEMENTATION 641

READINGS

8 *Setting Goals in Management by Objective* HENRY L. TOSI, JOHN R. RIZZO, and STEPHEN J. CARROLL 654
9 *How Companies Respond to Social Demands* ROBERT W. ACKERMAN 669
10 *Bridging the Gulf in Organizational Performance* JOHN B. MINER 686

CASES

19 Implementing IBM's System/360 Decision T. A. WISE 700
20 Ford Motor Co. WILLIAM M. CARLEY 715
21 United Technology, Inc. GEORGE A. STEINER 721

22 Small City (B)—The Ordinance GEORGE G. EDDY and BURNARD H. SORD 729

PART V

Policy/Strategy in Varied Contexts

Chapter 17
ENTREPRENEURSHIP 743
Chapter 18
SPECIAL ASPECTS OF POLICY/STRATEGY IN NOT-FOR-PROFIT ORGANIZATIONS 757
Chapter 19
CONTINGENCY THEORY OF POLICY/STRATEGY 773

READINGS

11 *Elementary Conditions of Business Morals* CHESTER I. BARNARD 784
12 *Business Payoffs Abroad: Rhetoric and Reality* PETER NEHEMKIS 801
13 *The Social Audit* GEORGE A. STEINER 825
14 *Toward a Contingency Theory of Business Strategy* CHARLES W. HOFER 842

CASES

23 Campaign GM GEORGE A. STEINER 870
24 South African Apartheid and Polaroid 877
25 World Mining and Chemicals, Inc. JOHN F. STEINER 879
26 Atlantic Manufacturing Company 884
27 Force Reduction at Machinery Systems GEORGE A. STEINER 886
28 Smokey Cigarette Company 889
29 DuPont's Refusal to Supply Certain Information 890

APPENDIX READINGS 893
A How to Evaluate a Firm ROBERT B. BUCHELE 893
B How to Read a Financial Report MERRILL LYNCH, PIERCE, FENNER & SMITH 915

REFERENCES 965

AUTHOR INDEX 997

SUBJECT INDEX 1009

PART

I

The Nature and Importance of Business Policy/Strategy

CHAPTER

1

Introduction

Most schools of business in the United States, as well as those in other countries of the world, have a capstone course in their curriculum that is concerned with "business policy." This book is designed for such a course. The nature of the business policy course, the changes taking place in the concept of such courses, and the objectives of the policy course, as well as the structure of the book are discussed in this introductory chapter.

THE BUSINESS POLICY COURSE

The impetus to the widespread introduction of business policy courses into school of business curriculums came in 1959 with reports sponsored by the Ford Foundation and the Carnegie Corporation of New York. Both reports were evaluations of course content in schools of business and both made recommendations about curriculum revisions which were designed to strengthen programs of study. The Gordon and Howell report [1959:206–207] * sponsored by the Ford Foundation, made the following recommendation:

> The capstone of the core curriculum should be a course in "business policy" which will give students an opportunity to pull together what they have learned in the separate business fields and utilize this knowledge in the analysis of complex business problems. The business policy course can offer the student something he (or she †) will find nowhere else in the curriculum: consideration of business problems which are not prejudged as being marketing problems, finance problems, etc.; emphasis on the development of skill in identifying, analyzing, and solving problems in a situation which is as close as the classroom can ever be to the real business world; opportunity to consider problems which draw on a wide range of substantive areas in business; opportunity to consider the external, nonmarket implications of problems at the same time that internal decisions must be made; situations which

* References, shown in square brackets, will be found on pages 965–996.

† Whenever *he* or *she* is used to refer to a person we mean either *he* or *she*. This is done without prejudice and only to avoid the awkwardness of saying each time he or she, his or her, or he/she.

enable the student to exercise qualities of judgment and of mind which were not explicitly called for in any prior course. Questions of social responsibility and of personal attitudes can be brought in as a regular aspect of this kind of problem-solving practice. Without the responsibility of having to transmit some specific body of knowledge, the business policy course can concentrate on integrating what already has been acquired and on developing further the student's skill in using that knowledge. The course can range over the entire curriculum and beyond [1959, pp. 206–207].

This point of view was also taken by the Pierson report [1959] sponsored by the Carnegie Corporation of New York. In 1969 the American Assembly of Collegiate Schools of Business included in its revised statement of curriculum standards for accreditation the provision that "study of administrative processes under conditions of uncertainty including integrating analyses and policy determination at the overall management level," be required of all students in business and administration programs.

Business policy courses have evolved in different directions but, generally, they can be characterized as capstone integrative courses much as Gordon and Howell recommended in their report [Mintzberg, 1971; Guth, 1971]. When details of course content and teaching methods are examined, however, there is a great diversity. So different are policy courses that Starbuck, with tongue in cheek, observed that: "Business policy is a course which appears near the end of a student's curriculum bearing the title 'Business Policy' " [1966, p. 357].

One common characteristic of many policy courses is a heavy reliance on business cases as subjects of study. Through the use of cases covering all aspects of management, students apply the skills they have learned, come to understand better the attitudes of managers, and pick up knowledge about management which derives from the case. The use of this method has a long tradition extending back to 1908 when the Harvard Business School first announced its intention of using cases in its classroom discussions [Copeland, in McNair, 1954].

NEW TRENDS IN POLICY COURSES

In recent years several trends in business policy courses are noticeable. First, the focus is on top management and the total organization, rather than on functional areas. Second, the core synthesizing concept of study is strategic management. Third, research findings about these two aspects of the area are introduced into policy course work. Fourth, policy issues and cases have been added for organizations in the nonbusiness sector. Fifth, while separate case books have long been available concerning business social responsibilities and business ethics the traditional policy course did not cover such subjects. The trend now is to introduce such cases in the policy course. Each of these trends will be examined now in more detail.

The View from the Top

The central view of this book is the role of the chief executive officer (CEO) of an organization as he looks at his total organization. The CEO is not necessarily singular but can be plural in the case of joint top executive authority in "offices of the president." The CEO can be plural, also, in the sense that different top executives may have types of plenary power over an organization under certain circumstances. So, in the present frame of reference, a CEO can be a top manager of an organization and not necessarily the *one* person who has that title. However, for ease of presentation the discussion here does adopt the singular mode.

The view of the top manager is unique. No one else in an organization has the same perspective. He alone is responsible for relating his organization to a changing environment. He alone is responsible for assuring the proper balance among various competing subsystems in his organization. He alone is responsible for determining the total thrust of the organization and for assuring that performance matches his design. Additional unique responsibilities of the CEO will be set forth in later chapters.

It is significant to note here that just as the role of the CEO is unique so is his way of thinking. Not all CEO's, of course, think alike, but there is a special way of thinking associated with the functioning of the top executive. It concentrates on the total enterprise rather than parts of it. Forrester [1964: 60] has correctly pointed out that an understanding of the functioning of a total business system does not merely extend the phenomena of simpler situations. "Entirely new phenomena take place." CEO's think in these terms. There are two types of management in an organization—strategic management that exists at the very top and all other management which might be called operational management. The thought processes, the attitudes, the perspective, the frames of reference, the methods of analysis, and the skills differ between the two.

To illustrate differences in perspective, consider the specialist versus the general top level manager. The specialist is an expert on a particular subject because his life has been devoted to mastering that subject. On other subjects he generally is no more informed than the average person. Specialists' thought patterns differ depending upon their specialties, but each specialist establishes standards for rationality drawn from his discipline and each seeks to decide matters in those terms. The standards may be equity, justice, and legal precedence (*stare decisis*) for the lawyer; cost reduction with acceptable quality for the engineer; quantitative solutions that optimize output for the operations research specialist; or profit maximization for the economist. The general top manager thinks in different terms. He must consider all relevant specialist criteria and then decide based on what is in the best interests of his organization as he sees those interests. What that means depends upon the organization, the problem, the philosophies of the manager, and pressures placed upon him.

In looking at the entirety of an organization, the top manager also approaches decision making differently than major division line managers. A major division line manager considers himself to be a part of a larger organization. But within the larger organization he thinks differently than the CEO at central headquarters. Indeed, the two may be and often are in conflict. For example, the divisional manager may wish a capital allocation to meet his needs which the CEO may not grant because of other higher level priorities of his total organization. Such conflicts are natural and understandable.

CEO's also think differently than functional departmental managers. Again, managers of such departments certainly consider themselves "team members" of a larger organization. But, again, their thought patterns are much different than those of top executives responsible for a total enterprise. For instance, sales managers tend to place greatest emphasis on increasing sales, market share, and reputation with customers. This emphasis, if unchecked, may be at the expense of profits. Financial executives, on the other hand tend to think in terms of profit, liquidity, low risk, and high return on investment. This viewpoint, if not balanced, may stifle growth and reduce risk taking and initiative. Research and development scientists may concentrate on new technical breakthroughs, top quality products, and research that interests them. This attitude, too, may result in costly research with limited applicability to the organization. Other functional departments have different driving motivations. All must be related to and integrated in the larger organization of which they are a part, and that is done by the CEO and his closely associated line managers and staff.

The student might ask at this point: "Why should I study the work and thinking of the top level managers of organizations? I will never get there." There are a number of answers to this legitimate question. To begin with, most business students will find their careers in organizations, especially large business organizations. Whether they become staff experts or general functional managers, the more they know about the top management of organizations the better they will be able to contribute. Also, the more they know about the top, the less frustrated they are likely to be in dealing with it. Although the focus is on top management, the analysis of cases, which will be discussed later, requires a perspective and methodological approach which students will find helpful in entering the world of organizations no matter at what level and job. For the student as well as the layman interested in policy, the study of top management can be stimulating in itself. We are dealing here with an extremely important talent in organizations which in one way or another has a very significant impact on our lives, individually and as a society. Finally, who knows which student will eventually wind up at the top of an organization? The policy course may help many to get there and to do a better job when they arrive.

Strategic Management, Strategy and Strategic Planning

Strategic management is a new name given to top management to distinguish it from operational management. Although the distinction between top management activities and operational management is not new [Goetz, 1963; Anthony, 1965] the name strategic management is new and certainly the recognition of its growing significance is of recent origin [Frankenhoff and Granger, 1971; Ansoff, 1972; Schendel and Hatten, 1972; and Irwin, 1974]. This concept is considered in detail in Chapter 3, but at this point a few aspects of it must be mentioned.

Schendel and Hatten [1972:5] define strategic management "as the process of determining and (maintaining) the relationship of the organization to its environment expressed through the use of selected objectives, and of attempting to achieve the desired states of relationship through resource allocations which allow efficient and effective action programs by the organization and its subparts." This definition is accepted here, with the observation that it describes a responsibility which top management has always had. Why then the new concept?

The emphasis on strategic management as distinct from operational management reflects the growing significance of environmental impacts on organizations and the need for top managers to react appropriately to them. As Organ [1971:74] has observed, ". . . there is a growing suspicion that the more relevant criterion of organizational effectiveness is not, as it used to be, that of efficiency, but rather that of adaptability to changes in the environment." Although strategic management, in Schendel and Hatten's terms, emphasizes adaptation to the environment, it does not neglect management of internal affairs. But the emphasis has shifted significantly from older concepts of the managerial job.

Strategy is the central and unique core of strategic management. Strategy refers to the formulation of basic organizational missions, purposes, and objectives; policies and program strategies to achieve them; and the methods needed to assure that strategies are implemented to achieve organizational ends. A more detailed examination of the meaning of strategy and policy will be given in Chapter 2, but the reader is asked to accept this definition in this introductory chapter. Again, because of its importance, the emphasis is on strategy (and policy) rather than on tactics. "Leaders will be judged," says Boettinger [1973:3] ". . . not by tactical nimbleness but by the robustness of their strategic decisions for the organizations they head."

In a growing number of corporations, particularly the larger companies, the framework by means of which strategy is devised is the formal long range planning process. This is a process that varies from firm to firm but, increasingly, has become inextricably interwoven with the entire strategic management process. In effect, strategic planning is a new way to manage.

The dominant themes of this book, the unifying threads are, therefore, strategic management, strategy (and policy), and strategic planning. The organizing framework of the book's contents is, centrally, the formulation and implementation of strategy (and policy).

Research on Organizational Policy and Strategy

One reason frequently used to justify exclusive use of cases in the policy course, although by no means the only reason, is that no underlying systematic body of theory exists upon which to build a different basis for teaching. It certainly has been true that research in the policy area has lagged. In light of the great significance of policy one may ask why there has been so little research until recently. The answer, says Bauer [1968:25] is that "precisely because the process is so complicated, it has been resistant to both adequate conceptualization and adequate research." Bauer's statement was made some time ago; since then there has developed a substantial body of research concerned with the formulation and implementation of organizational policy and strategy.

The pure case method certainly can be justified for policy courses when there is insufficient research and theory to teach, but that is no longer the case. Today cases alone cannot give students the understanding they should have about the strategy-policy-making processes of top managers. There is a growing body of research that can and should be used to strengthen and supplement cases. This is a position that a number of professors in the field have taken [Gordon, 1966; Mintzberg, 1973b; Glueck, 1972a; Anshen and Guth, 1973; Saunders, 1973; Paine and Naumes, 1974; Hofer, 1975a; Mintzberg, 1975b; to mention but a few]. This point of view, reinforced by some disillusionment with the pure case approach, has led to a spate of books of readings designed specifically for business policy courses for example, Gray, 1968; Bonge and Coleman, 1972; Klein and Murphy, 1973; and McCarthy, Minichiello, and Curran, 1975.

Although the body of research findings and theory concerning policy and strategy is inadequate in many ways, it has grown sufficiently to support the thesis that business policy has developed from a single capstone course to a discipline. A number of students in the field have expressed this view, such as Schendel and Hatten [1972]; Guth [1973]; and Greenwood [n.d.]. Many other scholars would agree with this position.

Business and Non-business Organizations

The primary focus of this book is on the business organization but not to the complete neglect of policy and strategy in nonbusiness organizations. Many of the accepted fundamentals about business strategic management and strategy are applicable to nonbusiness organizations. On the other hand, there are some significant differences between policy and strategy formulation and implementation in business and nonbusiness organizations. These are noted throughout the book but particularly in Chapter 18. If possible even more discussion of nonbusiness organizations would have been included, but limitations and higher priorities for space prevented it.

Social Responsibilities and Ethical Standards

Social responsibilities traditionally have been defined in terms of both economic and social goals of organizations. Until recent years, however, the greatest emphasis has been placed on the economic objective, namely, to be efficient in the production of goods and services that society wanted and at prices people were willing to pay. If this was done well, it was reasoned, profits would be maximized. Profit maximization, therefore, became the dominant goal of a business. Today, for many reasons which will be explained in some detail in Chapters 4 and 5, much greater emphasis is being placed on the social aspects of organizational obligations to society and to those working in the organizations.

This new emphasis is creating major policy and strategy problems for organizations for four fundamental reasons. First, society is putting greater and greater pressure on organizations to undertake social programs both voluntarily and in compliance with government legislation. Second, as an aftermath of Watergate and evidences of wrongdoing in some organizations, new attention is being paid by the public and organizational leaders to appropriate standards of ethics and morality in organizational management. Third, there is no simple answer to what the social obligations of a particular organization are or what the ethical standards should be. The result for every organization is considerable uncertainty about what policy and strategy really should be in this area. In a policy course these sorts of problems must be examined. Fourth, the net result is a need to rethink the profit objective. The profit objective is still dominant but becomes intertwined with social objectives.

OBJECTIVES OF THE ORGANIZATIONAL POLICY AND STRATEGY COURSE

The policy course has a focus and thrust that seeks to achieve a set of objectives different from any other course. Several writers have classified the objectives of the policy course into three categories: knowledge, skills, and attitudes [Christensen, Andrews and Bower, 1973; Glueck, 1972b; Broom, 1969, to mention a few]. To these may be added a few special instructor-student objectives. These general classes of aims are not, of course, unique to the policy and strategy course, nor are all the detailed objectives that may be listed under each. Together, however, they provide a set of objectives for a unique course of study. Some of the detailed objectives are as follows:

Knowledge

1. To understand the central significance of policy and strategy to top managers and their organizations. This means, among other things, an understanding of how environments, external and internal, affect the functioning of an organization. It means an ability to evaluate environment so as to detect opportunities and threats in it to which alert managers must respond. It means an understanding of the processes through which managers can best determine those missions and objectives their organizations should seek; it means the ability to formulate and evaluate the best policies and strategies to achieve these ends, and the methods to assure that policies and

strategies are implemented. An important aim of the course should be to underscore for the student the importance of implementation. The best of policies and strategies are ineffective if they are not implemented and problems of implementation are far too frequently underestimated, both in teaching management subjects and in actual practice.
2. To learn about and understand the interrelationships among subsystems in organizations and the problems top managers have in avoiding suboptimization of parts.
3. To learn the limits of specialized knowledge for strategic problems.
4. To understand better the uniqueness in settings and operations of different industries and individual companies.
5. Top managers of organizations have attitudes, values, and ways of thinking that are unique to them and which also have a distinctive impact on all processes and decision making. It is important that students understand and have an appreciation for this phenomenon.
6. To learn about and understand and appreciate the best research that has been done on the above subjects mentioned in items 1 through 5.

Attitudes

A central purpose of the policy and strategy course is to put the students "in the shoes of the top manager." This means a number of things.

1. Look at the subject matter from the point of view of a generalist, which a top manager is; rather than a specialist, which he is not. This attitude results in decision making on the basis of all relevant disciplines rather than on the basis of one alone. It means not hesitating to use judgment when facts are unknown or uncertain. Specialists tend to withhold decision pending the acquisition of more and more facts. The generalist knows there must be an end to the search for facts and does not hesitate to determine when fact gathering shall cease and decisions should be made.
2. Make decisions as a practitioner in contrast to a research specialist. General managers are pragmatic, results oriented, and realistic. The practitioner, perhaps more so than the specialist, is interested in identifying the right problem to solve rather than in finding a problem to solve. The practitioner is less interested (compared with the specialist) in an optimum solution than in an acceptable solution. The practitioner is constantly concerned with cost trade offs in terms of the timing of decisions, the nature of the solution, problems of implementation, and so on.
3. Make decisions from the perspective of the total organization in contrast to the point of view of subparts. The differences have been noted previously.
4. View the subject matter as a professional manager who accepts new research and specialists' dogma about decision making but refuses to be a captive of it. As Summer and O'Connell [1964:3] point out, scientific research findings and theories have great potential power in decision making

> but they also ". . . have serious, sometimes even dangerous, limitations for managers who must make decisions in large complex policy systems of today." The professional managerial mind understands both the power and the limitations of technology pertinent to his decision making and is able to bridge the gap between the two.

This attitude does not, of course, reject the scientific method *per se*. Indeed as Patz [1975] observes, a well-developed policy and strategy formulation and implementation process *is* the employment of the scientific method and is perfected by the more successful managers.

The professional manager keeps an open mind, mindful of the limitations of past knowledge and of the need to search for new knowledge that will aid him. He is alert to unexpected situations requiring new thinking. He accepts Hutchins' comment [1975:23] "If I had a single message for the younger generation I would say, 'Get ready for anything,' because *anything* is what's going to happen. We don't know what it is, and it's very likely that whatever it is it won't be what we now think it is."

Skills

Students in the policy and strategy course should be expected to demonstrate such skills as the following in dealing with specific cases and in using the research findings presented:

1. Size up quickly and accurately the situation presented in terms of identifying the core problems and/or issues; and in evaluating management's policy and strategy in relation to the environment, top management values, societal expectations, the financial position of the organization, and so on.
2. Analyze facts to identify opportunities and threats in the environment and the strengths and weaknesses of the organization so as to get in a position to appraise managerial behavior and/or prepare a situation audit useful in formulating, evaluating and implementing policies and strategies.
3. Identify policies and strategies which are appropriate to each situation and evaluate alternatives in terms of all relevant criteria, top management values, societal expectations, internal financial, production, technical and facility situation, and so on.
4. Recommend specific courses of action in terms of (when appropriate) detailed strategies and plans, organizational changes, financial requirements and implications, timing, personnel relations, etc.
5. Link theory and practice. Develop an understanding of when and how to use what tools, and their limitations, in particular problem solving situations.
6. Overall, to sharpen analytical skills acquired in functional areas—production, finance, marketing, operations research, personnel, etc.—in dealing with problems of the total organization. This is the skill of integrating the knowledge a student has so as to deal with a total enterprise.

Instructor-Student Objectives

There are several other additional overarching objectives of the policy and strategy course that should be mentioned. One is to stimulate students to think for themselves in dealing with specific business problems without depending upon the instructor for "the answer." Another is to help the student make a transition from the academic world to the world of operations by providing him with the opportunity to deal with problems, patterns of thinking, and so on, that are encountered in the organizational world. Finally, the policy course should seek to give the student a rich learning experience which is achieved with pleasure and high interest.

A NOTE ON CASE ANALYSIS AND CLASSROOM DISCUSSION

As students move to the analysis of the individual cases, they should draw upon the preceding text discussions and readings as appropriate. The Appendix readings (A and B) at the end of the book should also prove useful.

There is no correct way to analyze or discuss cases. For most problems which a manager faces there are a number of possible and equally acceptable courses of action. Often, too, the decision as to what is the best course of action rests on one's values.

Instead of looking for the "right" answer or one about which there is a concensus in the class, students should be more concerned about identifying the critical problem; finding feasible alternative courses of action; evaluating alternatives in terms of available knowledge, concepts, tested practices, lessons of experience, and relevant scientific techniques; testing alternatives against evaluations of company strengths and weaknesses; developing detailed plans to determine the credibility of chosen policies and strategies; matching potential gains against calculated risks; thinking through carefully the timing of action and how to make sure action is in conformance with plans; and so on.

More important than finding a "solution" is the analysis and interchange of ideas that takes place in the class discussion. There should be a maximum of discussion among students so that various views about the cases can be aired. Students need the opportunity to present their analyses and conclusions and to engage in debate with their peers in advancing their positions. The opportunity for students to think for themselves without domination from their peers and the instructor is important.

Students often find it interesting to "update" cases in the sense of finding out what really happened after the end of the case. This is, of course, interesting but not vital. What one person did in the past is not germane to the analysis of the case itself. It may be interesting for students to compare their recommendations with those decisions actually made, however. Yet if there is a difference between the two, not too much can be concluded from the variation because circumstances change very quickly, managers on the spot have more information at the time of a decision than students with only case materials, and, in any event, no one really knows what would have happened had a different decision been made by either the students or the practicing managers. More important than finding the solution which the managers actually adopted is the creativity, insight, and appropriateness of student recommendations made in light of the materials in the case and any other information that can be marshalled for dealing with the issue at hand.

Not all cases involve making recommendations. A number of them are concerned with problem identification. Some involve analysis of courses of action managers did take. Others are directed more at generating understanding of managerial problems than in reaching conclusions about what should be done. In a number of instances, cases have been disguised and it is not, therefore, possible to "update."

The role of the instructor will vary depending upon pedagogical preferences, the composition and size of the class, and the particular subject under discussion [Charan, 1975]. Usually, instruction is a combination of student-centered learning and instructor lecturing with the greatest emphasis on the former. Certainly, the instructor may expand upon and expound on the significance of research, such as that contained in this volume, as it relates to different incidents and cases. However, whatever lecturing is done at this point typically is intended to broaden and deepen the understanding of the students about issues related to and/or suggested by the cases. In addition, of course, time may be set aside in class for discussion of research and knowledge about policy and strategy without reference to any particular case.

In most instances the posture for the instructor with respect to cases is to stimulate a free and creative discussion by students without the instructor standing between them and their peers. Only rarely will the instructor accept the role of the "authority" in answering student questions about a case. This does not mean the instructor does nothing. He can and will stop a fruitless discussion and/or subtly redirect the discussion if the situation seems to warrant it. He may find it desirable to summarize a discussion up to a point in time. He may correct a misstatement of fact if no one else does. He may draw attention to areas of knowledge that are applicable to the discussion if it does not inhibit student discussion. Before cases are discussed he may emphasize that the student discussion must be as informed, creative, and rational as possible as opposed to being uninformed, off-the-cuff, and vague in analysis and recommendations.

There is no one correct way to discuss cases in the classroom. A few alternatives are as follows. An instructor may "lead" the discussion, perhaps for the first case, to emphasize different approaches to case discussion. If he "leads" a case he will seek to draw out the views of students about their perceptions of issues, their analyses of different aspects of the case, their opinions about what should be done, and so on. There is such a tendency, built into existing educational traditions, for students to look to the instructor for guidance, approval, and answers, that careful efforts may be required to avoid inhibiting the free thinking of students.

THE STRUCTURE OF THE BOOK

It is the authors' view, noted previously, that an impressive body of knowledge and research about organizational policy and strategy has evolved. This should be more closely intertwined than previously with the case materials used in the typical policy and strategy course. For the convenience of students and instructors this material has been organized in the text portions of this volume. Each part of the book is introduced with several of these text chapters. In all but the first part a set of appropriate readings then follows. Finally, once an adequate background has been developed, cases are presented to permit students to use the knowledge they have acquired in the preceding text chapters and readings. The general nature of the materials included in the various text, readings, and case sections dispersed throughout the book is as follows.

The Text Discussions

The text covers an enormous territory. Although the literature and research findings are not discussed in detail, all major relevant literature is included. This literature is placed in a conceptual framework and every effort is made to indicate its significance for policy and strategy.

In Part I the chapters deal with definitions of policy and strategy and describe the critical roles they play in the vitality of organizations.

Part II is concerned with overall forces affecting the formulation and implementation of strategy. The impact of changing environment on policy and strategy, the changing social role of business in society, and the impact of various managerial styles and organizational life cycles on policy and strategy are discussed.

The text chapters of Part III examine in depth the approaches to formulating business policy and strategy and the research that is of most significance in this process. Heavy stress is placed upon systematic strategic planning and the roles of people in this process.

Part IV deals with the implementation of policy and strategy. Here the preferred methods for implementation are examined. Again, there is blended into the discussion the results of research on operational systems and behavioral research concerned with people as they influence and are affected by implementation programs.

Part V considers policy and strategy in different contexts. One chapter is concerned with entrepreneurship. Another deals with the special aspects of formulating and implementing policy and strategy in nonprofit organizations. The contingency approach to developing theories of policy and strategy formulation and implementation is then discussed.

Throughout the various text portions, research in all areas relevant to policy and strategy is drawn upon; the major emphasis, however, is on what might be called operational theory and organizational theory. To oversimplify, the former is more concerned with what managers do (their functions and activities) and the second emphasizes the elements and processes that interrelate what they do. An attempt is made to marry these two approaches and also to blend into this body of thought relevant materials from other disciplines.

The Readings

Within the limited space available for text discussions it is impossible to explain in detail many highly significant aspects of organizational policy and strategy. Readings are therefore presented to provide additional depth of analysis of selected subjects.

An effort is made to provide as valuable a mix of readings as possible by using the following criteria: include a few so-called classic articles, examine only major aspects of policy and strategy, choose articles that are readable and not filled with jargon, present articles by authorities in their field and reproduce articles that not only will help to illuminate selected aspects of policy and strategy but also shed light on evaluation of the cases. The Appendix readings at the end are included specifically for the purpose of facilitating case analyses.

Cases on Policy and Strategy

The fundamental purpose of cases is, of course, to help students place themselves in the shoes of operating top managers of organizations. The idea is to provide students with the actual organizational settings, problems, and issues, so that they can apply their skills, attitudes, and knowledge in achieving objectives set for the policy/strategy course.

The cases have been chosen to present a suitable mix in light of the following criteria: a few so-called classic cases; a few large and complex cases; cases that require rigorous financial analysis; cases whose evaluations are solely qualitative and judgmental; predominantly undisguised real life cases; cases largely of recent origin; a mix of large, medium, and small company situations; a number of short "mini" cases; cases in the not-for-profit sector; cases covering managerial moralities, ethics, and social responsibilities; cases that focus on identifying, evaluating, and implementing policy and strategy; cases students have enjoyed discussing; and cases that represent a wide variety of industrial settings.

Questions and reading references have been included for some of the incidents and cases. Many classical case writers prefer not to do this because they believe this brings the case writer inappropriately into the evaluation and also destroys the illusion of reality. Yet for some cases, questions and references can be time savers in focusing attention on specific issues and sources of information. Nevertheless, for many cases, especially the larger and more complex ones, the approach is to follow the classical patterns and not raise questions at the end nor refer to specific references other than those cited in the case itself. In these instances, the students and instructor determine how the case is to be analyzed.

It should be noted that the concept of what constitutes a "case" used is rather broad. Classical case writers probably would not, for example, consider many of the short items to be cases. But if cases are designed to provoke thought about the formulation and implementation of policy and strategy in operating organizations, these items would qualify and so also might some of the readings.

WHAT THIS BOOK IS NOT

First of all, this is not a book on general management. It does not take the place of books dealing with the management of organizations and the way they function.

Second, it is not definitive in the areas it presumes to cover. Space limitations obviously restrict coverage of research, readings, and cases.

Third, this book is by no means an effort to substitute lecture and text for cases and discussions; it is an attempt to blend the best aspects of these approaches, however.

Finally, this book is not an attempt to train students to be chief executive officers. The intent is to permit them to simulate the position of the top manager so as to gain a better appreciation of his views, role, and functioning.

QUESTIONS

Discussion Guides on Chapter Content

1. Briefly trace the evolution of the business policy course.
2. What new trends are noticeable today in the content of business policy courses?
3. Define strategic management and explain how strategy and strategic planning are related to it.
4. What objectives do the authors establish for the business policy course? If achieved, how important may that be to you?
5. What guides and recommendations do the authors suggest for classroom discussion of policy cases?

Mind Stretching Question

1. A number of scholars and teachers today think that the study of business policy should not be confined to a single capstone course but should expand into a field of study. If you were developing a curriculum in a business school with this in mind, what would you include?

CHAPTER

2

The Nature of Policy / Strategy

INTRODUCTION

In the last chapter we noted a lack of concensus about the meaning of the words policy and strategy. In this chapter we present in detail what we mean by these as well as other closely related words.

In this general area there are serious semantic problems because words are sometimes used as nouns and sometimes as verbs. They are often used to signify concepts and at other times to denote specific actions. They are used interchangeably. Long usage has encrusted words in this area with implications and characteristics no longer applicable.

Policy and strategy are important words and change meaning with new developments. In this light we do not seek to forge definitions with which everyone will agree. That is impossible. Our purpose is to develop a general understanding of meaning upon which basis the remainder of the book can proceed.

STRATEGIC PLANNING, STRATEGIC PLANS, STRATEGY, AND POLICY

A useful starting point to clarify terms is our model of a company-wide planning process, shown in Figure 2-1. This is a conceptual as contrasted with an operational model and will be examined in detail in Chapter 7. This model displays a process that can be completed solely in the mind of one individual, and never written down on paper, or it can be pursued by many managers and staff on the basis of precise procedures that eventually produce detailed written plans. We are not so much interested in these processes at this point as in concepts.

This chart divides the entire planning process into three major types of planning, namely, strategic, medium range, and short range. Strategic planning as noted on the chart covers the entire process of determining major outside

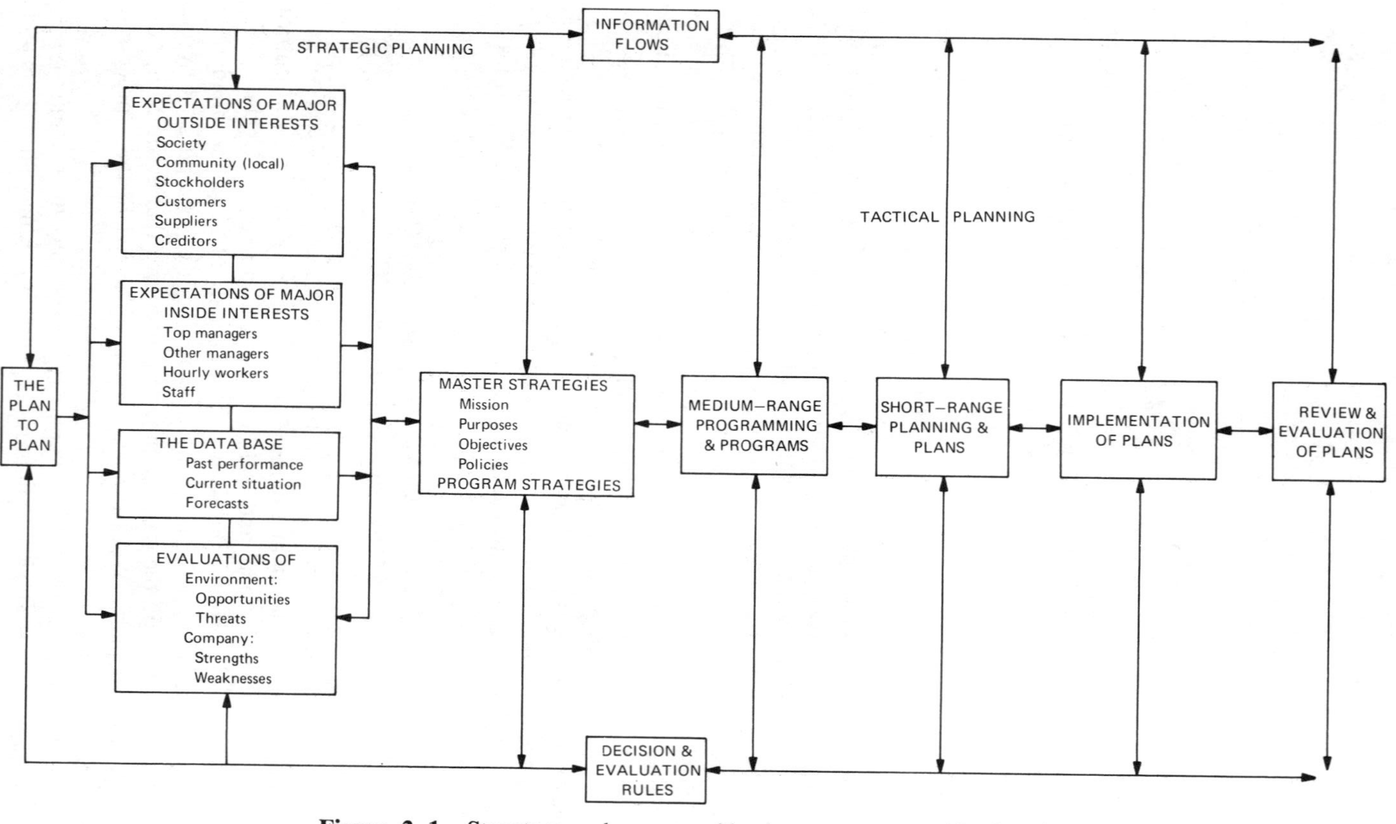

Figure 2–1 Structure and process of business company-wide planning.

interests focused on the organization; expectations of dominant inside interests; information about past, current, and projected performance; and evaluations of environmental opportunities and threats, and company strengths and weaknesses. With this data in hand managers are in a position to determine company missions, basic purposes, objectives, policies and program strategies. These results are called strategies by a growing number of scholars in the field [Ansoff, 1969:7; Cannon, 1968:xvii; Chandler, 1962:16; Christensen, Andrews, and Bower, 1973:107; Cooper and Schendel, 1971; and Newman and Logan, 1971:70–71].

Other equally distinguished scholars call the same set of elements "policy" [Glueck, 1972b:5].

A recent survey asked corporate planners ($N = 111$) what the word strategy meant to them. The conclusion was that "A near-consensus view would be that it includes the determination and evaluation of alternative paths to an already established mission or objective and, eventually, choice of the alternative to be adopted" [Brown and O'Connor, 1974:8]. This is what is meant by the specific word "strategies" shown in Figure 2–1. There obviously are different types of strategies, a matter which will be discussed later.

We accept the first broad definition but actually the choice is a matter of personal preference. In a sense, strategy is the more common term today for what used to be called policy. The word policy can be substituted in most of the above discussion for strategy. But, as will be shown, there are differences between policy and strategy that deserve attention.

The word strategy entered the literature and practice of management only in recent years. At first the word was used in its military sense to mean that which a manager does to offset actual or potential actions of competitors [Koontz and O'Donnell, 1955:504].

Then later the word was broadened to include major deployment of resources. More recently it has been broadened even further.

Our concept of strategy is more in line with its original meaning. Strategy derives from the Greek *strategos* which meant general. The word strategy, therefore, literally meant "the art of the general." It refers to that which is of major concern to top managements of organizations. Specifically, strategy is the forging of company missions, setting objectives for the organization in light of external and internal forces, formulating specific policies and strategies to achieve objectives, and assuring their proper implementation so that the basic purposes and objectives of the organization will be achieved.

Definitions cannot, unfortunately, be settled that easily. Before getting into details we should comment about the semantic problems in this field of study.

Semantic Confusion

Semantic difficulties exist in the field because there are many different definitions of terms used by various writers. This is due in no small measure to the fact that words like strategy, policy, objectives are "accordianlike" as

Andrews puts it [1971:27]. Each embraces a range of statements from broad and important to narrow and comparatively unimportant. For example, policies shade into procedures and procedures into rules. Strategies shade into tactics. Overall corporate objectives shade into minute budget ceilings. At the extremes it is easy to distinguish among these words, but as they shade into one another it is not.

In this field we also are confronted with an ends-means continuum in which words alter meaning as the decision making process proceeds. For example, suppose a company has an objective of sales growth of 25 per cent a year. Suppose also it decides to try to achieve this objective by acquiring other companies rather than through in-house research and development. It would be correct to say that acquisition was the strategy chosen by the company. Once that has been decided, however, seeking a company to acquire becomes an objective. The strategy choice then may be between acquiring a large rather than a small company. Suppose the decision is to acquire a large company. Search for a large company to acquire then becomes an objective, and so on. Depending upon inclination, the word policy can be substituted in this illustration for strategy. (For an extended discussion of this subject see Gross [1964:Ch. 19].)

Types of Strategies

There is no classification of strategies that is generally accepted. The following groupings are given to clarify some dimensions of strategies [Steiner, 1969:239–248, *passim*].

First, is classification based on scope. The single word strategy is unable to carry all the meanings in the definition given earlier. To help clarify meaning we suggest that there are *master strategies* [Newman 1971:70] that refer to the entire pattern of company's basic mission, purposes, objectives, policies, and specific resource deployment. McNichols [1972:11] calls these root strategies. They have also been designed as grand strategies. There are also *program strategies* which refer to the specific deployment of resources, physical and intangible, that are formulated to achieve basic organizational purposes. For example, if a company decided to increase its sales and profits by 20 per cent a year it might devise a strategy of increasing its internal research and development to produce new products. The specific plans to accomplish this could be called program strategies. As more detailed strategies are devised to implement major strategies, *substrategies* are developed first and then tactics. A substrategy in the preceding illustration might be to hire a scientist in a field of research not now pursued by the company. A tactic might be to offer a prospective scientist a new laboratory and congenial working place.

Second, strategies may be classified in terms of organizational level. In a divisionalized company one would find at least two levels, corporate headquarter strategies and divisional strategies. If the latter are developed in pursuit of the former they might be called *substrategies*.

Third, strategies may be classified as to whether they are concerned with material or nonmaterial resources. Most strategies deal with physical resources. But strategy can deal with the use of managers, scientific personnel, and other employees. Strategy can be concerned with styles of management, patterns of thinking, or philosophy about such matters as a company's attitudes towards social responsibilities.

Fourth, strategies may be classified as to purpose and/or function. For instance, growth is a major objective of most companies and there are many and preferred strategies to secure growth [Clifford, 1973b; and Gutmann, 1974].

Product-market strategies is another important classification. Included would be strategies designed to develop and exploit new products, strategies designed to expand sales and markets served, diversification strategies, and strategies related to product life cycle. For a good classification of such strategies see Luck and Prell [1968:177–188].

Financial strategies are vitally important to the survival and growth of a company. Indeed, all strategies are successful or unsuccessful depending upon the extent to which they affect the financial position of the company. This is an ultimate test of strategy. Here again, the area covered can be very broad. Financial strategies can include such areas as divestment of unwanted assets, customer credit, sources of funds, dividend policy, capital allocation, and transfer of balances among companies scattered around the world.

Fifth, are personal strategies of managers. The higher the level of the manager the more significant these strategies are to the life of an organization. Personal strategies are rules of thumb that capture a manager's values, motivations, protections from a hostile environment; methods to change their environment; techniques for dealing with people and getting things done; and ways to maximize their self-satisfactions and basic needs. These personal strategies constitute a fundamental, and generally unwritten, framework within which business strategy is developed. Classification of such strategies is a matter of personal choice. They may be aggressive, such as, divide and rule, strike when the iron is hot, divide and conquer, or in union there is strength. They may be mild, or passive, such as, time is a great healer, avoid action until success is certain, start small, or avoid decisive engagements when in a weak position [McFarland, 1967:159]. Other strategies may relate to timing, personal power, dealing with others, career paths, and so on. (For detailed classifications of manager's value systems see Lusk and Oliver [1974], England [1967], and Guth and Tagiuri [1965].)

An illustration of how personal values may affect a firm's strategy is that of a large research and development company which had most of its work in government contracts and was considering three strategies, as follows: (1) Try to triple sales over the next three to five years by expanding the research base and getting a larger share of growing government contracts; (2) achieve the same sales goal but through production of hardware, on the commercial market, which grows out of the research activity; and (3) aim for a slower growth rate and keep within the same type business.

Three vice presidents of the company had different values that had a bearing on the acceptability of these strategies. One was business-science oriented and wanted to make as much money as possible while still being part of an intellectually stimulating firm. He wanted profits but from an exclusively research company. Another had the value orientations of a materialist who wanted growth and profitability from widening markets and internal efficiency. He saw that the best path to this goal lay in the commercialization of hardware production. The third was more scientifically oriented. He wanted to continue present research activities and viewed with alarm getting into commercial production.

Taking these motivations and values into consideration, the president felt the best strategy would be to double sales over the next five years by continuing the business along the lines that had brought it to its present position. In this way he was best accommodating the values of his top executives [Guth and Tagiuri, 1965].

The Web of Successful Strategies

A successful strategy is usually not a single decision but a web of interrelated strategies, substrategies, sub-substrategies, policies, and tactics. For instance, in the mid-1950s when Timex rapidly increased its sales and profits the company followed three interrelated strategies all of which were essential for success. They were (1) produce an inexpensive disposable product that looked like an expensive watch; (2) undertake an effective national advertising campaign to promote the sale of the product; and (3) pursue a radical new approach to distribution (instead of depending upon jewelry stores for sales place watches in drug stores, grocery stores, department stores, garages, and so on). Each of these strategies, of course, had to be supported by interrelated substrategies, policies, and tactics.

The most successful companies generally are characterized by a succession of new and appropriate strategies. Sears Roebuck, for instance, has displayed over its corporate life a succession of new successful strategies. On the other hand, Coca-Cola until very recently was very successful with its strategy of a single product.

Strategy versus Tactics

Organizational decisions range across a spectrum having a broad master strategy at one end and minute tactics at the other. It is useful to distinguish between these two types of decisions because the way they are formulated and implemented are very different. The following distinctions are in no particular order of importance [Steiner, 1969b:37–39, *passim;* Steiner and Cannon, 1966:11–14; Anthony, 1964:18–24; Anthony, 1965].

1. *Level of conduct.* Strategy is developed at the highest levels of management (at headquarters and in major divisions) and relates exclusively

to decisions in the province of these levels. Tactics are employed at and relate to lower levels of management.

2. *Regularity.* The formulation of strategy is both continuous and irregular. The process is continuous but the timing of decision is irregular for it depends upon and is triggered by the appearance of opportunities, new ideas, management initiative, crises, and other nonroutine stimuli. Tactics are determined, for many companies, on a periodic cycle with a fixed time schedule, such as the annual budget process.
3. *Subjective values.* Strategic decision-making is more heavily weighted with subjective values of managers than is tactical decision-making.
4. *Range of alternatives.* The total possible range of alternatives from which a management must choose is far greater in strategic than in tactical decision-making.
5. *Uncertainty.* Uncertainty is usually much greater in both the formulation and implementation of strategy than in deciding upon and knowing the results of tactical decisions. Not only is the time dimension much shorter in tactical decisions but risks are more easily assessed than with respect to strategies.
6. *Nature of problems.* Strategic problems are generally unstructured and tend to be one of a kind. Tactical problems are more structured and often repetitive in nature.
7. *Information needs.* Formulating strategy requires large amounts of information derived from, and relating to, areas of knowledge outside the corporation. Most of the more relevant data needed relate to the future, are difficult to get with accuracy, and are tailored to each problem. In mind, for example, is information about competitors, future technology, social and political changes affecting corporate decisions, and economic developments altering markets. Tactical informational needs, in contrast, rely more heavily on internally generated data, particularly from accounting systems, and involve a higher proportionate use of historical information. For example, tactical plans to control production rest heavily upon internal records of past experience.
8. *Time horizons.* Strategies, especially when successful, are intended to, and do, last for long periods of time. However, sometimes the time dimension is very short. Tactics cover a shorter duration and are more uniform for all parts of an operating program, such as the contents of an annual budget.
9. *Reference.* Strategy is original in the sense that it is the source or origin for the development of tactics. Tactics are formulated within and in pursuit of strategies.
10. *Detail.* Strategies are usually broad and have many fewer details than tactics.
11. *Type of personnel involved in formulation.* Strategies for the most part are formulated by top management and its staff. The numbers of people

involved are comparatively few as contrasted with the formulation of tactics where large numbers of managers and employees usually participate in the process.

12. *Ease of evaluation.* It is usually considerably easier to measure the effectiveness and efficiency of tactics than of strategies. Results of strategies may become evident only after a number of years. Very frequently it is difficult to disentangle the forces that led to the results. In sharp contrast, tactical results are quickly evident and much more easily identified with specific actions.
13. *Point of view.* Strategies are formulated from a corporate point of view, whereas tactics are developed principally from a functional point of view.
14. *Importance.* Strategies, by definition, are of the highest importance to an organization. Tactics are of considerably less significance.

Blurring Differences

Both conceptually and operationally, the lines of demarcation between strategy and tactics are blurred. At the extremes their differences are crystal clear, as in the preceding comparisons. But these distinctions do not always hold. For instance, both in theory and practice, strategy gives rise to tactics, and tactics may be considered a substrategy which, in turn, employs tactics for execution. What is one manager's strategy is another's tactics; what is one manager's tactics is another's strategy. For example, strategies are developed in the strategic planning process at company headquarters. Substrategies within this strategic plan may then be pursued in the major divisions of the company. Concretely, a corporation may decide that its strategy is to penetrate the European market by divisional acquisitions of foreign companies. Part of the headquarters' tactical plan might be for the Electronics Division to buy a majority interest in a plant in Germany that produces a product similar to one of its own. But this may be considered a strategy by the Division. The Division may devise a tactical plan to acquire an interest in a specific plant through an exchange of stock rather than cash. From this illustration, it is clear that in an operational setting what is strategy and what is tactics may depend upon who is looking.

THE NATURE OF POLICIES

There is no concensus about the meaning of policy. Policies have characteristics that distinguish them from strategies, but there are times when it is difficult if not impossible to separate the two, as noted.

Policies are generally considered to be guides to action or channels to thinking. More specifically, policies are guides to carrying out an action. They establish the universe in which action is to be taken. This universe can be very broad if a policy deals, for example, with a general statement of managerial intent, such as, "it is our policy to be a good corporate citizen." The universe can be a much more restricted area for action in such a directive as, "It is our policy to retain 50 per cent of net earnings and to distribute the other half to stockholders in the form of dividends." Policies may be thought of as codes that state the directions in which action may take place. They set boundaries. Policies stand as ready guides to answering thousands of questions that may arise in the operation of a business.

Policies usually enjoy a long life. As a matter of fact there is too much of a tendency in business for them to live too long without review and revision. At any rate, policies are generally formulated with the long view in mind.

Policies direct action to the achievement of an objective or goal. They explain how aims are to be reached by prescribing guideposts to be followed. They are designed to secure a consistency of purpose and to avoid decisions which are short-sighted and based on expediency.

A business policy can be defined as management's expressed or implied intent to govern action in the achievement of a company's aims. This definition is at a high level of abstraction. It is necessary to dig deeper into the anatomy of a policy to understand its operational character.

Policy Verbs

Policies are generally expressed in a qualitative, conditional, and general way. The verbs most often used in stating policies are: to maintain, to continue, to follow, to adhere, to provide, to assist, to assure, to employ, to make, to produce, and to be. For example, "It is the policy of the Ajax Corporation to control the release to the public, employees, stockholders, and others all information that may disclose company plans, policies, and activities in such a way as to assure a favorable reaction toward the company, its interests, and its products." Or, "It is company policy to protect the assets of the corporation by having an adequate corporate insurance program."

Policy and Role Theory

From what has been said, it is clear that policy is quite important in role theory. For example, policies are means to ends and, as such, explain what people should do as contrasted with what they are doing. Policies, when enforced, permit prediction of roles with certainty [Miner, 1973a:113–114].

Procedures, Standard Operating Plans, and Rules

Procedures, standard operating plans, and rules, differ from policies only in degree. All provide guidance about how a particular problem shall be solved.

A procedure is usually considered to be a series of related steps or tasks expressed in chronological order and sequence to achieve a specific purpose. When a sequence of actions becomes well established and is, in a sense, a basic rule of conduct it is called a standard operating procedure. For instance, a series of steps in filling a customer order, in making a purchase of an office machine, in hiring an employee, or in handling crank letters, becomes a standard operating procedure when it is formalized. Procedures are methods, techniques and detailed ways by and through which policies are achieved.

Most companies have literally hundreds of standard operating procedures. Depending upon subject matter, of course, there are degrees of leeway in compliance. But most procedures specify patterns and/or steps of action that must be followed with minimum deviation.

Rules are prescribed courses of action which usually are stated in such a way as to leave no doubt about what is to be done. They are specific and permit a minimum of flexibility and freedom of interpretation. "Each operating division will be responsible for the direct export sales of its own products," is a rule. "All quantity discounts must be approved by the Vice-President, Sales," is a rule. Rules limit flexibility of managers. Rules cannot substitute for procedures and policies, nor vice versa. All companies, therefore, have the problem of developing a proper blend of policies, procedures, and rules.

Like strategies and tactics, rules and procedures and policies may be clearly demarcated by definition but in practice it may be difficult if not impossible to distinguish among them. A change in verb can blur the line of demarcation among these words. Or, the ends-means continuum noted earlier can create semantic problems. Also, as with strategies and tactics, much depends upon who is defining terms.

The Business Pyramid of Policies

It is clear from the preceding discussion that in every business there is a pyramid of policies. At the top of the pyramid are very broad fundamental policies concerned with company purpose, company thrust, and ways of doing business. At this point policies and strategies are indistinguishable. Falling below this level are policies of lesser scope and importance that shade into procedures and rules.

At lower managerial levels more attention is directed to implementation of higher level policies and controlling operations than to making subpolicies. When subpolicies are formulated the time horizon tends to be shorter and the policy statement tends to get more specific.

Although no company can or should have a policy to cover every action and contingency there is a tendency, particularly in the larger companies, to have an organized written register of policies. Problems that are unusual in a small company may come frequently enough to be covered by a policy in a larger company. In larger companies a structure tends to be developed, a comprehensive body, a more or less integrated set of policies and their derivatives, which becomes something like a legal system for management and other employees. These policies stretch from the highest level of generality in a company to low operating details. They may be broad in specification or specific, concrete or vague, quantitative or qualitative, flexible or inflexible, narrow or long in time, written or unwritten.

One distinction between policy and strategy in business operations relates to coverage. That which is usually spoken of as policy in business is pervasive and detailed. As noted in the following section virtually every area of a company's activities become covered with policies. Some policies, also, are extensive. A policy concerning conflict of interest in a large company, for example, may cover several printed pages.

Types and Classifications of Business Policies

Business policies may be classified in the same groupings as previously presented for strategies. Here again, however, there is no consensus.

First, policies may be classified in terms of scope and importance. One may speak of *master policy* or grand policy which covers the same area as *master strategy*. The two concepts are the same. At a lower level *program policies* can be identified. These are comparable to program strategies previously defined but are much more numerous in a company and cover many more activities. Program strategies are more selective. Then, of course, at lower levels of importance and scope are found procedures and rules.

Second, policies, like strategies, may be classified in terms of organizational levels. As Paul Appleby [1949] put it, everything decided at a particular managerial level, and above, is policy. Everything below is administration.

Third, policies, like strategies, may be classified in terms of material or nonmaterial subjects.

Fourth, policies may be classified according to purpose or function. In each of the following functional areas, for example, a large company will have policies: marketing, production, procurement, research, finance, facilities, personnel, public relations, law, dealings with foreign governments, and general management [Steiner, 1969b:272–273]. Some corporate policy manuals literally contain hundreds of policies covering activities in these areas.

Fifth, are personal policies of managers. A surprising number of companies have written creeds, philosophies, and standards of conduct that are policies. These creeds usually express the basic purposes of the companies and the beliefs of top managers about the ways in which the company will operate. They set forth moral codes of top management concerning such matters as honesty, integrity, fairness in dealings, efficiency, devotion to the public interest, devotion to profits, quality of work, and consumer service. Most creeds tend to be short rather than long. Some are for public relations purposes and others are taken very seriously as company policy [Steiner, 1969b:144–150, 158; Gross 1964:488; Thompson, 1958].

Public Policy

In the public sector the word policy attaches today to decisions and actions which are of the highest significance, widest ramifications, and longest time perspective. To be sure, they could be called strategy but the fact of the matter is they are not. When the President speaks of his major actions to deal with the energy problem or the economic problems of the United States he does not speak of "strategy" but of "policy." Most pieces of major legislation begin with a statement that explains the "policies" set forth in the legislation.

CONCLUDING COMMENT

In one sense the word policy is the older word for today's concept of strategy. But this is not quite so, for the words strategy and policy, as discussed in this chapter, do have some characteristics that differ. In this chapter we have pointed out the similarities and dissimilarities between the two words. We think the words are interchangeable when concerned with the major decisions of top managers but have different meanings at lower levels of organizational operations. Since the primary focus of this book is on the top levels of managers, the reader can decide whether he likes the sound of policy or strategy. For the purposes of this book we speak of policy/strategy. Behind that phrase, however, there are distinctions that have been set forth in this chapter.

QUESTIONS

Discussion Guides on Chapter Content

1. Distinguish among strategic planning, strategic plans, strategy, and policy.
2. What are some of the reasons for the semantic confusion concerning these words?
3. What classifications of strategies and policies do you see?
4. Explain the differences between strategies and tactics?
5. "Policy is quite important in role theory." Explain this quotation.

Mind Stretching Questions

1. If you were to try to straighten out the semantic problems discussed in this chapter what different words do you suggest for the major concepts?
2. Upon the basis of a little library research trace the evolution of the definition of the word strategy.

CHAPTER

3

The Central Role of Policy/Strategy in Organizations

INTRODUCTION

The conceptual understanding of policy/strategy presented in the last chapter will be expanded in the present chapter to examine why it is so important to organizations. It is our thesis that the policy/strategy responsibilities of top managers of an organization are of equal if not superior importance to all other responsibilities. In explaining why this is so, it is convenient to look at policy/strategy as a product of top management's strategic planning process. (We recognize, of course, that policy/strategy is a wider concept than strategic planning.) The chapter also will describe some successful and unsuccessful strategies.

TASKS OF TOP MANAGERS

Peter Drucker [1974:611] points out that there is no prescribed set of top management functions performed uniformly throughout industry. There are prescribed top management tasks, but these vary from one organization to another. Furthermore, says Drucker, these tasks are unique to top managements of organizations. This is true for public institutions as well as for business firms.

The tasks that Drucker identifies as belonging to top managers are as follows:

First, what we have designated as master policy/strategy.

Second, setting standards, as for example the "conscience" guides.

Third, is the "responsibility to build and maintain the human organization."

Fourth, assuring the proper relationships between the top managers and others, such as government, major suppliers, banks, other businesses, and so on.

Fifth, performing the countless "ceremonial" functions required of top managers.

Sixth, standing ready to lead when things go wrong. Drucker [1974:612] calls this a "stand-by organ for major crises."

There are other tasks, says Drucker, but this list serves to show that the tasks of top management are unique to it. Top management is a distinct type of work. "The ideal top management," he goes on to observe, "is the one that does the things that are right and proper for its enterprise here and now" [Drucker, 1974:613].

PRIMACY OF POLICY/STRATEGY

It is not our purpose to elaborate here on the functions of top management. More will be said about that in Chapter 6. Our intent is to note first of all the priority that Drucker gives to the policy/strategy function and to observe that the policy/strategy task influences and is influenced by the other functions. Other writers also emphasize the primacy of the policy/strategy function [Schendel and Hatten, 1972: Andrews, 1971; Frankenhoff and Granger, 1971].

The significance of master policy/strategy is framed in a comment made by Robert E. Wood when Chairman of the Board of Sears, Roebuck and Company. He said, "Business is like war in one respect, if its grand strategy is correct, any number of tactical errors can be made and yet the enterprise proves successful [Chandler, 1962:235]. He is saying that a company can be rather inefficient in its uses of resources but can be successful if its grand strategy is right. On the other hand, a company may be very efficient in organizing its production but will fail if its grand strategy is inadequate. Both, of course, are important but a company that has the "right" master policy/strategy can be inefficient and yet financially successful.

Business success generally is not the happy result of one accidental brilliant strategy. Rather, success is the product of continuous attention to the changing environment and the insightful adaptations to it. A classic illustration is Sears, Roebuck and Company which will be discussed later in this chapter.

The Policy/Strategy Process

In explaining further why master policy/strategy is so important, it is in order to comment on the strategic planning process where master policy/strategy is formulated. Details of this process will be given in Chapter 7 and following chapters. At this point it is only necessary to note that all companies have grand policies/strategies. In this regard, companies can be divided into two categories. First, there are those that live from day to day and whose policies/strategies are reactive to current events. The second group consists of those who seek to anticipate the future and to prepare suitable guidelines for making better current decisions. The second group can be divided again into two different types: those companies whose managers engage in what we call intuitive anticipatory planning, and those that do systematic formal planning. In Chapter 7 we shall say more about these two types, but at this point we wish to observe that the outcome of both types of planning are similar in that they produce grand policy/strategy, which involves an understanding of the organization's environment and the formulation of basic missions, purposes, objectives, and the policies and strategies to achieve the objectives. In the case of intuitive anticipatory planning, the results tend not to be written or are only sketchily written. The formal systems result in written sets of plans. It is rare to find a large company today, especially in the United States, Western Europe, and Japan, that does not have some sort of formal strategic planning system.

It is our thesis that to a large extent the success of a company will depend upon how well it formulates its policy/strategy in light of its evolving environment, how well it defines and articulates its policy/strategy, and how well it assures its implementation. Why is this so?

The Importance of Policy/Strategy

Simply stated, the elements of the strategic planning process, as shown in Figure 2-1, concern an understanding of the changing environment in which a company finds itself, the basic missions of the organization, basic company purposes, long range planning objectives, and program/policies and strategies. We shall comment on each of these elements.

The strategic planning process would be invaluable to a company if it did nothing more than force top management to be aware of its changing environment. As shall be shown in the next chapter, the environment of business is changing rapidly and it is opening up surprising new opportunities as well as spawning frightening new threats. Failure to adjust to either can bring disaster. The strategic planning process focuses attention on opportunities and threats, but it also asks fundamental questions the answers to which are indispensable to good management. In mind are questions such as: What are the basic strengths and weaknesses of our company? What are our competitors doing and likely to do? When will our present products require modification? What is our cash flow? What are our capital needs? Is our share of the market acceptable? Are we headed in the direction we wish?

The strategic planning process also addresses itself to defining the mission of the company. This includes the basic products and/or businesses of the company and the markets in which they are distributed. An understanding of mission permits management to deal explicitly with a number of fundamental strategic issues such as the following: What is the competitive area in which we find ourselves? What are the requirements for success in this competitive environment? Are we the proper size for success? What are our relative strengths and weaknesses in our basic businesses? Is our basic mission appropriate in light of our desires, capabilities, and opportunities?

The basic purposes refer to fundamental aims the company seeks for such factors as product quality, customer service, response to community interests, and ethical conduct. These ends are usually broadly stated, for example: "We seek to set the technical standard that other companies in the industry will strive to meet." Formulating purposes obviously forces top managers to come to grips with major questions, such as: What emphasis will be placed on customer service? In what ways will we try to capture consumer confidence? What will be our ethical posture with respect to customers, suppliers, employees, government and creditors? The answers to these questions will have profound impacts on operations.

A third major element of strategic planning is the formulation of specific long range objectives. Platitudes such as: "Our objective is to make a profit," do not provide proper direction for a company's activities. In the strategic planning process, specific objectives are set for sales, profits, share of market, return on investment, and other factors that top management thinks are important and for which it seeks measurement of progress.

A fourth component of strategic planning is the specification of program policies and strategies. These are the decisions concerning deployment of resources and guidelines developed to direct more detailed decisions in their implementation. They provide a framework within which managerial decisions throughout an enterprise can be made consistent with the basic missions, purposes, and objectives of the firm, as established by top management.

Overall, the singular significance of master policy/strategy is that it addresses itself to the core responsibility of top management, that is, to assure the success of the business today and tomorrow. To do this top management must be continuously involved in the process of surveying the environment, determining the nature of the business, setting goals for it, devising program policies and strategies to achieve objectives, and assuring that actions take place in such a fashion that the policies and strategies chosen really do result in the achievement of objectives and basic company purposes.

The strategic planning process provides a unified framework within which managers can deal with the major issues managers should face, for dealing with major problems that are unique to the company, for identifying more easily new opportunities, and for assessing strengths that can be capitalized upon and weaknesses that must be corrected. It can enable managers "without benefit of inspiration, to make solid contributions that would otherwise be lost" [Bower, 1966:50]. It is a training ground for managers to be better managers because it forces thought processes that are essential to better management and raises and answers questions that good managers must address.

STRATEGIC MANAGEMENT

So important is the foregoing that some scholars in the field suggest that a distinction should be drawn between the responsibilities of top managers in the formulation and implementation of policy/strategy and all other managers. It is suggested that what we have been discussing be called *strategic management* as distinct from *operations management* [Ansoff, 1972; Schendel and Hatten, 1972; Frankenhoff and Granger, 1971]. These writers do not suggest, of course, that tested theories, principles, and practices of management be abandoned. Rather they assert that there is a significant difference between management of the policy/strategy process and management in other areas of an organization. They say the label "strategic management" provides a new focus that highlights the significance of this process and its uniqueness compared with other managerial functions.

We think there is merit in this view and go one step further. We suggest that these new concepts be called *management by structured foresight.* This is a somewhat awkward phrase but it focuses on two major underlying principles, namely, structure and systematization of the policy/strategy framework, and decision-making based upon surveys of the future.

We are not saying that strategic planning is the same thing as strategic management. Rather, strategic planning is one major *aspect* of strategic management. The two are inextricably interrelated. It is wrong to speak of strategic planning as a "tool" of management or as a "technique" for decision making. It is a new concept of management. It is a new way to manage.

This does not mean, of course, any rejection of tested theories of effective management. They can all be embraced within these concepts. The concepts simply provide a new focus, a new emphasis, a new way of looking at top management of organizations. These views will be illustrated in later chapters. At this point a few illustrations of master policy/strategy that have been of critical significance in both the failure as well as success of companies will be presented to underscore the central role of policy/strategy in organizational life. Although the business literature is filled with simple statements of master policy/strategy of individual companies, there are comparatively few records of what may be considered a reasonably complete structured statement of policy/strategy. Companies understandably do not publish such statements. From an examination of the past records of individual companies, however, it is possible to obtain more than a superficial inference of master policy/strategy.

CROWN CORK AND SEAL COMPANY, INC.

About twenty years ago this company found itself in a financial crisis where it could not cover its preferred dividends. At that time, John F. Connelly, Chairman of the Board and a substantial stockholder, assumed the presidency of the company. He now is Chairman of the Board and President and the company has been very successful under his leadership. From his assumption of the duties of the President until 1974 sales have shown a steady rise from

$115 million in 1956 to $572 million in 1973. Profits have risen steadily and earnings per share have grown from a deficit in 1956 to $2.20 in 1974. Shareholder investment rose from $1.57 per share in 1956 to $15.10 in 1974. The following policies/strategies developed by the company were responsible for this performance, as revealed in case analysis of the company [Christensen, Andrews, and Bower, 1973:290–322]:

- Maintain a strong position in the production and distribution of cans, closures, and bottling machinery.
- Concentrate on producing cans for "hard-to-hold" products, such as beer and soft drinks, that require high strength in their containers and/or use conveniences in packaging such as aerosol dispensers and "tear-top" lids.
- Seek steadily rising sales and profit levels.
- Concentrate on reducing and holding down costs.
- Centralize the control function but make plant managers responsible for plant profitability.
- Maintain a geographic distribution of plants close to high-density population centers.
- Build plants abroad in areas where growth potential seems to be high.
- Develop wholly owned subsidiaries but have them operated by nationals in each country.
- Maintain technically advanced equipment in producing plants.
- Finance capital requirements through retained earnings and use of long-term debt.
- Maintain a high level of customer service.
- Be skilled at solving customer problems quickly.
- Invest in more equipment than is needed for standard production in order to assure quick service.
- Maintain sufficient research capability to solve customer problems and avoid unpleasant technical surprises but do not go overboard in supporting basic research.

SEARS, ROEBUCK AND COMPANY AND MARCOR

Sears' success over a long period of time supports the hypothesis that a corporation that can make the right strategic decisions at the right time can build a foundation of strength which can last for years. This company has faced stiff competition from its inception. It has competed against discounters and their price cutting, department stores, and foreign-favored nationals. Yet it has been highly successful.

In 1886 Richard Warren Sears saw an opportunity to sell a shipment of watches, which had been rejected by a Chicago wholesale jeweler, by mail-order to customers. This had not been done before. He was successful and expanded his success by adopting a strategy of selling at low prices, accepting a low margin of profit per item, and turning over merchandise fast through heavy advertising [Hidy and Cawein, 1967:72–73].

Beginning with the modern era of Sears, around 1925, there were a number of major strategic moves which maintained the momentum of the company, such as:

- The fateful decision in the mid-1920s to add retail stores to the original catalog business as the farm population came to town in automobiles.
- The decision to centralize merchandising (all buying, promotional, and advertising operations) in Chicago, and to control store operations from territorial headquarters—a unique management structure that forms the warp and woof of Sears today.
- The decision to control the cost, quality, and quantity of Sears' merchandise by having deliveries made to its own specifications. Sears today is responsible for the design details of 95 per cent of the goods it sells.
- The sweeping decision after World War II to expand aggressively, to relocate old stores, and to put new stores in new locations. Thus Sears very early preempted the prize locations as the population went from East to West and from the city to the suburbs.
- The decision in the mid-1950s to expand its sale of soft goods in retail stores, that is, to go to full-line department stores in place of the old hardware sort of stores featuring tools and fishing tackle.
- The more recent decision to play up style and fashion along with economy, a decision that has modernized Sears' image and, incidentally, made it one of the largest mink and diamond merchants in the country.
- The decision to set up a service organization, despite its low or zero profitability, to support the sales of Sears' durable goods.
- The decision to diversify into insurance and other financial services in the Allstate operation, which has possibilities of becoming as big as Sears itself one day.
- A series of decisions to invest in supplier corporations, which not only increased Sears' prime strength in distribution but has led to some sizeable capital gains.
- A series of decisions to invest heavily in superior personnel, in part through large-scale training programs . . . and related decisions to promote from within, to be generous with profit-sharing, and also to purchase Sears' own stock for the profit-sharing fund. . . . The result of such policies has been that Sears has superior management in considerable depth . . . [McDonald, 1964:120–123].
- The decision to develop entire shopping centers.
- The decision to develop entire communities, complete with residential areas, golf course, as well as shopping center.

- The decision to merchandize premium priced, and higher profit, as well as lower priced and lower profit merchandise.

During the recession of 1974–75, Sears lost many of its cost-conscious customers as a result of this policy/strategy of emphasizing higher priced, hence higher profit, merchandise. In 1975 Sears reverted to its older policy of concentrating on budget-minded shoppers [Elsner: 1975].

These policies/strategies were not, of course, suddenly and clearly defined. Some of them took years to clarify and implement. Cumulatively, however, they have formed a solid base for Sears' success.

In contrast, Montgomery Ward for years was a major competitor to Sears and, until the mid-1940s, was a very successful enterprise. Following World War II then Chairman of the Board Sewell Avery adopted a single strategy which left Ward at the post in the race with Sears. Avery expected that there would be a severe economic depression following the war. He reasoned that if he held the cash Ward had accumulated, he could expand at the pit of the depression with very low construction costs. This would, he reasoned, put him in a favorable competitive position. Unfortunately for Ward, but fortunately for the nation, there was no economic depression. Ward did not expand but Sears did. It took Ward more than 20 years to catch up with Sears, if that is the correct expression. Sears' sales in 1973 were almost $15 billion compared with Wards', now Marcor, of a little over $4 billion.

GENERAL MOTORS' PRICING POLICY

A classic example of a strategy that was the foundation of a highly successful business experience concerns GM's decision to avoid competing with Ford head-on and to produce different automobiles at varying prices. The decision was made prior to World War I at which time Ford had about 50 per cent of the automobile market divided between two cars, the high-volume, low-priced Model T and the low-volume, high-priced Lincoln. GM had approximately 12 per cent of the market. At the time the company had a line of ten cars, some of which were in the same price range, but none were at the low end of a price range. GM decided to compete over a wide range of prices (from $450 to $3,500 in six price classifications). The strategy was explained by Alfred Sloan, one of its architects, as follows:

"We proposed in general that General Motors should place its cars at the top of each price range and make them of such a quality that they would attract sales from below that price, selling to those customers who might be willing to pay a little more for the additional quality, and attract sales also from above that price, selling to those customers who would see the price advantage in a car of close to the quality of higher priced competition. This amounted to quality competition against cars below a given price tag, and price competition against cars above that price tag. Of course, a competitor could respond in kind, but where we had little volume we could thereby chip away an increase from above and below, and where we had volume it was up to us to maintain it. Unless the number of models was limited, we said, and unless it was planned that each model should cover its own grade and also overlap into the grades above and below its price, a large volume could not be secured for each car. This large volume, we observed, was necessary to gain the advantages of quantity production, counted on as a most important factor in earning a position of preeminence in all the grades" [Sloan, 1964:67–68].

In commenting on this strategy one of the authors said elsewhere: "Ford monopolized the low-price field, but General Motors' strategy was not to meet Ford head-on with the same type and price automobile; rather, the strategy was to produce a better car than Ford and price it at the top end of the low-price field. The price was near that of Ford's, but with the superior car the idea was that demand would be drawn from the Ford grade of car to the slightly higher price in preference to Ford's utility design. This strategy worked and was the basis for the rise of a major corporation. This was a strategy that Ford used after World War II [Steiner, 1969b:246].

IBM VERSUS RCA

In matters of master policy/strategy what is one company's formula for great success may be another's booby trap. This was the case with respect to RCA's entrance into the computer market with a policy/strategy to copy IBM's policy/strategy.

RCA decided to enter the computer business in 1957. It was a logical move since RCA had a strong electronics capability and the market for computers at the time promised to grow rapidly. IBM at the time held some 70 per cent of the market and its strategies reinforced one another. Its products were high quality and kept pace with technology. It emphasized solving both software and hardware problems of customers. IBM built a powerful and effective sales organization. It also decided to lease its equipment rather than sell it. One advantage of this strategy was that the machines could be depreciated more rapidly than they disappeared from the market. The result was a valuable asset that did not appear as an investment on the books of the company but produced substantial revenues.

RCA's strategy appeared to be that of competing "head-on" with IBM. RCA, for instance, introduced a series of computers aimed at capturing IBM's Series/360 users. RCA's machines had more capacity and were lower priced than IBM's series. This strategy failed, however, because RCA did not have as well-trained a sales force and stable of engineers as did IBM to deal with software and hardware problems of customers. In addition, IBM's customers were "locked in" because of past satisfaction with IBM's performance. Underneath it all, RCA committed itself to making its computer business a main thrust, but it appears the commitment was never really fulfilled. The result was that in 1971 RCA wrote off its computer business and took a loss between $400 and $500 million [Ross and Kami, 1973:70–76].

CONCLUDING COMMENT

Throughout the remainder of this book illustrations of the importance of the policy/strategy function of top management will be found. The next chapter will describe the rapidly changing environment of business, which not only complicates the problems encountered in formulating policy/strategy but underscores its significance to organizational fortunes.

QUESTIONS

Discussion Guides on Chapter Content

1. Why is policy/strategy of such great importance to an organization?
2. What are the major approaches to developing policies and strategies from which a manager may choose?
3. How does strategic management differ from operations management?
4. Describe some of the strategies behind the success of Sears, Roebuck and Company.

Mind Stretching Question

1. Choose one of the following organizations and with a little library research explain some of the recent strategies employed by the organization that brought either success or deep trouble:

   A & P
   AMTRAK
   General Motors Corp.
   W. T. Grant
   IBM
   Lockheed Aircraft Corp.
   Mattel
   New York City
   Pan Am
   Penn Central Railroad
   RCA
   Xerox

PART

II

Key Overall Forces in Policy/Strategy Formulation and Implementation

CHAPTER

4

The Changing Organizational Environment

INTRODUCTION

The most important single influence on organizational policy and strategy is the environment outside and inside the organization. The more complex, turbulent, and changing is the environment, the greater is its impact on human attitudes, organizational structures, and processes. Since today's environment has rarely been exceeded in complexity, turbulence, rapidity of change, and significance of change, all organizations, large and small, for their survival must pay more attention than ever before to their environments when formulating and implementing policies and strategies.

The purpose of this chapter is to develop a perspective about environment as a backdrop for the remainder of the book. The chapter will seek to do this first of all by presenting an overview of the interconnections between environment and organizational changes. Second, a brief factual review will be given of how major environments are changing. Third, we shall present a thumbnail sketch of the ways in which environment influences policy and strategy with respect to basic organizational design and fundamental organizational processes.

ENVIRONMENT AND ORGANIZATIONAL CHANGE

Scope of Environmental Impacts

Figure 4-1 is designed to reveal a number of relationships between an organization's environment and policies and strategies concerned with the functioning of the enterprise. First of all it is clear that an organization does not operate in one but in many environments. In the past, managers concen-

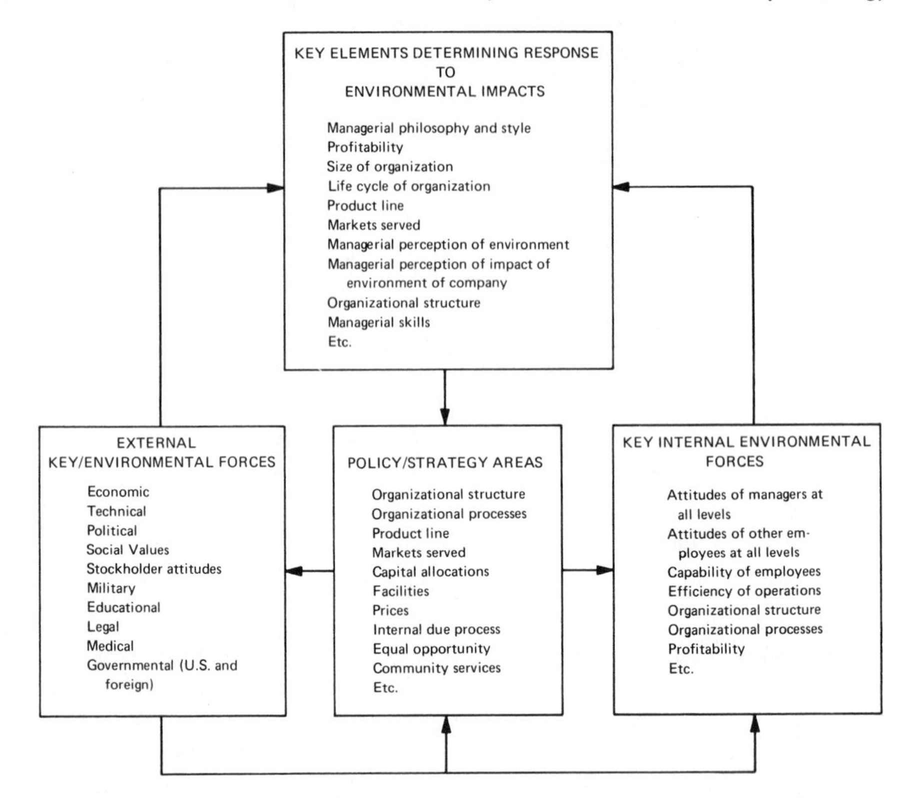

Figure 4–1 Environmental impacts on business policy and strategy.

trated attention on their economic and technical environments. In recent years, however, changes in human attitudes, social values, political forces, and legal liabilities have forced managers to broaden the scope of the environmental forces they consider.

Second, the forces in environments can affect many different parts of an enterprise. The influence is extremely complex. Some influences may be direct and dramatic, such as a sudden and unexpected change in a vital raw material availability and/or price in a foreign country. Other impacts are indirect, subtle, yet significant, such as changes in worker attitudes toward authority.

Third, the responses of an organization to environmental changes are not always obvious. Much will depend upon managerial philosophy, profitability, the life cycle of the organization, what managers see happening in the environment, how they perceive environmental forces affecting their organization, and so on. The profitability of an enterprise will also affect the way managers respond to outside pressures. For instance, two managers may recognize the importance of responding to society's demands for improving the quality of life in the community. One firm may be operating at a deficit and the other may be making handsome profits. This fact will influence their reactions.

Fourth, the influence process is extremely complex because most things influence all other things. To illustrate, managerial philosophy about the treatment of employees may be influenced by employee attitudes. Managerial philosophy may also influence employee attitudes. Factors in the external environment may influence managerial philosophies as well as employee attitudes. In addition, the interplay between policy/strategy decisions and the internal environment is constant. Changes in organizational structures and processes, for instance, will influence employee attitudes and vice versa.

Fifth, rates of change among different environments will vary. This is an obvious point but deserves mention. A company may find itself, for example, with a congenial economic environment but a hostile social environment. Such was the case of Eastman Kodak when in 1966 it became embroiled in a bitter fight with the black community [Sethi, 1974]. A number of classifications of environments based on rates of change have been suggested by scholars [Rhenman, 1973; Newman, 1971; Emery and Trist, 1965].

Finally, the influence of environment on business is not a unilateral force. Business firms individually and collectively have an important impact on environment. We shall return to this point later.

We turn now to demonstrating, by a few examples, major environmental forces that managers must take into account in formulating and implementing strategy for their enterprises. Much of the following is actual at the time of writing rather than hypothetical. We realize that the details of environmental change among the different sectors discussed in the following pages may be significantly different at the time the book appears (for example, the economic environment). We think, however, that at this point actual illustrations of complex environmental forces may better illustrate managerial problems in adapting policy/strategy to environment than conceptual hypotheses and theories. They will be presented later.

The Economic Environment

In the spring of 1975, the economic environment of business was more puzzling, uncertain, and threatening than at any other time in the preceding quarter of a century. The economy was in a recession and there were great uncertainties about the timing of a future upturn, whether an upswing would bring with it a return to double-digit inflation and double-digit interest rates, and whether profits would recover as fast as prices were expected to rise. There was grave doubt about whether price inflation would be brought under control within the next few years.

Over the longer time span, serious questions were raised about the ability of this nation to continue its past GNP rate of growth. It had been at an average annual real rate of around 4 per cent and there were predictions it might drop to 3.2 per cent. Such a drop would produce serious problems for business.

There were also huge uncertainties about the price and availability of oil. An international cartel formed by the Oil Producing and Exporting Countries (OPEC) had successfully boosted and maintained the price of oil at almost five times the precontrol price of around $2.10 per barrel. The result, among other things, was an enormous build-up of surplus cash in the hands of OPEC countries, the rise of serious financial problems for most nations of the world in meeting higher oil prices, and the creation of severe strains on the international trade and financial system.

To further illustrate the complexities of the business environment, it was noted in 1969 that the life cycle of products was shortening at the very time research and development costs were increasing and covering a longer period of time [Steiner, 1969b:555–560]. Wage rates for several years have been rising faster than productivity per man hour. Competition generally was becoming tougher both at home and abroad. Profits of business had been rising, but on a constant price basis they had been falling.

On the other hand, there are always elements in the economic environment that present profit opportunities. The mere size of the American market provides opportunities in mass production and marketing of products. New technologies are opening up new opportunities. Despite the fact that government is getting more involved in the operating details of business there are new profit prospects for business in government's growing expenditures to resolve some of our major socioeconomic problems, such as energy capacity, the lag in industrial productivity, transportation, housing, and technological development.

Government

For most businesses government is a partner—sometimes silent and sometimes highly vocal. Never before in our history, except in wartime, has government been so deeply involved in business as it now is.

The range of government relationships to business spreads from Christmas-like generosity to virtually complete regulation of all industry in time of national emergency. For most businesses the government, particularly the federal government, is one of the most significant influences on operations—growth, pricing, production, product quality, competition, wages, profits, investments, markets, and interest rates paid on capital. The impacts of government on business in recent years have increased in response to tough socioeconomic problems and rising demands and expectations of people for a better life.

Government supports business. To illustrate, it directly benefits business in making research grants, providing financial aids, negotiating tariff arrangements with foreign countries, purchasing the output of business, and commiting itself to a policy of producing economic growth and full employment of resources.

On the other hand, government restricts business. To illustrate, it directly regulates business in many ways—competition, prices, product quality, advertising, sale of securities, labor relations, and air pollution. There is a tendency in many areas, automobile safety for example, for government to get more deeply involved in business' operating details.

Business and government in the past have tended to be antagonistic towards one another. This condition still exists, but there seems to be a change taking place that is bringing about more cooperation between the two. This is illustrated by the government-business complexes developed by the National Aeronautics and Space Administration in its Apollo Program, the forming of COMSAT, and the production of military hardware in the aerospace industry.

This is not meant to imply that the governmental environment for business will necessarily become more friendly and stable. On the contrary, there is evidence that in its dealing with business the government is quite capable of lodging unexpected burdens on particular industries and companies.

The Legal Environment

A recent *Fortune* article was entitled "The 'Legal Explosion' Has Left Business Shell-Shocked" [Carruth, 1973]. The author pointed out that as recently as ten years ago the top legal worries of corporations centered on antitrust matters. Everything else was lumped together as a poor second. This is not so today. The *Fortune* article surveyed business and found eight major areas of legal concern: antitrust, securities and stockholder matters, consumerism, environment, fair employment practices, safety, government contracts, and wage-price controls. The latter do not exist at the time of this writing but are constantly being threatened when price inflation rates are high. The major source of business' legal problems stems from federal government activities.

Not only have legal actions risen substantially, but exposure of business has also increased. One manager lamented that, "the volume of laws and regulations is such that no one can comply faithfully with all rules. No large organization can effectively police all its employees" [Carruth, 1973:157]. Furthermore, it is far easier today for plaintiffs to sue and get redress for legitimate grievances against manufacturers than ever before [Berenson, 1972].

Technological Change

The businessman, no less than the ordinary citizen, is subject to "future shock," a term Toffler [1970:4] coined "to describe the shattering stress and disorientation that we induce in individuals by subjecting them to too much change in too short a time." The pace of technological change has increased rapidly during the past several decades and, although there are those who urge that it be slowed [Meadows, 1972; Mishin, 1971], it is likely to continue.

During the past few years we have had one spectacular technological development after another, for example, the computer, laser beams, xerography, miniature integrated circuits, color television, synthetic leather, birth-control pills, the discovery of DNA, nuclear power plants, human body organ transplants, artificial hearts, synthetic foods, new high-productive food grains, and two-way television. Within these developments are others as spectacular as the original invention. Today, for example, we have computers the size of typewriters with the capability of equipment that could only be housed in a two-story building 20 years ago. We are able to send men to the moon and return them safely to earth. We can send men to ocean depths unheard of only a few years ago. With new medicines we save millions of lives of people who would have died in the past.

The pace of technological change will continue in the future for several reasons. First, it is probably correct to say that more scientists and engineers are living today than ever lived before [Walker, 1968]. These people are busily engaged in refining past inventions and making new ones. Second, we are a technically oriented society and concentrate on the development of new technology. Third, most new inventions are "demand-induced" rather than "knowledge-induced." That is to say, most new inventions are stimulated by market opportunity, present or potential, which promises a profit [Schmookler, 1966]. Since the prospect is for rising new demands for goods and services it follows that technology to meet them will be forthcoming.

This outlook for continuing rapid technological change offers great opportunities as well as serious threats to the businessman. He has opportunities, of course, in finding new technical solutions to meet new demands and in identifying existing technologies that he can exploit. He faces threats in two ways. First, a technology may suddenly appear that makes his product obsolete. Second, new technology sets in motion forces that in turn result in changes in the values people hold. These value changes can be beneficial or threatening to business [Steiner, 1975b: 121–136].

THE CHANGING SOCIAL ENVIRONMENT

Changes in the social environment have, within the past half dozen years, introduced a new major force in the formulation and implementation of policy/strategy for all organizations, especially the large business firm. This has come as a direct reflection of social change and through the indirect impact of social change on economic, technical, and political forces of importance to business. So significant is this change and its impact on business that one observer speaks of the second American Revolution in a book with that title [Rockefeller, 1973]. We think the change is impressive enough to warrant saying that we are now, in this nation, redefining capitalism [Steiner, 1972b]. There are many facets to this phenomenon so the following sections are only illustrative.

New Demands on Business

Traditionally, business firms have been asked only to produce goods and services efficiently at prices consumers were willing to pay and within the rules of the game established by government and custom. If this was done well, said classical economists, firms then would maximize profits. The accepted goal of managers, therefore was to maximize profits in this way.

Efficient production is still demanded of business but in addition, especially for the larger company, the demand is that its management make decisions that help society to achieve the objectives it sets for itself. This is not a peripheral or modest addition to the agenda for business. It is, says Drucker [1969b:77], ". . . a demand that business and businessmen make concern for society central to the conduct of business itself. It is a demand that the quality of life become the business of business."

There is no concensus about what this means, but businessmen understand today that somehow or another the pressures must be met. As Reginald Jones [1974:5], Chairman of the Board of General Electric, expressed it:

> ". . . the basic strategy for corporate survival is to anticipate the changing expectations of society, and serve them more effectively than competing institutions. This means that the corporation itself must change, consciously evolving into an institution adapted to the new environment."

The response of corporations has taken many forms, ranging from doing nothing to undertaking elaborate programs to institutionalize the social point of view in the decision making process [Ackerman, 1973, 1975; Corson and Steiner, 1974]. An increasing number of large companies are surveying the demands of their constituents, sorting them out in terms of priorities, and making an effort to incorporate social priorities into the policy/strategy formulation and implementation process along with economic, technical, and legal considerations [Wilson, 1974a, 1974b].

Criticisms of Business

Never before in our peacetime history have businessmen thought more about their social obligations to society. Yet, paradoxically, criticisms of business have rarely been more widespread, and at no time in recent history has business been held in such low respect. A recent opinion poll revealed that 60 per cent of the American people said they had "little approval" of business [Benham, 1972]; in 1967 46 per cent held this opinion. Only 11 per cent of the population that was polled said it held business in "high approval," although 20 per cent approved in 1967. Such percentages indicate widespread dissatisfaction with business, and the situation exists for all organizations including government, universities, and churches.

Attitudes of Youth

Negative attitudes towards business are widespread among young people, so much so that among college students, especially those with better grades, large numbers are looking to professions other than management of business for their careers [Miner, 1974a:84]. Young people today display many values which, if held in the future, will raise serious problems for business. In a summary of a number of studies on this subject Miner [1974a] found the following; students do not want routine administrative work; they want freedom, social action, advancement, but, at the same time, are willing to give less in terms of loyalty, commitment, effort, and control over their behavior.

Young people resist authority. Miner [1974a:108] summarized research findings on this point as follows:

> "America's youth is becoming more negative to authority, less trusting of authority, less desirous of exercising authority, less accepting of the legitimacy of authority, more rebellious and defiant of authority, less tolerant of authority, less accepting of the moral values held by established authority, and more opposed to organizations viewed as authoritarian, and its behavior is frequently in opposition to existing authority. . . . There has been an increase in the freedom with which feelings and impulses are expressed and a greater self-indulgence; here, too, there is a sense of breaking away from controls, and often the uncontrolled expression is in defiance of, or in opposition to, authority."

Miner [1971a, 1974a] also found among various research reports that there has been a continuous decline in college students' motivations to manage. This may be a reflection of rejection of authority.

Changing Attitudes of Workers

Work in America observed that more than a hundred studies in the past 20 years have shown that blue-collar workers want "to become masters of their immediate environments and to feel that their work and they themselves are important—the twin ingredients of self-esteem" [O'Toole, 1973:13]. Some workers like routine jobs, but most want to avoid the oppressive features of work, such as coercion, monotony, and meaningless tasks. They want jobs with some prestige and self-determination of task. White-collar workers want the same thing but feel more strongly than blue-collar workers that their talents are not being used and that they are not being challenged intellectually.

Changing Attitudes of Managers

In a study of almost 3,000 American managers Tarnowieski [1973] found the definition of success was (in order of importance) achievement of goals (meaning a general reaching of all major aims); self-actualization; harmony among personal, professional, family, and social objectives; making a contribution to a greater good; happiness or peace of mind; greater job satisfaction;

self-respect and the respect of others; enjoyment in doing or in being; and job and financial security.

WORLDWIDE FORCES

To this description of environment there should be added worldwide forces. Possibilities for war exist, particularly limited war, and this casts a cloud of uncertainty on the total world environment. World population growth is projected to rise from over 3.5 billion today to about 7 billion in the year 2000. The rate of growth is slowing down in the industrial nations of the world but is still rapid in the less developed countries. Unchecked population growth can bring instability in political systems and tensions throughout the world as the rich nations get richer and the poor get poorer, and as underdeveloped nations face mounting food shortages.

There are offsetting counterforces. One is increasing efforts around the world to check population growth. New technology is creating new foods and higher yield grains. Industrial technology is spreading to underdeveloped countries and developed countries are still concerned about and are helping underdeveloped countries to achieve a better life.

Whatever one's perception of the state of the world environment, there is one thing certain about it; it adds to rather than reduces the risks and uncertainty in our domestic environment.

THE IMPACT OF BUSINESS POLICY/STRATEGY ON ENVIRONMENT

As noted earlier, the policies and strategies of business have a significant impact on environment. The majority of new technologies are introduced into the social system by business. The policy/strategy choices of business obviously have an influence on what is introduced, when, and how much. Business decisions concerning negotiations with labor unions, capital expenditures, transfers of foreign trade balances, foreign investments, and pricing certainly influence environment. Finally, it may be noted that business has lost power relative to other groups in influencing the various governments, but it still has significant power in legislative halls [Epstein, 1969, 1973, 1974; Steiner, 1975b].

THE FUTURE ENVIRONMENT

Most of the preceding discussion concerned current environments, but enough was said to indicate that the future environments of organizations are not likely to be calm. A few comments, added to what has already been said, will reinforce this conclusion.

Pluralism in this society is likely to expand rather than recede, which means further challenge to business power. An educated population will likely be more rather than less critical and demanding of all organizations, including business. Growing affluence will lead to less attention to material necessities and more to a richer life, self-satisfactions, and self-fullment. All organizations, including businesses, will be held accountable for their performance. For business this means accountability for social as well as economic performance. The economic environment will be supportive for business with a steady expansion of general economic activity. However, it will also be threatening because of serious problems associated with price inflation, growing scarcity of selected raw materials, problems in financing capital requirements, and so on.

We do not know precisely what the future holds for business as an institution and for individual business organizations, but certainly there will be continuing challenge to managers to adapt properly to rapidly changing environmental forces [Bell, 1973; Drucker, 1969a; *The Futurist,* 1967 to date; Kahn and Wiener, 1967; Kahn and Bruce-Briggs, 1972].

IMPACT OF ENVIRONMENT ON BUSINESS ORGANIZATIONS

Throughout the remainder of this book the many specific ways in which environment affects policy and strategy formulation and implementation will be examined. Here it seems appropriate to present a brief overview of different types of environmental impacts on business to underscore their significance.

Substantive Policy and Strategy Decisions

We need not dwell on the fact that the survival of business firms depends upon the way in which they respond to environmental changes. Well over a thousand automobile producers went bankrupt since the production of the first automobile because they could not compete in their environments. On the other hand, as noted above, Sears has been very successful over a long period of time because it altered its fundamental policies and strategies to meet changing environmental influences.

Business firms today, especially the larger ones, are developing major policies and strategies to respond to changing internal environmental forces, especially those emanating from changing attitudes and personal needs of employees. For instance, Xerox has instituted a sabbatical program for its employees to permit them to undertake their own initiated social programs in the community at full pay. More will be said later about changing business policy in response to employee interests.

Organization Structure Processes and Environment

In recent years scholars have been surveying the interrelationships between environment and organizational structures (for a review of the literature in this area, see Miles, Snow, and Pfeffer [1974] and Ouchi and Harris [in Strauss, Miles, Snow, and Tannenbaum, 1974]). These works have been helpful in providing us with a better understanding of the organization-environment interplay, but not much of the material is predictive for policy/strategy formulation and implementation processes in particular situations.

The first major analysis of the interrelationships among environment, strategy, and structure was that of Chandler [1962]. In a masterful analysis of 50 companies he concluded that strategy was directly related to the application of an enterprise's resources to market demand and that in turn brought major changes in organizational structures. He traced major stages in strategy and structure and found this sequence in the century following the Civil War. Companies expanded with single products and then consolidated to reduce costs per unit. This growth created the need for staff specialists and better coordinating mechanisms. As companies matured they decided to expand product lines and enter new markets. Such companies soon found it expedient to decentralize in order to operate more efficiently.

A step forward in facilitating cross-cultural comparative management studies was made with the work of Richman [1964] and Farmer and Richman [1965]. They hypothesized that the practices as well as the effectiveness of managers were a function of external environmental variables. They reasoned that interfirm differences could be explained by such variables in the environment and to advance analysis they, and others (for example, Schollhammer, [1969]), developed classifications of environmental variables affecting the management of business firms. Despite this early typology, research in the area "has not progressed beyond providing arbitrary classifications for separating environmental factors into certain groups: economic, social, cultural, etc. In other words, various environmental factors have not been operationalized, nor have testable hypotheses emerged from this approach" [Negandhi, 1975:336].

Lawrence and Lorsch [1967a; 1967b] demonstrated convincingly that environment affects the subsystems of a company differently. If an organization is to be effective, each of the subsystems must react appropriately to its environment, and they all must be properly integrated as they discharge their roles in different ways as determined by the environment.

Since the publication of these seminal works, an enormous number of studies built upon them has followed. Among other things, these studies have clarified the impacts of stable versus changing environments on different facets of organizations. For example, early theorists observed that organizations reacted to stable environments with centralized organization, highly specialized task orientation, close supervision of workers, a chain of command that is clear and observed, and inflexibility of procedures [Weber, 1946]. On the other hand, more recent research shows that the appropriate response to rapidly changing environments is decentralization, flatter organization structures (for example, wider span of control), dominance of organizational goal orientation, participation in decision making, and interpersonal managerial styles [Scott, 1973; Emery and Trist, 1965, 1973; Rhenman, 1973; Newman, 1971; Terreberry, 1968].

As researchers have probed deeper they concluded that the way in which organizations reacted to environment was much more complex than earlier researchers thought. Furthermore, they concluded that there was no one "right" way to respond to changing environments. Organizational design must be tailored to each situation [Negandhi, 1975; Lorsch and Morse, 1974; Miles, et al., 1974; Emery and Trist, 1973; Lorsch and Allen, 1973; Perrow, 1973; Rhenman, 1973; Child, 1972; Negandhi, 1970; Pugh, Hickson, Hinings, and Turner, 1969; Lawrence and Lorsch, 1967a, 1967b; Emery and Trist, 1965; to mention but a few].

In reviewing research on organization theory Perrow [1973:11] concluded that: "As the growth of the field has forced ever more variables into our consciousness, flat claims of predictive power are beginning to decrease and research has become bewilderingly complex." A good illustration of the precise responses to varied environmental changes is a detailed study of 140 Japanese company responses to environment made by Nagashima [1976]. We shall return to this subject in later chapters.

Gaps In Organizational-Environment Research

Most of the research on the environment-organization connection has attempted to relate broad variables in environment to particular types of organization structures and strategies, as illustrated by the preceding references. Not much has been done to relate specific types of environment phenomena to choices and preferred decisions at different points in the process an organization uses to relate itself to its environment. Very little has been done to show how different types of environments elicit particular types of program policies and strategies. Companies in an industry faced with the same economic environment, for example, do formulate some similar strategies in response. For instance, the unique set of environmental forces affecting the automobile industry today has resulted in the adoption of strategies that concentrate on smaller automobiles with engines that use gasoline more efficiently. Companies in an industry facing new government antipollution standards will tend to adopt comparable policies. Longitudinal research is virtually silent on such matters. Furthermore, most previous organization-environment research has taken the organization as static and has not addressed itself to how organizations continuously adapt to environment over time. The latter has been examined in the literature on corporate planning which, unfortunately, has not much influenced the organization-environment research.

With only a few exceptions, such as the work of Aguilar [1967] and the research dealing with perceived environmental uncertainty [Downey and Slocum, 1975], little has been done concerning the ways in which managers perceive the environment, in classifying these perceptions, or in explaining how different perceptions influence their decisions. There is literature on how organizations define their basic missions [Drucker, 1954, 1974] but nothing classifying the ways in which environment and missions are related. The same applies to fundamental company purposes, with the exception of social responsibilities. In that area the connection between environment and company response is more descriptive and normative than predictive [Committee for Economic Development, 1971; Corson, 1971; Davis and Blomstrom, 1971; Heald, 1970; Johnson, 1971; Moranian, Grunewald, and Reidenbach, 1965]. The same can be said for long-range planning objectives with the notable exception of Rhenman [1973].

Recent Past Versus Future Managerial Practices

Many other aspects of management practice, organizational structure, and organizational processes are influenced by environmental changes. The many environmental changes taking place today have profoundly affected the ways in which managers manage and organizations operate. There are deep and fundamental changes taking place in the business organization as a result of environmental forces and, as a result, future business organizations, especially of the larger companies, will operate much differently than their current-day counterparts. Table 4-1 summarizes some of the major changes likely to continue and is presented without further comment at this point.

CONCLUDING COMMENT

This short overview permits a few outstanding conclusions. First, the top management task in organizations, especially that related to the policy/strategy formulation and implementation task, is unbelievably complex and is destined to become more so because of rapidly changing, enigmatic, and uncertain environments. The environment will pose many more questions for managers than can be answered by the old quantitative economic calculus. Nonquantifiable parameters concerning political, social, ethical and human factors will be injected more and more into decision making [Wilson, 1974a, 1974b; Walton, 1969]. This all is further complicated by many changing attitudes of people in organizations.

Second, it must be quite obvious by now that the decisions made by top managers in the policy/strategy process, especially as they relate to environment, are the most critical decisions they are called upon to make. The only possible exception is the choice of other top managers to follow in their footsteps. Generally, however, that choice is the person whose capabilities

TABLE 4-1

Recent Past Versus Future Managerial Practices

RECENT PAST	TOWARD	FUTURE
1. Assumption that a business manager's sole responsibility is to optimize stockholder wealth; operational management dominant		Profit still dominant but modified by the assumption that a business manager has other social responsibilities; strategic management dominant
2. Business performances measured only by economic standards		Application of both an economic and social measure of performance
3. Emphasis on quantity of production		Emphasis on quantity *and* quality
4. Authoritarian management		Permissive/democratic management
5. Short-term intuitive planning		Long-range comprehensive structured planning
6. Entrepreneural managers who prosper by concentrating on exploiting opportunities they perceive in the environments		Renaissance managers who have the capability of entrepreneurs but who also understand political, technical, social, human, and other forces influencing their organizations
7. Control		Creativity
8. People subordinate		People dominant
9. Financial accounting		Financial, human resources and social accounting
10. Caveat emptor		Ombudsman
11. Centralized decision making		Decentralized and small group decision making
12. Concentration on internal functioning		Concentration on external ingredients to company success
13. Dominance of solely economic forecasts in decision making		Major use of social, technical, and political forecasts as well as economic forecasts
14. Business viewed as a single system		Business viewed as a system of systems within a larger social system
15. Business ideology calls for aloofness from government		Business-government cooperation and convergence of planning
16. Business has little concern for social costs of production		Increasing concern for internalizing social costs of production

SOURCE: Adapted from Steiner [1972].

best fit him or her to meet the challenges of the organization's environment.

Third, for the larger corporations, the line between public and private is becoming blurred. Indeed, as Harlan Cleveland [1973] has observed, managers of large private businesses will move further to the concept that they are responsible to people in general instead of to one or a few groups of constituents. On the other hand, government will contract with the private sector to undertake a growing proportion of the public's business.

QUESTIONS

Discussion Guides on Chapter Content

1. Discuss the conceptual interrelationships between a business' environment and its policy and strategy.
2. Explain briefly how the following domestic environments are changing for business: economic, government, legal, technological, social, worldwide forces. For each, appraise briefly whether the change is beneficial or threatening to business.
3. In what ways does business have an impact on its environment?
4. Explain in what ways environment has affected the way in which businesses are organized.
5. Explain briefly what is meant by each of the comparisons shown in Table 4-1 of the differences in management practices (past and future) brought about by changing environments. Can you add others to this table?

Mind Stretching Questions

1. You are now in the year 2000. Assuming that the practices of management of organizations change as asserted by the authors in Table 4-1, do you think the structures, operation, and role of the business institution will be radically different from today, only a little different from today, or about the same as today?
2. If you accept the changes in the way businesses will be managed in the future, as discussed in this chapter, how would you revise today's curriculum in schools of business to prepare students better to meet the needs and challenges of future business life?

CHAPTER

5

The Changing Social Role of Business

INTRODUCTION

It was noted in the last chapter that the sociopolitical environment of business is changing significantly and with it the role of business in society. This has introduced a new dimension of great importance in the formulation and implementation of policy and strategy. Three major interrelated parts of this new dimension are discussed in this chapter. First, are the imperatives that business managers respond positively to new sociopolitical demands for actions which further the social interest. Second, is the problem of measuring and forecasting forces in the organization's changing sociopolitical environment as a guide to this new decision making. Third, is the question of corporate reporting on social performance.

THE SOCIAL RESPONSIBILITIES OF BUSINESS

Managers of all organizations, including business institutions, have always had social responsibilities, but the meaning of this phrase and its importance in decision making is significantly different today than in the past. The following discussion applies to all organizations but the focus will be on business [Steiner, 1975b: 153–184 *passim*].

Shifting Managerial Philosophies

Traditionally, managers of business enterprises have been asked by society to concentrate on using efficiently the resources at their disposal to produce goods and services that consumers wanted at prices they were willing to pay. If this was done well, said classical economists, stockholder wealth would be maximized. This view came to mean that the managerial task was to maximize profits within, of course, the "rules of the game" laid down by law and custom. The decision making calculus focused on the short time span, and was predominantly economic with very little if any concern for social matters. This is the classical philosophy.

The first major break in this philosophy came in the 1930s when managers of large corporations asserted that they were obliged to make decisions in such a way as to balance equitably the claims on the enterprise of stockholders, employees, customers, suppliers, and the general public. Managers were considered to be trustees for these interests. If the balancing was done well, it was reasoned, the long-run profits of the corporation would be maximized. There were some who felt that actions not directly related to profits might be taken, but their acceptable range was negligible. This is the balanced-interest managerial philosophy.

Another major break from the older concept is now taking place. It is the socioeconomic managerial philosophy. In this view the business enterprise reacts to the total societal environment and not merely to markets [Jacoby, 1973:194]. There is no concensus about what this means. This view is rooted in the idea that there is a social contract upon which basis corporations function [Anshen, 1974]. Society grants corporations various rights and in turn expects them to operate in certain ways. In the past a corporation was only expected to use resources efficiently; now it is expected to assume social responsibilities that go well beyond mere efficiency. There is a growing recognition among corporate leaders, especially in the larger firms, that they do indeed have social responsibilities to try to meet some of society's new expectations, but there is no concensus about what to do. Although the policy/strategy implications are not clear in specific cases, there is no doubt that the underlying philosophy of managerial social responsibility identified here is distinctly different from the past views of balancing interests and of profit maximization [Adizes and Weston, 1973]. Today sociopolitical forces are as important to managerial decision making in the larger corporation as economic and technical forces.

These three views—the classical, the balanced-interest, and the socioeconomic—are not, of course, sequential. Among business managers and the general public each idea has some degree of acceptance as an operational philosophy [Richman, 1973]. Generally speaking the classical philosophy is more readily accepted for and among small enterprises and the social philosophy is more demanded of and accepted by managers of larger companies.

What Is Meant by the Social Responsibility of Business?

In the classical view, a business was acting in a socially responsible manner when it used efficiently the resources at its disposal. The current concept of social responsibility includes this action but much more. We define the new social responsibility from two points of view—the conceptual and in terms of specific programs.

CONCEPTUAL. At a high level of abstraction, business social responsibilities refer to "the businessman's decisions and actions taken for reasons at least partially beyond the firm's direct economic or technical interest" [Davis, 1960:70]. A broader view is that there are obligations to "pursue those policies, to make those decisions, or to follow those lines of action which are desirable in terms of the objectives and values of our society" [Bowen, 1953:6]. An even broader view is the following: "By 'social responsibility' we mean the intelligent and objective concern for the welfare of society that restrains individual and corporate behavior from ultimately destructive activities, no matter how immediately profitable, and leads to the direction of positive contributions to human betterment, variously as the latter may be defined" [Andrews, 1971:120]. Basically, these definitions say that business men in their decision making should consider the social interests of people in society.

SPECIFIC CORPORATE SOCIAL PROGRAMS. At an operational level, social responsibilities can be defined in terms of specific action programs which a corporation may take. Several lists of such programs have been compiled, the first by the Committee for Economic Development (CED) [1971:31–40]. There were ten categories and 57 separate programs in the CED list. Included were the classical responsibilities of business relating to economic efficiency and growth. Other categories were education, employment and training, civil rights and equal opportunity, urban renewal and development, pollution abatement, conservation and recreation, culture and the arts, medical care, and government. In a survey based upon this list respondents were asked what other programs might be included, and from this response these categories were added: product safety, advertising, consumer services, general community services, and improving employee self-satisfactions. McAdam [1973] compiled a more recent and longer list.

OTHER DEFINITIONS. There is no concensus about the definition of business social responsibilities. Different writers approach the subject from different points of view. For instance, social responsibilities have been defined in terms of ethics [Baumhart, 1968]; sociology [Bell, 1971]; aesthetics [Eells, 1968]; internalizing costs [Barkley and Seckler, 1972]; and how future society judges today's performance [Farmer and Hogue, 1973].

Most businessmen prefer words other than social responsibilities to describe the phenomenon. Some synonyms are: public policy, social action, social concern, social challenges, community activities, and public affairs.

SOCIAL RESPONSIBILITIES AND PROFITS. When speaking of social responsibilities many people, including managers, conclude that the pursuit of social responsibilities will *ipso facto* result in a reduction of short-range and perhaps also of long-range profits. This is not so. If one accepts our definitions, a corporation is acting socially responsibly when it improves its productivity and, other things being equal, that will raise both short- and long-range profits. But a corporation may undertake other programs that will raise profits rather than reduce them. For instance, assuring more due process, justice, equity, and morality in employee selection, training, promotion, and firing may well improve morale and productivity and, in turn, profits. Replacing a dangerous machine with a new one may not only eliminate an accident hazard but also raise productivity per man hour. Some social programs can, of course, reduce profits. If a firm installs expensive antipollution devices and the costs cannot be passed on to consumers, the company's profits will certainly be less than before.

The Case Against Business' Assumption of Social Responsibilities

Not everyone agrees that businessmen have social responsibilities beyond their classical function. Milton Friedman, a widely respected economist, is an outstanding protagonist of this view. He says:

> . . . there is one and only one social responsibility of business—to use its resources and engage in activities designed to increase its profits so long as it stays within the rules of the game, which is to say, engages in open and free competition, without deception or fraud. . . . Few trends could so thoroughly undermine the very foundations of our free society as the acceptance by corporate officials of a social responsibility other than to make as much money for their stockholders as possible. This is a fundamentally subversive doctrine [Friedman, 1962:133].

Friedman bases his position on a number of arguments. For example, he says that managers are employees of the owners of an enterprise and are directly responsible to the owners—the shareholders. Since shareholders want to maximize their wealth the managers should pursue that objective without deviation. He also says that if managers spend stockholder money without their consent that amounts to taxation without representation. More cogently, Friedman argues that if corporations pursue social responsibilities, which are really governmental responsibilities, their performance will tend to be measured by criteria used to judge performance of public officials. If so, the economic measure of performance will decline in importance and eventually economic efficiency will erode and society will lose. Friedman is joined by many others in such beliefs [Manne, 1972; Heyne, 1971, 1968; Levitt, 1958; Hayek, 1944].

The Case for Business' Assumption of Social Responsibilities

The number of people opposing such views is growing both in and out of the business world. Generally speaking, the case for the assumption of business social responsibilities is based on three interrelated core ideas. The first, simply put, is that society expects business to assume social responsibilities. Now, since the corporation is a creature sanctioned by society to achieve objectives set for it by society, the corporation must respond when society's will becomes manifest. Gerhard Bleichen [1972], Chairman of the Board of John Hancock Mutual Life Insurance Company succinctly put the position of business this way: ". . . it never occurred to me that there was a time when American business was at liberty to operate in conflict with the interests of society." Many businessmen accept the notion that the corporation operates under a franchise from society, and society can take that franchise away if business does not respond to its desires [Byrom, in Steiner, 1975a: Clapp, 1968].

Second, it is in the long-run self-interest of business to assume social responsibilities. This is inherent in the preceding position but can be expressed in different words. In a milestone policy statement of the CED, a group of prominent businessmen concluded: ". . . it is in the enlightened self-interest of corporations to promote the public welfare in a positive way" [Committee for Economic Development, 1971:25]. The statement continued: "Indeed, the corporate interest broadly defined by management can support involvement in helping to solve virtually any social problem, because people who have a good environment, education, and opportunity make better employees, customers, and neighbors for business than those who are poor, ignorant, and oppressed" [1971:26].

The same point holds with respect to other types of social responsibilities. For instance, corporations are understanding better that their best interests are served when corporate goals and personnel goals are in harmony. Arjay Miller [1966] says that a corporation cannot preserve stockholder equity in the long run without behaving with social responsibility.

Third, when business assumes social responsibilities it reduces the pressure for and incidence of federal regulations. In turn, the businessman will reduce his costs because regulation is generally expensive; he will retain some flexibility and freedom in making decisions; and he will restrain further concentration of power in government. Furthermore, says Anshen [1970], the businessman will retain a needed credibility with the public and will be invited to, not restrained from, participating in the political decision-making process when new legislation pertaining to business is being drafted.

Many other arguments are made to support business' assumption of social responsibility but only a few can be added here. Some say that businessmen are concerned citizens, as well as managers, and can be expected to use their corporate powers to help develop a better world. Some managers and scholars say that businessmen take social responsibility seriously in order to assure a legitimacy which today is tenuous and fuzzy. When managers find themselves in control of a giant company in which they possess small stock ownership, and no one else owns anything beyond a fraction of outstanding shares, to whom are they responsible? Finally, as Andrews [1971:133] points out: ". . . corporate executives of the caliber, integrity, intelligence, and humanity required to run substantial companies cannot be expected to confine themselves to their narrow economic activity and to ignore its social consequences."

An Assessment of the Argument

It is our judgment that arguments opposing the assumption of social responsibilities are weak on two grounds. First, they overstate the trend and ultimate magnitude of social responsibilities which businessmen voluntarily take on now and will undertake in the future. Second, they want corporations to do something they cannot do, and that is to ignore societal demands on them. This does not mean the arguments against social responsibilities are without any substance. They do contain warning signals that caution us against any excessive movement away from traditional economic motivations and measures of performance.

Opponents of the social responsibility doctrine like to point to the fact that stockholders are the legal owners of a corporation and that managers, by law and in conformance with the theory of the private enterprise system, must consider the interests of the stockholders as being preeminent. There are many who disagree. Wallich and McGown, for example, point out that this view rests on a simplistic notion of stockholder ownership. They say: "Once it is recognized that corporations are not usually owned by a group of investors who own shares in only one corporation, but by individuals who as a group typically own shares in a very large number of corporations, the whole concept of stockholder interest becomes extremely fuzzy" [in Baumol *et al.,* 1970:55]. If stockholders feel their interests are not being served, they sell their stock.

Opponents of business social responsibilities point to a conflict between socially responsible actions and profits. Earlier we noted that there need not be a conflict. A corporation can improve its profit position and at the same time be socially responsible.

The argument about whether businessmen have or do not have social obligations is by no means settled and will continue. For practical purposes, however, the issue is settled. Businessmen do have social responsibilities! There are questions of more immediate concern. Precisely what are the social responsibilities of a particular business? How can top managers institutionalize the social point of view in the decision-making processes of a company? How can and should a corporation account for its social performance? We shall address each of these questions but, before doing so, it is useful to distinguish among major types of business social responsibilities.

The Concept of Voluntarism

In the typical large corporation the totality of decision making which falls within the realm of social responsibility, as defined previously, may be classified into five categories, as follows: (1) decisions concerned with traditional economic and technical matters; (2) actions generated by irresistible internal human and organizational pressures; (3) responses to government laws, regulations, and other mandates; (4) responses to demands from powerful pressure groups, such as unions, which cannot be denied; and (5) voluntary socially oriented actions.

In the fifth class are new social programs introduced in the corporation and/or the addition of social dimensions to traditional types of decisions made in the other categories. Programs in this area can be divided into the following groups: those actions taken by managers to do more than the law requires, actions that recognize current public expectations and social demands, actions that anticipate new social demands and prepare in advance to meet them, and actions that serve to show that corporate managers are leaders in setting new standards of business social performance [Chamber of Commerce of the United States, 1973; Rockefeller, 1973].

No one knows precisely what volume of decisions, irrespective of how volume is defined, falls into the above categories. There seems little question about the fact, however, that the fifth area is growing in volume and significance in most larger and many smaller corporations.

The Business Response

There is no broad-based social pressure for every business, large and small, to assume all the social programs that well-meaning groups, as well as activists demand. The greater part of whatever pressure does exist is brought to bear on the larger businesses rather than on the small ones. However, even the larger firms are not expected to try to do everything. Individual companies can pick and choose those social actions they wish to take in response to society's demands.

Business has responded positively to the new societal demands for social programs. One evidence of this is the great increase in recent years of statements made by businessmen in their annual reports about their social programs [Coppock *et al.*, 1972].

Various polls have amplified the fact that large numbers of businessmen do not hold the classical view that their responsibility is to maximize stockholder wealth. Most executives today reject the view that "A corporation's duty is to its owners and only to its owners" [Ewing, 1971:147; Krishnan, 1973; Louis, 1969]. Even among businessmen who said in one poll that businesses' sole responsibility was to make a profit a majority claimed to have new social programs in full operation [Louis, 1969].

A comprehensive survey of almost 300 larger corporations showed a widespread commitment to social programs. Using the CED listing referred to earlier, respondents were asked to identify those individual programs to which they were making substantial commitments in time and money. A large number of companies were acting in every one of the CED programs. Table 5-1 shows the programs where most corporations are making heavy commitments [Corson and Steiner, 1974].

What Are a Corporation's Social Responsibilities?

As noted earlier there is an answer to this question at a high level of abstraction. There is no clear answer, however, at the operational or decision-making

TABLE 5-1
Rank Order Listing of Activities that Were Noted Most Frequently by Companies (N = 284) to Involve Significant Commitments of Money and/or Personnel Time

RANK *	NUMBER OF RESPONSES
1. Ensuring employment and advancement opportunities for minorities	244
2. Direct financial aid to schools, including scholarships, grants, and tuition refunds	238
3. Active recruitment of the disadvantaged	199
4. Improvement of work/career opportunities	191
5. Installation of modern pollution abatement equipment	189
6. Increasing productivity in the private sector of the economy	180
7. Direct financial support to art institutions and the performing arts	177
8. Facilitating equality of results by continued training and other special programs (civil rights and equal opportunity)	176
9. Improving the innovative and performance of business management	174
10. Engineering new facilities for minimum environmental effects	169

* Rank: (1) indicates highest commitment.

level. Each company is able to determine for itself how to respond to the many interests and pressures for social action that are focused on it.

This issue can be approached, of course, on a piecemeal basis. For example, many companies have established committees to identify the major social programs that the company should pursue on a voluntary basis. Some companies have given the responsibility for coordinating social responsibilities to one individual or a department [Corson and Steiner, 1974].

Another approach is to formulate a comprehensive set of policies governing social actions. This has the advantage of assuring an integrated set of actions if the policies are taken seriously. The sort of policy statement in mind might be given in the following way [Steiner, 1972a] with each item prefaced by, "It is the policy of this company . . ."

1. To think carefully about its social responsibilities. This policy does not commit a company to any particular social program, but it does say that the company feels its first social responsibility is to think carefully about its social responsibilities.
2. To make full use of tax deductibility laws through contributions, when profit margins permit. This policy simply takes advtange of the tax laws but does not commit the company beyond its current minimum philanthropy unless it feels that profit margins are high enough to warrant further giving.
3. To bear the social costs attendant upon its operations when it is possible to do so without jeopardizing its competitive or financial position. This policy says the company wishes to avoid the adverse side effects on society of its operations to the extent that it can do so.

4. To concentrate action programs on limited objectives. No company can take significant action in every area of social responsibility. It can achieve more if it selects areas in which to concentrate its efforts. This policy, therefore, sets limits on social programs.
5. To concentrate action programs on areas strategically related to the present and prospective functions of the business, to begin action programs close to home before acting in far distant regions, and to deal first with what appears to be the most urgent areas of concern to the company. This policy has many facets to it. For example, it does not say that a company should take only that action which is closest to its self-interest. It does say that it should concentrate its efforts in areas that will be importantly related to its survival and healthy growth. To implement this policy it will be necessary for a company to assess carefully the various expectations of its many constituencies, especially those close to it, lay out priorities for action, and then see to implementation. It says, for example, that it is much more important for a public utility to pay attention to what people in and out of the company expect by way of social action than to make contributions to charities far removed geographically from the company.
6. To facilitate employee actions that can be taken as individuals rather than as representatives of the company. This is an encouragement to try to free people who want to be released. A company should not force employees to go out in the community to do good deeds but there is a great opportunity for companies to encourage and provide means for their employees to pursue their community interests.
7. To search for product and service opportunities to permit our company and others to make profits while advancing the social interests; but not all social actions should be taken solely for profit. This policy recognizes that there are many things a company can do that are socially responsible and profitable. The combination should be encouraged.
8. To take actions in the name of social responsibilities but not at the expense of that required level of rising profits needed to maintain the economic strength and dynamism desired by top management. Actions taken in the name of social responsibility should enhance the economic strength of the company and/or the business community. The over-all mission of the company is two-pronged, as follows:

   To set forth and achieve corporate objectives that meet specified social challenges ranging from product quality to the "quality of life" requirements, both internally and externally.

   To increase the company's earnings per share at a rate required to meet share-owner/profit expectations and these new requirements.

   This policy does not replace traditional profit policy but expands it. Some companies, the Chase Manhattan Corporation [1971], for example, have embraced this policy.

9. To take socially responsive actions on a continuous basis rather than *ad hoc,* one at a time, or for a short duration. This policy is based upon the conviction that a company will be able to make a much greater impact, at less cost, with continuous as compared with on-again off-again actions.
10. To examine carefully before proceeding the socially responsive needs the company wishes to address, the contributions the company can make, the risks involved for the company, and the potential benefits to both the company and society. This is a warning to "look before you leap." In the past many companies got into trouble because they acted more on impulse than reason. This policy commits the company to take action that is organized, sensible, systematic, and extended over a period of time. It is the opposite of putting out fires or answering alarm bells in response to outside pressures and, after the pressures disappear, going back to practices existing before the stimulus. This policy says, "Let's make a careful cost/benefit analysis before making important commitments" [Steiner, 1972a].

If such policies are to result in action, they must be defined in more detail through subpolicies and substrategies. Reporting and control mechanisms must, of course, also be prepared, and managers then must exercise the necessary degree of surveillance and control. This process of institutionalizing the social point of view in the decision-making process is difficult and time consuming [Ackerman, 1973].

Although there are no rules that apply to individual companies in specifying what, when, where, and how much social responsibility should be introduced into the decision-making processes, there are a few generalizations that can give some guidance.

First, the larger a company becomes the more actual and potential influence it has over people and society. Society tends to take a greater interest in what the company does, and the company tends to think more carefully about its social responsibilities. In the words of jurists it tends to be "affected with a public interest." Society does not, on the other hand, expect many social responsibilities from very small corporations other than to produce goods and services efficiently within the law and codes of honesty and integrity.

Second, without regard to size, companies may have different degrees of power over individuals and communities. For example, company A may be smaller than company B, but company A may employ 90 per cent of the workers of town Y whereas company B employs only 1 per cent of the workers of the town. Both companies are planning to move. It would appear that, other things being equal, company A should give much more thought to its social responsibilities in moving than company B. This is what Davis [1960] calls a "socioeconomic responsibility" problem.

Again, although all this may be useful in helping a management that is trying to formulate social policies and strategies, it does not tell a company precisely what it ought to be doing. There is no easy answer to that question, and what may be a suitable answer today may well be insufficient tomorrow as the social environment changes.

Measuring and Forecasting the Changing Social Environment

As noted in the previous chapter the sociopolitical environment of business includes a wide spectrum of phenomena such as social attitudes and values, life styles, human expectations, political changes, legislative thrusts, and so on. It is clear that larger companies must consider such factors in decision making [Preston and Post, 1975]. If present trends continue, the measurement and forecast of such forces will stand beside the traditional economic and technical forecasts, with equal footing, in making major decisions in corporations.

This process is hobbled, however, by the lack of sociopolitical measuring and forecasting tools [Wilson, 1974a; Carroll, 1973]. Aside from speculation and general scanning of the environment the principal methods used today are trend projections, Delphi forecasting, scenarios, and "cross-impact analysis." General Electric has developed two new methods which have promise, namely the "probability-diffusion matrix," and the "values profile" [Wilson, 1974a]. Although progress is being made in this field, the state of the art is very low on the learning curve at the present time [Shocker and Sethi, 1973].

THE SOCIAL AUDIT

Corporate Accountability

Accompanying pressures for corporations to assume social responsibilities is the demand that they be held accountable for their social actions. Here, again, although there is some agreement on the principle of accountability, there is no concensus on what demands a particular company should recognize and be accountable for. The Standard Oil Company (N.J.), now the Exxon Corporation, recognized the general demand for accountability in these words: "Historically we have had a responsibility to account financially to our shareholders. Now there is growing pressure for a broader accounting to a wider audience" [*Roper Report,* 1971:2]. The Chamber of Commerce of the United States [1970:3] says this broader accounting is "a fundamental shift from the principle that all business is essentially private and accountable only to stockholders and the free marketplace to legal doctrines that make large enterprises, in particular, more and more accountable to the general public."

What Is a Social Audit?

In response to general pressures for corporations to assume social responsibilities and to be held accountable to constituent interests for their performance, companies have made reports of their social activities. These reports have been called social audits.

At a high level of abstraction there probably is agreement that a social audit is a report of social performance in contrast to a financial report which deals with economic performance. Consensus ends at this point.

There are two fundamentally different types of social audit. One type is required by government agencies to meet reporting requirements for such activities as equal opportunity, pollution abatement, and product performance. Reporting requirements vary widely. The second type covers social audits that concern social programs undertaken voluntarily. These vary from brief comments in annual reports to elaborate research reports [Corson and Steiner, 1974].

What Are Companies Doing?

Corporate social audits are a phenomenon of literally the past half dozen years, although the origins of the approach have been traced back to 1940 [Carroll and Beiler, 1975]. One survey asked corporations this question: "Has your company attempted within the period since January 1, 1972, to inventory or to assess what has been done in any of a series of 'activity fields'?" These fields were defined as the social programs listed by the CED and referred to earlier. A surprising 76 per cent of 284 responding firms answered affirmatively [Corson and Steiner, 1974:24].

The same survey asked respondents what purposes led their companies to make a social audit. In descending order of importance these were the responses: (1) to examine what the company is actually doing in selected areas, (2) to appraise or evaluate performance in selected areas, (3) to identify those social programs which the company feels it ought to be pursuing, (4) to inject into the general thinking of managers a social point of view, (5) to determine areas where our company may be vulnerable to attack, (6) to ensure that specific decision-making processes incorporate a social point of view, (7) to meet public demands for corporate accountability in the social area, (8) to inform the public of what the company is doing, (9) to identify those social actions that the company feels pressured to undertake, and (10) to offset irresponsible audits made by outside self-appointed groups [Corson and Steiner, 1974:33].

Major Policy and Strategy Questions

This entire subject is in a state of flux and corporations are at the very beginning of the learning curve [Bauer and Fenn, 1972]. The idea of a social audit raises a number of important policy/strategy questions for a large company, for instance: Should we undertake a social audit? Why should we do so? To whom should the audit be addressed? If it is addressed to constituents, how shall their interests be identified? What shall we do when constituent interests conflict? How complete shall the audit be? Should we make the audit public? How much should be made public? Who is to measure our social performance?

Different groups will see performance in different lights. Furthermore, there are no generally accepted measures of social performance. Scholars are beginning, however, to work on the measurement question [Sturdivant and Ginter, 1974].

David Rockefeller [1971] thinks the social audit is not a current fad. He says, "Because of the growing pressure for greater corporate accountability I can foresee the day when, in addition to the annual financial statement, certified by independent accountants, corporations may be required to publish a 'social audit' similarily certified." This day is some distance ahead, but we are moving in that direction. As this is being written the Securities and Exchange Commission is holding hearings on whether or not corporations should be obliged to disclose information about their social programs.

CONCLUDING COMMENTS

The role of the corporation, especially the larger one is undergoing significant change. No longer is society satisfied when it confines its efforts to being efficient. That is still required but, in addition, the corporation is expected to meet new and rising social demands of people. These new demands range from better working conditions in a company to helping society achieve the major objectives it sets for itself.

Not only are corporations expected to undertake social programs that, heretofore, they would not have thought of pursuing but they are also expected to inject into traditional economic and technical decision making a new social point of view. This has clearly added a new dimension to the traditional policy/strategy process. It has immeasurably complicated it because there are no hard and fast guidelines available to a company. Each firm must decide for itself.

An additional complication arises from the fact that corporations, like other institutions, are being held accountable for their social performance. A result of this is the development of the business social audit which is a report on a company's social performance. Here, again, no firm guidelines exist for the business in making a social audit.

QUESTIONS

Discussion Guides on Chapter Content

1. How have the fundamental philosophies of the business managerial role changed over the past 200 years?
2. What is meant by "the social responsibility" of business?
3. Explain the case against businesses' assumption of social responsibilities.
4. What is the case for businesses' assumption of social responsibilities?

5. How do you assess the arguments pro and con of businesses' social responsibilities?
6. In this debate does it make any difference whether one speaks about legally mandated responsibilities versus those voluntarily assumed by business?
7. Do you think the policy recommendations for social responsibilities stated in the chapter should be accepted by every business in the United States? Explain.
8. Argue the case pro and con that corporations should report publicly on their social activities as they do on their economic activities.

Mind Stretching Questions

1. Mr. Richard Gerstenberg, when Chairman of the Board of General Motors, said, "The most successful business in the years ahead will be the one that not only offers quality products at competitive prices, but also succeeds in matching its resources to society's changing demands, the business that is best able to give creative response to the social aspirations of the people it serves. Conversely, the business that fails in the years ahead will be the one that fails to understand how it is related to the society around it and will, therefore, overlook opportunities for services, for growth, and for profit." (Remarks made at the Institutional Investors Conference, General Motors Technical Center, Warren, Michigan, February 8, 1973.) Is he saying that the business that assumes its proper social responsibilities is likely to be the successful business? Do you agree?
2. John D. Rockefeller, III, examined the role of businessmen in their traditional economic activities and new responsibilities of a social nature and commented as follows: "The challenge is to be successful in business and in serving the needs of society. Is it unreasonable to assume that the same abilities and qualities apply in both cases? I think not." (John D. Rockefeller, III: *The Second American Revolution,* New York, Harper & Row, 1973, p. 95.) Do you agree with Mr. Rockefeller? Explain.
3. What major policy/strategy questions can you enumerate that will face the chief executive officer of a large company who decides that his managers should become more socially responsible?
4. Are social responsibilities and moralities the same?

CHAPTER

6

Managerial and Organizational Styles

INTRODUCTION

The environments that organizations face vary widely. This is in part a function of the type of organization and the particular industry that a company is in. It is also a function of the stage of development of the company and its current position in its organizational life cycle. These different environments call for different managerial styles, particularly at the top management level, if the company is to cope with its environment effectively. This pressure from the environment is one basis for variations in managerial styles and, thus, in the way companies operate.

Another basis for variation derives directly from within the organization and its members. People differ a great deal in many respects. Many different kinds of people become managers, and for one reason or another rise to top level positions. Thus, two companies in virtually identical environments can be run by chief executive officers who perceive their environments differently, value different things, have different kinds of knowledge and behave quite differently. (A variety of such factors, which may influence managerial decision making, are discussed in Chapter 10.)

These differences among people in their approaches to their jobs constitute differing *managerial* styles. To the extent there are consistencies within companies, so that certain styles tend to be pervasive, one may talk about *organizational* styles. Organizational styles are strongly influenced by top management and by the prevailing organizational climate, particularly by the value and reward structure components of that climate. Managerial and organizational styles in turn exert a great deal of influence on policy and strategy formulation and implementation.

MANAGERIAL JOBS

One approach to dealing with the managerial style question is through the analysis of managerial jobs. Once a knowledge of the range of managerial functions is developed, variations in the extent to which different managers emphasize certain functions and the appropriateness of such an emphasis to the particular situation can be examined [Osmond, 1971].

The Management Process Approach

The approach to the analysis of managerial work with the longest history is the management process approach, which views managing in terms of planning, organizing, and other similar functions. For many years this approach was almost entirely theoretical in nature, and the variety and number of functions considered really important in managerial work varied markedly from one theorist to another. More recently a solid underpinning of research has been developing, and certain managerial functions have been identified as playing a central role [Campbell *et al.*, 1970; Miner, 1971d, 1973a].

These primary functions are as follows:

1. Planning—including the planning of organization structures and decision making
2. Directing or supervising
3. Coordinating
4. Controlling—including evaluating and investigating for control purposes.

In addition it has been found that managers may spend considerable time in staffing and representing, although the emphasis on these two functions is not sufficient to justify classifying them as primary. Another function, negotiating, appears to be of importance only in certain kinds of jobs, such as among bank officers [Haas *et al.*, 1969].

If one studies people in upper level management positions, a tendency to concentrate time and effort on certain functions at the expense of others does emerge [Mahoney *et al.*, 1963, 1965]. There are relatively large numbers of top managers who concentrate primarily on planning—approximately 28 per cent in this study. Concentration in this area is much less at lower levels. A second sizable group of top managers (22 per cent) specializes in supervising and directing. These people do relatively little planning; however, this predominance of supervising is even more characteristic of lower management. Another 14 per cent at the top levels concentrate on either the investigative or evaluative aspect of controlling.

Yet top management is also characterized by a disproportionately large number of generalists who spread their time over many functions—20 per cent versus 9 per cent of lower level managers. None of these managers spend as much as 20 per cent of their time in a single function. Yet only staffing and representing receive very little attention.

Studies of this kind make it clear that managers at the top levels are by no means all generalists in their actual job behavior. This is not to say that a greater shift in the generalist direction might not be desirable. Any conclusion in this regard must await studies relating the use of managerial time to environmental and job requirements. However, the large amount of the top managers' time spent in planning does suggest that policy considerations are often of prime importance.

The Managerial Working Roles Approach

An alternative way of looking at managerial work has recently been developed by Mintzberg [1973a, 1975a] based primarily on his intensive study of five chief executives. Mintzberg is very much interested in developing an underlying theory for the field of business policy and in linking this theory into management theory in general. As a starting point he has focused on the working styles of managers. His approach differs from the management process approach because he starts his analysis of the managerial job from different premises and uses a different conceptual framework. That he comes out with a somewhat different result is not so much a repudiation of the process approach as a consequence of cutting up the pie differently in the first place. Yet the ideas that Mintzberg presents regarding the managerial job do provide some valuable insights into managerial styles and differential approaches to policy formation. The essence of his managerial work roles approach is stated in Table 6-1.

Clearly different managers may emphasize different combinations of these roles and, accordingly, exhibit widely varying managerial styles. Thus, one manager might devote a great deal of time and effort to the figurehead, liaison, monitor, spokesman, and negotiator roles. Such a person would be basically an outside manager; this approach could well be entirely appropriate in a company that had to cope continually anew with rapidly changing environmental events in order to survive. An inside manager on the other hand might focus almost entirely on the leader, disseminator, entrepreneur, disturbance handler, and resource allocator roles.

The perpetual disturbance handler is certainly different from the intracompany entrepreneur also. The number of different managerial styles that may emerge in response to the nature of managerial jobs is sizable. Whether a given style is appropriate can only be determined on the basis of a close analysis of the nature of the specific job and of the demands of that environment. In any event, the existence of different styles can make for extremely varied policies and strategies, as well as considerable variability in the extent to which policies and strategies are formulated at all. Emphasis on one or the other of the decisional roles can produce marked differences in the extent of planning, for instance.

TABLE 6-1
Ten Managerial Work Roles

ROLE	DESCRIPTION	TYPICAL ACTIVITIES
Interpersonal Roles		
Figurehead	Symbolic head; performs routine duties of a legal or social nature	Ceremony, status requests
Leader	Responsible for motivation of subordinates and for staffing and training	Almost all managerial activities involving subordinates
Liaison	Maintains network of outside contacts to obtain favors and information	Handling mail, external board work, telephone calls
Informational Roles		
Monitor	Seeks and receives information to obtain thorough understanding of organization and environment	Reading periodicals, observational tours
Disseminator	Transmits information received from outsiders or insiders to other organization members	Forwarding mail, review sessions with subordinates
Spokesman	Transmits information to outsiders on organization plans, policies, actions	Board meetings, handling mail
Decisional Roles		
Entrepreneur	Initiates and supervises design of organizational improvement projects as opportunities arise	Strategy and review sessions regarding change efforts
Disturbance handler	Responsible for corrective action when organization faces unexpected crises	Strategy and review sessions regarding disturbances
Resource allocator	Responsible for allocation of human, monetary, and material resources	Scheduling, requests for authorization, budgeting
Negotiator	Responsible for representing the organization in bargaining and negotiations	Collective bargaining, purchasing

SOURCE: Adapted from Henry Mintzberg [1973a:92–93].

INDIVIDUAL MANAGERIAL STYLES

Another approach to the study and analysis of managerial styles focuses less on the nature of managerial work and more on the nature of managers—their behaviors, predispositions, motives, attitudes, and values. This approach tends to yield somewhat different designations and descriptions of alternative styles than the managerial job approach.

Degree of Subordinate Concern

There has been a long history of research and writing in the leadership area that focuses on style variations associated with such terms as considerate, structuring, autocratic, democratic, laissez-faire, and the like [Miner, 1973a]. What these terms have in common is an emphasis on differences in the extent to which managers utilize styles that involve subordinates in the decision-sharing process and exhibit concern for subordinates as individuals. Style variations of this kind continue to provide a major area of study and to yield a wide range of research findings [Fleishman and Hunt, 1973; Hunt and Larson, 1974].

Attempts to synthesize this research abound. Thus, Hall, O'Leary, and Williams [1964] utilize concern for subordinate commitment and concern for decision adequacy to identify five prototype styles—eye-to-eye (commitment and adequacy of concern), good neighbor (commitment but not adequacy of concern), self-sufficient (adequacy but not commitment of concern), default (neither commitment nor adequacy of concern), and traditional (both commitment and adequacy of intermediate concern). Bowers and Seashore [1966] expand the number of underlying dimensions from two to four (support, interaction facilitation, goal emphasis, and work facilitation), and accordingly, introduce the possibility of a much more complex array of styles. What characterizes these efforts is a much greater concern with style variations from manager to manager than within the same manager from time to time. Also, there has been relatively little direct application to policy formulation and implementation. In recent years there has been some change in both of these situations, however.

Conditions for Sharing Decisions

It has become increasingly evident that managers do not stick entirely to one style, although because of personal predisposition or environmental pressures a particular style may predominate in their behavior. This viewpoint was expressed some years ago by Tannenbaum and Schmidt [1958], although empirical support has come much more recently. Basically Tannenbaum and Schmidt proposed a continuum of leadership behaviors:

1. Manager makes decision and announces it.
2. Manager sells decision.
3. Manager presents ideas and invites questions.
4. Manager presents tentative decision subject to change.
5. Manager presents problem, gets suggestions, makes decision.
6. Manager defines limits; asks group to make decision.
7. Manager permits subordinates to function within limits defined by superior.

Which of these approaches is taken is said to depend on

1. Forces in the manager including his value system, confidence in his subordinates, leadership inclinations, and feelings of security in an uncertain situation.
2. Forces in the subordinates including their need for independence, readiness to assume responsibility, tolerance for ambiguity, interest in the problem, identification with the goals of the organization, knowledge, and expectation of decision sharing.
3. Forces in the situation, including the type of organization, the effectiveness of the group, the nature of the problem and the pressure of time.

Research conducted since and elaborated in Chapter 12, indicates that variations in styles of the types indicated do occur within the repertory of a single manager as well as from individual to individual. Furthermore, a number of the forces discussed by Tannenbaum and Schmidt [1958] have been shown to condition the adoption of a particular approach [Heller, 1971; Vroom and Yetton, 1973; Vroom and Jago, 1974].

Leadership Style at the Policy Level

Increasingly, information is being developed on variations in styles of top level executives, especially the chief executive officer. One factor associated with the extent of decision sharing at the top appears to be the degree to which the company is involved in intense competition, and product competition in particular [Khandwalla, 1973a]. Where there is a great deal of competition the chief executive tends to delegate and share decisions more in areas such as raising long-term capital, selection of new investments, acquisition of subsidiaries, research and development, new product development, marketing strategy, pricing, top management staffing, and policy change. But it is also true that under highly competitive conditions this decision sharing is much more selective; some types of decisions are delegated and some are not depending on the circumstances involved.

However, it appears that where a company faces intense competition in its environment, the chief executive not only utilizes a more participative style in decision making but also introduces more controls to be sure the delegated decisions are made and carried out responsibly. Thus, where competition is high, one finds more use of statistical quality control in production, standard costs and cost variance analysis, use of operations research techniques in inventory control and production scheduling, flexible budgeting, investment evaluation by internal rate of return or present value methods, marginal costing for pricing and purchasing decisions, internal auditing, performance (operational) auditing, and systematic evaluation of managerial and senior staff personnel. In fact the tendency to use these controls when the competition gets heavy is even more pronounced than the tendency to delegate; and once again the use of the approach tends to be highly selective from one control to another depending on the situation.

Descriptions of individual chief executives make it apparent that sizable differences in style exists [Argyris, 1973a; Neuschel, 1969]. Yet these differences may be entirely appropriate to the external and internal environments with which an executive must cope. Both of the presidents described in Table 6-2 head profitable companies in spite of their very different styles and approaches to policy formation and implementation. Thus, their styles do appear to fit the needs introduced by the nature of company product lines, subordinate competence levels, organizational life cycle position, and the like.

Effective and Ineffective Styles

Although those writing about style variations associated with the degree of subordinate concern have generally favored greater participation in decision

TABLE 6-2
Descriptions of the Styles of Two Presidents

President Number 1
(45 years old; the company has sales of $225 million, has multiple products, and is divisionally organized)

Sparks subordinates by questioning mind, youthful energy, ideas, and efforts to stretch them.
Pushes executives to set high standards; is a tough evaluator and will replace mediocrity.
Decisions are fact-based and are made after discussions with subordinates.
Use of authority is reasonably permissive within limits of achievement goals; authority is more implied than used.
Seeks change, pushes for it, and is thorough in programming to carry it out.
Is deeply involved in planning, goal setting, and evaluation against targets, with the result that he has a good understanding of each business and has close, frequent contact with each key executive.

President Number 2
(53 years old; the company has sales of $325 million, has a single product, and is functionally organized)

Drives others by the sharpness and toughness of his thinking; he is respected but not held in affection.
Is highly demanding, critical, and imposes his own standards; becomes emotional over difficult people decisions and will by-pass but not fire the mediocre performer.
Makes decisions based heavily on intuition and long experience, which involve relatively little consultation with subordinates and which are held too steadfastly.
Is highly authoritarian, positive in point of view, and imposes decisions with force.
Although intellectually prepared for change, is fearful of it because of anticipation of mistakes and concern over organizational readiness.
In spite of efforts to delegate, maintains over-the-shoulder control; holds onto operations, although much thought is given to strategy.

SOURCE: Adapted from Robert P. Neuschel [1969:22].

making, delegation, and consideration for the needs of subordinates, the evidence does not indicate that such managerial styles invariably produce the best results [Miner, 1973a, 1974a]: that, clearly, is contingent on the situation.

On the other hand, certain categorizations of styles have been developed for the express purpose of contrasting one or more effective styles with certain characteristically ineffective ones. Thus, authoritarian and democratic leadership has been contrasted with a laissez-faire approach, where the manager essentially does nothing unless his subordinates ask him to. Bower [1966] has contrasted his programmed approach, where there is a will to manage an ongoing system, with *ad hoc* management, day-to-day management, piecemeal management, personal management, personal power management, and one-man management. All of the latter are described as "amorphous or mushy. They lack principle. They are indefinite and unclear. They are unfair to able people" [Bower, 1966: 12].

Another approach is set forth in Figure 6-1. Here the reconciler is viewed as exhibiting the most effective style, although the other styles may be reasonably appropriate in certain situations.

ORGANIZATIONAL STYLES

When managerial styles coalesce into a meaningful pattern at the upper levels of an organization, it is possible to speak of an organizational style. Not all organizations possess sufficient integration of managerial styles to specify *an* organizational style, although where there has been an extended history of interaction among a reasonably stable group of managers, some semblance of a characteristic style usually does develop. Beyond this, however, the nature, the degree of integration, and the extent of fit with organizational demands can vary tremendously from one company to another.

Variations in Organizational Style

The underpinning of an organizational style is some type of organizational ideology, value structure, or climate. Among the functions thus performed are [Harrison, 1972]:

1. Specifying goals and values toward which effort should be directed and by which success and growth should be measured.
2. Prescribing the social contract between individual and organization—what each is and is not supposed to do.
3. Indicating how control should be exercised over behavior—what is and is not legitimate.
4. Establishing which qualities and characteristics of people should be valued or rewarded and which should not.

THE OPPORTUNIST
Vacillates between idealism and realism in operating style.
Ignores or denies inconsistencies or hypocrisies in his behavior.
Compromises conflict which should be resolved
Has no strong affinity to either idealism or realism as the base of his behavior.
Seeks to reduce pressures.

THE REALIST
Reacts to the problem.
Is an autocrat; relies on the authority of power.
Yields to experience.
Is an artful practitioner of his specialty.
Is priority-oriented.
Is intuitive in his judgments.
Strives for optimal performance.
Employs resources.
Cuts the problem down to manageable size.
Is practical.
Reaches decisions quickly regardless of the information available.
Assumes the fact of resource scarcity and works around it.
Pursues attainable, tangible goals.
Seeks immediate results.

Style of Use of Cognitive Resources

Integrity of combined style

THE IDEALIST
Reflects on the problem.
Is a technocrat; relies on the authority of fact.
Sticks to principles.
Is a skilled technician.
Is process- and method-oriented.
Is systematic and rational in his judgments.
Strives for professional performance.
Creates resources.
Attacks the total problem.
Is theoretical.
Defers decisions until the information available is sufficient to support them.
Assumes that critical or scarce resources should be made plentiful and works to create them.
Sets the ideal as his goal.
Seeks high quality results.

THE RECONCILER
Accepts and works to integrate the contradictory traits of idealism and realism.
Can apply idealistic, realistic, or combined perspectives as the problem demands without gross inconsistencies.
Chooses subordinates in terms of the need for realistic or idealistic temperament based on the business situation.
Seeks balanced short- and long-range results.
Is the rarest managerial temperament of all.

Figure 6-1 Polarities of managerial temperament. [From Glenn A. Bassett: "The Qualifications of a Manager," *California Management Review,* Winter 1969, p. 38.]

5. Designating how people in the organization should treat each other—competitively, honestly, distantly, and so on.
6. Providing guides to appropriate methods for dealing with the external environment.

One typology of organizational styles based on variations in these factors is given in Table 6-3. The four alternative styles described are [Harrison, 1972]:

TABLE 6-3
Four Different Organizational Styles

A. INTERESTS OF PEOPLE

	SECURITY AGAINST ECONOMIC, POLITICAL, AND PSYCHOLOGICAL DEPRIVATION	OPPORTUNITIES FOR VOLUNTARY COMMITMENT TO WORTHWHILE GOALS	OPPORTUNITIES TO PURSUE ONE'S OWN GROWTH AND DEVELOPMENT INDEPENDENT OF ORGANIZATION GOALS
Power orientation	Low: At the pleasure of the autocrat	Low: Unless one is in a sufficiently high position to determine organization goals	Low: Unless one is in a sufficiently high position to determine organization goals
Role orientation	High: Secured by law, custom, and procedure	Low: Even if, at times, one is in a high position	Low: Organization goals are relatively rigid and activities are closely prescribed
Task orientation	Moderate: Psychological deprivation can occur when an individual's contributions are redundant	High: A major basis of the individual's relationship to the organization	Low: The individual should not be in the organization if he does not subscribe to some of its goals
Person orientation	High: The individual's welfare is the major concern	High: But only if the individual is capable of generating his own goals	High: Organization goals are determined by individual needs

B. INTERESTS OF THE ORGANIZATION

	EFFECTIVE RESPONSE TO DANGEROUS, THREATENING ENVIRONMENTS	DEALING RAPIDLY AND EFFECTIVELY WITH ENVIRONMENTAL COMPLEXITY AND CHANGE	INTERNAL INTEGRATION AND COORDINATION OF EFFORT—IF NECESSARY, AT THE EXPENSE OF INDIVIDUAL NEEDS
Power orientation	High: The organization tends to be perpetually ready for a fight	Moderate to low: Depends on size, pyramidal communication channels are easily overloaded	High: Effective control emanates from the top
Role orientation	Moderate to low: The organization is slow to mobilize to meet increases in threat	Low: Slow to change programmed procedures, communication channels are easily overloaded	High: Features a carefully planned rational system of work

TABLE 6-3—Continued

	EFFECTIVE RESPONSE TO DANGEROUS, THREATENING ENVIRONMENTS	DEALING RAPIDLY AND EFFECTIVELY WITH ENVIRONMENTAL COMPLEXITY AND CHANGE	INTERNAL INTEGRATION AND COORDINATION OF EFFORT—IF NECESSARY, AT THE EXPENSE OF INDIVIDUAL NEEDS
Task orientation	Moderate to high: The organization may be slow to make decisions but produces highly competent responses	High: Flexible assignment of resources and short communication channels facilitate adaptation	Moderate: Integrated by common goal, but flexible, shifting structure may make coordination difficult
Person orientation	Low: The organization is slow to become aware of threat and slow to mobilize effort against it	High: But response is erratic, assignment of resources to problem depends greatly on individual needs and interests	Low: A common goal is difficult to achieve and activities may shift with individual interests

SOURCE: ROGER HARRISON [1972:127].

1. *Power Orientation.* Such an organization attempts to dominate and control its environment. It makes every effort to avoid control by external law or power, and within the organization those who have power strive to use it.
2. *Role Orientation.* Such an organization attempts to be as rational and orderly as possible. The major concern is with legality, legitimacy, and responsibility.
3. *Task Orientation.* Such an organization devotes its energies to achieving a superordinate goal. The crucial consideration is that structure, functions, and activities are all evaluated in terms of contribution to some such goal—as for instance, profit.
4. *Person Orientation.* Such an organization exists almost entirely to serve the needs of its members. Person oriented organizations are evaluated as tools by their members. As a result, many have a short life because they outlive their usefulness to members.

It is apparent that different organizational styles among those proposed are differentially effective in alternative internal and external environments.

Another approach to the organizational style issue focuses entirely on alternative publics [Reimann, 1974]. For certain companies certain publics are more important and/or evaluated more positively than others. Large firms tend to view the national government and the local community relatively negatively as compared with small firms. Creditors are viewed more favorably by independent firms than in branch or subsidiary operations. Labor unions are consistently evaluated negatively. Clearly there is a great variation from firm to firm in the way that the top management group views and values different reference groups in the environment.

Similarly there are differences in those aspects of the firm's managers that are valued and then become part of the organization's style. The following are examples of valued characteristics in different firms:

1. A consulting firm [Miner, 1968a]
   - Emotional control
   - Desire to be with people
   - Low interest in implementation
   - Desire to be at the center of things
2. A bank devoted to growth [Miner, 1968a]
   - Youth
   - Noncomformity
   - Self-confidence
   - Dedication to problem solving
3. A department store [Miner, 1965]
   - Desire to compete
   - Desire to exercise power
   - Sense of responsibility
4. A large oil company [Miner, 1965]
   - Positive attitudes toward authority
   - Desire to compete
   - Desire to exercise power
   - Assertiveness
   - Desire to be at the center of things
5. A large city school district [Miner, 1967; 1968b]
   - Desire to compete
   - Assertiveness
   - Desire to be at the center of things

Not only do these organizations differ in the organizational style exhibited, but there also appear to be environmentally relevant differences—power motivation is not a consideration in the school district, where external power sources leave the administrators relatively powerless; problem solving is important in the growth-oriented bank; interaction with people is important in the client-oriented consulting firm, and so on. Data such as these suggest that forces in the environment do play an important role in molding organizational style.

The Office of the President

An approach to top level policy formation that relies heavily on an integrated organizational style is the office of the president or office of the chairman. Such an office may be described as follows:

The executives who formerly reported to the chairman or president personally now report to the office of the chairman as an entity. Plans and decisions that formerly were channeled only to the chairman and the president (and their assistants) now can be acted on by one to four more top men, each of whom is formally authorized to act for the office of the chairman. Within individual limits, each member of the office is free to make a decision that binds the entire corporation [Bagley, 1975: 104–105].

The objectives are to provide a greater total amount of work time for top level executives, to permit more time to be devoted to external affairs, to facilitate planning and to provide an expanded breadth of expertise. As companies become larger and larger the difficulty of getting decisions made or approved by one person increases. The office of the president is one way to speed up the decision process and provide organizational flexibility.

The actual forms that top level offices of this kind take vary considerably from company to company [Vance, 1972]. It is not always true that all members are completely coequal or that all can make decisions in all areas. The size typically varies from two to five people with the most common number being three. Individual company experience with the approach has also varied considerably; a number of firms have abandoned it whereas others have continued to use it effectively for a number of years. The absolutely crucial ingredient appears to be that an integrated organizational style exist so that members are able to predict each other's behavior and can in fact stand in for one another.

As Steinmetz and Greenidge [1970:31] have pointed out, the upper levels of management are likely to contain "ascendent-oriented people, who can be trusted to follow their own lead and work toward organizational goals." People of this kind are essential to the effective functioning of a collegial unit such as the office of the president. Since such people are more likely to be found at or near the top of most companies, the prospects for success when an office of the president is introduced tend to be good. However, the lack of an integrated organizational style can make these favorable prospects worthless. Without the constraints and unifying guidance provided by a consistent organizational style the probability that internal conflicts will blunt the potential effectiveness of a top level group are very high indeed [McDonald, 1972].

ORGANIZATIONAL LIFE CYCLES

The idea of an organizational life cycle and the view that there are significant stages of corporate development has been strongly influenced by Alfred Chandler's book *Strategy and Structure* [1962]. It is becoming increasingly clear that the strategies a company uses are influenced by its position in a developmental sequence, and that the appropriate managerial and organizational styles, the styles best suited to the current environment, also vary with the stage of development. In particular, companies at different stages face different competitive conditions in their markets and require different approaches to deal with them.

The Three-Stage Model

One widely utilized view of the developmental sequence represents company evolution as progressing from small to integrated to diversified; there is no implication that companies in the second stage need be any smaller than those in the third [Scott, 1973; Thain, 1969; Tuason, 1973]. The three stages are described in Table 6-4.

The basic theory is that as companies grow many tend eventually to resort to a diversified product mix as a protection against the vulnerability inherent in operating within a single industry. The development of the multiproduct strategy foreshadows the move to a diversified, decentralized structure based on product divisions. However, some firms continue to grow while remaining almost entirely within a single industry. Typically, these stage II firms have adopted a strategy of attempting to protect themselves by dominating their industries and to the extent possible controlling their markets. However, data indicate that firms moving on to stage III are more profitable by almost any criterion of economic effectiveness [Scott, 1973].

Companies at different stages of evolution tend to elicit different managerial and organizational styles. Often this means that those who have led the company at one stage may not be able to do so effectively at another; the probability that they will be replaced is high. In stage I a company requires a single guiding executive who basically operates a "one-man show." Such people tend to be rather authoritarian, to emphasize short term thinking, and to have an operating orientation. They will be considered in greater detail in Chapter 17 on entrepreneurship.

At stage II a group of managers with functionally specialized duties replaces the entrepreneur. Thus, there is a requirement that the chief executive be able to work with other members of the management team and utilize their talents effectively. Otherwise, the additional overhead for salaries will yield no benefits to the company. Clearly a managerial style change is called for.

The move into stage III may be through internal development of new products or by acquisition. In any event the move to a divisionalized structure calls for a general office that maintains more or less loose-reign control over operating units while stressing overall corporate planning. Thus, "the key skills necessary to be an outstanding general manager . . . shift from short-term operating ability in stage I to product-functional emphases in stage II and broad management abilities in investment trusteeship, diversification, and management supervision and development in stage III" [Thain, 1969:433]. It is not surprising that relatively few managers can transform their styles to meet all these varied requirements and thus to develop the various types of strategies their companies require. Yet if they do not change and are not re-

TABLE 6-4
Corporate Life Cycles: Three Stages and Company Characteristics

	STAGES IN CORPORATE LIFE CYCLE		
COMPANY CHARACTERISTICS	STAGE I COMPANY (OR SMALL COMPANY)	STAGE II COMPANY (OR INTEGRATED COMPANY)	STAGE III COMPANY (OR DIVERSIFIED COMPANY)
1. Product line	Single product or single product line	Single product line	Multiple product lines
2. Distribution pipeline	One channel or set of channels	One set of channels	Multiple channels
3. Organization structure	Little formal structure; one-man show	Specialization based on functional areas	Specialization based on market-product relationships
4. Intracompany product/service transactions	No pattern of intracompany transactions	Integrated intracompany transactions	Nonintegrated, pattern of transactions
5. R & D organization process	Not institutionalized; guided by owner-manager	Institutionalized search of product or process improvements	Institutionalized search for new products as well as for improvements
6. Performance measurements	By personal contact and subjective criteria	Increasingly impersonal, using technical/cost criteria	Increasingly impersonal, using market criteria (ROI, market share)
7. Rewards	Unsystematic and often paternalistic	Systematic with emphasis on stability and service	Systematic with variability related to performance
8. Control system	Personal control of strategic decisions	Personal control of strategic decisions	Indirect control based on analysis of "results"
9. Operating decisions	Personal control of operating decisions	Increasing delegation of operating decisions through policy	Delegation of market-product decisions within existing businesses
10. Strategic choices	Needs of owner versus needs of company	Degree of integration, market share objective; breadth of product line	Entry and exit from industries; allocation of resources by industry; rate of growth

SOURCE: Ramon V. Tuason [1973:37] as adapted from B. R. Scott [1973:137].

placed, the probability of company failure at the transition points from stage to stage is high [Clifford, 1973b].

Supplementary and Alternative Models

A number of writers have suggested stages supplementary to those of the three-stage model. Thus, Thain [1969] notes that stage IV may be a coalescing of major companies with government to formulate and implement national economic policy. Steinmetz [1969] stretches the three-stage model and proposes four stages to cover the same growth period—direct supervision, supervised supervisor, indirect control, and divisional organization. His concern is primarily with sources and methods of control; thus he focuses directly on the need for changes in style at various stages of small business growth. Greiner [1972] moves one step further to five stages, each with its own management style to achieve growth—an emphasis on creativity, direction, delegation, coordination, and finally collaboration. Between each stage, and thus precipitating each style change, a particular crisis is posited. These crises involve first leadership, then autonomy, then control, and finally red tape. Except for his stage V which involves a matrix of teams, a participative style and mutual goal setting, Greiner covers much the same ground as does the three-stage model. Whether stage V is in fact an evolutionary result or a desired alternative remains an open question at present; few if any examples exist.

Although varying in specifics, all of these models emphasize the style and strategy changes associated with growth and the problems resulting from these changes. A somewhat different concept of the corporate life cycle developed by James [1973] focuses more on the problems faced at each phase of evolution and also introduces the matter of decline. There are five stages as follows:

1. *Emergence.* There is almost invariably a shortage of liquid cash, a need to create consumer demand, and a need to expand production to meet this demand. Administrative processes are loosely defined and a flexible use of labor reduces dependence on more costly specialized personnel.
2. *Growth.* A point is reached where major refinancing becomes necessary and there may be some acquisitions as well. Extensions are made to the basic product line and overseas markets are evaluated. At the same time as new plants and machinery are purchased, control systems are strengthened and formal personnel policies instituted.
3. *Maturity.* Initially investments produce high returns, but over time higher unit production costs and overheads cut in. There is a tendency to become very conservative in marketing and to sacrifice opportunities. Unit production costs are increasingly affected by declining economies of scale and obsolescence of equipment. Conformity rather than individuality are rewarded and labor problems increase.
4. *Regeneration.* If regeneration occurs, it may be internal or external. Internally a company may divest itself of unprofitable subsidiaries, sell off assets, resort to rigid cost cutting, reduce labor use, and close some production lines. There is an attempt to reverse the decline in sales and profits of existing products and introduce new, profitable products. External regeneration may involve sacrificing a controlling interest, merger, being completely acquired, or government assistance.
5. *Decline.* As internal reserves are depleted, external financing becomes

> more difficult. The company is selling products that few want at excessive prices. Equipment becomes obsolete, production costs skyrocket, key personnel leave, and labor becomes increasingly militant.

Complete decline into liquidation is rare for the larger companies now, but in many cases external regeneration produces essentially the same result because the company does in fact lose its identity.

The Matter of Decline

Although the basic three-stage model does not concern itself with the final stages of the organizational life cycle, this latter period has been a matter of considerable discussion. Certain writers have argued that decline is not a basic characteristic of organizations, and that they typically tend to revive themselves by bringing in resources of a human, financial, and material nature from the environment, thus producing a state of negative entropy [Katz and Kahn, 1966]. Thus, it can be said that organizations lack the definite life cycle that their biological members possess [Rhenman, 1973].

Yet companies do decline and they do die, and experienced managers are characteristically concerned with warding off what they regard as the realistic possibility that this might happen. Their concern is entirely justified. An analysis carried out by the editors of *Forbes* [1967] reveals that of the top 20 companies in 1917 only 7 remained in that grouping 50 years later. Of the top 100, 43 dropped off the list and 28 of these disappeared entirely, either by merger or liquidation. Midvale Steel and Ordinance was number 8 in 1917, Cambria Steel was number 22, Central Leather number 24, Chile Copper number 29, Lehigh Coal and Navigation number 67, and so on. None exist today. Furthermore, a charting of the prior performance of companies that merge indicates that the great majority of the firms that have been taken over have been in a period of serious decline for some time [Vance, 1971].

Decline and death appear to be associated almost entirely with managerial failures [Editors of *Forbes*, 1967; Richards, 1973]. There is evidence that companies that decline and die tend to become involved in risks of such magnitude that alternative strategies are precluded. "Strategic decisions were undertaken for relatively large-scale activities even though potentially unsatisfactory performance would jeopardize the future viability of the complete enterprise" [Richards, 1973:42]. Overoptimism in forecasts was prevalent and contrary information tended to be suppressed, with the result that decisions were characterized more by dogmatism than rationality. Clearly the presence of managerial and organizational styles that were inappropriate to the demands of the environment and generated excessively risky strategies were crucial for failure.

Although organizations may not face inevitable decline, in the manner of human beings, since they can revitalize themselves by taking in new members, regeneration and protection against decline are not automatic processes. They require active intervention.

THE KEY ROLE OF PLANNING

The key requirement for coping with problems of decline just as with those of growth is that there be appropriate planning and effective implementation of these plans. By positioning itself in the corporate life cycle a company can identify upcoming problems and take steps in advance to deal with them.

Planning of this kind has a life cycle of its own [Ringbakk, 1972]. Studies indicate that those firms that do such planning experience better growth and greater profitability, but to achieve this level of sophistication requires from four to six years of prior effort and preparation.

Furthermore, plans cannot focus entirely on financial matters and material resources. It is absolutely essential that what is known about requisite managerial and organizational styles at various stages in the life cycle be built into the planning process. Managerial manpower planning must be carried all the way to the top so that steps can be taken to have the right kind of people available when they are needed. This may be accomplished through planning for some type of management development activity, so that existing managers are transformed to meet the demands of new developmental stages, or through a planned pattern of succession in the management ranks, including the very top.

QUESTIONS

Discussion Guides on Chapter Content

1. How do the management process and managerial working roles approaches to understanding managerial jobs differ?
2. Differentiate between managerial style and organizational style.
3. What is the office of the president idea? How does it work?
4. What are the different models of the corporate life cycle? How do they differ?
5. In what sense can it be argued that organizations are not subject to decline and death in the manner of human beings?

Mind Stretching Questions

1. Imagine yourself as the chief executive of a large corporation in a highly competitive industry and describe in detail the managerial style you would adopt. Why would you adopt this particular style?
2. In marketing it is common practice to speak of a product life cycle. Is this the same thing as an organizational life cycle? What is the relationship between the two? To what degree and in what way might each relate to organizational style?

Profiles of Chief Executive Officers

A. The Chief Executive Officer: Personal Management Styles*

There are thousands of corporations in the U.S., and no two are managed exactly alike. Each company has its own strengths and weaknesses, and each chief executive officer brings his own background and temperament to the job. The chief executives profiled here were picked because they represent markedly different ways of running a large company.

XEROX'S McCOLOUGH: ACTIVE IN POLITICS AND PUBLIC SERVICE

"The ceremonial role is very important for the chief executive officer in a large company," says C. Peter McColough, the 51-year-old chairman and CEO of Xerox Corp. "I think your major role is to be seen."

McColough manages Xerox so that he has to spend only half his time at the company's headquarters in Stamford, Conn. He spends the rest of his time visiting Xerox facilities in the U.S. and abroad and taking a more active role in politics (he is treasurer of the Democratic National Committee) and public service than does the typical CEO. "A company's reputation," he says, "good or bad, is made not only by the quality of its products and services but also by its people, especially its top people."

McColough acknowledges that he employs a fairly loose rein in running his $3-billion company. "I don't believe in abdicating," he insists, "but I've tried, I think successfully, to decentralize decision-making."

His Preserves

Yet McColough is still the boss, decentralized decision-making or not. "If something bothers me," he says, "I don't rely on the reports or what other top executives may want to tell me. I'll go down very deep into the organization,

* Reprinted from May 4, 1974 issue of *Business Week* (pp. 43–51) by special permission.

into certain issues and certain levels of people, so I have a feel for what they think."

He gets very deeply involved in the "important decisions that are really critical to the business." One such decision involved Xerox' move into computers five years ago through the purchase of Scientific Data Systems. "That was my decision, really," McColough recalls. "The basic decision and basic studies were done under my direction."

McColough also zeroes in on what he calls "sensitive decisions." In this category he includes anything that Xerox sends to the public and how the company treats its employees. He has always insisted, for example, that Xerox people at all levels travel first-class when on company business. "Some of my executives say that's a very small decision I ought not to be making," he explains, "but I do. That's my own management style."

And he reserves a veto power over the dismissal of any employee who has worked for Xerox for eight years or longer. "The case for dismissal must come to my office and obtain my written concurrence," he says emphatically. "I have a lot of opposition in the company on that procedure, but I don't care whether they like it or not. I believe in democracy—up to a point.

Reading Reports

Paperwork irritates McColough. "I refuse to let my day be run by letters and memos from other people in the company," he says. "I go through those pretty damn fast." Reports get much the same treatment. "I don't pay a lot of attention to them," he admits, "because I came that route. I know what a salesman can say. I also know that before I see them they go through 15 hands, and I know what they do to them."

McColough is a restless man with enormous reserves of nervous energy. Even when he is in Stamford, he spends one day a week in Manhattan, meeting with Xerox people and with people important to the company. He reckons that foreign travel alone amounts to "a couple of months a year."

He serves on only one outside board—First National City Corp., the company's lead bank. "I prefer to spend my time on charitable and political things," he says. In addition to his work with the Democrats, he is 1974 campaign chairman for the National Urban League. Moreover, he sees value to Xerox in all these activities. "A company like Xerox can't live in a stockade," he says. "I've spent more and more time on things that might affect society here and abroad because I think they affect Xerox and all our lives."

NORTHROP'S JONES: EASY COMMUNICATION AT ALL LEVELS

Thomas V. Jones, chairman and president of Northrop Corp., was a Rand Corp. planner in the 1950s when he visited the headquarters of the Strategic

Air Command. He was astonished to find that behind SAC's legendary tight discipline and high efficiency was an informal communications system.

"I was amazed at how relaxed things were," he recalls. "A sergeant could tell an officer exactly what he felt. There was cross-communication between officers." Discipline was tight, but it was largely a self-imposed discipline by people involved in their jobs and intensely proud of their organization.

That is precisely how Jones, a 53-year-old aeronouatical engineer, has tried to run things in the 15 years he has been CEO of Los Angeles-based Northrop. He shuns formalized reporting channels, encourages easy communication across managerial levels, and gets personally involved in every phase of his company's operations. The feeling he tries to stress at Northrop is that "everybody is safe in his job, there are no threats, everyone knows his responsibilities, so there is freedom of conversation. A match factory can afford to have barriers between people, but we can't." Northrop managers, says Jones, know they get "Brownie points for understanding, not for fighting, each other."

The result has been a consistently profitable aerospace company. It is best known for its fighter planes, but it also makes the fuselage for the Boeing 747 jumbo jet as well as communications and electronics gear.

Communicating

Unlike the CEO who believes in "picking a good man, standing back, and letting him do the job," says Jones, "I refuse to turn my back." He thinks that a highly involved CEO is good for company morale. And he feels that the weight of his office helps him solve problems quickly. If Northrop gets a new machine that proves costlier to operate than expected, Jones explains, "I go straight to the guys who are running it to find out why." When he learned recently of what appeared to be an unhealthy rivalry developing between two Northrop units, Jones immediately placed a conference call to the two unit heads and spent half an hour explaining that internal competition should be friendly.

Such "squawk-box meetings," as he calls them, are a basic Jones tool for dealing quickly with emerging problems and opportunities. With typical disregard for reporting channels, Jones will grab his phone, "loop" in four or five managers, and ask them to watch an evolving situation, keeping in touch with each other through frequent conference calls. The same uninhibited air pervades Northrop's home office. Its new headquarters, which Jones helped lay out, has open space and glass panels between offices.

Looking Ahead

Because of the long lead-time for Northrop's products, Jones puts heavy emphasis on planning. Once a year he and other Northrop executives discuss the 5- to 10-year outlook for the world economy and the mood in customer countries. This planning body is an ad hoc group whose membership changes from year to year and cuts across managerial levels, including anyone with something to contribute. "I don't believe in a formalized planning group," Jones explains.

The planners draw up "fundamental guidelines" on the political, military, and economic situation in the world and individual nations. These guidelines are circulated throughout Northrop to get employees thinking about basic trends and how they may affect the company's products and marketing efforts. "The trick is to make everyone in the company aware," Jones says.

Says Jones: "My antennae are always tuned to planning. I always fear that the company might head into a dead end."

CONNECTICUT GENERAL'S ROBERTS: A LOOSER GRIP ON LINE OPERATIONS

The average chief executive officer does not stay on the job for 12 years, but 59-year-old Henry R. Roberts has been running Connecticut General Insurance Corp. for that long. Indeed, after nearly a dozen years on top of the nation's eighth largest insurance company, Roberts turned CG's management structure completely around last year, changing the nature of his own job in the process. His Management Process Project reorganized CG along decentralized profit-center lines that are more typical of a manufacturing company than a financial services company.

The change did not come because CG was in trouble. In his 12 years, Roberts has pushed assets from $2.6-billion to $8-billion and profits from $16.6-million to $134-million. Still, Robert thought the old ways had become too stifling. "It's a little difficult," he says, "when you've seen yourselves as leaders to set the dial to zero again and say, 'O.K., now, what's wrong with everything we've been doing?' We've been doing a lot of that in the past year."

Robert's own job has changed in both structure and philosophy. For instance, today he concentrates on the decision-making at the top and delegates more. "I find myself leaving people freer," he says. "I'm following people less into their operations—which is hard for me to do because I'm fascinated by that."

Final Authority

That change in approach shows up in a lot of ways. Roberts has loosened his grip on line operations. "I tend to use the chief line people as sort of a management committee with me," he says. "It's taken a lot of experience for that approach to shake out as not entirely realistic. I can't ask those officers collectively to make tough decisions about one another. It isn't fair. I have to make those decisions."

And Roberts spends less time on outside activities than he used to. "On a priority basis," he explains, "keeping the business going and lively and vital ranks higher with me."

Most CEOs have been cutting back on staff jobs in recent years, and, "until recently," Roberts says, "I had always believed in minimal corporate staff. Now I'm beginning to appreciate better that, if it's organized properly and its activities are properly directed, a corporate staff can be extremely valuable. What I need is a good staff to make sure I have the whole picture and know what my options are."

Rivals Aetna Life & Casualty, Hartford Fire Inusrance, and Travelers have each molded their top echelons into a corporate office in which some of the duties of the CEO are divided among other managers. At CG, Roberts says, "The corporate office tends to be me and the corporate staff and, on a consultative and participatory basis, six major senior line officers. The concept of the corporate office per se is tending to strengthen, but it's really me, supported by corporate staff."

To make certain that each manager knows exactly where he fits into the structure, Roberts has taken the intriguing step of entering into contracts with his senior officers. These documents spell out, by mutual agreement, each man's authority and responsibility and what each man expects of the other. They also require Roberts to disclose, at regular intervals, his evaluation of each man's progress.

Interaction

The tall, lean, and balding Roberts may be the top man, but interaction with the people under him still figures importantly in his own management style. "I spend an awful lot of time talking to people about their roles," he says, "about the interrelationships of people within the organization." Roberts describes himself as a strong advocate of "humanics," which he defines as finding a way in which there will be a congruence between individual and corporate purpose." Says Roberts: "The old thesis was that everybody should know exactly what he was responsible for. I don't think that's realistic. We are too dependent upon one another."

In terms of actual managing, Roberts says there is very little he needs to decide on a day-to-day basis. Obviously he will have the final say on a major new commitment or a substantial change in plans, but his senior people make more routine decisions. If there is a question, CG's senior officers use what Robert's calls the "inform for hollering" device. "The officer involved informs me about what he's going to do—unless I holler. That's his way of testing me as to where my sense of that line is and making sure he's in order."

Roberts says that he lets more than half these decisions pass without hollering. The whole technique, he says, "makes it easier for me to do that because he has told me what he proposes to do. He's not asking. That's important. If people ask me what to do, it's going to be done my way."

GENERAL MILLS'S McFARLAND: TRAVELING LIKE MAD TO KEEP IN TOUCH

James P. McFarland sits at the head of a Danish-modern conference table, a collection of water colors and oils perking up the bland, fabric-covered walls of his suburban Minneapolis office. It is a comfortable setting from which to run General Mills, Inc.

But McFarland is restless. After six years as chairman he is in the midst of the second phase of the dramatic change he wrought at the Betty Crocker empire. The first was engineering tremendous growth through diversification that boosted sales from $668-million when he took over to $1.6-billion last year. Now he is meshing the new operations with the old.

To help him do it, two years ago McFarland set up an Office of the Chief Executive, effectively splitting many of his responsibilities with Vice-Chairman James A. Summer and President E. Robert Kinney. The new arrangement enables McFarland to continue what he calls "a more personalized approach to management" by relieving him of many operating details, but he still remains so busy that he has little time for playing his 20-handicap golf.

In setting up the Chief Executive's Office, McFarland is also thinking ahead to his retirement. The setup allows him and the board to appraise the performance of Summer and Kinney, both of whom have a chance at the top spot when McFarland steps down two years from now.

Diversifier

McFarland has taken General Mills, which as recently as the mid-1960s was primarily a flour miller and a maker of breakfast foods and cake mixes, into clothing manufacturing, hobby stores, sporting goods shops, children's games, restaurants, even a jewelry design firm. By two years ago he had slowed the diversification and set new priorities for digesting the businesses General Mills had acquired.

"To undertake a reversal of policy requires a good deal of skill and understanding," McFarland says. "There is no hallowed hall here, and you can't just put a bulletin out."

One way McFarland is tracking his managers' progress is through an elaborate performance monitoring system that he expanded and refined himself. It is basically a computerized financial reporting plan that also allows operating heads to measure their achievements against goals they helped establish.

McFarland receives monthly breakdowns of divisional operations and participates in the long-range planning sessions General Mills holds twice a year. But he says that most of his information and "feel" for the company comes in face-to-face meetings with divisional personnel.

"I try getting out to each operating unit at least once a year," he says, and his travel schedule often finds him on the road three days a week. "You can't run this company from this office."

Key Meetings

In addition, at least one member of the Chief Executive's Office—often McFarland himself—sits down every 10 days with 18 middle managers from the field. Each visitor makes a 10-minute presentation, followed by an open discussion.

Recent meetings have covered such diverse subjects as one division's problems with high employee turnover, profit margins on a product line, corporate responsibility, and the cost of financing growth. "It really keeps us aware of what our people are thinking and what's bothering them," McFarland says. As a result of these meetings, he is currently at work on three new projects.

One of the projects could lead to a whole new management program for General Mills. Divisions operating in a single geographical area do not coordinate their activities, one manager complained, and there is little chance to exchange ideas. So a regional coordinator was sent to Denver as a test. The program could ultimately be used around the country.

Says McFarland: "An intelligent, skilled organization does not follow blindly. Management is the utilization of resources to reach an objective. While you need controls at the top, there must be participation and autonomy as well."

SHELL'S BRIDGES: ADJUSTING TO A MORE VISIBLE ROLE

Harry Bridges fully expected to maintain the customary low profile of major oil company executives when he became president of Shell Oil Co. three years ago. But last fall, amid the public protests focused on the petroleum industry, Bridges found his job requirements had changed so dramatically that he took a two-day J. Walter Thompson Co. course in Chicago learning how to face television cameras, microphones, and aggressive reporters.

"I'm not a natural to appear on the television set or to be publicly interviewed," says Bridges, 58. "But it was a job that suddenly had to be done that you couldn't in all honesty just pass on to someone else."

There was little in Bridges' training to prepare him for his increasingly public role. Like many oil company executives, he started in the exploration side of the business and spent more than 30 years with the Royal Dutch/Shell Group in such places as New Guinea, India, Ecuador, and Canada. That wealth of technical and international experience has proven of little value to Bridges in coping with the grind of government thrust upon him by the energy crisis.

Fast Responses

His new, more visible role has required a radical professional and personal adjustment for Bridges. Keeping up with governmental and public developments affecting Shell and formulating the appropriate reaction consumes one-third of his time now, compared to 5% three years ago.

Thus Bridges spent a weekend early this year personally writing the copy for an advertisement that appeared in 425 U.S. newspapers explaining the company's position on the question of excess profits in the oil industry.

Timing

But Bridges has also had to cope with a major transition within the company itself. When he came to Shell from the top job at Shell Canada, Ltd., in 1970, the U.S. company was trying to develop its skill in foreign petroleum operations. It had become obvious that domestic crude oil, on which Shell was almost totally dependent, was peaking and that foreign sources would have to be tapped.

"In the past you could simply run your business as if it were three separate businesses—exploration-production, manufacturing-transportation-marketing, and petrochemical," Bridges says. "You didn't have to think so much at a corporate level about denying something to A so that B could be pushed a little more rapidly. With so many opportunities open to us now, we have to plan much more from a corporate point of view."

Bridges, for example, gets directly involved in such decisions as the timing of capital outlays for major expansion of refineries. Another Shell department might be competing for the same dollars for research on coal liquefaction or gasification. "You could say it is the role of a kind of referee who says, 'We don't want to go with this project because the timing is wrong.' These decisions occur almost every time we deal with long-range planning," he says.

And some operating matters still get close personal scrutiny from Bridges because they involve such sensitive subjects as pricing changes, or because of the possible economic impact on the company of a decision. "Exploration always takes me through what they intend to bid at offshore lease sales because of the possible commitment they are exposing," says Bridges, adding that $600-million might be exposed at a single sale. "I generally bless the plans."

B. Young Top Management: The New Goals, Rewards, Life Styles*

RICHARD S. RAVENSCROFT, PRESIDENT OF PHILADELPHIA NATIONAL CORP.: A BANKING INTELLECTUAL WHO 'RAMRODS THINGS THROUGH'

In an organization where the early morning talk over coffee generally revolves around last night's Phillies' baseball score or the skills of the Philadelphia Flyers hockey team, Richard S. Ravenscroft stands a bit apart. The 36-year-old president of Philadelphia National Corp., parent of the $4-billion Philadelphia National Bank, is more likely to be in his office, earphones on his head, listening to softly played classical music while he thinks about interest rates or the effect of regulation on the future of bank holding companies.

Ravenscroft earns $89,718 a year as the youngest president of a bank holding company in the U.S., and he is a fascinating study in contrasts. He is very much the bookish, pipe-smoking intellectual—whose quick mind frequently leaves co-workers miles behind—in an industry that is not much known for intellectual managers. He came to the bank 15 years ago, fresh out of Yale. But his college major was Amercian studies, not business, though he has since taken finance courses at the Wharton School. He lives on Philadelphia's Main Line but in a house that is decidedly modest. He shuns such traditional sports as golf for cycling on his 10-speed bike, and jogging.

But Ravenscroft has pushed hard since he joined PNB in 1960 to help launch Philadelphia Internation Investment Corp., an Edge Act subsidiary set up to invest in foreign banks and industrial companies. By 1966 he was president of PIIC, and in early 1974 he was named president of Philadelphia National Corp. "The corporation was always two steps ahead of me in new assignments and responsibilities," says Ravenscroft. "I was like a greyhound chasing a rabbit."

He has been and continues to be a brusque and demanding manager, pushing authority far down the chain of command and leaving it to lower level managers to sell their ideas all the way to the top. Ravenscroft thrived in that sort of environment and expects his subordinates to do so today.

Nowadays, Ravenscroft is busy trying to expand the holding company's nonbanking business and to cut the losses of the businesses it is already in, including an assortment of ailing mortgage and consumer finance companies and a factoring firm. Last year PNB earned $26.8 million over-all, but lost $1.1 million, or 19¢ a share, on its four nonbank subsidiaries.

* Reprinted from October 6, 1975, issue of *Business Week* (pp. 56–68) by special permission. © by McGraw-Hill, Inc.

Forcing Decisions

Ravenscroft's career at the bank was briefly interrupted by a year's stint in government. In 1969, he served as director of the policy division in the Office of Foreign Direct Investments. He returned to the bank in 1970, and under the sponsorship of both departing chairman John McDowell and the new chairman, G. Morris Dorrance, Jr., became executive vice-president with responsibility for the investment division, personnel, public relations, national, and correspondent banking. Last year, a shuffle handed Ravenscroft the presidency of the holding company.

As at most banks, work is often performed by, and credited to, committees rather than individuals, and Ravenscroft seems to accentuate the method. In a deceptively humble way, he constantly speaks in the collective "we" when referring to his own performance. "Ravenscroft never seems to make decisions," says one insider. "He forces decisions on others."

A Close Watcher

Ravenscroft freely admits that he leaves decisions to others. "That's what they're paid for," he says. "I try to give people more than they think they can handle, then watch them very closely."

But Ravenscroft is not always the understanding teacher. "He has no patience for stupidity," says one employee. "If you don't do your homework, he knows. You can't snow him. He even dresses people down publicly." To subordinates, Chairman Dorrance is aloof, Ravenscroft direct and sometimes brutal. "Ravenscroft ramrods things through," says one man.

Casual

Ravenscroft, who works from 8:30 A.M. to 5 P.M., pursues hobbies with the same intensity he shows at the office. A serious amateur photographer, he has shown and sold some of his work. Free time is jealously guarded for his wife and two children, the younger born just last spring. But Ravenscroft still takes home a full briefcase of work, which he reads to music from his eclectic collection of records and tapes.

At the office, Ravenscroft may be hard-driving, but his management still is distinctly casual. He is a bit irreverent about organizational trappings, frequently canceling his weekly staff meetings and dispensing with memos. "I like things to be out in the open," says Ravenscroft. "I'd much rather go see someone in his office. I can see the picture of his new dog, the amount of work on his desk. I like to see people in their lair."

WILFRED J. CORRIGAN, PRESIDENT OF FAIRCHILD CAMERA & INSTRUMENT CORP: 'CREATIVE TENSION' IN A GROWTH COMPANY

Steering his sleek, silver $14,000 Jensen Interceptor into his reserved parking stall at Fairchild Camera & Instrument Corp. in Mountain View, Calif.,

Wilfred J. Corrigan has definitely "arrived." At 37, he is president and chief executive of a $385-million-a-year company, the third largest in the semiconductor industry behind only Texas Instruments, Inc., and Motorola, Inc. With 16,300 employees and 20 manufacturing facilities in four states and seven countries under his tight command, Corrigan claims that this is "a fun-sized company," and for the first time in his fast-paced 15-year career he is comfortable in a job and not edgy about moving on to something "bigger and better."

For one thing, Corrigan is well paid for his 60-hour average work week. His annual salary, bonuses, and fees total $174,384. In addition, there is $58,580 in annual pension contributions and rights to purchase 60,000 shares of Fairchild stock at $18.38 to $28.41 per share. The company's stock has recently been trading at over $50, but Corrigan, who owned 6,250 shares last January, says that in the cyclical electronics industry, executives become blasé about the actual value of their holdings. "We've all felt wealthy at some point," he says.

In the semiconductor industry, salaries and incentives are often dazzling enough to both attract executive talent and keep it. "Once you are through the middle-management level and as your tax base goes up," says Corrigan, "material rewards become less of a driving factor." Far more important to this supremely self-confident chief executive is running a growth company and "managing change."

Keep Moving

Corrigan successfully steered Fairchild through the 1974–75 recession after becoming chief operating officer in 1973 and president in July, 1974. This summer he led the company from making just components to making end products when he announced a Fairchild line of electronic watches, and he has even grander plans for the company over the coming decade. Within those 10 years he expects it to move into the $1-billion class. "Whether a company or a country, you go either forward or backward; there is no way of standing still," he says.

That certainly has been Corrigan's personal and business philosophy. The son of a dockworker in Liverpool, England, Wilf (as he is still known to first- and second-tier Fairchild managers) knew from the age of 10 that he was going to leave England. One summer, between semesters spent earning a chemical engineering degree from the Imperial College of Science in London, Corrigan hitchhiked around the U. S. Favorably impressed, he later accepted a $7,000-a-year job as a product-line engineer in a Boston electronics plant over offers from a chemical plant in Germany and a gunpowder factory in Australia. Today about the only things Corrigan has from England are his Liverpool accent, his two-year-old sports car, and his wardrobe of $400 Savile Row suits.

Corrigan was recruited in 1961 by C. Lester Hogan, then executive vice-president of Motorola, as a junior-level engineer in the company's Phoenix semiconductor division. From his early Motorola days, Corrigan recalls, "I knew I wanted to be president of something." When Hogan resigned in 1968 to become president of Fairchild, seven of his lieutenants—including Corrigan—were quick to follow. Corrigan's title was group director of discrete devices. Says Hogan: "I knew he would be general manager of semiconductor component operations [Fairchild's largest division], but I felt Wilf had to earn his stripes first." Although Corrigan was cocky and occasionally insensitive to people's feelings, Hogan maintains that he had all the attributes of a top executive: "no-nonsense" toughness, stamina, a "mind like a sponge," and the uncanny ability to "always make the right decision." Corrigan became vice-president in charge of semiconductor operations in 1971 and chief operating officer in 1973. "I was grooming him for the top spot from the moment he arrived," says Hogan.

But it was Corrigan who finally took the initiative that actually put him in the presidency. He went over Hogan's head to Fairchild's Walter Burke, former chairman of the company and still president of a foundation that controls 13% of the company's stock, and threatened to resign if he were not named to Hogan's post. He got the job, and Hogan was moved upstairs to vice-chairman.

Stiff Payments

Corrigan's meteoric rise had its price. In 1970, when Fairchild was facing a recession, an internal liquidity crisis, and plunging sales and profits, Corrigan says he was working "literally all the time." He rarely saw his two sons and two daughters (now aged 7 to 13), and his Norwegian wife, Sigrun, was as "uptight" as he was. "When you're a workaholic," Corrigan recalls, "you tend to lose your mental equilibrium and go through periods when you feel persecuted." So Corrigan decided to put into Fairchild "whatever it takes" during the week but to save weekends for his family. With this two-dimensional view of life, Corrigan does not have time for the "trivia" of outside directorships, but he usually does manage to keep his weekend date with the family.

Although his wife has little doubt that work is the most important thing in Wilf's life, and Corrigan concedes that "it probably is," he still enjoys the time he spends at his seven-bedroom $200,000 home, an "English country cottage" in fashionalable Los Altos Hills, Calif., where he takes an occasional swim in his new pool.

At the office, where Corrigan still spends long days, he feels he is adept at delegating authority without abandoning it and at maintaining an efficient and responsive organization. There is a monthly review of the objectives of each of the 11 divisions, each product line, and each individual product, and Corrigan spends fully a quarter of his time in financial and planning reviews. He also devotes considerable attention to listening to customers, distributors, competitors, and lower-level managers. "It's dangerous when you hear just what you want to hear," he says.

A Tough Style

Corrigan has strong feelings about which management techniques work and which do not. One he rejects is "the Noah's Ark philosophy, where there are two managers in every chair." When a company is overly concerned about what happens when an officer leaves and "puts an organizational safety belt on everything," he says, it builds in political pressure and high overhead. "I don't believe in redundancy. We don't carry safety parachutes," he says.

What he does believe in is "creative tension," a state in which workers are under enough pressure to get their jobs done but not so much that it panics them. "I want to create enough tension to keep the adrenalin flowing, but I don't want to overdo it," says Corrigan. Says Vice-President Thomas A. Longo: "Wilf makes sure people don't get comfortable in their jobs."

A half-dozen vice-presidents and other top executives left in various shake-ups and resignations during Corrigan's rise to power, and only one other of "Hogan's heroes" still remains. One former division vice-president was fired without warning at 9:15 one morning and told to be out of Fairchild's headquarters by noon. He claims that Corrigan is not only bright and gutsy but also "very calculating and ambitiously ruthless—he is effective in cutting costs and people, but there is icewater in his veins."

With penetrating eyes, shortish hair combed straight back from his receding hairline, and a somewhat brittle manner, Corrigan does not exude warmth. Another former vice-president suggests that the "hard shell" might be a way Corrigan compensates for his youth. And Hogan thinks Corrigan is mellowing, no longer moving managers in and out as quickly as he was.

Not everyone agrees. In the past seven years there have been five managers of metal oxide semiconductors (MOS) products at Fairchild, and one former executive suggests, "If Corrigan doesn't see results in 18 months, he assumes it must be the guy who's running it rather than the fact that MOS is a long-term investment."

Industry analyst James R. Berdell of the San Francisco brokerage house of Robertson, Colman, Siebel & Weisel agrees that MOS is Fairchild's "Achilles heel" and adds that although Corrigan did well in the recession, "the jury is still out on how effectively he can run the company during an upturn."

Corrigan talks as though he expects a more or less unlimited upturn in his own business, which he grandly calls "the heartland of the universe." He says component companies like his will dominate the watch market and that sales of microprocessors—used in computers, auto and industrial controls, and cash registers—will grow from last year's $45 million to $300 million by 1980. He sees microprocessors being used in products as diverse as voice-activated typewriters and industrial robots. "Integrated circuitry is making possible products Flash Gordon would have ridiculed," says Corrigan. With such an electronic-oriented view of the world, it is no wonder Corrigan is happy in his job. "Why diddle around with things that aren't mainstream?" he asks. "There is no status quo in this business."

JOHN H. BRYAN, JR., PRESIDENT OF CONSOLIDATED FOODS CORP.: TAKING OVER AT NATE CUMMINGS' CONGLOMERATE

In business school, at the University of Virginia, professors accused John H. Bryan, Jr., of not being aggressive enough. Even after graduation, Bryan says, he set no conscious goals for himself. Indeed, since his family is well off, Bryan has never worried about salary and did not even discuss compensation for his present job until after he had taken it.

That may sound like a formula for going nowhere in today's competitive business world, but a year ago the 38-year-old Bryan was promoted from the presidency of Bryan Packing Co., the $160-million West Point (Miss.) meat-packing company founded by his father, to president and chief executive officer of its parent company, the $2.5-billion conglomerate, Consolidated Foods Corp. of Chicago.

The job, which carries a salary of $200,000 plus bonus, would have been a challenge to an executive with twice the experience of Bryan. Although sales have advanced steadily the past few years, earnings have sagged badly, dropping from a lackluster $72 million in the fiscal year ended June 30, 1974, to $50.6 million in fiscal 1975. And waiting in the wings, presumably ready to reassert himself if Bryan should falter, is the 78-year-old Nathan Cummings, Con Foods' founder and still honorary chairman, who until Bryan came along seemed altogether reluctant to let anyone else really manage the company.

"I have made it abundantly clear to him [Cummings] that I feel the charge of running the corporation and will do so," says Bryan. "But there was no point at which I felt compelled to say 'sit down, let's get this straight that I'm running the company.' You just begin doing it."

Early Experience

Already Bryan is refurbishing the troubled conglomerate. He ordered unprofitable operations such as Fuller Brush Co. and a furniture group sold, reorganized Con Foods' toy and home furnishing subsidiaries, and strengthened management controls throughout the company. He also has made a major effort to remake the board. Five outsiders are being added to Con Foods' 15-man board, including Paul W. McCracken, who was chairman of the President's Council of Economic Advisers in the Nixon years.

Despite his relative youth, Bryan had already piled up 16 years of experience in running a sizable company before he came to Consolidated Foods. Although his record was made in the meatpacking company founded by his father, it was impressive enough to catch the attention of the officers and directors of Con Foods, which acquired the company in 1968. That was the year Bryan formally became president of Bryan Packing, though he had been running the company for nine years before that.

"He's calm, deliberate, and has an excellent manner in dealing with people," says Tilden Cummings, a Con Foods' director, retired president of Chicago's Continental Illinois Corp., and no relation to Nathan Cummings. "He's not timid about facing problems."

Most of Bryan's management maturity can be traced back to the unique upbringing he received in his father's business. The oldest of four children, Bryan was born the day his father opened a small slaughtering plant next door to the family home in West Point, Miss., a town of 8,000.

"I grew up with the business, it was my playground," recalls Bryan. "My father was a very driving, determined person who just never suspected I might not be totally interested in the business." Yet Bryan was undecided about what he wanted to do, and after earning an economics degree at Southwestern at Memphis, he refused his father's entreaties to come back and run the store. Instead, he entered the business school at the University of Virginia to buy more time. A year later he gave in, and while finishing work for his MBA degree at Mississippi State University, took over operating control of the company.

"My father seemed instinctively to have confidence in me," says Bryan. "He wouldn't let me have any other office than his. He just left when I came in and got into other businesses."

Reorganizing

Working a 12-hour day that began at 7 A.M., Bryan boosted sales from $18 million when he took over to $160 million when he left last year. When he could not buy the company from other family members who shared in the ownership, he arranged the merger with Con Foods.

Today, Bryan still works 12-hour days. Taking the 7 A. M. train from his suburban Kenilworth, Ill., home, he is in his office by 7:45 and does not arrive home until about 8 P. M., sometimes by train, sometimes by limousine if he has missed the hourly train. He admits he is concerned that he does not spend as much time with his family—his four children range up to 15—as he did in Mississippi.

At home each night, Bryan plans his next day, breaking his activities into categories: what has to be done absolutely that day, and things to keep in mind. "I like to know what's coming up long- and short-term," says Bryan, who combats tension with spates of organizing.

Not surprisingly, Bryan began reorganizing Con Foods in the same meticulous way. At his first board meeting he listed six goals to be accomplished in his first months of office, including a review of the role of the corporate staff and a long-term expense reduction program.

Need for Controls

Bryan has a simple theory of management that involves three characteristics: leadership, financial control, and planning.

"The most important is the leadership aspect, the ability to select, organize, and motivate employees," he says. "You do that by having a genuine respect for people you work with."

Bryan has also installed financial controls and audit procedures the company was conspicuously lacking. "There is great strength in decentralization because of the motivation it fosters," he says. "But businesses are fragile things and you have to know what's going on. When several Con Foods' companies ran into trouble, the need for controls became evident." In the third quarter of fiscal 1975 Con Foods actually showed a net loss from continuing operations of $913,000 on sales of $570 million, compared with earnings a year earlier of $18 million on sales of $552 million. In the same quarter the company also provided for an estimated loss of $28.9 million on the disposition of Fuller Brush and four furniture companies.

But Bryan predicts that earnings in the current fiscal year—the first full year under the new management—will be "more respectable." He will not make projections, but some analysts forecast that earnings will rise from 1975's $1.63 per share to between $2 and $2.25. For a company the size of Con Foods, that still leaves a lot of room for progress. "It's a great company that got into trouble, and we had to take some corrective steps," he says. "But there is clearly optimism in the corporation today."

CASE 1

Aerosol Techniques, Inc.*

Charles W. Hofer

In January 1966, Mr. Robert Meyer, a 1965 Harvard MBA, joined Aerosol Techniques, Inc., as director of corporate development. While his immediate concern was the evaluation of numerous acquisition proposals that ATI had received, Mr. Meyer was also responsible for appraising over-all corporate strategy. Shortly after assuming his position, Mr. Meyer concluded that environmental trends might require a strategy change.

Founded in December 1955 by Mr. H. R. Shepherd, a chemist and biologist with aerosol R&D experience dating back to the end of World War II, ATI was a "contract filler," or producer and packager of items marketed to consumers by others. With 1965 sales of $47 million, or about 22% of the total contract filling market, ATI was the largest contract filler of aerosol products in the United States. Yearly growth since 1960 had averaged 46% for sales and 65% for profits. (For financial statements, see Exhibits 1 and 2.)

From the start, ATI's policy had been to emphasize service and development research for new products. As a result, about 95% of 1965 dollar volume was made up of products that ATI had developed in its laboratories either alone or jointly with customers. Mr. Shepherd indicated that ATI did not want to have to compete on a price basis, or to compete with customers by marketing products under its own name. Thus ATI's name was not on any products packed for other firms.

In 1965, ATI was the only contract filler with plants in each major section of the country. These provided an economic advantage over other contract fillers because of the relatively high cost of transporting filled aerosol containers. Nevertheless, Mr. Meyer was worried about ATI's strategy of developing and manufacturing aerosol products for national marketers because of several trends that had developed between 1960 and 1965. Of these, he felt the most important were a general decline in prices and profit margins for filling operations, and a tendency on the part of some national marketers to install their own aerosol filling lines as sales volume increased.

THE AEROSOL INDUSTRY

Aerosol products

The term "aerosol product" was used to describe any product packed in an aerosol container. The total item consisted of a pressurized container, a pro-

EXHIBIT 1

AEROSOL TECHNIQUES, INC.[a]

Balance Sheets for Years Ended September 30, 1960–1965
(dollars in thousands)

	1960	*1961*	*1962*	*1963*	*1964*	*1965*
Current assets						
Cash	$ 60	$ 449	$ 290	$ 359	$ 1,067	$ 1,433
Accounts receivable—net	461	832	1,279	3,373	4,924	6,566
Inventories—lower cost or market	465	238	468	2,136	2,329	3,098
Prepaid expenses	15	15	16	103	185	185
Miscellaneous	3	23	22	90	40	65
Total current assets	$1,005	$1,557	$2,076	$6,061	$ 8,544	$11,348
Fixed assets						
Land	0	0	0	13	13	179
Buildings	0	0	0	362	365	880
Machinery and equipment	479	496	541	2,024	2,497	3,226
Other	134	144	154	308	384	1,429[b]
	$ 613	$ 640	$ 695	$2,707	$ 3,260	$ 5,715
Less: accumulated depreciation and amortization	175	240	307	1,377	1,556	1,805
Total fixed assets	$ 438	$ 401	$ 388	$1,330	$ 1,704	$ 3,909
Other assets	19	18	24	155	75	125
	$1,462	$1,976	$2,488	$7,546	$10,322	$15,383
Current liabilities						
Notes payable	$ 0	$ 0	$ 0	$1,298	$ 1,500	$ 0
Accounts payable	596	527	758	2,480	2,842	4,151
Federal and state taxes payable	89	164	238	564	695	886
Other	179	209	200	388	396	1,318[c]
Total current liabilities	$ 864	$ 901	$1,196	$4,730	$ 5,434	$ 6,356
Long-term debt	217	98	34	241	200	3,152
Deferred federal taxes	36	43	47	53	55	60
Contingent deferred credit	0	0	0	355	257	184
Stockholders' equity						
4% voting, cumulative, preferred	0	0	0	715	715	715
Common stock: 10¢ par value	30	43	44	61	76	78
Capital in excess of par value	20	20	20	20	20	20
Paid in surplus	0	421	456	131	2,083	2,179
Retained earnings	295	450	691	1,240	1,480	2,639
Total stockholders' equity	$ 345	$ 934	$1,211	$2,167	$ 4,375	$ 5,631
	$1,462	$1,976	$2,488	$7,546	$10,322	$15,383

[a] Discrepancies may appear in totals as a result of rounding figures.
[b] Includes $934,000 for construction in progress.
[c] Includes $672,000 of current portion of long-term debt.

Source: ATI annual reports.

EXHIBIT 2

AEROSOL TECHNIQUES, INC.

Income Statements: 1960–1965*

(dollars in thousands)

	1960	*1961*	*1962*	*1963*	*1964*	*1965*
Net sales	$7,052	$7,734	$10,776	$21,327	$34,632	$46,975
Cost of goods sold, selling, administrative, and general exp.	$6,835	$7,415	$10,302	$20,159	$33,079	$44,705
	$ 218	$ 319	$ 475	$ 1,169	$ 1,553	$ 2,270
Other income	10	12	24	66	222	36
	$ 228	$ 331	$ 498	$ 1,235	$ 1,775	$ 2,306
Other deductions	27	16	11	85	104	124
	$ 200	$ 315	$ 487	$ 1,150	$ 1,671	$ 2,182
Provision for federal income taxes	99	159	247	567	751	980
Net earnings	$ 101	$ 156	$ 240	$ 583	$ 920	$ 1,202
% Sales	1.4	2.2	2.2	2.7	2.7	2.6

*Discrepancies may appear in total as a result of rounding figures.
Source: Various ATI annual reports.

pellant to supply the desired pressure, the usable product fill, and a cap and valve combination that controlled the release of the product and propellant. While almost any product that was liquid or gaseous at ordinary temperatures could theoretically be packaged in an aerosol container, in actual practice it was often difficut to "marry" the product, the propellant, and the cap and value into a workable combination. Nevertheless, by 1965 such diverse products as shaving cream, perfume, starch, furniture polish, hair sprays, and room deodorants were sold in aerosol containers.

Industry History and Growth

The first aerosol product was the "bugbomb" of which some 40 million units were produced for issue to servicemen during the last two years of World War II. When the war ended, the bomb was modified for civilian use.

While these first aerosols were high-pressure, refillable types which retailed for $3.98, myriad technical developments soon reduced both pressure and price. As a result, aerosol packaging spread to dozens of other products, as seen in Table 1. According to industry sources, aerosol packaging would continue to spread to other fields in the future.

Equally important to the rapid growth (about 17% a year between 1955 and 1964) of the aerosol market was the increasing penetration of aerosols as a packaging form in each of the above product areas. The percentage of room deodorants, shave lathers, and colognes packaged in aerosol containers increased from 0% in 1947 to 91%, 82% and 64%, respectively, in 1964 (see Exhibit 3). Moreover, some products, such as hair sprays, were made possible by aerosol packaging.

TABLE 1

	YEAR FIRST MARKETED IN AEROSOL PACKAGES
Room deodorants, lacquers, moth proofers	1948
Hair sprays, paints, automobile waxes	1949
Shave lather	1950
Whipped cream	1951
Perfumes	1954
Starches	1955
Glass cleaners	1956
Furniture waxes and polishes	1959
All purpose cleaners, antiperspirants	1962

EXHIBIT 3

AEROSOL TECHNIQUES, INC.

Percentage Penetration of Aerosols as a Packaging Form in Various Market Segments: 1951-1964 (per cents of dollar volume)

	1951	*1952*	*1953*	*1954*	*1955*	*1956*	*1957*	*1958*	*1959*	*1960*	*1961*	*1962*	*1963*	*1964*
Insecticides	30%	32%	37%	37%	39%	38%	39%	47%	47%	47%	47%	47%	48%	44%
Room deodorants	0	0	40	44	58	56	67	73	82	79	85	89	91	91
Shave lathers	0	12	29	38	47	51	59	60	65	69	71	79	81	82
Colognes	0	0	0	13	33	45	48	51	57	58	62	64	66	64

Source: *Eighth Annual Aerosol Market Report, 1964,* prepared by Freon Products Division of du Pont. Data supplied to du Pont by *Drug Trade News,* New York, New York.

In 1964, total sales of all aerosol-packaged products reached over 1.3 billion units. All but 6% of this total was made up of nonfood items, of which 46% were personal products, 30% household products, and 24% miscellaneous products (see Exhibit 4). Table 2 gives example of the types of products included in each category.

Industry observers expected each of these major categories to grow at least 8% a year during the coming decade. Du Pont, for example, in a 1965

TABLE 2

PERSONAL PRODUCTS	HOUSEHOLD PRODUCTS	MISCELLANEOUS PRODUCTS
Shave lathers	Room deodorants and disinfectants	Paints and coatings
Hair sprays and dressings	Cleaners (all types)	Insecticides
Medicinals	Household waxes and polishes	Automotive waxes
Colognes and perfumes	Starches	Veterinarian and pet products
Personal deodorants	Shoe and leather dressings	Industrial products
Other (shampoos, suntan preparations, hand lotions, etc.)		

EXHIBIT 4

AEROSOL TECHNIQUES, INC.

Du Pont Company Estimate of Aerosol Production (Nonfood Products Only)
(millions of units)

PERSONAL PRODUCTS	SHAVE LATHER	27.3	47.0	53.1	51.0	59.3	65.0	75.0	79.1	84.7	94.8	97.6	102.6	108.1
	HAIR SPRAYS & DRESSINGS	16.1	34.5	55.8	83.4	95.6	112.1	88.7	120.9	152.5	245.6	294.0	314.0	337.0
	DENTAL CREAMS						23.0	11.8	5.8	3.1	3.1	3.0	3.0	3.2
	MEDICINALS & PHARMACEUTICALS	0.8	1.1	1.5	2.4	6.2	8.1	10.5	12.3	19.5	36.9	39.8	45.6	49.4
	COLOGNES & PERFUMES	0.1	3.0	7.0	8.8	18.6	30.0	37.9	43.1	54.7	55.1	60.4	66.2	69.2
	OTHER[a]	3.8	4.4	7.2	7.7	7.1	9.6	12.9	18.7	18.5	36.9	38.5	47.1	52.8
	TOTAL	48.1	90.0	124.6	153.3	186.8	247.8	236.8	279.9	333.0	472.4	533.3	578.5	619.7
HOUSEHOLD PRODUCTS	INSECTICIDES[b]	47.0	47.0	57.0	61.4	50.7	71.3	78.9	92.5	87.3	89.2	73.2	75.1	76.4
	ROOM DEODORANTS	17.3	21.3	33.1	38.4	44.6	62.8	62.9	78.1	86.3	99.0	118.5	126.4	131.6
	SNOW	8.9	7.1	6.8	8.9	9.0	9.8	9.5	10.5	8.6	9.5	10.5	12.5	13.5
	GLASS CLEANERS				8.0	11.2	6.6	24.2	22.2	26.0	31.0	47.3	52.3	54.3
	SHOE OR LEATHER DRESSINGS				1.5	4.3	7.7	14.1	16.6	7.3	4.7	8.9	11.1	13.0
	WAXES & POLISHES (ALL TYPES)							12.1	40.6	42.1	52.9	50.9	57.8	61.0
	STARCHES								20.6	50.5	65.4	86.9	99.0	107.3
	OTHER	2.3	3.1	8.2	16.4	8.3	11.6	25.4	10.5	15.7	18.6	11.8	13.2	14.8
	TOTAL	28.5	31.5	48.1	73.2	77.4	98.5	148.2	199.1	236.5	281.1	334.8	372.3	395.5
ALL OTHER PRODUCTS	COATINGS	13.0	13.1	14.7	22.5	43.0	50.0	63.2	77.1	95.6	110.3	137.9	158.4	174.5
	VETERINARIAN & PET PRODUCTS	0.3	0.5	1.0	1.5	2.3	3.3	4.3	6.3	8.3	7.1	7.6	8.7	9.4
	AUTOMOTIVE PRODUCTS[c]											33.2	36.9	39.6
	MISCELLANEOUS PRODUCTS[d]	3.1	5.9	10.3	13.3	15.0	14.3	30.2	42.2	52.8	44.7	23.6	21.4	19.7
	TOTAL	3.4	6.4	11.3	14.8	17.3	17.6	34.5	48.5	61.1	51.8	64.4	67.2	71.0
	GRAND TOTAL	140.0	188.0	255.7	325.2	375.2	485.2	561.6	697.1	813.5	1004.8	1140.1	1251.3	1334.8

Source: *Eighth Annual Aerosol Market Report 1964,* prepared by the Freon Products Division of du Pont, p. 24.

[a] OTHER PERSONAL PRODUCTS include shampoos, sun tan preparations, personal deodorants, hand lotions, powders, depilatories, etc.

[b] INSECTICIDES include high pressure and low pressure products (including space, residual and moth proofers).

[c] AUTOMOTIVE PRODUCTS included in Miscellaneous products prior to 1963.

[d] MISCELLANEOUS PRODUCTS includ antistatic sprays, industrial applications, fire extinguishers, etc.

market report, forecast that between 1965 and 1967 sales of personal products would increase 14% a year, houshold products 12%, and all other nonfood products 10%.

Estimates of aerosol growth for foods were more uncertain. While sales of nonfood aerosols had increased more than 19% a year between 1955 and 1964, the sales of aerosol-packaged foods had increased less than 2% a year (see Exhibit 5). However, in 1963 and 1964, du Pont gained approval from the Food and Drug Administration for two new tasteless propellants. According to some industry sources, these promised to overcome previous technical problems and to open the way to aerosol packaging of a wide variety of foods

EXHIBIT 5

AEROSOL TECHNIQUES, INC.

Growth of the Food Aerosol Market

Year	*Sales (millions of units)*
1951	43
1952	50
1953	56
1954	60
1955	64
1956	69
1957	75
1958	80
1959	79
1960	59
1961	58
1962	63
1963	67
1964	75
1965	100

Source: *Eighth Annual Aerosol Market Report 1964,* prepared by the Freon Products Division of du Pont, p. 18.

—from staples such as peanut butter and cheese spread to additives such as vermouth. As a consequence, some industry sources were predicting in 1965 that the growth curve for food products would soon begin to resemble that of nonfood aerosols.

Reasons for Aerosol Usage

According to a study by the Freon Products Division of du Pont, there were three primary reasons for the use of aerosol packaging: (1) increased product effectiveness, (2) greater user convenience, and (3) time savings. The study noted that not all successful applications exhibited all three advantages; even where effectiveness was not improved, convenience alone was often enough to stimulate sales.

Nevertheless, aerosol packaging was relatively expensive (see Exhibits 6 and 7). Some observers felt that the cost would restrict the use of aerosol packaging for products with low profit margins.

Industry Structure

During World War II, the Bridgeport Brass Company produced most of the "bugbombs" used by the armed services. After the war, this company continued to make "bugbombs" which it sold through its regular sales force. Soon, however, Bridgeport, which had no product development activities, was

EXHIBIT 6

AEROSOL TECHNIQUES, INC.

Cost Estimates for Various Aerosol Products

Product type	*Starch*[a]	*Hair spray*[b]	*Shave cream*[c]
Product fill	1.0¢	4.0¢	1.5¢
Propellant	0.3	12.0[d]	0.1
Can[e]	7.0	6.3	5.0
Valve	3.0	2.6	3.0
Cap	0.5	1.0[f]	0.5
Carton[g]	0.6	0.5	0.5
Direct labor	1.0	1.0	1.0
Overhead	1.5	1.5	1.5
Profit (maximum)	1.0	1.0	1.0
Factory price	15.9¢	29.9¢	14.1¢
Approximate retail price	39¢	$1.00-$1.20	$0.79 to $1.00
Approximate retail price of comparable product (non-aerosol)	19¢ for 12 oz.	none available	$1.00 for 10 oz.

[a]16 oz. size, for laundry use.

[b]12 oz. size, alcohol-base, "most name brands."

[c]6 oz. size, "most name brands."

[d]Much more expensive than others shown because the product requires Freon as a propellant, which amounts to 70% of the weight of the contents. The propellants used in the other products shown are hydrocarbons, and are only 4% of the weight of the contents. Water-based hair sprays, with somewhat different characteristics, are available; these entail a lower propellant cost.

[e]Printed cans; no separate labels.

[f]More expensive only because usually fancier.

[g]Carton for a dozen cans.

Source: Estimates furnished by an industry source other than ATI. Estimates are for an established product with a volume per production run of about 25,000 units or more.

EXHIBIT 7

AEROSOL TECHNIQUES, INC.

Cost of a Typical Aerosol Food Product

Food Product: Pancake Mix

Cost	*Per Unit*
Direct labor	$0.04
Can (16 oz.)	0.09
Gas (nitrous oxide)	0.005
Valve and release	0.05
Product (pancake mix)	0.04
Overhead (interest and depreciation)*	0.01
Profit margin	0.015
Cost to marketer before distribution charges	$0.250

*Assumes an investment of $300,000 for a line that produces 9.6 million units a year for eight years with indirect labor and storage costs of $50,000 a year.

Source: Harvard Business School student reports conducted for ATI.

forced out of the aerosol market by contract fillers, which carried on intensive product development programs. These contract fillers were small, regional companies which would purchase the cans from national firms such as American Can Company, the propellants from firms such as du Pont and the caps and valves from small companies like themselves. They would then assemble these components, including the product fill, which they usually manufactured, into the final aerosol product. The contract fillers would then sell the finished product to marketing firms, which resold to retailers under their own brands. By 1950, at least 50 firms met the contract filler definition.

As the demand for aerosols grew, two changes occurred in industry structure. First, the contract fillers became larger through both internal growth and acquisition of other contract fillers. Second, some national marketers began to erect their own filling facilities since they felt their volume now warranted such a move. Such a marketer was called a "captive filler."

By 1964, output of nonfood aerosols was about evenly divided between captive and contract fillers (see Exhibit 8). Most industry observers felt a definite trend toward captive filling had not yet emerged among national marketers, however. While firms such as Colgate, S. C. Johnson, Alberto-Culver, Johnson & Johnson, Mennen, and Gillette had established their own filling lines, firms such as Procter & Gamble and Breck still relied on contract fillers. Moreover, most of the firms that had established their own filling lines still relied on contract fillers to supplement their own production during peak sales periods.

The difficulty of deciding between captive vs. contract filling was partly responsible for the lack of a definite trend. The economics of the decision required the marketing company to consider not only the cost of filling equipment and personnel, but also distribution costs, inventory costs (since the contract filler usually kept part of the inventory), and research and development costs (since many contract fillers developed new product formulations for the marketers). In addition, the marketing company had to consider noneconomic factors such as the need for security in protecting the product formulation and the need for tight quality control.

One industry source (not ATI) agreed that the issue of captive vs. contract filling was complex. He estimated, however, that a yearly volume of 5 million units in a standard product might be an "average breakeven point" as far as the economics of the filling operation were involved. Although some companies used captive operations for as few as 1 million units a year, and others used contract fillers for annual volumes as high as 10 million, he felt that these companies were clear exceptions and were probably influenced by other-than-economic factors. He also thought that it was becoming easier for companies to set up their own filling operations, since the necessary equipment could readily be purchased, and an increasing number of people with experience in aerosol filling operations were becoming available.

EXHIBIT 8

AEROSOL TECHNIQUES, INC.

ATI's Share of the Contract Filled and Total Aerosol Filling Markets: 1963–1964

	Per cent of market contract filled		*ATI share of contract market*		*ATI share of total market*	
	1963	*1964*	*1963*	*1964*	*1963*	*1964*
Household products						
Room deodorants	36.9%	22.1%	7.1%	17.0%	2.6%	3.7%
Cleaners	64.1	62.0	34.8	31.0	22.3	18.9
Waxes and polishes	18.9	22.1	28.9	23.5	5.5	5.2
Starch	82.9	84.0	26.7	25.0	22.2	21.0
Shoe and leather dressings	86.9	96.1	1.3	3.9	1.1	3.8
Other	69.4	82.0	21.5	5.7	14.9	4.7
Personal products						
Shave lather	23.0	37.0	7.1	1.6	1.6	.6
Hair spray	60.0	61.0	30.9	35.1	18.6	21.4
Medicinals and pharmaceuticals	63.0	68.8	13.9	21.4	8.8	15.0
Colognes and perfumes	51.0	38.1	15.9	31.0	8.1	12.0
Other	36.1	38.9	29.3	3.2	10.5	1.3
Miscellaneous products						
Insecticides	34.0	31.0	54.4	30.5	18.5	9.5
Coatings	52.0	41.0	4.5	4.3	2.4	2.0
Vet and pet products	96.3	77.5	3.9	1.4	3.8	1.1
Automotive and industrial	59.0	70.3	14.6	8.8	8.6	6.4
Other	–	36.7	–	10.3	–	3.8
Total	51.1%	50.4%	22.0%	21.9%	11.2%	11.1%

Source: ATI marketing statistics.

Other industry observers felt that many marketers would not go captive because of the low profit margins on filling. They reasoned that such marketers would be far more interested in new marketing opportunities which promised high margins than in a production activity with a rapid rate of technological change. (For further discussion of the advantages of using a contract filler, see Exhibit 9.)

Contract Fillers and Their Strategies

Although the aerosol filling industry had grown tremendously, it had nevertheless become increasingly competitive during the mid-1960s as the 98 independent contract fillers fought for a large but limited supply of contracts. The intensity of competition was suggested by the fact that three contract fillers had

EXHBIT 9

AEROSOL TECHNIQUES, INC.

Advantages of Using a Contract Packager

by

A. S. Pero

1. *Research & Development Advantages*
   a) Can draw from lab personnel already experienced in aerosols.
   b) Developments by fillers, either directly or in cooperation with other suppliers, are available promptly to marketers.
   c) Prevents added load being placed on marketers' lab facilities.
   d) Reduces marketers' outlay for research and development.
2. *Production Advantages*
   a) Can select latest and best equipment available for particular job required.
   b) Two or more products can be run simultaneously.
   c) Contract packagers offer facilities to cope with seasonal demands, or unexpected market fluctuations either of higher or lower volume than anticipated.
   d) Personnel of long, varied, and impartial experience available for quality control.
   e) Marketer can ask, and often gets, tighter specifications on his product.
   f) Supplier problems are handled by the filler.
   g) Can eliminate or minimize labor-management problems.
3. *Service Advantages*
   a) Marketer can warehouse both raw and finished materials, often at no charge, on filler's premises.
   b) Filler's trucking facilities can be used for drop shipments, emergency services, etc.
   c) Marketer can draw on know-how and information sometimes not available within his own organization.
4. *Economic Advantages*
   a) No money outlay for equipment and maintenance, plant building or expansion, or personnel and training of same.
   b) A contract packager is actually a co-op manufacturer who divides his labor, overhead, etc., among a wide group of customers and products.
   c) Working capital is conserved on material purchased by filler until product is completed.
   d) Material purchase are often less, due to filler's volume buying.
   e) Lowest costs on final product can be obtained through competitive bidding.
   f) Use of strategically located fillers can offer substantially lower shipping costs when products are to be nationally distributed.

How high a volume of product must an aerosol marketer be turning out before it pays him to consider doing his own filling?

Actually product volume is relatively unimportant in itself. More important is to seriously study the over-all advantages a good filler has to offer vs. the over-all advantages of the marketer doing his own work. Once this is determined, a further evaluation is needed on the aerosol product or products to be manufactured.

Is the product to be a low profit, highly competitive one? In this case a larger volume will be needed to justify the total expenditure involved. Or is the product a high profit one, in a noncompetitive line? In the latter, a lesser volume might justify doing one's own filling.

In general, a careful analysis of all factors involved by the marketer, in the light of his own capacities and business interests, should provide him with a satisfactory answer. A survey of the aerosol field today elearly indicates that most marketers have already decided it is to their advantage to have their aerosol lines produced by contract packagers. The aerosol filling industry is today so competitive that the margin above direct tabor is small enough to discourage not only the marketer's equipment plan, but also new competitive contract packagers as well.

Source: Article by A. S. Pero of the Fluid Chemical Co., Newark, N.J., Aerosol Age, June 1957, p. 28

been forced into bankruptcy in 1963, and Old Empire, Inc., of Clifton, New Jersey, one of the oldest and most respected names in aerosols, had also filed a bankruptcy petition.

On the other hand, several large companies entered the aerosol business through acquisitions. Borden's, for example, in 1963 and 1964 acquired Krylon, an aerosol paint manufacturer, and Aerosol Brands, a general contract filler. During the same period, Corn Products Company bought Peterson Filling in order to package its products in aerosol containers.

In an article in *Aerosol Age,* the industry trade journal, Mr. H. R. Shepherd, president of ATI, discussed the future role of the independent contract filler as follows:

> It is clear that in the future there will be only two types of contract fillers—first, the filler with national distribution and plants strategically distributed throughout the nation (or in several countries) which can adequately service a national or international marketing concern. The other type of successful contract filler will be the small filler, who can handle low volume runs of specialty products or products that are only beginning to be felt in the market-place. [2].

Vim Laboratories exemplified the latter type of company. One of the few publicly owned fillers, Vim had annual sales only slightly above $1 million. Custom filling represented part of its business, but the company's own specialty line, which included insecticides, paints, room deodorants, shaving cream, Christmas snow, insect repellent, sun tan lotion, and charcoal lighter, represented a significant portion of aerosol capacity.

George Barr & Company, which had been purchased by Pittsburgh Railways Company in 1962, was the second largest contract filler in the United States in 1965. Barr's 1962 sales had exceeded $15 million, but had not been reported separately since 1962. In May 1965, the company unveiled a new filling plant in Niles, Illinois, which was described as "the largest aerosol filling plant in the world." Barr's apparent strategy was to become a "packaging consultant." With this objective in mind, Pittsburgh Railways in 1963 and 1964 had acquired Advance Packaging Company, a filler of nonaerosol packages and Aero Valve Corporation, a manufacturer of caps and valves for aerosol containers.

Power-Pak, Inc., of Bridgeport, Connecticut, was a medium-sized contract filler. In 1962, Power-Pak formed agreements with three other contract fillers—one English, one Canadian, and one midwestern domestic—under which Power-Pak licensed these companies to use some of Power-Pak's product formulations. Power-Pak also performed R&D activities for these firms for a fee. While Power-Pak did not see any direct increase in the sales of its own products, Mr. Edward Helfer, Power-Pak's president in 1962, felt that this arrangement might lead to a penetration in continental Europe, which was just beginning to experience an aerosol boom similar to that in the United States between 1955 and 1960.

Industry Suppliers

The four principal components of an aerosol product—containers, propellants, caps and valves, and product fill—were supplied by diverse groups of companies.

The market for propellants was dominated by five large chemical companies: du Pont, Allied Chemical Corporation, Union Carbide, Pennsalt Chemicals Corporation, and Kaiser Aluminum & Chemical Corporation.

The market for aerosol containers was also dominated by large firms. Among the most important were Continental Can Company, Inc., American Can Company, Crown Cork & Seal Company, Inc., and National Can Corporation. Glass container manufacturers included Owens-Illinois Glass Company, Foster-Forbes Glass Company, and T. C. Wheaton Company.

Small companies, similar to many of the contract fillers, played an important part in the supply of caps and valves. The major supplier was Precision Valve Corporation, which had an estimated 50% of the market. The other half of the market was split among many suppliers.

The aerosol filler, contract or captive, usually produced the product fill. In the case of certain products, such as perfumes, however, the contract filler secured the product fill from the marketing company.

ATI HISTORY

Immediately after World War II, Mr. H. R. Shepherd joined the Bridgeport Brass Company as administrative assistant to the director of research. About a year later, he and three friends founded Connecticut Chemical Research Corporation. After eight years, Mr. Shepherd resigned to form his own company, Aerosol Techniques, Inc.

ATI was launched in 1955 with $20,000 capital invested by Mr. Shepherd, a $125,000 bank loan, and $600,000 in trade credit. Although contracts were obtained almost immediately to load hair sprays and colognes, ATI was $75,000 in the red after six months. At year's end, however, the company emerged with a modest profit of $5,000 on sales of $1.5 million. *Aerosol Age* reported as follows:

> During this stage of growth, Mr. Shepherd emphasized that the theme will be "give service—expand research—put profits into new equipment and technical development." . . . The company has started a research program with an eastern university on basic problems with aerosols. . . . A complete aerosol service center is a must for proper handling of customers in aerosol packaging, according to Mr. Shepherd [2].

By 1960, sales had risen to $7.1 million and net profit to $101,000. Although hair sprays remained ATI's most important single product, the line had been expanded to include shaving creams, toothpaste, furniture polishes, and other items. In addition, R&D laboratories had been established. A continuing effort was being made to improve formulae for customers and to develop or adapt aerosol packaging to new products. Though product diversification and research had reduced ATI's dependence on a few major clients, three customers still accounted for almost 60% of sales in 1960.

Although ATI lost an account which contributed 13% of 1960 sales because the customer went captive, the addition of new products and growth of established lines pushed 1961 sales to a new high of $7.7 million. Early in 1961, ATI issued 130,000 shares to the public, representing a 30% interest in the company, at $4.00 per share. This financing helped to alleviate the financial pressures caused by the company's tremendous growth. Even though ATI had decided to retain all earnings and to conserve funds for working capital by leasing rather than purchasing facilities, creditors were supplying over three-fourths of the firm's invested funds in 1960. In October 1961, the stock was listed on the American Stock Exchange.

In 1962, ATI's spectacular growth trend was resumed as sales reached $10.8 million and net income climbed to $240,000. In addition, ATI established a subsidiary, Aeroceuticals, Inc., to produce and market an assortment of ethical drugs which company R&D had developed for aerosol containers. Major reasons for this move were the high growth rate (over 40% per year between 1957 and 1962) of pharmaceuticals and the relatively high gross margin on these products.

In 1963, ATI moved into first place in the contract filling business with sales of $21.3 million and profits of $583,000, partly as a result of the acquisition of two contract fillers: Western Filling Corporation in Los Angeles, California, and Continental Filling Corporation in Danville, Illinois.

When acquired, Western had shown a rapid growth similar to ATI's. Sales had doubled between 1960 and 1962 from $2.3 million to $4.7 million, while earnings had increased from $19,000 to $278,000. The Western acquisition was basically an exchange of stock.

Continental's sales had fluctuated in the four years prior to the acquisition, dropping from $9.6 million in 1960 to $6.9 million in 1962, but recovering somewhat in 1963. Profits had declined continuously during the period, however, from $118,000 in 1960 to $5,000 in 1962 and then to a $27,000 loss in 1963. Because of this somewhat weaker record, the Continental acquisition was a cash and deferred payment agreement, even though Continental's capacity was somewhat greater than Western's: 40 million vs. 35 million units annually.

To finance these acquisitions, ATI negotiated a $1 million loan with its New York bank, and in November 1964 offered 80,000 shares to the public at $18.00 per share.

In 1964, ATI acquired Armstrong Laboratories, Inc. of West Roxbury, Massachusetts, through an exchange of stock. Armstrong's sales had been

$1.1 million in 1963, with profits of $52,000. Armstrong had already achieved a strong reputation as an aerosol producer specializing in pharmaceuticals and other close-tolerance filling operations. Armstrong had also opened a new building with advanced production and research facilities just prior to acquisition.

With this addition, ATI's sales increased to $34.6 million in 1964, with a net income of $920,000. This growth continued in 1965, with sales increasing to $47.0 million and profits to $1.2 million.

In December 1962 and again in December 1963, ATI declared 5% stock dividends.

ATI'S RECENT OPERATIONS

Product Line

ATI's 1965 product line consisted of over 200 products manufactured for nearly 150 customers. The largest customer, however, accounted for over 45 million units, or nearly 17% of 1965 production. In addition, the top five customers accounted for about 50% of ATI's production, and the top 10 for slightly more than 75%.

By product class, ATI was concentrated in personal products, which represented nearly 65% of 1965 volume—hair sprays alone accounted for over 45%. Household products were next in importance representing about 28%. Most of this was starches, which accounted for 15%.

John Thomson, corporate director of sales, indicated that ATI's product line strategy was to reduce the company's dependence on personal products by placing more emphasis on household products and pharmaceuticals. Nevertheless, Mr. Thomson indicated that ATI planned to continue its outstanding record in hair sprays and personal deodorants.

According to Mr. Thomson, coatings, paints, and food products represented special cases for ATI. While he felt that the market for coatings and paints would not grow as fast as other product categories, he indicated that they might become more important for ATI. However, he also indicated that if ATI decided to enter the coating and paint field at all, it would probably market as well as manufacture these products. This move would represent a major change in ATI's present strategy of not marketing products to end-use consumers.

In Mr. Thomson's opinion, food products represented a far more promising field for ATI. Up to 1965, ATI had not devoted much effort to this area because of the technical problems encountered in propellants and caps and valves. However, Mr. Thomson indicated that ATI would increase its effort in this direction as the food aerosol market developed—perhaps three to seven years from now, he believed.

ATI was also studying the possibilities of aerosols for the industrial cleaning and sanitation markets, Mr. Thomson said.

Marketing

ATI's sales objective was a volume of $100 million in contract manufacturing by 1969. To reach this goal, the company planned to broaden its line, particularly in the household products area, and to concentrate its selling efforts on national marketers in the continental United States. In this sales push, ATI planned to rely heavily on what it considered its two distinctive competences: low distribution costs resulting from having plants located in the East, Midwest, and the West Coast; and a continuing flow of new and improved products resulting from its R&D.

Mr. Thomson felt that ATI would have to price more competitively if it expected to hold its large national accounts. However, he felt the new plant being erected at Milford would allow production economies which would keep ATI competitive for at least the next five years. In addition, Mr. Thomson felt that ATI might acquire or build a southern production facility which would permit lower prices because of reduced distribution costs.

In 1963, ATI started to develop a corporate marketing staff to coordinate sales activity and develop marketing plans. One of the staff's first jobs was to develop a yearly sales forecast. This was accomplished through account-by-account analyses by each ATI salesman, which were later combined at headquarters into a national sales forecast.

Throughout 1965, the corporate marketing staff was assisting ATI's salesmen with major presentations to national marketing companies. These presentations represented a relatively new development for the industry. They were made to old customers whom ATI hoped to retain by developing new products for them, and to prospective customers who were either existing or potential aerosol marketers. As a result of one of these presentations, ATI developed a complete program—product, package design, and advertising theme—for marketing an aerosol hair spray for the American Home Products Company. Even though American Home had never marketed a hair spray before, this new brand, Sudden Beauty, became one of the top four hair sprays in 1965.

At the end of 1965, ATI had two men on its corporate marketing staff, four divisional sales managers, and six field salesmen. In addition to helping make the major presentations, the salesmen served as a liaison between the customer's purchasing, research, and marketing groups and the ATI organization.

Research and Development

In late 1965, ATI formed a new corporation called the Aerosol Techniques Research Center, Inc. This division was building a new research center in

Milford, Connecticut, which would eventually be staffed by 15 to 25 people headed by Mr. Clarence Clap, an ATI vice president formerly with Western Filling. At the same time, a new technical services department was formed under ATI vice president, Fred Presant, who had worked in the aerosol industry for 18 years. Technical services encompassed all the operating division's customer service, quality control, and product development laboratories. In Mr. Clapp's opinion, the new research center, combined with the technical services department, would give ATI the best research and product development activity among all contract fillers.

While the technical services department worked hand-in-hand with ATI's customers to improve product formulations, the research center was to be devoted solely to the development of new or improved products and new or improved technology in the aerosol field. According to Mr. Clapp,

> The direction of the research and development effort at the research center will be determined to a large degree by the market research department. Market research will be involved at both the initial and final stages of most projects. This is necessary because the ultimate dependence of our success rests with the consumer.

This policy implied that most projects chosen were expected to become commercially feasible within one to three years. Nevertheless, Mr. Clapp said that ATI would still have some commitment to "blue sky" projects, provided the financial commitments were not too heavy. He also indicated that ATI would seek technical assistance from its suppliers as much as possible, but, when necessary, would perform research in the areas of new containers, valves, and propellants. To help protect accomplishments, ATI planned to seek far more patents than in the past. When this was not possible, Mr. Clapp indicated that ATI would seek contractual agreements with its customers or utilize secrecy.

The contribution and importance of R&D to ATI's success up to 1965 is indicated by the company's record for new products and technical developments generated. These included the first personal deodorant, Right Guard; a patented water-based hair spray, which allowed cost savings of 10% to 30%; the first aerosol mouth freshener; the first dimethyl ether propellant system, which reduced costs because it was water-soluble; and the first aerosol barbecue sauce. In conjunction with a leading can company, ATI developed the first three-piece high-pressure container, which reduced costs since less propellant was required. ATI also developed new formulations which became leading products in their respective markets, e.g., Sudden Beauty hair spray, Dust and Wax furniture polish, Perform aerosol starch, and Fuller's oven cleaner. In addition, ATI had a complete cross-section of all types of aerosol products on the market in 1965, even though the company might not have been the original developer of some of these products.

Another indication of ATI's commitment to R&D was contained in Mr.

Shepherd's exposition on "The Contract Filler's Role in Aerosol Product Development," which appeared in the December 1963 issue of *Aerosol Age:*

In order to know of the future and to predict, within reasonable bounds, what we [the contract fillers] should be doing, we must understand the past and recognize the trends that are already discernible . . . we must understand what are the distinctive competences of the filler today and what these will be in the future. How should they be shaped and guided in order to continue the development of the aerosol industry? In the application of the resources at the disposal of the contract filler, how and when should these resources be allocated? How should they be developed? When I write of "resources," I mean things such as men, money and materials. I also mean the fund of knowledge and experience of the contract filler and new technological changes which shall come from the contract filler . . . I think we can expect to see a continual increase in the concentration of power in the hands of the marketing companies. We can expect to endure severe conditions of excess capacity and price competition among fillers. Because of these increasing economic pressures on marketers and contract fillers, there will be an even greater need for creative, new product and marketing concepts. In order to continue to play a role in the development of this industry, the contract filler must now begin to use effectively those distinctive competences and resources which he has developed over the years. These distinctive competences are first *creativity* and the *ability to innovate technologically*. The second distinctive competence . . . is that of the many years of experience in the organizations of the members of this industry. The next resource is that of having capacity to manufacture a wide spectrum of aerosol products. Next, those contract fillers who have moved toward putting facilities up in strategic locations in this country and on the continent, have moved toward offering more complete servicing of both national and international markets in terms of distribution. Finally, one distinctive competence which is not universally held by by contract fillers organizations is that of capably using new management techniques and tools.

Production

Aerosol products were manufactured in two basic ways in 1965. The slower but more accurate method was called cold filling. In this method, the propellant and product fill were liquefied by refrigeration and "poured" into the containers in carefully measured amounts. The cap and valve were then inserted by hand and sealed by machine, after which the filled containers were passed through a hot water bath to test for pressure leaks. Finally, labels were applied and the product was packaged for storage or shipment. The more rapid method was called pressure filling. In this method, the cap and valve were inserted in the container and then sealed at the same time a vacuum was created in the container. Next the product fill and propellant were injected through the valve into the empty container by the application of extremely high pressure. The filled container was then labeled and packaged for storage or shipment. In 1965, filling speeds of 200 cans per minute were considered high for aerosol production. However, speeds of 100 cans per minute had been considered high in 1960. Mr. Donald Schoonmaker, ATI's eastern division production manager, indicated that filling speeds might double again by 1970.

At the end of 1965, ATI had four plants with 21 filling lines located across the United States so as to insure national distribution at minimal cost. About 50% of ATI's equipment was new and 50% was relatively old. However, Mr. Schoonmaker said ATI's production efficiency was equal to or better than that of other contract fillers. Mr. Schoonmaker also felt that ATI had extremely good quality control, which he thought most contract fillers would be hard pressed to match. At this time, ATI's annual production capacity was about 390 million units.

Table 3 indicates the location and number of filling lines for each of ATI's four plants.

TABLE 3

Location	Number of Filling Lines	Approximate Annual Production Capacity (Millions of Units)	Warehouse Space (Thousands of Square Feet)
Bridgeport, Conn. (leased)	6	150	150
Los Angeles, Calif. (leased)	4	95	130
Danville, Ill. (owned)	6	100	100
West Roxbury, Mass. (leased)	5	45	35
Total	21	390	410

The Bridgeport facility, a converted piano factory, also contained the company's executive offices and research laboratories.

In June 1965, ATI began an expansion program designed to raise capacity to 430 million units by the end of 1966. This $4.2 million program included (1) a new building in Milford, Connecticut, to house the company's main offices and eastern division plant, replacing the overcrowded Bridgeport factory and offices; (2) a new research center, also located at Milford; (3) acquisition of a new building and property in Danville, Illinois, to double the facilities of the company's Continental Filling division; (4) addition of a production line and new warehouse area in Los Angeles to increase the capacity of the Western Filling division; and (5) completion of a new aerosol pharmaceutical development and filling installation at Armstrong Laboratories in West Roxbury.

All facilities were designed to permit the installation of additional lines in the future. Expenditures required to bring capacity into line with future sales targets were estimated as follows:

FISCAL YEAR	TARGET SALES (MILLIONS OF UNITS)	PRODUCTION CAPACITY * (MILLIONS OF UNITS)	CAPITAL EXPENDITURES TO OBTAIN ADDITIONAL CAPACITY (THOUSANDS OF DOLLARS)
1967	330	467	$480
1968	400	497	490
1969	460	532	520

* Reserve capacity in excess of sales targets was required to handle emergency orders and seasonal fluctuations.

According to Mr. Schoonmaker, expansion would be aimed at meeting the needs of national marketers who had medium-volume, high-quality, high-margin products. He felt this policy would enable ATI to make better use of its distinctive competences in R&D instead of having to sell on a price basis as was necessary on mass produced standardized products.

Organization and Control

In late 1965, ATI had four operating divisions in addition to the corporate staff and the research and technical services divisions. The name, location, and general managers of these divisions are listed in Table 4.

Each of these general managers was an ATI vice president. According to Mr. Rossetti, corporate treasurer, these general managers operated their divisions somewhat like independent entrepreneurs. For example, while the divisions sent monthly and quarterly profit reports to corporate headquarters, these reports were not standardized, and Mr. Rossetti said the divisional general managers were not evaluated on the basis of these reports. Nevertheless, Mr. Rossetti felt that the divisional general managers tried to maximize

TABLE 4

DIVISION	LOCATION	GENERAL MANAGER	PREVIOUS POSITION OF GM
Eastern division	Bridgeport, Conn.	John Kossak	Plant manager, General Foods, and operated own company
Western division	Los Angeles, Calif.	John Manara	President, Western Filling Company
Continental division	Danville, Ill.	Chris Canaday	President, Continental Filling Company
Armstrong Laboratories division	West Robxury, Mass.	Robert Armstrong, Jr.	President, Armstrong Laboratories

profits. The primary purpose of the reports was to enable the corporate staff to assist the divisional general managers by uncovering unfavorable performance trends.

In 1965, ATI did not employ a standard cost system or accumulate actual costs in such a way that it could estimate the relative efficiency of its different pieces of equipment or the relative profitability of its different products. While Mr. Rossetti indicated that such estimates might be desirable in the future, he felt it more important for ATI to keep up with rapidly expanding new product areas than to allocate its resources on the basis of estimated profitability.

In addition, since materials accounted for 85% of the total cost of finished products, Mr. Rossetti felt that costs could be effectively controlled by having efficient, modern equipment, by having careful quality control to minimize rejects and insure proper filling operations, and by purchasing high quality materials at competitive prices. In order to help control materials usage, ATI was installing an IBM 1401A computer at the end of 1965.

Financial Situation

To finance new fixed assets and increase working capital, ATI sold 80,000 shares of common stock to the public in October 1965 at $22.00 a share. An additional $3.0 million was raised by the sale of 5½% 25-year secured notes of subsidiaries to an insurance company.

PROBLEMS AND ALTERNATIVES AT THE END OF 1965

An internal policy memorandum issued in December 1965 stated,

> . . . ATI's position of leadership in the aerosol industry may not be sufficient to sustain ATI's objectives of $100 million in sales and 7% after taxes by 1969. This gap between our abilities and our goals has been brought about by factors underlying both the company's environment and the company's resources.

Environmental trends noted in this memorandum included the maturation of industry structure and aerosol technology, the increasingly heavy competition among contract fillers, the attendant threat to high-level profits, and the increasing power of the marketing companies. Mr. Shepherd commented as follows on these and other problems:

> Most of the problems ATI faces now—customers going captive and pressured profit margins—we faced 10 years ago and, in a sense, they're no more serious now than then. However, because of the trend toward competition on the basis of price, we are increasingly aware of the fact that ATI will have to become more formalistic and number-oriented—a prospect I would dislike *if* it saps creativity. Thus, if the only thing I can do is beat a competitor's price, I don't feel that I'm contributing much—and more to the point—I don't feel that ATI is contributing.

Our historical excellence is in creating profits for our customers through the kind of innovation which helped us to develop Right Guard for Gillette and, more recently, miniatures, a development which was written up in the *Wall Street Journal.**

Again, this trend toward a more formalistic organization will have to be balanced with what I believe are my responsibilities to the people who make up our organization and its social and business interrelationships. Up until now our creativity has given us an opportunity to allow the people within our organization to find their own particular niche—even though this process takes time and in the short run uses up profits. However, in a really price competitive market there would be no time for slack, no time for learning, and no opportunity for personal change. I believe that, in the long run, such an atmosphere would be damaging to our organization and to the interests of the company. So it is for this reason, in addition to our natural desire to achieve economic success, that we are looking at other businesses where we can use the technical and organizational creativity that we have developed over the past ten years.

This doesn't mean that we plan to de-emphasize the aerosol business altogether. However, we are considering other businesses which we might enter to hedge against the threats we see in the aerosol business. Ten years from now I expect that the aerosol business might be like the can business today: efficient production, tight control, low margins, and no fun—except when creating new opportunities for new products through technical and marketing research.

In looking at other businesses, there are three things I consider important. First, we should get closer to the consumer, where price isn't the only reason for survival. This is where the real opportunity for product innovation lies. Second, the acquired company should have good management so that we can build on them, rather than being forced to decimate the company and start from scratch. Finally, I would like to have a "feel" for the business.

As a result of environmental trends and Mr. Shepherd's concern about the future nature of the aerosol business, considerable attention was being focused on the question of what economic opportunities were available to ATI.

Although the European aerosol market was expanding rapidly, ATI paid little attention to expanding its operations overseas. However, it was considering strategies that would allow continued success in the domestic aerosol business. At the end of 1965, it had three groups of Harvard Business School

* "Marketing Miniatures: Now Products Come in One-Use Packages," *Wall Street Journal,* April 13, 1966:

Make way for the teeny-weeny economy size.

It contains one serving or application, and it's one of the hottest packaging concepts since the super-duper economy size. What's more, despite the increased cost per ounce the one-shot helping can prove to be a consumer's most economic buy.

* * * * *

Many of the goods are sold in pressurized aerosol containers. Aerosol Techniques, Inc., for example, is about to start commercial production of a breath freshener in a small aerosol container—not one shot but much smaller than any previous models—and is testing small containers of an antiperspirant, a man's hair spray, and a nasal spray.

students working on projects related to forward or backward integration. One group was considering possible acquisitions of plastic cap and valve manufacturers; even though this industry appeared at first glance to suffer from strong price competition and from profit margins lower than for contract filling. Another student group was concerned about the future of the food aerosol business. The third was studying markets for other types of packaging services that ATI might provide.

Possible Forward Integration

Some members of management felt that ATI should begin marketing products to the end-use consumer in order to get the higher profit margins associated with this business. There was, however, considerable concern lest such action cause ATI to lose some of its present customers, who would not want their supplier as a competitor. On the other hand, there had been little reaction from these same customers when ATI took Sudden Beauty hair spray to American Home Products, Inc., a company that had never been in the hair spray business, and essentially established AHP as one of the country's leading hair spray marketers. ATI's management also wondered whether ATI had the financial and managerial resources to market a consumer product nationally.

Diversification Guidelines

The major focus of ATI's attention, however, was directed toward diversification out of the aerosol business. According to the December policy memorandum,

> The need for an unconventional miracle is prompted by our objectives, by an assessment of the present economic progress of our aerosol business and by the question of whether ATI's strategy is viable for the next decade. . . . It is the contention of this paper that at least the following criteria must be met if a profitable diversification is to be achieved:
>
> 1. The company should promise a growth rate compatible with ATI's own rate of growth.
> 2. The company should promise a return on investment compatible with ATI's own ROI performance.
> 3. The company's management should not retard the growth of our own management structure.
> 4. The company should be a company to which ATI should be able to contribute synergetically so that there will exist the best possible opportunity for reaching the above listed financial criteria. In this context ATI's distinctive competences have been suggested as:
>   (a) Nationwide manufacturing and management facilities;
>   (b) A capacity to direct technological innovation toward supplying consumer and/or industrial needs;
>   (c) A strong series of relationships with the chemical industry; and
>   (d) A strong series of relationships with the financial community.
> 5. The company should be a company which has the capacity to contribute an

additional distinctive competence to ATI. Examples of the kind of contribution we have in mind are:

(a) A sales force for the sale of (say), industrial specialty chemicals;

(b) A technological niche in a nonaerosol packaging service so that ATI can be in a position to develop an integrated system of packaging services backed by nationwide manufacturing facilities, a nationwide sales force, unique packaging machinery of our own design, and a research facility specializing in formulation chemistry related to personal, household, pharmaceutical, and food products.

(c) The ability to manufacture nonaerosol personal products—e.g., specialty soap, eye makeup, lipsticks, etc.

6. The size of the company should be such as to make possible a noticeable contribution to ATI's earnings per share after taking into account the potential effect of a synergetic relationship. In this regard the generation of an incremental 10¢ per share in earnings would be considered by ATI to be a noticeable financial contribution.

Such opportunities could lie in industries as diverse as microencapsulation and radiation as well as in consumer and/or industrial packaging and/or product services, but what is most important for us to develop is a sense for the future and a technological and marketing ability to meet this challenge within the framework of the financial criteria listed above and our own resources.

The Quality Products Company

At the beginning of 1966, Mr. Meyer was engaged in the evaluation of over 20 possible acquisitions in light of the above guidelines for diversification. He indicated that the guidelines did not adequately emphasize the desire of ATI's management for developing an end-consumer marketing activity. According to Mr. Meyer,

ATI's management would like to reduce both the risks associated with being a one-product company and the risks associated with being solely a supplier to those companies which market a product to the end-consumer. While Mr. Shepherd would prefer to serve industrial end-customers, the real emphasis is to get closer to an end-use market where ATI can best exploit its distinctive creative and innovative talents and yet not prejudice its relations with its existing customers. In this connection, it will be an interesting task to identify the "legitimate" path between customer loyalty and new opportunities in those end-use markets suited to our strengths.

Presently we're not sure whether we should acquire several small companies or one large one. Having a family of small companies is certainly a situation which we have learned to live with in a constructive and profitable way. It is also true that having several associated companies might help us to solve some management problems if it becomes necessary to move toward more centralized management of our aerosol operations, since these associated companies might then provide a constructive way to utilize the talents of those of our present divisional managers who are experienced and gifted entrepreneurs. On the other hand, a large acquisition might be the essential step necessary to help us build a reputation of excellence in a new field and this strategy might have substantial appeal to the entrepreneur who looks forward to corporate size as a means of at long last achieving the institution of a stable enterprise.

Basically then, no acquisition is too big or too small. Rather different, and, at first sight, perhaps conflicting, criteria must be used to judge each individual case. Meanwhile, we are trying to use the time we have to test the assumption that we have the brains and feelings necessary for growth into a different and changing environment with a different and changing organization.

The Quality Products Company * was one of the more promising acquisition prospects that Mr. Meyer was considering. Quality Products was a small company in the women's hand lotion business. During the fiscal year ended December 30, 1965, Quality earned about $92,000 on sales of $2.3 million which represented an increase of $28,000 in profits and $300,000 in sales from the 1964 fiscal year (see Exhibits 10 and 11).

Quality specialized in the manufacture of high-grade women's hand lotions, which it then sold to various prestige marketing companies who marketed the products under their own brands. Quality also manufactured hand lotion

EXHIBIT 10

AEROSOL TECHNIQUES, INC.*

Quality Products Company
Income Statements
(dollars in thousands)

	1961	*1962*	*1963*	*1964*	*9 months 1965*
Income from sales	$1,258	$2,024	$1,890	$2,002	$1,744
Cost of sales	1,036	1,596	1,579	1,575	1,380
Gross profit	$ 222	$ 428	$ 311	$ 427	$ 364
Selling expenses	60	74	102	107	88
General and administrative	60	72	91	109	81
Other	3	2	9	7	7
Total deductions	$ 123	$ 148	$ 202	$ 222	$ 176
Income before officers' salaries, profit sharing and taxes	$ 100	$ 280	$ 109	$ 205	$ 188
Officers' salaries	58	58	58	61	60
Profit sharing	16	24	23	30	–
Federal and state income taxes	8	103	10	50	59
Net income	$ 17	$ 95	$ 19	$ 64	$ 69

*Discrepancies may appear in totals as a result of rounding figures.
Source: Quality Products annual reports.

* For reasons of security, ATI desired that the name of the company and the name of the industry be disguised. The basic characteristics of the company and of the industry (e.g., size, nature of competition, product-market characteristics, etc.) are not disguised, however.

EXHIBIT 11

AEROSOL TECHNIQUES, INC.*

Quality Products Company
Balance Sheet for Year Ending December 1965

Assets		Liabilities and Equity	
Current assets		Current liabilities	
Cash	$135	Accounts payable and accrued expenses	$105
Treasury bonds	2	Notes payable to bank	225
Accounts receivable	193	Other	3
Inventory	357	Taxes payable	72
Other	38	Total current liabilities	$406
Total current assets	$725	Deferred tax credit	11
Fixed assets (net)		Stockholders equity	
Machinery and equipment	$122	Capital stock $25 par value	$ 94
Laboratory equipment	1	Capital surplus	83
Furniture and fixtures	22	Retained earnings	356
Leasehold improvements	34	Total stockholders' equity	$533
Total fixed assets	$179		
Other assets	46		
Total assets	$950	Total liabilities and stockholders' equity	$950

*Discrepancies may appear in totals as a result of rounding figures.
Source: Quality Products 1965 annual report.

of normal quality, which it sold to various supermarkets on a private-brand basis. At the end of 1965, Quality was constructing a new plant in Philadelphia which would increase capacity from $2.5 million to $4.0 million and would make possible more efficient operations than the present three-building plant.

Quality's management felt that, as soon as the new plant had "shaken down," a minimum sales increase of $1.3 million could be expected on the basis of preliminary contacts it had made with potential customers. Quality's management also expected that demand for quality hand lotions would increase because of several trends: the increased wealth and general desire for luxury, the rapid growth of the fragrance market and the impact thereof on sales of higher priced hand lotions, and the public's increasing receptiveness to greater luxury in hand creams as a result of mass advertising by the larger manufacturers who were improving their lower priced, mass-marketed hand creams.

Mr. Meyer indicated that the proposed acquisition was not without risk, however. His primary concern was that almost 50% of Quality's 1965 sales came from one customer, and that this percentage was expected to increase to 75% after the new factory was in operation. Mr. Meyer felt that with Quality producing nearly 30% of this customer's requirements, representing $3 million in sales to Quality, there was some risk the customer might decide to manufacture for himself. Nevertheless, given the willingness of ATI's management to live with this kind of risk, which was common in the packaging industry, Mr. Meyer felt that the decision to acquire Quality would rest on the cost of the deal and the degree to which ATI's resources could help Quality to grow and to minimize its vulnerability to the decisions of its major customer.

Mr. Meyer also indicated that if ATI acquired Quality, it would probably try to purchase the quality hand cream division of one of the large national manufacturers that was located in the Midwest, giving ATI national coverage of the quality hand cream business. He felt the chances of negotiating this purchase would be better than fifty-fifty, since the national manufacturer had not exhibited a deep interest in this division for over 15 years.

REFERENCES

[1] *Aerosol Age,* July 1956.
[2] Shepherd, H. R.: "The Contract Filler's Role in Aerosol Product Development." *Aerosol Age,* December 1963.

CASE 2

Polaroid Corporation

*H. Deane Wong**

For 27 years Polaroid Corporation had successfully combined a genius for research with an aggressive bent for marketing to create a half-billion dollar market for instant photography. By 1973 Polaroid had achieved the second largest position in the domestic photographic industry and was heralded as one of the nation's most glamorous growth companies. Sales and profits grew rapidly between 1955 and 1965 at compounded annual growth rates of 23% and 28%, respectively. Profits reached a peak in 1969 of $146 million (2.19 per share) but dropped off in subsequent years despite steadily increasing sales. Nevertheless, the stock market continued to evaluate Polaroid's prospects at 60 times previous year's earnings as excitement over the company's revolutionary new instant photo camera, the SX-70, drove the stock price to 143 in 1973.

In the fall of 1974, the situation at Polaroid was clouded. Earnings were substantially down from 1973 levels (Exhibit A), and the SX-70 was still having difficulties—manufacturing problems, customer complaints, and shortages of film and cameras. Its P/E ratio had dropped to 17–20 times 1973 earnings.

EXHIBIT A

1974 Quarterly Earnings

	Earnings $ Millions	*% Chg. From 1973*
1st Quarter	$9.9	- 12%
2nd Quarter	$2.2	- 73%
3rd Quarter	$7.0	- 37%

Source: *Business Week,* Quarterly Reports of Corporate Performance, May 11, 1974; August 10, 1974; November 9, 1974.

* Reprinted by permission.

THE INDUSTRY

In 1973 the photographic industry was a $5.8 billion business. Average annual growth rate between 1967 and 1972 had been only 7% but increased to 10% in 1973 due to the expansion of discretionary income, new products, and technological advances in the amateur, professional, commercial, and industrial fields. The industry was dominated by Eastman-Kodak (Exhibit B) which had the broadest representation in the industry producing still cameras, film, home movie cameras, slide projectors, and photofinishing equipment and materials. It also had a significant fiber-chemical business. Polaroid, next in size, had a fair share of the amateur photo equipment market, matching Kodak's sales to United States amateurs of film and hardware in 1970.

The Amateur Photo Market

This sector of the industry, dominated by Kodak and Polaroid, accounted for nearly 40% of the total industry in 1973, with expenditures reaching close to $2 billion. The interest of the general public in photography was at its highest in 10 years.

Although economic climate clearly had an impact on this segment of the market, it was also one which was heavily dependent on technological innovation and introduction of new products to spur growth. The mid-60s was a period of explosive growth generated by introduction of some major product innovations. These included the Kodak Instamatic cartridge-loading camera of which ten million were sold in the first 26 months; the flash cube which sharply increased film usage and spurred the photo finishing industry; and the Polaroid Swinger, notable for being Polaroid's lowest priced camera (at $19.95) and for its "talking shutter" which said "yes" or "no" to light conditions. In the 70s Kodak introduced the Pocket Instamatic and Polaroid, its SX-70, both of which were major factors in broadening the amateur photo market.

Film was the single most important revenue source in the industry. Profit margins were high: Kodak, doing its own manufacturing, enjoyed a 70% pretax profit margin on film. Together Kodak and Polaroid accounted for 90% of the amateur film market, with Polaroid posting higher dollar sales of amateur film for still cameras than Kodak in recent years. "Production of film is a highly complex, precision automotated process . . . . Each new equipment product breakthrough usually requires an entirely new type of film" [Standard & Poor's *Industry Surveys,* 1974:L16].

Still camera sales were the second most important sales line. In 1973, "Polaroid's instant photography accounts for about one-third of all still cameras sold in the U.S.; of the remaining two-thirds, Kodak has 85%" [*Forbes,* Sept. 15, 1974:83]. Photo finishing, flash attachment products, slide projectors, and home movie equipment were the other major revenue producers in the amateur photo sector.

EXHIBIT B

Industry Data

	Interim or Annual Operating Data									Annual Earnings Per Share				
		Revenues (Millions)			Net Income (Millions)			Earnings Per Share						
	No. of Months	1973	1974	% of Change	1973	1974	% of Change	1973	1974	Year Ends	1970	1971	1972	1973
Bell & Howell	6 (Jun.)	197.0	227.0	+ 15.2	9.19	9.11	- .9	1.61	1.60	Dec.	2.02	2.50	3.00	3.36
Eastman Kodak	6 (Jun.)	1,704.3	1,965.8	+ 15.3	277.00	267.90	- 3.3	1.72	1.66	Dec.	1.50	2.60	3.39	4.05
Polaroid	6 (Jun.)	278.6	328.5	+ 17.9	19.60	12.10	- 38.0	.60	.37	Dec.	2.01	1.86	1.30	1.58

Source: *Standard & Poor's Industry Surveys*, 1974, Pg. L4

Since technological innovations played such an important part in sales growth, research and development (R&D) expenditures were high. In 1972 Kodak spent $215 million on R&D, 6.2% of its total sales; Polaroid spent $130 million, a whopping 23% of sales.

POLAROID'S HISTORY

Founded in 1937 by scientist-entrepreneur, Edwin H. Land, Polaroid's chief product was sun-glasses. But Land's major aim was to sell Detroit on putting polarized filters on every automobile. After the war and a flat "no" from the auto makers, Polaroid switched to the picture-in-a-minute camera, an invention of Land's, which started the firm's success story in 1947.

In 1963 Polacolor was introduced, a new color film that would emerge from the cameras as a color print 50 seconds after the shutter was snapped. It was a major scientific breakthrough because all the complexities of a photo-developing lab were squeezed into a small camera. More importantly, it cut Polaroid in, for the first time, to the big color film market. Also introduced that year was the Automatic 100, notable for its electronically controlled shutter, capable of automatically timing a flash or a natural exposure. A film pack was designed for the 100 that allowed pictures, both black and white and color, to develop outside the camera, eliminating waiting time between exposures.

The year 1965 marked Polaroid's first move into the mass market with the introduction of the Swinger, selling at $19.95. Previously, its lowest priced camera sold for $59.95. The Swinger gave Polaroid a product competitively priced with Kodak's Instamatic, and its price together with its ease of use put Polaroid, for the first time, deep into the vast and growing teenage market. In 1969 60% of all Americans 18 years old and under owned one or more cameras. In addition to conventional camera outlets, the Swinger was retained through more than 50,000 drug stores and also gave the discounters something to sell, a significant factor since the number of camera departments in discount stores had gone up 50% between 1964–1969. Five million Swingers were sold in the first two years boosting camera sales, and in 1965 for the first time, more of Polaroid's sales were from film than cameras, a desirable situation since film is a photographic equipment makers' stabilizing and high margin product. Three years later Polaroid introduced the Big Swinger, which produced a larger picture.

Closest to a breakthrough in the industrial field was Polaroid's introduction in 1966 of its ID-2 Land Identification System, which produces, within two minutes, finished, sealed identification cards with full color photographs of the subject.

In 1969, the 300 series was introduced, which included six cameras ranging from $199.95 to $29.95. One of these, Colorpak II at $29.95, was Polaroid's "expansion product," designed to widen its wedge in the low-price market. It was a big success; "nearly half of the four million Polaroids sold in the last 12 months were Colorpacks" [*Fortune,* November 1970:86].

Polaroid also in 1969 began to integrate backwards. Up to this time, Polaroid had farmed out the bulk of its manufacturing to U.S. Time, and Bell and Howell. The company had bought the negative stock for its color film from Kodak. In 1969 it began a $200 million expansion program and by 1972 had completed five new plants to produce color transparency film which could produce instant color slides; to produce new color negative film for a new camera, yet to be unveiled (the SX-70); to manufacture the new camera; and to assemble the new film packs. With this move, it became clear that Polaroid was no longer simply a specialty company, but one after the undisputed market leadership over Kodak in the amateur photographic market. The new plants made Polaroid a real manufacturer for the first time, with the goal of reducing costs and fattening future profit margins. Compared to Kodak's 70% pretax margin on film, Polaroid's was only 40–45%.

THE SX-70

The SX-70 will almost surely be the crowning scientific achievement of Land's distinguished career [*Fortune,* January 1974:147].

It is not just another camera. Its mere production must be counted as one of the most remarkable accomplishments in industrial history. Its development involved a series of scientific discoveries, inventions, and technological innovations in fields such as chemistry, optics, and electronics. Failure to solve any one of a dozen major problems would have doomed the SX-70. It comes very close to the ideal Land had set out to invent 30 years ago, "absolute one-step photography." The photographer composes the picture, focuses, and shoots. Shutter speed and aperture are electronically set. The picture is ejected immediately from the camera and starts to develop. There is nothing to throw away or peel off. The photo is sturdy, plastic-coated, and can be slipped into a pocket or purse at once.

Development began as a result of Land's desire to design a camera so different and so advanced as to set up a whole new patent wall and render obsolete other Polaroid cameras which any competitors may legally imitate. It was also designed to correct two persistent shortcomings in Polaroid's other cameras: a trail of refuse and a high decay rate of about 50%. This decay rate is the estimated rate at which Polaroid owners lose interest in instant photography and stop using their Polaroids. Kodak's estimated decay rate, by comparison, was only 9%; hence, Kodak's virtual monopoly on film sales. With the SX-70, Polaroid hoped to reduce its decay rate to 40%. Although the company has not officially released the project's cost, estimates range from $500–$600 million.

Land planned to produce 800,000 to 1.2 million SX-70s in the first year and 50 million over the next decade. His fantasy is "that this camera will be as widely used as the telephone" [*Fortune,* June 1972:31]. However, priced at $180, it was not exactly priced for the mass market. In 1972 the Wolfman Report showed that sales of *all* cameras over $100 totaled only 1.3 million that year. In January 1974, one year after its national introduction, the company announced that the SX-70 had passed the breakeven point—$350 million had been invested in R&D over a six-year span. At that point 470,000 cameras and 4½ million packs of film had been sold.

The project had been plagued from the beginning with problems. Scheduled for national introduction by Christmas 1972, it was only marketed in Florida by then; production and techniçal difficulties delayed its introduction nationwide until Fall of 1973. Even then, customers complained of focusing problems causing blurry pictures, dead batteries in film packs, and hardly the "exceptional clarity and brilliant color" of which the advertisements spoke. Since the batteries were an integral part of the film pack, a dead battery meant that the entire 10 picture pack would be ruined. By mid-1974 the battery problem had not improved much. Their relatively short shelf life (about five to six months) kept customers from buying a half a dozen packs at a time. Also inflation was curbing discretionary spending, making it difficult for dealers to sell the camera at their $179.95 list price. At that time, Polaroid was still struggling up the learning curve in its new plants. They were having reliability and yield problems so plant capacity was not fully utilized and production rates were erratic.

EXHIBIT C

POLAROID CORPORATION

Income Statements 1968–1973
Year Ending December 31
($ 000)

	1973	*1972*	*1971*	*1970*	*1969*	*1968*
Net Sales	$685,536	$559,288	$525,507	$492,095	$522,197	$443,895
Cost of Goods Sold	$358,277	$259,090	$243,397	$240,260		
Cost of Research, Engr.	$251,944	$237,577	$181,280	$140,451		
Selling Gen. & Admin. Exp.						
Operating Profit	$ 75,315	$ 62,621	$100,830	$111,384		
Other Income	$ 15,101	$ 11,869	$ 15,862	$ 15,640		
Earnings Before Taxes	$ 90,416	$ 74,490	$116,692	$127,024	$145,626	$135,053
Taxes	$ 38,598	$ 31,956	$ 55,674	$ 61,050	$ 74,445	$ 72,899
Net Income	$ 51,818	$ 42,534	$ 61,018	$ 65,974	$ 71,181	$ 62,154
Earnings Per Share	$ 1.58	$ 1.30	$ 1.86	$ 2.01	$ 2.19	$ 1.96

Source: Polaroid's 1973 Annual Report and Moody's Industrial Manual, 1974

EXHIBIT D

POLAROID CORPORATION

Balance Sheets 1968–1971
Year Ending December 31
($ 000)

	1973	1972	1971	1970	1969	1968
ASSETS						
Cash	$ 25,115	$ 16,758	$ 15,620	$ 14,403	$ 8,478	$ 8,843
Marketable Securities	$162,967	$199,912	$178,562	$196,389	$200,682	$ 81,283
Notes & Accts. Rec.	$265,622	$114,553	$115,476	$107,852	$100,203	$ 93,216
Inventories	$142,368	$ 88,125	$ 85,021	$ 55,778	$ 47,595	$ 41,910
Prepaid Expenses	$ 17,176	$ 7,919	$ 9,176	$ 6,089	$ 1,453	$ 1,619
Total Curr. Assets	$513,248	$427,267	$403,855	$380,511	$358,411	$226,871
Property, Plant, Eqmt.	$393,053	$354,774	$316,659	$258,879	$188,267	$144,569
Less: Depre. & Amort. Reserves	$164,719	$130,239	$103,387	$ 83,023	$ 63,197	$ 48,736
Investments in Foreign Subs.	$	$	$	$	$ 959	$ 4,226
TOTAL ASSETS	$741,582	$651,802	$617,127	$556,367	$484,440	$326,932
LIABILITIES						
Accts. Payable & Accruals	$ 83,312	$ 52,639	$ 45,127	$ 38,722	$ 44,044	$ 37,588
Provision for Taxes	$ 39,202	$ 22,196	$ 27,820	$ 24,595	$ 16,503	$ 18,366
Total Curr. Liab.	$122,514	$ 74,835	$ 72,947	$ 63,317	$ 60,547	$ 55,954
Common Stock	$ 32,855	$ 32,848	$ 32,840	$ 32,832	$ 32,828	$ 31,712
Add'l. Paid-In Capital	$121,999	$121,210	$120,455	$119,843	$119,725	$ 20,633
Retained Earnings	$464,214	$422,909	$390,885	$340,375	$271,340	$218,631
Total Stockholder's Equity	$	$	$	$	$	$
TOTAL LIABILITIES	$741,582	$651,802	$617,127	$556,367	$484,440	$326,930

Source: Moody's Industrial Manual, 1974 and Polaroid's 1973 Annual Report

FINANCE

Polaroid has been characterized by two unusual financial policies: no debt and no acquisitions. A seemingly prime rule of growth companies has been the use of capital leverage, yet Polaroid has financed its tremendous growth over the years entirely from earnings from operations. In 1969 when it needed money for its plant expansion program, it raised $100 million by sale of stock. The rest came from profits.

If Polaroid had chosen to, it could have expanded by using its high priced stock to buy other companies' assets and earnings at bargain rates. In 1966 its stock sold at 81 times previous year's earnings, and until 1974, had consistently sold above 60 times earnings. However, it has been a deliberate policy of Land's not to expand through acquisitions. When asked about it, Land's response was, "Why?" and that ended discussion of that question [*Forbes,* June 15, 1969:42].

PRODUCT PHILOSOPHY AND RESEARCH AND DEVELOPMENT

Land's product philosophy and attitude towards research were closely linked. Polaroid carried out "nearly pure research on a broad base, but concentrates application on a relatively few products. 'We do a few things magnificently.' " [*Business Week,* August 3, 1963:82]. This narrow product line policy had been consistent throughout Polaroid's history. With each new series of cameras, older models were discontinued: the Big Swinger replaced the Swinger, the Colorpack II replaced the Big Swinger.

Land also believed that a product should meet the "test of uniqueness" before it was brought to market. At the 1968 annual stockholders' meeting, he demonstrated a working model of a document copier, but it was never marketed.

> "We do not want to do what every Tom, Dick, or Xerox can do. Our company has been dedicated throughout its life to making only things which others cannot make. We proceed from basic science through applied science to highly desirable products" [*Forbes,* June 15, 1969:42].

As a result he insisted that his firm find its own opportunities for growth by way of research.

Land's goal had always been "to make a new kind of product—something people have not thought of as a product at all" [*Fortune,* July 1966:314]. He encouraged Polaroid's young scientists and engineers to spend up to one-fifth of their time on research of their own choice. Through research Land hoped continuously to develop new products for consumers, some not even demanded yet.

Cameras, film, and photographic accessories account for about 90% of Polaroid's total domestic sales with polarizer products and industrial items representing the remainder. Film sales account for well over 50% of the volume.

PRODUCTION

As stated earlier, production of the SX-70 cameras and film packs was Polaroid's first experience with mass production. As such, this presented a formidable managerial challenge to the company, compounded by the complexity of the totally new camera system of the SX-70 to be produced.

When Polaroid first announced its intention to manufacture its own color negative for the SX-70, Kodak expressed its doubts about Polaroid's ability to gear up for the exacting art of negative making and predicted many headaches in start-up of production. However, the color negative plant was a resounding success from the start. Usable negative was produced on the second run, and no major problems were encountered. The production line was run by digital minicomputers with older, proven analog controls operating alongside. Such automation was installed to assure standard quality of a finicky product, and also to give the plant flexibility to allow for changes in the production process. However, problems with the production of the film packs and cameras had slowed output to half the desired levels in 1974.

Although Polaroid produced its SX-70, it continued to use outside contractors to assemble earlier model cameras. Polaroid concentrated its manufacturing effort at the most critical value-added stage. It continued to farm out the high volume, repetitive manufacturing work "that others can perform just as well," consistent with Land's concept of uniqueness [*Business Week*, April 15, 1972:71].

MARKETING

Until 1960 Polaroid existed chiefly on a stream of remarkable cameras and film ideas from Land's laboratory. Land believed that the right product will sell itself. However, when sales reached $100 million and the instant color film had been perfected, Land beefed up marketing. The company's aggressive marketing and promotional abilities succeeded time after time in building a market where none existed before. For example, with the introduction of the 300 series and the Colorpack II in particular, Polaroid spent $2.2 million in a 12-day period for newspaper, magazine, radio, and television advertising. They estimated that the five-day TV introductory blast hit 96% of the population no fewer than seven times. Following this campaign, they spent an additional $10 million during the next three months and ultimately $22 million by year end on promotional advertising. In a relatively mature market where most of Polaroid's natural customers already owned earlier models, the marketing effort hoped to convince the consumer that there was enough difference between the old and the new to warrant replacement. In fact, 40%

of Colorpack II's initial sales were from Swinger and Big Swinger owners who had traded up. $9 million was spent on a barrage of advertising for the SX-70, with TV commercials featuring Lawrence Olivier.

Part of the marketing philosophy was that there is nothing like something new to stimulate public interest and sweep new buyers into a flagging market. Nearly every other year since 1963 Polaroid had introduced a new camera or series of cameras, with attendant improvements in the film.

Polaroid's salesmen were young and aggressive, not hand-holders like Kodak's. They were wedded to the discounters and drug stores in order to get Polaroid's cameras into as many hands as possible. In 1969 cameras, especially in the low-price market, were sold through discount stores (24%), conventional cameras outlets (26%), drug stores (17%), and department stores (16%). Kodak had at that time just moved into supermarkets, and Polaroid took steps to do the same, as supermarkets had started to gain in numbers as film outlets.

ORGANIZATION AND LAND

It is impossible to speak about the organization of Polaroid without talking about Land. Although he vigorously denied it, Polaroid was a one-man company, clearly bearing the stamp of its guiding genius scientist-inventor-president-chairman of the board-head of research-founder. The top management of Polaroid was imbued with science and in many ways resembled a university faculty. Land's ready access to top scientific circles at MIT and Harvard has served him well.

Polaroid was characterized by an associate of Land's as "80% Land's inventiveness and creative ability . . . . The frosting is that important disciplines such as marketing, personnel, patents, and finance have been in the hands of strong men" [*Business Week,* April 15, 1972:70]. One of Land's geniuses was to give good people the freedom to maneuver. Many of Polaroid's executives had been with Land from the early years, lending depth to the management team.

A strange blend of informality, paternalism, secretiveness, and experimentation was always characteristic of Polaroid. They never had an organization chart and "did not write long memos to each other" [*Forbes,* June 15, 1969:42]. It was not uncommon for Land to pop in on someone who was working on a project that had caught his attention for a moment.

Land was alternatively a shy scientist poring over a new discovery and a commanding chief executive. He has been described as "an industrial philosopher, humanistic employer, and final arbiter on Polaroid's crucial management decisions" [*Business Week,* March 15, 1972:73]. Once a year at the stockholders' annual meeting, he became a spellbinding showman as he described the wonders his laboratories had in store for the future.

He was a creative person with a suspicion that good, careful, systematic planning would kill a creative company. Whenever he worked on something that was wild and risky, like the SX-70, he was careful to insulate himself from anyone who was critical because he realized how easily it was, in the early stages, for a dream to be exploded.

OUTLOOK FOR THE FUTURE

Industry Outlook

In 1974 Standard & Poor's predicted "that the most fascinating and complex area in the amateur field now is instant photography" [Standard & Poor's *Industry Surveys,* 1974:L17]. With its SX-70 Polaroid had broadened this market and Kodak could no longer ignore the indications that instant photography was beginning to make inroads to conventional photography. Although Kodak hinted in its 1973 Annual Report that it could be entering the instant photo field soon, Land doubted that Kodak could close Polaroid's 22 year lead in instant photo technology. Polaroid's new cameras were protected by patents not due to expire until 1984.

U.S. Industrial Outlook predicted the following in its 1980 projections:

> The pocket cartridge load camera will increase its sales momentum, while the instant camera concept will revolutionize the camera industry. Next in sight are instant movie cameras and slide transparencies. The available light concept may eliminate the need for flash bulbs in still cameras. The long awaited home video system will become a reality as hardware prices decline. [*U.S. Industrial Outlook,* 1974:237].

At Polaroid

In late 1974 the jury was still out on the future of the SX-70. It was unclear whether market saturation had been reached or if subsequent resolution of both technical and production difficulties would change the picture significantly. It was even harder to predict what direct competition from Kodak could do the SX-70. It was clear that much was riding on Polaroid's performance as a large-scale manufacturer and on the market success of its new product. Heavy research and start-up costs had held 1971 and 1972 earnings down. And in 1974 analysts were predicting that earnings per share could drop below $1.00 a share.

Polaroid was reportedly continuing devolopment of an instant movie camera but received a setback in August 1974 when it was announced that Bell and Howell had withdrawn from an agreement with Polaroid to make the equipment for Polaroid's instant motion picture system. In late 1974 Polaroid introduced a new pack camera called Zip, selling for $13.95 which produced black-and-white pictures in 30 seconds.

Land gave no hint of retiring when he reached 65 in 1974, and said nothing about a successor except that one of the top two men at Polaroid should always be a scientist. It was hard to imagine Polaroid without Land. The scientist-industrialist would be missed especially in research where key Polaroid inventions were essentially Land's; he has been an unflaggingly productive inventor. In 1974 there was no Number 2 man evident, only a group of Number 3's. Land had assembled an impressive team around him, which as a group may be able to duplicate his personal talents.

REFERENCES

"A Sure Thing?" *Forbes,* June 15, 1973.

"Automated Cameras Catch the Customers." *Business Week,* August 3, 1963.

"The Blurry Picture at Eastman Kodak." *Forbes,* September 15, 1974.

Cordtz, Dan: "How Polaroid Bet Its Future on the SX-70." *Fortune,* January, 1974.

"The Dimensions of American Business: A Roster of the U.S.'s Biggest Corporations." *Forbes,* May 15, 1974.

"Dr. Land Redesigns His Camera Company." *Business Week,* April 15, 1972.

"Dr. Land's Latest Fantasy." *Fortune,* June 1972.

Karp, Richard: "The Clouded Picture at Polaroid." *Dun's,* November 1973.

"Kodak's Latest Hint." *Business Week,* March 30, 1974.

Moody's Handbook of Common Stocks: Third Quarter 1974. New York, Moody's Investors Service, Inc., 1974.

Moody's Industrial Manual. New York, Moody's Investors Service, Inc., 1974.

"Polaroid." *Forbes,* June 15, 1969.

"Polaroid Slumps." *Business Week,* July 6, 1974.

"Polaroid Snaps Into Color." *Business Week,* January 19, 1963.

"Polaroid Trains Lens on Quickie ID Cards." *Business Week,* October 1, 1966.

"Polaroid: Turning Out a Finicky Product." *Business Week,* December 8, 1973.

"Polaroid's Big Blitz." *Business Week,* March 1, 1969.

"Polaroid's Troubles with the SX-70." *Business Week,* June 8, 1974.

Siekman, Philip: "Kodak and Polaroid: An End to Peaceful Coexistence." *Fortune,* November 1970.

"The Singular Growth of Polaroid Corporation." *Fortune,* July 15, 1966.

Standard & Poor's Industry Surveys: Vol. 1. New York, Standard Poor's Corporation, October 1974.

Standard & Poor's Stock Reports. New York, Standard & Poor's Corporation, October 1974.

"Survey of Corporate Performance: Third Quarter 1974." *Business Week,* November 9, 1974.

"The SX-70 Makes It." *Business Week,* February 23, 1974.

U.S. Department of Commerce, Domestic & International Business Administration: *U.S. Industrial Outlook: 1974,* Washington, D.C., U.S. Government Printing Office, 1974.

CASE 3

Metropolis City Museum of Art

*Patrick H. Ela**

The Metropolis City Museum of Art (MCMA) has an administrative staff of 20. Included are a director, four curators, two co-office managers, three librarians, and a community relations liaison who also sits on the Board of Directors as a nonvoting member.

For the last century, the museum has depended upon its Board for primary financial support. Since 1870, the Board has raised over $20,000,000 for salaries, exhibitions, and various programs while building the collection from 20 to over 3,000 works of art.

The need for substantial monetary "pull" on the part of the 25 Board members has led to a situation where most of its members come from the ranks of big business and the well-established families of Metropolis. The average Board member is 67 years old and has an annual income of $100,000.

The basic objective of the Board is to maintain a high level of culture for the city. Mr. T. B. Walker, current Board Chairman, said at last year's annual fund-raising dinner that "The Board, as in years past, will do everything in its power to assure the continuation of high levels of taste and connoiseurship in acquisitions, and the maintenance of the aesthetic leadership of this community."

He continued by saying, "Despite the increased insurance costs which have cut this year's budget, we feel that our expenditures on new alarm systems, more security officers, and especially the new fences surrounding our museum are well spent. Our future Director, Mr. G. Y. Tal, will, I am sure, give us great assistance in our efforts to continue with our community's artistic growth, and as the cultural stewards of this great city, we will care for our legacy."

Walker ended his keynote speech by reminding his audience that "The Board had done all right in the past, gotten lots of money, bought lots of art, and served its community well. I guess you could say that we pretty much know what's good for this city. When my Daddy was Chairman of this Board, he told me that there would always be those who would try to change our system of doing things; but we've got a good system, and we're not going to give in to any unnecessary changes."

In December 1972, after three years of casual applicant screening, the

* Reprinted by permission.

Board hired Dr. G. Y. Tal as the new Director of the Museum. Tal's credentials were impeccable. He had received his Ph. D. in Art History from Harvard, directed three major American art museums from 1958 to 1966, and spent two years at Berlin's Dahlem Museum and three years at the Louvre in Paris as the "Professor in Residence." Since January 1972, Tal had worked as a consultant for the Association of American Art Museums, and as Executive Committee Chairman for the International Council of Museums (ICOM). He was also active in the formulation of a public education study. In his employment interview, Tal told the Board that he was "at a cross roads in life. I want to decide whether I will continue to work in a policy-making capacity, or return to museum directing. Tal was unconditionally hired for two years at $38,500 per year. After two years, the Museum Board would review his works, deciding whether they wished to keep him, and he would hopefully know if he wished to continue as a museum Director.

In addition to the normal fixed museum costs, the Board authorized a budget which would give Tal funding for three "special" shows per year, and $75,000 for yearly purchases of new works. Because of some letters about the museum's "social inactivity" in the Met *Times* (the local newspaper), the Board added a $10,000 per year stipend earmarked for "innovative activity in the community," which was renewable on a yearly basis, pending Board approval.

Tal's first action was to spend $5,000 on an audience survey. He wanted to find out who came to the Museum, how often, and why. Moreover, he wished to determine audience preferences and biases which he thought would be helpful in "innovatively" serving his community.

The survey, conducted by a professional polling organization, found that 2.8–3.2% of the city's 1.7 million people had been to the museum in the last five years. Of the roughtly 3%, Tal learned that only 20,000 people went regularly. The remaining 31,000 of the 3% said that the museum was only of slight interest. They felt that the shows were never varied, and that there was very little effort on the part of the museum to make its collections accessible to the public. One interviewee said about the museum, "The place seems too high brow, if you know what I mean. It's as if one has to wear a suit to look at the art works. Besides, except for the titles of the art works, the museum makes no attempt to tell us viewers anything about the art. Those so-called catalogues are too tough for me to try to understand and I took two art history courses in college."

Tal was upset by the results of the survey. He took his findings to the March Board meeting to see what could be done. The nonvoting community relations director, Mr. Forman, told him he was sure that the sample population in the study was invalid and unreliable; and that the whole survey was probably not representative of the population. "Anyway," he said, "there are probably not more than 3% of the population who know anything about art, so I say why bother with the riffraff. At the close of the meeting, T. B. Walker suggested to Tal that he "leave this marketing stuff to businessmen and get down to the business of running this art museum!"

Tal's reaction to the Board meeting was to call a meeting of his four curators. At that meeting the shows of the last five years were discussed as well as possible ideas for those in the next two years. The curators, almost in unison, said that the previous shows were primarily arranged around different groupings of the museum's permanent collection. The different art historical time periods (Ancient, Renaissance, etc.) were well represented, and the Board had often voiced the policy that "Our museum shouldn't buy works unless we are going to use them well and often." The resulting show format, they maintained, was therefore a logical extension of Board policy.

The curators were also asked what they felt the museum's role in the life of Metropolis was. The Curator of Ancient and Medieval Art said, "To collect and preserve the cultural heritage of ages past." The Curator of Renaissance and Baroque Art answered, "to gather important works and information so that interested citizens can learn about the not-too-distant past." The Curator of 18th and 19th Century Art felt that the museum was best described "as a sort of cultural warehouse." The last of the four, Mr. Branrye, Curator of 20th Century Art, said that it was the duty of the museum to interact with the citizenry of Metropolis in order to help them gain a workable knowledge of their lives through art. He added that "The museum should not be a mere storehouse of high cultural activities, nor should it be a simple library of paintings. Rather it should and must be a living, viable, and dynamic institution, through which cultural crossfertilization and growth can occur.

Tal especially liked Branrye's answer, and over the next two months began to work out the details for a show to be called, *The role of the museum in today's changing world.* The curators had expressed interest in and support of such a show but were somewhat apprehensive about the Board's reaction to the proposal, due to the fact that it would be a radical divergence from the normal permanent collection-type exhibition. Tal, on the other hand, felt that if they could get the plans rolling before they showed them to the Board the changes for success would be greater. "Leave the Board to me," he said, "my contract gives me three yearly shows of my own choosing."

On May 20, 1973, one week before the monthly Board meeting, Tal issued a press release to the *Times.* Therein he explained the purpose of the show, its didactic nature, and divergence from the past. He also spoke about the various uses such a show would have for the schools, artists, businessmen, and other cultural institutions.

The public reaction to the proposed show as evidenced by several letters to the Editor, some published, several not, was quite promising. Elated, Tal went to the May Board meeting and presented Mr. Walker with a show outline, budget, and copies of the public's reaction.

Walker was not at all pleased with the idea. "What is this place anyway," he asked, "an Art Museum or a college seminar! Here we spend millions of dollars collecting art works to be shown to the public and, without using a single one of them, you want to spend $80,000 to $120,000 for some new fangled show that's not even about art. He added, that he saw no need to diverge from the usual show format.

In rebuttal, Tal referred to the curators enthusiasm, the public's positive response, the results of the poll taken in January and February, and his own deep conviction that an art museum had to be in tune with, if not ahead of, the times.

Walker reiterated that the old way had been good enough. "Why," he asked, "spend money on building a collection, if you aren't going to use it?—The whole idea is crazy. Everyone knows you come to a museum to see art. That's how it's always been and always will be. We've had directors and curators in the past who've wanted to do all kinds of radical things, but we've always been able to make them see our side of things. We are certain, Dr. Tal, that you are a reasonable man, otherwise we wouldn't have hired you.

QUESTIONS

1. What are major managerial and artistic policy issues here?
2. Who is "in the right?"
3. Assuming, first, that you were Mr. Walker, and then Dr. Tal, what would you do between now and the proposed show opening date?
4. How do you think this situation will and/or should be resolved?

PART

III

Formulating Business Policy/Strategy

CHAPTER

7

Systematic Planning in Strategic Management

INTRODUCTION

A new comprehensive managerial planning system, called by many different names, has developed and spread rapidly around the world during the past twenty years. At the heart of the process is strategic planning. Although the process can be done informally, more and more companies, particularly the larger ones, find it is best conducted in a more formal and systematic fashion.

At the outset it is important to observe that there is no one way to introduce and use this new planning system. Each company is unique. We do know, however, that there are fundamental principles and practices that are needed for success. In this chapter we will summarize the nature of this system, how it operates, its importance to business, and the major pitfalls to be avoided in its operation. The literature in this field has been growing rapidly and now includes hundreds of articles and books. This chapter is a distillation of this literature and long experience with strategic planning systems.* (For literature surveys see Frazier [in Vancil *et al.*, 1969], Hussey [1974b], Mockler [1970], and Steiner [1969b].

WHAT FORMAL STRATEGIC PLANNING IS AND IS NOT

Intuitive-Anticipatory Versus Formal Long-Range Planning

There are a number of different approaches to the strategic decision-making processes of a company, as will be pointed out in Chapter 12. Here it must be noted that there are two basic types of strategic corporate planning. The first is intuitive-anticipatory planning. Although no one really knows the precise mental processes by which it is done, intuitive-anticipatory planning has

* This chapter mostly taken from George A. Steiner: *Comprehensive Managerial Planning*. Oxford, Ohio: Planning Executives Institute, 1972; and George A. Steiner: "Comprehensive Managerial Planning." In Joseph McGuire (ed.): *Contemporary Management: Issues and Viewpoints*. Englewood Cliffs, N.J.: Prentice-Hall, 1974.

several discernible major characteristics. Generally it is the work of one person. It may or may not, but often does not, result in a written set of plans. It generally has a comparatively short time horizon and reaction time. It is based upon past experience, the "gut" feel, the judgment, and the reflective thinking of a manager. It is very important. Many managers have extraordinary capabilities in intuitively devising brilliant strategies and methods to carry them out.*

In contrast, the formal planning system is organized and developed on the basis of a set of procedures. It is explicit in the sense that people know what is being done. It is research based, involves the work of many people, and results in a set of written plans.

These two systems of planning often clash. A manager who has been successful with his intuitive judgments is not likely to accept completely the constraints of a formal system. He may be uneasy with some of the new language and methods incorporated by sophisticated staff in a formal planning system. Or, he may feel a challenge to his authority as those participating in the system engage in the decision-making process.

There should be no conflict, however. These two systems should complement one another. The formal system should help managers to sharpen their intuitive-anticipatory inputs into the planning process. At the very least, the formal system should give managers more time for reflective thinking.

In a fundamental sense, formal planning is an effort to replicate intuitive planning. But formal planning cannot be really effective unless managers at all levels inject their judgments and intuition into the planning process.

Formal Comprehensive Managerial Planning Defined

The planning system that is the subject of this chapter has been given many names. We use synonymously: comprehensive corporate planning, comprehensive managerial planning, strategic planning, long-range planning, formal planning, over-all planning, corporate planning, and other combinations of these words.

Corporate long-range planning should be defined in at least four ways, each of which is needed in understanding it. First, it deals with the futurity of current decisions. This means that long-range planning looks at the chain of cause-and-effect consequences over time of an actual or an intended decision that a manager is going to make. If he does not like what he sees ahead, he then will change the decision. Long-range planning also looks at the alternative courses of action that are open in the future, and, when choices are made, they become the basis for making current decisions. The essence of long-range planning is the systematic identification of opportunities and threats that lie in the future which, in combination with other relevant data, provide

* We are using synonymously several words associated with creativity. Actually, there are differences among such things as intuition, judgment, hunch, instinct, invention, innovation, and entrepreneurship [see Steiner, 1969b:353–355].

a basis for management to make better current decisions to exploit the opportunities and avoid the threats.

Second, comprehensive corporate planning is a process. It is a process that begins with the development of objectives, defines strategies and policies to achieve objectives, and develops detailed plans to make sure that the strategies are carried out to achieve the objectives. It is a process of deciding in advance what is to be done, when it is to be done, how it is to be done, and who is going to do it.

Third, it is a philosophy. Many businessmen talk about corporate planning as being a way of life. Executives speak of assuring the proper climate in their enterprise to do the most effective corporate planning. This climate is a function of many forces among which is an attitude of wanting to do effective planning.

Fourth, comprehensive corporate planning may be defined as a structure of plans. It is a structure that integrates strategic with short-range operational plans. In this structure are integrated, at all levels, major objectives, strategies, policies, and functions of an enterprise.

All these characteristics of corporate planning will be further examined. Before looking at them, however, it is important to make a few comments on what long-range planning is not.

What Long-Range Planning is Not

Long-range planning does not attempt to make future decisions. Rather, planning involves choosing the more desirable future alternatives open to a company so that better current decisions can be made.

Comprehensive corporate planning is not forecasting product sales and then determining what should be done to assure the fulfillment of the forecasts, with respect to such things as material purchases, facilities, manpower, and so on. Corporate planning goes beyond present forecasts of current products and markets and asks such questions as: Are we in the right business? What are our basic objectives? When will our present products become obsolete? Are our markets accelerating or eroding? For most companies there is a wide gap between a simple forecast into the future of present sales and profits and what top management would like its sales and profits to be. If so, comprehensive corporate planning is a system that managers can use to fill the gap.

Comprehensive long-range planning is not attempting to blueprint the future. It is not the development of a set of plans that are cast in bronze to be used day after day into the far distant future. Indeed, much in long-range plans is obsolete when they are completed because the environment assumed in their plans has changed. On the other hand, long-range planning permits a company to "invent" its future. This means that a company, through the corporate planning process, tries to foresee the future it wants for itself. It then, very often, can fulfill the targets it sets for itself by the development of wise strategies and detailed plans.

Corporate Planning Models

A conceptual model of the corporate planning process was presented in Figure 2-1. This model was developed over a number of years during which one of the authors examined and helped to establish many planning systems. It can be concluded that companies that do effective strategic planning follow this model explicitly or implicitly. Yet, paradoxically, we have never seen an operational system diagramed in precisely the same way as Figure 2-1. Operational flow charts vary, depending upon differences among companies, but underneath, the basic elements of the model are found in the better systems. Conceptual models of leading authors in the field are quite comparable to Figure 2-1 [Anthony, 1965; Gilmore and Brandenberg, 1962; Ringbakk, 1972; Stewart, 1963; Humble, 1969; Cohen and Cyert, 1973].

In the following exposition we shall use Figure 2-1 to explain the planning process. It should be pointed out, however, that in actual practice the process is iterative and may begin at a different point. Also, in practice there is much back-and-forth analysis before decisions are made. For instance, a tentative objective may be established; then strategies are examined to achieve this objective. Depending upon the analysis of the strategies, the objective may be changed, and vice versa.

When a formal long-range planning system is first introduced in a company, especially a large one, it is advisable to determine precisely how the organization intends to operate the system. Most companies that have planning systems, especially the larger ones, have manuals that lay out procedures to be followed. These are plans to plan which will be discussed later.

THE STRATEGIC PLANNING PROCESS

As shown in Figure 2-1 the strategic planning part of the company-wide planning process includes five blocks to the left. We shall discuss each of these shortly, but before doing so a few characteristics of the strategic planning process should be mentioned.

First, it is quite obvious that the strategic planning process is the place where decisions of the highest significance to a company are made. Here is where the basic thrust and direction of the company is determined and the major approaches to proceeding along the lines set are decided.

Second, the time spectrum covered ranges from the very short range to infinity. Although the general thrust and content of strategic planning is long range, a decision can be made in this process to stop producing X product tomorrow or start to build tomorrow a new plant to produce Y product.

A third important characteristic is that, although the process may produce a written document on a periodic basis, such as once a year, the process is a continuous activity of top management, as illustrated in Figure 7-6. Top management cannot, of course, develop a strategic plan once a year and forget strategy in the meantime.

A fourth important characteristic of strategic planning, as compared with medium-range and short-range planning, is that the results are not usually neatly incorporated in a prescribed form. Medium-range and short-range planning result in numbers for specific functions for a prescribed period of time, as shown in Figure 7-2. Strategic planning covers any element of the business that is important at the time of analysis and embodies details that are of sufficient scope and depth to provide the necessary basis for implementation. The format for strategic plans is generally much more flexible and variable in content, from time to time, than for other type plans.

The Situation Audit

The four stacked blocks to the left of Figure 2-1 compose what has come to be called the situation audit or the planning premises. These blocks cover the identification and/or evaluation of information essential to making decisions described in the blocks to the right of them. The following discussion will present a few highlights of the nature of each of the major elements in this process. The discussion will combine fundamental concept, methodology, operational principles, and scholarly literature. The same thing will be done with other elements shown in Figure 2-1.

Expectations of Major Outside Interests

Up to a few years ago, in the academic as well as in the business world, a business was said to have but one socioeconomic purpose and that was to use the resources at its disposal as efficiently as possible in producing the goods and services that consumers wanted at prices they were willing to pay. If firms did this well, classical economic theory said they would maximize profits. Many people in both the educational and business world still think this is business' only responsibility. But more and more people in and out of business think that this is too narrow. For example, Edward N. Cole [1970:1], when President of General Motors Corporation said, "The big challenge to American business—as I see it—is to carefully evaluate the constantly changing expressions of public and national goals. Then we must modify our own objectives and programs to meet—as far as possible within the realm of economic and technological feasibility—the new demands of the society we serve." Any large company that begins its long-range planning solely on the basis of the short-range profit maximization principle as its only objective will inevitably wind up in a heap of trouble. As pointed out in preceding chapters many people and groups are interested in what larger corporations do, and the top managers of these corporations are wise in responding to their legitimate demands.

Expectations of Major Inside Interests

Similarly, as noted in preceding chapters, values, attitudes, and interests of individuals and groups inside a company must be understood and evaluated as significant premises for planning. The value systems of top managers particularly are basic and fundamental premises in any comprehensive corporate planning system. Sometimes executive values are written, but most of the time they are not written nor even articulated. Many of these values cannot be proven or disproven to be correct on the basis of numbers or even logic, yet they may determine basic long-range directions of a company. For instance, a chief executive may say, "I want my company to be the biggest in our industry in ten years." Or, he may say, "I want my company to be the technologically best in the industry." Or, he may say, "My goal is to make my company the biggest and the technically best company in my industry in the next decade." Each of these aims provides a very different frame of reference for doing corporate planning. Each is rooted in the value system of the chief executive officer in the company.

Not only do value systems influence objectives but they also influence all sorts of decisions made in the planning process. For instance, one executive may wish to do business with the Mexicans because he likes them. Another in the same industry may prefer not to extend his operations to Mexico. The reasons of both managers may have nothing to do with sales and profits but may be solely determined by the values each holds.

The Data Base

Included in the data base are facts about the past performance of the company, its current situation, and future prospects. Data about the past would cover such matters as sales, profits, return on investment, productivity, marketing systems, and so on.

The current situation could include the financial position of the company, market share, evaluations of managerial and employee skills, various measures of efficiency (for example, sales per employee, plant utilization, investment per employee), competition, constituent demands, government regulations, and so on. Forecasts would include sales, market conditions, and other economic conditions.

There are five major types of forecasts made in and for the planning process. First, are survey-research type forecasts that involve the integration of many different areas of knowledge. For example, a quality forecast of the automobile market will rest not alone on economic analysis but upon changes in social values, technology, politics, and pollution standards. Second, are economic type forecasts. Generally, the most often made forecasts are of sales. The tool kit of sales forecasters is very rich [Butler and Kavesh, 1974; Enrick, 1969; Chambers, Mullick, and Smith, 1971].

Technological forecasts are a third type of futures information being made by more and more companies. Work has advanced importantly in recent years about how to make acceptable forecasts of technology. The methodology ranges from mathematical formulas to informed judgment [Jantsch, 1967; Bright, 1968; Ayers, 1969; and *Technological Forecasting,* all issues].

Forecasting what competitors are likely to do is something that all companies should do systematically, but few do. For a large company a questionnaire to informed personnel is a simple and effective method to get such information.

Two other types of forecasts are now being made by a few very large companies but will be made increasingly by larger companies in the future. They are forecasts of social values and social indicators. By social values are meant attitudes and views people hold about such matters as social justice, comfort, human dignity, materialism, national pride, and so on. Everyone knows that values are changing importantly. A large company that can forecast changes in society's values that will affect it will obviously have an advantage [Baier and Rescher, 1969; Wilson, in Steiner, 1975a]. Social indicators are measures of phenomena associated with quality of life, such as personal safety, medical care, and different pollutions [O'Toole *et al.*, 1973; and Terleckyj, 1970].

Forecasts in these latter two areas will increase among the larger businesses and, for some, they will in the future stand beside the traditional economic forecasts as major considerations in corporate decision making. Important strides have been made in the past few years in making such forecasts [*The Futurist,* various issues]. The number of environmental forces, inside and outside, that may be of importance to a company is so great that it is necessary to determine which are most significant and to spend as much time and effort as possible in studying them. What is important to one company may be completely unimportant to another.

Opportunities, Threats, Strengths and Weaknesses

Figure 7-1 illustrates different ways a company can approach identification of opportunities, threats, and risks. Problem identification in the upper left hand corner refers to results of simple observation or deep analysis. For instance, a company may note that its profit margin for product X is falling. This is a problem, and the next step is to define precisely what is causing it. When that is understood, what can and should be done in the future to correct it becomes clearer. Some companies begin the planning process by identifying opportunities and threats in this way.

Another approach is to ask what are the basic missions and objectives of the company and then determine what opportunities are ahead to achieve them or which threats may thwart their fulfillment.

Opportunism is a third approach. For example, the analysis of diversification opportunities of some companies is dependent upon "what comes over the transom." In other words they wait to see what offers are made and then analyze each one. This is in contrast to a careful examination of opportunities in the environment to find the best possibilities for diversification. McDonnell-Douglas's movement into computer software systems resulted from such a systematic study.

Instinctive feel or intuitive insight into the future is always, of course, a potentially powerful approach.

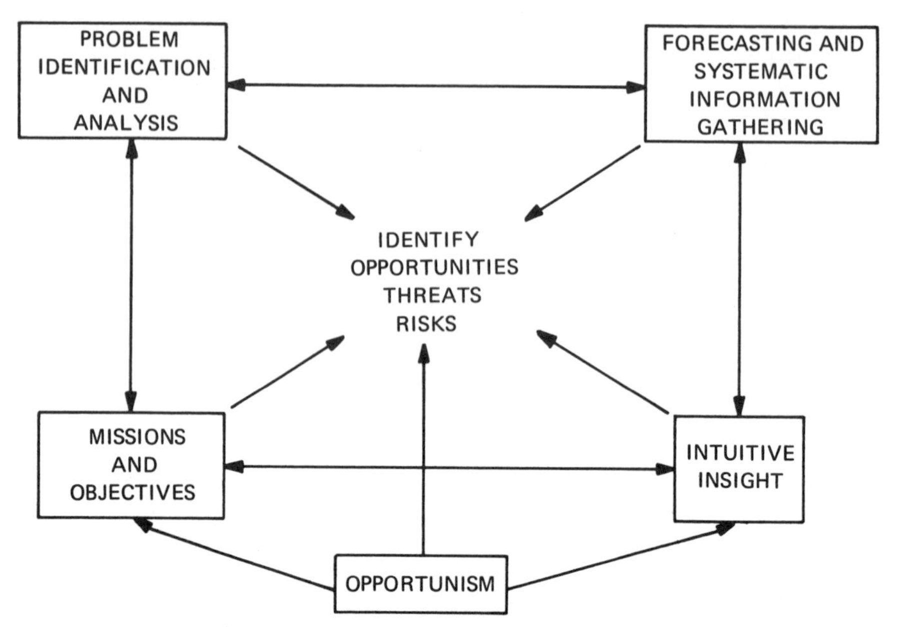

Figure 7-1 Opportunity-threat-risk analysis.

All of these approaches can result in a determination to make sophisticated forecasts and to gather masses of other information. They also can follow this activity or parallel it.

There is no single way to identify and analyze a company's strengths and weaknesses. They can, of course, cover a wide range from management talent to salesmen in the field. It is hardly necessary to comment that a company should move from its strength and avoid its weaknesses, and it should understand that a strength today may become a weakness in tomorrow's environment. Yet it is observable that companies fail because they ignored their weaknesses. Many have failed because they had a success syndrome which blindly assumed that present success was based upon a strength that would continue. Not enough companies systematically examine their strengths; fewer systematically study their weaknesses.

Throughout this process the objective is to ask the right questions, to identify the most important opportunities and threats, and to evaluate honestly and objectively company strengths and weaknesses. This is very difficult. The literature on how to solve a problem once it is discovered, for example, is mountainous. The literature on how to be sure to identify the right problem and how to see the best opportunity is small. This is too bad because a businessman runs a far greater risk in not finding the right problem or opportunity than in determining how to solve the problem or how to exploit the opportunity once it is identified. We shall return to this issue in the next chapter.

MAJOR ELEMENTS OF MASTER POLICY/STRATEGY

On the basis of the preceding analyses, the strategic planning process proceeds to hammer out basic missions, purposes, long-range objectives, and policies and strategies to achieve them. Each of these will be treated in turn.

Company Missions

Basic missions should be stated in both product and market terms. A company may say that it is in the business of producing air conditioners. However, it will be in entirely different businesses if it chooses to make air conditioners for office buildings, or for home cooling, or for automobiles. Deciding upon a basic mission is a fundamental step in planning. If the Baldwin Locomotive Works had said its mission was to make tractive power for railroads, instead of sticking with making steam locomotives, it probably would still be in business. A company that says it is not in the business of making bricks for construction but is in the clay products business for construction widens its opportunities as well as its threats. Too broad a mission, however, may be dangerous. For instance, it is doubtful whether a company making lead pencils should say its mission is changed to making communications equipment. There is a sort of iron law of product-market development that says the further a company gets from its present products and markets the less likely it will make a profit. However, if the product and market are very narrow, growth and prosperity can be enhanced by a judicious widening of the mission.

Purposes

The fundamental purposes of an enterprise can be thought of in two ways. First are the basic purposes society establishes for enterprises. As noted previously, the business institution has been created and supported by society to achieve objectives that society establishes for it. If managers of businesses, especially the large companies, ignore these societal purposes, the results may be more government regulation, at a minimum. So, planning must consider larger societal purposes of the enterprise.

Second are fundamental purposes that managers of an organization implicitly or explicitly determine. These purposes can include a range of subjects—from economic to ethic. Purposes are stated in broad terms and tend to have long lives. For instance, one company identified a basic purpose as follows: "To strive for the greatest possible reliability and quality in our products." Another said its purpose was "To be recognized as a company of dedication, honesty, integrity, and service." When taken seriously such purposes have powerful influence over company plans and activities.

Long-Range Planning Objectives

Although the purposes just described provide an important frame of reference for planning, they are not sufficiently focused to facilitate planning. More precise objectives are needed. These are the specific desired results to be achieved, usually in a specific time. They are important in the planning process because they are guides to developing specific actions to assure their fulfillment. Behavioral scientists also conclude they are important motivators of people in organizations because, generally, people in organizations like to try to achieve the objectives set for the organization. Objectives are also used, of course, as standards for measuring performance.

Objectives may be expressed for every element of a business considered important enough to be the subject of plans. There is no standard classification of objectives nor of the number of objectives a company should have. The common objectives found in long-range planning systems are sales, profits, margin, return on investment, and market share. These are usually stated in specific numbers and/or percentages of growth.

The number of possible objectives is very long, so each company must choose those it wishes to formulate. Objectives ought to be set for every activity that a company thinks is important and the performance of which it wishes to watch and measure. Peter Drucker [1954:63] says the following are such areas: market standing, innovation, productivity, physical and financial resources, profitability, manager performance and development, worker performance and attitude, and public responsibility.

Objectives can be based on different considerations. They may be dictated by top management without any research analysis, or they may be based upon thorough analysis. They may be extrapolations from the past or set to exploit a foreseen opportunity or to avoid a perceived threat. They may be derived from a settled strategy or designed to support other objectives.

However derived, objectives should exhibit a few major characteristics. First, they should be able to lead and motivate, and the more concrete and specific they are the more likely are they to have directive power. To say that "Our company seeks to make a good profit," is far less powerful than to say, "Our objective is to make $4 million in profits three years from today." Second, objectives should be actionable. Goals that are far too high or far too low do not lead to action. Objectives should be a little aggressive and require imagination and hard work to achieve. Third, objectives should be understood by those who are to develop means to achieve them. Fourth, objectives should conform to ethical and social codes accepted by society and by the business. Finally, objectives should correlate and be mutually supporting, to the extent possible. For instance, if the objective is to achieve a return on investment of 15 per cent, after taxes, by the end of five years, the target is much more likely to be achieved if sub- and subsubobjectives are linked to it. For instance, subobjectives might be: increase sales to $10 million in 5 years, raise gross profits to $2.5 million in 5 years, build modern facilities and operate them at capacity over the next five years, and upgrade and maintain a skilled work force in specified ways. These objectives might also be linked to subsubobjectives. For example, an increase in sales might be sought by setting specific objectives for market share, advertising expenditures, market penetration, product redesign, and research and development in specific directions. Similarly, subsubobjectives might be set for achievement of the subobjectives of gross profits, facilities, and work force. If the sub- and subsubobjectives are achieved, the achievement of the dominant objective is inevitable.

Program Policies and Strategies

Conceptually, of course, the next logical step is to develop specific policies and strategies to achieve the preceding objectives, purposes, and missions. The nature and significance of policies and strategies have been discussed previously. In later chapters we shall say much about the identification, evaluation, and implementation of policies and strategies. At this point it may be noted that there is no one way, no neat formula, by means of which program policies and strategies are formulated. We think that a systematic strategic planning process in a formal planning system is a preferred approach to the development of effective policies and strategies.

There are other approaches that can be pursued either within or outside of a formal planning system to the formation of program strategies. Intuition, as pointed out earlier, is an excellent approach if it is brilliant. For some activities, such as acquisitions, some companies use the *ad hoc* trial and error approach. A successful invention is an unexcelled strategy. Another approach is to determine the really significant factors that are important in the success of a particular business and concentrate major decisions on it. For instance, a new imaginative toy is a critically strategic factor in the success of a toy company, but superior technical and fail-safe qualities are of dominant importance to the success of an airplane manufacturer. Finding a particular spot, a propitious niche, where a company can give a customer an irresistible value that is not being satisfied, and at a relatively low cost, is a strategy that has made many companies rich. Finally, some companies are satisfied to follow the lead of other companies. That is their strategy.

MEDIUM-RANGE PROGRAMMING AND PROGRAMS

Medium-range programming is the process where specific functional plans are related for specific numbers of years to display the details of how strategies are to be carried out to achieve long-range objectives and company missions. Typically, the planning period is for five years, but there is a tendency for more technically advanced companies to plan ahead in some detail for seven or more years. Generally, the medium-range plans cover only the major functions and are quantified on comparatively simple forms, as shown in Figure 7-2. In many companies, especially large decentralized ones, functional plans are prepared only for major strategic programs [O'Connor, 1976]. In

ITEM	LAST YEAR	THIS YEAR FORECAST	NEXT FIVE YEARS				
			FIRST YEAR	SECOND YEAR	THIRD YEAR	FOURTH YEAR	FIFTH YEAR
SALES							
MARKETING EXPENDITURES							
ADVERTISING							
DISTRIBUTION							
UNIT PRODUCTION							
EMPLOYEES							
TOTAL							
DIRECT							
INDIRECT							
R & D OUTLAYS							
NEW PRODUCTS							
PRODUCT IMPROVEMENT							
COST REDUCTION							
NEW FACILITIES (TOTAL)							
EXPANSION PRESENT PROD.							
NEW PRODUCTS							
COST REDUCTION							
MAINTENANCE							

Figure 7–2 Division five-year plans.

most companies plans are translated into financial terms in the form of a pro forma profit and loss statement, as shown in Figure 7-3. Sometimes a *pro forma* balance sheet is also prepared. Sometimes, depending upon its importance, detailed forms are prepared for selected elements. This is especially true for facility programs.

SHORT-RANGE PLANNING AND PLANS

The next step, of course, is to develop short-range plans on the basis of the medium-range plans. In about half the companies that do formal planning, the numbers for the first year of the medium-range plans are the same as in the short-range yearly operational budget summaries. Some companies feel that tightly linking budgets and medium-range plans will help to make long-range plans realistic. Others feel that a tight relationship will divert attention from the long-range to current matters, such as return on investment. This is especially so if a manager's compensation is based principally on yearly return-on-investment performance. If the linkage is very loose, the long-range plan still can be reflected in and be of high importance to current budget making.

The current operating budgets will, of course, provide very great numerical detail as compared with the medium-range plans. Many more subjects will also be covered. The numbers of subjects will depend upon what management wishes to control in the short run. Some elaboration of this point is shown in Figure 7-4.

One should not leave this subject without at least commenting on the scope of short-range planning. Although strategic and medium-range plans may provide the framework within which short-range planning is done, the different types of short-range plans that can be affected cover a wide area. They can include production plans, such as plant location, facilities, work methods, inventory, employee training, job enrichment, management education, and negotiations with unions. Space limitations prevent any further examination of these types of short-range plans, their nature, or how they are prepared.

TRANSLATING STRATEGIC PLANS INTO CURRENT DECISIONS

Figure 7-4 shows that corporate strategies can be reflected immediately in current plans or used as a basis for the development of medium-range plans which, in turn, are the basis for annual or shorter plans. There are several additional features of Figure 7-4 worthy of note. In a divisionalized company where there is decentralized authority the general manager will be obliged to make studies of the environment for his product. This information will be used, with whatever directions he gets from headquarters about objectives and

DIVISION: ______________

	This Year	19__	19__	19__	19__	19__
SALES – UNITS						
GROSS SALES – DOLLARS						
ALLOWANCES						
NET SALES						
COST OF GOODS SOLD						
GROSS PROFIT ON SALES						
G & A EXPENSE						
SELLING EXPENSE						
ADVERTISING EXPENSE						
R & D EXPENSE						
TOTAL OPERATING EXPENSE						
OTHER CHARGES, NET						
INTEREST ON LONG TERM OBLIGATIONS						
OTHER						
INCOME BEFORE DEPRECIATION						
DEPRECIATION						
INCOME BEFORE OVERHEAD ALLOCATION						
ALLOCATION OF GENERAL OVERHEAD						
NET INCOME BEFORE TAXES						
RATE OF RETURN ON ASSETS						

Figure 7-3 Financial summary.

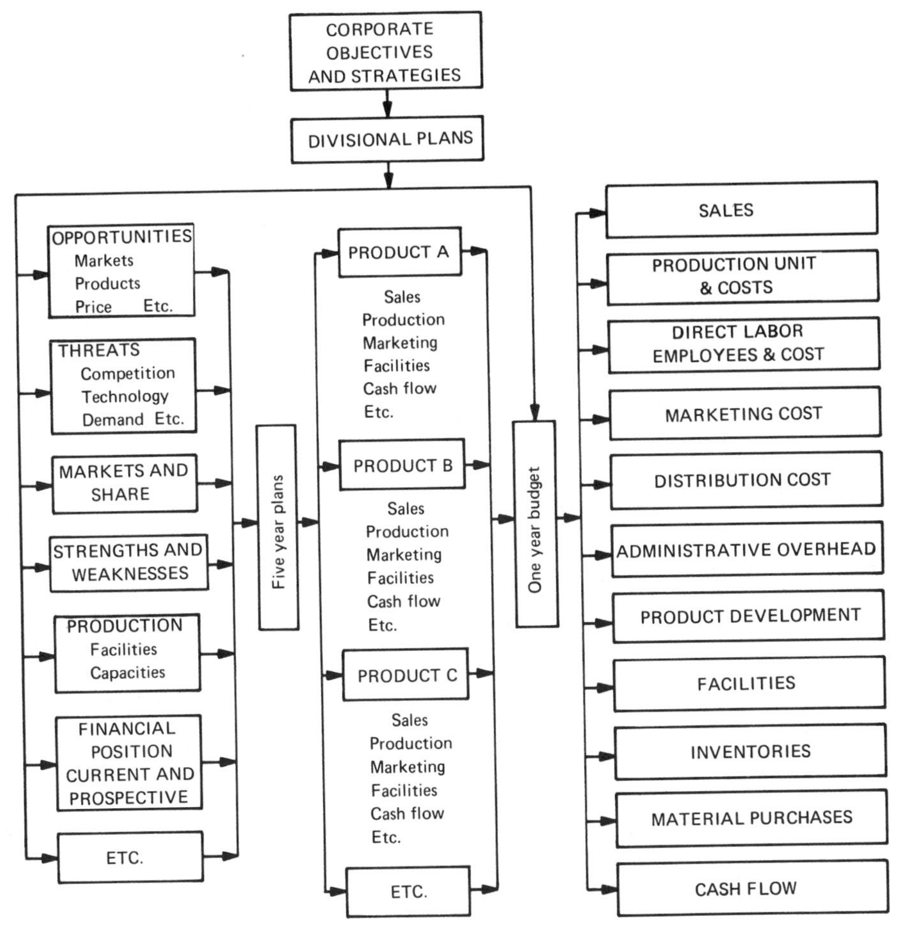

Figure 7-4 Relationship between strategic and tactical plans.

strategies, to make his medium-range plans. There should be, therefore, a close linkage between top management objectives and strategies and subobjectives and substrategies forged by the division manager.

Also, the details of the one-year budget are considerably different from the main categories of the five-year plans. The two can be the same, but the budget is more concerned with coordination and control of critical internal flows of resources. The subject matter of the short-range plans, therefore, will be focused on these concerns rather than on the more aggregative functions in the medium-range plans. The aggregates of the short-range plans, however, can relate to medium-range plans, as noted above.

In the formal planning process there is not a sharp distinction between strategic planning at one extreme and tactical planning at the other, or of planning at one end and control at the other. Each has a graduated impact throughout the planning process, as shown in Figure 7-5. This figure shows that traces of strategic planning are found in detailed short-range planning. Also, strategic planning and particularly medium-range programming is done in some reflection of control over operations.

OTHER ASPECTS OF THE PLANNING PROCESS

Planning Studies and Feasibility Testing

Planning studies can, of course, be made throughout the planning process. We have noted how important such studies are in examining the environment. They also, however, can be important in analyzing such matters as current inventory replacement policy or suitability of the present organization for planning.

Feasibility testing takes place throughout the planning spectrum. For instance, when lower level managers are examining different alternative choices, one may comment, "Method A has great profit potential, but I do not think the top management would like to use this method." He is obviously applying a feasibility test by appraising an alternative against the values of top management, as he understands them. At lower levels the testing can become completely quantitative and sometimes very sophisticated, as for instance in the applicability of a linear programming model to testing distribution routes for products to their markets.

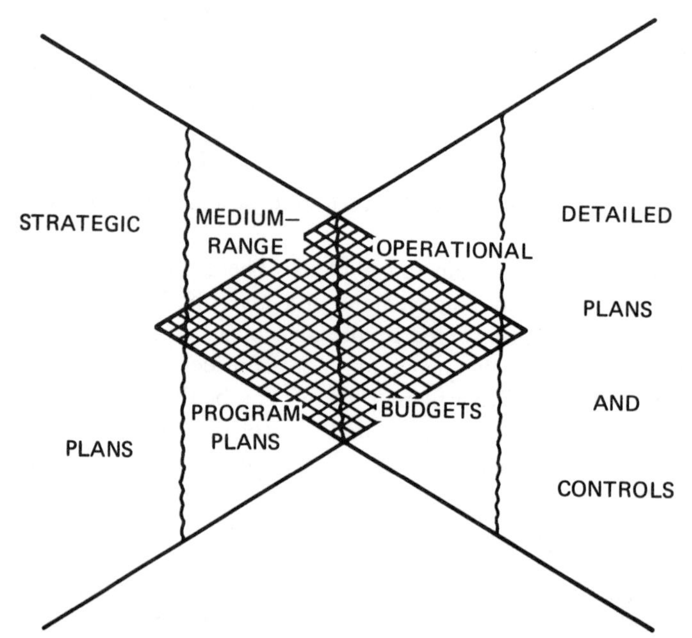

Figure 7-5 Intermeshing of long range planning and operational control.

Review and Evaluation

Plans that are developed should be reviewed and evaluated. There is nothing that produces better plans on the part of subordinates than for the top managers to show a keen interest in the plans and the results that they bring. When comprehensive formal planning was first developed some 20 years ago there was a tendency for companies to make written plans and not redo them until they became obviously obsolete. Now, the great majority of companies go through an annual cycle of comprehensive planning in which the plans are reviewed and revised.

Planning Tools

The range of tools available for making "rational" decisions in the planning process is very broad (see Table 9-1). It covers a spectrum from nonquantitative tools, such as intuition, judgment, and hunches, to very complex and highly sophisticated methods, such as systems analysis and computer simulation. In between are older quantitative methods like probability theory and linear programming.

Contingency Plans

Many corporations have contingency plans to meet emergencies. Strategic planning is done on the basis of the most probable events likely to occur. There are other possible events, however, that can open up great opportunities or pose serious threats to a company if they occur. Each company should ask itself some "what-if" questions and then briefly sketch out responses that are appropriate in the event the contingency takes place. For example, "What if a competitor suddenly drops his price 25 per cent?" "What if the government imposes an export tax on our product?" "What if a fire seriously damages our main plant?" The advantage of having such plans is obvious.

Contingency plans are much briefer than those discussed previously. The advantage of having such plans when catastrophe strikes is obvious.

We cannot do justice to this subject here, but there are several points that should be added to the present analysis. First, the applicability of different tools varies very much, depending upon where and when they are applied in the planning process. For example, a sophisticated quantitative forecasting technique, such as exponential smoothing, is not very effective in making a forecast with great unknowns, such as the market for aspirin in China. Second, it is very important for technicians to find major business problems that their methods can solve for managers rather than to try to find those problems their tools can solve easily. Third, there is currently increasing use of more sophisticated quantitative tools at higher levels of corporate planning. For instance, computer simulation and risk analysis is being used widely in strategic planning [Boulden and Buffa, 1970; and Miller, 1971]. Most of the computer simulation models are deterministic. They answer "what if" types of questions. But, increasingly, probability theory is being used in top-level decision making, as for instance risk analysis [Hertz, 1969]. In Chapter 9 more will be said about tools of analysis.

ORGANIZING THE PLANNING PROCESS

There is no single method, formula, or standard way to start and conduct a formal corporate planning system. What is done, to illustrate, is a function of such factors as managerial style, size of organization, whether the firm is centralized or decentralized, managerial authority extended to decentralized managers, types of problems the company faces, managerial knowledge, capital intensity, types of products, and services and managerial styles of top managers. So, each system is fitted to each company. There are no two exactly alike.

Before starting the planning process it is very important that top managers have a sound conceptual understanding of a long-range planning system (which we have tried to present in this chapter), an understanding of what a suitable system can do for them and their company, a clear concept of what they want the formal system to do for them and their company, and an understanding of how to set up the system and make it work effectively.

The Plan to Plan

There should also be a plan to plan, which should include first of all a strong statement of commitment of the chief executive officer. It should contain a glossary of terms to assure common understanding and avoid semantic debate. The information and documentation required should then be described. Time schedules should be included such as that shown in Figure 7-6 (a typical illustration). Finally, the statement should specify policies and procedures needed by those doing the planning, such as depreciation policy, interdivisional transfer policy, assumed price inflation rates, and so on. Beyond this, firms making a "plan to plan" can and do include many other things such as "how we became committed," "history of planning in our company," and "why we need to do better planning."

Four Fundamental Approaches

There are four fundamentally different approaches to doing formal planning. The first is the top-down approach. Comprehensive planning in a centralized company is done at the top of the corporation, and departments and outlying activities are pretty much told what to do. In a decentralized company, the president may give the divisions guidelines and ask for plans. The plans are reviewed at headquarters and sent back to the divisions for modification or with a note of acceptance. If the division plans do not add up to what top management wishes, additional corporate plans are then prepared which may concern acquisitions, divestment, or refinancing.

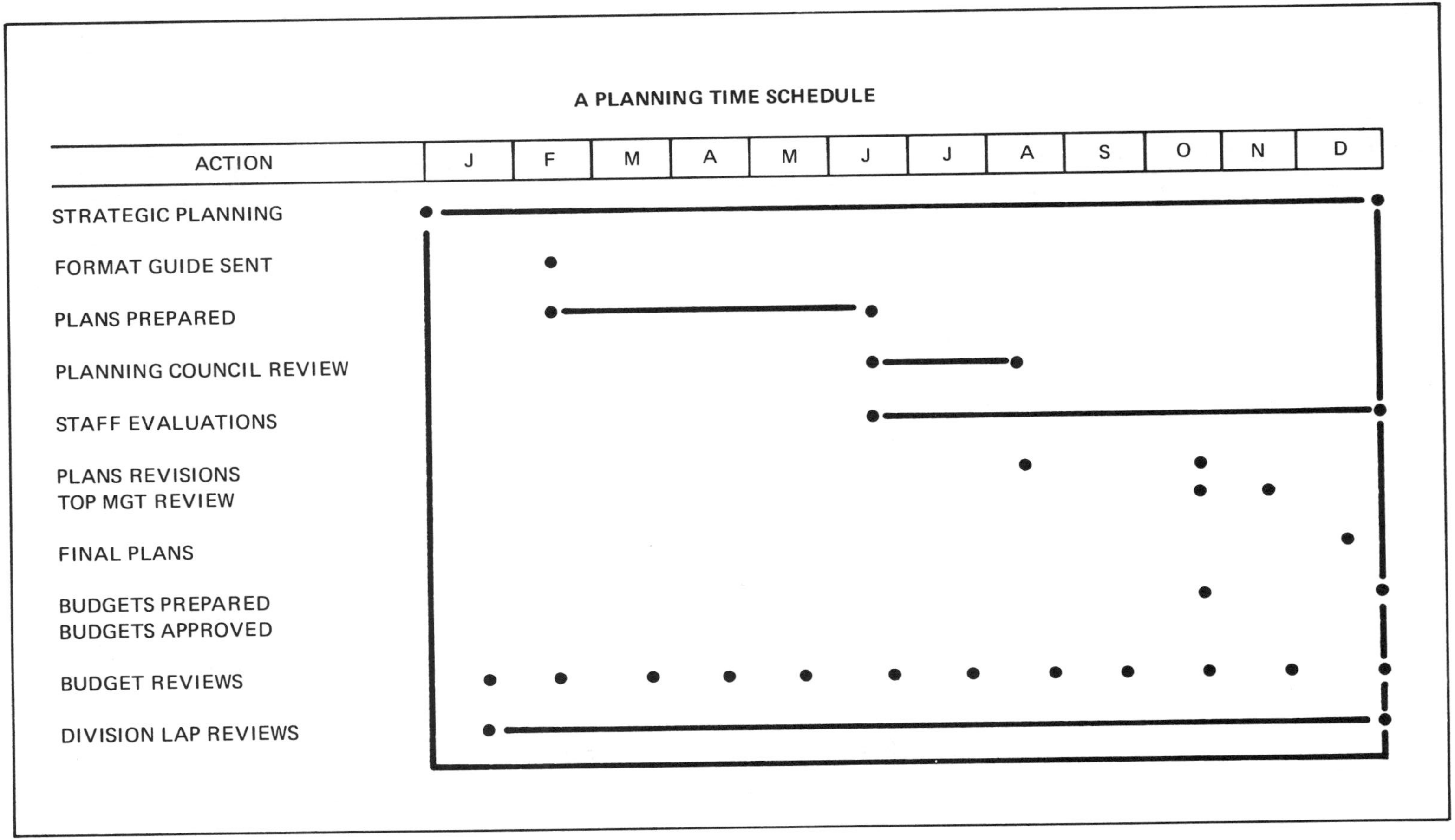

A PLANNING TIME SCHEDULE

ACTION
J F M A M J J A S O N D

STRATEGIC PLANNING
FORMAT GUIDE SENT
PLANS PREPARED
PLANNING COUNCIL REVIEW
STAFF EVALUATIONS
PLANS REVISIONS
TOP MGT REVIEW
FINAL PLANS
BUDGETS PREPARED
BUDGETS APPROVED
BUDGET REVIEWS
DIVISION LAP REVIEWS

Figure 7-6 A planning time schedule.

The second is the bottom-up approach. Here, top management gives the divisions no guidelines but asks them to submit plans. Information such as the following may be requested: major opportunities and threats, major objectives, strategies to achieve the objectives, and specific data on sales, profits, market share sought, capital requirements, and number of employees for a specified number of years. These plans are then reviewed at top management levels and the same process as noted in the top-down approach is then followed.

A third approach, of course, is to develop a mixture of the top-down and bottom-up approach. This is the method used in most large decentralized companies. In this approach, top management gives guidelines to the divisions. Generally, they are broad enough to permit the divisions a good bit of flexibility in developing their own plans. Sometimes a top management may hammer out basic objectives by dialog with division managers. Such objectives as sales and return on investments may be derived in this way, especially if the performance of the division manager is measured upon the basis of such standards.

Fourth, is the team approach. In smaller centralized companies the chief executive will often use his main line managers as staff in helping him to develop formal plans. In some very large companies the president will use his line managers in the same fashion. In many companies the president has a group of executives with whom he meets on a regular basis to deal with all the problems facing the company. In some companies, part of the time of this group is spent on long-range planning. Over time the group will develop written long-range plans.

Ten Alternatives

Within each of these approaches there are many alternatives of which we shall note ten, as follows:

1. *Completeness of Cycle.* When the process is begun it is not necessary to go through a complete cycle such as that suggested by Figure 2-1. Some companies begin by asking departments and/or divisions to supply top management with perceived opportunities and threats and with the strategies they suggest to exploit the opportunities and avoid the threats. Of course, once the system is in operation over several cycles all phases of planning in Figure 2-1 should be covered.
2. *Depth of Analysis.* Again, when starting, it is not necessary to require deep analysis of all aspects of the planning process. Too heavy a research work load can sink the process. As experience is gained, however, analysis should be as deep as required for each subject.
3. *Degree of Formality.* There is a wide spread of formality among planning systems in the United States. Among the larger companies, those having centralized organizational structures, comparatively stable environment, and homogeneous product lines tend to have less formal systems than

large diversified companies with decentralized and semiautonomous product division structures. High technology companies tend to have more formal systems than those employing low-level technology. Generally, the more flexible the system the better.

4. *Reliance on Staff.* Managers, of course, can determine how much planning they want to delegate to staff. Generally, the more managers do themselves the better.
5. *Corporate Planner or Not.* Larger corporations employ corporate planners to help top management with the planning process [Steiner, 1970; Vancil, 1967]. Smaller companies cannot afford this luxury.
6. *Linkage among Plans.* As noted previously some companies use the numbers of the first year of the five-year plan for their annual budgets. Other companies prepare budgets in light of the five-year plans, but the numbers are not identical.
7. *Getting the Process Started.* There are many ways to get the process started. For example, strategic planning may begin with an effort to solve a particular difficult problem, such as obsolescence of a major product. It may begin with a situation audit, or it may begin with a review of current strategy.
8. *Degree of Documentation.* A balance must be struck between too little and too much paper work.
9. *Participation of People.* Here, again, there is a choice. Top management can do the job itself, or it can elicit the help of many people.
10. *Role of the Chief Executive Officer.* The chief executive officer's role is critical and deserves a more extended comment.

The Chief Executive's Role

To begin with, the CEO (as used here this is shorthand for top management) should understand that the corporate planning system is his responsibility. What this means will vary much from case to case, but basically it means, as one CEO job description put it, "The CEO is the chief architect of the firm's future and the chief planner." In this role the CEO has several fundamental responsibilities, as follows: (1) make sure that the climate in the firm is congenial to doing effective planning; (2) make sure the system is organized in a fashion appropriate to the company; (3) if a corporate planner is employed, see to it that he is the right man for the job and he reports as close to the top of the firm as possible; (4) get involved in doing the planning; and (5) have face-to-face meetings with those who draw up plans for the CEO's review and approval.

The discharge of these responsibilities will vary much depending upon managerial styles. As noted in Chapter 6 there are different styles of managers. The permissive manager will operate differently than the entrepreneurial type. A manager who is a team leader will handle his responsibilities differently from the one who depends only upon his own council, and so on.

The roles of CEOs will vary over time. As the CEO and his staff become more experienced in planning, he may rely more on staff. Every company goes through a life cycle, as pointed out in Chapter 6, and the planning system reflects such change. CEO's tend to have different roles in complex organizations as compared with very simple ones.

Concluding Comment

Probably one of the most difficult problems in industry today with respect to formal planning concerns how the process is organized and pursued. It is an extremely difficult task for management, especially in a large corporation, to organize and implement a planning system that runs smoothly and fulfills its promise.

WHAT DOES A WRITTEN STRATEGIC PLAN LOOK LIKE?

There is no uniform format for a strategic plan. They vary much depending upon the company and its definitions. Conceptually, of course, the strategic plan includes the three main planning structures in Figure 2-1. Or, if one prefers, only that which is included in the area marked "strategic planning" is included in the strategic plan. We may identify three types of strategies plans.

First, are those of a centralized company. These might encompass the results of the three types of plan structures shown in Figure 2-1. Second are plans of decentralized companies. Each division will have its own plan. The central headquarters may aggregate the financial results of the divisional plans, add additional elements of concern to central headquarters such as divestment and acquisitions, and make some comments on the changing environment. That will be the strategic plan for the company. Third are the divisional plans. General Electric has divided its company into what are called strategic business units (SBU's). SBU's are distinct businesses, with their own set of competitors that can be managed in a manner reasonably independent of other businesses within GE. "The Strategic Plan," says GE, for SBU's comprises the following major elements [Cross, 1973; Salveson, 1974]:

"• A statement of the SBU's mission.
- The key environmental assumptions summarizing the external environment and its opportunities and threats.
- The key competitor assumptions.
- A list of constraints imposed from either inside or outside the company.
- The desired future position the SBU wants to attain—*its objectives*.
- The *goals* stated as specific time-based points of measurement that will be met in attaining the objectives.
- The course of action to be followed to achieve its objectives—*the strategy*.
- The programs—development and investment—critical to the strategy.

- The required resources and where they can be obtained.
- The contingency plans—which recognize that things might go wrong and what can be done to correct a situation.
- And finally, an indication in financial terms of the various elements of the strategic plan in a form that will allow them to be integrated with the existing operational control system."

THE VALUE OF FORMAL CORPORATE PLANNING

Comprehensive formal long-range planning has been growing in use throughout the world simply because managers find that it is valuable. There are many reasons why this is so, a few of which may be noted briefly.

As noted earlier in Chapter 3 long-range planning is essential to discharging top management's responsibilities. As companies become larger, the complexities of the task defy the capabilities of one or a few men to do it properly on an informal basis. System and formality are required, and the type of strategic planning process discussed in this chapter is employed.

The process is important because it asks and answers questions that good managers must address, such as: What is our basic mission and purpose? What are our competitors likely to do? What new product lines do we need? What opportunities are open to us to exploit? Where are the major threats to our business? What are our basic objectives? What strategies are best for us? Rapid environmental change alters answers to such questions as these rather quickly. That is why in most companies long-range planning is reviewed and revised on an annual cycle.

Planning enables a company to simulate the future on paper. If it does not like what it sees, it erases and starts over. This is much less expensive than letting the future evolve on an *ad hoc* basis. It applies the systems approach. It looks at a company as a system composed of many subsystems. Looking at the company in this way prevents suboptimization of parts. It forces a company to set objectives and clarifies future opportunities and threats. It links decision making between top and lower level managers. Lower level management decisions are much more likely to be made in conformance with the wishes of top management because plans are written and available to them. It sets standards of performance.

Long-range planning is a new and significant communications system. It permits people to participate in the decision-making process. People are more adaptable to change because they participate in making the change. It is a learning and mind-stretching exercise that increasingly is being recognized as a major tool for training managers [Camillus, 1975].

In sum, there are two types of values of comprehensive long-range planning —substantive and behavioral. Either set should be sufficient to convince management of the value of this new tool. When both are considered, it is easy to see why formal long-range planning has been introduced into most medium-sized and larger companies [Cetron, 1971]. More and more managers are agreeing with an old military assertion that says, "*Plans* sometimes may be useless but the planning *process* is always indispensable."

A few recent studies provide concrete evidence that long-range planning really pays off in cash. One study compared the five-year performance of firms that introduced formal planning with those that did not. It also compared the performance of the firms for the five years before introducing long-range planning with five years of long-range planning. Results were measured for sales, earnings per share, stock price, earnings on common equity, and earnings on total capital. In each instance those companies that did long-range planning had better performance in significant degree than companies in the same industry that did not formally plan. Also, in each case the record of the firms that did long-range planning was better after than before introducing the system [Thune and House, 1970; Gerstner, 1972; Herold, 1972]. Another study concluded that on virtually all relevant financial criteria companies that made acquisitions by a systematic planning approach did much better than those that went about it on an unplanned opportunistic basis [Ansoff *et al.,* 1970]. Some studies, however, cast doubt about the payoff of long-range planning [Rue and Fulmer, 1973; Fulmer and Rue, 1973].

It is our view that, other things being equal and especially for larger firms, formal systematic long-range planning will give a company an important edge over a competitor that does not have such a system. Our reason is that the success of a company is not due so much to the planning system as to the capabilities of managers. Our view is that better managers understand the significance to them of having an effective systematic planning system, and they devise a system to suit their needs.

LIMITS OF FORMAL PLANNING

Comprehensive corporate planning is not, of course, without its shortcomings. It is an intimate part of the managerial process, and if other parts of management are weak the planning process itself may be less than satisfactory. Long-range plans may not turn out well sometimes because of unexpected changes in the environment. Of fundamental importance, also, is the fact that long-range planning is virtually worthless in getting a company out of a major current crisis. Aside from such shortcomings, there are all sorts of problems that can arise in the development of a planning system. Many of these are suggested in the following analysis of pitfalls in planning.

Major Pitfalls in Planning

Despite the widespread use of formal long-range planning there is a good bit of dissatisfaction with the systems being employed. This has been documented in the literature [Bagley, 1972; Grinyer, 1973; Irwin, 1971; Kastens, 1972; Pennington, 1972; Ringbakk, 1971; and Warren, 1966]. There are many reasons for dissatisfaction, as explained in the works cited. One broad reason is that managers have fallen into pitfalls that must be avoided if planning is to be efficient and effective.

Steiner [1972c] developed 50 pitfalls encountered in planning and sought to identify the most important ones to be avoided. A survey was made among 600 companies and 215 usable replies were received. The ten most significant pitfalls that managers and planning staffs identified as the most important to avoid, if good results are to be achieved, are the following in descending order of importance:

- Top management's assumption that it can delegate the planning function to a planner.
- Top management becomes so engrossed in current problems that it spends insufficient time on long-range planning and the process becomes discredited among other managers and staff.
- Failure to develop company goals suitable as a basis for formulating long-range plans.
- Failure to assume the necessary involvement in the planning process of major line personnel.
- Failure to use plans as standards for measuring managerial performance.
- Failure to create a climate in the company that is congenial and not resistant to planning.
- Assuming that corporate comprehensive planning is something separate from the entire management process.
- Injecting so much formality into the system that it lacks flexibility, looseness, and simplicity, and restrains creativity.
- Failure of top management to review with departmental and divisional heads the long-range plans they have developed.
- Top management's consistently rejecting the formal planning mechanism by making intuitive decisions that conflict with the formal plans.

A world-wide survey showed a surprising concensus among managers and planners in different countries of the world that these ten pitfalls were, indeed, the most lethal to good planning [Steiner and Schollhammer, 1975].

Respondents in Steiner's study [1972c:32] were asked to rate their degree of satisfaction with their planning systems with the following response:

DEGREE OF SATISFACTION	PERCENTAGE OF RESPONSES
Highly satisfied	10.1
Above average satisfaction	34.1
Average satisfaction	32.2
Some dissatisfaction	15.2
Highly dissatisfied	8.5
	100.0

Respondents were also asked whether their companies had fallen importantly into any of the fifty pitfalls in the survey and, if so, whether that had an important adverse impact on planning. The conclusion was reached that "Without exception, those companies which said they had fallen completely into one of the top ten most important pitfalls to avoid were more dissatisfied than satisfied with their planning programs" [Steiner, 1972c:35].

FORMAL PLANNING IN SMALL COMPARED WITH LARGE COMPANIES

From the preceding section it should be obvious that there are literally thousands of different types of planning systems. Generally speaking planning is much less formal in small companies than in large ones. Smaller companies do not have the resources to be as thorough as larger companies. Among all companies, however, the thought processes of long-range planning are similar. Patz [1975] argues that the procedures followed in formal planning are the same as those prescribed in the scientific method. Only the names of the steps are different. For different types of planning structures for small companies see *Forbes* [1974], and Steiner [1967].

RATIONALITY AND IRRATIONALITY IN PLANNING

The Roman philosopher Seneca said, "Man is a reasoning animal." But Isaac Asimov [1975:46] commented, "What evidence he had for that assertion no one knows; certainly none has surfaced in the 19 centuries since his time." Asimov undoubtedly was referring to the large questions of man's governance. In our area of interest managers are rational and irrational—it is not always easy to decide which is which.

The planning system presented in this chapter is designed to try to inject more rationality into the decision-making process. It must be recognized, however, that many, and generally the most important, decisions made in this process cannot be settled on the basis of universal quantitative truths. The issues involve judgments, values, passions, and consequences that are very difficult to perceive. So, irrationality cannot be avoided no matter how carefully a formal planning system is erected. Anyway, the rationality or irrationality of any decision is often determined by who is looking [Steiner, 1969b:319–348]. Neverthless, good formal planning does move a company *toward* rationality; that is why companies that have formal planning systems have generally been found to perform better.

Planning and People

Throughout this discussion it is obvious that planning influences and is influenced by people, individually and in groups, in many different ways. One cannot speak of planning without understanding how people relate to the process. So important is this subject that Chapters 10, 11, and 12 are devoted to it.

TYPES OF STRATEGIC PLANNING SYSTEMS

This chapter, for the most part, has dealt with one type of comprehensive strategic planning system. It is quite true, as noted at several points, that the variations of the basic concept run into the thousands in practice. There are differences in completeness, documentation, and so on, as explained previously. There are variations in strategic planning processes that are more different in kind than degree. Ringbakk [1975] has identified five categories of strategic planning that are shown in Table 7-1 together with different characteristics, emphases, time horizons, formality of planning systems, and the responsibility of planners for each.

PLANNING IN NONPROFIT ORGANIZATIONS

It is our contention that the basic fundamental concepts, principles, and practices set forth in this chapter and the readings to which it refers apply to all organizations in society. With nonprofit organizations as with individual business enterprises, the problem is one of determining what system of planning is most appropriate to the characteristics of the organization. However, there are many characteristics of certain types of nonprofit organizations that complicate the organization and operation of comprehensive formal planning systems. We can note only a few illustrations here (others will be examined in Chapter 18).

Formal planning in a typical nonprofit organization, such as a hospital, city planning commission, or city, is complicated by fluid lines of authority and pressure. In the typical corporation the line of authority in planning runs from the CEO to functional and divisional units. The CEO may be assisted in his tasks by a planning committee, but he exercises authority over the committee. Boards of directors can override the CEO but generally do not do so. Pressures are exerted from outside groups but do not constitute, generally, a major challenge to the CEO's authority. This is oversimplified but illustrates authority relationships in a company so far as planning is concerned.

In nonprofit organizations the CEO is strongly influenced by what various authorities have decided or are likely to decide, for example, The Congress, The State Legislature, HEW, or the City Council. He will have far less control over his board of directors than the typical business CEO. The CEO may have a planning council but he will not control it. The council may have representatives from employees, the community, and the doctors in residence. They, in turn, are influenced by any individual or group affected by the decisions

TABLE 7-1
Characteristics of Categories of Strategic Planning

Characteristic	Posture Planning	Portfolio Planning	Business Area Strategic Planning	Action Planning	Programming
Purpose	Position firm vis-á-vis expected future environment	Balance business fields and create desired mix	Growth through expansion into (related) new products and markets	Coordinate; integrate; optimize	Maximize efficiency; base for control
Emphasis	Choose business fields; assess change; alter and expand firm	Allocate corporate resources; manage the mix and family of businesses	Product development; market development	Internal; unit-wide	Steering; fine-tuning
Time Horizon	15–20 years	5–10 years	3–5–7 years	Usually 3–5 years	1–2 years
Planning problem	Unstructured; qualitative; very new	Poorly structured; qualitative-quantitative	Somewhat structured; quantitative-qualitative	Structured; fairly quantitative	Highly structured; highly quantitative
Formal planning system	Generally lacking; people intensive; content dominates	Selectively emerging; some modeling; some numbers	Well developed; gap analysis; reasonably good numbers	Very well developed; procedure dominates; sufficient numbers	Routinized, EDP-based; standardized; nearly all numbers
Planners and responsibility	Top management; requires incremental resources at top of organization; small number involved	Senior corporate management; involvement by senior operating management; relatively small number involved	Senior operating management; involvement by functional areas	Operating management; unit-wide effort; large numbers involved	Technocrats; specialists

Source: Ringbakk [1975]

of the CEO. All these groups, in turn, seek to influence line and staff, the CEO directly, or the CEO through top legislative and administrative bodies [Webber and Dula, 1974].

Formal planning in the federal government is handicapped by many other constraints. For example, the time horizon of leaders is short—Congressmen, two years; Senators, six years; and Presidents, four years. The number of special interests focused on the policy formulation and implementation process is very large, especially with respect to important pieces of legislation. The decision-making process is political.

Such complexities as these become magnified, and others are added, when the organizational unit becomes the size of a city, state, or national government. Some of these organizations do have long-range plans but they are not as all inclusive for their domain as is formal business planning for a firm's activities.

Program Budgeting

During the past 15 years a new system has developed for improving decision-making in nonprofit organizations. It was first introduced into the U.S. Department of Defense in 1961, made mandatory for all major United States government agencies in 1965 by executive order (and later eliminated in the Nixon Administration), and has since spread to a wide variety of nonprofit organizations around the world [Novick, 1973]. The system has various names: program budgeting, the planning-programming-budgeting system (PPBS), and *rationalisation des choix budgetaires*.

Program budgeting is a systematic and formal system for making decisions about an organization's resource allocations to meet its goals. It takes as given the basic policies of the organization and establishes specific goals to be met in pursuing policies. Programs are then identified to achieve the goals. The major alternatives that are open in achieving goals, and the major issues involved in choosing from among them, are then identified and examined. Many analytical tools are used in the decision-making process but the cost/benefit method is central. By means of this technique the administrators in the organization seek to determine what benefits accrue from a given expenditure as compared to what costs. With this information in hand they are in a position to determine what resource allocation will yield the highest benefit in relation to cost [Novick, 1965, 1973].

This is an extremely powerful concept for governmental organizations. To appreciate it one must realize that up to very recent years the budgets of agencies of the federal government and most other governments were submitted line by line. To oversimplify, the agency budget would be specified in terms of pencils, typewriters, clerical personnel, and so on. This is still the way many budgets in nonprofit organizations, especially governments, are submitted. The PPBS says that an agency has programs, such as (for a municipal government): schools, hospitals, water treatment, police, and so on. Once these programs are established, budget expenditures attached to them should be aggregated for each of them. In this way, of course, total costs for schools, for hospitals, and so on, can be calculated. Conceptually, when the benefits are calculated for schools and hospitals, and so forth, the administrators are in a position to determine whether additional funds should be spent for schools, hospitals, or something else.

Program budgeting systems differ [Novick, 1973] but conceptually they have some characteristics comparable to the system described in Figure 2-1. They are both concerned with making better decisions in light of future environmental forces; they both involve participation of people; they are both recycled about once a year; they are both directed at achieving stated objectives; they are both conceived as being managerial learning processes; they both run into comparable problems in application, such as consumption of too much time by managers, a tendency to delegate too much to staff, a tendency to generate paper work, or problems of communications between managers and staff experts; and they must both operate in an atmosphere charged with interpersonnel political considerations. DeWolfeson found that practitioners of program budgeting identified much of the same pitfalls to be avoided as Steiner found in business planning.

On the other hand, there are important differences between program budgeting and formal long-range planning, both conceptually and in practice. For example, program budgeting rarely becomes involved in the formulation of an organization's basic missions, creed, or philosophy, whereas in a business planning system this is of dominant concern in planning. Objectives for PPBS are often dictated by legislative authority, which is less the case in business planning. The time horizon of business planning is usually longer than that of program budgeting. Program budgeting focuses essentially on programs, whereas formal planning deals with wider issues of strategy, policy, and plans implementation. Program budgeting is generally done with a top-down approach, whereas business planning can be and often is conducted on a bottom-up approach. Business planning, broadly speaking, is a much more enveloping, complex, and richer process from the point of view of an organization and the people in it than program budgeting in a nonprofit organization.

QUESTIONS

Discussion Guides on Chapter Content

1. Explain the difference between intuitive-anticipatory and formal systematic long-range planning. May they conflict in formal planning systems?
2. How do the authors define comprehensive managerial planning? What do they say it is not?
3. What is the "situation audit" made in planning and of what significance is it to identifying and evaluating strategies?

4. What are the distinctions among an organization's missions, basic purposes, and long-range planning objectives?
5. "The name of the long-range planning game is to translate strategy into current decisions." Comment.
6. The authors make clear that there is no one way to do long-range planning. Identify some major ways in which long-range planning systems may differ among organizations.
7. Identify the most important pitfalls that ought to be avoided in starting and doing long-range formal planning.
8. Explain in what fundamental ways planning differs in nonprofit organizations and business firms.

Mind Stretching Questions

1. Can business long-range planning philosophy and practice be applied to a person's career plans? How about a person's life plans?
2. What research would you suggest in the area of formal long-range planning to advance the state-of-the-art?

CHAPTER

8

Identifying Policies and Strategies to Evaluate

INTRODUCTION

In the strategic planning process the identification and evaluation of strategies/policies is, in many instances, a simultaneous activity. For purposes of exposition, however, we deal with identification in this chapter and evaluation in the next. Both the process of identification and evaluation may be done informally, as is often the case in very small companies. As companies become larger and more complex, however, the process becomes more formalized in a planning system like that discussed in the last chapter.

Following a short note on the importance of identification an analysis of conceptual and operational steps in identification is presented. This is followed with a discussion of selected approaches in the identification process. No one approach is necessarily superior to others, the approaches are not mutually exclusive but may be subsets of one another, and they may be used in various combinations. All can be accommodated in a formal strategic planning system. They can be considered both thought processes and procedures.

The range of alternatives open to managers in identifying policies and strategies is staggering. Some simplifying techniques must be used. The systematic planning process described in the preceding chapter is an important simplifying process. Within it, however, are many others which are discussed in this chapter. There has been some research on preferred strategies for selected activities, but it has not been extensive nor, for the most part, conclusive. Nevertheless, the results are useful in narrowing strategy identification problems and the relevant results will be cited here as well as in later chapters.

PROBLEM/OPPORTUNITY IDENTIFICATION VERSUS PROBLEMS/OPPORTUNITY SOLVING

Livingston [1971] reminds us that problem finding is more important than problem solving. For the manager this is obviously so, for an elegant solution to the wrong problem is far less advantageous to his company than a less-than-perfect solution to the right problem. Drucker goes one step further and concludes that a manager's problem-solving capability is exceeded in importance only by his opportunity-finding ability. Results in business are derived from finding the right opportunities to exploit, not from solving problems. He says, "The pertinent question is not how to do things right, but how to find the right things to do, and to concentrate resources and efforts on them" [Drucker, 1964:5].

Problems and opportunities are complementary. When problems arise, managers must seek ways (opportunities) to resolve them. When opportunities are discovered, there may be problems involved in exploiting them. So important is the positive connotation of opportunity (contrasted with the negative connotation of problem) that some managers do not speak of problems but only of opportunities [Ferrell, 1972]. To them a problem necessitates the discovery of the right opportunity to overcome it. In one company where this concept was held by the CEO, a manager was asked to present his situation to a group of other managers and began by saying, "When I came into this meeting I thought I had an insurmountable problem. Now I know I have an insurmountable opportunity."

CONCEPTUAL STEPS IN STRATEGY DEVELOPMENT

The literature of decision theory focuses on problem solving. We shall return to this literature in later chapters, but in this chapter the concept of problem solving as found in decision theory is the same as identifying opportunities, threats, strengths, and weaknesses. These may be called strategic challenges, as suggested by Hofer [1973].

We agree with Fleming [1966:56] that "The greatest need for creativity in decision making apparently comes during the search stage when the mind is challenged to find a new and different course of action." Our intent in the remainder of this chapter is to facilitate this creative activity by suggesting the different approaches that will stimulate it and also by illustrating preferred alternative courses of action in choosing strategies in particular situations.

There is no concensus about conceptual steps in formulating strategies. The views of two authors on this subject are presented for reference in Tables 8-1 and 8-2. Each is a logical process.

OPERATIONAL STEPS IN STRATEGY DEVELOPMENT

The steps presented in Tables 8-1 and 8-2 can, of course, be used in an operational setting just as they are given. It is not necessary in the development

TABLE 8-1
Steps in Strategy Formulation

1. Define the market
   (a) Purpose of item in terms of user benefits
   (b) Product scope
   (c) Size, growth rate, maturity stage, need for strategies
   (d) Requirements for success
   (e) Divergent definitions of above by competitors
   (f) Definition to be used by company
2. Determine performance differentials
   (a) Evaluate industry performance and company differences
   (b) Determine differences in products, applications, geography, and distribution channels
   (c) Determine differences by customer set
3. Determine differences in competitive programs
   (a) Identify and evaluate individual companies for their
      (1) Market development strategies
      (2) Product development strategies
      (3) Financing and administrative strategies and support
4. Profile the strategies of competitors
   (a) Profile each significant competitor and strategy
   (b) Compare own and competitive strategies
5. Determine strategic planning structure
   (a) When size and complexity are adequate
      (1) Establish planning unit in company
      (2) Make organizational assignments to product managers, industry managers, etc.

SOURCE: Adapted from Cannon [1968:86–100].

TABLE 8-2
Steps in Strategy Formulation

1. Identify and describe present strategy
   (a) Identify current scope of company activities; delineate customer/product/market emphasis
   (b) Examine past and existing resource deployment; determine where greatest sources of strength lie
   (c) Deduce basis on which company is competing; find competitive advantages or distinctive competence
   (d) Determine performance criteria, emphasis, and priorities governing strategic choices made in the past
2. Evaluate past performance
   (a) Compare the criteria used by management to choose (qualititative and quantitative) and stated targets and goals
   (b) Evaluate past performance for such elements as market share, return on investment and risk/reward tradeoff, and other parameters used to compare past performance with current targets
   (c) Compare these performance records with those of competitors
   (d) Compare past performance records with what could have been expected if company liquidated and funds used elsewhere

TABLE 8-2—Continued

3. Planning future strategy
   - (a) Examine environment rigorously to identify major opportunities, threats, changes in product life cycles, changes in customer desires, etc.
   - (b) Define future product/market scope and explain how current strengths can be exploited
   - (c) Determine future performance specifications and choice criteria (choice criteria are objectives)
   - (d) Develop plan for procurement and allocation of resources to achieve objectives

SOURCE: Adapted from Katz [1970:210–211].

of strategies to be strict about following either of these or other conceptual sequences.

Figure 8-1 is presented to illustrate the point that the strategic planning

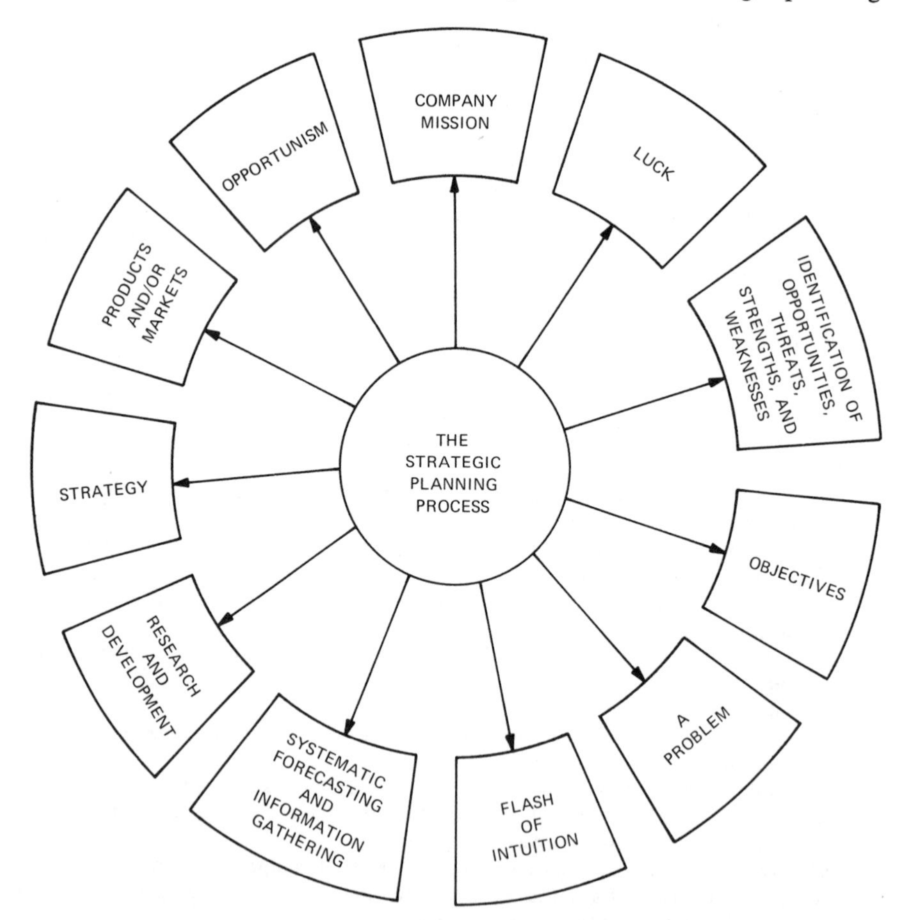

Figure 8-1 Starting points for formal strategic planning.

process can begin at any one of a number of points. The process of identifying strategies for evaluation can also begin at any point in the chart. Although points on the chart cover most of the typically used starting points, there are others, such as an actual or anticipated government regulation or a major change in an important environmental force (for example, war, new raw material supply discovery). Most of the approaches in Figure 8-1, and others, will be discussed later.

THE SITUATION AUDIT

Many conceptual and operational models of strategic planning begin with the situation audit. The result may be called the premises for planning meaning, literally, that which goes before. There is no standard definition of, or way to make, a situation audit, but it is indispensable to planning at all stages of the process.

The situation audit at a minimum covers boxes A through E in Figure 8-2. It can, depending upon one's definitions, encompass the second level of boxes in the chart. At any rate a major purpose of the audit is to provide a record of where the firm has been and where it is now in order to identify major strengths and weaknesses. This data base, plus projections into the future, is helpful in identifying opportunities and threats which, in turn, suggest strategies (see Figure 8-3). Once strategies are identified, they are evaluated on the basis of criteria some of which are derived from the data base formed in the situation audit.

The territory covered in the situation audit is so broad that each firm must determine what should be examined and in what depth. Obviously that which potentially is of the most significance to the company should have the highest priority. For an electric utility, for instance, industrial and residential demands for power are of the greatest importance. For a producer of automobiles consumer disposable and discretionary income is very significant. Depending upon importance, some information is derived from deep and costly research and some is estimated on the basis of general information in the minds of managers and staff.

The kind of data chosen for review in the situation audit, as well as the depth of analysis accorded to any one item, will depend upon asking questions such as: How important is this to the future of our company? Will the acquisition of this data help us do a better job of planning?

Another approach to the situation audit is to prepare a set of questions that top management thinks may stimulate the kind of thinking most needed to do a better job of planning. One such set of questions is given in Table 8-4.

If the situation audit is defined to include identification of strengths and weaknesses and/or opportunities and threats, these can be studied on the basis of the classification presented in Table 8-3 or the type of questions raised in Table 8-4.

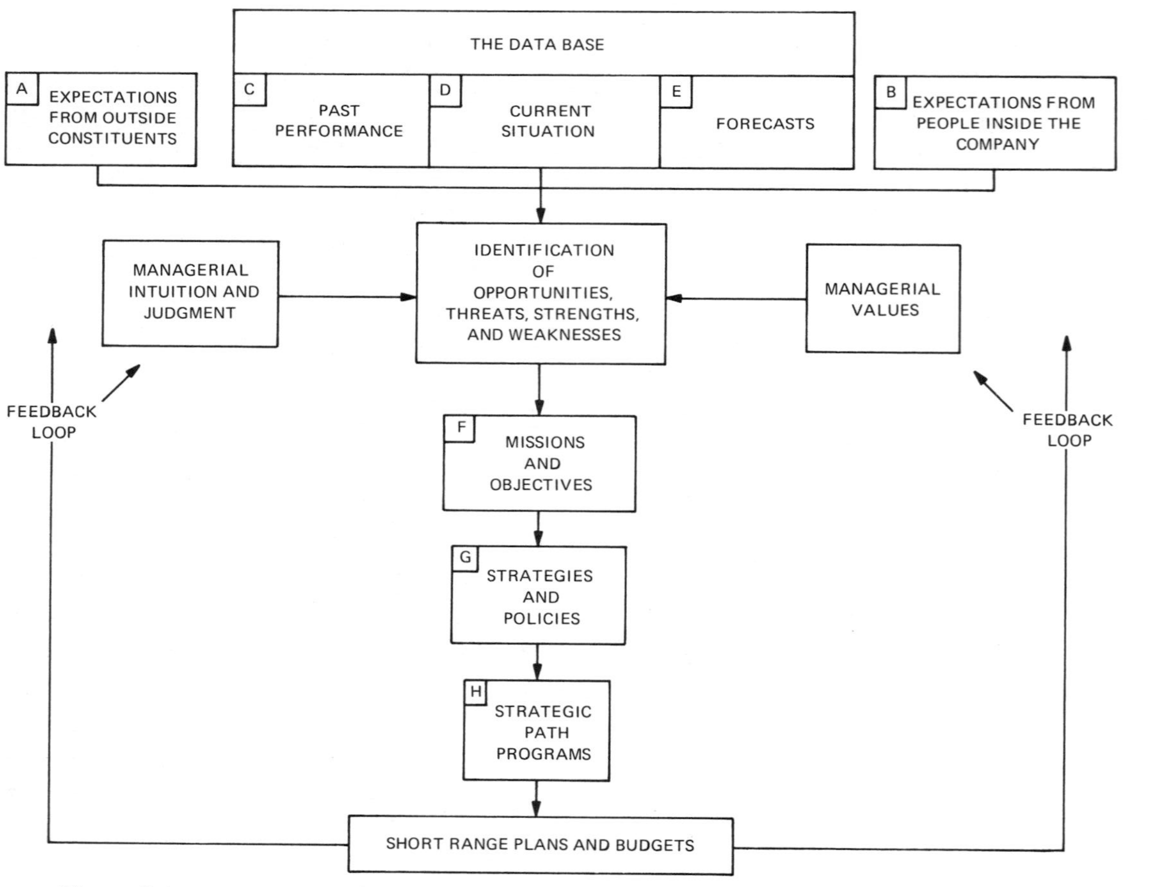

Figure 8-2 Corporate strategy: a conceptual development and implementation model (A).

TABLE 8-3
Classification of Information in the Situation Audit

1. Expectations from outside constituents
    - Stockholders
    - Suppliers
    - Customers
    - Government
    - Community
    - Creditors
    - Intellectuals
    - Etc.
2. Expectations from people inside the company
    - Board of Directors
    - Managers
    - Staff
    - Hourly employees
3. Past performance
    - Sales
    - Profits
    - Return on investment
    - Product development capability
    - Managerial skills
    - Labor relations
    - Public relations
    - Marketing capability
    - Etc.
4. Current situation
    - Financial
        - Profitability
        - Sales
        - Debt
        - ROI
        - Liquidity
        - Etc.
    - Resource use efficiencies
        - Sales per employee
        - Profits per employee
        - Investment per employee
        - Plant utilization
        - Use of employee skills
        - Etc.
    - Managerial capabilities
    - Staff capabilities
    - Evaluation of employees
        - Skills
        - Productivity
        - Worker satisfaction
        - Turnover
        - Etc.
    - Products/markets
        - Share
        - Strengths
        - Weaknesses
        - Etc.
    - Technology assessment
        - Impact on community
        - Technical strengths
        - Technical weaknesses
    - Competition
        - Price
        - Product/market
        - Technology
        - Etc.
    - Social policies
        - Conformance with pollution standards
        - Public image
        - Social demands on company
        - Evaluation of company voluntary programs
        - Etc.
    - Organizational structure
        - Suitability of
        - Strengths of
        - Weaknesses of
        - Etc.
5. Forecasts
    - Economic
        - Projected sales
        - GNP
        - Inflation rates
        - Market potential
        - Etc.
    - Competition
        - New products
        - Technology
        - Price
        - Etc.
    - Technology
    - Social Forces
        - Values
        - Attitudes
    - Political trends
    - Other
        - Population
        - International turbulence
        - Etc.

TABLE 8-4
The Situation Audit—Some Questions—An Exercise in Strategic Thinking

To evoke more substantial contributions to the planning process from the heads of the nine groups making up an industrial and consumer products company, a few years ago the firm's director of planning and market research prepared for the president a *list of 18 questions that group heads were to answer. The president pared the list to the nine set forth below.*

---

1. What steps can be taken to minimize effects of annual business cycles upon your profitability?
2. If you were to ignore the cost of entry, what new venture, new market, or new product line would you recommend entering, and why?
   (a) When you fully consider entry price, how does your answer change?
3. Are there competitive patents expiring that will enable you to take action previously denied to your group?
   (a) Are there new competitive patents issuing or likely to issue that appear to offer you problems? If so, are you considering requesting a license?
   (b) Are there company patents expiring in the five-year plan period that open doors for competitive action previously limited by our patent position?
4. As you ponder your competition and what action from each important competitor you might anticipate, what actions do you believe might occur in the next three years that would either hurt you or help you?
   (a) New technology or new product introductions?
   (b) Marketing programs or policies?
   (c) Pricing policies or practices?
5. Put yourself in your competitor's shoes. What market or product area in your group would you attack as the most vulnerable, and why? If you conclude that more than one warrants mention, do so.
6. What additional information or "intelligence" about your industry, competition, customers, trends, etc., would help your group be more effective in strategic or tactical planning?
   (a) If it might be possible to obtain any such information or intelligence from an outside source (Arthur D. Little, Stanford Research Institute, etc.), how much would you be willing to pay for it?
7. Consider the product life cycle as it applies to your key products.
   (a) Which do you identify as on the downgrade toward phasing out? Will any go out in the next three years?
   (b) Which do you identify as mature but still strong? Do they appear to be likely to remain for at least three more years?
   (c) Which do you identify as successfully introduced and on the upgrade toward a strong position in your industry? Are they enough to replace those in the first group?
   (d) Which have you recently introduced or are about to introduce that offer yet unproved promise?
8. In your opinion, are there unexploited opportunities for us to make more effective use of total division or total corporate strengths? If so, please describe.
9. Given freedom of action, would you increase your R&D budget beyond present levels? If so, how much and for what?
   (a) How about marketing?
   (b) If you did either of the above, how long would it take for results to show in increased profit and R.O.A.? One year? Two?

SOURCE: James K. Brown and Rochelle O'Connor [1974:10].

Information to develop the data in the situation audit can come from published sources [de Carbonnel and Dorrance, 1973] or from personal thinking and observation. Aguilar's classic study [1967] on scanning illuminates the latter. Aguilar studied 137 managers in 41 companies to determine what environmental information they sought and how they got it. He found that managers generally rely more heavily, by far, on personal than upon impersonal sources of information. The subordinates of managers constitute the largest single source of important external information, rather than internal reports and memoranda. ". . . the process for important external information appears to rely heavily on the manager's personal network of communications (including both private and organizational contacts) [Aguilar, 1967:68–69]. Larger company managers rely more heavily on internal sources of information than those in small companies.

The situation audit is a major generalized approach to identifying strategies for further evaluation. It also provides information to evaluate choices. What is discovered in the situation audit may raise issues that necessitate a strategic response and thus trigger a search for alternative strategies. Or, the audit may directly suggest a strategy to seize an opportunity, to avoid a threat, or to solve a problem, as the case may be. The situation audit may include or be supplemented by a number of specific approaches to strategy identification. Some of the more significant ones are presented in the remainder of this chapter.

"WOTS-UP" ANALYSIS SUGGESTS STRATEGIES

"WOTS-Up" is an anocrynom for weaknesses, opportunities, threats, and strengths. In Figure 8-3 we depict, simply, that WOTS-Up analysis suggests strategies and once strategies are identified their evaluation uses information employed in the WOTS-Up analysis.

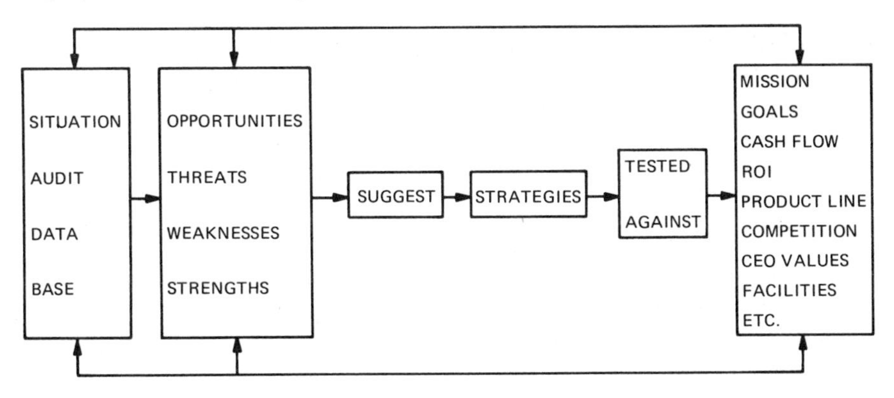

Figure 8-3 Strategies are derived from, but also tested against, analysis of opportunities, threats, weaknesses, and strengths.

Hofer's research [1973] supports the basic hypothesis of Figure 8-3 that strategies are directly suggested by strategic challenges identified in a WOTS-Up type of analysis. Furthermore, he concludes that different types of strategic challenges elicit different types of strategic responses.

There are a number of different types of WOTS-Up analyses. In the systematic audit, to illustrate, strengths and weaknesses are explicitly identified. A few illustrations of how they may suggest strategies follow. An audit of management reveals that the chief executive is 65 years of age, wishes to retire, and there is no one in the firm capable of taking his place. This is a weakness. Suggested strategies are to recruit a CEO from outside, to merge with another company, or to sell the business. Another example: the audit shows that 55 per cent of sales and revenues come from one product whose sales potential is projected to decline. This opens up a potential serious threat. This suggests many strategies, for example reduce dependence upon this product, remodel the product, add new more profitable products to the line, sell the product line and use the cash for the acquisition of new products, or engage in a cost-reduction program. Another audit may reveal that the company has a strong distribution system for its major product. This, of course, is a strength and opens up many opportunities. A suggested strategy would be to load comparable products on the system. A fourth audit may reveal that the firm has superior technical skills in the research and development department. An obvious suggested strategy would be to increase emphasis upon the development of new products and/or the redesign of old products to make them superior to those of competitors in the same price range.

Some companies begin strategic planning with a form, completed by the managers and staff of the company, that identifies an opportunity, a threat, a weakness, or a strength and suggests what ought to be done about it. These ideas are collected, classified, and evaluated.

One of the authors was associated with a large corporation that began its strategic planning process with a three-day meeting of selected managers and staff. At the meeting the major opportunities, threats, strengths, and weaknesses of the company were identified. Priorities were given to a selected few and they became the focus of staff research and valuation from which company strategies were eventually derived.

GAP ANALYSIS

In this approach the stimulus is an examination of whether an end that has been established is likely to be achieved. If not, the question becomes "What strategies and policies must be adopted to reach the sought ends?" Or, "should we modify our ends?"

Suppose, for example, that the basic mission of an aerospace firm is to produce military and commercial aircraft. If it is not making commercial aircraft the question will arise in the situation audit: Should we produce a commercial aircraft? If the answer is affirmative the decision is a strategic one. If the answer is negative and the decision is made to delete commercial aircraft from the basic mission statement this, too, is a strategic decision.

There may be a gap between mission potential and aspirations of management. For example, Gerbers' stated mission several years ago was: "Babies are our only business." When population forecasts revealed that the baby boom was over the company deleted "only" from the mission and proceeded to add other products to its line.

In preparing the situation audit, an elementary forecast is usually made for sales of current products as well as those that are projected to be added in the future. If the forecasts are not equal to the desired objectives of management, there obviously is a gap. This sometimes is called the "planning gap." It either must be filled with new strategies and policies or the aspirations of management must be lowered.

Figure 8-4 shows a thought process for identifying new strategies assuming given corporate objectives. It asks, simply, whether present or replacement products will meet the objectives. If the answer is yes, then there is no problem. If the answer is no, then there must be an assessment of capabilities against opportunities. If a match is found and the criteria for a positive decision are met, then there is no problem. If the answer is negative, the search goes on again and again until a strategy capable of meeting the objectives is found. If it cannot be discovered, the objectives must be lowered.

On the other hand, a comparable model may ask whether objectives are high enough in light of potential company product capabilities or acquisitions. Much the same thought process is involved in identification of strategies to determine whether to raise or to keep the objectives [Mason, Harris, and McLoughlin, 1971; Ansoff, 1965:203].

STRATEGY PROFILE

Another approach is to make a systematic examination of present company strategy—implicit and explicit [Ferguson, 1974]. Once this is done the logical question to ask is "where is it desirable to find new strategies?" Table 8-5 suggests a classification for identifying and analyzing a company's strategic profile. For example, the company may have a policy not to allow one customer to buy more than 15 per cent of the total sales of the firm. Excessive concentration of sales and profits in one customer can, of course, leave the firm vulnerable to a sudden drop in purchases of that customer. If the audit shows that one customer currently buys more than 30 percent of the total output of the company, one of two things or a combination of both, must take place: (1) the policy should be revised, or (2) new policies and strategies should be devised to reduce the concentration. There are many possibilities: an acquisition of

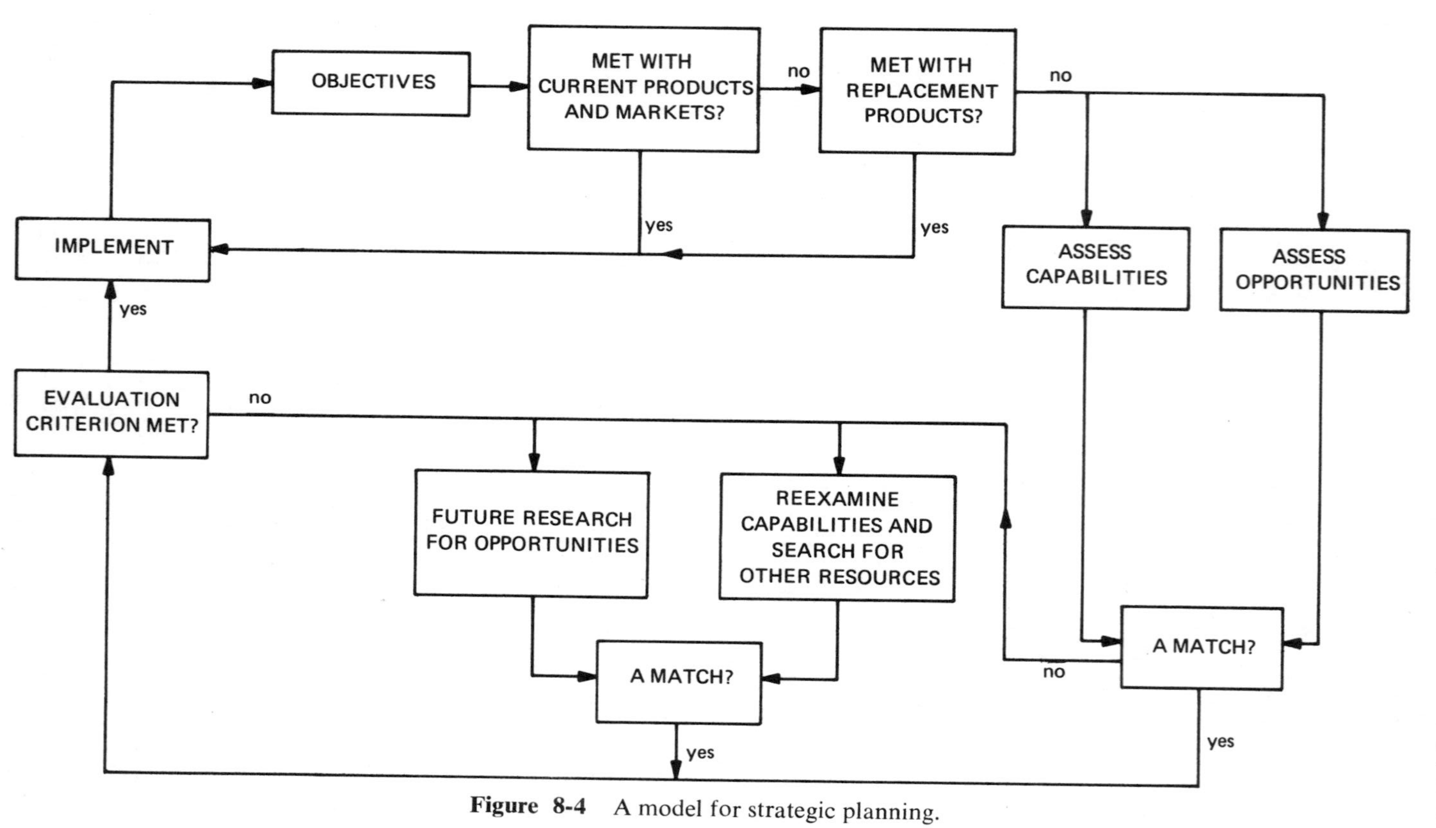

Figure 8-4 A model for strategic planning.

TABLE 8-5
Identifying and Analyzing a Company's Strategic Profile

1. Identify and measure dominant product/market concentrations
   (a) Sales by customer classification
   (b) Sales by major product group
   (c) Sales by channel of distribution
   (d) Sales by price/quality category
   (e) Sales by geographic distribution
2. Identify and measure units and/or activities receiving the greatest deployment of company resources
   (a) Distribution of assets among units and activities
   (b) Cash flows produced by each unit and activity
   (c) Focus of company discretionary allocations
3. Identify and measure major competitive advantages by comparisons with major competitors
   (a) Market share
   (b) Product quality
   (c) Product price
   (d) Product customer acceptance
   (e) Profit margin
   (f) Plant capabilities
   (g) Managerial capabilities
4. Identify financial strategies
   (a) Debt/equity ratio
   (b) Current asset and liability ratios
   (c) Dividend distribution
   (d) Cash position
5. Determine personal strategies of key executives
   (a) Risk orientation
   (b) Time horizon
   (d) Entrepreneural
   (c) Functional orientation: production, sales marketing, finance, etc.
   (e) Consensus
6. Determine analytical profiles of strategies
   (a) Timing of evaluations of strategies
   (b) Methods of evaluating strategies

another firm will by itself reduce dependence on the customer, the development of a new product not sold to the customer will have the same result, a conscious reduction of sales to the customer may be decided upon, or an aggressive campaign to penetrate new markets to raise total sales may be undertaken.

PRODUCT-MARKET MATRIX

Figure 8-5 displays in a simple fashion major strategic alternatives which every company must choose among concerning its product line and/or its markets. A company, for instance, can choose to stick with its present prod-

MARKET \ PRODUCT	PRESENT	RELATED	UNRELATED
PRESENT			
RELATED			
UNRELATED			

Figure 8-5 Product/market matrix.

ucts in its present markets. Or, it can decide to expand its line into either related or unrelated products. Similarly, it can choose to expand its present product line into other markets, or it can seek new markets for new products. Whatever it does will be a major strategic decision. The further the company moves from its present products and markets the more risky and expensive the move is likely to be. To illustrate the range of alternatives, suppose the company decides to increase penetration of existing markets with present products. Strategic choices are shown in Table 8-6.

Gutman [1964] found that 98 per cent of the companies he studied chose the sale of old products in old markets as the best strategy to growth. Morrison [in Mann, 1971] agrees but also observes that companies have shown outstanding growth by entering wholly new fields. In a study of Japanese companies Kono found that in the high-growth companies a major share of sales volume came from new products. Low-growth companies adopted a production-oriented strategy in contrast to the environment-oriented strategy of the high-growth companies [Kono, 1970]. Hofer's research takes him a step further. He concludes that, "the attempt to increase penetration of existing products for existing markets seems to succeed more often as a response to major increases in total demand than it does as a response to major changes in technology. By the same token, the development of new products for existing markets appears to be more successful as a response to major changes in technology than in horizontal diversification" [Hofer, 1973:51–52].

TABLE 8-6
Alternative Strategies for Increasing Penetration of Existing Markets With Existing Products

1. Expand the product's rate of purchase by present buyers.
   (a) Make existing designs obsolete.—If owners or consumers of the product become increasingly dissatisfied with the current or "old" style of the product that they own, because new ones are much more efficient, attractive, etc., the total market is expanded, and the best innovator captures the best share (if he promotes his products as well as any competitor). Of course, there are many forms of such product improvement, and it is a favorite strategy of durable-goods manufacturers.
   (b) Obtain sharper brand differentiation.—This may expand the total market little, if any, but increase the share sold by the seller making his product most conspicuously different (in appealing and acceptable ways). New designs or packages that provide truly greater satisfaction in use or enjoyment are obviously safer and more effective strategies than those that seek purely psychological differentiation.
   (c) Make the product more widely or conveniently available.—An example, and a method hardly exhausted by all appropriate products, is offering one's brand in vending machines, always available. Displays or packaging suitable for outlets that have not hitherto carried the product would be another way. And, sometimes an industry has not noticed shifts in buying habits and the traffic of potential buyers in types of outlets through which they have not distributed. Packages or forms of product with longer shelf life and less perishability, institution of mail-order delivery, and many other forms of such strategies may be found.
   (d) Increase the unit of purchase.—The well known "6-pack" and other multiple-unit packaging, as well as variety packs are examples of strategies that bring more usage by existing buyers who tend to consume more because they have more on hand and because they run out of the product less often.
   (e) Increase knowledge and recognition of the brand.—Here is universal strategy that tends to be sought by every contending brand. One firm's superior promotional skill or power may suffice to increase its penetration of the existing market, but this is unlikely to be a strong strategy unless coupled with differentiations that give value to the buyer.
2. Induce new uses of the product.
   (a) Add features or qualities serving additional uses.—This may be done in many ways, such as snow removal attachments for power mowers, pocket-sized packages of tissues, etc. Greater number of utilities for the buyer spells more sales.
   (b) Educate the buyer regarding additional uses.—Whether one is selling mending tape, sardines, or home power tools, it is very possible that good uses are not known to present buyers.
   (c) Proliferate.—Putting out the product in new models or forms, involving just moderate changes in the existing product, may enable the buyers to use it in more ways or more often, e.g., soft margarine, mentholated tobacco, child-sized aspirin tablets.
   (d) Provide services to encourage or enable new applications.—These tend to be more appropriate strategies for sellers of industrial and office equipment, but their use in such diverse fields as telephone service, encyclopedias, and insurance indicates that many lines may use such strategies to expand their products' uses and purchase.

SOURCE: David J. Luck and Arthur E. Prell, *Market Strategy*. © 1968, pp. 177–178. Reprinted by permission of Prentice-Hall, Inc., Englewood Cliffs, N.J.

Several researchers have devised classifications of product/market strategies. Foster [1970] suggests a set of preferred strategies. Prell and Luck [1968] list types of alternative product/market strategies. Hofer [1973] classifies all strategies, including product/market strategies, that can flow from analysis of strategic challenges.

Clifford examined over 700 rapidly growing companies, which he called "threshhold" companies, and concluded from their experience that the following were preferred product/market strategies [*passim,* 1973a:34–35].

1. Hold the expansion of product/market complexity to a pace and direction that can be managed effectively.
2. Obtain and hold niches in end-use markets where it is possible to maintain a profit performance superior to competition and to avoid retaliatory action from very large competitors.
3. Capitalize on the advantages threshhold companies have over their giant competitors, such as ability to grow in small markets, to enter large markets without affecting profitability, to make and attract acquisitions, and to react quickly to market demands.
4. Avoid areas where a threshhold company has disadvantages, such as markets demanding heavy capital investment for entry, products requiring high long-term research expenditures, and very large acquisitions.

PRODUCT LIFE CYCLES

A number of writers have identified the fact that products pass through a distinctive life cycle [for example, Dean, 1950; Forrester, 1959; Patton, 1959; Levitt, 1965; and Clifford, 1965]. Polli and Cook [1969] examined 140 nondurable goods categories and reaffirmed the existence of the product life cycle. In identifying strategies it is important for managers to ask what stage in the life cycle each product has reached because strategies which are successful in one stage can be disastrous in another. Figure 8-6 shows what may be a typical life cycle for a consumer durable good. (Life cycles of products have been shortening at the same time research and development costs have been increasing and spreading over a longer period of time. This is one reason why long-range planning is expanding in usage.)

In those companies blessed with above-average strategists, the curves in Figure 8-6 occur up to stage 4, at which time a product modification or a new product replacement is introduced, and a new life cycle is begun. In companies with the poorest strategies the classical life cycle does not occur because the life line never gets beyond stage 1, and the product is dropped.

In the research and development stage strategies relate to the precise product and technology to be developed, the timing of introduction of the product, the expenditures to be committed, and who is going to develop the prototype

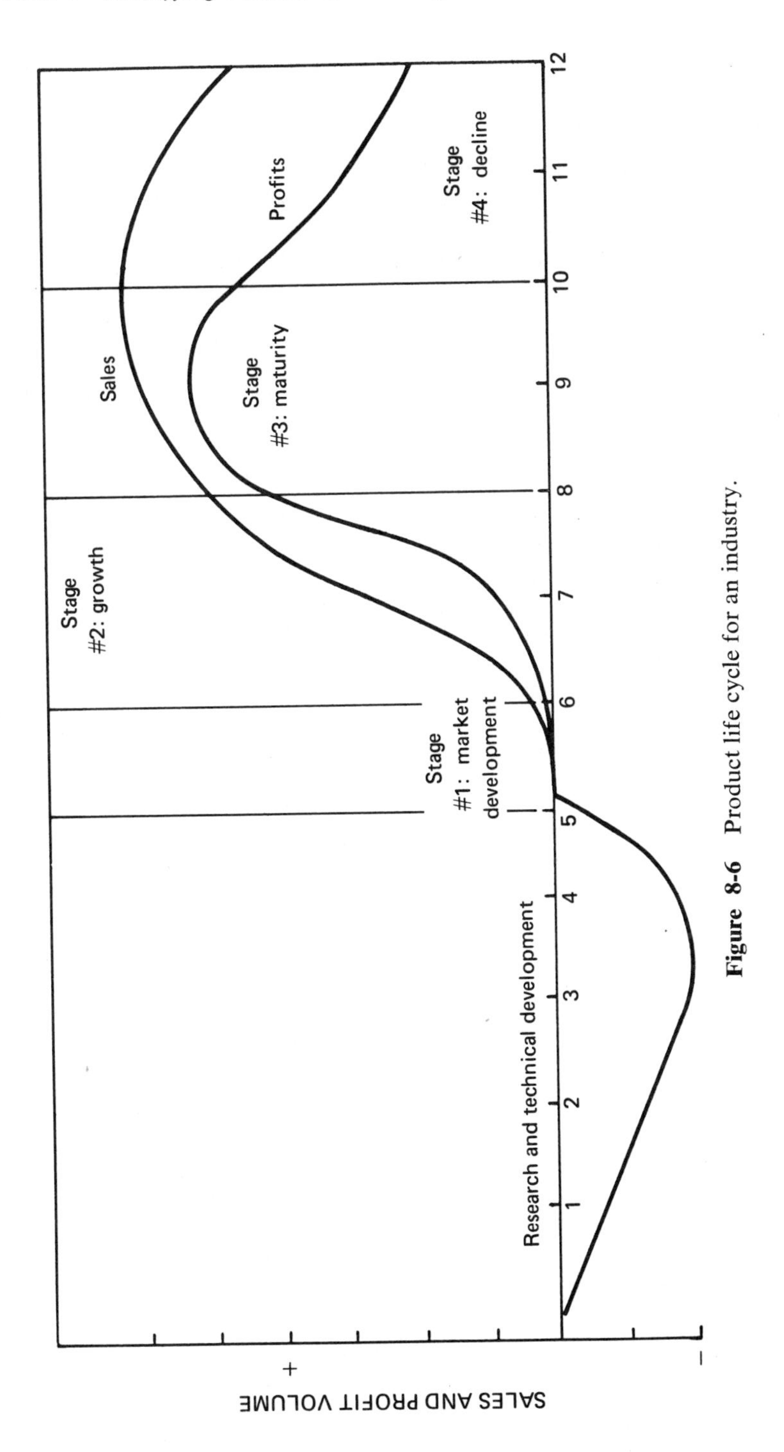

Figure 8-6 Product life cycle for an industry.

and lay plans for introducing the product on the market. In each case strategic decisions must be made.

Stage 1 is characterized by difficult problems in getting the product accepted and in achieving a break-even profit position. In stage 2 the product's sales take off and rise sharply. So do profits. Competitors then jump into the market and the originator, instead of trying to induce customers to try his product as he did in the early phases of stage 2, now faces a problem of getting consumers to prefer his brand. In stage 3 the market becomes saturated, price competition intensifies, manufacturers step up services, and the rate of sales growth slows down. Intense competition tends to turn down profits in the later parts of this stage. Then, in stage 4 sales decline and the drop in profits accelerates [Levitt, 1965]. Michael [1971] has concluded that products decline in different ways, which suggests different strategies for them.

It is obvious that in each stage a new set of strategies is required. We cannot here display alternatives in all areas, but to indicate the richness of possibilities an extended list is shown in Table 8-7 covering stage 3.

As a product moves through the different stages of its life cycle it has an impact on all areas of management decision making: for example, company missions, long-range strategic objectives, product design, pricing, packaging, distribution systems, production, promotion, information systems, personnel, facilities, cash flow, organization, and planning [Wasson, 1971; Fox, 1973; Rosen, 1974; and Hofer, 1975b].

PRODUCT PORTFOLIO APPROACH TO IDENTIFYING STRATEGIES

In this approach, probably first identified in its modern concept by Tilles [1966] and pioneered by the Boston Consulting Group, managers of companies with a variety of products in different life cycles, at growth rates and market shares, search for investment strategies to allocate resources among them to optimize company long-run profits [Moose and Zakon, 1971, 1972; Buckley, 1975; and Day, 1975].

The process begins with a distribution of company products in a matrix shown in Figure 8-7. Products having a high market share and prospective high market growth are likely to require capital over and above cash flow to maintain share. Eventually such products may become so-called "cash cows" with high share and low growth. In this category capital investment need not to be more than enough to maintain share, and cash spinoff can be great. When products fall into the category of low share and are in a high market growth area they tend to create problems such as: Should the company increase capital expenditures to try to increase market share? Or, should the products be allowed to decline and disappear? Should they be sold? If nothing

TABLE 8-7
Alternative Strategies for Stage 3 (Maturity) in the Product Life Cycle

1. Intensify brand promotion.
   (a) Use more intensive and brand-stressing advertising.
   (b) Make heavier point-of-sale effort.
   (c) Design more attractive and functional packaging.
   (d) Vary advertising messages and media for different market segments.
   (e) Offer more services with product.
   (f) Increase weight of expenditure on sales promotion rather than advertising, to hold customer loyalty rather than seek out new buyers.
2. Trade down.
   (a) Enter a "fighting brand" on the market at a lower price, to avoid jeopardizing an established premium brand.
   (b) Introduce lower priced models of an established brand.
   (c) Lower prices of the entire line, preferably as temporary promotions rather than imply line is worth lower value. Keep prices close to private labels.
   (d) Produce for private labels.
3. Proliferate (extensively or radically).
   (a) Offer more variety in features, flavors, designs, etc.
   (b) Seek more exclusive and innovative features.
   (c) Create more radical and distinct package designs.
   (d) Make more options available in accessories, designs, etc.
4. Trade up (strategy opposite to item 2).
   (a) Improve quality, appearance, etc. to offer better product.
   (b) Use prestige packages, brand names, etc.
   (c) Increase prices to cream market levels (to increase penetration of markets willing to pay higher prices, earning more margin on possibly lower sales and keeping greater differentiation over competitive products).
5. Increase product availability and point-of-sale service.
   (a) Use longer channels to make more available at wholesale level.
   (b) Open more distribution centers closer to point of use or sale.
   (c) Get into more outlets and different channels (e.g., vending machines).
   (d) Improve service offered by dealers (where applicable) or establish manufacturer-operated service centers.

SOURCE: David J. Luck and Arthur E. Prell, *Market Strategy*. © 1968, pp. 186–187. Reprinted by permission of Prentice Hall, Inc., Englewood Cliffs, N.J.

is done margins will be low and profits will be minimal or negative. Products that fall into the category of low share and low market growth are "dogs," which should be abandoned.

This analysis of alternatives is, of course, highly simplified. Issues become more complex, for instance, when the matrix is expanded to include moderate market share and moderate potential market growth rates. Greater complications arise when factors other than capital allocations and profit returns are considered in formulating strategy. Nevertheless, the fundamental idea of classifying products in terms of market share and market growth potential is powerful. This matrix helps managers ask pertinent questions about preferred strategies.

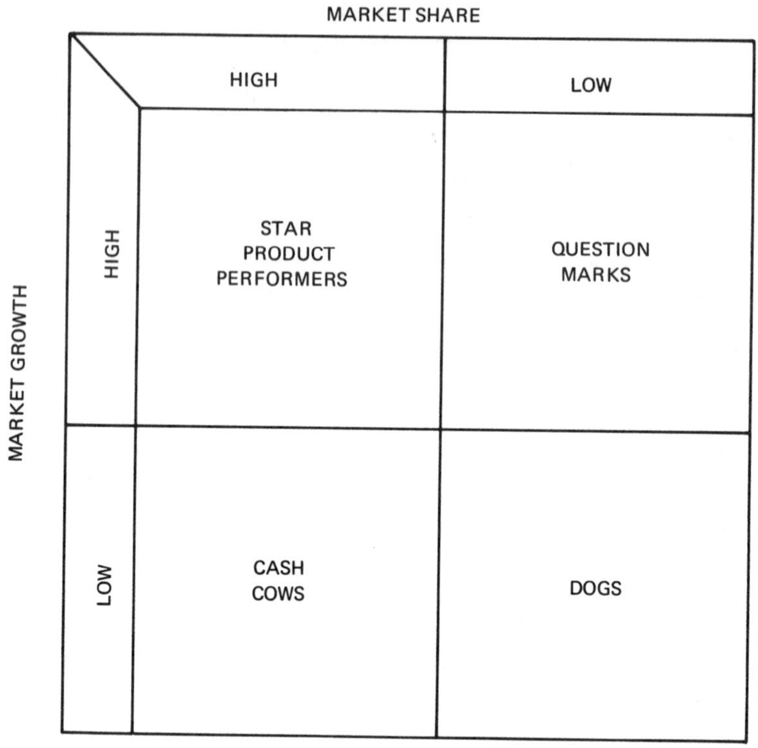

MARKET GROWTH \ MARKET SHARE	HIGH	LOW
HIGH	STAR PRODUCT PERFORMERS	QUESTION MARKS
LOW	CASH COWS	DOGS

Figure 8-7 Product portfolio matrix.

FINDING A NICHE IN THE MARKET

An unexcelled strategy is to find a niche in the market that no one else is filling. If a product can be developed and sold at a price that customers cannot resist, the result will be riches. To illustrate, a quarter century ago Baron Marcel Bich decided to make disposable ballpoint pens at a time when such pens were very expensive (around $12) and designed to last a lifetime. Societe Bic, the company built on this concept, has today captured one third of the world market for pens and has a market value of $315 million.

A strategy of picking propitious niches begins with an analysis of demand for products and services, weaknesses and strengths of the company in meeting the demand, and evaluation of the competition. Naturally, the best strategy will match company strengths with the requisites for success in filling the niche. A low potential for success is not attractive, even though company strengths match requirements for success in meeting demand. All possible limitations in filling a niche in a profitable fashion must be identified. Lockheed found a niche in the commercial transport market that could be filled with a medium-range wide-bodied jet and decided to build the L-1011. Then Douglas decided to build the DC-10 in direct competition with Lockheed. At the present time the market is not large enough to yield profits for these companies. A niche once filled successfully naturally attracts competition, as Hugh Hefner of *Playboy* can attest.

INVENTION

The creation of a new and better product or service is a superb strategy. The success of companies such as DuPont and 3M stems from the strategy of these companies of emphasizing research to produce new products that give them a commanding lead position in a market. There are few if any better strategies than to invent a new product that becomes a generic name, such as Coca-Cola, Smith Brothers cough drops, or Dixie Cups. Not all such inventions, however, were instant successes [Campbell, 1964]. Chester Carlson patented his xerography process in 1937 and tried without success to interest over twenty companies in the process, including such firms as Remington Rand and IBM. Finally, in 1944 he was supported by the Battelle Memorial Institute, but it was not until 1950 that the first machine was marketed. This machine became the strategic factor in the spectacular growth of Xerox.

COMPUTER MODELS

There are all types of computer models from which information is gathered to help identify strategies. Simulation modeling, for example, is widespread. An increasing number of companies are building computer simulation models of various degrees of complexity and comprehensiveness. The insurance industry, for instance, has developed a comprehensive computer simulation model that includes functional relationships among all significant factors involved in decisions such as rate structures, reserves, and demand elasticities. With such a model, managers are in a position to ask "what-if" questions of the computer and come to informed strategies with the answers [Life Office Management Association, 1970]. One of the earliest comprehensive simulation models was that of Rapoport and Drews [1962] made for the oil industry. A well-publicized early financial model made for the Sun Oil Company was reported by Gershefski [1968], its creator. The McKinsey computer simulation for mergers and acquisitions is given in Kraber [1970]. A compilation of computer simulation models, corporate and functional, can be found in Schrieber [1970]. Hamilton and Moses [1974] have developed a comprehensive model combining optimization and simulation. More will be said in the next chapter about simulation.

Another popular model is the econometric model. An econometric model of the United States, for example, is used by some firms to identify growing and declining industries from which appropriate strategies are identified for the company.

STRATEGIC FACTORS IN BUSINESS SUCCESS

There are strategic factors that will determine the success of any company in a particular industry and at a given stage in its life cycle. The economics, technology, and sociopolitical setting of the industry will determine what they are. One study identified 85 strategic factors that businessmen across all industries considered to be of major importance in company success. There was surprising consensus among survey respondents about the 10 to 15 factors that were most important across all industry. Respondents to the survey revealed close agreement about strategic factors governing success in particular industries [Steiner, 1969a].

Cohn and Lindberg [1974:5] identified the following factors as bearing critically on the survival and growth of small businesses: "A cautious attitude toward growth. A concern for liquidity. A focus on providing wanted products or services and satisfying work while keeping costs lean. Establishment and maintenance of an open system of communication and decision making. Creation of a rational organization. Control over certain functions. Economical use of time. Control of owner-manager subjectivity." A more comprehensive list of strategic factors responsible for the growth of larger firms was prepared by Guth [1972].

Clearly, managers can narrow the range of strategy identification by asking themselves what are the handful of strategic factors determining the success of their firm in their particular environment and then identifying those strategies capable of meeting the requirement. There is help for them in narrowing choice from research that has been done, but the predictive nature of most of the research is far from certain.

Cannon [1968] has classified strategies in all areas of business activity from which strategies may be selected. Glueck [1972a] has prepared a selected list of hypotheses from which preferred strategies may be chosen. These will be examined in Chapter 14. A number of scholars have derived strategies for success in particular situations and functions [Ansoff and Stewart 1967; The Boston Consulting Group, 1970; Chevalier, 1972; Fruhan, 1972; Khandwalla, 1973; Schendel, Patton, and Riggs, 1974; Schoeffler, Buzzell, and Heany 1974].

Space does not permit identification of the particular strategies suggested by these researchers. We do think it useful, however, to summarize the major findings of Schoeffler's group. He was director of the PIMS Project Team (profit impact of market strategies) designed to identify strategies of different businesses under different competitive conditions. His study of 620 diverse businesses concluded the following:

1. ". . . ROI goes up steadily as market share increases" [1974:141].
2. ". . . The higher the ratio of investment to sales, the lower ROI tends to be" [1974:143; confirmed by Buzzell, Gale, and Sultan, 1975].
3. "ROI . . . was highest for the largest companies and lowest for those in the 'average' group" [1974:144].

Altman and others (for example, Beaver [1966]) studied the use of *financial ratios* in conjunction with multivariate statistical techniques such as discriminant analysis to predict corporate failures. Altman [1968] found ($N = 66$) that five significant ratios could be used to *predict* corporate failure and bankruptcy. These were working capital/total assets, retained earnings/total assets, earnings before interest and taxes/total assets, market value of equity/book value of total debt, and sales/total assets. A prediction rate of 96 per cent was achieved one year before actual bankruptcy and 79% two years prior to bankruptcy.

Schendel and others tried to use these ratios to predict downturns in companies that had subsequent upturns. They were unable to find a significant pattern between these ratios and downturn. It is probable that the performance declines in the companies Schendel studies were not severe enough to give rise to significant changes in the financial ratios. They conclude, ". . . use of the ratio analysis designed by Altman for use in predicting corporate failure does not appear to be useable in prediction of decline or for control purposes" [Schendel, Patton, and Riggs, 1974:31].

There has been a good bit of descriptive literature on preferred strategies in particular functional areas. Earlier in this chapter some of the literature concerning the product/market mix and the product life cycle was noted. With no effort to be inclusive, but only for illustrative purposes, we may mention the following literature in other functional areas: strategies of multinational firms [Schollhammer, 1974; Dymsza, 1972]; marketing policies in multinational corporations [Gestetner, 1974; Holton, 1971]; research and development strategies [Ansoff and Stewart, 1967; Gibson, 1966]; vertical integration [Webster, 1967]; diversification [Kitching, 1967; Mace and Montgomery, 1962; Howell, 1970b; Ansoff *et al.*, 1970; Ansoff *et al.*, 1959; Steiner, 1964]; technological threats [Cooper *et al.*, 1973]; divestment strategy [Bettauer, 1967]; avoiding take-overs [Nesheim, 1970]; marketing [Luck and Prell, 1968; Kotler, 1970]; products [Way, 1975]; smoothing growth rates [Shank and Burnell, 1974]; research and development [Ansoff and Stewart, 1967; Twiss, 1970]; pricing [Oxenfeldt, 1975]; products [Day, 1975]; finance [Weston and Brigham, 1971; Shuckett and Mock, 1973]; and social policies [Steiner, 1972a, 1975a, and Rockefeller, 1973].

INTUITION

By intuition we mean innate or instinctive knowledge, a quick or ready apprehension, without obvious recourse to inference or reasoning. Many managers depend upon their intuition to a surprising degree in identifying the right strategy. For instance, Alfred Sloan said of Will Durant: "He was a man who would proceed on a course of action guided solely, as far as I could tell, by some intuitive flash of brillance. He never felt obliged to make an engineering hunt for the facts. Yet at times he was astoundingly correct in his judgment" [in Mihalasky, 1969:23]. Mihalasky [1969:23] suggests in his experiments that "some executives have more 'precognitive' ability than others—that is, they are better able to anticipate the future intuitively rather than logically and thus, when put in positions where strong data support may not always exist, will make better decisions." Although there probably is some truth to this statement, it is our view that the apparently "intuitive flash" is more the result of digestion of masses of information blended with experience, insight, and an intellectual capability of a manager to sift through the irrelevant and focus quickly on the critical. In some people this can be done very quickly in "the computer between the ears." There is no superior approach to superb strategy identification than a brilliant intuitive mind.

OTHER APPROACHES

Another approach to strategy identification is opportunism, or waiting until something happens and then reacting. During the past great merger wave many companies waited until opportunities came "through the transom" so-to-speak and chose strategies from this source. Some companies, as noted earlier, follow the leader. Luck plays a hand in strategy identification. Justin Dart recently explained the origin of his great success in business. Years ago he had high blood pressure and there was no drug available to suppress it. He found a small company where a remedy was being studied and invested $7,000 to push the research. That was the beginning of Riker Laboratories, which prospered and was later sold to Minnesota Mining and Manufacturing for $150 million [*Los Angeles Times,* May 5, 1974:48]. For still other approaches see Gregory [1967]; Kepner and Tregoe [1965]; and Allison [1971].

CONCEPT OF SYNERGY

Synergy is the process of putting two elements together to achieve a total greater than the sum of the individual parts. This has been called the "2 + 2 = 5" effect [Ansoff, 1965:75–102]. McDonnell's merger with Douglas Aircraft is an illustration of synergy on a large scale. A more simple illustration would be a motel owner who decided to build a restaurant close by. Each could contribute to the business of the other and net a total greater than they would achieve if operated independently.

There are many possibilities for identifying strategies that have a potential synergistic effect. The purpose in mentioning the subject here is simply to observe that the manager who is thinking about synergy is more likely to achieve it than one who is not.

A NETWORK OF STRATEGIES

In all of the above approaches the identification of a major alternative strategy immediately leads to the identification of substrategies and the formation of a network of strategies. For instance, when American Motors Corporation decided in 1957 to put all of its "chips" on the small Rambler automobile, that grand strategy was supported by strategies in all significant areas: production, advertising, plant divestment, cash utilization, cost control, and management.

THE ART OF ASKING THE RIGHT QUESTIONS

The art of asking the right questions runs throughout all of the preceding approaches. The simplicity of this approach should not distract one from its great power. The graveyard of unprofitable products is strewn with brilliant mechanical wonders that could not find a market. The reason is that managers asked whether a product could be produced rather than whether it would sell at the price required to make a profit.

Sven Lundstedt [1968:229] underscores the value of asking questions in the following passage:

> "Initial scientific questions, like first impressions, carry a great deal of weight in shaping the direction of a system of thought. Past experience suggests that more emphasis ought to be upon questions than upon method. If one discovers how to ask good questions (a substantive issue) and if one also learns how to determine if they are in fact also logical ones (a formal issue), the pursuit of scientific discovery in psychology in general is likely to be advanced."

This is equally true for those managers seeking to derive the very best strategies and polices for their organizations.

CONCLUDING COMMENT

Strategy identification reflects other considerations not examined in this chapter, such as cognate thought processes, managerial values, organization structures, company life cycles, and interpersonnel relationships. These aspects of the process of strategy/policy formulation and implementation will be examined in detail in other chapters.

Strategy identification is not a single and discreet step in management. It is iterative with other parts of the strategic decision-making process which will become clearer in the next chapter.

QUESTIONS

Discussion Guides on Chapter Content

1. Lay out the preferred conceptual steps in the formulation of strategy.
2. The president of General Motors Corporation asks you to tell him what information he should gather to make a situation audit prior to developing strategy. What would you suggest?
3. How can the "WOTS-Up" analysis help in identifying strategies?
4. Explain the product-market matrix and its role in strategy identification.
5. Illustrate how strategies may differ as a company's product goes through a normal life cycle.
6. Explain the meaning of "gap analysis."
7. Do you think the concept of "strategic factors in business success" is useful in strategy identification? Explain.

Mind Stretching Questions

1. You are asked this question by the president of a medium-sized corporation: "Out of all the research that has been done on identifying strategies, state ten major hypotheses that have been tested and found to be true and would be of the most importance to me in helping me to identify the right strategies for testing and evaluation." What would you reply?
2. Name several corporations that found successful strategies by finding niches in the market place and explain the strategies.

CHAPTER

9

Evaluating and Choosing Among Policy/Strategy Alternatives

INTRODUCTION

Approaches to identifying major polices and strategies were presented in the last chapter. Here, we address the question of their evaluation and choice.

In recent years there has grown up a body of literature concerning this process called "decision theory." Decision theory itself is not new. The "economic man" concept of the economist, for instance, was for generations the core of economic decision making. However, today's decision theory has broadened considerably beyond this narrow range, as will be illustrated in this and the following chapters.

It should be noted here that decision theory falls today into two broad classifications—normative and descriptive. Most relevant current research is of the normative type, and most of that is concerned with quantitative optimization models in monetary terms. One reason for the slow growth of research about decision making is that the real world is a very messy place. The processes are extremely difficult to unravel and trace, and universal generalizations of cogency are difficult to discover. This is truer the higher in an organization's hierarchy one probes and, generally, the more significant the decision is to the organization.

The purposes of this chapter are to examine the conceptual and operational processes of evaluation and choice of dominant policies and strategies; to illustrate the variety of disciplines focused on the strategic decision-making process; to illustrate the types of tools available for analysis, their strengths and weaknesses; and to present major overall tests for strategy evaluation and choice.

DECISION MAKING

Evaluation Does Not Always Follow Identification

It is worthwhile to point out that, when managers individually or in their planning processes identify alternative policies and strategies, the conceptual process of decision making calls for evaluation and choice. This does not always happen. Many managers fail to see that the end result of strategic planning is current decisions not just "plans." Some of the reasons why they do not leap to decisions once they have identified policies and strategies are as follows [Gerstner, 1972]:

Decision-making is risky. A major decision demands that executives take a stand. If they are wrong, their careers may be at stake. Making major decisions requires courage, and executives may prefer the safety of no decision.

Strategic decision making is fundamentally a creative process that is difficult. It demands a type of thinking and breadth of knowledge that many executives who have arrived at top management levels have neglected as they rose in the ranks because they devoted themselves to solving short-range problems in their narrow functional areas of expertise.

Most major strategic decisions are controversial and demand leadership to implement. How many times has one heard in corporations a statement such as this: "We ought to get out of that business." But nothing is done. Leadership is needed to decide to act and see that action is taken.

Finally, the promotion and evaluation systems in many corporations work against the making of significant decisions. Managers that show best short-run profit results tend to be promoted rapidly, which means that they may not be obliged to live with the medium- and long-range impacts of their decisions [Salveson, 1974]. As Gerstner notes [1972:9] ". . . incentive compensation is often tied either to short-term earnings performance or to stock-price movements, neither of which has anything to do with strategic success."

Planning, Decision, and Decision Making

The words planning and decision making are often used interchangeably, but there is a distinction between them. Planning is basically "an input-improving mediator that serves to establish role prescriptions" [Miner, 1973a:170]. In this sense it is decision making and certainly establishes not only a structure but a necessity for decision making. Decision making, however, covers a wider territory than planning. It touches all components of the management process. Most all that a manager does involves decisions, but decision making is not synonomous with management.

There is no agreement on what a decision is but few would object, we think, to this definition: "The generic concept of decision . . . is settlement, fixed intention, bringing to a conclusive result, judgment, and resolution. A decision is a choice made by a decision-maker about what should or should not be done in a given situation" [Steiner, 1969b:321].

There are many different classifications of decision in organizations, but we shall group them into creative, programmable, and negotiated. This present chapter will be concerned principally with the first type of decision. All types of decisions will be discussed further in Chapter 11. Decisions that result from the decision making process, will now be examined.

The Conceptual Process of Decision Making

The literature on decision making is filled with conceptual models. They range from simple to very complex models. The simplest ones usually follow fundamental steps, such as [Gibson, Ivancevich, and Donnelly, 1973:204]:

- Recognize the need for decision making.
- Consider and analyze alternatives.
- Select an alternative or strategy to attain a goal.
- Communicate and implement the decision.
- Evaluate and review.

In previous chapters a number of more complex conceptual decision-making models were presented. Other illustrative conceptual decision models with more or less complexity that are tailored to functional decisions are, for example, acquisitions [Boulden, 1969], divestment [Davis, 1974], sales pricing [Cyert and March, 1963:141], and product/market strategy [Ansoff, 1965: 202–203].

In Figure 9-1 we present the main classifications of phenomena together with the basic disciplines that have an impact on the decision-making process. Several features of this figure are noteworthy. First, at least six classifications of phenomena have significant influence on decision making in organizations. Second, a large number of disciplines relate to the detailed forces in the phenomenon classes. Third, not all conceivable disciplines that influence decision making in organizations are included on the chart.

SOME MAJOR CHARACTERISTICS OF THE OPERATIONAL STRATEGIC DECISION MAKING PROCESS

The Uniqueness of the Process

The decision-making process for the most significant decisions made by top executives will vary from organization to organization. Each process is unique because involved in the decision making will be managerial value systems and judgments; internal political forces; interpersonnel relationships; and individual managerial skills, capabilities, motivations, and values. In no two

Figure 9-1 An interdisciplinary framework of decision making. [Adapted from Harrison, 1975, p. 41.]

organizations will these be identical. Furthermore, major strategic decisions tend to be, but may not always be, unique to each organization. Grinyer and Norborn [1974] found, not surprisingly, that in United Kingdom companies the chief executive dominates decision making in major strategic fields of choice.

The Decision Making Process Is Very Complex

One of the authors had an opportunity to make major policy decisions in government organizations and concluded, after careful consideration, that even immediately following a top policy decision he could not reconstruct the detailed processes by means of which the decision was made. The forces, events, information flows, and thought processes were much too complex.

Former White House Press Secretary Moyers undoubtedly felt the same way in responding to an inquiry about how a particular decision had been made. He said: "You begin with the general principle that the process of decision making is inscrutable. No man knows how a decision is ultimately shaped. It's usually impossible even to know at what point a decision is made" [*Los Angeles Times,* January 23, 1966:1]. Efforts to describe the decision-making process from which major decisions have come underscore this point [Allison, 1971; Hitch, 1966; Bryan, 1964; and Bailey, 1950].

The Decision Making Process Is Iterative and Fluid

Major policy/strategy decisions are typically made only after long discussions among managers and staffs, reevaluations, checking and double checking, and jumping from one point in a conceptual decision-making process to another. This is undoubtedly what Marion Folsom, a top executive in business and government, had in mind when he said, "Decisions generally are the result of a long series of discussions by both line and staff people after the staff has collected the pertinent material. It is often hard to pinpoint the exact stage at which a decision is reached. More often than not, the decision comes about naturally during discussions, when the consensus seems to be reached among those whose judgment and opinion the executive seeks" [Folsom, 1962:4].

From company to company, and within the same company, the decision process is constantly changing. It alters with subject matter but also because of different individual and group involvements in the process.

While there may be a certain amount of formality to a planning process in a company, there can be and usually are informal communication and decision processes also at work. Grinyer and Norburn [1974:86] in their study of British corporations concluded that ". . . those involved in the real process of strategic decision making recognized that it is ultimately a political process in which power and influence of individuals change with the nature of the challenges to the company, with changing personal relationships, and with other factors like the health of top managers . . . informal political processes constitute the system by which decisions are really made." They go on to conclude that ". . . financially more successful companies tended to use more *in*formal channels of communication . . ." [Grinyer and Norburn, 1974:86].

Dominance of Nonquantifiable Element in Decision Making

Much of the literature of decision making emphasizes quantitative decision measures, and quantitative models and techniques to reach conclusions. This includes such measures as return on investment, maximization of output per unit of input, least cost, and profit maximation. For any major decision a manager will have available enormous quantities of factual information. Despite this quantitative emphasis in decision making the facts are, as observed by Greiner, Leitch, and Barnes [1970], that informed managers rely much more on qualitative than quantitative criteria in appraising performance, even when quantitative information is available and in use. Former Secretary of Defense McNamara validated this conclusion for a large and complex decision, that of the TFX airplane, in testimony before the Congress, as follows:

> "Fundamentally, we are dealing with a question of judgment. Granted there are specific technical facts and calculations involved; in the final analysis, judgment is what is at issue. . . . In this case we are faced with a situation in which judgments are pyramided upon judgments. . . . There is only one way I know to minimize the compounding error . . . and that way is to apply the judgment of the decision maker not only to the final recommendation but also to the underlying recommendations and factors" [*TFX Contract Investigation,* 1963:387].

This conclusion of the Secretary is even more significant given the fact that, for the first time in the history of the Department of Defense, he had established in the Office of the Secretary a large and distinguished staff of mathematicians and quantitative science experts specifically to help him make such decisions.

Two quantitative scientists accept this view and express it a little differently, as follows:

> "The contribution of quantitative techniques to decision making is largely in the appraisal step, the analysis of decision possibilities. Quantitative techniques are unable to suggest hypotheses or to define problems or to suggest alternatives. These abilities remain in the domain of personality, experience, and creativity. But once alternatives have been defined, these techniques can be powerful tools for making quick and accurate appraisals" [Emory and Niland, 1968:115].

Why is the preceding statement true? Fundamentally, it is because the "right" type of quantifiable information is not available; what is available is not convincing or creditable; but, more importantly, there are overriding considerations in decision making with which quantitative data cannot deal. Many major decisions must be made by managers that cannot be proven to be correct or incorrect by quantitative methods. An outstanding illustration is the definition of an organization's mission and purpose.

One of the most fateful strategic decisions a chief executive will make is to answer the question: "What is our business?" As Drucker [1974:79] points out, there never is one right answer and the answer, when derived, is seldom if ever the result of logical conclusions drawn from a set of "facts." The evaluation of alternatives and final choice is made solely on the basis of judgment.

No other strategic decision is as important as this one. This is so because, as described in Chapter 7, the mission establishes the lines of business and markets in which the firm will engage and the purposes will establish the main policies and standards of conduct for all employees both for economic and ethical activities. This is the foundation for determining specific objectives, resource priorities, strategies, plans, work assignments, organizational structure, and managerial tasks.

Strategies and policies may also be determined at lower levels, which spring from a manager's judgment rather than any set of facts that lead to the decision. For instance, irrespective of financial conditions an executive may decide from among one of the following strategies: invest for future growth, manage for earnings, or manage for immediate cash. Each of these choices will have a different impact on such decision areas as market share, pricing, promotion, existing product line, and new products [Gerstner, 1972].

RATIONALITY IN THE DECISION MAKING PROCESS

Types of Rationality

In theory, managers are the most successful stewards of their organizations when they make rational decisions either upon the basis of intuition, logical evaluation of facts, or both. But, when is a decision rational? In the simplest of terms a decision is rational when it effectively and efficiently assures the achievement of aims for which the means are selected. If a man is cold and wants to get warm it is rational for him to get close to a fire. If a man is in business it is rational to satisfy consumer wants at a profit.

Such simple concepts get complicated in organizational life. When Consolidated Edison of New York passed its dividend in 1974 for the first time in decades, the action was considered to be rational by management but the stockholders did not think so. The fact is that many individuals and groups are interested in every action a manager takes. Each has different aspirations, needs, and interests and views rationality in different ways. Even top managers of a business often disagree upon the rationality of a decision.

This suggests that rationality may be defined as the best selection of means to achieve an objective that is acceptable to the value system of the evaluator. The test of which means is best is, of course, determined by the same value system. For example, if the evaluator is a stockholder, his system of values may establish maximum rate of return on his investment as the desired objective. He can determine over time whether his objective has been met, but he will find it difficult to determine whether any particular decision is rational since its influence on the rate of return may be obscure. Suppose, for instance, management decided to maximize stockholder investment by building a new productive facility but the investment turned sour because a competitor got to the market first. Was the decision rational?

Different disciplines also look upon rationality in diverse terms. Rational action to the economist is that which maximizes profit. Chester Barnard [1954] defined rational decisions as being those which assured the communication, coordination, and motivation necessary to weld the organization into a cooperative effort to reach common ends. Quantitative scientists think of rational decision making as that which optimizes output per unit of input. Behavioral scientists look upon decision making as being rational when it meets certain human psychological needs. Environmentalists look at decisions in terms of impact on environment.

Simon suggests one way to avoid, or to clarify, complexities in determining whether a decision is rational or not is to think of different types of rationality. He says:

> ". . . a decision may be called 'objectively' rational if *in fact* it is the correct behavior for maximizing given values in a given situation. It is 'subjectively' rational if it maximizes attainment relative to the actual knowledge of the subject. It is 'consciously' rational to the degree that the adjustment of means to ends is a conscious process. It is 'deliberately' rational to the degree that the adjustment of means to ends has been deliberately brought about (by the individual or by the organization). A decision is 'organizationally' rational if it is oriented to the organization's goals; it is 'personally' rational if it is oriented to the individual's goals" [Simon, 1957a:76–77].

Filley and House [1969:125] suggest that, if managers sought to be completely rational, that would be an irrational objective. The preceding quotation supports this view.

It is obvious that there is no universal standard for judging rationality of managerial decisions. What is rational depends upon the evaluator. Much is to be said, however, for determining the rationality of managerial decisions in terms of the decision makers' own frame of reference [March and Simon, 1958]. Of course, frames of reference vary among individuals and organizations, as will be shown shortly.

Theories of rational behavior, rooted in classical economic theory, use the concept "comprehensive rationality." According to it a goal is established and rationality involves the choice of best alternatives, taking into account probabilities and utilities. Such choice requires knowledge of all possible alternatives, complete assessment of probabilities and consequences of each, evaluation of each set of consequences in achieving the objective, and choice of those alternatives that optimize goal achievement. Because a decision maker cannot comprehend all that this process would require, he forms simplified models of the real world and uses them to make decisions. Simon calls this "bounded rationality" [1957]. Theoretically, this process is not likely to produce as rational a decision as the first, but in practice it probably does and is much easier.

Organizational Models and Rationality

One's theory of the organization has much to do with his concept of what is rational behavior. Until the publication of *Organizations* by March and Simon [1958] and later *A Behavioral Theory of the Firm* by Cyert and March [1963] classical economic theory dominated organizational theory. A core concept of classical economic theory is that firms operate rationally when they seek to maximize profits under conditions of comprehensive rationality. Cyert, Simon, and March, on the other hand, view organizations as coalitions of participants with different motivations and limited ability to solve all problems simultaneously. Goals are formed in light of such constraints and achieved through a bargaining process.

Skibbins [1974] has identified seven different types of organizations and explains how differently they function, including the making of decisions. The most complete description and differentiation of major organizational models, especially with respect to decision making, is that of Allison [1971]. In a masterful study he explains the differences between what he calls "The Rational Actor," "Organizational Process," and "Governmental Politics" models. The first is patterned after the classical economic model, the second sees organizations as composed of different organizational units that have their own ways of doing things, and the third views organizations as institutions that get things done through political processes. The third encompasses the Cyert, Simon, and March model.

In sum, rational behavior as perceived from inside and from outside an organization depends upon the model that best explains the functioning of the organization.

Rationality of Profit Maximization

Central in decision making in "rational" business organizations is the goal to achieve profit maximization. Any decision is irrational in classical economic theory that does not serve to achieve this result. Hence, in economic theory, profit maximization is *the* goal of the firm.

There are many who challenge this notion of maximization. Anthony [1960] suggests the more usual objective is satisfactory return on capital employed. Alchian [1950] says the objective of firms is "realized positive profits." Steiner [1969b, 1971] says the goal is "required and steadily rising profits," and Simon [1957a], whose phrase has been most widely used, says it is "satisfactory profits."

Others challenge the idea that profit maximization is *the* goal of a firm. Mason [1958] quotes Keynes as saying the general stability and reputation of an institution is a higher goal. Baumol [1967] maintains that sales, subject to a profit constraint, is the objective. Clark [1961] says firms have many objectives, a fact that is amply clear from what has been said previously in this book.

METHODS OF EVALUATION

Tools for Evaluating Policy/Strategy

There is a wide range of tools available for evaluating policies and strategies. Since most readers of this book are familiar with the major ones, we shall not attempt to describe them in this section. Those who are not familiar with them can readily find descriptions in the literature either in depth or summary form [for example, in Harrison, 1975:217–254; Starr, 1971; Goetz, 1965; and Schlaifer, 1959]. Our purpose is to help the reader get a feel for the richness of the palette of tools available for evaluation, to cite the research that has been conducted concerning the usage of the newer quantitative tools, and to refer to research relating to strengths and weaknesses of some specific major quantitative evaluation methods.

Managerial Analytical Requirements

It should be observed that managers have different requirements for analyses of proposed policies and strategies. First, managers may ask staff to determine which among several alternatives will best achieve company profit and share of market goals. Second, a manager may have come to a decision in his own mind and may only seek confirmation by staff analysis. Third, a manager may want forecasts of environmental factors to be used as a basis for his own thinking. Fourth, a manager may have come to a conclusion but may desire staff analysis to show to members of his board of directors if they should inquire. Fifth, a manager may ask for staff analysis to help him identify possible strategies. For example, Sloan noted [1964:431] that for General Motors ". . . the basic decision to participate in the manufacture of diesel locomotives was largely based on product research by the staff."

Generally speaking, evaluation is continuous throughout a decision-making process which may take months or years. Problems arise in the process about which tools of analysis are most appropriate and the availability of data. There never is enough of the "right" data, and questions arise about how much time and effort should be spent on acquiring additional information.

The Spectrum of Analytical Tools

Table 9-1 lists a variety of major tools and techniques used in decision making. This is not an exhaustive list, but it is sufficient to reveal a wide range of possible analytical methods. Generally speaking the more unstructured the problem and the more significant it is to the organization, the greater will be the importance of nonquantitative techniques in decision making. When decisions are made solely or principally on the basis of routine quantitative analysis, decision making is generally moved from the strategic concern of top management to lower routine managerial levels.

Usage of Sophisticated Quantitative Tools In Strategic Decision Making

In recent years some very powerful quantitative tools have been developed that have great potential applications at the strategic decision-making levels of companies. Although their usage at these levels has increased, usage has not been close to the predictions of those most interested in their development.

A survey of 182 respondents revealed, for example, that the use of ad-

TABLE 9-1
A Classification of Major Tools and Techniques for Rational Decision Making in Business

1. Nonquantitative emphasis
   - (a) Creative mental processes (e.g., creativity, experience, judgment, hunches, intuition, brain storming)
   - (b) Finding the critical factor
     - (1) The limiting factor
     - (2) Simple decision chains and tables
     - (3) Asking the right questions
   - (c) Organization *per se* (e.g., planning organization and budget system)
   - (d) Rules-of-thumb
   - (e) Policies and procedures
   - (f) Simple problem-solving steps
   - (g) General knowledge of the field in which a decision is to be made (e.g., law, economics, physics, etc.)
2. General systems methods
   - (a) Problem design
   - (b) Nonquantitative simulation model building
     - (1) Logical-analytical frameworks
     - (2) Adaptive search
     - (3) Work flows
   - (c) Accounting systems and models
     - (1) Over-all accounting system
     - (2) Balance sheet and profit and loss statements
     - (3) Cash-flow analysis
     - (4) Accounting ratio analysis
     - (5) Break-even analysis
   - (d) Design of information systems
3. Older quantitative methods
   - (a) Marginal analysis
   - (b) Return on investment
     - (1) Average rate of return
     - (2) Present value methods
   - (c) Quantitative forecasting
     - (1) Trend extrapolation
     - (2) Exponential smoothing
     - (3) Correlation analysis
     - (4) Econometric models
     - (5) Input/output analysis
4. Nonquantitative forecasting
   - (a) Delphi
   - (b) Scenarios
5. Conventional scheduling models
   - (a) GANTT charts
   - (b) Milestone charts
   - (c) Critical path method
   - (d) Line-of-balance charts
6. Newer mathematical techniques
   - (a) Computer simulation
   - (b) Linear programming
   - (c) Dynamic programming
   - (d) Network analysis (pert/time and pert/cost)
   - (e) Heuristic problem solving
   - (f) Game theory
   - (g) Risk analysis
7. Complex methods combining many tools
   - (a) Systems analysis
   - (b) Cost-benefit analysis
   - (c) Social science research
   - (d) Formal corporate planning
   - (e) Program budgeting

SOURCE: Modified from Steiner [1969:336].

vanced mathematical tools in important decision making was low. The most often used tool was discounted cash flow (83 per cent), but no other tool was used by at least half the respondents [Coppinger and Epley, 1972]. This experience was corroborated in the United Kingdom by Rue [1974], and in the United States by Hall [1973], Miller [1971], and Reeser [1971]. Reeser concluded that ". . . subjective bases for decision making were mentioned over three times as frequently as sophisticated methods of analysis. When the academically unfashionable conventional methods of analysis are added to the subjective guides, the ratio to sophisticated techniques increases to 5.8:1" [Reeser, 1971:68]. However, Holmberg [1975] surveyed 89 public utilities and found considerable use of simulation models. His survey showed that 60 per cent of the respondents used simulation models in dealing with plant and equipment expansion and over 60 per cent used such models in plant and equipment improvement and financial matters.

Why has advanced mathematical technology not been used more at strategic decision levels? One reason, as noted repeatedly, is that many strategic decisions (for example, those concerning missions and purposes) are simply not amenable to quantitative analysis of any kind. Another reason is that managers are not usually faced with one simple choice between two clear-cut alternatives. They are faced with difficult trade-off choices among strategic paths, and the choice of path ultimately is based principally on judgment. For instance, a few types of trade offs managers face might be to build cash reserves versus investing in research, short-term profits versus long-term growth, profit margin versus share of market, profit versus nonprofit goals (for example, social responsibility), growth versus stability, profit versus complete product line, certainty of low return on investment versus possible but risky high return on investment, and satisfaction of firm goals versus those of dominant line managers. Even where decisions at top management levels involve quantitative analyses, they frequently are so complex that management science techniques do not have high prescriptive value. As one management science leader has stated, "What we still cannot do is to deal very rigorously with large sets of decisions under uncertainty, which means we can't deal very well with planning" [Hertz, 1973:61].

There are many other reasons, such as, managers do not take the time to participate in the making of complex models and therefore distrust the results. Since quantitative conclusions are less significant than nonquantitative considerations in making top-level decisions, managers do not feel the need for the precision of sophisticated mathematical models. Less rigorous estimates are acceptable. Managers distrust the reliability of information incorporated in models, especially data about the future, and therefore discount the results. Managers trust their intuition over mathematical models. These and other factors have been described by observers [Boulden, 1976; Drucker, 1973a; Grayson, 1973; Miller, 1971; Harvey, 1970; Enthoven, 1969; and Churchman, 1964].

In addition, is the fact that management scientists and managers have had difficult problems in speaking with one another and understanding each other's needs [McKenney and Keen, 1974; Grayson, 1973; Churchman and Schainblatt, 1965a, 1965b]. Hall [1973] argues that models are not used more by top managers because they are based upon false assumptions about how top managers make decisions.

On the other hand *Management Science, Operational Research Quarterly,* the *Journal of Industrial Engineering,* and *Long Range Planning,* include many successful applications of advanced techniques in decision making. It is easy to forecast that applications in the near term future will increase but that there will continue to be high skepticism about and only partial use, if any, of, these techniques in making the strategic decisions of most importance to companies.

Utility Evaluations of Individual Techniques

There has been comparatively little research about the value of particular types of analytical techniques in strategic decision making. Some examples of what has been done are as follows. Two excellent studies of the uses of forecasting techniques for different types of problems are Wheelwright and Makridakis [1973] and Chambers, Mullick, and Smith [1971]. Haitovsky, Treyz and Su [1974] conclude that econometric models have not demonstrated a superiority over simple projections in forecasting economic events. Gerstenfeld [1971] concluded that "There is a positive relationship between an industry's growth rate and the likelihood that its firms will use some technique of technological forecasting." Risk analysis has been used widely and successfully but it does have some drawbacks [Carter, 1972; and Cameron, 1972]. Two studies examined the places in strategic planning where optimization, simulation, and qualitative models should be used [Hammond in Vancil, 1972b; and Lorange, in Vancil, Aguilar, and Howell, 1969]. Hammond [1974] set forth some useful do's and don'ts for the use of computer models in planning. Ansoff [1965] criticizes traditional capital investment theory and suggests it be replaced with what he calls the "Adaptive Search Method." Evaluating potential decisions in terms of return on investment (ROI), made famous by Du Pont, is traditional in business. Dearden [1969] has argued that ROI should not have the universal applicability it has enjoyed in decision making, but Weston [1972] says the objections to ROI confuse goals and processes and once this confusion is erased, ROI does have applicability at all levels of decision making.

Fundamental Tests for Policies/Strategies

Tilles [1963] first suggested a series of overarching tests for strategies, an evaluation approach with which we agree. Following are 20 questions that must be raised at some point in the policy/strategy formulation process. They are simple questions. Yet, if they are not considered, and it is surprising how often they are not, a wrong strategic choice may be made. Once the question is raised its implications become obvious and, as a consequence, we shall not give detailed illustrations for each one. The list of questions is not all inclusive, of course.

1. Is your strategy in conformance with the basic missions and purposes of the company? If it is not, a new competitive arena may be entered with which management is not familiar.

2. Is your strategy consistent with the environment of the company? The Edsel was not, and it failed.
3. Is your strategy consistent with the internal strengths, objectives, policies, resources, and personal values of managers and employees? A strategy may not be completely in tune with all these elements, but major dissonance should be avoided.
4. Does your strategy balance the acceptance of minimum risk with the maximum profit potential consistent with the company's resources and prospects? This certainly was not the case with Lockheed's L-1011.
5. Does the strategy fit a niche in the market that is not now filled by others? Is this niche likely to remain open long enough to the company to return capital investment plus the required level of profit? Niches have a habit of filling up fast. When Lockheed made the decision to produce the L-1011, the airplane did fill a niche where no other manufacturer had a product. It was not long, however, before McDonnell-Douglas decided to produce the DC-10 a direct competitor to the Lockheed TriStar.
6. Does your strategy conflict with other strategies of the company?
7. Is your strategy divided into substrategies that interrelate properly? The Edsel did not fail solely because the economy moved into a recession in 1958 when the car was introduced but also, and probably more importantly, because mistakes were made in substrategies, such as the creation of too many car divisions and dealerships, hasty introduction of an untested automobile, and poor styling [Reynolds, 1967].
8. Has the strategy been tested with appropriate criteria such as consistency with past, present, and prospective trends; and the appropriate analytical tools, such as risk analysis, discounted cash flows, and so on?
9. Has the strategy been tested by developing acceptable and "doable" subplans for an extended period of time in the future?
10. Does the strategy really fit the life cycle of the company's products?
11. Is the timing of the strategy correct?
12. Does the strategy pit the product against a powerful competitor? If so, reevaluate carefully.
13. Does the strategy leave the company vulnerable to the power of one major customer? If so, reconsider carefully.
14. Does the strategy involve the production of a new product for a new market? If so, reconsider carefully.
15. Are you rushing a revolutional product to market? If so, reconsider carefully. This is what Rolls Royce tried to do and went bankrupt in the attempt [Ross and Kami, 1973].
16. Does your strategy follow that of a competitor? If so, reconsider carefully. This is what RCA did in following IBM and lost heavily.
17. Is it likely that you can get to the market first with your new product or service? This is a great advantage. The second firm to market has much less chance of high returns on investment than the first.

18. Do you really have an honest and accurate appraisal of your competition? Are you under- or overestimating competition?
19. Are you trying to sell abroad something you cannot sell in the United States? This is not usually a successful strategy.
20. Is your market share likely to be sufficient to assure a required return on investment? Market share and return on investment generally are closely related [Schoeffler, Buzzell, and Heany, 1974] but differ from product to product and market to market [Fruhan, 1972]. Have you calculated this relationship for market and product?

Have you also calculated the capital investment needed to achieve the projected market share? GE at one time felt that a business had to have a 15 per cent market share for success [*Business Week,* 1970], but RCA thought a 10 per cent share was the minimum [Smith, 1970]. Managers must clearly understand the capital requirements necessary to achieve what they calculate is a minimum market share. Aspiring for too much market share may consume such large capital commitments as to produce a Pyrrhic victory in the market place. This happened to both GE and RCA in the computer market [Fruhan, 1972].

A CASE STUDY IN POLICY MAKING

The range of evaluation processes is from purely mental activities (for example, defining company purposes) to mechanical automatic decision making (for example, computerized inventory replenishment policy). Space limitations prevent any detailed description at this point of decision-making processes between these two poles. For illustrative purposes, however, the following summary of steps taken in making a significant policy decision is presented.

"The Midwest Conglomerate Company is principally a maker of agricultural implements but has expanded into diversified product lines in electronics, automobile parts, electric motors, material handling equipment, and link belts. It has twelve major semi-autonomous divisions scattered throughout the U.S., and it has had a rapid growth during the past ten years.

Under a policy of encouragement to general managers to grow and increase profit through new and imaginative moves, the company found itself producing tractor parts in Brazil, steel in India, radios in England, and electronic components in Germany. All products produced abroad, while related to products made in the U.S., were really new to the company. Furthermore, it had a variety of equity holdings in different firms in other countries of the world. It seemed that, while the volume of sales of these foreign ventures was high relative to total sales, the current and projected profitability of all but one venture was negative. In short, the foreign investment program had gone sour.

The president of the company asked his long-range planning staff to examine the entire situation and report back to him. This touched off a major study which involved thousands of manhours.

The staff went through a research process which involved, generally, the following steps (many of the steps, of course, were pursued simultaneously):

First, the objectives of the company were reviewed to see whether foreign investment was necessary to reach projected sales and profit aims. The gap between projected objectives and growth from current products was examined to determine whether foreign investment or some other alternative might be a better means to fill the difference.

Second, a thorough examination was made of exactly what the company was doing in foreign countries, what the results were to date, and what the possibilities for the future might be. The staff visited each of the foreign outposts.

Third, the staff examined each of the present and projected product lines of the domestic divisions to see whether they might be sold or produced abroad with profit.

Fourth, an honest examination of the company's strengths and weaknesses in producing new products abroad was made.

Fifth, an exhaustive study was made of economic, political and social conditions in selected countries of the world to determine the climate of investment opportunity for the company. Indeed, this study resulted in a series of research reports of book length and high scholarly caliber.

Sixth, investment strategies were set forth and examined in depth. The strategies considered were: no investment abroad; permit divisions to expand abroad but only produce products sold successfully in the U.S.; permit divisions to produce abroad products complementary to or supporting the present product line; set up an international division to make investments of opportunity; merge with a large company in Western Europe; merge with a company in the U.S. with a strong foreign program; emphasize joint ventures as compared with fixed investment; concentrate in only one or two places in the world; invest all over the world; permit no small investments on the grounds that management does not have the time to devote to them; and concentrate only on big profit possibilities. Each of these strategies was examined on the basis of criteria including company know-how, financial measures, profitability, required flexibility, capability of staff in making acceptable studies, required management attention, sales potential, and general company product strategy.

Seventh, preferred strategies were discussed with all affected managers.

Eighth, all this information was studied and tentative conclusions were drawn.

Ninth, the staff undertook lengthy discussions with top management and other staff members about the results of the data and implications for policy.

Tenth, the staff formulated a series of recommendations which were presented to top management for approval.

In this particular case, as a result of this substantial research undertaking, the concluding policy was rather simply stated as a prohibition of the divisions of the company from engaging in foreign activities except for products which they have successfully produced and sold at a profit in the U.S." [Steiner, 1969b:277–279].

A CONTINGENCY THEORY OF CHOICE

Alfred Sloan in his book *My Years With General Motors* said, "No company ever stops changing. Change will come for better or worse. I also hope I have not left an impression that the organization runs itself automatically. An organization does not make decisions; its function is to provide a framework, based upon established criteria, within which decisions can be fashioned in an orderly manner. Individuals make the decisions and take the responsibility for them. . . . The task of management is not to apply a formula but to decide issues on a case-by-case basis. No fixed, inflexible rule can ever be substituted for exercise of sound business judgment in the decision-making process" [Sloan, 1964:443].

Clearly, at the strategic decision-making level each case is unique. Yet, there are underlying approaches to identifying preferred strategies, to evaluating the strategies, and to making the final choices. Research is no more than ankle deep in the search for tested theories applicable to this process.

QUESTIONS

Discussion Guides on Chapter Content

1. Are planning and decision making synonymous? Explain.
2. Do you think it would be correct to say that the higher in an organization a decision is made, and the more important the decision, the less likelihood the decision will be made upon the basis of quantitative analysis and/or a single discipline? Explain.
3. "Any important decision in an organization is irrational to someone." Do you agree or disagree? Explain.
4. Economic theory asserts that profit maximization is a completely rational goal of an enterprise, but there are many scholars who say that profit maximization as the single goal of an operating firm is irrational. Where do you stand and why?
5. Recent research reveals that sophisticated quantitative tools are not used nearly as much in strategic decision making as was predicted ten years ago. Why is this so?
6. The authors set forth 20 tests for evaluating policies and strategies. Do you think this is a valuable list? Explain. Pick out one of the tests and explain in detail why it might have great power in decision making.

Mind Stretching Questions

1. Return to "mind stretching question" 1 in Chapter 3. Can you relate the strategy or strategies you found in response to this question with one or

more of the 20 tests for policy/strategy in this chapter in such a way as to draw a conclusion about the correctness of the strategy?

2. Currently, the National Cash Register Co. is seriously considering producing computers. Which of the 20 tests for policy/strategy presented in this chapter do you think the management of NCR should consider carefully? Why?

CHAPTER

10

Individuals in Policy Formation

INTRODUCTION

Although individuals in policy-making positions are required to make decisions, this does not mean that policy formulation and decision making are identical. Policies are developed in an organizational context and thus evolve out of a political process that extends well beyond the boundaries of mere decision making. Bauer [1968] even goes so far as to argue that bargaining, not decision making, is at the heart of the policy process. In any event, when the general managers in charge of the product divisions of a company are vying for limited financial resources to expand production of their particular products, it is apparent that something more than is usually implied by the term decision making is involved.

Yet a knowledge of decision making, how it occurs and the factors that influence it, can contribute a great deal to understanding the policy process. This chapter focuses on the individual as a decision maker and the ways in which cognitive, emotional, and motivational factors may affect decisions. The prototype for this discussion would be the corporate chief executive officer laying down policy on a unilateral basis. Actually this does not happen as often as one might think. There is good reason to believe that it is most typical, within larger firms, of those who have put together and operated multiindustry conglomerates [Vance, 1971]. In many more-established firms, decision making often takes on something of a shared character. It is for this reason that the following chapter takes up the influences that groups such as boards of directors, executive committees, finance committees, and less formal coalitions of company officers may exert on top-level decision making.

What Is Decision Making?

Decision making has been defined as follows:

A conscious and human process, involving both individual and social phenomena, based upon factual and value premises, which concludes with a choice of one behavioral activity from among one or more alternatives with the intention of moving toward some desired state of affairs [Shull, Delbecq, and Cummings, 1970].

The crux of this definition as with the definition given in the previous chapter, is the idea of choice. When a manager decides to introduce a new product in one area rather than another or to accept certain union demands and not others during contract negotiations, he is making a choice. Putting it somewhat differently, he may also be said to be exercising judgment or attempting to solve a problem. What seems to be required for decision making to occur is that there be [MacCrimmon, 1974]:

1. A gap between the existing state of affairs and some desired state.
2. A focusing of attention on this particular gap.
3. A desire to reduce the gap.
4. Some possibility that the problem can be solved and the gap reduced.

It is apparent that policy formation does involve this kind of problem solving or decision making. Policies are developed to solve a problem or reduce a gap. If no one perceives the gap, or no one cares about reducing the gap, or no one believes it is possible to reduce the gap, then policy formation does not occur. If this happens with regard to a large number of problems or gaps, the company involved becomes very much like a rudderless ship. It simply drifts on a sea filled with treacherous and often-conflicting currents, constantly buffeted by the winds of uncertainty.

COGNITIVE FACTORS IN DECISION MAKING

Decisions and policies are expected to be, and usually are to a certain degree, rational—rational in the sense of contributing to organizational objectives or goals. This kind of rationality implies a clear logical link between what the company wants to do and what it decides to do; a decision maker who can make decisions with knowledge, intelligence, in an appropriate manner, and without distortions induced by values or motives that might lead him or her away from implementing such corporate goals as profit, growth, survival, and the like.

The Role of Knowledge

There is very little question that decisions require knowledge. This knowledge may reside in a person as a consequence of education and prior experience or it may have to be sought out. Search of this kind requires time, and managerial decision situations may not permit time. Thus, all in all, there would appear to be a clear advantage if production decisions were made by production people, marketing decisions by marketing people, and so on. That way the search for relevant information can be conducted in one's own mind, rather than over an extended landscape, and accordingly can be completed much more rapidly.

This becomes a problem primarily for those in general management. For such people the amount of knowledge needed and relevant to their work is tremendous, and the prospects for information overload overwhelming. Given the complexity inherent in such positions as chief executive officer, general manager, executive vice president, project manager, and the like, it is almost essential to resort to some kind of knowledge search, and in most cases this means relying on the judgments of staff specialists.

But people such as marketing research managers, research and development managers, and lawyers have quite different commitments, values, responsibilities, and personal objectives than general managers. They may well have the needed knowledge and still lack the loyalty or motivation to use this knowledge strictly for the accomplishment of company goals. In other words, their knowledge may not be brought to bear on the real problems of the company in a rational manner because of distortions introduced by functional, professional, and personal considerations.

This is the dilemma of the general manager or any manager whose responsibilities extend over multiple specialties and diverse expertise. He trusts his own knowledge, but he does not have enough of it; he rightly distrusts the knowledge of others, but this is where he can compensate for his own intellectual lacks. The possible solutions are to accumulate a great deal of the kinds of knowledge required by the job or to surround oneself with people he can trust. But without the knowledge to evaluate what one hears from advisors, how can trust be maintained? It follows that being an effective decision maker and policy maker requires a great deal of knowledge. The primary question is: What kind of knowledge is crucial?

BACKGROUNDS OF GENERAL MANAGERS. There is no simple solution that would permit us to sift the alternatives and say that some limited set of knowledge is all that is required of a policy maker. A study of the academic backgrounds of corporate top managements including chairmen of the board, presidents, and executive vice presidents yields the following diverse list [Bradish, 1970]:

Engineering and science	28%
Industrial management	14%
Accounting	13%
Liberal arts and social service	13%
Law	9%
Marketing	5%
Economics	5%
Miscellaneous	13%

There is good reason to believe that the ranks of the MBAs are furnishing an increasing proportion of chief executive officers and that college majors such as accounting and production are declining in numbers whereas finance majors are increasing [Steele and Ward, 1974]. Yet Livingston [1971] argues convincingly that much of the kind of learning that occurs in MBA programs is irrelevant to managerial decision making and executive success in any event. Nothing in the shifting trends of educational specialization appears to offer the prospect of identifying the knowledge required for policymaking.

If one goes to the functional experience background of chief executive officers, one finds much the same diversity as in college majors [Pohl, 1973]:

Finance	24%
Marketing	23%
General Administration	14%
Law	12%
Manufacturing	8%
Engineering and scientific	6%
International	1%
Other	12%

Pohl argues from these data and the fact that increasing numbers of financial executives are now being appointed to top posts that this particular type of knowledge is becoming increasingly crucial. Yet data presented by McDonald and Eastlack [1971] on the accelerating involvements of CEOs in new product decisions and development makes a convincing case for the crucial role of a marketing background, and Dalton and Miner [1970] have collected data suggesting that accounting knowledge may be the most important ingredient.

The most likely conclusion appears to be that relevant knowledge is what counts and that having it is a lot better than not having it. There is no one functional area of experience or type of major that will provide this knowledge. At the general management level at least, and to some extent below that level, better decisions will be made when the breadth as well as depth of knowledge is greatest. In any specific situation, at a point in time, however, some particular kind of knowledge may be crucial.

KNOWLEDGE DOES MATTER. That having knowledge within oneself, and thus being in a position to conduct an information search within, makes for greater competence in decision making may seem self-evident. If it is not, there are data to support this viewpoint. Whybark [1973] found that on a standardized set of business decisions, fifth year business students with a knowledge of forecasting and inventory theory came much closer to the criteria of success produced by an adaptive decision model than did second year students without such knowledge. One fifth year student did practically as well as the model; no second year students did.

In another study Moskowitz [1971] compared graduate business students and experienced R&D managers on a similar standardized decision task:

> Although both groups were highly motivated to perform well . . . , R&D managers were found to be more rational decision makers, superior information processors, and more risk-inclined than students, notwithstanding that [they] had no formal training in decision theory. R&D managers also appeared more interested, devoted more time . . . and *could better relate underlying concepts to actual decision problems as faced in practice.*

All in all it seems evident that the more one knows, which is relevant to on-the-job decisions, the better one will do. The problem is that a large amount of what is learned in school may not be very relevant to the managerial policy decisions against which the students may be gauged some 20 years or more later.

The Role of Intelligence

Intelligence refers to the degree or extent to which an individual is ready to learn new things rapidly and solve problems correctly. It is the developed capacity to grasp, relate, and use concepts, and thus to reason effectively. This is the type of capability needed to make rational decisions in pursuit of company goals, and there is good reason to believe that where the decision making process does utilize such a rational mode an organization is more effective [Price, 1968]. It would seem to follow that intelligence is an important ingredient of decision making; in part because it permits the accumulation of relevant knowledge more rapidly; in part because it facilitates making effective choices among multiple alternatives.

The available evidence reinforces this expectation. Studies have repeatedly shown that more successful managers and executives are typically more intelligent [Ghiselli, 1966; Campbell *et al.*, 1970]. In fact, it is practically impossible to arrive in the competitive world of top-level corporate decision making without a high level of intelligence. And those unintelligent few who do arrive are unlikely to remain long. Table 10-1 contains information on 39 company officers, mostly from the larger United States corporations. Their intelligence is compared with data for the total United States population age 10 and above [Miner, 1973b]. Roughly three-quarters of the presidents are in the top 3 per cent of the population and all are in the top 10 per cent. The company officers at a somewhat lower level score almost as well.

Although intelligence may contribute to other aspects of managerial performance, it definitely is a primary factor in decision making. On a standardized decision task more intelligent managers were found to process information more rapidly, to make more accurate decisions, and to be less willing to shift away from these accurate decisions on reevaluation [Taylor and Dunnette, 1974]. Intelligence appears to be particularly important in

TABLE 10-1
Intelligence Level of Company Presidents and Company Officers Below the Level of President Compared With the General Population

Intelligence Test Score Level	Per cent of General Population Sample at Given Level of Intelligence or Above ($N = 1500$)	Per cent of Company Presidents at This Level of Intelligence or Above ($N = 23$)	Per cent of Company Officers Below the Level of President at This Level of Intelligence or Above ($N = 16$)
20	0.4	26.1	12.5
19	0.9	65.2	18.8
18	2.9	73.9	68.8
17	5.3	95.2	75.0
16	10.1	100.0	81.3
15	15.1		93.8
14	22.1		100.0

evaluating information, integrating this information to make a correct choice, and judging the potential impact of adverse consequences.

The Role of Cognitive Style

In addition to knowledge and intelligence, the policy or strategy formulator should benefit from possessing a certain kind of what has come to be called "cognitive style." One approach in this area has stressed the importance of cognitive complexity [Schroder, Driver, and Streufert, 1967]. Cognitively complex people tend to search out and use a great deal of information in their thinking and to develop a variety of alternatives or choices based on this information. They are able to differentiate between aspects of a complex problem and to integrate these different aspects in achieving a solution.

This sounds very much like what is involved in developing policies and strategies. Certainly policy problems are typically complex and many faceted. One has to be aware that solving one problem in a particular way often only creates another problem. Preventing a strike by giving the union what it wants may well commit the company to costs in terms of wages and benefits that have major implications for production output, pricing, marketing, and practically every other aspect of the business. People who use a cognitively simple style may well not be able to cope with these interrelated problems effectively. At least, they do not perform as well on a standardized top management decision simulation as more cognitively complex individuals [Lundberg and Richards, 1972]. There is also good reason to believe that the ability to think using a complex style can be developed in business students through appropriately structured courses [Johnson and Werner, 1975].

A closely related view of cognitive style has been developed by McKenney and Keen [1974]. The most important distinction they make is between systematic and intuitive thinkers. Although both styles are viewed as appropriate under certain circumstances and in particular types of jobs, the manager engaged in policy formation should benefit most from using the more rational, less emotion-based systematic style. Such a style involves:

1. Looking for an explicit method of problem solving and making a plan of approach.
2. Defending solutions primarily in terms of the method used to reach them.
3. Defining constraints on what can be done at the beginning and discarding alternatives quickly.
4. Moving through a process that involves increasing refinement of analysis based on a systematic search for relevant information.
5. Not leaving things hanging, but rather completing all analytic steps that are begun.

The cognitively complex style and the systematic style appear to have much in common. Their use also assumes a level of intelligence adequate to the problem.

The Impact of Age

The preceding discussion provides some insight into how effective decision makers at the policy level think—how their minds work. A question might be raised, however, as to whether very many people are thinking this way by the time they get to policy level positions. Within the larger companies the average member of top management is in his or her early 50s, and it is very rare indeed for anyone to move to this level before age 35. If cognitive capabilities tend to decline with age, this could mean that the very people who need such capabilities most are least likely to have them; the frequently heard criticisms by the young of "irrational" decision making at the top might have some justification in fact.

It was indeed thought for some time that intelligence did decline with age in the adult population. However, this conclusion turned out to be an artifact of faulty research design. An extensive review of more recent research in which the earlier deficiencies have been corrected indicates that in the intelligence range characteristic of managers there is a rise in average intelligence level at least to the age of 50. After that there appears to be some leveling off; however, there is *no decline,* at least through to the usual retirement age in the mid-60s [Matarazzo, 1972].

Analyses that focus directly on decision making lead to much the same conclusion. In a study using a standardized personnel decision-making situation, older managers (up through their late 50s) were at least as capable as younger managers; in some respects they were more capable [Taylor, 1975]. Probably the reason younger people often *perceive* top management as acting irrationally is that the information available to them is not the same as that available to those at the top. A merger agreement that ultimately results in extensive personnel changes and layoffs (as most such agreements do), simply cannot make sense to anyone who is not privy to all the details of the company's financial position. Yet making such details available might well hinder the merger discussion and thus eliminate the possibility of choosing this alternative; many people would not fully understand them in any event.

VALUES AS INFLUENCES ON DECISIONS

A study conducted some years ago reported that United States business managers tend to have values that place strong emphasis on the economic, the political, and the scientific, as opposed to social, religious, and aesthetic considerations [Guth and Tagiuri, 1965]. It is apparent that such value orientations can influence the way in which decisions are made. A manager with predominantely religious values would be much more likely to be responsive to pleas for corporate contributions to a church-supported college than would a manager whose values were overridingly economic in nature.

The term *value* is often used in a loose manner without a clearly specified meaning. As a result, considerable confusion frequently exists as to what is really meant. The following definition, although somewhat cumbersome, does have the advantage of being comprehensive:

> To say that a person has a value is to say that he has an enduring prescriptive or proscriptive belief that a specific mode of behavior or end-state of existence is preferred to an opposite mode of behavior or end-state. This belief transcends attitudes toward objects and toward situations; it is a standard that guides and determines action, attitudes toward objects and situations, ideology, presentations of self to others, and attempts to influence others [Rokeach, 1973].

The Role of Values

The most extensive analysis of managerial values currently available has been conducted by Professor George England of the University of Minnesota [1973]. This research has clearly established the role that values play in decisions. Managers who value profit maximization strongly will not decide to commit funds to such things as cafeteria and rest room facility improvements if they can possibly help it. Managers who hold compassion to be an important value do in fact try to avoid the strategy of withholding part of a prospective employee wage increase when faced with the need to finance a research and development effort.

As these examples imply, certain kinds of values appear to contribute to executive success. In the United States this pattern is as follows:

Successful managers favor pragmatic, dynamic, achievement-oriented values while less successful managers prefer more static and passive values, the latter forming a framework descriptive of organizational stasis rather than organizational and environmental flux. More successful managers favor an achievement orientation and prefer an active role in interaction with other individuals useful in achieving the managers' organizational goals. They value a dynamic environment and are willing to take risks to achieve organizationally valued goals. Relatively less successful managers have values associated with a static, protected environment in which they take relatively passive roles and often enjoy extended seniority in their organizational positions [England, 1973].

It appears that what makes certain managers successful in policy positions is that they possess values that foster making decisions when decisions need to be made and taking risks when risk taking is called for rather than passively doing nothing. On the other hand, there remain major differences between those in leadership positions in different types of organizations, as the following listing of strongly held value objects among business and labor leaders attests:

BUSINESS MANAGERS	LABOR LEADERS
Owners	Blue-collar workers
Stockholders	Laborers
High productivity	Employee welfare
Organizational stability	Social welfare
Organizational growth	
Organizational efficiency	
Industry leadership	
Ambition	Trust
Ability	Loyalty
Skill	Honor

One might anticipate that the turbulent value climate of the late 1960s, both on campus and elsewhere, might have produced major changes in the values of business managers. A comparison of 1966 and 1972 data refutes this hypothesis, however [Lusk and Oliver, 1974]. The values of business managers remain as pragmatic as ever.

Managerial Values in Different Countries

Comparisons of managerial values in the different countries of the world have generally produced much greater similarities than one would anticipate. Apparently there is something about managing a company and surviving in that capacity that induces or attracts certain value patterns. Yet there are

TABLE 10-2
Values of Chief Executives in Various Parts of the World

	MEAN VALUE SCORE FOR *	
AREA	DIRECTING SUBORDINATES IN EXACTLY WHAT THEY SHOULD DO AND HOW TO DO IT	INVOLVING AS MANY PEOPLE AS POSSIBLE IN IMPORTANT DECISIONS
United States	6.5	4.0
Western Europe	4.7	4.1
Latin America	3.6	2.3
Asia	2.8	2.9

* Scored on a 1–7 scale, where 1 is "strongly agree" and 7 is "strongly disagree."
SOURCE: Adapted from Richard B. Peterson [1972:112].

differences, as a study of chief executive officers around the world demonstrates [Peterson, 1972]. In terms of decision making the Latin American and Asian CEOs value participative processes highly, but when it comes to directing, and thus implementing decisions, their values support a very close type of supervision (see Table 10-2). United States chief executives, on the other hand, reject this type of leadership style completely. One would expect from these data that the processes through which policy is made and the way in which it is implemented in various parts of the world would differ considerably.

Furthermore those values that are culture-based seem to have the capacity to carry over into new cultural contexts. Thus Japanese-American managers in Hawaii value long term employment commitments to the company, respect for the formal authority of a position, team performance as opposed to individual superiority, and paternalism in dealing with subordinates just as Japanese managers in Japan do [Kelley and Reeser, 1973]. What kinds of values are actually best in terms of effective, rational, goal-oriented decision making is not entirely clear. However, it does seem apparent that values that mesh with the existing culture are needed to gain the rewards of that culture, and that a degree of pragmatism of the kind United States managers value is needed to maintain flexibility in the face of varied cultural expectations.

RISK-TAKING PROPENSITY AND DOGMATISM IN MAKING DECISIONS

In addition to values, two other aspects of human personality have received considerable attention as they relate to making managerial decisions. These are a willingness, or perhaps even desire, to take risks and the tendency to hold dogmatically onto preexisting beliefs. Both characteristics have implications for policy formulation.

The Role of Individual Risk Propensity

Whether a propensity for taking risks is desirable in a policy maker depends very much on the situation. Because risk taking is closely allied to entrepreneurship and founding or investing in new enterprises, it has tended to take on very positive connotations in our society. Yet risk takers may not be the best decision makers. They tend to limit the amount of information they bring to bear on a problem and to reach decisions very rapidly [Taylor and Dunnette, 1974]. This is impressive if they are right, but the failure to search out needed information and consider multiple alternatives can be very costly; it all depends on the situation.

In situations where decisions should be made quickly, as in adapting price levels to those of competitors, risk takers can be expected to do well simply because high costs may be associated with decision delay. But the same approach to developing a corporate long-range plan can be disastrous; there are risks enough in such planning efforts without compounding them at the personal level. We find for instance that public school administrators are much less likely to take risks than business managers [Brown, 1970]. This seems entirely appropriate to the demands of the two decision environments. A risk-taking school administrator can quickly get in trouble with his school board, city government, and the parents, to the point where he is prevented from accomplishing his objectives. Thus, whether a high risk taker should make policy depends on the nature of the organization, its stage of development, the uncertainties inherent in its environment and a host of other considerations.

There is evidence that older managers tend to be less prone to take risks [Vroom and Pahl, 1971]. This is probably because they have more to lose and less to gain than younger managers. It is also true that companies differ in the extent to which their managerial ranks are staffed with risk takers. One would think that older, large companies which are firmly established in their industries would benefit most from the low propensity for risk associated with an older policy level group. Young companies without an established industry position, like young managers with few assets, may need to resort more to risk taking.

The Role of Dogmatism

The assumption underlying much of the research on dogmatism is that this characteristic will serve to distort decisions to make them conform to preexisting beliefs; thus policy makers should not be of a dogmatic nature. Yet existing data do not fully support this conclusion. Managers who tend toward dogmatism do make decisions more quickly and they do have considerable confidence in their decisions once made, nonetheless their decisions are not less accurate; if anything the reverse is true [Taylor and Dunnette,

1974]. Also dogmatism has no impact on decisions when the problem is unambiguous and the information clearly establishes the superiority of one choice over others; it does not override clear-cut, rational choices [Brightman and Urban, 1974].

How important dogmatism really is as an explanatory variable in executive decision making remains to be established; it may well have been overrated in the past. Probably the more dogmatically inclined manager is less likely to utilize a cognitively complex style in coping with multifaceted problems and is less effective in certain situations as a result. If so, the important thing to consider in selecting policymakers is cognitive style, not dogmatism *per se*.

CREATIVE MANAGEMENT DECISIONS

There is little question that creativity can be important in such scientific research areas as new product development and manufacturing equipment design. Studies conducted in the R&D context indicate that the scientist who is creative performs better when the job calls for and facilitates originality and innovation. But even in R&D, creativity can be a detriment; scientists who are creative tend to do poorly in the more restricted and controlled work situation, often of a development engineering nature, where innovation is difficult [Pelz and Andrews, 1966].

This conclusion, that creativity is not universally good, has important implications for management, especially at the policy level. It raises a distinct question as to whether creative people do contribute more effectively to the formulation of corporate policies and strategies and, if so, under what circumstances.

What Is Creativity?

For a plan, or a policy, or a managerial decision to be creative it must be original and different. But a unique idea is not necessarily a creative idea; it may merely be eccentric. Thus, a policy of paying employees only once a year to hold payroll preparation costs down would certainly be unusual, but in the world of today it is not very realistic. Insofar as policy making is concerned at least, creative means original *and* realistically related to achieving company objectives.

The kind of person who is creative in this sense can make a tremendous contribution to a company. However, this contribution may carry with it certain unexpected and undesired consequences. If these side effects are too marked and the situation is such that they assume considerable importance, then the costs of creative decision making may outweigh the benefits. To understand how this can happen it is necessary to know something about the characteristics of creative people [Barron, 1969; Tomkins, 1962].

For one thing, the creative manager must know a good deal about the particular area in which the decision making is to occur. To reinvent the wheel, not knowing that the wheel is already in widespread use, acomplishes nothing. Thinking at the forefront of knowledge requires knowing where the forefront is. Creative thinking is not a substitute for learning; it is a supplement. Accordingly, the creative manager has to want to learn and to have in fact done so.

Furthermore creativity appears to involve a feeling of excitement. Creative people do in fact get "wound up" over their ideas; thinking of this kind is exciting. As a result they tend to stick to problems they are trying to solve with a tenacity, even stubbornness, that may frustrate others. While other managers want to move on to new concerns, the creative member of a group may well refuse to leave the topic of his efforts. He may over time become quite unpopular because of such behavior.

There are other bases for unpopularity, also. Being creative often involves rejecting or ignoring the more conventional or stereotyped thinking of others. Creative people may appear hostile, conceited, contentious, domineering, nonconforming, and emotional, as well as having a tendency to live in the future and ignore the present and past. All of this implies a considerable potential for discord. Creativity is not merely an intellectual ability; it has major emotional and motivational facets as well. These latter seem to provide the necessary conditions for the creative problem-solving process to work. They also have a great capacity to disrupt the smooth functioning of a top management team. Thus, if such a team badly needs smooth functioning or its members cannot tolerate conflict and dissension, the creative ingredient in company decisions may well not be worth the cost.

Creative Managers and Creative Climates

There is a considerable body of research and writing that stresses the view that creative pontential will not come to fruition in a context that is inhibiting, restricting, and highly controlled [Taylor, 1972]. Among other things those who might *want* to stifle creativity should:

1. Stress that there is only one best way of doing things.
2. React quickly and negatively to any expression of new ideas.
3. Oppose anything they do not understand.
4. Emphasize that creativity brings only trouble.
5. See that rewards never go to creative people.
6. Keep creative individuals under tight control and, if that does not work, ostracize them.

Much of the writing on this subject deals with the climates that teachers create for their students and managers create for their subordinates. In general the thrust of this writing is that teachers and managers *should* foster learning and working environments that stimulate creativity [Korman, 1971]. All of this might appear to have very limited relevance for creativity at the policy level where there are no teachers and the policy makers are at the top level of management.

Yet there is a sense in which the findings regarding creative climates have considerable relevance. Company policies are made in a context of governmental laws and regulations. These provide the climate within which companies solve problems and make decisions. If this governmentally imposed climate acts on a whole industry, or on companies of a particular size or configuration, or on an individual company in certain ways, creative planning and policy making will be stifled just as surely as with school children or subordinate workers. Such a climate would include the following:

1. A stress on doing business one way and not any other way.
2. A proclivity for reacting quickly to suppress new approaches.
3. A tendency to oppose business strategies that are not clearly understood.
4. Indication that new business approaches can only lead to trouble.
5. Procedures that deprive creative managers of rewards for their ideas.
6. Close control over innovative companies or, if this fails, mechanisms for making it impossible for them to do business in the country.

Without much imagination one can easily think of many ways in which the legislative process and the executive enforcement agencies can serve to produce such consequences through the medium of antitrust laws, regulation of rates and profits, taxation, tariffs, labor legislation, and the like. Where such an unfavorable climate for creativity exists, introducing a creative element into the policy process may very well do more harm than good. Just as creative scientists can be expected to fail in highly restricted, controlled work situations, so too will creative policy makers.

Given this impact of climate, one would expect companies in the more controlled industries such as the utilities, transportation, and insurance to benefit very little if at all from creative management; the alternatives available are too limited or the incentives for seeking new alternatives too few. Similarly, creative approaches may only introduce problems in companies that have been under continued antitrust scrutiny, Securities and Exchange Commission investigation, and the like. For creative managers to develop plans and introduce policies that are new and different and effective, they must be, and feel, free to create.

DEVELOPING CREATIVITY. Creativity can help a company's decision-making processes when the conflict engendered is not too debilitating and when the external environmental climate serves to foster rather than inhibit creative ideas. This raises a question as to whether companies can do anything to increase the creative capabilities of those managers for whom this might appear to be an appropriate course of action.

The answer appears to be that techniques are available for this purpose and that they do seem to work well in most situations where they have been tried [Davis, 1973]. On the other hand, very little is known about their application to policy formulation. In general, it appears that the various approaches to creative training are effective because they induce values indicating that creative thinking is good and worth doing, foster a group attitude favorable to creativity and new ideas, and require participants to spend considerable time in searching for alternatives.

In many situations such an approach should facilitate decision making at the policy level, but not in all. Where the alternatives realistically available are sharply circumscribed and the situation calls for quick and unified action at the top, creativity training could well prove detrimental. Such might be the case if a company were faced with a determined take-over attempt or with drastic price cutting by a competitor. Planning activities, on the other hand, should be facilitated. In fact, it is in the planning sphere that the creative contribution seems most likely to be essential.

THE COMPLEXITY OF INDIVIDUAL INFLUENCES ON POLICY

The evidence is strong that individual decision-making capability may be influenced by knowledge levels, intelligence, cognitive styles, values, risk propensity, perhaps dogmatism, and creativity. These are the factors that have been studied in some depth. No doubt there are many other such factors that can assume a significant role that have not been studied as yet. The major implication of the existing studies is clear, however.

Relevant knowledge, intelligence, and certain kinds of values, particularly those in a pragmatic vein, appear to be essential to effective decision making in any policy context. But there are also a multitude of individual factors that may or may not be important depending on the situation. There are certainly policymakers who are better than others, and no doubt this is why some companies succeed and others do not. But it is also true that one organization may require a very different type of policymaker than another given its environment, existing top management, and other constraints.

The important conclusion that emerges from this analysis is that individual differences do matter. Some people are better at making a particular company's decisions than others, and it is in the interest of a specific company to find and develop such individuals. This leads to the question of how such individuals should be organized and how their thinking should be combined to produce the most effective result. This is the topic of the following chapter.

QUESTIONS

Discussion Guides on Chapter Content

1. What is decision making? How does it relate to policy?
2. What is the research evidence regarding the effects of knowledge and intelligence levels on decision making?
3. How may values influence decisions?
4. In what ways do risk-taking propensity and dogmatism appear to differ in their relationship to decision making?
5. It has been said that managing is not a creative art. Comment and document your answer.

Mind Stretching Questions

1. A number of characteristics of an individual have been discussed in this chapter as they relate to decision making. What other chracteristics do you feel are worthy of research investigation in this regard? Why?
2. It has been suggested that the values of the key decision makers in a company should be included in the assessments made by financial analysts. Does this make any sense? Why would anyone suggest this?

CHAPTER

11

Group Aspects of Policy Formation

INTRODUCTION

In the business world, and elsewhere, decisions related to policy formation and strategy typically are products of group interaction. Generally this group contains one person, perhaps the company's chief executive officer, who is in charge of the meeting, and the other members are individuals who report to this person on the organization chart. Thus the policy-making group has an inherent structure that is determined by the company's organization structure.

Although there are certainly many variations from company to company and situation to situation, it is common practice for such a group to utilize some type of staff work on a policy issue as a starting point. This report, which may be presented orally or in writing or both, usually spells out certain alternative choices and the pros and cons of each. However, in most cases the report concludes with a recommended decision. Not infrequently such reports are structured from the beginning so as to facilitate a particular choice, in spite of their seeming objectivity.

In any event, the report forms the basis for a group discussion in which members participate to varying degrees. The person in charge may act only in the role of a facilitator or catalyst for this discussion, but more often than not he is an active participant. He may very well be the most active participant. The final decision usually is made by the person in charge, but it may well be predetermined by a consensus within the group; decisions by voting tend to be rare, at least in the business world.

Although the staff reports may be primarily individual efforts and certain members of such a policy group may have given considerable individual thought to the issues, the decision-making process described is strongly interlaced with group interaction. This is even more true where a problem arises in the context of such a discussion and a decision is reached without benefit of staff input or individual investigation—a not uncommon occurrence.

The point is that decision making at the top levels of many organizations is very much a group process. This raises a question as to whether this is a desirable state of affairs and, if so, how this group process might best be carried out. Is the typical approach described here the best approach?

INDIVIDUAL VERSUS GROUP DECISIONS

Not all decisions are alike. Although typologies of decisions abound, one that appears particularly useful for understanding policy making differentiates between creative, programmable, and negotiated types [Shull, Delbecq, and Cummings, 1970]. Creative decision making is needed when there is considerable uncertainty surrounding the problem and new and original approaches are required. Programmable decisions are those to which a given technology may be applied and which are capable of some definite, clear-cut solution. Negotiated decisions imply the existence of conflicting factions, cliques or power centers, all of which must be to some degree satisfied in the final decision. A special case of negotiated decision making occurs when those who will implement the decision must get a decision they can "live with" in order for implementation to occur.

Creative Decisions

It does appear that the usual group discussion or meeting has the effect of inhibiting creativity; the group context simply does not permit realization of the full idea-producing potential of all the people participating. This is true for a number of reasons [Van de Ven and Delbecq, 1971]:

1. Interacting groups often become focused on one train of thought for long periods of time, to the exclusion of other alternatives.
2. Individuals tend actually to participate in the discussion only to the extent they view themselves as equally competent with others.
3. Even though more expert group members may not express criticism, others tend to expect that they will and thus hold back their ideas.
4. Lower level managers often are inhibited and go along with the ideas of their superiors, even though in their own minds they have better solutions.
5. Group pressures for conformity with the implied threat of some kind of punishment are almost inevitable.
6. More dominant individuals tend to monopolize and control the group with the result that the ideas of others are lost.
7. Groups as such tend to devote time to their own maintenance and survival and to the members' getting along with each other; this takes away from decision effectiveness.
8. Groups have a tendency to move to quick decisions, thus shortcircuiting the search for relevant information.

In meetings people tend to evaluate others and to expect to be evaluated, both in terms of their expressed ideas and in terms of their social skills. This can well create a less than optimal climate for creativity. As a result, the number of ideas dwindles and the quality of what ideas are produced tends not to be the best. It seems likely that these tendencies become particularly pronounced in well-established managerial groups where the existence of superior-subordinate relationships, competition among members, and the potential for long-term consequences all should militate against idea expression.

A STUDY COMPARING INDIVIDUALS AND GROUPS. An interesting example of this group inhibitation process, insofar as idea production is concerned, is provided by a study in which the participants were to offer ideas for "defining the job description of part-time student dormitory counselors who reside in and supervise student living units of university owned or approved housing." This is a difficult practical problem, producing considerable emotional involvement and controversy, that has no clear-cut solution. The participants in the study were student dormitory residents, student housing administrators, faculty members, and academic administrators [Van de Ven and Delbecq, 1974:605–607].

Three decision-making approaches were compared as follows:

Nominal Group Technique. Individual members first silently and independently generate their ideas on the problem or task in writing. This period of silent writing is followed by a recorded round-robin procedure in which each group member presents one of his ideas to the group without discussion. The ideas are summarized in a terse phrase and written on a blackboard. After all individuals have presented their ideas there is a discussion of the recorded ideas for the purposes of clarification and evaluation. The meeting concludes with a silent independent voting on priorities by individuals through a rank ordering or rating procedure.

Delphi Technique. A questionnaire designed to obtain information on a topic or problem is distributed by mail to a group who are anonymous to one another. The respondents independently generate their ideas in answering the questionnaire which is then returned. The responses are then summarized into a feedback report and sent back to the respondent group along with a second questionnaire that is designed to probe more deeply into the ideas generated in the first questionnaire. On receiving the feedback report, respondents independently evaluate it and respond to the second set of questions. They are requested to vote independently on priority ideas included in the feedback report and to return their second responses by mail.

Discussion Group Technique. Interacting group meetings begin with the statement of the problem by the group leader. This is followed by an unstructured group discussion for generating information and pooling judgments among participants. The meeting concludes with a majority voting procedure on priorities, or a consensus decision.

The result obtained when 20 separate groups of seven people each worked under each procedure are given in Table 11-1. The nominal and delphi groups, where people generated their ideas free of the inhibiting effects of group interaction, both produced a greater number of unique ideas for job activities that should be included in the job description. The nominal techniques in addition yielded a more positive evaluation of the decision-making process than the other two approaches.

This finding that creative thinking is more likely to flourish where individuals work independently of each other is typical. On the other hand, there is no implication that a single individual is likely to do better than many. Having more minds brought to bear on a problem does help, but it also makes a great deal of difference how those minds are organized and utilized.

MAKING CREATIVE DECISIONS. Say a manager is faced with the need to develop certain new products and to plan for the introduction of these products in the marketplace. He has a sizable staff of people who are familiar with those technologies that might be considered reasonably available to the company for producing new products. Instead of bringing these people together in a series of large meetings designed to hammer out the new product ideas, the manager would do much better to set his staff members working on the problem independently. What is needed initially is a large pool of potentially feasible ideas. When people work independently more and better ideas can be expected to emerge. When the same number of people operate in a discussion group setting, it is as if there were half as many people involved, or less [Bouchard, Barsaloux, and Drauden, 1974].

This superiority of individuals alone over groups extends to the use of subgroups as well. One might think that setting up three or four subcommittees or small project teams would generate more ideas because each subgroup would go off in a different direction and thus largely overcome the inhibiting effects of group discussion. This turns out not to be the case. The same number of people working alone do much better than the pooled result of subgroup efforts [Bouchard, Drauden, and Barsaloux, 1974].

TABLE 11-1
Relative Effectiveness of Nominal, Delphi and Discussion Groups in Defining the Job Descriptions of Student Dormitory Counselors

EFFECTIVENESS MEASURES	NOMINAL GROUPS	DELPHI GROUPS	DISCUSSION GROUPS
Mean number of ideas per group	33.0	29.0	18.0
Mean perceived satisfaction level per group	21.1	19.1	18.8

SOURCE: Adapted from Andrew H. Van de Ven and André L. Delbecq [1974:616].

However, once an idea base has been generated, the major need is for good, hard-headed arguments regarding the feasibility and profit potential of the proposed product. This kind of evaluative input to the decision process can be effectively developed through discussion. Group members may well stimulate each other and a general searching out of new information tends to occur; members can facilitate each other when the major goal is judgmental rather than creative [Gustafson *et al.,* 1973].

Perhaps the manager will get enough out of this type of discussion so that he can now proceed to develop his plan for introducing new products. On the other hand, he would probably benefit from obtaining independent evaluations from his staff of the various alternatives proposed. These evaluations would now reflect not only their previous views but the impact of what had come out during the discussions. Although many of the techniques used in research call for a search for consensus, voting, or some similar group-decision process at this point, this does not seem practical in many actual decision situations. To ask people to vote usually means that one intends to follow the results of the vote. For a number of reasons, including the constraints imposed by higher authority, it may not be possible or appropriate for the manager to do this. Yet he can utilize the independent evaluations to guide his own decisions.

Programmable Decisions

How much decision making of a policy nature really fits the requirements for a creative designation is an open question. In many cases there are so many constraints and restrictions operating that attempts to generate a list of new and original options are pointless [Steiner, I.D., 1972]. What is needed is to determine *the* best solution to the problem within the limited options available.

Research on these kinds of programmable problems, where there is an answer if it can only be found, does not indicate the same inhibiting effects of group interactions as with creative decisions. A person can be wrong in such a situation; but as long as he stays within the reasonable bounds established by the problem, he does not risk being labelled a "nut" by others. And these bounds are relatively easy to determine, in contrast with the creative decision situation where the high level of uncertainty involved makes it much more likely that one might burst forth with an "absolutely idiotic" idea.

Where the decision is one of making an economic investment under known constraints, such as deciding where among several alternatives to locate a new plant, or whether or not to manufacture a particular product batch [Schoner, Rose, and Hoyt, 1974], or involves troubleshooting an existing operation [Green, 1975], group discussion is at least as effective as a more individualized approach and it may be more so. These are cases where the alternatives are relatively clear. The real needs are to develop an appropriate method for coming to a decision, to apply sufficient judgment to know when a reasonably correct decision has been worked out, and to avoid adopting a poor decision. In these respects group decision and interaction can be very helpful, and the more traditional business decision-making approach appears to be entirely appropriate.

Negotiated Decisions

Negotiated decision making is by its very nature at least partly a group process. In general, we tend to view this type of decision situation as being limited to collective bargaining between union and management, purchasing negotiations, bargaining over conditions of sale, and certain similar activities. There is a tendency to consider negotiated decision making as something that only occurs across the boundaries of an organization. This impression is misleading. It is precisely the fact that so much decision making within organizations is of a negotiated nature that accounts for the widespread use of meetings and group discussions. Perhaps there is a greater use of this approach than there needs to be; perhaps even many negotiated decisions should not be considered as involving decision making in the usual sense of the term at all, being more in the nature of conflict reduction or coordination efforts. Be that as it may, negotiation does imply a group rather than an individual approach to the decision process.

One might expect, in companies, where authority generally resides at the top and is typically accepted as such, that there would be little need to negotiate decisions. This would seem to be particularly true at the policy level. Do top level executives really need to negotiate, say, with the somewhat lower level managers who will implement the policies? Within a relatively wide band of acceptable alternatives they probably do not, but one can imagine instances where this would not be true.

A company may, for example, be considered a pricing policy that involves a certain amount of subtle collusion with competitors or an arrangement with a union that is not specifically stated in the formal contract. Such strategies and policies can involve some personal risk to the managers who implement them. If these managers should not wish to assume these risks and in fact might consider resigning before doing so, then the decisions at issue had best become negotiated decisions. There is little point in establishing policies that no one is willing to implement.

Perhaps these are extreme cases, but negotiating decisions among managers at the same level is a common practice and where implementation is a major concern there must inevitably be some implicit, if not explicit, negotiation. We will return to this whole matter in later chapters dealing with policy implementation.

DO GROUPS TAKE MORE RISKS?

It is apparent that a great many business decisions are made in groups, whether or not they should be. Given this fact it becomes important to identify any special problems that may be associated with group decision making. Perhaps if one is aware that such problems are potentially present, it might be possible to avoid them.

Although a considerable amount of research has been done in recent years to identify dangers associated with group decision making, it is instructive to start by going back to an earlier period. Writing in 1921, Sigmund Freud had the following to say about individuals in groups:

> In a group the individual is brought under conditions which allow him to throw off the repressions of his unconscious instinctual impulses. The apparently new characteristics which he then displays are in fact the manifestations of this unconscious, in which all that is evil in the human mind is contained as a predisposition. We can find no difficulty in understanding the disappearance of conscience or of a sense of responsibility in these circumstances [Freud, 1960:9].

Several pages later Freud amplifies further:

> A group impresses the individual as being an unlimited power and an insurmountable peril. For the moment it replaces the whole of human society, which is the wielder of authority, whose punishments the individual fears, and for whose sake he has submitted to so many inhibitions. It is clearly perilous for him to put himself in opposition to it, and it will be safer to follow the example of those around him and perhaps even "hunt with the pack." In obedience to the new authority he may put his former "conscience" out of action, and so surrender to the attraction of the increased pleasure that is certainly obtained from the removal of inhibitions. On the whole, therefore, it is not so remarkable that we should see an individual in a group doing or approving things which he would have avoided in the normal conditions of life [Freud, 1960:22–23].

Freud is describing a process by which a "sharing of the guilt" occurs in the group setting. There may accordingly be a shift to greater irresponsibility in making decisions. Although Freud has not generally been credited in this regard, it is apparent that the irresponsibility and loss of conscience he describes can contribute to what has come to be called the "risky shift" in group decision making.

The Nature of Risky Shift

A sizable number of studies have demonstrated that there is a tendency for individuals to be more willing to accept high risk decisions after participating in a group discussion—decisions they would not have made previously. When this process appears, and it is by no means universal, the following phenomena seem to occur [Clark, 1971]:

1. The average preferred decision for the group as a whole shifts in a risky direction.

2. There is greater agreement in the group, converging on this more risky position.
3. No individual moves to a decision any more risky than that preferred by the riskiest group member before the discussion begin.
4. The preponderance of comments in the discussion tend to favor risk.

Although much of the research establishing this phenomenon has utilized decision situations far removed from the economic sphere and the policy-making context, there are more immediately relevant findings also. Risky shift has been found in making decisions about investments in new business projects, and the degree of risk taking tends to increase with the length of time spent in discussion [Streufert and Streufert, 1970]. Risky shift was also found in a study of stock market investment decisions made by business students majoring in the finance area [Deets and Hoyt, 1970].

Policy Implications

There is nothing in all this to indicate that risky decisions are necessarily bad; certain firms at certain points in their development need to take risks, even though they certainly would be expected to do all they could to minimize adverse consequences. Nor can it be assumed that discussion, among a group of top level executives for instance, will invariably yield a high risk decision. There are clearly many conformity pressures operating in any group situation, and a group composed of very cautious and conservative managers is unlikely to move very far in the direction of risk; in fact, many managers in this situation may move in the opposite direction after discussion. But given at least one advocate of a high risk course of action, the potentiality for risky shift becomes real [Roberts and Castore, 1972]. The group context does permit sharing the guilt or blame if the decision proves wrong.

This means that group composition becomes an important consideration. The potential for risky shift is only as great as the most risky position taken by a member going into the discussion, and the probability of occurrence is clearly related to the number of high risk advocates involved. Thus the risk level of policy recommendations from a committee, for instance, can be controlled by knowing something about the initial views of potential members and constituting the committee accordingly [Cecil, Cummings, and Chertkoff, 1973].

This type of outcome is not limited to the situation where a true group decision is made as with committee recommendations. A manager may become engaged in a discussion with a number of subordinates and subsequently shift to a riskier alternative than he would have selected without the discussion. This becomes increasingly true to the extent the subordinates favor high risk alternatives. The decision to fire an inefficient employee who also happens to be the son of a major customer is much more likely to occur after discussions with other managers at least some of whom favor the separation or some other such punitive action.

GROUP COHESION AND GROUPTHINK

In the case of risky shift the idea of sharing the guilt refers largely to the guilt associated with making an incorrect or wrong decision, not a bad decision in the sense of being legally or morally indefensible. Yet Freud's early insights appear to be at least somewhat, if not more, applicable to the latter situation and thus serve to emphasize another potential danger inherent in group decision making. Groups often produce a temporary loss of conscience; stable groups such as the top management of a company can maintain such an effect over a considerable period of time.

This effect tends to occur in the presence of a cohesive group; a group whose members experience a sense of emotional closeness that makes them stick together even when external pressures are working to break them up. The phenomenon has been labelled "groupthink" by Irving Janis [1972] who has documented it primarily with reference to decisions at the top levels of the federal government—the Bay of Pigs invasion of Cuba, the escalation of the Korean War, Pearl Harbor, and the escalation of the Vietnam War. He could now extend his analysis easily to the Nixon administrations' decisions *vis à vis* Watergate. Corporate examples of the same process abound, although reduced visability makes them harder to document.

Janis' point is that the more friendly and close the members of an in-group, the greater the chance that independent critical thinking and realistic moral judgment will be suspended in favor of group norms and conviviality. The result is groupthink, with the following consequences:

1. A belief in the group's basic morality so strong that ethical consequences of decisions are ignored.
2. A stereotyped view of some outside enemy (a competing firm) as evil, weak, or stupid.
3. A sense of invulnerability that encourages optimism and risk taking.
4. Efforts to rationalize so that warnings from outside are discounted and assumptions are not reconsidered.
5. Direct pressure on members not to express arguments against group positions under threat of being considered disloyal.
6. Self-censorship to the point where doubts regarding the wisdom of the group consensus are suppressed.
7. A shared sense of unanimity born out of the self-censorship and a view that silence must mean agreement.
8. The emergence of certain members who protect the group from informa-

tion that might interfere with the cohesion-induced irrationality, irresponsibility and immorality.

The overlap between risky shift and groupthink is obvious. Most important, both represent major threats to the integrity of decisions arising out of a group context. There are dangers inherent in a group approach above and beyond those noted in our consideration of the inhibitory effects on creative thinking. These dangers may not be insurmountable, but they often have not been surmounted. Perhaps with full knowledge of their potential impact, policymakers of the future can take steps to see that they do not emerge or that their consequences are minimized.

CONSTITUTING A MANAGEMENT TEAM FOR DECISION MAKING

Selecting the members of a group to control and adjust risk taking propensities is not the only way in which decision outcomes may be influenced by group composition. At least three other considerations appear to have an influence. One is the extent to which the members of a group are similar to each other, another is the degree of social skill possessed by the various people, and a third is the number of individuals involved. Although in many instances it is not possible to manipulate such factors, as in the case where those who are in certain positions must be included in a given discussion, there are other occasions when one has more discretion. This is true of many committees and project teams constituted for a specific purpose.

The Effects of Similarities and Differences

Groups may be constituted to contain people whose abilities, knowledge, attitudes, values, and personality characteristics are very similar or, on the other hand, sizable differences between members may be introduced. A considerable amount of attention has been given to such considerations in the research that has been done on group decision making [Filley, 1970; Steiner, I.D., 1972].

It is apparent that the more similar the members, the easier it is for them to work together, to understand each other, and to get right at the task at hand. Diversity is almost certain to bring on some conflict and misunderstanding. Groups in which there are large differences between individuals have a difficult time getting organized; sometimes they never do settle their differences sufficiently to get on with the job.

On the other hand, diversity brings varied abilities, information, viewpoints, and approaches to a problem. Where everyone has roughly the same background, knowledge, values, and the like, even if these are well focused in terms of the requirements of the specific problem, there is a paucity of resources for generating alternatives. It is like having a single individual rather than many.

In fact, there is a strong parallel between the similarity versus difference question and the individual versus group one. This parallel extends to the solution. Where the decision is essentially of the programmable type, similar individuals can easily get down to programming it. Alternatives are limited in any event, and people who think alike can usually find the right or best answer relatively quickly because they can focus their energies on the problem rather than on conflicts within the group.

Where the problem requires a creative decision, however, diversity has its value for the same reason that the average group is superior to the average single individual—more worthwhile alternatives are generated. Even the inhibitory impact of group discussion and the almost inevitable conflict between individuals are not usually sufficient to offset the advantages of greater resources. Thus, on creative decisions, constituting the group out of quite dissimilar people, even if the situation is such as to require initial and continuing face to face discussion, appears desirable. In particular, diversity in the degree to which members like to dominate or direct others is needed [Bither, 1971].

SIMILARITIES AND DIFFERENCES IN THE REAL WORLD. None of the research in this area has been conducted with ongoing groups in real organizations. A question arises as to how applicable it really is. Policy-making groups, for instance, are typically made up of people who have worked together for a long time and the company structure itself produces an inherent organization for the group. Thus, diversity may not have as much negative impact as in the newly formed groups used in the research. Once conflicts are ironed out and procedures for working together are established, they can remain in that status while the group tackles many problems over a considerable period of time.

In addition, there are often more pressing considerations than similarity and diversity that condition assignment decisions. Take for instance an engagement team in a management consulting firm. Such teams can number from three to ten or more consultants. They are put together to serve a particular client. One might think that similarity would be a helpful feature for an engagement team working on a routine cost reduction study, whereas diversity should be stressed in assigning consultants to a complex marketing strategy study. Perhaps this is the case, but it is in fact, impossible to accomplish. Consultants must be assigned in terms of what they know, engagements must be started as soon as possible after the client requests them, and consultants must be kept busy so that as much of their time as possible is chargeable to a client. This means that as soon as a person frees up some time due to the completion or changed requirements of one engagement he must be assigned to another team where his skills are needed. One cannot wait to put together teams of similar or dissimilar people; the firm would quickly go out of business.

The same situation arises in the corporate setting where prior assignments, travel commitments, the nature of positions, and the like, all may influence the way in which groups are constituted. Yet a familiarity with the results of research into the effects of group similarities and differences can be useful in the limited number of cases where the results can be put to use.

The Effects of Social Skill

There is good reason to believe that managers with highly developed social skills do better in group decision making. This has been demonstrated in creative decision contexts [Bouchard, 1969] and with standardized simulations of managerial decision situations [Bither, 1971]. Such people can be characterized as outgoing, self-assured, somewhat dominant and aggressive, and enthusiastic. They are probably least likely to be inhibited in their expression of ideas before a group. On the other hand, they are not necessarily people who prefer making decisions in groups; quite the contrary may well be the case [Karmel, 1973]. Also, there is reason to believe that younger people may be more likely to possess such social skills than those who are older [Webber, 1974].

The implication of these findings is that where possible, if group decisions are to be made, the groups should contain people with the social skills that facilitate interaction among members and the expression as well as effective utilization of ideas by the group. This sounds self-evident, yet in practice a sufficient number of decision-making groups are constituted of individuals who are uncomfortable, perhaps even quite anxious, in the group context to make the idea worth some repetition. There is no point having group decisions made by those who function at their worst in this type of social setting. Accordingly, if a top management group is to place heavy reliance on group decision making, social skill should be a criterion for selection to a position as an officer in the company.

The Effects of Group Size

The question of group size is of particular interest, not only in its own right but because it provides an indirect approach that can be used to deal effectively with the similarity-dissimilarity issue. There has been a continuing debate as to how large committees should be, how many people should serve on boards of directors, how large a group of subordinates should report to one superior, and similar problems [Cummings, Huber, and Arendt, 1974; Filley, 1970; House and Miner, 1969]. It is apparent that the answers in this regard are closely tied to both the nature of the decision to be made and the effects of similarities and differences among group members.

SIZE AND DIFFERENTIATION. Table 11-2 provides an indication of what can be expected to happen as the size of a decision-making group is increased. First of all, the *range* of any particular characteristic expands so that with eight people present it is almost triple that with only two. Thus, larger groups

TABLE 11-2
Group Size and Differences Among Members

GROUP SIZE	DIFFERENCE BETWEEN HIGHEST AND LOWEST SCORING MEMBERS	DIFFERENCE BETWEEN HIGHEST AND SECOND-HIGHEST SCORING MEMBERS	AVERAGE DIFFERENCE BETWEEN ADJACENTLY RANKED MEMBERS
2	0.88	0.88	0.88
3	1.35	0.67	0.67
4	1.68	0.59	0.56
5	1.94	0.54	0.48
6	2.14	0.51	0.43
7	2.30	0.48	0.38
8	2.44	0.46	0.35

NOTE: All differences are expressed in standard score units and represent averages that should be obtained when many groups of a specific size are randomly assembled from a population in which the measured attribute is normally distributed.

SOURCE: Ivan D. Steiner: *Group Process and Productivity*. New York, Academic Press, 1972, p. 128.

are likely to contain sizable differences with both the greater resources for problem solving and the greater potential for conflict that this implies. Second, as groups get larger, a member is more likely to find at least one other member who is quite similar to himself. As a consequence, there is an increasing probability of splintering and clique formation.

If the decision making required is at all complex, as many policy decisions are, small groups of three or so tend to do poorly [Holloman and Hendrick, 1971]. They need the range of talent that more people provide. On the other hand, this does not mean that size can be increased indefinitely with favorable results. Ultimately, the problems of coordination become overwhelming and decision quality suffers. In one study, groups of 11 were most effective; probably something in the range of 8 to 12 people is best for most continuing policy-making groups [Manners, 1975]. Such groups will find it difficult to come to complete agreement, but this should not be required if the person in charge takes responsibility for the final decision or even if a vote is employed. They are much more likely than either smaller or larger groups to develop an effective policy, however.

THE BOARD OF DIRECTORS. This matter of the relationship between group size and decision-making effectiveness is of particular significance in constituting corporate boards. Many such boards run well above the numbers that research suggests are optimal. In one study of 100 major corporations, the average board contained 13 people [Battalia, Lotz and Associates, 1969]. Insurance and banking firms are particularly likely to have large boards, and their is a marked tendency for firms with greater sales volume to have relatively larger boards [Pfeffer, 1972].

This problem of excessive size may well be increasingly compounded by recent pressures to place representatives of special interest groups such as racial minorities, consumer groups, students, ecologists, unions, and the like on corporate boards [Koontz, 1971]. The presence of such individuals, who represent specific constituencies, tends to shift decision making toward the negotiated form. It thus makes coordination even more difficult than the existence of a large number of board members would normally imply.

A major factor involved appears to be the degree of trust existing among board members. Where certain members represent outside constituencies and view it as their role to do so, others may naturally mistrust their commitment to company goals. Such a lack of trust within a group can seriously interfere with decision-making effectiveness when dealing with the type of problems with which boards of directors are concerned. This has been demonstrated in a study where groups of managers from the same company worked together to solve the joint problems of [Zand, 1972]:

1. Developing a strategy to increase short-term profits without undermining long-term growth of a medium-sized electronics company with a very low return on investment, outdated manufacturing facilities, whose labor force has been cut 25 per cent and whose top management personnel had been changed and reorganized two years before.
2. Obtaining commitment to implement such a program despite strong managerial disappointment because expectations of immediate investment for expansion and modernization would not be met.

In dealing with these problems the managerial groups with lower trust were much less effective in clarifying their goals, in using realistic information, in searching for solutions, and in obtaining commitment to implement solutions. It seems safe to assume that constituting boards to include individuals who do not have the interests of the organization as a major concern can only create just this lack of trust among those who are primarily committed to the organization; decision making will suffer accordingly.

INFLUENCES ON POLICY DECISIONS

This chapter and the one preceding have considered a great range of factors that may operate within the organization to influence the effectiveness of policy decisions. It is apparent that the capabilities and characteristics of individuals make a sizable difference and that in many cases it might be advisable for individuals to work on problems more independently than they normally do.

It is also apparent that if groups are to be used in connection with the decision process they often can be used more effectively than they usually are.

Such considerations as the risky shift phenomenon, groupthink, similarities and differences, social skills, group size, and trust can have a profound impact on the way in which organizational decisions are made and on the policies and strategies that are developed. With a knowledge of the ways in which these effects occur, it should be possible to upgrade policy and strategy decisions considerably. Against this backdrop the discussion in the next chapter considers the varied ways in which decision making does in fact occur.

QUESTIONS

Discussion Guides on Chapter Content

1. How do creative, programmable, and negotiated decisions differ?
2. What is the relative effectiveness of nominal group, delphi, and discussion group approaches to decision making? Define these approaches and cite the evidence.
3. What is risky shift? What are its policy implications?
4. What are the consequences of groupthink? Why would they not occur in a noncohesive group?
5. What is the evidence regarding the effects of similarities and differences within a group on decision effectiveness?
6. How does the size of a group affect its decision-making processes and capabilities?

Mind Stretching Questions

1. This chapter presents a great deal of evidence regarding the effectiveness of various group and individual decision-making approaches, but there are many loose ends as well. What additional questions need to be answered? What research is called for? How might this research be conducted?
2. If you were constituting an ongoing decision-making group such as the executive committee of a major corporation, how would you do it? What factors would you take into account?

CHAPTER

12

Alternative Approaches to Decision Making

INTRODUCTION

Given all the discussion about planning and decision making that precedes, it seems paradoxical to raise a question as to how important such activities are in the day to day life of top level managers. Yet this question has been raised, and there are a number of early studies which appear to indicate that, although managers often spend considerable time searching for information, they typically spend much less time actually making decisions [Dubin, 1962; Sayles, 1964]. This viewpoint has more recently been affirmed by Mintzberg [1973a:38]:

> The pressure of the managerial environment does not encourage the development of reflective planners. . . . The job breeds adaptive information manipulators who prefer the live, concrete situation. The manager works in an environment of stimulus-response, and he develops in his work a clear preference for live action.

Yet there are a number of studies which indicate that planning and decision making require considerable time of many executives, particularly those at the highest levels [Holden, Pederson, and Germane, 1968; Mahoney, Jerdee, and Carroll, 1965; Miner, 1973a]. The conflicting conclusions appear to reflect variations in methods of study and in the samples of managers considered. Direct observation of managers at work in their offices is not an approach conducive to revealing how much time these managers spend making decisions; one cannot see them think and, in any event, they may well do much of their thinking and planning outside the office. Only self-reports by the managers themselves can provide an indication of the time spent in decision making and planning, and when this approach is used many do emerge as devoting considerable time to such activities [Stieglitz, 1969; Heidrick and Struggles, 1972].

Yet there clearly are other top level executives who perform their jobs quite differently. They spend relatively little time in decision making; either they do not make many decisions, or they use approaches to their decisions that are not very time consuming. When studies utilize a rather small number of executives, there is always a good chance that a disproportionate number of those who spend little time on decisions will be included. This, too, appears to have contributed to the finding in some studies of a relatively low level of involvement in planning and decision making.

VARIATIONS AMONG MANAGERS

If nothing else the studies of managerial work point up the fact that major differences exist in the time managers devote to decisions. This is, of course, in part a consequence of the nature and consequences of the particular decisions to be made, a matter that will concern us later in this chapter. But it is also a consequence of the way in which specific executives and companies approach the decision-making process. One financial executive faced with the need to come up with a method of financing a projected expansion project may spend days evaluating the pros and cons of various alternatives; another, faced with the same problem, may hardly hesitate before attempting to work out details with a bank with which he has dealt on numerous occasions in the past.

The Formal Structured Approach

Planning and decision making that is formally structured follows procedures that have been laid down beforehand. Structured planning usually involves a number of people and an extensive search for information. Above all else it strives to be rational and systematic. When applied to the planning process this formal approach is usually referred to by some such terms as long-range planning, comprehensive planning, comprehensive corporate planning, integrated planning, overall planning, or corporate planning [Steiner, 1970]. In such cases it almost always eventuates in a written document.

However, a similar formal approach can be applied to any decision of consequence, including the development of policies. Staff reports may be prepared and a standard sequence of individual analysis followed by group analysis may be employed, especially if the decision is creative in nature. The crucial point is that the attack on the problem follows some systematic and explicitly stated procedure.

The Intuitive-Anticipatory Approach

In contrast to formally structured planning, the intuitive-anticipatory approach does not follow any explicitly stated process [Steiner, 1971]. In fact, no one really knows the precise mental processes and steps introduced. Generally only one person is involved, such as the chief executive officer. Although written documents may result, this tends not to be the case. Typically, the decision plan or strategy applies to events within a short time horizon. Executives who stress the intuitive approach are not usually prone to engage in long-term projections and planning for the far-distant future. Basically, what occurs is that the executive has a "gut" feeling that a particular alternative is the right one, based on past experience. How he got to this feeling and why this particular choice is the best one are things the manager cannot specify with any degree of certainty. He simply has a hunch that this is the thing to do, and he has developed considerable confidence in his hunches over the years.

Such an approach can involve a telescoping of years of observation and experience. Many managers have a great capacity to learn from their past failures and successes and to apply this knowledge to new, but similar, situations. If one can unravel all that is compressed into a single intuitive decision, a highly complex analytic process emerges. Attempts to do this and represent the thinking involved in the form of a computer program attest to this fact [Newell and Simon, 1972]. The result can be a brilliant strategy or a very insightful decision. However, because there is no way of checking on the logic and rationality of the various steps in the decision process, the potentiality for error is also very high. Furthermore, managers who have experienced some success with the intuitive approach often find it extremely personally satisfying, with the result that they may utilize it to the exclusion of other approaches more appropriate to a particular decision.

The Entrepreneurial Opportunistic Approach

There is also an approach that stresses finding and utilizing opportunity. The focus is on opportunity identification rather than problem solving. Such a manager is constantly searching for new types of business ventures, new products, and new markets. In many respects this approach is prototypic for the entrepreneur, and it usually involves the assumption of high levels of risk.

However, as Mintzberg [1973a] emphasizes, the entrepreneurial role is not limited to the small business enterprise. Managers in large organizations can become extensively involved in a variety of improvement projects—self-initiated change efforts designed to exploit opportunities. Again, this is an approach that may be totally alien to one manager, while representing the major thrust of another manager's efforts. As with the typical entrepreneur, such a manager is constantly on the alert to identify new opportunities both within the organization and outside and to develop methods of exploiting them.

The Incrementing Approach

The incrementing approach is best illustrated in the writings of Charles Lindblom [1959, 1965], who uses the term *disjointed incrementalism* to describe it. It is characterized as follows:

1. Rather than attempting a comprehensive survey and evaluation of alternatives, as in the formal structured approach, the decision maker focuses only on those policy alternatives that differ incrementally from existing policies.
2. Only a relatively small number of policy alternatives are considered.
3. For each policy alternative only a restricted number of consequences considered important are evaluated.
4. The problem is continually redefined, allowing for countless ends-means and means-ends adjustments, which make the problem more manageable.
5. Thus, it is assumed that there is no one right decision; there is a never-ending series of attacks on the issues at hand through serial analyses and evaluation.
6. As such the incrementing approach is remedial, geared more to the alleviation of present concrete imperfections than to the promotion of future goals.

Lindblom has referred to this approach as "muddling through." It is heavily concerned with obtaining agreement and seeks to simplify the decision process to make it more manageable or even manageable at all. Such an approach tends to result in decisions that are typically of the negotiated type.

The Adaptive Approach

The adaptive approach takes a somewhat different form as described by different authors. However, it has in common the idea of adapting or changing one's strategy depending upon the way existing circumstances are perceived. The adaptive search approach of Ansoff [1965] involves the following:

1. A successive narrowing and refining of decision rules depending upon the circumstances.
2. Thus, a cascade of decisions with feedback between stages.
3. A process of gap reduction within these stages. This involves:
   (a) Establishing a set of objectives.
   (b) Estimating the gap between the current position of the firm and the objectives.
   (c) Proposing one or more courses of action.
   (d) Testing these courses of action for their capacity to reduce the gap.
4. Adaptation of the objectives and the starting point evaluation.

Ackoff [1970] elaborates upon this adaptive approach with reference to the states of certainty; uncertainty, as ignorance regarding the future, resides in the decision maker's mind. Where near certainty exists, one can commit oneself to a given course of action consonant with the anticipated future. Where there is uncertainty, but it is possible to be relatively sure regarding the available possibilities, contingency planning is required; thus it is possible to quickly exploit the opportunities once the future becomes evident. Finally, where there is ignorance regarding an aspect of the future, responsiveness must be built into the system so that it can detect deviation from the expected rapidly and respond accordingly.

Under uncertainty and ignorance this adaptive approach involves relatively less attention to search and choice activities. Rather, there is more stress on building up a capacity to respond quickly when action is called for [Ackoff, 1970]. A manager utilizing such an approach needs to monitor his company's environment very closely to detect the first signs of change. He must then have the contingency plans or the capacity for response available, ready to bring to bear when the occasion calls for it; he must have the resources to implement the appropriate contingency plan or simply to respond in some manner.

Although such an approach does not require forecasting as such, it substitutes extensive monitoring and data collection. It is also costly in terms of planning costs (because many of the contingency plans may never be needed) and it often requires considerable stockpiling of resources. An example would be an approach that attempted to respond to any sign of a build up of competition in any local market area with a direct head-to-head challenge in kind to the particular strategy employed by the competitor. To be effective this would require a very rapid response and, thus, a standing inventory of money, people, and products.

Variations in the Ways Problems Are Perceived

The variations in approaches reflected in designations such as formal structured, intuitive-anticipatory, entrepreneurial opportunistic, incremental, and adaptive occur in terms of the way decisions are approached. These five do not exhaust all such possibilities, but they do serve to illustrate the great variability among managers. However, there is another source of variability that appears to be at least as important. This is a function of the way in which a problem is perceived.

An instructive example of how variable these perceptions may be is provided by a study of how different teams of individuals approached a simulated top management decision [Norman, 1967]. The teams had to react to a major reduction in materials requirements which produced a reduction of 25 per cent in direct manufacturing costs. Each of the nine teams tended to focus on a different aspect of the problem. The nine results were as follows:

Team 1 structured its decisions around its estimates of the changes in the total industry market.
Team 2 searched for an efficient level of sales in a given market.
Team 3 geared its decisions to a desired percentage of the market.
Team 4 focused on an efficient level of production and operating efficiency.

Team 5 tried to make and sell just as many units as possible.
Team 6 attempted to copy successful competitors.
Team 7 concentrated on pricing procedures that would yield the maximum revenue.
Team 8 established and held to a top industry price.
Team 9 focused on inventory and inventory control.

Each of these teams was faced with the same problem; yet each saw that problem differently and developed strategies accordingly. It is little wonder that the profitability of competing firms often varies so widely.

Decision Approaches in Small Business

In general, planning of a systematic, formal nature is much less prevalent in small firms than in larger ones. As a result, approaches such as the intuitive-anticipatory and the entrepreneurial-opportunistic are more characteristic, although variants of the incremental and adaptive approaches are also found. Yet even in the smallest organization it is important that the chief executive officer be engaged in planning, establish policies and strategies, and make decisions with planned objectives as well as realistic appraisals of the future in mind [Steiner, 1966].

Given that examining future consequences of present decisions, as well as choosing bases for making current decisions from among future alternative courses of action, are important to all managers and organizations, irrespective of size, a strong argument can be made for utilizing a more formal structured approach even in small firms [Steiner, 1967]. Because the small business has less capacity to control its environment and therefore is often at the mercy of events, truly long-range planning may not be fruitful; however, middle range efforts extending to two years or so can pay off. Many of the techniques of formal systematic planning and structured decision making are applicable in organizations of any size.

THE CONTROVERSY OVER DECISION APPROACHES

There has been much controversy over the years regarding how managers should and do make decisions. The position with the longest history is the one that emphasizes organizational rationality and the maximization of expected utility—the concept of *economic man*. This position, as noted in Chapter 9, has been attacked as unrealistic by both the incrementalists and advocates of so-called *administrative man,* who consider satisficing rather than maximizing as more characteristic of the real world of managerial decisions. These latter two positions have in turn come under attack on a variety of grounds including the view that both "muddling through" and satisficing settle for too little, and thus do not permit major change. Further confounding this picture is a considerable amount of uncertainty as to whether a given viewpoint is intended to be normative or descriptive or both.

Problems with the Maximizing View

The initial attacks on the maximizing concept by Herbert Simon [1957a] are well known. Essentially Simon felt that maximizing is not what managers actually do; rather they make the choice that occurs to them first and is at the same time good enough for the intended purpose (satisfice). These views seem to have evolved at the present time into the following three criticisms of the maximizing concept [Harrison, 1975:66]:

1. Although it is appropriate to consider firms and the individuals in them as having objectives, it is not true that these objectives are pursued in the maximizing mode.
2. The idea that firms or their decision makers have objectives for which a preference ordering of the states of nature always results in the choice of the most preferred alternative is unrealistic.
3. Maximizing is virtually impossible because the information required and the time and money to obtain it are limited.

All this does not necessarily say that some kind of maximizing is not, and should not be, what managers *strive* for. Thus, *good* decision making might be gauged in terms of the degree of approximation to, or effort expended to attain, the maximizing ideal. On the other hand, a normative theory of satisficing or muddling through would argue that all this effort to maximize is not worth the expenditure of energy and money involved.

Problems with Not Maximizing

Concerns over the incrementalist and satisficing approaches take both a normative and a descriptive tack [Etzioni, 1967; Michael, 1973]. Many feel that both approaches set only minimal standards for decision making, at least in terms of decision quality, and are to a large degree directionless. Even if decisions have been made this way in the past, they should not be in the future. Approaches of this kind are considered to be inconsistent with effective long-range planning and a structured formal approach to the planning process. Settling for satisficing and incremental change comes very close to encouraging nonrational and irrational decision making.

Furthermore, neither approach (satisficing or incrementing) seems adequate to the task of explaining how decisions in favor of major change occur. The incrementalist approach as such virtually precludes this possibility. The satisficing approach makes it very unlikely. Yet the annals of business history are full of instances where decision makers have instituted fundamental and far-reaching changes in their organizations [Chandler, 1962; Kakar, 1970; Sloan, 1964]. In view of the uncertainties that emerge from so much of the writing in this area, it is not surprising that solutions have increasingly been sought in research.

Studies of Real-Life Decisions

Although research on decision making has not always focused on top management policy making, there are a number of studies of the decision process in a context where the consequences are real and the incentive to do well sizable. This research clearly reveals that the alternative approaches previously considered are not sufficient to explain all of what actually happens when decisions are made. In particular, many people appear to be neither maximizers or satisficers, but rather are best described as confirmers or validators [Cecil and Lundgren, 1975; Soelberg, 1966].

Such individuals continue to search for information for some time after they have already located a satisfactory alternative, but they do not truly attempt to maximize. They tend to establish a preferred choice early in the decision-making process and then rapidly reduce the number of possible choices to two—the preferred alternative and one other. From then on the search process is devoted largely to validating or confirming the preferred choice.

The data seem to indicate that, where a decision makes several approaches feasible, some people will seek to maximize, some will satisfice, and some will validate or confirm early choices. Information on these three approaches as related to the decision to accept a job after graduating from college is given in Table 12-1. It is important to note that the maximizing mode is approximated by a sizable proportion of the students, although of course their search for alternative companies is ultimately limited by time constraints. Further-

TABLE 12-1
Alternative Approaches to a Job Choice Decision

Decision Approach	Characteristic Search Pattern	Choice Procedure	Per Cent of Individuals
Maximizing	Comprehensive—talk to as many companies as possible	Choose the company offering the most of what is wanted in a position	47
Validating or confirming	Moderate—continue searching until have two acceptable offers	Validate initial choice so as to justify it	30
Satisficing	Restricted—stop looking as soon as first satisfactory offer is received	Accept first satisfactory offer	23

SOURCE: Adapted from William F. Glueck [1974:80].

more, those students who have had more, and more diversified, work experience are the ones who are most likely to resort to maximizing [Glueck, 1974]. This would suggest that experienced policy makers may well be more likely to attempt to maximize than to settle for less demanding approaches.

Analyses of top level decisions related to major investments and to acquisitions indicate that extensive search extending over multiple levels of the organization can occur, but that there is a certain amount of negotiated decision making as well [Carter, 1971]. Furthermore, it is clear that top level decisions may be made with reference to goals other than profit maximization and that on occasion estimates of marginal costs and profits are only roughly made at best. Yet there is reason to believe that those firms which more nearly approximate a formal, structured, rational approach to decisions are more likely to be profitable [Stagner, 1969].

Data derived from this study of top-level decision making in over 100 firms are given in Table 12-2. From these data it would seem that, to the extent a firm can approximate the formal structured approach on most decisions, it will benefit accordingly. However, the goal pursued may not be profit at the expense of all else. At least one other goal is of considerable importance and that is the public image of the company. However, the data in this regard may well be reflecting the fact that such a concern for the realities of the social environment can contribute indirectly to profits. Always making decisions solely in an attempt to maximize the direct profitability of a particular decision may not always return the greatest profits overall.

TABLE 12-2
Characteristics of Decision Making in More Profitable Firms (N = 109)

There is a concern over formal steps in decision making at the top level including regular meetings, written records, and attention to formal routines.

Estimates of costs and anticipated profits to results from a decision are always carefully computed.

Discussions at the top level include all executives affected by the decision.

A top level policy committee or operating committee is actively used in the decision-making process.

Social interaction among top executives outside office hours and for nonbusiness purposes is frequent.

The chief executive is concerned about having detailed information on which to base decisions and wants substantial detail.

There is concern for going through channels and this communication pattern is always observed.

The preferred style of the chief executive is to talk with all interested managers together.

There are clear lines of authority that everyone knows and respects.

Importance is attached to the company image as seen by the public in making decisions and this often outweighs cost factors.

There is a high degree of satisfaction with the way in which decisions are handled.

SOURCE: Adapted from Ross Stagner [1969:10].

VARIATIONS IN APPROACH AS A FUNCTION OF THE NATURE OF THE DECISION

Several recent studies have made it increasingly clear that a single manager may vary considerably in his decision-making approach depending on the nature of the decision and the situation surrounding it. In fact such variability from decision to decision within the context of a manager's job tends to be at least as great, if not greater, than the variation in characteristic approach among a group of managers [Vroom and Jago, 1974]. To date these studies of variability in the approaches of individual managers have been concerned with the degree to which subordinates are included in the decision-making process. Hopefully at some later date they will be extended to other aspects of the decision process, such as the degree of formal structuring, the total amount of search for information, and so on.

Leadership Styles and Power Sharing Among Senior Managers

The major initial study of decision-based variability was conducted by Frank Heller [1971] using data provided by 260 senior managers in 15 large and successful companies. As indicated in Table 12-3 certain consistent preferences in style were found, with consultation being the approach most frequently used. However, when managers had large spans of control they tended to use the time saving approaches at the extremes (own decision and delegation) more frequently. Managers in the personnel area and in general management were more prone to use decision approaches involving power sharing, whereas those in the finance and production functions more frequently kept power to themselves. More experienced managers shared decisions more. The primary rationale for sharing a decision was to improve its technical quality.

Behind these general trends, however, was considerable variation dependent

TABLE 12-3
Use of Various Decision-Making Approaches as Reported by Senior Managers

Approaches to Decisions	Percentage of Time Used
The manager makes his own decision alone	15
Having made his own decision, the manager adopts some formal method of communicating the result to others	21
Prior consultation is used, but the final decision rests entirely with the manager	37
The decision emerges as the result of joint boss-subordinate discussion in which both take an approximately equal share	20
The senior manager delegates the decision to his subordinates	7

SOURCE: Adapted from Frank A. Heller [1971:xvi and 74].

on the nature of the decision and those involved. The managers did not use one preferred personal style irrespective of the nature of the situation. Senior managers gave their immediate subordinates considerable latitude in making decisions having an impact down the line; much less latitude when the decision involved only the senior manager and his subordinate. When the decision was of great importance to the company and a clear commitment to company goals was required, the senior managers typically made the decisions themselves; otherwise, they shared more power. If the senior manager perceived a sizable skill difference, such that the subordinate involved was less knowledgeable and experienced, there was little sharing in the decision process. More experienced subordinates were more likely to be included in decisions when appropriate.

Studies of Decision Quality, Acceptance, and Speed

A second series of studies has provided additional information on decision-based variability and on the factors that may influence this variability [Vroom and Yetton, 1973; Vroom and Jago, 1974]. Here also the major concern was with the degree to which the senior manager made the decision himself or involved subordinates. The alternative approaches considered were much the same as those used by Heller (Table 12-3). However, a greater variety of situational factors that might influence the choice of an approach was investigated. These were [Vroom and Jago, 1974]:

1. The quality requirements of the decision and thus the need for rationality.
2. The manager's own level of knowledge relative to the decision.
3. The degree to which the problem is structured.
4. The need for acceptance of the decision by subordinates in order to implement it.
5. The extent to which subordinates would in fact accept a decision made unilaterally by the manager.
6. The probability that subordinates share the organizational goals to be attained in solving the problem.
7. The likelihood of conflict among subordinates with regard to a preferred solution.
8. The availability of information needed for a high quality decision among subordinates.

As in the Heller research it was found that when the managers had the needed information they tended to make decisions themselves; the major reason for consulting subordinates was to obtain needed technical information to improve decision quality. Also managers do not share decision making with subordinates when there is reason to distrust the subordinates' commitment to organizational goals and thus to believe that they would favor decisions that would serve their own interests at the expense of the company.

The studies indicate that decision sharing tends to occur when quality is important, when the problem is unstructured (creative) in nature, when subordinate acceptance is crucial to implementation and the likelihood of acceptance of a unilateral decision is low, and when conflict among subordinates is absent. Time constraints do not appear to play a particularly important role in the choice of an approach.

The Role of Perceived Expertise and Power

One problem in interpreting the studies just reported is that managers may believe they are sharing decisions, and their subordinates may even believe it too, when this is not actually the case. Within decision-making teams, if one member is considered to be more expert, that person's views are very likely to prevail [Mulder, 1971; Mulder and Wilke, 1970]. Others will often change their positions to that of the expert even though ostensibly the decision making process is open and joint in nature. It does not matter whether the expert is really the best informed or not; the mere fact that he is believed to be tends to inhibit the expression of alternative views when creative decisions are to be made [Collaros and Anderson, 1969].

The consequence is that a senior manager may go into a meeting with his subordinates in search of information and alternatives for dealing with a problem that he poses and come out with nothing more than the solution that he had in mind himself originally. The mere fact that he poses the problem and elaborates its nature, coupled with the relative power inherent in his position, may be sufficient to bar any real sharing of the decision or even the presentation of realistic alternatives. Yet all those present may interpret the situation as one in which some sharing of decision making has occurred.

An antidote to this outcome seems to be introduced, however, when one or more of the subordinates is generally considered to have a major stake in the decision. Heller [1971] notes that senior managers tend to share decisions when these decisions are likely to affect not only the subordinate manager but those who work for him as well. Vroom and Yetton [1973] indicate much the same thing when they discuss decision sharing under conditions of a need for acceptance to facilitate implementation, and a concomitant uncertainty regarding acceptance without sharing. Patchen [1974] found the same tendency in studying varying influences on purchasing decisions; those who had a major stake in the decision were given an opportunity to influence it, and they did. What is involved in all of these instances is negotiated decision making occasioned by the existence of the power to withdraw commitment or contributions on the part of those at lower levels, combined with an implicit or explicit recognition that this could occur and introduce new problems of its own. Under such circumstances real decision sharing does appear to occur.

CONTINGENCIES IN DECISION APPROACHES

Taking a clue from the fact that managers tend to vary their approaches widely depending on the demands of the situation, it is now possible to gain further insight into the use of the various approaches to organizational decision making discussed at the beginning of this chapter. It would seem likely that, as companies face different types of decisions in different contexts, the same decision-based variability would occur. But it also seems probable that the environment one organization faces need not be the same as that another faces; in fact, we know this to be true [Inkson, Pugh, and Hickson, 1970; Lawrence and Lorsch, 1967a, 1967b; Pugh *et al.*, 1969]. Thus one would expect the predominant decision approach of organizations to vary depending upon variations in the environments in which they operate.

The formal structured approach, although probably desirable wherever it can be applied, seems most likely to be used in large companies that can exert at least some influence over their environments (suppliers, customers, governments, and so on) and thus stabilize them for purposes of planning.

The intuitive-anticipatory approach seems almost inevitable in very uncertain situations where the external world is changing rapidly and unpredictably and quick, risky decisions are better than nothing at all. To take an extreme case, many businesses face this kind of situation in wartime with the ebb and flow of the fortunes of battle. The use of the intuitive approach may not be highly desirable, and there are situations where it offers little hope of warding off failure, but it can on occasion be all there is.

The entrepreneurial-opportunistic approach appears most likely to emerge in the case of small firms faced with a need to make frequent changes in products or services because of rapid obsolescence or changes in profitability. Many small electronics firms lose their markets almost as soon as they develop them because the larger firms are attracted to these expanding markets and can achieve economies of scale that the smaller companies cannot. The need to seek new opportunities constantly is an almost inevitable consequence. Also there are certain entrepreneurs who are strongly oriented to the future and to the growth of their companies who appear to utilize the opportunistic approach consistently [Smith, 1967].

The incremental approach is generally associated with governmental organizations exposed to strong political pressures, that is, those operating in a democratic system. However, any organization that is highly institutionalized may resort to this approach frequently—utilities and regulated transportation companies for instance. Any organization that needs agreement among its multiple publics more than it needs rationality or decision quality is likely to resort to incrementalism.

The adaptive approach does not appear to be used widely or at least to be used widely in an effective manner. A number of companies do play "follow the leader" and attempt to adapt quickly to the strategies of an industry leader or a price leader. But they typically lack the resource reserves needed to utilize this approach competently, even if they do monitor industry changes correctly. The more such an adaptive decision maker lags behind in responding to the first cues that a change is needed, the less effective the approach. Furthermore, it is implicit in the adaptive approach that one does attempt to "zero" in on the more certain situations and exploit them to the utmost. This may require considerable ingenuity; it is very difficult to do well.

It seems apparent that there is no "one best way" for all companies, but there are better decision approaches given the constraints and characteristics of the situation. Even so, to the degree a formal, rational, structured approach can be used, the company will be likely to benefit.

QUESTIONS

Discussion Guides on Chapter Content

1. Define and describe each of the following approaches in decision making:
   (a) formal structured
   (b) intuitive-anticipatory
   (c) entrepreneurial-opportunitistic
   (d) disjointed incrementalism
   (e) adaptive search

2. Discuss decision making in small businesses.

3. What are the arguments pro and con on the maximizing approach to decision making?

4. What does the research evidence say about how decisions actually are made?

5. What factors influence the degree to which managers share their decisions with subordinates?

Mind Stretching Questions

1. Describe the decision-making approaches you would expect to find in each of the following organizations and indicate what aspects of their environments lead you to that conclusion:
   (a) U. S. Department of Labor
   (b) Princeton Manufacturing (a small R&D based firm)
   (c) IBM
   (d) AT&T

2. Think about some major decision that you have made recently. How did you go about it? How long and thoroughly did you search? Describe your search efforts and indicate when you made your decision. What do you think your characteristic decision approach is?

CHAPTER

13

The Roles of Consultants and Advocates

INTRODUCTION

Although in many firms the formulation of policies and strategies is entirely an internal affair involving members of the firm's top management, there are increasing instances where additional inputs to these decision processes are obtained. One such source is the outside consultant, operating either as an individual or as a member of a consulting firm. Another is the internal consulting staffs maintained by some, mostly larger, corporations.

To a considerable extent these external and internal consultants take on the role of advocates for particular positions and alternatives. They develop preferred solutions based on a study of the situation and a knowledge of approaches used by other companies. Then they attempt to persuade top management to their viewpoint. Advocacy of this kind may also be introduced by lower level managers and by individual members of the policy making group. What is inherent in all of these instances is that the individual is not in a position to make the decision himself and have it implemented. Thus, he must influence those who can decide to his viewpoint.

VARIETIES OF CONSULTANTS AND THEIR USE

Consulting services are available in a diverse array as a recent compilation by Hollander [1972] indicates.

Consultant suppliers of consulting services
- General management consultants
  - Nonprofit research institutes
  - General management consulting firms
  - Retired or former executives
- Specialized consultants

- Behavioral scientists
- Business historians
- Consulting engineers
- Design consultants
- Economists
- Educational consultants
- Electronic data processing consultants
- Financial, tax, and merger consultants
- Franchising consultants
- Health professions and facilities consultants
- Location, building, and industrial development consultants
- Minority enterprise development consultants
- Personnel and labor relations consultants
  - Executive recruiters
  - Minority employment counselors
  - Executive career counselors
- Physical distribution and transportation consultants
- Promotion and marketing consultants
- Public relations counselors
- Research and development consultants
- Security, protection, and related consultants

Other suppliers of consulting services
- Service businesses in general
- Accountants (management services)
- Advertising agencies
- Banks and financial institutions
- Buying offices
- Customers and distributors
- Data processing organizations
- Export organizations
- Government
- Internal consultants
- Labor unions
- Lawyers
- Real estate brokers, contractors, and landlords
- Suppliers and franchisors
- Trade and professional organizations
- University professors
- Volunteer organizations
- Wives and husbands (to their manager spouses)

This listing is by no means exhaustive, but it does provide an idea of the wide variety of consulting services available. Many of these sources do not exert their influence at the policy making level, however. This is particularly true of the specialized consultants and of certain of the suppliers of consulting services who are not *primarily* involved in consulting work. Yet even the general management consultants may on occasion deal with lower level problems.

Furthermore, the general management consultants do not typically handle all types of problems. Their work tends to concentrate in certain areas and there are a number of kinds of consulting services that are available only from the specialized sources. Table 13-1 contains data on the major focus of a series of 133 client engagements carried out by one office of a general firm. Many of these engagements also involve some degree of strategic planning in the area specified.

The Extent of Consultant Use

Surveys of consultant use suggest that roughly 75 per cent of all firms employ consultants of some kind on something approximating a regular basis [Bureau of National Affairs, Inc., 1971; Gustafson and DiMarco, 1973]. Use appears to be greatest in the personnel management and the accounting and finance areas. The larger companies are more likely to use consultants, and the primary source is a firm regularly engaged in some type of management consulting, although university faculty members and accounting firms are also used with some frequency.

Although surveys of companies tend to indicate that consultants are used primarily on lower level projects where specialized expertise is desired, these data appear to underestimate the policy level influence of the more prestigious

TABLE 13-1
Major Focus of Engagements Carried Out by a General Management Consulting Firm

FOCUS	PER CENT
Compensation—Primarily executive and sales	19
Organization planning	18
Market planning	10
Economic analysis and industry position	10
Electronic data processing and management information	9
General consultation	8
Cost reduction and profit improvement	7
Product marketing	4
Acquisitions and mergers	3
Inventory management and control	3
Facilities planning	2
Management controls	2
Production control	2
Pricing	1
Personnel relations	1
Office procedures	1

general management consulting firms. Higdon [1969] reports data indicating that these consulting firms are used almost universally by the larger corporations even though this use tends to be downplayed and in some cases actually denied. There is a tendency in this country at least for top management to conceal the extent of its reliance on outsiders in developing policies and strategies. On the other hand, in Europe just the reverse appears to be true; there engaging a well-known consultant is often a source of prestige in itself.

Satisfaction with Consultants

Perhaps the best summary of existing attitudes toward consultants is provided by a quote from Higdon [1969:89–90]: "If you approach three business executives, apparently at almost any level, you will find two inclined favorably toward management consultants and one who either doesn't use them, or won't use them, or refuses to talk about them." Among those who do use consultants over 80 per cent of all engagements elicit a generally positive evaluation of the services rendered [Bureau of National Affairs, Inc., 1971].

A frequently heard criticism of consultants is that they tend to view problems too narrowly through the prism of their own particular expertise and orientation, or as Leavitt [1966] puts it through their own "rose-colored blinders." On the other hand, the narrowness of some consulting recommendations may not be so much a function of the limitations of the consultant's perspective as of the way in which the problem is presented by the client and the limits placed on investigation [Wright, 1969]. Clients can force consultants into solutions that are not adequately tailored to the specific situation by over-stressing their own problem definitions and by preventing a broad analysis of the total context, ostensibly at least with the objective of keeping fees down. To the extent search is limited by whatever means, any attempt at rational decision making will suffer. This does not relieve a company of the need to monitor its consultants and check on their recommendations, however [Lebestky and Tuggle, 1975].

GENERAL MANAGEMENT CONSULTING

The greatest external influence on corporate, and probably also governmental, policy making comes from the general management consulting firms. In particular a handful of these firms appear to have obtained an especially strong position. Higdon [1969] identifies these as Booz, Allen & Hamilton; McKinsey & Co.; A.T. Kearney & Co.; Cresap, McCormick and Paget; and Fry Consultants.

How They Operate

The typical procedure when a firm of this kind is engaged is for a group of consultants to work together on the assignment. This engagement team may also include representatives of the client company. The approach is not unlike that under project management, with members rotating in or out of the engagement depending on the phase of the work involved and the type of skills required. Generally, there is an initial diagnostic phase involving considerable interviewing of managers at various levels in the company and perusal of company data, particularly financial data. In addition, efforts are frequently made to relate the company's current position to other companies in the industry or industries in which it operates. In essence what is done is a situation audit of the kind described in Chapters 7 and 8. Ultimately, recommendations are developed that are presented to top management in both oral and written form. In many instances these recommendations represent some form of strategic planning.

The degree to which the consultants become involved in the implementation of their ideas varies. If the proposals advocated are not accepted, of course the engagement ends at that point. If they are accepted, the consultants may monitor the implementation process providing advice at key points and even assist in doing the work. It is rare, however, for a consultant actually to manage the implementation, although this does occur. Basically consultants are planners, not doers. A particularly detailed description of a typical engagement designed to bring about a changed organization structure in an insurance company is provided in a book by Jeremiah O'Connell [1968] entitled *Managing Organizational Innovation.*

As indicated in Table 13-2 the duration of an engagement varies considerably, depending on the depth of the analysis undertaken, the degree of consultant involvement in the implementation phase, and the availability of individual consultants. Since one person may be working on a number of engagements at once, availability may be an important consideration. On the average an engagement typically runs seven or eight months, but the amount of consultant time billed within that period can vary sharply.

Similarly the number of consultants assigned to an engagement may range from one to fifteen or more, depending upon the specific circumstances. The

TABLE 13-2
Duration and Number of Consultants Involved for 133 Engagements

DURATION	PER CENT	NUMBER OF CONSULTANTS	PER CENT
3 months or less	16	1 or 2	13
4 to 6 months	29	3 or 4	37
7 to 9 months	23	5 or 6	25
10 to 12 months	12	7 or 8	12
13 to 15 months	8	9 or 10	4
16 to 18 months	3	11 or 12	4
19 to 24 months	6	13 or 14	4
Over 24 months	3	Over 14	1

typical engagement involves four or five individuals at some time during its course. Some of these may spend as little as an hour, providing advice on a particular aspect. But billings to a single engagement for one individual covering as much as 300 work days are not unheard of either; there is tremendous variability.

Staffing Procedures

The key to how most general management consulting firms operate, and a number of other consulting organizations also, is provided by a rule of thumb regarding the division of income from clients. One third is allocated for staff salaries, one third for administrative expenses and overhead, and the final third to profit [Higdon, 1969]. Profits are divided among the partners with greater proportions going to the more senior partners.

This approach to the division of income tends to foster a staffing strategy that limits the number of partners and attempts to keep the pay of nonpartners from becoming too high. One approach used to achieve these dual objectives is to institute an up or out policy under which nonpartners either become partners or leave the firm when their pay rises to a certain level.

Since those who enter the major firms currently tend to have graduate degrees, frequently from well-known business schools, it is not possible to attract them and keep the better people for any length of time without paying quite well. As a result, turnover can be rather rapid. As soon as an individual is judged to be unlikely to become a partner, efforts are initiated to terminate employment. In one major firm the separation rate per year among nonpartners has consistently run at around 14 per cent. Thus, the average consultant who is not elected to partnership stays a little over three years, and none stay more than nine years [Miner, 1973c].

Election as a partner tends to occur six or seven years after joining the firm when the individual is approximately 35 years old. One in six is elected; the remainder leave the firm. Thus as compensation levels begin to move up, the consultant either becomes a partner with the result that further increases in compensation are shifted to the profit category or he leaves and is replaced by a less high-priced person.

The Successful Consultant

Although information on the kind of people who make successful consultants (and obviously a great many do not) is limited, there are some data on this point [Miner, 1970a; 1970b; 1971a; 1971c]. The best consultants are planners and thinkers but not doers. Practical judgment and the ability to think logically and unemotionally are most important; to a lesser degree general mental ability and imagination are important also. In the social sphere the more successful consultants seem drawn to authority figures, do not like to be alone, and are attracted to relationships with others where they feel supported. But this support is desired for its own sake and is closely related to the attraction to people in positions of status and authority. These are people who are entirely capable of acting independently even though they seek close, approving relationships with those in authority. In addition, they are not attracted by groups of peers; they want to spend their time with those who are at the top, rather than with "the boys." They enjoy getting others to do what they want.

These characteristics appear to make considerable sense in a group of people who spend many of their working hours, and their nonworking hours as well, in social interaction with the leaders of large corporations. Also a group of people whose role requires them to problem solve and to plan at a very practical level, but in most cases to stop short of implementing their ideas. Theirs is the role of advocate and influencer, but moving too far in the direction of actually managing implementation can be viewed as a threat by company management and result in lost clients.

The data of Table 13-3 bring out certain other characteristics of successful consultants. There appears to be a consistent pattern of identification with and membership in prestigious organizations and groups—private preparatory schools, small private colleges, prestigious business schools, the Navy, Air Force, and Marines rather than the Army, and the management group in business. Coupled with this is evidence of considerable upward mobility relative to their fathers; successful consultants have fathers whose educational and occupational attainments have been at a relatively low level [Miner, 1971c]. All this suggests that a driving force for many good consultants is a strong desire to achieve and maintain elite associations. It would appear to be no coincidence that they have accepted employment with, and are behaving in a manner calculated to maintain their association with, a prestigious management consulting firm.

The characteristics that have been described apply to general management consultants in a major firm working primarily in the United States. How widely they apply to consultants generally is not known. It is clear, how-

TABLE 13-3
Statistically Significant Correlations Between Background Factors and Ratings by Superiors of Success as a Consultant

BACKGROUND FACTOR	CORRELATION
Prior experience as a manager in business	0.37
Prior service in the Navy, Air Force, or Marines	0.25
Holding a graduate degree from a well-known professional school	0.44
Holding an undergraduate degree from a small private college	0.30
Graduation from a private preparatory school	0.26
Father's level of educational attainment	−0.21
Father holds or has held a high level position in business	−0.52

SOURCE: Adapted from John B. Miner [1971c:373–374].

ever, that there are limits. Even within this firm, consultants working outside the United States, primarily in Europe, give evidence of succeeding on a somewhat different basis than those in the United States. In this type of client context, being a doer, as opposed to a planner, seems to be much more desirable. This finding is in line with known differences between managers and management systems in the United States and Europe [Kast, 1964].

UNIVERSITY PROFESSORS AS CONSULTANTS

A number of members of university faculties, especially professional school faculties, are actively engaged in consulting work. In a recent survey of Academy of Management members roughly 25 per cent of the professors reported outside income from consulting [Forsgren, 1974]. The extent to which these individuals were involved in consulting and the degree to which they typically provided input to corporate policy decisions varies considerably, however. Much of what university professors do is in some way related to their roles as teachers and is associated with a training or management development effort [McManus, 1973].

Within schools of business administration it is generally accepted policy to encourage faculty members to engage in consulting as a means of keeping informed regarding developments in the business world and also fostering favorable university business relations. Many universities do have policies that limit such consulting to one day a week, however [Roe, 1973].

Generally where companies use university professors as consultants, reactions are positive. On the other hand, management consulting firms are likely to be called upon more frequently than professors and on an overall basis appear to be somewhat preferred [Gustafson and DiMarco, 1973]. Among certain full-time practicing consultants, there is some resentment of professors because they are thought to represent unfair competition; according to this view professors are subsidized through their university salaries and therefore can afford to charge fees lower than those of the regular consultants, thus undercutting their competition. On the other hand, the well-known general management consulting firms have little concern in this regard, and those university professors who are most in demand as consultants charge fees that are fully comparable to those of the senior partners of major firms.

Actually, the primary role that university professors can play is to consult at the leading edge of new developments. Because professors are often researchers and developers of new knowledge, they may be able to provide information on matters that are as yet unknown to others. Furthermore, as a result of their teaching and theoretical interests they may be informed about certain areas well in advance of other consultants. It is in this "leading edge" role that university professors can contribute the most to policy formulation and the development of strategies. In this role the university professor can make a unique contribution.

ORGANIZATION-DEVELOPMENT CONSULTING

A considerable amount has been written in the past few years about the use of organization development in changing organizations. A number of books have been published describing how organization development is carried out and how consultants in this area operate. Some of the more recent additions to this literature are the books by Argyris [1971], French and Bell [1973], Golembiewski [1972], and Margulies and Wallace [1973].

A reading of books such as these reveals several facts:

1. The external consultant role is an important one in organization development. (All of the authors noted above are university professors involved in organization development consulting.)
2. Implementation is a major consideration in organization development. (Thus, we will return to this topic in the chapters that follow dealing directly with policy implementation.)
3. Matters of corporate policy and strategy formulation are not of central concern to many organization-development consultants. (The books noted above barely touch on these matters.)

Even though organization-development consulting and policy formulation are only partially overlapping activities, and the amount of writing on organization development as a whole appears to exceed by far the extent of actual utilization [Hollander, 1972], the organization-development approach does represent a new and different type of input to the policy process. As such it is important to understand what influences consultants of this kind can have on policies and strategies. Organization-development consultants are much like other consultants in their assumption of an advocacy role, but tend to differ considerably from other consultants in what they advocate.

Organization Development as Applied to Policy Formulation

When organization-development consultants do deal directly with policy matters and long-range planning, their approach leads them to involve people at lower levels in the organization much more than the general management consultants do. This is one of the major characteristics distinguishing the two consulting approaches. However, organization-development consultants who concern themselves directly with policy matters also are distinguished by a tendency to utilize an approach that is not nearly as typical of their fellow practitioners who do not have policy formulation as their central concern. The policy consultants utilize a systemic relations orientation in contrast to the more usual human relations orientation of other organization-development practitioners. These two orientations have been differentiated in the following terms [Ganesh, 1971:50]:

Systemic Relations Orientation

The change effort involves the total organization and the consultant works with top management on long-range problems that have implications for the entire organization.

The consultant works in the role of an outsider and neutral helper.

The consultant treats the total organization and its environment as the client system.

The commitment is long term and the consultant works with clients over a period of years with varying degrees of involvement.

The consultant's approach is task oriented.

Human Relations Orientation

The consultant considers organization development as a change effort involving small systems like groups and accordingly focuses more on the implications of the work for the groups themselves and less on implications for the rest of the organization.

The consultant works as an involved helper, as if he were another member of the organization.

The consultant relates as a person to individuals and to small groups as client systems.

Involvement is short term and of a specific type as, for instance, in T-groups and sensitivity training.

The consultant is people oriented rather than task oriented and, accordingly, there is a tendency to work on changes involving interpersonal relationships.

As described by Paine and Naumes [1974] the organization development approach to policy and strategy formation has five major characteristics. Several of these are not unlike those of approaches considered previously in this book. Thus, the effort involves a systematic diagnosis aimed at identifying relevant factors, and then the establishment of action steps that can be expected to lead to improved strategies and their implementation. In short the organization-development process is planned, just as many other policy formation efforts are.

Second, the organization-development approach to policy formation has organization-wide ramifications or, at the very least, ramifications for a major segment of the organization. This too is characteristic of other approaches to policy formation, but it is not nearly as characteristic of organization-development efforts that do not focus directly on policy matters.

Third, as in other approaches to policy development, top management involvement and commitment are important. Although top managers may be the analysts on certain occasions, it is more common for top management to endorse the combined efforts of external consultants and lower level groups.

Fourth, the approach achieves its ends through planned interventions using particular analytical and developmental tools. Here the organization-development approach to policy formation tends to part company with other policy formation approaches; it is more like other kinds of organization-development efforts. However, there is a somewhat greater emphasis on market, economic, and financial factors. The approach to problems is one of sharing information and attempts at solutions widely throughout the firm.

Finally, the approach focuses on coalitions and groups in the decision context rather than on individuals. There is a major concern with establishing problem-solving processes involving group and intergroup interactions out of which corporate strategies will emerge.

The important point here is that the consultant does not serve primarily as an advocate for a particular policy such as expansion through acquisitions, or promotion from within, or a major emphasis on leasing. His advocacy is generally limited to a particular approach to the policy formation process characterized by widespread involvement throughout the organization and a group emphasis in problem solving. "Outside advisors, assessors or consultants often share the responsibility with managers for the problem-solving and development process, but they also work with managers toward increasing the organization's own capacity to diagnose the external and internal environment and to develop and carry through strategic plans of action" [Paine and Naumes, 1974:178].

Values Inherent in Organization-Development Consulting

What has already been said makes it clear that organization development, whatever its central concern, tends to advocate a participative, democratic approach to the management of organizations. The values are humanistic rather than pragmatic, egalitarian rather than hierarchic, democratic rather than authoritarian. An analysis of the writings of prominent organization-development consultants reveals the following as characteristic orientations in introducing change [Miner, 1974a:192]:

1. A more democratic or participative set of values, which is antihierarchy, antibureaucracy, antiauthoritarian, and antiauthority.
2. A greater orientation to and consciousness of the immediate peer and work groups and a commitment to group sources of control.
3. Less individual competitiveness and less use of power by established authority; this has been called power equalization and is reflected in the emphasis on collaboration.

4. More stress on openness and free expression of feelings.
5. An emphasis on individual goals at the expense of organizational goals; thus an emphasis on humanism.

When the organization-development approach is applied to policy formation certain of these values may be muted to varying degrees, but they do not disappear. The reason is that these values tend to be strongly held by the organization-development consultants themselves.

A problem can thus arise when organization-development consultants become involved in the policy and strategy formation processes of certain organizations. The organization-development values often are not held by company managers, in particular top managers, or they are held to a much lesser degree. As a result the organization-development consultant may be met with considerable hostility, the attempt to introduce new approaches to policy formation may fail, and signs of internal conflict within the organization may abound [Evans, 1974; Kegan, 1971; Miner, 1973e]. Injecting organization-development consulting into the policy process of many companies is clearly fraught with many dangers, both for the company and for the consultant. It should be done only after considerable forethought as to possible consequences and their desirability.

THE ROLE OF THE INTERNAL CONSULTANT

The fact that general management consultants may work closely with members of the client company, incorporating them into the engagement team, has been noted. Actually the range of alternatives here is sizable, extending all the way from a completely external effort to a completely internal one. Furthermore, internal consultants may spend all of their time in a consulting role, thus operating in a manner completely analogous to external consultants, except that they serve only one client organization; or the consultant role may be a temporary one involving what amounts to a special assignment.

A number of firms develop special task forces to carry out assignments of exactly the same nature as those a general management consulting firm might undertake. In such cases there is a merging of consulting and staff work such that the two are almost indistinguishable. On occasion such a task force may be joined by an outside consultant. However, where the majority of those involved are insiders and most of the needed expertise rests in the inside group, the external consultant tends to become primarily a guider and expediter [Katcher, 1972].

There has been considerable argument over the merits of internal versus external consulting. A permanent internal consulting staff is not really feasible except in large multiinstallation companies. There must be enough to be done to keep the consultants busy on engagements that do, in fact, utilize their capabilities; otherwise the expense cannot be justified.

The use of internal consultant task forces requires that release time from other duties can be secured for those people who are in a position to make a significant contribution. When policy issues are involved, this may present a problem because those who can contribute the most may well be high-level managers, who have many other ongoing duties. In general it appears that internal consulting of the task force type is most appropriate when the time available is distinctly limited. Internal consultants have the advantage of at least some knowledge of the organization and the people in it. For an external consultant to acquire a comparable level of knowledge may require more time than there is available [Margulies and Wallace, 1973].

There is also reason to believe that internal consultants tend to be preferred to external ones, and probably should be, when an external consultant could constitute a major threat to the existing authority structure [Scurrah, Shani, and Zipfel, 1971]. On occasions an external consultant can achieve success in advocating a particular solution to a current problem and, at the same time, so effectively undermine certain top people in the company that they have difficulty dealing with and implementing solutions to other problems later on. If this seems likely, there may well be advantages in the long run to relying on the internal consultant approach.

CONSULTING AND ADVOCACY

As has been indicated, the consultant role in policy and strategy formation is essentially an advocacy role. Ultimately at some point the consultant has to advocate something, although this may be either an approach to problem solving, as with many organization-development consultants, or a specific problem solution.

When the consultant decides on what is to be advocated varies considerably. Some consultants have their minds made up at the outset; others search widely for information and spend long periods in diagnosis before taking a position. There is in addition the case where the role of the consultant becomes entirely one of advocacy; there is no direct problem solving at all.

This happens when a proponent of a given approach within the company either brings the consultant in specifically for the purpose of advocating that approach, and with that understanding, or so thoroughly convinces the consultant of the value of his approach that the consultant becomes an advocate for it. Consultants, particularly external consultants, can get results because of their prestige that company executives cannot. As Higdon [1969:94–95] points out "Actually it is the task of the consulting firm many times not merely to originate ideas, but uncover ones that have been lying around unnoticed. The executive who claims that his ideas have been pirated may have been unable previously to get the president to listen." Under circumstances such as these the consultant can perform a service for the client company, while operating entirely in the role of advocate, which far exceeds any contribution he might make as problem solver. This depends, of course, on whether a good solution is, in fact, already available in the company.

Techniques of Advocacy

Whether undertaken by an external consultant, an internal consultant, or an involved manager, there are approaches to advocacy that appear to facilitate the chances of success. A major contributor to knowledge in this area has been Frank Gilmore [1970, 1973a], who has worked out his approaches in considerable detail. It is his position that ". . . a report proposing a change in strategy must show that company developments and/or environmental trends challenge the validity of the present strategy; that the core of the strategy problem has been discovered; that the proposed new strategy appropriately meets the need for change; and that the proposed new strategy is practicable for the company" [Gilmore, 1973a:127].

In developing a proposal to advocate such a change, there are certain steps that should be followed, although as indicated in Figure 13-1 some shortcutting may be possible.

The first step is phrasing the proposal. This is a statement of what the company *should* do, such as market its products in certain foreign countries, which it has not previously considered. The second step involves discovering the major issues and deriving arguments to support them. Here the key questions are

1. Are there major challenges to the validity of current strategies?
2. Have the core strategy problems been identified?
3. To what extent does the proposed strategy meet the needs inherent in the current situation?
4. Can the proposed strategy really be implemented by the company? Is it practical?

Then it is necessary to marshal the evidence. Such support for the position advocated may derive from facts, generalizations, opinions, and assumptions, but to the extent data derived from scientifically valid research can be used one is in a better position. Contrary evidence should be acknowledged, and counter arguments presented whenever possible.

The fourth step, once the strategy is formulated, is developing a brief; in other words, organizing the arguments for the proposal in terms of an introduction, a body, and a conclusion. The key point is to present the arguments in a logical manner. These logical arguments are then rearranged for the purpose of appealing to the intended audience in the outline for the report. Here the crucial consideration is persuasion and emotional considerations,

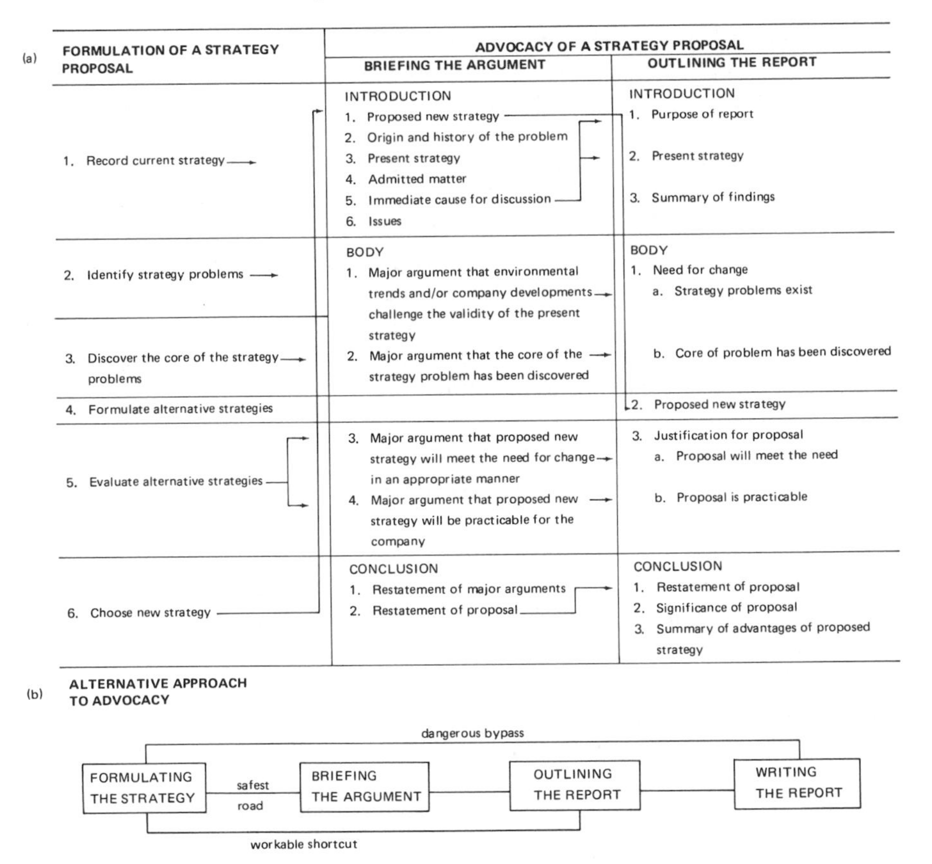

Figure 13-1 **(a)** Relation between formulation and advocacy of strategic proposals and **(b)** some alternative approaches to advocacy. [From Frank F. Gilmore: "Overcoming the Perils of Advocacy in Corporate Planning." *California Management Review,* Spring 1973, p. 136.]

human relations factors and cherished values become relevant. Knowledge of the audience is essential, and the presentation must now take this knowledge into account in addition to the logic inherent in the situation. These two steps, briefing the argument and outlining the report, are described in detail under the heading Advocacy of a Strategy Proposal in Figure 13-1. On occasion the brief can be bypassed, but the outlining stage should not be.

Finally the report must be written or the oral presentation developed. This is a matter of individual style, but the objective is to maximize the effectiveness with which both logical arguments and emotional persuasion are brought to bear. In many cases there is a need for both a formal oral presentation, where questions must be handled also, and a written memorandum. In the case of consulting engagements this kind of dual reporting, oral and written, is almost universal.

Consulting, Advocacy, and Policy Formation

The types of inputs to policy and strategy decisions considered in this chapter can be expected to increase in the future. As top level corporate decisions become more complex, it becomes increasingly important to include diverse inputs. The days when a single individual or a small clique could marshal all the information needed to cope with the multitude of problems companies face are disappearing rapidly. Consulting and advocacy are entirely consistent with the nominal approach to decision making. Since creative decisions are likely to be needed in increasing numbers and the nominal approach seems best suited to these decisions, it follows that consulting and advocacy should, and in all likelihood will, be a major component of policy and strategy decision making in the future.

QUESTIONS

Discussion Guides on Chapter Content

1. Look at the list of suppliers of consulting services at the beginning of this chapter and indicate for each whether you think the supplier exerts influence at the policy level?
2. How do the large general management consulting firms operate?
3. What are the characteristics of a successful consultant?
4. What special advantages and problems does the professor-consultant typically have?
5. What is organization-development consulting and how does it relate to policymaking?
6. What are the advantages and disadvantages of using internal consultants as opposed to external?
7. What are the techniques of advocacy?

Mind Stretching Questions

1. You are the chief executive of a large corporation and feel that you need assistance in strategy planning. What considerations would you take into account in deciding whether or not to use a consultant and in selecting a consultant? What would your decision regarding a consultant be? Why?
2. You are in charge of organization planning for a company and you believe the president's effectiveness is being hampered by too large a span of control (there are now 25 people reporting to him). How would you approach the job of advocating change? What would you propose? How would you propose it? What arguments would you use? Be specific and use your imagination.

Myth of the Well-Educated Manager*

J. Sterling Livingston

Foreward

This article discusses the inability of formal management education programs in both universities and industry to develop explicitly the traits, knowledge, and skills that are essential to career success and leadership in any business organization. In presenting a hard-hitting approach to education and management, this discussion brings us face to face with some of the facts of life about learning in the school room versus learning on the job. Although the author draws on the findings of others, many of the points and ideas expressed are the direct result of his own business observation and experience as a manager, entrepreneur, and teacher.

Mr. Livingston is Professor of Business Administration at the Harvard Business School. In his role as President of Sterling Institute and also as former President of Management Systems Corporation, he has actively managed hundreds of MBA graduates.

How effectively a manager will perform on the job cannot be predicted by the number of degrees he holds, the grades he receives in school, or the formal management education programs he attends. Academic achievement is not a valid yardstick to use in measuring managerial potential. Indeed, if academic achievement is equated with success in business, the well-educated manager is a myth.

Managers are not taught in formal education programs what they most need to know to build successful careers in management. Unless they acquire through their own experience the knowledge and skills that are vital to their effectiveness, they are not likely to advance far up the organizational ladder.

Although an implicit objective of all formal management education is to assist managers to learn from their own experience, much management education is, in fact, miseducation because it arrests or distorts the ability of managerial aspirants to grow as they gain experience. Fast learners in the classroom often, therefore, become slow learners in the executive suite.

Men who hold advanced degrees in management are among the most sought after of all university graduates. Measured in terms of starting salaries, they

* Reprinted from *Harvard Business Review,* January–February 1971, pp. 79–87 by permission of the publisher.

are among the elite. Perhaps no further proof of the value of management education is needed. Being highly educated pays in business, at least initially. But how much formal education contributes to a manager's effectiveness and to his subsequent career progress is another matter.

Professor Lewis B. Ward of the Harvard Business School has found that the median salaries of graduates of that institution's MBA program plateau approximately 15 years after they enter business and, on the average, do not increase significantly thereafter [21]. While the incomes of a few MBA degree holders continue to rise dramatically, the career growth of most of them levels off just at the time men who are destined for top management typically show their greatest rate of advancement.

Equally revealing is the finding that men who attend Harvard's Advanced Management Program (AMP) after having had approximately 15 years of business experience, but who—for the most part—have had no formal education in management, earn almost a third more, on the average, than men who hold MBA degrees from Harvard and other leading business schools.

Thus the arrested career progress of MBA degree holders strongly suggests that men who get to the top in management have developed skills that are not taught in formal management education programs and may be difficult for many highly educated men to learn on the job.

Many business organizations are cutting back their expenditures for management training just at the time they most need managers who are able to do those things that will keep them competitive and profitable. But what is taking place is not an irrational exercise in cost reduction; rather, it is belated recognition by top management that formal management training is not paying off in improved performance.

If the current economy wave prompts more chief executives to insist that management training programs result in measurable improvement in performance, it will mark the beginning of the end for many of the programs which industry has supported so lavishly in the past. As Marvin Bower has observed:

"One management fad of the past decade has been management development. Enormous numbers of words and dollars have been lavished on this activity. My observations convince me that, apart from alerting managers more fully to the need for management development, these expenditures have not been very productive" [3:171].

UNRELIABLE YARDSTICKS

Lack of correlation between scholastic standing and success in business may be surprising to those who place a premium on academic achievement. But grades in neither undergraduate nor graduate school predict how well an individual will perform in management.

After studying the career records of nearly 1,000 graduates of the Harvard Business School, for example, Professor Gordon L. Marshall concluded that "academic success and business achievement have relatively little association with each other" [16]. In reaching this conclusion, he sought without success to find a correlation between grades and such measures of achievement as title, salary, and a person's own satisfaction with his career progress. (Only in the case of grades in elective courses was a significant correlation found.)

Clearly, what a student learns about management in graduate school, as measured by the grades he receives, does not equip him to build a successful career in business.

Scholastic standing in undergraduate school is an equally unreliable guide to an individual's management potential. Professor Eugene E. Jennings of the University of Michigan has conducted research which shows that "the routes to the top are apt to hold just as many or more men who graduated below the highest one third of their college class than above (on a per capita basis)" [9:21].

A great many executives who mistakenly believe that grades are a valid measure of leadership potential have expressed concern over the fact that fewer and fewer of those "top-third" graduates from the better-known colleges and universities are embarking on careers in business. What these executives do not recognize, however, is that academic ability does not assure that an individual will be able to learn what he needs to know to build a career in fields that involve leading, changing, developing, or working with people.

Overreliance on scholastic learning ability undoubtedly has caused leading universities and business organizations to reject a high percentage of those who have had the greatest potential for creativity and growth in nonacademic careers.

This probability is underscored by an informal study conducted in 1958 by W. B. Bender, Dean of Admissions at Harvard College. He first selected the names of 50 graduates of the Harvard class of 1928 who had been nominated for signal honors because of their outstanding accomplishments in their chosen careers. Then he examined the credentials they presented to Harvard College at the time of their admission. He found that if the admission standards used in 1958 had been in effect in 1928, two thirds of these men would have been turned down. (The proportion who would have been turned down under today's standards would have been even higher.)

In questioning the wisdom of the increased emphasis placed on scholastic standing and intelligence test scores, Dean Bender asked, "Do we really know what we are doing?" [quoted in 1, p. 14].

There seems to be little room for doubt that business schools and business organizations which rely on scholastic standing, intelligence test scores, and grades as measures of managerial potential are using unreliable yardsticks.

Career Consequences

False notions about academic achievement have led a number of industrial companies to adopt recruiting and development practices that have aggravated the growing rates of attrition among bright and young managerial personnel. The "High Risk, High Reward" program offered by a large electrical manufacturer to outstanding college graduates who were looking for challenging work right at the beginning of their careers illustrates the consequences of programs that assume that academic excellence is a valid yardstick for use in measuring management potential:

Under this company's program, high-ranking college graduates were given the opportunity to perform managerial work with the assistance of supervisors who were specially selected and trained to assess their development and performance. College graduates participating in the program were assured of promotion at twice the normal rate, provided they performed successfully during their first two years. Since they were to be "terminated" if they failed to qualify for promotion, the program carried high risks for those who participated.

The company undertook this High Risk, High Reward program for two reasons: (1) because its executives believed that ability demonstrated by academic achievement could be transferred to achievement in the business environment, and (2) because they wished to provide an appropriate challenge to outstanding college graduates, particularly since many management experts had contended that "lack of challenge" was a major cause of turnover among promising young managers and professionals.

The candidates for the program had to have a record of significant accomplishment in extra-curricular activities, in addition to a high order of scholarship, and had to be primarily interested in becoming managers. Young men were recruited from a cross section of leading colleges and universities throughout the nation.

Although they were closely supervised by managers who had volunteered to assist in their development, at the end of five years 67% had either terminated voluntarily or had been terminated from their jobs because they had failed to perform up to expectations and were judged not capable of meeting the program's objectives. This rate of attrition was considerably higher than the company had experienced among graduates with less outstanding academic records.

ARRESTED PROGRESS AND TURNOVER: Belief in the myth of the well-educated manager has caused many employers to have unrealistic performance expectations of university graduates and has led many employees with outstanding scholastic records to overestimate the value of their formal education. As a consequence, men who hold degrees in business administration—especially those with advanced degrees in management—have found it surprisingly difficult to make the transition from academic to business life. An increasing number of them have failed to perform up to expectations and have not progressed at the rate they expected.

The end result is that turnover among them has been increasing for two decades as more and more of them have been changing employers in search of a job they hope they "can make a career of." And it is revealing that turnover rates among men with advanced degrees from the leading schools of management appear to be among the highest in industry.

As Professor Edgar H. Schein of the Massachusetts Institute of Technology's Sloan School of Management reports, the attrition "rate among highly educated men and women runs higher, on the average, than among blue-collar workers hired out of the hard-core unemployed. The rate may be highest among people coming out of the better-known schools" [19:14]. Thus over half the graduates of MIT's master's program in management change jobs in the first three years, Schein further reports, and "by the fifth year, 73% have moved on at least once and some are on their third and fourth jobs" [19:95].

Personnel records of a sample of large companies I have studied similarly revealed that turnover among men holding master's degrees in management from well-known schools was over 50% in the first five years of employment, a rate of attrition that was among the highest of any group of employees in the companies surveyed.

The much publicized notion that the young "mobile managers" who move from company to company are an exceptionally able breed of new executives and that "job-hopping has become a badge of competence" is highly misleading. While a small percentage of those who change employers are competent managers, most of the men who leave their jobs have mediocre to poor records of performance. They leave not so much because the grass is greener on the other side of the fence, but because it definitely is brown on their side. My research indicates that most of them quit either because their career progress has not met their expectations or because their opportunities for promotion are not promising.

In studying the career progress of young management-level employees of an operating company of the American Telephone & Telegraph Company, Professors David E. Berlew and Douglas T. Hall of MIT found that "men who consistently fail to meet company expectations are more likely to leave the organization than are those who turn in stronger performances" [2:36].

I have reached a similar conclusion after studying attrition among recent management graduates employed in several large industrial companies. Disappointing performance appraisals by superiors is the main reason why young men change employers.

"One myth," explains Schein, "is that the graduate leaves his first company merely for a higher salary. But the MIT data indicate that those who have moved on do not earn more than those who have stayed put" [19:90]. Surveys of reunion classes at the Harvard Business School similarly indicate that men who stay with their first employer generally earn more than those who change jobs. Job-hopping is not an easy road to high income; rather, it usually is a sign of arrested career progress, often because of mediocre or poor performance on the job.

WHAT MANAGERS MUST LEARN

One reason why highly educated men fail to build successful careers in management is that they do not learn from their formal education what they need to know to perform their jobs effectively. In fact, the tasks that are the most important in getting results usually are left to be learned on the job, where few managers ever master them simply because no one teaches them how.

Formal management education programs typically emphasize the development of problem-solving and decision-making skills, for instance, but give little attention to the development of skills required to find the problems that need to be solved, to plan for the attainment of desired results, or to carry out operating plans once they are made. Success in real life depends on how well a person is able to find and exploit the opportunities that are available to him, and, at the same time, discover and deal with potential serious problems before they become critical.

Problem Solving

Preoccupation with problem solving and decision making in formal management education programs tends to distort managerial growth because it overdevelops an individual's analytical ability, but leaves his ability to take action and to get things done underdeveloped. The behavior required to solve problems that already have been discovered and to make decisions based on facts gathered by someone else is quite different from that required to perform other functions of management.

On the one hand, problem solving and decision making in the classroom require what psychologists call "respondent behavior." It is this type of behavior that enables a person to get high grades on examinations, even though he may never use in later life what he has learned in school.

On the other hand, success and fulfillment in work demand a different kind of behavior which psychologists have labeled "operant behavior." Finding problems and opportunities, initiating action, and following through to attain desired results require the exercise of operant behavior, which is neither measured by examinations nor developed by discussing in the classroom what someone else should do. Operant behavior can be developed only by doing what needs to be done.

Instruction in problem solving and decision making all too often leads to "analysis paralysis" because managerial aspirants are required only to explain and defend their reasoning, not to carry out their decisions or even to plan realistically for their implementation. Problem solving in the classroom often is dealt with, moreover, as an entirely rational process, which, of course, it hardly ever is.

As Professor Harry Levinson of the Harvard Business School points out: "The greatest difficulty people have in solving problems is the fact that emotion makes it hard for them to see and deal with their problems objectively" [11:109–110].

Rarely do managers learn in formal education programs how to maintain an appropriate psychological distance from their problems so that their judgments are not clouded by their emotions. Management graduates, as a consequence, suffer their worst trauma in business when they discover that rational solutions to problems are not enough; they must also somehow cope with human emotions in order to get results.

Problem Finding

The shortcomings of instruction in problem solving, while important, are not as significant as the failure to teach problem finding. As the research of Norman H. Mackworth of the Institute of Personality Assessment and Research, University of California, has revealed "the distinction between the problem-solver and the problem-finder is vital" [15:242].

Problem finding, Mackworth points out, is more important than problem solving and involves cognitive processes that are very different from problem solving and much more complex. The most gifted problem finders, he has discovered, rarely have outstanding scholastic records, and those who do excel academically rarely are the most effective finders.

The importance of a manager's ability to find problems that need to be solved before it is too late is illustrated by the unexpected decline in profits of a number of multimarket companies in 1968 and 1969. The sharp drop in the earnings of one of these companies—Litton Industries—was caused, its chief executive explained, by earlier management deficiencies arising from the failure of those responsible to foresee problems that arose from changes in products, prices, and methods of doing business.

Managers need to be able not only to analyze data in financial statements and written reports, but also to scan the business environment for less concrete clues that a problem exists. They must be able to "read" meaning into changes in methods of doing business and into the actions of customers and competitors which may not show up in operating statements for months or even for years.

But the skill they need cannot be developed merely by analyzing problems discovered by someone else; rather, it must be acquired by observing firsthand what is taking place in business. While the analytical skills needed for problem solving are important, more crucial to managerial success are the perceptual skills needed to identify problems long before evidence of them can be found by even the most advanced management information system. Since these perceptual skills are extremely difficult to develop in the classroom, they are now largely left to be developed on the job.

Opportunity Finding

A manager's problem-finding ability is exceeded in importance only by his opportunity-finding ability. Results in business, Peter F. Drucker reminds us, are obtained by exploiting opportunities, not by solving problems. Here is how he puts it:

"All one can hope to get by solving a problem is to restore normality. All one can hope, at best, is to eliminate a restriction on the capacity of the business to obtain results. The results themselves must come from the exploitation of opportunity. . . . 'Maximization of opportunities' is a meaningful, indeed a precise, definition of the entrepreneurial job. It implies that effectiveness rather than efficiency is essential in business. The pertinent question is not how to do things right, but how to find the right things to do, and to concentrate resources and efforts on them" [5:5].

Managers who lack the skill needed to find those opportunities that will yield the greatest results, not uncommonly spend their time doing the wrong things. But opportunity-finding skill, like problem-finding skill, must be acquired through direct personal experience on the job.

This is not to say that the techniques of opportunity finding and problem finding cannot be taught in formal management education programs, even though they rarely are. But the behavior required to use these techniques successfully can be developed only through actual practice.

A manager cannot learn how to find opportunities or problems without doing it. The doing is essential to the learning. Lectures, case discussions, or text books alone are of limited value in developing ability to find opportunities and problems. Guided practice in finding them in real business situations is the only method that will make a manager skillful in identifying the right things to do.

Natural Management Style

Opportunities are not exploited and problems are not solved, however, until someone takes action and gets the desired results. Managers who are unable to produce effective results on the job invariably fail to build successful careers. But they cannot learn what they most need to know either by studying modern management theories or by discussing in the classroom what someone else should do to get results.

Management is a highly individualized art. What style works well for one manager in a particular situation may not produce the desired results for another manager in a similar situation, or even for the same manager in a different situation. There is no one best way for all managers to manage in all situations. Every manager must discover for himself, therefore, what works and what does not work for him in different situations. He cannot become effective merely by adopting the practices or the managerial style of someone else. He must develop his own natural style and follow practices that are consistent with his own personality.

What all managers need to learn is that to be successful they must manage in a way that is consistent with their unique personalities. When a manager "behaves in ways which do not fit his personality," as Rensis Likert's managerial research has shown, "his behavior is apt to communicate to his subordinates something quite different from what he intends. Subordinates usually view such behavior with suspicion and distrust" [13:90].

Managers who adopt artificial styles or follow practices that are not consistent with their own personalities are likely not only to be distrusted, but also to be ineffective. It is the men who display the "greatest individuality in managerial behavior," as Edwin E. Ghiselli's studies of managerial talent show, who in general are the ones "judged to be best managers" [8:236].

Managers rarely are taught how to manage in ways that are consistent with their own personalities. In many formal education and training programs, they are in fact taught that they must follow a prescribed set of practices and adopt either a "consultative" or "participative" style in order to get the "highest productivity, lowest costs, and best performance" [12:11].

The effectiveness of managers whose personalities do not fit these styles often is impaired and their development arrested. Those who adopt artificial styles typically are seen as counterfeit managers who lack individuality and natural styles of their own.

Managers who are taught by the case method of instruction learn that there is no one best way to manage and no one managerial style that is infallible. But unlike students of medicine, students of management rarely are exposed to "real" people or to "live" cases in programs conducted either in universities or in industry.

They study written case histories that describe problems or opportunities discovered by someone else, which they discuss, but do nothing about. What they learn about supervising other people is largely secondhand. Their knowledge is derived from the discussion of what someone else should do about the human problems of "paper people" whose emotional reactions, motives, and behavior have been described for them by scholars who may have observed and advised managers, but who usually have never taken responsibility for getting results in a business organization.

Since taking action and accepting responsibility for the consequences are not a part of their formal training, they neither discover for themselves what does—and what does not—work in practice nor develop a natural managerial style that is consistent with their own unique personalities. Managers cannot discover what practices are effective for them until they are in a position to decide for themselves what needs to be done in a specific situation, and to take responsibility both for getting it done and for the consequences of their actions.

Elton Mayo, whose thinking has had a profound impact on what managers are taught but not on how they are taught, observed a quarter of a century age that studies in the social sciences do not develop any "skill that is directly useful in human situations" [17:19]. He added that he did not believe a useful skill could be developed until a person takes "responsibility for what happens in particular human situations—individual or group. A good bridge player does not merely conduct post mortem discussions of the play in a hand of contract; he takes responsibility for playing it" [17:32].

Experience is the key to the practitioner's skill. And until a manager learns from his own firsthand experience on the job how to take action and how to gain the willing cooperation of others in achieving desired results, he is not likely to advance very far up the managerial ladder.

NEEDED CHARACTERISTICS

Although there are no born natural leaders, relatively few men ever develop into effective managers or executives. Most, in fact, fail to learn even from their own experience what they need to know to manage other people successfully. What, then, are the characteristics of men who learn to manage effectively?

The answer to that question consists of three ingredients: (1) the need to manage, (2) the need for power, and (3) the capacity for empathy. In this section of the article, I shall discuss each of these characteristics in some detail.

The Need to Manage

This first part of the answer to the question is deceptively simple: only those men who have a strong desire to influence the performance of others and who get genuine satisfaction from doing so can learn to manage effectively. No man is likely to learn how unless he really wants to take responsibility for the productivity of others, and enjoys developing and stimulating them to achieve better results.

Many men who aspire to high-level managerial positions are not motivated to manage. They are motivated to earn high salaries and to attain high status, but they are not motivated to get effective results through others. They expect to gain great satisfaction from the income and prestige associated with executive positions in important enterprises, but they do not expect to gain much satisfaction from the achievements of their subordinates. Although their aspirations are high, their motivation to supervise other people is low.

A major reason why highly educated and ambitious men do not learn how to develop successful managerial careers is that they lack the "will to manage." The "*way* to manage," as Marvin Bower has observed, usually can be found if there is the "*will* to manage." But if a person lacks the desire, he "will not devote the time, energy and thought required to find the way to manage" [3:6].

No one is likely to sustain for long the effort required to get high productivity from others unless he has a strong psychological need to influence their performance. The need to manage is a crucial factor, therefore, in determining whether a person will learn and apply in practice what is necessary to get effective results on the job.

High grades in school and outstanding performance as an accountant, an engineer, or a salesman reveal how able and willing a person is to perform tasks he has been assigned. But an outstanding record as an individual performer does not indicate whether that person is able or willing to get other people to excel at the same tasks. Outstanding scholars often make poor teachers, excellent engineers often are unable to supervise the work of other engineers, and successful salesmen often are ineffective sales managers.

Indeed, men who are outstanding individual performers not uncommonly become "do-it-yourself" managers. Although they are able and willing to do the job themselves, they lack the motivation and temperament to get it done by others. They may excel as individual performers and may even have good records as first-line managers. But they rarely advance far up the organizational hierarchy because, no matter how hard they try, they cannot make up through their own efforts for mediocre or poor performance by large numbers of subordinates.

Universities and business organizations that select managerial candidates on the basis of their records as individual performers often pick the wrong men to develop as managers. These men may get satisfaction from their own outstanding performance, but unless they are able to improve the productivity of other people, they are not likely to become successful managers.

Fewer and fewer men who hold advanced degrees in management want to take responsibility for getting results through others. More and more of them are attracted to jobs that permit them to act in the detached role of the consultant or specialized expert, a role described by John W. Gardner as the one preferred increasingly by university graduates [7].

This preference is illustrated by the fact that although the primary objective of the Harvard Business School is to develop managers, less than one third of that institution's graduates actually take first-line management jobs. Two thirds of them start their careers in staff or specialized nonmanagerial positions. In the three-year period of 1967, 1968, and 1969, approximately 10% of the graduates of the Harvard Business School took jobs with management consulting firms and the management service divisions of public accounting firms. A decade earlier, in the three-year period of 1957, 1958, and 1959, only 3% became consultants.

As Charlie Brown prophetically observed in a "Peanuts" cartoon strip in which he is standing on the pitcher's mound surrounded by his players, all of whom are telling him what to do at a critical point in a baseball game: "The world is filled with people who are anxious to act in an advisory capacity." Educational institutions are turning out scholars, scientists, and experts who are anxious to act as advisers, but they are producing few men who are eager to lead or take responsibility for the performance of others.

Most management graduates prefer staff positions in headquarters to line positions in the field or factory. More and more of them want jobs that will enable them to use their analytical ability rather than their supervisory ability. Fewer and fewer are willing to make the sacrifices required to learn management from the bottom up; increasingly, they hope to step in at the top from positions where they observe, analyze, and advise but do not have personal responsibility for results. Their aspirations are high, but their need to take responsibility for the productivity of other people is low.

The tendency for men who hold advanced degrees in management to take staff jobs and to stay in these positions too long makes it difficult for them to develop the supervisory skills they need to advance within their companies. Men who fail to gain direct experience as line managers in the first few years of their careers commonly do not acquire the capabilities they need to manage other managers and to sustain their upward progress past middle age.

"A man who performs nonmanagerial tasks five years or more," as Jennings discovered, "has a decidedly greater improbability of becoming a high wage earner. High salaries are being paid to manage managers" [9:15]. This may well explain in part why the median salaries of Harvard Business School graduates plateau just at the time they might be expected to move up into the ranks of top management.

The Need for Power

Psychologists once believed that the motive that caused men to strive to attain high-level managerial positions was the "need for achievement." But now they believe it is the "need for power," which is the second part of the answer to the question: What are the characteristics of men who learn to manage effectively?

A study of the career progress of members of the classes of 1954 and 1955 at the Graduate School of Industrial Management at Carnegie Institute of Technology showed that the need for achievement did not predict anything about their subsequent progress in management [4:9]. As Harvard Professor David C. McClelland, who has been responsible for much of the research on achievement motivation, recently remarked:

"It is fairly clear that a high need to achieve does not equip a man to deal effectively with managing human relationships. . . .

"Since managers are primarily concerned with influencing others, it seems obvious that they should be characterized by a high need for power and that by studying the power motive we could learn something about the way effective managerial leaders work" [14:2].

Power seekers can be counted on to strive hard to reach positions where they can exercise authority over large numbers of people. Individual performers who lack this drive are not likely to act in ways that will enable them to advance far up the managerial ladder. They usually scorn company politics and devote their energies to other types of activities that are more satisfying to them. But, to prevail in the competitive struggle to attain and hold high-level positions in management, a person's desire for prestige and high income must be reinforced by the satisfaction he gets or expects to get from exercising the power and authority of a high office.

The competitive battle to advance within an organization, as Levinson points out, is much like playing "King of the Hill" [10:53]. Unless a person enjoys playing that game, he is likely to tire of it and give up the struggle for control of the top of the hill. The power game is a part of management, and it is played best by those who enjoy it most.

The power drive that carries men to the top also accounts for their tendency to use authoritative rather than consultative or participative methods of management. But to expect otherwise is not realistic. Few men who strive hard to gain and hold positions of power can be expected to be permissive, particularly if their authority is challenged.

Since their satisfaction comes from the exercise of authority, they are not likely to share much of it with lower level managers who eventually will replace them, even though most high-level executives try diligently to avoid the appearance of being authoritarian. It is equally natural for ambitious lower level managers who have a high need for power themselves to believe that better results would be achieved if top management shared more authority with them, even though they, in turn, do not share much of it with their subordinates.

One of the least rational acts of business organizations is that of hiring managers who have a high need to exercise authority, and then teaching them that authoritative methods are wrong and that they should be consultative or participative. It is a serious mistake to teach managers that they should adopt styles that are artificial and inconsistent with their unique personalities. Yet this is precisely what a large number of business organizations are doing; and it explains, in part, why their management development programs are not effective.

What managerial aspirants should be taught is how to exercise their authority in a way that is appropriate to the characteristics of the situation and the people involved. Above all, they need to learn that the real source of their power is their own knowledge and skill, and the strength of their own personalities, not the authority conferred on them by their positions. They need to know that overreliance on the traditional authority of their official positions is likely to be fatal to their career aspirations because the effectiveness of this kind of authority is declining everywhere—in the home, in the church, and in the state as well as in business.

More than authority to hire, promote, and fire is required to get superior results from most subordinates. To be effective, managers must possess the authority that comes with knowledge and skill, and be able to exercise the charismatic authority that is derived from their own personalities.

When they lack the knowledge or skill required to perform the work, they need to know how to share their traditional authority with those who know what has to be done to get results. When they lack the charisma needed to get the willing cooperation of those on whom they depend for performance, they must be able to share their traditional authority with the informal leaders of the group, if any exist.

But when they know what has to be done and have the skill and personality to get it done, they must exercise their traditional authority in whatever way is necessary to get the results they desire. Since a leader cannot avoid the exercise of authority, he must understand the nature and limitations of it, and be able to use it in an appropriate manner. Equally important, he must avoid trying to exercise authority he does not, in fact, possess.

The Capacity for Empathy

Mark Van Doren once observed that an educated man is one "who is able to use the intellect he was born with: the intellect, and whatever else is important" [20:13]. At the top of the list of "whatever else is important" is the third characteristic necessary in order to manage other people successfully. Namely, it is the capacity for empathy or the ability to cope with the emotional reactions that inevitably occur when people work together in an organization.

Many men who have more than enough abstract intelligence to learn the methods and techniques of management fail because their affinity with other people is almost entirely intellectual or cognitive. They may have "intellectual empathy" but may not be able to sense or identify the unverbalized emotional feelings which strongly influence human behavior [18:155]. They are emotion-blind just as some men are color-blind.

Such men lack what Norman L. Paul describes as "affective empathy" [18:155]. And since they cannot recognize unexpressed emotional feelings, they are unable to learn from their own experience how to cope with the emotional reactions that are crucial in gaining the willing cooperation of other people.

Many men who hold advanced degrees in management are emotion-blind. As Schein has found, they often are "mired in the code of rationality" and, as a consequence, "undergo a rude shock" on their first jobs [19:92]. After interviewing dozens of recent graduates of the Sloan School of Management at MIT, Schein reported that "they talk like logical men who have stumbled into a cell of irrational souls," and he added:

"At an emotional level, ex-students resent the human emotions that make a company untidy. . . . [Few] can accept without pain the reality of the organization's human side. Most try to wish it away, rather than work in and around it . . . . If a graduate happens to have the capacity to accept, maybe to love, human organization, this gift seems directly related to his potential as a manager or executive" [19:90].

Whether managers can be taught in the classroom how to cope with human emotions is a moot point. There is little reason to believe that what is now taught in psychology classes, human relations seminars, and sensitivity training programs is of much help to men who are "mired in the code of rationality" and who lack "affective empathy."

Objective research has shown that efforts to sensitize supervisors to the feelings of others not only often have failed to improve performance, but in some cases have made the situation worse than it was before [6]. Supervisors who are unable "to tune in empathetically" on the emotional feelings aroused on the job are not likely to improve their ability to empathize with others in the classroom [18:156–157].

Indeed, extended classroom discussions about what other people should do to cope with emotional situations may well inhibit rather than stimulate the development of the ability of managers to cope with the emotional reactions they experience on the job.

CONCLUSION

Many highly intelligent and ambitious men are not learning from either their formal education or their own experience what they most need to know to build successful careers in management.

Their failure is due, in part, to the fact that many crucial managerial tasks are not taught in management education programs but are left to be learned on the job, where few managers ever master them because no one teaches them how. It also is due, in part, to the fact that what takes place in the classroom often is miseducation that inhibits their ability to learn from their experience. Commonly, they learn theories of management that cannot be applied successfully in practice, a limitation many of them discover only through the direct experience of becoming a line executive and meeting personally the problems involved.

Some men become confused about the exercise of authority because they are taught only about the traditional authority a manager derives from his official position—a type of authority that is declining in effectiveness everywhere. A great many become innoculated with an "anti-leadership vaccine" that arouses within them intense negative feelings about authoritarian leaders, even though a leader cannot avoid the exercise of authority any more than he can avoid the responsibility for what happens to his organization.

Since these highly educated men do not learn how to exercise authority derived from their own knowledge and skill or from the charisma of their own personalities, more and more of them avoid responsibility for the productivity of others by taking jobs that enable them to act in the detached role of the consultant or specialized expert. Still others impair their effectiveness by adopting artificial managerial styles that are not consistent with their own unique personalities but give them the appearance of being "consultative" or "participative," an image they believe is helpful to their advancement up the managerial ladder.

Some managers who have the intelligence required to learn what they need to know fail because they lack "whatever else is important," especially "affective empathy" and the need to develop and stimulate the productivity of other people. But the main reason many highly educated men do not build successful managerial careers is that they are not able to learn from their own firsthand experience what they need to know to gain the willing cooperation of other people. Since they have not learned how to observe their environment firsthand or to assess feedback from their actions, they are poorly prepared to learn and grow as they gain experience.

Alfred North Whitehead once observed that "the secondhandedness of the learned world is the secret of its mediocrity" [22:79]. Until managerial aspirants are taught to learn from their own firsthand experience, formal management education will remain secondhanded. And its secondhandedness is the real reason why the well-educated manager is a myth.

REFERENCES

[1] Athos, Anthony G., and Lewis B. Ward: "Corporations and College Recruiting: A Study of Perceptions." Unpublished study being prepared for the Division of Research, Harvard Business School.

[2] Berlew, David E., and Douglas T. Hall: "The Management of Tension in Organization: Some Preliminary Findings." *Industrial Management Review*, Fall 1964.

[3] Bower, Marvin: *The Will to Manage*. New York, McGraw-Hill, 1966.

[4] Dill, William R.: *GSIA Alumni—Their Progress and Their Goals*. Carnegie Institute of Technology, 1962.

[5] Drucker, Peter F.: *Managing for Results*. New York, Harper & Row, 1964.

[6] Fleishmann, E. A., E. F. Harris, and H. E. Burt: *Leadership and Supervision in Industry: An Evaluation of a Supervisory Training Program*, Monograph No. 33. Columbus, Ohio, Bureau of Education Research, The Ohio State University, 1955.

[7] Gardner, John W.: "The Anti-Leadership Vaccine." *1965 Annual Report*, Carnegie Corporation of New York.

[8] Ghiselli, Edwin E.: In Wolfle, op. cit.

[9] Jennings, Eugene E.: *The Mobile Manager*. Ann Arbor, Mich., Bureau of

Industrial Relations, University of Michigan, Graduate School of Business Administration, 1967.

[10] Levinson, Harry: "On Becoming a Middle-Aged Manager." *Harvard Business Review,* July-August 1969.

[11] Levinson, Harry: *Executive Stress.* New York, Harper & Row, 1970.

[12] Likert, Rensis: *The Human Organization.* New York, McGraw-Hill, 1967.

[13] Likert, Rensis: *New Patterns of Management.* New York, McGraw-Hill, 1969.

[14] McClelland, David C.: "The Two Faces of Power." Unpublished manuscript, Harvard University, September 15, 1968.

[15] Mackworth, Norman H.: "Originality." In Wolfle op. cit.

[16] Marshall, Gordon L.: "Predicting Executive Achievement." Unpublished doctoral thesis, Harvard Business School, June 1964.

[17] Mayo, Elton: *The Social Problems of an Industrial Civilization.* Boston, Division of Research, Harvard Business School, 1945.

[18] Paul, Norman L.: "The Use of Empathy in the Resolution of Grief." *Perspectives in Biology and Medicine,* Autumn 1967 (The University of Chicago Press).

[19] Schein, Edgar H.: "How Graduates Scare Bosses," *Careers Today,* Vol. 1, No. 1.

[20] Van Doren, Mark: *Liberal Education.* Boston, Beacon Press, 1967

[21] Ward, Lewis B.: "Analysis of 1969 Alumni Questionnaire Returns." Unpublished report to the Faculty, Harvard Business School, 1970.

[22] Whitehead, Alfred North: *Aims of Education and Other Essays.* New York, Macmillan, 1929.

[23] Wolfle, Dael (ed.): *The Discovery of Talent.* Cambridge, Mass., Harvard University Press, 1969.

Reforming the Strategic Planning Process: Integration of Social Responsibility and Business Needs*

Ian H. Wilson

One of the prime organizational imperatives for the development of a responsive, operational 'corporate social policy' must be reform of the strategic planning process. Indeed, I would argue that this reform is *the* essential prerequisite to making that true integration of social responsibility and business needs, without which a social policy is all too liable to turn into an empty public relations gesture.

I should point out, at the outset, that there are *other,* important reasons for reforming the business planning process in most companies; and there are other aspects of reform than those I shall mention. What is included in this paper must *not,* therefore, be construed as the total picture of strategic planning, reformed or otherwise.

Before going on to delineate the nature of the reform I have in mind, I should perhaps indicate the reasons for my focus on the strategic planning process. In brief, my reasoning is as follows:

1. *The pace, complexity and pervasiveness of change dictate some important shifts in business planning.* Because change is so rapid, planning must be more farseeing, operating with a more distant time-horizon than previously (i.e. it must, in the first instance, focus on strategy, not on tactics). Because change is multi-dimensional and complex, planning must consider a broader set of inputs than previously (more on this later). Because of the uncertainties caused by change, planning must be better prepared to deal with 'alternative futures' (i.e. contingency planning must be more detailed and explicit).
2. *The concept of corporate social responsibility is being broadened and deepened.* Up until recently it was defined almost exclusively in quantitative, material terms (i.e. improving the material standard of living for the

* SOURCE: *Long Range Planning,* October, 1974, pages 2–6. Reprinted by permission.

majority), with lesser degrees of emphasis on certain 'peripheral' areas of corporate performance (e.g. educational and cultural support, community activities). Now, however, the corporation's social charter is being redefined to include a range of qualitative expectations concerning the scope and objectives of a company's business, its style of operations, its governance, its support for social objectives.

3. *Questions of social responsibility are no longer peripheral, but central to decisions about corporate planning and performance.* This is not to say that the corporation has, or should, become a non-profit charitable institution. Indeed, to argue—pro or con—in those terms would be to misconstrue the new social charter as being merely an extension of the old, peripheral 'do-good' concept. Rather, this proposition asserts that social responsibility and business needs are now so intertwined that they cannot logically be separated; and that both factors must be weighed, simultaneously, at the primary level of corporate planning—that is, the formulation of strategies and the process of resource-allocation. Or to put the matter another way: virtually all business decisions are now infused with social significance; and, on the other hand, matters of social responsibility are now of such importance and concern to management that they must be handled in a business-like manner. If, as has been said, 'social responsibility is too important to be left to the PR staff', it is equally true that strategic business decisions are too important (to the corporation) to be made without reference to the potential impact of changing societal conditions.

THE NEED FOR A 'FOUR-SIDED FRAMEWORK'

Obvious though this last assertion may appear, it is a fact that virtually all that passes for long-range planning today still ignores or minimizes this vital ingredient. Typically, corporate planning is based essentially on only two sets of inputs—economic and technological. Thus, economic forecasting will supply, at the macroeconomic level, projections of future Gross National Product, consumption and investment expenditures, productivity, inflation, and so on; while marketing research will focus more sharply on analyses of the relative attractiveness of mature, developing and potential markets. Technological forecasting is expected to supply as planning inputs predictions about state-of-art developments in new products, new systems, new materials; forecasts of completion dates for the company's development projects; and assessments of competitors' technical competence, domestically and world-wide.

These two areas, supplemented by financial forecasts (which are, after all, also economic forecasts—at the microeconomic level), have been presumed to give us all the hard data we need for planning purposes. For the rest, great reliance has been placed on the assumption of 'other things being equal'. Yet, if businessmen have learned one thing from the tumultuous sixties, it surely should be that other things have an uncomfortable habit of *not* being equal. An otherwise soundly conceived plan based on these two sets of conventional inputs can be very vulnerable to attack on its open flanks—the social and political flanks—for it is there that the tumult and the change has perhaps been greatest, from a business point of view.

Both business logic and changing public expectations would seem to suggest that strategic plans should be formulated only within a framework of four major parameters—social, political, economic, technological. (In fact, even this is a simplistic model; and we have elaborated on it in our planning system at General Electric.) On the one hand, business planning has always been concerned with the assessment of risk; if there are now new dimensions to risk, it is a matter of elementary prudence to introduce a new element to the forecasting process. On the other hand—and perhaps more germane to our discussion today—if public expectations of corporate performance are now broader and more sophisticated, strategic planning should establish a broader set of performance criteria and goals, and seek more sophisticated data on the two new parameters (social and political) which, I have suggested, must be added to the planning framework.

Rather than further elaborate the theory, let me illustrate it by the example of what we are trying to do in this regard at General Electric. We have made it a requirement that the first step in the planning process should be the development of a long-term environmental forecast; and that this forecast should make explicit the environmental assumptions upon which all corporate strategies—marketing, manpower, technological, financial and 'social'—should be based.

In developing this required long-term forecast for our planning cycle last year we produced nine separate views of aspects of the future business environment—'tunnel visions' of the future—dealing with probable developments in nine distinct spheres: international, defense, social, political, legal, economic, technological, manpower and financial. In each of these segments we tried to (a) give a brief historical review (1960–1970) as a jumping-off point for our analysis of the future; (b) analyze the major future forces for change—a benchmark forecast for 1970–1980; (c) identify the potential discontinuities, events which might have low probability, but high significance for General Electric; and (d) raise the first-order questions and policy implications suggested by these forecasts.

These were, by definition, *segmented* views of the future: as such, they would have been quite inadequate for planning in a world and society in which the *interrelatedness* of trends and institutions is a distinctive characteristic. To pull together the separate forecasts in these nine segments, and to blend quantitative and qualitative data, we used cross-impact analyses and scenarios as integrative mechanisms for our work.

From the hundreds of specific trends and events identified in the nine environmental segments we identified the 75 or so that had the highest combined weighting of probability and importance. (Some events that were quite probable had little significance for General Electric; while others of low probability would have critical importance should they occur.) A cross-impact analysis examined these 75 trends/events, asking 'If event A occurs, what will be the impact on the other 74? Will the probability of their occurrence increase? decrease? remain the same?' In effect, this process enabled us to build sets of 'domino chains', with one event triggering another, and then to construct a small number of consistent configurations of the future.

It is essential, as I have noted, to deal with 'alternative future', rather than rely on a single, simplistic set of environmental assumptions. The use of multiple scenarios, of the type developed by Herman Kahn, is a useful technique for presenting such alternatives, and for integrating the 'hard' data of technological, economic and financial forecasting with the 'soft' data of social and political analyses. In the end we developed four alternative scenarios; and—as a commentary on the uncertainty of the future—we rated even our benchmark (or 'most probable') forecast no better than a 50 per cent probability.

There are many advantages, it seems to me, in commencing the strategic planning process with an environmental analysis such as this. In terms of defining corporate social policy, the utility of this analysis lies in:

- making explicit *all* the environmental assumptions on which corporate planning and policy-making should be based;
- integrating the 'social' factors and the 'business' factors into the planning framework;
- confronting future corporate problems as a system of interrelated issues and pressures (i.e. seeing them 'as a piece', rather than piecemeal), with all their attendant complexities and 'trade-offs';
- identifying the spectrum of probable future constraints *and opportunities* for corporate performance;
- providing an opportunity, early in the planning cycle, for determining needed corporate responses to changing conditions.

Social responsibility is, I believe, best defined in terms of *'social responsiveness'*—that is, in the ability of the corporation to respond, constructively and opportunely, to changing societal needs and expectations.

BROADENING THE CONCEPT (AND EVALUATION) OF 'STRATEGY'

The societal needs and expectations can be for new goods and services, in either the public or the private domain; or they can be for new 'styles' of corporate performance and policy. Together, they form a total package of expectations; togther they constitute the charter according to which society expects the corporation to perform. The interlocking nature of these expectations is the fundamental reason why the planning framework must be enlarged to include new inputs and new perceptions of the future. It is also the reason why we need to conceive of 'strategy' in broader terms.

It is not merely that we must have a more distant time-horizon for our strategy, though that is undoubtedly true. To try to ensure that our short-term actions do not lead us ultimately into traps or blind alleys, we surely do need to speculate about the future ten years hence at least. More fundamentally, however, we must rid ourselves of the dangerous notion that strategy applies only to the economic and technological aspects of a business.

In our approach to strategy we currently suffer from the same sort of limitation that, I suggested, afflicts our planning framework. We are prepared, that is, to acknowledge the necessity for strategy as it applies to investment, technology, production and marketing. For the other aspects of a business, we seem content to rely on tactics and improvisation. However, if I am anywhere near being right about the pace and nature of the change in public expectations of corporate performance, such an approach—or lack of an approach—is almost precisely designed to maximize the amount of *re*action in corporate policy-making, and minimize the number of corporate initiatives; to maximize the constraints and added costs on the business, and minimize the opportunities for creating new markets, utilizing new resources, willing new vitality and new public acceptance.

In General Electric we have defined strategy as 'that activity which specifies for a business a course of action that is designed to achieve desired long-term objectives in the light of all major external and internal factors, present and future'. In such a definition there is no restriction on the scope of objectives and courses of action, limiting them only to, say, financial goals, technological objectives and marketing strategies. It implies, indeed encourages, the notion that we need strategies for the *totality* of a business including, importantly, strategies for manpower development, for labor-management relations, for organization development, for business–government relations, for community action programs, and for dealing with the developing issues of corporate governance.

This broader definition of strategy is underscored when one considers that the first element of strategy must be a definition of 'mission'. The mission of a business determines its long-term goals and objectives: it, at once, raises questions about the scope and nature of a company's activities, about the 'style' of its operations, about the proper 'mix' of objectives. Add to this the fact that an important end-result of strategic planning is the allocation of corporate resources, and it becomes even clearer that *all* elements of strategic alternatives must be considered, simultaneously and on an equal footing, if we are to arrive at a balanced and viable set of corporate objectives. In developing a course of strategic action it is necessary to discuss the allocation of manpower resources as well as of financial and facilities resources; to confront social and political constraints as well as competitive forces; to determine what is appropriate social action as well as adequate market penetration; to access management style as well as the styling of products. These are *all* matters of strategic importance to the corporation; and the strategic planning process must, therefore, be made to embrace them all.

There is a third and final enlargement of scope that is needed to reform the strategic planning process, and that is the criteria used for strategy evaluation. In assessing the relative merits of alternative strategies we are used to considering their impact on corporate growth; market position; return on investment; cash flow; and earnings per share. However, in view of what I have termed the new dimensions to risk, we need to add to these criteria an assessment of each strategy's social responsiveness, political viability and employment attractiveness.

To understand the significance of these new criteria, consider some of the questions that might be asked under each of these headings:

1. Social Responsiveness

- To what extent will the strategy increase the company's ability to contribute toward the attainment of national goals and the serving of 'social needs' markets?
- Will the strategy increase or decrease involvement in products and manufacturing facilities that are inherently more polluting?
- What impact will the strategy have on the company's 'social legitimacy', i.e. its recognition and public acceptance as a major social asset?

2. Political Viability

- Will prospective expansion of government regulations and controls tend to raise the level of risk, and so impair the attractiveness, of the strategy?
- Will the strategy raise or lower the level of exposure to antitrust action?
- How will the policies and programs needed to implement the strategy impact on the acceptability of corporate objectives to government leaders?

3. Employment Attractiveness

- Will the strategy tend to enhance the company's public and campus image as a good place to work?
- Will the strategy tend to enhance the company's ability to attract needed talents and skills?
- Will the challenge and excitement of the corporate mission and objectives tend to increase employee morale, and so the level of commitment and productivity?

If society is going to evaluate corporate performance against a broader set of criteria, it surely makes good business sense for management to ward off future problems—or to seize anticipated opportunities—by building these criteria into its own strategy evaluation process. The fact that there are no simple, quantifiable answers to such questions certainly complicates the task: however, it in no way diminishes the need for it.

SOCIAL PRESSURES AND CORPORATE PRIORITIES

In a pluralistic society such as ours it is predictable that the criteria by which corporate performance is judged at any one time will be many and varied. The social pressures on the corporation will also shift over time. In the face of such variety and shifting, it is essential that there should be located in the strategic planning process some systematic means of assigning corporate priorities to these pressures. Almost certainly the demands that are made on the corporation at any one time will exceed its ability to respond, equally and effectively, to all: it is doubtful if the corporation can ever be *all* things to *all* men—and women. Furthermore, there is a legitimate question to be raised about the societal ranking of these demands: not every demand is equally valid, or pressed with equal vigor.

In an effort to meet this need for priority-analysis, we are experimenting with a systematic screening and analysis procedure whose main elements are shown in Figure 1. Essentially, this is an attempt to supply a rational, systematic and (as nearly as possible) objective evaluation of social pressures, with a view to determining priorities for corporate response in the development of strategy or making of policy.

The first step in the process is the building-up of an inventory of social pressures as expressed in the major complaints commonly made about corporate performance. At this stage we have aimed to be as comprehensive and inclusive as possible, preferring not to omit any, and have grouped the pressures into eight principal categories: Marketing/Financial, Production Operations, Employee Relations/Working Conditions, Governance, Communications, Community and Government Relations, Defense Production, and International Operations.

Next comes the identification of the major demands and hazards associated with these complaints. In this context, 'demands' are defined as the range of solutions advocated to remedy the defect that is complained about (e.g. Federal chartering, to curb 'market power'; stringent emissions standards, to control pollution; job enlargement, to upgrade the challenge in 'boring, dehumanizing work'). 'Hazards', on the other hand, are the adverse consequences that might flow from inadequate corporate response to some of these demands: a good example would be the progressive alienation of employees, and lowering of productivity, that would flow from failure to meet the new and growing demands for 'meaningful, significant work assignments'. At this state of our research the total number of identified demands and hazards is on the order of one hundred.

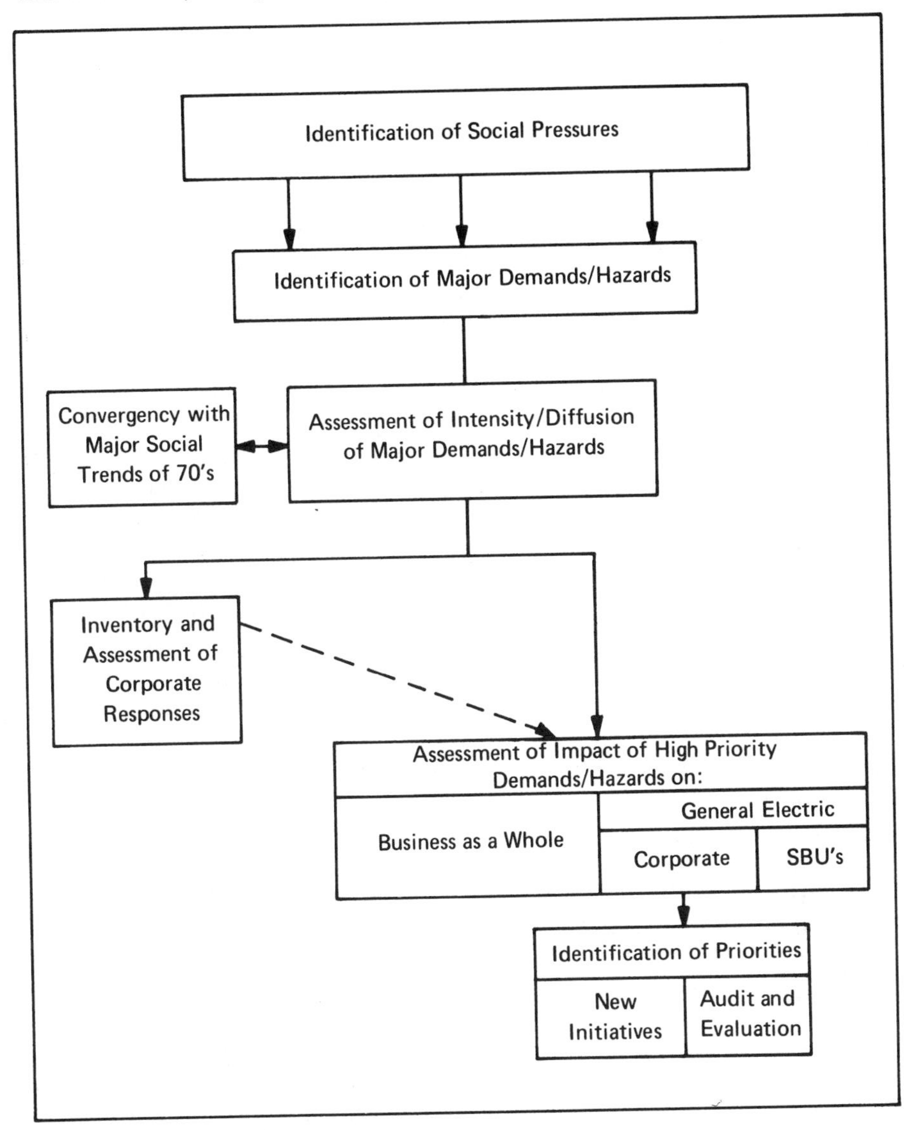

Figure 1 Social pressures on business. A systematic analysis for corporate priorities.

The third step is a two-phase screening process that is performed on each one of these demands and hazards. In an effort to arrive at their relative societal validity and ranking, we have assessed each one in terms of:

(a) its *'convergence' with the major social trends of the seventies*. To what extent are *thirteen* major trends * likely to accelerate or impede the reali-

* Increasing affluence; Rising level of education; Proliferating technology; Emergence

zation of each demand or hazard? The impact of each trend on each demand is assigned a numerical score from 1–10, either positive or negative depending on whether the impact is accelerating or impeding. An aggregate 'convergence' score is then computed for each demand/hazard.

(b) *the intensity/diffusion of pressure behind it.* To what extent are fourteen major constituencies/pressure groups † of the corporation likely to press for this demand? Each demand is ranked 4–3–2–1 according to whether it might be included in the top, second, third or bottom quartile of each group's demands and interests. An aggregate 'intensity/diffusion' score is then computed for each demand.

As a result of this third step it is possible to plot each demand on a scoring sheet using the two aggregate scores for 'convergence' and 'intensity/diffusion'. It may appear that we have become obsessed with quantification, but we fully recognize that this numerical scoring is only a means to the end. The important point is, *not* the precise score assigned to each demand, but its final position *in relation to the median* score on both axes. In other words, our purpose is to identify, and focus on, those demands that fall in the 'high/high' quadrant of the chart, scoring high on both convergence with major trends and intensity/diffusion of pressure.

The fourth and fifth steps are then performed only on these high priority demands. (This is not to say that we can wholly ignore demands falling in the other three quadrants, only that they would, on current assessment, appear to have a lower order of societal validity and ranking.) These two assessment steps deal with:

- the impact of these demands on the business community as a whole, and on General Electric (at both the corporate level and on the Strategic Business Units, the operating components of the company);
- an inventory and evaluation of corporate responses (to date) to these demands.

So far the impact analysis has been done only on a rudimentary basis, assessing the high priority demands on a low to high impact scale; and the evaluation of corporate responses is in process, and is, in a sense, a never-ending task.

The outcome of this whole process should be at least an approximation to

---

of 'post-industrial society' (services economy); Growing interdependence of institutions (incl. business–government partnerships); Increasing emphasis on individualism; Growing pluralism (groups, organizations) and diversity of life styles; The 'equality revolution'; Growing emphasis on 'quality of life' (ecology, culture, education, Maslow's Levels 4 and 5); Redefinition of work/Leisure patterns; Continued increase in foreign competition; Growing/changing role of government; Continued urbanization.

† Consumer Groups; Share Owners; Government; Unions; Blue Collar Workers; Managers and Professional workers; Small Business; Minorities; Women; College Youth; Environmental Groups; Populists; Academic Critics; 'Moralists'.

a set of corporate priorities on social pressures which should be factored into strategic planning and decision making. Based on the evaluation of corporate responses to date, it should also be possible to differentiate between those areas in which new initiatives are clearly called for, and those in which the main need is continuing audit and evaluation of existing responses.

CONCLUSION

In these cursory remarks about some needed changes in the strategic planning process, my focus has been (a) on some changes needed to reflect social factors more adequately in decision making, and (b) on methodology, process, system. Nothing that I have proposed will *guarantee* the development of a 'corporate social policy' which all, or most, might consider adequate to the times: it will, however, make it more likely. I have, after all, been dealing with only one of many organizational imperatives: these reforms are, therefore, necessary, though not sufficient prerequisites. The basic fact remains: if ever social responsibility factors and 'traditional' business needs are to be considered on anything like an equal footing, they must be integrated at that stage of corporate planning that determines strategies, policies and resource-allocation.

READING 4

What Program Budgeting Is and Is Not*

David Novick

During the 1960s the concept of program budgeting generated substantial interest, speculation, experimentation, and literature in business and at all levels of government throughout the western world. With the widespread introduction of this new management idea after the middle of the decade, a great variety of activities were undertaken in its name. Some of the proposals, however, bore little resemblance to it other than the use of the words *program budgeting* as part of an argument for changes in management that were not at all program budgeting or the planning-programming-budgeting system. (PPBS).†

WHAT PROGRAM BUDGETING IS

Program budgeting is a management system that has ten distinctive major features. These are:

1. Definition of an organization's objectives in terms as specific as possible.
2. Determination of programs, including possible alternatives, to achieve the stated objectives.
3. Identification of major issues to be resolved in the formulation of objectives and/or the development of programs.
4. An annual cycle with appropriate subdivisions for the planning, programming, and budgeting steps to ensure an ordered approach and to make appropriate amounts of time available for analysis and decision making at all levels of management.
5. Continuous reexamination of program results in relationship to anticipated costs and outcomes to determine need for changes in stated programs and objectives as originally established.
6. Recognition of issues and other problems that require more time than is available in the annual cycle so that they can be explicitly identified and

* *Current Practices in Program Budgeting (PPBS),* edited by David Novick. Copyright © 1973, The Rand Corporation, published by Crane, Russak and Company, Inc., New York, N.Y. 10017. Reprinted by permission.

† PPBS is the more common usage in the United States and many other countries. Programme budgeting is widely used in England. In France, it is "Rationalization des Choix Budgetaires" (RCB). Program budgeting (PB) will be the preferred usage herein.

set apart from the current period for completion in two or more years, as the subject matter and availability of personnel require.

7. Analysis of programs and their alternatives in terms of probable outcomes and both direct and indirect costs.
8. Development of analytical tools necessary for measuring costs and benefits.
9. Development each year of a multiyear program and financial plan with full recognition of the fact that in many areas resource allocations in the early years (e.g., years one through five) require projections of plans and programs and their resource demands for ten or more years into the future.
10. Adaptation of existing accounting and statistical-reporting systems to provide inputs into planning and programming, as well as continuing information on resources used in and actions taken to implement programs.

The General Approach

Traditional budgeting is aimed largely at efficiency in carrying out specific tasks. It is an appropriation rather than a policy-making approach. Program budgeting sets its sights on larger purposes, the objectives of an organization. These are stated in terms of available alternatives, which in turn are appraised in cost-benefit considerations. Once the issues involved in establishing policy are illuminated, the decision makers can better make the overall decisions. When these are placed in a context of available resources, the next steps to efficiency in operation or performance can be taken as they usually are. That is, in the terms of the traditional budget.

To carry out the major objectives of program budgeting, three general areas of administrative and operational activities are involved. These are program format, analysis, and information and reporting.

1. *Program format* concerns the organization's objectives and the programs established to meet them. Program budgeting begins with an effort to identify and define objectives and to group the organization's activities into programs that can be related to each objective. This aspect of the system is revolutionary, since it requires groupings by end product or output rather than, as in traditional budget practice, by line items of input arranged in terms of object classes, administrative organizations, or activities. The new method allows us to look at *what* is produced—output—in addition to *how* it is produced—which *inputs* we consume.

One of the strengths of program budgeting is that it cuts across organizational boundaries, drawing together the information needed by decision makers without regard to divisions in operating authority among jurisdictions. Examining a program as a whole has its obvious advantages. Contradictions are more likely to be recognized, and a context is supplied for consideration of changes made possible only by cutting across existing agency line barriers.

The purpose of program budgeting is to identify and understand relationships and interdependencies. That is, to consider individual items in terms of related activities and the totality. For example, in planning for a local government, the program budget considers not only the customary issues of land utilization, aesthetics, and architectural design, but goes beyond them into the economic and social consequences of the physical changes in structures, streets, and neighborhoods. Once such effects are identified, decisions can be reached on whether or not the output is worthwhile, and if it is, how much of the organization's limited resources should be appropriated to it.

The program-budgeting summary document presents resources and costs categorized according to the program or end product to which they apply. This contrasts with traditional budgets that assemble costs by type of input—line item—and by organizational or object categories. The point of this restructuring of budget information is that it focuses attention on competition for resources among programs and on the effectiveness of resource use with programs. The entire process by which objectives are identified, programs are defined and quantitatively described, and the budget is recast into a program-budget format is called the format or structural phase of program budgeting.

An outstanding feature of program budgeting is an emphasis on analysis at all stages of activity. Although it is sometimes not recognized, the developments of the appropriate format or structure in and of itself requires analysis. The examination of an organization's objectives and the identifying of its programs and program elements can constitute a major contribution to improvement of management even when the more complete analytical capability contemplated in the program budget is not fully developed.

One product of the structural phase is a conversion matrix or crosswalk from the budget in program terms to the traditional line-item, organization, and object-class budget. In program budgeting, organization gives way to program, and line-item detail is aggregated into summary figures more appropriate to policy-making decisions.

For example, the wages and salaries figure for the environment program in Figure 1 is not only the sum of personnel service payments in the program elements which constitute environment-oriented activities in water, air, land, pollution, etc., but also an aggregation of pieces of the wages and salaries data in each operating department whose activities contribute to environmental control. If Figure 1 were not abbreviated, the illustration would include the contributions from other departments and supporting services such as central electronic data processing. Detail is not the purpose, however, and such activities are instead grouped into a general support program.

Program structures rarely conform to the appropriation pattern or to the organizational structure. Therefore, the program presentation of activities and resource requirement cannot be interrelated with budget data on appropriation and/or organization except by the crosswalk. As indicated earlier, the program structure provides insight into the objectives of the organization; and the allocation of budget authority to programs provides a measure of the

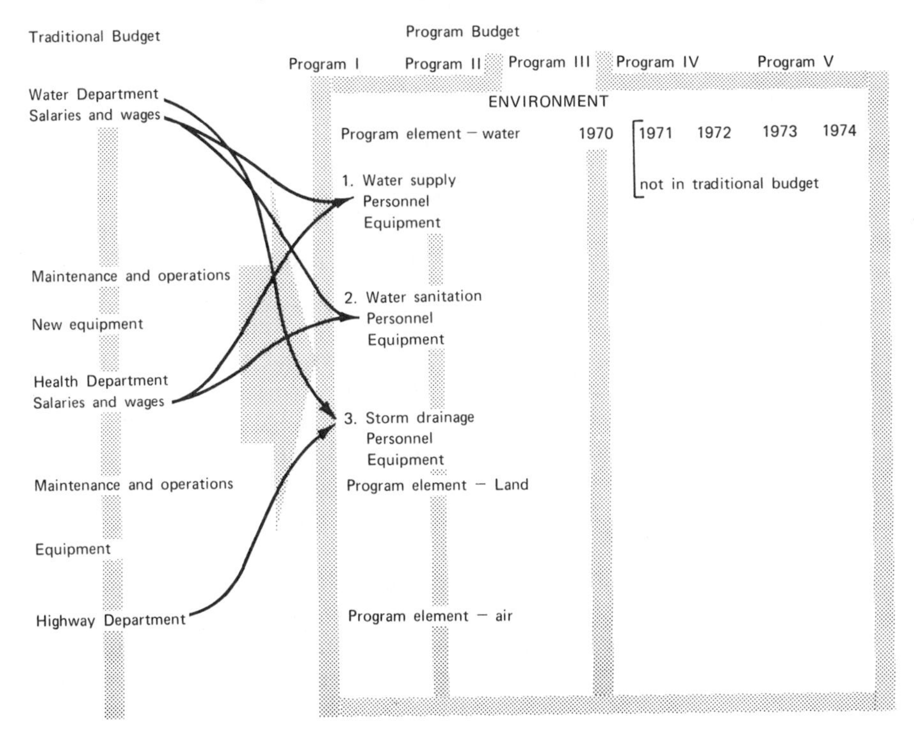

Fig. 1 reproduced from *Management: A Book of Readings* by H. Koonz and C. O'Donnell, 3rd ed. copyright 1972 by McGraw-Hill Inc. Used with permission of McGraw-Hill Book Company

Figure 1 Crosswalk: traditional line-item budget to new program budget.

organization's priorities. The selected agency budgets grouped by program categories in the U.S. federal budget documents are an example of the crosswalk at a very high level of aggregation [1].

The crosswalk prepared for the members of the Pennsylvania Legislature as part of their program budget for 1971–1972 may be the most useful illustration available. It is set out in terms of organizations, appropriations, Commonwealth (of Pennsylvania) major programs, and program subcategories [2].

To aggregate the multitude of line items of the traditional budget or even the summaries of its operating departments into their program-element contributions or costs, it is necessary to make allocations, and some of them may be rather arbitrary ones. The important features of the crosswalk are (1) to have the two documents balance no matter what the dimensions of the classifications, and (2) to ensure that decision makers and reviewing entities can identify next year's traditional budget in program terms, and vice versa.

By use of the crosswalk we also are able to convert data in existing records and reports into that needed for program planning. It permits program decisions to be translated into methods already in use for directing, authorizing, controlling, recording, and reporting operations. If the management methods currently being used in any of these areas are inadequate or unsatisfactory, they should be improved, whether or not the organization has a program-budgeting system. In any case, the program budget must derive its information and relationships from existing management records and practices and must rely on them for the implementation of the programs [3].

2. The second area of the general approach is *analysis*. The program-budgeting method of decision making subsumes a systems-analysis capability with which the resource and cost implications of program alternatives and their expected "outputs" or accomplishments may be estimated, examined, and compared. When a system-analysis capability does not exist or is inadequate, it should be created or upgraded, since analysis is the most important part of this approach to management decisions. A wide range of techniques is employed in these program analyses, including statistical analysis, modeling, gaming, simulation, operations analysis, and econometrics. Both the resource-cost side and the benefit-effectiveness side of program consequences are analyzed.

Quantification is sought wherever possible, but many matters do not readily lend themselves to quantitative measurement. In these instances, qualitative analysis is required. In every case, whether the analysis is quantitative, qualitative, or an appropriate mixture of the two, there is to be explicit identification of the problem, the alternative ways of resolving it, and an attempt to measure the cost and effectiveness of each possibility.

Program analysis is not confined to predetermined alternatives; development of new and better alternatives is part of the process. It is likely that analysis of possibilities A, B, and C will lead to the invention of alternatives D and E, which may be preferable (more cost effective) to the original candidates. Therefore, the analysis part of program budgeting cannot be viewed merely as the application of a collection of well-defined analytical techniques to a problem. The process is much more flexible and subtle, and calls for creativity by the managers and the analysts and interaction between analysts and decision makers during the process.

3. The third part of the program-budgeting system deals with *information and reporting*. The accounting and related statistical-reporting systems identify information for all activities of the organization. Neither new accounting nor new statistical-reporting systems are called for. Instead, reidentification or restructuring in the existing systems is required for utilization of information in the planning and programming parts of the new activity. When program determinations are made, the reporting requirement imposes on existing systems the need to provide continuing information (usually monthly and/or quarterly) on the use of resources and the operational steps taken in the implementation of the programs.*

* Complete enumeration on a periodic basis is not always required. For example, sample surveys might be used.

Although the accounting and statistical reports of necessity are carried on in terms of actions in the current calendar, the reporting provision must require and provide specific identification of today's activities in terms of impact in both the balance of the current year and the future years of the multiyear plan.

Information and reporting is an important part of the total system since (a) accounting for appropriated funds is a requirement in any government or business, (b) knowing and measuring progress towards stated objectives is important, (c) analysis for the future can only be based on measurements derived from past experience, (d) much of the mystery of traditional budgeting derives from the esoteric nature of the reports, and (e) a huge mass of data is now produced by modern record-keeping practice, office machines, and the computer in the name of information and reporting. (Instructions for preparing documents and forms used to collect, store, and report information are procedures and are not included here. Any good program structure can readily be converted to the coding of any accounting, statistical, or reporting system.)

All of the ideas in program budgeting are best developed when they are adapted to the special requirements of the organization introducing the new methodology. This is even more true of the information and reporting activities, since here it is definitely a matter of adapting an ongoing accounting, statistical, or reporting system to meet the program-budgeting requirements.

A brief summary that relates the areas of operation to the major features of program budgeting and to the kinds of documents the system produces is sketched in Figure 2.

Main Features	*Operation Areas*	*Representative Documents*
Define objectives Determine programs Assign activities to programs Establish plan-program-budget cycle	Structural Aspect	Multi-year program and financial plan
Develop cost/benefit measurement methods Identify and apply criteria	Analytical Aspect	Program memoranda including alternatives Issue Analysis Special studies
Use existing reporting system Update programs	Data and Information Aspect	Accounting and statistical reports Program change proposals

Fig. 2 reproduced from *Management: A Book of Readings* by H. Koonz and C. O'Donnell, 3rd ed., copyright 1972 by McGraw-Hill Inc. Used with permission of McGraw-Hill Book Company.

Figure 2 Sketch of program budgeting.

REASONS FOR PROGRAM BUDGETING

The primary reason for program budgeting is that it provides a formal, systematic method to improve decisions concerning the allocation of resources. Obviously, these allocation problems arise because available resource supplies are limited in relation to the demands for them. This leads to a need for making choices among demands in terms of what to do, how much to do, and when to do it.

Program budgeting is designed to open up debate on these questions and put the discussion on a new basis. It does this by requiring explicit identification of all actions—ongoing or new proposals—in terms of programs related to stated objectives. This enables the top decision makers to act in terms of the total organization rather than on the basis of ideas limited by individuals or operating units. The orientation of this new method is to plan the future in both short-term and long-range aspects, and to make decisions on what is to be done.

A second reason for program budgeting is that planning should be carried on with adequate recognition of what costs are. When an organization's plans call for more resources than it has or is likely to have available to it, planning becomes a game not played for "keeps." An organization that is unable to carry the costs of its objectives should revise its objectives; otherwise it will be wasting some of its substance. Resource considerations introduce realism into planning.

Since as many alternative plans as possible should be examined at the planning level, resource considerations should be in highly aggregated terms. We should use "in the ball park" estimates of costs to facilitate examining a large number of possibilities in a reasonably short period of time. In program budgeting the name of the game is "alternatives" and we seek a menu of the most relevant ones.

When we have selected the most promising plans from that list, we analyze them in a less aggregative but still not completely detailed form. This is programming. Here activities are identified and feasibility is established in terms of capability, resource requirements, and timing of each one of the alternatives. The selection is linked to a budgetlike process because the final budget decisions determine the allocation of resources not only for the next year but in many cases make commitments for many years into the future.

To formulate a single program requires that we make decisions on feasibility, resource demands, and timing. Even so, data used for programming are still not as detailed as next year's budget. The budget is an operating and financial document and, as such, must give great detail for inputs like personnel, supplies, and equipment, and assignment of such resources to administrative units. That kind of detail overwhelms decision making and makes unmanageable a process designed for choosing among alternatives.

The third basic reason for program budgeting is that it provides for a basis of choosing between available and feasible alternatives, a choice that takes place at the conclusion of programming. At that point the issues involved have been illuminated. The decision makers can exercise their judgment and experience in an appropriate and informed context, as they determine "what to do."

Given these decisions, the details of "how to do it" can then be laid out. This is the point at which performance budgeting, management by objective, work measurement, and other methods of improving efficiency take over. In program budgeting the focus at this point is on annual allotment of funds for the next step to be taken along a path that has been thoughtfully set by policy makers at all levels. Probably more important, the direction of the path and the distance to be covered in the next year will have been established after the consideration of a number of possible futures for the entire government or business organization.

This means that program budgeting is not designed to increase efficiency in the performance of day-to-day tasks, nor is it designed to improve administrative control over the expenditure of funds. It is instead a recognition of the fact that more money is wasted by doing the wrong thing efficiently than can be wasted by doing the right thing inefficiently. In short, program budgeting aims at the decision-making process; that is, top level determination of what to do, how much to do, and when to do it, rather than deciding on how to carry on day-to-day operations, decisions which are best made by those who are closest to the activity.

WHAT PROGRAM BUDGETING IS NOT

Some systems that have been called program-budgeting systems may be useful improvements, but they do not deal with choosing objectives, developing plans through systematic analysis of costs and effectiveness, resource allocation, and the other major decision areas which are its essentials. These include:

1. Reorganization plans justified on the basis that the organization must fit the program structure.
2. New accounting or statistical systems that identify program elements.
3. Management-information systems undertaken as a substitute for major PB features.
4. Elaborate new personnel recruiting, education, or training undertaken without developing the PB organization and procedures which will utilize them effectively.
5. Extensive use of the words *program* and *program budgeting* in existing documents and procedures in lieu of developing and introducing the PB concepts and required changes.
6. Treating performance budgeting and other methods for improving adminis-

tration of specific tasks as a substitute for PB treatment of major decision-making problems.

THE GENERAL DISCLAIMER

In both government and business, responsibility for the work required to accomplish a coherent set of objectives is divided among a number of organizations. In government, for example, programs with objectives for health and education are distributed among a dozen bureaus and independent agencies as well as levels of government. The activities of each are sometimes complementary, sometimes in conflict. As a result there is no overall coordination of the resource allocations relevant to program objectives.

Since program budgeting cuts across organization and administrative lines, there are cases where this has been translated to mean that the activity is limited to the structural phase and resultant reorganization to fit the new identification or programs. This is not only an incomplete view of what is involved but also a most undesirable one.

It should be recognized that the PB management concept calls for continuous reexamination of program results and for reidentifying and restructuring programs and objectives. Normally, this would be done on an annual basis. One can readily visualize the chaos that could result in administration and operations if organizational changes were required for every change in program format.

> *The program budgeting system is not a re-organization plan nor does it seek or require changes in organization to fit the program structure.**

In the same way, the information and reporting requirement of program budgeting, with its emphasis on accounting and recurring statistics, has sometimes been translated into the need for the development of a new accounting system or a major change in the existing one. As indicated in the preceding discussion of organization, programs can be expected to change or, at a minimum, be modified on a recurring basis. This makes it not only unnecessary but undesirable to change the accounting or the reporting systems to conform to the currently identified program structure.

The emphasis on maintaining existing accounting and reporting systems derives from the recognition of two major factors. First, temporary change is always undesirable and since programs and objectives are both subject to change, molding them to fit the format developed at any one point in time provides only limited advantage and has all the disadvantages that will be

* Change in organization may be desirable, but it is not one of the general principles of program budgeting. For a discussion of the organization implications of program budgeting see R. J. Mowitz, *The Design and Implementation of Pennsylvania's Planning, Programming, Budgeting System.* The Pennsylvania State University, 1970, pp. 39–41. Also, for the impact in terms of President Nixon's reorganization proposals in 1971, see Chapter 26.

encountered when they must be changed to fit the next development of the format. The second reason is that both the operators and the decision makers are knowledgeable about the existing system and therefore find it more comfortable to do their work in a situation in which changes have been kept to a minimum and are of a kind that are made essentially once and for all time.

Another reason for not making frequent changes is that in providing information for the inputs into the planning and programming process, and in reporting on actions taken in the execution of programs, the emphasis on detail is different from that in traditional line-item budgets. As we move through the process from the lowest level of operation and decision up through the higher levels of executive decision making, there is a steadily increasing need to present aggregated instead of detailed information. The important new development for accounting and statistical reporting is to ensure that, as we move up the ladder and aggregate the data, the units of record do not lose integrity through the continuing introduction of judgment or "fudge factors."

*Program budgeting is not a new accounting system nor does it necessarily require changes in the existing accounting and statistical reporting systems to fit the program structure.**

What is needed is an examination of both the accounting records and the basic records from which statistical reports are drawn to ensure that these can in fact be translated into the required inputs in planning, programming, and budgeting activities as well as in recording and reporting. This means an emphasis on units of account that are "pure." That is, units that can be carried upward in the accounting or statistical-reporting system as is and do not require the introduction of adjustments when accumulated into more aggregative units of information.

Program budgeting is not a management-information system, even though a good MIS is very useful to its operation.

Management-information systems have come into fashion recently. As a result, in many cases the development of program budgeting has been regarded as synonymous, with the installation of a new computer system and the related techniques for making management data more readily available—and nothing more. Although a good MIS is always desirable and can be used to very good advantage in the working of a program-budgeting system, it lacks the planning emphasis and surely does not include the appropriate recognition of the development of programs, the analysis of alternatives, and the development of all of the related analytical activities and tools that are so important in the concept of program budgeting.

Although program budgeting, because of its emphasis on analysis, frequently calls for individuals with an analytical approach and/or training,

* Changes in the accounting or reporting systems may be desirable and in fact may be suggested by the program-budgeting analyses, but they are not required by this management system.

program budgeting requirements are not met just by introducing elaborate new personnel recruiting, education, or training efforts. For the most part, what is needed is some redirection of existing personnel and the kind of education and training essential for this purpose. But the program requirements will not be met just by new personnel policies and activities.

The word *budget* in program budgeting, or the planning-programming-budgeting system, sometimes leads to the assumption that, if the title *program* is introduced into the existing budget documents, the result is in fact a program budget. Obviously, the word *program* is available for anyone to use in any manner that he sees fit.

The emphasis on program in this new system is on output, or end-product measurement, rather than on the inputs as they are emphasized in traditional budget-making. Therefore, whether the existing budget is the straight line-item type, performance oriented, or based on organization and object class, adding the word *program* in selected places or in the title does not make it a program budget and in no way accomplishes the purpose of program budgeting.

It is especially worth noting that program budgeting is not performance budgeting. Performance budgeting developed mainly in the 1930s and has had a major impact at the state and local government levels. It has also been used extensively in business. The performance budget is a way of choosing between a series of alternative ways of "how to do" a specific task. It does not provide for evaluation of the importance of the task in terms of either the total program or individual programs designed to meet a set of goals. In short, it is a way of choosing among alternative means available for doing a task rather than a way of determining whether the task should be performed at all or, if it is to be undertaken, the amount of it that is required.

Program budgeting recognizes the need for administrative and organizational budgets as well as performance budgeting and does not contemplate that they be abandoned or relabelled. Instead, it requires that they be used in conjunction with the PB by means of the crosswalk.

The program budget has a time element that extends beyond the typical next-year's budget. The multiyear program and financial plan lays out not only next-year's financing but also the estimates of funding that would be required for future years on the basis of decisions already made when the final action is taken. In this sense, next-year's budget is an important first step in the operation of the multiyear program, and the five and ten year projections represent the "spend-out" implications of decisions made to date.

This does not mean making fundamental changes in existing budget practice. In the traditional line item, object-class, performance, or organization and activity budget, there is a need for detailed identification by object or activity classes which requires, as we have seen, more detail than is either necessary or possible to use as we move up to the policy level in the decision process. For this reason, the primary change is in adding program budgeting to the traditional annual-budgeting process. This permits the development of the multiyear program and financial plan at a high level of aggregation from which a "crosswalk" can be made to the traditional one-year, line-item budget by object class.

THE CONTRAST IN BRIEF

In short, program budgeting is characterized by an emphasis on objectives, programs, and program elements, all stated in output terms. Cost, or the line items of the traditional budget, is treated at an appropriate level of aggregation which ensures that plans and programs are developed with adequate recognition of their resource implications.

Analysis and the use of a large variety of analytical techniques are the backbone of this new system of management. PB requires explicit identification of assumptions, the development of all relevant options and alternative outcomes to the extent that time and personnel permit. PB's process of analysis forces recognition of the organization and operation line-cutting features of programs. In the same way, the analytic process forces translation of a broad goal, like better education, into operational terms like courses, students, teachers, libraries, etc., that identify both the purposes of the education process and the resources that can reasonably be made available for it. Analysis takes many forms and places substantial emphasis on the use of such tools as computers and mathematical models. However, the computer and the model are simply part of the kit of tools for analysis; they are not the decision makers.

Program budgeting also places a new emphasis on continuous reporting of both the accounting and statistical type, including ad hoc data-collection methods when appropriate. These serve the purpose of providing the inputs into the next planning and programming cycle, as well as of measuring how the determinations on resources and program are being carried out (progress reporting).

New organization charts, accounting systems, personnel recruitment and training systems, management-information systems, or the generous use of the word *program* in traditional budgets are not in themselves program budgeting. They cannot promise the improvement in decision-making that is the primary goal of the program-budgeting process.

REFERENCES

[1] *Special Analyses,* Budget of the U. S. Government, pp. 289–317, U. S. Government Printing Office, Washington, D. C., 1971.

[2] *Commonwealth of Pennsylvania,* Program Budget Vol. 1, pp. 261–314 (also see pp. 67 and 68), July 1971–June 1972.

[3] Schick, Allen: *The Use and Abuse of Program Structure,* International Federation of Operational Research Societies, Washington, D. C., 1976. This work gives a different point of view.

Shaping the Master Strategy of Your Firm*

William H. Newman

Every enterprise needs a central purpose expressed in terms of the services it will render to society. And it needs a basic concept of how it will create these services. Since it will be competing with other enterprises for resources, it must have some distinctive advantages—in its services or in its methods of creating them. Moreover, since it will inevitably cooperate with other firms, it must have the means for maintaining viable coalitions with them. In addition, there are the elements of change, growth, and adaptation. Master strategy is a company's basic plan for dealing with these factors.

One familiar way of delving into company strategy is to ask, "What business are we in or do we want to be in? Why should society tolerate our existence?" Answers are often difficult. A company producing only grass seed had very modest growth until it shifted its focus to "lawn care" and provided the suburban homeowner with a full line of fertilizers, pesticides, and related products. Less fortunate was a cooperage firm that defined its business in terms of wooden boxes and barrels and went bankrupt when paperboard containers took over the field.

Product line is only part of the picture, however. An ability to supply services economically is also crucial. For example, most local bakeries have shut down, not for lack of demand for bread, but because they became technologically inefficient. Many a paper mill has exhausted its sources of pulpwood. The independent motel operator is having difficulty meeting competition from franchised chains. Yet in all these industries some firms have prospered—the ones that have had the foresight and adaptability (and probably some luck, too) to take advantage of their changing environment. These firms pursued a master strategy which enabled them to increase the services rendered and attract greater resources.

Most central managers recognize that master strategy is of cardinal importance. But they are less certain about how to formulate a strategy for their particular firm. This article seeks to help in the shaping of master strategies. It outlines key elements and an approach to defining these. Most of our illustrations will be business enterprises; nevertheless, the central concept is just as crucial for hospitals, universities, and other nonprofit ventures.

A practical way to develop a master strategy is to:

- Pick particular roles or niches that are appropriate in view of competition and the company's resources.
- Combine various facets of the company's efforts to obtain synergistic effects.
- Set up sequences and timing of changes that reflect company capabilities and external conditions.
- Provide for frequent reappraisal and adaptation to evolving opportunities.

NEW MARKETS OR SERVICES

Picking Propitious Niches

Most companies fill more than one niche. Often they sell several lines of products; even when a single line is produced an enterprise may sell it to several distinct types of customers. Especially as a firm grows, it seeks expansion by tapping new markets or selling different services to its existing customers. In designing a company strategy we can avoid pitfalls by first examining each of these markets separately.

Basically, we are searching for customer needs—preferably growing ones—where adroit use of our unique resources will make our services distinctive and in that sense give us a competitive advantage. In these particular spots, we hope to give the customer an irresistible value and to do so at relatively low expense. A bank, for example, may devise a way of financing the purchase of an automobile that is particularly well-suited to farmers; it must then consider whether it is in a good position to serve such a market.

Identifying such propitious niches is not easy. Here is one approach that works well in various situations: Focus first on the industry—growth prospects, competition, key factors required for success—then on the strengths and weaknesses of the specific company as matched against these key success factors. As we describe this approach more fully, keep in mind that we are interested in segments of markets as well as entire markets.

The sales volume and profits of an industry or one of its segments depend on the demand for its services, the supply of these services, and the competitive conditions. (We use "service" here to include both physical products and intangible values provided by an enterprise.) Predicting future demand, supply, and competition is an exciting endeavor. In the following paragraphs, we suggest a few of the important considerations that may vitally affect the strategy of a company.

ELEMENTS OF DEMAND

Demand for Industry Services

The strength of the desire for a service affects its demand. For instance, we keenly want a small amount of salt, but care little for additional quantities. Our desire for more and better automobiles does not have this same sort of cut-off level, and our desires for pay-television (no commercials, select programs) or supersonic air travel are highly uncertain, falling in quite a different category from that of salt.

Possible substitutes to satisfy a given desire must be weighed—beef for lamb, motorboats for baseball, gas for coal, aureomycin for sulfa, weldments for castings, and so forth. The frequency of such substitution is affected, of course, by the relative prices.

Desire has to be backed up by **ability to pay,** and here business cycles enter in. Also, in some industries large amounts of capital are necessarily tied up in equipment. The relative efficiency, quality of work, and nature of machinery already in place influence the money that will be available for new equipment. Another consideration: If we hope to sell in foreign markets, foreign-exchange issues arise.

The **structure of markets** also requires analysis. Where, on what terms, and in response to what appeals do people buy jet planes, sulphuric acid, or dental floss? Does a manufacturer deal directly with consumers or are intermediaries such as retailers or brokers a more effective means of distribution?

Although an entire industry is often affected by such factors—desire, substitutes, ability to pay, structure of markets—a local variation in demand sometimes provides a unique opportunity for a particular firm. Thus, most drugstores carry cosmetics, candy, and a wide variety of items besides drugs, but a store located in a medical center might develop a highly profitable business by dealing exclusively with prescriptions and other medical supplies.

All these elements of demand are subject to change—some quite rapidly. Since the kind of strategic plans we are considering here usually extends over several years, we need both an identification of the key factors that will affect industry demand and an estimate of how they will change over a span of time.

SUPPLY SITUATION

Supply Related to Demand

The attractiveness of any industry depends on more than potential growth arising from strong demand. In designing a company strategy we also must consider the probable supply of services and the conditions under which they will be offered.

The **capacity** of an industry to fill demand for its services clearly affects profit margins. The importance of over- or undercapacity, however, depends on the ease of entry and withdrawal from the industry. When capital costs are high, as in the hotel or cement business, adjustments to demand tend to lag. Thus, overcapacity may depress profits for a long period; even bankruptcies do not remove the capacity if plants are bought up—at bargain prices—and operated by new owners. On the other hand, low capital requirements—as in electronic assembly work—permit new firms to enter quickly, and shortages of supply tend to be short lived. Of course, more than the physical plant is involved; an effective organization of competent people is also necessary. Here again, the case of expansion or contraction should be appraised.

Costs also need to be predicted—labor costs, material costs, and for some industries, transportation costs or excise taxes. If increases in operating costs affect all members of an industry alike and can be passed on to the consumer in the form of higher prices, this factor becomes less significant in company strategy. However, rarely do both conditions prevail. Sharp rises in labor costs in Hawaii, for example, place its sugar industry at a disadvantage on the world market.

A highly dynamic aspect of supply is **technology.** New methods for producing established products—for example, basic oxygen conversion of steel displacing open-hearth furnaces and mechanical cotton pickers displacing century-old hand-picking techniques—are part of the picture. Technology may change the availability and price of raw materials; witness the growth of synthetic rubber and industrial diamonds. Similarly, air cargo planes and other new forms of transportation are expanding the sources of supply that may serve a given market.

For an individual producer, anticipating these shifts in the industry supply situation may be a matter of prosperity or death.

CLIMATE OF INDUSTRY

Competitive Conditions in the Industry

The way the interplay between demand and supply works out depends partly on the nature of competition in the industry. **Size, strength,** and **attitude of companies** in one industry—the dress industry where entrance is easy and style is critical—may lead to very sharp competition. On the other hand, oligopolistic competition among the giants of the aluminum industry produces a more stable situation, at least in the short run. The resources and managerial talent needed to enter one industry differ greatly from what it takes to get ahead in the other.

A strong **trade association** often helps to create a favorable climate in its industry. The Independent Oil Producers' Association, to cite one case, has been unusually effective in restricting imports of crude oil into the United

States. Other associations compile valuable industry statistics, help reduce unnecessary variations in size of products, run training conferences, hold trade shows, and aid members in a variety of other ways.

Government regulation also modifies competition. A few industries like banking and insurance are supervised by national or state bodies that place limits on prices, sales promotion, and the variety of services rendered. Airlines are both regulated as a utility and subsidized as an infant industry. Farm subsidies affect large segments of agriculture, and tariffs have long protected selected manufacturers. Our patent laws also bear directly on the nature of competition, as is evident in the heated discussion of how pharmaceutical patents may be used. Clearly, future government action is a significant factor in the outlook of many industries.

CRUCIAL FACTORS

Key Factors for Success in the Industry

This brief review suggests the dynamic nature of business and uncertainties in the outlook for virtually all industries. A crucial task of every top management is to assess the forces at play in its industry and to identify those factors that will be crucial for future success. These we call "key success factors." Leadership in research and development may be very important in one industry, low costs in another, and adaptability to local need in a third; large financial resources may be a *sine qua non* for mining whereas creative imagination is the touchstone in advertising.

We stressed earlier the desirability of making such analyses for narrow segments as well as broad industry categories. The success factors for each segment are likely to differ in at least one or two respects from those for other segments. For example, General Foods Corporation discovered to its sorrow that the key success factors in gourmet foods differ significantly from those for coffee and Jello.

Moreover, the analysis of industry outlook should provide a forecast of the **growth potentials** and the **profit prospects** for the various industry segments. These conclusions, along with key success factors, are vital guideposts in setting up a company's master strategy.

The range of opportunities for distinctive service is wide. Naturally, in picking its particular niche out of this array a company favors those opportunities which will utilize its strength and bypass its limitations. This calls for a candid appraisal of the company itself.

POSITION IN MARKET

Market Strengths of Company

A direct measure of **market position** is the percentage that company sales are of industry sales and of major competitors' sales. Such figures quickly indicate whether our company is so big that its activities are likely to bring prompt responses from other leading companies. Or our company may be small enough to enjoy independent maneuverability. Of course, to be most meaningful, these percentages should be computed separately for geographical areas, product lines, and types of customer—if suitable industry data are available.

More intangible but no less significant are the relative standing of **company products** and their **reputation** in major markets. Kodak products, for instance, are widely and favorably known; they enjoy a reputation for both high quality and dependability. Clearly, this reputation will be a factor in Eastman Kodak Company strategy. And any new, unknown firm must overcome this prestige if it seeks even a small share in one segment of the film market. Market reputation is tenacious. Especially when we try to "trade up," our previous low quality, service, and sharp dealing will be an obstacle. Any strategy we adopt must have enough persistence and consistency so that our firm is assigned a "role" in the minds of the customers we wish to reach.

The relationship between a company and the **distribution system** is another vital aspect of market position. The big United States automobile companies, for example, are strong partly because each has a set of dealers throughout the country. In contrast, foreign car manufacturers have difficulty selling here until they can arrange with dealers to provide dependable service. A similar problem confronted Whirlpool Corporation when it wanted to sell its trademarked appliances publicly. (For years its only customer had been Sears, Roebuck and Company.) Whirlpool made an unusual arrangement with Radio Corporation of America which led to the establishment of RCA-Whirlpool distributors and dealers. Considering the strong competition, Whirlpool could not have entered this new market without using marketing channels such as RCA's.

All these aspects of market position—a relative share of the market, comparative quality of product, reputation with consumers, and ties with a distributive system—help define the strengths and limitation of a company.

SERVICE ABILITIES

Supply Strengths of a Company

To pick propitious niches we also should appraise our company's relative strength in creating goods and services. Such ability to supply services fitted to consumer needs will be built largely on the firm's resources of labor and material, effective productive facilities, and perhaps pioneering research and development.

Labor in the United States is fairly mobile. Men tend to gravitate to good jobs. But the process takes time—a southern shoe plant needed ten years to build up an adequate number of skilled workers—and it may be expensive. Consequently, immediate availability of competent men at normal industry wages is a source of strength. In addition, the relationships between the company and its work force are important. All too often both custom and formal agreements freeze inefficient practices. The classic example is New England textiles; here, union-supported work habits give even mills high labor costs. Only recently have a few companies been able to match their more flourishing competitors in the South.

Access to **low-cost materials** is often a significant factor in a company's supply position. The development of the southern paper industry, for example, is keyed to the use of fast-growing forests which can be cut on a rotational basis to provide a continuing supply of pulpwood. Of course, if raw materials can be easily transported, such as iron ore and crude oil by enormous ships, plants need not be located at the original source.

Availability of materials involves more than physical handling. Owernship, or long-term contracts with those who do own, may assure a continuing source at low cost. Much of the strategy of companies producing basic metals—iron, copper, aluminum, or nickel—includes huge investments in ore properties. But all sorts of companies are concerned with the availability of materials. So whenever supplies are scarce a potential opportunity exists. Even in retailing, Sears, Roebuck and Company discovered in its Latin American expansion that a continuing flow of merchandise of standard quality was difficult to assure, but once established, such sources became a great advantage.

Physical facilities—office buildings, plants, mines—often tie up a large portion of a company's assets. In the short run, at least, these facilities may be an advantage or a disadvantage. The character of many colleges, for instance, has been shaped by their location, whether in a plush suburb or in a degenerating urban area, and the cost of moving facilities is so great that adaptation to the existing neighborhood becomes necessary. A steel company, to cite another case, delayed modernizing its plant so long that it had to abandon its share of the basic steel market and seek volume in specialty products.

Established organizations of highly talented people to perform particular tasks also give a company a distinctive capability. Thus, a good research and development department may enable a company to expand in pharmaceuticals, whereas a processing firm without such a technical staff is barred from this profitable field.

Perhaps the company we are analyzing will enjoy other distinctive abilities to produce services. Our central concern at this point is to identify strengths and see how these compare with strengths of other firms.

FINANCES AND MANAGEMENT

Other Company Resources

The propitious niche for a company also depends on its financial strength and the character of its management.

Some strategies will require large quantities of capital. Any oil company that seeks foreign sources of crude oil, for instance, must be prepared to invest millions of dollars. Few firms maintain cash reserves of this size, so financial capacity to enter this kind of business depends on: an ability to attract new capital—through borrowing or sale of stock—or a flow of profits (and depreciation allowances) from existing operations that can be allocated to the new venture. On the other hand, perhaps a strategy can be devised that calls for relatively small cash advances, and in these fields a company that has low financial strength will still be able to compete with the affluent firms.

A more subtle factor in company capacity is its **management.** The age and vitality of key executives, their willingness to risk profit and capital, their urge to gain personal prestige through company growth, their desire to insure stable employment for present workers—all affect the suitability of any proposed strategy. For example, the expansion of Hilton Hotels Corporation into a world-wide chain certainly reflects the personality of Conrad Hilton; with a different management at the helm, a modification in strategy is most appropriate because Conrad Hilton's successors do not have his particular set of drives and values.

Related to the capabilities of key executives is the organization structure of the company. A decentralized structure, for instance, facilitates movement into new fields of business, whereas a functional structure with fine specialization is better suited to expansion in closely related lines.

PICKING A NICHE

Matching Company Strengths With Key Success Factors

Armed with a careful analysis of the strengths and limitations of our company, we are prepared to pick desirable niches for company concentration. Naturally, we will look for fields where company strengths correspond with the key factors for success that have been developed in our industry analyses described in the preceding section. And in the process we will set aside possibilities in which company limitations create serious handicaps.

Potential growth and profits in each niche must, of course, be added to the synthesis. Clearly, a low potential will make a niche unattractive even though the company strengths and success factors fit neatly. And we may become keenly interested in a niche where the fit is only fair if the potential is great.

Typically, several intriguing possibilities emerge. These are all the niches—in terms of market lines, market segments, or combinations of production functions—that the company might pursue. Also typically, a series of positive actions is necessary in order for the company to move into each area. So we need to list not only each niche and its potential, but the limitations that will have to be overcome and other steps necessary for the company to succeed in each area. These are our propitious niches—nestled in anticipated business conditions and tailored to the strengths and limitations of our particular company.

An enterprise always pursues a variety of efforts to serve even a single niche, and, typically, it tries to fill several related niches. Considerable choice is possible, at least in the degree to which these many efforts are pushed. In other words, management decides how many markets to cover, to what degree to automate production, what stress to place on consumer engineering, and a host of other actions. One vital aspect of master strategy is fitting these numerous efforts together. In fact, our choice of niches will depend in part, on how well we can combine the total effort they require.

Synergy is a powerful ally for this purpose. Basically, synergy means that the combined effect of two or more cooperative acts is greater than the sum which would result if the actions were taken independently. A simple example in marketing is that widespread dealer stocks combined with advertising will produce much greater sales volume than widespread dealer stocks in, say, Virginia and advertising in Minnesota. Often the possibility of obtaining synergistic effects will shape the master strategy of the company—as the following examples will suggest.

COMBINATION OF SERVICES

Total Service to Customer

A customer rarely buys merely a physical product. Other attributes of the transaction often include delivery, credit terms, return privileges, repair service, operating instructions, conspicuous consumption, psychological experience of purchasing, and the like. Many services involve no physical product at all. The crucial question is what combination of attributes will have high synergistic value for the customers we serve.

International Business Machines, for instance, has found a winning combination. Its products are well designed and of high quality. But so are the products of several of its competitors. In addition, IBM provides salesmen who understand the customer's problems and how IBM equipment can help solve them, and fast, dependable repair service. The synergistic effect of these three services is of high value to many customers.

Each niche calls for its own combination of services. For example, Chock Full o' Nuts expanded its restaurant chain on the basis of three attributes: good quality food, cleanliness, and fast service. This combination appealed to a particular group of customers. A very limited selection, crowded space, and lack of frills did not matter. However, if any one of the three characteristics slips at an outlet, the synergistic effect is lost.

ADDING TO CAPABILITIES

Fuller Use of Existing Resources

Synergistic effects are possible in any phase of company operations. One possibility is that present activities include a "capability" that can be applied to additional uses. Thus, American watch companies have undertaken the manufacture of tiny gyroscopes and electronic components for spacecraft because they already possessed technical skill in the production of miniature precision products. They adopted this strategy on the premise that they could make both watches and components for spacecraft with less effort than could separate firms devoted to only one line of products.

The original concept of General Foods Corporation sought a similar synergistic effect in marketing. Here, the basic capability was marketing prepared foods. By having the same sales organization handle several product lines, a larger and more effective sales effort could be provided and/or the selling cost per product line could be reduced. Clearly, the combined sales activity was more powerful than separate sales efforts for each product line would have been.

VERTICAL INTEGRATION

Expansion to Obtain a Resource

Vertical integration may have synergistic effects. This occurred when the Apollo Printing Machine Company bought a foundry. Apollo was unsatisfied with the quality and tardy delivery of its castings and was looking for a new supplier. In its search, it learned that a nearby foundry could be purchased. The foundry was just breaking even, primarily because the volume of its work fluctuated widely. Following the purchase, Apollo gave the foundry a more steady backlog of work, and through close technical cooperation the quality of castings received by them was improved. The consolidated set-up was better for both enterprises than the previous independent operations.

The results of vertical integration are not always so good, however; problems of balance, flexibility, and managerial capacity must be carefully weighed. Nevertheless, control of a critical resource is often a significant part of company strategy.

UNIQUE SERVICES

Expansion to Enhance Market Position

Efforts to improve market position provide many examples of "the whole being better than the sum of its parts." The leading can companies, for example, moved from exclusive concentration on metal containers into glass, plastic, and paper containers. They expected their new divisions to be profitable by themselves, but an additional reason for the expansion lay in anticipated synergistic effects of being able to supply a customer's total container requirements. With the entire packaging field changing so rapidly, a company that can quickly shift from one type of container to another offers a distinctive service to its cusomers.

International Harvester, to cite another case, added a very large tractor to its line a few years ago. The prospects for profit on this line alone were far from certain. However, the new tractor was important to give dealers "a full line"; its availability removed the temptation for dealers to carry some products of competing manufacturers. So, when viewed in combination with other International Harvester products, the new tractor looked much more significant than it did as an isolated project.

NEGATIVE SYNERGY

Compatibility of Efforts

In considering additional niches for a company, we may be confronted with negative synergy—that is, the combined effort is worse than the sum of independent efforts. This occurred when a producer of high quality television and hi-fi sets introduced a small color television receiver. When first offered, the small unit was as good as most competing sets and probably had an attractive potential market. However, it was definitely inferior in performance to other products of the company and, consequently, undermined public confidence in the quality of the entire line. Moreover, customers had high expectations for the small set because of the general reputation of the company, and they became very critical when the new product did not live up to their expectations. Both the former products and the new product suffered.

Compatibility of operations within the company should also be considered. A large department store, for instance, ran into serious trouble when it tried to add a high-quality dress shop to its mass merchandising activities. The ordering and physical handling of merchandise, the approach to sales promotion, the sales compensation plan, and many other procedures which worked well for the established type of business were unsuited to the new shop. And friction arose each time the shop received special treatment. Clearly, the new shop created an excessive number of problems because it was incompatible with existing customs and attitudes.

BROAD COMPANY GOALS

Summarizing briefly: We have seen that some combinations of efforts are strongly reinforcing. The combination accelerates the total effect or reduces the cost for the same effect or solidifies our supply or market position. On the other hand, we must watch for incompatible efforts which may have a disruptive effect in the same cumulative manner. So, when we select niches—as a part of our master strategy—one vital aspect is the possibility of such synergistic effects.

Master strategy sets broad company goals. One firm may decide to seek preeminence in a narrow specialty while another undertakes to be a leader in several niches or perhaps in all phases of its industry. We have recommended that this definition of "scope" be clear in terms of:

- Services offered to customers.
- Operations performed by the company.
- Relationships with suppliers of necessary resources.
- The desirability of defining this mission so as to obtain synergistic effects.

But master strategy involves more than defining our desired role in society. Many activities will be necessary to achieve this desired spot, and senior executives must decide what to do first, how many activities can be done concurrently, how fast to move, what risks to run, and what to postpone. These questions of sequence and timing must be resolved to make the strategy operational.

STRATEGY OF SEQUENCE

Choice of Sequence

Especially in technical areas, sequences of actions may be dictated by technology. Thus, process research must precede equipment designs, product specifications must precede cost estimation, and so forth. Other actions, such as the steps necessary to form a new corporation, likewise give management little choice in sequence. When this occurs, normal programming or possibly PERT analysis may be employed. Little room—or need—exists for strategy.

Preordained sequences, however, are exceptional in the master strategy area. A perennial issue when entering a new niche, for instance, is whether to develop markets before working on production economies, or vice versa. The production executive will probably say, "Let's be sure we can produce the product at a low cost before committing ourselves to customers," whereas the typical marketing man will advise, "Better be sure it will sell before tooling up for a big output."

A striking example of strategy involving sequence confronted the Boeing company when it first conceived of a large four-engine jet plane suitable for handling cargo or large passenger loads. Hindsight makes the issue appear simple, but at the time, Air Force officers saw little need for such a plane. The belief was that propeller-driven planes provided the most desirable means for carrying cargo. In other words, the company got no support for its prediction of future market requirements. Most companies would have stopped at this point. However, Boeing executives decided to invest several million dollars to develop the new plane. A significant portion of the company's liquid assets went into the project. Over two years later, Boeing was able to present evidence that caused the Air Force officials to change their minds—and the KC 135 was born. Only Boeing was prepared to produce the new type of craft which proved to be both faster and more economical than propeller-driven planes. Moreover, the company was able to convert the design into the Boeing 707 passenger plane which, within a few years, dominated the airline passenger business. Competing firms were left far behind, and Convair almost went bankrupt in its attempt to catch up. In this instance, a decision to let engineering and production run far ahead of marketing paid off handsomely.

No simple guide exists for selecting a strategic sequence. Nevertheless, the following comments do sharpen the issue:

- Resist the temptation to do first what is easiest simply because it requires the least initiative. Each of us typically has a bias for what he does well. A good sequence of activities, however, is more likely to emerge from an objective analysis.
- If a head start is especially valuable on one front, start early there. Sometimes, being the first in the market is particularly desirable (there may be room for only one company). In other cases, the strategic place to begin is the acquiring of key resources; at a later date limited raw materials may already be bought up or the best sites occupied by competitors. The importance of a head start is usually hard to estimate, but probably more money is lost in trying to be first than in catching up with someone else.
- Move into uncertain areas promptly, preferably before making any major commitments. For instance, companies have been so entranced with a desired expansion that they committed substantial funds to new plants before uncertainties regarding the production processes were removed.
- If a particular uncertainty can be investigated quickly and inexpensively, get it out of the way promptly.
- Start early with processes involving long lead-times. For example, if a new synthetic food product must have government approval, the tedious process of testing and reviewing evidence may take a year or two longer than preparation for manufacturing and marketing.
- Delay revealing plans publicly if other companies can easily copy a novel idea. If substantial social readjustment is necessary, however, an early public announcement is often helpful.

In a particular case, these guides may actually conflict with each other, or other considerations may be dominant. And, as the Boing 707 example suggests, the possible gains may be large enough to justify following a very risky sequence. Probably the greatest value of the above list is to stimulate careful thought about the sequence that is incorporated into a company's master strategy.

RESOURCE LIMITATIONS

Straining Scarce Resources

A hard-driving executive does not like to admit that an objective cannot be achieved. He prefers to believe. "Where there's a will there's a way." Yet, an essential aspect of master strategy is deciding what can be done and how fast.

Every enterprise has limits—perhaps severe limits—on its resources. The amount of capital, the number and quality of key personnel, the physical production capacity, or the adaptability of its social structure—none of these is boundless. The tricky issue is how to use these limited resources to the best advantage. We must devise a strategy which is feasible within the inherent restraints.

A household-appliance manufacturer went bankrupt because he failed to adapt his rate of growth to his financial resources. This man had a first-rate product and a wise plan for moving with an "economy model" into an expanding market (following rural electrification). But, to achieve low production costs, he built an oversized plant and launched sales efforts in ten states. His contention was that the kind of company he conceived could not start out on a small scale. Possibly all of these judgments were correct, but they resulted in cash requirements that drained all of his resources before any momentum was achieved. Cost of the partially used plant and of widely scattered sales efforts was so high that no one was willing to bail out the financially strapped venture. His master strategy simply did not fit his resources.

The scarce resource affecting master strategy may be managerial personnel. A management consulting firm, for instance, reluctantly postponed entry into the international arena because only two of its partners had the combination of interest, capacity, and vitality to spend a large amount of time abroad, and these men were also needed to assure continuity of the United States practice. The firm felt that a later start would be better than weak action immediately —even though this probably meant the loss of several desirable clients.

The weight we should attach to scarce resources in the timing of master strategy often requires delicate judgment. Some strain may be endured. But, how much, how long? For example, in its switch from purchased to company-produced tires, a European rubber company fell behind on deliveries for six months, but, through heroic efforts and pleading with customers, the company weathered the squeeze. Now, company executives believe the timing was wise! If the delay had lasted a full year—and this was a real possibility—the consequence would have approached a catastrophe.

Forming Coalitions

A cooperative agreement with firms in related fields occasionally provides a way to overcome scarce resources. We have already referred to the RCA-Whirlpool arrangement for distributing Whirlpool products. Clearly, in this instance, the timing of Whirlpool's entrance into the market with its own brand depended on forming a coalition with RCA.

EXAMPLES OF COALITIONS

The early development of frozen foods provides us with two other examples of fruitful coalitions. A key element in Birdseye master strategy was to obtain the help of cold-storage warehouses; grocery wholesalers were not equipped to handle frozen foods, and before the demand was clearly established they were slow to move into the new activity. And the Birdseye division of General Foods lacked both managerial and financial resources to venture into national wholesaling.

Similarly, Birdseye had to get freezer cabinets into retail stores, but it lacked the capability to produce them. So, it entered into a coalition with a refrigerator manufacturer to make and sell (or lease) the cabinets to retail stores. This mutual agreement enabled Birdseye to move ahead with its marketing program much faster. With the tremendous growth of frozen foods, neither the cold storage warehouse nor the cabinet manufacturer continued to be necessary, but without them in the early days widespread use of frozen foods would have been delayed three to five years.

Coalitions may be formed for reasons other than "buying time." Nevertheless, when we are trying to round out a workable master strategy, coalitions —or even mergers—may provide the quickiest way to overcome a serious deficiency in vital resources.

THE RIGHT TIME TO ACT

Receptive Environment

Conditions in a firm's environment affect the "right time" to make a change. Mr. Ralph Cordiner, for example, testifies that he launched his basic reorganization of General Electric Company only when he felt confident of three years of high business activity because, in his opinion, the company could not have absorbed all the internal readjustments during a period of declining volume and profits.

Judging the right time to act is difficult. Thus, one of the contributing factors to the multimillion-dollar Edsel car fiasco was poor timing. The same automobile launched a year or two earlier might have been favorably received. But buyer tastes changed between the time elaborate market research studies were made and the time when the new car finally appeared in dealer showrooms. By then, preference was swinging away from a big car that "had everything" toward compacts. This mistake in timing and associated errors in strategy cost the Ford Motor Company over a hundred million dollars.

A major move can be too early, as well as too late. We know, for instance, that a forerunner of the modern, self-service supermarket—the Piggly Wiggly—was born too soon. In its day, only a few housewives drove automobiles to shopping centers; and those that could afford cars usually shunned the do-it-yourself mode so prevalent today. In other words, the environment at that time simply was not receptive to what now performs so effectively. Other "pioneers" have also received cool receptions—prefabricated housing and local medical clinics are two.

NO SIMPLE RULES

The preceding discussions of sequence and timing provide no simple rules for these critical aspects of basic strategy. The factors we have mentioned for deciding which front(s) to push first (where is a head start valuable, early attention to major uncertainties, lead-times, significance of secrecy) and for deciding how fast to move (strain on scarce resources, possible coalition to provide resources, and receptivity of the environment) bear directly on many strategy decisions. They also highlight the fundamental nature of sequence and timing in the master strategy for a firm.

Master strategy involves deliberately relating a company's efforts to its particular future environment. We recognize, of course, that both the company's capabilities and its environment continually evolve; consequently, strategy should always be based, not on existing conditions, but on forecasts. Such forecasts, however, are never 100 per cent correct; instead, strategy often seeks to take advantage of uncertainty about future conditions.

This dynamic aspect of strategy should be underscored. The industry outlook will shift for any of numerous reasons. These forces may accelerate growth in some sectors and spell decline in others, may squeeze material supply, may make old sources obsolete, may open new possibilities and snuff out others. Meanwhile, the company itself is also changing—due to the success or failure of its own efforts and to actions of competitors and cooperating firms. And with all of these internal and external changes the combination of thrusts that will provide optimum synergistic effects undoubtedly will be altered. Timing of actions is the most volatile element of all. It should be adjusted to both the new external situation and the degrees of internal progress on various fronts.

Consequently, frequent reappraisal of master strategy is essential. We must build into the planning mechanisms sources of fresh data that will tell us how well we are doing and what new opportunities and obstacles are appearing on the horizon. The feedback features of control will provide some of these data. In addition, senior managers and others who have contact with various parts of the environment must be ever-sensitive to new developments that established screening devices might not detect.

Hopefully, such reappraisal will not call for sharp reversals in strategy. Typically, a master strategy requires several years to execute and some features may endure much longer. The kind of plan I am discussing here sets the direction for a whole host of company actions, and external reputations and relations often persist for many years. Quick reversals break momentum, require repeated relearning, and dissipate favorable cumulative effects. To be sure, occasionally a sharp break may be necessary. But, if my forecasts are reasonably sound, the adaptation to new opportunities will be more evolution than revolution. Once embarked on a course, we make our reappraisal from our new position—and this introduces an advantage in continuing in at least the same general direction. So, normally, the adaptation is more an unfolding than a completely new start.

Even though drastic modification of our master strategy may be unnecessary, frequent incremental changes will certainly be required to keep abreast of the times. Especially desirable are shifts that anticipate change before the pressures build up. And such farsighted adjustments are possible only if we periodically reappraise and adapt present strategy to new opportunities.

Master strategy is the pivotal planning instrument for large and small enterprises alike. The giant corporations provide us with examples on a grand scale, but the same kind of thinking is just as vital for small firms.

AN EXAMPLE

A terse sketch of the central strategy of one small firm will illustrate this point. The partners of an accounting firm in a city with a quarter-million population predicted faster growth in data processing than in their normal auditing and tax work, yet they knew that most of their clients were too small to use an electronic computer individually. So they foresaw the need for a single, cooperative computer center serving several companies. And they believed that their intimate knowledge of the procedures and the needs of several of these companies, plus the specialized ability of one partner in data processing, put them in unique position to operate such a center. Competition was anticipated from two directions: New models of computers much smaller in size would eventually come on the market—but even if the clients could rent such equipment they would still need programmers and other specialized skills. Also, telephonic hook-ups with International Business Machines service centers appeared likely—but the accounting firm felt its local and more intimate knowledge of each company would give it an advantage over such competition. So, the cooperative computer center looked like a propitious niche.

The chief obstacle was developing a relatively stable volume of work that would carry the monthly rental on the proposed computer. A local insurance company was by far the best prospect for this purpose; it might use half the computer capacity, and then the work for other, smaller companies could be fitted into the remaining time. Consequently, the first major move was to make a deal—a coalition—with the insurance company. One partner was to devote almost his entire time working on details for such an arrangement; meanwhile, the other two partners supported him through their established accounting practice.

We see in this brief example:

- The picking of a propitious niche for expansion.
- The anticipated synergistic effect of combining auditing services with computing service.
- The sequence and timing of efforts to overcome the major limiting factor.

The project had not advanced far enough for much reappraisal, but the fact that two partners were supporting the third provided a built-in check on the question of "how are we doing."

REFERENCE

This article is adapted from a new chapter in *The Process of Management*, second edition, published by Prentice-Hall, Inc., in 1967. Executives who wish to explore the meaning and method of shaping master strategies still further can consult the following materials: E. W. Reilley, "Planning the Strategy of the Business," *Advanced Management*, XX (Dec. 1955), 8–12; T. Levitt, "Marketing Myopia," *Harvard Business Review*, XXXVIII:4 (July-Aug. 1960), 45–66; F. F. Gilmore and R. G. Brandenburg, "Anatomy of Corporate Planning," *Harvard Business Review*, XLI:6 (Nov.-Dec. 1962), 61–69; and H. W. Newman and T. L. Berg, "Managing External Relations," *California Management Review*, V:3 (Spring 1963), 81–86.

READING 6

Impact of Social Sanctions on Product Strategy*

George Fisk

As enchantment with the production of technically feasible products gives way to concern over the diminishing "quality of life," the weight of U.S. public opinion is shifting to focus on the social benefits and costs of a technological society. Without conscious direction from a single source, American society is erecting barriers to further technological developments unless products offered have desired impacts on the ephemeral and largely undefined quality of life now replacing the pursuit of affluence as a top national priority. These barriers to unplanned technological development are being created largely by the exercise of three classes of social sanctions: life styles, social values, and national priorities.

Since product strategies are the means by which new technologies are introduced, this aspect of management is directly affected by social sanctions. As used here, the term product strategy refers to the determination of what products to produce and market, what mix of products to include in a product portfolio, and what products to delete or what production divisions to acquire or divest from the parent company. The details of product search and evaluation and the route to commercialization are included with elements of marketing as product tactics and are not considered further.

Social sanctions are simply rewards or penalties imposed in response to behavior of the managers who direct product strategy. Sanctions are positive and benign when the value for price is satisfactory to the consumer, when production and sale do not adversely challenge the interests of powerful groups, and when the product does not provide incentives for government restrictions. Sanctions are negative when a consumer suffers a loss or when, even if the consumer is satisfied, society incurs social costs as in the case of automobile emissions. Product managers need to know how social sanctions can affect their decisions; knowledge of sanctions is also valuable to special interest groups and government agencies responsible for their administration.

A few large firms have set up environmental study groups in recognition of the growing influence of forces external to the firm. For example, General Electric has established a business environment study group whose task is to

* Reprinted from the *Journal of Contemporary Business,* Winter 1975, pp. 1–19. Reprinted by permission.

keep top management appraised of changes in their operating environments [1]. Most firms do not follow this practice until a crisis forces a decision, but by that time it is often too late to prepare for an impending change without major disruption or cost. For firms willing to organize a business intelligence or environmental surveillance group, adaptive planning is simply a matter of phasing the analysis and evaluation stage into the product strategy sequence.

What benefits can environmental study groups offer to justify their costs? As diagrammed in Figure I, these groups supply data that permit management to plan; in effect, they are "decision insurance departments," giving management the information it needs to adapt to forces beyond its ability to control. Even AT&T, General Motors, and other corporate giants must adapt to the impact of social sanctions. As recent experience has sadly demonstrated, most large corporations repeatedly are caught unprepared to deal with social sanctions. Unless top management believes in, finances, and uses the results of business environment study groups, such groups have extremely limited value to line product managers.

Most environmental analyses continue to focus on technological and economic forecasts, the traditional elements of business environment closely watched by management. Product managers are seldom as familiar with the impacts of social sanctions as they are with these more familiar elements of their environment. However, once a social sanction is introduced, its impacts are widely felt. Hence, tracing these impacts is an important analytical task in providing information needed for designing product strategy. For firms of significant size as well as for public interest groups, this article examines methods for analyzing and evaluating the impacts of social sanctions on product strategy.

SOCIAL SANCTIONS AS DETERMINANTS OF PRODUCT DECISIONS

This analysis focuses on the social sanctions listed in Step 2 of Figure I: life styles, social values, and national priorities. These "states of the business environment" are treated here as social sanctions whose impacts motivate product management decisions. Impacts are simply the rewards or penalties regarded by product managers as benefits or costs. By imposing benefits or costs on managerial behavior, social sanctions direct managers to choose payoffs that reduce costs or increase benefits to acceptable levels. Thus, social sanctions are influences that determine product strategy decision processes to a greater or lesser extent depending on circumstances unique to specific products.

Managers are accustomed to dealing with the impacts of social sanctions on an *ad hoc,* opportunistic basis. While this orientation is rooted in inability

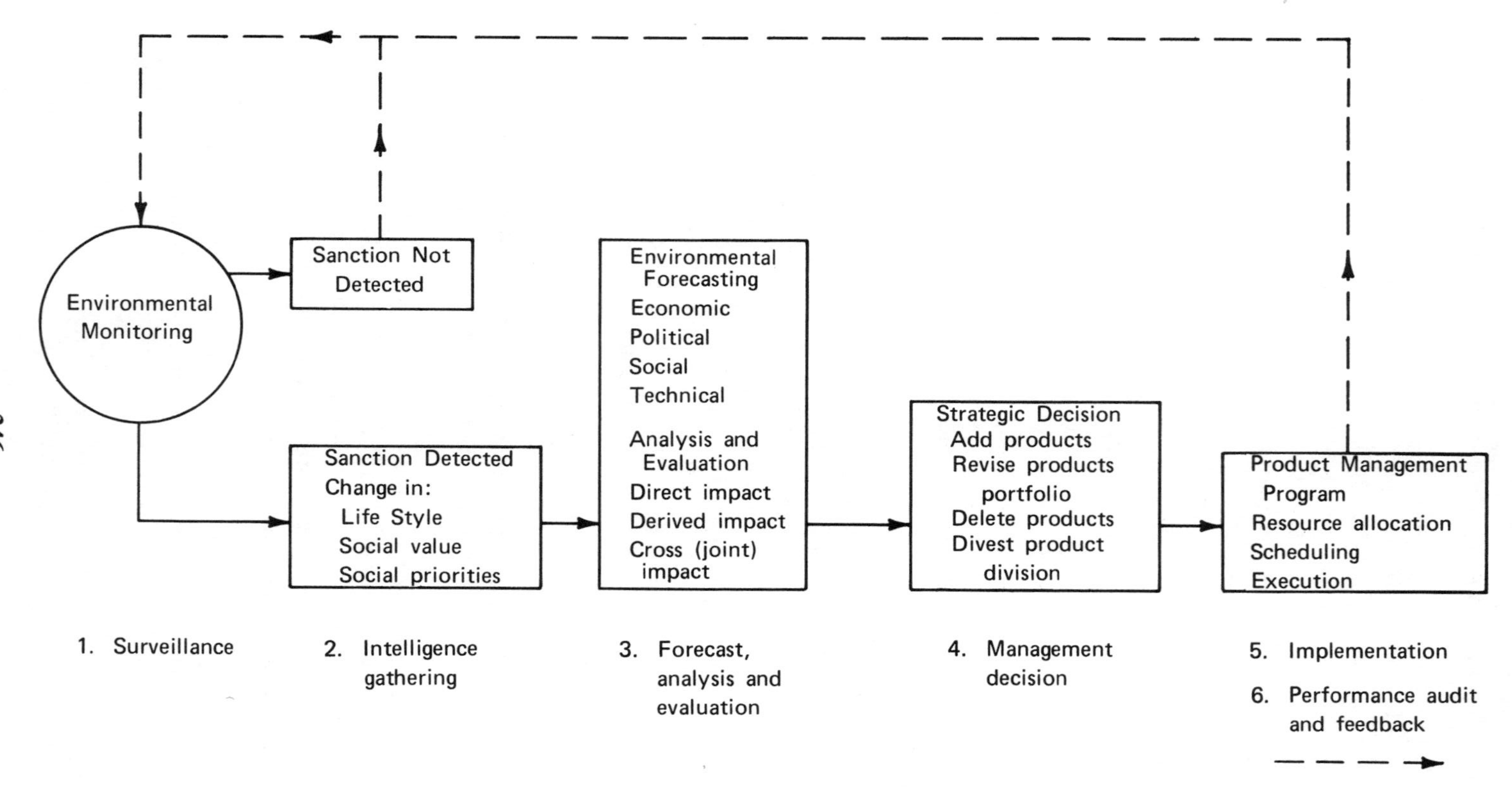

Figure 1 Stages in an adaptive product strategy.

to foresee far into the future, it limits the application of experience to specific cases instead of extending it to a generalized mode of response. If specific impacts are regarded as elements in an interacting system of impacts, product strategies can be chosen that are managerially more effective and socially more responsible.

For example, in Table 1 sanctions are analyzed by level of impact. Although each of the three sanctions is examined in general terms rather than with respect to impacts on specific classes of products, the next section focuses on two bellwether industries: automobiles and drugs. For the moment, consider impacts as elements of an interacting system.

A sanction directly influences product strategy, either by promising rewards or imposing penalties. For example, under life styles, an increase in purchases leads to increased market share and, ordinarily, to decreased costs, thus enabling producers to lower prices and increase volume until cost per unit is as low as the extent of the market will permit. Such an impact has a derived consequence. For example, pollution and resource depletion increase at the same time as gross national product increases. These derived "spillovers" also have consequences that include the imposition of further sanctions by public interest groups, by government or both. Thus, a positive sanction can evoke positive and negative impacts at the same time, and among these impacts are the imposition of further sanctions.

Also shown in Table 1 under Life Style Sanctions is a drop in consumption. This could be caused by many influences, e.g., adverse business conditions or a change in tastes. In the illustrative case the immediate cause is monopolistic pricing and supplier-controlled shortages. The direct impact of shortages on producers who need materials in controlled supply forces them to introduce close substitutes at hand in the short run and to mobilize research and development efforts to find substitutes in the long run. The derived "spillover" effect is to raise the level of scientific and technological development. Technological advance usually carries new health, safety, and environmental hazards so cross-sanction impacts are likely consequences. Among these cross sanctions are coalitions of public and private interest groups including environmentalists, labor, and consumerists seeking to force government to impose more rigorous controls. At the same time, political pressure is likely to force government to act to protect the environment, workers, and consumers so that synergistic reinforcement of cross-sanction impacts direct product strategies toward desired social goals and national priorities.

Table 1 provides further positive and negative sanction illustrations stemming from social values and national priorities. Social values that trigger direct impacts may be held by religious groups, labor groups, farm groups, ethnic groups, public interest groups, or other organized power blocs that can mobilize public opinion. National priorities usually are expressed in budgets, subsidies tax levels, legislation, court and administrative decisions or, as illustrated, by contract awards and regulatory rulings. Since the illus-

TABLE 1
Behavioral Impact of Social Sanctions
Analyzed by Level of Sanction
Level of Impact

Social Sanction	Direct Product Impact	Derived Spillover Impact	Cross-Sanction Impact
Life style—positive			
Increase in dollar value of purchases by consumers	Increase in market share for product leads to reduction in production cost per unit, leads to strategic decision to lower prices to increase volume until total combined unit cost of production and distribution is at the minimum dictated by extent of the market	Pollution and accumulation of waste and accelerated depletion of resources	Wastes and pollution generated by rising consumption encourage environmentalists to agitate for new legal restraints Government enforcement of pollution regulations raises producer costs
Life style—negative			
Monopolistic price fixing and control over supplies of basic materials lead to decrease in consumption (i.e., milk, sugar, coffee, oil, metals)	Product designers substitute materials for price-fixed commodities; management institutes R&D programs to find new components whose supply is assumed at acceptable costs	Scientific and technological advance produces safety and health hazards (e.g., plastics, asbestos fiber, radioactive materials)	Government intervention to protect environment; occupational health and safety leads to lawsuits by public interest, consumer, worker and industrial user groups
Social sanction—positive			
American Society For Testing Materials sets voluntary quality safety specifications	Producers adopt industry-recommended quality and safety standards	Accident rates drop insurance; demand for hospital and medical services reduced; insurance company profits rise	Consumer purchases increase driving unit cost of production down

Social sanction—negative Consumers' Union files complaint on misleading and deceptive advertising with Federal Trade Commission	Producer forced to reengineer product to conform to advertised performance claim or to modify advertising	Consumer brand loyalty shifts changing volume-price-product differentiation competition	Consumer purchases decline driving cost of production up
National priorities—positive Military R&D contract for cost plus profit	Advanced engineering designs developed in new weapons systems	Production technologies advanced with diverse civilian applications; raises capability to earn foreign exchange	Increase in taxes curbs consumer spending/public spending for peace-time programs
National priorities—negative Consumer Product Safety Commission empowered to remove hazardous products from market	Product planners organize product safety committees to plan, trace and recall campaigns; quality controls tightened	Improved products may be more durable as well as less hazardous; poor consumers priced out of market in short run	Consumerists shift attention from product hazards to price levels and value-for-pride antimonopoly legislation

trations in Table 1 do not explain fully how these social sanctions can modify product strategy, amplification of these concepts should prove helpful.

Life Styles

The goals people strive to achieve in interacting with others can be defined as their life style [2]. To move around in space and time and to express themselves as they would like to, people use goods and services as instrumentalities. Therefore, when they enter the market to acquire these instruments, patronage increases. Patronage raises market share and profits for some producers and reduces it for others; thus, purchasing goods to express one's life style has the effect of a positive sanction in encouraging producers of desired goods to produce more. On the other hand, not buying penalizes producers of unwanted goods who are encouraged to produce less. The very basis of the theory of free and open competition rests on these market sanction powers of so-called "consumer-sovereignty." In high-level technologies, consumer sovereignty regulates production of inscrutable goods poorly. This explains why other sanctions must be invoked, e.g., industry self regulation, in the interest of product safety and fair dealing, or government regulation.

Despite conspicuous failures, consumer choice in the marketplace remains the most powerful single sanction available to unorganized consumers to direct business to produce products of desired quality and design. For example, consider the impacts of purchasing patterns that stem from changes in U.S. consumer life styles:

- The quest for self expression and authentic living that has magnified demands for "natural foods," "country homes" and outdoor camping and hiking equipment and led to the decline in sales of traditional home furnishings.
- The urge to save time by homemakers entering the labor market as manifested by the rapid acceleration of sales of drip dry clothing, prepared foods, frostfree refrigerators, and other costly items for which lower cost alternatives are readily available.
- The rapid rise of service industries relative to durable and nondurable goods. People stay in school longer despite the expense because they believe that it raises their productivity and earning power. Self improvement and health maintenance enable people to attain a higher degree of self fulfillment over a longer life span.

When individual desires are expressed accurately in the marketplace as purchases, consumers can vote for massive adjustments in product management, such as

- Market exit of high-cost, inefficient producers.
- Introduction of technically more effective new products.

- Continuous improvements in service after sale via manufacturer warranty programs.
- Multinationalization of production facilities and flow of desirable product designs across national boundaries.
- Redirection of private sector resources from low labor saving component to high labor saving component products.
- Mobilization of private sector capital to produce wanted but unavailable public sector goods capable of gratifying unmet individual consumer demands.

Changes in consumer life styles that change product management behavior express a high order of sanction power. However, life-style sanction power is too limited to serve many social needs. Indeed, although the free market was not developed for this purpose, its critics are seldom challenged when they introduce this assumption. Within the range of its capabilities, the free market offers extremely effective positive and negative sanctions. However, since it cannot meet all social expectations, supplementary sanctions are required to channel product management to achieve desired social goals. Among the most effective supplementary sanctions are those that express social values of power blocs and the political consensus expressed in laws and government action as discussed below.

Social Values

Social values are norms that provide group members with standards of behavior. The attitude of a loyal farm union member towards consumers who buy nonunion grapes or vegetables; the views of a conservationist on strip mining to produce coal; and the selective patronage campaign of a black minister to encourage employment of minorities in local industries are examples of social values whose attainment evokes strong emotional support.

These examples also illustrate the motivating power of social values to enforce sanctions. Social values endow members of groups with the will power to persist in lobbying, in lawsuits and in public demonstrations. Sometimes they include violence to achieve conformity to group norms as in the case of terrorist activities.

The will to serve specified social values undergirds the perceptible shift in allocation to a higher proportion of public goods expenditures as national income rises. Among the major impacts of sanctions that serve social values are the following modifications of product strategy:

- Expansion of human capital investment training programs and related software industries.
- Expansion of health-related geriatric and medical care programs and related capital investments in plant and equipment.

- Expansion of protective services including environmental, police, and fire protection.
- Organization of countervailing power blocs to challenge industry safety standards development and product practices in fields such as automobile design, utility pricing, fossil and nuclear fuels, new product introduction of drugs and foods, etc.

Not all social sanctions are designed to serve the public interest. Indeed, many are intended to carve out vast exemptions from measures intended to serve the general welfare. For example, resale price maintenance remains legal in a number of states, despite general agreement that antitrust legislation should be enforced to assure consumers' choice among price-competitive products. Similarly, union featherbedding and make-work rules still apply in industries where the supply of workers is too limited to serve effective demands. Protective tariffs and oil depletion allowances, cost-plus contracts in military goods production, and numerous other arrangements exist because the countervailing power of special interest groups exceeds that of an unorganized and largely apathetic electorate.

Despite the exercise of sanctions to serve special interest groups, sanctions that express values of general welfare are slowly bending product strategies in directions favored by public opinion. When demanded by a sufficient proportion of the electorate, social values acquire the force of laws.

Social values are having major "cross-sanction impacts" on consumer life styles and on national priorities. Beginning with Ralph Nader's consumer safety crusade, momentum for enforcing fair dealing with consumers has increased steadily, as evidenced by the establishment of consumer protection agencies. In addition, the rush to save the environment, sometimes without consideration of benefits relative to economic and social costs, has led to the enactment of stringent environmental protection legislation. Enactment of additional environmental protection measures, including returnable beverage container legislation and hazardous product limitations, is likely in the future.

National Priorities

The rewards and penalties imposed by taxes, subsidies, budgets, and laws represent the wishes of citizens able to express their perceptions of the relative importance of social goals and values through political action. Social values have, on occasion, changed product management behavior more effectively than laws that are unenforced or budget-starved by political foes in legislatures. However, when laws are enforced, their sanction power is fully capable of imposing fundamental shifts in product strategy design.

Perhaps the most fundamental change imposed by the power of national priorities in recent decades is the shift in emphasis from the production of private goods to public goods and services. By aggregating individual demands for educational services, transportation, health-related services, housing, etc., the federal government has used its power to tax to reconstruct the balance of public versus private market demands. Pollution control and healthcare delivery systems exemplify this enormous power.

Older, long-standing public concerns include full employment, the maintenance of free and open competition, economic growth and development and the concomitant rising standards of living. Table 2 displays these social values which were expressed as national priorities during the Era of Affluence, during which product differentiation, planned obsolescence, and two cars in every garage represented the common denominator described as "the American Dream." When the U.S. imagination was captured by the concept of "spaceship earth" at the time of the first moon landing, the penalties for rapid economic growth were felt sufficiently to mobilize the consumerist and environmentalist groups. Rising political pressures in the mass media, in presidential campaigns, and in Congressional appropriations and legislative actions gave rise to the priorities of a conservationist era, as displayed in Table 2.

The shift in expenditures for health services, crime control, and environmental protection is symbolic of the changing emphasis in national priorities. These positive sanctions are accompanied by increasingly stringent negative sanctions as resource imports are curbed by international political and economic pressures. No great insight is required to extend into the future the probable impacts on product management of these changing priorities. When auto firms such as Ford falsify emission control reports or when General Motors' catalytic converters add to the retail price of autos more than consumers can pay, cross-sanction impacts are imposed, not on the government that requires the cost-generating pollution controls but on the product managers whose designs are unacceptable. Derived spillovers, such as massive

TABLE 2
Shift in U.S. National Priorities Since World War II

HIGH PRIORITY NATIONAL GOALS	
ERA OF AFFLUENCE, 1945–1970	CONSERVATIONIST ERA, 1971–
Affluence: The American Dream	Economic stability—stable GNP
Economic growth and development	Equal job opportunity for minorities
Full employment	
Maintenance of vitality of competition	Environmental protection and conservation of scarce resources
High-level mass consumption: "war on poverty"	Demand for improved "quality of life"
Consumer sovereignty but let the buyer beware	Consumer protection from unfair methods of competition and hazardous products—let the seller beware

unemployment in the auto industry and in the rubber and machinery industries that supply the auto industry, have only the most indirect impacts on the legislators whose actions triggered these consequences.

Because spillover effects of changing national priorities are serious and often unforseeable, they will be considered far more carefully in the future by planners in government and in the industries affected. In particular, consumer protection poses counterintuitive threats to the very consumers it should protect because product trace and recall programs must be paid for by the prices consumers pay. The poor, already impoverished the most by inflation, may yet be called on to pay for the higher costs of consumer protection.

Finally, both government and industry have a major stake in learning more about the impacts of national priority changes on product strategy. While futures analysts and technological forecasters have some knowledge of these impacts, little is known about means for supressing their undesirable consequences and encouraging their benign impacts. Consequently, as the United States moves toward the steady state "recycle society," numerous small-scale pilot projects will be needed to prevent the mindless technological innovation that has brought so many unwanted consequences to American life in the recent past.

TRACING THE IMPACTS OF SOCIAL SANCTIONS ON PRODUCT STRATEGY

Adaptive product strategies seek to convert potential penalties into rewards by analyzing and evaluating impacts of sanctions for decision making, as shown in Figure I. To illustrate impact analysis and the evaluation process for tracing implications, two bellwether industries are analyzed. Table 3 analyzes social sanction impacts on automobiles, and Table 4 provides contrasts by analyzing the impacts on prescription drugs. Together these tables present limiting historical cases of managerial freedom to plan product strategy. The automobile industry represents the zenith of managerial freedom in product strategy. Cars are designed to please the consumer who buys and uses them. In contrast, the drug industry represents an industry in which the buyer and user traditionally have little impact on either the product or brand chosen. Federal legislation has constrained the freedom of product planners in the drug industry since the first Pure Food and Drug Act of 1906. Legal regulations are now so restrictive that prescription drugs product introductions are becoming a rarity. In comparison, until Ralph Nader wrote *Unsafe at Any Speed,* virtually all legislation, federal as well as local, was designed to accelerate the distribution and use of automobiles at the expense of other transportation and communication modes. A sharp reversal in public policy only recently has halted further increases in production and distribution of automobiles. Despite such reversals, the legislation, taxation, and land use patterns of virtually all U.S. communities identify automobile operation as an extremely high consumer priority—overriding the interests of property and home owners, cultural values, economic efficiency, and personal safety of citizens subject to pollution and traffic accidents.

To trace the impacts and their implications for these two industries, Tables 3 and 4 analyze impacts by type of sanction and level of impact. Column 1 of each table shows model social sanctions. For example, Column 1 of Table 3 shows that consumers want to economize on gasoline consumption. The shift in purchases from big to small cars produces direct impacts on product design: Smaller cars will sell more than big cars, so Detroit designers introduce mostly small cars as shown in the Direct Impact column 2, Table 3. Meanwhile, many other environmental impacts are building up simultaneously. High levels of pollution force Washington to enact and enforce clean air legislation. Added costs of pollution control and safety equipment augment rising price levels, fueling a double digit inflation and massive inventory buildup of unsold cars. Column 3 shows the resulting unemployment as a derived spillover.

Cross-impact pressures backed by the economic dislocations force the President and Congress to retreat from earlier stringent environmental protection programs. Derived spillovers, illustrated in column 3, and cross impacts on government action, shown in column 4, have still further joint impact reverberations, as shown under Social Value and National Priorities impact analyses.

In the drug industry, longer experience with governmental legislation and regulation previously has led to diversification, multinationalization, divestiture, and heavy research and development plus time-consuming safety testing procedures that are virtually unknown in the auto industry. Because of the importance of prescription drugs to the "quality of life" along the health dimension, the drug industry is undergoing strenuous intrinsic product differentiation based on U.S. Pharmaceutical standards imposed by HEW regulations rather than on extrinsic image-related promotional and packaging differentiation. In the drug industry, generic product performance is required by government regulation, not by consumer preference. Quite possibly, as EPA requirements for miles-per-gallon and emission levels are refined, a similar return to price rivalry and intrinsic product performance characteristics as the basis for consumer preference may overtake the automobile industry.

In both tables, impacts are shown within as well as between categories. Some impacts clearly set up event chains that create opportunities for new directions in product planning. Others merely provide early warning of contingencies to be prepared for, such as the product trace and recall programs. Few firms prepare adequately despite plenty of advance warning. In either case, the analysis provides management with information needed to shape product strategy, and it also provides interested groups with estimates of derived and cross impacts of actions undertaken to serve the interests they represent.

TABLE 3
Analysis of Social Sanctions Impacts on Automobile Product Strategy

Social Sanction *	Direct Product Impact	Derived Spillover Impact	Cross-Sanction Impact
Life style			
Shift in purchases to small-size "big cars" and compacts	Nine of 11 U.S. new cars are small cars	Reduction of materials requirements spreads unemployment in rubber-related supplying industries	Reduced output alleviates pressure by environmental activists for more rigorous measures; drop in employment forces government to increase public spending on unemployment benefits and de-emphasize other national budget priorities such as inflation control
Consumer expectations that fuel will be rationed, anticipation of economic uncertainty about future	Drop in sales of new automobiles; economy in miles per gallon and lowest maintenance costs emerges as principal buying motivations	Decreased use of automobiles for pleasure, recreation, travel, and vacation depresses industries based on automobile use	
Social values			
Scientific community analyzes environmental consequence of automobile emissions in professional engineering and medical journals	Stimulates mobilization of environmental action groups seeking auto design modification and substitution of mass transport	Intellectual leaders call for substitution of electronic communication for transportation of people	Power blocs organize to design public transit facilities to replace passenger automobiles
Public interest research groups (PIRG) demonstrate that rigorous auto emission standards can be met at low cost	Environmentalists pressure EPA to maintain strict air pollution requirements	High annual price increase to cover emission controls and safety equipment curbs new car sales; increase triggers widespread unemployment, shrinkage of scarcities and back orders in supplier industries	EPA regulations stiffened to include indirect air pollution impacts including urban land use for parking lots, shopping centers, high rise dwelling limited

Consumerists press for more stringent safety measures on new cars that are "unsafe at any speed"	Manufacturers organize product safety committees to trace and recall defective cars; safety and performance reliability emphasized in product design	Emergence of safety consciousness among consumers forces technological innovations stressing safety	Consumer Product Safety Act enacted in 1972 to reduce product-related accident hazards
National priorities			
National speed maximum of 55 mph to conserve fuel	Automobile replacement rate drops as cars last longer; aggravates unemployment generated by consumer uncertainty	Accidental auto death rates drop and insurance company profits rise	Some return to older U.S. life style as race for the suburbs slows as population begins fuel conservation practices; population redistribution affected by rising transportation costs forces substitution of transportation outlays for other expenditures in short run.
Devaluation to restore "favorable balance of trade"	Imported autos priced above U.S. prices, but suitability of imported designs maintain market penetration of imports	Inflationary pressure on economy of rising new car prices reduced as foreign manufacturers stabilize or cut prices	U.S. consumer shift from credit purchases to saving higher proportion of income

* Direction of causality is from left-hand column to right-hand column throughout table.

TABLE 4
Analysis of Social Sanctions Impacts on Prescription Drug Product Strategy

Social Sanction *	Direct Product Impact	Derived Spillover Impact	Cross-Sanction Impact
Life style			
Consumer expectation of conformity of prescription drugs to USP standards is rising	Increased purchase of generic instead of brand-name prescription items leads to	Improved public health reduces mortality and illness rate, raises profitability of insurance companies using outdated mortality tables	Mandatory enforcement of generic drug prescriptions by HEW and public assistance agencies
Increasing proportion of total consumer expenditure allocated to health maintenance in private sector as GNP rises	Posting of prescription prices in large-volume drug stores and	Increased health and earning power of labor force	Drop in prices of prescription drugs reduces consumerist and government action to enforce additional legislation to revitalize competitive pricing
	Shifts manufacturing output to high-volume, low unit profit lines away from high-markup, low-volume, brand-name prescriptions	Reduction in number of prescription pharmacies serving drug consumers	
Social values			
American Medical Association refuses paid drug advertising in AMA journal	Drop in sales of brand-name prescriptions and reduction in number of medical expansion of potential markets for new uses of existing drugs	Improved diagnosis and prescription by physicians using non-advertised drug information sources	Cumulative impact of restictions on prescription advertising improves efficiency of "industry self regulation"

Consumerist agitation for more stringent "drug-safety" laws	Drop in drug-related accidents and sharp drop in domestic U.S. sales of new products	Decrease in health-related public assistance and insurance claims	Consumer ability to use prescription drugs is enhanced, hence, consumer sovereignty becomes more effective sanction
	Sharp increase in R&D costs and costs of testing of new uses of drugs by manufacturers		
National priorities			
Federal Trade Commission requires substantiation of advertised drug claims, corrective advertising and proscribes deceptive advertising	Increase in product testing costs and decline in advertising and detail man promotion sampling costs	Expansion of nonregulated product lines	Interaction between FDA an FTC regulations encourages industry self regulation
Patent office review and limitation of patents	Decrease in number of new products stimulates efforts to diversify by drug producers; acquisition of product lines in chemicals and medically related nondrug lines such as pesticides, medical instruments adapted as a product strategy	Expansion into multinational, joint-venture, licensing operations; dropping unprofitable lines on which patents have expired	National health insurance proposals specify allowable charges for lowest-price, generic product prescription
Increase in health-related expenditures by government	Rise in basic research on public health problems including drug addiction, alcoholism and nicotine addiction	Rise in R&D by manufacturers for new products designed for public health problems	Emphasis in public spending shifts from institutionalization to community services with medication

* Direction of causality is from left-hand column to right-hand column throughout table.

IMPLICATIONS

Arnold Toynbee long ago pointed out that civilizations fail when they continue to respond to changed conditions by means that are no longer appropriate. This lesson has applications for product managers, for public interest advocates, and for government lawmakers. Detroit shows strong inclinations to cling to product strategies that were effective in the affluent 1960s. Social responsibility stockholder groups and others tend to focus on particular issues without regard to unanticipated and unwanted "counterintuitive" derived or cross impacts of sanctions. Government lawmakers often enact conflicting legislative measures, failing to consider the system of action for which they are legislating or the system of impacts which their actions generate.

Analysis and evaluation of these problems, as is well known, is not sufficient to solve them. Management has to mobilize resources and allocate them in risky strategies. But to do this by blind adherence to habitual modes of action without analysis is patently unwise. Adaptive product strategies are more likely to be effective when premised on reports of environmental surveillance and performance auditing groups within the corporation then when the all too common "groupthink" management processes are employed. These work well enough as long as no major discontinuities intervene to change environmental states, but their inadequacy is demonstrated in every major U.S. industry.

Recommendations for intensive research in the environmental area are often dismissed as trite, even at the highest scientific policy levels [3]. As the sociotechnical structure of U.S. society grows ever more interdependent with that of the rest of the world, the need to anticipate possible rewards and penalties of social sanctions becomes more urgent. Like the weather, everyone talks about the need for data on the impact of sanctions but no one does very much to implement its production. As the experience of General Electric and a few other firms suggests, environmental study groups can provide management with alternatives to "groupthink" strategies. In view of the usefulness of impact analysis to government and public interest groups, the organization of nonpartisan research groups from the ranks of university and research institute personnel would be one way to start this new "institution building" process. American society already has paid a high price for social sanctions that have been imposed without consideration of their complex interactions. The means are at hand for research if the common will can be mustered.

A second implication concerns the mechanism for change. Traditionally, negotiation in economic matters has taken place in free markets. Consumer life styles dictate the rise and decline of product acceptability. Still valuable for imposing sanctions on private goods, life styles and market-determined values are being supplemented increasingly and even replaced by the nonmarket benefit and cost calculations appropriate for public goods. Without the impartial check on values provided by market-determined prices and sales, some kind of shadow pricing allocation system is needed for public goods. At present the countervailing power of competing interest groups leaves the bulk of the population unrepresented by sanction power. Either some approximation of market transactions by electronic voting on such matters or the organization of ombudsmen is needed to represent the "silent majority" whose seeming apathy may be attributable to factors other than disinterest. If the politicization of product strategy alternatives does take place, new forms of representation will have to be worked out to assure that decisions are indeed the "will of the people" and not that of those whose interests and social values are at stake.

Finally, one benign consequence of analyzing changes in life styles, social values, and national priorities is that these sanctions and their impacts are exposed more fully to public scrutiny. At present, few people know with exactitude their own social values. Even the great national debate over national priorities inaugurated by President Eisenhower has long since faded to a low murmur. If the only "spinoff" impact of studying the adaptive product strategy process were to heighten public awareness of these important issues and firm the sense of national purpose, the benefits would, be very large relative to any conceivable costs.

REFERENCES

[1] Wilson, Ian H.: "Socio-political Forecasting: A New Dimension to Strategic Planning." *Michigan Business Review,* July 1974, pp. 15–25.

[2] Myers, James H. and Jonathan Gutman: "Life Style: The Essence of Social Class." In William Wells (ed.): *Life Style and Psychographics,* Chicago, American Marketing Association, 1974, p. 237.

[3] Reissman, Leonard: "Social Sciences, Future Tense." *Science,* December 20, 1974, p. 1077.

Computers: Snow White and the Seven Dwarfs (RCA, GE, Univac, Control Data, NCR, Burroughs, Xerox)*

Joel E. Ross and Michael J. Kami

"Do you know we actually had two guys whose job it was to keep us out of the computer business? It probably saved us half a billion dollars. The worst thing we could have done is gone down that road."

—Harold Geneen
Chairman, IT&T

How many directors, chairmen, and other top executives have wished that they had adopted the philosophy of this incredible manager, Harold Geneen? Consider the corporate giants that have tried to edge into the mainstream of computer manufacturing, only to back off or fail miserably. RCA, General Electric, Westinghouse, Hughes Aircraft, Bendix, Ratheon, General Foods, and Philco-Ford are among these. Is it, as a top computer executive admitted, "because companies failed to realize that computers were a business and not a technological romance?" Or is it because, once again, we see corporate giants overlooking management basics? Perhaps it is both.

Something indeed did go wrong, as we can see from examining fact and fiction:

FICTION	FACT
"Except for a minority of skeptics, computer men believe their business is entering an era in which all but the incompetent or the inordinately unlucky are destined to fare handsomely." —*Fortune,* August 1968	As of 1972, the rate of shipment of computers has not improved since 1968. Hundreds of software firms dropping out.

* From the book *Corporate Management in Crisis: Why the Mighty Fall* by Joel E. Ross and Michael K. Kami. © 1973 by Prentice Hall, Inc. Published by Prentice-Hall, Inc., Englewood Cliffs, New Jersey.

FICTION	FACT
"We intend to be the Ford of the computer business." Bill Norris, Chairman Control Data Corp. (1967)	In 1971, return on equity was 2.9% and company ranked *sixth* in the industry.
"We aim to achieve a strong second place." Van Aken, General Mgr. Computer Dept., GE (1964)	Called it quits in 1970. Merged into Honeywell-GE and got 18.5% on a temporary basis before phasing out.
"We expect to be second only to IBM and we expect to be profitable." Robert Sarnoff President, RCA (1968, 1969)	Called it quits in computers in 1971. Loss $490 million.

Except for IBM and Control Data, the major firms in the computer industry are multiproduct, and computers represent only one operation of several. If this were not true, many of them would have been unable to survive the fumbles, the management errors, and the strategic blunders involved.

The computer industry is like no other. It is not the technical hardware of the nature of the product that concerns the major computer makers but a matter of *survival strategy*. In an industry so big and with so many participants, it might seem that the companies would have a wide range of strategies available to them. In fact, their *only available strategy is to react to IBM!* The manner in which the individual firms have reacted is largely the subject of this chapter.

You might ask, why study IBM? The answer lies in the nature of the industry. IBM is the "fortress" and all assaults upon it have failed. The history of business in the United States contains many examples of companies who succeeded by a ferocious determination to make headway against what seemed to be insuperable competition. But no industry has thrown up a company so formidably powerful in everything that counts as IBM—and things aren't going to get better!

So if we can discover what makes IBM tick, and its *competition* fail, some valuable lessons will have emerged; perhaps some lessons for those inside as well as outside the industry. We note particularly that despite the track record of some of the big giants (GE, RCA, Univac), a number of smaller firms (Texas Instruments, Fairchild Camera, etc.) have plans for cracking the nut. Our advice: read the story of Snow White (IBM) and the Seven Dwarfs (RCA, GE, Univac, Control Data, NCR, Burroughs, Xerox).

FORTRESS IBM

"If I found it necessary to raise some money, I would liquidate a painting or a jewel rather than sell a share of my IBM."

—Stockholder comment (to loud applause)
Stockholder Meeting—April 26, 1971

Perhaps this stockholder's loyalty is overstated. Or is it? Three months later, Tom J. Watson, Jr., 57, announced that he was relinquishing the offices of chairman and chief executive of IBM. This move marked the end of a great tradition of Watsonian leadership that guided IBM from a tiny, disorganized tabulating-equipment manufacturer to its present position among the very top industrial corporations of the world. And incidentally, if you had joined Tom Watson, Sr., in 1914, when he founded the Computer-Tabulating-Recording Company and bought 100 shares for $2,750, your investment would have risen to over $25 million.

In 1960, hardly a decade had passed since the installation of the first business computer. Yet IBM had moved into a position of competitive strength unparalleled in business history. They had over 70 per cent of the market, a position they have yet to relinquish. Moreover, this market share gives them 90 per cent of the profits.

It is a case history in outstanding management to examine those policies that put this company where it is. These policies can then be compared to the failures in order to see why they failed.

Service

IBM has a widespread advertising slogan today: *"We sell solutions, not just computers."* This philosophy is not new; it has been with the company since inception, and perhaps more than any other policy has accounted for the success of the company. Purchasers of computers know that support services (programming, software) are more important than the machine. Moreover, they know that they can get these services from IBM when needed. The "We sell solutions" approach results in a "multiplier" effect on sales. The real selling begins after delivery of the machine. Maintaining the world's largest stock of software, programmers, and educational facilities, IBM invites customer personnel, from top management to machine technicians, to spend some time at one of their several training facilities. After this, the salesman and systems engineer show the customer how the computer can solve more and more problems. The chances are good that, with proper follow up, the customer will discover sufficient new applications that will cause him to buy *additional* capacity. This process continues until the customer is "locked in" to the combination of IBM hardware and service.

Selling

If there is one corporate philosophy that has pervaded IBM from the beginning, it is the notion that the company is a sales organization—a philosophy that has given the company their prominent position despite the fact that they were never regarded as a pacesetter in the technology of computer hardware. No computer manufacturer has had much fear of the technical aspects of IBM because all manufacturers could design just as good or perhaps better machines. However, they couldn't match IBM in *selling* the machine.

From the beginning, Tom Watson, Sr. adopted the policy that a salesman who lost an order without exhausting all the resources the company had to offer deserved to be drawn and quartered. This company way of life was a serious one and was reflected in the organizational maximum that few men could rise to line executive positions unless they had spent some time selling.

In summary, IBM's marketing strategy was simple but effective, and could be expressed in the two-part approach: "We sell solutions and not computers," and "after the sale, hold the customer's hand." This strategy confused and confounded the competition because it had built a fortress that others were unable to assault. This frustration was expressed by one competitor in the mid-sixties after IBM had produced their now famous System/360 series: "And now IBM is selling real computers—alas!"

Lease versus Buy

Aside from their marketing strategy, the next most important reason for IBM's relentless hold on the industry is financial—and this in turn is due to their long-time policy of leasing rather than selling their machines. The idea is to keep title to most, if not all, of your output by leasing for a monthly fee. The advantage is that you can depreciate this investment on an accelerated four-to-six year basis, thus making the investment disappear from the books much faster than the machines disappear in the field. The result is a huge bank of hidden assets in the form of fully written-off equipment that does not appear on the balance sheet, but is still earning revenues.

In the industry, this bank of leased equipment is known as a "rental deck" and has been the major stumbling block (next to marketing strategy) for other manufacturers. Not even RCA or GE could afford the fantastic sums necessary to "carry" such an investment until it began to pay off. IBM, on the other hand, has a "rental deck" in excess of $20 billion despite the fact that it is carried on the books at only $3 billion. This deck is known in the industry as "IBM's bank" and it is a *money machine* unique in the history of U.S. industry. In one recent year, the company drew $5.5 billion of its $7.5 billion in revenues from this "money machine." As one frustrated competitor quips, "What makes IBM such a fortress is cash, resources, cash, liquid assets, earnings, and cash."

Organization

In these days of the real blunders—Convair, Edsel, Lockheed's C5A, and RCA's computers—it is to the credit of IBM's tight organization that their biggest product blunder was a mere $20 million mistake called STRETCH, a giant computer in 1960–61 that didn't sell or perform to expectations. To the credit of the organization, the company and Tom Watson learned a lot: "Our greatest mistake in STRETCH is that we walked up to the plate and pointed at the left-field stands. When we swung, it was not a homer, but a hard line drive to the outfield. We're going to be a good deal more careful about what we promise in the future."

IBM has always maintained and deserved an image of a chillingly efficient organization, one in which plans were developed logically and executed with crisp efficiency. Despite this image of efficiency, the company has not been impersonal. Indeed, it is hard to find a company in which the employees are so totally dedicated to the organization. In the case of its salesmen, the dedication borders on idealization. To quote a dated metaphor of a successful former sales executive, "Going to work for IBM is like joining the New York Yankees."

Much of this credit goes to Tom Watson, Sr., a businessman who linked his moral beliefs to management principles. When Tom Watson, Jr. took over from his father in 1956, the evangelical atmosphere and missionary zeal remained, but was overlaid with a new dedication to the disciplines of science. These various facets of the company (reflected in the motto—THINK) combine to provide an organization that facilitates the practice of good management principles.

Product

IBM's approach to, and success in, their product lines reflects the efficient organization described above. Their products have been developed very carefully but have not been particularly spectacular. It must be recalled that with over 70 per cent of the market, they are competing largely with themselves in introducing radical product departures. It is somewhat like the quandry faced by the auto industry when they introduced the minicar, a product that competed directly with the Maverick, Mustang, Camaro, and Duster.

The company's decision to produce the System/360 series of computers was the biggest commercial project in business history. At about $5 billion, it was even greater than the SST (later abandoned).

The decision to produce the System/360 has emerged as the most crucial and portentious, as well as the riskiest judgment of recent times. It has been called IBM's $5 billion gamble, or "bet your company," in view of the likelihood of corporate failure if the gamble didn't pay off. Fortunately it did, and this is a credit to the company's organization and good management.

The success of this product decision made the next one easy; the introduction of the System/370 series in 1971. This "fourth generation" of computer hardware is destined to further solidify IBM's hold on the industry —a hold that is not so much the result of superior products, but the strategy of "selling the hell" out of these products.

RCA: NUMBER ONE IN ELECTRONICS (BUT NEVER IN COMPUTERS)

"If you want to go into the computer business, ask David Sarnoff. He had all the right reasons to go in to it."

—Anonymous RCA competitor
1971

If anyone should have gone into the computer business it was RCA. In 1957, under pressure to protect its reputation in industrial electronics and tempted by the potential of the multi billion dollar computer market, RCA took the plunge. On and on they plunged, from 1957 through 1971, through rivers of red ink, recurring rumors that they were dropping out of the business, countless staff reorganizations, a failing reputation in electronics, and finally a disaster in 1971. When the final score is added up, the product write-off for RCA—somewhere between $400–500 million—could exceed any other single loss in history.

What went wrong? Did RCA fail in the fundamentals of management that IBM was so successful at?

Strategy

Shortly before disaster hit in 1971, the top management of RCA was paying lip service to a strategy that included computers as the main thrust of the company. For public consumption it was announced that their most serious efforts were going into computers and electronic data processing (EDP) and that they expected to be second only to IBM. However, there was never a *commitment* to this strategy. The computer division was looked upon as just another profit center of many other profit centers, and for years there was an uneasy but unsaid feeling that the eventual demise of the division was a matter of time.

The *specific strategy* for the computer division was ill-conceived and too long overdue for change. This strategy was simply to *mimic IBM!* It was amusing in the industry and probably worked to RCA's disadvantage. They bore the brunt of such industry jokes as this one: "RCA computer manuals are just as good as IBM's—they even have the same spelling errors."

This "head on" strategy fired its last broadside in 1970 when L.E. Donegan, General Manager of the division (and an ex-IBM supersalesman) came up with his strategy of "interception." This approach attempted, by underpricing

IBM, to persuade existing users of IBM equipment to make a changeover to RCA's equipment. The idea was to offer them an alternative to the additional cost of moving up to the then newly introduced line of IBM System/370 machines. The strategy, as one Honeywell executive said, "Doesn't seem credible in the long run." *It wasn't!*

Selling and service

It was never a secret at the level of RCA's top management that marketing and service operations were far behind those of IBM. They probably also recognized the need to improve these operations. Whether from lack of control at the top (RCA's executive vice-presidents ran their divisions as independent dukedoms) or lack of commitment to strategy, the changes came too late and with too little detailed consideration.

In 1969, when Robert Sarnoff took over as chairman from "the General," he determined to close the gap between RCA's marketing and its recognized technological ability. Unfortunately, before this strategy was "geared up" with a sufficiently trained field force, the disaster had struck. Comparing RCA's sales force to that of IBM was like comparing the Boy Scouts to the U.S. Marines.

Pricing

In implementing their strategy of "going head on with IBM," RCA designed (in copy-cat style, it was said) a series of computers aimed directly at Series/360 users. RCA's had more capacity, was priced lower than IBM's new series, and RCA offered the potential user a very attractive price on changeover. This tactic failed because: (a) RCA didn't have the trained sales force and systems engineers to deliver the goods, and (b) IBM's loyal customers were "locked in" to IBM because of past good results.

Organization

It is doubtful whether RCA ever made the organizational commitment to become successful in computers. They assumed that they could pirate from and mimic IBM. This approach got them off to the wrong start when RCA hired a management consultant whose close relationship with IBM was presumably on a confidential basis. Thereafter, IBM management resolved to "kill RCA."

The organization of RCA could best be described as "loose." Vice-presidents of divisions "just dropped in" to see General Sarnoff to talk over problems, and this "let's talk it over" approach to problem solving was widespread in this $3 billion company. Ironically, when an operations staff was organized, among their first recommendations was one to get out of the computer business. This leads to the speculation that a good organization would have prevented the costly entry into the business in the first instance.

Control

A number of things indicate that the operations of the computer division were out of control. The news that RCA was abandoning computers came after close of business on a Friday afternoon, immediately following a board meeting where the decision was made. Second, the decision to quite computers came just a few months after the appointment of Julius Kippelman as fiscal officer of the Computer Systems Division. "He went out to the field and found out what the real story was, and it was a lot worse than corporate knew." To say that there was confusion in RCA is to underestimate the lack of control over operations. It appears once again that the multi-product conglomerate type of organization that prevailed at RCA inhibited the type of control system that would have forewarned of impending disaster in time to take alternative measures.

GENERAL ELECTRIC

In March 1970, the "gunslinger" Wall Street analyst Martin Simpson remarked, "GE is sick, sick, sick. It's an overextended behemoth. They lost the strongest man they had in the computer area in an airplane crash." Later in September of that year, GE effectively called it quits in the computer business by merging with Honeywell and forming Honeywell-GE, an operation that gave GE an 18.5 per cent interest. This merger is also destined for mediocrity if we believe one computer software executive, who snapped, "It's putting a sick heart in a cancerous body."

Of all those major companies that entered computer manufacturing, only RCA was in a better position to profit than General Electric. They got off to a late start in 1959 after landing a $30 million job from the Bank of America. At that time it looked like they had everything going for them. Despite the fact that GE has long been regarded as one of the best managed corporations in the world, they bit the dust in computer manufacturing with a loss measured in the hundreds of millions. What happened?

GE's downfall came as a result of managerial factors essentially the same as those at RCA. First, they figured they would make a killing in computers. Before they woke up to the fact of what it took to compete with IBM, it was too late. Although GE, like RCA, had the technical excellence and the hardware, every bit as good as IBM's, they did not have the sales and service organization to support it. Neither did they have the corporate dedication or commitment to these two important factors.

Second, GE, like RCA, was a varied and multiproduct company and was not organized to give computers the attention they deserved. Fred Borch, GE's Chairman, reflected this fact in his post mortem comment: "The major thing we've learned (from computer fiasco) is that the minute we identify one of these ventures as one of the few honest-to-God opportunities around, I would hope my successor would put the top guy he can find in charge of it, irrespective of its size at the time. It may be a little $20 million peanut. But, if that peanut could be $500 million one day, then the top man ought to pretend it is $500 million right now, and give it the $500 million kind of organization, of talent."

Managers and potential managers should take note of Borch's comment about organization. In GE's case it led not only to the computer debacle, but to perhaps even greater mistakes in the areas of nuclear power plants and jet aircraft engines, big losses for GE. Only an $8 billion giant could survive managerial blunders of such magnitude.

SPERRY RAND-UNIVAC

"For the first twenty years of the electronic computer's hectic history, Univac racked up an unenviable record of snatching defeat from the jaws of almost certain victory."

—*Business Week*

Although Sperry Rand has not gone out of the computer business and has no plans to do so, its Univac Division (as in RCA and GE) has lost almost enough money to sink the parent. This is remarkable in view of the fantastic head start Univac had on the industry. By 1952 they had fully two-thirds of the computer brains and design talent in the United States, and by 1955 had developed and sold three of the now-famous Univac I's to the government. They could have emerged as the giant of the industry if good management fundamentals had been followed.

The near downfall and subsequent distant second-place finish of Univac can be attributed to confusion caused by managerial shortcomings—confusion about organization, management, and marketing.

Univac's organization has never been clear from the time in its early life when its irreplaceable group of scientist and design talent split up over internecine warfare (one of the group, William Norris, quit and started Control Data Corporation, of which Norris is still president). The organization structure itself was weak, unclear, and without lines of authority.

Confusion in the management of the firm as well as in the group of top managers has also been evident. In 1964, *Fortune* remarked that few enterprises have had such incredibly bad management. Controls were nonexistent, planning was done on a day-to-day basis; profit planning and control were largely overlooked. It was said that top management came up from the ranks of carbon paper and Cardex and that they didn't understand computers and were consequently afraid of them.

Marketing could never approach that existing at IBM. This selling climate is reflected by the remark of a recent design chief, who remembered the days in the early fifties when the Univac I was manufactured, and three of them sold to the government: "then we sat there and wondered if anybody would ever buy another one." As late as 1958, the forecast of the market potential for the Univac: a total of twenty machines could be sold!

In conclusion we find in the case of Univac an organization and top management that treated the computer somewhat in the nature of a stepchild, and did not organize for it. After all, the computer was just one of many products. In the post-1965 period much of this changed at Univac. A new chairman began to establish plans and set performance standards in order to achieve them. A market strategy has been developed which puts hardware and design experience to use in large complex operations such as airline management, areas in which the future of time sharing and other complex and profitable operations lie. Moreover, the long-needed emphasis on marketing and services is developing. Univac may be on the road to recovery.

CONTROL DATA CORPORATION (CDC)

Like most companies, CDC has its good and bad points. However, CDC knew the computer business well and has been in perhaps the best position to profit from it. Their failure to achieve their potential can be traced to the usual oversight in management fundamentals.

Founded in 1957 by William Norris, its current Chairman and a man who learned about computers as vice-president of Univac, CDC raised revenues from practically nothing in 1958 to over $570 million in 1969.

Unlike the rest of the industry, Norris avoided the strategy of "going head-on with IBM." Instead, he adopted the strategy of "hitting IBM where they are weakest," in large-scale computers, time sharing, and big installations where IBM's equipment could not do the job. The rifle approach to the market was based on its ability to produce the biggest, most powerful, most sophisticated computer in existence. Except for some acquisitions in related fields (including Commercial Credit Corporation to finance their "rental deck" of computers), CDC stayed pretty much in the computer industry. Norris believed that the relative failure of the big multimarket companies (RCA, GE, Univac, etc.) was due to their lack of attention to their computer products. He was fond of saying, "To run a computer company, it is necessary to have top executives who understand computers."

His product and market strategy, plus his insistence on strict standards of costing and pricing, made CDC a profitable company in its early life. However, their computer expertise notwithstanding, the management of the company fumbled the ball because they did not understand or practice the basics of good management. Aside from the autocratic, one-man rule of Norris (one vice-president said, "People learn what he wants to hear and then they play it back to him"), CDC's failure to achieve their potential can be traced to *planning and control:*

(a) The assumption that the sophisticated users of their equipment would be able to design and produce their own software and spare CDC this expense. This turned out to be a false premise.
(b) "Running scared" and price-cutting their magnificent 6600 computer based on a mere announcement of a new line (360 series) by IBM, *despite* the fact that IBM didn't deliver for three years.
(c) A complete bust in their market forecast. The forecast in 1970 was that business would keep on booming, and as a result inventory was doubled to exceed $300 million. When sales went down, profits were drastically cut not only due to falling sales, but by reason of increased financing costs.

LESSONS TO BE LEARNED

The computer industry is like no other. It has one big winner (IBM), one potential winner (CDC), and a number of others trying to cut their losses or carve out a small niche. From the short history of this industry we can draw some valuable principles of management for the future:

Don't go to war with a popgun. If you go head-to-head with the proven leader, be prepared to bring up your heavy artillery.

Make a commitment to a chosen product or market. Whether or not you are a conglomerate or a multiproduct company, if you decide to assign substantial resources to new projects/products/markets—make the necessary corporate commitment to see it through. Either get in or stay out of the business.

Don't get seduced by the prospects of a sexy new product, particularly if it is a high technology area or if it is capital intensive. Look before leaping.

Avoid a "copy-cat" strategy. Develop your own corporate personality, image, strategy, and policies. If you want to "mimic" the leader, be sure you can deliver the goods.

Organize for a commitment. If you're going to be in a market for long-run profitability, commit the necessary personnel and other resources and organize to get the job done. Some computer manufacturers either treated the product as a sideline or never really believed they were in the market to stay.

CASE 4

Illini*

George A. Steiner

THE COMPANY AND ITS BACKGROUND

The Illini Farm Equipment Company was founded in Peoria, Illinois, in 1878 and did well until the depression of 1929. It was badly hurt in the depression and found its sales dropping from $35 million in 1929 to $5 million in 1932. The company recovered, however. By 1970 its sales were $50 million. Thereafter, the company ran into trouble and found its sales dropping to $30 million in 1972 and $20 million in 1975. Profits as a percentage of sales fell from 6.1 per cent in 1970 to 3.2 per cent in 1972 and in 1975 the company incurred its first deficit since the depression of the 1930s. Even more alarmingly, Illini's share of the market fell drastically.

The Super Illini tractor, first introduced in 1935, is the company's principal product. It is available in either a standard or row-crop tread width. The company makes power-take-off implements for use with its own tractors or those of other makes. The principal implements made by the company are disc and moldboard plows, disc harrows, row crop cultivators, mowers, forage harvesters, hay balers, pull and self-propelled combines, ensilage harvesters, and corn planters. Most of the company's sales are for agricultural uses; about 10 per cent of its sales come from tractors used for light industrial purposes.

Illini products have always enjoyed a good reputation, but they have not been in the forefront of technological developments in recent years. Nor is the implement line regarded by dealers as sufficiently complete. The basic complaint about the Super Illini tractors is that they are underpowered.

Illini has a number of manufacturing facilities in different states and Canada. All plants are reasonably modern and well maintained. Production costs, however, have fluctuated widely with changes in volume of product demanded.

Illini distributes its products through 32 company-owned sales branches in the United States and Canada. There are also 19 independently-owned distributors serving small geographical areas. The branches keep inventories of company products and parts. Branch managers are responsible for getting dealer outlets in their regions and supervising dealer sales and service func-

* Suggested by "Hawkeye," *SRI Journal,* Fourth Quarter 1961. Reprinted by permission.

tions. The almost 3,000 franchised dealers retain Illini products, primarily, although about one fourth handle related lines.

Illini has been a consistent, but not a large, advertiser. To save money, however, advertising was cut back in 1973, 1974, and 1975.

Branches and distributors are required to submit each month a three-month forecast of anticipated sales to dealers.

The firm has not pushed hard in foreign markets. A dealer in Mexico did well until export restrictions forced him into another business in 1965. Licensing arrangements have been made in Great Britain, Canada, and West Germany.

The company has four subsidiaries. Many years ago a small company in Montreal making mining equipment was acquired because it was felt that the power plants used in the Illini tractors could be adapted to the mining equipment. This did not happen and the mining-equipment company operates independently of other Illini divisions. Its sales and profits trends have been at about the average for the industry in the past two decades. Joe Plowman is president. His predecessor when a young man was a ski-buff and, on one of his trips to Colorado, acquired a controlling interest in the Denver Ski Lifts Construction Co. In the past few years it has just about broken even. During the Korean War the Aerojet Fastener Company of St. Louis was acquired, but in recent years has shown increasing deficits. A subsidiary making grinding wheels was acquired in Philadelphia from the son-in-law of Joe Plowman who wanted to go into teaching. This company has lost money from the day it was purchased.

The financial policy of the company has been conservative. Growth has been financed through retained earnings and the company has no long-term debt. At the present time its receivables are high because of the generous terms given to purchasers and, as a result, its cash position is low. Because of stable dividends the stock of the company has enjoyed the favor of institutional investors until recently. A number of firms have made overtures to the company looking toward a merger, but Joe Plowman has never considered them seriously.

In 1973 Joe Plowman established a Corporate Planning Committee composed of the top management of the company. He also went so far as to name a Director of Planning. Precisely why Joe Plowman did this is not clear and probably was not clear in his own mind. He said that he favored looking ahead, but spent most of his time dealing with day-to-day problems. He knew that some of his competitors were doing long-range planning and he had the uneasy feeling that he, too, should be doing it, but he was never really sure what he and the others should do. So, the long-range planning function drifted.

It is now September 1976 and you are about to attend what euphemistically might be called a meeting of the Illini Planning Committee. Before doing so, however, meet the top management of the company.

THE TOP MANAGEMENT

Joe Plowman, a kindly man about 55, is the fifth president of the company. He has spent all of his life with the company, reveres those presidents who preceded him, and is not frequently given to strong authoritarian orders or decisions. He has served in different functional areas of the company, is fairly well educated, and is oriented towards engineering and manufacturing.

Ralph Appleman, is Vice President Administration. He is 50 years of age and has been with the company for a quarter of a century. He is well liked, conservative, and quiet. He was Financial Vice President before assuming his new position.

John Dollarfield, 40 years of age, is the present Vice President Finance. Before coming to Illini he was controller of four other companies and has gained a wide experience. He is bright and hard working.

Roy Steele, is 60 years of age and has been with Illini most of his working life. He is the Chief Engineer.

James A. Boelter is 63 and also has been with Illini most of his working life. Now, the Vice President Manufacturing, he has the reputation for being outspoken, short tempered, a driving manager, but honest. He is exceptionally loyal to the company.

George M. Hartley is a young engineer aged 32 who, before being named the Director of Planning, was Plowman's assistant for a few years. He reports to John Dollarfield.

William Sellers is Vice President Marketing. He has been with the company for 23 years. Before joining Illini he was sales manager for a large electrical firm. He has the reputation for being a very good salesman and for knowing intimately the details of Illini's field operations.

Edward Travelard is 52 years of age and is the Vice President International. He has moved around in the sales department of Illini for 20 years before assuming his present position. He is aggressive, imaginative, and hard working.

Wilson S. Bright is 40 and Manager of Research and Development. He has been with the company for only 2 years. Before that he was assistant director of research and development for an automotive company.

THE MEETING OF THE PLANNING COMMITTEE

Appleman (Adm): We better get started. This is the first meeting of this Committee for some time. Last month's meeting had to be cancelled because so many of you couldn't make it. Bill (Sellers) how was New York? I wish I could get around like you salesmen . . . (laughter) . . . All fun no work is fine if you can get it.

Sellers (Mktg): Ralph I don't like that crack. You know damn well how hard I work. I did seen one good show, though.

Boelter (Mfg): If you guys are going to horse around I'll leave. I've got work to do.

Appleman (Adm): You're right Jim. George (Hartley) has a report to make on our long-range plans and we ought to get on with things. George (Hartley) how about it?

Secretary enters: Mr. Dollarfield, (Fin) there is a long distance call for you.

Plowman (Pres): Who is calling?

Secretary: Mr. Martinson from New York.

Dollarfield (Fin): Joe, Martinson and I are negotiating that lease on our Denver property.

Plowman (Pres): John, unless it is of the highest urgency I would rather you stay here. We are having tough problems and we should be talking about them, not night clubs, and not racing to the telephone. Miss Williams (Sec), please do not interrupt us again with telephone calls. I don't care who calls. Last week at our directors meeting I was really taken over the coals for our poor performance and we're going to do something about it.

Sellers (Mktg): Well, Joe, you know how bad the weather has been lately, and farm prices have not gone up with our costs. Farmers just aren't buying.

Plowman (Pres): Our competitors are selling in the same market as we are and they are not hurting as much as we are.

Boelter (Mfg): Well, I'll tell you one thing that is hurting us . . . those lousy forecasts of sales . . . we can't maintain an efficient production run with the bad forecasts we get.

Sellers (Mktg): Wait a minute Jim. No one could have forecast accurately in the last couple of years. I don't think we did any worse than our competitors.

Steele (Egr): How can we make money if we can't raise our prices? Our tractors are worth 10 per cent more than we're charging.

Sellers (Mktg): We would lose more money if we raised our prices. Our competitors have cut prices more than we have. One of the reasons our forecasts were off was because we did not anticipate that our competitors would cut prices as much as they did. They took some of our market.

Boelter (Mfg): I'll match anybody in the field on costs. I can get my costs lower than anybody's. But how in the hell can I cut costs with the screwed up forecasts you guys give me? And look at the heavy inventories we are asked to carry so that you guys can promise instant delivery to anybody that wants anything.

Dollarfield (Fin): You fellows are partly right and partly wrong. We have been in a tough situation during the past year. With declining total demand we have been faced with relatively increased inventories. And, with slowing demand and uncertainties in the market our production costs have risen because of lower and uneven output.

Steele (Egr): Well, there's one thing we better do damn fast and that's to get better equipment. Half our plant is obsolete.

Travelard (Intl): That may be so but I think our biggest problem is that we had better beef up our tractors. The designs are obsolete.

Steel (Egr): Hold on a minute. We're as good as any. Our stuff is good, real good.

Appleman (Adm): Maybe we do need some retooling and maybe we do need more research and development. But how can we put money into these areas when our cash is low and our profits are slipping badly. This would increase the red ink.

Boelter (Mfg): We wouldn't be too bad off if we were not losing our shirt in that fastener plant that John (Dollarfield) suckered us into buying in St. Louis.

Dollarfield (Fin): Now just wait a minute Jim. It is true that we are losing some money now in that plant but just wait and see what will happen over the next five years. We have some great plans for that company. Anyway, you must admit that our Montreal plant is doing OK.

Steele (Egr): What plans are you talking about? If you are thinking of using the fasteners from that plant that you talked with me about for our equipment forget it. I told you it would not work.

Dollarfield (Fin): I remember our conversation but I talked with Miller (General Manager of St. Louis plant) and he thinks the wrinkles can be ironed out.

Steele (Egr): You're both dreaming.

Plowman (Pres): This talk doesn't seem to be getting us anywhere, except hot under the collar. I think we have a fine team here if we can just begin to pull together. I'd like to talk about doing this better than we have in the past. Maybe the best way to start is to talk about what long-range planning we ought to be doing. I know that Ralph (Appleman) has been thinking about this. So has George (Hartley). Well, I guess we all have been doing some long-range planning but we haven't put it together very well.

Hartley (Planner): I think we have a good start in long-range planning with this Planning Committee. As pointed out we need better forecasts. We should begin with a review by this committee of our sales forecasts and then start our long-range planning. I'm not sure just what all the details should be but this should be a starting point.

Sellers (Mktg): You are right George but what is the time horizon you are talking about? If you have in mind next year's forecast to be used by Jim (Boelter) in planning his production line, we are already doing that. As I said before, our problem during the last couple of years has been unexpected events which were not easy to forecast. If you mean the long-range future I don't see how we can do much. How can we see ahead five or ten years from now if we can't see ahead very good for one year?

Boelter (Mfg): Personally, I don't think we have much of a problem. If I can get some decent sales forecasts, minor retooling, and better workers, I can send out the front door tractors and other equipment that can't be beat. If we can only get good forecasts we can develop our plans for manpower, raw materials, components, inventories, and tooling with real precision. Oh boy how we could plan if we could get good sales forecasts.

Travelard (Intl): I have been doing a good bit of long-range planning in my Division. You may remember our talk about six months ago about expanding foreign sales. Well, I have had three of my best staff working on this and they have come up with a pretty good plan. I'll send it to you. If we follow it we will increase our foreign sales from $1,000,000 today to well over $25,000,000 in ten years and our profits will grow even faster. I talked briefly with John (Dollarfield) about getting on with this and he is now looking at the financial aspects of it. I sure would like to have a chance to present this plan to this Committee when we have finished it.

Steele (Egr): That sounds interesting. But I don't see how your staff could get very far without talking with me or my people about design changes. We can't ship our equipment anywhere without thinking about environmental conditions that need changes in engineering.

Travelard (Intl): We know that and have not ignored it. We simply have been so busy with other parts of the plan that we weren't able to talk with you about them. But we sure planned to plug into your operation.

Steele (Egr): This is not the right approach. What we need is for George (Hartley) to lay out a detailed plan that we can discuss and agree upon. If we can settle on detailed and precise plans for the next five or so years I don't see how we can miss. We have worked together well in the past and can do it again.

Plowman (Pres): What do you mean by detailed plans?

Steele (Egr): My thought is, once and for all—for five years away—to figure out what we will produce, the people we will employ, how much money will be spent on facilities (buildings and tooling), and anything else which has to be coordinated with production. Once we have firmed up our plans and everyone agrees, then let's freeze them and everybody put his shoulder to the wheel and make sure we operate on the basis of those plans. Maybe again in five years we can do the same thing for the next five or so years.

Dollarfield (Fin): Maybe we can make a plan and stick with it until it needs change. But five years is a long time and many things can happen to necessitate a change in plans. How do you account for that?

Steele (Egr): Well, if the change is great I guess the plans will have to be changed. But I still think if our plans are prepared carefully and in detail that we won't always be faced with the need for changing them, as Jim (Boelter) now does.

Appleman (Adm): I don't like much the idea of a big comprehensive plan that Roy (Steele) suggests. I think we should pick out a few good strategies and plan around them. For example, we have started an acquisition program. Some of it has been successful and some of it has not. Well, if we still want to stick with this strategy let's make some plans to make it work. Let's decide to redesign our Super Illini tractor and plan around that?

Bright (R&D): I find myself in agreement with that. We are committed to and R&D program. But we have not settled on how big it ought to be or what areas we should be working it. This is such an important area not only for our own future but also to avoid unpleasant surprises from competitors. It is a major area in which we ought to day some plans.

Plowman (Pres): We've done a lot of talking this morning. But I have not heard anything that will get us moving on long-range planning. We've got to develop our programs and see that they are carried out.

Appleman (Adm): Joe, I don't think you are being entirely fair. This is a dog-eat-dog business. We have had some rough years, but we'll pull out of it. Wait and see.

Boelter (Mfg): If we perform like we have in the last year or so we'll see this company go down the tubes.

Sellers (Mktg): Just give me a better tractor at a lower price and you'll see what my men can do.

Plowman (Pres): Here we go again! I am certain we can reverse past trends. But we can't do it sitting around talking like this. We have had some good planning sessions, we have done a lot of talking.

Boelter (Mfg): You can say that again. Too much talking and not enough work.

Plowman (Pres): We've done more than that. I can remember that last year we got together a good set of long-range objectives and strategies to achieve them. George (Hartley) I don't know where they are but find them and we'll take another look at them. Long-range planning is important to this company and I consider it to be my major responsibility at this time. I think we can pull together and lay some good plans. Let's adjourn this meeting and get to work.

QUESTIONS

1. Does the management of Illini have a good concept of what long-range planning really is? Explain.
2. What wrong concepts do the managers have? Are anti-planning biases present?

3. Define formal long-range planning?
4. What answers should formal long-range planning give to this company?
5. How would you suggest that long-range planning get started and proceed in this company?

The Ecological Monitoring Corporation (EMC)

*H. Scott Watson**

This case concerns the development of a long-range plan for EMC. The company was founded in 1969 by Chester Smith. The initial capitalization was $400,000 paid by the founder and his associates. The per share price of stock at the time was $1.00. In its three year history the company has grown to about $1,000,000 in annual sales. The company has accumulated $44,000 of earnings. Currently, equity is $444,000. The company has not lost money in any past year.

The company income is from the sales of a laboratory model water pollution tester, based primarily on electronic design, and the sale of reagent chemicals consumed by the users of the tester. The tester is Smith's patented design. The chemicals are currently purchased from outside suppliers and relabeled for sale as the company's own product.

Chester Smith has done no long-range planning in the past except on a few occasions he has given thought to the future in a vague sort of way. Up to the present time his day-to-day activities have been successful. But now he thinks that if he continues in his present line of business his sales and profit growth will be limited. He, therefore, is now convinced that he must engage in a more formal long-range type of planning.

This case represents one approach to the development of a formal plan. To simplify matters, a complete long-range plan for the company is not presented. Rather, only one program is selected for development and it, together with existing programs, constitutes the basis for the development of the plan. It should be recognized that even in a simple plan for a small company developed by the method presented here, there will be multiple programs comparable to the one illustrated here for various functional areas, such as production, finance, marketing, manpower, and so on. Enough is presented here, however, to illustrate the comparative simplicity of the approach and precisely how the plan can be developed.

* Reprinted by permission.

A CATALYTIC APPROACH TO COMPREHENSIVE BUSINESS PLANNING

There are nearly as many techniques for constructing business plans as there are people involved in planning activities. The major elements involved in business planning, however, are straightforward and conceptually simple to describe.

- The environment in which the business operates must be analyzed and assessed.
- The status of the business in this environment must be objectively assessed and clearly defined.
- The resources available to the business must be realistically evaluated and stated.
- The desires and needs of the stakeholders in the business must be understood, evaluated, and synthesized into a balanced set of goals for the business.
- The alternative strategies available to the business must be identified and the most appropriate strategy to achieve its goals must be selected.
- The tactics for implementing this strategy must be selected.
- The tactics for implementing this strategy must be defined.
- The criteria for assessment of progress must be established.

The technique described here is a catalytic approach. It is based on the concept that only the group responsible for implementing the plan is capable of developing the most appropriate plan, since only that group can derive the plan most suitable to the group dynamics arising out of the interaction of that group's intellects and personalities.

The planning technique constitutes the use of a series of catalytic devices to structure and channel the group's interactions and creative efforts into a sequence of tasks insuring a logical progression toward a comprehensive plan. The devices used are of three types, a human moderator, procedures, and forms. These three devices all contribute to fostering communication and creative group dynamics, maintaining a logical sequential progression of effort, and insuring the completeness of information used and developed.

The role of the human moderator is that of catalyst, buffer, advisor, and whip. For greatest effectiveness he should not be an intimate member of the planning group because he must maintain objectivity and authority at all times. Obviously he must be experienced and expert in the planning process and must have a broad knowledge of business and financial operations. The moderator's role is best filled by a staff member normally somewhat removed from the planning group or by an outside consultant. The individual chosen must possess acute sensitivity to human interaction and group response and be capable of firm persuasion. The moderator's function is clear and the remaining discussion will deal with the procedures and forms and their implementation.

Catalytic planning, as used here, breaks down into three phases of implementation. Phase one involves the preparatory collection of the data base regarding the environment, status of the business, resources available, and the goals of the stakeholders. Phase one is referred to as the Situation Audit, i.e., determining what the current situation of the business is relative to the environment in which it operates.

Phase two is the Plan Development, the application of creative group effort to define a path for the future starting with Situation Audit as the point of departure.

Phase three, Plan Assembly, involves the organization and summarization of the information produced during Plan Development into a comprehensive set of working documentation. This documentation is preferably divided into three parts; the Strategic Plan which summarizes the overall strategy and objectives, the Development Plan which delineates the tactical plans for implementing those activities of a developmental nature that are being instituted as a result of the planning, and the Operations Plan which defines the tactical plans for continuation of existing activities.

SITUATION AUDIT

Preparing the planning data base involves four basic analyses. They are (1) Stakeholders Analysis, (2) Sales Trend Analysis, (3) Resources Analysis and (4) an analysis of strengths and weaknesses that we call WOTS UP Analysis for lack of a sensible acronym. WOTS UP stands for Weaknesses, Opportunities, Threats, and Strengths Underlying Planning.

These analyses are performed by the specific managers of the unit undertaking planning that have the closest relationships with the various activities involved. Usually this involves having different managers complete parts of each analysis and where more than one manager has special knowledge of a specific area, all those with such knowledge should cooperate in completing those parts of the analyses.

The Situation Audit analyses involve the completion of relatively detailed sets of forms for each analysis. The forms will not be reproduced here because of their length and straightforward nature. The points they cover will be described in general, however.

Stakeholders Analysis

The purpose of this analysis is to determine the desires of and current state of relations with each of the six stakeholders in the business. The stakeholders (those that have a stake in the performance of the business) in any business are

1. Owners (stockholders in a corporation—may include top management)
2. Employees (may also include top management—possibly need consideration as a subgroup)
3. Customers
4. Suppliers
5. Financial institutions (lenders)
6. Society (community)

For each of these groups, an analysis of what they desire from the business and their present state of satisfaction or dissatisfaction with the performance of the business relative to those desires is prepared. Some of these desires are in direct conflict with one another, of course, so they must all be balanced out into an expression of a set of goals that would provide the greatest possible level of satisfaction for all concerned. Almost without fail, the Stakeholders Analysis will clearly indicate a growth strategy as the only satisfactory approach for increasing the satisfaction of each of the stakeholders. The result of the Stakeholders Analysis is an expression of the goals for the business for the planning period and an understanding of the feeling of each of the stakeholders concerning the progress of the business toward those goals.

Sales Trend Analysis

Determination of the sales trend usually begins with a sales forecast prepared by the marketing and sales managers. The forecast is then analyzed to separate out those portions of the forecast sales based on implicitly assumed developments such as product improvements and market development efforts assumed, but as yet undefined. Assumed new product developments, diversification moves, and sales into new marketplaces must be identified and separated out also. The sales trend forecast left, then is that deriving from current operations of the business. One of the purposes of the planning activity is to identify and define the programs necessary to bring about the additional sales based on assumed developments.

Resources Analysis

Business resources include people, facilities, and finances. The purpose of the Resources Analysis is to define the quantity and quality of each of these resources that the business has at its disposal, and to analyze the efficiency with which the business has characteristically utilized these resources in the past. The utilization efficiencies are indicated by such statistics as sales per employee, direct employees per manager, support personnel per manager, square feet of space per employee, capital investment per employee, excess production capacity, return on invested capital, leverage, and other balance sheet and income statement ratios. The Resources Analysis provides information as to the limiting effect of the availability of resources on the plans to be developed or the necessity to include plans to obtain additional resources and provides departure guidelines for the efficiency with which these resources can be converted to output by the business. This analysis should be carried out with a thoroughness governed by common sense and reasonable expenditure of time and effort.

WOTS UP Analysis

The catalytic backbone of the planning data base resides in this analysis. The idea is to gather observations of the strengths, weaknesses, opportunities, and threats facing the business. For this purpose a wide range of participation is desirable. Participants should include top management, the members of the planning team, members of middle management, directors and secretaries and production supervisors if practical. For this purpose a form must be used. The form in Exhibit 1 is the result of much experience with this activity and numerous modifications.

The procedure for carrying out the analysis involves indoctrination meetings for the participants in groups of 5 to 15, at which the moderator explains the planning purpose of the WOTS UP Analysis. Following a brief explanation of the form the moderator should create a few example forms and then insist that each participant fill out at least one form for practice on the spot. These are collected by the moderator and critiqued for the group. Participation in this analysis must be guaranteed anonymity and open communication must be established with any fear of retribution absolutely eliminated. After the moderator is sure that each participant understands the form and how to use it, he specifies the date for final input, preferably 3 to 7 days, and establishes ballot box collection points for the WOTS UP forms. These forms provide the initial set of planning issues that will be used to kick off the activity in the Plan Development phase.

Taken together, the four analyses produced in the Situation Audit accomplish fulfillment of the first four major elements of business planning defined at the beginning of this discussion. With the guidance provided by the Stakeholders, Sales Trends, and Resources analyses and the planning issues provided by the WOTS UP Analysis the planning team is prepared to undertake phase two of the catalytic planning procedure.

PLAN DEVELOPMENT

Greatest effectiveness is achieved in phase two if it can be accomplished in a concentrated group effort conducted on consecutive days until complete. If done in this fashion, preferably even in a location away from the business so that interruptions can be held to a minimum, the entire Plan Development

EXHIBIT 1A

WOTS UP PLANNING ISSUE **ISSUE NO. 16**

TIME CONSUMED IN BRINGING SAMPLES TO TESTER IS HURTING ACCURACY

OPPORTUNITY		STRENGTH	
THREAT	X	WEAKNESS	

STATMENT OF ISSUE

An increasing number of users of our pollution tester are getting inaccurate test results because they are taking too long to get the sample to the tester. They are attempting to save money by using slower transportation to bring the samples to the lab. This could hurt our market due to poor test results.

OBSERVATION BASED ON

Observation of users of our testers and a few complaints from customers about the high cost of getting samples to the testers within the 8 hour requirement.

WE SHOULD

EXHIBIT 1B

WOTS UP PLANNING ISSUE **Issue No.** 34

FIELD POLLUTION MONITORING WILL INCREASE OUR MARKET

OPPORTUNITY	X	STRENGTH	
THREAT		WEAKNESS	

STATEMENT OF ISSUE

Several potential customers are planning to put pollution monitoring teams into the field for monitoring of different locations on a sampling basis within the next year.

OBSERVATION BASED ON

Articles in January Issue of Environment Magazine and proceedings of Pollution Control Association 1971 Conference.

WE SHOULD

EXHIBIT 1C

WOTS UP PLANNING ISSUE **Issue No. 67**

PORTABILITY WOULD IMPROVE OUR PRODUCT

OPPORTUNITY	X	STRENGTH	
THREAT		WEAKNESS	

STATEMENT OF ISSUE

The ability to take the pollution tester to the site for use rather than having to bring collected samples to the lab. for testing would result in more accurate tests, large time savings and better public relations for our customers.

OBSERVATION BASED ON

Discussions with existing and potential customers.

WE SHOULD

Develop a portable version of our tester.

can be accomplished in 5 or 6 days with an experienced moderator. Use of a remote location does, however, require careful attention to backup material so that information needed during the sessions isn't found to be "back at the ranch."

Such a concentrated approach is not necessary to the technique, but does facilitate it because it prevents the chain of thought and the group dynamic interaction from being broken and having to be reestablished several times. Total time consumed in the Plan Development process is likely to double if approached on a piecemeal schedule, although the result is not impaired.

Preparation for phase two on the part of the planning team (those 5 to 9 managers who will be responsible for implementing the plan and desired staff personnel) involves digesting the results of the Stakeholders, Sales Trend, and Resources analyses so that the data and guidance contained in them will be fresh in their minds. The moderator should initiate the session by briefly explaining the procedure to be followed in order to prevent confusion from developing over the direction of the process.

The procedure begins with a rotational reading aloud of each of the planning issues collected on the WOTS UP forms and classifying each of them by consensus into one of the six functional areas of business. These are (1) Product (or Engineering or R&D), (2) Process (or Production or Manufacturing), (3) Marketing (or Customer), (4) Sales (or Distribution), (5) Finance and (6) Administration (or Management). To further facilitate separation of the issues and to profile the attitude of the business entity, the issues are also classified as present or future within each functional area.

Next the issues from each functional area are studied and segregated further into smaller families of closely related issues. Often a family is characterized by all issues describing faults in a functional activity related to one product line or by all issues describing opportunities to expand into a particular market, etc. At this point a Tactical Program TD form (Exhibit 2) is filled out for each family of planning issues. The form requires that a title, describing an action program envisioned to address the issues contained in the family, be generated to identify the Tactical Program. Rough estimates of the current status of the proposed action, its effect on sales or profits, its cost and required schedule are made at this time. Suggestions as to assignment of responsibility are also given.

Having identified the Tactical Programs raised by the planning issues, the thrust of the process turns to conscious, rather than subconscious, attention to strategy development. The list of Tactical Programs and the goals from the Stakeholders Analysis provide the framework from which to derive the guiding strategy for the planning activity. At this point the moderator provides a general review of business strategy types and discusses the classifications and implications of the various diversification strategies. Taking into account the Sales Trend and Resources as well, the group derives the most appropriate strategy for the business and themselves, as managers. The strategy is arrived

EXHIBIT 2

Tactical Program I D

TITLE Develop Portable Pollution Tester NO. E–1

Specific Issues included Larger market, better accuracy, lower cost of use.

Issue numbers: 16, 67, 34

STATUS OF SOLUTION

FUNCTION / STATUS	END RESULT & APPROACH	BUDGET OR METHOD OF FINANCE	ORGANIZATION & ADMINISTRATION
PROBLEM ILL DEFINED Definition needed			
PROBLEM DEFINED Concept of solution needed	X		
CONCEPTS ON HAND Data needed		X	
DATA ON HAND Evaluation needed			
EVALUATION MADE Decision needed			
DECISION MADE Work program needed			
WORK PROGRAMMED Ready to go			
IN BEING			X

PRIORITY

AT STAKE (Sales or Profits)	COST TO SOLVE (Expense or Captial)	REMARKS
$ 1 Million Sales next yr.	$50 Thous.Dvlpmt.Exp. $ 5 Thousand capital	Sales of 200 Units at $5,000/Unit

DECISION DEDLINE (Date)	LEAD TIME (Months)	REMARKS
1 month	6 months	

ACCOUNTABILITY

KEY RESPONSIBILITY	DELEGATABLE TO:
V. P. Engineering	Director Product Development

ACCOUNTABILITY GUIDELINES:

- [X] Functional Involvement
- [ ] Personal Interest
- [ ] Freedom from Bias
- [ ] Adequate Attention
- [ ] Special Competence
- [ ] Fresh Approach
- [ ] Georgraphy
- [X] Magnitude of Risk

COMMENTS:

Believe a portable is possible with integrated circuit technology. Think it would double our market for testers.

at by adding, deleting, consolidating, and modifying titles of Tactical Programs, creating new TPID forms for each change, until the list of action programs is descriptive of a strategy with which the group is satisfied (Exhibit 3). The strategy thus derived is then described concisely by the group writing technique, an orderly process of creative group dynamics through which precise descriptions can be quickly developed (Exhibit 4).

EXHIBIT 3

Tactical Program Index

Program No.	*Title*
Product	
P-1	Develop Portable Pollution Tester
Marketing	
M-1	Develop Market Research Activity
Distribution	
D-1	Expand Sales Representative Coverage
Manufacturing	
Mf-1	Purchase Wave Soldering Equipment
Finance	
F-1	Arrange Financing for Growth
Administration	
A-1	Develop Acquisition Program for Chemical Capability
Operations	
O-1	Continue Sales of Labratory Pollution Tester Model M-1
O-2	Continue Sales of Tester Chemicals

With the strategy defined, the effort moves to detailed development of program plans for each of the Tactical Programs now constituting the strategic plan. The planning team is subdivided into small groups of two or three members each, closely related in functional expertise. The small groups take the Tactical Program ID forms (with the associated planning issues) related to their respective functions and proceed to develop and define detailed action program plans on Tactical Program Plans forms (Exhibit 5).

When this effort is complete, the planning team reconvenes and thoroughly reviews each plan, modifying if necessary, until the group reaches consensus acceptance of all the Tactical Program Plans. During the review process, summaries are compiled for a master schedule, a master list of planning assumptions, a total sales summary (Exhibit 6) and a consolidated expense and

EXHIBIT 4

Statement of Strategy

BECAUSE WE RECOGNIZE that pollution testing is a rapidly growing market area,

IT IS OUR STRATEGY TO pursue aggressively the development of new products to fulfill the needs of this marketplace.

BECAUSE WE RECOGNIZE that the parameters of this marketplace are still developing and undergoing constant change,

IT IS OUR STRATEGY TO establish and maintain a market research capability to provide accurate and timely analyses of the needs and potential of the market.

BECAUSE WE RECOGNIZE that the scope of the marketplace encompasses all of the developed nations,

IT IS OUR STRATEGY TO develop and maintain sales coverage throughout the United States, Europe and Japan.

BECAUSE WE RECOGNIZE that simultaneously increasing production rates and achieving corporate profit objectives required the latest in production capability,

IT IS OUR STRATEGY TO maintain a production facility equipped to take advantage of the most up to date and economical production methods.

BECAUSE WE RECOGNIZE the necessity of sufficient financing to achieve corporate growth objectives,

IT IS OUR STRATEGY TO develop financial relationships capable of supplying our full capital needs.

BECAUSE WE RECOGNIZE the opportunity to achieve greatly increased profit on our chemical sales to users of our equipment,

IT IS OUR STRATEGY TO acquire a chemical manufacturer as a wholly owned subsidiary.

---

capital budget (Exhibit 7). Assignments of responsibility for the Tactical Programs are made and accepted at this time as well.

The next step, utilizing the Sales Summary and Budget Summary and arriving at the necessary assumptions relative to work cash, inventory levels, etc. (Exhibit 8), is the compilation of pro forma Profit & Loss Statements and Balance Sheets for the plan (Exhibit 9). Compiling the financial statements is an iterative process solving for the unknowns of long term debt level or excess cash from profits. Quantitative objectives can now be stated and related to the Stakeholders Analysis goals (Exhibit 10).

EXHIBIT 5

Program Title Develop Portable Pollution Tester **Prog. Plan No.** E-1
Exec. Responsibility V.P. Engineering Day [X]
Assignee Director Product Development Ops [ ]

Work Statement:

Phase 1
Assign 4 man development team:
a) Analyze present tester to determine possibilities of miniaturization and reduction of power consumption.
b) Perform human factors, analysis to define desirable size, weight and configuration of portable model.
c) Review (a) and (b) and determine parts of tester that must employ modified concepts of operation to fulfill requirements of (b).
d) Develop concepts for parts needed as determined by (c).
e) Prepare Conceptual Design Report.

Schedule:

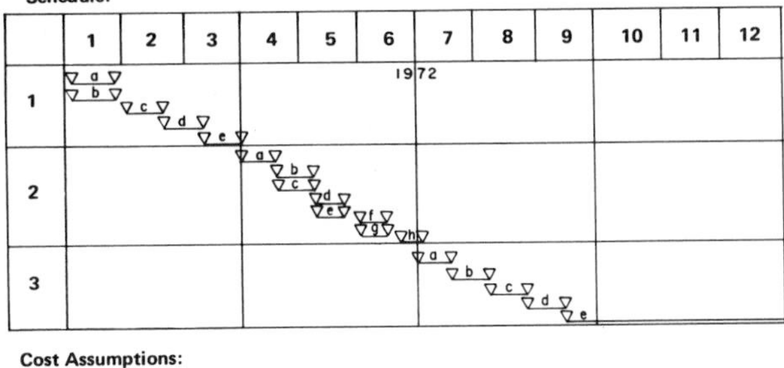

Cost Assumptions:

Phase 1 & 2: 4 man team at average cost of $1,500/man/month.
$5,000 in portable electronic test equipment for field tests.
$3,000 for parts and outside fabrication for prototype.

Phase 3: $3,000 new production equipment. Preproduction units cost $5,000 each.
Production and Selling: Direct Material—21%, Direct Labor—11%, Manufacturing Overhead—20%, Selling Costs—21% & G & A—9% = 82% of Sales

Phase 2
a) Perform necessary design work for portable prototype.
b) Construct prototype.
c) Purchase necessary test equipment for field tests.
d) Field test prototype.
e) Prepare Field Test Report.
f) Perform manufacturing engineering analysis.
g) Develop manufacturing procedures.
h) Prepare Manufacturing Cost Analysis Report.

Cost Budget:

Cap.	$	8,000
Exp.	$	36,000 + 13,000 + 127,000 = 176,000

Results:

1	Conceptual design for portable tester.
2	Design prototyped, tested and manufactured engineered.
3	Full production established.

Performance Assumptions:

Phase 1: Satisfactory portable unit can be developed through miniaturization of standard. model using integrated circuitry and moderately limiting lower threshold of dection.

Phase 2: Preproduction units will function as demonstrators for first sales.

Phase 3: Sales will reach 20 units/month in 6 months, then increase at 15%/year for 3 years.

Phase 3
Transfer to Manufacturing:
a) Establish pilot production line.
b) Produce 5 preproduction testers.
c) Field test preproduction units.
d) Establish full production line.
e) Produce portable pollution testers.

Performance Budget:

Sales	$	155,000
C.Red.	$	

Control:

Mi.	1) Conceptual Design Defined - March 15 2) Prototype Complete - May 15 3) Field Test Complete - May 31	4) Preproduction Units complete - July 31 5) Full Production - Aug. 31
Dec.	1) Go Ahead Decision - April 1 2) Go Ahead Decision - June 1	
Rep.	1) Conceptual Design Report - March 31 2) Field Test Report - May 31 3) Manufacturing Cost Report - June 30	

EXHIBIT 5 (continued)

1	2	3	4	5	6	7	8	9	10	11	12	1st ½	2nd ½	1st ½	2nd ½	2nd ½	1st ½
					19	73						19	74	19	75	19	76

980,000	1,120,000	1,290,000	1,480,000

1,195,000	1,370,000	1,570,000	1,800,000

EXHIBIT 6

Sales Summary

($)

		1972	1973	1974	1975	1976
P-1	Portable Pollution Tester	155,000	1,195,000	1,370,000	1,570,000	1,800,000
O-1	Laboratory Pollution Tester	1,700,000	900,000	700,000	500,000	300,000
O-2	Tester Chemicals	500,000	700,000	1,100,000	1,700,000	2,100,000
	Total Sales	1,355,000	2,795,000	3,170,000	3,770,000	4,200,000

PLAN ASSEMBLY

The final phase in the planning activity involves the assembly of the documentation produced in the session into three working plan documents. The strategy statement, master summary information, statement of objectives and compiled financial proformas constitute the Strategic Plan.

The Development Plan is composed of the Tactical Program Plans for development efforts (each with their TPID forms and planning issues for reference) segregated into functional sections. A Control Sheet is prepared for each section with the title of each plan included in the section, the first milestone in each plan, the date it is to be accomplished, and the person responsible for the program. The Control Sheets facilitate monitoring the progress of the plan. As each milestone is completed, the Control Sheets are updated to show the next milestones.

The Operations Plan is assembled in the same fashion as the Development Plan except that it contains the Tactical Program Plans that apply to the continuation of existing business operations.

QUESTIONS

1. Compare the steps in this plan with the conceptual model of a comprehensive corporate plan presented in Chart 2-1 of Part I. Are all the boxes in Chart 2-1 explicitly or implicitly incorporated in this planning process?
2. Appraise EMC's plan in terms of "doability" for a small company like this? Is it too complex?
3. If you think the process is too complex for EMC or another small company, how would you go about making the work easier and still, hopefully, achieving the same substantive results?

EXHIBIT 7

Budgeted Resource Allocation
($)

No.	Title	Operations 1972	Operations 1973	Operations 1974	Operations 1975	Operations 1976	Development 1972	Development 1973	Development 1974	Development 1975	Development 1976
P-1	Develop Portable Pollution Tester						176,000 8,000	980,000	1,120,000	1,290,000	1,480,000
M-1	Develop Mkt. Research Activity						24,000 2,000	18,000	18,000	18,000	18,000
D-1	Expand Sales Rep. Coverage						3,000				
Mf-1	Purchase Wave Soldering Equip.						30,000		60,000		
F-1	Arrange Financing for Growth										
A-1	Develop Acquisition Prog. for Chemical Capability						5,000	25,000 500,000			
O-1	Continue Sales of Pollution Tester Model M-1	595,000	765,000	595,000	425,000	255,000					
O-2	Continue Sales of Tester Chemicals	450,000	630,000	825,000	1,275,000	1,575,000					
	Total Expense	1,045,000	1,395,000	1,420,000	1,700,000	1,830,000	208,000	1,023,000	1,138,000	1,308,000	1,480,000
	Capital						40,000	500,000	60,000		

EXHIBIT 8

Financial Assumptions

	1972	1973	1974	1975	1976
Current Assets					
Cash	5%	5%	5%	3%	3%
Accts. Recv.	10%	10%	10%	15%	15%
Inventory	10%	10%	10%	8%	8%
Current Liabilities					
Accts. Payable	10%	10%	10%	9%	9%
Accrued Exp.	4%	4%	4%	4%	4%

Depreciation Schedule

10 Year Life – Straight Line

	1972	1973	1974	1975	1976
Base ($450K)[a]	45,000	40,000	35,000	30,000	25,000
1972 ($40K)	2,000	4,000	4,000	4,000	4,000
1973 ($500K)		25,000	50,000	50,000	50,000
1974 ($60K)			3,000	6,000	6,000
1975 (0)				–	–
1976 (0)					–
	47,000	69,000	92,000	90,000	85,000

[a]Investment made in year shown. See Exhibit 7

EXHIBIT 9

Profit and Loss, and Balance Sheet, Statements
($ 000 omitted)

	1972	1973	1974	1975	1976
GROSS SALES					
Net Incomes	1,355,	2,795,	3,170,	3,770,	4,200,
Cost of Operations	1,253,	2,418,	2,558,	3,008,	3,310,
Depreciation	47,	69,	92,	90,	85,
Interest (8%)	θ	34,	34,	13,	θ
GROSS PROFIT	55,	274,	486,	659,	805,
PROVISION FOR TAXES (50%)	27,	137,	243,	329,	402,
NET PROFIT	28,	137,	243,	330,	403,
CAPITAL INVESTMENT	40,	500,	60,		
CURRENT ASSETS					
Cash	68,	140,	159,	247,	711,
Receivables	135,	280,	317,	566,	630,
Inventory	135,	280,	317,	302,	336,
FIXED ASSETS					
Plant & Equip.	497,	997,	1,057,	1,057,	1,057,
LESS RESERVE FOR DEPR.	167,	236,	328,	418,	503,
NET FIXED ASSETS	330,	761,	729,	639,	554,
TOTAL ASSETS	668,	1,461,	1,522,	1,754,	2,231,
CURRENT LIAB.					
Trade Payables	135,	280,	317,	339,	378,
Accrued Exp.	54,	112,	127,	151,	168,
Tax Payable	7,	38,	61,	82,	100,
FIXED LIAB.					
Debt	θ	422,	165,	θ	θ
NET WORTH					
Stock	400,	400,	400,	400,	400,
Earned Surplus	72,	209,	452,	782,	1,185,
TOTAL NET WORTH	472,	609,	852,	1,182,	1,585,
TOTAL LIAB. & NET WORTH	668,	1,461,	1,522,	1,754,	2,231,

EXHIBIT 10

Quantitative Objectives

	1972	1973	1974	1975	1976
Earnings/Share $/Share	0.07	0.34	0.61	0.82	1.01
Return on Equity, %	5.5	22.5	28.5	27.9	25.4
Return on Sales, %	2.6	4.9	7.7	8.8	9.6
Sales/Equity Ratio	2.9	4.6	3.7	3.2	2.7
Leverage, %	0	70%	19%	0	0
Dividends, %	0	0	0	0	0

CASE 6

Stouffer Foods Services Group* Division of Litton Industries

John Doutt and Joseph Latona

In the Litton Industries Annual Report for 1967, it was stated that shortly after the close of the fiscal year, Stouffer Foods Corporation joined Litton. It was observed at that time that "Stouffer's experience in the processing, packaging, and marketing of food, coupled closely with Litton's capabilities in electronic cooking technology should produce major advances in the fast-growing markets for home, commercial, and institutional food preparation." By the end of 1968, the management stated that Stouffer produced 141 frozen foods in quantity for hospitals, schools, hotels, clubs, and airlines and that Stouffer operations had been expanded to include food servicing for hospitals, schools, and industrial plants. During that year, a $9 million frozen food processing plant was opened in Solon, Ohio, and that began the direct marketing of frozen-food products, continuing to expand its share of the $3.3 billion frozen food market.

In addition to their retail, commercial, and institutional markets, by 1969 the Stouffer Restaurant and Inn Division had expanded to include 53 restaurants and 9 inns in major cities throughout the midwest and eastern parts of the United States. The Stouffer Restaurant organization had been built over a period of years and the basic strategy throughout its growth had been an emphasis on assured high-quality foods, moderate prices, and portion control.

The organization of Litton Industries was structured to divide the business into four basic divisions, which in turn had a number of separate operating companies that produced a variety of manufactured goods and services. Stouffer's Foods was a part of the "Professional Services and Equipment" Division. See Exhibit I for a financial indication of the size and profitability of these divisions.

Financial indications of Stouffer's growth and profitability are as indicated in Exhibit II.

EXHIBIT I

LITTON INDUSTRIES

Sales and Operating Profits by Division
Fiscal Year, 1970
(all figures in millions of dollars)

Division	Sales	Operating Profit
Business Systems and Equipment	$701	$46
Defense and Marine Systems	618	54
Industrial Systems and Equipment	714	54
Professional Services and Equipment	397	39

Source: Annual Report

EXHIBIT II

Sales, expenses and profits of Stouffer's Foods Services Group
1968 - 1973, Fiscal Year

	52 Weeks Ended July 28, 1968	52 Weeks Ended Aug. 3, 1969	52 Weeks Ended Aug. 2, 1970	52 Weeks Ended Aug. 1, 1971	52 Weeks Ended July 30, 1972	26 Weeks Ended Jan. 30, 1972	26 Weeks Ended Jan. 28, 1973
	(unaudited)		(thousands of dollars)			(unaudited)	
Sales and Service Revenues							
Sales	$ 29,423	$ 34,408	$ 39,893	$ 42,912	$ 52,824	$ 23,528	$ 30,898
Service Revenues	66,130	70,096	70,561	67,109	70,735	35,006	37,239
	95,553	104,504	110,453	110,021	123,560	58,534	68,137
Cost and Expenses							
Cost of sales (exclusive of depreciation)	19,037	21,841	24,717	26,962	33,563	14,803	19,079
Cost of service (exclusive of depreciation)	54,595	59,545	58,764	56,768	59,969	30,115	31,411
Marketing, general and administrative (exclusive of depreciation)	13,637	14,661	17,154	16,905	20,174	9,947	12,115
Depreciation	2,372	2,985	3,025	3,078	3,256	1,626	1,700
Litton management fee	997	1,070	1,202	1,151	1,250	587	694
Interest expense	23	84	542	342	324	200	270
	90,661	100,186	105,404	105,206	118,536	57,278	65,269
Earnings before Taxes from Continuing Operations	4,892	4,318	5,049	4,815	5,024	1,256	2,868
Taxes on Income	2,290	2,183	2,441	2,128	2,285	555	1,286
Net Earnings from Continuing Operations	2,602	2,135	2,608	2,687	2,739	701	1,582

Source: Unpublished preliminary stock prospectus.

MANAGEMENT BY LITTON INDUSTRIES

One of the more important management devices employed by Litton was the "Opportunity Plan." The problems of assuring growth and innovation in a company manufacturing over 78 product lines and including services such as the motel industry were in part solved by the systematic application of the "Opportunity Plan" which the Litton Industries management had developed and refined over a period of years. This was a part of the management benefits which any organization operating under the Litton conglomerate received and for which they paid 1 percent of sales; see Exhibit III for an actual accounting of this arrangement.

EXHIBIT III

Financial Accounting of Litton Management Fee 1968 - 1973

	52 Wks. Ended Jy. 28, 1968	52 Wks. Ended Aug. 3, 1969	52 Wks. Ended Aug. 2, 1970	52 Wks. Ended Aug. 1, 1971	52 Wks. Ended Jy. 30, 1972	26 Weeks Ended Jan. 30, 1973	Jan. 28, 1973
	(thousands of dollars)						
Litton Management Fee	$ 997	$1,070	$1,202	$1,151	$1,250	$ 587	$ 694

Source: Unpublished preliminary stock prospectus

DESCRIPTION OF LITTON'S OPPORTUNITY PLANNING

The basic premise of Litton's opportunity planning model was that planning was considered as a line, not a staff, function. The model consisted of the following three parts or phases:

1. Opportunity Framework Review
2. Opportunities for Internal Development
3. Opportunities Through Acquisition

The Opportunity Framework Review

The major objective here is to create a better understanding of what the business was all about and to utilize this knowledge to identify areas of opportunity. This review is not merely a presentation but above all an opportunity for thinking creatively together as well as a forum for discussion.

The four chief objectives of this review are to:

1. Develop a basic rationale, i.e. why does the division exist?
2. Determine the division's position in the market place, i.e. who are the customers and competitors? What is the sales structure and strategy?
3. Determine capabilities, i.e. what are the division's principal strengths and weaknesses in relation to the competition?
4. Determine opportunities, i.e. what are the major areas of opportunities that exist for your division as a result of the above analysis?

The following diagram reveals the relationships of these four objectives.

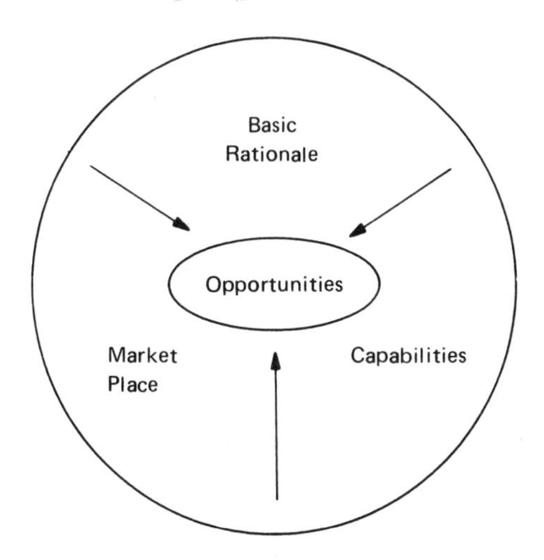

DIAGRAM I

Interaction of the Four Objectives in the Opportunity Framework Review

Opportunities for Internal Development

This phase concerns itself with the problems of
—identifying the areas of potential internal development and
—determining what resources and in what quantity should be applied

The four chief objectives of this phase are to:

1. Develop a basic rationale or concept, i.e. what are the main ideas and chief feature of this opportunity?

2. Analyze the market, i.e. customers, competition, sales strategy.
3. Determine capabilities, i.e. what capabilities do we have and need? What are our strengths and weaknesses compared to the competition?
4. Develop a general strategy based on sound business and analyses.

The main thrust here is a plan of action, anticipated results and adequate back-up to assure success.

Opportunities Through Acquisition

This phase would follow the same general approach outlined in the preceding sections. Basically the goals are to:

1. Develop a rationale as to why the acquisition should be made.
2. Determine the market characteristics of the acquisition . . . customers, competition, etc.
3. Determine the capabilities, strengths, weakenesses and competitive posture of the proposed acquisition.
4. Develop a general strategy for realizing the potential growth that the acquisition would represent.

Early in 1968, the Stouffer Foods division prepared an opportunity plan which described the specific reasons and expectations they perceived for moving into the frozen baked goods market segment. In previous years, they had developed a line of frozen prepared foods including entrees, side dishes, and meat pies. It was estimated by Sales Area Marketing, Inc., that the frozen baked goods market in 1968 was about $285 million and would amount to $400 million by 1973. It could be segmented into three major categories as follows:

a. sweet goods—manufactured by such companies as Sara Lee, Pepperidge Farm, Morton Foods, and some private label producers.
b. pies—manufactured by such companies as Mrs. Smith, Banquet, Morton Foods, and many local pie companies.
c. bread and rolls—products not especially successful in frozen form.

It was decided that sweet goods and pies offered the greatest opportunity, although it was recognized that there had been strong companies who had attempted to enter these markets and had not been successful. For example, Pepperidge Farm had attempted to market their parfait and their layer cakes (this latter with some success), and a number of companies had tried to compete with Sara Lee by lowering their price a few cents per item. For the most part, this approach had not been successful.

In attempting to evaluate the reasons for the many failures experienced by large and successful companies, Stouffer management believed that essentially four factors accounted for this. These included the failure to make good-quality items, the duplication of items already on the market and not needed (especially by the retailer as he looked at the limited space in his frozen food case), items that had low market potential and infrequently used, and lack of advertising support.

In examining the record of Sara Lee, a company with sales of over $80 million in 1968 and producing 30 baked-goods items, it was noted that about eight items accounted for the bulk of their sales. These could be grouped into three broad categories: breakfast items, dessert cakes, and cheese cakes.

Stouffer market research revealed new demographic patterns in the population and also new patterns of family living, including:

1. "Fractionated meals" within a family wherein different members of the family chose to eat at various times of the day.
2. Individualized tastes wherein different members wanted to eat different items during the same meal, if it was not inconvenient to the homemaker.
3. A desire for more variety of new products and creative serving ideas and
4. A rising affluence particularly concentrated in the well-educated, upper middle class.

It was decided that Stouffer's should enter both the sweet goods and pie markets, and the opportunity plan that was presented to the top management of the Litton Industries Corporation is described in the following section.

THE OPPORTUNITY PLAN

As indicated earlier, the key to the decision process in the Litton Industries organization was the opportunity plan and its presentation to top management. The essential aspects of the plan as presented in 1968 are described here in condensed fashion.

The basic focus of the introductory sections of the presentation was to demonstrate Stouffer's proven competence in the frozen food industry and to estimate their potential in the markets in which they had already established themselves. Exhibit IV presents this information.

The plan went on to state that their 1968 frozen-food line consisted of fish quality entrees, side dishes, and meat pies; that their market was primarily high income, well educated, people over 35 years of age with smaller families; in addition they had developed skills in institutional food servicing, systems and "spot automation" (a term indicating the use of an automatic oven or process within a traditional food servicing system); and finally, that they had developed regional market acceptance for a line of sauces and dressings.

The plan continued with a statement entitled, "Our Evolving Potential." Included were the statements that the company was known for high quality

EXHIBIT IV

Frozen Food Industry Sales Volume and Stouffers' Share

	Total Dollar Volume 1968 in Millions	Stouffers' Share 1968[a]
Total Foods	$107,391	0.03%
Frozen Foods	3,440	0.87%
Frozen Prepared Foods	1,225	2.46%
Frozen Entrees, Side dishes & meat pies	355	8.45%
Frozen Entrees	155	12.93%

(Note: Frozen Entrees are included twice in order to conform to industry classification data) - But extent of duplication in reporting not clear.

[a]By 1970 when the Stouffers' Foods sought funds for plant expansion, they were able to present the following figures suggesting their level of achievement in these markets: Total Food, 0.04%; Frozen Foods, 1.13%; Frozen Prepared Foods, 3.07%; Frozen Entrees, side dishes and meat pies, 9.08%; and Frozen Entrees, 17.14%.

Source: Company records and commercial reporting services.

foods and that this reputation was not limited to frozen foods. Moreover, the division was believed to be strong enough to develop several brand names if the opportunities should suggest this approach. Again, the company had demonstrated ability to design and market food systems, components, and equipment. It was held that they had developed a highly efficient marketing organization.

Market segments for the years 1968 and estimated for 1973 were presented in bar chart form as presented in Exhibit V.

In outlining the basic strategy to be pursued, the company listed five aspects they chose to emphasize as of 1968. They are presented in Exhibit VI.

Strengths and weaknesses of the present organization were set forth in candid fashion and with some effort at objectivity. They are presented in Exhibit VII.

A ten-year projection covering the years 1963 to 1973 was graphed, and it suggested an average annual increase of 27 percent if the present product lines were to be continued. But if certain new lines were to be added, the

EXHIBIT V

Market Segments for the Frozen Food Industry in 1968 and Projected for 1973 ($ in millions) Stouffer Share of Market Blocked

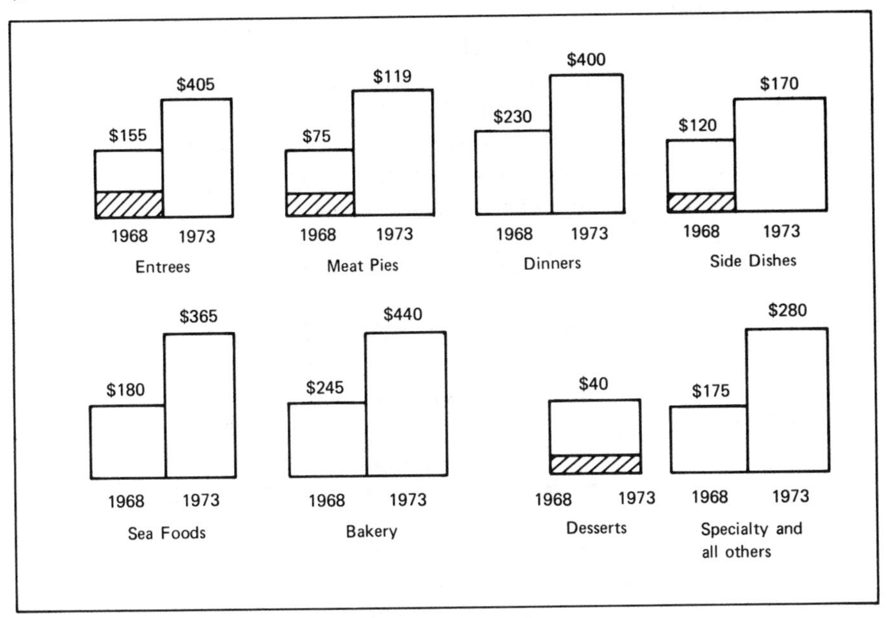

Source: Commercial reporting services

EXHIBIT VI

Basic Strategy for Stouffer Frozen Food Division 1968–1973

1. Double existing retail volume by 1973 through improved market penetration and new product development.
2. Enter new food product markets by internal development, and acquisition.
3. Reduce costs by manufacturing consolidation and marketing efficiencies.
4. Build aggressive marketing and manufacturing teams to meet opportunities.
5. Concentrate U.S.A. – then International.

Source: Company Opportunity Plan

average annual increase could amount to as much as 35 percent. In either case, the greatest increase in sales was depicted as occurring in the period 1970 through 1973.

A final point developed in the opportunity plan was the projected future

EXHIBIT VII

Strengths and Weaknesses of Stouffers' Foods as of 1968.

Strengths

1. Highest quality food preparation.
2. Strong franchise with current users.
3. Efficient production and distribution.
4. Capacity available for sudden sales spurts.
5. Aggressive young management.
6. Important line for brokers.
7. Priced for good usable gross profits.
8. Excellent trade reception for new items.
9. Non-union.
10. Ability to put together broader food system than any other competition.
11. Restaurant association reputable.

Weaknesses

1. Operating at 45% capacity.
2. Undeveloped consumer franchise. (acceptance and opportunity)
3. Product line too limited.
4. Considered high priced.
5. Considered small portions.
6. Too few food systems in operation.
7. Adequate replacements not trained.

Source: Opportunity Plan

growth of Stouffer's Foods from 1968 to 1973. This was shown by product classification, and included estimates of what Stouffer's might hope to achieve if they were to acquire certain competitors in the field.

In Exhibit V, Stouffer's clearly identified where they thought their best opportunity was by graphing "Bakery" dramatically in bright red blocking. Accordingly, approval was given for the purchase of Hanscom Bakeries, an established eastern company, and in May of 1969, negotiations were completed.

Consequent experimentation with a line within the frozen fruit pies category proved that this was not acceptable as prepared by Stouffer's, primary reasons apparently being the absence of a bottom crust which the customer had come to expect and possibly some problems of freezer storage in upright freezers where freezing and thawing in the upper shelves tends to change the consistency of the pie crust (top layer).

The frozen sweet-goods effort resulted in a more successful experience for Stouffer's, and Exhibit VIII presents their Bakery product line.

EXHIBIT VIII

Product Line, Stouffer's Bakery Foods, 1972

Item
Devil's Fudge Cupcakes
Cream Filled Cupcakes
Iced Yellow Cupcakes
Lemon Filled Cupcakes
French Crumb Cakes
Almond Crunch Cake
Chocolate Chip Cake
Orange Danish
Chocolate Rum Danish
Apricot Danish
Cinnamon Raisin Danish
Twisted Coffee Cake
Glazed Pecan Danish
Coconut Lemon
Macaroon Crumb Cakes
Blueberry Crumb Cakes
Apple Pecan Streusel
Garlic Bread

Source: Company Records

By way of comparison, Sara Lee had established a broader line. This is presented in Exhibit IX.

Some perspective on the market penetration of Stouffer's bakery division can be obtained by a study of the graphs in Exhibit X.

Exhibit XI details performance of Stouffer's bakery division for the fiscal year 1972 as compared to percent of quotas and percent changes over previous year's sales.

QUESTIONS

1. Should an opportunity plan be based on an explicit statement of an appropriate corporate strategy? If so, what conceptual framework would you advance to the management of Stouffer Foods to help them develop a corporate strategy? If not, how would you suggest they begin the development of an opportunity plan?
2. What do you make of the scope of the opportunity plan developed by Stouffer's? Is it sufficiently encompassing and comprehensive? Are there

EXHIBIT IX

Product Line
Sara Lee, 1972

Item	*Item*
Cream Cheese Cake, Large	Maple Crunch Coffee Rings
Cream Cheese Cake, Small	Almond Coffee Rings
Pineapple Cheese Cake	Pound Cake
Blueberry Cheese Cake	Chocolate Swirl
Strawberry Cheese Cake	Raisin Pound
Cherry Cheese Cake	Brownies
Danish Royale	Banana Cake
Pecan Coffee, Large	Orange Cake
Pecan Coffee, Small	Devil's Food Cake
Apricot Danish	Chocolate Cake
Cinnamon Nut	German Chocolate Cake
Apple Danish	Golden Cake
Caramel Pecan Rolls	Butter Gems (cookies)
Cheese Danish	Croissant
Cherry Danish	Parkerhouse
Streusel, Large	Finger cookies
Streusel, Small	Sesame
Blueberry Coffee Rings	Chicken (bag)
Raspberry Coffee Rings	Cinnamon Rolls

Source: Information from Commercial Reporting Services

any points of information you would like to have added before using it as a top management decision making system?

3. Is the opportunity plan as here presented sufficiently explicit in its assumptions and precise in its measurements to serve as a useful guide to management in evaluating a proposed course of action?
4. Would you think that the top management of Litton would expect more or less development of an opportunity plan coming from a division with which they might be more familiar (industrial product and not a consumer item)?
5. The opportunity plan is part of a package of management services that Litton provides in exchange for the 1 per cent (of sales) management fee. How would you go about assessing the value of a device such as the opportunity plan if you were Stouffer's?
6. What do Exhibits X and XI reveal? Has Stouffer's penetration proven their basic strategy correct? Is the opportunity plan now justified? What factors enter into successful market penetration?

EXHIBIT X

Composite Market Share of Major Baked Goods Producers, Late 1971 – Early 1972
(Based on data gathered from four major cities in the east)

DOLLAR BASIS

	1971 August September	1971 October November	1972 December January	1972 February March
Total (000)	1709	1865	3888	4317
All Others	34.6%	35.3%	44.1%	48.4%
Sara Lee	48.7%	47.4%	42.8%	38.3%
Stouffer	16.7%	17.3%	13.1%	13.3%
Volumes				
All Others	$592	$659	$1714	$2088
Sara Lee	$832	$883	$1664	$1653
Stouffer	$285	$323	$ 510	$ 576

UNIT BASIS

	1971 August September	1971 October November	1972 December January	1972 February March
Total (000)	2277	2559	4933	5357
All Others	40.4%	41.8%	45.7%	50.6%
Sara Lee	43.1%	41.3%	40.6%	35.4%
Stouffer	16.5%	16.9%	13.7%	14.0%
Volumes				
All Others	920	1068	2251	2712
Sara Lee	982	1057	2003	1894
Stouffer	375	434	679	751

Source: Commercial Reporting Service

EXHIBIT XI
Sales Analysis – Bakery Division
SALES ANALYSIS

BAKERY – YTD JULY – 1972

(add 000 to dollar sales)

Area	*Quota*	*Actual*	*% of Quota*	*L.Y. Sales*	*% of Change*
Region 1	$ 730.0	$ 705.3	96.6	$ 641.6	9.9
Region 2	1573.3	1564.7	99.5	653.9	139.3
Region 3	236.5	328.2	138.8	95.8	242.6
Region 4	655.2	739.3	112.8	260.5	183.8
DIVISION A total	$3195.0	$3337.5	104.5	1651.8	102.1
Region 5	$ 690.6	$ 587.8	85.1	291.9	101.4
Region 6	1191.8	1320.1	110.8	880.4	49.9
Region 7	353.4	776.7	91.0	138.0	462.8
Region 8	177.0	161.6	91.3	–	–
DIVISION B total	$2912.8	$2846.2	97.7	1310.3	117.2
Region 9	$ 878.1	$1121.7	127.7	.6	–
Region 10	306.0	182.5	88.6	78.1	133.7
Region 11	–	–	–	–	–
Region 12	–	–	–	–	–
Region 13	–	–	–	–	–
DIVISION C total	$1084.1	$1304.2	120.3	78.7	1557.2
Total Retail Bakery					
GRAND TOTAL	7191.9	7487.9	104.1	3040.8	146.3

Source: Commercial Reporting Services

CASE 7

Ski-Kit, Inc.*

Robert Williams

SKI-KIT, Inc., a California corporation, was founded in August of 1974 to market SKI-KIT luggage. Prior to its incorporation, SKI-KIT, Inc. had been a "dba" and a partnership during the market research and product development stages.

SKI-KIT luggage was invented by Mr. Fred McAlister who, not only as a skier but also as a concerned airline pilot, recognized the need for total in-transit ski equipment protection and convenience. He perceived that the luggage (Exhibit A) should be made of lightweight molded plastic or aluminum, use the skis as a reinforcing frame, be large enough to pack skis, boots, clothing, and accessories, and be versatile enough to pack other sporting goods when not used for ski equipment. Three years perviously Mr. McAlister had applied for a patent, built several prototypes and, on a limited basis, personally conducted some market research. He then realized SKI-KIT luggage would have to be produced either in high volume or in a very limited, garage-type operation. In April of 1973, Mr. McAlister contracted with DYNO Enterprises, a market and product development consulting firm, to determine the market potential and the best approach to pursue.

EXHIBIT A

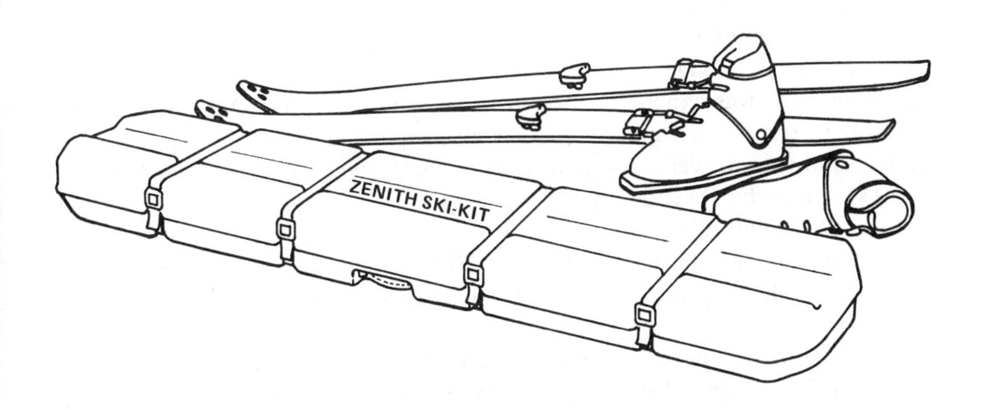

* This case was prepared by the author under the direction of Hans Schöllhammer and Arthur H. Kuriloff for their book *Entrepreneurship and Small Business Management*, Santa Barbara, Wiley/Hamilton, 1977. Reprinted by permission from the authors.

BUSINESS FEASIBILITY STUDY

DYNO Enterprises was essentially a two-man firm consisting of Mr. Joe Ciarica, president, and Mr. Bob Wilhelm, associate consultant and MBA candidate in the University of Southern California Business Development and Entrepreneurship Program.

Over the next five months they proposed to investigate all aspects of the product, the ski industry, and the ski market. A business feasibility study would then be developed to analyze the market, and the technical and financial potential of SKI-KIT luggage. This would determine the need for the product, its ability to satisfy the need, and the sales volume at which it would be profitable. If the results proved acceptable, a business plan would be implemented.

DYNO Enterprises decided that a questionnaire to 3,000 United States Ski Association members would provide the necessary information on skiers' interest in the concept. An additional 500 people including ski industry executives, retailers, ski officials, distributors, competitors, travel agents, ski resorts' managers, ski magazine personnel, and other skiers would be contacted.

Experiencing a return of 23% of the questionnaires, the partners tabulated the following results:

Skiers Acceptance of SKI-KIT

1. 79% of the skiers who responded were in favor of SKI-KIT and its one-piece durability.

Skiers Dissatisfaction with Current Protective Coverings

2. 80% of the skiers desired improved luggage equipment.
3. Nearly 85% of the skiers indicated dissatisfaction with the ski protection techniques employed by commercial carriers.

Ski Equipment Damage

4. Ski damage was experienced by 40% of those surveyed. Automobile and airplane travel cause most of the "beyond repair" damage to skis.
5. Bus and train travel cause almost as much damage as the airlines but not as severe as the "beyond repair" category.

Present Protective Covering

6. Of those skiers suffering ski damage, 70% owned some kind of protective covering; the majority of these were vinyl bags.

Another important result indicated how much a skier was willing to pay for SKI-KIT luggage. The percentage breakdown was as follows:

PRICE RANGE ($)	PERCENTAGE
50–65	58
66–81	20
82–97	8
98–113	2
greater than 114	1
no reply	11
	100

Realizing that SKI-KIT was a new concept, and initially limited low volume production would require a higher selling price than desired in the long run, Ciarica and Wilhelm were satisfied with the 11% acceptance in the $82 and up categories. Their marketing strategy was now coming into focus. They believed that the serious, affluent skier would buy it at the initially high selling price. Then, by exposure, word-of-mouth, and a lower price through high volume production, SKI-KIT would be purchased by the occasional recreational skier who represented the mass market.

Desirable Features

Analysis of the questionnaires showed that the respondents thought durability the most important SKI-KIT feature, followed by transit protection, equipment safety, lightweight, hard-covered, convenience (one-piece), protective lock, slimline design, ability to satisfy airline requirements, and compact storage (off season).

SKI INDUSTRY

After investigation of the industry using information from Ski Industries America (SIA, the Ski Industry's trade association), *Ski* magazine and *Skiing* magazine, DYNO compiled the following information:

The retail trade sales volume in skis was expected to grow from $405 million during the 1972–73 ski season to $1,070 million during the 1979–80 ski season [1]. This represented an average annual growth rate of approximately 13%.

A 1972–73 *Ski* magazine survey showed that well over half the skiers surveyed had purchased new ski equipment: 61% bought skis, 59% bought boots, 78% bought ski clothing, and 71% bought other new equipment. This "other new equipment" (which would be SKI-KIT's classification) comprised 46% bindings, 38% poles, 18% car ski racks, and 37% goggles.

Of those skiers responding to the SKI-KIT questionnaire, 58% valued their equipment at $500–$1,000; 20% at $1,000–$1,500; 7% at $1,500–$2,000; 4% at greater than $2,500. There was no correlation between the value of the skiers' equipment and their interest in buying SKI-KIT luggage.

According to an executive of SIA, the total amount spent on ski equipment (equipment, travel, lodging, etc.) for the 1972–73 ski season was $1.74 billion and would increase an average of 13.3% through the 1979–80 ski season to $4.65 billion.

Checking channels of distribution, DYNO discovered approximately 180–200 ski equipment distributors. Less than 10% had sales in the multimillion dollar category, approximately 75% were in the $6,000,000–$1.5 million category, and the balance had sales of $500,000 or less. The major national and regional distributors operate on a 33–35% gross margin; a national sales force with administrative facilities but not buying and stocking merchandise operates on a 20–25% gross margin; and independent representatives on a regional basis operate on a 6–15% gross margin depending on the product. Retail shops expect a 35–50% gross margin depending on the merchandise.

Ciarica and Wilhelm found from a *Ski* magazine survey that skiers purchase their equipment at the following retail outlets:

RETAIL OUTLET	PER CENT
Ski shop	70
Sporting goods store	26
Department store	7
Discount store	2
Mail order	1
Other	4
	110*

* Exceeds 100% because of multiple answers.

Of the almost 6,000 retailers selling ski equipment, approximately 80% are specialty ski shops.

On the basis of this industry information, DYNO concluded that with industry and retail sales growing at an average annual rate of 13% and with a high percentage of skiers making yearly purchases, the potential of SKI-KIT looked bright. The data pointed to the desirability of focusing sales on the specialty ski shop. This would require a sales force capable of contacting specialty ski shops successfully.

Ski Market

According to a 1970 *Ski* magazine survey, the demographic data for a typical skier are the following: Skiers' average income was $21,113; skiers' average age was 29.5 years. Approximately 3 times as many men as women ski; 50% of the men were single and 50% were heads of household. The occupational status breakdown showed skiers were: 33% professionals; 12%

semi-professionals; 12% proprietors and managers; 18% clericals and sales personnel; and 12% craftspeople and supervisors.

Not only is the ski market an affluent one but it is also very close knit. According to *Skiing* magazine,

". . . the serious skier is the hub around which the entire skiing market revolves. The serious skier sets the trends which others follow. Their influence is felt not only in the sale of skiing clothing and equipment . . . .

Word-of-mouth influence is the crucial factor for the successful movement of goods in the ski market. Skiers participate in the sport in a very concentrated area. From the time they leave their home to the actual skiing and staying in a ski location, they are in constant communication and association with each other.

. . . sell the serious skier and you win the best customer there is for everything skiers use. More importantly, you gain the skiing markets best 'salesman' . . . using and recommending the products he knows and believes in, as others emulate his example and follow advice."

According to an SIA executive, growth of the ski population may be shown and projected as follows:

YEAR	HARD-CORE, SERIOUS SKIER *	PERCENTAGE INCREASE	OCCASIONAL SKIER †	PERCENTAGE INCREASE
1970–71	3,273,700 +	9.75	2,119,200 +	9.75
1971–72	3,633,900 +	9.90	2,352,300 +	9.50
1972–73	4,033,600 +	10.20	2,611,000 +	9.80
1973–74	4,477,300 +	10.00	2,898,200 +	12.25
1974–75	4,969,800 +	9.75	3,217,000 +	7.50
1975–76	5,515,500 +	9.50	3,570,900 +	9.50
1976–77	6,123,200 +	9.75	3,963,700 +	9.80
1977–78	6,796,700 +	9.80	4,399,700 +	10.00
1978–79	7,544,400 +	9.80	4,883,700 +	9.75
1979–80	8,374,300 +	10.00	5,420,900 +	9.50

* Hard-core serious skier: Those who ski 12 or more days per year.
† Occasional skier: Those who ski fewer than 12 days per year but visit ski areas and purchase clothing and equipment.
NOTE: The two groups are considered independent markets by the industry. Estimates as of September 17, 1970.

On the basis of information from a 1970–71 survey of 1,000 skiers by *Skiing* magazine, DYNO discovered that on a relative scale, 15% of the skiers traveled to Europe, 55% to other states outside their home state, and 30% traveled to Canada. DYNO further determined that 15% travel by airline, 4% by train, 16% by bus, and 67% by automobile.

Interestingly, ski trip duration varied as between DYNO's questionnaire results and *Ski* magazine's survey of 1971–72. DYNO's percentage breakdown was

DURATION	PER CENT
1 day	16
2 days	35
3–5 days	30
6–7 days	10
greater than 7 days	12
	103*

* Exceeds 100% because of multiple answers.

Ski magazine's survey showed far greater emphasis on one- and two-week vacations. In any event, skiers would be carrying a considerable amount of equipment and luggage awkwardly, and SKI-KIT luggage would quite easily eliminate the need of all other baggage.

Several other important marketing aspects DYNO considered were the retail and consumer buying cycles and the accounts receivable policy. *The Sporting Goods Dealer* magazine indicated that the majority of sales to retailers were in March, April, and December. March and April were important because of the trade shows and December because of Christmas and the peak of the ski season. The consumer buying cycle followed the ski season with December being the most important month followed by November, October, January, and February. SKI-KIT luggage would therefore expect its strongest sales commencing in October and increasing through December, then tapering off in January to practically nothing during the summer months.

From various ski manufacturers and distributors, it was found that accounts receivable were dated December 10th. However, the majority of revenue did not come in until January, February, and March. This meant that a manufacturer or distributor wrote orders at the March and April shows, produced an inventory against these orders, and shipped the merchandise in late August through September. The manufacturer thus had to carry the receivables from date of shipment for several months—sometimes to March. This was not viewed favorably by DYNO but there appeared to be little alternative than to sell to financially sound retailers, keep close watch on accounts receivable, and offer favorable cash discounts to entice early payment.

One of the most important aspects of DYNO's feasibility study was the analysis of the competition. DYNO divided the competition into two categories: indirect and direct. The indirect competition consisted of airline cardboard cartons or plastic bags, and vinyl or canvas bags. Since the airlines discontinued using cardboard boxes because of the expense, and the plastic bags offered no protection at all, as DYNO's questionnaire had indicated, competition from the airlines appeared to be no problem.

The sales of vinyl and canvas bags over the past couple of years had increased tremendously, pointing out the trend to cover and protect ski equipment. The industry retail sales for these bags were approximately $4 million in 1972 with the average retail price for a ski bag at $12 to $15, boot bag at $10–$12, and a carry-all bag at $10–$20. Therefore, the total price for all bags was approximately $32–$47 not including a car rack, which was also needed. These bags, according to the DYNO questionnaire, offered little protection and no convenience.

A thorough search within the industry for direct competition showed that there had been seven previous attempts at hard-shelled luggage. They consisted of two imported models, several homemade models, and the attempt of a major U.S. ski manufacturer. None of these units were now on the market. The viewpoint of the ski executives interviewed was that a need might exist, but the market potential was too small for them to pursue. Most individuals who had made their own units still believed in the concept. Previous attempts had many things in common but not the advantages of SKI-KIT luggage. The most important deficiencies compared with SKI-KIT included:

1. Carried skis and poles only.
2. No patented feature.
3. No research directed towards consumer demand.
4. No market plan.
5. Poorly designed.

Ciarica and Wilhelm concluded, that the primary advertising and promotion thrust should be geared to the skier, who would in turn create a consumer demand at the retailer level.

TECHNICAL PRODUCTION AND PRODUCT DESIGN FEASIBILITY

On the basis of information gathered, DYNO believed that SKI-KIT would be purchased by the serious and affluent skiers for the first couple of years. At low volume production, the cost versus performance difference between aluminum and plastic appeared insignificant. Aluminum was considered to be more prestigious (according to DYNO's questionnaire, the three most important SKI-KIT features—durability, transit safety, and equipment safety—also pointed to aluminum). Therefore, DYNO concluded that SKI-KIT should be produced out of aluminum for the first two years. In the third year a plastic SKI-KIT should be introduced to the mass ski market. This would allow time to investigate the many different kinds of plastic processes.

With this in mind, DYNO surveyed 24 plastic and metal fabricators in Southern California. This effort revealed 15 different candidate materials and processes for SKI-KIT construction. These processes had a variety of cost/performance trade-offs (Exhibit B).

EXHIBIT B

Comparative Manufacturing Economics

Process	Material	Estimated Per Unit Costs (Total Assy.)	Estimated Tooling Costs	Estimated Production Facility Costs	Advantages	Disadvantages
Thermoforming	ABS	$30 – $40	($5,000/mold)	($100,000–$150,000)	(Durable, Lightweight) (Flexible Operation)	(Expensive per unit (costs. Poor Full (production expenses
	HDPE	$25 – $30	($20,000 total)	($100,000–$150,000)	(Good Initial) (Production)	(Less Expensive than (ABS but high for PE
Profile Extrusion	Vinyl	$25 – $30	$2,000–$5,000	$0.5 to $1 mm	(Good struct'l design)	(Weight incr., Labor (intensify with con- (siderable part (assy.
	ABS or HDPE	$30 – $35	$2,000–$5,000	$0.5 to $1 mm	(Low start-up costs)	
	Aluminum	$30 – $40	$1,000–$3,000	$1 mm	(Good flexibility) (to operations)	
Injection Molding	ABS	$13 – $20	($ 60,000 to) ( ) ( )	($0.6 to) ( ) ( )	–Highest Quality Plastic Process & Material –Low Unit Cost	–High tooling Costs –High minimum volumes
	PE or PP	$10 – $15	( ) ($100,000)	( ) ($1 million)	–High Quality –Inexpensive –Durable, Lightweight	–High tooling Costs –High min, volumes
Blow Molding	PE or PP	$15 – $20	($15,000 to) ( )	($0.5 to) ( )	–Air Mold modification of Blow mold provides good volume economies and excellent structural properties	–Conventional Blow Molding has major technical difficul- ties with quality –Surface detail fair
	ABS	$18 – $25	( ) ($25,000)	( ) ($1 million)		
Rotational Molding	PE or PP ABS	$17 – $24	$8,000 to $15,000	$0.5 to $1 million	–Inexpensive per unit and tooling costs –Good flexibility in process for limited production quantity	–Serious Weight Pen- alty of up to 7% weight increase –Wall Thickness req'd greater fr quality; fair surface detail
Structural Plastic Foam Molding	Open–Cost	$13 – $20	$3,–$5,000 Total: $12,–$20,000	$20,–$50,000	–Cheap start-up costs –Fair quality surface expected	–Questionable street integrity, Extensive tests req'd –Wt. Penalty Expected
	(N2 VCC (Pressure (PE	$14-– $18	$10,–$15,000 (Total)	VCC license + $,5 to $1 mm	–Poor quality surface –Low volume economics –Durable container	–Up to 7 % weight penalty –Surface finish mold
Fiber Reinforced Plastic	Fiberglass + Polyester or Epoxy	$17 – $30	$3,–$6,000 Total $15,000 - $25,000	$20,000 to $40,000	–Lightweight –Flexible operations –Low start-up costs	– Labor intensify –High costs for req'd surfaces
Cold Forming	6063 Alum.	$25 – $45	$20,000 - $35,000	$.5 to $1 mm	–Readily coatable surface for better inventory flexibility –Durable, high prestige unit	–High percent costs –Mass Mkt acceptance for metal ltd.

SKI-KIT could be tooled for production in aluminum in the range of $3,000 (extrusion) to $30,000 (cold forming); in plastic for as little as $2,000 to $30,000 (FRP, foam molding, extrusion) to $15,000 to $25,000 (thermoforming, air molding, rotational molding, or structural foam molding); or as high as $50,000 to $95,000 (injection molding). The per unit cost varied from $10 to $15 (injection molding) to $40 to $45 (thermoforming).

It was clear to the DYNO partners that the selection of optimum manufacturing technique depended on market strategy. Therefore, the most practicable approach would be to select initially the manufacturing process that offered the most flexibility and the least start-up costs with no attendant sacrifices in quality. Choice of initial process appeared to be open as several product design firms stated the patent would be easy to adapt to metal or plastic.

Taking all this into account, DYNO formulated a business plan—a step-by-step process on how to launch what appeared to be a potentially successful venture.

BUSINESS PLAN

Marketing Strategy

DYNO believed that the marketing strategy should be heavily weighted towards the skier, but major sales effort by a sales force should be launched at the same time.

During the feasibility study DYNO had sent letters to the major airlines. They had received positive responses from most of the airlines, expressing an interest in the DYNO questionnaire and SKI-KIT luggage. DYNO believed that a leasing program could be developed in which SKI-KITs would be leased or sold to the airlines, which would provide SKI-KITs for their passenger skiers. The distribution points would be at ski shops or travel agencies.

Other areas of strategy would be in promotion. The first phase would be extensive use of free promotion through the major ski and related publications. Over 100 U.S. ski writers would be contacted. The releases would consist of the typical product release and also editorials analyzing the results of the SKI-KIT questionnaire. This free publicity would indirectly stimulate demand.

DYNO believed the most direct way to expose SKI-KIT was to give presentations at ski clubs. In Southern California alone there were over 11,000 members in 67 United States Ski Association clubs. A representative from each club could solicit orders and submit them to retailers. This concept would be developed in all nine regions across the United States.

National trade shows in Las Vegas and Boston, and regional shows would be attended and orders taken. Primary emphasis would be placed on those regional shows where maximum results could be realized. There were a number of other shows geared toward professional skiers and ski patrolmen, which would also be attended.

A limited number of SKI-KIT packs would be made available as gifts and donations. They would be given to the most influential people in the industry and used as prizes at the consumer ski shows.

Paid advertising would be limited to the several major ski consumer and trade publications. Cooperative advertising with original equipment manufacturers and major retail shops, and other important purchasers would be used extensively to get maximum exposure at least cost, and to gain recognition by association with known products and retailers in the industry.

DYNO next laid out a time schedule of major events to be accomplished each quarter for the following year-and-a-half.

Fourth Quarter 1973—September–December

1. Conclude business arrangement for necessary financing and manufacturing.
2. Contact airlines for leasing program.
3. Schedule presentations to ski clubs.
4. Send out new product releases.
5. Produce brochure.
6. Design metal SKI-KIT.
7. Apply for foreign patents.

First Quarter 1974

1. Finalize details for airline leasing program.
2. Conclude arrangements with a distributor.
3. Prepare for and attend SIA trade show in Las Vegas.
4. Fabricate metal prototypes.
5. Commence tooling for full production of metal SKI-KIT.
6. Contact suppliers for material requirements.
7. Initiate limited production scheduling.

Second Quarter 1974

1. Implement mechanics of commercial carrier arrangement.
2. Attend regional ski shows.
3. Make presentations to ski clubs in key cities.
4. Commence designing plastic SKI-KIT.
5. Initiate full production for metal SKI-KIT.
6. Conclude all foreign licensing programs.
7. Schedule cooperative advertising programs.

Third Quarter 1974

1. Finalize plastic design.
2. Execute foreign licensing program.
3. Fabricate metal SKI-KIT according to sales schedule.
4. Implement cooperative advertising programs.

Fourth Quarter 1974

1. Presentations to ski clubs.
2. Publicize plastic SKI-KIT to all news media.
3. Prepare full plastic production.
4. Continue cooperative advertising programs.

First Quarter 1975

1. Organize a cooperative program between ski clubs and ski shops.
2. Prepare for and attend trade shows with new plastic product design.
3. Compare tooling and material arrangements for full production of plastic SKI-KIT.

Second Quarter 1975

1. Update previous SKI-KIT operations for future implementation.

Financial Projections

DYNO utilized their questionnaire results and the SIA ski population projections to calculate SKI-KIT sales projections. The formula used was the following:

23% return on questionnaire × 79% stated they were in favor of the SKI-KIT concept × number of hard-core serious skiers and occasional skiers (table footnote 2). This total was then multiplied by a reasonable market share percentage for varying degrees of success (table footnotes 3, 4, 5).

Calculations For Sales Projections

YEAR	HARD-CORE SERIOUS AND OCCASIONAL SKIERS [1]	POTENTIAL SKI-KIT MARKET [2]	SKI-KIT UNITS		
			MOST PESSIMISTIC	MOST PROBABLE [4]	MOST OPTIMISTIC [5]
1974–75	4,500,000	806,000	3,000	3,500	6,000
1975–76	5,000,000	895,000	9,000	20,000	26,500
1976–77	5,500,000	993,000	15,000	50,000	93,000
1977–78	10,100,000	1,816,000	36,000	68,000	110,000
1978–79	11,200,000	2,015,000	40,000	78,000	120,000
1979–80	12,400,000	2,237,000	50,000	90,000	145,000
1980–81	13,800,000	2,473,000	40,000	90,000	150,000
1984–85	18,400,000	3,303,000	40,000	90,000	150,000

NOTES TO TABLES

[1] The number of hard-core serious skiers is indicated as the total for the years 1974 through 1977 ski season (first 3 years). The remaining years include both serious and occasional skier population.

[2] See calculation formula.

[3] Most pessimistic estimates are based on a market share of 1% to 2% of total SKI-KIT potential and/or market penetration of less than 0.5% of the total ski population.

[4] Most probable estimates are based on a market share of 3% to 4% of total SKI-KIT potential and less than 1.0% of total ski population.

[5] Most optimistic estimates are based on a market share of 6% to 8% of total SKI-KIT potential and less than 2.0% of total ski population.

DYNO believed that the "Most Probable" business analysis (Exhibit C) would be the most likely to occur. They estimated the sales price breakdown to be the following:

SKI-KIT	1974–75	1975–76	1976–77	1977–78	1978 & ON
Metal	$165	$150	$140	$140	$140
Plastic	85	85	80	80	80

EXHIBIT C

SKI-KIT, INC.

Pro-Forma Cash Flow

Most Probable Forecast

	1974	1975	1976	1977	1978	1979-84 annual entries
Cash-In (1) (2)						
Metal	$248,000	$ 585,000	$1,411,000	$2,117,000	$2,205,000	$2,646,000
Plastic	15,000	434,000	1,210,000	1,512,000	1,764,000	2,016,000
Leasing	60,000	488,000	1,000,000	1,680,000	2,500,000	3,000,000
Total Cash-In	$323,000	$1,507,000	$3,621,000	$5,309,000	$6,469,000	$7,662,000
Cash-Out						
Cost of Sales	215,000	888,000	1,400,000	1,810,000	2,055,000	2,266,000
Gross Operating Cash	108,000	619,000	2,221,000	3,499,000	4,414,000	5,396,000
Indirect Expense						
Marketing						
Leasing	15,000	100,000	200,000	350,000	500,000	600,000
Promotion	20,000	35,000	80,000	100,000	125,000	125,000
Warehousing, Shipping, Delivery @ 3% of Total Cash-In	10,000	45,000	109,000	159,000	194,000	230,000
Commissions @ 20% Total Cash-In	65,000	301,000	724,000	1,062,000	1,294,000	1,532,000
Technical						
Product Development (3)	10,000	4,000				
Overhead						
Legal	3,000	1,000	1,000	1,000	1,000	1,000
G&A @ 5% Total Cash-In	16,000	75,000	181,000	265,000	323,000	383,000
Management (DYNO)	18,000	25,000	40,000	50,000	50,000	50,000
Sub-Total Indirect	157,000	586,000	1,335,000	1,987,000	2,487,000	2,921,000
10% Contingency	16,000	59,000	134,000	199,000	249,000	292,000
Total Indirect	173,000	645,000	1,469,000	2,186,000	2,736,000	3,213,000
Net Cash (Out)	(65,000)	(26,000)	752,000	1,313,000	1,678,000	2,183,000
Capital Investment (Tooling and Start-up)	75,000	100,000	140,000	75,000	75,000	75,000
Net-Net Cash (Out) (Expensing all tooling)	(140,000)	(126,000)	612,000	1,238,000	1,603,000	2,108,000
(1) Sales Schedule (units/year)						
Metal	3,500	9,000	20,000	30,000	33,000	38,000
Plastic	500	12,500	30,000	38,000	45,000	52,000
Total	4,000	21,500	50,000	68,000	78,000	90,000
(2) Wholesale Price Schedule ($/unit)						
Metal	99.00	90.00	88.20	88.20	88.20	88.20
Plastic	51.00	51.00	50.40	50.40	50.40	50.40
(3) Product Development Costs do not include $40,000 tooling expenditures during 1973						
(4) Retail List Price ($/unit)						
Metal	165	150	140	140	140	140
Plastic	85	85	80	80	80	80

DYNO's basic thought about the metal/plastic ratio was that the commercial carriers would probably be more inclined to use the plastic version for its overall durability while the skiing public would lean toward the metal fabrication. Leasing arrangements with the airlines and ski retail shops were figured at $5.00 per usage for both metal and plastic units. The usable life of each leased unit was considered to be one year.

YEAR	LEASE PRICE	NUMBER LEASED	USAGE 1 UNIT PER YEAR	LEASED UNITS METAL	LEASED UNITS PLASTIC
1974–75	$5.00	1,200	10	1,000	200
1975–76	5.00	6,500	15	2,500	4,000
1976–77	5.00	10,000	20	4,000	6,000
1977–78	5.00	14,000	24	6,000	8,000
1978–79	5.00	18,000	30	8,000	10,000
1979 & on	5.00	20,000	30	8,000	12,000

DYNO used the following cash analysis to determine the overall profitability of a leasing arrangement in which the SKI-KIT luggage principal would be the lessor. However, they decided that the leasing program should be financed by an independent agency at a 20% rate, which would include all administrative duties associated with the leasing operations.

	1974–75	1975–76	1976–77	1977–78	1978–79	1979 & ON
Total Leased Units	1,200	6,500	10,000	14,000	18,000	20,000
Cost of Goods Sold	$64,000	$265,000	$280,000	$370,000	$480,000	$520,000
Leasing Costs	$15,000	$100,000	$200,000	$350,000	$500,000	$600,000
Total Costs	$79,000	$365,000	$480,000	$720,000	$980,000	$1,120,000
Total Revenues	$60,000	$487,500	$1,000,000	$1,680,000	$2,500,000	$3,000,000

The cost of Goods Sold schedule below, outlined the direct manufacturing costs. The initial costs of $45 in plastic and $55 in metal should reduce to $18 in plastic and $35 in metal in larger volume runs.

SKI-KIT	UNIT COST	TOTAL COST	UNIT COST	TOTAL COST	UNIT COST	TOTAL COST	UNIT COST	TOTAL COST	UNIT COST	TOTAL COST
Plastic	$45	$ 22,500	$35	$437,500	$40	$800,000	$35	$950,000	$35	$1,155,000
Total Costs		$215,000		$887,000	$20	$600,000	$20	$760,000	$20	$ 900,000
Metal	$55	$192,500	$50	$450,000		$1,400,000		$1,810,000		$2,055,000
			Metal		$35	$1,330,000				
			Plastic		$18	960,000				
			Total cost			$2,290,000				

DYNO figured the marketing costs (commissions) to independent representatives would be 10% for the first 2 years and 7% thereafter. The retail outlet gross margin would be on the basis of a 35% markup. An additional set of calculations was made under the heading, "Conservative-Most Probable," which added an additional 20% commission to be divided among the distributor/sales representatives and/or the retail outlets (all calculations were made on a mark-down basis using end retail price as a base). A markup percentage would tend to be 5% to 10% higher and more in line with previously discussed gross margins.

"Most probable" case showed mass SKI-KIT acceptance by the second or third year (1976–77). DYNO's rationale was that the plastic units would be more popular, particularly for the leasing arrangements. Also, the lowest possible sales price of $80 in plastic and $140 in metal would be achieved in that year.

A financial analysis (Exhibits C and D) showed that between $350,000 and $600,000 would be required over a 2½ year period to finance SKI-KIT adequately. The overall breakeven point would occur at about the fourth year of operation. The overall long term profitability (greater than 5 years) showed a pretax profit/sales ratio of 10%–25%.

DYNO concluded the "Most Probable" case represented a realistic analysis of the SKI-KIT operation. The 2–3 year mass market acceptance was considered conservative in view of the impulsive buying characteristic of the ski market. Also, the 3%–5% SKI-KIT market penetration and the overall 1%–2% total ski market penetration were considered well within realistic probabilities.

DYNO then used the information from a ski magazine survey to determine where the highest concentration of serious skiers was. This identified the primary revenue-producing regions in which to concentrate their sales effort.

AREA	PERCENTAGE
Alaska and Southern states	1
Northern states	1
Rocky Mountain states	3
Pacific Northwest	4
Central	10
Intermountain	12
Far West	22
Eastern	48

With the 200-page Business Plan complete, DYNO was ready to make presentations to raise capital or to find a manufacturer to provide working capital and to produce SKI-KIT. DYNO projected that at least $100,000 would be needed for initial start-up cost and working capital during the first ski season. This would carry the project to the second quarter of 1974, at which time a "go/no-go" decision would be made on the basis of actual sales and market acceptance. If the decision were a "go," then an additional $150,000 to $500,000 would be required.

FINDING CAPITAL/MANUFACTURER

In September of 1973, DYNO ran an advertisement in the "Business Opportunities" section of the *Wall Street Journal,* which read:

> "Recently completed nationwide market test by outside firm demonstrated over 79% market need and acceptance for new plastic and/or metal ski luggage product. Designed to contain all necessary ski equipment in one piece, lightweight luggage eliminating multiple luggage pieces and assured durable protection and convenience. U.S. patent issuing within month; now filing foreign patents. Seeking business arrangements regarding commercialization or patent sale. Complete thorough business development feasibility study available to principals only."

DYNO received twelve inquiries from this advertisement, mostly from business brokers. One inquiry was from a major leisure-time company. However, none proved fruitful. At the same time, DYNO was giving presentations to Southern California corporations with the capabilities of financing and producing SKI-KIT luggage. Finally, in October, a licensing agreement with Zenith Manufacturing Co., Inc—a well-known Southern California specialized aluminum container producer for military, industrial, and consumer products—seemed certain. Zenith's only concern was how SKI-KITs they manufactured would be distributed.

DYNO presented three alternatives, each one showing a different means of distribution, profit, and market participation. The choices were to use a national distributor, use a regional distributor, or develop an independent sales force. A national distributor was the safest but least profitable because Zenith would be acting almost as a contract manufacturer, receiving a manufacturing profit only. On the other hand, using independent representatives was the most profitable but riskiest because it meant producing SKI-KITs without any assurance of selling the inventory. Developing an independent sales force appeared too difficult and time consuming to be worth the effort. Zenith elected to go with an intermediate plan: Use regional distributors and participate in both manufacturing and marketing profits. DYNO was retained to coordinate the marketing operation.

Zenith acquired exclusive manufacturing and marketing rights under a licensing agreement. They agreed to pay a 5% royalty to Mr. McAlister, the inventor, throughout the life of the patent. Zenith also agreed to pay the product design expense, to produce promotion brochures, and to determine if SKI-KIT could be tooled and manufactured in production quantities at a

EXHIBIT D

BUSINESS PLANNING SCHEDULE (From Schedule B Pro-Forma — Most Probable Case)

(Technical and Marketing Plans — Expense Schedule)

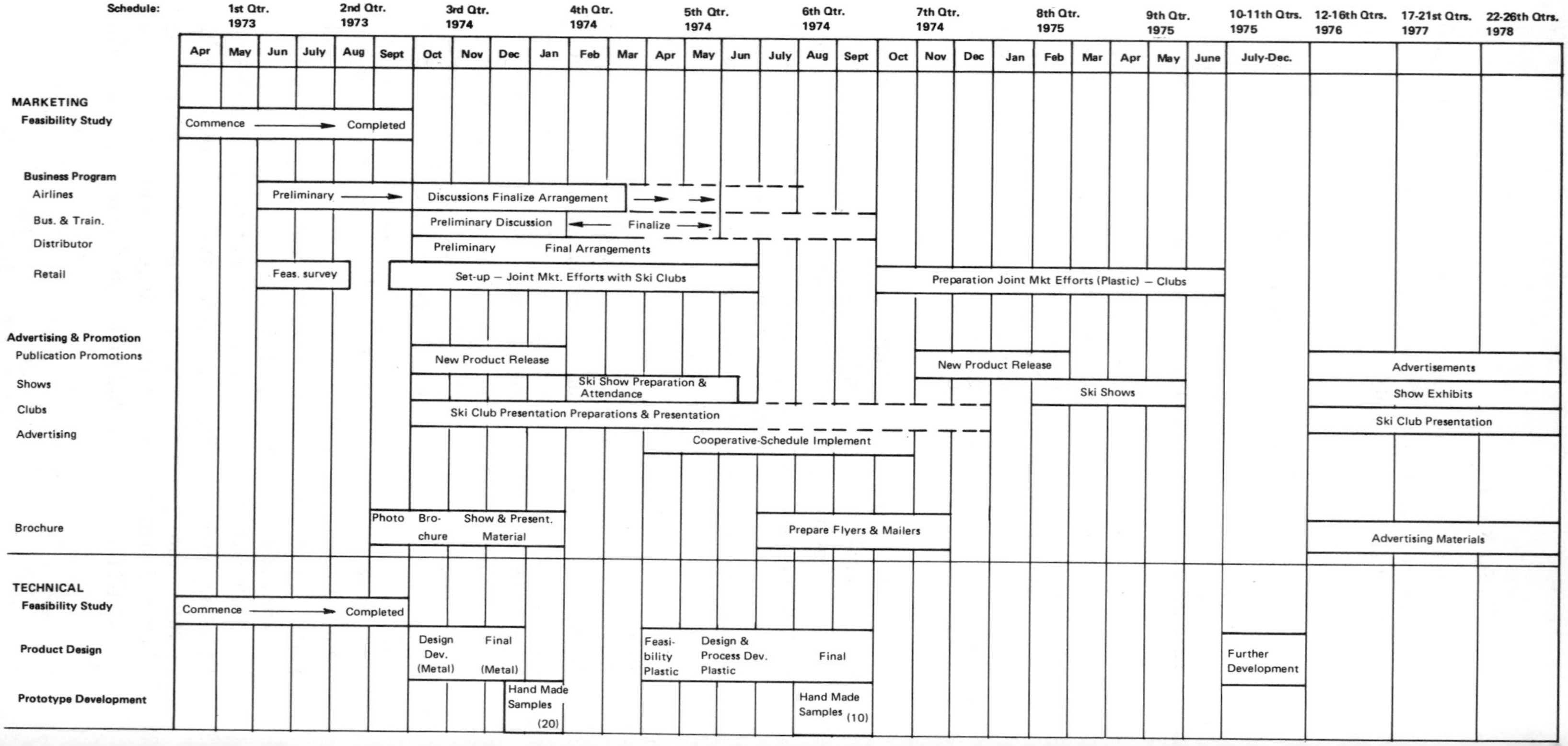

Schedule:	1st Qtr. 1973			2nd Qtr. 1973			3rd Qtr. 1974			4th Qtr. 1974			5th Qtr. 1974			6th Qtr. 1974			7th Qtr. 1974			8th Qtr. 1975			9th Qtr. 1975			10-11th Qtrs. 1975	12-16th Qtrs. 1976	17-21st Qtrs. 1977	22-26th Qtrs. 1978
	Apr	May	Jun	July	Aug	Sept	Oct	Nov	Dec	Jan	Feb	Mar	Apr	May	Jun	July	Aug	Sept	Oct	Nov	Dec	Jan	Feb	Mar	Apr	May	June	July-Dec.			
MARKETING																															
Feasibility Study	Commence → Completed																														
Business Program																															
Airlines			Preliminary →				Discussions Finalize Arrangement						→ →																		
Bus. & Train.							Preliminary Discussion				← Finalize →																				
Distributor							Preliminary			Final Arrangements																					
Retail			Feas. survey			Set-up — Joint Mkt. Efforts with Ski Clubs													Preparation Joint Mkt Efforts (Plastic) — Clubs												
Advertising & Promotion																															
Publication Promotions							New Product Release													New Product Release									Advertisements		
Shows											Ski Show Preparation & Attendance												Ski Shows						Show Exhibits		
Clubs							Ski Club Presentation Preparations & Presentation																						Ski Club Presentation		
Advertising													Cooperative-Schedule Implement																		
Brochure						Photo	Bro-chure	Show & Present. Material								Prepare Flyers & Mailers													Advertising Materials		
TECHNICAL																															
Feasibility Study	Commence → Completed																														
Product Design							Design Dev. (Metal)	Final (Metal)					Feasibility Plastic	Design & Process Dev. Plastic			Final											Further Development			
Prototype Development									Hand Made Samples (20)								Hand Made Samples (10)														

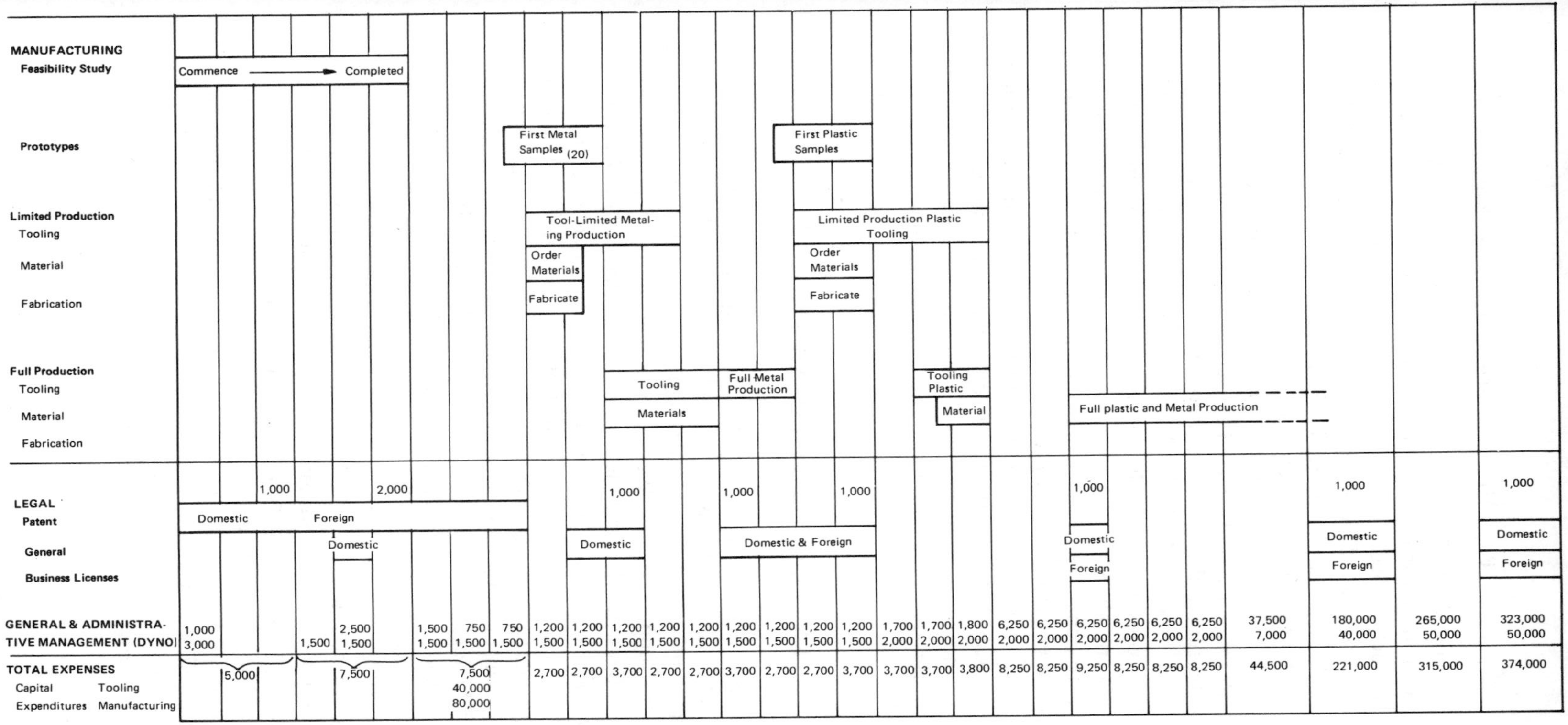

	1	2	3	4	5	6	7	8	9	10	11	12	13	14	15	16	17	18	19	20	21	22	23	24	25	26	27	28	29	30	31
MANUFACTURING																															
Feasibility Study	Commence ——→ Completed																														
Prototypes									First Metal Samples (20)								First Plastic Samples														
Limited Production																															
Tooling										Tool-Limited Metal-ing Production							Limited Production Plastic Tooling														
Material										Order Materials							Order Materials														
Fabrication										Fabricate							Fabricate														
Full Production																															
Tooling												Tooling			Full Metal Production					Tooling Plastic											
Material												Materials									Material			Full plastic and Metal Production — — —							
Fabrication																															
LEGAL			1,000			2,000						1,000			1,000			1,000						1,000					1,000		1,000
Patent	Domestic			Foreign																											
General					Domestic						Domestic				Domestic & Foreign									Domestic					Domestic		Domestic
Business Licenses																								Foreign					Foreign		Foreign
GENERAL & ADMINISTRATIVE MANAGEMENT (DYNO)	1,000 3,000			1,500	2,500 1,500		1,500 1,500	750 1,500	750 1,500	1,200 1,500	1,200 1,500	1,200 1,500	1,200 1,500	1,200 1,500	1,200 1,500	1,200 1,500	1,200 1,500	1,200 1,500	1,700 2,000	1,700 2,000	1,800 2,000	6,250 2,000	6,250 2,000	6,250 2,000	6,250 2,000	6,250 2,000	6,250 2,000	37,500 7,000	180,000 40,000	265,000 50,000	323,000 50,000
TOTAL EXPENSES		5,000			7,500			7,500		2,700	2,700	3,700	2,700	2,700	3,700	2,700	2,700	3,700	3,700	3,700	3,800	8,250	8,250	9,250	8,250	8,250	8,250	44,500	221,000	315,000	374,000
Capital Expenditures — Tooling								40,000																							
Capital Expenditures — Manufacturing								80,000																							

total manufactured cost of $40. If this could be done, twelve prototypes would be produced in time for the March SIA trade show, tooling would be fabricated, and production begun. DYNO would be responsible for coordinating all aspects of product development, setting up national distribution, and making sure SKI-KIT was in the trade show.

The minimum performance agreement stated that Zenith was required to sell a minimum 1,000 SKI-KITs during the first 18 months of the agreement ending May 31, 1975 and 3,000 SKI-KITs per year each year thereafter. Zenith would also be required to pay Mr. McAlister, in the form of a rebate, $30,000 for his prior expense. If Zenith failed to meet such minimums, Mr. McAlister had the right to convert the exclusive licensing agreement to a nonexclusive agreement allowing him to seek other licensees; in return, he would be required to repay Zenith $25,000 out of SKI-KIT net sales at a 5% rate. There were no minimum royalty payments.

Lastly, Zenith decided to fabricate the first SKI-KITs out of plastic rather than metal. They reasoned that, in the short run, subcontracting the thermoforming operation and fabricating in-house would be less expensive than forming aluminum. Besides, they questioned the technical feasibility of manufacturing in metal.

EXTERNAL ENVIRONMENT

At almost the same time of the signing of the licensing agreement, the Arab oil embargo surfaced and conditions grew steadily worse as 1973 drew to a close. Gasoline and plastic prices shot dramatically upward and a general reduction in plastic supplies on the West coast compounded the difficulties of the situation. As one executive for the Society of the Plastics Industry, Inc. stated, "I firmly believe that Southern California stands ready to have its entire manufacturing industry grind to a halt within the next few months unless something is done to reverse the trend in the resin shortage for the plastics industry." Fortunately, ABS high-impact, low temperature plastic was selected for SKI-KIT luggage fabrication. This material was available but was one of the most expensive plastics on the market. It had increased 50% in price in only three months.

By the end of 1973, the shortages were at their worst and a recession looked imminent. In addition, the ski industry was going through its third successive year of poor snow conditions in the Eastern and Mid-Western United States, forcing retailers into bankruptcy and creating the highest level of accounts receivable the ski industry had ever experienced. In early 1974 Zenith's management was becoming concerned, but they were assured that serious skiers will find a way to ski regardless of the economic conditions. Besides, there was plenty of snow in the Western United States. Skiers could travel by commercial carrier, which suited SKI-KIT's purpose perfectly.

Following the Business Plan, DYNO did a feasibility study to determine the trends in the size of ski equipment in order to fix the SKI-KIT luggage dimensions. After speaking with major ski and boot distributors and measuring existing equipment, DYNO and Zenith concluded that luggage 84 in. (214 cm.) × 15 × $6\frac{3}{4}$ in. would capture at least 95% of the market.

With these results, Zenith contracted with a well-known design firm to do the product design, determine the cost of materials, and fabricate a production prototype. The firm designed into the SKI-KIT a car rack, interior bracing pods (as covered by the patent), shoulder strap, and luggage handle. Zenith wanted a prestigious looking plastic case, so aluminum extrusions, latches, and hinges were added to the unit. These additions increased the labor and material costs as well as the weight. The finished product weighed 18 pounds.

The production prototype cost $49.50 to make, almost $10 over the agreed upon $40, but Zenith decided to continue with the project. With G&A and R&D expenses for the year, the wholesale price would increase considerably, as shown in the following cost breakdown:

Cost Breakdown

		Anticipated Units Produced	
	1,000	2,000	3,000
Material			
Labor and Overhead: 1.5 hours @ $9.00	$36.00	$36.00	$36.00
per hour	13.50	13.50	13.50
Subtotal	49.50	49.50	49.50
G&A @ 10%	4.95	4.95	4.95
Subtotal	54.45	54.45	54.45
R&D			
Sales—DYNO $10,000 (contract to coordinate marketing program)			
Promotion 5,000 (brochures, travel, etc.)			
Design firm 10,000			
Prototype 4,000			
29,000	29.00	14.50	9.65
Production tooling $10,000			
(amortized over 5,000 units)	2.00	2.00	2.00
TOTAL	85.45	70.95	66.10
Zenith's profit @ 15%	12.81	10.64	9.91
	98.26	81.59	76.01
McAlister's royalty @ 5%	4.91	4.08	3.80
TOTAL (distributor price)	$103.17	$85.67	$79.81

On the basis of an annual production of 3000 units the retail price would be $200, giving the wholesaler a 40% gross margin at the wholesale price of $120. The distributor price would be $80, at a gross margin of 33⅓% on the wholesale price.

Dyno was disappointed that Zenith intended to amortize the tooling and R&D costs over so few units. They also believed that labor and overhead costs were too high. By making a nominal adjustment in quantity of units and cutting labor and overhead costs somewhat, Dyno believed the retail price could be reduced to about $115, still too high but considerably closer to the questionnaire results. Zenith was unwilling to reduce the distributor price below $80, the 3,000 unit production level. Zenith's management stated that if the product could not sell at a profitable price, then SKI-KIT was not a viable product.

MARKET DEVELOPMENT

A trademark determination and distributor search was made during the cost studies. Out of 90 names compiled, SKI-KIT was voted by Zenith management to be best. Zenith's name would precede SKI-KIT to assure it from being too generic.

From November to February continuous efforts were made to conclude arrangements with a distributor. Over 50 distributors and independent representatives were contacted; all declined because the inquiries were too late in the season, because they did not believe in the concept, or because it was too expensive. In early February, an Eastern distributor consented to show Zenith SKI-KIT in the Chicago National Sporting Goods show in mid-February. After evaluating the retail interest they would decide whether they and their Western associate would distribute it.

Few retailers of skis were at the National Sporting Goods show, but most of the major mass merchandisers attended. All mass merchandisers expressed interest in SKI-KIT luggage but stated it was far too expensive. Throughout the entire show, this was always the major complaint. To a lesser extent, weight and bulkiness were also mentioned. Since the SIA show was only three weeks away, it was too late to make any changes. DYNO also was not very impressed with the Eastern distributor and would try to find another one prior to the ski show.

In the following two weeks all efforts to interest a distributor failed. At the last possible day DYNO reached an informal agreement with Sako Industry Sports, Inc., one of the largest ski distributors in the United States. They agreed to show SKI-KIT in the ski show, evaluate the results, and decide whether to distribute it. They warned, however, that because of lack of time prior to the show, their salesmen would not have proper knowledge and few positive results were expected until September when their salesmen visited the ski retailers. Sako also questioned the need for SKI-KIT and said the price was definitely too high.

At the Ski Industries America show, SKI-KIT luggage stirred a lot of interest among the retailers but few orders were written. They said the price was far too high. They were not sure who among their regular clientele would buy it, and they would prefer to talk to a Sako salesman when he visited their shop in September, or wait until a customer asked for a SKI-KIT. At the show, there was also considerable interest from European, Japanese, and Canadian distributors. However, because of high shipping costs, SKI-KIT would have to be licensed to be manufactured in foreign countries.

The DYNO partners then redesigned SKI-KIT, eliminating all latches, hinges, and extrusions thereby utilizing the patented concept to its fullest. A drawing was made and displayed at the SIA Boston ski show, where the new SKI-KIT was priced at $137.50 retail, $82.50 wholesale, and $60.00 distributor price. It received more favorable acceptance but very few orders. Back in Los Angeles, a prototype was made using straps and buckles rather than the previous hardware. This not only reduced the manufactured cost but also reduced the weight to 15 pounds. Bob Wilhelm went to the San Francisco regional ski show with the prototype, received very little sales support from Sako, returned to Los Angeles convinced SKI-KIT would sell at the lower price, but that it would be necessary to find a new distributor.

Meanwhile, Zenith was growing disappointed, not seeing the expected sales results they were assured would be forthcoming. DYNO argued that it was the price that was still too high, and Zenith remarked they were led to believe skiers were affluent and the price should not be a critical factor. If the price was the major factor, then the product was not viable. Zenith's management stated despite the lack of sales force and the high price, they would probably produce 500 units in an attempt to recover some of their R&D costs, but they would allocate very little money for promotion and advertising.

Founding of Ski-Kit, Inc.

Confronted with the possibility of not recovering the capital already invested and of never seeing SKI-KIT luggage on the market, Mr. McAlister and DYNO evaluated the following alternatives:

1. Continue the licensing agreement with Zenith and hope that the first 500 units would be easily sold and more produced.
2. Mr. McAlister would look for a new licensee/subcontractor, even though he would be required to pay Zenith $25,000 at 5% of net sales.

3. Acquire the licensing rights from Zenith and raise enough capital for Mr. McAlister to start his own manufacturing facilities.
4. Sell the manufacturing, technical, marketing information, and patent rights.
5. Scrap the entire project and use it as a tax write-off.

McAlister and DYNO reasoned that the fifth alternative would always be available. Because the patent would become more valuable the more developed the product, the fourth alternative was also a last resort. The third alternative would require at least $100,000 immediately, which would be extremely difficult to raise in the existing economic situation. The first and second alternatives therefore seemed the most feasible.

McAlister contacted several of his friends and received an $11,000 loan commitment; he got commitments from other friends for approximately $90,000 more at a future date. McAlister and Zenith then discussed a new business arrangement. Zenith was willing to let McAlister have only the marketing rights; Zenith would retain the manufacturing rights.

The following amendment to the licensing agreement was made:

1. For McAlister's initial $25,000 investment, Zenith would provide a $2.00 trade discount on the first 12,500 SKI-KITs purchased by McAlister.
2. Zenith would not participate in any leasing revenues.
3. Zenith would agree to sell a minimum of 500 SKI-KITs the first year, ending May 31, 1975 and 1,000 SKI-KITs each succeeding year, ending May 31. In any year McAlister was not the distributor, he agreed to give Zenith an additional year to sell the minimum quantity.
4. McAlister would still receive the 5% royalty on all SKI-KIT sales.

A distributor agreement was also signed by McAlister and Zenith. This agreement read as follows:

1. McAlister agrees to spend, in addition to purchasing the SKI-KIT luggage, $15,000 annually for advertising, and promotional materials or services.
2. McAlister agrees to purchase from Zenith a minimum of 500 SKI-KITs by May 31, 1975 and 1,000 SKI-KITs in each succeeding year ending May 31. If these minimums are not met, Zenith has the right to terminate the distributor agreement.
3. Zenith agrees to produce a minimum of 500 SKI-KITs and sell them to McAlister at $58 each. Zenith's price to McAlister for SKI-KITs in subsequent years shall include a 15% pretax profit. Included in Zenith's cost will be the recovery of $35,000 in development costs; this will represent $5.00 a unit on the first 7,000 units.
4. After the initial 500 units, if McAlister places a firm order with Zenith, McAlister will determine design and quantities to be manufactured.

CORPORATE STRUCTURE AND OPERATIONS

With these agreements signed, Zenith began gearing up for production and McAlister began organizing SKI-KIT, Inc. He retained Mr. Bob Wilhelm to organize and manage the company. Two of McAlister's friends who provided loans became corporate officers; legal counsel was retained for proper incorporation; and an accounting firm was hired to establish an accounting system.

McAlister's lawyer stated the best plan was to incorporate as a small business corporation capitalized at 500,000 shares with a par value of $1.00 per share. Stock would be issued on a private placement basis to McAlister's friends.

A total of 326,806 shares would be distributed accordingly:

Stockholder	Corporate Office	Per Cent of Equity	Shares of Stock	Dollar Value of Stock	Reason
Fred McAlister	President Chairman of the Board	51	166,161	166,161	prior advances prior services patent values
Bob Wilhelm	Executive Vice Pres., Director	7	22,807	22,807	prior services
Bill DuVaugh	Vice Pres. Advertising Promotion, Director	5	16,290	16,290	prior advances prior services
Bob Nemon	Treasurer	5	16,290	16,290	prior advances prior services
Charlotte Castle		1	3,258	3,258	prior advances prior services
Joe Ciarica			1,000	1,000	prior services
Jim Sabot	Secretary				
McAlister's friends		31	100,000	100,000	investors

SKI-KIT, Inc. now became the legal entity to market SKI-KIT luggage.

Mr. Wilhelm would be the only individual to receive money for his services and Ms. Castle would act as the secretary until SKI-KIT, Inc. had sufficient funds to hire one.

SKI-KIT, Inc. revised the *pro forma* financial projections to show that in the first full year of operation they would gross $337,000 (3,600 SKI-KITs by direct sales, wholesale, foreign licensing, export, and commercial carrier) and incur at $6,000 loss. The second year revenues would rise to $937,000 (10,000 SKI-KITs) and pretax profits of $103,000. The third year of operation would have sales of $2,342,000 (25,000 SKI-KITs) and pretax profits of $475,000. On the basis of these projections, SKI-KIT, Inc. would need slightly more than $100,000 in working capital during the first year of operation. A loan would be needed to finance SKI-KIT, Inc. during the slow period from April to July.

All business operations would be conducted from an office SKI-KIT, Inc. rented. However, Zenith would warehouse the SKI-KITs and drop ship orders according to SKI-KIT, Inc.'s instructions. Zenith would then bill SKI-KIT, Inc. 60 days from the end of the month in which the SKI-KIT luggage was shipped.

Consumers buying directly from SKI-KIT, Inc. would be required to pay in advance of shipment by check, money order, or major credit card. Because of SKI-KIT, Inc.'s modest capital support, adverse economic conditions, and poor credit rating of many ski retailers, orders by retailers would require 50% down payment and the balance according to normal ski industry terms.

MARKETING

SKI-KIT management rationalized that the ski market was faddish and fashion conscious with respect to color; SKI-KIT luggage should also follow this market characteristic. Instead of offering SKI-KIT in white only, they added yellow, orange, blue, and green. This would cost SKI-KIT, Inc. several dollars more per unit but they would pass the cost on to the consumer. The car mounting straps and shoulder strap would be optional features priced separately to keep the price of the SKI-KIT luggage as low as possible.

Because the major retail shows were over and it was too close to ski season to hire and train a national sales force, SKI-KIT, Inc. would have to devote the majority of its efforts to direct consumer marketing. This would not only generate needed sales at the highest profit margin but would also provide maximum national exposure at least cost. It would also create a consumer demand at the retail level.

An advertising agency was retained for three months to develop a national advertising campaign. This would include full-page advertising in a major consumer ski magazine, advertising in retail trade magazines, local advertising, product brochures, and contacts with other ski companies for cooperative advertising.

The final arrangements between SKI-KIT, Inc. and three airlines and a car rental company proved to be somewhat disappointing because these commercial carriers did not purchase any SKI-KITs nor did they want to participate in a leasing program the first year of SKI-KIT's operation. Their decisions stemmed from SKI-KIT's being a new product and consumer acceptance not yet proven. They believed the total ski equipment damage incurred during transit was not significant enough to warrant an investment in SKI-KITs; their budgets had already been approved and it was too late to make any major changes.

These commercial carriers did include SKI-KIT luggage in their promotion programs to analyze consumer interest. If there were sufficient interest, they would then create a more elaborate program during SKI-KIT's second year of operation. The first year promotional programs included the commercial carriers' endorsements by displaying SKI-KIT luggage at 23 consumer ski shows across the United States. One airline gave SKI-KITs away as a grand prize for a consumer game they sponsored. This same airline also promoted it in their inflight magazine and used SKI-KIT luggage as an employee sales incentive. A second airline had their ski team carry it to all ski races they participated in to promote the airlines' new color and logo. A third commercial carrier, an international airline, offered SKI-KIT as an optional purchase to skiers traveling on their ski charters to Europe. They also demonstrated SKI-KIT luggage while promoting their ski vacations to all ski clubs in the Southern California area.

Other promotion programs included:

1. Endorsements by three major professional and amateur ski associations providing international exposure and credibility to the skier population.
2. Giving SKI-KITs to ten movie stars, for product identity.
3. Demonstration of a SKI-KIT on television.
4. Endorsement of SKI-KIT by an international travel tour organization.

One-hundred new product releases were sent out to the major national magazines and largest newspapers in the United States. These releases were eventually printed in all the major ski publications, and several major international general interest publications.

October is the beginning of the ski season. Consumer ski shows begin then and go on through late November. SKI-KIT Inc. presented SKI-KIT luggage in San Francisco, Los Angeles, Chicago, and New York, and the commercial carriers displayed it in other consumer shows.

At the first show in San Francisco, SKI-KIT management were shocked to discover another ski manufacturer with similar ski luggage. It was the same color, and had almost the same dimensions and general appearance. However, its quality was far inferior to SKI-KIT's. A skier could not pack his boots in it and there was no car mounting feature. This luggage was priced under $100 at retail. SKI-KIT management learned that Zenith's plastic supplier had told this competitor about SKI-KIT four months prior to the ski show.

SKI-KIT at first wanted to take legal action against the competitor. However, on second thought SKI-KIT management decided that their competitor did not pose a threat during the first year because they had an inferior product, no sales force, and no advertising or promotional effort. In the future SKI-KIT would be so advanced in marketing and product development that they would not have to worry. Also, if the competitor were selling its product in the future, it would actually improve SKI-KIT's position because competition would help to create a consumer demand, increase the overall market share for ski luggage, and provide the consumer the opportunity to see SKI-KIT's superior quality.

Skiers at all the consumer shows indicated that SKI-KIT luggage was a highly desirable product and they would very much like to own one—but could not afford it. This convinced SKI-KIT management that they had a good product, but that they would have to find a way to reduce the price.

Sales and Financing

The original loans were spent rapidly on start-up for organizational and advertising costs. More capital would be needed for SKI-KIT to survive until their stock permit was issued, and income from sales of the product was generated. McAlister and several of his friends together lent SKI-KIT an additional $12,900.

In October, the full-page advertisement was printed and several promotional programs were initiated. Sales were a disappointing $1,000. By November, a sales force for California had been established to sell to retail ski shops. The advertisement, product releases, and retail SKI-KIT displays were widely seen by skiers. SKI-KIT sales displays increased sales to $9,000; the majority of these sales were directly to the consumer. SKI-KIT experienced a flurry of orders in late November and through December; skiers called by telephone from across the United States and Canada, causing sales to jump to $15,199.

Unfortunately, skiers wanted their SKI-KITs immediately or before Christmas. Many of these orders were impossible to deliver in that short time. Normal shipping to the East Coast was 4 to 6 weeks but SKI-KIT's carrier developed a backlog because a competing truck company went on strike. SKI-KIT management was forced to spend a considerable amount of time on customer relations.

Future of Ski-Kit, Inc.

SKI-KIT management was pleased with the December sales but they knew sales would taper off substantially in the following months because of the seasonal characteristic of the sport.

The financial statements for the first quarter of operation (Exhibit E)

EXHIBIT E

SKI—KIT, INC.

Statement of Income and Retained Earnings (Deficit)
From October 1, 1974 to December 31, 1974
(Unaudited)

SALES, net	$ 25,199
COST OF SALES	14,940
GROSS PROFIT	10,259
OPERATING EXPENSES	
Advertising	33,878
Consulting fees	5,305
Show expense	1,903
Freight and delivery	599
Amortization of organization costs	249
Depreciation	12
Sales promotion and entertainment	255
Professional fees	250
Miscellaneous	219
Office	696
Telephone	1,547
Travel	651
Rent	1,310
Commissions	175
Equipment Rental	32
Bank charges	58
Dues and Subscriptions	10
	47,149
INCOME (LOSS) BEFORE TAXES ON INCOME	(36,890)
TAXES ON INCOME (Note 1)	200
NET LOSS	(37,090)
RETAINED EARNINGS - OCTOBER 1, 1974	—
RETAINED EARNINGS (DEFICIT) - DECEMBER 31, 1974	$ (37,090)

EXHIBIT E (continued)

SKI-KIT, INC.

Balance Sheet
as of December 1, 1974
(unaudited)

Assets

CURRENT		
Cash		$ 9,515
Accounts receivable		5,102
Advances to officers		221
TOTAL CURRENT ASSETS		14,838
PROPERTY AND EQUIPMENT, at cost		
Net of accumulated depreciation of $12		1,374
OTHER		
Unamortized organization costs	$ 4,722	
Deposits	262	4,984
		$ 21,196

Liabilities and Stockholders' Equity

CURRENT LIABILITIES	
Accounts payable and accrued expenses	$ 33,574
Loans payable	4,500
Taxes other than income	412
TOTAL CURRENT LIABILITIES	38,486
ADVANCES FROM INCORPORATORS	19,800
COMMITMENTS AND CONTINGENCIES (Note 2)	
STOCKHOLDERS' EQUITY	
Common stock, authorized 500,000 shares; par value $1 each issued and outstanding, none	–
Retained earnings (deficit)	(37,090)
	$ 21,196

EXHIBIT E (continued)

SKI-KIT, INC.

Statement of Changes in Financial Position
October 1, 1974 (Unaudited) December 31, 1974

SOURCE OF FUNDS	
Advances from incorporators	$ 19,800
APPLICATION OF FUNDS	
From operations	
Net loss	
Non-cash charges against income	37,090
Depreciation and amortization	261
	36,829
Purchase of equipment	1,386
Organization costs	4,971
Deposits	262
	43,448
(DECREASE) IN WORKING CAPITAL	$ (23,648)
INCREASE (DECREASE) IN COMPONENTS OF WORKING CAPITAL	
Cash	$ 9,515
Accounts receivable	5,102
Advances to officers	212
Accounts payable and accrued expenses	(33,574)
Loans payable	(4,500)
Taxes other than on income	(412)
(DECREASE) IN WORKING CAPITAL	$ (23,648)

EXHIBIT E (continued)

SKI-KIT, INC.

Notes to Financial Statements
December 31, 1974
(unaudited)

NOTE 1: **SUMMARY OF SIGNIFICANT ACCOUNTING POLICIES.**

INVENTORIES

Inventories are stated at the lower of cost (first-in, first-out method) or market.

DEPRECIATION

Depreciation and amortization is computed using the straight-line method for both book and tax purposes.

FISCAL YEAR END

The company has adopted June 30 as its accounting year end.

INCOME TAXES

Investment tax credit is treated as a reduction of tax expense in the year the related asset is placed in service (flow-through method).

Income for financial reporting and tax purposes will be substantially the same.

NOTE 2: The company is presently contemplating suit against one of its creditors because of various deficiencies in their performance. There is approximately $6,000 in dispute.

Payment to a national organization to promote SKI-KIT luggage has been terminated becuase they have not complied with the agreement. To date, SKI-KIT, Inc. has paid $1,000 and the unpaid portion of $9,000 was not included in the accounts at December 31, 1974.

showed SKI-KIT, Inc. to be in a precarious position. SKI-KIT, Inc. management knew they had to do the following:

1. Maintain the previously high level of sales for the next two quarters. This was necessary not only for needed revenue, but also to sell the balance of the 500 units required to retain the exclusive distributorship.
2. Continue efforts to get the stock permit issued.
3. Reduce the retail price to under $100.
4. Establish national distribution and warehousing.
5. Broaden the product mix to include other ski items and counter-seasonal products.

Sales for the next three months totaled only $5,000, which meant that 30% of the inventory still remained. Complications with the stock permit further delayed its issuance. Other means of acquiring capital were pursued, but venture capital companies, which at one time had invested in leisure companies, were no longer investing in anything. Several banks indicated that they were no longer granting SBA loans because of the uncertain economic situation.

Private investors showed interest but took too long to make a decision. And SKI-KIT principals, having already lent $50,400, were not willing to lend any more or secure a loan with their personal assets.

Not until after the major ski retail show in March was SKI-KIT, Inc. able to establish a firm relationship with a national ski equipment distributor with warehousing. At about the same time, SKI-KIT management succeeded in obtaining new manufacturing costs from another manufacturer. This allowed the retail price to be reduced to $99.

SKI-KIT, Inc. also succeeded in acquiring the rights to represent several other ski products and a full line of tennis gear and clothes. The only goal not achieved was raising the capital to keep the company going.

The principals now came to believe that their only alternative was to sell the company. The national sales force was queried to determine how many SKI-KITs they could sell during the next ski season. An analysis of the sales for the first year showed that 70% were direct sales to the skier and 30% were sales made through retail shops. From this information financial *pro formas* were made, showing the following:

	1975–76	1976–77	1977–78
Units	7,000	12,000	20,000
Sales	$364,500	$556,000	$814,000
Pretax profits	$ 25,760	$ 91,000	$139,000

The sell-out proposal SKI-KIT, Inc. offered was a small upfront cash or equivalent stock payment partially to compensate for SKI-KIT principals' loans. In addition, the buyer would assume all SKI-KIT, Inc. liabilities and pay a 5% royalty on net sales for the life of the agreement.

After a three-month search, SKI-KIT, Inc. began negotiating with a leisure-time company. This company gave their own buy-out proposal stating they would give no upfront cash or stock, assume no liabilities, and would pay only a 5% royalty. SKI-KIT, Inc. was again confronted with a most precarious situation, which would require a decision very soon.

CASE 8

Kramer Carton Company*

Richard Hill

HISTORY

Background of President A. J. Kramer

A. J. Kramer, President of Kramer Carton Company, was born in 1897. He left school during the eighth grade, this being the extent of his formal education. He lived on a farm in Ohio with his grandparents from age 10 to 15 years old, leaving them to join his father who worked at Kalamazoo Vegetable Parchment Company in Kalamazoo, Michigan. His father was able to get him a job at the company wrapping bundles. He eventually became a sheeter operator and soon was promoted to printing press operator.

During the time Kramer was at Kalamazoo, Mr. Kindleberger, the owner and chief salesman of the company, developed wax paper and implemented a parchment paper process for packaging lard and butter. The company originally employed ten to twelve people, but by the time Kramer was hired, Kindleberger had twenty personnel.

At the age of eighteen, Kramer took a chemistry course through International Correspondence School as his immediate goal for the future was to become a chemist. He set up a chemistry laboratory at home in the attic to experiment with his new found interest.

When World War I began, Kramer enlisted and was placed in the Army Signal Corps. He was trained in radio/teletype communications through a special course at Indiana University. Upon termination of the war, he was released from the Army and had to decide whether or not to remain at the university to complete his degree. This would have taken one year of additional study; however, due to his recent marriage and birth of a son, Donald J. Kramer, he was forced to leave school and obtain a job.

While Kramer was in the Army, his father had quit his job at Kalamazoo Vegetable Parchment and had gone to work for Sutherland Paper Company. Kramer joined his father at Sutherland and became a foreman in the Parchment Division at the age of twenty-two. He was in charge of the printing department and also ran a press. This division of the company was sold to

* This case was prepared from a report made by Neal Morgan, James Swallow and Gil Victor.

Kindleberger of K.V.P., and Kramer was transferred to the carton department.

During this period, Kramer worked for Mr. Brisbois who was Plant Manager for Sutherland. Brisbois went to California in 1925 to join National Paper Products Company (eventually to become Fibreboard Corp.). He offered Kramer a job as foreman of the carton department with National Paper Products. When Kramer came to California, he brought his cutting man and gluing man from the Sutherland plant. In addition, he brought his "little black book" containing all his knowledge and the rules of the printing and cutting and gluing he had learned up to this point.

Kramer was in charge of the carton plant in Stockton, California, and was earning $350 per month. When he took over the plant, he "closed it down by firing everybody who knew anything" and then reopened it with the people he had brought with him, training his own men. According to Kramer, "In those days you could do that, but now you can't due to the Unions, etc." In Kramer's viewpoint, he brought the know-how of the folding carton business to Northern California; and while at the plant, Kramer introduced cost reduction programs for three of National's plants in his capacity as efficiency man for the company.

Kramer rose to the position of Assistant General Manager of three plants and helped the company develop corrugated plants in Los Angeles and Antioch. While in this position, an instance arose that helps to characterize him. He tolerated the supposed inefficiency of a crippled foreman, but then decided that he had to fire him. This resulted in a strike by the twenty-five personnel who worked for the foreman. Kramer stated, "I got up on a table to try to convince them to stay, but about half of them left."

In 1923, Kramer found out there were virtually no more advancement opportunities in the National hierarchy. He answered an advertisement in a trade magazine and was subsequently hired as a plant manager of a cardboard box plant in Indiana. His annual salary was $10,000 plus 2 per cent of the profit. After three months, he was making good progress: "Firing like hell, as always, because I couldn't get many people to do what I wanted. I finally had to fire Joe, the Italian line foreman, but he went over my head to Mr. Kline, the company owner in Chicago. Mr. Kline came down to the factory one afternoon to inform me that he had rehired (his friend) Joe. I said, 'I'm running this business' and Kline answered, 'I own this business.' So I said, 'It's either Joe or me.' " Kline told Kramer "If you want to run a business you better own it." Kramer then returned to National to take over the Antioch Carton and Corrugated Plant, replacing the two men who ran it. This was for a monthly salary of $400. He observed that there were major problems in the Antioch plant; therefore, he reorganized the plant, rearranging the flow of work, and fired everyone but two of a total of thirty people. He kept a "lazy" Texan machinist because he had imagination. Mr. Kramer thought he would devise the "easiest" way to do a job.

During the next thirteen years from 1929 to 1942 with Fibreboard he became President of the Antioch Chamber of Commerce, and an active member of the Lion's Club, American Legion, and Boy Scouts of America. Mr. Kramer felt that he was a civic leader. He also took correspondence courses in foremanship and plant management at Alexander Hamilton. He invented a number of items used in the paper box industry and obtained patents on a milk carton, a fibre drum, an oil carton, an egg carton, and other containers.

EXHIBIT 1

KRAMER CARTON COMPANY

PAPER BOX MANUFACTURERS
Of Folding Cartons

We Manufacture

CAKE BOXES
Lock Corner and Automatic, Plain and Printed,
with or without windows applied

BAKERY SUPPLIES
U Boards and Automatic Trays
Machine Lock Trays
Glued, Tapered and Nested Trays

CLOTHING BOXES
Lock Corner and Automatic, Plain and Tinted

MILLINERY BOXES
SAUSAGE AND MEAT CARTONS
Automatic glued 1 pc and 2 pc

MEAT BOARDS

CHICKEN BOXES

ICE CREAM CARTONS
Stock and/or Special Print Designs
Special Made To Order Cartons Of All Kinds

WE SPECIALIZE in
DEVELOPING NEW IDEAS
IN THE PACKAGING LINE

IF YOU HAVE A PACKAGING PROBLEM
WE CAN HELP YOU

In 1929 when he recognized that he could not advance with Fibreboard he decided that he would open his own business. In 1936, with $5,000 capital and his patents he attempted to start a paper-carton business. He was unfamiliar with all the items that he should accomplish for this venture; therefore, he obtained the services of an attorney and a promoter. Effectively they spent his $5,000 and the venture terminated. He, therefore, remained at Fibreboard, but kept looking for the opportunity to go into business for himself.

History of Kramer Company

In September, 1941, Mr. Kramer approached several smaller cardboard plant owners to purchase their companies. The contacts did not result in acquisition because of his lack of capital. Later that year he was approached by Mr. Bockman, owner of Bockman Printer and Box Company. Mr. Bockman had a terminal illness and wanted to dispose of the business to provide financial security for his family. Bockman offered to sell for $10,400. Kramer had no capital but sold his home. His equity was $1,500 which served as a down payment. On November 1, 1941, the sale was finalized. During the negotiation Kramer got good accounting, legal, and banking advice. The sales agreement allowed for clear title to the property which allowed him to mortgage his equipment, thus providing working capital of $4,000. When he took over the company it had seven employees and annual sales of $24,000. Some of the equipment in use was 30 years old.

Initially, Mr. Kramer performed the function of manager of operations as well as the salesman. During the first full year of operations which was the first year of World War II, sales were in excess of $48,000 doubling Bockman's 1941 figure.

While expanding in the next few years, Kramer ran into a major difficulty. Zellerback Paper Company, his primary paper supplier, stopped the line of credit to Kramer thus forcing him to restrict his production due to the lack of raw materials. He was guaranteed eight tons per month allotment of paper by the Federal government.

Even with the allotment, it was very difficult to arrange for a permanent supply. Mr. Kramer thought he could overcome this by increasing his quantity of output. In early 1943, he obtained a large order from J.C. Penney to furnish a carload of boxes. He didn't have enough supplies to meet this order; therefore, he contacted Pacific Paperboard Company of Longview, Washington, and made the following agreement: He would buy a full carload of paper, if Pacific would continue to supply him on a regular basis. Since Mr. Flood of the Pacific Paperboard Company was just beginning his business, this arrangement was more than satisfactory. As Kramer was able to meet this order, he eventually got all of Penney's West coast carton business.

During the war, Kramer produced paper coat hangers which mounted to 50 per cent of his sales, but after the war people went back to using wire hangers. He felt that he could have made a million dollars on these hangers had he been able to get enough paperboard. Also, during this time, he continued to do a limited amount of printing using Bockman's old equipment.

From 1942 to 1949 sales increased and the company expanded steadily. In 1949, he employed from 25 to 30 men and women with sales in excess of $300,000 and a net worth that had grown from $1,500 in 1941 to an excess of $100,000.

In December, 1949, there was a large setback. A major fire destroyed the original plant in downtown Sacramento. The company's offices were moved to the home of the president. Two buildings were rented for temporary operating space. Some used equipment was purchased and some rented on a temporary basis. Other competitors were contacted to help fill their orders until he could purchase more equipment. Then in May, 1950, the company moved to its present location.

PRODUCTION

Plant

At the time of the fire, Kramer Carton Company had a signed contract to have built a 20,000-square-foot plant which it was going to lease from the builder and owner, Mr. Harold. Although much of Kramer's operating capability was lost as a result of the fire, Mr. Harold built the building since it could be used for other purposes if Kramer Company could not recover from its losses. The building was only a 100-foot by 200-foot shell; therefore, Mr. Kramer had to finish it by installing wiring and plumbing and providing building maintenance in accordance with the terms of the lease agreement. This building now serves as the basic production area and office area.

In 1952, another 20,000-square-foot building was constructed. Approximately two thirds of the building is used to store finished goods. The remainder contains production equipment.

In 1957, a 20,000-square-foot building was taken over from a neighboring lumber company that went out of business. This is used for raw materials. An additional 8,000-square-foot warehouse, also used for finished goods, was added to these facilities in 1967.

All of the above facilities provide a total of 68,000 square feet, which, in 1971, is leased from Mr. Harold for $2,750 per month. The lease has essentially been in effect for twenty years. Kramer initially wished to purchase the land and buildings but did not feel that there was sufficient capital available to do so. In 1971, Mr. Kramer considered buying the property (land and buildings) for $500,000; however, his banker suggested that the monthly lease payments may have been more economical than purchase.

Production Process

In the process of producing clothing boxes, meat boxes, ice cream boxes, and most other types of printed boxes, it is necessary to process many different types of raw materials. To make a finished product, three basic types of equipment are used: (1) Printing machines which print labels on the boxes; (2) Presses which cut and perforate the basic cardboard sheets; and (3) Folding and gluing machines.

As shown in Exhibit 2, Kramer Carton Company uses the following machines for the operations indicated: (1) One Koeing-Baur, high speed, dual-output printer; (2) Two printing machines using the dry offset printing (without water) method; (3) Two machines which have the capability of printing and cutting at the same time; (4) A dying machine used for background coloring of the boxes; (5) Two machines which can fold and glue

EXHIBIT 2
Factory Layout

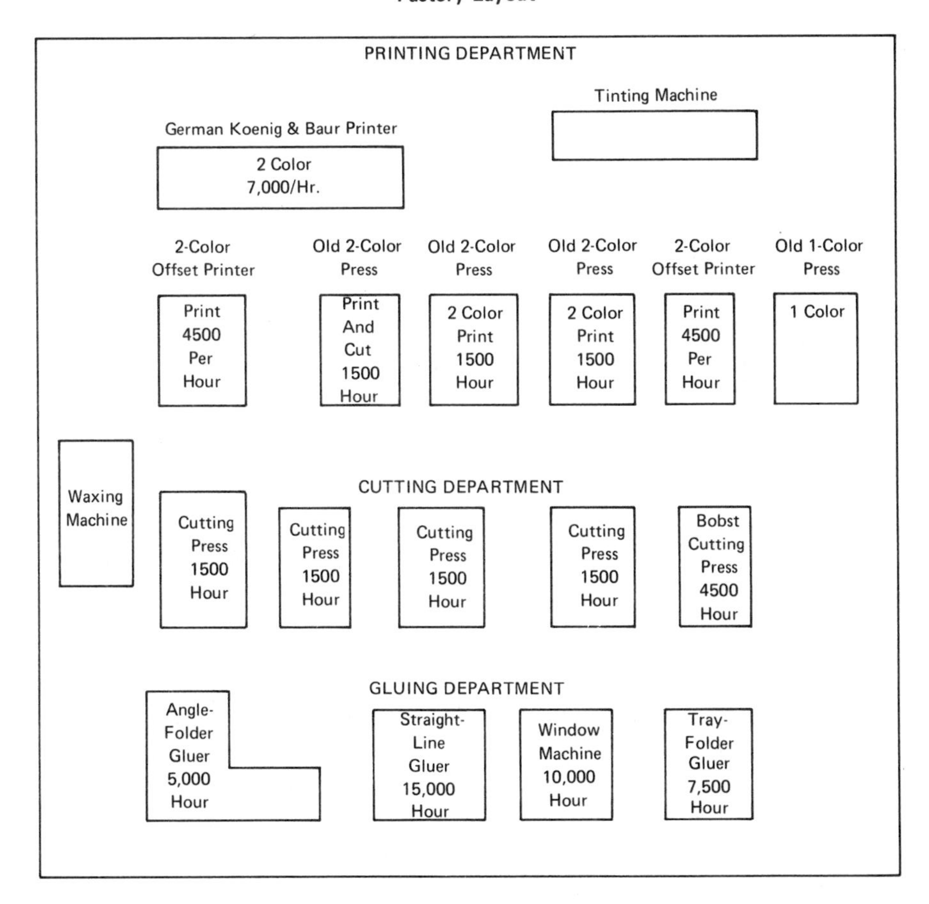

simultaneously; (6) One machine for only folding; (7) One window machine that cuts and glues in transparent windows and waxes. This represents a total of ten major machines in use. There are also various smaller support machines.

Kramer, in 1968, visited the Wurzburg, Germany, Koeing-Baur factory which produces heavy equipment for the paperboard container industry. He bought the new printing press at a cost of $160,000. This new machine permits the simultaneous printing of two colors and produces a total output of 7,000 units per hour with a set-up time for each new job of two to three hours. The two-color, 40-year-old letter press printers operate at a rate of 1,500 units per hour, requiring 10 to 12 hours of set-up time. Until ten years ago, they were satisfactory. Now, most companies are using high-speed presses. Mr. Kramer stated that the old printers are only used on one shift. Before, without the new machine, they were used on two shifts.

Two-color, offset printing will produce 4,500 units per hour. Most large cardboard manufacturers use the wet, offset printing process. However, Mr. Kramer believed that the letter press and dry offset gives more accurate registration and color distribution than wet offset process.

Mr. Kramer felt that he would not junk the old equipment as it could be used on certain jobs economically and kept more men employed.

Mr. Kramer stated that he could purchase another German printer and eliminate all other printers. This would decrease the total amount of equipment required, reduce the floor space used, reduce maintenance, cut costs, and increase production. This has not been accomplished as Kramer does not feel he wants to make the additional cash outlay at this time.

The offset printing machines require two half-cylinder master plates. In order to obtain a new master plate, Kramer must send the design to a company in San Francisco for special fabrication. Plates for the new machine can be made in-house.

Kramer stated that the company used to manufacture laminated, aluminum paperboard but recently discovered that he could buy it cheaper from Kaiser Corporation because of the waste in his shop. Now he buys paper laminated with aluminum, prints it, cuts it, and glues it; and the folder-gluer (and stacker) finishes the product. These aluminum boxes are principally used for packaging baking products.

The process for producing a paperboard box is basically composed of the following steps:

1. Designing the box to include size, shape, weight, and art scheme.
2. Preparing a master printing plate and a master cutting and folding plate. These typically print, cut, or fold several boxes simultaneously.
3. Setting up the appropriate machines.
4. Operating the machines in the following sequence: Printer, Cutter, Folder, Gluer.
5. Shipping.

Kramer in 1925 designed a job scheduling board which is still used today. The order and its specifications are written on a card and the card placed on a rack opposite the name of the machine which is to be used on the job. The operator can quickly see daily what jobs must be done on what machines in what order. He takes the card for the job and after performing it returns the card to the proper place on the rack. Kramer, his son, and the estimator control the board and the system works very well.

Inventory

Kramer carries a raw materials' inventory of many-sized rolls of cardboard. Since the cutting machines cut the proper length, the only economies which can be achieved are to minimize the excess waste of the cut. There is presently a $380,000 inventory, 50 per cent raw materials and 50 per cent finished goods. Inventory is controlled through a perpetual inventory system but supplemented with three or four annual checks. In the estimating procedure, there is a 3 per cent average waste factor calculated which includes the amount recovered by reselling the scrap waste. Recovery costs range from $20 per ton for corrugated cardboard to $90 per ton for white paper.

Raw material inventory is based upon width, thickness, quality, and variety. The level of inventory for each item is based upon experience. Raw material inventory is of two types; rolled-paper cardboard and precut flat sheets.

Of any one type of cardboard there may be as many as 15 different widths. It had been suggested that a standard width should be used to minimize inventory and reorder costs. Mr. Kramer rejected this idea based on his experience although no quantitative analysis was performed. A former employee tried to establish his own box company with a lower inventory, and eventually went out of business. Kramer claims the failure was a result of the lower inventory.

Kramer spent $1.25 million on raw materials in 1970. Purchase terms are generally on a 1 per cent/twenty/net 30. He thought if he had his own paper mill he could save $10 to $40 per ton. His major competitors have vertically integrated companies containing their own paper mills and are able to buy paper at a cheaper price per ton. Because of this, he attempted to arrange for finances to buy a mill in 1960 through the Small Business Administration; however, the request was not approved.

Presently, Kramer's suppliers are located in Lewiston, Idaho; Tacoma, Washington; Los Angeles, California; Port Angeles, Washington; and other states on the Gulf of Mexico. Mr. Kramer stated that he did not have a complete breakdown of raw materials' sources by location, quantity available, type, or unit price.

Cost Estimating

When an order for boxes is received in the factory from salesmen, the estimator estimates all costs and establishes machine requirements for production (see Exhibit 3). Net costs of the job are calculated through a proprie-

EXHIBIT 3

Date ______

Name and Description ______

Quantity ______

Estimated By ______

Caliper and Grade of Stock ______ Colors ______

Cost Per Ton ______	Per M
Rate ______ Unit ______ Amount ______	
Stock	
Waste	
Ink	
Wax	
Glue	
Containers or Wrappers	
Electros	
Print M.R.	
Print Run	
R.S.H.	
Composing—Lino.	
Die Making	
Cutting M.R.	
Cutting Run	
Stripping	
Glueing	
Waxing	
Ream Cutting	
Wrapping	
Freight	
Selling and O.H.	
Cost	
Profit	

Selling Price Total ______

EXHIBIT 3 (continued)

QUOTATION

KRAMER CARTON CO.

1800 61st Street Phone 457-5701 Sacramento, CA

We are pleased to quote you a price of $ ______________________
for the following:

Our quotation covers only the work mentioned above. Any addition to or alteration of the work quoted on will be charged for at the regular rate per operation.

Kramer Carton Co.

Date ____________________ By ______________________

tory empirical formula developed by Mr. Kramer. Mr. Kramer's view was that "We still do estimating the old-fashioned way, but it works pretty good."

Some of the factors considered in the formula are the freight costs of raw materials and finished products, wax, glue (amount per square inch) wrappers, dye, waste factors, the cost of the plate, the size of the run, the possibility of subsequent runs, direct labor, machine costs, and overhead. The waste factor used in the calculations varied between 2 per cent and 5 per cent which was a function of the designer's layout. Mr. Kramer felt that any small businessman who did not understand his costs would not be successful. A typical example of the complexity of the estimating process was a job layout for the packaging of various kinds of ammunition. This job required ten different-size boxes with 69 different-size labels. Mr. Kramer acts as the senior estimator on key jobs and he exercises his final authority over the estimation of any job he chooses.

Since every employee fills out a time slip for each job, the labor costs are easily identified. In the end, the total cost estimate must allow for profit and it always allows for the subjective estimate of a potential competitor's bid.

MARKETING

Kramer's Marketing Process

The company markets its products in seven Western states and Hawaii. Total sales for various years are shown in Exhibit 6. Sales representatives are located in Los Angeles, Honolulu, and San Francisco. Robert Larson, Kramer's son-in-law handles the territory bounded by the Oregon border; Reno, Nevada; and Bakersfield, California; including Sacramento, California. There are also four jobbers who account for 10 per cent of the total sales. The jobbers receive commissions from $2\frac{1}{2}$ per cent to 10 per cent, depending on the size of the order.

All sales are made to industries that use paperboard packaging for their products on the basis of 1 per cent/ten/net 30. Applications for credit by purchasers are all approved by Mr. Kramer. If he deems necessary, he will go to the Sacramento Credit Managers' Association for further verification. Often, Mr. Kramer has an intuitive feeling if an account will not pay.

Mr. Kramer feels that the company needs several large-volume sales orders with a low-profit margin-key account like Continental Baking Company, a cupcake maker. Such accounts insure continuous utilization of employees and machines. About 30 per cent of the business is large-volume low-profit. The balance is in small- and medium-sized orders with better profit margins. This product mix allows an economical production flow and insures a profit.

Competition presents a difficult situation now because of the very large cardboard box manufacturers such as Container Corporation.

ORGANIZATION AND PERSONNEL

The organizational structure is described by Exhibit 4. The informal organization is shown in Exhibit 5. In addition there is an office staff headed by Mr. Fessia, the estimator and lifelong friend of Donald Kramer. It consists of six other employees, one of whom is part-time. Functions performed by this staff are the planning and writing up of factory orders, billing and invoicing, sales record keeping, payroll, personnel records, accounting, and correspondence. Mr. Kramer feels that one of his reasons for success is the low overhead resulting from his small office staff. In addition to these employees, he recently hired an individual to install a cost accounting system. He is not an accountant as Kramer felt he could not afford one, so he trained him.

For the entire organization, the list of employees is presented as of 1971:

No. of Years in Employment		No. of People
0–5		17
5–10		23
10–15		14
15–20		14
20 +		9
Mgmt. + Sales		18
	TOTAL:	95

The minimum female hourly wage is $2.76 per hour. The minimum male hourly wage is $3.04 per hour. Hourly employees are in a company union, and both employees and Kramer appear to be satisfied with pay rates. Although Kramer felt that the union constrained his management of the company, his dynamic personality effectively controlled the elected union representative. The union contract is negotiated annually, with a 6 per cent per year cost of living increase in the contract. This increase has been passed on in increased prices to the consumer or balanced by reducing costs elsewhere. The company union maintains an affiliation with the National Printing Specialties and Paper Products Workers Local 460. One employee belongs to the Machinists' Union and two of them belong to the Photo-Engravers' Union.

EXHIBIT 4

KRAMER CARTON COMPANY
Formal Organization
1971

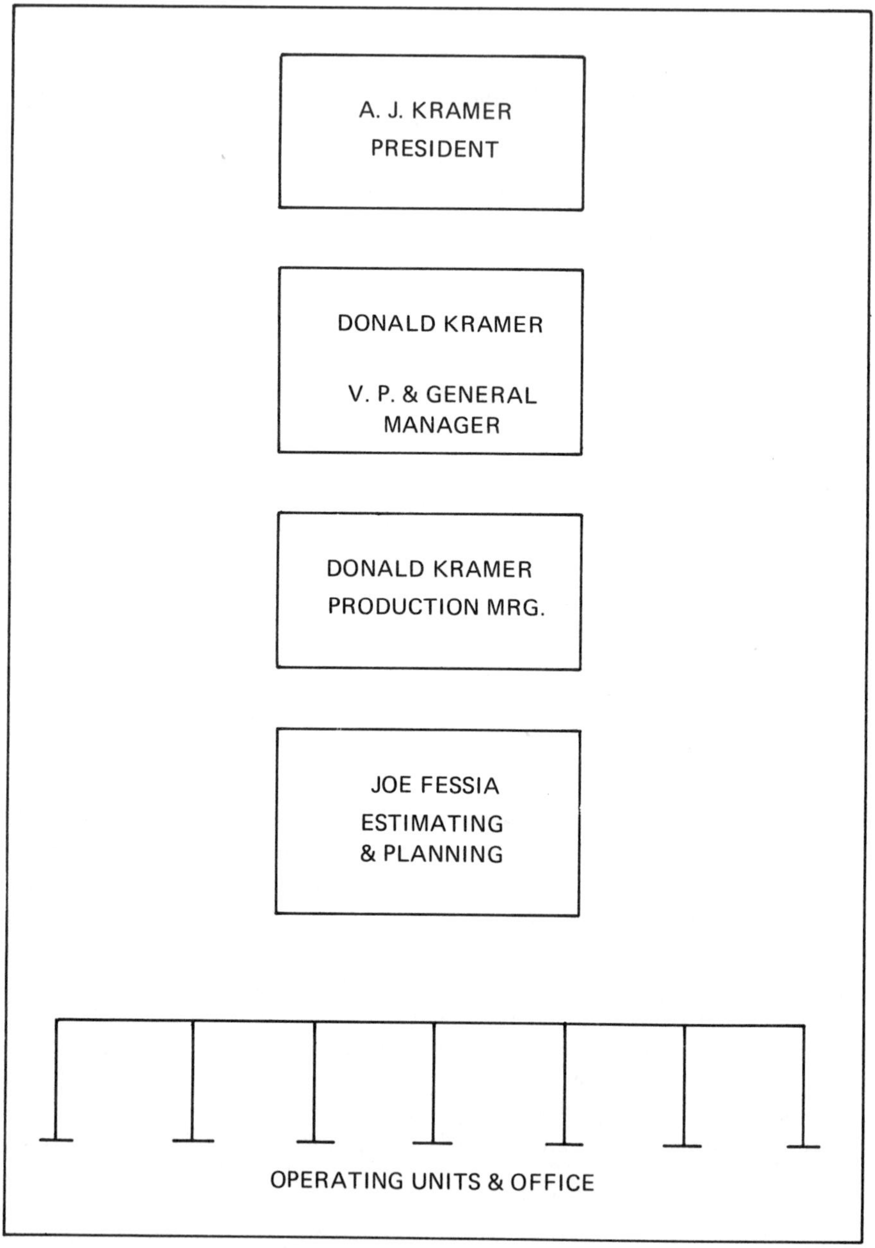

A. J. KRAMER
PRESIDENT

DONALD KRAMER
V. P. & GENERAL MANAGER

DONALD KRAMER
PRODUCTION MRG.

JOE FESSIA
ESTIMATING & PLANNING

OPERATING UNITS & OFFICE

EXHIBIT 5

KRAMER CARTON COMPANY
Informal Organization
1971

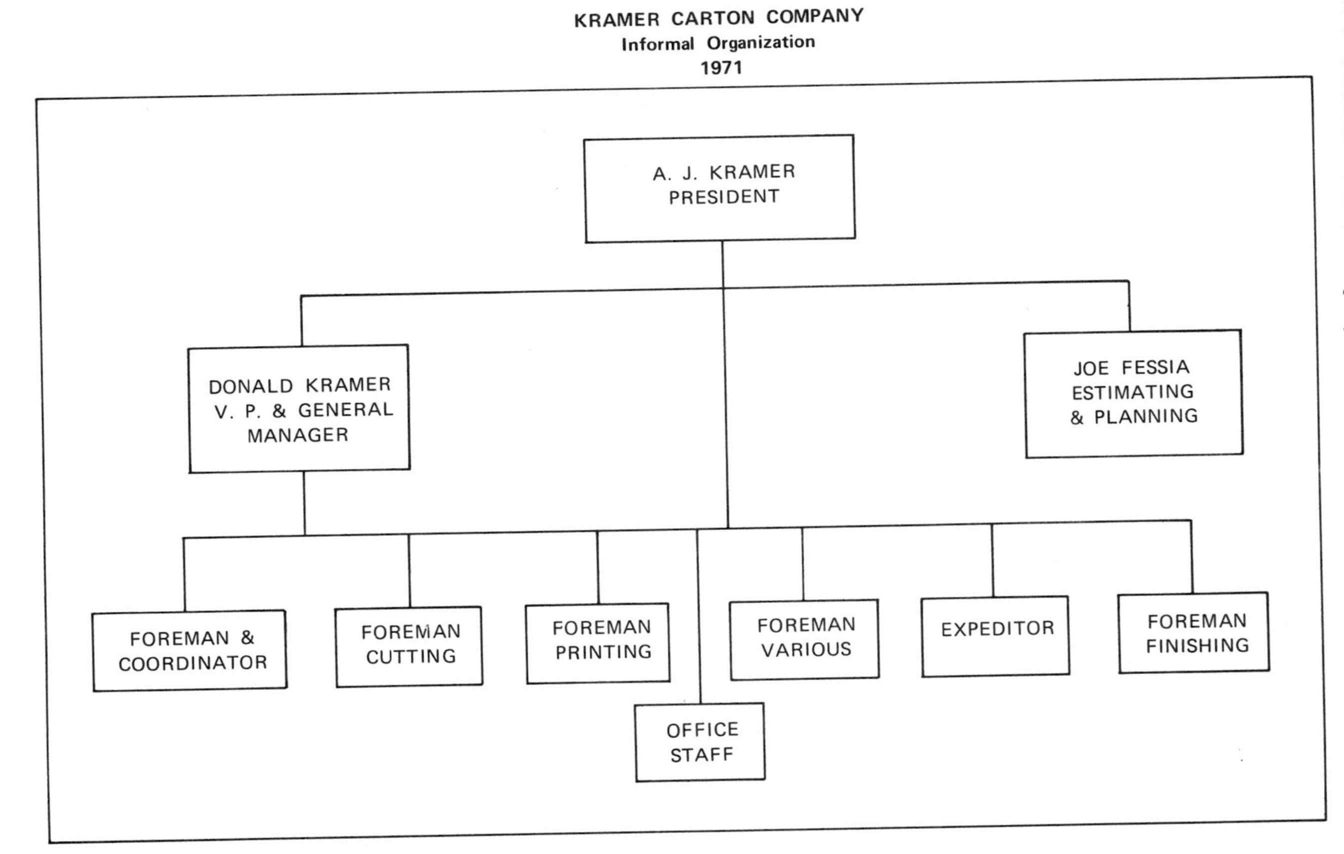

FINANCE

When the company incorporated in 1961, it issued 22,000 shares of $10.00 per share common stock. In 1971 this stock is now held by four groups:

President	A. J. Kramer	16,782 Shares
Vice President	Donald Kramer	1,291 Shares
Secretary/Treasurer	V. Larson (A. J. Kramer's daughter)	1,320 Shares
Three Key Employees		1,900 Shares
	TOTAL:	21,239 Shares

A profit-sharing plan was also established in 1961. Ten key employees were given the option to purchase company stock at a par value $10.00 per share. This was done through a payroll deduction plan in which the employees could have up to 20 per cent of their payroll directed to stock. It also required the employee to redeem or sell the stock back to the company upon his termination of work. This is done at the book value on that date. As of November 30, 1970, the book value was $22.00 per share.

There have never been any dividends declared or paid on the stock: however, to compensate key employees who owned stock, the company has paid an average annual bonus of 6 per cent on the book value. Kramer had always felt that profit sharing was the key to employee incentive; however, after he tried to use the system to finance expansion and boost incentive, he discovered the plan would not work on a company-wide basis.

In 1960, Kramer attempted to expand his company by acquiring a paper mill which he estimated would have cost 1 to 1½ million dollars. The Small Business Administration would not grant a loan nor would any banks; therefore, the idea was abandoned. Through 1971, Kramer has used the policy of keeping the business family controlled and did not go out for additional equity financing. As far back as 1960, he has had offers by investors to buy stock.

Kramer's financial data are shown in Exhibits 6 through 10.

Kramer commented that city and county taxes, primarily on inventory, amounted to $14,000 per year. These, he indicated, were too high and he would consider moving at least outside of the county and possibly go to Reno. There he would buy land, erect a building, sell it, and lease it back. Kramer had also to consider the following: The company is surrounded by a public utility. The utility's property is bounded on the other sides by a railroad and freeway. Any further expansion by the utility would be done by acquiring the property from Mr. Harold, under the right of eminent domain.

EXHIBIT 6

KRAMER CARTON COMPANY

Comparative Profit and Loss Statement

	11-30-70	11-30-69	11-30-68	11-30-67	11-30-66
Sales	$2,721,126	$2,296,209	$2,239,291	$2,311,620	$2,197,165
Less: Cost of Goods Sold	2,172,214	1,839,494	1,831,318	1,847,453	1,823,140
Gross Profit	548,912	456,715	407,973	464,167	374,025
Expenses:					
Freight out	118,231	101,210	98,563	100,098	102,417
Selling expense	117,802	121,475	103,251	101,258	104,366
General and administrative	187,501	165,474	166,701	143,297	142,157
Total expenses	423,534	388,159	368,515	344,653	348,940
Operating profit	125,378	68,556	39,458	119,514	25,085
Other income:					
Interest earned	4,252	5,116	4,711	3,911	2,117
Discount earned	3,889	3,117	3,001	3,329	3,276
Miscellaneous	240	–	–	–	–
Total other income	8,381	8,233	7,712	7,240	5,393
Other expenses:					
Discount allowed	23,403	15,823	16,012	13,429	21,672
Interest expense	12,882	14,721	15,726	3,120	3,311
Donations	1,306	916	1,260	875	1,117
Officers' life insurance	3,624	3,624	3,624	3,624	3,624
Miscellaneous	7	–	–	–	–
Total other expenses	41,222	35,084	36,622	21,048	29,724
Net Profit Before Taxes	92,537	41,705	10,548	105,706	754
Taxes	45,332	16,682	2,844	51,796	233
Net Profit	$ 47,705	$ 25,023	$ 7,704	$ 53,910	$ 521

Kramer Company has never had a financial manager. Mr. Kramer feels that there is no need for one, that he could handle this function himself.

PRODUCT DEVELOPMENT AND INNOVATION

In 1964, Mr. Kramer had an idea which he thought would help to smooth production and increase profits. He wanted to manufacture styrofoam egg carton fillers which would eliminate the familiar egg carton. The project included designing the machine to produce the fillers. The development covered a period of 1½ years and $150,000 was expended before Mr. Kramer finally conceded that the high waste factors would not permit efficiently machining and, as he later admitted, the filler could not be used by the large

EXHIBIT 7

KRAMER CARTON COMPANY

Comparative General and Administrative Expense

	11-30-70	11-30-69	11-30-68	11-30-67	11-30-66
Manager's salary	$ 48,500	$ 48,000	$ 42,000	$ 42,000	$ 36,000
Salaries	100,219	79,862	77,347	72,501	68,702
Payroll taxes	3,762	3,594	3,471	3,396	3,048
Telephone	9,322	11,601	13,972	7,651	5,948
Taxes and licenses	86	104	174	64	82
Office supplies and expense	6,019	4,712	7,132	3,595	6,310
Dues and subscriptions	1,503	1,921	1,417	962	2,350
Depreciation	1,747	1,747	1,221	942	942
Legal and accounting	2,750	2,500	5,300	2,000	2,000
Insurance	710	921	644	676	857
Pension	4,388	3,788	3,702	3,591	3,472
Bad depts	8,490	6,717	10,321	5,919	12,381
Miscellaneous	5	7	–	–	15
Total general and administrative	$187,501	$165,474	$166,201	$143,297	$142,157

EXHIBIT 8

KRAMER CARTON COMPANY

Comparative Selling Expenses

	11-30-70	11-30-69	11-30-68	11-30-67	11-30-66
Salaries	$ 53,068	$ 61,017	$ 47,382	$ 45,001	$ 51,719
Commissions	12,432	10,321	10,279	10,444	9,911
Payroll taxes	1,625	1,540	1,471	1,457	1,291
Auto and travel	16,713	17,997	15,421	14,998	15,071
Promotion and entertainment	31,567	27,672	26,541	26,872	24,334
Advertising	1,614	2,112	1,417	1,721	1,253
Depreciation	630	630	630	570	570
Insurance	153	186	110	195	117
Total Selling Expense	$117,802	$121,475	$103,251	$101,258	$104,366

chicken farmers who had automatic egg-packing equipment. The later fact he did not discover until the final product was tested by an egg packer.

In 1966, the second development project he attempted was the styrofoam plate. The plate machine was supposed simultaneously to form five styrofoam plates which could be used on picnics or in ultrasonic ovens. The styrofoam plate with a plastic coating would also be helpful for camping since it could be used several times. The machine to manufacture the plates was estimated to cost $25,000. But, before the final design was completed, a total of $150,000 was expended. A distributor, Zellerback, had agreed to handle the

EXHIBIT 9

KRAMER CARTON COMPANY

Comparative Cost of Goods Sold

	11-30-70	*11-30-69*	*11-30-68*	*11-30-67*	*11-30-66*
Materials	$1,255,419	$1,013,040	$1,062,943	$1,159,201	$1,090,641
Wages	664,472	567,885	516,507	472,193	508,628
Payroll taxes	31,839	27,382	25,473	23,808	24,525
Supplies	44,692	39,871	41,712	34,510	39,717
Repairs and maintenance	47,118	41,910	53,229	44,801	50,096
Personal property tax	13,510	10,440	9,673	9,595	9,109
Depreciation	32,143	31,796	16,911	3,914	4,117
Rent	35,275	35,275	34,975	33,675	33,525
Insurance	21,016	18,742	18,004	16,981	16,442
Utilities	10,476	8,921	8,762	8,849	8,312
Services	212	521	1,217	54	15
Employees' pension and welfare	46,042	43,711	41,912	39,872	38,014
Total Cost of Goods Sold	$2,172,214	$1,839,494	$1,831,318	$1,847,453	$1,823,140

products. Kramer figures that if he could make eight good plates every 30 seconds he could produce them for 2 cents each. However, the styrofoam plates could not compete in the principal market area with regular paper plates because of the inefficiency of the machine. These above two projects cost approximately $300,000 over a period of three years. Therefore, Kramer said, he will be more careful before going into a new venture in the future—especially if it is out of his line.

Over the past several years, Mr. Kramer thought he should consider automating some of the company functions for two basic reasons: first, it would ensure continuous operation upon his death and second, it would reduce the number of clerical workers in the front office. He had contacted several computer service bureaus but thought their prices were too high and they would be less responsive to his demands for completion of particular jobs especially payroll and billing. In April, 1971, IBM announced a new computer especially designed for small business environments. The computer was called IBM System 3, Model 6. It had an impressive program repertoire which could be purchased from the company.

Available Programs

- Invoicing
- Invoice Register
- Inventory Management Report
- Inventory Sales Analysis
- Sales Analysis

EXHIBIT 10
KRAMER CARTON COMPANY
Comparative Balance Sheet

	11-30-70	*11-30-69*	*11-30-68*	*11-30-67*	*11-30-66*
Current Assets					
Cash	$ 22,456	$ 13,721	$ 38,797	$ 60,193	$ 21,321
Accounts receivable (net)	230,223	166,214	152,321	161,723	176,389
Inventory	371,374	305,856	256,211	222,003	186,410
Advance to employees	1,326	26,321	22,821	8,321	1,673
Prepaid Expense	36,094	51,714	29,711	41,037	39,711
Total current assets	661,473	563,826	499,861	493,277	425,504
Machinery,,Equipment and Leasehold (Net)					
Machinery and equipment	172,144	198,611	216,821	77,311	70,009
Leasehold improvements	147	2,156	4,217	4,562	4,651
Auto	2,807	4,667	6,427	1,716	2,912
Office furniture and fixtures	2,200	2,823	3,571	4,499	3,683
Total machinery, equipment and leasehold	177,298	208,257	231,036	88,088	81,255
Other Assets					
Deposits	21,125	23,750	18,750	18,750	18,750
Surrender value—life insurance	20,105	17,250	15,010	13,240	11,725
Investment—country club	1,800	1,800	1,800	1,800	1,800
Total other assets	43,030	42,800	35,560	33,790	32,275
Total Assets	$881,801	$814,883	$766,457	$615,155	$539,034
Current Liabilities					
Notes payable	$ 27,000	$ 21,086	$ 24,327	$ 15,671	$ 14,912
Accounts payable	174,006	141,318	126,488	112,040	135,640
Contracts payable	32,297	37,187	15,495	–	–
Accrued expense	48,971	29,919	42,886	23,711	16,824
Taxes payable	35,048	19,721	5,744	47,910	3,133
Total current liabilities	317,322	249,231	214,940	199,338	170,509
Long Term Liabilities					
Notes payable	14,895	14,895	5,086	5,086	5,086
Contracts payable	80,716	117,903	133,398	–	–
Total long term liabilities	95,611	132,798	138,484	5,086	5,086
Total liabilities	$412,933	$382,019	$353,424	$204,424	$154,174
Capital					
Capital stock issued	$221,110	$221,110	$221,110	$221,110	$221,110
Retailed earnings	247,758	211,744	191,923	189,621	142,329
Total capital	$468,868	$432,854	$413,033	$410,731	$363,439
Total Liabilities and Capital	$881,801	$814,883	$766,457	$615,155	$539,034

- Trial Balance
- Inventory Analysis
- Accounts Payable—Vendor Analysis
- Accounts Payable—Cost Requirements
- Payroll Register
- Labor Distribution—Work in Progress
- Labor Distribution—Completed Job Summary
- Economic Order Quantity Analysis
- Production Waiting Line Problem (Queueing)
- Standard Deviation and Variance
- Graph and Forecast Display
- Mfg. Routing and Cost Estimating
- Forecasting and Inventory

The purchase price of the computer was $60,000 and all of the programs were available for $10,000 total or through a lease arrangement. Mr. Kramer could lease both the computer and the programs and break even in 40 months. Another $2,000 in initial training was required along with $2,500 in supplies and support equipment. Mr. Kramer was reasonably sure this system would meet his objective but after losing so much in the new product development area he was not sure what he should do.

PACKAGING INDUSTRY

Nature of the Market

For many years, expanding markets, new materials, and consumer preference for disposability have enabled the packaging industry to grow at a rate considerably faster than either the population or the industry; this trend should continue. For other areas, future gains will primarily reflect continued price increases rather than any substantial rise in consumption.

The market for packaging materials ranks as one of the most important sectors of the U.S. economy, with sales in 1970 indicated at about $20.6 billion, against an appropriate $19.5 billion in 1969. The sales breakdown is about as follows: paper and paperboard containers, 37 per cent; metal containers, 20 per cent; glass containers, 9 per cent; flexible packaging materials, including wrapping paper, cellophane, and polyetheylene, 8 per cent; component materials, including adhesives, tapes and labels, 5 per cent; closures, 3 per cent; wooden containers, 3 per cent; aerosols, 2 per cent; cargo or bulk containers, 1 per cent; and miscellaneous, 9 per cent. The sales breakdown, while not significantly different during the past ten years, does show that certain areas, such as aerosols and plastics, have recorded relatively sharp gains, whereas the market share of paper and paperboard has declined somewhat. By 1980, sales of the packaging industry could well grow to $30 billion, with the greatest percentage gains most likely posted by plastic packaging materials.

Consumer preference for disposability seems to be one of the keys to product marketability. Therefore, technology faces the problem of meeting this preference with economical containers that can be readily disposed of without posing pollution problems.

Plastics should continue to grow relatively faster than the industry as a whole, especially if both major soft drink companies should decide to use plastic bottles. Light weight, flexibility in shape, and good protection against breakage favor plastics as a packaging material, sometimes at the expense of more established materials such as paper and paperboard.

Still a relatively expensive packaging material, aluminum is also recording sharp growth as a container for beer and soft drinks. As in the case of plastics, light weight is a primary reason.

The three leading segments—paper and paperboard, metal containers, and glass bottles—have been experiencing a squeeze on profit margins resulting from rising costs of wages, freight, and fuel.

The major factor with long-range implications is the rising demand for better pollution controls. While most companies in the packaging industry are not direct pollutants of the atmosphere or water, their products are solid wastes that also present problems of effective municipal disposal. Legislation has been passed in isolated cases and is proposed on a much greater scale to cope with this problem of solid waste pollution. Proposals range from banishment to taxation. Recycling has been offered as a solution and, to a limited extent, seems plausible. Farther out, new packaging materials possessing shorter life spans in terms of biodegradability may prove necessary.

Disposal of all packing materials results in some form of solid waste pollution. Paper and paperboard products are the primary pollutants, and attempts are being made to alleviate this situation by increasing the recycling or use of waste paper. At present, the low price for waste paper precludes any major solution. Over a period of time, however, a tight world supply situation for pulp could force prices of waste paper upward, thus enhancing the profitability of waste paper reclamation, as well as accelerating trends towards this adoption by paper manufacturers. A breakthrough on the brightness problem for recycled papers, one reason why much of waste paper goes into newsprint, could expand markets.

Consumer Demand

Increased competition from alternative packaging materials, especially plastics, has slowed the rate of growth in demand for paper and paperboard, but this segment commands only slightly less than what its share of the total market was 12 years ago. This slower expansion rate will most likely continue over the foreseeable future, indicating a slight decline in market position.

Based upon the indicated dollar value of shipments, paper and paperboard containers held an estimated 37 per cent of the packaging market in 1970, compared to 38 percent in both 1968 and 1969. Demand for the various grades within this group differs greatly, however. From 1968 through 1970, the dollar value of shipments of major paper products posted the following percentage gains: grocery, variety, and miscellaneous bags, 54 per cent; folding paper boxes and cartons, 63 per cent; sanitary food containers, 104 per cent; rigid paper boxes, 108 per cent; and solid fibre and corrugated shipping containers, 109 per cent. Shipments of items such as glassine, waxes, or parchment bags, and paper shipping sacks were relatively flat or lower over this period. The over-all growth in shipments of paper and paperboard during this 12-year span was almost 87 per cent.

The year-to-year gain in value of shipments in 1970 is indicated at only 3.5 per cent or lower, reflecting higher prices, thus emphasizing this segment's dependence on economic expansion. Growth rates in the future will vary for different products, with that for corrugated shipping containers being perhaps up 6 to 7 per cent annually, depending upon the extent of gains in economic activity and technological innovations. Folding cartons, on the other hand, will most likely post smaller percentage gains, since increased inroads by plastics can be expected. Fibre cans, now a small factor, could maintain strong growth, bolstered by expanded outlets.

Plants and Equipment Outlays

Capital spending among companies in the paper container group is cyclical in character, since the economics of the business require that additions to capacity be made in relatively large increments. Since it often takes several years to absorb the expanded capacity, expenditures normally decline following a major expansion program, but lately return to the level of prevailing before the expansion program. Moreover, because of the protracted rise in the per-ton cost of new capacity, each expansion cycle is likely to carry capital expenditures to new highs.

Sales Record

Demand for cartons, boxes, and other paper and paperboard packaging materials is closely geared to general business activity. Widening uses and applications during the postwar years, coupled with large-scale expansion of facilities and/or acquisition of smaller concerns, permitted the large firms to score sales increases even during recessionary periods. The economic slowdown reduced demand in 1970.

Profit Margins

Extremely sharp price competition in the industry made for relatively wide year-to-year swings in margins of most companies for some years through 1963, since producers attempted to operate primary and converting facilities full capacity in the face of widespread price weakness. Margins in that period were well below those experienced during the mid-1950s. In 1964, 1965, and 1966, operating results were bolstered by firmer prices, increased efficiency, and high operating rates. This pattern was interrupted in 1967 as demand weakened. Profit margins improved in 1968 and were favorable in 1969, but sluggish demand constricted spreads in 1970.

Net Income Ratios

The percentage carry-through of sales to final profits trended downward in the decade through 1963, reflecting pressure on operating margins, increased depreciation charges, and higher interest expense. Most companies experienced significantly higher net income-to-sales ratios in the 1964–66 period, but ratios declined somewhat in 1967, reflecting some weakness in demand and higher depreciation and interest charges due to recent expansion programs. Ratios of net income to sales recorded some improvement in 1969, as strong demand bolstered operating rates (see Exhibit 11).

EXHIBIT 11

Profit Margins (%)
Operating Income as a Percentage of Sales

	COMPOSITE DATA					Paper Containers					
	425 Industrials	Paper Containers	Glass Containers	Brown	Diamond Int'l.	Federal Paper Board	Fibre-Board	Hoerner Waldorf	Inland Container	Maryland Cup	Stone Container
1969	15.4	12.5	13.8	6.3	16.0	10.9	12.3	18.2	9.0	18.7	9.0
1968	15.8	12.9	14.0	5.3	17.0	12.1	12.8	18.2	9.2	19.2	8.7
1967	15.5	12.8	13.4	7.1	16.6	11.8	11.3	17.8	10.1	18.3	10.3
1966	16.4	13.4	13.5	6.7	16.7	11.1	11.3	18.1	11.3	20.5	10.0
1965	16.3	12.8	13.5	6.9	17.1	11.0	11.1	19.1	12.0	19.8	8.7
1964	15.9	12.8	12.2	8.0	15.8	8.9	13.4	18.0	12.3	19.4	8.0
1963	15.7	13.1	12.1	8.6	14.3	10.8	13.1	17.2	13.1	18.4	10.8
1962	15.2	13.6	12.2	8.4	14.7	11.7	11.3	12.9	13.9	17.9	12.2
1961	14.7	13.5	12.2	10.8	14.8	11.6	11.1	11.0	12.8	18.0	12.5
1960	14.7	13.3	10.4	10.6	13.8	9.4	10.3	11.9	14.7	16.5	10.4

Net Income as a Percentage of Sales (%)

	COMPOSITE DATA*					Paper Containers					
	+425 Industrials	Paper Containers	Glass Containers	Brown	Diamond Int'l.	Federal Paper Board	Fibre-Board	Hoerner Waldorf	Inland Container	Maryland Cup	Stone Container
1969	5.7	4.2	4.6	0.8	7.2	3.2	3.8	5.1	5.8	5.1	3.5
1968	6.1	3.4	4.9	def.	7.3	3.6	4.6	6.5	5.8	6.3	4.3
1967	6.1	4.2	5.0	0.4	7.3	3.9	2.5	6.4	6.4	7.0	5.2
1966	6.6	4.6	5.3	1.8	7.9	3.5	3.4	8.0	6.3	8.0	5.2
1965	6.8	4.2	5.1	2.6	7.6	3.4	3.1	7.7	6.2	8.1	5.0
1964	6.6	4.1	4.3	3.3	6.3	2.4	3.8	9.0	5.9	7.6	4.0
1963	6.2	3.8	3.8	3.5	5.7	2.9	3.3	7.7	6.6	6.8	3.5
1962	5.9	4.2	3.8	1.3	5.7	3.8	2.3	5.6	6.5	6.7	4.3
1961	5.7	4.2	3.7	2.6	5.5	3.9	2.0	3.9	7.2	6.9	4.3
1960	5.7	4.2	3.1	2.3	5.4	4.6	1.9	4.5		6.5	3.6

*Based on Standard & Poor's Industry Group Stock Price Indexes.

CASE 9

Two Contrasting Strategies

Following are two cases concerned with growth and market share. They are presented together because comparisons between them, which the student is asked to make, display major lessons for the strategist. What are they?

A. The Mattel Debacle: How It Took Shape*

Robert A. Rosenblatt

The top executives of Mattel Inc. were a desperate group of people in December, 1970.

They had promised Wall Street analysts that the giant toy company would enjoy its sixth straight year of record profits when the fiscal period ended January 31.

But sales were slumping badly. Mattel's "Hot Wheels" cars had been the hit of the 1969 Christmas season; this year of 1970, however, the market was flooded with Hot Wheels, and they weren't moving from store shelves.

During a December strategy meeting, the top executives discussed ways of boosting sales to meet the target for the year. Somebody suggested a "bill and hold" program, under which Mattel would solicit additional orders from its customers, and hold the goods for future delivery.

"Bill and hold" is a legitimate device—only if the orders are real and the goods are segregated in a warehouse.

Mattel's salesmen swarmed out to see customers, pleading, begging, cajoling for millions of dollars worth of orders. Customers who didn't need toys until the next fiscal year were persuaded to book their orders in advance.

Salesmen told customers, "Don't worry about those orders, you can cancel them later."

In one case, orders were written up at a value of $615,000, but later shipped at a true selling price of $185,000.

This spasm of activity in the final month of the fiscal year boosted pretax profits by more than $7 million, enabling Mattel to dazzle Wall Street and its stockholders with another earnings record.

The only flaw was that the sales failed to meet "any minimal legal or accounting standards," according to a special investigative report issued last week. A whopping 80% of the orders generated in January were quietly cancelled a few months later during the new fiscal year.

Such is the description of Mattel's affairs contained in the 500-page special report. It was prepared at a cost of more than $500,000 by independent lawyers and accountants. Mattel's management agreed to this probe as part of a settlement with the Securities & Exchange Commission, which had accused the Hawthorne-based company of issuing false earnings releases.

The SEC also forced Mattel to appoint a majority of outsiders to the board of directors. This was an unusual step, and might set a pattern for future cases in which the SEC fears wrong-doing by top management.

The special report detailed a history of scandalous activity during the 1971 and 1972 fiscal years, with massive falsification of sales and profit figures.

The report lays most of the blame for Mattel's manipulations at the feet of the company's founders, Ruth and Elliot Handler, and their former executive vice president, Seymour Rosenberg. It shouldn't be assumed that the three officials are responsible for all the problems, but there are enough indications to justify a lawsuit against them by Mattel, the report says.

Along with the special counsel's report, Mattel last week announced an agreement to settle five class action lawsuits filed by stockholders against the company and some top officials.

Mattel will distribute $30 million among shareholders who lost money because the firm issued phony earnings releases. The proposed settlement is the biggest ever in a securities case, according to Thomas S. Loo, an outside director.

The Handlers and Rosenberg will make major contributions toward the cost of the settlement. Mattel's independent directors decided that all other defendants in the suits—current and former officers of the company—had acted in good faith except the Handlers and Rosenberg, the special report says.

The Handlers will give Mattel 2 million shares of stock, and refund $112,000 in legal fees paid on their behalf by the company.

Mattel stock last sold on the New York Stock Exchange in September, 1974, at $2 a share, and traded in the $3 range in the over-the-counter market until an SEC ban in July. If trading resumes at $3 a share, the Handlers' settlement will be worth $6 million. Director Loo believes this would be a record repayment to any U.S. company by former executives accused of wrongdoing in management activity.

Rosenberg, who resigned from Mattel in 1972, will cancel a severance pay agreement giving him $45,000 a year through 1987. He will also pay Mattel $100,000 in cash and reimburse the firm for $94,000 in attorney's fees.

The settlement, which must be approved by a federal judge, protects Mattel, the Handlers and Rosenberg from stockholder suits. It eliminates possible action by Mattel against the three former executives, or counter-suits by them against the company. By making big contributions toward the settlement, the Handlers and Rosenberg avoid long and costly litigation. They also gain further protection—the settlement provides that Mattel will defend them against other lawsuits.

Anyone who bought Mattel stock between May 1, 1968, and Dec. 31, 1974, and can prove a loss will be entitled to a share in the settlement.

The settlement will be small compared with the potential losses. Mattel stock climbed from $18 a share at the start of 1967 to $105 in June, 1968, split two shares for one, climbed to $73 in 1970 and again split two-for-one, and reached another peak of $52 in 1971. The shares slid downhill after that, and never recovered.

The Mattel debacle was painful for many people: the numerous stockholders, past and present; the Wall Street securities analysts who believed the company's forecasts; the Handlers, who were the biggest financial losers because they had the largest block of stock; and Rosenberg, whose reputation as a top acquisition-minded executive was virtually destroyed.

"We are deeply, deeply distressed and I don't know how else to say it," says Ruth Handler, who along with her husband Elliot, spent nearly three decades building Mattel into the world's biggest toy company. "It's a very sad feeling but life has to go on," says Elliot.

Their feelings are mixed, some sadness, some bitterness. On Oct. 17 they resigned from the board of Mattel, severing all connections with the company they started in a converted garage in 1945.

Since 1973, they had been figureheads, with no real power, because the banks who loaned Mattel large sums of money didn't want the Handlers running the company.

"I'm shocked and discouraged and disheartened by the whole thing," says Rosenberg. "It's sad to to see the Handlers receiving this kind of treatment. They built one of the great American companies."

Asked what went wrong at Mattel, Rosenberg says, "I'm not sure what happened."

Neither the Handlers nor Rosenberg will discuss the charges against them in the special report. Their lawyers won't let them talk about it until the court settlements are final.

The report acknowledges that the people named didn't have a chance to cross-examine those who accused them of wrong-doing, and didn't examine any documents or papers used in the investigation.

The Mattel story, as told in the report, is a case study of what happens when business becomes obsessed with growth for its own sake, when executives work with one eye on the stock ticker.

Between 1948 and 1965, Mattel was strictly a toy company, with no plans for doing anything else. In 1966, the company changed its objectives, according to a memo from the office of President Ruth Handler: "It is felt that the basic corporate objective should be to increase earnings per share in a manner which will foster further growth and enhance our stockholder investment."

Growth should be internal, by selling more toys, and external by acquiring other firms, the memo said. It spoke of increasing sales by 10% a year, and aiming for net profits of 5% of sales.

The Handlers looked for someone to bring this about, and found Seymour Rosenberg, who had a glittering reputation at Litton Industries, where he worked on acquisitions.

"Rosenberg had such a hot reputation that Mattel stock jumped after they announced he was coming over from Litton," recalls a Mattel supplier.

The special counsel's report on Mattel puts it more formally: "The financial community viewed Rosenberg's association with Mattel as bringing to the company a degree of financial sophistication that it previously lacked."

Rosenberg immediately began talking with analysts, inviting them to Mattel's offices, and outlining the company's prospects. The analysts pushed Mattel stock as a good buy.

Between 1968 and 1971, with Rosenberg playing the key role, Mattel bought five companies: a circus, a pet supplies firm, and producers of playground equipment, magnetic recording tape and plastic hobby kits.

Mattel "was operating in much the same manner as it was when it was a small company," says the special counsel's report. "Formal organizational lines of communication were often ignored. Decisions of varying degrees of magnitude were made by a small group of people."

Growth was the operative word at the company; more sales, generating more profits would raise the price of the stock, making it easy to buy new companies, providing even more sales and profit. . . .

Yet much of this growth was illusory, a creation of "improper and unjustified accounting" methods, according to the special report issued last week.

Starting with the quarter ended May 2, 1970, the report says, Mattel used these devices to reach its sales goals:

A senior management executive would decide on the targets for the quarter.

Then the accounting department was given instructions to reach the target. For the quarter ended May 2, for example, sales had to show a 22% gain over the prior year.

This goal was reached by shifting second quarter sales back into the first quarter to inflate the total.

For the six months ending Aug. 7, 1970, the accounting department's target was a sales gain of 26% and an earnings per share jump of 41%.

Expenses were purposely understated by $6.6 million—the company simply deferred advertising and overhead expenses until later in the year.

The technique for this report and other false figures followed a basic rule. Take the target profit and work backwards, changing the records and books until the numbers jell to produce the desired profit.

Mattel's executives were casual in their approach to the company's figures. "Give me another million," a vice president once told an accounting manager, according to the special report.

Always, the accountants were pressured by management to produce figures that would look good to securities analysts following Mattel's stock.

One manager in the accounting department told the special investigators that "a few members of management had a pre-eminent concern over Mattel's Wall Street image, and that a senior executive was locked into his representation that he could favorably affect Mattel's stock price."

According to the report, the pressure for profits led to numerous abuses in fiscal 1971 and 1972:

- Sales of the Ringling Bros. circus, a subsidiary, were purposely understated for the first quarter of 1971 to produce the image of a big jump the following year.
- The company skipped its contribution to the employe profit-sharing plan in 1971 to increase earnings although 1971 was the best year ever.
- Royalties owed to inventors were understated by $3 million.
- Mattel shipped 5 million Hot Wheels cars near the end of fiscal 1972, losing $400,000 on the sale, but didn't record the loss until the next fiscal year.
- A single order for $4.8 million worth of toys was counted twice in the sales total for the quarter ended May 1, 1971. The mistake was discovered before the quarter ended, but not corrected until the next quarter.

Arthur Spear has been president and chief operations officer at Mattel since 1973. He was executive vice president for operations when the books were being falsified.

Spear says he never felt any pressure in the company for performance to impress Wall Street. He concentrated on his responsibilities for manufacturing. "I don't recall being too conscious of anything except the job to be done."

He says he had no idea the numbers were false. "There were regular meetings reviewing the company's financial performance. I was not privy as to how they arrived at those numbers. I had no cause to question the information being reviewed."

The responsibility for the financial manipulations goes to the top of the company, according to Spear.

"These things clearly can't and don't originate at lower and middle management levels."

Spear has installed an elaborate financial superstructure and internal reporting system as safeguards against another outbreak of phony numbers.

During its growth surge, from 1967 through 1971, Mattel's sales grew to $299.2 million from $137.2 million, while profits soared to $17.4 million from $3.3 million.

Fiscal 1971 was the best year, also the year when extensive accounting manipulation first began. The company reported pretax profits of $34 million; as much as $15 or $20 million may have been created by improper accounting devices, according to a special auditor's investigation.

During fiscal 1972, a dock strike hurt the flow of supplies, Mattel's product sales slipped, and even improper accounting couldn't produce a profit. The company reported a net loss of $31.2 million on sales of $206.4 million for the year.

The figure before taxes was a loss of $59 million, but the complexities of the financial finagling make it impossible to know what the real loss was, according to the auditors.

Mattel couldn't find a toy to match Hot Wheels for generating profits. Although sales improved somewhat in the 1973 and 1974 fiscal years, the company suffered aggregate losses of $37.8 million.

The SEC began investigating the company in 1973, after Mattel issued contradictory press releases about its expected earnings.

Last year, the SEC accused the company of issuing false earnings figures in 1971 and 1972. The company agreed to accept a majority of outside directors approved by the SEC, and to hire outside lawyers and accountants to investigate the financial activities of those years.

The result was last week's report, accompanied by Mattel's agreement to pay $30 million to settle shareholder actions, plus the parallel settlements between the company, the Handlers and Rosenberg.

Completion of the special auditor's report satisfies the SEC requirement that the public be informed of what really happened at Mattel during the years of hidden scandal.

Now, the company can file updated financial statements with the SEC, and ask for resumption of trading in its shares. The last earnings statement covered the nine months ending Nov. 2, 1974. Mattel had a net profit of $2.6 million on sales of $243.9 million for the period.

Ruth and Elliot Handler want Mattel to succeed, even thought they won't be part of the business.

"It is a good company, it is a solid company and it must survive," Ruth Handler said during an interview in their penthouse apartment in Century City.

"That company is like our child and that company must live."

B. Hewlett-Packard: Where Slower Growth Is Smarter Management*

RELYING ON PREMIUM PRODUCTS RATHER THAN TRYING TO COMPETE ON PRICE

David Packard, chairman of Hewlett-Packard Co., stretched his six-foot-five frame after lunching with a score of his middle managers recently and then proceeded to set the record straight on the company's strategy for survival in the fast-changing world of high-technology electronics. The leading producer of electronic instruments and a major force in minicomputers and calculators had grown too fast in the boom years of 1972–73, Packard declared.

He ticked off the disturbing results. Inventories and accounts receivable got out of hand, products went into production before they were fully developed, and prices were set too low. The problems were well in hand now, but Packard wanted to be sure that the lesson was understood.

"Somewhere we got into the idea that market share was an objective," Packard told his attentive audience, jingling a pocketful of coins for emphasis. "I hope that's straightened out. Anyone can build market share, and if you set your prices low enough, you can get the whole damn market. But I'll tell you it won't get you anywhere around here."

Packard's feisty speech was part of a year-long campaign he and President William R. Hewlett have been waging to reemphasize the principles they laid down when they launched their unique partnership 36 years ago. The fact that Hewlett and Packard had to initiate and lead the drive personally shows clearly why some company watchers are beginning to worry about what will happen to the high-flyer once its two founders depart.

The style and leadership of the two men are intertwined with the major policies of their company to a far greater degree than are those of the top managers at most major corporations. Now both Hewlett and Packard are nearing retirement age, and they have started moving younger managers into positions that hint at a line of succession. A major task will be to make sure that their philosophies and strategies are deeply ingrained before they leave.

But it will be a tough act to follow. "Hewlett and Packard are unique people," declares Galen Wampler, who follows the company closely as an analyst for Creative Strategies, Inc. "The company needed a technology innovator like Hewlett, but it also had Packard, a man with a lot of business

* Reprinted from the June 9, 1975 issue of *Business Week* by special permission.

sense." Thomas J. Perkins, a venture capitalist who was once a top H-P executive, points out that Hewlett and Packard have been personally responsible for many of the company's new products and diversification moves. "They are extraordinary entrepreneurs," he says.

Pricing for profit

The fundamental tenet on which they have built the company—and the point they have strongly reemphasized to their managers during the past year—is that rather than compete on price, H-P must concentrate on developing products so advanced that customers are willing to pay a premium for them. "After a few excursions in the opposite direction," says Hewlett, "we're found that this philosophy fits our style of operation."

So now, at a time when other companies are dropping prices to boost sales and cutting research spending to boost earnings, Hewlett-Packard is taking the opposite tack. It has raised prices by an average of 10% over the last year, and it has increased spending on research and development by 20% to an $80-million annual rate.

If the strategy works, H-P will slow the pace of growth that more than doubled sales in the past three years, but its profitability will continue to improve. So far, this is exactly what has happened. Last week, H-P announced that first-half sales were up 14% to $460 million, while profits jumped 21% to $42 million. Several analysts now predict that H-P will reach $1 billion sales for the first time in the fiscal year that ends next October.

Even more dramatic than the first-half results was H-P's balance sheet turnaround. A year ago, net short-term borrowings totaled $118 million, and the company was planning to resort for the first time to long-term debt. Instead, Packard toured the divisions to impose new asset-management discipline. Reaction was quick: inventories were slashed, accounts receivable were tightened, and hiring was frozen. As a result, H-P is now almost completely out of the banks. "This is nothing short of astounding," says Michael R. Weisberg, an analyst at William D. Witter, Inc.

To spend or not to spend

The sail-trimming at Hewlett-Packard reflects one response to the unique dilemma that managers of high-technology companies must resolve in these days of accelerating technical change, intensified competition, and economic uncertainty. On the one hand, recession conditions create great financial dislocations for companies used to growing fast, and product development is a tempting area for temporary cutbacks. Notes Jeremy G. A. Davis, vice-president and general manager of the Boston Consulting Group's Menlo Park (Calif.) office: "The weaker the company, the more pressure there is to slash R&D spending."

On the other hand, some companies producing advanced electronic products feel that they must increase their research spending during a recession to be ready for the onslaught of price cuts and new products that will accompany the next upturn. "Our development spending is up 60% over last year," says Andrew S. Grove, executive vice-president of Intel Corp., a fast-growing semiconductor company that has prospered by introducing significant new products. "We are buying our position in the upturn," he declares. Packard agrees. "The main determinant of our growth," he says, "is the effectiveness of our new-product program."

In betting large sums on the inventiveness of their engineers, companies like Hewlett-Packard and Intel are counting on developing products that cannot be quickly imitated. The classic example is H-P's hand-held scientific calculator, the HP-35, which was introduced early in 1972 and did not have a serious competitor until Texas Instruments, Inc., introduced an electronic slide rule of its own last year.

In H-P's last fiscal year, according to estimates by Creative Strategies, the HP-35 and its later variations accounted for sales of $120 million and pretax earnings of $40 million. Whether that kind of success can ever be duplicated seems open to question in light of the increasing competitive pressures in virtually every niche of high-technology electronics. "The pioneer has very little lead time now," says Davis of Boston Consulting. "Instead of several years to get down that experience curve, he may have only a few months."

What is happening is that the management of technology—not only in electronics but also in pharmaceuticals, chemicals, and other specialities—is no longer an art but a discipline that is becoming better understood by a growing number of companies. Furthermore, the specialization that once separated an instrument maker from a computer company or a component supplier has melted away in recent years as semiconductor devices have taken on new complexity and instruments have been combined with calculators and computers in an endless array of specialized systems. Semiconductor houses, such as Texas Instruments and National Semiconductor Corp., are integrating forward into end products, and instrument companies, such as Tektronix, Inc., and Varian Associates, are making their own data-processing equipment. The result is an open-ended array of potential competitors in almost every area of advanced electronics.

An increasingly common tactic to achieve dominance is to price a new product in relation to the manufacturing costs that the producer expects to achieve when the product is mature. Popularized by the Boston Consulting Group and exploited by such companies as TI and Digital Equipment Corp., "experience curve pricing" puts a premium on achieving market share early in the game. Other industries follow similar strategies, but one consultant points out: "Nobody is moving faster on the experience curve than the high-technology electronics companies, and the consequences of being late are most severe in that business."

A good strategy

Against that background, H-P's decision to eschew market share in favor of a concentration on profitability seems fraught with risk. But Packard and Hewlett do not see themselves as risk takers, and their philosophy makes sense for a company that can consistently produce truly innovative products. "If you have a new product that makes a contribution," says Packard, "it's easy to sell all you can produce at a respectable price. Then as you actually achieve cost reductions, you can lower the price accordingly."

H-P's leadership position in instruments has paid off handsomely as the company has diversified into computers, calculators, and components. "Measuring instruments have to be better than the products they measure," Packard explains. "From the beginning, we've had to keep a good base of technology." That is something of an understatement, says one former H-P executive. "Along with Bell Labs, they get the cream of the crop of bright young engineers," he claims. "And they provide an environment that is very rewarding."

Innovative products have been the cornerstone of H-P's growth since 1939, when Hewlett engineered a new audio oscillator and set up shop with Packard in a Palo Alto garage. The product was cheaper and easier to use than competing oscillators, and it was quickly followed by a family of test instruments based on the same design principles. During World War II, H-P developed some high-speed microwave instruments—"because we didn't know any better," Packard claims—and used that technology to ride the postwar boom in communications.

By the 1950s, H-P was churning out up to two dozen new products every year, including the first high-speed electronic counter and an oscillator that automatically swept through a range of frequencies. "Hewlett and Packard had the fortune or wisdom to get into the electronics business when it was just starting to boom," remarks one observer.

But H-P's strategy of product dominance did not always succeed. Despite heroic efforts, H-P has never managed to shake the grip held by Tektronix on oscilloscopes, the ubiquitous instrument used in every lab to display electronic signals on a cathode-ray tube. "We delayed our entry in that business too long," Packard admits, "and the first scope we introduced wasn't a better product." And in minicomputers, H-P missed an opportunity to catch up with Digital Equipment Corp. in the early 1970s by failing to move technology into the marketplace at a competitive pace. "Despite the fact that we are second in the market," says Paul C. Ely, Jr., general manager of H-P's Computer Systems Group, "our impact hasn't been felt."

Nevertheless, H-P's diversification has been a success by most standards. In the last fiscal year, the original test and measurement instruments accounted for only half of H-P's sales of $884 million. Data products, including minicomputers and calculators, brought in $326 million. Medical electronics, a field H-P entered largely by acquisition, added $76 million and analytical instruments another $39 million. Much of this growth has come in the last three years, spurred by both the world economic boom of 1972–73 and the success of new products, such as the minicalculator. Sales soared by nearly 30% in 1972 and to almost 40% the following year. "It was a seller's market," Packard says.

At first, growth was welcome. H-P had been sharply affected by the computer and aerospace downturns in 1970, while Packard was serving as No. 2 man in the Defense Dept. Earnings actually declined slightly in fiscal 1971 in spite of such measures as company-wide pay cuts.

But the boom also brought problems, including a rapid increase in inventories and an unaccustomed influx of new employees. By the end of 1973, H-P's short-term debt load was big enough to force a decision. "Some of us thought we should convert to long-term debt," Packard says, "but I began to think about it, and I concluded that we hadn't been on the right track."

"The problem with debt," says Hewlett, "is that you eventually have to pay the piper. It's more comfortable to have zero debt when you have to increase inventories to keep people working." Adds Packard: "My philosophy goes back to the Depression. I don't want to be in debt if a downturn comes."

The situation came to a head while Packard was visiting H-P's German subsidiary in January of last year. "Somebody got up and said we should transfer more products to Europe to gain market share," recalls Ely. "Dave laid into that concept so hard that the audience was aghast." What troubled Packard, apparently, was the prospect that H-P would become so dependent on growth that it would slip away from the principles that he and Hewlett have expounded over the years.

As it happened, H-P's belt-tightening effort turned out to be the perfect preparation for the general recession that hit last fall. With hiring virtually flat for most of last year, H-P's productivity improved rapidly.

The change in the cash position saved $5 million annually in interest charges, and prices on products such as oscilloscopes were pushed upward, off-setting price declines in calculators and computers. As a result, earnings jumped ahead in the face of slowing sales. "Packard put the emphasis on control at all levels," says Creative Strategies' Wampler. "That's the watchword for the future."

CASE 10

American Motors Corporation 1972–1975

*Karen Boulton and Steven M. Green**

OVERVIEW

At the end of its 1975 fiscal year, American Motors Corporation (AMC) reported a $27.5 million loss. Thus ended four turbulent years. These years, 1972–1975, are the focus of this case.

Although there were significant increases in their dollar sales volume, spiraling costs of materials and labor, government mandated engineering changes, and an international oil crisis lessened any chances AMC had to achieve profitable operations. Also, during these four years, the changes in consumer preferences were the most marked in the history of the automotive industry.

As AMC entered 1976, it faced major challenges in both marketing and financial areas. The strategies it employed to meet them had to encompass product planning, engineering, marketing, production, international operations, finance, and competition.

CORPORATE PHILOSOPHY

Insight into the overall corporate philosophy of AMC is perhaps best exemplified by an excerpt from its 1972 annual report as follows:

". . . a way of life for American Motors in the automotive industry (is) what we termed our philosophy of difference. It means finding niches in the market that are not being fully served and then applying the company's skills and resources to servicing them. It means doing things differently and distinctively—with a willingness to assume the risks of innovation."

Broadly interpreted, AMC felt that rather than meet its competition in the automotive industry head on by producing like models, it would instead try to produce vehicles which were designed for smaller market segments that were not being adequately served by the Big Three automotive manu-

* Reprinted by permission.

facturers. In the years prior to 1972 this philosophy manifested itself through production of compact and intermediate size vehicles. Prior to the 1960s the market which was being addressed by the Big Three consisted primarily of intermediate compacts and full-size cars. In recent years, however, the Big Three were producing compact and intermediate automobiles in direct competition with AMC. Even so, AMC continued to concentrate on smaller and hopefully more profitable segments of the automotive market. AMC's president, William Luneburg, stated: "We are not shooting with a shotgun, we are shooting with a rifle" [33].

In addition to this automotive product orientation, AMC's philosophy was further extended to encompass a goal of vertical expansion and integration to get a greater control over its supply of components for vehicle production [9].

There was also a thrust to nonautomotive diversification. In the years 1972–1975 there were several significant acquisitions, noted in Exhibit I.

Although AMC sought growth in the automotive market, it had reservations about excessive concentration on growth without regard to profitibility. Chairman Roy Chapin said "When you get beyond a certain size the economies of scale do not continue ad infinitum" [19].

EXHIBIT I

American Motors Expansion and Diversification

1972

AM Data Systems
AM Leasing Corporation
Coleman Products
Manufacturer of wiring looms and harnesses for use in AM vehicles.

1973

Evart Plastics
Totally supply plastic components for American Motors vehicles
Mercury Plastics
Windsor Plastics
Mercury and Windsor provided materials for American Motors vehicles and also to other consumer products manufacturers.

1974

Wheel Horse Products
Manufacturers of lawnmowers, small tractors and other items of lawn care equipment. Also included the acquisition of G.E. Outdoor Products Division.
Coleman Plant Number 2
Expansion of the wiring facility.

PRODUCT LINE

The overall trend in AMC's product mix from the early 1970's through the 1976 lineup showed a substantiation of its marketing philosophy, i.e., it could best succeed in the marketplace by catering to the individual interested in smaller cars. As shown in Exhibit II there were significantly fewer models in 1976 than in the 1972 model year. Most noticeable was the elimination of the Ambassador product line which was an intermediate size vehicle, although, it was primarily marketed at the low end of the full size market. The introduction of the Pacer in 1975 gave AMC two comparable entries into the subcompact market.

Essentially the Hornet and Gremlin were mechanically identical vehicles. The Hornet was available in a two-door and a four-door sedan, a four-door stationwagon and a two-door "hatchback," which was a two-door sedan with a large rear cargo door fashioned in the fastback style.

The Gremlin was, for all practical purposes, a Hornet stationwagon that had 12 in. removed from its midsection resulting in a two-door, 96-in. wheelbase, subcompact size stationwagon.

The Matador product line consisted of a coupe, a sedan, and a stationwagon.

The Pacer was a unique vehicle introduced in March of 1975. It required all new tooling for AMC at a cost of $60 million. It was designed to permit production of other derivative vehicles from its basic components. Thus, it would parallel the Hornet/Gremlin in concept.

Sales information for the various product lines and total AMC offerings are shown in Exhibit III.

AMC was not unique in the automotive industry in its desire to attract young buyers. It was felt, and had been historically shown to be true, that brand preferences were established early in life and when the performance

EXHIBIT II

Passenger Car Models

	1972	1973	1974	1975	1976
Hornet	3	4	4	4	4
Gremlin	1	1	1	1	1
Matador	3	3	3	3	3
Ambassador	3	3	2	0	0
Javelin/AMX	2	1	1	0	0
Pacer*				1	1

*Introduced spring, 1975

EXHIBIT III

AMC Sales

	1971	1972	1973	1974	1975*
Ambassador		41,000	30,000	12,000	0
Hornet		89,000	139,000	132,000	71,000*
Gremlin		100,000	133,000	120,000	50,000*
Pacer†					150,000*
Matador		47,000	54,000	83,000	60,000*
Javelin/AMX		26,000	27,000	18,000	0
Total AMC	253,000	303,000	383,000	365,000	331,000*
Total Domestic Built U.S. Sales		8,900,000	9,600,000	7,700,000	6,600,000
AMC % of U.S. Domestic (Does not include imports)		3.4%	4.0%	4.7%	5.2%
Jeep			46,000	64,000	75,000*
Foreign Sales	58,000	59,000	67,000	96,000	

*Projected for calendar year
†Introduced March, 1975

of the product was satisfactory, consumers tended to stay with that automotive product.

In 1967 the average age of the buyer of an AMC product was 62 years [33]. In 1974, showing the strong effect of AMC's orientation towards smaller and more youthful products, the average age had dropped to 35.

DEALER NETWORK

During the years under consideration, AMC changed its strategy regarding the dealer network from growth in numbers to an emphasis on fewer dealers having higher quality. AMC recognized that any significant gains in vehicle sales must be accompanied by a well run and responsible dealer network which could meet the needs of the auto buying public.

The results in the change of policy are shown in Exhibit IV. At first glance, the decrease in the number of dealerships might indicate some cause for alarm. However, this was in keeping with AMC's avowed intentions of having fewer but better dealers. Additionally, it afforded dealers an opportunity to sell more vehicles per dealer and hence acquire a greater return on investment. In 1974 the annual report indicated that AMC dealers had the highest return on investment in the automotive industry. It was also stated

EXHIBIT IV

Number of AMC Dealerships

1971	*1972*	*1973*	*1974*	*1975*
2,044	1,951	1,930	1,881	1,797

Source: *Automotive News*

that since 1970 AMC had invested over $40 million in new and improved dealer facilities.

AMC still had not achieved its objective of placing dealerships in each of the key marketing areas it desired to reach.

FOREIGN MARKETS

In the early 1970s international economic pressures, materials and oil shortages contributed to a concerted effort on the part of AMC to develop and further cultivate foreign markets. The strength of the growth in foreign sales is shown in Exhibit III.

Contributing to this growth was a policy by AMC to achieve a "partnership approach" in the nations where its sales horizons were being expanded. This produced a beneficial effect of providing responsible foreign management, insight into local customs, as well as obtaining the blessings of the foreign governments concerned.

Between 1973 and 1975, United States exports of AMC rose by over 30 percent. In 1975, Jeep exports alone were up 42 percent [11]. New markets which AMC was rapidly cultivating for its four-wheel drive Jeep vehicles included both the Mid East and the Far East.

Additionally, in late 1975, AMC introduced right-hand drive versions of the Pacer and Jeep Wagoneer into Great Britain. In September of 1975, AMC's Mexican affiliate began production of new Pacer models in Mexico City with equipment specifically designed for that country [31].

One of the key success measurements for any auto company is the number of "conquest sales" which are achieved by a given model. This is an indication of how many people bought products whose prior automobile had been from another manufacturer. The Hornet and Gremlin in 1973 achieved conquest rates of 70 and 85 percent respectfully [9].

PRODUCT AND MARKETING PROMOTIONS

AMC achieved a significant marketing and competitive advantage with the introduction of the Buyer Protection Plan in 1972. Essentially, this plan completely guaranteed all AMC vehicles for a period of 12 months or 12,000 miles for all defects excluding tires. This plan was unique in the industry at that time and afforded a degree of product warranty coverage unmatched by the competition. It additionally included, at most participating dealerships, free loaner cars for the period of time required to effect repair. In 1973 the Buyer Protection Plan was upgraded with trip interruption insurance, which provided up to $150.00 for expenses incurred, should overnight repairs be required while the individual owning the vehicle was away from home. An optional two year and 24,000 mile Buyer Protection Plan was offered at a cost of approximately $150.00. Of this $100.00 was the approximate cost of required routine maintenance during this time period. Hence, the corporate officers argued that the real cost of this program was only $50.00.

In 1973, 25 percent of those individuals visiting AMC dealerships stated that the Buyer Protection Plan was the reason that they came in [9]. In 1974, 60 percent of sales were to buyers new to the company and half of them stated the Buyer Protection Plan was responsible for their purchase of an AMC vehicle [10].

At the end of 1975 AMC was preparing to offer a broader service plan to be put into effect in January of 1976 [2]. Essentially, this Service Protection Plan would guarantee all dealer service for three months or 3,000 miles and the costs of the service would be estimated in advance as a maximum. The impetus behind this addition to the Buyer Protection Plan was given by R. William Nealy, Group Vice President, North American Marketing, as follows [2]:

> "When the BPP was instituted by American Motors Corporation four years ago, it was a total corporate-wide commitment to render the best possible protection for the buyers of American Motors Corporation cars . . . ."
>
> "We are continuing to explore other avenues to protect consumer's interest—ways that are just as meaningful, simple and positive as the Buyer Protection Plan."

AMC also utilized automobile racing as a form of product promotion. In 1970 it entered a pair of Javelins in the Trans-Am Racing circuit. These racing efforts were continued through the mid-70s. It is worthy to note that AMC was serious enough regarding its racing policy to make significant styling changes in the 1974 Matador in order to secure a more streamlined shape which would be beneficial on the racing circuits.

At the end of 1975 AMC indicated that its racing plans would include European type rallys in which Jeep vehicles would be entered. AMC considered these efforts in organized competition to be beneficial in capturing the imagination and enthusiasm of the youthful segments of the car market [4].

AM GENERAL

In 1971, AMC established a wholly owned subsidiary which was called AM General. Its purpose was to compete for sales in the military and mass transit markets as well as others for specialized vehicles. In 1972 it obtained a contract to develop a prototype mass transit bus and in 1973 it obtained its first contract to produce 620 of these buses for the Washington, D. C. Transit Authority.

In the years 1971 through 1973 this division made significant contributions to the profit picture of AMC through the production of $2\frac{1}{2}$ and 5 ton tactical vehicles. In 1972, for example, the contribution of AM General was 22% of the total profit picture. Also in 1972 AM General obtained a $122 million contract for the production of postal vehicles which were essentially a derivative vehicle of the Jeep CJ-5.

In 1973, however, revenues were down significantly for the AM General division. This was expected and was due to a reduction in the production of tactical vehicles for the United States government [9]. In 1973 AM General expanded into other product lines through the introduction of a new power module concept for motorhome manufacturers. Although prototypes existed the unit was not tooled or put into production because of the 1973/74 oil crisis and deterioration in the motorhome industry.

In 1974 AM General showed a loss which was attributed to the start-up costs for the mass transit program. On the bright side for this division, 870 additional bus orders were obtained in 1974 as was a contract for 350 experimental electric delivery vehicles for the U. S. Post Office. In 1975 over 1,000 additional bus orders were obtained along with a $54 million contract for the production of tactical vehicles for Morocco [11].

At the end of 1975 AMC was optimistic regarding its decision to enter the mass transit field. It felt that AM General's bus offered product superiority and could anticipate significant future sales.

JEEP

In 1970 AMC purchased Kaiser-Jeep and began a slow process of integrating Jeep's marketing and production functions where possible with existing AMC lines.

At the end of 1975 there were essentially three different types of Jeeps available. This included the traditional Jeep which was an offshoot of the World War II military vehicle. It was available in two wheel bases, the CJ-5 or the long wheel base CJ-7. Recent product improvements included V-8 engines, automatic transmissions, and full-time four-wheel drive. These vehicles were aimed at the serious off-road enthusiast market.

Also in the Jeep lineup was the Wagoneer series, which was more of a stationwagon on a long wheel base chassis. It still retained the four-wheel drive feature which was considered by Jeep executives as one of its trademarks. In 1975, a shorter wheel base version of this wagon was introduced to compete with the market led by Chevrolet Blazer. In 1972 and 1973, Jeep had addressed itself to this recreational use marketplace with the Commando. Production was suspended, however, because of poor sales.

Jeep also produced a pick-up truck which was available only in a four-wheel drive version. This truck shared sheet metal and components with the Wagoneer.

As shown in Exhibit III, the Jeep division experienced significant sales gains throughout the period under review despite downward market pressures. Much of this was attributed to a strong growth in the four-wheel drive and recreational use markets as well as continued growth in AMC's exports of the Jeep. In 1973 Jeep had 17 percent of the four-wheel drive market and became fully integrated into the operating structure of AMC [21].

PERSONNEL

Up until the second week in November, 1975, the top personnel at AMC had remained virtually the same since the beginning of the period under consideration. The new post of Vice Chairman was created and named to this position was R. William McNealy, Jr., who had formerly been the Group Vice President, North American Marketing. Another significant promotion was that of Gerald C. Meyers, who was named Executive Vice President, having formerly been Group Vice President, Product. In their new capacities, McNealy reports to Roy Chapin, the current Chairman, and Meyers reports to President William Luneburg. Industry observers anticipate that these men will become the next Chairman and President, respectively of AMC. At the end of 1975 Mr. Chapin was 60 years old and Luneburg was 63. McNealy is 48 and Meyers is 47 years of age [27].

FINANCE

The 1972 to 1975 time period produced a wide range in the financial picture for AMC. In 1972 and 1973 the company felt that it had "a strong financial position and flexibility in evaluating opportunities and moving on them" [8]. In 1973 it paid off $25 million in short-time loans on AM General. Finances would have been even more favorable in 1973 had AMC been able to produce more cars. The inability to produce these cars was caused by materials shortages.

Another problem contributing to decreased economic success in 1973 was the nation's economic stabilization policies which restrained price adjustments that AMC felt were necessary to cover increased costs of materials and labor. AMC spent $177 million on new plants and manufacturing facilities during the period 1967 to 1973. In 1974 and 1975 the company suffered financially due to the general economic recession and increased costs for materials and labor. In 1975 major cost-cutting programs were initiated but could not overcome severe financial losses in the first half of 1975 [11].

In 1975 AMC had a $27.5 million loss for the year which was actually a recovery from a loss of $53.4 million in the first six months of the fiscal year ending March 31, 1975. AMC blamed a significant part of its loss for the year on the combined effects of the recession and the United Auto Workers strike in September and October of 1974. Chapin and Luneburg were "cautiously optimistic" about the 1976 fiscal year [3].

Further details on the financial cross section of AMC are shown in Exhibit V.

EXHIBIT V

Domestic vs. Foreign Sales

	1972	*1973*	*1974*	*1975*
Domestic	9,960,000	9,630,000	7,330,000	6,450,000
Imports	1,530,000	1,720,000	1,370,000	1,550,000
% Imports	15.3%	17.8%	18.7%	24%

It should be noted that the bulk of the tooling costs for the Pacer (60 million) was spent in 1973 and 1974.

THE MARKETPLACE THROUGH 1975 AND BEYOND

The years 1972 to 1975 were turbulent and demanding for the automobile industry. In addition to increasingly large inroads being made by foreign manufacturers into the United States automobile market (Exhibit VI) the auto makers were also faced with a variety of sometimes conflicting requirements of the United States government.

Basically the governmental requirements were broken down into two areas, those covering automobile safety and those covering emissions. The emissions laws required that exhaust pollutants be cleaned up in excess of 95 percent of the preregulatory levels. These mandates imposed great strains on the manufacturers to fulfill the requirements and still maintain other product improvements.

There were numerous safety requirements including vehicles capable of sustaining 5 mile per hour collisions front and rear without any damage to

EXHIBIT VIA

AMERICAN MOTORS CORPORATION

Consolidated Statement of Changes in Financial Position
(dollars in thousands)

	1971	*1972*	*1973*	*1974*
Sources of Working Capital				
From Operations:				
Earnings before extraordinary items	$10,177	$ 16,457	$ 44,526	$ 27,546
Depreciation, amortization of plant	22,354	37,477	34,454	39,707
equipment, tools & dies	–	–	–	–
Amortization of good will and debt	13,774	561	561	2,039
discount	–	–	–	–
Deferred income taxes	514	–	–	12,693
From Operations	$46,819	$ 54,495	$ 80,280	$ 81,985
Extraordinary Credits	–	13,700	41,450	–
Proceeds from Insurance of Bonds	–	36,947	–	23,504
and Notes	–	–	–	–
Issurance of Capital Stock-Conver-	–	–	–	–
sion and acquisitions			13,438	17,503
Total Working Capital	$ 46,819	$105,142	$135,168	$122,992
Applications of Working Capital				
Cash dividends paid	$ –	$ –	$ –	$ 5,678
Additions to property, plant and	27,240	30,663	68,120	95,064
equipment	–	–	–	–
Payments and maturities of Notes	–	5,696	–	–
Investments in subsidiaries	–	–	21,492	28,096
Conversion of Long Term Dept.	–	--	8,032	10,672
Other	5,406	10,796	6,958	6,499
Total Application of Working Capital	$ 32,646	$ 47,155	$104,602	$146,009
Net Increase (Decrease) In Working Capital	$ 14,173	$ 57,987	$ 30,566	($ 23,017)

Source: American Motors Annual Reports, 1971-1974

safety related items on the vehicle (this would include lights, etc.). At the same time government pressure was being exerted on the manufacturers to produce cars which would obtain fuel economy 40 per cent greater than that achieved in 1974 [29].

Many manufacturers felt that the threat of subcompact imported cars was one of the most significant factors in automotive marketing at the end of 1975. Detroit executives were pondering the reasons why buyers were switching to the smaller imports over American compacts.

Ford Motor Company initiated a special program in California to determine buyer motives and desires for compact and subcompact cars. In California in

EXHIBIT VIB

AMERICAN MOTORS CORPORATION 1971–1974

(dollars in thousands)

	1971	1972	1973	1974
Assets				
Current Assets				
Cash and marketable securities	$ 18,239	$100,892	$109,430	$ 75,767
U.S. government receivables	45,644	32,090	10,219	–
Notes and accounts receivables	65,877	60,600	83,758	71,479
Refundable federal excise taxes	45,550	–	–	–
Accounts receivable from	10,997	11,964	13,727	33,318
affiliated companies	–	–	–	–
Inventories	172,340	165,990	201,303	298,617
Prepaid expenses	6,345	7,420	8,631	6,701
Deferred income tax charges	–	–	23,178	27,272
Total Current Assets	$323,992	$378,956	$450,246	$513,154
Investments and Other Assets				
Investment in subsidiaries	$ 11,524	$ 13,616	$ 51,765	$ 75,367
Miscellaneous investments	21,458	27,599	11,971	13,911
Deferred charges and other non-	–	–	–	–
current assets	–	1,132	4,615	5,002
Total Investments and Other Assets	$ 32,982	$ 42,347	$ 68,351	$ 94,280
Property, Plant and Equipment				
Land	$ 6,718	$ 6,843	$ 7,199	$ 7,352
Buildings and Improvements	100,304	104,654	114,133	123,802
Machinery and equipment	222,834	221,070	257,698	320,202
Less accumulated depreciation	170,648	180,429	191,438	202,812
Total Property, Plant and Equipment	$159,208	$152,138	$187,592	$245,544
Unamortized and Debt Expense	$ 7,020	–	–	–
Goodwill from Acquisitions	$ 2,210	$ 2,210	$ 6,766	$ 10,337
Totai Assets	$525,412	$575,651	$712,955	$863,315

	1971	1972	1973	1974
Liabilities and Stockholders' Equity				
Current Liabilities:				
Short-term bank borrowings	$ 25,248	$ 25,000	$ –	$ –
Accounts payable	148,396	148,523	183,179	278,341
Accrued expenses	49,350	50,273	68,849	68,240
Taxes on income	5,278	5,509	17,309	8,414
Current portion of long-term debt	5,308	1,252	957	942
Total Current Liabilities	$233,580	$230,557	$271,294	$356,117
Long-Term Liabilities:				
Long-term debt	$ 42,969	$ 67,966	$ 64,316	$ 78,895
Other liabilities	34,846	32,940	33,743	31,205
Deferred income tax credits	–	–	–	14,126
Total Long-Term Liabilities	$ 77,815	$100,906	$ 98,059	$124,226
Stockholders' Equity:				
Capital Stock	$ 42,326	$ 42,328	$ 45,167	$ 48,911
Additional paid-in capital	104,125	104,137	114,736	128,494
Earnings retained for use in	–	–	–	–
business	67,566	97,723	183,699	205,567
Total Stóckholders' Equity	$214,017	$244,188	$343,602	$382,972
Total Liabilities and Stockholders' Equity	$525,412	$575,651	$712,955	$863,315

Source: American Motors Corporation Annual Reports 1971–1974.

1975 the sale of imported cars was approaching 50 per cent of the market [38].

Although AMC had addressed itself to the subcompact market with the Pacer and the Gremlin, consumer acceptance of these vehicles in the marketplace was not as high as desired. The reasons for this, as stated by AMC's management, was that the weight of the vehicle was so high that good gas economy comparable with the imports was unattainable [36]. This was an intrinsic drawback with the inherent design of the vehicle which utilized large expanses of glass.

Consequently, AMC began plans to produce a true subcompact type vehicle. This vehicle would require a new four-cylinder light-weight power plant for propulsion. In an effort to keep tooling costs as low as possible, AMC entered into an agreement with Volkwagenwerk AG to use, and later to build in the United States, the latest V.W. Audi engine [11]. Industry observers anticipated this would give AMC an opportunity to produce a true subcompact in either 1979 or 1980 [1].

This would give AMC a direct competitive entry with the 1976 Chevrolet Chevette which is a true European size subcompact and the announced 1977 Ford subcompact [24].

Industry observers were confident that the 25 per cent share of market which the imports achieved during 1975 would decrease as domestic "minicar" subcompacts, such as the Chevette, became more readily available. At the end of 1975, Chevrolet was planning to begin producing the Chevette at a second plant and was also planning on a subcompact vehicle which would function as a two-seater commuter type automobile.

In addition to the Chevette and proposed 1977 Ford subcompact, Chrysler Corporation was also known to be working on a minicar.

GM was known to be working on plans to reduce the size of all its models in the coming years [37, 41]. In 1977 the full-size cars would be reduced to the approximate size of the current intermediates while in 1978 the intermediates would be similarly reduced.

All of this activity was a direct consequence of changing consumer desires and motives which were aroused during the 1973/74 oil crisis. Consumers exercised their prerogatives by purchasing vehicles which were lighter in weight and produced higher miles per gallon figures than their predecessors. The smaller imports were also considerably less expensive than many of the domestic offerings. Much of the approximate 20 per cent increase in automotive prices from 1973 to 1976 was attributable to government mandated requirements. Consumer backlash was beginning to mount against these requirements to the extent that certain dealer groups initiated petitions that were circulated throughout the United States (see Exhibit VII).

AMC also had plans for a 1976 introduction of a station wagon version of its successful Pacer. This would then parallel the mechanical similarities between the older Gremlin and Hornet station wagon lines. It should be noted that many industry observers had anticipated that the Pacer would be pro-

EXHIBIT VII

PETITION TO

MEMBERS OF THE SENATE AND THE HOUSE OF REPRESENTATIVES
OF THE UNITED STATES OF AMERICA

PLEASE DON'T MAKE ME PAY $1,247.00* FOR FEDERALLY MANDATED AUTO EQUIPMENT I DIDN'T ORDER!

We, as American consumers and civic minded citizens, urge you—our representatives in Congress—to enact a five-year moratorium on the enforcement of previously legislated, but not yet implemented, controls, standards and devices on new motor vehicles. Additionally, we request similar action regarding new or pending regulatory legislation involving motor vehicles.

Federally mandated requirements on new vehicles already have had substantial effects on automotive and related industries, perpetrating a negative impact on the entire American economy.

It is our hope and contention that this moratorium would provide adequate time for research, development and the in-depth testing required to ensure worthwhile improvements in the performance, economy and safety of motor vehicles.

(*) Estimated average of the three major manufacturers' costs for federally required equipment, 1975 through 1980.

NAME	ADDRESS	CITY, STATE, ZIP

Petitions submitted by: ________________
Group/Organization: ________________
Address: ________________
Phone: ________________

Please mail, when completed, to:
CONSUMERS FOR ECONOMIC RECOVERY
230 N. Michigan Ave.-Suite 3000 Chicago, Illinois 60601
312/782-2618

duced as an updated replacement for Gremlin. However, the strong shift in consumer preferences to smaller cars indicated that it would still be profitable to retain the Gremlin in the product line after the introduction of the Pacer.

The prospect of significantly changing market trends also affected Jeep and AM General divisions. At Jeep, the management recognized that its existing lines of Wagoneers and trucks were heavy and out of date for the market conditions of the 1980s. A decision would have to be made soon as to what direction new vehicles must take [36].

Certain industry observers [39, 42] were confident that the truck market would continue to experience the very high growth rate that had been seen during the 1972–1975 time frame. It was even predicted that by 1980, 50 per cent of the vehicles on the road would be trucks.

Some executives at AMC were critical of the decision not to produce a two-wheel drive pick-up truck in the early 1970s [36]. The two-wheel drive personal use truck market had been one of the strong areas of sales growth. The Jeep division had to decide whether or not to change its marketing philosophy from only producing four-wheel vehicles to producing two-wheel vehicles also.

The prospect of mass transit posed a bright picture for the AM General division which at the end of 1975 produced its "second generation of mass transit buses." Although this was certainly beneficial to the AM General division, many industry observers still felt that the effect on automobiles sales of mass transit would not be significant [29].

AMC closed its 1975 fiscal year with an optimistic projection for 1976. It anticipated producing 400,000 passenger cars and 80,000 Jeeps. As stated by Chairman Roy Chapin, "The important thing is that American Motors has weathered one of the most critical periods in automotive history, and we are emerging from it in a stronger competitive position than before it occured.

"We're not underestimating the future but we're ready for it. Our basic directions are set and we believe they are sound."

HENRY FORD ON AUTOS
A LOOK DOWN THE ROAD

Interview With the Chairman, Ford Motor Company

Q Is the time coming when people will drive their cars until they're ready for the scrap heap?

A Anything is possible, but I doubt it. There are certain buyers who buy new cars just because they are new cars. If they can afford it, they still will. They're going to keep their cars longer, but not that long.

There's another factor at work—longer periods for repaying loans. If a buyer goes to a finance company, he will probably spread out his car repayments now to 42 or 48 months, instead of 36. That frequently means he's going to keep his car another year while paying off his debt.

Q The emphasis this year seems to be on smaller cars and on fuel economy. Is that just a passing phase?

A No—all our products are going to get lighter and smaller and more fuel-efficient. For good and sufficient reason, the consumer wants to have a lighter, smaller car to drive—one with better fuel economy. That is the wave of the future.

Q What about cars for big families or for people who have to drive half a dozen kids or more to a Little League game? Will the auto industry meet their needs?

A When large cars get smaller, they're still going to be relatively large six-passenger cars. They're going to be smaller on the outside, with less overhang front and rear, less width and bulging out on the sides. They're going to be more slab-sided. Standard-sized cars are going to be 600 to 900 pounds lighter and 2 feet shorter.

There will be six-passenger cars—no question about that—but they won't be as big as what's on the road today. I don't know whether they will come in two-door and four-door models as well as station wagons, or just four-door models and wagons. But the lines will be simplified.

Q Will horsepower be cut back, too?

A Yes. The engine sizes are going to come down because of the lighter weight of the car. Axle weights, the whole mechanical side is going to come down as well. Therefore you're going to get more fuel economy with less horsepower.

Q Will the trend to small cars affect big luxury autos?

A Yes. Some of the big luxury cars, as we know them today, are not going to be in existence in four or five years. We're seeing news that the Imperial is not even going to be sold this model year. Cadillac has already brought out the Seville as a hedge against the future.

The big cars are going to go the way of all flesh—lighter and smaller.

Q How big a jump did Chevrolet get on the rest of the field in coming out with a new small auto—the Chevette?

A They got a big jump. They obviously made the decision to bring out the Chevette during the time of the Arab oil embargo in late 1973. They needed all this time to order the machine tools, prepare the plans to build a special engine, lay out the assembly plants.

Q Were they doing all this in secret?

A Well, rumors get around. The minute you order an engine line, the engine-line manufacturer starts to talk. We knew they were going to make a four-cylinder engine, but we didn't know exactly what kind of car it was going to turn out to be. What helped them get a jump was that they have a similar car in other countries, so that the car was already basically engineered.

Q How well do you think the Chevette will sell?

A I assume it's going to be accepted very well. It's in a size range that people seem to want to buy.

To me, it's a far more acceptable car than many of the imports. It's competitive in price. It's a more-stable car than many of the small imports. I think you're going to feel more comfortable in that car than in some imports. Therefore, I think it would have great appeal.

Q When will Ford come out with a direct competitor of its own to the Chevette?

A I'm not sure I would use the word "direct," but we have a car which we're bringing out in Europe in the fall of 1976. We're planning to import that car into the United States sometime in 1977.

Q Do you foresee new types of power plants in automobiles in the future—some alternative to the standard gasoline engine?

A A new power plant can't come until the industry knows what the Government's requirements on emission controls are going to be some years down the road. We can't afford to make any major change in power plant now because we don't know what emission standards we will have to meet in the near future. Beyond that, if the Government would tell us we have a certain number of years of stability—no change in emission requirements—then we can make some choices.

Most of the new power plants under consideration are going to take an awful lot of money to develop, though. We have rights, for example, to the Stirling engine in this country, and we've been told that it will cost a billion dollars to develop—and that doesn't include the cost of putting it in production.

Q Why does it take an auto maker so long to come out with a small car?

A Because of the gestation period for making a car. If you start from the ground up—with engineering, new machine tools and other preparations to make long in advance—it's going to take three years minimum, and probably more.

Q It's been 15 years or more since the Volkswagen invasion. Some people say U.S. auto makers should have moved faster on small cars—

A Well, we thought the Pinto and Vega were the right answers. Those cars have been on the road a number of years. We started out as early as 1959 with a Ford Falcon, and General Motors had the Corvair. That's when we started to think small and get the size down.

But we have a terrible habit in the automobile industry: We start out with a small car, and every time we change its styling, it gets bigger and heavier. I hope we've learned a lesson now, because all the facts point in the other direction. If we haven't learned, we're going to go broke.

Launching a new car, however, is difficult. You've got to decide what the public is going to want 2, 3, 4 years ahead of time. You've got to decide the basic size of the vehicle, and then whether to use facilities you have in place to build them or go for something all new. In the case of Chevette, Chevrolet went for a tremendous investment, several hundred million dollars.

You've got to have a lot of capital available to undertake such a project. If you've got a capital problem and a profit problem, you're going to be careful about what you do. So maybe we didn't move quickly enough.

Q Do you think the American public will go for a car even smaller than the Chevette?

A In my own mind, I am not really sure if the public will buy a car that small in large quantities. The big question today is: Is Chevette small enough, or is there a market for a car below Chevette in size?

Look at the Volkswagen Beetle. It's smaller than Chevette, but it's on the way out. So we'll have to find out whether Americans, across the board, are ready to go to that smaller-size car.

Q Why do imports, over all, take so big a share of the American market? Is owning an import a status symbol?

A I think it's a matter of a preconceived image of size, price, fuel economy, maintenance costs. Imports do have a certain image, yet, but I think the status-symbol aspect is less than it used to be.

We think we can build cars just as fuel-efficient as foreign manufacturers. In fact, we are in most areas except for the very small cars. We think our quality is as good as theirs—a lot better than some of the imports.

Some of the advantages of imports are purely image and not fact. But that doesn't make any difference. If it's image in the marketplace, that's what people go and buy, regardless of the facts.

Q Looking beyond the 1976 models, do you think Detroit will move away from extensive year-to-year model changes?

A We won't have model changes for change's sake. If we have to modify a car to meet some new Government requirement, we might make other changes at the same time. You get two changes for the price of one, so to speak. Why not make the car look different?

Q How many different models does the Ford Motor Company have today?

A We have 18 car lines with many different models.

Q Does the American public demand so many models from all the manufacturers?

A Take a look at other industries—apparel, television, refrigerators. They all do the same things we do. Television manufacturers put out all kinds of sizes and shapes of television sets.

The consumer is looking for certain things, and if the consumer is willing to buy, we should make it for the consumer. This economy of ours has grown for many different reasons, but maybe it has grown in part because the producer has decided to offer many lines.

Q Is that going to come to an end?

A Yes, partially. Cost is one reason. You're going to see a big change in our industry in the next five years. You're going to see a lot of car-line names dropped, and far fewer series within car lines.

You're going to get more interchangeability of parts throughout cars, again for cost reasons.

Q Will all this mean that we won't be seeing those $200 or $300 raises in car prices year after year?

A I can't answer that. But I would assume that if labor costs keep going up, if material costs keep going up, if all our other costs keep going up, we're going to have to charge more per car.

Now, we don't want to charge more, but our returns at the moment—whether measured on assets or sales or invested capital—are minimal. And with the capital requirements and the problems we face because of Government-mandated equipment we must put on cars, we have a problem on prices.

Q What kind of engine is the Stirling?

A An external-combustion engine—which has lots of problems. It has a great future, but it needs a lot of work.

We're also forging ahead on turbines as fast as we can with the money we have available. But when you talk about spending a billion dollars for something that won't be ready to put in a car until 1985 at the earliest, well, you think twice before you invest that kind of money.

Q Is it fuel economy that's spurring this research?

A Yes, these engines have fuel economy combined with low emissions potential. Some use different kinds of fuels, less-expensive ones than gasoline.

Q Do you think it is important to find a replacement for gasoline? Is the gasoline crisis a permanent one?

A There's only so much oil in the ground. The supply is not inexhaustible, and if we had anything like the growth rates in oil consumption that we were expecting a few years ago, we would be facing a severe problem 30 to 50 years from now.

But with slower economic growth on a worldwide basis and more efficient fuel use in the United States, the time frame may be stretched. Therefore, the pressure to go to a completely new engine will be lessened. One of our projects, for example, is a refinement of the internal-combustion engine. We're working with Japanese Honda on something quite similar to their CVCC engine. It runs on gasoline.

Q Do you expect gas prices to rise much in the future?

A Personally, I don't think it's going to be a major increase. At least, it will be minimal in the next two to three years. Long term, we think the price of gas will go up, and our company is basing its plans on that assumption.

Q What would happen to the price of gasoline if domestic oil prices were fully decontrolled all at once?

A We don't really think that would shoot prices up substantially—maybe a nickel a gallon, or less if the $2-a-barrel duty on imported oil comes off at the same time.

Q You've mentioned your concern about Government auto standards a number of times. Is it Washington or Detroit that is going to dictate how cars are to be designed?

A Washington certainly dictates a good part of what the design is going to be. If they dictate emission standards, then they dictate an awful lot of things about the car. And now we're faced with another problem: Congress is talking about dictating fuel economy, requiring cars to give an average 20 or 21 miles a gallon by 1980, and 28 by 1985.

The automobile is being hit from both sides. If you have controls to lower emissions, those controls mean less fuel economy. So we're being put in a difficult situation—not insoluble but very difficult.

The President has asked us—and we have agreed—to improve gasoline mileage by 40 percent from 1974 to 1980 models. That's voluntary. But I don't think we can make the targets that Congress is talking about—unless we get a fixed, reasonable emissions target in the near future. And the sanctions are just stupendous if we miss—as high as 300 million dollars after taxes under certain conditions.

I'd like to repeat that what we need is a pause for a period of time on Government action so that we can rationalize what we are doing, then do work for the future that will make sense in the long run, but from a fuel-economy and from an emissions-control standpoint.

Q Will the auto industry be asking labor to improve its productivity to keep some control on costs?

A Productivity is a responsibility of management, as I see it. We can't blame lower productivity on the union or the workers. We've got to blame it on ourselves in the industry and our company.

We're highly automated, and to increase productivity, we need additional capital. At the moment, much of our capital is going into other things: 20 per cent in 1976 will be to meet Government laws on emission controls, clean air, clean water, job safety.

If we could get sales back up to 1973 levels—11.8 million for the model year for the industry as a whole—that would mean a dramatic improvement in productivity. We're only utilizing 70 per cent of our capacity now.

Q Turning to another area, Mr. Ford, are you concerned by the prospect of foreign manufacturers coming into the U.S. to build their cars here?

A I don't think so. Volvo is building a plant here, and Volkswagen is considering a move, too. They might lower their costs and increase their profits that way, but I don't think it necessarily means their volume would be any higher. As a matter of fact, it may be a good thing for the country because it would provide more employment.

What bothers me is the fact American companies don't get a fair shake overseas as exporters. Practically all foreign countries have so many import regulations and taxes and duties that it makes it impossible for a U.S. manufacturer to export in any volume except to the Caribbean.

REFERENCES

[1] "AMC Minicar." *Motor Trend,* December, 1975, p. 12.

[2] "AMC Prepares to Offer Broader Service Plan." *Automotive News,* October 27, 1975.

[3] "AMC Suffers $27.5 Million Loss for Year." *Los Angeles Times,* November 13, 1975, Part III, p. 12.

[4] "AMC Switches Racing Plans." *Automotive News,* November 10, 1975, p. 22.

[5] "American Flits Ahead." *Time,* November 24, 1971, pp. 78–80.

[6] *American Motors Corporation Annual Meeting and First Quarterly Report to Stockholders, February, 1975.*

[7] *American Motors Corporation Annual Report,* 1971.

[8] *American Motors Corporation Annual Report,* 1972.

[9] *American Motors Corporation Annual Report,* 1973.

[10] *American Motors Corporation Annual Report,* 1974.

[11] *American Motors Corporation Nine Months Report to Stockholders,* August 1975.

[12] *American Motors Corporation Six Months Report to Stockholders,* May 1975.

[13] "American Motors' Crucial Year." *Business Week,* October 3, 1970, p. 17.

[14] "American Motors' Road Looks Bumpier." *Business Week,* April 24, 1971, p. 23.

[15] "Autos: Shifting Down for the '70s." *Time,* February 23, 1970, pp. 80–81.

[16] "Automakers Want More Price Relief." *Business Week,* March 16, 1974, p. 28.

[17] *Automotive News 1974 Almanac Issue,* April 24, 1974.

[18] *Automotive News 50th Anniversary—Prologue to the Future,* August 27, 1975.

[19] "Chapin of American Motors." *Forbes,* May 15, 1974, p. 87.

[20] "Debuts for Subcompacts." *Time,* September 21, 1970, p. 92.

[21] "Detroit De-emphasizes the Styling Game." *Business Week,* April 3, 1971, p. 16.

[22] "Detroit's Gamble to Get Rolling Again." *Time,* February 10, 1975, pp. 68–73.

[23] "Getting the Lead Out." *Time,* February 23, 1970, pp. 81–92.

[24] "Henry Ford on Autos—A Look Down the Road." *U.S. New & World Report,* October 20, 1975, pp. 25–28.
[25] "Imports Race for the Middle Market." *Business Week,* April 3, 1971, p. 15.
[26] "Lifting the Lid on Autos." *Time,* December 24, 1973, p. 76.
[27] "McNealy, Meyers Rise Close to Top at AMC." *Automotive News,* November 17, 1975, p. 1.
[28] "Pacer May Signal New Wave of Cars." *Autoweek,* October 25, 1975, p. 4.
[29] "Rivals Thrive During the GM Strike." *Business Week,* October 3, 1970, p. 17.
[30] "Safety Upstages Styling." *Time,* August 23, 1971, pp. 50–51.
[31] "Small-Car Market Share Up Again." *Automotive News,* October 27, 1975, p. 3.
[32] "The Hard Sell on MPG." *Time,* April 1, 1974, p. 74.
[33] "The New Pacesetter." *Time,* March 25, 1974, p. 82.
[34] "The Painful Change to Thinking Small." *Time,* December 31, 1973, pp. 18–25.
[35] "Why Detroit Failed to Sway the EPA." *Business Week,* May 20, 1972, pp. 29–30.

Interviews

[36] Fred Bennie, Advertising Manager, Jeep Division, American Motors Corporation.
[37] Bob Cook, General Manager, Oldsmobile Division, General Motors Corporation.
[38] Edsel Ford, Marketing Department, Ford Motor Company (son of Henry Ford II).
[39] Steven Gifford, Light Truck Product Planner, Ford Motors Corporation.
[40] Frank Hedge, Vice President, Public Relations, American Motors Corporation.
[41] Bob Lund, General Manager, Chevrolet Division, General Motors Corporation.
[42] J. R. Williams, Administrator Truck Merchandising, Chevrolet Division, General Motors Corporation.
(These meetings were held during the fall quarter of 1976 with discussions either related to or specifically concerning the topic of this case study.)

CASE 11

A. H. Robins Co.*

Victor F. Zonana

At noon today, A. H. Robins Co. will hold a luncheon for Petersburg city officials at the local Ramada Inn to announce plans for a $6 million chemical plant and service facility here.

As business news goes, the announcement wouldn't normally rate much attention. A. H. Robins, a big pharmaceutical concern headquartered in Richmond about 30 miles north of Petersburg, has made far larger investments. Other companies across the nation in the next few days doubtless will unveil bigger plans.

But the story of how A. H. Robins came to make its investment here is nonetheless worth telling. It's a tale of more than a year of intensive planning, of intracompany warfare and of unexpected economic and business developments—as well as of how real people make real decisions in the real world "that you'd never learn about at Harvard Business School," as one Robins insider puts it. Among other things, Robins started out planning to build or buy a plant of its own; it wound up, almost at the last minute, in a joint venture with a big West German pharmaceutical concern, Boehringer Ingelheim Associated Cos.

IMPORTANT DECISIONS

The story is also important for what it tells of the problems that businessmen face these days in trying to decide whether to commit funds to capital projects, whatever their size. The level of capital spending this year and next is likely to be a key factor in determining whether and how fast the American economy recovers from its worst recession in decades. Last month, the Commerce Department projected that 1975 capital spending would plummet 11.5% below last year's, and most economists are cautious about next year's outlook.

The story of the A. H. Robins project actually begins in 1958, when company chemists first synthesized a white powdery chemical called methocarbomal. A muscle relaxant, methocarbomal was patented and sold in pill form under the name Robaxyn after receiving government clearance. Contracts

* Reprinted with permission from *The Wall Street Journal,* October 22, 1975.

were given to several chemical makers to supply Robins with raw methocarbomal, since the company only made finished pharmaceuticals.

Robaxyn was a big success. By 1967, Robins believed it was buying enough methocarbomal to consider making the chemical for itself. The company was also purchasing large volumes of glyceryl guaiacolate (GG) for its Robitussin cough medicine, and since methocarbomal was a derivative of GG, manufacture of the two petrochemicals seemed desirable, according to William L. Zimmer III, Robins' 63-year-old president.

DELAYED BY FDA STUDY

But the idea hit a snag and was shelved in 1970 when the Food and Drug Administration's Drug Efficacy Study, and industry-wide review of pharmaceuticals, gave methocarbomal a "questionable" rating. Although the FDA eventually cleared the chemical in 1974, the review kept methocarbomal, along with Mr. Zimmer's idea of manufacturing it and GG, under a cloud for four years.

The idea was revived by the 1973–74 oil crisis and the resulting shortages of petroleum-based chemicals. "Skyrocketing chemical prices were cutting into our profit margins," Mr. Zimmer says, noting that the price of methocarbomal shot up more than 40% in 1974 alone. Even worse, at times methocarbomal and GG were unavailable at any price; the costly production closedowns that ensued "were cutting into the lifeblood of our business," Mr. Zimmer says. He says he decided in April 1974 that Robins "would no longer be a pawn of the market."

On May 16, 1974, Robert G. Watts, senior vice president, sent a memo to the heads of seven corporate divisions. "Mr. Zimmer has requested that immediate attention be given to the feasibility of the manufacture of selected chemicals," the memo stated. It announced creation of a secret, high-level task force to "be responsible for providing recommendations for compounds to be considered, acquisition possibilities, site selection and facilities, as well as financial justification for same."

TWO TEAMS SET UP

The task force met June 1, 1974, and was quickly broken down into two subgroups, one to study the acquisition of a chemical plant and the other to look into building one from scratch.

The "build" unit, headed by Mr. Watts, a tough 42-year-old ex-Navy officer, sought out six process engineering firms and was approached by dozens more. "These engineers have a grapevine that's incredible," Mr. Watts says. "You talk to one and they all come along." In early October the group settled on Lockwood-Greene Engineering Co., Atlanta.

In March 1975, Lockwood-Greene delivered to Robins an inch-thick, $16,000 volume that detailed design criteria, the chemical-making process, an equipment list, environmental impact statement, project schedule, drawings and, most important, a preliminary cost estimate. The engineering firm calculated that a plant making 200,000 pounds of GG and 500,000 pounds of methocarbomal annually, Robins' projected 1978 needs, would cost $6 million, plus 30% or minus 20%.

Robins' officers calculated that the same amounts of chemicals would cost $6,050,000 if purchased on the open market, but that it could be manufactured for only $3.5 million. Based on a $6.2 million capital outlay ($6 million for the plan and $200,000 for the land), the pretax return on investment (compared with continued outside purchases) would exceed 40%, and the investment would pay for itself in less than three years.

Meanwhile, consultants for the "buy" team identified over 100 existing plants that seemed to meet Robins' needs. Of these, about 20 were actually contacted by the company and three strong candidates ultimately emerged. One was Hexagon Laboratories Inc., New York, which later was acquired by the West German concern that eventually became Robins' partner in the joint venture in Petersburg.

Hexagon was up for sale and it was already a big supplier of methocarbomal to Robins. Little plant modification would have been necessary. "But Hexagon was in the Bronx and there was no room for possible expansion," Ernest L. Bender Jr., senior vice president of Robins, says. Also, a Robins spokesman notes, "Hexagon's plant was unionized, and we've always tried to steer clear of unions." The buy group finally settled on a plant in Sheboygan, Wis.

The "build" and "buy" units developed a keen rivalry, with personal reputations and egos becoming involved in the outcome. "The acquisitions people were desperate for something big," Mr. Watts asserts. "They really wanted another feather in their cap." One member of the acquisition team retorts that Mr. Watts wanted to build a plant "so that he could have another picture hanging on his wall." (Mr. Watts' office wall bears architectural renderings of plants he has been responsible for in Puerto Rico and Richmond.)

Mr. Zimmer minimizes the effect of the rivalry; he says he had hoped for just such "creative tension." But in the meantime, more serious questions were being raised—including doubts about whether Robins should get into the chemical business at all.

A CASE OF COLD FEET

Carl Lunsford, vice president in charge of chemical research—and one of the discoverers of methocarbomal in 1958—had begun to develop cold feet about the project. He suggested that the proposed plant be scaled down by about half.

"You just don't go out and build a chemical plant," he recalls saying. "It takes expertise and technical know-how. Since this was our first move into a new area, I thought it would be well to leave room for a third party to supply us. There's always the possibility for a plant going down because of fire or some other catastrophe."

Mr. Lunsford's hesitation came on the heels of a study commissioned by Robins from Chase Manhattan Bank. The Chase analysts argued that Robins shouldn't go through with the project because of the cyclical nature of the chemical business. By prudent hedging operations—buying supplies when prices were low—Robins could assure itself of the necessary raw materials, they said.

Mr. Zimmer, still vividly remembering the 1973 oil embargo, rejected the Chase argument out of hand. "Any savings we'd obtain would quickly be lost if supplies were interrupted," he says. Of Mr. Lunsford's objections, Mr. Watts says dryly: "I think our suppliers convinced him."

Ironically, however, it was Mr. Lunsford's vision of the course Robins should take that came closest to what actually happened—although not necessarily for the reasons he cited.

ECONOMIC ILLS NOTED

Planning for the project was coming to a head in the midst of a precipitous decline in the economy. "Some of our meetings were pretty strained," one insider recalls. "Inflation was rushing along and the recession just kept getting worse. Some of us felt we were just spinning wheels, that the state of the economy—the sheer uncertainty of it all—would preclude a big commitment of capital."

G. E. R. Stiles, vice president and treasurer, says those who were worried about the recession were overruled because a company can't look at short-term fluctuations in determining capital spending policies. "This is long-term planning," he says. A recession, he adds, "is a one-to-three-year thing. When you're talking about a new plant, you're talking 10 to 20 years." Besides, Robins was able to minimize the recession's impact because a strong balance sheet allowed the company to finance the project internally rather than compete for funds on the capital markets.

By last March, the management team had studied its "build" and "buy" options for about 10 months, and a showdown was slated. The proponents of purchasing the Sheboygan plant made a persuasive presentation. The next day, the "build" forces counterattacked with an equally persuasive proposal, aided by an artist's sketch, for a custom-built facility in Virginia. The costs were about equal.

DECISION: TO BUILD

The decision, by Mr. Zimmer in consultation with Chairman E. Claiborne Robins Sr., went in favor of the "build" team. "We really wanted that damned plant in Virginia," Mr. Zimmer says. "That way we can run down and touch it just to make sure it's there every one in a while." Virginia industrial development officials were asked to help choose the site; they assigned the project the code name "Operation Dogwood" and soon narrowed the search to nine possible locations.

But no sooner had the decision seemingly been made between "buy" and "build" than a third possibility arose. Hexagon Laboratories, the Bronx concern considered as a potential purchase possibility, had been acquired in February for $4 million by Boehringer Ingelheim, a big pharmaceutical and chemical concern based in Ingelheim, West Germany. Subsequently, Hexagon officials had gotten wind of Robins' plans for a captive soure of methocarbomal and GG, and two Hexagon representatives were dispatched to Richmond in April in an effort to keep the Robins' business.

Hexagon offered to build a plant in Virginia and negotiate a long-term sales agreement with Robins. Robins, which had gone this far down the road, demurred. Hexagon offered Robins an equity interest in the plant as a sweetener. Mr. Zimmer struck: "I said 50% or nothing at all. Take it or leave it."

"I almost dropped my teeth," recalls Mr. Lunsford, who was at the meeting and saw a joint venture with an experienced chemical concern as the solution to his fears about building a chemical plant. Mr. Lunsford worried that Mr. Zimmer's insistence on a half interest might be unacceptable to Boehringer.

But Boehringer eventually agreed to the transaction. Most of the plant's output would be sold to Robins, profits would be divided equally, and Robins would have an option to buy Hexagon's share after an unspecified period of time. The package neatly disposed of nearly all the objections that various Robins factions had about the build or buy options. Among other things, for example, it will allow Robins to hold capital spending next year to about $7 million, the same as this year, because Robins' share of the project will result in an outlay of only about $1.5 million to $2 million next year, with the remainder in 1977. The plant is slated to open in early 1978.

"We'd have probably gone ahead alone and built a new plant," Mr. Zimmer says, "but the joint venture sure makes us feel more confident about this project."

QUESTIONS

1. Do you think that Mr. Zimmer's approach to decision making in this case was rational? Was it appropriate to the situation?
2. What were the main factors that Robins Co. had to take into consideration in making the "right" decision?
3. What nonquantitative considerations seemed to be governing throughout the decision-making process?

CASE 12

Tasty Foods, Inc.

Tasty Foods, Inc., offers consumers an impressive array of food products including cookies and crackers, jellies and jams, canned vegetables and soups, candy, packaged cheeses, pies, condensed milk, etc. During the 1960s the company diversified into a variety of consumer products which included glues, masking tapes, paints, and stationery supplies.

The Company is now reassessing its strategies. In the following matrix the president has set forth basic assumptions held in the past and the major strategies of the company which were implied and adopted by the "givens." Now, the president and his staff have determined that the old premises no longer are suitable and that new "givens" must be considered. What strategic implications would you suggest to the president as possibly appropriate in light of the new premises?

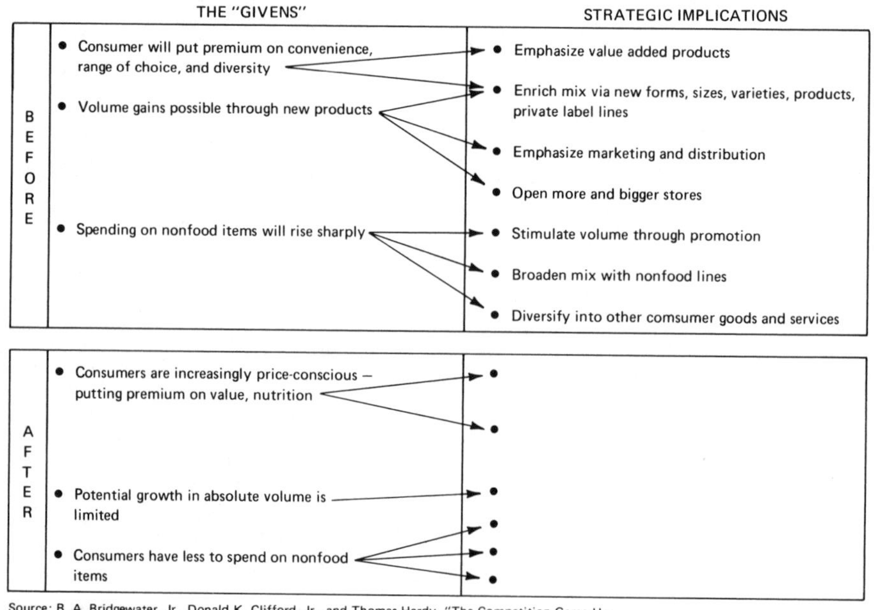

Source: B. A. Bridgewater, Jr., Donald K. Clifford, Jr., and Thomas Hardy. "The Competition Game Has Changed," *Business Horizons*, October 1975, p.11.

CASE 13

White Motor Corporation*

William Schlender and
Eleanor Brantley Schwartz

REDESIGN

When Semon "Bunkie" Knudsen [1] flew to Cleveland from Detroit in May, 1971, to take the chief executive position at White Motor, the company needed $290 million in bank loans just to stay in business. After three years of declining earnings, White was $21 million into the red. Just in the middle of their expansion in farm equipment, the bottom fell out of that market and left White dealers with over $130 million of unsold farm machinery. Equipment installation had been halted on a $45 million engine plant in Canton, Ohio. White trucks were steadily losing market share. All but five of White's 22 top executives had left. With no money, no organization, and no staff, Knudsen assumed the chief executive spot with little margin for error but with plenty of opportunities for error. He began a systematic program to put White Motor back into a profitable direction. Twelve strategic problem areas were pinpointed: finances, organization, liquidity, new models, marketing, balance sheet, sales, inventory, financial, forecast, the Italian plant, and the Canton plant.

The entire business world watched: Can Knudsen do it? Can he turn White Motor back into a going company?

BACKGROUND (1900–1971)

The White Motor Company began in 1900 as a producer of horseless carriages. The first White steamer, the Stanhope, was produced that year and a later version was Teddy Roosevelt's official White House car. By 1906 White's auto sales were twice those of the nearest competitor. White left the passenger car business in 1918 to specialize in the truck business and remained a relatively small manufacturer of heavy-duty trucks until the 1950s.

* Distributed by the Intercollegiate Case Clearing House, Soldiers Field, Boston, Mass. 02163. All rights reserved to the contributors. Printed in the U.S.A. Reprinted by permission.

[1] See Appendix A for a brief background of Knudsen.

Today White is engaged principally in the manufacture and sale of three groups of related products:

1. Heavy-duty trucks, consisting of trucks manufactured by White and sold under the names "White," "Autocar," and "White Western Star," and trucks purchased by White and sold under the name "White-Freightliner."
2. Industrial and construction equipment, including diesel, gasoline, and natural gas engines for stationary, marine, and locomotive applications, compressors, and "Euclid" off-highway dump trucks.
3. Farm equipment, including tractors, combines, and planting and tillage equipment, sold in North America under the names "White," "Oliver," "Minneapolis-Moline," and "Cockshutt."

The truck group comprises about 65 per cent of White Motor's total sales; the construction and industrial equipment group accounts for almost 18 per cent of total sales; and the farm equipment group accounts for about 17 per cent.

HOW WHITE MOTOR GREW

White management's attitude about being a small company changed in the fifties. Along with the rest of the trucking industry, White Motor was hit hard by the 1949 downturn in the economy. White stock slipped to the $13–14 level, compared with a book value of $56 per share. This made White vulnerable to corporate raiders. Being what *Forbes* called a "loaded laggard,"[2] White feared being swallowed by a big company. White decided that the best way to avoid this was to swallow first: grab other loaded laggards and become big on its own.

ACQUISITIONS PROGRAM

White grew phenomenally through its acquisitions. The major role in White's expansion was played by Robert F. Black, Chairman and Chief Executive Officer, and John N. Bauman, President of White from 1956 to 1969 and Chairman of the Board for one year, before retiring in 1970.

(1) Truck Industry

With the decision to grow through an aggressive acquisition program,[3] the logical area for expansion was the truck building industry. Moreover, White

[2] A company whose stock price has lagged behind the value of its assets—making it a prime target for bargain hunting conglomerates.

[3] See Appendix B for the five guidelines that constituted White's acquisition philosophy.

Motor foresaw that the heavy-duty truck market, then only 2 per cent of total 1950 unit sales, would quadruple in the fifties and sixties.

Sterling Motor Company, a heavy-duty truck operation, was purchased in 1951 only to be liquidated two years later. Sterling's potential in the heavy-duty construction and West Coast Markets was difficult to attain, both because of an outmoded product and an internal management resistant to change. In addition, a vastly superior competitor, Autocar Company,[4] became available to White Motor. Thus, Autocar (with five times Sterling's sales volume, a better product, and better distribution) was acquired by White and Sterling was liquidated.

Autocar had two major problems: uneconomic production and a top-heavy distribution organization. The uneconomic problem was solved by selling the antiquated multistory plant at Ardmore, Pennsylvania, and building a compact, efficient one-story plant on property Autocar already owned in Exton, Pennsylvania. The answer to the distribution problem was to integrate Autocar sales and service functions into existing White branches and dealers. Autocar began to show a good profit as a manufacturing operation exclusively.

In 1959, the assets of Reo Motor, Inc., a truck manufacturing firm, was acquired. Reo's benefits included a gasoline engine, one hundred additional dealers, and a large government contract. In 1958, White had acquired the assets of Diamond T Motor Car Company. The company was small, but the Diamond T heavy-duty truck was among the most respected in the industry. These two marginal truck divisions were merged into one strong truck operation, the Diamond Reo Division, in 1967.

White Motor's last truck acquisition, an effort to broaden its distribution base, was not as successful a venture as the previous acquisitions. Montpelier Manufacturing Company produced a $3,000 multistop delivery truck, which White dealers, accustomed to the $15,000 jobs, were not particularly delighted to sell. Despite several years of hard work to put Montpelier at a break-even point, White management "walked away without looking back" when the plant burned in 1965.

(2) Farm Equipment Industry

With the urge for continued growth, White began to look to an unfamiliar segment of industry for expansion and purchased the farm machinery assets of the Oliver Corporation. Then, rather than develop a grain harvesting combine for Oliver, White bought Cockshutt Farm Equipment, Limited, of Canada, a company already producing a good combine. In January, 1963, White acquired Motec Industries, Inc., and its Minneapolis-Moline farm equipment business, which became a member of the White farm group. Minneapolis-Moline had operated in the red during three of its last five years.

[4] A long-time leader in the extra heavy-duty truck field and solidly positioned with over-the-road, construction, and West Coast diesel models.

White raised many eyebrows when it ventured into the then severely depressed farm equipment industry. Even the industry giants were suffering a profit squeeze because of the competition. Marginal producers such as Oliver, Cockshutt, and Minneapolis-Moline were barely hanging on. The White management, however, saw the farm market as cyclical and about ready for an upturn. Their research indicated that the farm machinery market had a decidedly favorable shortage of farm labor, the national and worldwide population explosion, and the huge replacement market. Furthermore, White management felt that the industry's distribution, engineering, and manufacturing techniques were akin to those of the heavy-duty truck business as well as the fact that the industry was undergoing a competitive shakedown making a number of small established manufacturers susceptible to acquisition on advantageous terms. The assets of these small, marginal companies were purchased at bargain prices with the idea of combining them into a more efficient larger operation.

(3) Industrial Power Equipment Industry

White saw the engine as another logical area of company diversification, and in 1955 bought a division of National Supply Company, an oil-field supplier. Because the oil market was diminishing, White redesigned the engine to become a major supplier of engines for government missile and rocket programs. Also, a line of compressors was developed with the engines for the gas and petrochemical industries, two prime engine markets.

With the advent of the total-energy concept in the early sixties, White began supplying engines for total-energy installations. In 1966, White acquired Robert E. Hattis Engineers, Inc., of Chicago, moving from an engine supplier in this industry to that of a "source of complete total energy systems"—from feasibility study through design and construction to actual plant operations.

At the end of 1966, White purchased the Hercules Engine Division of Hupp Corporation. Hercules Engine, though it had a substantial backlog of military contracts, was known mostly as a marginal supplier of some commercial engines to original equipment manufacturers. Though White found this market and the Hercules operation satisfactorily profitable, another purpose of White's purchase was to acquire a competent staff and experienced work-force for a new engine plant for production of a family of farm-tractor and truck engines.

Another venture in June, 1968, the purchase of the Euclid Division of General Motors Corporation, significantly broadened White Motor's product line in the highly specialized off-highway trucking field. With this purchase, White's industrial group included four divisions: Hercules (producer of engines up to 200 h.p.), Euclid (a world leader in off-highway hauler products —rear dumps and bottom dumps for quarrying, mining and construction—

for 40 years), Alco [5] (producer of diesel engines 800–4500 h.p.), and White Superior (maker of engines and compressors in the 400–2400 h.p. range—in diesel and in natural gas fuels).

The Trucking Industry Problems

The truck manufacturing company acquisitions of the fifties were intended to increase White's market share in the business it knew best—heavy-duty trucks. They did increase its market share of heavy-duty trucks. When, however, White moved manufacturing of the Diamond T from Chicago and produced both Diamond T and Reo trucks in the Lansing, Michigan plant in an effort to maximize efficiency, they began to be assembled the same way. Nearly identical, the two trucks began to compete with each other rather than with other manufacturers, which resulted in poor sales for both divisions during the booming truck market of 1959 to 1966. To correct this, the two divisions were combined into one operation with one nameplate—Diamond-Reo.

Also, part of an internal growth plan was to increase the truck market share by cutting into the competitor's share of the market,[6] put its sights on two factions of the mass-produced market: the light-heavy market [7] and the heavy-duty truck fleet market.[8]

White's light-heavy entry was aimed at the farm delivery market and dubbed "The Trend." It was marketed at all their various dealerships as the White Trend, the Reo Trend, the Diamond Trend, the Oliver Trend, and the Minneapolis-Moline Trend. White sold only 1500 of the 5000 Trends it produced (under all nameplates). Analysis subsequently attributed The Trend's low sales to three reasons:

1. White again competed against itself by producing one truck with several labels.
2. Dealers were moved into the hotly competitive light-truck class where the mass producers had a distinct advantage.
3. The Trend received a cool response from its dealers. The competition made it relatively unprofitable to sell.

The fleet market was dominated by the mass producers, particularly Ford. In catering to this market, White had to economize and standardize production to meet the stiffer competition. The custom work took on a secondary im-

[5] American Locomotive Company.

[6] The company made its start and drew its best profits from the owner-operator who was willing to pay a higher price for a truck customized to his needs. He might require, for instance, a heavier axle or a wider wheelbase for his particular truck. He couldn't get this type of service from the mass producers, such as Ford and General Motors.

[7] Trucks used for short-haul and in-city cartage.

[8] Companies with several trucks as opposed to the single owner-operator.

portance and gap between custom trucks and mass produced trucks narrowed. The close relationship between truck maker and truck buyer dissolved. Many of White's loyal owner-operator buyers took their business elsewhere.

As a whole, the sixties were booming years for truck sales. Even though hampered with marketing problems, the cumulative sales of the entire truck group increased each year, except for 1964 and 1967. These two years were relatively poor for trucks in general. White remained in its position of number two independent producer of heavy-duty trucks, only behind International.

The Farm Equipment Industry Problems

White Motor's main marketing strategy for the sixties, however, did not involve trucks, but revolved around the farm equipment assets of the three companies it had acquired (Oliver Corporation, Minneapolis-Moline, and Cockshutt). These companies were not combined into one line, but continued to operate as three separate divisions.

Although at the time of acquisition the farm equipment industry was experiencing serious problems, White management was convinced that the farm cycle was about to change. The farm equipment business did show substantial gains until 1968, when it took a severe nosedive. Marginal producers were in trouble, and White owned only marginal producers. White's share of the farm market declined and White lost $20 million in 1970 as opposed to a net income of $12 million for the previous year. This situation was due almost exclusively to the $43 million loss for the Farm Group. White dismissed the downturn as temporary and kept building up dealer inventories, tying up huge amounts of capital. When the market failed to rebound as anticipated, the company was forced to cut prices and sustain heavy losses.

Meanwhile, an engine plant had been built in Canton, Ohio, at an estimated cost of $45 million. The plant's profit potential was centered around volume. For instance, according to one analysis,[9] "to make the plant break even 25,000 farm tractor engines must be built a year." The way the economy was going in 1969, only about 18,000 could be sold. Since White would operate at a loss at that level, the plant, virtually fully equipped and nearly ready to operate, remained idle.

Hard-pressed for cash after the farm market downturn, White agreed to a merger with White Consolidated, the Cleveland-based sewing machine company turned conglomerate. The Justice Department, however, indicated its opposition to the merger by obtaining a temporary injunction. At this point, the company had neither financial nor managerial resources. At the edge of liquidation, the outside directors in an emergency meeting selected Semon E. Knudsen as Chairman and Chief Executive.

[9] "White Upon White," *Forbes,* November 1, 1970, p. 20.

NEW MANAGEMENT ACTION

The first action was to rebuild White's financial strength. Knudsen obtained a line of credit for $290 million, something White's previous management had been unable to do.

The next item was to put together an organization. Knudsen hired some of the best talent (see Appendix C for the management team).

The balance sheet was "cleaned up" by writing off obsolete inventory and other items. An improved financial forecasting system was put into operation.

The new management then attacked the marketing problems. In July, 1971, the overlapping and duplication of heavy-duty truck products was eliminated by selling the Diamond-Reo Truck Division. The four remaining lines were combined under one marketing group so that White's trucks were available in a full line, with each nameplate directed to specific segments of the market: the top-of-the-line Freightliner for owner-operators; White and White Western Star for owners and for fleet use; and the Autocar, a construction truck. White's advertising theme, the "Big 4," was more than advertising and promotion identity. It indicated that White's previously splintered sales and marketing activities by nameplate were brought under coordinated direction.

Expenditures for research and development were sharply increased for the development of new products and the improvement of existing ones. A total of 16 major new products was introduced in 1972 and early 1973, including two new White trucks: the Road Commander and the Road Boss.

The Road Commander, a newly styled heavy-duty truck, was part of a vigorous program to regain the owner-operator market. The Road Commander generated 75 per cent more orders in 1972 over 1971 than the model it replaced and contributed significantly to record sales in 1973. The Road Boss, introduced in early 1973, received tremendous enthusiasm. It soon was the hottest conventional heavy-duty truck in the marketplace. Western Star, showing the fastest growth rate of White's nameplates, received a new look by midsummer of 1973. At Autocar a new construction model—XK94—was being tested in 1973. This model with offset cab would allow for the installation of a greater range of engines and take on competitor Mack truck which in 1973 had this particular market to itself.

White developed an entire new family of heavy-duty trucks and tractors that, hopefully, would be better than anything the competition had. Heavy-duty truck industry registrations from 1955 to 1972 more than tripled from 50,000 to 157,000. The long-term growth trend was 6 per cent to 7 per cent annually with 200,000 registrations clearly indicated by 1980. White wants at least 20 per cent of that market.

Restructuring and consolidation of the farm group was initiated. The two farm lines (Minneapolis-Moline and Oliver) were combined. The new management admitted White could make money in the farm equipment business but did not anticipate it to dominate White's total operation. The year 1973 promised a strong market; the North American farm backlog of tractor orders from dealers was three times that of the year before. Farmers ended 1972 with record farm income. It appeared that farm income would rise another 10 per cent in 1973. With the demand for United States crops, particularly by such countries as Russia and China, farmers' net income was expected to move to a new all-time-high record. The growth trend for farm income appeared very good for a sustained period of time. North American farm sales for the first four months of 1973 totaled $64.8 million compared with $51 million one year earlier—an increase of 26.9 per cent. The goal in 1973 was to move from 1971's deficit of $7 million to a profit of $4.7 million in 1973. In 1972 White had 4.8 per cent of the United States farm tractor market; the 1973 goal was six per cent.

Product development work in the Farm Equipment Group moved ahead for tractors, combines, and implements and for construction units and fork-lift trucks. The new management felt that the trend to larger farms meant larger equipment was needed. Model 2255 with 150 h.p. was brought to market in Fall 1972 with a heavy promotion program; the 150 h.p. Class Minneapolis-Moline tractor was in full production. Three new combines, a small skid-turn loader, and a heavy-duty four-wheel drive backhoe as well as a 6,000-pound capacity fork-lift were among new offerings.

A program was launched to increase White's international operations:

1. *Arbos, the Italian operation, had generated losses (e.g., $1.4 million loss in 1970; $2.8 million loss in 1972) since its 1966 purchase.* Although more than 400 new combines in inventory and in the field were rebuilt by the end of 1972 at the cost of over $1 million, this action restored credibility and brought new sales opportunities. A new combine line was introduced to correct design weaknesses; a new forage harvester was in production; and a new management team was installed. By 1973, the Italian subsidiary was made a branch of the North American Farm Equipment Group.

2. *Australian operations were in a loss position.* The COE truck design was unsatisfactory; trucks in the field were being returned for quality problems. A poor reputation was closing off new orders, and dealers were discouraged. Corrective actions included rebuilding all trucks in the field. The Road Commander was introduced. A Euclid Division was added to the Australian operation; plant facilities were expanded to handle the Division and the increased truck activity. A farm operation was started to import and distribute farm equipment in Australia. Plans eventually included bringing in farm equipment on a CKD basis and assembly along with some local components. Orders at the time were substantially in excess of past performance.

3. *Export sales departments of domestic divisions had no legal or financial support, and little liaison and coordination from Erieview headquarters, for their export sales activities.* To support export sales, an International Finance Department was organized to work with domestic divisions on financing,

credits, and collections on international sales. A full-time lawyer with the International Department was to support the domestic divisions in the legal area, particularly with respect to contracts, distributor agreements, and license arrangements. The International Department had a marketing manager to assist the divisions in market planning and distribution problems. The aim of the International Department was not to tell the export sales departments of the domestic divisions how to function but to coordinate division activities and supply expertise and guidance for areas in which there was a specific corporate interest and where the domestic activities were not always able to have this expertise available.

In June, 1972, White bought a $2 million plant in Canada for expansion of its Euclid off-road machinery division.

Total 1973 foreign sales, including foreign subsidiaries and exports would be over $72 million (up from $57 million in 1972 and $54 million in 1971). White's international business at the time amounted to 6 per cent of its gross.

OVERALL RESULTS

During 1972, sales rose by 13 per cent while profits rose by 191 per cent. Total profit in 1972 was $7.1 million. These earnings were achieved despite the loss of truck production caused by a supplier strike and truck component shortages as well as the costs of the idle Canton plant and a strike at the Hercules Engine Division.

The earnings outlook for 1973 were even better. Second-quarter earnings in 1973 increased 161 per cent to $4,986,000 (57 cents a common share) from $1,907,000 (22 cents a share) in 1972. 1973 second-quarter sales were $308,291,000 as compared to 1972 second-quarter sales of $235,516,000. After income tax reductions, White Motor's six-month earnings were $10.9 million ($1.23 a share).

Two years after Knudsen became Chairman, White had little or no short-term debts, adequate funds for current programs, and unused borrowing capacity to handle new capital expansions.

The declining trend in truck market penetration had been arrested. White had increased its share of the total heavy-duty truck market from 13.4 per cent in 1971, to 13.5 percent in 1972, and to 14.8 per cent for the first five months of 1973. White truck registrations were up 25 per cent in 1973 against a 14 per cent gain for the industry as a whole. Sales of heavy-duty trucks were limited only by White's production capacity. A new plant was under construction in Virginia to increase production.

Also in 1973, farm operations were in the black with a 33 per cent increase in sales over 1972. The biggest problem was production capacity. White management saw farm sales limited only by its ability to produce as much as they can sell. In support of this, Euclid Division-Canada, a plant opened in January, 1973, had sold out its entire production through March, 1974. Profits were significant from the farm equipment operations at the end of 1973 as the backlog and incoming orders were converted to shipments.

Appendix A

ABOUT SEMON KNUDSEN

Knudsen learned about the automobile industry at an early age; his father, William S. Knudsen, was president of General Motors Corporation from 1937 through 1940. Knudsen graduated from Massachusetts Institute of Technology in 1936. By 1956 he had earned an outstanding reputation as an engineer and was elected a GM vice president. Knudsen enhanced his managerial reputation, first as the general manager of the Pontiac Division and later as the leader of Chevrolet. In each case, he led his division to record sales and profits. In 1967 he was elected an executive vice president and a member of the board of directors.

After being passed over for the GM presidency, Knudsen shocked the automobile community by resigning from GM and accepting the job as president of Ford Motor Company. Allegedly, his aggressive take-charge management style upset Ford's established executives and led to his ouster only 19 months after he began.

Knudsen was soon back in the vehicle business, however. He and several business colleagues founded a motor-home company, Rectrans, Inc. Rectrans was merged with White Motor Company when Bunkie became chief executive officer of White in May, 1971.

Appendix B

WHITE'S ACQUISITION PHILOSOPHY *

Five principles that White's management evolved to govern their acquisition program:

1. A good offense is not only the best but, perhaps, the *only* secure defense—

* J. P. Dragin, Executive Vice President, White Motor Corporation, "Charting an Acquisition Course," an address made at a seminar on Mergers and Acquisitions, Los Angeles, California, March 13, 1968.

coupled with constant attention to increasing the profitability of existing operations.

2. Corporate acquisitions should follow a predetermined plan which:
   (a) specifies industries within which the company's existing know-how and experience are directly applicable;
   (b) pinpoints market segments within those industries which offer the prospect an average return;
   (c) fits acquired operations into a company-wide profit pattern.
3. Make acquisitions only in specific situations which afford exceptional profit potential because they couple a low purchase price with the virtual certainty of near-term operating improvement. (i.e.—a company which cannot compete economically as an independent entity and thus can be had at a bargain price but which can make a significant contribution to earnings once properly meshed with other White Motor operations functioning in the same general field.)
4. Carefully evaluate the top and middle management of each acquisition prospect; give preference to those in which competent leadership is available internally at either first or second levels.
5. When a mistake is made (as any company with a continuing acquisition program occasionally will make) get rid of it at the first reasonable opportunity.

An acquisition program must achieve a synergy—which may be basically financial in nature, as a result of leveraging securities; alternatively, it may be fundamentally operating (i.e., improving operations and profitability). White motor chose the operating synergy. In acquiring companies within the same industry, White management looked primarily for opportunities to consolidate their manufacturing facilities and distribution organizations while improving over-all product lines and the product development function.

Appendix C

MANAGEMENT

Directors

Semon E. Knudsen, Chairman of the Board, President and Chief Executive Officer

D. O. Andreas, Chairman of the Board, Archer-Midland-McDaniels

George V. Brown, Vice President, Secretary and General Counsel

H. Stuart Harrison, President and Chief Executive Officer, The Cleveland Cliffs Iron Company

James A. Hughes, Chairman of the Board and Chief Executive Officer, Diamond Shamrock Corporation
Robert E. Hunter, Chairman of the Board and Chief Executive Officer, The Weatherhead Company
George F. Karch, Honorary Chairman, The Cleveland Trust Company
John R. Kramer, Executive Vice President, Operations Staff
Arnold P. Moran, Executive Vice President, Financial Staff
J. B. Poole, Chairman of the Board, Poole Broadcasting Company
James F. Preston, Jr., Partner, Squire, Sanders & Dempsey
Charles E. Spahr, Chairman of the Board and Chief Executive Officer, The Standard Oil Company (Ohio)

Executive Officers

S. E. Knudsen, Chairman of the Board, President and Chief Executive Officer
J. R. Kramer, Executive Vice President, Operations Staff and Director
A. P. Moran, Executive Vice President, Financial Staff and Director
D. V. Johnson, Group Vice President, Industrial
R. E. Kidder, Group Vice President, Farm Equipment
C. A. Kiorpes, Group Vice President, Trucks
J. G. Musser, Jr., Group Vice President, Engineering and Recreational Products
G. V. Brown, Vice President, Secretary, General Counsel and Director
J. C. Curran, Jr., Vice President and Treasurer
H. G. Henning, Vice President, Manufacturing
S. H. Mieras, Vice President, International
S. Petok, Vice President, Public Relations and Advertising
H. H. Phillips, Vice President, Personnel and Industrial Relations
A. F. Atwood, Vice President and Controller

APPENDIX D

WHITE MOTOR CORPORATION
AND CONSOLIDATED SUBSIDIARIES

Ten-Year Summary
(in thousands — except per share amounts)

	1972	1971	1970 (4)	1969	1968	1967	1966	1965	1964	1963
Results for the Year										
Net Sales										
Truck	$611,390	$522,310	$507,710	$613,164	$518,552	$431,782	$508,890	$407,647	$340,793	$375,569
Industrial and Construction	181,950	189,335	201,996	191,643	135,335	106,549	48,152	36,573	23,936	38,522
North American Farm	142,347	117,901	93,478	137,515	190,271	225,249	221,620	193,976	186,003	161,423
European Farm	7,649	8,321	6,922	8,133	6,869	6,235	—	—	—	—
	$943,336	$837,867	$810,106	$950,455	$851,027	$769,815	$778,662	$638,196	$550,732	$575,514
Income (Loss) before Extraordinary Income (Loss)	$ 7,069	$ 2,430	$ (20,969)	$ 17,516	$ 23,020	$ 28,856	$ 32,089	$ 22,400	$ 18,056	$ 15,781
% of Sales	.7%	.3%	(2.6)%	1.8%	2.7%	3.7%	4.1%	3.5%	3.3%	2.7%
% of Total Shareholders' Equity (1)	3.7%	1.2%	(9.1)%	8.1%	11.2%	15.3%	19.5%	14.9%	12.6%	11.9%
Net Income (Loss)	$ 8,610	$ (13,487)	$ (20,969)	$ 12,435	$ 23,020	$ 28,856	$ 32,089	$ 22,400	$ 18,056	$ 15,781
% of Sales	.9%	(1.6%)	(2.6)%	1.3%	2.7%	3.7%	4.1%	3.5%	3.3%	2.7%
% of Total Shareholders' Equity (1)	4.5%	(6.6%)	(9.1)%	5.7%	11.2%	15.3%	19.5%	14.9%	12.6%	11.9%
Cash Dividends										
Preferred Stock	$ 1,064	$ 1,064	$ 1,064	$ 532	$ —	$ —	$ —	$ —	$ 229	$ 274
Common Stock	—	—	3,264	13,036	13,068	11,831	9,671	7,859	6,598	5,937

APPENDIX D (continued)

Property, Plant and Equipment Additions — Gross										
Current Operations	$ 8,283	$ 9,971	$ 59,705	$ 19,794	$ 13,802	$ 12,571	$ 13,878	$ 10,720	$ 6,537	$ 4,450
Corporate Acquisitions	—	—	—	6,289	11,224	1,220	3,734	—	381	2,411
Depreciation	8,975	9,282	8,618	9,191	8,222	8,391	6,521	5,141	4,922	5,315
Interest Charges	13,916	14,741	15,778	10,635	7,296	5,109	3,377	2,701	2,704	3,323
Balance Sheet (December 31)										
Working Capital	$213,923	$132,241	$122,406	$171,898	$178,261	$145,588	$143,355	$129,332	$123,047	$121,660
Current Ratio	2.3 to 1	1.5 to 1	1.4 to 1	1.7 to 1	2.0 to 1	1.9 to 1	1.9 to 1	2.0 to 1	2.3 to 1	2.2 to 1
Long-Term Debt	155,706	105,108	114,423	83,968	82,176	39,524	36,376	31,011	35,604	38,395
Preferred Shareholders' Equity	15,767	15,767	15,767	15,767	—	—	—	—	—	4,810
Common Shareholders' Equity	206,037	175,601	189,676	214,109	216,599	206,203	188,371	164,939	149,936	138,216
Total Capital (2)	377,510	296,476	319,866	313,844	298,775	245,727	224,747	195,950	185,540	181,421
% of Long-Term Debt to Total Capital	41.2%	35.5%	35.8%	26.8%	27.5%	16.1%	16.2%	15.8%	19.2%	21.2%
Shares Outstanding										
Preferred	158	158	158	158	—	—	—	—	—	48
Common	8,232	6,964	6,929	6,511	6,538	6,519	5,887	5,831	5,794	5,754
Number of Common Shareholders	23	24	28	25	25	26	25	22	20	17
Per Common Share (3)										
Shareholders' Equity	$ 25.03	$ 25.22	$ 27.37	$ 32.88	$ 33.13	$ 31.63	$ 29.09	$ 25.71	$ 23.53	$ 21.84
Income (Loss) before Extraordinary Income (Loss) —										
Assuming No Dilution	.79	.19	(3.27)	2.60	3.52	4.43	4.95	3.49	2.80	2.45
Net Income (Loss) — Assuming No Dilution	.99	(2.09)	(3.27)	1.83	3.52	4.43	4.95	3.49	2.80	2.45
Cash Dividends	—	—	.50	2.00	2.00	1.82	1.50	1.23	1.05	.95

(1) Percentage is based on the balance at the beginning of the year.
(2) Total Capital is the sum of Long-Term Debt and Shareholders' Equity.
(3) Adjusted to give retroactive effect to Common Stock Distributions as follows: Two for one Common Stock split in 1963 and 10% Common Stock dividend in 1967.
(4) Figures for 1970 have been restated to include Rectrans, Inc.

CASE 14

Durard Plastics Company*

Thomas S. Dudick

The Durard Plastics Company's products consist of plastic molding, metal stamping, and related hand assembly operations. The product line includes such items as push buttons for radios, plastic knobs for appliances, plastic bottles with caps, electric shaver parts, small radio cabinets, and a variety of metal parts used in the appliance industry.

The management of this company wanted to increase its share of the market. It planned to achieve this goal through the purchase of established companies as well as through internal expansion. As each acquisition was digested, the plan was to move the operations to the town of Durard, for which the parent company was named.

The management of the company was disappointed in its progress—and changed general managers three times during a six-year period. The chronology of events leading to management dissatisfaction was as follows:

PURCHASE OF ACME PLASTICS AND EXPANSION FROM WITHIN

Acme Plastics became a part of Durard in August of the first year. This acquisition resulted in a substantial increase in sales volume as well as profits. Since plans called for all Acme activities to be moved to Durard, a building expansion program was undertaken. This was completed in the spring of the second year, and the move was made. Concurrently with the completion of this move, 12 injection molding presses were purchased and set up in the expanded plant. The combination of the Acme move and the establishment of an injection molding department proved to be "too big a bite." Since only key supervisory personnel of the Acme Company were transferred, critically needed skills, such as setup men and die and mold repair men, were in short supply. Utilization of equipment, which had normally been running at 95 per cent, now dropped to an average of 45 to 50 per cent. The new injection molding presses ran less than 25 per cent of the time for several months following installation while "bugs" were being taken care of and operators and setup men trained.

* "A Backward Look at Forward Planning." Reprinted by permission of *Management Adviser,* January–February 1972, pp. 16–19.

Naturally, these problems reflected themselves in reduced sales volume as well as reduced profits. As a result, the second year ended with a loss.

Sales had slipped throughout the second year because of the company's inability to make shipments to customers. Some improvement was experienced during the third year. Utilization of the equipment transferred from Acme increased to 75 per cent—somewhat short of the desired 90 to 95 per cent. The newly purchased injection molding equipment still lagged at 65 per cent of production goals rather than at the anticipated level. The company believed it would take from six to nine months more before utilization of the equipment could attain optimum levels. The profit outlook still was not good, but improvement seemed in sight. Because the Durard Company was in sound financial condition, it was able to weather the storm. Under similar conditions other companies would have failed.

PURCHASE OF THE PIC COMPANY

The general manager, who had been with Durard two years, had been released and replaced by a new man. The new man was advised of the company's interest in growth and of the recent problems that had been encountered.

Shortly after taking over, the new general manager learned that the PIC Company, which was in financial straits and losing money, could be purchased at a bargain price. This purchase would permit Durard to get into another related product line immediately and pick up PIC's customers. With the Acme move out of the way, the decision was made to purchase PIC and to transfer the operations to Durard as soon as possible.

Within two months, the unprofitable hand assembly items were moved. It was felt that the high labor rates paid at PIC's former location made profits there out of the question. The substantially lower rates in the Durard area should help considerably. Although the rates were lower, management miscalculated on two other counts:

1. Purchasing and production scheduling personnel were unfamiliar with the new product line. Bills of material were incomplete because PIC personnel had carried this information "in their heads" rather than in documented records.
2. The Durard plant could not accommodate the PIC press operations. The trouble was not lack of space but the wrong type of floor construction. PIC's heavy presses required heavily reinforced floors.

PIC press operators and tool shop men were leaving as soon as they could find other employment—knowing that their tenure was limited. Downtime on presses, because of shortage of skilled personnel, increased astronomically. Plans for the second Durard expansion were hurriedly made, but actual work could not start because of an unexpected strike that closed down all construction in the area. Finally, with the settlement of the strike, construction began late in the year. Durard made a small profit that year, but its working capital was becoming strained.

The second expansion was completed late in the spring of the fourth year. Production schedules were firmed up and certain PIC items were now running at high volume. But then problems began to mount again. The tools used at PIC were of a poor quality—no longer meeting the tighter requirements of the industry, which had greatly increased the use of automated assembly equipment. As a result, many fabricated parts that did not meet the finer tolerances that were required had to be scrapped or reworked.

It was obvious that a substantial retooling program was required. In the meantime, productivity had dropped and production schedules had to be "juggled" frequently to satisfy specific customer demands. The tooling program would require from 15 to 18 months before it could be completed. Also, production output continued to drop with a resultant slippage, of course, in sales and profits. To add to the problems, a business recession developed near the end of the fourth year during what was normally a high volume production period. Although the recession was relatively mild, productivity continued to slip while the company frantically tried to find competent tool makers to speed up the retooling program. At this point the general manager was relieved of his responsibilities and still another new man was brought in.

The new general manager, Norm Bayard, was somewhat surprised to learn that his predecessors had had such a short tenure. He realized that if he mechanically picked up the reins, without some deeper investigation, he might fall victim to the same problems that had resulted in the release of his predecessors.

In his "get acquainted" interviews with the members of his staff, he decided that he would attempt to determine exactly what the problems were and how they might have been prevented—or, at least, greatly minimized. He sensed that some of the staff would, undoubtedly, in the role of "Monday morning quarterbacks," apply the 20/20 vision of hindsight to impress the new boss. To avoid being misled, Norm double-checked all statements that were made. If he was told that bad tools had been at fault, he asked such questions as

- Were the tools poorly designed or were they merely worn out and in need of maintenance?
- Could better maintenance have prevented the problem?
- Was it possible that only some of the key high volume tools were the source of the problems? In that case, would the availability of a duplicate set of tools have allowed for the needed maintenance?

By asking questions such as these, statements could be pinned down to more factual data. Without being obvious, Norm gradually accumulated a "bank" of information which was correlated with past sales. To this he added the data accumulated during his own tenure. The pictorial diary was then prepared. Since growth was being emphasized by the company, two projections were made for the balance of the ten-year period. These were based on

- Rate of growth for the first three years.
- Rate of growth for the first five years.

The first three years would project the trend if the high rate of sales increase experienced in the first three years could be duplicated. The five-year period, on the other hand, was a more conservative estimate because it reflected the problems incident to the PIC move and the effect of a business recession. The favorable effect of a major competitor's strike, which occurred in the sixth year, was not included because this was considered to be a nonrecurring windfall.

Corrective programs that had been instituted by Norm and his predecessor gradually began to take hold. Although production volume continued to slip, defective production was reduced materially. It was now only a matter of time before the problems of tooling and setup would be corrected. The Durard Company had profited immensely from the long strike of its competitor because it was able to take business on a more selective basis and set up certain equipment to run continuously, day-in and day-out. One-shift operations were expanded to two shifts and the work week was extended to 45 hours. Sales and profits soared—somewhat relieving a serious shortage of working capital.

Norm felt that the pictorial diary of problems experienced by the Durard Company could serve a two-fold purpose:

1. It would provide a history of past events and demonstrate their effect on operations.
2. The availability of this type of data would be helpful in management meetings to reinforce the need for solid planning.

It seemed that the two previous general managers had moved too quickly to fulfill the company's desire for growth—with the consequence that the company's working capital had been seriously impaired. As a result of this and the other observations made by Norm, it was decided to set forth specific policies for expansion.

QUESTION

What policies do you suggest for this company to guide its future expansion in such a way as to avoid the problems encountered in the past?

CASE 15

Drexler Technology Corporation*

Paul L. Goodman and
Carlton A. Pederson

It was June, 1972. Jerry Drexler, President of Drexler Technology Corporation, was concerned about the future direction of his firm. Although Drexler Technology had exhibited substantial growth since its founding, the future market for its products appeared to be ultimately limited and, therefore, desired growth seemed difficult to obtain, even for a company which excelled in its product and service. Jerry wondered whether or not it was time to diversify.

HISTORY AND PRODUCTS OF THE COMPANY

Drexler Technology Corporation was incorporated under the laws of the State of California in July, 1968, to acquire and hold small high-technology companies, providing them with common financial resources and management. (See Exhibit 1 for a graphical representation of the corporate structure.)

In February, 1969, Drexler acquired all the outstanding stock of Microfab Systems Corporation, a California corporation organized in January of 1968 to manufacture and sell photomasks to the semiconductor industry for use in the manufacture of integrated circuits. In January, 1969, Microfab organized Precision Photoglass, Inc., as a wholly owned subsidiary for the purpose of purchasing high resolution photographic plates from Eastman Kodak Company. In June, 1969, Drexler invested $543,000—more than half of its net worth—in Photophysics, a company which had developed a new electrographic process for making hard copy prints from cathode ray tube (CRT) and microfilm displays. Photophysics was not acquired and run by Drexler, but remained an independent affiliate whose only connection with Drexler was the fact that Drexler's investment accounted for 42 per cent of its outstanding shares, or 544,000 shares which had a present market value of over $3,000,000.

EXHIBIT 1

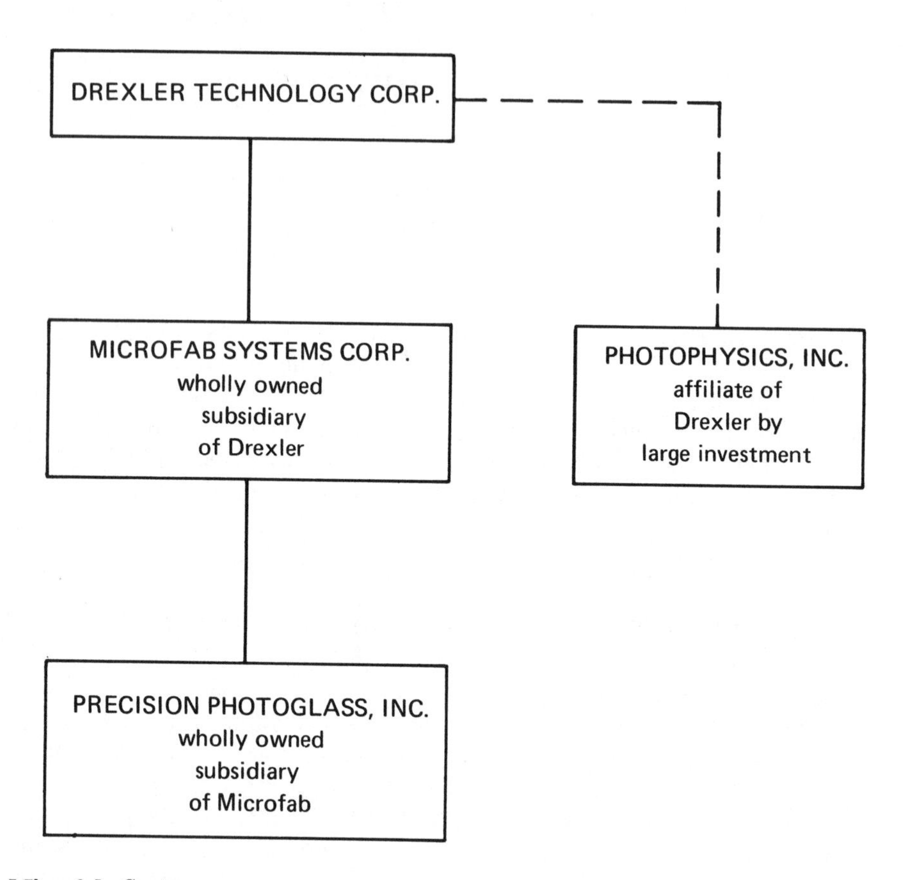

Microfab Systems

Integrated circuits are produced through a highly refined photoengraving process in which silicon wafers coated with photosensitive chemicals are exposed to ultraviolet light through photomasks. Microfab Systems supplied photomasks to semiconductor manufacturers for this process. Although most semiconductor manufacturers have their own inhouse facility for producing photomasks, many contract out photomask work because they lack sufficient facilities, have a peak load problem, or need special expertise.

Production of photomasks involves a high degree of precision. The circuit design is generally reduced 400–500 times and photographically projected on the surface of a high-resolution glass plate coated with emulsion or metal plating. The image is repeated many times on the photoplate, producing a grid of tiny circuit dies generally one- or two-tenths inches square. The plate is then developed to produce a photomask.

In a continuing effort to improve this process, Microfab developed a computerized system to produce photomask designs from IBM cards, punched paper tape, or magnetic tape.

Precision Photoglass

This subsidiary provided "blank" photoplates to customers who made photomasks. It was incorporated to take advantage of a special discount given by Eastman Kodak to companies that were distributors of photoplates but not manufacturers of photomasks. Precision Photoglass cut the photoplates into various sizes, ultrasonically cleaned them, and stacked the plates into special packages to facilitate handling. It produced photoplates coated with photographic emulsion or chromium. Since their introduction in 1970 the chromium-clad plates increased in importance. Whereas emulsion plates could only be used about 10 times in processing the silicon wafers, the chromium plates could be used several hundred times and also produce finer geometric patterns. In 1972 Precision Photoglass introduced a transparent iron oxide photoplate, making the alignment of masks in the engraving process easier. Despite their advantages, however, metal-clad plates could not be used in the production of all semiconductor devices.

Precision Photoglass developed a line of instruments for semiconductor manufacturers. Early in 1972 it introduced a micromeasurement readout for microscopes. Another instrument, a semiautomatic photomask contact printer, was introduced in mid-1972. The printer, selling for about $13,500, manufactured production copies of master photomasks.

Precision Photoglass sold its products to Microfab Systems for use in the manufacturing of photomasks, and as an intermediate product to manufacturers of integrated circuits.

FINANCIAL HISTORY OF DREXLER

The financial history of Drexler is one of innovation and close acquaintance with financing procedures, as well as an ability to take advantage of a securities market which favored new issues of promising companies. The following quote from *Forbes'* July 15, 1969, issue explains how Drexler took advantage of this market condition:

> . . . Consider the case of a typical California scientific company, Drexler Technology, Inc. It is the creation of a New York-born Californian named Jerome Drexler, an electrical engineer who learned management at Stanford and Harvard. Drexler, formerly of Varian Associates, started manufacturing micrographic masks for integrated circuits. In March 1968 he and his partners raised $500,000 on their own. The original $500,000 started to run thin at a time when the business was starting to expand. In a less speculative era, Drexler and friends might have had to give away a big piece of the equity to refinance. But with institutions panting for action in hot new companies, he had a better alternative. He persuaded

New York's Value Line Development Capital Corporation to buy $200,000 in convertible preferred. On the strength of the Value Line participation, he had little trouble selling another $300,000 worth of preferred. The buyers were both institutions: Wells Fargo Investment Co., a small business investment company owned by the big California bank, and C.I.T. Financial. Drexler gave up only about 10% of his equity through conversion privilege.

In August 1971, Drexler handled its own issuing of 200,000 shares of common stock at $2.50, and went public. Another issue of common stock was registered with the Security Exchange Commission in June 1972. This issue was for 320,000 shares to be exchanged for the outstanding convertible preferred shares. (A complete set of financial statements is included in Exhibit 2).

DREXLER'S MARKET AND COMPETITION

Spurred by a high degree of technical innovation in the semiconductor industry, the photomask market grew significantly from 1967 to 1972 with all indications that the trend would continue. Its growth in the several years preceding June 1972 was closely linked to the growth of the integrated circuit production volume which had expanded at a rate of more than 20 per cent per year from 1967 to 1972. Its earlier growth was linked to the production of transistors (and other discrete semiconductor devices) which were growing at a much slower rate. In June 1972, about 85 per cent of all photomasks produced were for integrated circuits. Of considerable importance in evaluating the photomask market was the fact that it required about 30 times as many photomasks to produce one million integrated circuits as it did to produce one million transistors.

For the fiscal year ended March 31, 1972, approximately 63 per cent of Drexler's sales were for photoplate packages. These photoplate packages were prepared by Precision Photoglass. The technology involved in manufacturing these packages was developed by Drexler as part of its program for improving its own photomask manufacturing techniques. The remaining 37 per cent of Drexler's sales were for photomasks manufactured to the customer's specifications by Microfab from photoplates supplied by Precision Photoglass.

Drexler sold its products to approximately 103 customers, of which eight accounted for about 67 per cent of the total sales for the year. International markets had grown steadily and for fiscal 1972 included 17 companies in 7 countries. These international markets accounted for $350,000 worth of sales which was approximately 8 per cent of the total sales of the company.

Drexler competed in the manufacturing and sales of its photoglass, metal-clad plate, and photomask products with approximately ten firms, some of which were considerably larger than Drexler in both size and financial re-

EXHIBIT 2

Consolidated Balance Sheet

March 31, 1972
with comparative figures for 1971

Assets	**1972**	**1971**
Current assets:		
Cash	$ 212,970	16,063
Accounts receivable, net of allowance for doubtful accounts (1972, $24,000; 1971, $12,500)	714,468	484,597
Inventories, at lower of cost (first-in, first-out) or replacement market	477,008	297,976
Other current assets	13,144	7,697
Total current assets	1,417,590	806,333
Fixed assets, at cost (Notes 2 and 3):		
Equipment	796,345	646,702
Furniture and fixtures	9,028	5,939
Leasehold improvements	87,703	72,114
	893,076	724,755
Less accumulated depreciation	342,841	225,859
Total fixed assets	550,235	498,896
Investment in common stock and debt of Photophysics, Inc. net of allowance for loss (Note 4)	180,039	3,305
Other assets:		
Deferred income tax benefit	74,821	–
Organization expense	506	2,437
Deferred product development costs (Note 5)	–	67,246
Deposits	35,435	16,453
Patent costs	1,553	–
Total other assets	112,315	86,136
	$2,260,179	1,394,670

See accompanying notes to consolidated financial statements.

EXHIBIT 2 (cont.)

Consolidated Balance Sheet

Liabilities and Stockholders' Equity	1972	1971
Current liabilities:		
Due to banks (note 2)	$ 248,202	228,501
Accounts payable	307,662	203,672
Current portion of lease and purchase contracts payable	53,685	47,375
Accrued liabilities	78,807	59,748
Income taxes payable	82,178	103,016
Reserve for relocation and consolidation	65,000	—
Total current liabilities	835,534	642,312
Long-term liabilities:		
Deferred income taxes payable	—	45,402
Due to banks—long-term portion (Note 2)	32,862	60,873
Lease and purchase contracts payable	104,616	38,721
Total long-term liabilities	137,478	144,996
Stockholders' equity (Note 6):		
Cumulative convertible voting preferred stock, $1 par value; authorized 1,000,000 shares (500,000 shares designated as 5% Series A); issued 327,000 shares of 5% Series A	327,000	327,000
Common stock, $.20 par value; authorized 3,000,000 shares; issued in 1972, 1,105,000 shares; 1971, 915,000 shares	221,000	183,000
Additional paid-in capital	919,468	514,469
Retained earnings (deficit)	(180,301)	(417,107)
Total stockholders' equity	1,287,167	607,362
Commitments and contingencies (Notes 6 and 10)		
	$2,260,179	$1,394,670

See accompanying notes to consolidated financial statements

EXHIBIT 2 (cont.)

Consolidated Statement of Operations
Year ended March 31, 1972
with comparative figures for 1971

	1972	1971
Net sales	$4,604,579	3,069,077
Cost of sales	3,242,415	2,059,704
Gross profit	1,362,164	1,009,373
General, administrative, selling and research and development expenses	966,782	743,004
Operating profit	395,382	266,369
Other income (expense) net (Note 7)	(116,642)	64,781
Income before income taxes	278,740	331,150
Income taxes (Note 8)	94,774	166,049
	183,966	165,101
Equity in net (losses) of common stock investment in Photophysics, Inc. (Note 4)	(132,000)	(8,000)
Provision for possible loss and adjustment thereto relating to debt of Photophysics, Inc. (Note 4)	219,000	(197,777)
Income (loss) before extraordinary item	270,966	(40,676)
Extraordinary item:		
Loss on discontinued product line, net of taxes (Note 5)	34,160	–
Net income (loss)	$ 236,806	(40,676)
Per share of common stock and common equivalent share (Note 9):		
Income (loss) before extraordinary item	.22	(.04)
Extraordinary item, net	(.03)	–
Net income (loss)	$ .19	(.04)
Per share of common stock assuming full dilution (Note 9):		
Income (loss) before extraordinary item	.19	(.04)
Extraordinary item, net	(.02)	–
Net income (loss)	$ .17	(.04)

See accompanying notes to consolidated financial statements.

EXHIBIT 2 (cont.)

Consolidated Statement of Stockholders' Equity
Year Ended March 31, 1972
with comparative figures for 1971

	1972	1971
Preferred Stock:		
Beginning and end of year	$ 327,000	327,000
Common stock:		
Beginning of year	183,000	183,000
Par value 190,000 shares sold during year	38,000	–
End of year	221,000	183,000
Additional paid-in capital:		
Beginning of year	514,469	514,469
Net proceeds in excess of par value from sale of 190,000 shares of common stock	403,864	–
Repurchase of special stock options on common stock	(1,030)	–
Other	2,165	–
End of year	919,468	514,469
Retained earnings (deficit):		
Beginning of year	(417,107)	(376,431)
Net income (loss)	236,806	(40,676)
End of year	(180,301)	(417,107)
Total stockholders' equity	$1,287,167	607,362

See accompanying notes to consolidated financial statements.

Accountants' Opinion

Board of Directors
Drexler Technology Corporation:

We have examined the consolidated balance sheet of Drexler Technology Corporation and subsidiaries as of March 31, 1972 and the related statements of operations, stockholders' equity and changes in financial position for the year then ended. Our examination was made in accordance with generally accepted auditing standards, and accordingly included such tests of the accounting records and such other auditing procedures as we considered necessary in the circumstances.

In our opinion, such financial statements present fairly the consolidated financial position of Drexler Technology Corporation and subsidiaries at March 31, 1972 and the results of their operations and the changes in stockholders' equity and financial position for the year then ended in conformity with generally accepted accounting principles applied on a consistent basis after giving retroactive effect to the inclusion, which we approve, of the results of operations of Photophysics, Inc. on an equity basis, as explained in Note 4 to the consolidated financial statements.

San Francisco, California
May 24, 1972

EXHIBIT 2 (cont.)

Statement of Consolidated Changes in Financial Position

Year Ended March 31, 1972
with comparative figures for 1971

	1972	1971
Funds provided:		
Income (loss) before extraordinary item	$ 270,966	(40,676)
Charges (credits) not requiring working capital:		
Depreciation and amortization	120,546	135,233
Loss on write down of microfiche equipment	62,000	–
Provision (benefit) for deferred taxes on income	(120,223)	45,402
Provision for loss on Photophysics, Inc. common stock and debt	(87,000)	205,777
Other	2,125	–
Working capital derived from operations before extraordinary item	248,414	345,736
Ex Extraordinary item:		
Income tax benefit resulting from loss on discontinued product line	31,532	–
Working capital derived from operations and extraordinary item	179,946	345,736
Proceeds from sale of 190,000 shares of common stock, net of selling expenses	441,864	–
Increase in long-term debt	120,318	–
Proceeds from sale of equipment, net of gain	438	51,537
	$ 842,566	$ 397,273
Funds used:		
Repurchase of stock options	960	–
Deferred product development costs	–	67,246
Investment in common stock and debt of Photophysics, Inc.	89,734	31,221
Increase in long-term deposits	18,982	10,987
Additions to plant and equipment	232,421	200,784
Reduction of long-term debt	82,434	69,822
Increase in working capital	418,035	17,213
	$ 842,566	397,273

See accompanying notes to consolidated financial statements.

EXHIBIT 2 (cont.)

Statement of Consolidated Changes in Financial Position

Year Ended March 31, 1972
with comparative figures for 1971

	1972	1971
Changes in working capital:		
Increase (decrease) in current assets:		
Cash	196,907	(15,292)
Accounts receivable	229,871	151,481
Inventories	179,032	23,685
Prepaid expenses	5,447	(7,883)
	611,257	151,991
Increase (decrease) in current liabilities:		
Notes and contracts payable	26,011	126,806
Accounts payable	103,990	(37,323)
Accrued expenses	19.059	16,477
Federal and State taxes on income	(20,838)	51,818
Reserve for relocation and consolidation . .	65,000	–
Estimated liability for replacement of returned goods	–	(23,000)
	193,222	134,778
Net increase in working capital	$ 418,035	17,213

See accompanying notes to consolidated financial statements.

EXHIBIT 2 (cont.)

Drexler Technology Corporation and Subsidiaries
Notes to Consolidated Financial Statements
March 31, 1972

1. **Principles of Consolidation**

The consolidated financial statements include the financial position and the results of operations of Drexler Technology Corporation (the Company) and its wholly owned subsidiary, Microfab Systems Corporation and its wholly owned subsidiary, Precision Photoglass, Inc. All significant intercompany transactions have been eliminated.

2. **Due to Banks** is composed of the following:

	Total	Current portion	Long-term portion
Indebtedness under a line of credit secured by accounts receivable (currently 6¾%)	$220,000	220,000	–
Installment note, 6% due 1972	11,200	11,200	–
Installment note, 10½% due 1971-1975	49,864	17,002	32,862
	$281,064	248,202	32,862

The notes are secured by certain equipment.

The above borrowings are payable in the following amounts for the annual periods ended March 31, 1973–$248,202; 1974–$18,876; 1975–$13,986.

3. **Fixed Assets** are being depreciated over useful lives ranging from 5 to 10 years using the double-declining balance and straight-line methods of depreciation. Depreciation of $118,643 during the year ended March 31, 1972 and $132,886 during the year ended March 31, 1971 was changed to operations.

Certain items of equipment, in addition to that mentioned in Note 2, secure notes arising from lease and purchase contracts in the amount of $157,820 excluding interest.

4. **Investment in Common Stock and Debt of Photophysics, Inc.**

The Company's investment in Photophysics, Inc. common stock has been adjusted to give retroactive effect to the losses of Photophysics, Inc. on the equity method of accounting.

In addition to providing for losses on investment in common stock, management has provided for possible losses on investments in debentures, notes, and accrued interest receivable.

The Company converted a $300,000 subordinated debenture, which was fully reserved for possible loss in prior years, into common stock as of February 11, 1972. The common stock received from this conversion was valued at the cost of the debentures converted and the reserve for loss was eliminated. This transaction increased the Company's investment in common stock which was then reduced for equity method loss resulting from the operations of Photophysics, Inc. during the year ended March 31, 1972.

Income resulting from the net increase in investment in common stock of $168,000 was partially offset by additional provisions for possible loss on Photophysics, Inc. debt of $81,000.

(Charges) and credits to income during the periods presented were as follows:

	1972	1971
Losses under the equity method of accounting	$ (132,000)	(8,000)
Provision for possible loss and adjustment thereto relating to debt of Photophysics, Inc.	219,000	(197,777)
	$ 87,000	(205,777)

The investment in and receivable from Photophysics, Inc. at March 31, 1972 and March 31, 1971 were as follows:

	1972	1971
Photophysics common stock (454,000 shares in 1972; 254,000 shares in 1971)	$168,000	32,000
6% ten year, subordinated debentures, convertible into 250,000 shares of common stock at $1.20	–	300,000
6% ten year, suboridanted debentures, convertible into 90,000 shares of common stock at $2.40	216,000	216,000
6% unsecured note receivable, due March 31, 1973	93,540	–
Accured interest receivable	19,414	23,221
	496,954	571,221
Allowance for loss	316,915	567,916
	$180,039	3,305

The Company owned 42% and 44% of the outstanding common stock of Photophysics, Inc. at March 31, 1972 and March 31, 1971, respectively. The Company also owned all of the outstanding subordinated debentures of Photophysics, Inc.

5. **Discontinued Product Line**

The Company discontinued publication of the "Decision Matrix Monthly Publication Service" in September of 1971. The loss, net of income tax effect of $31,532, is composed entirely of the write off of deferred product development costs relating to that publication service.

6. **Stockholders' Equity**

No cash dividends can be paid on common stock without first paying a cash dividend (5% per annum on Series A preferred stock) on the par value of the said series of preferred shares. The preferred stock dividend is cumulative subsequent to November 13, 1970. The Company has not paid cumulative dividends of $22,530 on the Series A preferred stock as of March 31, 1972.

The Company may purchase all or part of the preferred shares outstanding at any time for par value plus accumulated unpaid dividends. Preferred shares may, at any time, be converted into common shares on a share for share basis. The Company has a sufficient number of authorized common shares available for such conversion.

EXHIBIT 2 (cont.)

Notes to Consolidated Financial Statements

Under the Company's Employee Stock Option Plan certain key employees of the Company held at March 31, 1972, stock options to purchase an aggregate of 159,566 shares of the Company's common stock. The outstanding options are generally exercisable in cumulative installments over a period of three years beginning two years from the date of the granting of the option. The option price is not less than 100% of the fair market value on the date the option is granted as determined by the Stock Option Committee of the Board of Directors.

The plan provides for the granting of both qualified options expiring five years from the date of grant and non-qualified options expiring ten years from the date of grant. Of the outstanding options 113,566 are qualified and the remaining 46,000 options are tandem options in which the employee is granted both a qualified and a non-qualified option covering the same shares and the exercise of one option terminates an equal number of shares under the other option.

It is currently contemplated that if options are exercised, the par value of the shares issued will be credited to "Common Stock" and the excess of the option price over par value will be credited to "additional paid-in capital." No charges are made to operations when the options are granted and it is not currently contemplated that charges will be made to operations if options are exercised.

As of March 31, 1972, there were warrants outstanding to purchase approximately 29,000 shares of the Company's common stock at approximately $3.70 per share subject to investment letter restrictions. These warrants expired on May 17, 1972.

There were special options to purchase 20,600 shares of the Company's common stock at not less than $4.25 per share issued to employees of Photophysics, Inc. These options were all repurchased during the year ended March 31, 1972.

The Company has a sufficient number of authorized shares available to provide for the exercise of such options.

7. Other Income and Expense

The other income and expense in 1972 and 1971 were as follows:

	1972	1971
Interest income (Photophysics, Inc,)	$ 29,734	36,561
Gain on sale of common stock (Photophysics, Inc.)	60,000	–
Write down of microfiche equipment to realize value	(62,000)	–
Relocation and consolidation reserve	(65,000)	–
Gain on sale of fixed assets	–	17,038
Current year's operating expenses of discontinued Decision Matrix Publication	(80,406)	–
Miscellaneous other income	1,030	11,182
	$(116,642)	64,781

8. Income Taxes (Note 8)

Federal income taxes were reduced by realization of investment tax credit of $28,912 in 1972 and $2,800 in 1971.

The Company has consistently followed the flow-through method of accounting for investment tax credit.

In 1972 the provision for income tax is net of deferred tax benefits of $120,223 which are primarily caused by expensing for financial statement purposes only a $62,000 write down of equipment, a $65,000 provision for consolidation and relocation and the accrual of state income tax expense.

Such provisions for 1971 included net deferred taxes payable of $45,402 resulting from expensing research and development costs for tax purposes only which was partially offset by the accrual of state income tax expense.

9. Earnings (Loss) Per Share

Per share of common stock and common equivalent share data are based on the weighted average of common shares outstanding and common equivalent shares deemed to be outstanding during the periods presented. 125,000 shares of $1 par value cumulative convertible preferred stock has been considered to be the equivalent of common stock from the time of its issuance in 1969. The number of common equivalents also includes shares subject to stock options granted at a price less than the current fair market value of the Company's common stock. The increase in the number of common shares was reduced by the number of common shares which are assumed to have been purchased at the fair value or fair market value with the proceeds received upon the exercise of the options. The anti-dilutive effect of the common equivalent shares reduced the net loss by $.01 per share in 1971.

Per share of common stock assuming full dilution was determined as above and giving effect to the conversion of the remaining 202,000 shares of convertible perferred stock.

10. Commitments

The Company has entered into lease agreements for buildings and equipment which have total aggregate annual payments of approximately $165,000 decreasing in annual amounts to March 31, 1976.

The Company is the guarantor on a bank load to Photophysics, Inc. secured by a portion of their equipment. The loan balance at March 31, 1972 was $41,688.

sources. Eastman Kodak, a major competitor for sales of photoglass products, was also Drexler's major supplier of high resolution photographic plates. Approximately half of Drexler's major customers were located outside the San Francisco Bay Area. Competitors located in these other regions enjoyed a substantial advantage in competing for the business of these customers.

In order to stay competitive Drexler needed continually to evaluate new technologies. These included diazo photomasking, projection printing of photomasks, and silicon transparent photomasking, all of which held the potential for new products which may have rendered Drexler's products obsolete.

According to Merrill Lynch, Pierce, Fenner & Smith, sales of electronic-component products were expected to continue growth. These sales were led by integrated circuit sales which were expected to rise more than 15 per cent in 1972. The following quote is from the Merrill Lynch Aerospace and Electronics research discussion 19, May 12, 1972:

> Electronic-component sales—an important indicator of electronic-product sales—declined in 1971 to $4.6 billion compared with $4.8 billion in 1970. Although component sales rose in the second half of 1971, increases over year-earlier levels did not begin until the fourth quarter and were not sufficient to offset the declines registered in the previous three quarters.
>
> Semiconductor sales declined by about 5% in 1971 to $1.17 billion compared with $1.23 billion in 1970. We estimate that total U.S. factory sales of semiconductors will rise by 10% or more to $1.3 billion in 1972. The resumed growth of electronic-components sales is being led by integrated-circuit sales, which rose modestly in 1971; and we estimate that they could rise more than 15% in 1972 to $510 million vs. $443 million in 1971. The integrated-circuit-sales increase in 1971 largely reflected sharp gains reported for MOS * sales, which rose more than 60% to about $100 million vs. $61 million in 1970. For 1972, we estimate that MOS sales will rise about 25%. Some estimates for MOS sales in 1972 range as high as 40%. We believe, however, that the expected slowdown in the growth of custom MOS chips for calculators—the largest current market for MOS chips—will not be offset as rapidly as expected by increases in the use of MOS chips for other electronic functions, particularly the computer-memory market.

Since Drexler was incorporated to purchase and hold small, high technology companies, many other markets for both component parts and/or end user products were available. A few of those potential markets appeared to be:

- Microfiche Information Retrieval Equipment
- Photo-Optical Instruments
- Special Purpose Light Sources

* MOS—metal oxide silicon. In early 1972 there were two types of integrated circuits, both used for memory and logic circuits, MOS and bipolar. Generally speaking, MOS integrated circuits are slower than the bipolar and, therefore, are more heavily used in equipment where milliseconds do not matter, such as calculators.

- Microwave Devices
- Micropublications
- Calculators
- Minicomputers
- Photographic Equipment
- Educational Games
- Educational Devices

THE PROBLEM FACING DREXLER

A year prior to June 1972, the Directors and senior officers of the company had decided that if Drexler Technology was to realize dynamic growth it would have to move into end user products rather than just stay in the photomask business. But that decision had been made when the semiconductor industry had been somewhat depressed and no one realized just how much growth was available to Drexler Technology in the photomask business. Jerry Drexler knew that during the past twelve months Drexler Technology had grown by 50 per cent and that it seemed almost certain that it would experience another 35 to 40 per cent growth in the next twelve months.

Several facts came to mind as Jerry considered the problem. Jerry was free from the operating routine and had the time to devote to the future direction of the company. In order for a small company to grow it had to have acceptance in the financial community and the fact was that photomasks had not been a glamorous business and it was easier to raise money for companies making end user products. The market for photomasks and related materials was ultimately limited. Drexler could not become a $50,000,000 company by staying solely in this business. The calling in of 320,000 shares of convertible preferred stock would remove all the outstanding "junior debt" and put the company in a better position to raise capital for further development.

If a diversification program was to be considered, Jerry recognized the need for more effective marketing. Drexler had more than enough ability in the area of new product development; however, it did not have the marketing ability or distribution channels necessary to market successfully an end user product. To build up such a capability internally would take a disproportionate amount of time and, therefore, Jerry felt the most effective answer was to acquire a company which already had adequate marketing capability, probably a company with a weak or mature product which could use additional products.

In the short run it appeared that Drexler should look into its present market, develop better service, and add other products for use by the semiconductor industry. The immediate growth potential was there. But top management and Directors were anxious to identify specific opportunities for additional markets for component parts and for end user products. Long run growth seemed to point toward such diversification; however, diversification should be into a market which offered growth at least equal to that already available to Drexler or else it would be hard to justify putting time and resources into it. Jerry felt that the present business could be at the $10,000,000 level within two to three years and, as a ball park figure, the total sales of any new businesses should be able to equal that if they were worth entering.

Succinctly, should Drexler put its time and resources into diversification or should the company put more effort into increasing its share of the market for its present products? There would not be enough resources available to do both. If the latter option is selected, than the prior one could be reconsidered in a year or so. But if the prior option is selected, then several other questions immediately appear:

What kind of business opportunities should they consider? To what extent should they consider a lucrative business opportunity that could distort the image and possibly lower the P/E of Drexler Technology? How large a sales goal should be set for end user products versus present products? Given built-in growth of Drexler over the next two years, should Drexler give up its shares to acquire a new business or should it borrow capital and acquire companies for cash?

What should Drexler's strategy be with respect to growth? Should the company attempt to become high specialized, emphasizing computer and information technology industry? Should the company concentrate its efforts on the application of new technology (developed by others such as IBM) to specific needs in the market place? Should the company attempt to develop a broad line of products which will develop sufficient sales volume to justify the establishment of a nation-wide sales and service organization? If so, what products should be considered?

CASE 16

Heublein, Inc.*

Charles W. Hofer

With growth in sales and profits since 1959 far outstripping the liquor industry's "Big Four," Heublein, Inc., producer of Smirnoff vodka and other liquor and food items, had moved up to become the fifth largest liquor company in the United States by 1965. (See Exhibit 1 and 2 for Heublein financial statistics.)

TABLE 1 †

Industry Rank in 1965	Company	1964 Liquor Sales (Millions)	1965 Total Sales (Millions)	Total Sales Gain 1959–1965 (Per Cent)	Profit Gain 1959–1965 (Per Cent)
1	Distillers Corporation	$718	$1,005	37	52
2	Hiram Walker	498	530	28	46
3	National Distillers	430	829	44	24
4	Schenley Industries (est.)	390	461	0	33
5	Heublein, Inc.	123	166	89	259

† Derived from various company annual reports.

Mr. Hart, Heublein's president since 1960 and a former executive vice president of international marketing for the Colgate-Palmolive Company, commented on the company's business as follows:

> Although liquor products account for most of our sales at the present time, we consider ourselves in the consumer goods business, not the liquor business. Liquor is a consumer good just like toothpaste and is sold the same way.
>
> To be successful in this business, you need three things: a good product, distribution, and advertising. You must have a good product. If you don't, the consumer will find you out and you will not get any repeat purchases. You also need good distribution so the consumer will be able to get your product easily and conveniently. Finally, you must have a good convincing story to tell the consumer about why he should buy your product and you tell it through advertising.

EXHIBIT 1

HUEBLEIN, INC. (A & B) (Condensed)

Consolidated Balance Sheets as of June 30

(dollars in thousands)

ASSETS	*1955*	*1960*	*1963*	*1964*	*1965*
Current assets:					
Cash	$ 2,298	$ 3,925	$ 2,744	$ 3,357	$ 3,338
Time deposits	–	–	6,000	1,750	–
Marketable securities	9	4,883	1,000	–	4,048
Investment in whiskey certificates	–	593	1,069	150	–
Accounts and notes receivable	5,157	12,426	17,835	18,668	19,010
Inventories	5,825	8,269	9,127	13,347	16,323
Prepaid expenses	297	382	356	325	548
Total current assets	$13,586	$30,479	$38,130	$37,597	$43,267
Long-term assets:					
Property, plant and equipment—net	$ 3,254	$ 5,793	$ 6,363	$ 7,339	$ 7,502
Deferred charges, other assets and goodwill	223	416	1,068	3,659	5,383
Total long-term assets	$ 3,477	$ 6,209	$ 7,431	$10,998	$12,885
Total assets	$17,063	$36,688	$45,561	$48,595	$56,152

LIABILITIES AND STOCKHOLDERS' EQUITY	*1955*	*1960*	*1963*	*1964*	*1965*
Current liabilities:					
Notes payable to banks	$ 2,000	–	–	–	–
Accounts payable	687	$ 1,933	$ 2,078	$ 2,417	$ 3,584
Federal income tax	531	2,857	3,607	4,129	4,701
Accrued liabilities	513	2,688	4,044	5,175	5,774
Cash dividends payable	98	299	733	721	986
Long-term debt due within one year	301	631	777	850	1,013
Total current liabilities	$ 4,129	$ 8,408	$11,239	$13,292	$16,059
Long-term liabilities:					
Long-term debt due after one year	$ 4,699	$ 5,388	$ 3,239	$ 2,416	$ 1,403
Deferred federal income tax	–	–	154	248	316
Minority interest	–	–	–	272	–
Total long-term liabilities	$ 4,699	$ 5,388	$ 3,393	$ 2,936	$ 1,719
Stockholders' equity	$ 8,235	$22,892	$30,929	$32,368	$38,374
Total liabilities and stockholders' equity	$17,063	$36,688	$45,561	$48,595	$56,152

Source: Heublein records.

In 1965, Heublein's management had three long-range goals: (1) to make Smirnoff the number one liquor brand in the world; (2) to continue a sales growth of 10% a year through internal growth, acquisitions, or both; and (3) to maintain Heublein's return on equity above 15%.

As one means of meeting these goals, a major specific acquisition oppor-

EXHIBIT 2

HEUBLEIN, INC. (A & B) (Condensed)

Consolidated Statement of Income for Year Ending June 30
(dollars in thousands)

	1955	1956	1957	1958	1959	1960	1961	1962	1963	1964	1965
Net sales	$37,222	$68,543	$82,064	$87,839	$87,647	$103,169	$108,281	$116,142	$121,995	$135,848	$165,595
Cost of sales	29,503	53,219	63,234	67,231	67,276	78,028	80,419	85,793	89,500	99,575	121,503
	$ 7,719	$15,325	$18,830	$20,608	$20,372	$ 25,140	$ 27,862	$ 30,349	$ 32,495	$ 36,273	$ 44,092
Expenses:											
Selling and advertising	$ 4,650	$ 8,013	$10,617	$12,613	$12,710	$ 14,276	$ 16,089	$ 16,444	$ 18,271	$ 20,477	$ 24,551
Administrative and general	1,479	2,288	2,699	2,822	2,561	2,783	3,205	4,111	3,710	3,485	4,257
	6,130	10,301	13,315	15,434	15,271	17,060	19,293	20,555	21,981	23,962	28,808
	1,590	5,024	5,515	5,176	5,100	8,080	8,569	9,794	10,514	12,312	15,284
Other†	189	316	407	519	638	293	168	199	(339)	(18)	(112)
	1,401	4,708	5,109	4,654	4,462	7,788	8,401	9,595	10,852	12,330	15,397
State and federal income taxes	733	2,531	2,697	2,524	2,399	4,232	4,587	5,188	5,830	6,516	8,021
Net income	$ 667	$ 2,177	$ 2,411	$ 2,130	$ 2,063	$ 3,556	$ 3,814	$ 4,407	$ 5,022	$ 5,814	$ 7,376

*Cost of sales includes federal excise taxes on the withdrawal of distilled spirits from bond. For the fiscal year 1965, these totalled $90 million.

†Interest income, interest expanse, and miscellaneous.

Source: Heublein records.

tunity was being considered in the fall of 1965. The potential acquisition (Hamm's Brewing Company) raised a number of short-term as well as strategic issues, however, which Mr. Hart wanted to consider carefully. Hamm's was almost as large as Heublein in sales, and therefore the impact of the acquisition on Heublein was certain to be significant. The beer and liquor industries were in many respects similar, but Heublein had had no direct experience in the beer industry. Mr. Hart emphasized that the kinds of companies being sought were not just profitable financial deals, but rather firms in which Heublein's management believed it could improve operations. Heublein's acquisition policies had been explained more fully by Mr. Hart in a 1965 presentation before the Los Angeles Society of Security Analysts:

> Frankly; we take a long hard look at any potential acquisition. We ask ourselves: "Will the new product or company we acquire have a potential at least equal to existing Heublein products, in order not to dilute present equity? Will new products lend themselves to our channels of distribution and marketing techniques? Will these products have sufficient gross margin to allow for our type of distribution, advertising, and merchandising?"

The question of the potential of Hamm's acquisition will be explored in more detail following a description of Heublein's current position, strategy, and the trends in their basic markets.

Market

Between 1955 and 1964, U.S. consumption of distilled spirits [1] increased from 199 million wine gallons to 277 million, or 39% (see Exhibit 3). By the latter year, some 60 million Americans—about 53% of the adult population—drank some sort of alcoholic beverage. These Americans spent $6.5 billion for liquor, about one-third of the amount spent for public elementary and secondary school education. Excise taxes [2] on these sales provided the Federal Government with about $2.5 billion in 1964, more than any other single source of revenue except for personal and corporate income taxes.

Rising sales of liquor could be attributed to various causes, including a rising population, increased personal discretionary income contributing to a slightly higher per capita consumption; changing social mores; the declining proportion of people in "dry" states; and changes in the population make-up by age group. Mr. Edward Kelley, Heublein's executive vice president, felt

[1] Several terms in common use in the industry require definition:

Proof is a term used to specify the proportion of alcohol in a product. The proof number is equal to twice the percent of alcohol (by volume) in the product.

A *proof gallon* is any volume which contains the same amount of alcohol as a gallon of 100 proof spirits.

A *wine gallon* is a gallon by volume (regardless of proof). Thus a gallon (five fifths) of 80 proof vodka would be one wine gallon but only 8⁄10 proof gallons.

[2] The federal excise tax on distilled spirits was $10.50 per proof gallon in 1965.

the growth in liquor consumption between 1955 and 1964 was primarily the result of the increase in per capita consumption, which appeared to be related to the growth in personal discretionary income, and the spread of drinking to more segments of the population and on more occasions, resulting from the trends of social living habits.

Predicting the future in relation to income and demographic changes, industry sources looked forward to an even faster growth in consumption from 1965 to 1970 than from 1955 to 1964: 4.5% or more a year, compared with 3.6%. Since the Bureau of the Census forecast that the 25 to 54 age groups would increase an average of nearly 17% between 1970 and 1980, many industry observers felt the picture beyond 1970 looked better than that between 1965 and 1970.

Market Changes

Demand for the various categories of liquor was changing as well as growing between 1955 and 1964 (see Exhibits 3, 4, and 5). Thus there was a dramatic shift in consumer preference to straight whiskeys, imported whiskeys and the nonwhiskeys, and away from the blended and bonded whiskeys. While some

EXHIBIT 3

HEUBLEIN, INC. (A & B) (Condensed)

Liquor—Consumption vs. Population

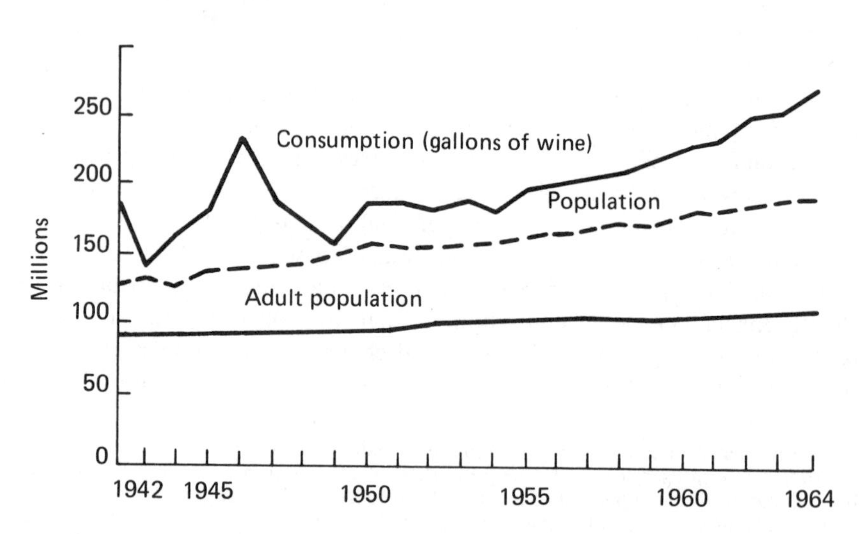

Source: Garvin Jobson Associates, Inc., *The Liquor Handbook, 1965;* cited by Glore Forgan, Wm. R. Staats Inc., in *Heublein, Inc.,* December 1965.

EXHIBIT 4

HEUBLEIN, INC. (A & B) (Condensed)
Whiskey Consumption Trend, 1955-1964
(expressed as a three-year moving average)

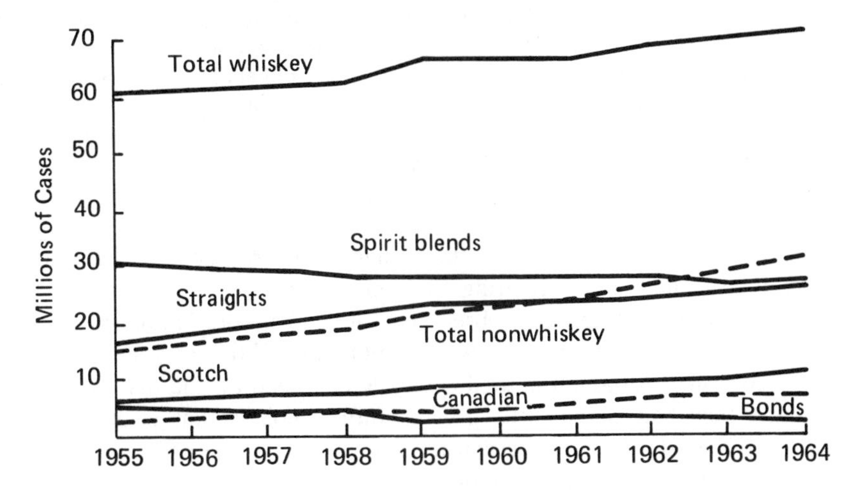

EXHIBIT 5

HEUBLEIN, INC. (A & B) (Condensed)
Nonwhiskey Consumption Trend, 1955-1964
(expressed as a three-year moving average)

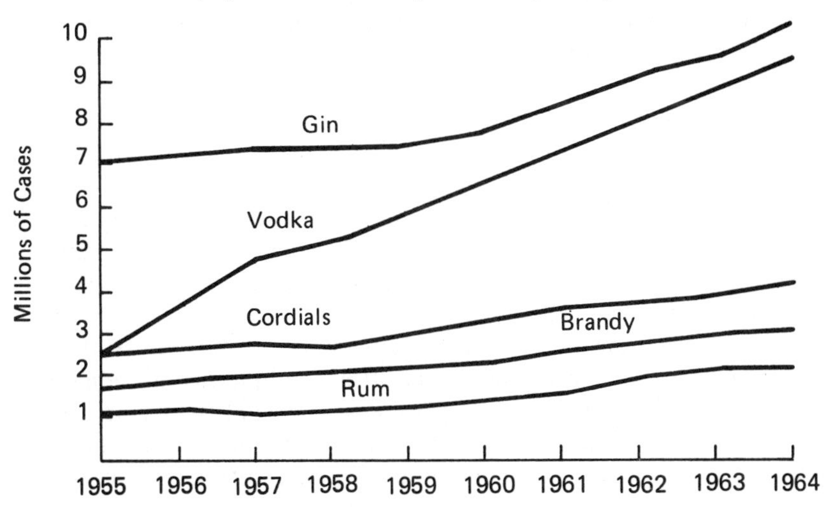

Source: Gavin Jobson Associates, *The Liquor Handbook*, 1965; cited by Glore Forgan, Wm. R. Staats Inc, in *Heublein, Inc.*, December 1965.

observers felt this represented a return to the pre-World War II relationship which provided straight whiskeys with a slight edge over blended whiskeys, most industry sources felt the shift in consumption reflected a trend toward lightness in liquor taste. According to Roger Bensen:

> The most probable reason [for the trend toward lightness] is that people drink mainly to satisfy social and status needs and for effect and not inherently for taste. The taste of many liquors is something which new drinkers find difficult to assimilate. Hence, they turn to various cocktails or mixed drinks to disguise the original flavor of the liquor product. And to complete the pattern, people achieve further fulfillment of social and status needs by using the newer, more current, more exotic liquors and cocktail formulations as a vehicle for their drinking.[3]

Some of the most important of these changes are reflected in the following figures for distilled spirits entering trade channels:

According to many industry observers, one of the more important developments in the liquor industry between 1960 and 1965 was the growth of bottled cocktails. Although bottled cocktails had been on the market for over 50 years, they had shown little growth until 1960. In that year, Heublein, which had almost 100% of the market at that time, developed a new product formulation, package, and promotional campaign for its line of bottled cocktails. By 1965, volume had increased 100% to an estimated 1.9 million wine gallons, as Distillers Corporation, Hiram Walker, Schenley, and others entered the market. Nevertheless, Heublein, whose volume increased 60% during the period, still had 55% of the market in 1965. The convenience, low consumer price (only a few pennies more than comparable drinks mixed at home), and trend toward lightness caused one liquor authority to predict that bottled cocktails might represent close to 10% of the industry's volume by 1975.

Trends in Competition

Between 1955 and 1965, the majority of the companies in the liquor industry followed one of two broad strategies. Most of the medium-sized companies aggressively marketed their products in traditional ways. They did not increase, decrease, or change their product line, nor did they attempt to diversify out of the liquor business. None of these companies had a complete line of liquor products, and some had only one or two products. Several of these companies, however, experienced extremely rapid growth during this period. Their success could generally be attributed to having a leading product in one or two of the more rapidly growing segments of the liquor market.

The four major distillers also marketed their products in traditional ways. However, with the exception of Hiram Walker, each of these companies attempted to diversify out of the liquor industry through acquisitions between

[3] Roger Bensen, *Heublein, Inc.*, Investment Research Dept., Glore Forgan, Wm. R. Staats Inc., December 1965, p. 21.

TABLE 2

PRODUCT TYPE	VOLUME 1955 (MILLIONS OF WINE GALLONS)	VOLUME 1964 (MILLIONS OF WINE GALLONS)	MARKET SHARE 1955 (PER CENT)	MARKET SHARE 1964 (PER CENT)	CHANGE IN VOL. 1955 TO 1964 (PER CENT)
Whiskeys					
Bonded	12.9	7.9	6.3	2.8	(39)
Straight	46.1	69.6	22.7	24.3	51
Blend	81.5	74.7	40.0	26.1	(8)
Scotch	12.3	28.3	6.0	9.9	130
Canadian	9.2	17.2	4.5	6.0	87
Total all whiskey	161.5	197.9	79.5	69.1	22
Nonwhiskeys					
Gin *	20.7	31.1	10.2	10.9	50
Vodka *	7.0	28.1	3.4	9.8	302
Rum	2.7	5.9	1.3	2.1	119
Brandy	4.6	8.7	2.3	3.0	89
Other	6.6	14.6	3.3	5.1	121
Total nonwhiskeys	41.8	88.4	20.5	30.9	111
Total distilled spirits	203.3	286.3	100.0	100.0	41

* Gin and vodka were unique among the distilled spirits since they required no aging. The principal distinction between gin and vodka was that the juniper berry flavor was added to grain neutral spirits to produce the former, while as many flavor-producing ingredients as possible were filtered out from grain neutral spirits to produce the latter.

1955 and 1965. Even with this diversification, however, liquor accounted for the major portion of the sales of each of these companies in 1965. Moreover, with the possible exception of National Distillers, the major distillers no longer seemed to be interested in further diversification outside of the liquor business in the middle 1960s. Rather they began to compete more vigorously in all segments of the liquor market during 1964 and 1965, particularly the more rapidly growing segments. This increased competition, coupled with the trend toward lightness, caused John Shaw of Equity Research Associates to predict that:

> Marketing efforts will become more consumer-oriented, stressing "appetite appeal" in much the same way as the food industry. Over all, advertising and promotional costs can be expected to trend higher, as brand competition remains intense.[4]

Thumbnail sketches of a few of the companies that have grown rapidly or that competed directly with Heublein are given below.

[4] John Shaw, "Trends in the Liquor Industry," *Equity Research Associates,* August 30, 1965, p. 6.

James B. Beam Distilling Company was a medium-sized liquor company that specialized in the production and marketing of premium Kentucky straight bourbon whiskey. Nearly 80% of Beam's $92 million sales in 1965 were derived from its Jim Beam brand, which was the second largest selling straight bourbon whiskey in the country. As a result of the expansion of the straight whiskey market, Beam was able to increase its profits by over 20% per year between 1953 and 1965.

Paddington Corporation [5] was the exclusive importer of J & B Rare Scotch whiskey, the number two brand of Scotch in 1964. Although J & B was Paddington's only product, the company sales and earnings growth were the highest in the industry between 1960 and 1964. In the latter year, Paddington earned 37.5% on its stockholders' equity, and gross sales reached over $125 million.

Distillers Corporation-Seagram's, Ltd., a Canadian-based corporation, was the largest worldwide producer and marketer of distilled spirits in 1965. Although 80% of Seagram's $897 million in 1964 gross sales came from whiskeys, the company also had a complete line of the nonwhiskeys. The breadth of its product line allowed Seagram's to take advantage of changing consumer preferences. Seagram's VO, for example, was the major recipient of the growing demand for Canadian whiskey. However, the company also changed old products or introduced new products in response to changing consumer preferences. When sales of Calvert Reserve had declined for over seven consecutive years, Seagram's replaced it with a restyled "soft whiskey," Calvert Extra, in the spring of 1963, and experienced an immediate sales gain of over 17%. In 1964, Seagram's withdrew Lord Calvert, a premium blended whiskey, and replaced it with Canadian Lord Calvert, a moderately priced Canadian whiskey bottled in the United States, to take advantage of the trend toward bulk imports. In addition, Seagram's introduced nine new liquor products between 1961 and 1964 to capitalize on the trend toward lightness. Among these were two Scotches (100 Pipers and Passport) and four liqueurs as well as a gin, a vodka, the first Hawaiian rum, and a line of Calvert bottled cocktails.

Schenley, the fourth largest liquor company in 1964 with gross sales of $406 million, had one of the lowest growth rates in the liquor industry between 1955 and 1964. The company's gross sales decreased about 3% during that period, even though Schenley had three of the top ten straight whiskey brands and had made several nonliquor acquisitions. However, in 1964, Schenley acquired Buckingham, the importer of Cutty Sark, the number one brand of Scotch, and introduced a line of bottled cocktails. As a result

[5] Paddington Corporation was acquired by Ligget & Myers Tobacco Company in April 1966. L & M also acquired Star Industries, a wholesale liquor distributor, liquor importer, and owner of 40% of Paddington's voting securities, at the same time. In 1964, Star's net sales (sales less federal and state excise taxes) were $82 million. During the same year, L & M had net sales of $293 million and total assets of $401 million.

of these actions, several industry observers were predicting a turn around at Schenley by 1967.

Methods of Distribution

Distribution of liquor took two basic forms at the beginning of 1966. In 18 "control states," a state-regulated agency was responsible for the distribution and sale of distilled spirits. In these states, the marketer usually sold the product to the state agency at the national wholesaler price and allowed the state to distribute the products as it saw fit. These states often had laws which restricted the type of point-of-promotion advertising that a company could undertake. In the other 32 states, called "open states," distribution was accomplished through wholesalers who redistributed the product to the retailers who sold the product to the ultimate consumer. From 1958 to 1964, the number of these independent wholesalers declined almost 43%, so there were only 2,305 wholesalers left in 1964 who were licensed by the Federal Alcohol Administration to deal in distilled spirits. This trend, which was similar to that in other consumer-product industries, was primarily caused, according to industry observers, by a serious profit squeeze on the wholesaler as his costs of operation increased while the retail prices of inexpensive liquors declined because of intense competition—a situation which was aggravated by the spread of private labels. While distillers had not felt the effects of this squeeze by 1964, there was a feeling among some industry observers that distillers might have to lower their prices to wholesalers or lose lower volume lines if the trend continued.

Cost Structure

The cost of producing liquor products, excluding federal and state taxes on the raw materials, was relatively low compared to the retail selling prices. For example, high-quality vodka reportedly cost about 61 cents a fifth to produce, and retailed at $5.75. Federal taxes on raw materials, were often not much different for high-priced and low-priced liquors, even though they were often made by different processes. The different methods of production resulted in differences in taste and quality between the high-priced and low-priced liquors, however.

HEUBLEIN'S HISTORY

The House of Heublein was founded in 1859 in Hartford, Connecticut, by Andrew Heublein, a painter and weaver by trade. At that time, the House of Heublein was a combination restaurant, cafe, and small hotel. By 1875, Andrew's two sons, Gilbert and Lewis, were running the business. They branched out by conducting a wholesale wine business in addition to expanding the original operations. In 1892, through a combination of fortuitous circumstances, Heublein invented the bottled cocktail. From this time until the start of national prohibition, Heublein's principal business was the production and sale of distilled spirits.

In 1907, Heublein began importing Brand's A-1 steak sauce and later, when World War I disrupted the importation, acquired the manufacturing rights to the product in the United States. When prohibition forced Heublein to close down its liquor plant in 1920, the company transferred key personnel to food operations. Until the repeal of prohibition in 1933, A-1 steak sauce was Heublein's principal product.

In 1939, John Martin, Heublein's president and one of the company's principal stockholders, acquired the rights to Smirnoff vodka from Mr. Rudolph Kunett. Although Heublein sold only 6,000 cases of Smirnoff that year, a carefully planned promotional campaign, which was put into operation immediately after World War II, aided in boosting the sales of Smirnoff to over one million cases per year by 1954. As the vodka market expanded, Heublein introduced Relska vodka in 1953 and Popov in 1961 to have entries in the middle- and low-price segments of the market.

Although Smirnoff's remained Heublein's principal product from 1959, when it accounted for over 67% of sales, to 1965, when it accounted for 51% of sales, Heublein began to diversify its product line and to expand its international operations in the former year.

Heublein used both internal growth and acquisitions to broaden its product line. In 1960, Heublein began a campaign to increase the sales of its bottled cocktails by introducing new kinds of cocktails and promoting the entire line more heavily. As Heublein's sales began to increase, other distillers, principally Distillers Corporation, began to market their own cocktails. By 1965, bottled cocktails sales exceeded 850,000 cases a year, more than double the 1960 sales. At that time, Heublein still claimed 55% of the market.

In 1961, Heublein made two acquisitions which strengthened its specialty food line. Timely Brands, which manufactured and marketed a complete line of ready-to-use, home dessert decorating products including Cake-Mate icing and gels, was acquired in June. In July, Heublein acquired Escoffier, Ltd. of London, England, makers of 23 famed gourmet sauces and specialties.

Heublein made two more acquisitions during this period, both of which were designed to broaden and strengthen Heublein's liquor line. In April 1964, Heublein acquired Arrow Liquors Corporation for an estimated cost of $5.7 million. Arrow's principal products were its line of cordials, including Arrow Peppermint Schnapps, Arrow Blackberry Brandy, and its domestically bottled, bulk-imported Scotch, McMaster's. According to Mr. Edward Kelley, the three principal reasons for the Arrow acquisition were that Heublein expected the cordial and Scotch markets to grow in the future, that Arrow had products that were among the leaders in these markets in the control states, and that Arrow had a small but extremely competent management.

In January 1965, Heublein acquired Vintage Wines for approximately $2.2 million. Vintage, whose sales were about $4 at the time of the acquisition, was integrated with the Heublein Liquor Division. Vintage's principal product was Lancers Vin Rose, and imported Portuguese wine that accounted for about 50% of the company's sales.

The expansion which occurred in Heublein's international operations consisted primarily of the establishment of franchise operations in 21 additional foreign countries. This raised the number of such operations from 11 in 1959 to 32 in 1965.

HEUBLEIN'S RECENT OPERATIONS

Financial Situation

During the 1965 fiscal year, Heublein earned $7.4 million on sales of $166 million, which represented about a 19% return on stockholders' equity. Between 1959 and 1965, Heublein's sales growth, profit growth, and return on equity far exceeded the average of the four major distillers (see Table 1). In addition, even though Heublein was spending nearly twice as much (as a percentage of sales) on advertising as the average of the four major distillers, and had increased the company's dividend payout ratio to 50% of earnings, the company had a cash flow of $8.6 million in 1965, about 22% on equity, which compared favorably to the 9% average of the four major distillers.

Product Line

At the end of 1965, Heublein was marketing well over 50 products through its four divisions. While vodka was the company's principal product, accounting for 62% of 1965 sales, the company's product base had been broadened considerably since 1960 by acquisitions, internal growth, and new marketing agreements (see Exhibit 6 for sales mix trends). Heublein's product-line strategy was to market high-quality consumer products which provided the high margins necessary to support intensive advertising. Heublein aimed its promotions of these products at the growing, prosperous, young adult market. The company was also interested in phasing out some of its less profitable lines whenever possible.

The liquor products division accounted for over 80% of Heublein's 1965 sales. Its principal product was Smirnoff vodka, the fourth largest selling liquor brand in the United States in 1965, with estimated annual sales of 2.3 million cases. Company officials expected that Smirnoff, with its faster rate of growth would move ahead of the third place brand (Canadian Club: 2.4 million cases) and second place brand (Seagram's VO: 2.5 million cases) within three years.

In 1965, Smirnoff had 23% of the total vodka market and outsold the second place vodka brand by over four to one. In addition, Smirnoff was the

EXHIBIT 6

HEUBLEIN, INC. (A & B) (Condensed)

Heublein Sales Mix for Selected Years

	Smirnoff vodka	*Other vodka*	*Total vodka*	*Other alcoholic beverages*	*Food*	*Total*
1965	51%	11%	62%	30%	8%	100%
1964	58	12	70	21	9	100
1963	62	12	74	16	10	100
1962	63	11	74	16	10	100
1961	64	11	75	19	6	100
1960	67	9	76	18	6	100
1955	61	2	63	32	5	100
1950	27	–	27	63	10	100

Source: Heublein records.

only premium-priced vodka on the market in 1965, since Wolfschmidt, formerly another premium-priced vodka, had lowered its wholesale price in 1964 in an effort to stimulate sales. After considering this action, Mr. Hart decided the appropriate response was to raise Smirnoff's wholesale price $1 per case and to put the additional revenue into advertising. Although Wolfschmidt's sales more than doubled, this increase appeared to come from the middle-priced segment of the vodka market, since Smirnoff's sales also increased 4% over the previous year and was running over 10% ahead in 1966. Smirnoff also appeared to be immune to the spread of the hundreds of private-label vodkas, since company officials felt that these products obtained their sales from the 15% to 30% of the vodka market that was price conscious.

As a result, many industry observers expected Smirnoff to dominate the vodka market well into the future, particularly since Smirnoff could, on the basis of its sales volume, afford to spend $7 to $8 million on advertising, while its closest rival could afford to spend only $2 million before putting the brand into the red.[6, 7]

Relska, a medium-priced vodka, and Popov, a low-priced vodka, were produced and sold primarily to give Heublein's distributors a full line of vodka products. They accounted for 11% of company sales in 1965. They

[6] Roger D. Bensen, *Heublein, Inc.*, Glore Forgan, Wm. R. Staats Inc., December 1965, p. 25.

[7] In 1963, according to the *Liquor Handbook*, Heublein spent $1.4 million to advertise Smirnoff, while total advertising for all other vodka brands during the same year was $1.2 million.

were cheaper to produce than Smirnoff but were not as smooth to the taste, according to company officials.

Heublein bottled cocktails sold an estimated 500,000 cases in 1965, about 55% of the bottled cocktail market. Nevertheless, Heublein was beginning to receive competition from the national distilling companies, particularly Distillers Corporation, whose U.S. subsidiary, Seagram's, was marketing a similar line. Mr. Hart, however, welcomed this competition. He commented to the Los Angeles Society of Security Analysts in 1965:

> We believe the idea of bottled cocktails has not been completely sold to the American public. We were therefore delighted when we learned that one of the major companies in the liquor industry was introducing a new line of cocktails and that there would be heavy expenditures in advertising and merchandising to promote their usage to the public.[8]
>
> We are of the opinion that, as the cocktail market expands, our share will decrease, but Heublein cocktails will continue to be the leader and that our cases will show remarkable increases.

Mr. Hart explained to the casewriter that distribution was one of the principal reasons Heublein would keep its number one position:

> We secured distribution in 1960 when the other companies weren't too interested in cocktails. Since a distributor will usually carry only two or three lines, this means that he will have Heublein and Calvert or Heublein and Schenley: in other words, Heublein and somebody else. . . . In addition to being first, Heublein's wide line will also help us get and maintain distribution.

In 1965, Heublein's bottled cocktail line included Manhattans, Vodka Sours, Extra Dry Martinis, Gin Sours, Whiskey Sours, Side Cars, Vodka Martinis, Daiquiris, Old Fashioneds, and Stingers.

During 1964, the liquor products division re-introduced Milshire gin. For years, Milshire had been a regional gin selling about 100,000 cases a year. However, in 1963 the promotional budget was deemed sufficient to devote some real attention to Milshire. To prepare for this, the old inventory was sold off, the product was reformulated, and the package was redesigned. The principal difference in the product was that its botanical and aromatic content was lowered since it was filtered through activated charcoal in a process similar to that used to make Smirnoff. The net effect of this was to make the gin "lighter." Sales for 1964 increased to 150,000 cases, a significant jump, but still very far behind the 2.1 million cases of Gordon's, the leading brand.

In 1966, Heublein reached an agreement with Tequila Cuervo S.A. to be the exclusive U.S. marketer of Jose Cuervo and Matador tequilas and a

[8] Heublein spent $2 million advertising its line of bottled cocktails in 1965. Seagram's spent $1.5 million advertising its Calvert line the same year.

cordial based on the same spirit. Heublein planned to market these products on a nationwide basis through the liquor products division.

The liquor products division also marketed Harvey's sherries, ports, and table wines; Bell's Scotches; Gibley's Canadian whiskeys; Byrrh aperitif wine ("Byrrh on the rocks, please"); and the products of Vintage Wines, Inc.

The Arrow division accounted for about 10% of Heublein's sales in 1965. The division's principal products were Arrow cordials, liqueurs, and brandies, and McMaster's Scotch. Arrow's distribution system was particularly strong in the control states. In addition, Arrow's distribution in the open states was strengthened in 1965, when Heublein discontinued the production of its line of Heublein cordials and substituted the Arrow line.

Although the sales of the food division more than doubled between 1961 and 1965, it accounted for only 8% of the company's 1965 sales. Nevertheless, A-1 steak sauce was the company's number two profit producer in 1965, second only to Smirnoff vodka. Other food products included Cake-Mate icings and gels, Escoffier sauces, Grey-Poupon Mustard, and Maltex and Maypo cereals. In 1965, Heublein reached an agreement with the Coastal Valley Canning Company of California to distribute and market Snap-E-Tom Tomato Cocktail. Snap-E-Tom was a tomato juice flavored with onion and chili pepper juices. It was designed for the pre-meal juice and the cocktail mixer markets, both of which had high profit margins.

Marketing

The casewriter felt that Heublein's unique advertising and promotion policies and campaigns set Heublein apart from the other liquor companies (see Exhibit 7 for the advertising expenditures of various liquor companies). Heublein considered liquor to be a branded consumer product, and viewed

EXHIBIT 7

HEUBLEIN, INC. (A & B) (Condensed)
Advertising Expenditures of Major Liquor Companies for 1965

Company	*Advertising (million)*	*Sales (million)*	*Advertising as a percent of sales*
Distillers Corp. Seagram's Ltd.	$43,750	$762,520	5.7%
Schenley Industries	23,100	380,200	6.1
National Distillers & Chemical Corp.	19,668	810,900	2.4
Hiram Walker-Gooderham & Worts, Ltd.	17,750	498,174	3.6
Heublein, Inc.	17,495	165,522	10.6

Source: *Advertising Age,* January 3, 1966, p. 46.

itself as a marketer of high-quality consumer products rather than as a liquor company. As a result, Heublein developed intensive advertising campaigns to sell its products for the growing, affluent young adult market, since it believed it was easier to get a new customer in this market than to get a 40-year-old Scotch drinker to switch to vodka. Because of the importance attached to advertising, Heublein spent 10.6% of sales for advertising in 1965, nearly double the 5.7% of Distillers Corporation.

In addition, Heublein was an aggressive innovator among liquor industry advertisers. In the 1950s, industry self-regulation prohibited depicting a woman in an advertisement for a liquor product. In 1958, Heublein advised the Distilled Spirits Institute that it believed this ban on the portrayal of women was "obselete, hopelessly prudish, and downright bad business." Finally, the DSI agreed, and Heublein became the first liquor company to portray women in its ads under the new DSI self-regulation, an advertising practice later followed by nearly every major distiller. Heublein also pioneered a change in DSI regulations to permit liquor advertising in Sunday supplements. At the end of 1965, Heublein was pushing for the use of liquor advertisements on radio and TV similar to beer and wine advertisements.

Another unique feature of Heublein's marketing was the promotions it used. These were designed to appeal to the young adult group and used celebrities and off-beat approaches to gain attention. An example of this approach was the Smirnoff Mule promotion launched in May 1965. The promotion, Heublein's largest for a single drink, was designed to catch the discotheque popularity on the upswing. The total investment was about $2.0 million for advertising, merchandising, and sales promotion. *The New York Times* commented that:

> Included in the Smirnoff advertising mix are a drink, called the Smirnoff Mule; a song and dance, called simply The Mule; a recording called Skitch Plays "The Mule"; a copper-colored metal mug in which to drink the Smirnoff Mule and a recent phenomenon called the discotheque . . . [Heublein's advertising agency] the Gumbinner-North Company has recruited such vodka salesmen as Skitch Henderson, Carmen McRae, and Killer Joe Piro to put it over. . . . In addition to Smirnoff ads, The Mule will be featured in local advertising by the 7-Up people.[9]

Distribution

Heublein sold its products directly to state liquor control boards in the 18 control states and approximately 235 wholesale distributors in the 32 open states and the District of Columbia. Food products were sold through food brokers and wholesalers. It was Heublein's policy to strive to create mutually

[9] Walter Carlson, "Advertising: Smirnoff Harnesses the Mule," *The New York Times*, June 27, 1965.

profitable relationships with its distributors. For example, one of the reasons for the creation of Popov vodka was to give Heublein's distributors a low-priced vodka brand to sell.

International Operations

At the end of 1965, Heublein was involved in three types of overseas activities. The largest and most important was its licensing operation. Distillers in 32 foreign countries were licensed to manufacture and market Smirnoff vodka. Among the countries in which Heublein had such franchises were Austria, Denmark, Greece, Ireland, New Zealand, South Africa, and Spain. When selecting a franchise holder, Heublein looked for a local distiller who had good production facilities and who was a good marketer in his country. Heublein felt this policy allowed them to get established faster than if Heublein tried to set up its own plant. Heublein also felt it improved relations with the local government.

Under these franchise agreements, the distiller produced the neutral spirits in the best way possible in his country. To maintain quality control, however, Heublein installed and owned the copper filtration units and shipped the charcoal to these locations from Hartford. This was done at cost. The contracts called for a license fee (about 10% of sales) and also stipulated that certain amounts be spent by the franchisee for advertising. Usually, during the first three or four years, Heublein would add its 10% license fee to these advertising funds in order to help build up the business. Plans were under way at the end of 1965 to begin operations in six more countries, including Ecuador, India, and Nigeria.

Heublein also exported Smirnoff, primarily to military bases overseas. In addition, Heublein opened an operation in Freeport, Jamaica, in 1965, to produce Smirnoff and other Heublein liquor products, and to market these products to customers such as ship's chandlers and diplomatic agencies who could purchase tax-free liquor.

Between 1961 and 1965, Heublein's export sales increased 99%, royalties from licenses 145% and profits from international operations 458%. In 1965, net export sales stood at $1.2 million and profits before taxes from international operations, including license fees, were $880,000.

Production

At the end of 1965, Heublein owned and operated three plants throughout the United States, with an annual capacity of 20.0 million wine gallons for all product lines, and was building a plant in Detroit to replace the old Arrow plant. This plant was to cost $4.5 million and to have an annual capacity of 5.5 million wine gallons. When completed, this plant would give Heublein a total annual capacity of 25.5 million wine gallons. All these plants were highly automated.

Heublein had about 975 employees in 1965, of whom slightly less than half were hourly employees. In 1965, labor costs were only 3% of the total cost of sales.

Heublein did not produce the grain neutral spirits for its gin and vodka production, but rather purchased these requirements on contract and the open market from four distillers. Heublein maintained facilities in the Midwest for the storage of 8.0 million proof gallons, however, in case none of these suppliers could meet Heublein's stringent quality requirements. At 1965 consumption rates, this represented about a one-year supply.

According to Heublein, even the high-quality grain neutral spirits it received from its suppliers contained too many impurities for direct use in Smirnoff. The first step in Smirnoff production was, therefore, to redistill these grain neutral spirits. At the end of the redistillation, the alcohol was 192 proof. It was then blended with distilled water to reduce the mixture to 80 proof. This mixture was then filtered slowly through 10 copper tanks which contained over 14,000 pounds of activated charcoal. The filtering process required eight hours. According to company officials, it was during this process that the vodka became smooth and mellow and acquired its mild, but distinctive taste. The only remaining step was to bottle the finished product, since vodka required no aging.

Heublein also redistilled the grain neutral spirits used in the production of its charcoal filtered Milshire gin. However, the company did not redistill the liquors (purchased on the open market) used in the production of Heublein cocktails.

Most of the food products were manufactured at Hartford or at the plant in Burlington, Vermont. Heublein insisted on the same high-quality standards in the purchase of raw materials and production of its food products that it required in its liquor production.

THE PROPOSED HAMM ACQUISITION

Early in the fall of 1965, Heublein's top management was seriously considering the possible acquisition of the Theo. Hamm Brewing Company. They were particularly interested because they felt Hamm's could profit immensely from what they felt was Heublein's major strength—the ability to market a consumer product extremely well. If the acquisition were consummated, Heublein would become the first company to engage in the production and sale of both beer and liquor.

Under the proposed agreement Heublein would acquire all of the outstanding shares of Hamm's common in exchange for 420,032 shares of Heublein's 5% preferred, and 200,031 shares of Heublein's 5% convertible preferred. Both preferreds had a par value of $100; the latter was convertible into three shares of Heublein common, subject to certain provisions against dilution of earnings. Although Hamm's stock was held by a family group and did not have a market price, Heublein's board estimated that the aggregate fair value was in excess of $62 million, or book value (see Exhibit 8). The proposed agreement stipulated that each class of preferred would have the right to elect one member to Heublein's board. In addition, it was provided that the $25 million of securities indicated on the Theo. Hamm Brewing Company consolidated balance sheet as of 9/30/65 would be liquidated and used to buy out dissident Hamm's stockholders prior to the acquisition

EXHIBIT 8

HEUBLEIN, INC. (A & B) (Condensed)

Theo. Hamm Brewing Company Consolidated Balance Sheets
(dollars in thousands)

	Nov. 30 1964	*Sept. 30 1965*
Current Assets		
Cash	$ 3,475	$ 3,153
Certificates of deposit	2,000	500
Commercial paper and marketable securities (at cost)*	26,560	24,044
Accounts receivable (net)	5,452	7,959
Inventories	5,352	6,479
Prepaid expenses	898	891
Total current assets	$43,737	$43,027
Investments and other assets	6,467	6,536
Property, plant, and equipment (net)	26,381	26,930
	$76,585	$76,493
Current Liabilities		
Trade accounts payable	$ 2,639	$ 2,926
Salaries and wages	1,207	1,304
Customers' deposits	932	1,151
Miscellaneous accounts payable and accrued expenses	470	1,301
Taxes other than taxes on income	2,038	2,299
Federal and state taxes on income	2,657	2,559
Dividends payable	1,538	660
Sinking fund deposits due in one year	100	100
Total current liabilities	$11,580	$12,302
Eight percent debenture bonds	1,400	1,400
Stockholders equity		
Capital stock	55,083	26,432
Capital surplus	–	26,273
Earned surplus	8,521	10,086
	$76,585	$76,493

*The market value of these securities was $28.1 million in 1964 and $25.7 million in 1965.
Source: Heublein Acquisition Study.

by Heublein. This would have the effect of reducing Hamm's working capital and stockholder equity before the purchase by about $25 million.

Hamm's History and Competitive Position

Hamm's was a family-owned brewing company. During the five years preceding the proposed acquisition, sales and profits had remained relatively stable (see Exhibits 9 and 10). However, since industry sales had increased slightly more than 11% during this period, Hamm's market share had declined from 4.5% to 3.7%. In addition, Hamm's return on sales had lagged behind the industry leaders (see Exhibits 11 and 12).

Hamm's sold three brands of beer at the end of 1965: Waldech (premium price), Hamm's (premium and popular price), and Buckhorn (lower price). The 1964 sales breakdown among these brands had been 17,800 barrels[10] for Waldech, 3,624,700 barrels for Hamm's, and 57,800 barrels for Buckhorn, for a total of 3,700,300 barrels. In addition, Hamm's had produced some beer for sale to F. & M. Schaefer Brewing Company under the Gunther brand in 1964.

In 1965, Hamm's beer was sold in 31 states and the District of Columbia. Most sales, however, were made in the midwestern, western, and southwestern parts of the United States. Hamm's relied exclusively on 479 independent wholesalers for its distribution, most of whom carried other brands of beer. Although any of these wholesalers could terminate his relationship with Hamm's at will, none of them accounted for more than 2.5% of Hamm's 1964 sales.

According to some industry observers, Hamm's four breweries were one of its principal assets. Three of these were owned outright, while the fourth was leased. The location and annual productive capacity of each of these plants was as follows:

LOCATION	ANNUAL PRODUCTIVE CAPACITY (BARRELS)
St. Paul, Minnesota	2,550,000
San Francisco, California	1,000,000
Los Angeles, California	500,000
Houston, Texas (leased)	450,000
	4,500,000

According to industry estimates, the cost of replacing Hamm's 1965 capacity would be about $135 million, or more than double the proposed purchase price. This estimate was based on the industry rule of thumb which set the

[10] A barrel was equivalent to 31 U.S. gallons.

EXHIBIT 9

HEUBLEIN, INC. (A & B) (Condensed)

Theo. Hamm Brewing Company Consolidated Statement of Income
(dollars in thousands)

	Years ended November 30					*(Unaudited) ten months ended September 30*	
	1960	*1961*	*1962*	*1963*	*1964*	*1964*	*1965§*
Revenues:							
Sales less allowances	$119,881	$115,874	$114,885	$119,584	$124,233	$106,109	$109,449
Interest	161	240	270	575	958	748	941
Dividends	81	62	50	51	61	58	42
Other	283	95	175	196	351	301	359
	$120,407	$116,272	$115,380	$120,405	$125,602	$107,217	$110,791
Costs and expenses:							
Cost of goods sold*	$ 89,843	$ 86,314	$ 86,595	$ 90,878	$ 95,388	$ 81,004	$ 84,597
Selling, delivery, advertising, general and administrative expenses	16,263	17,065	16,200	18,534	21,423	18,196	19,026
Interest:							
Long-term debt	235	164	120	120	120	100	100
Other	8	159	2	16	13	12	–
	$106,349	$103,702	$102,918	$109,548	$116,945	$ 99,312	$103,723
Earnings before taxes on income	$ 14,057	$ 12,570	$ 12,462	$ 10,857	$ 8,657	$ 7,905	$ 7,068

EXHIBIT 9 (continued)

Taxes on income:							
Federal	$ 6,750	$ 6,150	$ 6,100	$ 5,100	$ 3,900	$ 3,550	$ 3,000
State	450	400	400	275	300	275	522
	$ 7,200	$ 6,550	$ 6,550	$ 5,375	$ 4,200	$ 3,825	$ 3,225
Net earnings (excluding the operations of the Eastern division and related distributing subsidiaries)	$ 6,857	$ 6,020	$ 5,962	$ 5,482	$ 4,457	$ 4,080	$ 3,843
Loss on operations of Eastern division and related distributing subsidiaries less applicable income tax benefits†	1,092	1,717	2,124	1,408	–	–	–
Net earnings	$ 5,765	$ 4,303	$ 3,838	$ 4,074	$ 4,457	$ 4,080	$ 3,843
Preferred stock dividend requirements	210	210	210	210	210	175	142
Earnings applicable to common stock	$ 5,555	$ 4,093	$ 3,628	$ 3,864	$ 4,247	$ 3,905	$ 3,701
Per common share (dollars)							
Earnings applicable to							
Common stock‡	$2.14	$1.57	$1.40	$1.49	$1.63	$1.50	$1.40
Cash dividends declared	–	–	.40	.95	$1.25	.50	.75

*Cost of goods sold includes federal and state excise taxes of between $32 and $38 million for each of the above periods.

†In 1960, the company acquired brewing facilities in Baltimore, Maryland, which were sold in 1963 for $6 million, the approximate net carrying amount of the facilities. Applicable income tax benefits ranging between $1.2 and $2.1 million have been netted against loss on operations of Eastern division and related distributing subsidiaries for the years 1960–1963 inclusive.

‡Earnings applicable to common stock are based on the number of shares outstanding at the end of each period as adjusted for the recapitalization during the year ended November 30, 1961.

§Earnings for the 10 months ended September 30, 1965 were adversely affected by nonrecurring legal and centennial expenses aggregating approximately $400,000.

Source: Heublein Acquisition Study.

EXHIBIT 10

HEUBLEIN, INC. (A & B) (Condensed)

Heublein, Inc. and Theo. Hamm Brewing Company
Pro Forma Combined Statement of Income
(dollars in thousands)

Heublein *Hamm*	*June 30, 1960* *Nov. 30, 1960*	*June 30, 1961* *Nov. 30, 1961*	*June 30, 1962* *Nov. 30, 1962*	*June 30, 1963* *Nov. 30, 1963*	*June 30, 1964* *Nov. 30, 1964*	*Ten months to* *Sept. 30, 1965*
Net sales	$223,050	$224,156	$231,027	$241,579	$260,082	$249,056
Cost of sales	167,872	166,732	172,389	180,378	194,963	187,059
Selling, general and administrative expenses	33,323	36,359	36,755	40,515	45,385	43,164
Other income (deductions):						
Interest and dividend income	352	417	444	865	1,287	1,217
Interest expense	(560)	(595)	(363)	(344)	(342)	(215)
Miscellaneous — net	198	85	93	503	308	320
	(10)	(93)	174	1,024	1,253	1,322
Income before income taxes	21,845	20,972	22,057	21,710	20,987	20,155
Provision for income taxes	11,432	11,137	11,688	11,205	10,716	9,966
Net income before loss on discontinued operations of Hamm	10,413	9,835	10,369	10,505	10,271	10,189
Loss on discontinued operations of Hamm, less applicable income tax benefits	1,092	1,717	2,124	1,408	—	—
Net income	9,321	8,118	8,245	9,097	10,271	10,189

EXHIBIT 10 (continued)

Deduct pro forma adjustments						
Interest and dividend income	219	275	290	591	981	950
Interest expense	1,209	983	975	501	122	85
Income taxes	(738)	(638)	(652)	(549)	(496)	(418)
	690	620	613	543	607	617
Pro forma net income	8,631	7,498	7,632	8,554	9,664	9,572
Preferred dividend requirements:						
Heublein:						
5% preferred stock	2,100	2,100	2,100	2,100	2,100	1,750
5% convertible preferred stock	1,000	1,000	1,000	1,000	1,000	833
	3,100	3,100	3,100	3,100	3,100	2,583
Pro forma earnings applicable to common stock	$ 5,531	$ 4,398	$ 4,532	$ 5,454	$ 6,564	$ 6,989
Pro forma earnings per share (dollars):						
Assuming no conversion of convertible preferred stock	$1.15	$ .91	$ .93	$1.12	$1.37	$1.43
Assuming full conversion of convertible preferred stock	1.21	1.00	1.01	1.18	1.40	1.43
Actual Heublein earnings per share*	.74	.79	.91	1.03	1.21	1.30

*Heublein shares outstanding in June of 1965, 4.9 million; approximate market price/share in 1965 (to September) $26–$27.

Source: Heublein Acquisition Study.

EXHIBIT 11

HEUBLEIN, INC. (A & B) (Condensed)

Beer: Larger Markets, Tougher Competition*

> The bigger it gets, the rougher it gets. That sums up the brewing industry, which has just had its best year ever. But no one brewer had an easy time of it, and the competition will get even stiffer in the years ahead.
>
> by Kenneth Ford, Managing Editor

No one in the brewing industry had anything but kind words last week for the nation's growing number of young adults.

Not only were they quaffing their share of brew and more besides, but even more significant, they appeared willing to cast aside some old-fashioned concepts about beer being a "blue-collar" drink.

For the nation's 190 brewers (four fewer than the year before) the moral was that patience pays off. All during the long, dry decade of the Fifties the industry watched total consumption lag behind population growth and per capita consumption remain static at a low level. Brewers pinned their hopes on the vast crop of war babies of the Forties, hoping that when they reached drinking age they would set off a beer boom, but also fearing they might move from the innocence of Coke to the decadence of Martinis in one easy step.

They didn't. When the 1963 figures were totaled up at this time last year, there were clear signs that the brewing industry was on the move at last. No one outside the industry realized how fast it was moving until the 1964 totals came in last month.

The results: total sales (consumption) climbed to 98.5-million barrels, up five per cent from 1963s 93.8-million barrels. Per capita consumption, the more meaningful measure of marketing effectiveness, jumped to 15.7 gallons, up 2.6 per cent from 1963s 15.3 gallons. Both gains were the best year-to-year increase posted by the industry since 1947.

It is a certainty that the industry will cross the 100-million barrel barrier in 1965. The only question is whether it will reach 101-million or 102-million barrels. No one will be unhappy if it doesn't go that high—the industry's most optimistic forecasters hadn't expected it to reach the 100-million barrel level until 1967.

But though the over-all industry outlook is sudsy, neither leaders nor laggards are finding it easy selling.

Competition has never been fiercer. The nation's top 10 brewers have staked out 57.7 per cent share of the total market, selling 56.6-million barrels of that 98.5-million total. The next 14 ranking brewers take 25.4 per cent of the total, or 25-million barrels. All together, the top 24 brewers, each doing better than one-million barrels apiece, account for 82.9 per cent of total sales, some 81.6-million barrels.

But even what would be a normally respectable gain was not enough to hold the previous year's position, much less advance, in the top 24 standings.

Losses and gains

Carling dropped in 1964 from fourth to fifth; Hamm from seventh to eith; Rheingold from tenth to 11th; Lucky Lager from 13th to 16th; Pearl from 17th to 18th; Narragansett from 19th to 21st and Jackson from 23rd to 24th. Yet five had made sales gains—Carling's posted a 1.7 percent increase; Rheingold a 3.1 percent increase; Pearl a 5.4 percent increase; Narragansett a 2.8 percent increase; and Jackson a 2.2 percent increase.

The leading brewers had set such a blistering pace that merely running to keep up just wasn't fast enough.

First-place Anheuser-Busch (Budweiser Busch Bavarian-Michelob) achieved a 10.1 percent gain that carried it across the 10-million-barrel level, an industry record, and gave it a 10.5 percent share of the total market. A-B phenomenal performance was the culmination of

*Printer's Ink, February 12, 1965. Reproduced by permission.

EXHIBIT 11

HEUBLEIN, INC. (Continued)

Competition keen in East, too

Throughout the East, competition was similarly strong. Philadelphia-based Schmidt (Schmidt-Prior-Valley Forge) gained 13.3 percent, Baltimore-based National climbed 21.5 pereent, and Manhattan-based Ruppert, strong in New England, moved ahead 22.5 percent. Rochester-based Genessee (up 20.2 percent) cemented its already strong position in upstate New York.

One result of this fierce competition was increased ad budgets. With most brewers offering what economists call "poorly differentiated products" i.e., sameness—images were the most important function in marketing. Most brewers, in Printer's Ink's annual marketing survey, of course declined to give data on ad expenditures, though a few admitted increases ranging from 4 to 6 percent. However, the industry operates on a so-much-per-barrel basis in its ad budgeting. *Printer's Ink's* study of beer advertising expenditures (October 2, 1964, page 25) found the industry average was 96-cents a barrel for the four measured media. This would put total spending in a 98.5-million barrel year at $94.4-million in those media. This, however, is only about one-third of total expenditures. Big chunks of money go for "rights" to broadcast sports events, a staple of beer marketing. For instance, Schlitz, now building a new brewery in Texas, paid out $5.3-million for rights to the Houston Colts games.

"It's all part of becoming a new resident of the area," a Schlitz spokesman explained. "We want to get known fast and this is how you do it."

So important are sports sponsorship that they significantly influence marketing strategy. For example, Schmidt's bought the old Standard Beverage plant in Cleveland from Schaefer (which then bought the old Gunther plant in Baltimore from Hamm). Schmidt originally intended to use the Cleveland brewery to supply its markets in Western Pennsylvania and Western New York state and had no immediate intention of entering the northeastern Ohio market. But the opportunity arose to buy a participation in radio-sponsorship of the Cleveland Browns games. Schmidt's bought it and entered the market immediately.

Can U.S. compete aboard?

For the past few years, American brewers have enviously watched the success of imported European beers in the U.S. The European imports sell less than 1 percent of the total sold in the U.S. but their profit margins are far better than the domestic brewers achieve on a unit basis. Would the same not hold true for U.S. and Canadian beers overseas? It is also a way to rise above the cannibalistic competition in the U.S. The other way is to increase the beer consumption of the American drinker. Though 1964s 3.3 percent increase in per capita consumption was the best in recent years, the industry lags far behind the high of 18.7 gallons set in 1945 or even the post-war 18.4 gallons quaffed in 1947.

New products may help. Schlitz, Pabst and National are now strongly promoting malt liquor brands. A-B's Mechelob and Hamm's Waldech in the super-premium class are upgrading beer's image and adding a new group of customers.

But it is a packaging development that may be of the most far-reaching significance. This is the home keg or draft beer that fits neatly into the family refrigerator. In the consumption battle, beer's increase in share must come from soft drinks, coffee, tea, and such—not merely from population growth or competitors' customers.

In the decade ending in 1963, beer consumption increased only 12 percent while the population grew 19 percent. Soft drinks shot up 48 percent, soluble coffee 158, and tea 20 percent confirmed beer drinker guzzles about six quarts a week on a yearly averaged-out basis. That's about two and a half 12-ounce cans at a time.

What the industry must attract is the glass-at-a-time sipper. That's not much at a time, but there are an awful lot of them and enough sips by enough people can boost beer back near the 20 gallons per capita consumption level of pre-World War I days.

It will take a revolution in American beer-drinking patterns to do it, but it could happen.

EXHIBIT 11

HEUBLEIN, INC. (Continued)

marketing programs set in motion as long as a decade ago. Basically, these concentrated on development of marketing executives, achieving the best possible communication with its 900 wholesalers throughout the country and expanding plants into growing markets. (Its new Houston brewery will be ready next year.)

Though A-B is one of the heaviest advertisers in the industry, it makes only evolutionary changes in its advertising program from year to year. "Where There's Life There's Bud" (1963) became "That Bud, that's beer" (1964) and now becomes "It's Worth It, It's Budweiser" (1965).

Expansion-minded Schlitz, eyeing the heavier-beer-drinking Canadian market (per capita consumption 16.4 gallons) tried to migrate north by buying control of Canada's Labatt Brewing, but found itself ensnarled in anti-trust actions and other legal complications. The time and attention it had to devote to these were reflected in only a 5.3 percent gain, in contrast to 1963s 13 percent gain.

Another 11.6 percent gain like the one Pabst made last year might well knock Schlitz out of second-place. And fast-rising Falstaff is a factor that Schlitz and Pabst marketing executives both must reckon with in the year ahead.

Falstaff surprised everyone by clipping Carling out of fourth place in the breweing industry. Carling had made sixteen consecutive sales gains that brought it up from 19th in the industry and was generally conceded to be the brewer to watch. Controlled by Canadian entrepreneur E. P. Taylor, its marketing strategy is based on two rules: build plants where the markets are growing (it now has nine in the U.S.) and advertise heavily.

But it was Falstaff's ambition and innovation that carried it ahead. It markets only one brand of beer, Falstaff, in 32 states westward from Indiana. These states have 45 percent of the nation's population but consume less than 45 percent of total beer production.

A competitor to respect

"If we were in the other 18 states, we'd be selling 10.5-million barrels instead of 5.8-million," says George Holtman, vice president, advertising. Holtman's boast is not idle. That Falstaff is a competitor to respect is attested to by Hamm's decline of 2.5 percent. Both collided competitively in the Midwest generally and the Chicago market in particular. Falstaff began moving into Chicago three years ago and the 1964 figures reflect its arrival. Similarly, it began moving into the West Coast in recent years where traditional beer sales patterns are changing, too. Lucky Lager, long the leading West Coast brand, slumped 15.1 percent, dropping below the two-million barrel level under the impact of competition from Falstaff and other interloping brewers. Among them: the Schlitz-Burgemeister brand team, Falstaff, Budweiser, and Carling. The latter is going to build its own brewery in the San Francisco area, which should make conditions in the important California market (it accounts for about 7.5 percent of total consumption alone) even more competitive.

But the moral is not that the big bad national brands come in and knock off the poor little locals. Washington-based Olympia, strong in the Northwest, and Dever-based Coors both are making significant progress on the West Coast. Olympia scored a 22.1 percent increase, and Coors, long the strong man of the Rocky Mountain empire, boosted advertising budgets by 11 percent and barged into California. Result: a 12 percent sales increase.

In the big New York market it was a locally-based brewer that led the pack—Brooklyn's F&M Schaefer Brewing. Schaefer soared to 4,250,000 barrels up 10.1 percent, while Newark-based Ballantine dropped 3.9 percent and Rheingold, up 3.1 percent, slipped out of the to ten and found its claim to being top brand in the New York metropolitan area under severe pressure.

Ballantine, long handled by the Wm. Esty Co., is now looking for a new advertising agency. Rheingold, sold by the Liebmann family to Pepsi-Cola United Bottlers, switched agencies again. In recent years it has gone from Foote Cone & Belding to J. Walter Thompson, back to FCB, and is now at Doyle Dane Bernbach. Rheingold, under the aegis of its new management, reportedly was moving ahead at year's end behind a barrage of television and radio spots.

EXHIBIT 12

HEUBLEIN, INC. (A & B) (Condensed)

Returns on 1964 Sales of Leading Brewers

	Total revenues (000)	*Pretax net (000)*	*Profit margin (percent)*	*Barrels sold (000)*	*Pretax returns/ barrel*
Anheuser-Busch	$491,384	$39,312	8.00	10,235	$3.84
Schlitz	311,394	28,277	9.08	8,266	3.42
Pabst	227,610	20,421	8.97	7,444	2.74
Falstaff.	211,943	13,604	6.42	5,815	2.33
Hamm	125,602	8,657	6.89	3,719	2.33

Source: Company annual reports.

costs of new plant construction at $30 to $35 per barrel at the end of 1965.

Like Heublein, Hamm's purchased most of the raw materials needed for its production—malt, barley, hops and corn grits—from various independent suppliers. About one-fourth of the malt and hops requirements were met by wholly owned subsidiaries, however.

The Brewing Industry

At the end of 1964, the beer market was approximately the same size as the distilled spirits market, or about $6.4 billion a year (see Exhibit 13). In addition, from 1960 to 1964, the beer market had grown at approximately the same annual rate as the liquor market, i.e., at about 2.5%. Per capita beer consumption had increased moderately during the period.

EXHIBIT 13

HEUBLEIN, INC. (A & B) (Condensed)

Alcoholic Beverages—Consumer Expenditures, 1942-1964

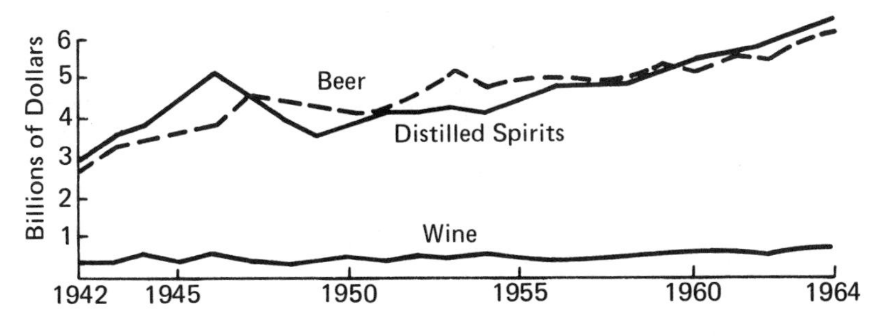

Source: *The Liquor Handbook, 1965;* cited by Glore Forgan, Wm. R. Staats Inc., in *Heublein, Inc.,* December 1965.

Since people began consuming beer at a younger age than liquor, industry observers expected beer consumption to increase as much as, if not more than, liquor consumption through 1970. Most of this increase was expected to be in the sale of packaged beer since the sale of draught beer had decreased from 22% of total beer sales in 1955 to 19% in 1964.

The same observers felt that brand loyalty was not as strong for beer as for liquor. Nevertheless, the economies of high-volume production and the use of high dollar advertising (see Exhibit 14) seemed to be causing

EXHIBIT 14

HEUBLEIN, INC. (A & B) (Condensed)

Advertising Expenditures of Major Vrewers in 1965

Company	*Advertising (000)*	*Sales (000)*	*Advertising percent of sales*
Jos. Schlitz Brewing Ço.	$ 34,200	$311,375	11.0
Anheuser-Busch, Inc.	32,500	491,384	6.6
Pabst Brewing Co	15,900	227,610	7.0
Carling Brewing Co.	15,500	412,306	3.8
Falstaff Brewing Corp.	15,000	211,943	7.0

Source: *Advertising Age*, January 3, 1966, p.46.

a gradual concentration of the beer industry, for the number of breweries operated in the United States decreased from 329 to 211 between 1953 and 1963. Moreover, the percentage of sales accounted for by the largest brewing companies had recently been increasing (see Exhibit 15).

EXHIBIT 15

HEUBLEIN, INC. (A & B) (Condensed)

Market Share of Major Brewers (percent)

	1964	*1963*	*1962*	*1961*	*1960*	*1959*	*1958*	*1957*	*1956*	*1955*	*1954*	*1953*	*1952*	*1951*
Top 25	83.7	82.2	79.9	77.4	75.1	73.8	70.5	69.2	67.5	64.3	62.1	61.3	60.2	57.5
Top 10	57.7	56.8	55.0	52.8	51.4	50.0	45.9	45.2	44.4	42.7	40.1	40.1	40.8	39.2

Source: Research Company of America.

RECOMMENDATION

Mr. Hart knew that the negotiations with Hamm's had been proceeding for some time, and that any significant modifications in the proposed terms were unlikely. He also felt that there was little additional information available which would be important, and that the Heublein directors would be expecting his recommendation soon.

CASE 17

Amtrak

*J. Russell Roy, Robert Hickcox and David A. Brock**

In May, 1975, the National Railroad Passenger Corporation, popularly known as Amtrak, completed its first four years of operation. This event was commemorated by a front page feature in the *New York Times* "Amtrak, at Age 4, Still Problem-Ridden" [1].† Amtrak is a quasipublic corporation chartered by Congress to rescue the Nation's ailing passenger train service. The corporation, funded initially through federal allocations and private railroad contribution, was expected to be a profit making venture by 1973–74. Instead, Amtrak has experienced mounting losses and is not expected to be profitable until 1980. In addition, Amtrak has been plagued by problems ranging from antiquated equipment and unsafe track beds, to broken air conditioning and vermin infestation, to late service and incorrect reservation bookings. As a result, critics in Congress, the railroad industry, and among the general public are becoming increasingly sceptical of the feasibility of Amtrak's operations and of railroad passenger service.

RAILROAD PASSENGER SERVICE

In his report "Railroad Train Deficit" of September, 1958, Interstate Commerce Commissioner Howard Hosner had a dismal view of passenger train service:

"For more than a century the railroad coach has occupied an interesting and useful place in American life, but at the present time, the inescapable fact . . . seems to be that in a decade or so this time-honored vehicle may take its place in the transportation museum along with the stagecoach, the sidewheeler, and the steam locomotive" [2].

Indeed, since 1920, passenger train utilization declined from over 20,000 passenger trains producing 47.4 billion passenger miles and carrying 77 per cent of the intercity passengers to about 150 passenger trains having 4.3 billion passenger miles and carrying less than 1 per cent of the inter-city passengers [3].

* Reprinted by permission.

Railroad passenger service has operated at a deficit since 1927, with the exception of the World War II period. In 1957, a record deficit of $723.7 million was recorded [4]. Thereafter, the deficit declined, generally as a result of the increase in mail revenues and an increasing number of discontinued trains. The operating losses for 1966 were slightly over $400 million [5], for 1967 they were about $480 million, and for 1968 they were about $600 million [6]. In addition to the increasing losses, passenger revenues were declining rapidly, as was service, as shown in Table 1. Passenger train service was losing its share of intercity passenger travel to other transit forms, primarily the automobile and the airplane (This is shown in Table 2.). It appeared that the era of railroad passenger service had run its course.

Throughout the 1960s Congress had been considering a number of bills and made a number of studies to try to save this mode of transportation. In the late 1960s, under increasing pressure from various environmental groups, the National Association of Railroad Passengers and the Railroad Industry; Congress held hearings on a number of proposals. These included:

- Providing passenger service in those areas where public agencies were willing to provide some operating funds.
- Chartering a private corporation to provide passenger service on a number of selected routes.
- The creation of a car pool operated by the Department of Transportation (DOT), which would lease cars to the railroads, and thereby help subsidize the railroad expenses.

In October of 1970 the Rail Passenger Service Act of 1970 was passed and signed by the President. This Act chartered the National Railroad Passenger Corporation. This corporation, which was to consolidate and operate the passenger service from the subscribing railroads, signaled the start of a new era in railroad passenger service.

THE LEGISLATION

Amtrak's charter states that "The Corporation shall be a for-profit corporation, the purpose of which shall be to provide intercity rail passenger service, employing innovative operating and marketing concepts so as to fully develop the potential of modern rail operating service in meeting the Nation's intercity passenger transportation requirements" [7]. Amtrak was also allowed to begin car-ferry service except in areas where contracts existed at the time of the Act. Excluded from Amtrak's operations were short-haul services and commuter service.

Under the provisions of the Act, the federal government was to provide funds up to $175 million primarily to cover start-up costs through the first

TABLE 1
Railroads, Class I Line-Haul—Selected Passenger Statistics: 1950 to 1973

Item	1950	1955	1960	1965	1970	1972	1973
Average miles of road operated	146,468	119,745	94,117	76,993	49,533	29,398	28,286
Passenger revenue . . . mil. dol.	813	743	640	553	420	407	443
Revenue per passenger-mile:							
Incl. commutation passengers . . . cents	2.56	2.60	3.01	3.18	3.90	4.76	4.76
Excl. commutation passengers . . . cents	2.74	2.70	3.03	3.14	4.02	5.31	5.19
Revenue passengers carried . . . millions	486	432	326	299	284	261	254
Revenue passenger-miles . . . millions	31,760	28,525	21,258	17,389	10,770	8,560	9,298
Average distance . . . miles	65.3	66.0	65.2	58.2	37.9	32.8	36.6
Revenue passenger-miles per train-mile	88.5	95.2	100.9	100.9	117.1	140.3	153.0
Revenue passenger-miles per car-mile	17.0	17.8	19.3	19.5	25.8	33.3	34.2
Passenger-train miles . . . millions	358	299	209	172	92	61	61
Passenger-carrying car-miles . . . millions	1,870	1,602	1,101	885	417	257	272
Train-miles per train-hour	37.4	39.8	40.7	41.3	40.1	38.3	37.6

SOURCE: *Statistical Abstracts of the United States,* U.S. Government Office, 1974, p. 569.

TABLE 2

Volume of Domestic Intercity Passenger Traffic, by Type of Transport: 1950 to 1972

[In billions of passenger-miles, except percent. Airways, prior to 1950, and other types of transportation, prior to 1960, exclude Alaska and Hawaii. A passenger-mile is the movement of 1 passenger for the distance of 1 mile. Comprises public and private traffic, both revenue and nonrevenue.]

Year	Total Traffic, Volume	Private Automobiles		Airways [1]		Bus (excludes schoolbus)		Railroad [2]		Inland Waterways [3]	
		Volume	Percent of Total	Volume	Percent of Total	Volume	Percent of Total	Volume	Percent of Total	Volume	Percent of Total
1950	508	438	86.20	10	1.98	26	5.20	32	6.39	1.2	0.23
1955	716	637	89.01	23	3.18	25	3.56	29	4.01	1.7	0.24
1958	760	685	90.14	29	3.75	21	2.73	24	3.11	2.1	0.27
1959	765	687	89.89	33	4.26	20	2.66	22	2.93	2.0	0.26
1960	784	706	90.10	34	4.33	19	2.47	22	2.75	2.7	0.34
1961	791	714	90.18	35	4.37	20	2.56	21	2.59	2.3	0.30
1962	818	736	89.95	37	4.58	22	2.66	20	2.47	2.7	0.33
1963	853	766	89.83	43	5.02	23	2.64	19	2.19	2.8	0.32
1964	896	802	89.53	49	5.49	23	2.61	18	2.05	2.8	0.32
1965	920	818	88.86	58	6.31	24	2.58	18	1.91	3.1	0.34
1966	971	856	88.19	69	7.14	25	2.53	17	1.78	3.4	0.35
1967	1,021	890	87.18	87	8.55	25	2.44	15	1.50	3.4	0.33
1968	1,079	936	86.80	101	9.38	25	2.27	13	1.23	3.4	0.32
1969	1,138	977	85.86	120	10.54	25	2.19	12	1.08	3.8	0.33
1970	1,185	1,026	86.60	119	10.01	25	2.14	11	0.92	4.0	0.34
1971	1,230	1,071	87.11	120	9.76	26	2.07	9	0.73	4.1	0.33
1972 (prel.)	1,300	1,129	86.82	133	10.24	26	1.97	9	0.66	4.0	0.31

[1] Includes domestic commercial revenue service and private pleasure and business flying.
[2] Includes electric railways. [3] Includes Great Lakes.

SOURCE: U.S. Interstate Commerce Commission, *Annual Report*, and *Transport Economics*, monthly.
SOURCE: *Statistical Abstracts of the United States*, U.S. Government Office, 1974, p. 547.

two years of operation. Amtrak was to assume the operation of the passenger service from the private railroad companies who subscribed to the service. Subscribing railroads were to purchase some of Amtrak's stock and lease its equipment to the corporation. The amount of stock that could be purchased was determined on the basis of the railroad's passenger service deficit during the year ending December 31, 1969. As an incentive for the railroads to subscribe to this service the nonsubscribers were required to operate their passenger trains until January 1, 1975. Of the 23 companies that offered passenger train service, 20 joined the Amtrak plan. In effect, this enabling legislation created an experimental two-year period in which the nationwide passenger service network would remain reasonably intact.

This initial legislation created a 15-person Board of Directors: eight appointed by the government, four by those holding preferred stock, and three from those owning common stock. Additionally, there was a 15-person panel of financial advisors: six from the railroad and banking industries, two from DOT, and seven from the general public.

FUNDING

The Railroad Passenger Act of 1970 provided the following funding:

- The federal government was to provide $9 million in grants for various operating and development costs.
- The federal government was to provide $100 million in loan guarantees.
- The subscribing railroads were to supply $5.5 million per month in exchange for stock in the operating company.
- Common stock was to be sold only to the railroad companies subscribing to the service.
- Preferred stock could be issued when Amtrak deemed it necessary. At that time it would be sold to any person or organization that was not a railroad nor controlled any railroads.
- No individual could own more than 10 percent of preferred stock, no railroad could own more than 33 percent of the common stock.
- Additional guarantees of $200 million in loans were secured.

The Railroad Passenger Act of 1970 was revised in 1973 by the Amtrak Improvement Act of 1973. It required the corporation to initiate at least two new routes a year. These routes were to be designated by the Secretary of Transportation and could be discontinued only if he found that they did not serve "The public convenience and necessity. . . ." Otherwise, after two years these experimental routes were to be added to the "basic system." Other parts of this Act provided that the Amtrak budget would be submitted directly to Congress: the DOT would no longer control the corporation's spending; and the Office of Management and the Budget would no longer be able to withhold funds.

In related legislation, in 1972, an additional $179 million subsidy was provided while the loan ceiling was raised to $200 million. In 1973 another $154.3 million subsidy was appropriated and the loan ceiling was raised to $500 million. By the summer of 1974 Congress was considering a $200 million subsidy and raising the guaranteed loan ceiling to $900 million.

In March 1975 DOT sent to Congress the Amtrak Improvement Act of 1975 which called for a change in the basic approach to federal funding. Rather than loan guarantees, the plan calls for direct grants totalling $465 million for a four-year capital improvement program covering both rolling stock and roadbeds. It is believed that direct grants will save Amtrak interest payments. The plan also calls for direct operating subsidies which DOT estimates will amount to $315 million in fiscal 1976, and rise to $330 million by 1979 [8].

In April 1975 the House approved a $1.12 billion package consisting of $873 million to cover operating deficits through September 1977, and $245 million for new equipment and capital improvements. The intent is to give Amtrak greater operating flexibility than the prior annual subsidies. The bill has been sent to the Senate where quick passage is expected [9].

OPERATIONS

In May 1971, despite numerous problems obstructing the beginning of service, the first train ran on schedule. Roger D. Lewis had been named the president of the new corporation. The management had developed a basic strategy to insure Amtrak's success during its first two years of experimental operation. This strategy called, first, for the improvement of service and related items not requiring much money, hopefully to stop the decline in railroad passenger travel and in the long run to reverse this decline. Secondly, Amtrak management sought to obtain sufficient funds for new cars and locomotives with the aim of increasing passenger traffic. Finally, management wanted to earn public support required to generate the funds sufficient for massive roadbed improvement necessary for high speed operation.

In spite of everyone's hopes Amtrak has experienced increasing operating deficits. For the year ending December, 1972, there was a net loss of $147.5 million on operating revenues of $162.6 million. At year-end 1973 the the deficit was $158.6 million on revenues of $202 million (see Exhibit 1). At year-end 1974 losses amounted to $272.7 million on revenues of $256.9 million (*1974 Annual Report Amtrak*).

EXHIBIT 1

NATIONAL RAILROAD PASSENGER CORPORATION

Balance Sheet
Assets
December 31, 1973 and 1972

	1973	1972
	(thousands of dollars)	
CURRENT ASSETS:		
Cash	$ 5,386	$ 1,450
Temporary cash investments, at cost	3,000	5,300
Accounts receivable -		
Railroad capital payments (Note 2)	21,046	64,731
Railroad operations, net (Note 4)	21,981	4,467
Customers and other	15,560	1,712
Federal grants	2,000	9,600
Materials and supplies	6,250	2,018
Prepayments and deposits	539	422
Total current assets	75,762	89,700
PROPERTY AND EQUIPMENT (Note 5):		
Passenger cars and locomotives (Note 3)	125,144	42,088
Other	8,257	1,307
	133,401	43,395
Less - Accumulated depreciation and amortization	6,191	1,532
Net property and equipment	127,210	41,863
OTHER ASSETS:		
Railroad capital payments, due January through April, 1974 (Note 2)	–	21,898
Miscellaneous	2,769	–
Total assets	$205,741	$153,461

Source: Annual Report, National Railroad Passenger Corporation, 1973.

EXHIBIT 1 (continued)

NATIONAL RAILROAD PASSENGER CORPORATION

Balance Sheet
Liabilities and Capitalization
December 31, 1973 and 1972

	1973	1972
	(thousands of dollars)	
CURRENT LIABILITIES:		
Accounts payable	$ 6,594	$ 3,513
Amounts due on purchases of property	2,123	7,129
Accrued expenses	7,108	1,669
Deferred ticket revenues	4,474	7,532
Total current liabilities	20,299	19,843
LONG-TERM DEBT:		
Notes payable, due December 31, 1975, interest at approximately 1/2% above Federal funds rate (Note 3)	78,600	–
Capitalized lease obligations (Note 5)	28,751	–
	107,351	–
CAPITALIZATION (Notes 1 and 2):		
Preferred stock, par value $100 per share, 1,000,000 shares authorized	–	–
Common stock, par value $10 per share, 40,000,000 shares authorized -		
Issued and outstanding	83,429	52,143
Subscribed	10,428	41,714
	93,857	93,857
Capital surplus -		
Railroad capital payments	103,238	103,238
Federal grants	278,712	175,612
	381,950	278,850
Accumulated deficit (Note 4)	(397,716)	(239,089)
Total capitalization	78,091	133,618
Total liabilities and capitalization	$205,741	$153,461

EXHIBIT 1 (continued)

NATIONAL RAILROAD PASSENGER CORPORATION

Statement of Operations
for the Years Ended December 31, 1973 and 1972

	1973	1972
	(thousands of dollars)	
OPERATING REVENUES	$202,093	$162,576
Operating expenses:		
Maintenance of way and structures	4,495	4,958
Maintenance of equipment (Note 5)	65,515	60,001
Traffic	26,517	20,142
Transportation	158,244	129,403
Dining and buffet service	33,285	28,030
General	30,466	37,038
Taxes on payroll and property	21,604	15,727
Equipment rents	5,194	5,798
Total operating expenses	345,310	301,097
Operating deficit (Note 4)	143,217	138,521
General and administrative expense	10,759	7,462
Interest expense	4,651	1,528
Net deficit	158,627	147,511
Accumulated deficit, beginning of year	239,089	91,578
Accumulated deficit, end of year	$397,716	$239,089

EXHIBIT 1 (continued)

NATIONAL RAILROAD PASSENGER CORPORATION

Statement of Changes in Financial Position
for the Years Ended December 31, 1973 and 1972

	1973	1972
	(thousands of dollars)	
USES OF FUNDS:		
Net deficit	$158,627	$147,511
Depreciation	(4,850)	(1,427)
Total cash used for operations	153,777	146,084
Increases in accounts receivable from operations	31,362	4,467
Purchases and refurbishments of property	59,268	28,309
Other changes in working capital	8,840	12,321
Total uses of funds	253,247	191,181
SOURCES OF FUNDS:		
Railroad capital payments received	65,583	65,529
Borrowings of long-term debt	78,600	–
Federal grant funds received	110,700	129,300
Total sources of funds	254,883	194,829
INCREASE IN CASH AND TEMPORARY CASH INVESTMENTS	$ 1,636	$ 3,648

EXHIBIT 1 (continued)

NATIONAL RAILROAD PASSENGER CORPORATION

Balance Sheet

for the Year Ended December 31, 1972

(dollars in thousands)

CURRENT ASSETS:	
Cash	$ 1,450
Temporary cash investments, at cost	5,300
Accounts receivable –	
Federal grants	9,600
Railroad capital payments, due within one year (Note 2)	64,731
Other	1,712
Advances for railroad operations, net	4,467
Materials and supplies, at cost	2,018
Prepayments and deposits	422
Total current assets	89,700
PROPERTY AND EQUIPMENT, at cost:	
Passenger cars and locomotives (Note 3)	42,088
Furniture, fixtures and leasehold improvements	1,307
	43,395
Less Accumulated straight-line depreciation and amortization	1,532
Net property and equipment	41,863
RAILROAD CAPITAL PAYMENTS, due January through April, 1974 (Note 2)	21,898
Total assets	$153,461

EXHIBIT 1 (continued)

NATIONAL RAILROAD PASSENGER CORPORATION

Balance Sheet
for the Year Ended December 31, 1972
(dollars in thousands)

CURRENT LIABILITIES:	
Accounts payable –	
Passenger service provided by railroads	$ –
Corporate operations	3,513
Amounts due on purchases of property	7,129
Accrued expenses	1,669
Deferred ticket revenue	7,532
Total current liabilities	19,843
NOTES PAYABLE (Note 3)	–
CAPITALIZATION (Notes 1 and 2):	
Preferred stock, par value $100 per share, 1,000,000 shares authorized	–
Common stock, par value $10 per share, 40,000,000 shares authorized –	
Issued and outstanding	52,143
Fully paid, in process of being issued	–
Subscribed and unpaid	41,714
	93,857
Capital surplus –	
Railroad capital payments	103,238
Federal grants	175,612
	278,850
Accumulated deficit	(239,989)
Total capitalization	133,618
Total liabilities and capitalization	$153,461

EXHIBIT 1 (continued)

NATIONAL RAILROAD PASSENGER CORPORATION

Statement of Operations
for the Year Ended December 31, 1972
(dollars in thousands)

Railway Operating Revenues (Note 5)	$162,576
Operating Expenses:	
Services provided by railroads (Note 5)	
Maintenance of way and structures	4,958
Maintenance of equipment	58,572
Traffic	6,821
Transportation	127,728
Dining and buffet service	28,030
General	36,896
Taxes on payroll and property	15,169
Equipment rents	5,798
	283,972
Services provided by the Corporation	17,125
Total operating expenses	301,097
Deficit from operations	138,521
Corporate Expenses	
General and administrative	7,462
Interest	1,528
	8,990
Net deficit	147,511
Accumulated deficit, beginning of year (represents net deficit since commencement of operations on May 1, 1971, to December 31, 1971)	91,578
Accumulated deficit, end of year	$239,089

EXHIBIT 1 (concluded)

NATIONAL RAILROAD PASSENGER CORPORATION

Statement of Sources and Applications of Funds for the Year Ended December 31, 1972
(dollars in thousands)

SOURCES OF FUNDS (Note 1):	
Federal grants received or receivable	$138,900
Railroad capital payments becoming due within one year	65,700
Total sources of funds	204,600
APPLICATIONS OF FUNDS:	
Operations -	
Net deficit	147,511
Depreciation and amortization	(1,427)
Funds used for operations	146,084
Repayment of notes payable	25,000
Investment in passenger cars and locomotives	27,106
Investment in other property	1,203
Total applications of funds	199,393
INCREASE IN WORKING CAPITAL	$ 5,207
SUMMARY OF CHANGES IN WORKING CAPITAL:	
Increase in current assets -	
Cash	$ 148
Temporary cash investments	3,500
Accounts receivable	10,795
Advances for railroad operations	4,467
Materials and supplies	508
Prepayments and deposits	422
(Increase) decrease in current liabilities -	
Accounts payable	349
Amounts due on purchases of property	(6,434)
Accrued expenses	(1,016)
Deferred revenue	(7,532)
Increase in working capital	$ 5,207

EQUIPMENT AND ROADBED

Amtrak leased or bought most of its original equipment from the railroad companies. It began its operations with 1,275 cars and 326 locomotives. By July 1974 Amtrak had 2,082 cars and 451 locomotives. Although Amtrak had bought what it felt to be best cars, most were over twenty years old. Amtrak started an extensive program of refurbishing the cars but in late 1973 changed the refurbishment program to emphasize major overhauls [10]. Most of the cars required overhauls which cost more than $50,000 per car [11]. Even with the initiation of this program, the vast majority of the cars were substandard. In an effort to upgrade its equipment, Amtrak started an extensive purchasing program. Through 1974 Amtrak had ordered a total of 201 locomotives of which 40 had already been delivered. These were mostly to replace existing equipment rather than expanding it. Also, by this time Amtrak had ordered 257 coaches, two of which had been delivered. The lead time on these deliveries was averaging a little more than a year [12]. Amtrak has proposed purchasing 435 new cars and 25 locomotives in addition to those previously ordered so as to double ridership for fiscal year 1979. Included are 235 double-deck long-distance cars and 200 single-level metroliners. It should be noted that the double-level cars can only be used on the long-distance western routes.

The tracks on which Amtrak operates are leased from and shared with other railroad companies. The vast majority of these trackbeds are old and greatly deteriorated. Amtrak has little to no control over the condition of these tracks because of the leasing arrangements. The deteriorated tracks are the result of neglect of the railroad companies—primarily because of their financial difficulties, and from the heavy usage of these tracks by freight trains. As a result, Amtrak has been forced to operate its trains at greatly reduced speeds for safety reasons. Additionally, scheduling of trains is a problem. Railroad companies do not divert their slower freight trains to allow the Amtrak trains to pass them. As mentioned previously, a key strategy of Amtrak is to provide fast, regularly scheduled service. The track conditions limit 100 mile per hour operations to a few short distances. This problem has caused Amtrak to have a very poor on-time performance. In 1973 61.7 percent of its trains arrived on time. In 1974 this figure increased to 75.3 percent. The performance, however, was very erratic; for example, the New York to Chicago line had on time 53.2 percent in March of 1974 and only 1.8 percent in February 1975.

Amtrak has proposed a five-year program to spend $1 billion on track and roadbed improvements. It has been proposed that this be funded through direct federal grants rather than through loan guarantees. Of this proposed allocation $21.6 million has been approved for the improvements in the Northeast Corridor.

MARKETING AND SERVICES

In late October 1970 the initial system was announced and is shown in Exhibit 2. The strategy in determining routes was one of cutting back on those passenger lines having the greatest losses so that efforts could be concentrated on those that could give the greatest profit. Criteria other than the probable profitability of the route included: how the route fit into the nation's transportation needs, the service demands on each route, the route cost of service, population area served, the adaptibility of the route to the total rail network, the flexibility of route management by Amtrak, and the extent of capital improvements needed.

As soon as the company could finance its own operations, passenger routes were to be expanded to meet anticipated growing customer needs. The number of trains were cut from 366, as operated by the independent companies, to 150 operated by Amtrak. Amtrak did provide service to those areas not included in the routes only if local government agencies were willing to pay two thirds of the additional costs incurred.

By the summer of 1974 there was modification of the routing strategy. At that time Transportation Secretary Brinegar was expected to announce a change in guidelines in order to remove most, if not all, long distance routes. He believed that Amtrak should concentrate on shorter, more profitable routes like those characterized by the Northeast Corridor. Later, shortly after assuming the role of president, Paul Reistrup announced Amtrak's decision to concentrate on shorter routes [13].

The Amtrak marketing department attempted to link the passenger with service. One way to do this was through advertising. Harold Graham, Amtrak vice president of marketing, commented, "Advertising is very necessary because we still have the basic problem of getting the people to try the product" [14]. Another program to improve service, as mentioned previously, was a massive program to refurbish the interiors of the cars. The Amtrak management felt that people would use the service if the trains were clean, comfortable, safe, well lighted, air conditioned, and served good food. Also important to this strategy was providing good service; consequently, stewards and stewardesses were put on the cars.

Amtrak has problems in drawing customers to the trains and keeping them. An early Metroliner survey showed that the idea of passenger train service was well received by most people but it was not seen as a realistic alternative to the passenger car or airplane. [15]. In mid-1972 the results of a Harris survey showed that the majority of the public believed rail passenger service had a place in a balanced national transportation system, including a majority who supported it even if massive federal support was required. The same survey, however, pointed out that most people felt that passenger train service had deteriorated considerably! The major complaints focused around

EXHIBIT 2

INTERCITY RAIL PASSENGER ROUTES

National Railroad Passenger Corporation

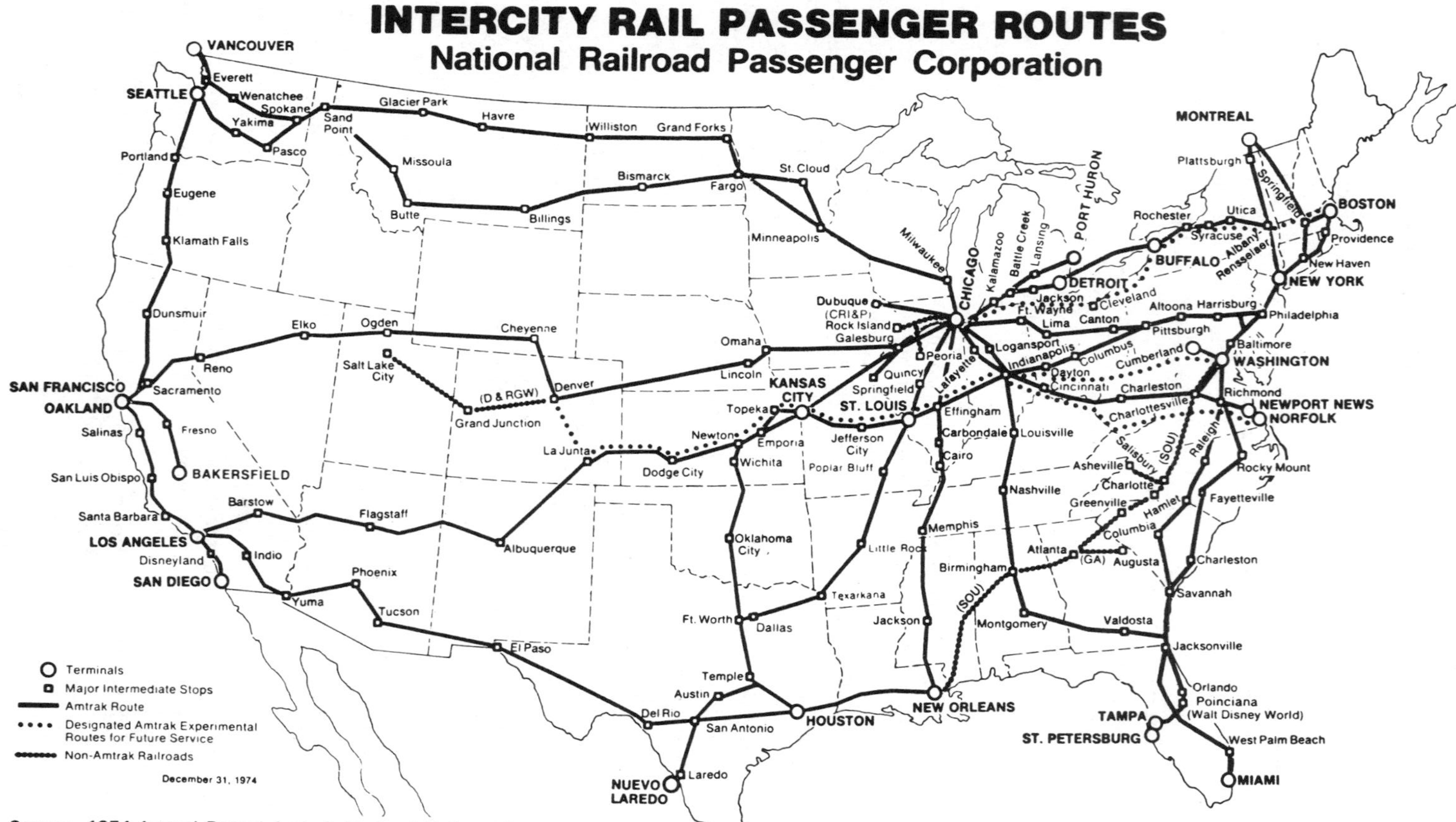

Source: *1974 Annual Report Amtrak,* National Railroad Passenger Corporation.

speed, flexibility, good quality food, comfort, service, and safety. Exhibits 3 to 5 give the results of the Harris survey. A recent study shows that passengers are still complaining of surly attendants, poor food, broken air conditioning units, poor baggage handling, vermin infestation, late arrivals, uncomfortable and dirty cars, and improper reservations [15]. Amtrak clearly had a disparity between its publicized and achieved service.

The results of a Harris study (Exhibit 4) led Amtrak to concentrate on three major market segments; the under-30 age group, the college educated, and those earning more than $15,000. Market penetration in these groups at the time was about 6.5 percent but was about twice that of other groups and had the best growth potential. A *New York Times* survey of Amtrak passengers on the other hand (Exhibit 6) showed that the majority of passengers were over 50 years of age and had incomes of less than $15,000. The segments towards which Amtrak directed its marketing strategy were, therefore, just the opposite of what they should have been.

The energy crisis in the winter of 1973–74 greatly changed the outlook for passenger rail service. The oil shortage had drawn so many people to Amtrak's service that traffic levels increased to heights not expected until 1976 [16]. At this time Amtrak also instituted a computer reservation system similar to that used by American Airlines. Problems resulted from difficulties with this reservation system [17] and from the shortage of train equipment. Though the overall loading factors were at about 42 percent, at peak hours the loading could surge to over 100 percent [18]. Amtrak simply did not have the train capacity to accommodate these peak level demands.

When Amtrak instituted its service in 1971 the passenger rail fare structure was a mass of various different regional, interregional, local, and other types of tariffs. Amtrak made major fare improvements and brought East and West Coast fares more in line with each other. Also, uniform family plans were developed for the United States as a whole. In October 1973 and again in March 1974, fares were raised 5 percent to offset higher material and labor costs [19]. These costs had been growing at an annual rate of 7.5 percent for the entire system. In June 1974 the fares were raised again an average of 20 percent primarily on the transcontinental routes. This was due in part to rising costs, but also was instituted in order to discourage some passengers due to lack of capacity during peak periods. Amtrak planned to decrease these fares at an appropriate time in the future. In the past Amtrak had more than doubled business on its Seattle-Los Angeles route with an experimental reduction of fares by 20 per cent.

GENERAL ORGANIZATION

With the creation of Amtrak in May of 1971 Roger Lewis took charge as president. He came to Amtrak from his position as president and chairman

EXHIBIT 3

Difference that Various Improvements in Train Travel Would Make in Deciding Whether to Travel by Train

	A Great Deal Difference %	Only Some Difference %	No Difference at All %	Not Sure %
If trains almost always ran on time	61	25	12	2
If the time of a train trip were reduced by 50%	56	23	18	3
If trains were new and were kept sparkling clean	56	30	13	1
If train attendants were friendly and attentive to your needs	54	30	13	3
If train terminals were modern and efficient	53	31	13	3
If there were a terminal located at a place convenient to where you live	52	27	19	2
If overnight trains had showers and modern up-to-date Bathroom facilities	50	30	18	2
If long distance trains provided facilities for carrying Automobiles so that you could take your car with you	43	20	34	3
If low-cost rental cars were available to you when you arrived at your destination	35	29	33	3
If there were new railroad cars with modern, stylish decoration	31	34	34	1
If there were three classes of travel -- first class, coach, and economy	29	33	34	4
If trains offered more entertainment such as new movies	23	29	46	2
If you could purchase tickets by using any major credit card	22	20	52	6
If trains had telephones so that you could make calls along the way	18	24	57	1
If attendants wore colorful, new uniforms	14	24	60	2

Source: *Annual Report, National Railroad Passenger Corporation, 1972, p.34.*

EXHIBIT 4

Key Attributes Motivating Inter-City Travel and the Potential Attraction of Train Travel in Building its Market Share on Them

		Train Rating		Train is Best Way to go			
13 Top Motivators for Travel	**Very Important %**	**Positive %**	**Negative %**	**Total Public %**	**18 to 29 %**	**College %**	**$15,000 and Over %**
Positive for train travel							
Cost of trip	63	36	28	13	10	12	11
Personal comfort	46	45	31	19	11	16	13
Safety	41	67	11	36	29	33	31
Look out and see interesting things en route	31	63	18	38	31	43	43
Arrive rested and relaxed	13	50	26	18	14	15	13
Be able to get up and walk around	13	61	18	62	61	65	63
Arrive on time	9	42	31	16	12	17	13
Friendly, helpful employees	8	40	27	11	6	8	6
Negative for train travel							
Reach destination quickly	19	35	41	5	3	3	2
Flexible when can leave	15	25	42	8	6	6	6
Quality food available	18	32	39	15	9	13	11
Good food at reasonable prices	17	23	36	13	11	12	9
Modern washroom facilities	9	33	33	16	11	14	13
Average potential penetration on all items				21	18	20	18
Current penetration by rail service				4	6	7	6

Source: Annual Report, National Railroad Passenger Corporation, 1972, p. 36;

of the Board of the General Dynamics Corporation and took a considerable cut in salary to accept the post. Mr. Lewis preferred to delegate most of the operating decisions to other parts of the management structure. As a result, the functionally structured departments tended to compete with each other at each other's expense. The result was to drag down the overall performance of the corporation.

EXHIBIT 5

Best Way to Travel: Summary Table
(Total Public)

	Air %	Train %	Bus %	Not Sure %
Cost of trip	29	13	44	14
Personal comfort	67	19	6	8
Safety	35	36	10	19
Chance to look out and see interesting things	15	38	39	8
Reaching destination quickly	86	5	3	6
Good quality food available	63	15	4	18
Good food at a reasonable price	50	13	7	30
Flexibility on when to leave	50	8	19	23
Arrive rested and relaxed	67	18	4	11
Being able to get up and walk arroumd	22	62	5	11
Knowing you will arrive on time	52	16	10	22
Modern washroom facilities	57	16	4	23
Friendly, helpful attendants	66	11	5	18
Helpful to young children	53	15	5	27
Chance to rest and talk to other travelers	35	32	13	20
Place of departure easy to reach	34	15	31	20
Luggage handling facilities	48	14	11	28
Fast information and reservation facilities	65	9	6	20
Helpful to older people	55	15	5	25
Convenience of charging the cost of the trip	49	6	4	41

Source: Annual Report, National Railroad Passenger Corporation, 1972, p. 32.

Members of the Congress think that Amtrak's troubles stem in no small degree to a failure of management, and much of that responsibility can be laid on Mr. Lewis. So unhappy was the Congress with Mr. Lewis that in 1972 that body tried to force him to quit by cutting his salary in half. On the other hand, Mr. Lewis blames many of Amtrak's problems on the Congress. "You think the Lord Jesus had troubles?" as asks. "You should see us going up the hill with our crosses on our backs" [21]. This is an interesting comment in light of the fact that the Congress was more sympathetic to Amtrak than the Executive Branch.

EXHIBIT 6

Profile of AMTRAK Passengers on Long-Haul Trips

Coach Passengers	80%
Non Business Travelers	90
Traveling with Family	50
Women	60
Not Employed	60
Family Incomes Under $15,000	70
Over 50 years old	60
Under 30 years old	20
A majority of AMTRAK passengers refuse to fly.	

Source: *The New York Times,* May 1, 1975.

In March of 1975 Mr. Lewis resigned and Paul H. Reistrup assumed the position of president of the corporation. Reistrup had been senior vice president for traffic at Illinois Central Railroad, and, although only 42, had wide experience in railroading. A West Pointer, Reistrup left the army in 1957 to join the Baltimore & Ohio Railroad where he was given credit for solving that road's passenger service problem [20].

One of the important differences between the operation of Amtrak and that of other railroad companies is its quasipublic nature. As a federally funded business the management of the company faces a unique organization and decision-making structure—the United States Congress. By law, Amtrak officials must have their operating budgets approved by the Congress. Amtrak's funding proposals are often severely cut by the Congress. Influential Congressmen have often pressured the corporation into instituting special routes in their home states or to pet areas, despite their unprofitability. The Board of Directors is chosen, in part, by the President of the United States with the approval of Congress. Rate structures, the creation and maintenance of routes and other major operating and financial decisions must be approved by the Congress or other governmental agencies. Finally, the DOT and the Interstate Commerce Commission (ICC) exercise a great deal of informal control over Amtrak decisions. Many of Amtrak's problems stem from the fact that Congress and the Executive Branch cannot agree regarding the usefulness and functioning of Amtrak and how it should be funded.

A majority of members of the Congress think that Amtrak should be subsidized but neither the Nixon nor the Ford administrations agree. Executive Branch officials have rejected equipment purchases beyond the next fiscal year and take the hard-nosed position that Amtrak should not do any long-range planning because eventually it should be self-supporting or go out of business [22].

All of these factors create a cumbersome situation under which the Amtrak management has limited control and ability to manage the company properly.

EXTERNAL COMPETITIVE FACTORS

A major competitive threat to Amtrak, of course, continues to be the airplane, the bus, and the private automobile. Total travel costs to customers are quite comparable between the airlines and Amtrak. One top executive of a bus line commented that if the Congress would give his company the subsidy enjoyed by Amtrak, he would carry passengers for free! Cost comparisons to travelers between the private passenger car and Amtrak vary much depending upon the number of persons carried, distances travelled, whether cost comparisons include total or out-of-pocket expense of car owners, and the types of accommodations enjoyed on long trips. Cost comparisons of fares and total costs to Amtrak, however, raise different competitive issues. For example, on a typical day only about 200 through passengers ride the Floridian. When someone pays $120 for a Chicago-St. Petersburg roomette, Amtrak subsidizes the trip by $264. The federal government would save money if instead of subsidizing Amtrak it gave each passenger on the Floridian a first class air fare plus $100 in cash [23].

REFERENCES

[1] *New York Times,* May 1, 1975, p. 1.
[2] "Railroad Passenger Train Deficit." Report proposed by Howard Hosmer, Hearing Examiner, *et al.,* Docket No. 31954, 1958.
[3] *Journal of Commerce,* September 14, 1974, p. 3.
[4] Hilton, George: *The Transportation Act of 1958.* Bloomington, Indiana, Indiana University Press, 1969, p. 136.
[5] *Ibid.*
[6] Patton, Edwin P.: "A Plan to Save the Passenger Train." *Business Horizons,* February 1969, p. 7.
[7] Huddleston, W., and Siegel, M.: "Amtrak: The Pointless Arrow." An unpublished paper, UCLA Graduate School of Management, December 10, 1974.
[8] *Railway Age,* March 31, 1975, p. 23.
[9] *Wall Street Journal,* April 25, 1975, p. 23.
[10] *Trains,* December 1975, p. 16.
[11] *Trains,* May 1973, p. 12.

[12] From the Senate Hearings on Amtrak, p. 1055.
[13] *Wall Street Journal,* January 30, 1975, p. 11.
[14] *Railway Age,* "A Smoother Track Ahead for Amtrak?", January 10, 1972, p. 26.
[15] *Railway Age,* May 11, 1970, p. 25.
[16] Loving, Rush: "Amtrak is About to Miss the Train." *Fortune,* May 1974, p. 23.
[17] *New York Times,* May 1, 1975, p. 1.
[18] *Railway Age,* April 26, 1971, p. 11.
[19] *Wall Street Journal,* March 21, 1974, p. 14.
[20] *New York Times,* January 9, 1975, p. 51.
[21] Loving, *op. cit.,* p. 274.
[22] *Ibid.*
[23] "Track to Nowhere." *Forbes,* December 15, 1975.

CASE 18

The Mississippi Test Facility

*Edmund R. Gray and Raymond V. Lesikor**

HISTORY

On October 25, 1961, the National Aeronautics and Space Administration (NASA) announced the location of the Mississippi Test Facility (MTF) in Hancock County, Mississippi. This new installation was created purely in response to President Kennedy's mandate to put a man on the moon before 1970.

The decision to build the new facility was made by NASA officials in the belief that it was necessary in achieving the organization's moon-landing goal. They reasoned that launch, manufacturing, and development facilities for large launch vehicles would pace the lunar landing program. Thus, bringing these facilities on line was necessary to meet the program deadline. The plan was to manufacture the stages at one site, test them at a second location, and launch them at a third. At this time, the first and third sites were already in operation. Stages were being manufactured at the Michoud plant near New Orleans, and the Atlantic Missile Range (later named Kennedy Space Center) was in operation in Florida. These two facilities needed only modifications to fit into the new plan. The test site had to be built from scratch.

Selection of the Mississippi location for the new test facility was primarily a matter of logistics. The extremely large size of the space vehicles was expected to bring about difficult transportation problems. Movement by water appeared to be the best solution. With availability of water transportation the determining factor NASA concluded that the Michoud–MTF–Atlantic Missile Range trail offered the best available option. The Mississippi location was only 45 miles from Michoud; and it was connected with Michoud by intercoastal waterway and with Florida by way of the Gulf of Mexico. Land for the new facility was acquired in 1962 by the U.S. Army Corps of Engineers. Site development and construction was done in 1963. On April 23, 1966, MTF became operational when a S-II prototype was static fired for 15 seconds.

At the beginning the stated mission of MTF was that of serving as a static site for Saturn and Nova-Class stages. In the early 1960s a Nova program

* Reprinted by permission.

was being planned as a follow-on to the Saturn program. Nova was to be a much bigger and more powerful Saturn—the first stage was to develop 12 million pounds of thrust (compared to Saturn's 7½ million pounds) and the second stage 4 to 5 million pounds (compared to Saturn's 1 million pounds). The scenerio for Nova was that it would be used for direct assent missions to the moon and for the exploration of near planets and deep space.

MTF was planned and constructed with the testing of the huge Nova stages in mind. The Nova program, however, was cancelled in 1964, two years before MTF became operational, with the decision to ascend to the moon in stages; i.e., earth orbit to moon orbit. With this decision the $400 million facility which was under construction was left with the sole long-range objective of static testing Saturn launch vehicles.

Another significant factor related to the early history of MTF was that at the same time MTF was under construction NASA was building other test stands for Saturn stages—one at Huntsville, Alabama, and another at Santa Susana, California. The principal reason given for this duplication was time pressures of the moon program. In support of this action, Dr. VonBraun testified that it would take about 18 months longer to build operational test stands in Mississippi than in Huntsville because Huntsville already had the basic utilities and data centers. Hence, in order to meet the projected launch schedule, the first S-IC stand was built in Huntsville. A similar reason was given for building the two S-II test stands at Santa Susana. The first three S-ICs were static fired at Huntsville but no S-IIs were acceptance tested at Santa Susana.

Ancillary arguments were also made for the construction of the duplicate stands. These stands were to be used for R&D purposes and hence should be located near where the engineering work was being done, i.e., Huntsville and Seal Beach, California. Moreover, because of the proximity of private residences, it would not be desirable to utilize these stands for acceptance testing. Finally, it was suggested that in addition to their R&D role, these stands were considered as backups for the MTF stands.

In the first two years of its operation MTF became NASA's largest testing site for large rocket stages. Principally, it was used for the static firing[1] and check-out of the first (S-IC) and second (S-II) stages of the Saturn V, the large launch vehicle of the Apollo Program. After being built at Michoud, S-IC stages were transferred by water to MTF for static firing, returned to Michoud for refurbishing and post-firing checkout, and then sent to Florida. S-II stages were shipped from their Seal Beach, California, manufacturing

[1] Static firing means the rocket stages are run through full-strength, full-duration, "hot" firings; but instead of being launched, they are held captive by the huge test stands. The economics of rocketry demand that everything humanly possible be done before ignition occurs, and the holddown mechanisms let go, to assure that the launch vehicle will perform satisfactorily. When there are human passengers, this factor becomes increasingly more significant. Static firing allows engineers to assure the flight worthiness of a stage before it is launched.

site by Navy LSD through the Panama Canal to the Michoud Assembly Facility. Here they were reloaded on a river barge and transported to the S-II test stands at MTF. After testing, the stages were refurbished and checked-out in the S-II Vertical Check-Out Building at MTF. Then they were barged to Michoud, reloaded on an ocean vessel, and shipped to Kennedy.[2]

In summary, MTF was a product of the enthusiasm and optimism of the early space program. Economy was of secondary importance; a lunar landing by the end of the decade was the primary consideration. Moreover, the proposition that the country and the Congress would continue indefinitely the high level of funding for space exploration went unquestioned.

DESCRIPTION OF THE FACILITY

Land

Situated in the piney woods and marshlands of Hancock County, Mississippi, MTF includes a fee area of 13,424 acres (about 5 square miles) surrounded by an acoustical buffer zone of an additional 128,526 acres. NASA owns the fee area outright. The buffer zone it controls through easements which it secured. The buffer zone extends into Pearl River County, Mississippi, and Saint Tammany Parish, Louisiana. It is inhabited by livestock and wildlife, with some farming and lumbering permitted; however, no one is allowed to reside in the area because of the possible danger from sound waves created during testing.

Plant

MTF is carried on the NASA books as a capital investment of $350 million. Replacement cost estimates run as high as $400 million. The site has three test stands: two single-position stands for testing the S-II, and one huge dual-position stand for testing the first stage for Saturn V launch vehicles (this stand is the largest static testing facility in the United States). In addition, there are approximately 20 support and service buildings, an extensive canal system, a railroad, and a navigation lock that provides access from the Pearl River to the MTF canal system. It should also be noted that MTF utilizes the services of the $50 million Slidell Computer Center for computations beyond the limits of its own computers. Organizationally, however, the Slidell center is attached to the Michoud Assembly Facility.

$250 million of the $350 million investment at MTF is considered single-

[2] The third stage (S-IVB) of Saturn V is manufactured and assembled by McDonnell Douglas Corporation at Huntington Beach, California. It is shipped by air to the Sacramento Test Facility for acceptance testing and then shipped by air to the Kennedy Space Center.

purpose facilities; i.e., it can only be used for rocket testing. The other $100 million represents more flexible facilities.

Personnel

MTF is the first major NASA facility which is predominately contractor operated. A relatively small contingent of NASA personnel (75–85) are assigned to MTF. They have overall management and supervisory responsibilities, make final evaluation of test results, and issue flight worthiness certificates to the stage contractors, who conduct their own tests.

The General Electric Company (GE) is by far the largest single employer at MTF. GE, under a prime contract with NASA, maintains the facility and provides test, technical, and site services to all tenants.

North American Rockwell, Inc., under a prime contract with NASA, is responsible for the design, development, manufacture, and testing of S-II Stages. To perform its testing and checkout function, this firm maintains a force at MTF. The Boeing Company, which is responsible for the S-IC Stages, likewise has personnel stationed at MTF.

Personnel from North American's Rocketdyne plant (for engine checkout), various subcontractors and elements of other government agencies, such as the U.S. Air Force Material Quality Branch, which is in charge of quality assurance of material from all prime contractors for the government, are also domiciled at MTF.

NASA ORGANIZATIONAL STRUCTURE

MTF, of course, is but one of the many facilities in the NASA organization. Thus, for our purposes it may be helpful to know just how MTF fits into the total organization.

NASA is headed by an Administrator who is appointed by and reports directly to the President. The NASA organization at the top level consists of three units: (1) the Office of the Administrator, (2) a group of staff officers reporting to the Administrator, and (3) four line offices reporting to the Administrator (see Exhibit 1). Three of these offices—the Office of Manned Space Flight (OMSF), the Office of Space Science Applications (OSSA), and the Office of Advanced Research and Technology (OART)—may be considered program offices out of which the major NASA programs are run. The fourth office—Office of Tracking and Data Acquisition—is basically an auxiliary department which provides tracking and data acquisition services for the other offices. OSSA administers the unmanned space flight programs and OART administers NASA's more basic research programs.

OMSF is by far the largest office in terms of both funds and personnel and the one with which we are most concerned, since it is in the direct

EXHIBIT I

NATIONAL AERONAUTICS AND SPACE ADMINISTRATION

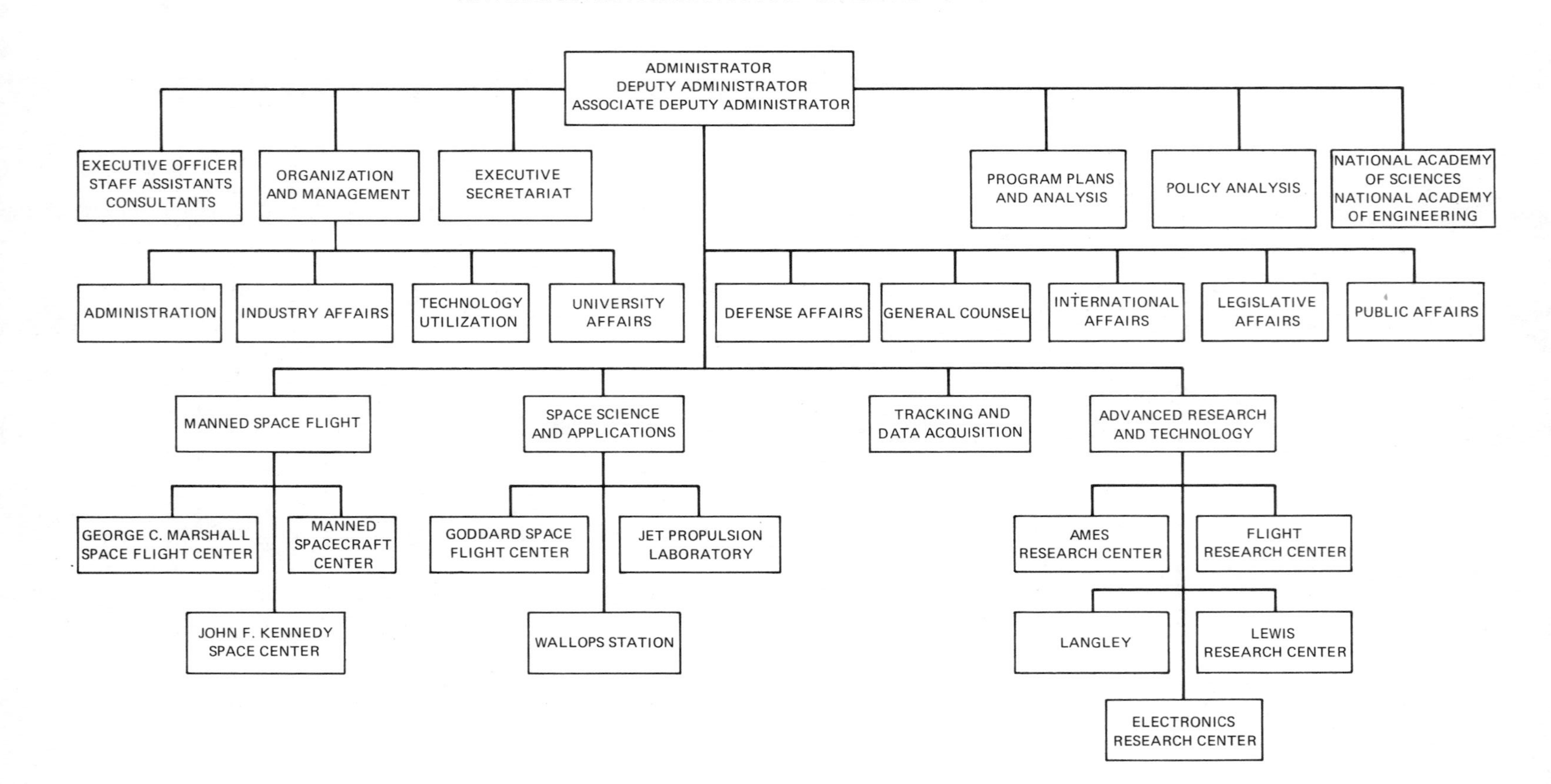

scalar chain to MTF. As can be seen in Exhibit 1, there are three centers—George C. Marshall Space Flight Center (MSFC), John F. Kennedy Space Center (KSC), and Manned Spacecraft Center (MSC)—reported directly to the Associate Administrator of Manned Space Flight. Briefly, MSC is responsible for all spacecraft activities and KSC is responsible for all launch activities.

MSFC is the center with which we are concerned here. Its mission is the management of all research, development, and procurement activities for launch vehicle and space transportation systems including related support equipment and facilities. Four major departments—Program Development, Science and Engineering, Program Management, and Administration and Technical Services—report to the director of MSFC (see Exhibit 2).

Program Management, formerly Industrial Operations, is the department with which we are primarily concerned because it runs the Saturn program. Moreover, the Director of Program Management is the direct line superior of the MTF Manager (see Exhibit 2). The formal organization structure of MTF is depicted in Exhibit 3.

IMPACT ON SURROUNDING COMMUNITY

MTF has had a significant impact on the surrounding community. The impact area includes Hancock, Pearl River, and Harrison Counties, Mississippi, and Saint Tammany Parish, Louisiana. The principal effect, however, has been in Hancock and Pearl River Counties, which have had a history of economic stagnation prior to the arrival of NASA.

MTF's physical impact on the local area was immediate. The towns of Gainesville, Logtown, Santa Rosa, Westonia, and Napoleon were eliminated to make way for the facility. The 850 families living in these towns were required to relocate [Holman, 1967:91].

The economic impact of MTF, however, is more far reaching. According to Holman's study the NASA test program brought about 2,530 new non-local employees to the facility by 1966. In addition, approximately 2,210 local residents were hired by the facility. Conservatively, Holman estimates that 900 of these 2,210 were not employed previously. Hence, MTF directly increased employment in the impact area between 1963 and 1966 by over 3,400 jobs [Holman, 1967:117–120]. These employees were typically white-collar or technical workers albeit a sizable number (over 1,000) were temporary construction workers. The average salary of MTF employees in 1966 was approximately $10,000 [Holman, 1967:103].

In addition to the increase in direct employment there was a concomitant increase in the service sector of the economy. Holman estimates this to be in excess of 2,100 jobs. Hence, MTF brought approximately 5,500 new jobs to the area by 1966 [Holman, 1967:121].

EXHIBIT II

NATIONAL AERONAUTICS AND SPACE ADMINISTRATION

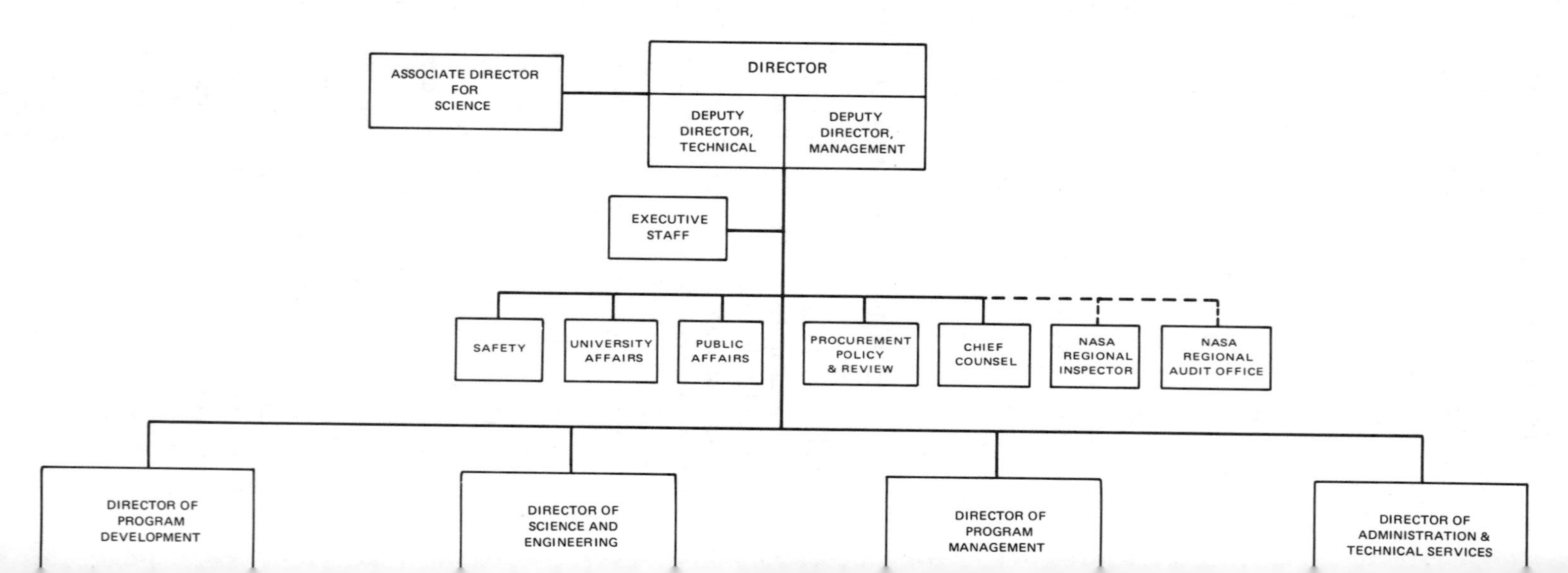

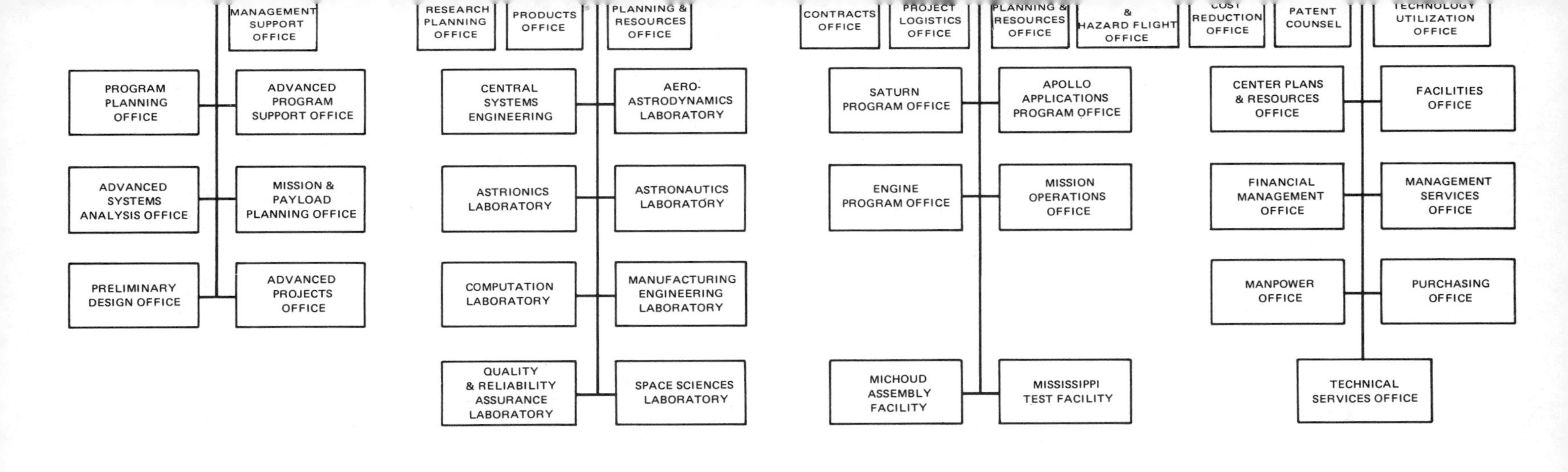

MANAGEMENT SUPPORT OFFICE
PROGRAM PLANNING OFFICE
ADVANCED PROGRAM SUPPORT OFFICE
ADVANCED SYSTEMS ANALYSIS OFFICE
MISSION & PAYLOAD PLANNING OFFICE
PRELIMINARY DESIGN OFFICE
ADVANCED PROJECTS OFFICE
RESEARCH PLANNING OFFICE
PRODUCTS OFFICE
PLANNING & RESOURCES OFFICE
CENTRAL SYSTEMS ENGINEERING
AERO-ASTRODYNAMICS LABORATORY
ASTRIONICS LABORATORY
ASTRONAUTICS LABORATORY
COMPUTATION LABORATORY
MANUFACTURING ENGINEERING LABORATORY
QUALITY & RELIABILITY ASSURANCE LABORATORY
SPACE SCIENCES LABORATORY
CONTRACTS OFFICE
LOGISTICS OFFICE
RESOURCES OFFICE
& HAZARD FLIGHT OFFICE
SATURN PROGRAM OFFICE
APOLLO APPLICATIONS PROGRAM OFFICE
ENGINE PROGRAM OFFICE
MISSION OPERATIONS OFFICE
MICHOUD ASSEMBLY FACILITY
MISSISSIPPI TEST FACILITY
REDUCTION OFFICE
PATENT COUNSEL
UTILIZATION OFFICE
CENTER PLANS & RESOURCES OFFICE
FACILITIES OFFICE
FINANCIAL MANAGEMENT OFFICE
MANAGEMENT SERVICES OFFICE
MANPOWER OFFICE
PURCHASING OFFICE
TECHNICAL SERVICES OFFICE

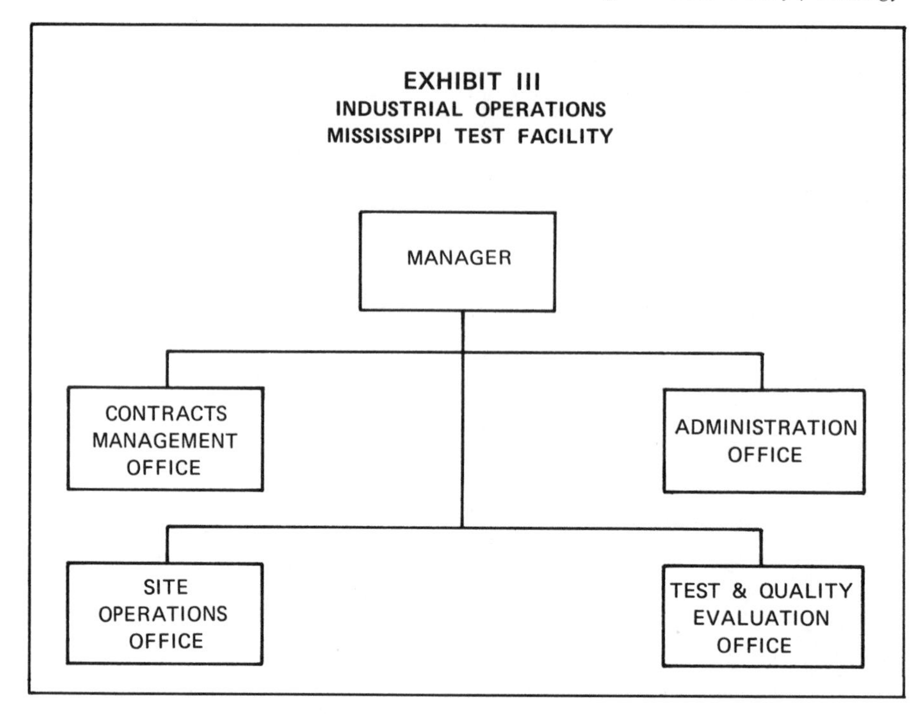

To attract the needed highly educated and skilled employees to the area, it was felt that the community would have to provide improved public services. Hence, NASA officials conducted a vigorous public relations program aimed at inducing the community to expand and modernize its services (schools, roads, sewage system, etc.). As a result Hancock County alone floated a $200 million bond issue which it expected to repay from an expanded tax base.

The new jobs created at MTF had a significant effect on the economic activity in the surrounding community. To illustrate, between 1962 and 1965 disposable income rose by about 35 per cent in both Hancock and Pearl River Counties [Holman, 1967:103]. During the same period retail sales increased threefold in Hancock County and almost doubled in Pearl River County [Holman, 1967:107]. Between 1962 and 1964 demand deposits in federal and state chartered banks more than doubled in Hancock County. In practical terms this means that the money supply in the county approximately doubled during this period. In Pearl River County during this same period demand deposits grew by $1.7 million [Holman, 1967:103–105]. Furthermore, Professor Holman estimates the NASA-generated income led to an additional 340 housing starts in the years 1964 and 1965 (almost double what they would have been otherwise in a major portion of the impact area) [Holman, 1967:108]. Sales tax revenue gives still another indication of economic activity. In Hancock County between 1965 and 1966 it rose by about 225 per cent and in Pearl River County increased by approximately 69 per cent.

Hence it is clear that MTF has had a tremendous economic impact on a surrounding community which had been basically stagnant for decades. Since 1966, however, there has been a steady decline in employment at MTF. Almost all construction contractors departed by the middle of 1967. (More importantly, however, the service and stage contractors have decreased their working force at MTF fairly steadily since mid-1967. Although there are no studies presently available on the situation, it is fairly obvious that since there is nothing else in the immediate area to take up the employment slack the local economy is being placed under a severe strain.

THE MANAGER'S QUANDRY

The present manager of MTF came to the site from a high-level staff position at MSFC in 1966 at a time when the construction program was seriously behind schedule. Largely through his efforts, schedule slippages were rectified and the MTF was able to play its destined role in America's space program.

Now in 1968, with most of the early "bugs" in the technical systems and coordination problems among the various domiciled organizations worked out, the facility is operating smoothly. The manager is uneasy however. He looks out his office window surveying the $400 million facility under his direction. "Can it be," he ponders, "that this magnificant facility has already served its usefulness? Could it be all over so soon?"

As he considers this all-important question, he recalls how it had become apparent to him as early as 1967 that the site was operating considerably below its potential capacity. In fact, he noted then that the only time his personnel were fully occupied was for the five-day period centering around the firing of a stage. The remainder of the time was "valley" time in which the work force had little to do. In fact, a 1968 confidential report by General Electric showed that the site was being used at only 30 per cent capacity.

Because of this apparent inactivity, the manager had made a proposal to Marshall Space Flight Center (MSFC) that all NASA rocket testing be consolidated at MTF. In his proposal, he had demonstrated how such a plan would eliminate valley time and could save $17 million a year. But MSFC rejected the proposal.

Now in 1968 the future of MTF appears even more dismal. All Saturn tests are scheduled to end in 1970. No follow-up mission is scheduled. In fact, there is little reason to believe that MTF will ever receive another mission. And without a mission to support it, MTF must be closed down (NASA's budgeting is by program).

Even if there were to be a program scheduled immediately, it would be too late to solve MTF's problem. It takes a minimum of three years (usually longer) from the time NASA approves a program for the hardware to be made ready for acceptance testing.

With this dismal outlook facing his facility, the manager ponders the effects of closing this $400 million facility. He thinks of what it will mean to the workers at the facility—how they will have to pull-up roots and move on. It bothers him more as he recalls how he and others worked to get many of these people to come down to this location.

His thoughts turn also to the people in the community. Once Hancock County had been among the poorest in Mississippi; and now it is one of the wealthiest. He thinks, also, of how the citizens had voted bond issues to finance public services for what they had thought was to be a growing community. He cannot help but think of the families, communities, and towns that have been forced to move from the area to make way for the facility.

Then quite naturally he thinks of the effects on himself. What will happen to him? Will he be retained as manager of a "mothballed" facility? Will he be sent to another NASA facility and have to sell his house, leave his friends, and move?

He thinks also of the national interest. Is it wise to desert a facility that has cost so much? Has the nation received a fair return from its investment in the facility? Is it possible that the facility should never have been built?

PART

IV

Implementing Policy/Strategy

CHAPTER

14

Organizational Structures and Processes for Implementing Policies and Strategies

INTRODUCTION

President Kennedy once said that "Our responsibility is not discharged by the announcement of virtuous ends." He spoke often of the problems he had in moving the huge bureaucracy of government to act when he made a decision. For instance, even during the crucial events associated with the Cuban missile crisis, several times he ordered the withdrawal of United States missiles from bases in Turkey, in the clearest language, yet they were not removed [Allison, 1971]. To formulate policies and strategies without assuring their implementation is an exercise in futility.

The implementation of policies and strategies is an extremely complex problem in all organizations, especially larger ones. Ackerman [1975], for instance, concluded after in-depth studies of two organizations that it took six years to assure effective implementation of top management policies associated with social programs. When George Romney was Chairman of the Board of the American Motors Corporation he made the decision to produce a small compact automobile. It took him seven years and involved some dramatic personnel changes in the company before he succeeded in implementing his strategy [Christensen, Andrews, and Bower, 1973].

Implementation of policies and strategies is concerned with the design and management of systems to achieve the best integration of people, structures, processes and resources, in reaching organizational purposes. The scope of managerial activities associated with implementation is virtually coextensive with the entire process of management.

Obviously, space does not permit an examination in any depth of the range of theory and practice that is embraced. Our focus will be limited to three major aspects of implementation: organization structure and processes; major coordinating, control, and motivating systems; and the role of people in implementation. The present chapter will deal with organization, the following with systems, and the next with people. Obviously all three interrelate but they are segregated here for purposes of exposition.

PERSPECTIVE ON THE AREA OF IMPLEMENTATION

Since implementation encompasses all functions of management, of both strategic and operational management, no simple statement of what is involved can be sufficient. To narrow the focus and establish a framework for the discussion, Table 14-1 presents major responsibilities of managers in implementing policies and strategies. The list is not intended to describe procedural steps for implementation. Rather, the list is designed to present major considerations involved in designing and managing implementing systems. A comparable list can be found in other writings [for example, Christensen,

TABLE 14-1
Major Managerial Responsibilities in Implementing Policy/Strategy

1. Divide the key tasks and sequences of steps to be performed to carry out policies and strategies in a fashion required to achieve objectives.
2. Determine who is responsible for major specific tasks that must be discharged, steps that must be taken, and decisions that must be made.
3. Determine the major organizational structures within which implementation will take place, e.g., functional departments or decentralized product divisions.
4. Determine the resources (physical and human) necessary to implement policies and strategies and assure their availability when needed.
5. Determine types of performance required by organizational units and individuals and the dates when specific activities must be accomplished.
6. Determine the personal motivation and incentive systems to be employed.
7. Analyze the key interrelationships among people, organizational units, and activities within units that require coordination and determine the appropriate systems to assure their proper coordination.
8. Assure the proper degrees of participation in the formulation and operation of implementing systems and processes.
9. Establish appropriate information systems to assure accurate measurement of performance against standards so that corrective action can be taken when required.
10. Adopt training programs to develop the technical and managerial skills needed in implementation.
11. Assure that managerial leadership is effective in motivating and leading the organization in implementing policies and strategies in such a way as to achieve organizational ends in the most effective and efficient fashion.

Andrews, and Bower, 1973; Newman, Summer, and Warren, 1972; Andrews, 1971].

A quick glance at the list reveals a number of important characteristics of policy/strategy implementation. First, it is clear that the focus is on design and integration of major mechanisms, philosophies, structures, and personal interrelationships. Second, many different disciplines are involved in the design, operation, and use of integrating systems. Third, conflicts inevitably arise and must be resolved. Conflict resolution is a key consideration in implementing about which there has been much research [Miner, 1973a:394–422]. Fourth, the discharge of the responsibilities listed requires the exercise of all functions of management.

Problems of implementation will differ depending upon many variables. Stages of organization development will influence implementation problems [Thain, 1969; Scott, 1973; and Newman, 1971]; stability or instability of environments [Lawrence and Lorsch, 1967; Lorsch and Allen, 1973], types of organizational structures [Buckley, 1971], interdependencies among organizational units [Thompson, 1967], personnel interrelationships [Lorsch and Morse, 1974], environmental competitive conditions [Negandhi and Reimann, 1972], and cultural forces [Farmer and Richman, 1964], to mention just a few variables to illustrate the point.

ORGANIZATIONAL STRUCTURE AND PROCESSES DEFINED

There is no concensus about the meaning of "organizational structure," or "organizational processes." Organizational structure generally refers to the more or less fixed and formal relationship of roles and tasks to be performed in achieving organizational goals, the grouping of these activities, delegation of authority, and informational flows vertically and horizontally in the organization. Implementation of strategy, however, includes much more than this. It involves various mechanisms to coordinate, influence, and control these activities, such as planning, interpersonnel relationships, and incentive systems; managerial styles; and control mechanisms. These are called organizational processes. Each of these elements must be appropriate to the design problem and, for best results, the mixture of all elements must be appropriate. Our interest in this chapter is primarily on structure, but we shall also touch upon organizational processes.

INTERDEPENDENCE OF STRATEGY AND STRUCTURE

In summarizing the long experience of his consulting firm in devising strategies and organizing companies Cannon [1972:30] said: "The experience of McKinsey supports the view that neither strategy nor structure can be determined independently of the other. . . . If structure cannot stand alone without strategy, it is equally true that strategy can rarely succeed without an appropriate structure. In almost every kind of large-scale enterprise, examples can be found where well-conceived strategic plans were thwarted by an organization structure that delayed the execution of the plans or gave priority to the wrong set of considerations . . . good structure is inseparably linked to strategy. . . ." He then goes on to say that structure must reflect an organization's basic mission as well as goals and strategic programs of top management.

But structure is influenced by a great many other considerations, as noted previously. From research and thinking on the subject there has evolved "a contingency theory" of organizations to which we now turn.

A CONTINGENCY THEORY OF ORGANIZATIONAL DESIGN

In the past there have been schools of thought that claimed to have had the correct prescription for the best organizational structures and processes. The classical writers on management, for example, felt that over many years there had been developed a set of principles which, if properly applied, would determine the structural design best suited to achieve the purposes of the organization [for example, Gulick and Urwick, 1937]. Early behaviorists insisted that better results would be achieved when organizational structure and process followed certain prescribed concepts about individuals [for example, Likert, 1961; McGregor, 1960]. More recent research supports the thesis that there is no one "right" or "best" way to organize for effective results. This is called "a contingency theory of organizations." These words to describe the theory were first used by Lawrence and Lorsch [1967] but the ideas underlying the concept have been supported by many other researchers and observers [Lorsch and Morse, 1974; Clifford, 1973a; Cannon, 1972; Negandhi and Reimann, 1972; Thompson, 1967; Woodward, 1965; and Chandler, 1962].

"The basic assumption underlying the theory," say Lawrence and Lorsch [1967:157], "is that organizational variables are in a complex interrelationship with one another and with conditions in the environment." Organizations must be designed according to the tasks they are trying to perform.

Although many observers agree with the basic theme of the contingency theory, they concur from different perspectives. For example, Clifford examined 103 rapidly growing companies and concluded that "The 'right' structure for each company at any point in time is a function of five determinants: corporate objectives and plans . . . the number of distinct businesses making up the company . . . the key factors for success in each major line of business . . . organizational principles (adopted by the company) . . .

and management capabilities, style, and personality . . ." [Clifford, 1973a: 26–27].

The contingency theory will appeal to the practitioner of the art of organizational design. However, the body of research it has produced, although valuable both as a guide to understanding organizations and to designing them to implement strategy, is unable to prescribe the "right" structure, not to mention processes, in any given situation. As Cannon [1972:32] commented: "The theoretical propositions about broad organization structure are still so general that they offer little help in specific situations. And where the theory can be more precise, it is often at a level of detail that is not germane or at least not central to the basic organization problems. So the organization designer, be he manager or consultant, finds himself in the middle, as it were, and has no choice but to rely on empirical approaches." Perrow [1973] has voiced the same conclusion.

This means for the student of strategy, of course, that the theoretical constructs of the relationships between strategy and structure are helpful in understanding organizational-environmental relationships but are far from sufficient to explain detailed differences in organizations or to identify what specific organizational structures are most appropriate to the successful implementation of specific strategies. Each case must be considered alone. Nonetheless, there are theories and lessons from experience that are helpful both in explaining the interrelationships between strategy and organization structure and in predicting success or failure with different structures. We now proceed to presenting some highlights of the research undertaken in this area.

EVOLUTION OF MAJOR ORGANIZATIONAL STRUCTURES

The first comprehensive analysis of the interrelationships among environment, strategy, and organizational structure was made by Chandler in 1962. He compared the history of organizational change among 50 large companies during the century following the Civil War. His major conclusions were as follows:

> "The comparison emphasizes that a company's strategy in time determined its structure and that the common denominator of structure and strategy has been the application of the enterprise's resources to market demand. Structure has been the design for integrating the enterprise's existing resources to current demand; strategy has been the plan for the allocation of resources to anticipated demand" [Chandler, 1962:476].

Chandler also found that our present-day large companies evolved through four stages. They all tended to move sequentially through these stages, but the timing differed among companies in different industries with different environments.

He found that the large American industrial enterprise was born and grew in the post-Civil War years. The rapid industrialization and urbanization of the nation of that period opened up new opportunities and enterprises began to acquire new productive facilities, a labor force, and trained supervisory personnel to exploit them. Consolidations of companies permitted the new firm to produce higher volume at lower costs per unit. This was a period of great growth for such companies.

The second stage began when these vertically integrated companies found it increasingly imperative to coordinate better their activities in order to meet customer needs and maintain profits. The old organizational structures and administrative methods could not meet these needs. A new centralized, functionally departmentalized administrative structure was therefore created. Technical specialists were trained to coordinate various functional activities and the central headquarters installed control mechanisms to assure the integration that was needed to meet customer needs. This was a complex communications network that linked together all the activities in the industrial process to customer demands.

The third stage began when large companies found that opportunities for expanding their markets with their present products were declining as were possibilities for reducing costs per unit. So, these companies began to increase the number of products in their product line, to expand their overseas activities, and to produce new products for new markets.

The fourth and final stage began when these companies discovered that their old functional organizational structures and processes were inadequate to coordinate the activities involved in the production and sale of diverse products in different markets. They established new divisions in which all activities associated with a major product or product line were placed under the authority of a division manager. A central headquarters remained, of course, to assure the necessary coordination among the divisions and to make those strategic decisions that were required to assure a strong growing enterprise. The product-division structure was first introduced in the early 1920s.

The timing of these stages varied from company to company and industry to industry. By and large, however, the fourth stage began in the early 1920s after DuPont established (in 1921) the product-division structure. Many companies continued with functional organizations until recent years, and the substantial increase in the product-division structure among large companies did not take place until the post-World War II period.

Several recent studies have documented this thrust [Fouraker and Stopford, 1968; Wrigley, 1970; Channon, 1973; Scott, 1973; and Rumelt, 1974]. Rumelt surveyed approximately 200 of the largest companies in the United States (from the *Fortune* 500 list) and found that between 1949 and 1969 those having product-division organizations rose from 20.3 per cent to 75.9

per cent of the total. Those that were functionally organized fell from 62.7 per cent to 11.2 per cent of the total. Most of the decrease was due to the fact that previously functionally organized firms became product-division firms, rather than dropping from the top 500 list [Rumelt, 1974:65]. These are very substantial changes.

Rumelt also reached valuable conclusions about the performance of different types of organizational structures. Following Wrigley [1970] he divided firms into the following classes, depending upon strategies employed [Rumelt, 1974:29–32]:

1. Single Business: those whose revenue comes from one business.
2. Dominant Business: those for whom 70 per cent or more of revenues come from one business.
   (a) Dominant-Vertical: vertically integrated firms for whom 70 per cent or more of total revenue comes from one business.
   (b) Dominant-Constrained: those nonvertical firms that have expanded by emphasizing a dominant original strength, skill, or resource and whose activities are related one to another and to dominant business (the constraint).
   (c) Dominant-Linked: nonvertical firms that have expanded by building upon several skills, strengths, or resources and where the preponderance of activity is not directly related to the dominant business but is related to different activities of the firm.
   (d) Dominant-Unrelated: nonvertical firms whose diversified activities are not related to the dominant business.
3. Related Business: nonvertically integrated firms whose dominant business produces less than 70 per cent of total revenue and whose other activities are related to the dominant and other businesses.
   (a) Related-Constrained: related business firms that have diversified by relating new businesses to a particular skill or resources but where each activity, as a result, is related to almost all other activities.
   (b) Related-Linked: related business firms that have expanded by relating the new business to an old strength or skill but not always the same one.
4. Unrelated Business: nonvertical firms that have diversified into unrelated businesses.
   (a) Acquisitive Conglomerates: firms that have aggressive programs for acquiring unrelated businesses. Criteria for aggressiveness are (1) average growth rate in earnings per share of over 10 per cent annually in the past five years, and (2) issued new equity shares with total market value at least as great as the total amount of common dividends paid during the period.
   (b) Unrelated-Passive: those conglomerate firms that do not qualify as acquisitive conglomerates.

Rumelt [1974] came to the following major conclusions about the financial performance of these structures:

- Product-division firms showed average growth rates in earnings per share substantially higher than did the nondivisionalized firms [1974:107].
- No science-based company moved into the maturity and decline phase of its life-cycle without diversifying and adopting a multidivisional structure [1974:109].
- "Related Business firms will, on the average, have higher profitability, higher rates of growth, and higher price-earnings ratios than other categories of firms" [1974:114].
- "Related-Constrained firms will outperform Related-Linked firms in these (above) measures" [1974:114].
- "Divisionalized Related Business firms will outperform those that are functionally organized" [1974:114].
- The Related-Constrained and Dominant-Constrained firms are top performers in almost all measures—growth, return on equity, earnings per share [1974:123]. (Controlled diversity pays off. It may be that controlled diversity itself is not the cause of high performance but rather that high performance eliminates the need for greater diversification.)
- Both the Acquisitive conglomerates and Unrelated-Passive firms had average returns on capital not much different from the overall averages of all firms [1974:115].

Perhaps the most significant finding of Rumelt [1974:121] was that "the (above) categories did separate firms into groups that displayed significant and consistent differences in financial performance."

Channon [1973] studied the largest 100 firms in Great Britain and found trends in organization structure, between 1950 and 1970, very similar to the Rumelt results. He also concluded that British firms did not achieve all the advantages of divisionalization because they did not develop the proper mechanisms, knowledge, and skills to implement their structural strategy [Channon, 1973:220–227].

Scott [1973] studied trends in structure in four European countries (United Kingdom, France, Germany, and Italy) and found comparable organizational structural trends. His data revealed a significant increase in multidivisional companies and a sharp decline in single product firms. He concluded that diversification alone is not responsible for divisionalization. Under conditions of low competitive pressures, a strategy of diversification can be managed in a number of ways. However, when competition becomes intense managers turn to the divisional structure because it is the most effective way to manage a diversified firm.

Following the work of Chandler [1962], Scott [1973] formalized and tested a three-stage model in which the stages follow one another sequentially in the development of organizations. Stage I is an organization with a single product or single line. In stage II the firm expands the products in the single product line. In stage I there is little or no formal structure, for everything centers in one person. In stage II there is specialization based on function, and in stage III specialization is based on product-market relationships. Many other structures and processes in an organization differ depending upon which stage a company happens to be in. Chapter 6 contains an extended discussion of organizational life cycles.

PROGRAM STRUCTURES AND BUSINESS UNITS AS INTEGRATING FORMS

Corey and Star [1971:52] conclude that the greatest single influence on business organizational structures is the market environment. To exploit strategies for that market, most companies have created program structures. In their survey of over 500 companies they found 77 per cent with such structures. "A program is a total strategic plan for serving a particular market segment. It provides for product design, pricing, channels of distribution, advertising, promotion, and field selling; for product supply and customer service" [Corey and Star, 1971:2]. Those firms that produce a diverse product line for homogeneous markets generally use a product-market program manager. Those that have a homogeneous product line to sell in diverse markets typically have market program managers. Those with both diverse lines and markets are likely to have both types of managers. Companies generally form divisions, product departments, or business units to house one or more programs.

Coordination of activities is accomplished principally through product managers, who integrate marketing and production programs; interface managers, who guide the allocation of resource efforts to programs; resource scheduling activities; and planning. Among all the areas of responsibility which different product and market managers assume, planning is dominant above all others. Indeed, the central integration and resource allocation device is annual and long-range planning. Corey and Star [1971:53] found that "the type of program structure (product, market, or both) which a business has is a function of the type(s) of diversity with which it is faced." They also found that "businesses with program organizations seem to have been considerably more successful in developing and introducing new products than businesses without program organizations" [Corey and Star, 1971:54].

INTERRELATIONSHIPS AMONG ENVIRONMENT, STRUCTURE, INTEGRATION, AND PERFORMANCE

Around 1960 a number of studies discovered that successful organizations in different industries had different organizational structures [for example,

Woodward, 1958, 1965] and that organizational structures differed depending upon the organization's environment [for example, Burns and Stalker, 1961]. These led to a synthesis in Lawrence and Lorsch's *Organization and Environment* published in 1967, the highlights of which are presented here.

Lawrence and Lorsch studied in depth six firms in the plastics industry and two firms in each of the container and foods industries. One of the two was a high performer and the other a low performer, as measured in terms of profits, sales, and new product introduction. Their interest was centered on the way in which the environment affects functional units in an organization, the requirements for integration among the units, and the impact on performance in the way the organization responds. They drew the following conclusions:

- Among primary functional units—sales, production, and research and development—there was differentiation attributable to the particular environment of each. (Differentiation means variations in the way people are oriented towards goals, time, and interpersonnel relationships, as well as in the formality of organization structure.)
- The greater the differentiation the more is the need for integration. (Integration too is "the quality of the state of collaboration that exists among departments that are required to achieve unity of effort by the demands of the environment" [Lawrence and Lorsch 1967:11]. The organizations with the most successful performance records were those that have achieved the highest degree of integration and are also the most highly differentiated.
- Classical organization theorists said that integration is accomplished through rational processes, such as issuing orders through the managerial hierarchy and observing lines of authority. Lawrence and Lorsch said that integration is not achieved automatically but comes only when there is a resolution of the conflicts that exist in organizations. There are many means to do this, such as integrating committees and collaboration of people in different functional units.
- In highly dynamic environments they found that high performance organizations had to be highly differentiated and highly integrated. In more stable environments there could be less differentiation, but there still had to be a high degree of integration [Lawrence and Lorsch, 1967:108]. The greater the differentiation the more difficult is the task of integration. However, the devices and methods to secure integration among subsystems involves a great deal of mutual adjustment and communications. In a later study of 26 social service organizations Osborn and Hunt [1974:243] concluded that the applicability of classical formality, centralization, and nonparticipation "may be effective over a broad range of environmental conditions."

In a more recent study Lorsch and Allen [1973] confirmed Lawrence and Lorsch's earlier findings and added further details in an in-depth study of four conglomerate firms and two vertically integrated companies. Major findings of this study are as follows:

- The greater the differentiation among interdependent functional units the greater is the problem of integration. But the higher the quality of integration the better is the performance of the organization. This is generally true, but in conglomerates Lorsch and Allen concluded that there is a limit to integration between divisions and central headquarters. For conglomerates, where divisions need have no contact with one another, an attempt to install highly complex integrative devices may be counterproductive [Lorsch and Allen, 1973:181]. Where divisions do interrelate in their productive processes more complex integrative devices do pay off.
- Within divisions, and at the corporate level, the more complex the pattern of interdependence, the more complex the integrative devices will tend to be. Similarly, the more complex the interdependence and degree of differentiation in a vertically integrated company, the more complex will the integrative mechanisms tend to be. Again, as noted, if integrative devices become too complex, the effect will be counterproductive. An excess or a deficit of integrative effort, relative to the degree of interdependence, will produce less effective relationships among functional units.
- In organizations where there exist "appropriate patterns of differentiation and integration, there will tend to be a higher quality of information flowing downward from headquarters to the divisions and upward from the divisions to headquarters" [Lorsch and Allen, 1973:184]. Also, in such organizations conflict resolution will tend to be accomplished by face-to-face dialogue among managers which seeks to evaluate all available relevant information before decisions are made. In addition, patterns of influence will tend to coincide with the focus of available information.
- In conglomerates facing greater uncertainty and diversity but lower interdependence among divisions the performance evaluation system tends to be based upon financial and explicit end-result standards. Furthermore, monetary rewards are directly linked to results. In vertically integrated firms, with lower uncertainty and high interdependence, the performance evaluation systems tend to be more informally administered and there is a looser linkage between monetary rewards and achieved results. Among the more successful conglomerates, the reward system contained multiple criteria and tried to balance long-run and short-run considerations.
- Economic performance will be better when it achieves the proper differentiation required by the environment and introduces the proper integrative devices, integrative effort, and decision-making processes consistent with the information-processing requirements set by the environment.
- Economic performance of an organization will be higher the better is the organization-environment fit. This means that the proper differentiation in subunits must exist and that the proper integrative devices, integrative

effort, and decision-making processes are installed and are consistent with the information-processing requirements of the environment.

The net of all of this, in the words of Lorsch and Allen [1973:167] is that "Control and coordination of the total enterprise are most effectively facilitated when top management chooses a set of organizational devices which are congruent with the particular constellation of environmental factors faced by the firm."

Newman [1971] has speculated on the impact of different environments on major functions of a company. He says that three types of response flow from three different environments. In the "stable" environment the need for change in firm response is rather infrequent. The firm response is one of "required flexibility" when the environment forces more frequent change, but the problems are still familiar. When the environment requires even more frequent change, and when sometimes the problems are unprecedented, the requirement is for an "adaptive" mode. In each situation the tendency is to produce a specific type of response among the major functions of management: organization, planning, leading, and controlling. Table 14-2 shows the different impact Newman sees for these different functions depending upon environmental change.

Steiner and Ryan [1968] examined the managerial attitudes and techniques employed by 18 project managers in the aerospace industry who were given a responsibility for producing a new high technology product to meet a new requirement. Each manager was given a rather free hand by the government and his own top managements. It was found that each had the same fundamental management attitudes and employed similar managerial methods. Furthermore, they were able to produce a prototype product at a time and cost that was one third that of project managers who operated under conditions of greater control and supervision from top managers.

INTEGRATION AND DECENTRALIZATION

Firms that have introduced the product-division structure of organization have had difficult problems in determining the degree of integration that should be maintained between the divisions and central headquarters. In commenting on this question Sloan, for many years the top executive of General Motors, said: "Having . . . established techniques of control in the particular areas of appropriations, cash, inventory, and production, the general question remained: How could we exercise permanent control over the whole corporation in a way consistent with the decentralized scheme of organization? We never ceased to attack this paradox; indeed we could not avoid a solution of it without yielding both the actual decentralized structure of our business and our philosophy of approach to it" [Sloan, 1964:139–140]. He went on to say that the solution was to review the effectiveness of divisionalized operations on the basis of return on investment. But subsequent analysis has shown that this standard has significant weaknesses [Weston, 1972; Dearden, 1969].

The issues in integration between headquarters and decentralized divisions cover a broad spectrum of managerial philosophy, tasks facing both areas, interpersonnel relationships, integration mechanisms, and environments (internal and external). In this light there can be no universal solution.

Aside from the research noted there has been other work that throws light on preferred courses of action in designing organizational structures and processes. To illustrate, Dale [1952] has laid out the spectrum of choice with respect to authority relationships. Lorsch and Allen [1973:139] concluded that the better the integration between corporate headquarters and divisions the higher the performance of the company. They also identified the mechanisms that managers in the companies surveyed considered to be the most significant in achieving desired integration. Planning systems were among the more prominent integrating mechanisms. Greiner examined 58 companies and concluded that the more the planning is systematized into the organizations the more effective it is; the more explicit goals are for an organization the higher is the estimate of effectiveness for the organization [in Aguilar, *et al.*, 1970:98]. Dearden concluded that "a decentralized profit center system . . . requires a more sophisticated and expensive budgeting and planning system to overcome the problems of communication, coordination, and evaluation than profit decentralization creates" [Dearden, 1962a:147; 1962b].

There have been a number of contributions of a very specific nature to this general question, only a few of which can be illustrated. Solomons' [1965] research has detailed the methods used to measure and control the performance of decentralized divisions. Vancil [1972a] has described an allocation of funds methodology to assure better planning and control of product development. Soden [1972] has described causes of failure and their solutions in establishing computerized information systems linking headquarters with divisions.

The mixture of integration devices is as important as the mechanisms chosen. A number of companies, for example, have experienced grave problems in, first of all, making the decision to decentralize and, having made the decision, to manage properly the decentralized firm. On the first instance management, not used to delegating authority and responsibility, may not make the transition. Many entrepreneurs who built a company have not been able to do so and, as a result, have had the traumatic experience of being asked to resign by their boards of directors. Once decentralization has been undertaken, there are factors that must be considered in designing and employing integrating mechanisms. Many companies have lost the effective-

TABLE 14-2
Typical Features of Management Structures For Three Types of Technology

	Features That Distinguish Management Structures	Nature of Technology *		
		Stable	Regulated Flexibility	Adaptive
Organizing	Centralization versus decentralization	Centralized	Mostly centralized	Decentralized
	Degree of division of labor	Narrow specialization	Specialized, or crafts	Scope may vary
	Size of self-sufficient operating units	Large	Medium	Small, if equipment permits
	Mechanisms for coordination	Built-in, programmed	Separate planning unit	Face-to-face within unit
	Nature and location of staff	Narrow functions; headquarters	Narrow functions; headquarters and operating unit	Generalists at headquarters; specialists in operating units
	Management information system	Heavy upward flow	Flow to headquarters and to operating unit	Flow mostly to, and within, operating unit
	Characteristics of key personnel	Strong operators	Functional experts in line and staff	Analytical, adaptive
Planning	Use of standing plans: Comprehensiveness of coverage	Broad coverage	All main areas covered	Mostly "local," self-imposed
	Specificity	Detail specified	Detail in interlocking activities	Main points only
	Use of single-use plans: Comprehensiveness of coverage	Fully planned	Fully planned	Main steps covered
	Specificity	Detail specified	Schedules and specs detailed	Adjusted to feedback

	Planning horizon	Weekly to quarterly	Weekly to annually	Monthly to three years or more
	Intermediate versus final objectives	Intermediate goals sharp	Intermediate goals sharp	Emphasis on objectives
	"How" versus results	"How" is specified	Results at each step specified	End results stressed
Leading	Participation in planning	Very limited	Restricted to own tasks	High participation
	Permissiveness	Stick to instructions	Variation in own tasks only	High permissiveness, if results OK
	Closeness of supervision	Follow operations closely	Output and quality closely watched	General supervision
	Sharing of information	Circumspect	Job information shared	Full project information shared
	Emphasis on on-the-job satisfactions	Limited scope	Craftsmanship and professionalism encouraged	Opportunity for involvement
Controlling	Performance criteria emphasized	Efficiency, dependability	Quality, punctuality, efficiency	Results, within resource limits
	Location of control points	Within process; intermediate stages	Focus on each processing unit	Overall "milestones"
	Frequency of checks	Frequent	Frequent	Infrequent
	Who initiates corrective action	Often central managers	"Production control" and other staff	Men in operating unit
	Stress on reliability versus learning	Reliability stressed	Reliability stressed	Learning stressed
	Punitive versus reward motivation	Few mistakes tolerated	Few mistakes tolerated	High reward for success

* "Technology" as used by Newman includes "all sorts of methods for converting resource inputs into products and service for consumers. The inputs can be labor, knowledge, and capital as well as raw materials" [1971:12].

SOURCE: William H. Newman: "Strategy and Management Structure." *Academy of Management Proceedings,* August 1971, pp. 15–18. Reprinted by permission of the Academy of Management.

ness of decentralization because their design and management of integrating mechanisms was faulty. This happened in Great Britain as noted previously [Channon, 1973].

MANAGERIAL PHILOSOPHY AND STRUCTURE

Structure is usually determined by environmental conditions, but it can be influenced by other forces. Simonetti, for instance, found a direct relationship between managerial philosophy and structure in Italian companies. He compared American subsidiaries in Italy with similar domestic firms. The differences he found he explained in these words: "Most American subsidiaries studied were structured around a philosophy of competence and responsibility, permitting a high degree of specialization, well-defined areas of responsibility, a general sense of personal accountability, and an overall structure based on decentralization. Generally, the Italian company is characterized by a greater degree of control, less delegation, hierarchical density, and centralization" [Simonetti, undated]. Vancil [1973] also has observed how managerial philosophy, which may or may not correspond to environment, can influence structure.

CONCLUDING COMMENTS

This review has touched only the most dominant conclusions of research dealing with organizational structure and processes concerned with implementation of policy and strategy. Although there has been a great deal of research there are few prescriptive guides that managers may employ to be assured they have the "right" structure and mix of procedures. Each case must be designed in light of the unique circumstances surrounding it. It is clear from much of the research, however, that long- and short-range planning is a major integrative methodology. We now turn to how planning implements policy and strategy.

QUESTIONS

Discussion Guides on Chapter Content

1. Discuss important problems that you think managers in most companies have when trying to be sure that strategies are implemented. Generally, how are the problems overcome?
2. Identify some of the key factors in organizations that will influence the manner in which strategies are implemented.
3. Explain the "contingency theory of organizational design."

4. Describe the major conclusions that scholars such as Chandler, Rumelt, Scott, and Lawrence and Lorsch have discovered about the interrelationships between strategy and organization structures.
5. The studies of Newman and of Lawrence and Lorsch, come to conclusions about the impact of different environments on management and organizational structures. Compare the conclusions of these scholars.

Mind Stretching Questions

1. In what major ways would you expect that environments in which United States based multinational companies operate will have a different impact on strategy of organizational structures, and the implementation of strategies, than the environment in the United States?
2. If you were to undertake research building upon the work of the scholars discussed in this chapter what hypotheses would you recommend for testing?

CHAPTER

15

Formal Systems for Implementing Policies and Strategies

INTRODUCTION

The focus in this chapter is on a few major more or less formal systems for implementing policies and strategies, namely, planning and budgeting, the network of policies and standard operating procedures, management by objectives, scheduling, and communications. These systems were chosen for analysis because they are virtually universally used, they are fundamental, and they are generally structured. This contrasts with various types of interpersonal mechanisms, which will be discussed in the next chapter.

Most emphasis in this chapter will be on the planning systems. Justification for this lies in the fact that the single most significant mechanism used in organizations, especially the larger and more complex ones, to translate strategy into current decisions, is the linkage among different plans.

The emphasis of this chapter is also supported by Lorsch and Allen [1973] in their study of four companies with decentralized organization structures. They identified major integrating devices that were perceived by managers as playing the most significant role in corporate-divisional relations as follows:

Annual budgeting system
Approved system for major capital and expense items
Formal goal-setting system, performance evaluation, and incentive compensation system
Group vice presidents
Direct managerial contact
Monthly budget reviews
Five-year planning system

Other devices that managers identified as of importance, but not as frequently cited, were quarterly budget forecast; monthly operating reports; cash management system; approval system for hiring, replacement, and salary changes of key division personnel; divisional "specialists" in corporate controller's office; annual meetings between corporate and divisional general managers; group management committees; technical evaluation board for capital projects; permanent cross-divisional committees; line management task forces; and *ad hoc* cross-divisional meetings for functional managers [Lorsch and Allen, 1973:59]. Their listing of and significance attached to integrative devices for vertically integrated companies was quite similar to this list [Lorsch and Allen, 1973:129].

Obviously, relationships among people rank high in the important integrative devices. One cannot, of course, implement a planning system or a system of management by objective without interpersonal dealings.

INTEGRATING AND IMPLEMENTING SYSTEMS

On the Nature of Integrating Systems and Their Design

It is worth repeating here what was said previously that, first of all, major systems such as those discussed in this chapter must be tailored to each organizational situation. There are many ways to organize, introduce, and use each of these systems, and the "right" design must be found for each situation for best results. Second, the forces that influence design are the same as those discussed in connection with organizational structual design, plus many more.

The influence of one dimension, not discussed in detail previously—interdependence of subunits of an organization—will illustrate the point. Thompson [1967] identified three major types of interdependence, as follows:

Pooled interdependence—units having virtually no needed contacts, such as a conglomerate with unrelated divisions.

Sequential interdependence—an organization where the output of one major unit is the input for other units, such as is the case in vertically integrated companies.

Reciprocal interdependence—instances where outputs of each unit are the inputs for other units, such as single product companies which produce components for their end item.

The design, introduction, implementation, costs, problems, and usage of major systems will vary depending upon which type of the above interdependence exists.

Coordination Takes Place Throughout the Planning Process

Integrated corporate planning has two significant dimensions. First, plans are coordinated, more or less, from the top levels of an organization down through the lower levels. Second, plans are coordinated at different levels. Both dimensions were explained in Chapter 7. One result of a conscious effort to perfect such coordination is that the formulation of strategy takes place with some reference to circumstances surrounding its implementation, even at low levels of an organization.

To illustrate the first dimension of coordination, the Monsanto Chemical Company decided several years ago to enter the detergent field with a branded product. This strategy was well timed and in line with the company's resources. It was not implemented, however, because it aroused strong opposition from consumer product companies who were major customers for Monsanto's detergent materials. To illustrate the second dimension of coordination, Rolls Royce did not interrelate properly its marketing planning for the RS-211 engine, designed for the Lockheed L-1011 airplane, with research and development engineering and, as a result, went bankrupt [Ross and Kami, 1973].

Typically, in most organizations that have a formal planning system, there are three sets of plans, as described in Chapter 7—strategic, medium range, and short range. In theory, each relates to the other and each has some degree of internal coordination. Complete and detailed coordination and integration within and among these sets of plans would be extremely difficult. As a consequence managers are wise when they coordinate only that which is necessary to the achievement of the major organization aims. This will, of course, vary from case to case. There has been a little, but not much, research on this point as will be noted.

Nature of Implementation Plans

Implementation plans translate strategic plans into current decisions. The process is that of making medium-range functional plans and using them as bases for making short-range plans and decisions. In this section our focus is on medium-range plans.

Figure 15-1 shows how different medium-range plans may be interrelated. Each company must decide for itself whether plans will be prepared for each of the subjects shown in the chart, in what detail, and with what coordination with other plans. There is no rule or formula governing such decisions. There are some minimums, however, that each company should consider. For example, a medium-range marketing plan of a manufacturing company should interrelate, at a minimum, with production and product development plans. Depending upon circumstances it might be wise to extend the interrelationship to other functional plans, such as facility plans. The medium-range marketing plan should be developed within the overall objectives and strategies of the company and in relationship to other functional plans at the same level of planning.

The objectives, strategies and detailed plans will depend upon the functions of the marketing manager. Functions of marketing managers vary much from firm to firm, but if the job descriptions of a number of them were

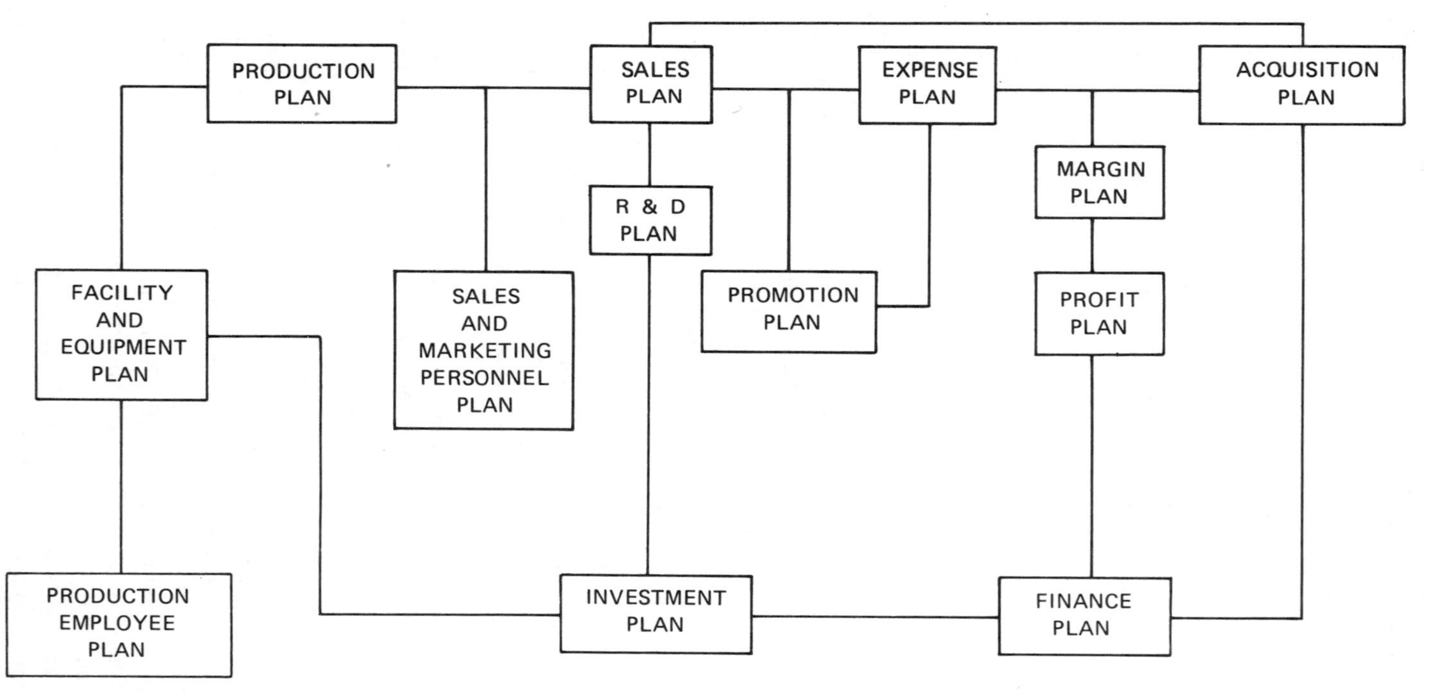

Suggested by Alfred Friedrich, "Planning in a German Steel Company," *Long Range Planning*, December 1972.

Figure 15-1 Medium range programming of the strategic path. [Suggested by Alfred Friedrich: "Planning in a German Steel Company." *Long Range Planning*, December 1972.]

aggregated the range of activities would encompass the four P's identified by McCarthy [1964:36] to classify marketing functions—product, place, promotion, and price. Each of these, of course, covers a wide range of possible detailed activities. For instance, under product might be included plans for adding, dropping, or modifying product lines; branding, packaging, standardizing, and grading. Place refers to distribution channels to get the right product at the right place at the right time. Promotion is concerned with communicating with customers, such as through advertising, developing salesmen, etc. Pricing involves not only the actual price of a product but costs, volume, product mix, promotion, and so on.

Vancil [1972a] has illustrated in detail how in one company headquarters and divisions integrated new product development planning. Howell [1970b] has set forth a detailed model to assure the proper integration of acquisitions with other functional plans, and Corke [1970] has developed a model explaining the ways in which production planning can be interrelated with other plans. The ways in which a German engineering company interrelates functional plans is examined by Heckman [1971].

In theory, the more stable the environment the more appropriate are extensive interrelationships among functional plans. The more unstable the environment the less appropriate is comprehensive integration of such plan [Lawrence and Lorsch, 1967; Lorsch, 1965]. The extent and degree of integration among companies has not been measured but our empirical observations lead us to conclude that perhaps one third of medium to large companies have moderately well-integrated operational plans beyond 12 months. Vancil [1970a] surveyed 29 companies concerning the extent to which they prepared the following functional plans: financial, marketing, manufacturing, facilities, and manpower. Almost half said they included them all, 41 per cent said some, and 10 per cent said few. His study did not ask whether these were coordinated but the presumption seems to be that there were some interrelationships.

In the same survey, this time with 48 responses, Vancil asked whether financial statements were part of the documentation of the long-range planning effort. To prepare financial plans presumably would require coordination of functional plans. He found that only 2 per cent had no financial statements, 14.6 per cent had only financial ratios, 14.6 per cent prepared their statements in the same detail as the annual budget [Vancil, 1970].

BUDGETS: A MAJOR INTEGRATING MECHANISM

Nature and Purpose of Budgets

Peter Drucker once observed: "The test of a plan . . . is not how good the plan is itself. The test is whether management actually commits resources to action which will bring results in the future. Unless this is being done, there is no plan. There are only promises and hopes" [in Ewing, 1972:5]. A dominant method to make commitments to assure action is a budget.

Budgets are formal statements of policies, plans, and goals that are designed to assure that actions are taken within specified boundaries laid down by top management and upon the basis of which performance can be measured. Three basic purposes are expressed in this definition. Budgets are based upon plans, as explained previously, and are plans in themselves. Budgets conceptually express detailed plans that interrelate various functional activities in such a fashion as to assure the most effective and efficient utilization of resources to achieve the objectives sought. This means that budgets interrelate such activities as production, raw material purchases, inventories, facilities, labor requirements, and so on. Budgets are vehicles for assuring the proper coordination of activities. Budgets set standards for performance and when management monitors activities there will be control over performance. Budgets not only facilitate but force integration of functional activities to achieve predetermined objectives.

In 1958 a survey of 386 correspondents in 35 companies showed that budgets were virtually universal [Sord and Welsch, 1958]. Since then the budget has become even more entrenched and comprehensive in scope.

Types of Budgets

Although budgeting is universal in usage there is no uniform pattern of budgets. In Figure 15-2 a comprehensive pattern of interrelated budgets in a manufacturing company is shown. Notice the dominant position of the cash budget, which is typical in industry.

Jerome [1961:109] observed that: "To freeze a plan and to put a dollar sign on it is the essence of budgeting. But as soon as plans are frozen, the attitude and behavior of everyone concerned with the plans have a way of freezing too." Managers adopt a number of methods to assure flexibility in budgets. Among these are supplemental budgets, which provide funding above budget ceilings; alternative budgets, which may be applied when different environmental conditions occur; and variable expense budgets, which relate such elements as raw material purchase, inventory, direct labor, and supervisory costs to fluctuations in customer demand and production runs [Steiner, 1969b:301–305]. In addition to such budgets top management injects flexibility into budgeting through its own activities and by instilling flexible thinking in the minds of all managers.

Linkage

The linkage between short-range budgets and medium-range plans is not uniform either in theory or practice. There is a tight linkage when the numbers used in budgets are identical with the numbers in the first year of multiple-year medium-range plans. There is a loose linkage when medium-range plans are only used as a frame of reference for preparing budgets.

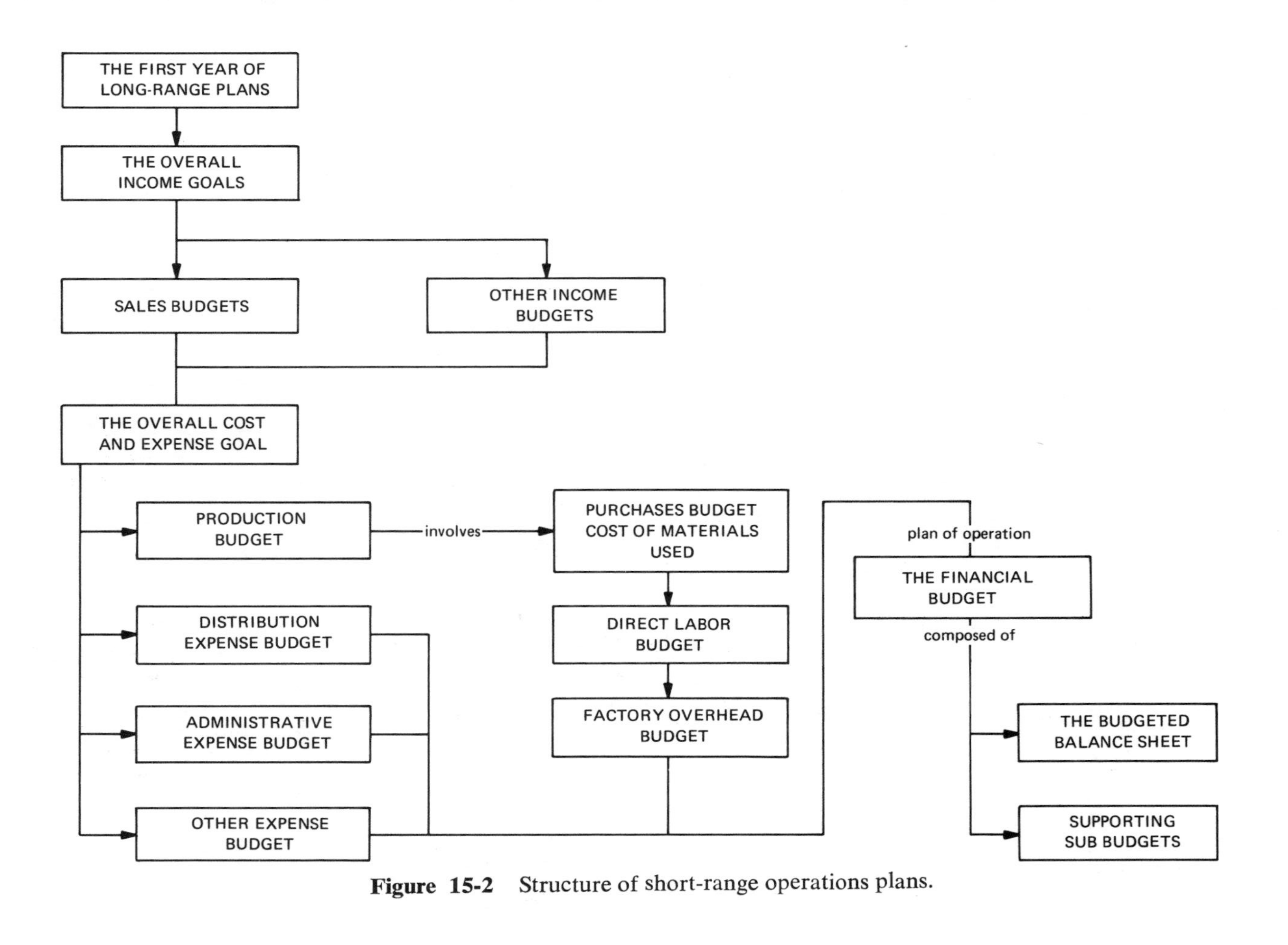

Figure 15-2 Structure of short-range operations plans.

From Vancil's studies [1970a] of linkage it can be concluded, although the data are not precise, that in about half the companies in the United States the linkage is probably tight. Vancil's survey showed that operating managers said the linkage was tighter than did the corporate planners!

When the linkage is tight the top management of a firm in effect is saying to managers that the long-range planning process is serious and not a game. There are disadvantages, however. If the focus is sharp and intense on short-run budgets, the manager whose budget is under survey naturally will pay attention to the short run and neglect the long run. This is especially so if his performance is measured on short run criteria. In addition, short run orientation tends to induce risk aversion [Vancil, Aguilar, and Howell, 1968]. For such reasons about half the firms in the United States have a loose linkage between budgets and medium-range plans.

Another reason for not using a tight linkage is that, between the time the medium-range plans are made and the actual short-range budgets are prepared, basic assumptions upon which plans rest may have changed. The first draft of the budget may reveal relationships unforeseen at the time the strategic guidelines and subsequent medium-range plans were prepared. Wisdom would, of course, suggest appropriate adjustments.

IBM at one time had a tight linkage between medium-range and short-range plans but because of such difficulties moved to a looser linkage.

Several points should be made about linkage. First, budgets typically are prepared for each month for one year. Second, the details in budgets are far greater than in the first year of a medium-range plan; that is, budgets not only cover more activities but break them down in far greater detail. Third, as noted before, complete coordination of all major functions either in a medium-range plan or in the budgeting system is ill advised. The degree of integration will depend upon many factors, such as stability of environment, complexity of task, and interdependency of organizational units.

In sum, budgets are the most universally used and central basis for translating strategic decisions into current actions. They are key means by which top management states its intentions in quantitative terms, provides for the coordination of selected functions, and establishes bases for controlling and measuring performance.

Managerial Influence on Plans and Capital Allocations

There has been a little research on the relationships among managers in the implementation process. McDonald and Eastlack [1971] in a study involving 211 chief executive officers concluded that firms that were most successful were those where top management got involved in both the formulation and implementation of strategy. This was found also by Sylvester [1970] in a study of commercial projects undertaken in the areospace industry.

On a five-point scale Vancil [1971:284] found that managers ($N = 89$) said the mean was 4.43 for the influence of division managers in the final version of the division plan and 3.72 for corporate managers. Pfeffer and Salancik [1974] studied university departments and concluded that the more powerful the department the less the budget was limited to departmental work. Bower [1970] also found that powerful divisional managers were likely to get top management's approval of their capital requests. He concluded: "That boards and appropriations committees in most companies recognize the extent to which they have delegated their capital appropriating powers is evidenced by the very low rate of project rejections which characterizes their actions" [Bower, 1970:15]. Pondy and Birnberg [1969] also discovered that managers with the highest profits and most convincing proposals get the largest budget allocations. However, managers with less profitable projects are favored when they present biased cases with strong pleas.

This strength of divisional managers in the planning process is understandable because they have power and they are strongly motivated. This may well lead to presenting top management with biased cases. It may also lead to disaster, which was the case with the powerful Convair Division of General Dynamics and the financial disaster of the 880 and 990 airplanes [Newman and Logan, 1971]. This research also underscores the fact that planning and budgeting are undertaken in a political climate and decisions may be made on political as well as economic grounds.

Monitoring Deviation from Plans

The typical textbook on management states that controls are installed to assure minimum deviation from plans. In practice this is not the case. In a study of 41 companies Henning [1964] found that performance was compared against standard in only one standard out of five. Furthermore, he found little difference in this practice between large and small firms [Henning, 1964]. In a study of 75 utility firms in the United States Holmberg [1974] found that a significant proportion of the firms surveyed did not formally compare the various long-range plans to actual results. Finance and equipment plans were more frequently compared with actual results than in other areas. Other studies also indicate the absence of formal mechanisms for monitoring long-range plans against results in other areas [Vancil, 1970b].

Anthony [1965:28–29] takes the position that the aim of management control is not to assure that the results of operations conform as closely as possible to plans. He asserts: "To the extent that middle management can make decisions that are better than those implied in the plans, top management wishes it do so. And the middle managers can in fact make better decisions under certain circumstances; to deny this possibility is implicitly to assume that top management is either clairvoyant, or omniscient, or both, which is not so" [Anthony, 1965:29]. Top management wants middle managers to react to what is happening in the world and not to follow blindly a preestablished plan. Plans are made at one point of time on the basis of various assumptions. When the premises change so should the plans. "The practical implication of the foregoing statements," says Anthony [1965:29] "is that conformance to plans is *not* the standard against which performance should be measured."

This question often arises: Should actual performance be compared with the original budget or with a later revision? There is no argument about whether an original budget should be adhered to when it fails to meet current conditions. As a result, many companies revise budgets quarterly, and sometimes monthly. But which budget should be used to measure performance? If actual performance is compared with the original budget, managers are measured on what they originally agreed to do. To use the revised budget is to accept an excuse for missing the original target. To use the revised budget as a standard of comparison, however, is to accept the reality of change and the irrationality of clinging to an outmoded target. Some companies resolve the problem by comparing current actual performance against both the original budget and the revised "forecast" [Solomons, 1965:240].

Participation and Budget Achievement

A number of research studies have focused on relationships between participation and the making and acceptance of policies. Some of the results of these studies were examined in Chapters 11 and 12, and the topic will receive more extended consideration in Chapter 16. Less research has been conducted which deals specifically with the budget process, although a few such studies do exist.

In one early study Argyris [1952] concluded that a lack of participation in the budget process resulted in very low levels of commitment to achieve budget targets. A decade later Sord and Welsch [1964] surveyed 204 lower level supervisors and concluded that budgets were resented by many who did not participate in making them. On the other hand, it is apparent that people without major interests in the accounting area, such as certain engineers, may actively resist efforts to get them to participate in establishing budgets because this is not the way they wish to spend their time [Wallace, 1966].

Certain studies have appeared to indicate a relationship between participation and goal setting of the kind involved in budget preparation. Several support the view that participation in goal setting is positively related to goal acceptance [Dunbar, 1971; Locke, 1966; Raia, 1966], and there are other studies that suggest that, at least in certain people under certain circumstances, participation in decision making, including budgeting, can act as a motivator for improved performance [Lowin, 1968; Stedry, 1967; Vroom, 1960]. Yet there are as many studies that raise questions about these performance effects of participation [Morse and Reimer, 1956; Powell and Schlacter, 1971; Tosi, 1970], and it appears that goals set by others can have positive effects just as participative goal setting does [Bryan and Locke, 1967].

In an extensive research effort, which focused more directly on budgetary considerations and covered 23 plants and almost 350 managers, Searfoss and Monczka [1973:543] tested four hypotheses about budgets with these results:

First, the hypothesis was supported that "perceived participation in the budget process and motivation to achieve the budget are positively related."

Second, the hypothesis was supported that "a positive relationship exists between perceived participation in the budget process and the position in the organizational hierarchy."

Third, *not* supported was the hypothesis that "the positive relationship between perceived participation in the budget process and the motivation to achieve the budget will increase when the need for independence increases."

Fourth, *not* supported was the hypothesis that "the positive relationship between perceived participation in the budget process and the motivation to achieve the budget will decrease when the level of authoritarianism increases."

These findings indicate that, where acceptance of budget figures is a major problem and managers lack motivation to stay within their budgets, the use of participation can help with these problems. However, obtaining the needed sense of participation may be easier at higher levels of management than at lower.

Probably the area of budget preparation is a particularly favorable one for the use of participation, at least within the ranks of management, because separate and distinct budgets are prepared for a great variety of organizational units. More comprehensive or organization-wide decisions and policies cannot be broken down into separate decisions differing from unit to unit, a problem treated in greater detail in the next chapter.

There is evidence that in one setting increased participation may raise motivation, whereas in another setting the impact on motivation may be negative [Mitchell, 1973]. Thus, the positive findings in the area of budget *acceptance* should not be generalized to task performance more generally or to other contexts; nor should findings with regard to participation in other situations be applied uncritically in the budgetary area. Even within the budget area there are limits to what can be achieved through participation [Caplan, 1971].

Tosi examined the many studies concerning the motivations of budgets and concluded: "From these studies, and an abundance of other data on target setting, goal clarity, and similar concepts, it can be concluded that the motivating effect of the budget derives from simply the fact that it is a statement of explicit goals" [in Chandra and Singhvi, 1975:66].

OTHER INTEGRATING AND IMPLEMENTING SYSTEMS

The Network of Policies and Standard Operating Procedures (SOP)

As noted in Chapter 2, policies and procedures provide a network of strands that bind together the activities of an organization. A large organization must have literally hundreds of interrelated polices and procedures. When procedures are formalized, they become SOP and serve to guide routine actions of all types. There can be no effective implementation of policies and strategies without this network.

Management by Objectives (MBO)

Drucker [1954] is widely credited with first publicizing the MBO approach which originated in management practice. A considerable body of research and knowledge has been accumulated since regarding this approach [Carroll and Tosi, 1973; Raia, 1974]. Today most large companies utilize some type of MBO system and usage is growing in medium- and small-sized companies. The approach is also applicable to, and has been employed in, nonprofit organizations [Brady, 1973].

Originally, MBO was a system designed to improve measurement of individual performance [McGregor, 1957]. However, the MBO process has evolved until today it is a system that seeks to "integrate management processes and activities in a logical and consistent manner. These include the development of overall organizational goals and strategic plans, problem-solving and decision-making, performance appraisal, executive compensation, manpower planning, and management training and development" [Raia, 1974:15]. In this more advanced role, MBO obviously can be a significant integrating force in effective implementation of master policies and strategies.

There are many different names given to the approach under consideration, and there are many different ways it is accomplished in organizations [Raia, 1974]. Nevertheless, there is a good likelihood of agreement that any advanced MBO system would include the conceptual processes shown in Figure 15-3. Individual goals are set in relationship to company goals and strategic plans, actions are planned and individuals attempt to exercise self-control in their performance, and performance is reviewed and measured. The entire system is interrelated and coordinated with other major managerial systems, such as compensation programs, training efforts, and career planning. Individual goals and the actions to attain them are characteristically established for periods of one year or less.

Studies have been conducted that support the view that MBO can be a significant process for improving implementation of plans [Carroll and Tosi,

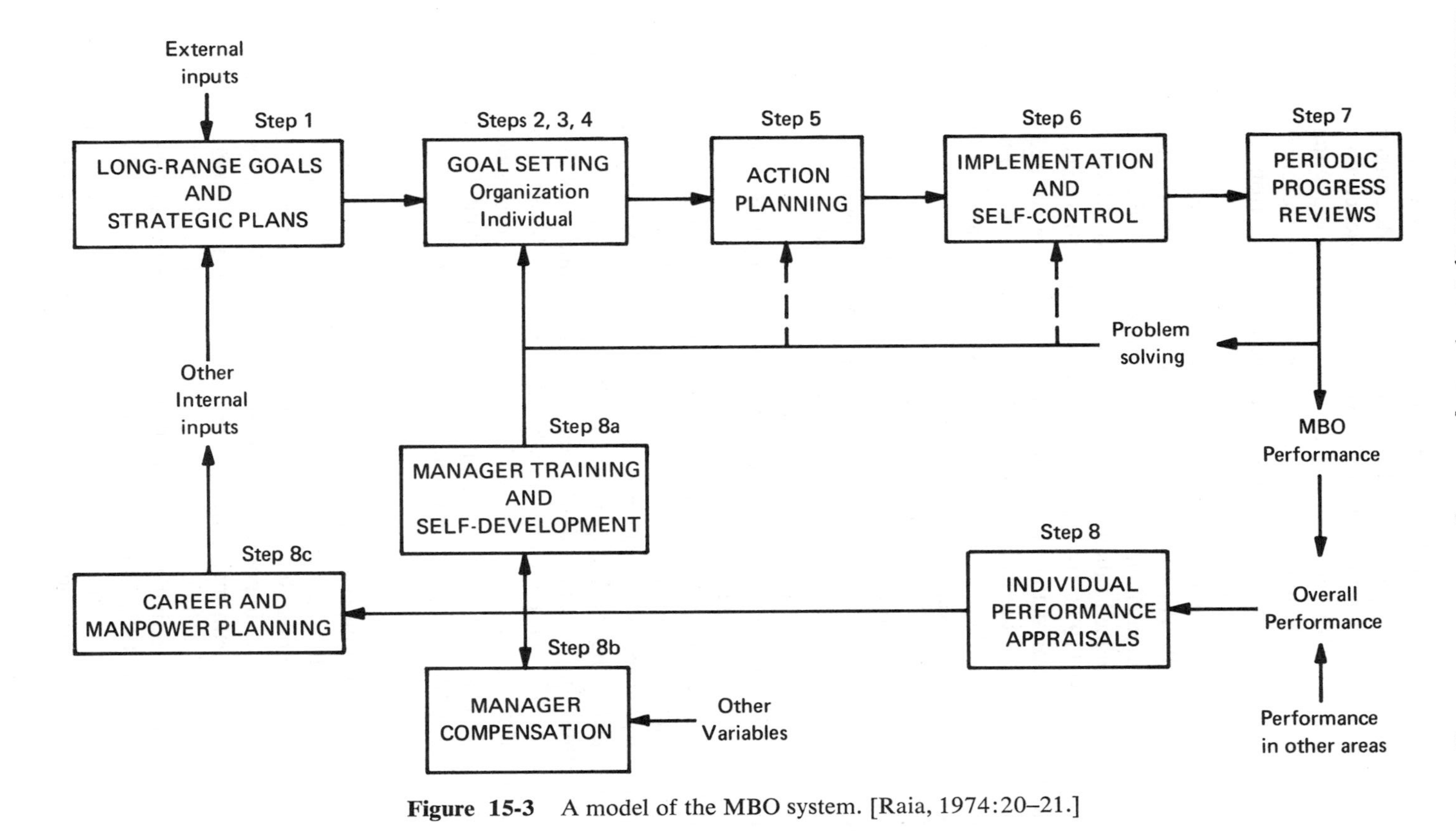

Figure 15-3 A model of the MBO system. [Raia, 1974:20–21.]

1973; Howell, 1970a; Raia, 1966]. Many other benefits have been attributed to the effective operation of an MBO program. Thus McConkey [1973:27] in a 20 year reassessment of reported company experience concluded that ". . . practicing MBO in depth does result in improved communication, coordination, control, and motivation of managers. These desirable ends are considered the minimum an organization should expect from its MBO efforts. . . ."

Like formal planning, however, MBO is conceptually simple but deceptively difficult to do well. There are many pitfalls that need to be avoided for a successful application of an MBO system to occur and sizable numbers of companies have indeed fallen into them [Humble, 1970; McConkey, 1972]. Carroll and Tosi [1973:107] in their assessment of MBO experience, conclude that ". . . unless the various organizational systems are tied into MBO, it will be very difficult to carry out the MBO process." They also note, as does Raia [1966], that there is a tendency for MBO programs to become less effective after the first year or so of application.

Although the use of MBO has been associated with a participative style of management by certain writers [McConkey, 1973; Raia, 1974], the available evidence does not support the view that extensive use of participative procedures in establishing objectives is a *necessary* condition for the effective use of MBO. Superior-set objectives can achieve the same effects [Carroll and Tosi, 1973]. This finding is consistent with that of Bryan and Locke [1967] on goal setting outside the MBO context.

MBO has been described as a new way to manage. Drucker [1974:442] concludes that ". . . management by objectives and self-control may properly be called a philosophy of management . . . it insures performance by converting objective needs into personal goals." Some would view this as an overly enthusiastic interpretation. There are serious questions as to whether MBO in actual application does involve this much self-control and in fact whether self-control can ever be relied upon to achieve organizational goals [Miner, 1976]. Nevertheless, the approach is an important one among the wide variety of tools for policy implementation available.

Scheduling Models

It should be mentioned here, although no detailed analysis will be attempted, that a number of scheduling models have much to contribute to implementation. As noted in Table 9-1 there are a number of conventional scheduling models of importance in integrating activities, such as milestone charts and critical path methods. Network models, such as Program Evaluation and Review Technique (PERT), are powerful tools for integrating extremely complex activities. Developed to coordinate the Polaris submarine weapon systems in 1958, this technique is credited as having played a major role in the success of that program. There are today many variations of PERT in use. To these tools should be added systems and simulation models

[Steiner, 1969b]. Milliken and Morrison [1971] have made a detailed evaluation of such tools as they are used in the aerospace industry.

Communications Systems

Communications may be considered at four different levels of analysis. One is intrapersonal, which relates to how an individual takes in, processes, and produces communications. A second is interpersonal, which deals with interactions between individuals and groups. Third, is the flow of communications in channels in organizations, both formally and informally. Fourth, are systems of data flow including computer applications [Miner, 1973a:361]. The more efficient these systems are the better will be implementation of policies and strategies.

The design of the information system will have important implications for policy and strategy formulation, as well as its implementation. This is clear from the discussions in Chapters 7, 8, 9, and the present chapter.

It should be obvious, but it does not seem to be to some observers, that there is and can be no such thing as *the* management information system [Dearden, 1972]. There are many different systems which may or may not relate. These systems are designed to provide managers with information needed in discharging their responsibilities, which range from making current decisions about nonrecurrent problems to reporting to government agencies in prescribed terms. The systems are constantly changing, and it is rare to find a management that is satisfied with its management information systems.

The notion of the single system has given way to the concept of individual systems using a common data base. This is a more realistic approach [Tipgos, 1975].

Another thrust of research about management information systems concerns the relationship between information systems, such as computer models, and the realities of organizational needs for and uses of information [Hammond, 1974; Hall, 1972].

Another thrust, based upon the original work of Marshak [1968], concerns the value of adding information in information systems [Gallagher, 1974]. New research is also being conducted on behavioral factors in the design of information systems [McKenney and Keen, 1974]. Finally, as evidenced in many articles in *Management Science,* work is being pushed in developing more complex information models.

A Note on Other Mechanistic Systems

In organizations with complex and interrelated processes there are found many other types of systems for assuring proper coordination. In mind, for example, are computerized network systems, incentive contracting, make or buy models, quality assurance systems, and so on. For an analysis of such systems, including an evaluation, in the aerospace industry see Milliken and Morrison [1971].

A Note on Comprehensive Treatments of Control Systems

Most books on managerial processes, theory, and practice include sections on planning and control to implement plans. There have been comparatively few books that deal only with planning and control as related activities or solely with control. One of the earliest books in the field was Goetz's *Management Planning and Control* [1949]. After a long time span this was followed by Jerome's *Executive Control* [1961]. Shortly thereafter there appeared Anthony's *Planning and Control Systems* [1965], which emphasized planning more than control. More recent editions parallelling more closely the contents of this chapter, but in much greater coverage and detail of methods of implementation of plans, are Mockler's *The Management Control Process* [1972] and Newman's *Constructive Control* [1975].

QUESTIONS

Discussion Guides on Chapter Content

1. Identify some significant managerial devices for integrating activities in organizations to assure the implementation of strategies.
2. How do you visualize differing integrating systems among Thompson's three types of organizational interdependence?
3. Specify how a planning system can assure the proper implementation of strategic decisions.
4. How are budgets used as integrating mechanisms?
5. Studies have shown that the strongest divisions and divisional managers tend to get the most generous capital allocations from headquarters. Why do you think this is so?
6. In management's efforts to control operations to meet plans, do you think actual performance should be compared with the original budget plan, with a later revision, or with neither?
7. Discuss the more significant research findings related to achieving budgeted goals and the participation of people in the budgetary process.
8. Explain the meaning of MBO and how it can serve to assure better implementation of policies/strategies.

Mind Stretching Questions

1. Identify four or five different managerial styles that might be adopted by the chief executive officer of an organization and explain how implementation systems may vary depending upon the style.
2. Discuss this subject: "The Politics of Managerial Control."

CHAPTER

16

The Role of People in Implementation

INTRODUCTION

When policies are formulated, strategies are developed, and plans are established, there is a definite assumption that what is decided will in fact be done. To the extent such decisions are clearly and effectively stated they can be translated into specific organizational structures and formal systems for implementation. Each individual member of the organization who is touched by a policy is in effect provided with information as to how he or she is expected to act so that the policy may be carried out. These role prescriptions or implementation plans vary from individual to individual, depending on the particular nature of the job, but in the end when all are put together it is intended that they add up to effective policy implementation.

Unfortunately, effective implementation is not entirely a matter of decision-making factors; concrete, clear, explicit, and comprehensive role statements do not guarantee that policies will be implemented. The people who make up an organization vary widely in terms of their motives, values, capabilities, and so on. Often they cannot or simply do not wish to implement a policy, or do what is required to implement it. There is no certainty that job behavior will match the requirements that have been established. It is this problem introduced by the people who work in a company, rather than problems inherent in the policy formation process itself or in the organization structures and formal systems introduced to implement policy, that will be of concern in this chapter.

PARTICIPATION AND POLICY IMPLEMENTATION

Human behavior on the job is a complex result of many factors, and all of these can contribute to job behavior which departs from role expectations and thus to failures of implementation. A recent analysis identified 35 types of factors that might contribute to this result [Miner, 1975].

However, those factors falling in the broad area of motivation have been very much at the forefront insofar as discussions of policy implementation are concerned. Thus, the desires, wishes, needs, and values of those who must implement policies will provide the primary focus in the ensuing treatment.

Participation and the Acceptance of Decisions

For a number of years a group of very productive and widely read authors have been advocating participation as the answer to the implementation problem. Among them are Argyris [1970, 1971], Likert [1961, 1967], and McGregor [1960, 1967]. According to this view the way to get people to accept a decision and have a desire to implement it is to involve them in the decision-making process itself, so that they can come to view the decision as at least in part their own. The basic assumption is that people will *want* to do what they themselves have *decided* to do. The argument is a cogent one, so much so that many people tend to think of participation almost automatically whenever questions regarding problems of implementation are raised.

Furthermore, a number of well-conducted research studies tend to support this argument [Bass and Leavitt, 1963; Maier, 1970]. Consistently in these studies of small group decision making, acceptance has been higher for participative decisions, or where the individual made his own choice, as opposed to the condition where outsiders did the planning or chose the problem solution.

Managers clearly do vary their styles as they are exposed to real implementation problems of various kinds [Bons, Bass, and Komorita, 1970]. In addition, they report using participation more and thus engaging their subordinates in the decision-making process more, when they foresee problems in getting a decision actually carried out [Vroom and Yetton, 1973; Vroom and Jago, 1974]. On balance, there is sufficient evidence available to recommend the use of participation when, for some reason, the individual manager foresees trouble in getting his subordinates to accept a decision in a particular area.

Participation at the Policy Level

However, there are a number of considerations that raise questions regarding the widespread use of participation at higher levels, on policy issues. For one thing top level managers are very loath to resort to participation when the decisions are of great importance to the company, presumably because they tend to suspect the motives of subordinates and believe the recommended policies may be more in the self-interest of the recommenders than in the interest of the company [Heller, 1971]. Also, there is consistent evidence that top level decisions are likely to be implemented somewhat more than lower level decisions, and that even participative decisions benefit from top level support; role prescriptions accepted at high levels and promulgated with the idea that sanctions will be mobilized behind them do tend to gain greater acceptance [Bell, 1968]. Thus, there may be less need to use participation on top level policy issues.

All this suggests that hierarchy never does totally disappear, even when widespread participation in policy making is the accepted norm. Data from studies of conventional American business firms as well as socialist organizations in Yugoslavia and Israel support this conclusion [Tannenbaum *et al.*, 1974]. Top managers may be willing to coöpt other members of the organization to the extent necessary, but they do not go all the way to power-equalization [Denhardt, 1971]. Presumably there are good reasons for this fact.

The problem appears to be that findings regarding the value of participation in small groups, or with reference to specific decisions where implementation by the particular individual consulted is crucial, do not appear to be as applicable to policy issues at the top levels of large organizations. Thus a chief executive who shares decisions with his "cabinet" may gain support for implementation at that level but no further.

However, implementation requires support at many levels further down. Should all these levels participate in the decision to gain their acceptance? Is it even possible for them to participate really? Do they have the expertise to participate or even to feel they are participating? Does not the sheer weight of large numbers create a situation where each individual's influence on a decision is so small that there is little incentive to implementation? In short, can the implementation advantages of participation be obtained throughout large groups and organizations, and is real participation possible under such circumstances?

The data available suggest that the answer is a very qualified yes at best [Tannenbaum, *et al.*, 1974]. Top level policy implementation problems cannot be fully solved through participation. Expertise differentials and influence diffusion are simply too great for the advantages of participation found in small group or in one-to-one situations to apply in most cases. Attempts to solve this problem by viewing the company as a series of interlocking small groups (the linking-pin concept proposed by Likert [1961]) simply misrepresent the facts. When a chief executive shares decisions with his vice presidents and policy is established, there is no possibility that managers at the next lower level can either make these decisions themselves or share them with their subordinates. Large organizations and the managerial hierarchies they inevitably produce preclude a total reliance on participation to achieve effective implementation.

THE LARGER ISSUE OF ORGANIZATIONAL COMMITMENT

The underlying principle in the use of participation is that a person who is involved in making a decision will feel committed to it and will want to see it implemented. In small homogeneous groups this seems to work in the sense that decision acceptance does occur, although greater productivity or output need not occur [Stogdill, 1974]. The point is that resistance to implementation is defused. In large organizations, where policies apply to very sizable numbers of people and where certain individuals are likely to exert undue influence on decisions because of their relevant expertise, the use of participation in policy making does not appear to work as well.

Yet the idea of commitment is an important one for policy implementation. What seems to be needed is for the members of the organization to be committed to it and to its objectives so that they will accept policies, strategies, and plans that appear to be in the organization's interest. The concept of organizational commitment draws upon the principles inherent in participation, but broadens them to apply to the organization as a whole, rather than to each decision separately. This broadened perspective makes organizational commitment a very important factor in policy implementation.

The Nature of Organizational Commitment

Although definitions of organizational commitment do vary somewhat [Buchanan, 1974], the three major components appear to be [Buchanan, 1975]:

1. A sense of identification with the organization's objectives such that individual and organizational goals are closely aligned.
2. A sense of involvement and psychological immersion in one's work resulting in considerable enjoyment.
3. A sense of loyalty, perhaps even affection, toward this particular organization as a place to spend one's time and work.

Such a commitment tends to be present in older, more senior employees who are at higher levels in the organization; also in those who basically trust their organization, who have a clear understanding of what they are expected to do, and who desire to exert influence [Hrebiniak, 1974]. Interestingly, employees having a high level of organizational commitment do tend to be relatively satisfied with the extent of participation they experience [Alutto and Acito, 1974].

Further data on factors associated with organizational commitment are given in Table 16-1. The four organizations described there are taken from a total of eight that were studied—five federal government agencies and three large corporations. As Table 16-1 indicates, managerial commitment was consistently higher in the private sector than in government [Buchanan, 1975].

Given this knowledge of what is associated with organizational commitment, it makes sense that effective policy implementation is more likely in organizations that possess high levels of commitment and among those particular members that have the greatest commitment. The problem is that some organizations, such as the federal government agencies, are distinctly

TABLE 16-1
Average Scores for Factors Differentiating between Two Organizations Having Managers with High and Two with Low Levels of Commitment (Out of a Total of Eight Organizations Studied)

	LOW COMMITMENT LEVELS		HIGH COMMITMENT LEVELS	
FACTOR	GOVERNMENT AGENCY	GOVERNMENT AGENCY	LARGE CORPORATION	LARGE CORPORATION
Commitment score	101.5	99.2	141.3	142.3
Feeling that present job is accepted as important	18.9	19.4	29.4	29.3
People worked with during first year had mostly positive attitudes to organization	16.5	18.5	22.8	21.8
Feeling that organization has fulfilled initial expectations	16.3	14.4	24.3	28.0
Managers are *expected* to be personally committed to organization	13.8	12.9	16.3	17.3
Given challenging work to do during first year with organization	12.7	13.9	17.6	15.4
People currently working with have mostly positive attitudes to organization	16.2	19.0	19.7	22.5
People currently working with friendly and close-knit	12.7	12.2	22.4	22.6

SOURCE: Adapted from Bruce Buchanan [1974:539–540, 1975:72].

NOTE: The factors noted are the seven out of the thirteen studied which clearly differentiated between high- and low-commitment organizations as defined by the overall Commitment Score. Thus, these factors serve to define the components of organizational commitment.

lacking in this regard and that commitment is less likely among younger people in lower level positions. These individuals simply do not have the same identification with the company's mission, the same involvement in their work, and the same sense of loyalty.

Inducing Organizational Commitment

There clearly are major differences among people in the propensity for feeling a strong sense of commitment to an organization. Some people are averse to any such feeling with regard to any organization, including their native country. Others hold certain values that conflict with a particular organization's mission so strongly that identification with that organization may be impossible. Strong environmentalists do have problems in the wood products and coal industries, vegetarians find identification difficult in meat packaging firms, and so on. The answer in these cases is to try not to hire people who have little chance of developing commitment in the first place.

Another important consideration appears to be to avoid overstaffing, so that job challenge may be maintained and organizationally meaningless make-work avoided [Buchanan, 1975]. People should be told about the relationship between what they are doing and organizationally relevant ends, even if this seems obvious. Furthermore, attention should be given to their work, and responsibilities expanded at periodic intervals. Above all it is important not to induce unrealistic expectations that may result in later disillusionment with the firm. Companies should convey the message that organizational commitment is expected, and top level managers should be very careful not to act in their own self-interest at the expense of the firm. A poor model at the top will almost guarantee it at lower levels.

All this does not imply that organizational commitment is a panacea for all policy implementation problems. In spite of what has been said, too little is known about how to induce it. Some organizations do not appear to be able to use this approach effectively, and it is not entirely clear why. Certainly there are large and probably increasing numbers of employees with whom this method of achieving policy implementation simply will not work.

LEGITIMATE AUTHORITY AND THE INDUCEMENT—CONTRIBUTION BALANCE

The traditional approach, should other approaches either fail or appear to have little chance of succeeding, has been to implement policies through the use of hierarchic authority and by varying positive and negative sanctions. The use of hierarchic control in this manner to get policies carried out has continued to receive widespread usage [Miner, 1973a] in spite of its general unpopularity even among many managers who apply it [Haire, Ghiselli, and Porter, 1966], and a long-standing attack by human relations advocates [Roethlisberger and Dickson, 1939; Whyte, 1955]. Argyris [1957, 1964, 1973b] for example, has repeatedly argued that exposure to hierarchic control in this manner is debilitating to the individual and stunts psychological growth. Certainly writers in this area have produced convincing evidence documenting their view that the use of formal authority often elicits a response from the informal organization which effectively serves to undermine policy implementation.

Yet the fact that the use of authority continues to be a major, if not the major, method of implementing policies does bear some testimonial to its effectiveness. There are occasions when there appears to be no alternative available, and at such times effective managers will use all the authority they can bring to bear rather than see important policies go unimplemented [Bower, 1966]. Certainly experienced managers do view the use of authority as an effective way of getting policies carried out, while recognizing that there are certain negative side effects and that total implementation is unlikely. Studies have repeatedly demonstrated that changes initiated by top management and promulgated down through the managerial hierarchy do produce results [Dalton, Barnes, and Zaleznik, 1968; Guest, 1962; O'Connell, 1968].

It should be recognized, however, that in any society which protects the rights of individuals, hierarchic organizational control can never be complete and total. Top management cannot get people to do anything; only what those people are willing to do without taking some counteraction that is definitely not desired by the company, such as leaving employment, bringing suit against the company, engaging in sabatoge, or enlisting strong union support.

In this sense the response to authority is to some degree negotiated. A lower level manager may have the weight of support from higher authority behind him, but his subordinates have the weight of society's laws and values to call on also. Thus, the views regarding the upward flow of authority, expressed originally by Barnard [1938] and Simon [1957a] and elaborated more recently by social exchange theorists, do fit the realities of the organizational authority situation [Jacobs, 1971].

Companies must offer inducements to get people to do the sorts of things necessary to have policies implemented, and the use of authority must be viewed as legitimate in terms both of its source and of its nature. The organization gives something; in return it obtains a willingness to contribute in a manner specified by legitimate authority up to a certain maximum. Beyond that the organization will have to give more.

One major thing that companies give as an inducement is money; there is no question that in doing so they can motivate people and get them to contribute [Lawler, 1971; Tosi, House, and Dunnette, 1972]. The problem is that in building the inducement-contribution balance primarily around money one is forced to rely largely on authority to implement policy. Organizational commitment appears to be a contribution that is elicited more by other types of inducements, such as a feeling that one's work is important and challenging.

Also, the effective use of sanctions to implement policies requires that the rewards be firmly placed behind behavior that is desired. All too often, as Haire [1964] and more recently Kerr [1975] have pointed out, the behavior actually rewarded turns out to be different from, if not directly antithetical to, that which the policies imply. Table 16-2 contains data taken from one division of a large manufacturing firm concerning the extent to which lower level employees perceive that rewards are placed behind risk taking and nonconformity. In this particular company it is the policy to encourage employees at all levels to take appropriate risks and to think originally and creatively about developing new approaches to the work. In fact the reason for collecting the data of Table 16-2 from employees was to determine if this policy approach was being effectively implemented [Kerr, 1975].

Clearly, it was not. Sizable proportions of the employees indicated that taking risks was, in fact, disapproved by their supervisors rather than being

TABLE 16-2
Extent to Which Lower Level Employees Expect Approval or Disapproval for Certain Risk and Conformity—Related Behaviors (N = 127)

	PER CENT EXPECTING		
BEHAVIOR	DISAPPROVAL	NOT SURE	APPROVAL
Making a risky decision based on the best information available at the time, but which turns out wrong.	61	25	14
Setting extremely high and challenging standards and goals, and then narrowly failing to make them.	47	28	25
Setting goals which are extremely easy to make and then making them.	35	30	35
Being a "yes man" and always agreeing with the boss.	46	17	37
Always going along with the majority.	40	25	35
Being careful to stay on the good side of everyone, so that everyone agrees that you are a great guy.	45	18	37

SOURCE: Steven Kerr: "On the Folly of Rewarding A, While Hoping for B." *Academy of Management Journal,* December 1975. Reprinted by permission of the Academy of Management.

rewarded and that conformity was a source of positive reward. In no case did a majority describe their work situation as one where risk taking was definitely rewarded and the nonconformity required for creative, new decisions fostered. Somehow the reward system had become disengaged from the policy system. This appears to be a rather frequent occurrence; the contributions induced by rewards are not those the policies presuppose.

IMPLEMENTING AFFIRMATIVE ACTION POLICIES: AN EXAMPLE

In the past few years one of the most active areas of policy formation and implementation has been that of equal employment opportunity. Under pressure from various government agencies and the courts, which are in turn backed by a variety of newly enacted laws and executive orders, many companies including practically all of the large ones, have introduced staffing policies revised to foster affirmative action in the hiring and upgrading of women and/or minorities [Miner and Miner, 1977]. These policies have presented some very difficult implementation problems and thus provide fertile ground for illustrating implementation approaches.

Problems and Methods of Implementation

Affirmative action policies typically establish certain goals for hiring minorities and women so as to create employment percentages roughly comparable to appropriate labor force statistics. Those statistics may be for the local labor force, the national labor force, the proportion of college graduates in the labor force, and so on, depending on the occupational and geographical groups involved.

These policy goals often have proved difficult to achieve for a variety of reasons, among them a lack of job qualifications on the part of minorities and women, a lack of requisite motivation in these groups, and the existence of strong stereotypes and prejudices among those currently employed [Bureau of National Affairs, 1971]. On the latter score for instance, it has been found that white supervisors are more likely to resort to firing, suspension, written warnings, and formal disciplinary actions for the same infractions with black subordinates than with whites [Kipnis, Silverman, and Copeland, 1973].

Yet a number of companies have achieved some success in implementing affirmative action programs. They have done this in part by instituting a variety of special recruiting, selection, training, counseling, and other services through the personnel department, as indicated in Table 16-3 [ASPA-BNA Survey, 1973]. Personnel managers have generally been very sensitive to the negative consequences for a company associated with a lack of compliance with governmental regulations in the equal employment opportunity area. Many have worked hard in support of these special programs out of a strong sense of organizational commitment and a feeling of responsibility for protecting the company against the sizable financial costs that may accrue if affirmative action goals are not met.

TABLE 16-3
Special Programs Introduced to Meet Affirmative Action Goals of 113 Companies

	PER CENT
Special recruiting efforts for minorities generally	84
Special recruiting efforts for minorities in higher positions	64
Changed selection criteria to achieve affirmative action goals	62
Special recruiting efforts for women in higher positions	45
Special counseling for minority workers	34
Special training provided for minorities after hiring	28
Special training provided for minorities to facilitate upgrading	28
Special training provided for women to facilitate upgrading	21
Special training provided for minorities to prepare them for managerial jobs	20
Special services such as day care centers provided for women	2

SOURCE: Adapted from ASPA-BNA Survey [1973:3–6].

Within the line organization some companies such as General Electric have achieved success in implementing affirmative action policies by establishing specific goals for every manager in the company who has responsibility for hiring and firing [Pinckney, in Steiner, 1975a; Purcell, 1974]. Rewards and punishments then are tied to these goals through management appraisal and compensation systems that give specific attention to the affirmative action implementation factor.

One of the most important considerations in whether minority employees from disadvantaged backgrounds perform effectively and stay employed appears to be the degree of support they experience from supervisors and fellow workers [Friedlander and Greenberg, 1971; Goodman, Salipante, and Paransky, 1973]. Obviously such support is difficult to achieve when prejudice against them is widespread, and in fact under such conditions the first black employees in a given group may experience considerable difficulty. However, with continuing contact between blacks and whites the effects of prejudice do tend to dissipate [Palmore, 1955]. Thus, policy implementation in this area may require that the top managers who introduced the policy maintain a continuing close tie between inducements, such as pay and promotions, and contributions to the end of facilitating the hiring and retention of minorities. Given the existing laws and the effects that penalities may have on company profits, the area of affirmative action is clearly one where the use of managerial authority is an appropriate method of inducing change.

The extent to which such authority may be needed appears to vary, depending on the extent of resistance generated by existing prejudices and stereotypes. One large firm reports a successful introduction of blacks into sales and repair positions involving considerable customer contact, which had previously been considered very sensitive on this issue. The managers responsible for actually implementing the change were in fact highly supportive and acceptance by fellow employees and customers was good. Subsequent performance levels for the blacks were equal to those of whites and retention rates somewhat better [Kraut, 1975].

Minorities and Women as Managers

Because employment *level* as well as employment is a consideration in governmental enforcement efforts, many affirmative action policies have resulted in goals being established for the movement of minorities and women into management positions. Much of what has been said previously with regard to implementing affirmative action policies in general applies with equal force to the promotion of increasing numbers of minorities and women into management.

There is, however, a special problem with regard to black managers that requires consideration. Under some circumstances there appear to be few differences between black and white managers [Hill and Ruhe, 1974]. However, other studies have reported less effective performance for black managers while raising serious questions about the performance evaluation procedures themselves. In one instance it was clear that the overall evaluations of black managers were heavily influenced by social considerations, such as acceptance by others, personal example set, self-confidence, and friendliness [Beatty, 1973]. In another study it became apparent that such evaluations of social and human relations skills are highly susceptible to influence by racial attitudes and biases. More prejudiced evaluators tend to rate black managers as being poor in this particular regard [Richards and Jaffee, 1972]. The two studies combined indicate that careful attention must be given to the criteria and standards applied to the evaluation of black manager's performance. Without this, bias rather than behavior can be the major determinant of evaluations, and affirmative action policies may fail, not because blacks are kept from promotion into management but because they are not retained there, or are not moved up when their performance warrants [Fernandez, 1975].

In implementing policies that expand managerial opportunities for women, the primary problem appears to be one of obtaining acceptance for legitimate authority. Many males and females, too, view managing as essentially a male occupation [Schein, 1973, 1975]. Thus, the female manager may find it difficult to exercise authority that males are more easily accorded. Methods of dealing with this problem include placing women in charge of subordinates who are considerably less expert with regard to the work to be done, training female managers to plan in advance how they will handle authority problems, placing women managers in occupational areas where sex-typing is at a minimum, and providing supportive supervision [Brenner, 1972]. As with minorities it is not enough merely to implement affirmative action policies by making the initial promotion; something must also be done to assure that many of those promoted actually stay in management.

It is apparent that affirmative action policies, like many other policies, are not easy to implement. There are often major sources of resistance at lower levels and these may manifest themselves in many different ways. Where such resistances exist their manifestations must be identified and dealt with, usually through appropriate use of legitimate authority and inducements. To the extent organizational commitment can be mobilized, it can make a useful contribution to implementation in the affirmative action area, as in any policy area. The important need is that the relevance of affirmative action for company goal-attainment be clearly spelled out and understood. Participation has not been widely utilized in this type of policy implementation, but there is some evidence that it might prove useful in gaining acceptance for changes in the composition of work groups [Marrow and French, 1945].

EXCEPTIONS TO POLICY AND IMPLEMENTATION

The discussion to this point has concentrated entirely on the implementation of existing policies, strategies, and plans. However, there are instances where in spite of cogent arguments for maintaining a policy in general there do appear to be good reasons for making specific exceptions. Thus, a company having a basic policy of expansion through acquisitions, and with a very small research and development investment, might still make an exception to the standard expansion policy should an extremely promising product emerge unexpectedly from internal research efforts. Similarly, an exception to a policy of promotion from within might be made should a situation arise where the best internal candidate for a position was an unlikely prospect at best, and highly qualified alternative candidates were readily available in the industry.

The argument against making exceptions to policy is that they may undermine implementation of existing policy where that policy is entirely appropriate. If people can point to exceptions they may use these as a basis for arguing against implementation in other instances, or they may simply not implement because they feel the policy has limited validity due to past failures to implement. Such an undermining of policies can occur; the threat is real. Yet the need for some mechanism to permit exceptions so that capitalizing on special circumstances is not precluded is just as real [Miner, 1975].

Exceptions to policy should be made only in the presence of convincing evidence in their favor. They should be made only at the highest levels or by special units or committees to which such powers have been delegated. They should be recorded in writing and if a number of exceptions to a particular policy are required this very fact should serve as a basis for reevaluating the policy. To the extent exceptions are limited in number, obtained only with high level, formal approval, and based on explicit, rational considerations, undermining of policy implementation on a general basis should not be a problem. Otherwise, there is a distinct possibility that implementation may be gradually eroded over time.

QUESTIONS

Discussion Guides on Chapter Content

1. What problems are involved in using widespread participation to facilitate implementation of major corporate decisions?
2. What is organizational commitment and how does it facilitate implementation?
3. Where and when would one expect to find high levels of organizational commitment?

4. How does the inducements-contributions balance relate to implementation?
5. What are the limits on the use of managerial authority in the United States?
6. Discuss the matter of "exceptions to policy."

Mind Stretching Questions

1. We have considered the matter of implementing affirmative action policies. Select some other major policy and discuss the implementation problems you would foresee and the methods you would use to deal with them.
2. What are the various things that those at lower levels may do to impede the implementation of top management policies? Why would they do these things? Is such behavior irrational?

Setting Goals in Management by Objective*

Henry L. Tosi, John R. Rizzo, Stephen J. Carroll

Management by objectives (MBO) is a process in which members of complex organizations, working in conjunction with one another, identify common goals and coordinate their efforts toward achieving them. It emphasizes the future and change, since an objective or goal is an end state, or a condition to be achieved or have in effect at some future time. The emphasis is on where the organization is going—the what and the how of its intended accomplishments. Objectives can be thought of as statements of purpose and direction, formalized into a system of management. They may be long range or short range. They may be general, to provide direction to an entire organization, or they may be highly specific to provide detailed direction for a given individual.

One purpose of MBO is to facilitate the derivation of specific from general objectives, seeing to it that objectives at all levels in the organization are meaningfully located structurally and linked to each other. Sets of objectives for an organizational unit are the bases which determine its activities. **A set of objectives for an individual determines his job,** and can be thought of as a different way to provide a job description. Once objectives are determined and assumed by organizational units and by individuals, it is possible to work out the means or performance required for accomplishing the objectives. Methods of achieving objectives, resources required, timing, interactions with others, control, and evaluation must have continuing attention.

Objectives May or May Not Require Change

The goal or end-state may be one of insuring that no change occurs—for example, an important recurring organizational operation. However, the emphasis still remains on change and the future, and "no change" conditions can be thought of as making finer change discriminations in the management process. However, MBO is deemed most appropriate in situations where activities tend not to be recurring or repetitious, where change toward new or improved conditions is sought. Typically, these would be innovative endeavors, problem-solving situations, improvements, and personal development.

Objectives May Originate at Any Point in the Organization Structure

Quite naturally, they should be derived from the general purposes of the organization, and consistent with its philosophy, policies, and plans. It is beyond the scope of this paper to discuss the details of policy formulation and planning. Rather, it is recognized that these activities take place and that the setting of objectives can, and often does, occur in concern and consonance with them. For example, plans can specify the phasing and timing of organizational operations, out of which are derived objectives for those involved in implementing them. Objectives are not considered as substitutes for plans, but rather as a basis for developing them. Stating objectives accomplishes the following:

1. Document expectations in superior-subordinate relationship regarding what is to be done and the level of attainment for the period covered by the goal.
2. Provide members with a firmer base for developing and integrating plans and personal and departmental activity.
3. Serve as the basis for feedback and evaluation of subordinates' performance.
4. Provide for coordination and timing of individual and unit activities.
5. Draw attention to the need for control of key organizational functions.
6. Provide a basis for work-related rewards as opposed to personality-based systems.
7. Emphasize change, improvement, and growth of the organization and the individual.

OBJECTIVES AS MEANS-END DISTINCTIONS

The formulation of objectives throughout an organization represents a kind of means-end analysis, which is an attempt to factor general requirements into specific activities. Means-end analysis starts "with the general goal to be achieved, (2) discovering a set of means, very generally specified, for accomplishing this goal, (3) taking each of these means, in turn, as a new sub-goal and discovering a more detailed set of means for achieving it, etc" [1].

MBO is predicated on this concept. It is assumed that a means-end analysis can occur with a degree of precision and accuracy. The end represents a condition or situation that is desired, a purpose to be achieved. Here, the concept of *end* is equated with *goal* or *objective.* Objectives may represent required inputs to other sectors of the organization. They may be specific achievement levels, such as product costs, sales volume and so on. They may also be completed projects. For instance, the market research department may seek to complete a sales forecast by a particular date so the production facilities may be properly coordinated with market demands. Objectives, or end states, are attained through the performance of some activity. These activities are the *means* to achieve the *end*. It is important to distinguish between ends and means in the use of the "objectives approach" since there are implications for measurement and assessment which will be discussed later in the paper.

It is obvious that a malfunction or break in such a process may lead to major problems in implementing management by objectives. It is for this reason that commitment, effort, support, and use by top management is critical at all levels to obtain consensus of objectives, cooperation in achievement, and the use of objectives as criteria for evaluation. But there are some problems in doing this. This paper is directed toward these: stating objectives, areas they should cover, the question of measurement, as well as some suggestions for dealing with them.

THE OBJECTIVE

The objectives for any position should reflect the means-end distinction discussed earlier. The first critical phase of objectives-setting is the statement which describes the end state sought. It should be

- Clear, concise and unambiguous.
- Accurate in terms of the true end-state or condition sought.
- Consistent with policies, procedures, and plans as they apply to the unit.
- Within the competence of the man, or represent a reasonable learning and developmental experience for him.
- Interesting, motivating, and/or challenging whenever possible.

Some examples of goal statements might be written as: increase sales by 10 per cent; reduce manufacturing costs by 5 per cent; reduce customer complaints; increase sales by 5 per cent by December 1; increase quality within a 5 per cent increase in production control costs; develop understanding and implementation of computer techniques among subordinates.

Notice that these goal statements have at least two key components. First, each clearly suggests an *area of activity* in which accomplishment occurs. Second, some clearly specify a level of achievement, the quantity or deadlines to be met. We will refer to the desired level of achievement as *performance level*. The need for this distinction is obvious. It indicates the evaluation criterion by specifying the *level* or the condition which should exist. This has clear implications for both measurement and appraisal. Before discussing these implications, however, a more detailed examination of the scope and types of objectives in the MBO process is required.

Scope and Type of Objectives

It would be difficult to conceive of developing objectives for a manager which would cover each and every area of responsibility. The structure of most jobs is simply too complex. Yet once objectives are set for a position, they should comprise the major description of the job, and their achievement in light of what is known about total job requirements should be assessed. A sense of interference or conflict between objectives and other job requirements should be prevented.

Two major types of objectives may be delineated: *performance* objectives and *personal development* objectives [2]. *Performance objectives* refer mainly to those goals and activities that relate to the individual's position assignment. *Personal development* goals have to do with increasing the individual's skills, competence, or potential. Delineating types of objectives in this manner, more importantly, allows for an assessment of how MBO is being used and what emphases are deriving from it. For instance:

- Once all objectives are set for a person, a basis exists to ensure that there is a "balance" of different types, that he is problem solving, developing, and maintaining critical functions.
- Some estimates can be made regarding the importance of objectives and consequences of failure to achieve them. For example, a man who fails on a difficult creative objective should not be evaluated the same as one who fails to maintain a critical recurring operation.

Performance Objectives

This type is derived directly from the job assignment, from the major areas of responsibility and activity of the individual that he must sustain or manage. Among them would be the maintenance of recurring or routine activities, the solving of problems, or the creation of innovative ideas, products, services, and the like. Some of these may take on the form of special activities or projects not normally part of the job. That is, even though they are part of the normal job requirements, they are goals which may take on special importance for a number of reasons—emergencies, changes in priorities, or simply management decisions.

A special activity for one position may be routine for another. A special project goal for a lower-level manager might be a routine goal for his boss Developing a computer-based information system for personnel records may be a highly creative objective for the personnel department, yet should probably be considered a routine goal for a systems analysis group.

Discretionary Areas and Other Problems

By its very nature, organization imposes restrictions on individuals. The structure of an organization defines legitimate areas of influence and decision making for an individual. Specialization and definition of function tend to limit decisions and activities to those defined for the incumbent.

If the objectives process is intended to, and does, facilitate subordinate participation and involvement, we must recognize the implicit nature of power. A lower-level manager cannot *legitimately* influence goal levels and action plans in areas in which he has no discretion, unless he has the *approval of his superior.* Therefore, it is necessary to spell out areas in which the subordinate has some latitude so that he knows what his decision limits are. Otherwise he may be misled into believing that he can participate in departmental and organizational decisions which have been defined, either procedurally or by managerial fiat, as being outside his discretion area. When you expect to participate and then cannot, negative consequences may occur. It is for this reason that it is important to determine and *communicate to the subordinate* what these discretion areas are.

One way to define discretion areas is to determine whether an individual should influence means or ends. If the activity operates primarily across the boundaries of the organization and is affected by conditions beyond its control, then the individual charged with performing it may be in a better position to determine both the goals (or ends) and the most appropriate manner to achieve them. For instance, the marketing executives in constant touch with the external environment are in a better position to determine possible sales penetration and programs than others in the organization. However, not having discretion over goal levels should not preclude involvement in goal setting. Here the MBO process should focus on developing the best *means* (later called action plans) for goal attainment.

High levels of skill and technology required in a particular function may make the specialist better able than a nontechnical person to assess what can be done in a technical field. Thus, he should be involved in determining goal levels, as well as in carrying out activities. This is not to suggest that organizational constraints and requirements be entirely removed. Budget limitations, sales quotas, and production requirements are boundaries or restrictions which may not be removed but may have to be made more flexible.

If performance levels are set, for any reason, at higher organization levels, then there is little option but to focus on the determination of the "best" activities to achieve these levels. Internal definition of goal levels will most probably be for activities which function primarily within the boundaries of the organization. The assumption, of course, is that the one defining the objective, or level, is either competent to do so or must because of its critical importance.

An important limitation on discretion is organizational level. The lower the organizational level, the more and more narrow the zone of a manager's discretion. That is, the manager at the lower levels is responsible for fewer, more specific, and more measurable activities and can commit smaller quantities of resources than those at higher levels [3].

Another factor which causes variation in the discretion range for a particular job is the changing competency levels of the incumbent. A person learning a job may need more guidance from the superior. However, as his skills increase, the superior may spend less time since the subordinate can capably handle more activities and make more decisions. The objectives approach, incidentally, may help the superior make assessments of the subordinate's competence to expand the decision area. As a subordinate becomes more successful in achieving goals, additional and more challenging goals within the parameters of the job could be added. When the incumbent can perform these adequately, then consideration should be given to possible promotion and transfer.

What about those decision areas beyond the discretion limits? We are not suggesting that the subordinate should have no part in these decisions. His role may be contributing information and assistance, such as providing inputs to the decision-making process of the superior, which the superior may choose to accept or reject. But this type of activity must be differentiated from *goal setting participation,* in which the individual *has something to say about the final shape and form* of the goals and activities. However, discretion boundaries are not rigid. While a particular decision may fall within the discretion range under normal circumstances, emergencies might develop which would result in the decision being made by the boss. These conditions cannot be foreseen, and consequently not planned for.

PERSONAL DEVELOPMENT OBJECTIVES

First, it is important to stress that these must be based on problems or deficiencies, current or anticipated, in areas such as improvements in technical skills or interpersonal problems. They may also be directed at developing one for movement within the organization. The critical nature of these objectives lies in their potential as means to combat obsolescence under a rapid expansion of knowledge, to prepare people for increased responsibility, and to overcome problems in organizational interactions.

Setting development goals is probably more difficult than setting performance goals, since they are personal in nature and, as such, must be handled with care and tact. This difficulty may be avoided by simply not setting them. It could be argued that they should be avoided since they are an intrusion into the individual's privacy by the boss or the organization. However, when perceived personal limitations hinder effective performance, the problem must be treated.

Thus, if at any time the superior believes an individual's limitations stand clearly in the way of the unit's goal achievement, it should be made known to the individual. He may not be aware that he is creating problems and would gladly change—if he knew. Many technically competent people have been relieved from position because of human problems they ostensibly create. Many might have been retained had they only known that problems existed or were developing.

Personal development objectives should be a basic part of the MBO program, *when there is a need for them.* But, if they are included only to meet formal program requirements and are not problem-based, little value will obtain. Then personal improvement goals will probably be general and ambiguous, tenable only if the organization wishes to invest in "education for education's sake." For other than a philosophical or value-based justification, personal development should attack deficiencies related to performance, containing specific action proposals for solving the problems. This may be done in the following manner.

PINPOINT A PROBLEM AREA. Parties involved in goal setting should continually be alert to negative incidents resulting from personal incapacities. The boss is in a particularly important position for recognizing problems. When situations occur which he believes are due to either personal or technical limitations, he should be aware of who was involved, and make some determination of the cause of these problems. Other individuals in the unit may bring problems to the fore. Those with whom an individual interacts may be in a reasonably good position to judge his technical competence or to determine when problems are due to his behavior. If colleagues are continually complaining about another person, additional investigation into the problem is warranted. Perhaps the most important sources of these negative incidents is the subordinate himself. He may be very aware of problems in which he is involved and by discussing them may determine those in which he has been the primary cause.

These negative incidents should be relatively significant in effect and frequency and not simply a single event that has caused some notice to be taken. This does not mean, however, that an important incident which occurs one time should be overlooked if it suggests serious deficiencies.

There are at least three areas in which personal development objectives should be set.

- **Improve interpersonal relations.** Inability to maintain reasonably effective working relationships may be due to a person's lack of awareness or his inability to cooperate. This may arise from personality deficiencies or simple lack of awareness of his impact upon others. He may be unable to recognize that he is precipitating problems.
- **Improve current skills.** A manager may be, for instance, unable to prepare a budget or to engage in research because he has not had adequate training

in these areas or because his training is not up to date. His general performance may be acceptable, but his skills should be improved.

- **Prepare for advancement.** Another possibility covers either technical or human skills required for different or higher level positions. These are truly developmental goals which focus on preparation for advancement. There are many ways in which they may be achieved. In some cases the individual may be given advanced work assignments; in others, they may be achieved by exposure in training situations to new concepts. In any event, they represent a *potential* problem area.

ASSESS THE CAUSES OF THE PROBLEM. Once it has been established that a problem exists, the cause needs to be determined. Causes should be sought jointly, a result of investigation and discussion by both the superior and subordinate after both have thought of possible causes.

The possible causes of problems may be grouped into three general categories:

- **Procedures and structure.** The structure of the organization itself may induce disturbances. Interpersonal conflict may develop because of the interdependence of work activities. For instance, if formal requirements cause a delay in information transmission, those who need it may develop negative attitudes and feelings.
- **Others with whom an individual must work.** Problems with subordinates or managerial peers of the goal setter may be caused by personality incompatibility or lack of certain technical skills. While this may represent an important cause of problems, it is too easy to blame negative incidents on others.
- **The person himself.** The *individual* may have habits and characteristics which are not congruent with those of subordinates or colleagues. Or, he may lack the technical skills requisite to carry out certain responsibilities.

Attempting to define problems and causes facilitates converting development objectives into achievable goals. Like other objectives, they can be general (attend a sensitivity training course or role-playing seminar), or more specific (attend XYZ course in financial planning, use PERT techniques on Project X).

Self-improvement goals may be designed to improve current performance, or may be specifically intended to develop skills required at higher levels, or in different jobs (where it may be impossible to describe the end state of affairs to be achieved because success can be determined only in the future, or in other positions).

For development objectives it is necessary simply to rely upon the determination that the action plan has been carried out and that the individual has learned something. Suppose, for instance, that a development goal for an engineer destined to be a supervisor read as follows: "To meet with members of the financial, marketing, and production groups in order to learn how product release schedules affect their areas." Currently, he may have to know little about this since he may now have little impact on product release schedules. The question is, "How do you know that the activity produced the desired learning?" You don't. At some point in time, the superior, who presumably has some knowledge in the goal area, should discuss the results of the meeting with the subordinate, emphasizing particularly the important points that should have been learned. If this is done the subordinate will have the learning experience of the meeting and the reinforcement from discussion.

There is obviously no way to determine if these activities will improve the current, or future, performance of the manager. Managerial judgment is important here. We must simply assume that the superior is able to work with the subordinate to define activities of value in future work assignments.

Finally, it should be clear that performance and development objectives may well be derived from and related to management training and development efforts. These efforts must account for current organizational problems and future needs, and treat development as an integrated organization-wide effort. MBO should therefore be integrally tied to them.

PERFORMANCE REQUIRED: THE ACTION PLAN

Some of the problems inherent in MBO can be overcome by stating and discussing the specifics of the performance required to accomplish an objective. Earlier, the differentiation of means and ends was stressed. The goal statements reflected the ends: here, the performance or "action plan" refers to the means to accomplish an objective. It describes the manner in which it is to be attained. These means reflect alternatives which lead to the desired end and performance level.

The action plan may be brief statements, but it should summarize what is to be done. The action plan for a complex activity should be broken down into major subprograms and should represent the "best" alternative, of possibly many, which would achieve the goal level. The action plan provides an initial basis for a total action program for the individual or department. These action plans might be stated in the following manner:

- **For the sales increase**—develop more penetration in a particular market area by increasing the number of calls to dealers there.
- **For the reduced manufacturing costs**—analyze the overtime activities and costs and schedule more work during regular hours.

Subordinates may base their own action plans on those developed by their manager, using his plan to guide their own roles in the unit's effort. Thus, clear differentiation of means from ends can facilitate lower level use of the objectives process.

Including both means and ends permits comparing performance with some criteria and determining if events occurred which are presumed to lead to a desired outcome. It is important to recognize the distinction between measuring an objective and determining if an event has occurred. If we are unable to quantify or specify the goal level adequately, then we simply *assume that the desired goal level will be achieved* if a particular event or set of activities takes place. For example, while it is very difficult to measure if a manager is developing the talents of subordinates by means of any hard criteria, we can determine if he has provided them with development opportunities. If they have participated in seminars, attended meetings, or gone off to school, it may be *assumed* that the development activity is being properly conducted.

Some further benefits and opportunities provided by adequate attention to an action plan are as follows:

1. Aids in search for better, more efficient methods of accomplishing the objective.
2. Provides an opportunity to test the feasibility of accomplishing the objective as stated.
3. Develops a sounder basis to estimate time or cost required and deadline for accomplishment.
4. Examines the nature and degree of reliance on other people in the organization toward coordination and support needed.
5. Uncovers anticipated snags or barriers to accomplishment.
6. Determines resources (manpower, equipment, supplies, facilities) required to accomplish the objective.
7. Facilitates control if the performance is well specified and agreed upon; reporting need only occur when problems arise in implementing. This is a form of planning ahead; when plans are sufficiently complete, only deviations from it need be communicated.
8. Identifies areas in which the superior can provide support and assistance.
9. Facilitates the delegation process.

DETERMINE COORDINATING REQUIREMENTS AND CONTINGENCIES. Successful achievement or failure of an objective may depend upon the contribution and performance of other individuals or departments. Therefore, since they may be extremely critical to successful performance, they must be considered.

Some contingencies apply to all objectives and need not be documented on each. For example, delays in the availability of resources, change in support or priorities from higher management, equipment failures, delayed information or approval, and the like, which are unplanned, should relieve some responsibility for objective accomplishment.

Other contingencies, specific to the objective, should be discussed. Among these might be inadequate authority of the subordinate, lack of policy covering aspects of the objective, possible failure to gain other's cooperation, known delays in the system, and so on. Once these are uncovered, several actions are possible:

- Reexamination of the objective (e.g. alteration of a deadline) when and if the contingency occurs.
- Commitment of the superior to aid by overcoming or preventing the contingency.
- Revision of the performance required to accomplish the objective.
- Establishment of a new objective. If a contingency is serious enough, an objective aimed at overcoming the problem may be justified.

MEASUREMENT AND APPRAISAL

Management by objectives carried with it most of the familiar difficulties and complications of measurement and appraisal processes. Its emphasis on performance, as oppossed to personality traits or criteria presumed related to performance, makes it potentially more effective. But this potential cannot be realized unless measurement and appraisal are reasonably valid, reliable, objective, and equitable.

Means, Ends, and Evaluation

Performance evaluations should rarely be based only on whether or not the objective was accomplished, or on the sheer number accomplished. They should include:

1. Quantitative aspects. (Was cost reduced 5 per cent as planned?)
2. Qualitative aspects. (Have good relations been established with Department X? Has an evaluation technique been established?)
3. Deadline considerations. (Was the deadline beaten? Was it met?)
4. Proper allocation of time to given objectives.
5. Type and difficulty of objectives.
6. Creativity in overcoming obstacles.
7. Additional objectives suggested or undertaken.
8. Efficient use of resources.
9. Use of good management practices in accomplishing objectives (cost reduction, delegation, good planning, etc.)
10. Coordinative and cooperative behavior; avoidance of conflict-inducing or unethical practices, etc.

Evaluation and measurement, therefore, require considering both means and ends, being concerned with both the objective (number, type, difficulty, etc.) and the means to its achievement (cost, cooperativeness, time consumed, etc.). Unless this is done, an important opportunity to communicate expectations, feedback performance results, and setting effective goals may be lost. It must be fully understood that evaluation has obvious links to action plans, as well as to desired end states.

Further Consideration in Measurement

Some goals lend themselves more easily than others to measurement—scrap rates, production costs, sales volume, and other "hard" measures. These measures pertain most to lower organizational levels and to areas such as production, marketing, or other major functional activities of the organization and least to most staff and specialist units. The measurement problem often reduced to finding the appropriate, agreed-upon criterion for each objective, realizing that some will apply to many situations while others are unique to a single objective.

We have already detailed the distinction between performance and personal development objectives. Another distinction relevant to the measurement problem is the difference between routine and special project objectives. Classifying objectives according to these types permits some important refinements in evaluation and control. By examining the nature of the mix of objectives for a set of positions it is possible to determine any or all of the following:

- The extent to which each individual has some personal development objectives.
- That sufficient problem-solving or innovative activities were forthcoming in units where they might be required.
- The priorities for performance or personal development objectives.

Routine objectives are basic to the job, a core part of the job description. How should they be measured? The most appropriate method for evaluating if an individual has achieved them is first to insure that he is aware of these activities and required levels. The manager must tell the subordinate—early in the relationship—what the activities of the job are and what the desired level of performance is. Evaluation should not occur after a period of service unless there has been previous discussion of criteria.

At the same time that the criteria are being specified, acceptable tolerance limits should be developed. Measurement of the routine should be a major part of the objectives process, yet it should be of most concern *when performance falls outside acceptable levels.* Essentially, we are proposing that minimum performance levels be set for routine activities. Therefore, evaluation of routine goals is *by exception,* or when these standards are not met. Naturally, the ability to manage by exception demands good plans or clear standards from which exceptions can be specified in advance. Odiorne cites the following example:

> The paymaster, for example, may report that his routine duties cluster around getting the weekly payroll out every Friday. It is agreed that the measure of exception will be zero—in other words, the boss should expect no exceptions to the diligent performance of this routine duty. Thus, the failure any week to produce the payroll on Friday will be considered an exception that calls for explanation by the subordinate. If the cause were reasonably under his control or could have been averted by extra care or effort, the absence of the payroll will be considered a failure on the part of the subordinate [4].

What about Superior Performance?

When a subordinate frequently exceeds the performance levels, the manager should let him know that his outstanding performance has been noticed. Positive feedback should occur, especially to let the individual know when he is performing his major job responsibilities exceptionally well.

Generally, routine job responsibilities or goals are expressed as job standards, or other "hard" performance measures. Although appraisal and evaluation essentially compare performance to the standard, this may be relatively short sighted and suboptimal. Recall that the manager should also evaluate the activities or the manner in which performance was carried out. Often costs may be reduced by foregoing other expenditures, which may have negative long-run effects. There can be substantial distortions of behavior when only quantitative criteria are used in measurement.

Problem-solving, special project, or *creative objectives* are more difficult to quantify than the essentially routine. If the ends are truly creative, determining an adequate performance level may necessarily rely on intuitive judgment. Since innovation and invention are needed in their very formulation, we cannot generally measure results in these areas adequately, or directly. It is usually possible, however, to judge if an activity has been performed appropriately even though the ends, or the performance levels, are neither quantifiable nor measurable. Furthermore, constraints may be set on the activities. We can assess that they have occurred by some specific point in time or that a specific dollar amount has been expended. Thus, we are not only concerned with whether or not events have occurred, but also within some tolerance limit such as of target dates, budget constraints, or a quality assessment by the manager. It becomes possible under these conditions to establish review points, thus giving attention to the outcomes of activities when they occur. Deliberations on these outcomes can serve to re-evaluate both objectives and means. Thus changes are possible, and both flexibility and control are assured where they appear to be most needed—where predictions, plans, and standards could not be specified or articulated in advance.

Deadlines and budget constraints can be strictly specified in some cases and not in others. A great deal depends on:

- The importance of the objective.
- The ability to determine the time or costs required in performance.
- Whether or not written plans or objectives of other people require coordinated completion dates.
- The amount of time and money the subordinate will spend on the particular objective under discussion.
- The predictability of problems or barriers to accomplishment.

Discussing these constraints allows greater understanding between superiors and subordinates and establishes their use in evaluation. Expectations become known; realities can be tested. Deadlines and costs should be viewed as "negotiable," and should be reasonably and rationally arrived at whenever possible. Deadlines especially should not be set simply to insure that action is initiated.

We wish to re-emphasize the importance of this criterion problem. A fundamental requirement for MBO is the development and use of sound criteria for evaluation, appraisal, and feedback. This is critical to achieve meaningful changes in behavior. "Hard" criteria must be used with extreme care. They are best viewed as ends or levels; they indicate nothing about attaining either. "Soft" criteria involve not a particular level of achievement, but determination that an event or condition has or has not occurred. These soft criteria are a vital and fundamental part of MBO. Without them, the approach cannot be well implemented.

To some managers, the development and communication of goals comes naturally. There are those who are able intuitively to determine and specify appropriate measures, criteria, goals, and the most satisfactory methods for achieving them. They innately sense what must be observed and measured and communicate this effectively to subordinates. This, of course, is the behavior which management by objectives seeks to develop and reinforce.

SUMMARY

Research and experience strongly support the relationship between the degree of a subordinate's acceptance of the objectives approach and his perception of its support and reinforcement from top management [5]. Organization support is critical for two reasons.

- Top management may be an important reference group for lower level managers. Ambitious employees are likely to emulate managerial behavior. They identify with the top management and act similarly. If top management uses a particular method of managing, lower level managers are likely to use it also.
- Consistent factoring and communication of goals to lower organizational

levels is necessary. The general objective of the organization must be continually broken down into smaller and smaller units. The boss must learn what is expected, must communicate this to his subordinates, and must work with them to achieve these objectives. If this process breaks down at any point, then the whole approach is difficult to use.

Objectives must be written down for the entire organization, but the degree of detail and precision cannot easily be specified. This may be a matter for organizational policy and procedure, or it may be determined by mutual superior-subordinate agreement. However this is resolved, the varied aspects of objectives-setting should be attended to, discussed, and resolved as fully as possible to benefit from the MBO process.

Most important is that the approach must be intrinsically built into the job of managing. It must be related to other organizational processes and procedures, such as budgeting. It should be fundamentally incorporated into planning and development activities. It should be one of the major inputs to the performance appraisal and evaluation process. If not, it is likely that unless a manager intuitively uses this approach, it is easier to do other things. There are costs involved in MBO. There must be some value or payoff which managers can recognize; otherwise they will view it as a waste of time.

REFERENCES

[1] J. March and H. Simon: *Organizations.* New York, Wiley, 1958, p. 191.

[2] These categories are similar to those proposed by Odiorne. See his *Management by Objectives.* New York, Pitman, 1964, especially Chapters 7, 8, & 9.

[3] H. Tosi and S. Carroll: "Some Structural Factors Related to Goal Influence in the Management by Objectives Process." *Business Topics,* Spring 1969, pp. 45–50.

[4] Odiorne, [ref 2] p. 104.

[5] H. Tosi and S. Carroll: "Managerial Reactions to Management by Objectives." *Academy of Management Journal,* December 1968, pp. 415–426.

How Companies Respond to Social Demands*

Robert W. Ackerman

FOREWORD

As concerns of society like clean air, fair employment, and honesty in packaging are thrust on U.S. business with growing intensity and frequency, corporations are finding it very difficult to integrate responses to these demands into their regular operating procedures. This is especially true of the large, decentralized companies, whose profit-center managers are reluctant to change their procedures as long as they are judged on their bottom-line performance. This article is based on a year of intensive study of a number of large companies that are wrestling with this problem. The author analyzes the painful response process that starts with futile attempts from the top to accomplish change and ends (if the organization is adaptive) with the institutionalization of the new corporate policy at the operating level.

The president of a consumer goods company and the manager of one of its divisions were confronted recently with different but equally uncomfortable problems.

The former had been an early supporter of fair employment, especially in respect to minority hiring and training. He devoted much time to federal and state commissions locating job opportunities for minorities in the business community. The company from time to time had assisted minority enterprises in various ways and, on his initiative, had accepted a government contract to operate a job training center.

The president had communicated in strong terms his commitment to a policy of equal employment at all levels in his organization, and he had received general support for it. Despite these efforts, he felt that the company's record in hiring blacks and other minority group members and advancing them into management positions left much to be desired.

He pondered how to close the gap between his public statements and the indications he received of actual performance. He also worried about the impact—tangible and intangible—of stricter government enforcement.

The division manager's problem was in some respects more difficult. He managed one of seven operating units in the company and was responsible

* From *Harvard Business Review,* July–August 1975.

for six plants, several dozen sales offices, and 2,200 employees. Each year, he and his management group assembled a plan that included a financial projection supported by an environmental analysis and a strategy for achieving the goals. After negotiations, top management and division management agreed on somewhat revised figures as the division's performance commitment for the coming year. Although the division manager took pains to keep the president and others on the corporate staff alerted to major strategic developments or changes in the forecasts, he was expected to take responsibility for managing the business.

The division manager understood and agreed with the president's position on equal employment. In view of the diversity of attitudes and values in his organization, he became convinced that the only way of implementing the president's policy was to agree on minority hiring and advancement targets with each of his manufacturing, sales, and administrative managers, and to hold them accountable for the results.

He had not, however, taken this step. He rationalized that the plants operated against very tight budgets; as long as a plant performed well on this measure, the plant manager knew he would win praise, earn pay raises, and preserve his relative autonomy. For several reasons the division manager was unwilling to disturb this arrangement by appearing to put limits on the plant managers' autonomy in choosing their subordinates. He was equally reluctant to insist on the hiring of minority salesmen, thus risking damage to the sales managers' commitment to meeting volume targets. At least for the time being, the task of establishing standards and getting action was left to government enforcement agencies.

This familiar illustration is not unique to this company or issue. By rearranging the situation, I could present comparable cases for other organizations struggling with pollution control, occupational health and safety, consumerism, and so forth.

The U.S. corporation is faced with a twofold dilemma:

- The organizational innovations enabling it to manage growing product diversity and to adapt to technological, economic, and competitive change may inhibit effective responses to societal concerns.
- The need or desire to absorb a growing array of societal demands into its operations—affecting product design and marketing policy, to name just two—may reduce its effectiveness as a producer of goods and services.

When a company falls victim to either of these dangers, the cause, in my view, lies in the difficulty of the management tasks involved, rather than moral or ideological intransigence. In the long run, the more successful corporations will be those that can achieve both social responsiveness and a good economic performance.

In the remainder of this article, I shall first sharpen the issue by providing a framework for thinking about the managerial problems created by social responsiveness. Then I shall describe the response patterns I observed during a year of field research in corporations attempting to implement programs covering a variety of social concerns. Finally, I shall offer suggestions for improving the management of this difficult process.

My primary concern will be with the large U.S. corporation. This is not because small enterprises are lacking in social or economic impact, but because the concentration of resources in large companies and the prominence of their chief executives often endow them with positions of leadership and make them inviting targets for critics. Moreover, for larger companies the internal dilemmas are the most acute.

A POOR FIT

Periodically in our history, the scope of corporate accountability has been extended. The rapid expansion of the labor movement in the 1930s is one obvious example among many manifestations of social change that businessmen had to assimilate during the Depression years. So, if the responsive corporation managed to adapt to them without serious damage, is not our problem today merely one of relearning the solutions to old problems? I think the answer is *no*—not so much because of the intensity of public expectations as because of the radically changed configuration of today's large corporation.

According to recent studies, the divisionalized organization has rapidly replaced the functionalized organization as the dominant formal structure among the largest U.S. industrial corporations [1]. Exhibit I shows the dramatic shift.

EXHIBIT I

Structure of the Fortune "500" Companies in Three Time Periods

Organization structure	Estimated percentage of companies		
	1949	1959	1969
Functional	62.7%	36.3%	11.2%
Functional with subsidiaries	13.4	12.6	9.4
Product division	19.8	47.6	75.5
Georgraphic division	.4	2.1	1.5
Holding company	3.7	1.4	2.4
Total	100.0%	100.0%	100.0%

The adoption of the divisionalized structure, a result of the sharp swing toward diversification, has been accompanied by important modifications in the internal dynamics of the corporation and in the assignment of responsibilities for responding to environmental change [2].

But the results have not always been satisfactory. A prime reason is the poor fit of social responsiveness into the modus operandi of the decentralized company. In its attempt to fashion flexible and creative responses to changing social demands, top management faces three main problems. I have summarized these in Exhibit II and shall explain them in some detail:

1. *The separation of corporate and division responsibilities is threatened.* In the illustration cited at the beginning of this article, the barriers between corporate and division officers had been built on mutual consent. The division manager, in exchange for the opportunity to run his own show and the promise of rewards if he did it well, had shouldered the responsibility for achieving agreed-on results. The president was then relieved of the task of formulating and implementing strategy in a number of (possibly unfamiliar) businesses and devoted his attention to matters of companywide interest.

However, as a result of the president's public statements and actions concerning equal employment, the world assumed he was responsible for seeing that it was accomplished in his organization. Successes or failures anywhere in the corporation reflected on him. Yet performance in employment opportunity—as in most areas of social concern—was closely related to operating decisions that had been delegated to managers down the line.

How can any president ensure an effective corporatewide response without interfering with his division managers? Should he choose to use the influence of his office, what effect would it have on the commitments he could expect for the achievement of corporate financial goals? Sharing the responsibility for social responsiveness may entail making traditional responsibilities more ambiguous. That is a result which most managers naturally want to avoid.

2. *The financial reporting system is inadequate.* Divisionalized companies rely heavily on sophisticated financial reporting systems to monitor the performance of operating units. Indeed, the flow of plans, budgets, and accounting reports often constitutes the primary dialogue between corporate and division offices.

However reliable the reporting system may be in measuring operating unit performance against financial goals, not only is it ineffective in measuring social responsiveness, but by and large it is irrelevant. Analysis of a division's financial statements provides little indication of its effectiveness (however that may be judged) in controlling waste emissions, providing safe working conditions, or manufacturing safe products.

Aggregation of the direct costs of programs related to social commitments is getting increased attention. For instance, one large packaging company isolates the projected expenditures for pollution control equipment in the capital budget (though the associated operating costs are not reflected in the

EXHIBIT II

Critical Aspects of Managing Corporate Responses to Social Demands in a Decentralized Company

Existing management patterns	Problems in responding to social issues
Allocation of responsibilities	
Corporate level: secures division performance commitments and monitors the results, while fostering operating autonomy.	A corporatewide responsibility is implied, with the demand or desire for a corporatewide response. But that response involves operations and implementation is possible only at divisional levels.
Divisional level: formulates strategy for the division's business and accepts responsibility for achieving the results.	
Management through systems	
Division performance is monitored by financial reporting systems that are:	Social costs and benefits are often not amenable to financial measures or planning.
related to division commitments	Current expenditures are real; long-run benefits are uncertain.
amenable to corporatewide aggregation	Benefits may be general and not related to the spending unit.
reasonably simple to communicate and understand.	
Executive performance evaluation	
Performance of assigned responsibilities — often measured through the financial reporting system — is reinforced by incentive compensation and is the determinant of career paths in the organization.	Benefits of social responsiveness may appear in time frames longer than the manager's tenure in his job.
	Current expenditures of time and money may penalize the financial performance to which the organization is committed.
	Trade-offs are required which involve values and judgments on which managers may reasonably differ.

projected income statement). A bank keeps track of expenses associated with its community relations program. The results, however, are at best incomplete, even on the cost side, and little progress has been made in the measurement of social benefits. Nor are substantial breakthroughs to be expected in the near future [3].

The obvious alternative is to create new measures of social responsiveness for each area of concern. Aside from whatever methodological problems such an attempt might pose, the result would be an enormous increase in the complexity of managing the organization—assuming that each reporting system was taken seriously. That, again, is a result most managers would prefer to avoid.

3. *The executive performance, evaluation, and reward process is challenged.* This dilemma is in part an outgrowth of the first two and is perhaps the most difficult to resolve.

In the case of the company whose situation was described at the beginning of this article, the division manager participated in setting the standards to be used in evaluating the performance of his unit, and he secured commitments of support from his subordinates. He was not assuming that their behavior was predicated solely on the desire to meet the budget; their needs and satisfactions were defined in much broader and subtler ways. So he did not evaluate their performance solely in terms of the bottom line. Yet financial appraisal was an important tool for securing the subordinates' support in the pursuit of the division's strategy. The division manager was reluctant to insist on minority hiring and advancement quotas which he felt would introduce new restrictions, ambiguities, and, possibly, discord into the process of evaluating his managers.

How can an organization obtain its middle managers' support for social responsiveness if their careers do not in some explicit way depend on it? A division manager in a large electronics company made the point to me very clearly: "Look, let's start with the idea that I don't need pollution control equipment or minorities to run my business. If the company wants me to do these things, they'll have to make it worth my while."

PATTERN OF RESPONSE

There is an argument that appears to justify ignoring the administrative implications of managing corporate responsiveness. It holds that social expectations for business's behavior become legitimate only when the government requires compliance, and to the extent that governmental regulations exact penalties, a social issue is converted into an economic one and so can be managed just like any other business problem. The fallacy in this reasoning lies in the premise that corporate *action* on social issues is either voluntary or required. In fact, during the period when responsiveness is most important, it is neither.

For every issue there is a time period before it becomes a matter of social concern, and espousing the issue may even arouse economic and social sanctions. There is also a time when its acceptance is so widespread that adherence is an unquestioned part of doing business. (Child labor laws create little anxiety in 1973.)

Between those two points there is a period of uncertainty as to the strength and durability of public support for the issue, standards of socially acceptable behavior, timing of desired conformity, and the technologies or resources available for complying. This period might be called a zone of discretion, in which the signals the company receives from the environment are unclear. It cannot avoid responding in some way, but it still has discretion in the timing and strength of the response.

The history of federal air pollution control legislation is one current example. The first national standards and enforcement provisions appeared in the 1963 Clean Air Act; it was another four years before the Air Quality Act strengthened them; and three more before nationwide ambient air standards were established, to be fully effective in 1975. Regulations have also been imposed at the state and local levels, frequently permitting variances for those facilities with the "latest available technology"—itself a changing standard. So for many years, while the federal legislation was evolving, corporations were engaged in activities affecting air quality and had choices whether to alter them.

A number of social issues have progressed so far through the zone of discretion that their final dimensions are beginning to take shape. Equal employment and ecology are two examples, although even in these instances great uncertainty remains as to the intensity of enforcement and the ultimate standards to be applied. Other issues are much less well defined.

Based on intensive observations in several companies that have been recognized as leaders in managing those social issues of particular relevance to their businesses, I think a common response pattern is developing. (The nature of these particular issues creates differences, but the similarities are far more noticeable.) There are three phases to this response process, spanning a period of at least six to eight years. The first two phases are necessary but insufficient in themselves for an effective response. I shall discuss each in turn.

1. A Policy Matter

First, the chief executive recognizes the issue to be important. He may rationalize his interest as a matter of corporate responsibility or as far-sighted self-interest. Either way, it coincides with his recent experience, often outside his business milieu. One chief executive I know became concerned about minority opportunities during the widespread urban disturbances in the mid-1960's, when a riot took place near the company's headquarters. Several years earlier, some personnel managers had tried to generate his interest in the issue, but they had got nowhere.

The chief executive's involvement is marked by several activities. Initially, he begins to speak out on the issue at meetings of industry associations, stockholders, and civic groups. He becomes active in organizations and committees involved in studying the issue or influencing opinion on it. He may also commit corporate resources to special projects, such as ghetto businesses, waste recovery plants and training centers.

Soon he perceives the need for an up-to-date company policy, which he takes pains to communicate to all managers in the organization. Responsibility for implementing the policy is assigned as a matter of course to the operating units as part of the customary tasks performed in running the business.

The directives from top management, couched in terms of appeals to long-term benefits and corporate responsibility, fail to provoke acceptable action or achievement. Heads nod in agreement, but the chief executive's wishes are largely ignored. Managers in the operating units lack evidence of the corporation's commitment to the cause; responsibilities are unclear, score-cards are lacking, and rewards for successes or penalties for failures are absent. The managers view as foolhardy any attempt to implement the policy at the risk of sacrificing financial and operating performance.

2. Onus on the Specialist

The first phase may last for months or even years. The key event heralding the beginning of a new phase is the president's appointment of a staff executive reporting to him or one of his senior staff to coordinate the corporation's activities in the area of concern, help the chief executive perform his public duties, and, in general, "make it happen." The new manager, often a specialist in his field, carries one of a variety of titles that have recently appeared on organization charts: vice president or director of urban affairs, environmental affairs, minority relations, consumer affairs, and so on.

The vice president of urban affairs views the problem as essentially a technical one that can be attacked by isolating it and applying specialized skills and knowledge to it. He begins to gather more systematic information on the company's activities in the area and matches these data with his assessment of environmental demands. If his responsibility includes minority relations, he gets personnel statistics from the operating divisions and attempts to pinpoint where problems exist in minority representation. During the audit process, he also develops methods for systematically collecting information, which he plans to use as a control device in the future. Finally, he mediates between operating divisions and external organizations, including government agencies, that are pressing for action.

But these efforts, while not without impact or merit, do not elicit the response envisaged in the corporate policy. The staff manager's attempts to force action are so alien to the decentralized mode of decision making that he becomes overburdened with conflict and crisis-by-crisis involvement. The only arrows in his quiver, aside from his own powers of persuasion, are the corporate policy and the demands of outsiders. But line managers may consider neither one credible. One environmental control director commented to me:

> "We find ourselves in a 'damned if you do, damned if you don't' situation a lot of the time. We get accused by the regulators of backsliding when we argue that the company is doing the best it can. Then when we argue for a program inside the company, we get accused of giving money away. The operating managers fail to see that if they don't take steps now, the cost in the long run could be a lot greater. They hear the wolves howling out there, but they only notice the ones that get in and not the ones we're keeping outside."

Consequently, if staff proposals interfere with its operations, middle management stands aside and lets the staff take responsibility (or blame) for the results. Faced with a choice between supporting his senior line executives (who have major operating responsibilities and probably a long history of sound judgments) and his new urban affairs vice president, the chief executive usually backs up the former.

Nevertheless, the job done by the corporate specialist is essential for the eventual implementation of the policy. He crystallizes the issue for top management. He also unearths and collects a great deal of information that serves to clarify what will be expected of the corporation in the future and the techniques or technologies that will be available to fulfill those expectations.

3. Organizational Involvement

The chief executive recognizes at this juncture that responsiveness entails a willingness to choose among multiple objectives and uses of resources. Fundamentally, such judgments are a general management responsibility. Top management sees the organizational rigidities to be more serious than previously acknowledged; they cannot be waved away with a policy statement nor can they be flanked by a specialist.

Instead, the whole organizational apparatus has to become involved. In this third phase, the chief executive attempts to make the achievement of policy a problem for all his managers. That is accomplished by institutionalizing policy, which I take up next.

INSTITUTIONALIZED PURPOSE

In the cases I have observed, the chief executive's problem was not winning acceptance of the new company policy; in numerous instances, managers down the line were found who, from a personal standpoint, wished the policy had been stronger. Rather, the problem was in the institutionalization of the policy—that is, working it into the process through which resources were allocated and ultimately careers decided.

A well-known characteristic of large organizations is that, unless somehow provoked to do otherwise, they tend to approach today's problems in the same way that worked yesterday, even though the context in which the new problems arise may be different. A study of the Cuban missile crisis ascribed this phenomenon to "standard operating procedures" that are enormously useful in simplifying complex problems and organizational interaction [4].

To illustrate, companies with strong unions and a long history of successful labor-management relationships develop routines for processing employee grievances that grow out of the union experience. If a complaint arises alleging plantwide discrimination, both union and management try to rephrase it in traditional terms; then they can handle it in their usual fashion.

However, the minority employees may feel that their situation will not receive the special attention they believe it warrants if they rely on a decision-making process that has failed to satisfy their needs in the past. Consequently, they avoid the union and attempt to communicate directly with executives many levels above those managers normally responsible for employee grievances. The normal reaction in such instances is to rule the employee's tactic inadmissible and insist that they "play by the rules."

This phenomenon helps to explain the stability (stated negatively, the unresponsiveness) of most large organizations. For the chief executive of the decentralized corporation, the problem of securing responsiveness to social issues is compounded by the rules governing the interrelationships between corporate and division levels. The rules state that while the chief executive is obtaining and evaluating divisional results, he is not to meddle in the divisions' standard operating procedures. If he wants to change those procedures to coincide with the spirit of the new corporate policy, he presumably must attempt it indirectly by changing the standards for judging performance.

The chief executive does indeed try to play by the rules. This letter, written by one president to his subordinates, is a graphic illustration:

> "The most significant change this year—the one that is basic to all others—is to place responsibility for achieving equal opportunity objectives where it rightfully belongs: with operating management, with each of us. Achieving these objectives is as important as meeting *any other* traditional business responsibility.
>
> "It follows, of course, that a key element in each manager's overall performance appraisal will be his progress in this important area. No manager should expect a satisfactory appraisal if he meets other objectives, but fails here."

If one talks with operating managers shortly after such an announcement has been made, one finds interest in the policy but considerable skepticism about the corporation's will to enforce it. They detect gaps between pronouncement and performance:

- Since reporting on implementation of, say, a minority hiring quota, cannot be integrated directly into the financial control system, it must be communicated separately. Consequently, it must compete for attention with the regular reporting system. In view of the technical problems likely to be encountered with the new procedure and the central position and historic importance of the old one, the competition may be very one-sided.
- It is doubtful that a manager who has met his economic targets will be criticized, let alone severely punished, for failure to perform adequately in the area of social concern. The president may be uttering strong words on appraisal, but it is the manager's immediate boss several layers down, not the president, who appraises him.

Creative Function of Trauma

In due course, a test case is encountered, though at the time it may not appear to be particularly significant. The institutionalization of purpose may hinge on the creative use of trauma. The trauma results not from the problem posed in the test case, but from the organizational dynamics through which the problem is resolved. Top-level executives suspend the rules governing their relationship with the operating divisions. For a brief period, division executives lose control of their operations: their decisions are countermanded and staff managers reporting to their superiors exercise inordinate influence in directing the outcome.

The whole affair is very unsettling for the divisions. Worst of all, questions are raised in the operating executives' minds about who really is responsible for managing the divisions' response and what the consequences may be if it is not them.

For instance, shortly after the letter quoted earlier had been sent, a smoldering controversy about minority relations erupted in a small service unit four levels down in a division. Eventually, no fewer than seven levels of line management, from the first-line supervisor to the president, were involved with their associated staffs in attempting to settle it. For a two-week period, the normal chain of command was tenuously observed. Then, the president intervened directly by issuing a decision that overturned the one announced by his subordinates. By his own forceful action, he dramatically illustrated the quality of management he expected in response to employee problems.

Intervention from the top level may not have been executed effectively in the test case, but that is not the issue. The experience has had two very beneficial results:

1. The managers in the division realized that to prevent such a fracas from recurring, they must be responsive to the issue in the future. That may

mean incorporating action programs related to the issue into the division's strategy and modifying the process of evaluating the managers who are positioned to influence responsiveness directly.

2. The company has provided clues to the new standard operating procedures that it wants adopted to establish the policy in the operating units. The policy has been tested and a precedent established that can serve as a guide for its implementation throughout the corporation.

The response patterns I have described may appear to be chaotic, and, in fact, they were often characterized as such by the managers involved. Yet there is underlying order and logic to the process.

Exhibit III illustrates how a policy problem is converted into a managerial problem through the process of institutionalization. During these three phases of involvement of the organization, concern for responding to the social issue spreads from the chief executive to middle-level managers. The awareness of a social need that produced the policy is enriched by the infusion of new skills and finally matures into a willingness on the part of the middle-level managers to commit resources and reputations to responsible action.

The process receives strong impetus from the changing and increasingly

EXHIBIT III

Conversion of Social Responsiveness from Policy to Action

Organizational level	Phases of organizational involvement: Phase 1	Phase 2	Phase 3
Chief executive	Issue: Corporate obligation	Obtain knowledge	Obtain organizational commitment
	Action: Write and communicate policy	Add staff specialists	Change performance expectations
	Outcome: Enriched purpose, increased awareness		
Staff specialists		Issue: Technical problem	Provoke response from operating units
		Action: Design data system and interpret environment	Apply data system to performance measurement
		Outcome: Technical and informational groundwork	
Division management			Issue: Management problem
			Action: Commit resources and modify procedures
			Outcome: Increased responsiveness

demanding environmental conditions that often parallel the response pattern in this manner:

- *Phase 1*—social concerns exist but are not specifically directed at the corporation.
- *Phase 2*—broad implications for the corporation become clear but enforcement is weak or even nonexistent.
- *Phase 3*—expectations for corporate action become more specific and sanctions (governmental or otherwise) become plausible threats.

UNDESIRABLE CONSEQUENCES

While the particular response pattern may eventually produce acceptable results, it is often inefficient and entails some undesirable side effects:

1. If the six- to eight-year cycle that I have observed in relatively successful instances is typical, the elapsed time required may be excessive. Unless social issues can be processed with reasonable speed, they may pile up and ultimately put the company in a position where it cannot function effectively in its traditional role as a producer of goods and services.

2. Until the final phase, operating managers are not intimately concerned with the issue; specialists direct the responses. The legal staff and the environmental control director work out compliance schedules for pollution control, the minority relations specialist communicates with factory personnel managers about affirmative action programs, and so forth.

But without middle-level management commitment, it is likely that the specialists will interfere with operating activities, misapply resources, or be ineffective in securing results. That is, in the two examples I just cited, compliance schedules do not mesh with planned capital spending programs, and minority relations seminars are taken lightly. Deservedly or not, the specialist often shoulders the blame.

3. Performance evaluation is usually skewed to distributing penalties for failures rather than rewards for successes. Moreover, the process is very unsystematic; it relates not so much to consistent performance against objectives as it does to poor handling of particular conspicuous situations. The manager cited for polluting a stream or charged with discrimination may find his career badly tarnished. His counterpart, who fails to construct and implement an effective environmental program or meet his hiring and advancement goals—but is not guilty of an overt action—may escape sanctions.

The excuse normally given is, "We needed an example for the rest of the organization." Perhaps so, but it is unfortunate that such sacrifices must be made when the entire organization is trying to learn how to respond effectively to a new set of problems.

NEEDED: RESPONSE PROCESS

Issues of social concern are generally recognized as certain unrelated environmental phenomena demanding substantive corporate responses of some kind. Product safety, equal employment, ecology, and work safety each require a particular set of activities that change over time and are dealt with separately. A more sophisticated concept calls for a systems approach to the environment through which the interrelationships among issues are explored and the likely trends and impacts predicted [5].

A third way of viewing corporate responsiveness focuses on organizational requirements. Social issues arise not as discrete events but as a flow of events which may or may not be closely related, but which share a call on corporate attention.

They are at different stages in the zone of discretion. The outlines of some, such as air pollution control, have been well described; while the shape of others, such as "the new work force," is still murky. For example, referring to the evolving regulations covering noise levels, an experienced engineer charged with applying federal environmental standards in his company commented to me. "If the company gave me $10 million to spend on getting noise levels down to 90 decibels, I wouldn't know how to spend it." He had neither the technology nor the directions for using it.

Guidelines for Strategy

From an organizational standpoint, the need is for a response process through which issues can be recognized and formed into policy, implications and possible solutions explored, and, finally, plans generated to govern action. The challenge for management is to facilitate a means of organizational learning and adaptation that will permit flexible and creative responses to social issues as they arise. In the divisionalized organization, that assignment will not be easy; some preliminary suggestions on the nature of such a process follow.

DO NOT OVERLOAD THE RESPONSE PROCESS: The process for responding to social demands described in this article is a reasonable way of approaching a difficult managerial problem. There is, however, a real danger of overloading the process. The time and energy of the chief executive are limited. So are the tolerance and capacity of the organization for wrestling with the environmental uncertainties that accrue to the ones who take forceful action. Top management should balance the numerous social demands pressing on the organization and the social goals it seeks. It should give priority to those areas that are most likely to have an impact on the company's business and should try to maintain a low profile on the others.

To ease the problems of implementation, top management must anticipate the transition from one phase to the next and clearly communicate to middle-level management the ground rules for managing the new phase.

USE SPECIALISTS EFFECTIVELY: New skills and knowledge are particularly necessary in the formative stages of the company's response. It must scan an unfamiliar environment, master new technologies, and collect and analyze a vast amount of information, both internally and externally. The staff specialist has the difficult task of developing approaches to this environment and designing systems to permit the planning and evaluation of programs for adapting to its needs. Although the specialist's role as an agent of change is vital, there are two dangers to be considered:

- Operating managers often resist or even ignore the specialist's advice. This is predictable; after all, he is usually a purveyor of bad tidings. Furthermore, since his is a new field, he may be new to the organization and therefore lack the mutual trust built up over time with the operating executives. Worse, he is both highly visible and largely void of influence other than having the proverbial "boss's ear," which can be seldom used and then only with caution. Clearly, the specialist is vulnerable and needs support from the top if he is to be successful.
- The specialist may keep his hand in the issue too long. His vantage point at the corporate level and his inclination to tackle the job himself may impede the assumption of responsibility and commitment by operating managers. Independent responses at the middle levels are essential for effective action.

The staff specialist's role in implementation of new policy should be temporary. Top management support during the critical second phase is necessary, but as soon as responsibility and accountability have been lodged with operating managers, the staff specialist's involvement should be limited to providing technical advice as requested.

But he has a crucial, broader role in the organization. If he has managed his relationships in the organization well, he will be immensely useful in equipping it to respond to the next social issue. For instance, the specialist who has been concerned with air and water pollution has skills in engineering, environmental analysis, and government relations that may prove to be very useful in working with, say, the occupational health and safety issue. He can become a multipurpose corporate change agent.

FORMULATE RESPONSE STRATEGIES: To plan a rational sequence of activities in support of goals in areas of social concern, a response strategy is necessary. Placing the responsibility for formulating these strategies with middle-level managers who also set operating strategy exploits, rather than subverts, the organizational strengths of the decentralized company. The procedure of goal setting and strategy evaluation is second nature for both corporate-level and operating managers.

Insisting on a direct parallel between social response strategies and the more familiar business strategy yields three benefits:

1. The response becomes anticipatory and not merely reactive.
2. The response demands a level of analysis that is too often lacking when resources are allocated to social problems. It may not be possible, or in the long run even worthwhile, to measure social costs and benefits in economic terms; however, requiring rigorous justification for the action to be taken makes the best use of the information and analytical tools available.
3. The articulation of a strategy provides the basis for subsequent measurement and evaluation.

COMPLICATE THE EVALUATION PROCESS: This final suggestion is, in my judgment, the most important but the least likely to happen of the four. It is commonplace to hear managers describe their jobs as being more complicated now than in the past. One division vice president summed it up this way: "Business used to be fun. But now there are so damn many people around demanding this and that, I just don't enjoy it any more."

Ironically, while the job of the manager—especially those in the middle levels—has been growing more complex, the basis on which his performance is evaluated has often become simpler. The reason, of course, lies in the need for a lowest common denominator that can be used for allocating resources and making comparisons among units operating in different businesses and geographical environments. The financial plan serves these purposes admirably.

If the corporation is to be socially responsive, however, this divergence may have to be arrested. Top management may have to tolerate a greater degree of complexity in the measures it uses to evaluate the performance of middle-level executives. The path need not lead to more subjective or less results-oriented evaluations. Indeed, if attention has been paid to setting strategy in areas of social concern, the power of the results orientation may actually increase over a procedure that does not subject social programs to planning and analysis. Economic performance no doubt will always remain the dominant yardstick (and with good reason), but it should be augmented to reflect the greater complexity and scope of middle management's responsibilities.

IN CONCLUSION

There are hopeful signs that large corporations in this country are developing processes for converting the rhetoric of corporate responsibility into meaningful action. The burden for implementing corporate policy on social issues is ultimately placed on middle-level managers, the same managers who are primarily responsible for planning and directing the operations of the business. Through the creative and persistent leadership of top management, the barriers to incorporating social change in the decentralized company can be overcome.

The response to social demands is not without human cost. Managers' careers have been tarnished by the bad luck of getting caught up in conspicuous incidents that may be learning experiences for the organization, but at their expense. Does somebody have to get hurt? Unfortunately, the answer all too often is *yes*. An urgent challenge for the top managements of large corporations is to make their organizations more understanding of the human costs of change as well as the demands of society.

REFERENCES

[1] Richard P. Rumelt: "Strategy, Structure, and Economic Performance." Unpublished DBA dissertation, Harvard Business School, Boston, 1972.

[2] For a discussion of this transition, see Bruce R. Scott: "The Industrial State: Old Myths and New Realities." *Harvard Business Review,* March-April 1973, p. 133.

[3] See Raymond A. Bauer and Dan H. Fenn, Jr.: "What *Is* a Corporate Social Audit." *Harvard Business Review,* January-February 1973, p. 37.

[4] Graham Allison: *The Essence of Decision: Explaining the Cuban Missile Crisis*. Boston, Little, Brown, 1972.

[5] Herman Kahn and B. Bruce Biggs: *Things to Come: Thinking about the 70s and the 80s*. New York, MacMillan, 1972, Chapter 1.

Bridging the Gulf in Organizational Performance*

John B. Miner

FOREWORD

There is a gulf, contends this author, between the so-called "principles of management" theory, which has failed to deal adequately with problems of managerial motivation, and the various alternatives advanced that emphasize motivation above all else. In suggesting how this gulf can be bridged, he offers a new approach based on the assumption that a business organization's effectiveness depends on the ability to integrate the efforts of its members with its goals of continued existence and profitability.

How can a business organization maximize its effectiveness within the constraints of its environment? This question has long been the primary concern of traditional management theory. The so-called "principles of management," with their emphasis on planning, organizing, directing, staffing, and controlling, have won widespread acceptance because they recognize the overriding significance of top management decisions in the areas noted, and because they provide the means for precise and unambiguous specification of managerial roles. Yet in one respect traditional management theory has proved deficient. It has failed to deal adequately with the problems of managerial motivation, and with the use of incentives to guide managerial behavior.

Behavioral scientists have offered alternative approaches that compensate for this deficiency with a vengeance. They have emphasized motivation above all else, thrusting top management decisions, corporate goals, and role prescriptions into the background.

Can the gulf be bridged? I believe it can, and in this article I shall suggest how.

INTEGRATIVE APPROACH

My approach to organizational analysis and diagnosis is basically motivational, but it relates motivation to company goals and clearly defined job

* From the *Harvard Business Review*, July–August 1968.

requirements. It draws on traditional techniques of personnel selection and performance rating, and it combines this emphasis on measurement with the organizational point of view associated with Mason Haire, Harold Leavitt, James March, and Herbert Simon. The resulting tools for achieving effective utilization of *human* resources can provide a useful supplement to the economic and accounting procedures management uses to guide the company's utilization of *financial* resources.

The approach to be considered rests on the assumption that *an organization is likely to be effective and successful to the degree it can integrate the efforts of its members with its goals*—in the case of a business, the goals of continued existence and profitability. Anything that tends to thwart integration by diffusing the efforts of individuals is assumed to reduce or jeopardize organizational success.

Starting from this premise, I shall discuss six specific conditions for organizational effectiveness, which may be regarded as revised or supplementary "principles of management." These conditions, in effect, establish the groundwork for a behavioral science approach to organizational analysis and diagnosis. I shall then show how this approach might be applied in two companies —one small, one large—and how important strategies for change might be developed by its use.

Supporting Evidence

Since the six conditions to be discussed are firmly rooted in my basic premise, let us consider some of the evidence supporting it. First, of course, the integration concept is central to a large body of management theory, both past and present [1]. Recent research into organizational and managerial processes provides another line of support. Thus, Stanley Vance's work at the University of Oregon indicates that the more profitable companies within an industry tend to have a greater proportion of inside directors who are officers [2]. Clearly, a predominantly inside board should contribute to integration in pursuit of corporate goals. Again, preliminary results of a study currently being conducted by Paul Lawrence and Jay Lorsch at the Harvard Business School indicate that higher integration among functional departments is a characteristic of more successful firms [3].

To determine the extent to which the conditions for organizational effectiveness are satisfied in a particular organization, certain data will have to be obtained for each manager included in the analysis. These include, first, performance ratings by all superiors familiar with the man's work; second, current managerial level and current total compensation; third, assessments of the man in terms of whatever biographical, intellectual, motivational, and emotional characteristics appear to be relevant to successful performance in the company.

SPECIFIC CONDITIONS

Before proceeding to a discussion of how integration theory can be profitably used in organization analysis, let us first list and then consider the six conditions for organizational effectiveness which it implies. These are (1) *rater reliability,* (2) *halo realization,* (3) *reward consistency,* (4) *multiple criteria,* (5) *concurrent validity,* and (6) *goal relevance.*

Rater Reliability

Individuals in positions of authority should be in basic agreement on who is a good performer and who is not. Traditional industrial psychology has used the term *rater reliability* to denote consistency of results obtained with particular rating forms and appraisal procedures. There is evidence, however, that such consistency of agreement (or the lack of it) is a function of the organization as well as of the evaluation instruments employed. Research I conducted in four school districts indicates, for example, that consistency of ratings obtained by the use of a given rating scale may range from only moderate to very high, depending on the degree of integration in the district [4].

A consistent value climate in a company enables managers to develop a clear picture of desired behavior patterns and to act accordingly. Without such a climate, individuals may be pulled in conflicting directions by the disparate values of different superiors, with a corresponding loss of integration in individual efforts. Hardly anyone can maintain a consistent pattern of behavior in support of company goals when one top executive condemns the very actions that are praised and supported by another.

All too often the vice presidents of a corporation will isolate themselves from each other and develop unrelated value structures. When top managers disagree on who are the good performers, anything that might foster job-related interaction at the top of the organization can provide a valuable antidote. The virtue of such techniques as management by objectives, family group sensitivity training, and superior-group appraisal is that they contribute to an integrated value climate by encouraging such job-related interaction.

Halo Effect

Consistency of values will be reflected not only in high agreement on who are the good performers, but also in a general tendency to see individuals as good or bad in an overall sense: to view each man's work as a whole and to react to him as a total person. This implies that the truly effective organization should have a clear picture of the "competent performer," a standard against which a man can measure himself and consider himself valued or not valued. Markedly different evaluations of different aspects of performance are likely to impair a man's self-esteem unnecessarily and to make him uncertain how to behave.

This does not mean that uneven performance should be minimized or ignored. People do, of course, perform some parts of their jobs better than some others, and these variations should be identified for such purposes as establishing development needs. But since a man cannot be simultaneously rewarded by a salary increase or promotion for one aspect of his work and penalized for some shortcoming, it is important that the evaluation process that precedes penalty or reward reflect a single overall performance judgment of the man as a whole.

In the past this integrative tendency in performance measurement has been termed the *halo effect* and regarded as something to be avoided or minimized. Scales that produced high correlations among ratings for various items of performance were considered imperfect, and complex procedures were devised to avoid or correct the deficiency.

From the organizational viewpoint, however, consistent evaluations of different aspects of behavior are highly desirable. In general, as psychologists have repeatedly noted, this halo condition does appear to be realized in most companies. Yet studies indicate that some organizations are characterized by rather low consistency among ratings of various aspects of managerial performance. This is true, for instance, of Company B, to be discussed in the latter part of the article. A rating procedure that prevents halo from being noted when it is present deprives the organization analyst of important information regarding the company's value climate.

Reward Consistency

Integration in pursuit of organizational goals implies a *reward consistency* —that is, a close relationship between job grade or level and total compensation. When, for seniority or other reasons, people at lower levels earn more than their superiors, the patterns of reinforcement lack integration because of the inconsistent reward structure. Hence, people in the organization lack a clear guide to action. Monetary and status rewards should operate together to reinforce the same kind of behavior.

Thanks presumably to job evaluation procedures, executive compensation plans, and the like, the consistency of reward condition seems to be rather widely satisfied in U.S. industry, with compensation closely tied to job level in most cases. Where this condition does not prevail, shifts in organization, revised compensation procedures, and/or personnel changes can help to achieve a better integrated reward structure.

Multiple Criteria

Traditional personnel psychology has long been concerned with what has been termed the *multiple criteria* problem. In order to determine what test scores, interview responses, or application-blank items might be used to select people for a certain kind of work, "validity studies" had to be devised to relate the test, interview, and application-blank data to some criterion of job success. But what criterion? The various criteria were often entirely unrelated, and validity was observed to vary, depending on whether promotion, or performance rating, or some other criterion was used as a measure of success.

How could these disparities among different success indexes be eliminated? Could a single all-purpose criterion be achieved and, if so, how? Once again the emphasis was on consistent measurements. Multiple criteria were viewed as a measurement problem, a source of error. Little thought was given to the possibility that differences in the consistency of results obtained with various criteria might reflect important differences among organizations.

A fourth condition of effectiveness, then, is congruence between value and reward structures. Among people of similar age and job level, those who are most highly valued in the organization should be most highly rewarded. This condition should hold among the top and middle managers of practically all companies, and for the management groups as a whole in many.

Experience indicates that while various value indexes often are closely related (condition 2) and reward indexes are even more likly to be congruent (condition 3), true integration of value and reward structures is unsual. The multiple criteria problem almost always reflects such value-reward disparities. In some organizations, studies have even revealed a slight tendency to provide greater rewards to the least-valued managers. These cases are admittedly the exceptions, but the denial of rewards to many individuals who are considered very good managers is apparently a common feature of organizational life. This conclusion is not limited to my own studies; other analyses have produced the same result [5]. Where this condition prevails, motivation to contribute to company goals will inevitably suffer.

VALUED-REWARD DISPARITIES: Why should less-valued individuals be rewarded while others who are considered outstanding are in effect penalized? One reason is probably reluctance to remove rewards once they are granted. Promotions and pay increases are, of course, far more common than demotions and pay reductions, and people are rarely dismissed for failing to perform at a level commensurate with status and monetary rewards. Thus the reward structure may remain static while individual behavior and even company value structures are changing. Many company presidents have successfully sold their organizations on new value climates emphasizing creativity and emotional freedom, and the like, without doing anything to bring established reward structures into line so as to reinforce these new values in behavior.

That less-valued performers may continue to be rewarded (i.e., promoted), with resulting disparities, is illustrated in Exhibit I. These data derive from a recent study in which I evaluated the management appraisal system of a large manufacturing company. The appraisals represent the pooled judgments of

EXHIBIT I

Management Appraisals Compared with Subsequent Promotions

Overall effectiveness
100%
90—
80—
70—
60—
50—
40—
30—
20—
10—
0—

Division A (60 men)
Promoted within 3 years 48%
40%
8%
19%
Not promoted 52%
33%

Division B (100 men)
Promoted within 3 years 39%
27%
12%
18%
Not promoted 61%
43%

Division C (76 men)
Promoted within 4 years 25%
11%
14%
37%
Not promoted 75%
38%

Division D (157 men)
Promoted within 3 years 24%
15%
9%
33%
Not promoted 76%
43%

Division E (90 men)
Promoted within 18 months 17%
13%
4%
30%
Not promoted 83%
53%

Key
Rated high
Rated low

Overall effectiveness
100%
90—
80—
70—
60—
50—
40—
30—
20—
10—
0—

Division A
Promoted within 3 years 48%
43%
5%
14%
Not promoted 52%
38%

Division B
Promoted within 3 years 39%
19%
20%
9%
Not promoted 61%
52%

Division C
Promoted within 4 years 25%
16%
9%
22%
Not promoted 75%
53%

Division D
Promoted within 3 years 24%
14%
10%
22%
Not promoted 76%
54%

Division E
Promoted within 18 months 17%
11%
6%
19%
Not promoted 83%
64%

several superiors who were familiar with each manager's work. The periods over which promotions were studied varied among the divisions; so did the number of openings which developed during the follow-up period. Ideally, one would expect to find very few low-rated men promoted, at least as long as a sizable number of high-rated managers remained unpromoted.

In Division C, however, promotions were actually more often given to managers rated low in overall effectiveness than to those rated high, and many good men remained unpromoted. In the other departments the situation was not quite so bad, but there were several other instances of marked divergence from the ideal pattern of value-reward congruence, to the detriment of organizational integration.

Concurrent Validity

Congruence between value and reward structures should be reflected not only in a close relationship between value and reward measures, but in a tendency to value and reward the same characteristics. In my work to date, I have been primarily concerned with personality characteristics, although biographical data and mental abilities may be equally significant.

It is easy enough to discover whether *concurrent validity* in fact prevails in an organization. One first identifies the *valued* characteristics by relating measures of various personality and character traits to job effectiveness ratings. *Rewarded* characteristics are then identified by correlating the same measures with salary and grade level. (Reasonably accurate measurement of the various characteristics is assumed.) The approach is the same as that used by the personnel psychologist in carrying out a concurrent validity study to establish a selection procedure. Only the interpretation is different. Instead of emphasizing the measures—that is, distinguishing "good" tests or determining which scores indicate job success—the concern is with determining what personal characteristics of the individual are valued and rewarded in a particular organization.

Ideally, to maximize integration, the highly valued characteristics—those closely related to ratings of competence—should be the rewarded characteristics, given similar ages and job demands. Yet my own research results indicate that the reward structure often fails to reinforce significantly the value structure [6]. As will be seen, this is the case in the comparative examples that I shall present a little further along in this article.

THE ORGANIZATIONAL UNCONSCIOUS: The characteristics identified by concurrent validity analysis are not necessarily the socially desirable "good" qualities that most managers normally associate with success. This type of analysis can, to be sure, reveal such qualities to be important; but it may pinpoint qualities that many managers would rather not recognize as part of the organization's value and reward structures. It thus reveals aspects of organizational character that might otherwise continue to influence decisions and policy formulation unbeknown to those making the decisions. In a sense it exposes the organizational unconscious.

The value and reward structures that gradually emerge in a company are an amalgam of separate decisions by many individuals, who are guided largely by forces of which they are unaware. When managers having like personality characteristics and behavior patterns are consistently praised and/or rewarded, a particular type of organizational character emerges. Yet the executives at the top may not be aware of the real reasons why they are singling out certain individuals for approval and reward. It is these reasons which are brought to the surface by concurrent validity analysis.

RESISTANCE TO CHANGE: While individual resistance to change, as a function of individual motives, can occure under any conditions, concerted group-supported action may often, on a deeper level, be a sign that the proposed innovation is in conflict with an existing value structure. For example, in a company where close social relationships are valued, a change in office assignments that physically separates people who are accustomed to frequent contacts is likely to meet with resistance. On the other hand, in a company with a different value structure, the same change might be accepted with equanimity or even welcomed.

All of this suggests the wisdom of attempting directed organizational changes only with full knowledge of the existing value structure. Such knowledge would permit the contemplated change to be designed and presented in such a way as to support rather than oppose this structure. Or, to take a different tack, the value structure could be altered to bring it into line with the subsequent innovation.

Typically, such changes in value structure come about when several members of the top executive group are replaced. The new top executives introduce new performance criteria, and a different value climate develops. Alternatively, management development techniques such as sensitivity training can be used to change the value structure without actually changing personnel.

Whether the innovation is to be adapted to the value structure or this structure adjusted to the desired change, organizational diagnosis is an important precondition. This is particularly true where massive reorganization is contemplated. Whether a decentralization move, for example, will succeed or merely produce confusion largely depends on the existing value structure. Equipped with a thorough knowledge of this structure at the outset, management is less likely to stumble over unanticipated and perhaps insurmountable barriers to directed organizational change.

Goal Relevance

In considering the final condition of *goal relevance* for organizational effectiveness, it will be useful to turn back briefly to my basic premise. I have considered the assumption that integration fosters the effective pursuit of organizational goals. In addition, I have dealt with the meaning of integration within the value structure, within the reward structure, and between the two. But what about the integration of these structures with goals? Cannot a business be perfectly integrated behind an inappropriate objective—such as keeping a particular clique in power—which has nothing to do with the organization's economic function? Clearly, the answer is *yes*.

It is important, therefore, to consider the characteristics—be they character traits, mental abilities, biographical factors, or whatever—that are valued and rewarded in a company in terms of their relevance for goal attainment. A company whose survival depends on swift adjustment to advances in knowledge and technology cannot afford to undervalue and/or penalize high academic qualifications in its managers. Again, a company that markets heavily to minority groups will jeopardize its long-term profitability if its value and reward structures are integrated in support of discrimination. Many similar examples could be cited. The point is simply that value and reward structures should reinforce legitimate organizational goals and objectives.

COMPARATIVE EXAMPLES

The six specific conditions just discussed, in effect, serve to establish the groundwork for a behavioral science approach to organizational analysis and diagnosis. Now let us see how this diagnostic approach might be applied in two companies—one small, one large—and how important strategies for change might be developed by its use.

Essential Precondition

Exhibit II presents an analysis of the two companies in the terms I have discussed. In the case of Company A, a small, marketing-oriented organization, all the managers were included in the analysis; in Company B, a large financial firm, the analysis was based on a representative sample including about three fourths of those at the middle management level and above. The valued and rewarded characteristics, which were measured by appropriate psychological tests, are listed in order of the size of the correlations; only statistically significant relationships are presented.

In objective terms, Company A seems to be the more successful of the two organizations. It also exhibits greater integration in terms of the halo effect, reward consistency, concurrent validity, and probably rated reliability, although on this data are not available for Company B.

Taken as a whole, Company A emerges as an organization with high integration *within* its value and reward structures, respectively, but considerable disparity *between* the two. The relationship between age and reward is sizable; between age and value, minimal. This suggests that the two may be products of different time periods, and that the familiar reward lag may be

EXHIBIT II

Specific Conditions Compared with Degree of Integration

	Integration	
Condition	**Company A**	**Company B**
Rater reliability	Very high	(No data)
Halo effect	High	Low
Reward consistency	Very high	Moderate
Multiple criteria	Low	Low
Concurrent validity	Very low	None
Valued characteristics:	Emotional control Desire to be with people Low interest in bard work Desire to be at the center of things	Youth Nonconformity Self-confidence Interest in hard work (especially problem solving)
Rewarded characteristics:	Age Independence Desire to avoid people Low self-confidence Low interest in hard work Low assertiveness Emotional control Anxiety	Age Anxiety Desire to avoid people Independence Intelligence
Goal relevance	Value structure reasonably good; reward rather poor	Value structure reasonably good; reward structure rather poor

operating. Emotional control and low interest in hard work are characteristic of both; but while the value structure stresses social interaction, the reward structure does just the reverse. In general, Company A tends to reward rather negative characteristics, with the exception of independence. The value climate, with its emphasis on social relationships, is more positive and also more congruent with the goals of the organization.

Company B, in contrast, clearly lacks integration in pursuit of its goals. Compared with Company A, it comes off rather poorly. The correlations under the concurrent validity condition are much lower than in Company A—

a further indication of the difference in integration. Valued characteristics differ completely in the two companies, but the reward structures are somewhat more similar, both favoring age, anxiety, desire to avoid people, and independence. But Company A rewards a number of characteristics that Company B does not. All in all, it seems clear that a man who succeeds in one company might very well not succeed in the other.

All my analyses of organizational structure and character to date have disclosed similar patterns. Not only are value and reward structures characteristically at odds, in that valued characteristics tend not to be rewarded and vice versa, but factors that make for success, as measured by indexes of value and reward, frequently differ from one organization to the next. Many companies, moreover, seem to be doing a poor job of attracting, retaining, and developing managers who possess the characteristics conducive to success.

Consider the comparative two-company data presented in Exhibit III. It is evident that Company A has disproportionately large numbers of managers who possess characteristics which, whether or not they are valued, are most unlikely to be rewarded. Company B, on the other hand, has accumulated proportionately more men who are very likely to be considered ineffective managers but who may, or may not, be rewarded.

How this happens is not entirely clear. One may hazard a guess that the company, lacking consistent and effective selection procedures, may in effect leave managerial selection too much in the hands of the potential candidate himself. After all, what company a man goes to work for is often as much or more *his* decision than that of his employer. His decision, in turn, may be influenced by any number of factors, one of which is likely to be the existing "image" of the company. Since the company image is typically shaped by

EXHIBIT III

Managerial Characteristics and Value-reward Correlation

Predominant differentiating characteristics	Correlation with Value	Correlation with Reward
Company A		
Desire to be with people outside of work	Plus	Minus
Interest in hard work	Minus	Minus
Self-confidence	Neutral	Minus
Company B		
Low interest in hard work	Minus	Neutral
Conformity	Minus	Neutral
Lack of self-confidence	Minus	Neutral

public relations efforts to influence the product market, it may often influence the labor market inappropriately. This would explain the predominance of certain differentiating managerial characteristics in Companies A and B.

Strategy for Change

Up to this point, I have emphasized description in presenting an analysis of Companies A and B in terms of integration theory. Such a diagnostic approach is an essential precondition for change. Actually, to bring about the appropriate change, and thereby to achieve a more effective organization, a strategy for change must be developed.

In the case of Company A, where a number of the conditions for effectiveness already exist, it is important that efforts to improve integration where it is lacking do not disturb these existing assets. Except for its negative emphasis on hard work, the value structure appears to be sound for a company of this kind. However, a change in the hierarchy is needed to move managers with valued characteristics into positions of greater status and reward. At the same time, the company needs a more effective selection procedure that will emphasize the characteristics of emotional control and a desire to be at the center of things, rather than extreme self-confidence.

An appropriate strategy to accomplish these changes might be to introduce an attractive early retirement plan, supplemented by some shifts in the organizational structure to open up more high-level positions to individuals with valued characteristics who are also interested in hard work. A change in the reward structure as it relates to work motivation should eventually have some impact on the value structure as well. More drastic organizational surgery, such as demotion or firing of top level people, might disrupt the existing integration.

To obtain more potential managers whose characteristics match the newly integrated value-reward system, it might be best to attempt a deliberate restructuring of potential job candidates' image of the company, perhaps by rewriting recruiting literature and using public relations techniques. Interview guides should be changed to stress the desired characteristics, and psychological test batteries should be revised accordingly.

Company B presents a more complex problem. Its value structure appears to be its major source of strength. The valued characteristics are consistent with innovative behavior. It is not clear, to be sure, that such behavior is really necessary in this particular kind of company, but in any event resistance to change should not be severe. In fact, if changes are presented as creative solutions to real problems, they should win acceptance rather easily.

The first step in Company B, then, would probably be to move a number of younger managers with valued characteristics into positions of greater responsibility. If a few demotions and/or dismissals should be necessary for this purpose, the company's value structure would probably support such action, and there is little need to be concerned about preserving existing integration. Intelligence, currently a rewarded characteristic, should be retained as a promotion criterion.

While these personnel changes are being carried out, studies aimed at achieving a full integration of compensation and executive grade level should be undertaken. Since youth is currently valued in Company B, while age is rewarded, it may be necessary to move a number of younger men up rather rapidly, or to hire from the outside. Since both approaches tend to stress the reward consistency condition, particular care should be taken to ensure the adequacy of individual compensation.

Given the fact that value and reward structures have been made reasonably congruent and the reassignment process has been completed, attention should turn to a consistent and stable value climate. Top-level managers should be encouraged to spend considerable time discussing performance standards, personal effectiveness, and compensation rewards with their subordinates. If a management by objectives approach should fail to achieve the desired results, then family group sensitivity training might be instituted.

CONCLUSION

The approach to improving organizational effectiveness I have discussed in this article uses integration theory to develop guidelines for organizational change which differ somewhat from the principles of management that have traditionally guided organization planning. Primarily, they supplement the principles, but in certain respects they replace them. Their novelty lies in (a) their emphasis on precise measurement of variables and in (b) the importance they attribute to managerial motivation. Like the traditional principles of management, however, they emphasize specific actions to achieve company goals, top management orientation, and clearly defined job requirements.

To analyze an organization adequately in terms of integration theory, various kinds of information are needed. First of all, personal ratings need to be obtained from the whole top echelon of the company. Each manager should rate as many subordinate managers as he can on a number of specific aspects of performance. Salary information and grade level should be recorded for each manager studied. In addition, data on age, education, and other biographical factors should be obtained, along with intelligence test scores. If organizational character is to be considered, tests or other assessment measures of personality are needed. All this information is then put into the form of a correlation matrix. Partial correlations, with age differences removed, must then be computed to determine whether the multiple criteria and concurrent validity conditions have been met.

With these correlational data in hand, specific prescriptions for improving organizational effectiveness may be developed. The actions taken can now be coordinated with the existing value structure and can be focused directly on known problem areas in order to increase the degree of integration behind company goals. A follow-up measurement and analysis can subsequently determine the extent to which the changes made have actually contributed to the objective.

REFERENCES

[1] See Edgar M. Schein: *Organizational Psychology*. Englewood Cliffs, New Jersey, Prentice-Hall, Inc., 1965, pp. 97–98; and Sherman Krupp: *Patterns in Organizational Analysis*. New York, Holt, Rinehart & Winston, 1961, pp. 169–170.

[2] *Boards of Directors: Structure and Performance,* Eugene, Oregon, University of Oregon Press, 1964.

[3] "Differentiation and Integration in Complex Organizations." *Administrative Science Quarterly,* June 1967, pp. 27–28.

[4] See John B. Miner, *The School Administrator and Organizational Character*. Eugene, Oregon, University of Oregon Press, 1967.

[5] Mason Haire, E. E. Ghiselli, and M. E. Gordon: *A Psychological Study of Pay*. Washington, D. C., American Psychological Association, 1967, pp. 15–16.

[6] Miner, *op. cit.,* pp. 68–79.

CASE 19

Implementing IBM's System/360 Decision*

T. A. Wise

When Tom Watson Jr. made what he called "the most important product announcement in company history," he created quite a stir. International Business Machines is not a corporation given to making earth-shaking pronouncements casually, and the declaration that it was launching an entirely new computer line, the System/360, was headline news. The elaborate logistics that IBM worked out in order to get maximum press coverage—besides a huge assembly at Poughkeepsie, IBM staged press conferences on the same day in sixty-two cities in the U.S. and in fourteen foreign countries—underscored its view of the importance of the event. And the fact that the move until then had been a closely guarded secret added an engaging element of surprise. But it was the magnitude of the new line—Watson called System/360 "a sharp departure from the concepts of the past"—that was really responsible for the reaction that ran through the computer industry. No company had ever introduced, in one swoop, six computer models of totally new design, in a technology never tested in the marketplace, and with programing abilities of the greatest complexity. Once the announcement was made, it is no wonder that, in the scattered locations where IBM plans, builds, and sells its products, there was, on that evening of April 7, 1964, a certain amount of dancing in the streets.

By now, two and a half years later, it would seem that there was good reason for the celebrations. As *Fortune* related in Part I last month, IBM was staking its treasure (some $5 billion over four years), its reputation, and its position of leadership in the computer field on its decision to go ahead with System/360. The current rate of shipments of the several models in the series is probably running close to 1,000 computers a month. Authoritative forecasts indicate that, on the basis of orders already on the books, over 26,000 members of the System/360 family will be operating around the world by the end of 1968. If these forecasts are correct, some $10 billion worth of IBM's new computing equipment will be in the field then. Even allowing for the fact that as many as 10 to 20 per cent of the customers now signed up

* "The Rocky Road To The Marketplace," *Fortune,* October 1966. Reprinted by permission.

may cancel their orders, the results in hand by the end of this year would stamp the whole 360 venture as very successful.

The final verdict on IBM's wisdom, however, depends on a series of factors more complicated than the number of shipments. The programing of System/360 is one enormously difficult area and here much remains to be accomplished before the project can be rated a complete success. Moreover, there have been new developments in tchnology since System/360 was launched in 1964; will they enable competitors to leapfrog into something better? And the managerial and organizational changes that were brought about by the company's struggle to settle on, and then to produce and market, the new line are still having their effects. In each of these several aspects, past, present, and future are closely intertwined.

THE RISING COST OF ASKING QUESTIONS

No part of the whole adventure of launching System/360 has been as tough, as stubborn, or as enduring as the programing. Earlier this year, talking to a group of IBM customers, Tom Watson Jr. said ruefully: "We are investing nearly as much in System/360 programing as we are in the entire development of System/360 hardware. A few months ago the bill for 1966 was going to be $40 million. I asked Vin Learson last night before I left what he thought it would be for 1966 and he said $50 million. Twenty-four hours later I met Watts Humphrey, who is in charge of programing production, in the hall here and said, 'Is this figure about right? Can I use it?' He said it's going to be $60 million. You can see that if I keep asking questions we won't pay a dividend this year."

Watson's concern about programing, of course, goes back to the beginnings of the System/360 affair. By late in 1962 he was sufficiently aware of the proportions of the question to invite the eight top executives of IBM to his ski lodge in Stowe, Vermont, for a three-day session on programing. The session was conducted by Fred Brooks, the corporate manager for the design of the 360 project, and other experts; they went into the programing in considerable detail. While the matter can become highly technical, in general IBM's objective was to devise an "operating system" for its computer line, so that the computers would schedule themselves, without manual interruption, and would be kept working continuously at or near their capacity. At the time it announced System/360, IBM promised future users that it would supply them with such a command system.

Delivery on that promise has been agonizingly difficult. Even though Tom Watson and the other top executives knew the critical importance of programing, the size of the job was seriously underestimated. The difficulty of coordinating the work of hundreds of programers was enormous. The operating system IBM was striving for required the company to work out many new ideas and approaches; as one company executive says, "We were trying to schedule inventions, which is a dangerous thing to do in a committed project." Customers came up with more extensive programing tasks than the company had expected, and there were inevitable delays and slowdowns. Even today, the difficulties of programing are preventing some users from getting the full benefit from their new machines. By IBM's own estimates, the company won't have most of the bugs out of programing the larger systems until the middle of 1967—at least a year behind its expectation.

In technology, IBM was also breaking new ground. During the formative years of the decisions about the technology of System/360, a lengthy report on the subject was prepared by the *ad hoc* Logic Committee, headed by Erich Bloch, a specialist in circuitry for IBM. Eventually, the Logic Committee report led to the company's formal commitment to a new hybrid kind of integrated-circuit technology—a move that, like so many other aspects of the 360 decision, is still criticized by some people in the computer industry, both inside and outside of IBM.

The move, though, was hardly made in haste. The whole computer industry had raced through two phases of electronic technology—vacuum tubes and transistors—between 1951 and 1960. By the late 1950's it was becoming apparent that further technological changes of sweeping importance were in the offing. At that time, however, IBM was not very much of a force in scientific research, its strengths lying in the assembling and marketing of computers, not in their advanced concepts. The company's management at the time had the wit to recognize the nature of the corporate deficiency, and to see the importance of correcting it. In 1956, IBM hired Dr. Emanuel Piore, formerly chief scientist of U.S. naval research. Piore became IBM's director of research and a major figure in the technological direction that the company finally chose for its System/360.

THE COLD REALITIES OF CHOICE

Under Piore's direction, IBM's prestige in both pure and applied research rose dramatically. The company gained recognition as a leader in electronics, physics, and mathematics. It made efforts in many directions, including an important inquiry into cryogenics—the behavior of materials at extremely low temperatures. At temperatures close to absolute zero (—459.7°F.) the resistance to electricity of certain metals, such as lead and tin, virtually vanishes. This means that cryogenic computer circuitry could be much faster, and the power required much smaller. Between 1958 and 1961, IBM spent between $10 million and $15 million, including some government funds, in an attempt to perfect a computer technology based on cryogenics; at one point the company made what some regarded as an alarming laboratory discovery of a cryogenic process that might eventually make the manufacture of computers so cheap that IBM's profits would become very thin. (Watson turned to his marketing and manufacturing experts to find out what the company might do if this process were perfected. They assured him it was not about to happen.) For a long time some people at IBM remained convinced that cryogenics would revolutionize their company and their industry. But when the company started working toward the practical choice of a technology for System/360, it leaned more heavily on its engineers than on its research scientists, and cryogenics died a sudden death.

In the end, as the report of the Logic Committee showed, the choice narrowed to two technologies. One was monolithic integrated circuitry: putting all the elements of a circuit—transistors, resistors, and diodes—on one chip at one time. The other was hybrid integrated circuitry—IBM rather densely termed it "solid logic technology"—which means making transistors and diodes separately and then soldering them into place. In 1961 the Logic Committee decided that the production of monolithic circuits in great quantities would be risky, and in any case would not meet the schedule for any new line of computers to be marketed by 1964.

There was little opposition to this recommendation initially, except among a few engineering purists. Later, however, the opposition strengthened. The purists believed that monolithic circuits were sure to come, and that the company in a few years would find itself frozen into a technology that might be obsolete before the investment could be recovered. However, the Logic Committee's recommendation on the hybrid approach was accepted; since that time, Watson has referred to the acceptance as "the most fortunate decision we ever made." But some of the critics, at least, still persist in their disagreement with that judgment: their position is that if IBM had put into monolithic circuits the effort is devoted to the hybrids, there would have been a monolithic success, and both company and industry would be better off.

THE SECRETS CIRCUITS HIDE

The decision to move into hybrid integrated technology accelerated IBM's push into component manufacturing, a basic change in the character of the company. In the day of vacuum tubes and transistors, IBM had designed the components for its circuits, ordered them from other companies (a principal supplier: Texas Instruments), then assembled them to its own specifications. But with the new circuitry, those specifications would have to be built into the components from the outset. "Too much proprietary information was involved in circuitry production," says Watson. "Unless we did it ourselves, we could be turning over some of the essentials of our business to another company. We had no intention of doing that." In addition, of course, IBM saw no reason why it should not capture some of the profit from the manufacturing that it was creating on such a large scale.

The company's turn to a new technology jibed neatly with a previous decision made in 1960 by Watson at the urging of the man who was then IBM president, Al Williams, that the company should move into component manufacturing. By the time the decision to go into hybrid circuits was made, IBM already had started putting together a component manufacturing division. Its general manager was John Gibson, a Johns Hopkins Ph.D. in electrical engineering. Under Gibson, the new division won the authority, hitherto divided among other divisions of the company, to designate and to buy the components for computer hardware, along with a new authority to manufacture them when Gibson thought it appropriate.

This new assignment of responsibility was resented by managers in the Data Systems and General Products divisions, since it represented a limitation on their authority. Also, they protested that they would be unable to compare the price and quality of in-house components with those made by an outside supplier if they lost their independence of action. But Vincent Learson, then group executive vice president, feared that if they kept their independence they would continue to make purchases outside the company, and that IBM as a consequence would have no market for its own component output. He therefore put the power of decision in Gibson's hands. IBM's board, in effect, ruled in Gibson's favor when, in 1962, it authorized the construction of a new manufacturing plant, and the purchase of its automatic equipment, at a cost of over $100 million.

While IBM was making up its corporate mind about the technology for System/360, the delegation of specific responsibilities was going ahead. Learson designated Bob Evans, now head of the Federal Systems Division, to manage the giant undertaking. Under Evans, Fred Brooks was put in charge of all the System/360 work being done at Poughkeepsie, where four of the original models were designed; he was also made manager of the over-all design of the central processors. The plant at Endicott was given the job of designing the model 30, successor to the popular 1401, which had been developed there. And John Fairclough, a systems designer at World Trade, was assigned to design the model 40 at the IBM lab at Hursley, England.

Out of the Hursley experience came an interesting by-product that may have significant implications for IBM's future. With different labs engaged in the 360 design, it was vital to provide for virtually instant communication between them. IBM therefore leased a special transatlantic line between its home offices and the engineers in England, and later in Germany. The international engineering group was woven together with considerable effectiveness, giving IBM the justifiable claim that the 360 computer was probably the first product of truly international design.

While dovetailing plans for the 360, IBM also became involved at first hand with an international communication system for the processing of information. In 1961, IBM used 28,900 miles of domestic telephone circuitry; by 1966 it was using 380,000 miles, and two voice channels across the Atlantic. On the basis of that volume, IBM last year petitioned the FCC for the right to by-pass the common carriers, AT&T and ITT, and have direct access to the comsat satellite. The petition was turned down in July of this year.

But the experience opened a new window to the future for the company. IBM now has the vision of the communication of tomorrow, with machines talking to machines across the oceans. What that will mean in terms of the dollar volume of the market is still conjectural, but IBM feels sure it is a market that does not have to be controlled completely by the entrenched carriers. IBM makes a careful distinction between data transmission—the simple function of carrying electrical impules—and data transformation, which it defines as the analyzing, correlating, and sorting of those impulses. IBM does not want to be considered merely the manufacturer of a device that would be only a part of the common carriers' communication system, and so subject to conventional regulations and tariff schedules. It sees itself playing a critical role in a brand-new kind of international data communication, composed of computers that work and talk with each other. And in such a vision compatibility is a necessary element. Compatibility is just what System/360 possesses.

IN A TUG-OF-WAR, ENOUGH ROPE TO HANG YOURSELF

Even in a corporation inured to change, people resist change. By 1963, with the important decisions on the 360 being implemented, excitement about the new product line began to spread through the corporation—at least among those who were privy to the secret. But this rising pitch of interest by no means meant that the struggle inside the company was settled. The new family of computers cut across all the old lines of authority and upset all the old divisions. The System/360 concepts plunged IBM into an organizational upheaval.

Resistance came in only a mild form from the World Trade Corp., whose long-time boss was A. K. Watson, Tom's brother. World Trade managers always thought of European markets as very different from those in the U.S., and as requiring special considerations that U.S. designers would not give them. Initially they had reservations about the concept of a single computer family, which they thought of as fitted only to U.S. needs. But when IBM laboratories in Europe were included in the formulation of the design of some of the 360 models, the grumblings from World Trade were muted. Later A. K. Watson was made vice chairman of the corporation and Gilbert Jones, formerly the head of domestic marketing of computers for the company, took over World Trade. These moves further integrated the domestic and foreign operations, and gave World Trade assurance that its voice would be heard at the top level of the corporation.

The General Products Division, for its part, really bristled with hostility. Its output, after all, accounted for two thirds of the company's revenues for data processing. It had a popular and profitable product in the field, the 1401, which the 360 threatened to replace. The executive in charge of General Products, John Haanstra, fought against some phases of the 360 program. Haanstra thought the new line would hit his division hard. He was concerned, from the time the System/360 program was approved, about the possibility that it would undermine his division's profits. Specifically, he feared that the cost of providing compatibility in the lower end of the 360 line (which would be General Products' responsibility) might price the machines out of the market. Later he was to develop some more elaborate arguments against the program.

For a while, some parts of IBM's marketing organization also resisted the new course. The marketers' concern was centered on one aspect of the 360 program: the central processor—i.e., the computer and its memory without any peripheral equipment—would sell for less than those in other IBM lines. Some salesmen assumed that the difference threatened their commission structures. At IBM, salesmen are given quotas expressed in points, with one point representing one dollar's worth of additional net monthly rental income. If a salesman receives a quota of 1,000 points, and then manages to persuade a customer to replace equipment renting for $4,000 monthly with something renting for $5,000 monthly, he has met his quota (and earned a commission). Salesmen were haunted by the notion that lower prices would depress commissions. But this fear gradually dissolved, as it became clear that the lower prices for central processors would be more than offset by heavier sales of peripheral equipment—which were implied in the System/360's expanded capabilities.

THE BATTLE OF SAN JOSE

Long after the company's SPREAD committee had outlined the System/360 concept, and it had been endorsed by IBM's top management, there were numerous development efforts going on inside the company that offered continuing alternatives to the concept—and they were taken seriously enough, in some cases, so that there were fights for jurisdiction over them. Early in 1963, for example, there was a row over development work at IBM's San Jose Laboratory, which belonged to the General Products Division. It turned out that San Jose—which had been explicitly told to stop the work—was still developing a low-power machine similar to one being worked on in World Trade's German lab. When he heard about the continuing effort, A. K. Watson went to the lab, along with Emanuel Piore, and seems to have angrily restated his demand that San Jose cut it out. Some people from San Jose were then transferred to Germany to work on the German machine, and the General Products effort was stopped. In the curious way of organizations, though, things turned out well enough in the end: the German machine proved to be a good one, and the Americans who came into the project contributed a lot to its salability. With some adaptations, the machine was finally incorporated into the 360 line, and now, as the model 20, it is probably selling better than any other in the series.

In the fall of 1963, Tom Watson acted in several ways to speed up work on the 360 program. First of all, he announced the abolition of the corporate management committee, a group of top executives functioning as the chief policy makers of the company. While the move was not formally linked to the 360, the fact was that Watson had become impatient with the excessively crowded agenda of the committee during the years when the 360 was being developed. He believed that too many of the vital decisions about the program were being "bucked upstairs" when they could have been settled at a lower level; abolishing the committee would force these earlier settlements.

Watson also made some new management assignments that reflected the impact of the 360 program on the corporation. Learson was shifted away from supervising product development and given responsibility for marketing, this being the next phase of the 360 program. Gibson took over Learson's former responsibilities. The increasing development of IBM into homogeneous international organization was reflected in the move up of A. K. Watson from World Trade (he is now corporate vice chairman); he was succeeded by Gilbert Jones, former head of domestic marketing. Piore became a group vice president in charge of research and several other activities.

One reason for Watson's interest in speeding up the 360 program in late 1963 was an increasing awareness that the IBM product line was running out of steam. The company was barely reaching its sales goals in this period. Some of this slowdown, no doubt, was due to mounting rumors about the new line. But there was another, critical reason for the slowdown: major customers were seeking ways of linking separate data-processing operations on a national basis, and IBM had limited capability along that line. Finally, IBM got a distinctly unpleasant shock in December, 1963, when the Honeywell Corp. announced a new computer. Its model 200 had been designed along the same lines as the 1401—a fact Honeywell cheerfully acknowledged—but it used newer, faster, and cheaper transistors than the 1401 and was therefore priced 30 per cent below the IBM model. To make matters worse, Honeywell's engineers had figured out a means by which customers interested in reprograming from an IBM 1401 to a Honeywell 200 could do so inexpensively. The vulnerability of the 1401 line was obvious, and so was the company's need for the new line of computers.

It was around this time that some IBM executives began to argue seriously for simultaneous introduction of the whole 360 family. There were several advantages to the move. One was that it would have a tremendous public-relations impact and demonstrate the distinctive nature of IBM's new undertaking. Customers would have a clear picture of where and how they could grow with a computer product line, and so would be more inclined to wait for it. Finally, there might be an antitrust problem in introducing the various 360 models sequentially. The Justice Department might feel that an IBM salesman was improperly taking away competitors' business if he urged customers not to buy their products because of an impending announcement of his own company's new model. IBM has long had a company policy under which no employee is allowed to tell a customer of any new product not formally announced by the management. (Several employees have, in fact, been fired or disciplined for violating the rule.) Still, introducing a long line of computers in sequence might put pressure on salesmen, many of whom would be closely questioned by anxious customers, to violate the rule. Announcing the whole 360 line at once would dispose of the problem.

LEARSON STAGES A SHOOT-OUT

Beginning in late 1963, then, the idea of announcing and marketing the the 360 family all at once gained increasing support. At the same time, by making the 360 program tougher to achieve, the idea gave Haanstra some new arguments against the program. His opposition now centered on two main points. First, he argued that the General Products manufacturing organization would be under pressure to build in a couple of years enough units of the model 30 to replace a field inventory of the 1401 that had been installed over a five-year period. He said that IBM was in danger of acquiring a huge backlog, one representing perhaps two or three years' output, and that competitors, able to deliver in a year or less, would steal business away.

Haanstra's other objection in this period related especially to the 360-30, a model that IBM hoped to sell heavily to its old 1401 customers. The trouble was, Haanstra said, that the 360-30 was noncompatible with the 1401; meanwhile, Honeywell's 200, which was being sold with that company's new reprograming techniques, might tempt as many as three quarters of the 1401 users—unless IBM extended and improved its 1401 program. Specifically, he proposed a modernized version, using advanced transistor technology, the 1401-S.

But Haanstra's argument was countered to some extent by a group of resourceful IBM engineers. They believed that the so-called "read-only" storage device could be adapted to make the 360-30 compatible with the 1401. The read-only technique, which involved the storing of permanent electronic instructions in the computer, could be adapted to make the model 30 act like a 1401 in many respects: the computer would be slowed down but the user would be able to employ his 1401 program. IBM executives had earlier been exposed to a read-only device by John Fairclough, the head of World Trade's Hursley Laboratory in England, when he was trying (unsuccessfully) to win corporate approval for his Scamp computer.

Could the device really be used to meet Haanstra's objections to the 360-30? To find out, Learson staged a "shoot-out" in January, 1964, between the 1401-S and the model 30. The test proved that the model 30, "emulating" the 1401, could already operate at 80 per cent of the speed of the 1401-S—and could improve that figure with other adaptations. That was good enough for Learson. He notified Watson that he was ready to go, and said that he favored announcing the whole System/360 family at once.

"GOING . . . GOING . . . GONE!"

Haanstra was still not convinced. He persisted in his view that his manufacturing organization probably could not gear up to meet the production demand adequately. On March 18 and 19, a final "risk-assessment" session was held at Yorktown Heights to review once again every debatable point of the program. Tom Watson Jr., President Al Williams, and thirty top executives of the corporation attended. This was to be the last chance for the unpersuaded to state their doubts or objections on any aspect of the new program—patent protection, policy on computer returns, the company's ability to hire and train an enormous new work force in the time allotted, etc. Haanstra himself was conspicuously absent from this session. In February he had been relieved of his responsibilities as president of the General Products Division and assigned to special duty—monitoring a project to investigate the possibility of IBM's getting into magnetic tape. (He is now a vice president of the Federal Systems Division.) At the end of the risk-assessment meeting, Watson seemed satisfied that all the objections to the 360 had been met. Al Williams, who had been presiding, stood up before the group, asked if there were any last dissents, and then, getting no response, dramatically intoned, "Going . . . going . . . gone!"

Work on the pricing of the 360 line had already begun. IBM's marketing forecasters go through what is termed a "pricing loop" in determining the optimal price of their products. A price is first set tentatively on a model. Then the marketing organization gives an estimate of the number of models it can sell at that price. This estimate is fed back to the manufacturing group, which must itself estimate whether, given that volume of production, manufacturing costs might be lowered enough to warrant a lower price. This whole cycle is repeated several times, until the most desirable balance between price and volume is achieved. In the case of the 360, the pricing sessions were fairly hectic. One participant recalls, "We reviewed the competitive analysis for perhaps the fifteenth time. We had to take into consideration features that could be built in later with the turn of a screwdriver but that were not to be announced formally. We were pulling cost estimates out of a hat."

The April 7, 1964, announcement of the program unveiled details of six separate compatible computer machines; their memories would be interchangeable, so that a total of nineteen different combinations would be available. The peripheral equipment was to consist of forty different input and output devices, including printers, optical scanners, and high-speed tape drives. Delivery of the new machines would start in April, 1965.

THE NATURE OF THE RISK

With the April 7 announcement, IBM was at last irrevocably committed to the risks that it had always recognized to be inherent in the 360 program. But in the summer of 1964 management was confident that it had made the right decision and had ample resources to see the program through. It was so confident, in fact, that it decided IBM did not need all the cash it had on hand. Cash balances had been increasing for several years, and were approaching \$1 billion at the end of 1963; meanwhile, there had been some trend toward increased purchases of equipment instead of rental, and so it was assumed that the need for cash would decline. For these reasons the company decided to prepay \$160 million of loans from the Prudential Insurance Co., bearing an average interest rate of $3\frac{1}{2}$ per cent; Prudential waived the stipulated premium for prepayment. This stands as one IBM decision about which there is, in retrospect, no controversy—it was a mistake. In 1966 the company has had to establish bank lines of credit totaling the same \$160 million, and has to pay about two percentage points more for any of the funds that are used.

The basic announcement of the new line brought a mixed reaction from the competition. The implication that the 360 line would make obsolete all earlier equipment was derided and minimized by rival manufacturers, who seized every opportunity to argue that the move was less significant than it appeared. IBM's new technology was criticized for being less than pure microcircuitry. The competition also voiced doubts that IBM could achieve any meaningful degree of compatibility in its line; that was unfeasible, they said, and even if achieved, it would be uneconomic for many customers.

Despite these depreciatory words, the competition was concerned enough about the System/360 to respond to its challenge on a large scale. During the summer of 1964, General Electric announced that its 600 line of computers would have time-sharing capabilities. The full import of this announcement hit IBM that fall, when MIT, prime target of several computer manufacturers, announced that it would buy a GE machine. IBM had worked on a time-sharing program back in 1960 but had abandoned the idea when the cost of the terminals involved seemed to make it uneconomic. GE's success caught IBM off base and in 1964 and 1965 it was scrambling madly to provide the same capability in the 360 line. Late in 1964, RCA announced it would use the pure monolithic integrated circuitry (i.e., as opposed to IBM's hybrid circuitry) in some models of its new Spectra 70 line. This development probably led to a certain amount of soul-searching at IBM.

In the end, however, IBM seems to have decided that the threats posed by these new entries in the market were not disastrous. The company felt that the turn to monolithic circuitry did not involve capabilities that threatened the 360 line; furthermore, if and when monolithic circuitry ever did prove to have decisive advantages over IBM's hybrid circuitry, the company was prepared—the computers themselves and some three quarters of the component manufacturing equipment could be adapted fairly inexpensively to monolithics. As for time sharing, any anxieties IBM had about that were eased in March, 1965, when Watts Humphrey, a systems expert who had been given the assignment of meeting the time-sharing challenge (he is a nephew of President Eisenhower's Treasury Secretary, George Humphrey), got the job done.

The competitive challenge and its own new capabilities led IBM to announce some additions to the 360 line in 1964 and 1965. One important addition was the model 90, a supercomputer type, designed to be competitive with Control Data's 6800. Another was the 360-44, designed for special scientific purposes. Also, there was the 360–67, a large time-sharing machine. Another, the 360-20, represented a pioneering push into the low end of the market. None of these are fully compatible with the models originally announced, but they are considered part of the 360 family.

THE FLYING SUITCASE SQUAD

It looked, at this point, as if the 360 program was well under control. Then some quite unforeseen troubles broke out in the manufacturing operation. One of the steps in making semiconductors was accomplished by an evaporation process, and the company had used small-capacity evaporators to test the technique. But when large-capacity evaporators were introduced to meet mass-production requirements, the IBM engineers at East Fishkill, New York, ran into some problems, which had to do with metallurgical changes that took place in the larger units. Production at East Fishkill came to a virtual standstill. The company immediately rounded up all the smaller evaporators it could find and used them to work production back up to about 50 per cent of the original goal. By the end of 1965 the metallurgical problems were finally solved—but by that time the original delivery schedule was unsustainable. IBM had intended to deliver 1,000 of the new computers by December 31 but settled for 837.

Production of the 360 line was also held up by a maddening series of shortages. There were, for example, critical shortages of epoxy glass, copper laminate, and contact tabs. The tabs carry the connection between the printed circuits and the modules. Manufacturers of these tabs were scattered around the eastern part of the U.S., and none of them were prepared for the kind of demand IBM was unleashing in their markets. In some periods of acute tab shortage, teams of IBM engineers were being yanked off their jobs and sent to work with the suppliers to expedite production. IBM representatives suddenly began appearing at tab plants late in the evening or early in the morning, with suitcases. They would pack all the tabs they could and then fly back to Endicott to keep the production line moving.

Around mid-1965, however, the company gradually became aware that production problems were not its only, or even its greatest, obstacle to getting the 360 program on schedule. While there had been no disposition to underrate the technical difficulties in preparing the programing, no one, it appears, foresaw the appalling management problems that would be associated with them. Part of the management problem was that programers who were desperately needed to develop improved software for the 360 line all during 1963 and 1964 were still spending a great deal of time improving the programs associated with the company's older computers. In any case, there was no real yardstick by which management could gauge the time and manpower required to develop the software for a unique venture like the System/360. Early this year the burden of this problem was thrust on Watts Humphrey, fresh from his triumph on time sharing.

The first thing Humphrey did was to order a complete review of all proposed programs; the second was to eliminate some of the more elaborate functions that had been promised. In IBM's rather euphemistic terminology, some thirty-one technical capabilities were "decommitted." This move helped to break one bottleneck, but it represented only a minor gain in the total software campaign.

IBM had several managers trying to get the 360 program back on the track in 1964–65. Gibson, who had succeeded Learson in the job, was replaced late in 1964. His successor, Paul Knaplund, lasted about another year.

SHARING THE BAD NEWS

In March, Tom Watson Jr. visited California to address a meeting of "Share," which is a group of users of IBM equipment who meet from time to time to exchange information and opinions about IBM products. Some of the Share members had helped IBM develop its new 360 computer language, and Watson doubtless felt a special obligation to be candid to the group; in any case, he made no effort to paper over his company's problems. Some of his listeners were then grumbling about the postponements of hardware delivery announced the previous October. Watson acknowledged the dissatisfaction of his customers, referred to the problems with software, and even conceded that the momentous decision to announce the entire 360 package at once in April, 1964, may have been "ill advised."

A month later there was another unscheduled development. Watson surprised the financial community by asking his stockholders for $371 million of equity capital. This financing partly reflected the needs that arose out of heavy demand for the 360 line, and in a sense, therefore, it was good news for the stockholders. In the prospectus, however, there was one item of unalloyed bad news: the company had suffered heavy setbacks at the high end of the 360 line—i.e., in its efforts to bring forth a great supercomputer in the tradition of Stretch. It was writing off $15 million worth of parts and equipment developed specifically for the 360-90.

There were signs at about this time that the 360 program was still generating major reshufflements of divisions and personnel. A new management committee had been formed. The corporate staff had been split into two sections, each headed by a group vice president. Dr. Piore had been freed from operational duties and responsibilities and given a license to roam the company checking on just about all technical activities. Some of his former duties are now in a division headed by Eugene Fubini, a former Assistant Secretary of Defense and the Pentagon's deputy director of research and engineering before he joined IBM in 1965. Fubini was one of the first outsiders ever brought into the company at such a high executive level (he is a group vice president); his appointment would seem to confirm the continuing rise in influence of the technical men. Another change represented a comeback for Stephen Dunwell, who had managed the Stretch program and had been made the goat for its expensive failure to perform as advertised. When IBM got into the 360 program, its technical men discovered that the work done on Stretch was immensely valuable to them; and Watson personally gave Dunwell an award as an IBM fellow (which entitles him to work with IBM backing, for five years, on any project of his choosing).

Still another change involved a new management review committee composed of the two Watsons, Learson, and Williams, which was created to help the chief executive run the corporation. Williams, who long had been planning to retire at fifty-five, was prevailed on by Watson to stay as chairman of the executive committee. Finally, Learson, the man who had sparked the 360 from the outset, was named president.

THE FUTURE OF A LINE

System/360 has undergone many changes since the concept was originally brought forth back in 1962 and even since Watson's announcement in 1964.

Today nine central processors are being offered in the 360 line; some of them have memories that are much faster than those originally offered. The number of input-output machines jumped from the original forty to over seventy.

These changes should not be veiwed as surprising because the 360 family was designed to be adaptable to new technologies and new kinds of peripheral equipment, and has been made adaptable to time sharing. It is still unclear how much of the equipment will ultimately provide this feature. IBM estimates that time sharing will account for about 30 per cent of the computer market; other manufacturers think it may take over the whole market.

To date, the 360 program seems, with one large reservation, to be a considerable success. The reservation concerns programing, where a lot of problems are yet to be licked. The company is currently investing very heavily in money and manpower to get them licked: some 2,000 programers and "support personnel" are on the job, and the cost of this effort may run over $200 million.

The payoff on the 360 program will take years to measure, of course. The payoff will involve not only direct System/360 orders (which have been pretty breathtaking so far), but the entire expansion of computer applications implicit in the line's burgeoning capabilities. The program has pushed IBM itself into feats of performance in manufacturing, technology, and communications that its own staff did not believe were possible when the project was undertaken. Because of the 360, the company is a more sophisticated and more thoroughly integrated organization than it was in 1962.

At the same time, the massive difficulties associated with the project, and the retreats from some of the original goals, have led many businessmen to see IBM in a new light. The difficulties have done something to that extraordinary IBM mystique of success. The mystique is probably gone for good —although the successes may just go on becoming greater and greater.

Ford Motor Co.*

William M. Carley

To hear officials of some multinational companies talk, there is a surefire success formula for any large corporation with global facilities. First of all, they say, the multinational should unify its product lines around the world to obtain mass-production efficiency. Second, it should make its parts wherever such manufacturing is most economical. Third, it should focus its sales efforts on countries where markets are growing fastest. The result, say the formula's proponents, is a maximization of profits.

If all this sounds reasonable, not to say obvious, one might consider the fact that Ford Motor Co. has been following just that formula in recent years and is finding that the scheme isn't as surefire as it seems. This by no means implies that the giant auto maker is thinking of abandoning its integrated approach; however, it does mean that Ford is finding some major flaws in the approach—a finding that is emphasized by talking to Gerd Maletz, an owner of one of the biggest Ford dealerships in Germany.

"Take spare parts," Mr. Maletz says. "An engine for one Ford model now must come from Britain, and we may wait months for it. And if the British workers are on strike—and they're always on strike—we wait and wait and wait. We could get a German engine in a couple of days."

RUNNING INTO PROBLEMS

Nor does Mr. Maletz think much of the quality of the cars produced by Ford's integrated manufacturing plants in Europe. "If you buy a new Granada (the top of Ford's European line), for the first 10,000 kilometers it seems very quiet, smooth, and solid," he says. "But then there's a rattle here, and something goes wrong there, and you begin to run into all kinds of problems. We're having trouble selling the car."

In short, the integration of international operations can bring a host of problems along with the benefits. For Ford, integration in Europe has meant some huge cost savings. At the same time, however, the move has meant snarled production lines, soured labor relations, quality and delivery problems, and, in some countries (especially Germany), a major decline in market share.

And the experience has had a major impact on the totality of Ford Motor

* Reprinted with permission of *The Wall Street Journal,* February 20, 1974.

Co. Last year, Ford's European operations accounted for about 25% of the company's world-wide production of 5.7 million cars and trucks. Ford's two principal European subsidiaries, Ford of Britain and Ford of Germany, together accounted for 20% of their parent's 1972 revenues of $20.2 billion and about 14% of the company's profit of $870 million. If it weren't for all the problems in Europe, these percentages, especially the contribution to profit, would have been much larger.

Be that as it may, many multinational companies around the world still favor integrating their far-flung operations, and this is particularly true of those American multinationals that went on a shopping spree for foreign companies in the 1960s. "We have no choice," says a vice president of one American company that plans to follow Ford's footsteps in integrating European operations. "We have to have common products so we can go for cheap mass production. It's too expensive to manufacture on a country-by-country basis—you can't do that much longer without going broke."

A MATTER OF ECONOMY

Maybe not. But this vice president, as well as other officials connected with American multinationals, would do well to take a close look at the experience of Ford, which decided on integration in 1967. At the time, the company's rationale for so doing seemed sound indeed: Integration would avoid unnecessarily duplicating the amount—some $100 million—that it costs to engineer and produce a new auto model. "There's no sense spending that a dozen times or more for each country in Europe, when you need spend it only once," explains Gordon Guthrie, general sales manager of Ford's German subsidiary.

So Ford decided to produce just one European line in place of the completely different cars that used to be turned out by its British and German plants. And the single line began to reduce costs in another way, since the company began to buy parts in bigger volumes—meaning lower prices—from its outside suppliers.

Along with its integration of production, Ford also moved to shift its marketing emphases from countries like Britain, where auto sales were languishing in the 1960s due to government credit controls, to countries like France and Italy, where sales were growing. "In countries where markets were static, we had some of our strongest and most imaginative management teams; in other countries where the opportunities for expansion were greater, we had much smaller resources," Stanley Gillen, then chairman of the integrated operation (called Ford of Europe), told a company management meeting in 1971.

To achieve integration, Ford began to weave a complex manufacturing web that stretched from its big plants in Britain and Germany to its smaller units in Belgium, France, Ireland, the Netherlands and Portugal. It was planned that some units would make parts, some would assemble finished autos and some would do both, with the entire operation being directed from Ford of Europe's headquarters in Warley, outside of London.

THE EARLY STAGES

But even in the very early stages, there were problems. One Ford executive, an American who moved from Detroit to Britain to help set up Ford of Europe, says he quickly ran into nationality differences. "It was easy to get our British people to agree (to a plan), but five minutes later they were always back questioning it," the American recalls. "It seemed almost impossible to get the German Ford people to agree to anything; but once they did, they just kept marching even if they were marching right off the end of the earth."

The first all-new auto launched by Ford of Europe was a medium-sized car that was called the Cortina Mark II in Britain and the Taunus in Germany. The launch, which began in 1970, was a disaster, and the aftereffects are still plaguing Ford. "There's no question we screwed that one up," Mr. Guthrie concedes.

The fiasco stemmed partly from British inexperience with the metric system. Ford's British workers had just converted to that system, long used by Germany and other Continental countries; but, say one of the British workers, "we were still thinking in inches." As a result, the British and German parts often didn't mesh. "The doors didn't fit, the bonnet (hood) didn't fit, nothing fit," says Arthur Naylor, a metal finisher in Ford's Dagenham, England, body plant.

It has also been argued by British workers that some of the German-designed parts were too precise. "Our men often work with a one-sixteenth-inch tolerance, but on the German engine-suspension system, we had to work down to two- or three-thousandths of a bloody inch," contends Jock Macrae, a union shop steward at Dagenham. "The Germans wanted an engineering job done on the production line, and that's impossible."

Because of all the snafus, the Cortina-Taunus assembly line in Dagenham barely moved along. By January 1971, when some kinks had been ironed out, the line was speeded up—much to the displeasure of some workers, Mr. Macrae says. Coincidentally, Ford's wage contract was expiring at the time; and on January 29, 1971, unions struck Ford in Britain, halting production for nine weeks. It wasn't until September, nearly a year after initial production of the new car had begun, that Dagenham hit peak production. Ford says the peak should have been reached in two months.

But the problems attendant to the Cortina-Taunus launch have had an even longer-lasting impact in Germany. First of all, of course, there were the immediate effects of the British strike. "Britain struck, our plants went down and we fell flat on our tails," says a former executive of Ford's German operation. "Our dealers were crying for cars and they couldn't get them." But even after the strike was over, production problems led to quality problems, and consumer tests in Germany showed that the public thought the Taunus rated low on quality.

To avoid a second fiasco, especially in quality-conscious Germany, the launch of Ford's next new car was delayed until April 1972, six months later than had been planned. This car was the top-of-the-line Granada (a less luxurious and somewhat less powerful version of the same car is called the Consul), and the delay, if necessary, was nonetheless costly. For one thing, four months prior to the Granada's debut, General Motors Corp.'s German subsidiary, Opal, came out with its new Rekord line, which quickly snatched sales from Ford. But another damaging factor was that by delaying mass production until April, Ford of Germany missed the peak springtime selling season.

As a result of these problems, a Ford official concedes, "the Consul-Granada never has picked up sales momentum." Underscoring his words is the fact that the Consul-Granada production line in Germany was closed for a week last December due to slow sales.

FIVE YEARS, FIVE CHAIRMEN

Ford of Europe has also been entangled in organizational problems, one being leadership. There have been five chairmen of Ford of Europe in five years, making continuity of policy difficult. (The current chairman, William Burke, previously headed Ford's Asian and Pacific operations.) Creation of Ford of Europe has also meant that some British executives have had to move to Germany and vice versa, which sometimes hasn't pleased all the executives. "They called me the 'slave trader,' " says a former Ford man who ordered some transfers.

The new layer of bureaucracy, which was felt by some Ford executives in Britain and Germany to have reduced their access to corporate decision makers in Detroit, has also created ill will. And there have been bitter fights over pricing, with Ford of Europe pushing higher prices to maximize profits at the same time that some operating companies were trying to price their cars lower to be more competitive in the market.

In fact, Ford of Europe, which was supposed to improve communications, has instead created some bottlenecks of its own. "Everything, including hiring a single worker, has to go to Warley (Ford of Europe headquarters) for approval, and it can take forever," says Heinz Allrup, who represents workers at Ford of Germany plants. He cites the case of a foreman who died six months ago. "We just got permission to fill his job," Mr. Allrup says.

Another example: One day last year a Ford of Europe man walked into a

German plant and announced that a department employing over 100 men would be closed. A worker's representative got on the phone to Hans-Adolf Barthelmeh, the chairman of Ford of Germany, and asked what was going on. It was the first time Mr. Barthelmeh had heard of the move. (The closing was later rescinded.)

"GENERAL ANIMOSITY"

Hans-Adolf Barthelmeh is no longer with Ford of Europe, nor are several other executives who chafed at the integrated operation's various communications gaps and arbitrary transfers. But integration has also caused disaffection at nonexecutive levels. "There is a general animosity toward Ford of Europe," says Mr. Allrup, the German workers' representative. The reasons for this animosity are multifaceted. German workers, for example, are angry over layoffs stemming from British strikes. (Ford's Cologne plant recently said it would lay off 4,450 workers in the weeks ahead, with one of the cited reasons being the British three-day workweek. British workers, on the other hand, are fearful of losing jobs to Germany.

But Ford of Europe's problems go beyond its work force. Take, for example, the case of its marketing plans. The German subsidiary was to have fed cars into France and Italy; however, Ford officials say they have found it difficult to sell in France, since they are competing against government-owned Renault, which doesn't need to make any profit and can thus cut prices to the bone. And Ford says it's also difficult to sell in Italy, where Fiat, which specializes in the tiny cars preferred by Italians, holds a massive 60% of the market. Another hurdle: The German mark has gained in value against both the franc and the lira, making the German-made Fords more expensive in both France and Italy. In any case, Ford's share of the European market has declined since integration—from 14.5% in 1965 to 11.7% in 1972.

Ford's integration in Europe hasn't had any clear-cut impact so far. More than anything else, profits seem to react to such factors as strikes and the presence or absence of credit controls. Earnings of both Ford of Britain and Ford of Germany have shown wide fluctuations; and Ford of Germany's profits since integration have never equaled its pre-integration peak year of 1966, when the company earned $70.9 million (in 1972, it earned $58.5 million).

With all these problems, does Ford still feel that integration was the right choice? The answer seems to be a resounding yes—if only because of the cost savings attained by integrating. "We're still one of the most profitable auto operations in Europe," says Walter Hayes, vice president of Ford of Europe, "and we're still No. 2 in auto sales (behind Fiat), so we must be doing something right." And he adds that a lot of Ford of Europe's problems—such as communications and labor strikes—would have existed even without integration.

In the end, Mr. Hayes believes, the prime value of Ford of Europe's integration may prove to be more flexibility in management and operations. "We aren't thinking like Texans in Texas anymore," he says. "We're thinking like Americans who consider all the states as their market, and this will help us do better in the future."

QUESTIONS

1. Ford Motor Co., made a major policy decision to unify product lines around the world, to make spare parts where it could do so the cheapest, and to focus its efforts in the fastest growing markets. What are the claimed advantages of such a strategy?
2. Identify some of the major problems Ford ran into in trying to implement this policy.
3. What major policies would you recommend to overcome the principal problems Ford encountered in implementing this policy?

CASE 21

United Technology, Inc.

George A. Steiner

George Stoner, General Manager of the Medical Instruments Division of United Technology, Inc. and Vice President, UTI, had just come from Robert Bellman's office and was angry, puzzled, and frustrated. Stoner and Bellman had examined together the third quarter 1975 performance figures of Stoner's Division. (Bellman was Stoner's immediate superior and Group Vice President of the Measuring Instrument's Group of UTI, as shown in Exhibit I,) Stoner's profits were 19 per cent under target and Bellman made it clear that Stoner should take action to turn around his situation by the end of the year or his performance appraisal for the year and bonus would be poor. In Bellman's tone of voice Stoner detected more sinister threats.

Stoner was not too concerned about Bellman's threats since UTI had only recently acquired a small laboratory developed by Stoner and two of his friends. The purchase price added importantly to Stoner's financial security

EXHIBIT I

MEASURING INSTRUMENTS GROUP
Robert Bellman
Group Vice President

CONTROLLER
Arthur Price

MARKETING
James Dinmore

PERSONNEL
Stanley Webb

ENGINEERING
Neal Kelley

INDUSTRIAL INSTRUMENTS DIVISION
Lundy White

MEDICAL INSTRUMENTS DIVISION
George Stoner

MILITARY INSTRUMENTS DIVISION
Willis Gorman

MARKETING MANAGER
Allan Page

PRODUCTION MANAGER
Eugene Handley

NEW PRODUCT MANAGER
Kenneth Brown

COST CONTROL MANAGER
John Foley

although it did not make him independent. Beyond that, Stoner knew he was a brilliant technician and could readily command a high salary in the industry. His pride was hurt. He knew he was not the best manager in the world, but he was learning. Furthermore, his expectations of working as a division manager with UTI were apparently out of line with what he thought he had been told and with cold reality. If not that, then something had happened between the time he was brought to UTI and his current situation. Bellman and other top managers of UTI were delighted to have Stoner because he brought a new technology which UTI needed and wanted, and they frequently publicly told Stoner this. It was obvious that they had great respect for his technical capabilities. Stoner knew he could get profits back on target but to do so by making "blind" cost cuts might create difficult problems. He could also reduce his research and development expenditures, but that would endanger future new products and probably put his long-range sales and profits goals well out of reach. This prospect bothered him. What should he do?

UTI

In 1925 Randy Jackson designed a new drill for oil exploration which was cheaper and more efficient than those then in use. The little company he started to produce the drill prospered and today has become a multinational corporation with sales in 1974 of $1.8 billion.

UTI has organized its activities around three major areas. First is oil drilling equipment, which includes a wide range of products from drills to ocean exploration platforms and rigs. Second is power generating equipment, which includes products ranging from small motors and generators to steam generating plants for electricity production. Over 80 per cent of UTI's sales and profits come from these two groups. Third is measuring instruments.

Up to the spring of 1975 the Measuring Instruments Group contained two divisions, namely Industrial Instruments and Military Instruments. The Industrial Instruments Division produced a broad range of products from household thermometers to aircraft scanning instruments used by controllers at commercial airports. The Military Instruments Division made such products as night sensoring devices, radar and submarine detection devices.

While UTI had always kept close control over capital expenditures, it did encourage division managers to develop new products which, if promising, were supported by top management. As a result of this policy, these two divisions had, over the years, developed a number of instruments now used by the medical profession. Among the more important ones are patient monitoring systems, especially heart, pulse, and blood pressure monitoring systems; operating room equipment of all types; disposable clinical thermometers; and a variety of laboratory medical testing and measuring devices.

In 1973 UTI's Corporate Planning Department carefully surveyed the market for medical instruments and concluded that this product group was destined to expand at a rate above the Gross National Product. UTI's medical products enjoyed a quality reputation, but it was also concluded that if UTI was to compete successfully in this market it had to acquire new technical capability which would give its products an edge.

DYNAMETRICS

George Stoner received his electronic engineering degree from UCLA after which he joined the Semiconductor Division of Fairchild Camera. While there he became convinced that new developments in integrated circuits could and would revolutionize instruments used in the medical profession. Warren Webber, a young medical doctor, agreed with him and they formed Dynametrics in 1968 to develop new solid state and computer-based patient monitoring systems. Their ideas and technology were excellent, but their manufacturing and marketing skills were weak. The administrator of St. Joseph's Hospital in San Francisco became interested in the new system and suggested that Dynametrics contact Robert Bellman, head of the Measuring Instruments Group of UTI. They did and UTI formed a joint venture with Dynametrics to produce and market new high technology patient monitoring systems. Dynametrics provided the scientific and technical skill, and UTI added manufacturing and marketing capabilities. The new systems were a great success and Dynametrics operated profitably.

In 1970 George Stoner, who was the chief executive officer of Dynametrics, became interested in applying laser beam technology to medical systems. Stoner was not an expert in this field but thought its potential was great. As a result, he asked Wendell Brozen, a professor at Stanford University, to join Dynametrics to help develop laser beam technology in medical instruments. Brozen joined Dynametrics part time and was successful, with Stoner, in developing a new revolutionary eye surgery machine.

UTI ACQUIRES DYNAMETRICS

In 1974 UTI made a series of decisions, all of which were related. It decided to expand in the medical instruments field. It decided to acquire new technology in this field because it had very little in UTI and that which was available was locked into more important profit areas. It decided to acquire Dynametrics and to merge the facilities of Dynametrics with all other products being produced in the medical area in UTI in a new organization to be called the Medical Instruments Division.

When Stoner was first approached, he was cool to the merger idea. He was his own boss in a profitable company. The atmosphere at Dynametrics was relaxed, congenial, and scholarly. Why move? The longer discussions continued with UTI, however, the more Stoner warmed to the idea of a merger. He saw that if he was to become an important producer in the field he had to have capital backing which he did not have. He had to have manufacturing and marketing talents which Dynametrics lacked, although it was developing capabilities in these areas. He also became enamored with the idea of someday heading a large company such as UTI. Finally, UTI offered Stoner and Dr. Webber $2,000,000 for their equity in Dynametrics which they found attractive.

Stoner knew that UTI set aggressive goals which, in the past, at any rate, were achieved through imaginative yet tough management. UTI's management had demonstrated skill in identifying new product leaders and in exercising the controls required to make them pay off. Stoner's dealings with UTI had been mutually profitable, comfortable, and congenial. In his merger negotiations with UTI there seemed every reason to expect they would continue this way. So, in the end, Stoner agreed to the merger, and to his becoming Vice President and General Manager of the new Medical Instruments Division (MID). All of the employees of Dynametrics, including Brozen (part-time), agreed to follow Stoner.

STONER'S TRANSITION

Dynametrics was moved to a new building which could readily accommodate its facilities as well as those transferred from other areas of UTI. The paper work associated with the move, together with organizational problems, occupied most of Stoner's attention from the Fall of 1974 when the merger was completed to the Spring of 1975.

During this period of time Stoner was also introduced to key management goals and methods of UTI. "We pride ourselves on our management-by-objective system," Kenneth Wonderman, the president and chief executive officer of UTI, told Stoner one day at lunch. "It begins," he explained, "with the 'Three Stars.' They are a 10 per cent average annual rate of growth of sales, an 11 per cent annual return on assets employed, and a 12 per cent average annual increase in net profits. We sometimes call this our 10-11-12 formula," said Wonderman.

"This is an aggressive rate of growth," added Bellman who was also present, "but we have achieved these objectives over the past twenty years. We have found that we are able to make these targets only by being 'tough nosed'." Stoner raised his eyebrows at this comment, but Bellman continued: "We work with our profit center managers in setting fair objectives for their performance and then hold them to the goals set."

Bellman went on to explain to Stoner other aspects of UTI's MBO. "We believe," he said, "in delegation of authority. We like to set up profit centers as low down the line as possible and let managers manage. Some profit centers can do better than UTI's sales and profit goals; some cannot meet them in any particular year. But, if a profit center fails to meet the company's targets over a period of time we either change managers or get rid of the division. We have maximum participation of all concerned in setting our sales, ROA and profit objectives," he went on. "We have tight controls to check on performance but we also try to keep them at a minimum. If targets are met, our reward system is generous. Altogether," said Bellman, "we encourage a high degree of self-management, innovative thinking, an eye on the future, and effective managerial control." While this was not exactly the way Dynametrics was run, it sounded acceptable and challenging to Stoner.

Stoner soon learned that the cornerstone of UTI's MBO system was a five-year long-range plan to which annual budgets were tightly linked. He had been given the usual set of policy and procedure manuals when he joined UTI but did not have time to study them. At the suggestion of Bellman he invited Harry Lester, the Director of UTI's Corporate Planning Department, to explain to him the company's long-range planning system. At about the same time Arthur Price, the Measuring Instruments Group Controller, discussed budgetary procedures with Stoner.

Since Stoner was so new to UTI and MID was so recently formed Bellman suggested that Lester help Stoner as much as possible to work through the first five-year plan and that a task force be established to work on the budget for the first half of 1975. Stoner readily agreed to this arrangement. Bellman invited Stoner to seek his aid whenever desired and said that he clearly understood the difficult situation in which Stoner was placed and did not expect a perfect long-range plan and 1975 budget. "Actually," said Bellman, "all that is needed now is a rough five-year plan sort of laying out directions." We all will pitch in to help block out a budget for the first half of 1975. After that you can stand on your own feet." He added, "No one expects the first half 1975 budget to be a masterpiece. Let's consider it a ballpark working document."

Revised Five-Year Plan and New Budget For Second Half 1975

In April 1975, the UTI's Corporate Planning Council issued its call for long-range plans to be completed in December for use in preparing 1976's budgets. At that time, Bellman told Stoner that he should begin preparing his budgets for the second half of 1975 and also his long-range plans for 1976 and beyond, in conformance with the company's time schedule. Bellman was friendly but made clear that this budget should be well thought out and defensible. He concluded the conversation by saying: "If I or my staff can be helpful in any way don't hesitate to call upon us. Working up these documents is tough, and it takes time to learn to develop numbers you will stand by."

Stoner looked upon the challenge with enthusiasm for he had many ideas and felt his Division would soon be a rising star at UTI. First off he revised his five-year plan, although he was unable to get into as much detail as he wanted. Based upon the experience for the first half of 1975 and what he hoped to do in the second half he prepared sales, profit, and ROA objectives shown in Exhibit II. He thought he could achieve UTI's sales and profit goals in 1976 and 1977 but thereafter he had to add new products to the line as well as improve current products if he was to reach the three overall company goals. If, however, he could maintain high research and development expenditures in 1975, 1976, and 1977 it would pay off handsomely in high sales and earnings thereafter. His plan reflected this strategy.

Stoner asked John Foley, his manager of Cost Control to head up a small staff group to help him prepare his second half 1975 budget. Other members of the group were Allan Page, MID Marketing Manager; Eugene Handley, MID Production Manager; and Kenneth Brown, MID New Product Manager. They consulted freely from time to time with various members of Bellman's staff, especially a representative from the Controller's Department and Group Marketing. It was not easy collecting all the necessary information since it had been scattered around UTI. But for the products which UTI had been producing, they felt they had creditable sales projections and cost estimates. It was more difficult to make projections for new products which Stoner was introducing into the product line, especially a new computer-based monitoring system for hospitals which could instantaneously show a long list of a patient's conditions at the press of a button; a more advanced laser-beam surgeon's tool; a new light-weight long-life pacemaker; and a new artificial heart. Nevertheless, he felt he had developed a budget which could be defended. It is shown in Exhibit III.

Bellman congratulated Stoner on his first budget, but he and his staff sug-

EXHIBIT II

MEDICAL INSTRUMENTS DIVISION

Five Year Sales and Profit Goals
1976 - 1980
($000 omitted)

GOAL	1975 (projected)	1976	1977	1978	1979	1980
SALES	14,360	15,796	17,376	19,460	21,795	25,500
PROFITS	2,850	3,192	3,575	4,110	4,725	5,670
ROA %	9.7	10.5	11	12	12.5	15

EXHIBIT III

MEDICAL INSTRUMENTS DIVISION

Proposed and Approved Budgets for July-Dec 1975
($000 omitted)

	PROPOSED	*APPROVED*
SALES	7,360	8,190
DIRECT PRODUCTION COSTS		
LABOR	800	900
MATERIALS	2,410	2,610
OTHER	125	175
MARKETING	950	1,220
R&D	900	700
GROUP ENGINEERING	175	250
GROUP MARKETING	300	400
OVERHEAD	150	160
OTHER	50	75
PROFIT	1,550	1,700
ROA (annual % rate)	8.9	9.7

gested some modifications. "Your budget," said Bellman, "reflects a somewhat different strategy than I would pursue, but if that is what you want, let's talk about it." The discussion with Bellman and his staff was amiable but Bellman was persistent. For instance, he raised questions about Stoner's heavy emphasis on R&D for two new products he had not heard Stoner talk about before—the pacemaker and artificial heart. Also, Bellman felt the marketing and engineering budget should be raised if the higher sales levels were to be met. Bellman urged higher sales and profit numbers partly because he really felt Stoner could achieve them but more to get Stoner's ROA closer to the company objective. Stoner was impressed with Bellman's experience and knowledge and was willing to compromise with Bellman's recommendations. The agreed budget is shown in Exhibit III.

Budget Versus Performance

Early in October 1975 Stoner was called into Bellman's office to review third quarter operations. Sales were 9 per cent below budget and profits were 19 per cent under target. Furthermore, the annual rate of ROA dropped to 7.6 per cent. Bellman expressed disappointment and made it clear to Stoner that fourth quarter performance ought to be more in line with the approved budget. The 9 per cent drop in sales below the budgeted figure was due to a slower industry growth rate than had been projected and to several problems which delayed shipment of new expensive patient monitoring systems. Stoner was not disappointed with his performance. Indeed, he was pleased. He felt that he had managed his controllable costs pretty well. True, he increased his R&D expenditures, but progress with his new products seemed to warrant it. The big problem, as Stoner saw it was the increase in group engineering and marketing over which he had little control.

Stoner was not sure what to do, if anything. Things ought to work out, he thought. But, if the fourth quarter was like the third quarter, his performance rating would not be good since UTI measured performance solely on the "bottom line." He would not get a bonus at this rate. This did not bother him, but a potential adverse performance rating did. In the long run UTI would thank him for the new revolutionary and certainly highly profitable products he was introducing into the line. What was that worth?

EXHIBIT IV

Budget Variance
3rd Q 1975
($000 omitted)

	BUDGETED	*ACTUAL*	*VARIANCE*
SALES	4,100	3,784	- 9.2
DIRECT PRODUCTION COSTS			
LABOR	450	410	- 9
MATERIALS	1,300	1,170	- 10
OTHERS	80	72	- 9
MARKETING	640	575	- 11
R&D	350	410	+ 17
GROUP ENGINEERING	130	150	+ 15
GROUP MARKETING	190	230	+ 21
OVERHEAD	80	75	—
OTHER	35	30	—
PROFIT	845	662	- 19
ROA (annual % rate)	9.7	7.6	

CASE 22

Small City (B)—The Ordinance*

George G. Eddy and Burnard H. Sord

"My God! I never expected anything like this!" exclaimed Mayor Edward Burns as he replaced the telephone receiver in its cradle following a vitriolic conversation with one of the town's most prominent citizens. His sigh was more like a groan as he stared at the city documents spread before him on his well-ordered desk. The documents in question represented a city ordinance on regulating privately owned waste disposal systems that the City Council had passed several months before without apparent opposition of substance. Now, however, it seemed as if his telephone would never cease ringing, as one irate resident after another called him to complain. Some of the complainers were fairly restrained, although obviously angry, but many were not even civil; one caller's language was so foul, the Mayor, who was a relatively mild man, lost his own temper and shouted back before banging his telephone down. He began to wonder if the abuse would ever cease. He put the ordinance down and picked up another document. It was a petition signed by more than 200 residents demanding the ordinance be rescinded. Opposition was mounting, and there were mutterings of suing the city to overturn this regulation. The next meeting of the City Council promised to be the stormiest in his two years of office.

Held in the elementary school auditorium, the meeting attracted a full house of community dwellers. Almost before the Mayor could gavel the meeting to order, Mr. Reginald Jackson was on his feet demanding to be heard. He wanted to present to the City Council his latest petition against the ordidance, and to mention several of the prominent citizens who had signed it, he declared. The Mayor deferred to his request, and when Mr. Jackson had finished with his enumeration, he suddenly launched into a highly emotional tirade which impugned the competence and the motives of the Mayor directly and the council in general.

When Mr. Jackson finished he turned to another man who was seated nearby and they spoke for a few moments. Turning back to the Mayor and the Council, who were seated at a long narrow table at the front of the audience, Mr. Jackson announced he wished to introduce a Mr. Royce, a lawyer retained by an unidentified group of protesting residents. Immediately, Mr. Royce began to dissect the ordinance in a manner that one Councilman later described as aggressively hostile. This sparked a series of heated exchanges with several of the Council, including the Mayor. In the background, private discussions sprang up throughout the assembly, making it difficult to understand what the lawyer was stressing. He concluded abruptly with a threat of suit to overturn the ordinance, and almost as promptly another man began to speak.

At this point, the Mayor had to gavel for order for none of the Councilmen could hear or learn the identity of the new speaker. After a moderate degree of silence was obtained, the Council discovered another lawyer was on the attack. He rambled on, interminably, frequently alluding to the unfortunate "necessity" to institute suit unless the Council retracted the obviously ill-conceived and "illegal" statute. From time to time the City Attorney made comments but few seemed to heed him. Finally, after a blistering exchange between the second lawyer and a Councilman, the former sat down. The Mayor, obviously experiencing difficulty in remaining calm, reiterated his belief in the need for such an ordinance to protect and preserve the quality of the environment. He stressed what he considered to be the essential aspect: the city needed to take the initiative and institute appropriate controls on individual home septic systems before some state agency, such as the Water Quality Control Board, interceded and imposed its own directives. Sample tests taken on a randomly selected basis throughout the community, the Mayor continued, revealed that certain pollution was occurring; he highlighted the serious deficiencies attending septic systems, even when constructed and maintained on the most ideal basis.

The Mayor, believing he had touched on all significant matters (see Exhibit 1), concluded with the following observations: "I think everyone will agree that our terrain and soil characteristics make septic tanks, as a proper waste disposal method, highly suspect. Nevertheless, this is what we have, and as I've said previously, if we don't provide for proper controls the State will force our hand by requiring we install a central waste disposal collection system. I've tried to point out to our citizens that that could be prohibitively expensive. Additionally, since we live here on a layering series of rock strata, the blasting and all that goes with construction would seriously and permanently disfigure our landscape. One of the main attractions of our community is just that landscape, and our underlying objectives always have been to preserve it in its natural state to the maximum extent feasible. I'm convinced that by instituting the measures embodied in our ordinance we can forestall the need for a central collection system for many, many years to come. Really, I believe it is the only way. . . . Now I'd like to call on Mr. Henry Blackmore to comment on the objections many of you have raised concerning the manner in which his firm, Brownlee Engineering, has been conducting septic system inspections."

As Mr. Blackmore began to speak, the Mayor realized with dismay that this engineer was not really going to allay the suspicions of the majority of

EXHIBIT 1

Events and Conditions Leading to the Drafting and Adoption of the Water Pollution Control and Abatement Ordinance

1. Small City relied entirely on private septic systems for the disposal of household waste.

2. Due to the failure of some home owners in matters of care and maintenance of their private sewage disposal systems, Small City was cited on several occasions in local newspapers as a source of water pollution.

3. The State Water Quality Acts of 1967 and 1969, with adoption of additional codes in 1971, provide, among other things, for a fine of $1000 for each violation and each day a separate violation to be applicable to both industrial and municipal corporations, as well as individuals involved in actions of negligence which result in the pollution of streams and lakes.

4. Approximately one-third of Small City was situated within a special zone designated for attention by the Water Quality Control Board to insure proper measures were taken to prevent water pollution. This was because this portion of Small City's topography and soil characteristics and proximity to Lake Blue made it particularly susceptible as a water pollution contributor if septic systems were used.

5. Administration of the granting of permits, the design and supervision of construction of septic systems in Small City had been accomplished for many years by officials of the Health & Sanitation Department of Big City. In the past two years, the Mayor, some Councilmen and private citizens of Small City believed they had reason to question how effectively these functions were being performed by Big City. Such concern had its origin in such as the following:

a. Apparent indiscriminate issue of permits for septic systems on all lots on application by builders or owner irrespective of the size, slope of the surface, soil thickness and relationships to ravines, and other critical criteria required to be analyzed by the codes established by the State Department of Health.

b. Public utterances by employees and others associated with the Big City Health Department, indicting Small City for its sanitation problems – particularly the odor and visible seepages of effluent in numerous instances from septic systems previously approved by Big City officials.

6. Studies of the sanitation situation, problems and possible alternative solutions commenced prior to the present term of the Mayor. Such studies were under the supervision of a professionally qualified sanitation engineer who lived in Small City.

7. Nothing in the body of municipal law within the State, or rulings by the courts related directly or specifically to the regulation of existing septic systems. The State had, however, authorized cities to take appropriate and necessary measures to control pollution in pertinent Acts passed by the State Legislature in 1971. These Acts also defined functions and authorities of the Water Quality Board. The legal basis for entry on private property for inspections in the face of opposition by the owner was contained in the Fourteenth Amendment to the State Constitution. A warrant to permit such inspections could be issued on the basis of complaints by neighbors offended by unsanitary conditions.

8. Suggestions to the Municipal League, lawyers and legislators that the authority for control of septic systems be definite and specifically spelled out in legislation had not been received with any degree in interest to date.

those present who had been contending, among other allegations, that the Brownlee firm was not doing its inspections in a thoroughly professional manner. While the focal point of citizens' anger seemed clearly the $50 inspection fee—"It's just another damn tax on top of already damn taxes, and for what?"—the quality of these inspections was drawing extensive ire. Several residents were shouting now, completely drowning out Mr. Blackmore's rather feeble attempts to explain the firm's methods, that they would not tolerate "inspections" made by some damned, college-kid hippie who ambled haphazardly over their property, while his flashy girl friend sat impatiently waiting for him in a small foreign car, occasionally tooting the horn while the radio blared on.

Stirring uneasily in the midst of such a hostile audience, Mayor Burns concluded that this just did not seem to be his night. As the interruptions to Mr. Blackmore gained momentum, the Mayor wondered if he should call upon Mr. George Anderson at all. Mr. Anderson was a representative of the State Water Quality Control Board that Burns had asked to attend for the purpose of reinforcing the city's position that it was well within its rights to regulate individual spetic systems in the community. While Mr. Anderson had seemed to be a forthright and positive person during private discussions with the Mayor, the Board also was coming under increasing attacks in neighboring communities lately for its stringent water control rulings. Mayor Burns had not seen Mr. Anderson respond on his feet before an unfriendly group, and this meeting was getting out of hand. In a few moments the Mayor knew he had to make a number of important decisions.

Suddenly there was an unexpected quiet in the auditorium. Everyone was eyeing Mayor Burns. Clearly, he was expected to speak.

* * * *

A small community of some 1500 residents and 600 homes, the city encompassed approximately 2000 acres of wooded, rolling hills. One of the city's boundaries was shared by Big City with a population of over 100,000 people. Small City received water and electricity from Big City utilities, and the majority of Small City homeowners worked in Big City. The dense vegetation, steep hillslopes, canyons, and numerous creeks provided a particularly scenic, rural environment. For years Small City operated with a voluntary contribution program to pay city expenses. Although some residents contributed nothing, enough home owners sent the city sufficient funds to provide for the very simplest demands for services. With the rapid growth of Big City and the realization of the need for some modern city planning, the Council agreed that a tax program was needed to give Small City fiscal responsibility. In May of 1970, the Council passed a tax program of 25 cents on $100 with a 75% evaluation. The intent of such a program was to take care of road repairs and maintenance and the modest salaries of paid officials (the Secretary-Treasurer, Police Chief, two policemen, and the City Attorney) and Small City's share of developing a master plan in conjunction with Big City on a pro rata funding basis as sponsored and largely funded by the Federal government. Small City was administered by the Mayor and five Councilmen, all elected officials. The organization chart is outlined in Exhibit 2.

The major areas of concern to the residents and Small City's administrative body were: (1) preservation of the environment; (2) control the density by requiring one-acre minimum lot size; (3) protecting residential property from encroachment by commercial, industrial, and apartment intrusions by means of a zoning and planning commission; (4) establish standards for the development of subdivisions; and (5) development of an appropriate master plan to help insure an orderly and systematic growth in keeping with the natural environment. Details of such concerns and the manner of implementing them are contained in Exhibit 3.

In consonance with its understanding of the views of the community about preserving the environment and the concomitant necessity for control over water pollution, the Council passed an ordinance designed to regulate septic systems. This ordinance was intended to outline applicable standards for the operation of individual, privately constructed septic systems. Additionally, it provided for an inspection schedule and related fees. Believing the most economical and efficient manner for implementing this regulation was by

EXHIBIT 2
Organization of the City Government

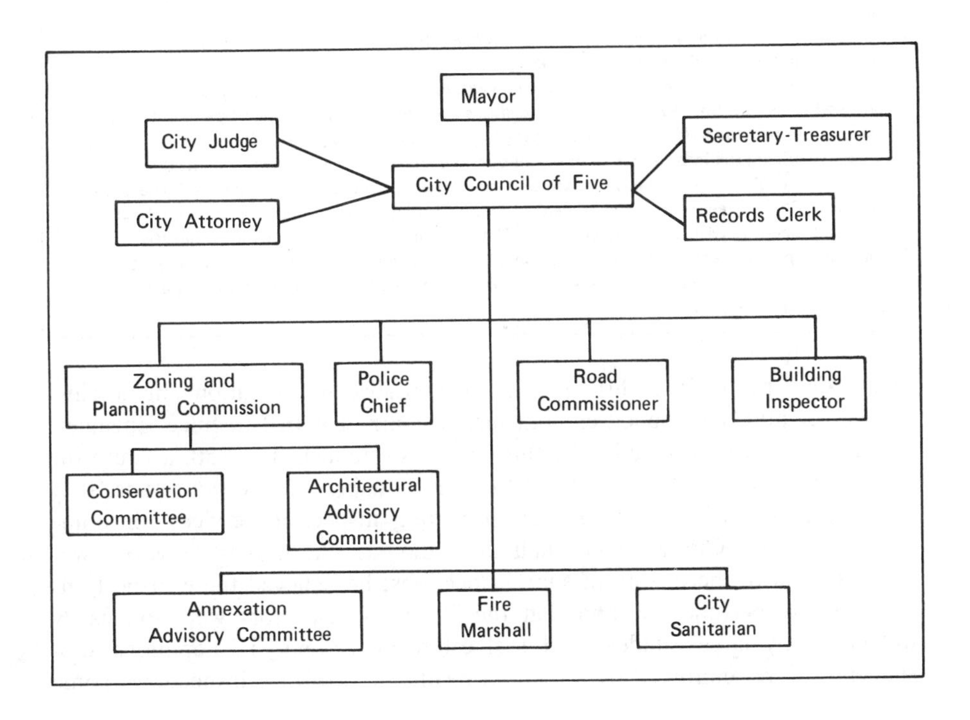

EXHIBIT 3

Preservation of the City Environment

The City Council, recognizing the value of Small City from an ecological and scenic point of view, had taken several actions to protect the quality of the environment:

1. A one-acre minimum lot size was established for two reasons: (1) to protect the land from unplanned, uncontrolled development which would have resulted in destruction of the environment; and (2) to prevent a proliferation of septic tanks with the possibility of a resultant pollution of Lake Blue, as Small City drained directly into these bodies.

2. The City Council applied for a Federal 701 planning grant through the Governor's Planning Office, and was on the list for funds in 1972. Although no efforts had as yet been made to contact planning consultants, two highly reputable firms had already asked to be considered because of their interest in the exciting possibilities here for the new type of "open-space planning," which could make Small City an example for the entire state. It was to be hoped that land developers and real estate people would see the advantages to them in working in an area that had a protected environment and was planned properly. Other areas in the United States, such as Columbia, Maryland, to cite one example, that have done open-space, quality planning, have been enormously successful financially for the developers and real estate people.

The cheap operator, who attempts to make a "quick killing" and get out, it not interested in the long-range welfare of the community and usually fights any and all restrictions designed to establish quality and environmental integrity. It was hoped that the good sense of the community at large could overcome this type of activity.

3. The City Council passed an Ordinance strictly controlling the size and location of all signs in Small City, eliminating neon flashers and other tasteless exhibitions.

4. An Architectural Advisory Committee was established under the Zoning and Planning Commission to offer free architectural advice to business enterprises interested in building in this community.

5. Under study in the Zoning and Planning Commission were two ordinances aimed at quality control:

(1) An off-street parking ordinance which, among other things, would require a landscaped strip between the road and a parking lot.

(2) A cluster-enabling ordinance, which would permit houses in a subdivision to be grouped so as to economize on roads and utilities and yet, with an average of one house per acre, would provide land in the development for open spaces and green belts.

6. Realizing the importance of going all-out to protect the scenic environment, the City Council in 1968 activated the Conservation Committee. In the Chairman's words, "The Conservation Committee went to the citizens of Small City last year with a series of eight neighborhood meetings with 125 in attendance. There was an endorsement of the committee's plans to support the rural atmosphere of Small City and the encouragement of green belts through the one-acre minimum, conservation easements, and the establishment of green belts through a city plan."

means of a professional firm possessing expertise in sanitation engineering, the Mayor and the Council entered into a contract with Brownlee Engineering. The fee for an inspection by this firm was established at $50, a figure the Mayor and the Council considered to be reasonable. At the same time, they recognized that Big City had been providing inspection services for home owners in Small City for about half that amount. The Mayor, however, was dissatisfied with the quality of such inspections; he believed these inspections were largely perfunctory, and that the Big City inspectors were too easily influenced by large builders and real estate developers. His opinions subsequently were reinforced by the initial results of Brownlee inspections; some

15% of those inspected were classified as defective, and all these had been approved initially by Big City inspectors from the Health Department. Additionally, investigations by the Small City Health Officer disclosed that nearly 50% of effluent from waste disposal systems were contaminated. This effluent was sampled from ditches alongside city roads.

This new ordinance, which required each home owner to apply for a license to operate his septic system, was passed by the Council without any complaints of note by community residents. Within a month after the Council action, the Mayor wrote each home owner a personal letter, calling attention to the following:

"Your City Council, after publishing notice in the official newspaper (The Big City Daily) and after notice posted in public places of a public hearing on December 7th, adopted Ordinance No. 34. This Ordinance deals with water pollution control and abatement within our City. It provides an organized approach to the task of obtaining compliance with the requirements of the Water Quality Board.

"Over 500 private sewage disposal systems are in operation within our area. This area is drained by streams that are tributary to Lake Blue. The probability of water contamination without strict regulation of the use of our disposal systems is high."

The Mayor went on to emphasize that this ordinance was passed only after careful and extensive consideration of the facts and alternatives and that a reputable law firm had been employed to draft the ordinance, which was designed specifically to assure compliance with the requirements of the State Water Quality Board. "Since the estimated cost of funding and construction of an organized collection system," he continued, "is out of our financial reach with our present tax base, and also for the near future, the only open course of action was to adopt our Ordinance No. 34. The Ordinance provides for the payment of fees of $50 for inspection and licensing of private disposal systems. The term of the license for a system will be for five years. This cost of $10 per annum may be compared with the alternative cost of an organized system which would have a minimum effect of quadrupling our present tax rate. Our estimates of the cost of an organized collection system take into account the effects of Federal grants of 55% of the cost of certain parts of the system."

Included in this same letter was notice that the firm of Brownlee Engineering had been engaged to assist in implementing the ordinance, and that the latter authorized the formation of a Water Pollution Control and Abatement Division for Small City.

Approximately a month after the distribution of the Mayor's letter, each home owner received one from Brownlee Engineering, which contained an application form each property owner was requested to complete. See Exhibit 4. The letter also pointed out that "due to the number of inspections to be made, it will be impossible to make every inspection in the presence of the

EXHIBIT 4

EXISTING SYSTEM

APPLICATION FOR PRIVATE SEWAGE FACILITY LICENSE

APPLICATION NO. ______________________

Amount Enclosed $ ______________________

DO NOT WRITE IN THIS BLOCK

$ ____________ Fees Enclosed
Application ( ))
Inspection ( )
Percolation Tests ( )

PLEASE DRAW A LAYOUT OF YOUR LOT AND SEWAGE SYSTEM ON THE BOTTOM OF THIS PAGE

TO THE CITY: I hereby make application to operate a private sewage facility within the jurisdiction of the City as required by the City Ordinance No. 34 passed December 7, 1971.

(All information below must be completed)

Property Owner: ____________ ____________ ____________
(Last) (First) (Middle)

Mailing Address: ____________ ____________
(Number) (Street)

Telephone Number: ____________

Subdivision: ____________ ____________ ____________ ____________
(Name) (Section) (Block) (Lot)

Type Dwelling: House ( ) Mobile Home ( ) Other ( )

Average Number Occupants: ____________ Days per year used ____________

ALL APPLICANTS please write TOTAL no. of items below & leave blank for "none."

1. Bedrooms ____	4. Lavatories ____	7. Kitchen Sinks ____	10. Garbage Disposals ____
2. Commodes ____	5. Showers ____	8. Clothes Washers ____	
3. Urinals ____	6. Bathtubs ____	9. Auto. Dish Washer ____	11. Grease Traps ____

(Sewage System Information)

APPLICANTS for EXISTING SYSTEM LICENSE ONLY please complete this block

Septic Tank Information

1. No. of separate systems at this location: ____

NOTE: If more than 1 system, give same info. as below for tank & field on back of this form.

2. Nearest water well or cistern distance ____ ft.
3. Distance to organized sewer collection system line: ____ ft.
4. Tank capacity: ____ gal.
5. Yr. installed ____
6. No. of tank compartments: ____
7. Name the Installer: ____________
8. Tank made of: (check one)
   ( ) prefab metal
   ( ) prefab concrete
   ( ) concrete poured in place

Absorption Field Information

1. Type field: ( ) Trench or ditch system ( ) Absorption Bed System
   a. Trench size: (Wd)____ in. X (Dp)____ inches X (Total Lg.) ____ ft. (OR)
   b. Bed Bottom-Size: (WD) ____ ft. X (Lg.) ____ ft.
   c. Distribution Pipe Size: ____ inches dia.
   d. Kind of Pipe: ( ) Vitrified Clay ( ) Concrete, ( ) Plastic
2. Distance from Field to Nearest Lake Shore: feet

EXHIBIT 4 (cont'd.)

Authorization is hereby given to the City, Water Quality Board, the State Dept. of Health, the engineers, Brownlee Engineering, and to their agents or designees, singularly or jointly, to enter upon the above described property during daylight hours for the purpose of making soil percolation tests, inspecting private sewage systems, or for any reason consistent with the water quality program of the Water Quality Board, the State Dept. of Health and the City.

____
SIGNATURE OF APPLICANT

Date: ____________________, 19 ________

LAYOUT SPACE
For Property Outline, Size and Improvements Location.

In addition to other information requested on other side, please indicate:
1. *Direction of North at property.*
2. *Direction and Distance from Field to nearest Lake Shoreline.*

EXAMPLE

property owner" and further that "after an inspection of your property has been made, an evaluation of the system will be made. This evaluation includes an analysis of the size and adequacy of the system to serve the apparent loading. Our findings and recommendations will then be given to your City Council who will decide whether or not to issue a license. You will be notified of their decision by our firm."

Soon thereafter, Brownlee commenced the inspections. As they continued, the grumblings mounted, soon to take the form of bitter, complaining telephone calls to the Mayor and his wife if she happened to answer the telephone. When the Mayor realized how extensive the dissatisfaction had become, and that only a relative handful of property owners had submitted applications for septic tank inspections, he called upon the Council to (1) exclude those property owners whose septic tank systems were less than two years old, (2) reduce the inspection fee by $5, and (3) extend the deadline for submitting applications. In a series of public meetings commencing two months after Ordinance 34 was passed, the Council passed such amendments.

Public furor did not subside. Complaints poured into the Mayor's ear about the "excessive" fee for the inspections and the "substandard" performance of Brownlee Engineering. Several citizens began to collect signatures on petitions demanding the repeal of Ordinance 34, although no one could be found who disagreed with the objective of controlling and abating potential water pollution attributable to septice tank systems.

Soon the rhetoric opposing the ordinance became charged with invective, with the principal target being the Mayor. So pronounced did it become that Mayor Burns nearly decided not to run for reelection, due to be held less than three months subsequent to the passage of Ordinance 34. Refusing to be intimidated, however, by what he considered to be a small clique of perpetual malcontents, the Mayor decided to run again. Self-reliant and wealthy, the Mayor had been in responsible positions for many years prior to his retirement as a professional man. Unusually energetic and susceptible to challenges, Mayor Burns prided himself on his ability to identify a major problem, assess pertinent alternatives and promptly and decisively make a decision. He had moved to Small City about ten years ago, buying several large lots atop a prominent hill.

As soon as his desire to try for another term was public knowledge, his opponents—some of whom had lived in the community for over twenty years and were large property owners in and around Small City—commenced a bitter campaign to defeat him. The Mayor discovered that he was being accused of incompetence, stupidity, contempt for his fellow citizens, misuse of his office for alleged personal gain, and almost every other ulterior motive that could be conceived. Despite this well-organized attack, the Mayor won re-election—by a margin of less than 15 votes. The central issue was Ordinance 34, its components contending it was both illegal and unnecessary. Regarding the latter claim, many agitated residents could not understand why Small City property owners could not continue to use the relatively inexpensive services of the Big City Health Department inspectors.

Shortly after his re-election, the Mayor presided over the Council meeting, before the largest gathering of community residents he had ever seen, to reexamine Ordinance 34 (Exhibit 5).

EXHIBIT 5

Pertinent Extracts from Ordiance No. 34

SECTION 1. Definitions. For the purpose of this Ordinance, certain terms, words, and phrases are defined as follows:

1.4. *Septic tank* means a vented, watertight tank, which serves as a sedimentation and sludge digestion chamber, which is placed between the house sewer and the soil absorption field.

1.5. *Septic tank system* means a system for disposing of sewage through soil absorption and consisting of the following components, the house sewerethe septic tank, and the soil absorption field.

1.6. *Soil absorption field* is that part of a septic tank system consisting of drainage tiles and surrounding permeable soil used for the subsurface disposla of septic tank effluent.

1.7. *Private sewage facilities* means septic tanks, pit privies, cesspools, sewage holding tanks, injection wells used to dispose of sewage, treatment tanks, and all other facilities, systems, and methods used for the disposal of sewage.

* * *

SECTION 5. *Water Pollution Control and Abatement Division.* The Water Pollution Control and Abatement Division is hereby created to administer the licensing, investigative and administrative functions provided herein. Appeal of an action by this Division shall be to the City Council. The Mayor is authorized to appoint a person as the head of this Division and to provide such Staff as necessary to carry out its functions. The Mayor is authorized, with the consent of the City Council, to contract with private firms for administration of this Ordinance.

* * *

SECTION 6. *Schedule of Fees.* The following fee schedule is adopted for the inspection and licensing services of this Ordinance:

6.1. Septic Tank Systems

a. *Single-Unit (family) Structure.*

(1) Existing Non-Licensed Systems
$ 5.00 – Application Fee
$45.00 – Inspection Fee

(2) New Systems
$ 5.00 – Application Fee
$75.00 – Inspection Fee (includes one set of six percolation tests)

(3) Transfer of License
$ 5.00

* * *

SECTION 7. *Rules Covering Licenses for Private Sewage Facilities.*

7.1. *Term of Licenses.* Licenses for private sewage facilities issued under this Ordinance, other than temporary and conditional licenses issued pursuant to this Ordinance, shall be effective for a term of five (5) years. Licenses may be renewed for successive terms of five years if the City finds that the lot or tract in question may continue to be served by the private sewage facility without causing pollution or injuring public health. Any license issued under this Ordinance shall automatically terminate if there is a subdivision of the property served by the private sewage facility, if the property is used for a purpose other than described in the license, or if the loading of the system is significantly increased beyond that stated in the license. In addition, any license issued hereunder may be amended, vevoked, or suspended for good cause.

* * *

SECTION 8. *Private Sewage Facility License Procedure.* The following procedures shall govern the issuance of licenses for private sewage facilities under this Ordinance:

8.3. Within sixty (60) days after receipt of an application, the City will cause to be performed such inspections and tests as may be deemed ncessary, which may include percolation tests as provided in *A Guide to the Disposla of Household Sewage* published by the State Department of Health, site inspection and other such tests and inspections as the City may consider appropriate. If the Cityh approves the application, it shall so notify the applicant who may then proceed with the construction of the private sewage facility in accordance with the plans submitted with the application. If the application is disapproved as submitted, but the City is of the opinion that a private sewage facility of a different design may be constructed on the property, it shall advise the applicant in writing of the changes necessary to obtain a license.

* * *

SECTION 10. *Existing Private Sewage Facilities.*

10.1. Private sewage facilities existing within the City as of the date of passage of this Ordiance are required to obtain a conditional license. Applications for such licenses shall be made within sixty (60) days after the effective date of this Ordiancne. For good cause, the City may permit late filings of such application. However, the City reserves the right to invoke the penalties herein even if a late filing is permitted.

10.2. Any license issued under the authority of this Section shall be temporary and conditional and shall be for a period not to exceed five (5) years.

10.3. Any license issued under this provision shall automatically terminate if the system is changed, if the loading on the system is significantly increased from that existing at the date of issuance of the license, or if the property served by this system is subdivided or resubdivided.

* * *

SECTION 17. *Penalties.* Any person who violates any of the provisions of this Ordinance is guilty of a misdemeanor, and upon conviction shall be punished by a fine not exceeding $200.00 for each offense. Each day of violation constitutes a separate offense.

PART

V

Policy/Strategy in Varied Contexts

CHAPTER

17

Entrepreneurship

INTRODUCTION

This and the following chapters deal with policy considerations outside the framework of the established business corporation, which has been the major focus of the discussion to this point. There are two particular types of organizations that require consideration, each of which is treated in a separate chapter. The first is the new business venture headed by, and in the early stages almost synonymous with, a single entrepreneur or a small entrepreneurial group. The second is the not-for-profit organization of which government is the prime example.

Chapter 6 raised the issue of entrepreneurship briefly in several connections. One involved the concept of a corporate life cycle. Entrepreneurial organizations are at stage I and are in a state of emergence; they are led by a certain type of individual who may have to be replaced by a different kind of person in later stages of the firm's development. It is this type of person, who founds an organization, and the company thus created that concerns us here.

Chapter 6 also introduced the term entrepreneur in describing a managerial role involving the initiation and design of organizational improvement projects [Mintzberg, 1973a]. Other writers have also tended to identify entrepreneurship with managing to varying degrees. Thus, Anyon [1973:49–50] says ". . . . an entrepreneur and a general manager may become almost synonymous. Entrepreneurship remains, however, only one aspect of the total of management challenges involved in the running of an organization." Palmer [1971] defines entrepreneurship with reference to decision making under conditions of great uncertainty and thus makes it as much a part of managing any large corporation in an erratic and unpredictable environment as it is of managing a new business venture.

Certainly the parallel between entrepreneurship and certain kinds of general managerial activities, such as initiating improvement projects and coping with uncertain environments, cannot be denied. However, for the present purpose a definition that focuses directly on the emerging business is more to the point. The discussion will be concerned with established firms only in the case of new businesses that are funded by an existing corporation—the special field known as *venture management*.

Entrepreneurship and the Policy Discipline

The inclusion of the topic of entrepreneurship within the broad rubric of business policy reflects a growing trend. In fact, the founding of new businesses has become the primary focus of some business policy courses. Popp and Hicks [1973] describe an experiential business policy course in which groups of students either started or conducted feasibility studies preliminary to doing so. The new businesses included an arts and crafts dealership, a tutoring service, a company selling packaged pecans to school groups, a car pool matching service, and an automobile shopping service. Although the companies experienced varying degrees of success, student reaction to the emphasis on entrepreneurship in a "living case" was overwhelmingly positive.

Courses such as this appear to be proliferating at a rapid rate in business schools across the country, largely in response to student demand [Vesper and Schlendorf, 1973], Topics covered include new venture initiation, management of small companies, entrepreneurial development of emerging economies, minority entrepreneurship, psychology of the entrepreneur, economic and social impact of entrepreneurship, and entrepreneurial history. Although objectives such as building knowledge about the legalities of incorporation, learning from the experiences of current entrepreneurs, and inspiring interest in becoming an entrepreneur are prevalent, many courses focus directly on the design of specific venture projects by student teams.

CHARACTERISTICS OF THE SUCCESSFUL ENTREPRENEUR

Although characteristics of individual managers and in particular the style with which they approach their jobs exert important influences on policy formation and implementation generally, these individual characteristics become absolutely crucial in the case of the entrepreneur. In the small emerging firm, typically lacking both financial and human resources, if the talent needed for survival and growth is not inherent in its entrepreneurship, success is unlikely. In the early years the person and the organization are very much as one.

Achievement Motivation and the Entrepreneur

A sizable amount of study has been devoted to the question of the relationship between entrepreneurship and the desire to achieve. The data consistently indicate that people who found new businesses where none existed before and make them survive have high levels of achievement motivation [Hines, 1973; Hornaday and Aboud, 1971; Hornaday and Bunker, 1970]. Table 17-1 contains data from the Hines [1973] study which was conducted in New

TABLE 17-1
Achievement Motivation Levels of Entrepreneurs Compared With Other Occupational Groups

Occupational Group	Number	Mean Score	Per Cent Low	Per Cent High
Entrepreneurs	80	5.5	14	36
Engineers	74	4.7	19	24
Accountants	68	4.6	25	29
Middle managers	93	4.0	37	15

SOURCE: Adapted from George H. Hines [1973:314–315].

NOTE: Achievement scores can vary from zero to eight. A low score is defined as falling in the range zero through three; a high score in the range six through eight.

Zealand. Achievement motivation was measured by a questionnaire which assigned scores in terms of the following characteristics:

1. A tendency to have difficulty relaxing on holidays.
2. A tendency to become annoyed when people are late for appointments.
3. A dislike of seeing anything wasted.
4. A dislike of getting drunk.
5. A tendency to think about work matters outside working hours.
6. A preference for competent but difficult work partners over congenial but incompetent ones.
7. A tendency to become angry over inefficiency.
8. A long standing pattern of working hard to be at the top in one's area of endeavor.

Endorsing six or more of these items was interpreted as indicating high levels of achievement motivation, while endorsing three or less was considered indicative of low levels. The entrepreneurs endorsed these statements significantly more often than any of the other occupational groups and were particularly high on achievement motivation relative to the middle managers.

This finding that achievement motivation is related to entrepreneurship extends not only to those who found businesses but to other managers in whose jobs the entrepreneurial role predominates [Litwin and Siebrecht, 1967]. Furthermore, entrepreneurs who have high levels of achievement motivation tend to head firms that grow more rapidly in terms of such indexes as sales volume, number of employees, and total investment in the business than do companies headed by entrepreneurs with lesser achievement needs [Hundal, 1971; McClelland and Winter, 1969; Wainer and Rubin, 1969].

These links between achievement motivation and entrepreneurship appear to take the following form:

1. Individuals differ in the degree to which achievement is a major source of satisfaction.
2. Highly achievement motivated people have certain characteristics:
   (a) They are more concerned with achieving success than avoiding failure and thus do not concentrate their energies around warding off adversity.
   (b) They tend to give close attention to the realistic probabilities for success associated with different alternatives.
   (c) They much prefer situations where they themselves can influence and control the outcome rather than having success depend on chance factors.
   (d) They are strongly future-oriented and are willing to wait for rewards.
   (e) They prefer situations where there is a clear criterion of whether they are succeeding.
   (f) They prefer situations involving clear-cut individual responsibility so that if they do succeed that fact can be attributed to their own efforts.
3. These characteristics are inherent in the entrepreneurial job and thus people with high achievement motivation will be attracted to this type of work and, because they fit its requirement more closely, will be more likely to achieve success (business growth).

Achievement-oriented people of this kind should be highly rational decision makers and in this respect one would expect them to make good corporate managers as well. However, their strong need for individual credit may make it difficult for them to cooperate with others in their activities. This and other considerations to be taken up in the next section make it unlikely that most effective entrepreneurs will make effective corporate managers. It is for this reason that most expanding companies require changes at the top as they move through the various stages of their development.

The Enterprising Man

In addition to the work related to achievement motivation, the only other major program of study dealing with the characteristics of entrepreneurs is one initiated at Michigan State University by Collins and Moore. Their major publication, entitled *The Enterprising Man* [1964], dealt with the results of interviews and psychological tests obtained from 150 entrepreneurs in the state of Michigan whose firms have survived the first trying years.

The most striking finding from this research was that the entrepreneurs "had difficulty throughout their lives in playing the role of employee and subordinate. . . . These men came to realize that they can never adequately measure up to the demands placed on them by other people's organizations . . . they cannot go on accepting situations in which their security is dependent upon forces outside themselves . . . they cannot adjust to older and superordinate figures." [Collins and Moore, 1964:133] As a consequence of this inability to handle authority relationships effectively, the entrepreneurs drifted from one organization to another experiencing a number of failures enroute. Finally they solved this problem by going into business on their own, where they would be accountable to no one but themselves. In this sense founding a company represents an escape, but is also a creative act which does in fact appear to provide a satisfying and rewarding solution to their personal problems.

Collins and Moore [1964:245–246] sum up their findings as follows: "Our study suggests that the 'carriers' of the basic entrepreneurial values of our society tend, paradoxically enough, to be those who are marginal to the established social networks. They are those who for social, psychological, ethnic, or economic reasons, cannot make a go of it in existing social structures." Interestingly enough this picture coincides in a number of respects with that presented by Vance [1971] in his portrayal of the men who have been the dominant force in putting together the large conglomerates that have come on the business scene in recent years. He says, "Tracing the education and experience backgrounds of these eminent leaders, it is rather astounding to note that they, as a group, are definitely not in the pattern prescribed by James Burnham's *Managerial Revolution* . . . the heads of major nonconglomerate firms . . . tend toward the high image, well-educated, socially prominant, civicly active, scientific, and professional managerial types. The new conglomerators, relatively speaking, are not of that ilk. They do, however, bring to mind the almost forgotten breed of entrepreneurs, the Henry Fords, John D. Rockefellers, J. P. Morgans—the men who built our enterprise system" [Vance, 1971:62 and 70].

The picture that Collins and Moore present is also consonant with another finding in the research literature. Entrepreneurs consistently have been found to have a low level of need for support from others [Hornaday and Aboud, 1971; Litzinger, 1965]. They care little about being treated with understanding, receiving encouragement from others, and being treated with kindness and consideration. One can assume that when it comes to authority figures such as superiors in a company not their own, they may even feel acutely uncomfortable about receiving this kind of support. Certainly the lonely world of the entrepreneur is no place for the person who requires constant encouragement from other people.

Although most research on entrepreneurs has failed to differentiate subtypes, there are some data on this point derived from a further analysis of the Collins and Moore interview materials [Smith, 1967]. Two types of entrepreneurs were identified, as follows:

1. *Craftsman.* Characterized by narrowness in education and training, low social awareness and social involvement, a feeling of having little com-

petence in dealing with the social environment, and a limited time orientation.

2. *Opportunistic.* Characterized by breadth in education and training, high social awareness and involvement, high confidence in his ability to deal with the social environment, and an awareness of and orientation to the future.

These types of entrepreneurs were found to head very different kinds of firms. Characteristically the craftsman entrepreneurs had introduced few changes. The firm's customer mix, product mix, and production methods were much the same as when the company started. Production is concentrated at one location, sales are restricted to the company's own state, and plans for change and growth are lacking. Such a firm was defined as *Rigid.* In contrast *Adaptive* firms, most commonly headed by an opportunistic entrepreneur who perceives and reacts to a much broader range of his culture, had undergone considerable change and diversification and there were plans for even more.

The nature of this relationship between type of entrepreneur and type of firm is set forth in Figure 17-1. The conglomerator described by Vance [1971] provides a good example of the opportunistic entrepreneur who heads an adaptive firm. In the Smith study, firms of this kind under an opportunistic head had 12 times the sales of the rigid companies under a craftsman entrepreneur.

Although many of the cases included in Figure 17-1 do serve to substantiate the hypothesized fit between individual and firm and there are no cases where the craftsmen had highly adaptive firms and the opportunistic had very rigid ones, there is a clustering concentrated slightly to the left of the center of the figure which suggests a possible third type of entrepreneur. Further analysis reveals that the 10 circled cases do have a great deal in common. Smith [1967] suggests the name *Inventor-Entrepreneur* for them. All had taken out a large number of patents. Such an entrepreneur is described as follows: "It appears that his orientation is not to attempt to build a business or to turn out the best product. Rather, his major concern seems to be to develop an organization, not as an end in itself, but rather as a vehicle to allow him to invent and produce various products" [Smith, 1967:89]. Whether this organization turns out to be rigid or adaptive depends on the nature and number of products involved.

It thus appears that there are distinct differences among entrepreneurs. Probably it is the opportunistic type who is most likely to found a company that grows sufficiently to have a life cycle of the kind described in Chapter 6. It is likely also that achievement motivation is a particularly relevant consideration among opportunistic entrepreneurs.

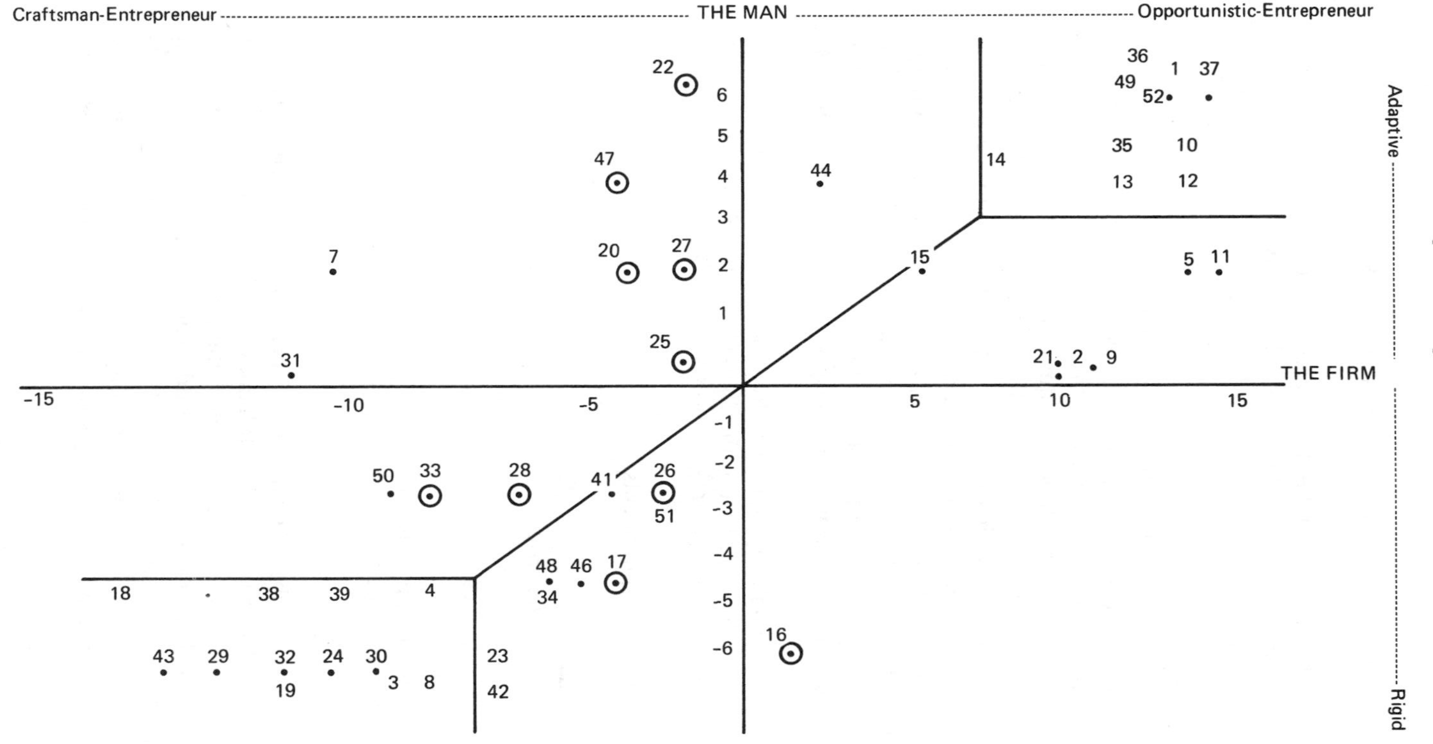

Figure 17-1 The relationship between type of entrepreneur and type of firm (as indicated by the positioning of their numbers) $N = 52$ entrepreneurs and their firms. From Norman R. Smith, *The Entrepreneur and His Firm: The Relationship Between Type of Man and Type of Company*. © 1967. Reprinted by permission of the publisher, Division of Research, Graduate School of Business Administration, Michigan State University.

INITIATING A NEW BUSINESS

With some knowledge of what kind of people start new businesses and why they do it, it is now feasible to look into what is involved and some of the problems that may arise.

Factors to be Considered

The entrepreneur's job is indeed that of a generalist. Depending on the circumstances he may be called upon to make decisions in any area of business expertise. Since he rarely possesses all the knowledge he would like to have, typically does not have the time to acquire this knowledge, and either does not have access to or cannot afford the advice of specialists in the area, a truly systematic approach to decision making can only be approximated at best. As noted in Chapter 12, decision making under these circumstances tends to be of the entrepreneurial opportunistic and intuitive anticipatory type. The kind of person who finds it difficult to take any risks and needs all the facts before reaching a decision will do better operating in some specialized functional area of an established business rather than as an entrepreneur [Anyon, 1973].

Some idea of the complexity and the diversity of the decisions an entrepreneur faces may be obtained from the following list of factors that must be considered in starting a business [Grieco, 1975:32]:

- Determining the capital requirements.
- Obtaining legal assistance.
- Researching the market.
- Locating the business enterprise.
- Securing personnel.
- Providing physical facilities.
- Creating a profit plan.
- Determining accounting procedures.
- Determining risk and insurance coverages.
- Determining information needs.

Generally, in order to obtain financing for his business, an entrepreneur must develop a detailed business plan [Shames, 1974]. Such a plan must cover the areas noted above in considerable detail; normally, it will project the company over a three to five year period. Thus, although many small businessmen resist formal planning [Steiner, 1967], the realities of the investment capital markets are increasingly requiring it, at least at the time the business is emerging. Among the questions such a business plan must answer are the following:

- What are the objectives of the business?
- What is the precise nature of the market?
- What competitor firms now exist and what are their strengths and weaknesses?
- What are the anticipated selling prices and how do these compare with current prices?
- What are the exact specifications of the product or service?
- What patents are held?
- What are the key technologies and skills required?
- What alternative distribution channels are available?
- What capital equipment is needed?
- When and how will additional funds go into the venture in the future?
- What staffing and space requirements will exist at various points in the future?
- What business locations are proposed and why?
- What cash flow positions are projected for various points in the future?
- What profit and loss positions are projected at various points in time?
- What ownership position is anticipated and how might this change over time?

Preparing such a plan well and implementing it with some degree of success, requires that a tremendous amount of energy be focused on the new enterprise. Presumably it is the function of a high level of achievement motivation that it does in fact bring this needed energy to bear.

Problems of Growth

Assuming that a new business survives, and only about 50 per cent do, growth will inevitably bring with it new problems even in the early stages [Steinmetz, 1969]. Many of these problems relate more to the implementation of policies and strategies than to their formulation. As the business grows it becomes increasingly difficult for the entrepreneur to supervise all employees directly and maintain personal relationships with them. This changing relationship with employees is disturbing to many entrepreneurs, a feeling which becomes accentuated as informal organization develops among employees and in many cases as organizational commitment declines. Ultimately, the work force may be unionized. The shift from owner to manager that occurs with growth introduces a whole host of implementation problems.

A second problem area relates to partners. In the early period when it is crucial to obtain customers, get production moving, purchase supplies, and pay off short term notes, many entrepreneurs tend to lose or trade away considerable control over the firm. Partners may be brought in for purposes of obtaining their skills or their money. However, once the firm has hurdled the problems of getting started, the need for these individuals is less and the primary entrepreneur typically tries to get rid of them in order to reassert control over his business. "At the interpersonal level, he must get rid of those people who have, during this transitional phase, either supported him or used his temporary position of weakness to intrude upon him. He must get rid of these figures for two reasons. At the interpersonal level he must get rid of them because they block the further development of the entrepreneur's own career and the development of the firm. At the level of internal dynamics, he must get rid of them because they inhibit him, restricting the autonomy for which he constantly searches" [Collins and Moore, 1964:196].

Multiple partners tend to eat into profits and to restrict the amount of money available for reinvestment in expansion. Furthermore the achievement motivated entrepreneur wants to be able to attribute success to his own efforts and he wants no restrictions on his authority and opportunity to achieve personally.

This process of getting rid of partners can be a difficult one, and the resulting turmoil can pose a major threat to the survival of the business. Personal enmities are almost inevitable, although when provisions for buying out partners are included in the agreements establishing the business, they may occasionally be avoided.

A final problem area related to growth involves legal and governmental requirements. When a firm is small it is typically exempted by statute from many regulations, especially with regard to personnel practices, which apply to larger firms. Furthermore, governmental enforcement agencies characteristically have limited financial and manpower resources and, accordingly, focus their efforts on larger companies where a greater return on the investment of their efforts can be anticipated [Miner, 1973d]. Small companies being less visible simply are not held to the same stringent compliance requirements that larger ones are, and knowingly or not many entrepreneurs do ignore regulations that apply to them.

With growth, however, this situation changes. Increasing numbers of laws do apply and restrictions and red tape escalate. Many of the restrictions are costly. Furthermore, anonymity is no longer possible; compliance becomes necessary. All this poses many problems for expanding businesses because of costs, because of the need for know-how, and because of the increased staffing required to process forms and meet reporting requirements. This kind of government control is onerous to most entrepreneurs. In their efforts to avoid it as their firms grow they may create some serious problems for their companies.

VENTURE MANAGEMENT AND ENTREPRENEURSHIP

The discussion to this point has focused primarily on new enterprises initiated by the entrepreneur. Increasingly, however, the initiative for such ventures is coming from another source, either from large corporations or from independent small business investment companies [Ammer, 1970]. In both instances investment capital is provided by the larger organization, and an active effort is made to put this capital behind as promising new ventures as can be found. Often the new venture involves producing and marketing an invention. In any event, venture management means a new business or technology or service that did not previously exist in the sponsoring company. It is an alternative strategy to that of acquisition.

The Structure and Development of Venture Efforts

Generally as companies move into the venture management field they go through an evolutionary process [Shames, 1974]. The initial effort utilizes a relatively informal task force. If this succeeds and the company decides to invest further, a venture management department is established with its own budget. The final stage of development is a venture management company managed separately from the sponsoring company.

All of these forms, whether task force, department, or separate company, are essentially entrepreneurial in that a new line of business is started where none existed before. Occasionally, this is true also of joint ventures, where two or more companies merge their efforts in order to combine skills or spread risks. However, more frequently the new joint venture is merely an extension of what the companies have been doing all along, and thus does not represent a *new* business. Such is the case, for instance, in the many joint ventures of the oil industry where companies pool their resources to undertake exploration and test drillings. It is also true of those combined efforts by companies headquartered in different countries, which serve to pool know-how and access to markets within a common industry.

Typically companies will staff a new venture with a team of senior managers who span the areas of needed expertise. Usually there are three or four such individuals and areas such as marketing, production, and finance are represented [Parker, 1973]. This means that more systematic, formal decision-making approaches are possible than is the case in a company started by a single entrepreneur. There is not only a greater range of expertise available within the venture but the resources of the parent company are available as well. On the other hand, this team approach does involve greater start-up costs.

The evaluation of ideas for a new venture characteristically is carried out against the twin criteria of estimated potential return and the estimated capacity of the sponsoring company to create and support the particular type of venture in terms of the resources available to it. Initial ideas for consideration may stem from within the company, the R&D department for instance, or from the outside. Companies known to be active in venture management are often approached by inventors with ideas to sell or license. Once an idea is thought to be worth considering, a senior management team is established and it is this team that prepares the business plan. If the plan is approved and implemented through the medium of a separate company with the parent firm having the major ownership position, the members of the original team usually are given some equity position in the venture.

The Parent Company—Venture Firm Relationship

One thing on which there is widespread agreement is that the relationship between the sponsoring company and the new venture is a delicate one [Parker, 1973; Shames, 1974; Wilemon and Gemmill, 1973]. The reason is that if the person put in charge of the venture is a true entrepreneur and the type of individual who is most likely to make the venture a success, he is also likely to have characteristics that militate against strong control on the part of the parent company. His high level of achievement motivation means that he will be the type of person who wants to achieve success through his *own* efforts, not the efforts of the sponsoring company and its chief executive. Furthermore he is likely to have a strong distaste for bureaucratic constraints and to want to escape from authority relationships which make him uncomfortable.

The implication is clear that the nature of the venture manager is a key ingredient for success and that if one has a good manager for this purpose he should be given considerable freedom. The primary control should be in terms of the amount the parent company is willing and able to invest. Should the venture grow to sizable proportions and become firmly established, it will usually be desirable to replace the original manager simply because he is an entrepreneur and not a manager of ongoing organizations. At this point some companies sell off the new venture, thus taking a sizable profit. In other cases

TABLE 17-2
Areas of Decision Making Freedom for Venture Managers

AREA	PER CENT WITH CLEAR AUTHORITY
Recommending promotions	96
Rating performance	92
Assigning personnel	83
Assigning priorities	79
Terminating projects	79
Allocating funds	78
Determining salaries	71
Hiring personnel	71
Firing personnel	67
Directly promoting personnel	57
Undertaking new projects	63

SOURCE: Adapted from David L. Wilemon and Gary R. Gemmill [1973:52].

a new *managerial* team is installed. In either instance it is appropriate to have the venture manager start over again on yet another new business.

Although research data on venture managers are limited as compared with what is known about the more conventional type of entrepreneur, it is apparent that venture managers are not typical managers. Furthermore, as contrasted with product managers they do in fact experience much fewer bureaucratic controls [Hlavacek and Thompson, 1973]. On the other hand, as indicated in Table 17-2, some venture managers do operate without the kinds of decision-making discretion that the independent entrepreneur has. These data derive from venture managers in 24 companies [Wilemon and Gemmill, 1973]. A number of these managers are restricted in the personnel actions they can carry out and in their freedom to initiate new projects. These restraints may, of course, be entirely acceptable if the particular managers involved are not achievement motivated, enterprising men. If they are of a truly entrepreneurial bent, however, the parent company controls can only mean trouble.

MINORITY ENTREPRENEURSHIP

In recent years there has been a special emphasis on the development of new enterprises by minority group members. In the past this type of entrepreneurship has been quite limited, but concerns for social responsibility and the problems of the ghetto have provided a new stimulus. The federal government has been actively encouraging the development of minority enterprises and a number of companies have become involved in venture management efforts involving minorities [Cross, 1969; Haddad and Pugh, 1969].

Although many such efforts face almost insurmountable obstacles and it is certainly too soon to evaluate the net effects of what has been done, one conclusion is emerging quite clearly already: There is a distinct need to identify and develop minority group members who are capable of playing the entrepreneurial role with skill and effectivness.

To this end programs have been undertaken to assess and develop achievement motivation among blacks who are in, or are interested in going into, business for themselves. The initial impetus for this training came from efforts undertaken in underdeveloped countries, and in particularly in India [McClelland and Winter, 1969]. From research conducted in India it became apparent that achievement motivation could be developed or aroused in certain people and that many of these people did subsequently start new businesses or markedly expand existing ones. More recently similar results have been obtained with black ghetto residents [Timmons, 1971].

The approach appears to be a promising one, and there are a number of considerations that suggest that, in spite of its currently limited scale, minority entrepreneurship ultimately may become a significant economic factor in this country. As Collins and Moore [1964] point out, most entrepreneurs of the past have been to varying degrees on the fringes of the larger society. Many are foreign born (20 per cent in the Collins and Moore sample) and many more had foreign-born parents (another 35 per cent of the Collins and Moore group). They tend to come from families that are not well off financially. In a very real sense they have little to lose and much to gain from undertaking the creation of a new business.

To the extent these types of considerations apply to minority group members these groups may represent fertile ground for the nurturance of entrepreneurship. For this to happen, however, the primary rationale for the new business must be personal economic accomplishment, not the creation of new jobs for ghetto residents. Furthermore, these businesses will actively have to seek and obtain markets in direct competition with existing businesses and in many cases outside the ghetto environment where money is currently too scarce to permit sizable profits.

Data currently available indicate that black entrepreneurs who are successful differ little if at all from their successful white counterparts with regard to the characteristics which make for success in establishing new business ventures [Hornaday and Aboud, 1971]. Developing the policies and strategies that will make a new firm survive and prosper, and successfully implementing them, requires a certain kind of person; it appears to make no difference whether that person is black or white.

QUESTIONS

Discussion Guides on Chapter Content

1. How is achievement motivation related to entrepreneurship?
2. "Entrepreneurs . . . cannot make a go of it in existing social structures." Explain and comment.
3. What are the different types of entrepreneurs? What kinds of firms do they head?
4. What is the nature and role of a business plan?
5. What problems are associated with the growth of an entrepreneurial company?
6. How does venture management relate to entrepreneurship?
7. What are the special problems of minority entrepreneurship?

Mind Stretching Questions

1. Do you think you are the kind of person who would enjoy being an entrepreneur and do well at it? Why do you feel as you do?
2. If you were teaching a course in business policy would you include entrepreneurship as part of the subjectmatter, and if so, what approach would you use? Explain the reasons for your decision.

CHAPTER

18

Special Aspects of Policy/Strategy in Not-for-Profit Organizations

INTRODUCTION

From time to time in preceding chapters reference was made to the policy/strategy process in nonbusiness institutions, which we shall call not-for-profit (NFP) organizations. Much of what was said in these chapters about policy/strategy in business institutions applies to NFP organizations. However, there are fundamental differences between the two sectors. In this chapter some of the principal similarities will be noted, but the emphasis will be placed upon the major differences between the two sectors.

THE NFP SECTOR

What Is The NFP Sector?

The NFP can be divided roughly into two distinct groups of organizations. The first encompasses governments and the second includes all other organizations. The differences among these organizations are probably greater than differences among companies in the private sector, as diverse as they are. The government spectrum ranges from the federal government to state and local governments. The range of organizations in the federal government is from the Congress, the Executive Branch, and the Supreme Court to special agencies of the government such as the Tennessee Valley Authority, the Panama Canal Zone, and shipbuilding yards.

Other organizations in the NFP sector include savings and loan associations, trade associations, chambers of commerce, professional societies, farmers' cooperatives, trade unions, private colleges and universities, foundations, hospitals, churches, and museums. These organizations are like private institutions in that they are not a part of government. However, they perform a public service and are not operated for profit which, of course, makes them different from private firms.

Some of these institutions are quite similar in structure and operation to private enterprises. Such, for example, are transportation systems of cities, toll roads, and state liquor stores. Many of these organizations have boards of directors like private companies.

Importance of the NFP Sector

We need not elaborate the point that government is the most dominant institution in society. Its policy/strategy making processes literally may mean the difference between life and death to all of our institutions and to each of us personally. Government is also growing rapidly in terms of expenditures, jobs, laws, and administrative regulations.

There has been substantial growth in our nongovernment public service institutions in recent years, especially in the areas of health. Business is still, of course, a major institution in society, but it is declining in importance relative to these other NFP institutions as measured by employment, power, control of capital, and expenditures.

On Comparing Private and NFP Organizations

Before proceeding with a detailed discussion of the major aspects of NFP policy processes that differ from those in the private sector, a few comments about comparing the two sectors provides a useful perspective.

First, our interest focuses on the formulation, implementation, and evaluation of policy/strategy, and most of what follows will be concerned with this process. In private institutions, particularly the larger ones, these processes frequently take place in the comprehensive strategic planning process. There is no comprehensive integrated long-range national strategic planning process in the federal government, and there are grave reservations about the advisability of introducing such a system at the present time [Steiner, 1975c]. The nearest approach to such a system was the introduction of a planning-programming-budgeting system (PPBS) into the federal government by President Johnson in 1965. This system was abolished by President Nixon when he assumed office and was replaced with a management-by-objective system. This MBO system has some long-range planning characteristics, but it is concerned with individual agencies not with the entire federal government [Fri, 1974]. On the other hand, PPBS is being introduced into more and more state and local governments [Novick, 1973].

Among the nongovernment institutions in the NFP there is a new thrust to develop a type of formal strategic planning quite comparable to that employed in private industry. This trend will grow because the Social Security Administration in mid-1974 made institutional planning mandatory for participation in Medicare and Medicaid. This new regulation is part of Public Law 92-603 and requires that hospitals prepare an overall plan and budget for operations and capital expenditures. The latter must cover a three-year period and be reviewed annually and updated. However, despite this mandate, Glueck and Mankin [1975] studied 15 Missouri hospitals and found that they did not formally plan their strategies in much detail.

The fundamental processes of formal strategic planning used in the private sector, and the lessons learned from that experience, are highly applicable to institutions in the NFP. This is especially so with respect to the many non-government organizations, but it is also applicable to the federal government [Steiner, 1975c]. A number of writers have explained how corporate long-range planning processes apply to different types of NFP organizations. Cartwright [1975] has dealt with the subject for local governments, McKay and Cutting [1974] for educational institutions, Hussey [1974a] for a church, Peters [1974] and Webber and Dula [1974] for hospitals, and Hardy [1973] for nonprofit organizations generally.

Although certain of the fundamental approaches, methods, and processes of corporate planning are applicable to planning in the public sector, there are many important differences. These will be highlighted in the following pages. The degree of similarity and/or dissimilarity varies much depending upon the type of institution. A government-owned and operated electric utility may have a strategic plan comparable to that of its private counterpart. Strategic plans in government organizations, however, tend to be less like those in even the huge private corporations.

The policy processes in an organization take place, of course, within a larger management context. A great many of the fundamentals of operational management of private organizations apply to public organizations, and vice versa [Drucker, 1973b, 1974; Koontz and O'Donnell, 1972; and Kast and Rosenzweig, 1970]. It should be noted, too, that a massive literature is developing that compares the functioning of all types of organizations [for example, Burack, 1975; Etzioni, 1975; Miles, 1975; Rogers, 1975; Gibson, Ivancevich and Donnelly, 1973; Leavitt, Dill and Eyring, 1973; Miner, 1973a; Levinson, 1972]. Obviously space does not permit any penetrating comparisons between the private and NFP sectors with respect to the generic nature of organizations nor the ways in which they are managed. This larger comparative field should be noted here but, again, our focus is on the process of formulating, implementing, and evaluating policy/strategy.

FORMULATING POLICY

Politics and Pluralism in Public Sector Policy

Some years ago in a very perceptive book Appleby [1949:153] said, "Everything having to do with the government and everything the government does is political, for politics is the art and science of government." This means for this discussion that decision making in government is essentially forged on the political anvil. Here is a major difference with business decision making. Although it is quite true that decision making in business, especially in the larger corporation, is based considerably more on political and social considerations than current academic decision theorists admit, the core determinant is still economic.

Another fundamental feature of our political democracy is pluralism. A pluralistic society is one in which many individuals and groups have power that can be, and is, used to influence decision making in government. This is not only permitted but encouraged by the Constitution of the United States. No one group has overwhelming power over all others, but each may have at least an indirect impact on all the others. The basic purpose of this Constitutional right to influence government was originally designed to limit the power of the federal government. But it also has served to decentralize power, to assure a check on and balance of power, and to prevent the tyranny of a majority over a minority. Here, too, is a major difference with business decision making. Whereas business firms, especially the larger companies, must today respond to the demands of various interests focused on the enterprise, there is no legal compulsion for managers of private companies to entertain or respond to the demands of such interests. In a public institution these demands are heard, and the way in which they are weighed on the political scale decides public policy.

Drucker illustrates this dissimilarity with private firms in this way. A company with a market share of 20 per cent must pay attention to customers in this market segment. Along with stockholders these are the two primary constituents of the company. The other 80 per cent of the market can be ignored. In a public service institution, whether a government or a voluntary hospital, management must be concerned with 100 per cent of its constituents [Drucker, 1973b].

Furthermore, any group of constituents with even moderate power can, for a time at least, block action. To illustrate, President Johnson two years before he left office directed that a predominantly low-income housing development be created in the District of Columbia called the Fort Lincoln Housing Project. Despite the President's strong support, the resistance of local groups and then conflicts among government agencies blocked the program. Incoming President Nixon abandoned the project [Derthick, 1970]. Although it may be an oversimplification, it can be asserted with some truth that "a politics based on concensus by the relatively few (in the past) has given way to a politics of conflict engaged in by a great many" [Stedman, 1975:24]. This certainly complicates the decision-making processes in public service institutions. This fact of life affects all organizations in the public sector—from the federal government to "businesslike" organizations.

Determining Missions, Purposes, and Long Range Objectives

The processes of formulating basic missions, purposes, and objectives is significantly more difficult in public service organizations than in private organizations. The Constitution of the United States, of course, sets forth a comprehensive set of missions, purposes, and objectives for this nation but no integrated, more detailed network of these aims exist. The first and only attempt to establish a set of long-range consistent national goals, for instance, was made by the Eisenhower Administration in 1960 (President's Commission on National Goals). The basic reason that this work has not been updated is not lack of interest but the extraordinary difficulty in achieving any sort of consensus of goals except at very high levels of abstraction.

The federal budget in a very real sense is a statement of national goals and priorities, but it is comparatively short-range in focus, although it naturally has significant long-range implications. It is also an extraordinarily complicated document with an endless array of explicit and implicit goals.

Even in comparatively small and "businesslike" public service institutions, such as a hospital, problems of formulating basic missions, purposes, and objectives are very complex. Such questions as these, for example, are difficult to answer. Should a hospital be the service facility for physicians? If so, which physicians? Or, should the purpose be to respond to the health needs of the community? What are they? Whose needs? Should the focus be on preventive medicine or administering to those people with current health problems? Each of these basic missions can be defended, and each would get support from major constituents of the hospital.

Coming to an agreement about which missions and purposes are of highest priority is a complex and difficult task because different constituents hold values that do not readily change. In reviewing the introduction of management by objective into British hospitals, Charnock [1975] found that among physicians, to mention but one powerful constituent group, there appeared to be no adjustment of their values to changing societal values concerning health services. Physicians were still committed, he said, to optimizing their subsystems [Charnock, 1975].

Getting Problems on the Policy Agenda

There is a major difference between the way problems get to the attention of management in public as contrasted with private organizations. In business, problems come to the attention of management when something happens to alter importantly those established measures of performance used in business, such as market share, sales, profits, return on investment, cash flow, and so on. In government, the process is much different and far more complex. In a classical treatment Truman [1951] observed that when the equilibrium of a group is seriously disturbed the group exerts pressure on government to preserve equilibrium. This is still true but as Jones [1970] points out, there are many other ways problems attract the attention of government. Self-appointed advocates for groups (such as consumers or those interested in preserving the environment) often are successful in getting their issues on the policy agenda of government. Individual legislators, of course, can initiate legislation, and the executive branch is constantly seeking new policies to resolve existing and anticipated problems. This process of stimulating policy development is fundamentally different from that of business firms.

Disjointed Incremental Policy Making

In Chapter 12, the so-called "disjointed incremental" approach to policy making in government was discussed. With such an approach, policy makers take one little step at a time. Something is tried, then altered, then tried in a slightly different form. All the while the policy makers seek compromises with powerful interest groups until the bargaining process produces a result acceptable to all having power or until those who are dissatisfied are unable or disinterested in obstructing a decision. This is also called by Lindblom [1959] "muddling through." In an earlier paper Lindblom [1955:5] took the position that bargaining in government was akin to Smith's "jiggling of the market." A good bit of policy/strategy decision making in private enterprises can be described in this fashion, but it is not as pervasive in comparison to total decision making as in public service organizations. In public policy decision making, for instance, nonincremental alternatives are generally not within the range of choice. This is so because party politics is generally based on incremental differences in policies, not radical change. In private industry, however, no reasonable alternatives are eliminated in the policy/strategy decision-making process.

Policy and Learning

Closely associated with the idea of muddling through and the group decision-making character of policy formulation is the idea that, in the governmental sector, formulation of policy is often tentative and incremental because the state of knowledge is inadequate to be clear and precise. The democratic process is a learning process, and this fact applies to both the formulation and implementation of policy. Schattschneider [1969:89] expresses the idea this way:

"Every statute is an experiment in learning. When Congress attempts to deal with a new problem it is likely to pass an act establishing an agency with vague powers to do something about it. The new agency makes an investigation, it issues some literature about its functions, invites comments by interested parties, assembles a library of information, tries to find some experts, tries to get people to do something about the problem, and eventually reports back to Congress, recommending some revisions of the statute. Thereafter the problem is passed back and forth between Congress, the President, the agency, interested people, the public. It is debated, criticized, reviewed, investigations are made, the statute is revised, over and over again, sometimes for years, before a policy is evolved."

Frequently the Congress and the executive agencies of government keep the issue open deliberately precisely because the "answer" is not obvious and/or discussion is required to reach a needed concensus. Furthermore, there are very few decisions which, because of this process, are irrevocable.

Group Decision Making

In the Congress, decision making cannot be said to rest ultimately with one individual. Decisions are compromises among many. In the Executive Branch of government, however, one man is often responsible for a decision. More frequently than not, however, the decision is recommended by a group assigned the responsibility to do so. This process is pursued in the private sector but generally not as extensively as in the public sector. The result is that in the public sector there is greater dependence on group decision making with all the strengths and weaknesses of that approach. In Chapter 11 the strengths and weaknesses of group decision making were examined. It was found that grave dangers rest in group decision making for a number of cogent reasons described there. Janis [1972] and Allison [1971], as noted earlier, linked a number of major fiascos in government policy to what Janis calls "groupthink" which stresses the weaknesses in group decision making. The linkage, however, admittedly is imperfect [Janis, 1972:11]. Nevertheless, the conclusion may be tentatively set forth that the possibility of serious policy errors may be greater in public service institutions because they engage more in group decision making.

Policy Analysis

Major business policy/strategy decisions contain a good bit of judgment and reliance on unquantifiable considerations. But, generally, major decisions also rest on quantified economic analysis. In the public service area more decisions rely more heavily on judgment and nonquantifiable factors. In examining in detail the Congressional decision-making process with respect to foreign aid, for instance, Geiger and Hansen observed that in the Congress "the role of rational intellectual considerations is much less important than is commonly supposed and that it would not be greatly enhanced by changes in the volume and nature of information per se . . ." [in Bauer and Gergen, 1968:363].

Because decisions are ultimately made on "political grounds" it cannot be said that rational calculation is absent in making the decisions. Actually, relevant information and quantifiable calculations are being more and more used and are sometimes decisive in policy formulation [U.S. 90th Congress Research and Programs Subcommittee, 1967; Hitch, 1966]. This technology is becoming encompassed in a new discipline called "policy science" [Brewer, 1974; Fisher, 1974]. The methods and tools of business analysis, such as return on investment, are generally inapplicable in the NFP. But comparable, although less precise, tools and processes have been developed such as cost/benefit analysis, system analysis, operations analysis, cost-effectiveness analysis, and program budgeting [Fisher, 1974].

The ultimate test of a "good" policy is conceptually the public interest. But this is an elusive test and differs much among decision makers. There are daily instances where disagreements about what is the public interest sharply distinguish positions taken by the President and Congressional leaders. Within the Congress as well as in the Supreme Court, there is not always a consensus about what the public interest is. Lindblom [1959:81] says that "The test of a 'good' policy is typically that various analysts find themselves directly agreeing on a policy (without their agreeing that it is the most appropriate means to an agreed objective)." This may serve for large overarching policies, but there are more rigorous tests that can be applied to policies of lesser magnitude, such as a program to improve highway safety, or to meet demands for new airports.

Although quantitative approaches to policy analysis are growing in usage, there are still many who caution against placing too much reliance upon them for public policy making. Strauch, for instance, is highly critical of quantitative methodology as a tool for the analysis of what he calls "soft" or "squishy" problems (that is, without any well-defined mathematical formulation that unambiguously captures the substantive problem) [Strauch, 1974]. When these limitations are neglected, he says, serious distortions in policy can result.

In sum, the role of analysis in policy making in the NFP sector is different than in the private sector. Much depends, however, upon the level of policy and the organizational setting in which it is made. In both sectors, however, at high levels of policy there is no *best* solution to a policy problem. In both sectors the less significant the policy problem is, the more likely the decision makers will be to rely on pertinent information and quantitative analysis.

Policy Versus Means

The conventional view of problem solving is that means are adjusted to ends, or, policies/strategies are sought that will achieve identified objectives. As noted previously, however, strategies can bring a redefinition of objectives in business. In government, more frequently than in business, ends of public policy are governed by means. For instance, U. S. Navy shipbuilding yards were originally established to build ships. With the decline in the demand for ships, the production of ships became a means to achieve a different end, namely, that of providing employment for shipyard workers.

Also, in the public sector more than in the private sector, making a policy, any policy, is sometimes more important than the wisdom of the substance of the policy. This results from the fact, for example, that great pressures exist on politicians to meet their promises to deal with urgent demands.

Complexity of Policy Making

In the larger public service institutions, it is obvious that policy making is far more complex than in the largest private organizations. George M. Humphrey left the Hanna Company to join President Eisenhower's cabinet and to apply his no-nonsense managerial decision making capability to straightening out the government. Later, in discussing his experiences he said:

"Government is vast and diverse, like a hundred businesses all grouped under one name, but the various businesses of government are not integrated nor even directly related in fields of activity; and in government the executive management must operate under a system of divided authority . . . when a government executive decides on a course of action not already established under law, he must first check with other agencies to make certain his proposal does not conflict with or duplicate something being done by somebody else. It is common in government, much too common, for several agencies to be working on different facets of the same activity. The avoidance of overlapping or conflict calls for numerous conferences, for painstaking study of laws and directives, for working out plans in tedious detail so that what one Cabinet officer does will not bump into what another is doing—or run counter to our interests and activities abroad. . . .

Before coming to Washington, I had not understood why there were so many conferences in government, and so much delay. Now I do. Everything is more complex. . . ." [Humphrey, 1954:31].

Comparable problems exist in smaller public service organizations. Figure 18-1 shows the range of influences on an administrator of a public hospital. To begin with, his board of directors is probably appointed by an elected official and will owe some allegiance to that official. Board members are influenced by individuals in various government agencies and by hospital employees. The planning committee of the hospital is composed of managers and staff working in the hospital as well as representatives of outside interests. Their role on the committee is to represent those outside interests. In sum, everyone is able to influence everyone else in the operation of the hospital. No strong influence can be ignored and consensus on major issues is difficult to achieve. Furthermore, actions decided upon must not conflict too much with other organizations.

Although managerial skills which can be successfully applied in the private sector may also be transferrable to the public sector, the transition is not easy. One of the authors has spent a number of years in the federal service and has

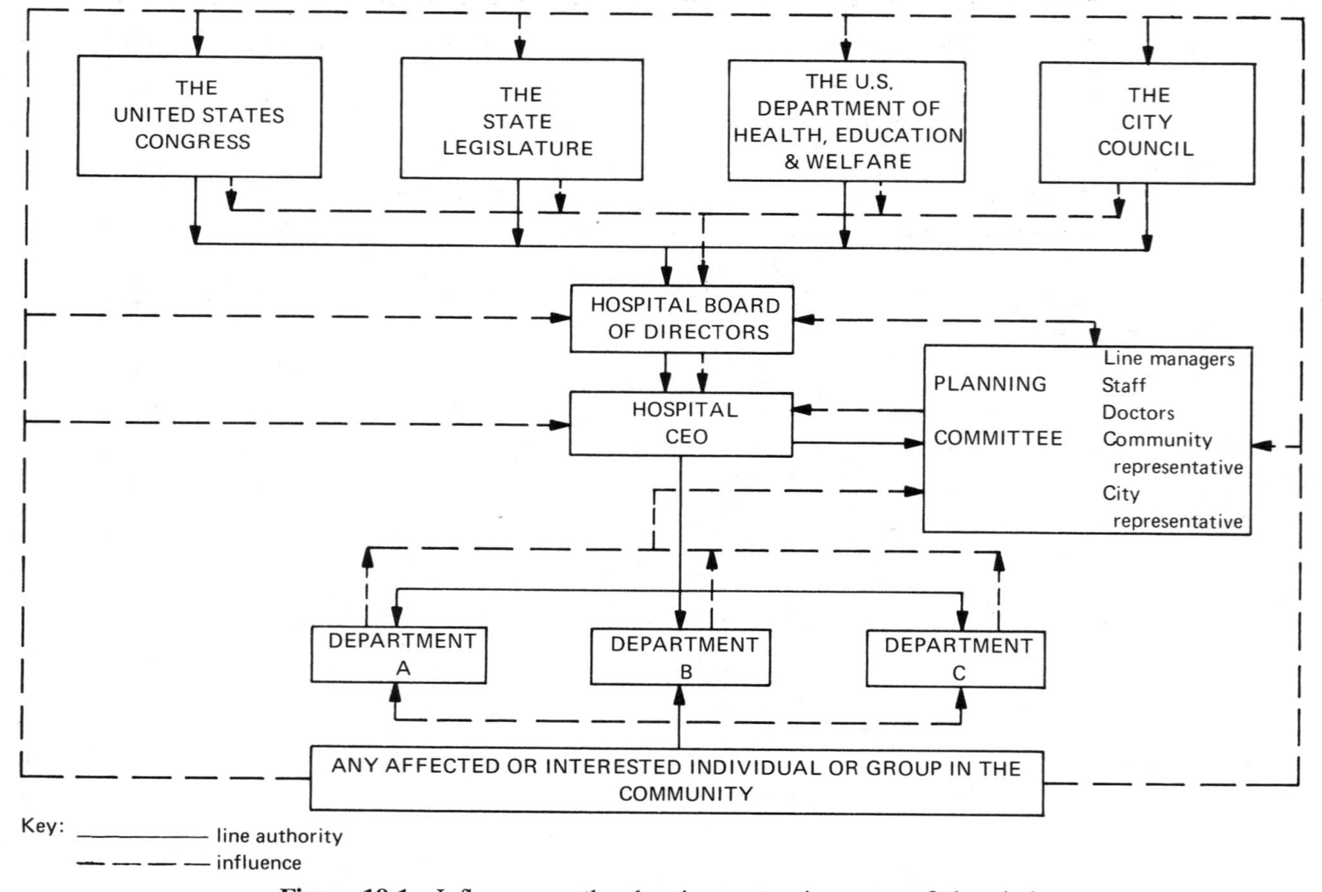

Figure 18-1 Influences on the planning process in a nonprofit hospital.

watched successful business managers enter into public service with visions of using "sound business methods" to improve the public service. He saw many of them in a short time become frustrated, angry, and depart because they could not adapt their managerial skills to the new demands of the public service institution they joined. On the other hand, many businessmen have made the adjustment and have used well the managerial skills they learned in business. Much or little is transferrable, depending upon the situation.

IMPLEMENTING POLICY

Implementing policy/strategy in a private business is not easy, as discussed in earlier chapters. However difficult it may be in even the largest corporation, it is more complicated in government and other public service organizations for all the reasons given previously plus many more. In business there are common systems and procedures used to administer actions. There are no such common systems and rules in government agencies. Edelman explains what often happens in government, as follows:

> "Politics always involve conflicts. For the individual decision-maker group conflict means ambivalence, and ambivalence can be described in behavioral terms as the concomitant of taking of incompatible roles. . . . Enforcers and 'enforced' alike assume both the role of the potential violator and the role of his victim. Out of their responses to such mutual role-taking come the rules as actually acted out: the specification of the loopholes, penalties, and rewards that reflect an acceptable adjustment of these incompatible roles" [Edelman, 1964:51].

Edelman used law enforcement to explain what happens, but his analysis applies to many other government activities as well.

In the public service sector, as in business, human problems complicate the implementation process. For example, Brady [1973] says that difficulties he encountered in introducing MBO in the Department of Health, Education, and Welfare were largely "people" problems. It is more difficult to discharge inefficient employees under the Civil Service than in business. Political influence in hiring and promoting is probably greater in the public service sector than in business. The typical administrator in the public service sector is far more a politically sensitive animal than his counterpart in the private sector [Boise, 1975; Bernstein, 1958].

EVALUATING RESULTS

In business the evaluation of the results of policy, at least in incremental periods of time—such as months, quarters, or years—are measurable, for the most part, in quantitative terms. This is not true in government. No single or set of quantitative evaluation measures exist.

We have already noted that the extent to which the public interest is met is an ultimate measure of performance. We noted, too, how difficult it is to apply. Another final measure, much like the public interest, is what Appleby [1949:131] calls political efficiency, or that which gains the consent of the governed. Jones [1970:109] speaks of the same measure as "support for the authorities" as being applicable to all decision makers in the public service sector. He quotes Rourke with approval as follows: ". . . there are three vital centers from which political support may be drawn: the outside community, the legislature, and the executive branch itself. All these sources of political strength may be cultivated simultaneously, and usually are. . . . Basic to any agency's political standing in the American system of government is the support of public opinion" [Rourke, 1968:3].

Jones goes on to say that an evaluation of policy consequences on this standard would require answering a long list of extremely difficult-to-answer questions, such as [Jones, 1970:109]:

"1. How specific publics define the problems which policy is designed to affect.
2. The awareness of existing policy by specific publics.
3. The extent to which existing policy is associated with specific authorities.
4. Opinions toward existing policy.
5. Whether, and to what extent, opinion is divided within a public or between publics that are affected.
6. Whether, and to what extent, existing policy affecting one problem is considered significant enough for publics to grant or withhold political support."

To answer such questions, says Jones, would necessitate the establishment of a new government agency. Even if the evaluation process were undertaken, the results would be ambigious in recommending policy changes. This is so because of widespread differences in perception of what the basic problem is, disagreement on the effects of policy, and so on.

As a result, the evaluation process in government is not routine as in business. It varies depending upon policy and the level of activity. At lower levels of government and for most nongovernment public service organizations annual reports of activities are rather standard. The standards of measure, however, are not common to all.

Drucker [1973b] observes that some differences in the measurement of performance result from the fact that in private organizations income is derived from sales to satisfied customers whereas in NFP organizations income is received in budget allocations. Desirable objectives in such organizations, he says, associate with getting higher budgets. Efficiency and cost control are not considered virtues. Rather, spending total budget allocations is a prime objective. Such gamesmanship goes on in business, but not to the same degree. The point Drucker is making is that the public agency begins to serve its own internal needs rather than those of its constituents.

MANAGERIAL CAPABILITIES AND VALUES

There is a widespread belief that business managers are generally more capable than managers in government. This is said to be due to the fact that in government there are greater political influences on managers, the civil service regulations constrain them, they have less freedom to act, and they are not invigorated by the rigors of economic competition. Miner's [1974a: 64] research tends to support this view, although, of course, there are many exceptions to it.

Findings of a recent study that compared values of managers entering or reentering the profit and nonprofit sectors suggest that in the future the quality of managers in nonprofit organizations may improve considerably [Rawls, Ullrich, and Nelson, 1975]. In this study 142 persons were evaluated and the following conclusions were reached:

1. Individuals favoring the nonprofit sector were more dominant and flexible than those favoring the profit sector.
2. Those preferring the nonprofit sector had greater capacity for status, social presence, and concern for personal relations. They expressed lower preference for obedience, responsibility, ambition, a comfortable life, cleanliness, and economic wealth.
3. Those preferring the nonprofit sector placed greater value on helpfulness, cheerfulness, and forgiveness.
4. Nonprofit sector aspirants expressed a greater need for power and a lesser need for security than those going into the profit sector.
5. Those individuals considered to be change agents were mostly destined for the nonprofit sector.

This study shows clearly that for the subjects examined there are significant differences in personality, values, and behavioral characteristics between those destined for the nonprofit as contrasted with the profit sector. Furthermore, the comparisons are, in part, just the reverse of those that stereotypes of the past have asserted. If the results of this study are correct, and persist, we may see some substantial changes in the ways in which our public service institutions are managed.

CONCLUDING OBSERVATIONS

An experienced manager has concluded that there are fundamental differences between administration in business and government, as follows:

"It is exceedingly difficult clearly to identify the factors which make government different from every other activity in society. Yet this difference is a fact and I believe it to be so big a difference that the dissimilarity between government and all other forms of social action is greater than any dissimilarity among those other forms themselves. Without a willingness to recognize this fact, no one can even begin to discuss public affairs to any good profit or serious purpose" [Appleby, 1945:1].

As this chapter explains there are some very significant differences in formulating, implementing and evaluating policy between private and public sector organizations. Table 18-1 summarizes in simplified form some comparisons highlighted in the chapter. Yet, as also explained, there are fundamental similarities between organizations in the two sectors in the policy process.

TABLE 18-1
Comparisons of Business and Not-For-Profit Organizations

Basic purpose	Profit	Advance the public interest
Objectives	Few	Many
	Have general concensus	No concensus
Organizational structure	Decentralized in most large companies	Generally a centralized bureaucracy
	Many large companies	Many extremely large organizations
Decision-making processes	ROI a dominant standard	Evaluating tools more blunt
	Quantitative evaluating tools widely used	Qualitative evaluating tools widely used
	Economic standard dominant	Political standards dominant
	Decisions centered in one person	Group decision making predominates
	Integrated decision making	Piecemeal decision making
	Wide policy choices considered	Policy choices narrow
Dominant constituents	Stockholders and customers	Any interest group can influence decisions
Environment	Competitive and turbulent	Monopolistic and relatively stable
Implementation of decisions	Lines of authority reasonably clear	Chain of command not clear and confused
	Common implementing mechanisms	No standard implementing systems
Source of income	Satisfied customers	Budget allocations
Measures of performance	Principally economic and quantitative, e.g., return on investment	Political and not well defined, e.g., public interest, political efficiency

SOURCE: Suggested by Paine and Naumes [1974:58–59].

QUESTIONS

Discussion Guides on Chapter Content

1. What is the not-for-profit sector?
2. Set forth fundamental dissimilarities between policy/strategy formulation and implementation in the not-for-profit sector and in the profit sector.
3. What are some major similarities in policy/strategy formulation and implementation in the private and not-for-profit sector?
4. It is often said that managers in private industry are more capable than those in government. Do you agree or disagree?
5. Assume that you are the chief executive of a not-for-profit hospital. What differences would you expect to find in formulating and implementing a long-range planning program in contrast to, say, a chief executive in a manufacturing company having about the same revenues and number of employees?

Mind Stretching Questions

1. "A basic difference between decision making in the private and in the public sector is that in the former a central standard for rationality is economic theory whereas rational action in the public sector is based upon political theory. Do you agree or disagree? Explain.
2. Is a growing pluralism likely to accentuate differences between the private and public sector in the formulation and implementation of policy/strategy?
3. "The differences in policy/strategy formulation and implementation between large and small corporations are much less than among different types of organizations in the not-for-profit sector." Do you agree or disagree with this assertion? Explain.

CHAPTER

19

Contingency Theory of Policy/Strategy

INTRODUCTION

At various points in the preceding discussions a contingency theory approach has been advocated and various proposals of this nature have been considered. For instance in Chapter 4 certain environmental contingency variables were discussed with the major emphasis placed on variables that have been of concern to those working in the field of organization theory. Also as noted further in Chapter 14 environmental contingencies of this kind play an important role in the design of organizations, and thus in the implementation of strategies through the medium of organizational structure.

Although applications of the contingency approach to problems of organizational planning and design appear to have the longest history, there have been relatively recent applications in other areas as well. Thus, as indicated in Chapter 8, a number of scholars have attempted to specify appropriate strategies to be used in a given set of circumstances (but not in others). Similarly Chapter 12, in considering the various decision-making approaches, provides evidence that there is no "one best way" for all circumstances; the appropriate approach will vary with the nature of the situation, and in particular with the characteristics of the firm's external environment.

This final chapter seeks to focus more directly on this contingency theory approach, to evaluate it in the context of existing research, and to derive from this analysis some conclusions regarding the future of the policy discipline. The fact that the authors choose to mold this discussion around a contingency theory theme is indicative on the one hand of their profound belief in the need to develop sound theory in this most practical of all areas and, on the other hand, of their conviction that something approximating a contingency approach is most likely to provide an effective means to this end, at least for the present.

CONTINGENCY THEORY AND LIMITED DOMAIN THEORY

The appeal of contingency theory is that it appears to provide a middle ground between the extreme situationist view that every situation is unique and that therefore theoretical generalization is well nigh impossible, and the view that organizational functioning can be fully explained in terms of broad general truths and principles, a view that is not born out by the evidence [Miner, 1973a]. Furthermore, the contingency approach potentially provides a means of "getting a handle on" the almost unlimited complexity of the open system concept, which views organizations in terms of the constant dynamic interaction of internal subsystems and environmental variables [Kast and Rosenzweig, 1973]. Unfortunately, as Moberg and Koch [1975] point out this potential has not as yet been fully realized. Yet the potential is there. Current difficulties appear to relate to efforts to achieve too much too fast, and thus to an oversimplification of the problem, and to a premature settling on key contingency variables.

These points, and at the same time the true nature of the contingency approach, may be illustrated with reference to a contingency theory of leadership developed by Fiedler [1967]. The reason for choosing this particular theory is that it has been stated in comprehensive form and has been in existence long enough to elicit a sizable body of research. (In fact this is one of the very earliest contingency theories.) A similar situation does not yet exist with regard to any of the contingency theories in the field of policy/strategy.

The essential point of Fiedler's theory is that the particular leadership styles that will lead to success and to failure are contingent upon three aspects of the leadership situation: (1) whether leader-member relations are good or poor, (2) whether the structure of the tasks to be performed is high or weak, and (3) whether the leader's position power is strong or weak. With a knowledge of these three variables, according to the theory, one can specify what kind of a leader will prove effective. Taking these three variables and specifying two theories for each, the theory yields eight situations and thus eight subtheories. Together these eight subtheories specify a comprehensive theory of leadership.

The difficulty with this approach is that when subjected to research test some of the subtheories seem to hold up much better than others [Miner, 1973a]. Furthermore, there is a serious question whether these three contingency variables are the right ones. In particular it appears that specific inclusion in the theory of variables drawn from the wider organizational context in which leadership occurs is essential to effective prediction.

As a theoretical and research strategy, it might be more appropriate not to attempt to develop a comprehensive theory immediately but rather to focus on a limited domain that appears particularly amenable to understanding. Thus, using the Fiedler subtheories as an example, the octant specified by good leader-member relations, high task structure, and strong leader position power might be explored in considerable detail. This could be done with a view to determining key aspects and causes of these three variable states and how they might interact with leader behavior and various indexes of success over time. To the extent one focuses on one important theoretical area in this manner, ignoring other areas and thus producing a less than fully comprehensive theory, the theory is best described as a limited domain theory. However, in the literature such theories are not always clearly differentiated from the more comprehensive contingency theories.

The main virtue of limited domain theories is that they simplify the theoretical task to a point where it is amenable to precise conceptualization and intensive research investigation. Key variables delimiting the domain, which may later be expanded into true contingency variables, can be clearly identified. Over time as various domains are explored, the matrix of possible domains is gradually filled in, until a comprehensive contingency theory emerges. Ideally the domains explored initially will be those where the prospect of establishing valid theories is greatest *and* where the most important practical contribution can be made. One definition of the latter would be a domain in which the greatest number of organizations fall for the longest periods of time.

The obvious difficulty with the limited domain approach to developing contingency theories of policy/strategy is that many top executives and their firms will be left without precise theoretical guidance for some time to come. Yet, as will become evident in the following discussion, this is the general state of affairs for *all* organizations at the present time, in spite of the fact that serious attempts at theoretical generalizations are now beginning to appear for the first time. No discipline can move to complete understanding instantaneously. The task must be divided into manageable segments and subjected to intensive study over time. This is what the limited domain approach to the development of valid contingency theory attempts to accomplish.

APPROXIMATIONS TO CONTINGENCY THEORIES OF POLICY/STRATEGY

It has been evident for some time that the strategies and policies that are appropriate for one firm under one set of circumstances are very different from those another firm, in different circumstances, should use. In fact it is this very fact that fostered the use of the case approach in teaching business policy. Each situation was seen as unique, and the way to have the student fully comprehend this uniqueness was to expose him or her to a variety of cases.

In its original form this approach made no attempt at the development of theoretical generalizations, but more recently various writers have proposed sets of contingency hypotheses derived from case analysis. This approach to the development of theory is very much in the tradition of the business policy field.

A second approach to the formulation of contingency theories of policy/strategy is more consistent with the view that the policy field is closely intertwined with management and organization theory [Mintzberg, 1973b]. This approach draws heavily upon the research related to organization structure and in fact derives its contingency variables from this source.

Theories Based on the Case Tradition

As might be expected those theories that have developed out of the case tradition tend to be quite complex. There are a number of contingency variables and many hypotheses. The objective is to retain the richness of the basic case materials in the theory to the extent possible.

A recent formulation by Hofer [1975] provides a typical example. This theory attempts to develop strategies that are appropriate at different stages of the product life cycle. The variables considered are as follows:

Market and consumer behavior variables—buyer needs, purchase frequency, buyer concentration, market segmentation, market size, elasticity of demand, buyer loyalty, seasonality, cyclicality.

Industry structure variables—uniqueness of the product, rate of technological change in product design, type of product, number of equal products, barriers to entry, degree of product differentiation, transportation and distribution costs, price/cost structure, degree of technological change in process design, experience curves, degree of integration, economics of scale, marginal plant size.

Competitor variables—degree of specialization within the industry, degree of capacity utilization, degree of seller concentration, aggressiveness of competition.

Supplier variables—degree of supplier concentration, major changes in availability of raw materials.

Broader environmental variables—interest rates, money supply, GNP trend, antitrust regulations, growth of population, age distribution of population, regional shifts of population, life style changes.

Organizational characteristics and resources—quality of products, market share, marketing intensity, value added, degree of customer concentration, discretionary cash flow, gross capital investment, length of the production cycle, plant and equipment newness, relative wage rate.

Descriptive propositions are developed for each stage of the product life cycle. Thus, for example:

In the maturity stage of the life cycle, the major determinants of business strategy are the nature of buyer needs, the degree of product differentiation, the rate of technological change in process design, the degree of market segmentation, the ratio of distribution costs to manufacturing, value added, and the frequency with which the product is purchased.

Normative contingency hypotheses are then formulated using these major determinants. An example for the maturity stage is

When (1) the degree of product differentiation is *low*
(2) the nature of buyer needs is primarily *economic*
(3) the rate of technological change in process design is *high*
(4) the ratio of distribution costs to manufacturing value added is *high*
(5) the purchase frequency is *high*
(6) the buyer concentration is *high*
(7) the degree of capacity utilization is *low*

Then businesses should

(a) allocate most of their R&D funds to improvements in process design rather than to new product development
(b) allocate most of their plant and equipment expenditures to new equipment purchases
(c) seek to integrate forward or backward in order to increase the value they add to the product
(d) attempt to improve their production scheduling and inventory control procedures in order to increase their capacity utilization
(e) attempt to segment the market
(f) attempt to reduce their raw material unit costs by standardizing their product design and using interchangeable components throughout their product line in order to qualify for volume discounts

Other sets of strategies of a quite different nature are proposed for different combinations of states of the contingency variables. Furthermore, the relevant contingency variables themselves change at different points in the product life cycle. Obviously this is far from a parsimonious theory, but it does retain much of the richness of its case origins.

The Hofer approach to theory construction relies heavily on the inductive skills of the theorist. In contrast Miller [1975] has used a type of statistical factor analysis of case data to achieve similar results. He defined nine different scenarios—five for successful and four for unsuccessful firms—in terms of such variables as environmental stability and hostility, use of controls, environmental scanning, delegation, technocratization, availability of resources, bureaucratic constraints, strategic innovation, length of time horizons, multiplexity, extensiveness of analyses, risk taking, and so on. Again the number of contingency variables emerging is quite large.

Theories Derived from Organization Theory

The approach to theory construction which draws upon organization theory for its key contingency variables is considerably more parsimonious than the preceding, but may suffer from limited predictive power to the extent these key variables fail to subsume these proposed by case-oriented theorists such as Hofer and Miller. An example of this approach is provided by Anderson and Paine [1975] who have developed a theory based on two environmental contingency variables. The first is the perceived uncertainty of the environment (certain or uncertain) and the second is the perceived need for strategic change (high or low). In both cases the relevant perceiver is the strategy maker (singular or plural). Different strategies are proposed for the resulting four quadrants.

Thus, under conditions of perceived environmental certainty and low need for change, strategies would stress defending the domain, expansion in "sure bet" areas only, integration to protect supplies and markets, efficient technological processes and maintenance of market share. In contrast where uncertainty and high need for change are perceived strategies would emphasize divestiture and selective acquisition, diversification, new ventures, and entrepreneurial risk taking. Similar guides to strategy formation as well as typical planning modes, organizational forms, and information search behaviors are presented for the other quadrants.

A somewhat different theory has been proposed by Cook [1975] using perceived environmental press (hostile or benign) and organizational responsiveness orientation (stable or dynamic) as the contingency variables. It is posited that benign environments elicit approach behavior and hostile ones avoidance; stable organizations elicit conventional strategies and dynamic ones creative strategies. Four basic hypotheses are thus derived:

1. Stable organizations facing benign press tend to enact intensification (approach/conventional) strategies.
2. Dynamic organizations facing benign press tend to enact proactive (approach/creative) strategies.
3. Stable organizations facing hostile press tend to enact reactive (avoidance/conventional) strategies.
4. Dynamic organizations facing hostile press tend to enact mediative (avoidance/creative) strategies.

Unlike the authors of the preceding theories, Cook has conducted an empirical test using 14 supermarket chains as a data base. The results do in fact provide impressive support for the hypotheses, at least in a descriptive sense. Whether strategies of the type specified yield more effective organizational performance under the indicated contingency conditions is yet to be determined.

Random Lists of Hypotheses

There are in addition certain unintegrated lists of hypotheses drawn from various sources that have been proposed primarily to stimulate thinking and research. Typical of these is the list of 71 hypotheses developed by Glueck [1972a]. Many of these hypotheses are stated in the general form, but a number are of a contingency nature. Contingency variables proposed are the degree of dependency of the firm; the extent to which the company is entrepreneurial; complexity of product line, technology, and environment; industry; the presence of long linked, mediating, or intensive technology; market share; stage of the product life cycle; growth rate of the market; volatility of the market; and company size.

Some of these hypotheses refer to a specific theoretical domain rather than subsuming the full variable range as in true contingency theory. Some derive from organization theory and some from case experience. The variable terminology, lack of logical relationships among the hypotheses, and on occasion the total failure to maintain internal consistency almost automatically invalidate such a list as theory. The list is merely what the author originally presented it as—an attempt to get things started.

THE NEED FOR RESEARCH TESTS

It is clear that the policy field is moving toward conceptual maturity. In fact, it is beginning to develop an overabundance of hypotheses, although not of logically consistent theories dealing with causal relationships among key variables. The problem is that the research which should serve to cull out incorrect hypotheses is lacking. Thus, more and more hypotheses pile up with no basis for differentiating among them. This is why the authors have not set forth *a* contingency theory, or even *a* set of limited domain theories, in this chapter or the preceding ones. The state of our knowledge at the present time is simply not such that this can be done with any degree of certainty. Guides for managerial strategy and policy formation which have a sufficient grounding in research to justify recommending them to practitioners are not yet available. In a few years, assuming that the current progress continues, there may well be such guides, but not at present. The data to make an accurate choice from among conflicting theoretical statements simply are not available.

Research Problems and Problems with Research

One of the major problems of the policy field is its grounding in and long-term commitment to the case approach. In terms of teaching and learning this is a real asset; in terms of theory construction and research it is not, simply because those who have learned to be good case writers and analyzers have not at the same time learned to value research and to be good collectors and analyzers of statistical data. The two skills are not the same [Schendel, 1975; Schendel and Hatten, 1972]. "There is a need to empirically test concepts and hypotheses to evaluate their applicability to real circumstances. Models do need to be tested for their worth. It is fair to say that policy is long on models and short on empirical results" [Schendel, 1975:15].

An example of the kind of exploratory research that is currently needed is provided by a study conducted by Hofer [1973] using data derived from business case histories written up in *Fortune* from 1960–72. Although, as Hofer himself notes, the study has its drawbacks in terms of scientific precision and rests on certain assumptions that may not hold entirely, the following conclusions are supported by the data:

". . . when environmental opportunities abound and/or when resources are more than sufficient for the needs of existing product/market areas, the Firms studied typically sought to increase the scope of their present operations in some way, while, when the opposite conditions applied, they more typically curtailed increases in the present scope of operations and pursued changes in their functional policies and/or conglomerate diversification . . . the development of new products for existing markets and/or increased penetration of existing products for existing markets were almost always among the top two or three responses. . . . the attempt to increase penetration of existing products for existing markets seems to succeed more often as a response to major increases in total demand than it does as a response to major changes in technology. By the same token, the development of new products for existing markets appears to be more successful as a response to major changes in technology than is horizontal diversification [Hofer, 1973:51–52].

In conjunction with findings such as those of Cook [1975] reported previously these results provide a good beginning in gaining an understanding of the marketing strategies companies do and should develop when faced with varied environmental circumstances.

As research of this kind increases, however, there are certain pitfalls that must be avoided. One is that hypotheses should not be tested using the same case data that were used to generate them in the first place. Another is that when hypotheses are derived from analyses of a set of cases by factor analysis or some similar technique, the hypotheses cannot be assumed to be true because they derive from data; they must be tested on another independent data set. Another is that causation cannot be attributed to a particular independent variable unless other correlated variables are controlled either statistically or experimentally. And yet another is extrapolating from limited data to widespread applications. Pitfalls of this kind have marred research in the past; they are in fact inevitable in an emerging field. But to obtain valid answers to important research questions they need to be kept to a minimum.

Stages of Research

As research in a field develops it tends to appear first in the form of surveys dealing with practice, attitudes, and intentions; then in the form of correlational or correlation-type analyses relating key variables to each other; and finally in the form of experimental studies that establish *causal* relationships [Miner, 1973a]. The field of policy/strategy is now moving into the second of these phases, although certain of its subareas are still in the initial, survey phase. On the other hand, some areas such as that of behavioral decision theory (see Chapters 10, 11 and 12) are in fact well into the experimental phase.

The problem in these more advanced areas is that they have gotten to the point where causal statements can be accepted as fact through a heavy reliance on laboratory studies. The causal statements are true as far as they go, but many may need serious modification when injected into the context of an ongoing organizational setting. The ultimate need is for field experiments where key variables are manipulated and the behavior of dependent variables is observed. Such studies are very difficult to conduct with adequate controls; they should not even be attempted until the key variables have been established with high certainty by research of lesser degrees of elegance. Yet in the end, if solid guidelines for managerial practice in the policy/strategy field are to be established, such studies will be required. It is apparent that the road to understanding through scientific research is not a short one.

THE EMERGENCE OF A DISCIPLINE

For many years the field of business policy has been represented by a single capstone course in the undergraduate and MBA curriculums, which relied heavily on case materials and which was taught by people from diverse backgrounds and with varied areas of functional specialization. Now this situation is changing and it is changing very fast. The policy/strategy field is emerging as a full-fledged discipline in its own right. A number of considerations attest to this. Perhaps the most important of these is that some 300 pages of text can be written here describing existing knowledge, theory, and research in the field, and still only the surface has been scratched. As noted in Chapter 1, the policy/strategy discipline has developed its own body of knowledge, its own theory, and it is spawning its own research. At the same time it is reaching out and providing a scholarly home for certain subdisciplines that have previously been largely in academic limbo. The key point is that it is no longer drawing primarily on other disciplines and functional fields to create an unstable amalgam of theories, hypotheses, and data with little apparent relationship to one another. It is now a discipline that is generating its own indigenous knowledge and within which certain individuals find their primary professional identity.

Further evidence for this view derives from the fact that increasing numbers of universities are providing coursework at the doctoral level to train teachers and researchers in the field. In most cases such efforts currently are represented by one or two courses within a doctoral program in management or organizational behavior. In such cases the major thrust of the training is outside the policy field, although an individual may develop an individual specialization of this kind through reading, research, and in particular the choice of a dissertation topic. However, an increasing number of business schools are offering a full-scale Ph.D. program designed for those who wish to make an academic career of the policy discipline [Hofer, 1975a]. This is a most encouraging development; it reflects a considerable degree of disciplinary maturity.

The core of the discipline is the organization-environment interaction as reflected in the decision-making process, the development of strategies and policies, and in planning. Policy implementation is at the interface with the management and organizational behavior areas and the development of knowledge in this regard no doubt will continue to be shared with these disciplines. At the same time certain areas of study that have not previously had a secure disciplinary home appear to be finding this home in the policy/strategy context. Among these are subject matter areas that have been variously labeled business and environment, business and government, business and society, social responsibility, management consultation, entrepreneurship, and behavioral decision theory. All of these areas have major contributions to make to our understanding of the total process surrounding policy and strategy. This is not to say, however, that these subject matter areas do not have a sufficient separate identity to warrant independent courses and even, in some cases, independent programs of study.

Increasingly, the student will have something of a major practical importance to learn in this area to supplement the traditional development of analytic skills that the study of cases provides. The source of this knowledge will be the theory and research of the policy/strategy discipline. As indicated in the first chapter, the objectives of the policy/strategy course are to help students develop their analytical skills, improve their knowledge, and develop appropriate and relevant attitudes. The burgeoning theory and research make the accomplishment of all three of these objectives now increasingly feasible.

QUESTIONS

Discussion Guides on Chapter Content

1. Distinguish between contingency theory and limited domain theory.
2. In what ways do contingency theories of policy/strategy derived from the case approach differ from those derived from organization theory?
3. What are the special problems in developing a sound research base that appear to be plaguing the policy field at the present time?
4. "The policy/strategy field is emerging as a full-fledged discipline in its own right." Comment.

Mind Stretching Questions

1. What do you think will be the state of the policy/strategy field in the year 2000?
2. In what areas of policy/strategy study does the need for more research seem greatest? Why are these areas relatively lacking in sound research?
3. "Theory is fine for ivory-tower academics, but it has no relevance for the practical businessman or businesswoman." Comment.

Elementary Conditions of Business Morals*

Chester I. Barnard

This subject has been selected as consonant with the purpose of the founder of the Barbara Weinstock Endowment [1]. Although "Business Morals" is somewhat broader than "The Morals of Trade," the phrase he used includes the latter. Please note also that I am not talking about "Principles of Business Morals" but "Elementary Conditions" and that the emphasis is empirical rather than theoretical or philosophical. What follows is not an essay in sociology, social psychology, or the philosophy of ethics, nor is it a theological discussion of virtue and sin in or of business organizations. What follows is the result of reflection upon long personal experience in a wide variety of organizations—business, governmental, and philanthropic—with extensive opportunity for observation, although of course I have benefited from the views of many others expressed in conferences and in books. I should therefore like the privilege of being quite informal and at times quite personal.

It may help to understand the significance of our subject and my purpose if I summarize briefly my experience in reaching my present views of it. Apropos is a letter I received recently from a student in a technical school in Sydney, Australia. Evidently he had been required to read at least one of my books and had been assigned as a topic for a paper "Barnard's Biography." He said he could find nothing about me in Sydney except in *Who's Who,* which told him little. Therefore, would I kindly write an autobiographical sketch that would tell him "how you got that way." I shall now state "how I got this way."

In 1937 I delivered eight lectures at the Lowell Institute in Boston under the title "The Functions of the Executive." On the initiative of the Harvard University Press I agreed to convert these lectures, which were orally extemporaneous, into a book. This was published in the fall of 1938 under the same title. Perhaps a more nearly appropriate title would have been "The Sociology of Formal Organizations," but such an effort was far from my mind, and such a title would have seemed bombastic to me and to others as well. I was merely trying to describe or state the nature of the essential tool or apparatus with, through, or by which executives have to work, as an indispensable

 Reprinted from the *California Management Review,* Vol. I, No. 1, pp. 1–13, by permission of the Regents.

introduction to the discussion of the practice of management and the problems of leadership.

From this study emerged two leading ideas pertinent to this lecture, although I was not aware of this until after publication. The first is that every formal organization is a social system, something much broader than a bare-economic or political instrumentality or the fictional legal entity implicit in corporation law. As social systems, organizations give expression to or reflect mores, patterns of culture, implicit assumptions as to the world, deep convictions, unconscious beliefs that make them largely autonomous moral institutions on which instrumental political, economic, religious, or other functions are superimposed or from which they evolve.

The second idea is that to a large extent management decisions are concerned with moral issues. Undoubtedly long before recognizing this I had had numerous experiences exemplifying it; but I had never distinguished between decisions of a technical or technological character, subject to factual and reasoned conclusions, and those involving a less tangible sensing of values. But this idea of moralities in organizations was one of issues arising within organizations, with little or no reference to prevalent moral conceptions in the great societies within which these formal organizations exist, nor did it take into account the obligations of incorporated organizations as legal entities.

Recognition of the fact that cooperation among men, through formal organizations of their activities, creates moralities was to me, in 1938, a startling conception. One of its implications was that modern Western civilization is morally complex, far beyond other civilizations. This view seemed to me to be confirmed by the marvelous orderliness and stability of our society. Another implication was that conflicts and misunderstanding of moral positions, as contrasted with conflicts of economic or power interests, must have greatly increased and that frustrations, confusions, and uncertainties with respect to right and wrong surely were magnified. However, all this increased my perplexity concerning the reasons why Judeo-Christian ethics, the Ten Commandments, the Sermon on the Mount, the Golden Rule, seemed to have so little application or relevance to the moral problems of the world of affairs. I did not know then that others recognized this, as I subsequently discovered. For example, Professor Frank H. Knight in his essay "Conflict of Values: Freedom and Justice" says:

> All will agree that literal individual liberty must be limited by law, by enforced law. We need not here debate against anarchism; nor, we should hope, against the view (though held for many centuries by official Christianity) that laws and governments "would be" superfluous if men were not sinful. A pure personal-relations ethic, of whatever form, can hardly furnish rules for such activities as international trade, or any dealings with people too numerous and remote to have reality for us as individuals, with the unborn, or for the future of cultural values; in fact, any rules for organizing work or play [2].

And Mrs. Alfred North Whitehead is reported to have remarked: "They may finally succumb and learn to like the poison after they have been sufficiently tainted. . . ."

"On the credit side," said Whitehead, "I notice that a large part of what is written for the serious columns of your newspaper is to set before the readers their responsibility for maintaining the social system. The aspects of this are various, but that in the end is what it all comes to: the readers are being reminded that the preservation of a social system depends on them. Now responsibility for a social system is the groundwork of civilization. Without a society in which life and property are to some extent secure, existence can continue only at the lowest levels—you cannot have a good life for those you love, nor can you devote your energies to activity on the higher level. Consequently, a sense of responsibility for the continuance of a social system is basic to any morality. Now this form of responsibility is almost entirely absent from Christianity. Jesus hardly mentions it, except for one or two remarks."

"And one of these," said Mrs. Whitehead, " 'Render unto Caesar,' was evasive."

"There were historical reasons for this lack, I grant you," he continued. "The Hebrews had no independent state to govern, and a man cannot be blamed for failing to consider what there was in his period no occasion for considering. He said what an able thinker might be expected to say. His historical situation did not elicit a code of ethics concerned with responsibility for a social system; but the absence of such responsibility has been a characteristic of the Jews for centuries. That is one reason for their unpopularity. You may say that the way they have been treated in many of the countries of their sojourn has not permitted such participation, and I quite agree. But that absence has involved Christianity in an almost perpetual self-contradiction. It held that the externals of life are not worth caring about and at the same time insisted on types of moral conduct which cannot be observed—without perishing—unless the externals of life are sufficiently well organized. A society run on strictly Christian principles could not survive at all" [3].

The approach of war and then war duties prevented much reflection upon these matters, though experience during this period seemed to confirm my previous conclusions about the essentially moral character of behavior in formal organizations.

I began to get a little more insight into this subject in 1944 when I attended a conference of what was then called "A Commission on a Just and Durable Peace," an activity of the Federal Council of Churches of Christ in the United States of America. It was held at Cleveland, Ohio, under the chairmanship of Mr. John Foster Dulles. About half the delegates were clergymen and most of the remainder were church people. It was concerned primarily with international relations; but in the various sectional meetings I observed that whenever the discussion related to public or business affairs, the assumptions as to the nature of such affairs seemed to me quite unrealistic. Whenever an attempt was made to apply a moral precept, it seemed to me substantially irrelevant;

and what seemed to me the essential moral dilemmas of business and public affairs were evidently not contemplated at all.

Why? Because, I thought, the facts of business life were not available. This seemed to be to some extent a matter of communication and of semantics. The theologians were talking in terms of a nomadic and simple agricultural life—of sheep and lambs, of shepherds—in an industrial age in which the majority had no experience of rural life. But the fault was not so much that of the theologians and the clergy. The doctrine of the economists concerned with highly abstract aggregates of behavior, with its highly artificial assumptions of the maximizations of profits as the principle of economic behavior, was not merely misleading but abortive; and they had neglected the study of business as such, of the entrepreneurial functions and its history. And the men of affairs, though some were highly loquacious, were singularly inarticulate except in the technical language of their heterogeneous shops. There are reasons for this inarticulateness to which I shall refer later. Suffice it to say that in my estimation empirical studies of behavior in business and affairs, of organizations, and of the moralities they create, were needed, stated in language facilitating communicating with those whose concern is with general problems of ethics.

However laborious the path by which I reached this view, it was not new. For a number of years the Federal Council of Churches had maintained a Department of the Church and Economic Life which had shown concern for the empirical facts, though its approach was primarily from the religious side; and it had little money for the expensive research required. Mr. Paul G. Hoffman, one of my predecessors on this platform, then Chairman of the Committee for Economic Development, was much interested in these efforts which I suppose were somewhat analogous to those of his committee. He offered to attempt to raise money for the research requirements if I would do likewise; but my suggestion was that at least initially funds should be sought from the most neutral sources, that is, the foundations, since many controversial questions would be involved, the treatment of which should not be biased by the source of funds, whether from private individuals, corporations, or labor unions. Subsequently the Federal Council made application to the Rockefeller Foundation for support. More than $200,000 in two appropriations was made available, resulting in the production of a series of books published by Harper & Brothers. In them there is not much reflection of empirical research, but an illuminating presentation of the approaches and considerations involved in understanding the problems of business morality.

My purpose in this introduction has been to indicate the nature of the problem of business morality, the confusion that exists about it, its importance, and something of what has been attempted recently to secure enlightenment in a field that is obscure. What I wish to do in the following discussion is to sketch some of the elementary conditions of behavior in business relevant to moral questions.

DEFINITION OF MORALITY

The ideas that there may be numerous systems or codes or attitudes of morality and that cooperation in formal organizations creates such systems or codes or attitudes are not common. And much behavior that is determined by moral attitudes is not recognized as such. I therefore should attempt some approximate definition of morals, morality, and associated concepts. I mean by moral behavior that which is governed by beliefs or feelings of what is right or wrong regardless of self-interest or immediate consequences of a decision to do or not to do specific things under particular conditions. To some extent questions of right or wrong in business are strictly personal—honesty, abstinence from violation of the rights of others, conformance to rules of decency, Golden Rule in regard to the interests of others, charity—the questions with which traditional religious or philosophical ethics are concerned. Most modern concrete business behavior, however, is not of direct personal interest. Rather, business morality relates to "good of the organization," "interests of society," prescriptions of law. The fact that personal interests are not involved leads many to fail to recognize that adherence to organizational interests, to correct procedure, as in the courts—for example, in application of the first ten amendments—becomes not technical, but moral in the sense just stated. I shall set forth some of these moralities in the next section of this paper entitled "Varieties of Moralities."

The propensity toward ideal behavior stated without regard to ethical foundations in religious doctrine or to philosophical precepts is so deceptively simple that it raises the possibility that to emphasize the moral character of so large a part of modern business behavior is to paint the lily of what after all may be only "practical" behavior. Why, to the laymen, does business practice so often seem either immoral or amoral? In part the remainder of this lecture is concerned with this question; but it may be useful to give here some brief general comments suggesting why moral business behavior is not always recognized as being moral.

First, a perfectionist standard is not a valid criterion of moral behavior. Moral ideals, when expressed in general terms rather than in action in concrete situations, are necessarily abstract, and attainment may fall far short of the abstract ideal. This does not mean that failure is evidence of immorality, but that moral achievement is in part dependent on concrete conditions which vary widely. This is perhaps only to say that the degree of "temptation" to deviance must be taken into account. The test is not whether moral error is committed, but whether when committed it is so recognized with accompanying apology, regret, or remorse. However, the situation is one where the professor of a moral standard is vulnerable to criticism, extremely difficult to meet where technical considerations are involved. It explains why so often I have heard men say that they were operating frankly on the basis of self-interest or for economic or even legal reasons when I knew this was not the case.

Second, the more moral organized behavior becomes the more frequently will conflicts arise, not only between moral principles, but between such principles and those of technical (accounting, financial, legal, organizational) and technological character. This will be further discussed later. Suffice it to say here that the situation is one easily interpreted as one of incessant conflict to defeat moral principles, and to obscure their constructive influence.

Finally, and perhaps more important, is the fact that explicitly moral terms are not much admitted in business or public affairs. The terms most used are "loyalty," "responsibility," "duties," and "obligations." Though such terms are ambiguous (*e.g.,* "responsibility" is often used to mean "legal liability" where no moral question may be involved) they are in fact loaded with moral implications. These being the terms currently used, I shall from here on largely use them instead of "moral" or "morality" as being more convenient and as lending themselves perhaps to more easily intelligible discussion.

VARIETIES OF MORALITIES IN BUSINESS

To give more meaning and substance to general remarks already made and to suggest what is meant by "elementary conditions" of business morality, I shall now present several classes of responsibility readily distinguishable in any large organization and only somewhat less easily recognized in other organizations, even though small. I am not attempting here to be comprehensive or to present a selection based on a thoroughgoing taxonomic study of the moralities of business. Indeed, I think that would be impossible at the present time. Much observation and analysis will be required before this can be done. There is little explicit knowledge of this subject. Such understanding of it as there is, is a matter of intuitive familiarity with specific organizations, specific operations, and specific conditions. Thus the moral climate in different organizations varies greatly, so that a thoroughly competent executive, administrator, or employee transferring from one to another will require as much time "to learn the ropes" of the moral climate as of the technical situation—and may never "learn the ropes"; this is, the loyalties and responsibilities of a transportation organization, of a publicly regulated electric power organization, of one manufacturing shoes and one manufacturing dangerous chemicals, of a distributor of automobiles and a distributor of nylon stockings, are radically different.

In the discussion that follows I have arranged the topics roughly from the general and simple to the more specific and complex. First I shall discuss personal responsibility, then representative responsibility, then personnel responsibility, then corporate responsibility, then organizational responsibility, followed in order by economic, technical and technological, and legal responsibility.

Personal Responsibility

A necessary, but by no means a sufficient, foundation of business morals is the character of individuals as such. The basis of character may be the inculcation of the ethics arising from religious or philosophical doctrines and the mores of the society in which the individual develops. The requisite character includes: avoidance of criminal acts, gross and public immoralities and in particular stealing and lying; a willingness to recognize the interests of others to the extent of ordinary courtesy; and, finally, a willingness to discharge commitments, that is, to perform duties accepted, to honor promises.

Representative or Official Responsibility

One of the important, if not the dominant characteristic of modern Western society, as contrasted with ancient, or with Western societies of one hundred or two hundred years ago, is the extent to which concrete behavior of individuals has become representative rather than personal. By "representative" is here meant "on behalf of other," that is, not by the actor personally, but "in accordance with the aims or goals or by the methods determined by others." From the point of view of this lecture the most significant aspect of this radical change of conditions is the wide gap between the ethics of personal behavior and those of representative behavior. This seems to be well recognized only with respect to the decisions of trustees and of directors of corporations, and of other agents either of individuals or of firms or of corporations. In these technical functions it is well understood that a trustee may not do things which an individual may do, and must do things which an individual is not required to do. These are matters governed by deeds of trust, wills, statutes and court law, and the law of agency. The limits so fixed usually leave wide latitude for the exercise of judgment, but even so that judgment is to be divorced from personal interest entirely.

The field of representation or official behavior covered by legal prescriptions is only a small part of the total of the behavior on behalf of others. Every act of a trustee, director, officer, or employee is officially representative action, not personal, and the ethics of personal behavior are not identical, except coincidently, with the ethics of representative behavior. This seems to be recognized generally only with respect to a few kinds of action. Morally and legally it is not permissible for one to kill another (except in self-defense) yet the policeman, the soldier, and the executioner may and sometimes must kill in the discharge of duties, usually without any implication of immorality. Indeed, failure or refusal to do so would often be regarded as immoral. On the other hand, so far as I know, no one may legally steal on orders, except perhaps in foraging for military purposes. Yet there are circumstances where it would be immoral, from the standpoint of responsible representative behavior, not to do things immoral and even illegal from a personal point of view.

The representative character of organized behavior is the basic condition of the numerous special moralities. It affects not only such behavior directly, but also strictly personal behavior. For example, the housewife purchasing from a chain store is affected by the impersonal morality of the store, and often there is a conflict not so much of interest as of moralities involved.

Personnel Loyalties

Representative behavior is the ethical ground upon which is erected a sometimes elaborate structure of moralities in organized cooperation. Perhaps the most pervasive and important of these moral structures is that of personnel loyalties. Superficially these appear as personal loyalties, but they are not, and it is this fact which gives them their special moral character.

In formally organized activities the principal personnel relationships are those between superiors and subordinates and between those of coordinate status (fellow workmen). This relationship involves loyalties to individuals *acting in their official capacities.* Loyalty in this context means recognition of the responsibilities of others and the desire to support others in the discharge of those responsibilities, often by means thought to be erroneous and contrary to self-interest. Spontaneously constructive efforts largely grow out of such loyalties, and they constitute a very large part of the cohesiveness of organizations.

The highly moral character of these relationships will not be understood unless it is recognized that subordination is not a criterion of personnel loyalty. Mere acceptance of orders, the making of prescribed reports, the effective performance of specified functions are all consistent with essential disloyalty, and, indeed, can be a method of sabotage.

Nor should personnel loyalty be confused with personal loyalty as involved in the ordinary social relations of individuals. One kind of loyalty does not involve the other. In fact they are usually incompatible. This is readily seen where there is a change of official status or relationship, for example, in cases of retirement, termination of employment, promotion. It is probably very much the exception when two persons bound by mutual official loyalties remain close personal friends after the termination of official relationship—for example, when one retires. One reason for this is the restricted extent to which any individual can maintain close personal contact with others. Another is that close official relationships paradoxically are largely private and confidential. Thus where A and B are mutually loyal in an official relationship, and by the turn of events C replaces B, then A's loyalty to C requires severance of his loyalty to B. He cannot communicate to B what has become confidential with respect to C, and there is no longer the degree of common interest permitting intimate communications. Thus it would usually be regarded as very bad taste at best for A to discuss C's performance with B. Many a workman promoted to foreman has found, to his dismay, that his loyalty to a fellow workman is of a radically changed character.

Corporate Responsibility

The social invention of the limited liability corporation, whether for business or other purposes, is, in my view, more important than any single scientific or technological discovery in making possible either utilization of discoveries or especially mass production or mass distribution. It is also an important factor in economic and social stability. Yet the corporation, as something having the attributes of a personality, is a legally authorized fiction. The concrete physical activities underlying it are those of individuals or organized groups. But a myth or fiction accepted widely as a basis for individual behavior becomes a social reality. Corporations can sue and be sued; can have title to property; are responsible to public authority, for example, in the matter of taxes; can be given privileges, for example, the right of eminent domain. Although there can be nothing to a corporation except its organization, there is imputed to it not only legally but popularly a special responsibility as if it were a person; hence there can be attributed to it moral or immoral action.

The imputation of moral responsibility—not merely legal liability and privilege—can be realized only in the concrete action of trustees, officers, and employees. The moral decisions they must make, however, are not of the order of personal morality, nor of official organizational morality, but of a fictitious entity where responsibility and obligations are in many respects outside the possibility of relevance either to individual or to organizational morality.

The responsibilities of corporations, aside from the obligation to conform to their charters and the law, are of two kinds: (1) those which may be called internal, relating to the equitable interests of stockholders, creditors, directors, officers, and employees; and (2) those relating to the interests of competitors, communities, government, and society in general.

Organizational Loyalties

Corporate entities, including not only formal corporations, and enterprises of partnership and of individual proprietors but also government departments, and educational institutions, have no reality except as they relate to coordinate activities (whether directed, spontaneous, or autonomous) which as a whole we call organizations. The ethical problems of organizations, that is, their duties and obligations, are most conveniently considered as like those of formal corporations already discussed, although in some peripheral areas one must recognize that there is sometimes a moral situation of an organization distinct from that of the corporate entity. On the other hand there is a moral situation with respect to individuals and also to groups or communities related to organizations as entities with which we are now concerned. Many individuals feel an obligation to what they conceive to be an entity—an organization—that transcends personal interest or advantage. In extreme cases this loyalty has involved great personal sacrifices "for the good of the organization" that become matters of public knowledge; but for the most part this kind of loyalty is not publicly recognizable. It is sufficiently recognized so that elaboration of the idea is not necessary here; but it is not sufficiently recognized to make superfluous some comments about it. Naive critics and cynics fail to recognize the high moral character of organization loyalties, their importance, and the ethical problems involved. This is probably due principally to the following circumstances:

1. With some exceptions, particularly in the fields of religion, education, philanthropy, and politics, individuals become attached to organizations for reasons of nonmoral incentives. It is not easily recognized that loyalty develops afterward.
2. At any given time the members of an organization include many who have no loyalty to an organization.
3. Concrete expressions of organization loyalties relate chiefly to action in small groups (subsidiary organizations) that are overlooked or discounted.

Economic Responsibility

We are so accustomed to think of economic behavior in terms of calculation, supply and demand, efficiency, maximization of profits, that we leave out of account economic morality. It has many forms from the simple conviction that one should discharge obligations with respect to debts to a moral horror of waste or of inefficiency. When I was a boy, repeatedly dinged into my ears was the aphorism "Willful waste makes woeful want," which I seldom hear nowadays. Waste was not merely economically inept, it was sinful. With this embedded in my moral sense, no economic or political argument can convince me that the destruction of food stocks to maintain prices is morally defensible. A trivial example is my perpetual annoyance at the appalling waste of electric current for lighting, manifest in every organization with which I have or have had any connection. I do not doubt that such waste is going on right now on this campus at Berkeley. In one organization for which I had responsibility I found that the annual electric bill was about $5,000. I estimated that at least half was wasted, but I decided that to correct the situation involved a nagging pressure to change habits that would cost more than it was worth. I should have to suffer in silence. But I could not resist from time to time visiting empty offices and switching off the blazing and useless lights.

The moral horror of waste and patent inefficiency is, of course, often reenforced by economic sanctions such as the danger of losses or bankruptcy, a fact that leads many to assume that conservative and efficient management is merely a matter of effective calculation. This is too limited a view. Calculation is not a sufficient basis.

Technical and Technological Responsibility

Another type of morality is that to which I give the title "Technical and Technological Responsibility." It is commonly assumed that this kind of responsibility is involved in the work of the creative artist, the first-class artistic performer, the experimental scientist, an artisan such as a first-class toolmaker. It is not so widely appreciated that the adherence to high standards of performance is a common characteristic of many kinds of technical and technological work, including the management of human relations in cooperative enterprises. This failure to recognize one of the most important factors in business operations is due perhaps to the difficulty of making explicit the standards of performance in much technical work. The reality of the moral factor in much work commonly regarded as merely technical is manifest when, as a matter of deliberate policy, the attempt is made to reduce standards, say, for economic reasons. The accountant, the engineer, the manager, all resist such efforts not as a matter of insubordination, conscious unwillingness to conform to prescriptions, but as moral reaction to doing things wrongly.

The significance of this reaction may be illustrated by the following case. A manufacturer was engaged in producing a certain type of vehicle of very high quality, using the best materials and a high grade of precision workmanship so that each unit was to a considerable extent equivalent to a custom job. It was decided to produce the same type of vehicle by mass production methods, using materials of lower quality and less precision in mechanical work. The manufacturer attempted to do this in the same plant, merely lowering standards and using some new machines, but with the same organization. The attempt was a failure. The old organization simply could not produce effectively with lower standards, so that finally a new plant in a distant city with a new organization was set up to produce the cheaper product. Note that this is not a case where new skills had to be learned. In general, less skill and less time were required. The acceptance of lower standards was morally repugnant.

In the converse case, where an attempt might be made to change from a low quality product to a higher one, the moral resistance to the change would be evident—it would often seem wasteful and even silly to those affected.

Legal Responsibility

The last type of morality I wish to present I have called "Legal Responsibility." By this I mean much more than a propensity to conform to statutes, court decisions, regulatory rules. I include also the rules of internal and private character that are important aspects of the operations of formal organizations. No doubt much conformity is a reflection of interest in avoiding sanctions or liabilities, but the morality I am speaking of transcends this interest. Its basis is the deep belief that the kind and degree of order involved is not only indispensable to effective cooperation and the proper distribution of specific responsibilities, but also is essential to equity and justice, and that the flouting of legal prescriptions is destructive of integrity and morale in an organization. Therefore, immediate or even ultimate advantage or disadvantage of any specific requirement is irrelevant.

I hope that this incomplete description of some of the kinds of morality involved in business organization is sufficient to convince you that the moral factors are of predominant importance. Clearly they are complex, some being quite independent of others, some closely connected and interdependent, and most of them imponderable. But little reflection is needed to see that they involve many inconsistencies and contradictions, so that the conflict of responsibilities is a characteristic condition of cooperative efforts. To this important subject I turn next.

CONFLICTS OF RESPONSIBILITY

Experience, or even contemplation and imagination, suggests that if there are simultaneously in effect different sets of moralities, then there is likely to be ethical conflict or dilemmas of loyalties and responsibilities. This situation is certainly a characteristic of decisions in the world of affairs; but its nature is concealed by the labels by which it is described, such as "personality conflicts," "conflicts of interests" (economic, political, or prestige). It is also concealed by the privacy with which the struggles for the discharge of conflicting responsibilities are veiled. Men seem unwilling or unable to reveal moral struggles, and often seem forced to concoct rationalizations of their decisions instead of "the real reasons."

In what follows I shall attempt to state briefly the nature of a few types of moral conflicts to suggest the kinds of conflicts which we should look for in a study of the ethics of practical affairs. But first a few general remarks are desirable to avoid confusion.

The first is that most of the moral systems in effect, unlike the Ten Commandments or the Sermon on the Mount, are not explicitly formulated or coded. They are "feelings" or "attitudes" made evident by overt action (or restraint) or overt (i.e., verbally expressed) decisions. This is an important fact suggesting the great difficulty of understanding the moral situation. It is due not merely to the limited ability of most people for self-analysis and to their inarticulateness, but also to the fact that morals are in many respects felt to be private, not appropriate or seemly for public expression.

The second general remark is that it is important to distinguish two classes of moral conflicts. The first I shall call "objective conflicts or contradictions"; the second, "subjective conflicts or dilemmas." In the first class inconsistency of behavior is not recognized or admitted by those "guilty" of it, but it is apparent to observers. One of the interesting instances of it is the propensity of businessmen to effect purchases or consolidations of competing enterprises, although persistently extolling competition. These opposing views are sincerely held, and the contradiction simply not realized, for in the concrete situation not to try to effect consolidation would seem to be a dereliction in one's duty to stockholders, or to heirs, or to the organization, or to the discharge of other obligations.

This kind of objective conflict is commonly observed in many other circumstances including the conduct of individuals of high moral or religious convictions. What is involved is not insincerity or hypocrisy. This kind of conflict can lead to personal recrimination and lawsuits, but not to personal frustrations and anxieties.

The most crucial testing of behavior from the standpoint of morals in business comes from conflicts of responsibility. Almost every moral issue in matters both large and small arises from such conflicts, although in business they are most frequently not recognized, or at least not expressed as such. I should like to explain the nature of such conflicts by three illustrations. Those I have chosen relate to large and complex problems having a certain dramatic character, which make them serve better as illustrations, but it should be remembered that the nature of these conflicts could be exemplified in the thousands of moral dilemmas, hidden from public view or discussion, that are the main burdens of the administrators of affairs.

A friend who was employed in the American military government of Sicily dropped in to see me after his return to his usual academic functions. I asked him what he had been doing in Sicily, and he said he had been engaged in making public opinion polls for the American military government among the Italian citizens of Palermo. It developed that when the American forces had taken over, practically all the inmates of the prisons were released on the mistaken assumption that they were political prisoners regarded as enemies of the Fascist regime. Consequently, there were released not merely political prisoners, but also thieves, burglars, rapists, and murderers who then proceeded in their usual practices to the terror of the civilian population. The attempt to bring this situation under control by arbitrary methods, such as arrest and incarceration on suspicion without trial, was opposed by the legal authorities of the army as un-American and in violation of the Bill of Rights. I suppose there is no one in my audience who, like myself, does not regard the Bill of Rights as the most fundamental legal basis for political and social security. When the citizens of Palermo were consulted, many suggested that arbitrary methods of arrest and detention were the only way to get the situation under control. When it was suggested to them that with such methods serious injustice would inevitably be done to a number, if not to many individuals, to this the pertinent reply was made that failure to establish control of the lawless behavior of many ex-prisoners inevitably resulted in a far greater injustice to the many victims of these criminals. This certainly could be true. The situation, therefore, presented a moral dilemma of the most crucial character. Under such conditions, should procedures we usually regard as of fundamental importance to maintain be abandoned to prevent the great injustice perpetrated by failure to maintain law and order? The right of the President to suspend the writ of habeas corpus under certain conditions involving a great moral responsibility, is recognition of this type of dilemma, which is experienced every day in the conduct of affairs.

My second illustration relates to problems of engineering where moral questions to the uninitiated would not seem to be prominent. That this is not so can readily be appreciated by considering what are ultimately moral problems, what are called "margins of safety." It costs money, frequently very substantial amounts, to introduce factors of safety to offset uncertainties of future conditions, errors of calculation, and the like. When it can be assumed that the economics are such that no great question of practicability is involved, there is no great problem. It is merely one of efficiency in engineering. But where the cost of factors of safety is such as to make the economic feasibility of an engineering enterprise doubtful, the problem is different, for the decision must then be whether to deprive the community of a service or the entrepreneur of an opportunity, or to take the risks of failure.

The question just discussed leads easily not only to that of accident control which comprises the question of safety factors in structures and electrical and chemical systems, but also to matters of personnel and discipline. Whenever there is a serious accident of catastrophic character in which many are killed, the public reaction frequently is that such accidents should be prevented at no matter what cost. It is easy to see, however, that in many situations the reduction of possibilities of inadvertent occurrences can be obtained, if at all, only at very great expense in the introduction of material factors of safety and by excessive inspection, testing, and policing. Many of the services we now have would not be economically feasible if the "Safety First" slogan was excessively applied, especially in the early stages. Consequently, those who make decisions in such matters are confronted with moral issues. To what extent is one morally justified in loading a productive undertaking with heavy charges in the attempt to protect against a remote possibility, or even one not so remote?

METHODS OF RESOLVING CONFLICTS OF RESPONSIBILITIES

Reflection would suggest, and experience shows, that although conflicts of responsibilities are recognized as presenting moral issues, a condition of moral tension in a business, or any other kind of organization, can become unbearable and disruptive, leading to severe political types of controversy and opposition. It therefore becomes important to discover and develop methods of resolving such conflicts. No comprehensive discussion of the techniques of such resolutions can be given here, but a few words should be said about three of the main types of solution of this general problem.

The first may be called the judicial method. This essentially is the process of narrowing and delimiting the areas of responsibilities, thus restricting the incidence of conflict.

The second method of resolving conflict is that of reconciliation, the process of demonstrating that apparent or alleged conflicts of responsibility are pseudo-conflicts based on false assumptions or ignorance of the facts. This is a process continually in use in organizations; it is frequently expressed as "changing the point of view." It also frequently involves redefinition of jurisdictions.

The third method of resolving conflicts of responsibilities may be called that of the invention of concrete solutions. Thus, where a proposal which seems desirable from one standpoint appears to involve consequences that are seriously deleterious in some respects, the solution may be to discover or construct another proposal which will effectively accomplish the ends initially desired without involving the deleterious effects to be avoided. This may be illustrated by the analogy of certain drugs which initially may be of great value in the therapy of a particular disease, but which have side-effects that may be harmful or even fatal if their use is long continued. This prevents a dilemma for the physician and often for the patient. It leads to efforts, often successful, to discover derivative or analogous drugs having the desired therapeutic properties, but not having the undesirable side-effects. The development of Novocain as an alternative to cocaine is one of many instances that could be adduced. The need for invention of alternative means is one of the chief reasons for the effort to secure people of great ability, for alternative solutions call for imagination, fine discrimination, and persistence. Many of the moral collapses of individuals in active affairs result from their being placed in positions involving moral dilemmas which they have insufficient ability to resolve by invention and construction.

CONCLUSION: THE SIGNIFICANCE OF THE DISCUSSION

Rather than presenting a summary of the discussion, I think it might be more useful if I made a few remarks regarding the significance or the pertinence of this discussion to the problems of our times. This is partly because it seems to me that any summary at this time would lead to easy generalizations and much oversimplification. I have barely touched upon, have merely assembled some illustrations of, an underlying situation and a set of problems which it seems to me no one adequately comprehends.

This at least partly results from the increased importance and complexity of moral behavior. Unlike many of the jeremiads of today, what impresses me the most in the present situation is not the confusion, the frustration, and the irresponsibility to which so much attention is given, but rather the enormous increase in responsible behavior that has attended the growth of modern civilization and its technological expression. Despite the wars of recent years and the conflicts of many kinds of which we are almost pathologically conscious, the fact is that a network of social behavior of enormous size and complexity is carried on daily and largely autonomously with relatively few errors or failures, although it is the errors and the failures that occupy us almost entirely in the news reports.

This increase in the magnitude and the complexity of moral behavior is first the result of increased specialization, especially in economic activities and in the machinery and materials which are employed for materialistic purposes. Attention is increasingly given to the technical knowledge now required and to the technical skills arising from specialized experience. The moral factor involved in these activities seems to be almost entirely neglected. Yet the dependability with which the burden of specialized activities is carried on, and the dependability which we ascribe to those who do the carrying on, is the most essential aspect of modern civilization.

Thus in earlier periods morals were confined to a relatively small range of alternatives which were conspicuous by the fact that they could be more or less rigidly adhered to and enforced. Needless to say this is so little appreciated with respect to specialized functions that it is extremely difficult to convey the nature of the moral problems involved except to those who have knowledge of the specific functional problems. Indeed, it seems to me that the most important of our problems is to convey an understanding of the moral issues that are involved, rather than the technical and scientific questions to which so much of our educational and training processes are directed.

This matter takes on the increasing importance with respect to one of the crucial problems of our times: how to secure the essential degree of coordination of a vast system of activities while securing the degree of decentralization and autonomy essential to initiative and, indeed, to responsible behavior. It is almost obvious that those who are not capable of dependable behavior cannot be entrusted with the making of local decisions. Yet, if this cannot be done the burden placed upon centralized authority for securing appropriate behavior over vast areas is in fact an impossible one. The span of control is so limited that despite methods of specialized training and the inculcation of the appropriate points of view authority could not sufficiently operate if it were not for the development, whether inculcated or spontaneous, of the moral sense to which we broadly give the name "sense of responsibility." Responsibility cannot be arbitrarily delegated and, therefore, a high degree of effective autonomous behavior cannot be secured except as responsibility is freely accepted. When so accepted the possibility of effective autonomous behavior is realized.

It should also be noted that it is the moral problem that leads to much frustration and even to pathological behavior. This seems to me to have been largely neglected by psychiatrists who have been concerned with other factors in personal behavior. It has been well and illuminatingly discussed by Eliot D. Chapple in an article entitled "Contribution of Anthropology to Institutional Psychiatry." This neglect is to some degree responsible for the neglect of the moral factor by those in responsible management positions, a neglect that perhaps is reinforced by the relative ease with which technical problems can be approached.

Another aspect of this subject which deserves emphasis is that it indicates the importance of communication from within and to without in a specialized organization. Again and again it has been made clear to me that public misunderstanding is due largely to lack of appreciation of the moral elements involved in specialized activities and the extreme difficulty of conveying to outsiders what these moral elements are.

It must occur to anyone who considers this subject that we are in a state of considerable ignorance. It simply is not known to any wide degree what are the number and the character of the moral problems that are faced by those who do the world's work. It is here, I think, that the universities in the future will have a great opportunity, for I doubt if those within our organizations can be sufficiently adept and objective to give appropriate study to the nature of the moral problems which they face. . . . Nevertheless I think a deep reflection upon the nature of business activities will indicate that this is inevitably the kind of investigation that is required.

REFERENCES

[1] This paper was first given as a Barbara Weinstock Lecture on Morals of Trade at the University of California, Berkeley.

[2] In *Goals of Economic Life,* ed. A. Dudley Ward, New York, Harper & Brothers, 1953, pp. 203–230.

[3] *Dialogues of Alfred North Whitehead. As Recorded by Lucien Price.* Boston, Little, Brown & Co., 1954, pp. 261–262.

[4] In *Human Organization,* XIII, 2, (Summer, 1954), pp. 11–15.

Business Payoffs Abroad: Rhetoric and Reality*

Peter Nehemkis

An investigation begun in 1974 by the Securities and Exchange Commission into illegal corporate contributions to former President Nixon's 1972 reelection produced a serendipity effect: the revelation that a number of prominent American corporations engage in overseas payoffs.

The disclosure that U.S. corporations operating abroad pay—or are solicited to pay—bribes in order to obtain or engage in business, or to procure favorable tax and other administrative decisions from foreign governments, has opened a Pandora's box of complex and troublesome issues, which affect U.S. foreign relations, national security, and the investment and marketing policies of American international companies.

Since the SEC's inquiry, the Internal Revenue Service and the Departments of State and Defense have launched their own probes—the former to determine whether overseas payoffs were deducted as "business expenses," the latter to ascertain the legitimacy of commissions paid to middlemen in negotiating the sale of military aircraft and hardware. The Senate Foreign Relations subcommittee investigating multinational corporations and other congressional panels were quick to hold public hearings on the leads developed by the SEC.

Also confronted with difficult decisions as a consequence of the SEC's investigations are the outside members of the boards of directors whose managements, without their prior knowledge or approval, may have countenanced overseas payoffs. What is the extent of their fiduciary responsibility, they ask, to have known of this practice in the past or to ascertain whether it now prevails and to disclose it? The SEC believes that directors are accountable for a company's conduct. But the outside directors wonder if the price of their directorial inquisitiveness, ironically, will produce a swarm of stockholders' suits.

Nor are members of the legal profession immune from perplexing dilemmas. Are corporate counsel under a duty to reveal information to which they are privy with respect to bribes? Will this breach the confidential attorney-client relationship? Is it the lawyer's responsibility to discover whether such payments have in fact been made by his client and to report them? To whom? Some lawyers fear that forcing them to perform policing functions in the business world will destroy the confidentiality essential to their primary responsibility—advising the client and representing his interests.

Corporate auditors have long been a target of criticism by successive SEC members and staff for the limited reach of the audit certificate. They are now feeling the heat of the SEC's censure for continuing to use an audit procedure that is too random to discover the concealed payoff and whose standards of financial "materiality" exclude such transactions.

Whether the customary audit procedures can be extended or expanded raises practical cost/benefit questions. An improved audit can be many times more costly than the actual payoff unearthed. When and if such payments are—or can be—found to exist, is it the auditor's obligation to disclose them to the board of directors (as the SEC believes he should)? Why, the embattled auditor asks, should he be expected to act as a surrogate of corporate morals?

LET THERE BE LIGHT

"Sunlight" is a widely used word among officials of the SEC. It derives from a maxim of Supreme Court Justice Louis D. Brandeis, who wrote, "Publicity is justly commendable as a remedy for social and industrial disease. Sunlight is said to be the best of disinfectants; electric light the most efficient policeman." [1]

A "cleansing effect" can be obtained in the universe of corporate enterprise—so the watchmen of the securities markets believe—by focusing the spotlight of publicity on the corporation's financial transactions. Full disclosure has been the prophylaxis used by the SEC to safeguard the investor against misleading or untruthful information. [2]

To enable investors to reach informed decisions, the SEC has promulgated two pivotal disclosure forms—8-K and 10-K. Form 8-K is used for filing a monthly "current report" in which the registrant is expected to supply information on any new developments pertaining to such matters as changes in the control of the company, acquisition or disposition of assets, significant litigation to which the corporation is a party, and other "material" financial data. The 10-K form is an "annual report" designed to pick up previously unreported legal, business, and financial activities of the registrant—activities which, if disclosed, are presumed to enable an investor to keep informed on what management is doing with his money. Both reports must be filed by corporations subject to the SEC's jurisdiction, that is, those whose stock is traded on the New York Stock Exchange and other registered exchanges. For all practical purposes, every major U.S. corporation is obligated to file these two reports.

But how much light? The gravamen of the SEC's injunctive actions against five—at this writing—corporate offenders is their failure, among other things, to disclose on one of these forms the use of corporate funds to buy the favor of government officials and politicians of ruling and governing parties in exchange for special treatment. Members of the SEC's enforcement division are reported to believe that, when a company receives substantial benefits as a result of a payoff, or if its continued operations are subject to extortion, investors are entitled to know.

Widening the circle of disclosure to encompass under-the-table payments overseas has engendered both approval and criticism. To the increasingly vociferous critics of the multinational corporation, payoffs to foreign officials or political parties strengthens the demand for stringent regulations. Hence the tightening of the screws by the SEC is applauded. On the other hand, a White House aide is reported to see a "revolution" in the SEC's views of what constitutes material information that can influence investment decisions. Others assert that the SEC has embarked on a typical American exercise in ethnocentrism—imposing its own moral judgments on foreign governments and U.S. international corporations.

Actually the commissioners are not united in their stance regarding disclosure of overseas payments. A minority of the members perceive the issue with an uncluttered moral simplicity: transgressors should disclose their sins of omission and commission; in telling the truth, they must bear the consequences. The majority, on the other hand, recognizes that full disclosure, including the names of recipients, their official positions, and the sums paid to them, can be harmful to U.S. foreign relations and jeopardize U.S. investments abroad.

Despite the accusation of its critics—and, indeed, of the moralists within the commission—the majority members do not believe that the SEC has a mandate "to enforce, even indirectly, through compulsory disclosure, all of the world's laws and all of its perceptions of morality and right conduct." As former chairman Ray Garrett said, "some forebearance not only seems implicit in our governing statutes, but also may be essential to enable us to do a competent job of investor protection." [3]

BUYING FAVORS

Bribery is an institutionalized fact of international business life. It is to be sure no more prevalent in other industrialized countries—Italy is an exception—than it is in the United States. Bribery is, however, pervasive throughout virtually the entire Third World of Latin America, the Middle East, Africa, and Asia. [4]

It has also appeared in the Soviet Union (where as a warning to other Soviet trade officials—and to foreign businessmen who deal with them—the former head of the furniture import corporation was recently executed by a firing squad for accepting $150,000 in bribes from a Swiss supplier), and in the Eastern Communist bloc (where, for example, Yugoslav officials doing business with West European firms demanded—and received—bribes, which were deposited in Swiss bank accounts).

In the morass of global palm greasing, a distinction must be made between two types of payoffs: the "lubrication" bribe and the "whitemail" bribe.

THE LUBRICATION BRIBE

The lubrication bribe usually involves payment of relatively small sums of "speed money" to make the wheels of administration turn more rapidly. In the days of the rule of the political boss and the dominance of the political machine in the big American cities, this kind of money transfer was known as "honest" graft. (This is not to suggest that bribes, big or small, are no longer familiar to American cities. Payoffs in New York City, for example, are said to be endemic.)

Third World countries are awash in administrative bribing. Payments are made to the customs official to accelerate his paperwork to allow a shipment of machinery, raw material, or semi-finished components to move from dock-side to plant. (There is, to be sure, a suspicion that the slowdown is designed to produce a payoff.) The gratuity is used to encourage a clerk in one of the ministries to reshuffle his papers to find an application—on file for months—for a construction permit. An under-the-table payment facilitates issuance of a permit to allow the entry of company personnel—an engineer, a cost accountant, a marketing specialist. A tip helps to obtain the requisite authorization for foreign exchange for needed imports or repatriation of dividends.

The lubrication bribe expedites clearances that ought to be made available to business enterprise as a matter of convenience but that in practice require a "token of appreciation." In the former British West African colonies, for example, the foreign firm that doesn't "dash" the local functionaries will eventually be unable to operate. The West African dash system of payoffs is so widespread that foreign companies treat it as a routine business expense. The ostensible reason for the ouster of the Nigerian regime led by Major General Yakubo Gowan by another army faction was that too many high officials had their fingers in dash. The new military regime has mounted a broad attack—so, too, had its predecessor—against corruption. In an unprecedented step for black Africa, the new military leadership has dismissed hundreds of civil servants and required all high-ranking military officers and civilian officials to disclose their finances.

Kenyan government officials are wont to request "contributions" from foreign business executives for hospitals, churches, and charities. In return, they promise smooth sailing in the establishment of a business or its unhampered continuance. When these requests are granted—not all are—they can sometimes run into six figures.

Elsewhere in East Africa, with the notable exception of Tanzania, bribery is so rampant that the elite class of government officials has earned the derisive Swahili term "Wabenzi." (*Wa* is a prefix that means group of people. *Benzi* is a root word coined from Mercedes Benz cars, the hallmark of virtually all elite Africans.)

Latin America is another world region in which the payoff is pervasive. Venality flourishes betcause of a symbiotic relationship between business enterprise and government. Businessmen perceive those in the seat of power in statist governments as the dispensers of privileges and exemptions. Most public officials see themselves in the same light.

The bribe—known variously as *mordida* ("the bite") in Mexico; *pajada* ("a piece of the action") in Honduras; *jeitinho* ("the fix") in Brazil—ensures, on the one hand, flexibility in the application of administrative discretion, and on the other hand, the opportunity for business growth in competition with state-owned corporations. In consequence, the private and public sectors are bound to each other by a profitable cash nexus.

The Confucian tradition. Graft, it should be remembered, has different moral sanctions in different cultures. Corruption in the Far East stems largely from the Confucian tradition, which countenanced the use by the world's first elite civil servants of public office for personal aggrandizement—acceptance of gratuities supplemented low government salaries. In Japan, and other Asian countries that were formerly British-ruled territories, *kumshaw* (literally "thank you"), "tea money," or an actual gift to an official symbolizes the difference in status between the one who does the asking and the one who confers the favor.

In passing, it should also be mentioned that in Malaysia and Singapore civil servants are expressly forbidden to accept gifts or other perquisites of office. The climate of honesty created by Prime Minister Lee Kuan Yew—an authentic Chinese Puritan—in his island city-state causes even a policeman to think twice before accepting a cigarette from the owner of an illegally parked bicycle. Lee has pointedly admonished his Third World colleagues, particularly those from Africa, that "instead of dams and power stations, roads and railways, we have Rolls Royces and executive mansions, not to mention golden bedsteads." But in nearby Indonesia, high-ranking military officers and civilian officials in the government accept gifts in cash or stock in foreign companies as the quid pro quo for helping them "adjust" to the Indonesian business climate.

India is, perhaps, a classic illustration of an environment in which the lubrication bribe is indispensable for the survival of private business enterprise —indigenous and foreign. In India's socialist-oriented society, the civil servant is vested with discretionary power to grant or withhold permits for almost every commercial activity. Hence, at every stage of the administrative process there is scope for bribery. "Not a single file can move if the clerk's palm is not greased," a correspondent for the *Hindustan Times* once wrote —before India's press was muzzled by Madame Gandhi's authoritarian rule.

India's political "democracy" was built on corruption. Payoffs, shakedowns, and gaining access to illegal wealth—known as "black money"—occupies much of the time and energy of the government's ruling Congress Party. Bribery of government officials bought official tolerance of hoarding, adulterating, smuggling, and black-marketing.

The corruption factor has to be taken into account before a management decision is reached on penetrating the Indian market. Once a foreign company is established there, only the corporate Quixote will believe it can remain outside the mainstream of corruption with which Indians have lived for centuries.

The envelope. Earlier it was suggested that Italy is *sui generis* among the European countries in the use of the lubrication bribe. Italy's colossal bureaucracy makes the employment of *bustarella* (an envelope stuffed with varying amounts of 10,000 lire notes, each worth about $17) mandatory for the Italian business enterprise—and, indeed, for the citizen who can afford it —to overcome the chronic governmental chaos.

In his illuminating book *The Italians,* Luigi Barzini points out that his country's regulatory structure is a "tropical tangle of statutes, rules, norms, regulations, customs, some hundreds of years old, some voted last week by Parliament and signed this very morning by the President." [5] Within the vast, inchoate Rome bureaucracy no one knows for certain which laws are still valid and what some of them really mean.

This Byzantine web of statutory ambiguities, inconsistencies, and contradictions—all subject to the interpretation of poorly chosen, wretchedly underpaid and badly organized bureaucrats, whose primary loyalties are to the political parties and only secondarily to their government—can only be made to function by means of *bustarella.* In other words, corruption makes an inefficient and chaotic social system work.

THE WHITEMAIL BRIBE

Though there may be official tolerance in Washington for the lubrication bribe, there is a definite reluctance to condone the whitemail variety. The reason is not hard to find. The latter type of payoff generally involves an elaborate system for concealing the use of large sums of corporate cash. These payments are invariably accompanied by false accounting, fictitious bookkeeping entries, and bogus documentation. To generate the cash needed for the big payoff, it is usually necessary to resort to legerdemain transfers of funds between subsidiaries, employment of dubious consultants, and routing money through overseas bank accounts. In a word, the corporation's internal system of financial accountability is distorted by a small number of high-ranking managers, whose actions are cloaked in secrecy.

When viewed in the abstract, such transfers of corporate funds are indefensible. When seen in the context in which they take place, however, there may be a reasonable doubt as to whether to condemn them.

In the discussion that follows, three major SEC prosecutions are analyzed. This will serve to place in perspective the "pressures"—psychological, cultural, and political—which impelled a course of conduct now under criticism.

The banana tax: the case of United Brands. To offset soaring petroleum prices that were bankrupting their economies, the seven banana-producing countries of the Western Hemisphere, under the initiative of Costa Rica's outgoing president, Jose Figueres, and the Marxist-oriented Panamanian dictator, General Omar Torrijos, met in Panama in March 1974. Their objectives were to establish a "banana cartel," modeled after the Organization of Petroleum Exporting Countries (OPEC); raise the export price of bananas, unchanged for about twenty years; and break the control over banana production held by the big three fruit companies—United Brands Company (whose Central American banana division is the old United Fruit Company), Standard Fruit Company (a subsidiary of Castle & Cook, Inc.), and Del Monte Corporation.

Present at the Panama meeting were Colombia, Ecuador, Guatemala, Costa Rica, Honduras, Nicaragua, and their host, Panama. Together, these seven countries account for 80 percent of the world's banana production—250 million of the 350 million crates of bananas exported annually to the consumer markets of the United States, Canada, and Europe.

The "Saudi Arabia" of the banana-producing countries is Ecuador, the world's largest source of supply. Hence, Ecuador's adherence to the proposed price-fixing-production-curtailing pact was crucial. Ecuador refused to join the other producing countries in imposing an export tax of $1 a crate. She agreed, however, to raise her own export tax from 21 cents per crate to 41 cents, but almost immediately made the decision inoperative by announcing that exporters would be compensated by 50 percent of the value of the tax. Moreover, Ecuador declined to meet with the other producing countries at the next scheduled meeting (to be held at the end of March in Bogota, Columbia). Ecuador's refusal to participate with the other banana producers in an OPEC-inspired cartel doomed the idea of a Union of Banana Exporting Countries.

The "banana war"—as it was called in the Central American press—was reduced to individual country skirmishes. Costa Rica, Honduras, and Panama began negotiating their own tax increases—Guatemala, Colombia, and Nicaragua had none in effect at that time—with the big three multinational companies.

In April, Honduras announced an export tax of 50 cents on each forty-pound box of bananas, although it was not to take effect until June. The proposed tax would have increased United Brands' costs by some $15 million.

The new levy could not have come at a worse time for United Brands:

- The banana market in the U.S. was already oversupplied as a result of the industry's increased shipments during the early months of 1974.
- Hurricane Fifi had swept through Central America during the fall, severely damaging 85 percent of the company's own and associated producer acreage in Honduras. The loss of crops and facilities amounted to $19.5 million.
- The John Morrell meat-packing division of United Brands had sustained a $6 million loss from increased cattle-feeding costs.
- Combined Central American banana export taxes, increased labor costs, and other charges amounted to around $18.8 million.

The company reported an aggregate loss of $43.6 million and was forced to omit dividend payments on its preferred and preference stock. To cover these losses and to provide the company with additional working capital, Eli Black, then chairman, was obliged to sell United Brands 62 percent interest in Foster Grant, Inc., a sunglasses and plastics producer.

The bribe. In August 1974, Black wrote to his shareholders that the Panamanian tax of $1 per box, the Costa Rican tax of 25 cents a box, and the Honduran tax of 50 cents "violated and breached the provisions of existing agreements with these countries." He also said that the company realized the need of the banana-producing countries for additional revenue, and he intended to negotiate with them to arrive at a reasonable formula.

Later that same month the company announced that it had reached an understanding with Honduras whereby the export tax would be reduced to 25 cents a crate, with yearly escalations beginning in 1975 depending upon market conditions. The reduction in the impost represented a saving of $7.5 million. The price for the favorable governmental action was the payment to Honduran officials of $2.5 million.

In September the company arranged for the deposit in Swiss banks for the account of designated officials of the Honduran government—understood to be the former president and the minister of economy—the sum of $1.25 million, to be deposited in the spring of 1975. Corporate funds for the initial payoff were obtained from United Brands' subsidiaries. Fictitious entries were made in the company's books to conceal the sources and the use of the funds. [6]

Four months later, early in February 1975, Eli Black jumped to his death from his forty-fourth floor office in mid-Manhattan. The SEC began looking into the operations of the company following the suicide of United Brands' chairman, a routine type of investigation when there is an unusual death of a chief executive. Also looking into the affairs of United Brands Company were several members of the staff of the *Wall Street Journal*. Their story of the payment of the bribe was published on April 25—well before the SEC had completed its investigation.

With the fat thus in the fire, United Brands' board of directors issued a statement that they had belatedly learned of the payoff, which had been authorized by its late chairman, but which they had not approved.

The evidence is conflicting on whether the initiative for the bribe came from the company or from Honduran officials. Several high-ranking executives of the banana division have asserted that they were solicited by the former Honduran minister of economy for a $5-million payoff in return for a tax reduction—a charge that is denied by Abraham Bennaton, the former minister. Another version has the late Eli Black himself meeting with former president Lopez and making the proposal for the bribe—an allegation that is vehemently denied by the Black family.

Such is the bare recital of the events that rocked the company's management and board of directors, induced the suicide of its former chairman, caused a *coup d'etat* in Honduras by junior army officers that ousted President-General Oswaldo Lopez Arellano, and produced a change in the ownership pattern of the company's investment in Honduras and a multiplicity of lawsuits by the federal government and stockholders. (As if the company did not have enough troubles, it has been charged by the European Economic Community with antitrust violations.)

There is an aspect of Greek tragedy in this human drama. Eli Black was a rabbi by training and a businessman by inclination. A sensitive man with a social conscience, Black believed that he could straddle the spiritual and temporal worlds and do justice to both. Events—his own actions—proved him wrong.

Under his leadership, the company sought to eradicate the lingering image of the old United Fruit Company as a swashbuckling corporate pirate. Black sought to promote community development programs for the people of the region in home improvement, nutrition, child care, education, and other fields of social betterment.

For the moralist on the sidelines, the payment of a bribe is a simple issue: it is improper conduct and therefore must be condemned. Yet to the individual at the head of a corporation, under relentless pressure from stockholders and the financial community to increase earnings and his own reputation as a successful professional manager hanging on the outcome, a payoff, though deplorable, may offer a means to buy time while the company recovers from a temporary illness.

The question remains: were United Brands' investors really benefited by telling the world of the payment of a bribe?

Keeping friends and influencing people: the case of the oil companies' political contributions. Congressional hearings as a rule are not intended to serve as political science seminars. More often they are a legislative version of an American morality play. At the raised dais—now familiar to millions of American television viewers of the Senate Watergate hearings—sit the "tribunes of the people," the forces of "good." Seated below them are the witnesses, who, if they are executives of the big oil companies, occupy a place equivalent to that of Satan in medieval times.

Conforming to this stereotype were the public hearings held in the ornate Senate Caucus Room in mid-July 1975 by the Senate subcommittee investigating overseas payoffs by multinational corporations. The substantial contributions to the Italian political parties made by the Italian affiliates of Exxon Corporation and Mobil Oil Corporation were excoriated by the subcommittee's chairman, Senator Frank Church (Democrat, Idaho), as "bribes" for obtaining special favors. Not so, responded Mobil Oil's executive vice president for international operations; his company's political contributions were made "to support the democratic process." In an Italian context, the distinction may have been without a difference, except that in the American news lexicon, "bribe" is a pejoratively loaded word.

Few high-ranking business executives are endowed with the politician's contrived bonhomie and the forensic skills needed for dominating a legislative committee before whom they appear as witnesses—usually reluctant witnesses. Most end their ordeal wearing a dunce cap. Yet the experienced New York or Washington political law firm can usually arrange helpful stage props for its clients.

Instead of acting the part of "culprits"—political contributions by corporations are not forbidden under Italian law—the witnesses from Exxon and Mobil, nudged by leading questions planted with friendly members of the panel, could have used the hearings as a forum for a realistic discussion of the political facts of life in Italy. They could have shown that:

- Nearly all Italian politicians and certainly all the political parties (from the ruling Christian Democrats to the coalition groupings of Social Democrats, Socialists, Republicans, and Neo-Fascists to the Communists) are tied to the *bustarella* system. (Some knowledgeable observers believe that the Communists are indirectly financed by Italian big business through the brokerage fees earned in arranging deals with Communist bloc countries. The Socialists are said to earn similar fees for arranging ventures with Yugoslavia and Communist China.) [7]
- Members of Parliament are expected to kick back up to 50 percent of their salaries—about $2,000 per month—to their respective parties. With the galloping inflation, the high cost of living, and large families to support, most of the deputies and senators have to "put the arm" on the one certain source of supplemental income—business enterprise, both domestic and foreign.
- The larger parties run schools and youth centers, publish newspapers and journals, and maintain their own publishing houses for the printing of party

books, pamphlets, and tracts. Most, if not all, of these activities operate at a loss. The scale of election spending—by Italian standards—is massive.

- The losses are made up in large part by the private and state-owned corporations—the Fiats, Olivettis, Pirellis, Montedisons, ENI (State Hydrocarbon Corporation—the huge state oil company), IRI (Industrial Reconstruction Institute), *Confindustria* (General Confederation of Italian Industry), and the Italian subsidiaries and affiliates of major international corporations from Western Europe, Japan, and the United States. (In 1974 a law was enacted by the Italian Parliament granting public subsidies of about $75 million annually for all political parties. The 1974 law continues to recognize the legality of contributions made by corporations, but for the first time requires disclosure of the recipients of such contributions. Prior to this—by mutual understanding of donors and donees—it was the practice to conceal the names of the recipients. This led to disguising such payments on the corporate books so that they could not be identified by the prying eyes of the tax inspectors. In a candid letter to his fellow Exxon employees, dated July 14, 1975, the now retired chairman, J. K. Jamieson, acknowledged that adherence to this practice by Exxon's affiliate, Esso Italiana, was a "mistake.")
- Oil is big business in Italy. She has the largest refining capacity in Western Europe. Middle East oil is processed not only for the large Italian market but for the other Common Market countries as well. The Italian affiliates of the international oil companies are important sources of political contributions to the parties. For example, from 1963 until 1972, Exxon contributed $29 million to the major non-Communist parties, mainly through party-owned newspapers. Contributions by foreign business enterprises (such as Esso Italiana claims to have made) to newspapers owned by the big private or state corporations—*La Stampa* (by Fiat), *Il Giorno* (by ENI), *La Notta* and *Il Giornale* (by Pesanti and Italcementi)—also end up in the coffers of the political parties.
- The Italian business community supports the political parties—even the powerful Communist Party as insurance against the not-too-distant day when it will share in or take over the Rome government—for the same pragmatic reasons as obtain among the other parliamentary democracies of Europe and Japan and in the United States: to influence party attitudes and to exert leverage over party votes. But in Italy there is also an additional reason for contributing to the parties; the secretaries-general of the major parties have more influence with the rank and file of the bureaucracy (who are beholden to the parties for their part-time jobs) than the regular government ministries. In consequence, a telephone call from party headquarters works a miracle in cutting red tape.
- Political contributions to the major parties provide the leverage for the award of lucrative government contracts, public utility franchises, subsidies, protection against import competition, and other favors that a friendly

government can confer. (Exxon's controller, Archie Monroe, testified that his company's contributions were allocated to "categories relating to business objectives," such as efforts to reduce or defer taxes, obtain refinery licenses, win permission to import natural gas and secure favorable locations for service stations.)

Financing the Italian political parties has helped to keep the political damage to private business enterprise within tolerable limits, and through the majority ruling party—the Christian Democrats—for thirty years has ensured the preservation of the status quo—a condition that the Christian Democrats seem less and less able to continue as Italy is increasingly racked by civil violence and class warfare.

The moral—and, perhaps, the ultimate irony—of the presentation would have been the depiction of the plight of the oil companies after they ceased making any contributions to the political parties last year in the wake of an investigation of alleged bribery of Italian politicians.

With the goose no longer laying golden eggs, the Italian politicians applied their own pressure— they refused to grant authorization to the companies for price increases to reflect increased crude costs. The consequences were predictable: Profit margins were severely crimped; the affiliates piled up sizable losses; and several of the companies may be forced out of the Italian market.

The elicitation of these facts would have portrayed Italian politics as not greatly different from American politics. Special interest groups in Italy slip cash to politicians in the same way that milk producers in the United States, for instance, finance Democrats and Republicans to fix milk prices, or the unions finance Democrats to see things labor's way.

It is no secret that the subcommittee's chairman, Senator Church, a latter-day populist, attacks the multinational corporation because it is not an instrument of the political sovereignty of the state. For the doctrinaire populist and political moralist, as Professor Peter Drucker observes, "the crime of the multinational corporation is that it is not [also] an instrument of American morality." It eludes the populist critic that the multinational corporation cannot fulfill either of these functions because it operates in a myriad of cultures and under diverse environmental—economic, sociological, political, and governmental—constraints. In consequence, "it must fit itself . . . to the prevailing legal and moral beliefs of the political sovereignty in the country where it operates." [8]

An evangelical fervor that insists on carrying the torch of American moral values, albeit in disarray at home, into every foreign environment in which the U.S. international corporation does business will not everywhere be appreciated. In many countries, a display of American corporate righteousness will be resented as presumptuous. And to the crescendo of grievances, real or fancied, against the multinational corporation there will be added still another: "moral imperialism."

The shakedown. When does a donation to a political party cease to be a contribution and become extortion? When the individual making the request is the late S. K. Kim, financial chairman of South Korea's Democratic Republican Party. "He happens to be as tough a man as I've ever met. I have never been subjected to that kind of abuse," Bob R. Dorsey, chairman of Gulf Oil Corporation, told the Senate subcommittee on multinational corporations.

An American public that thought it had heard the last word on the rascality of its own politicians was given a behind-the-scenes glimpse of raw, Oriental political power, as Gulf's chairman described how he was strong-armed into making $4 million available to South Korea's ruling and governing party.

Dorsey testified that Kim had extracted the payments under "severe pressure" and under conditions that amounted to "what is basically blackmail." Kim's threats, Dorsey said, "left little to the imagination" as to what would happen to Gulf's $300 million investment, most of it in refining and petrochemicals, if "the company would choose to turn its back on the request.

Gulf gave the party $1 million in 1966, "based upon what I sincerely considered to be in the best interest of the company and its shareholders," Dorsey said. In 1970, Dorsey met personally with Kim, who demanded a payment of $10 million for the 1971 election campaign. "I had heated discussions with officials of the party and flatly rejected both the intensity of the pressure being applied and the amount demanded," he stated. Kim's $10 million was haggled down to $3 million.

Gulf's chairman informed the subcommittee that he was told "that all foreign companies in Korea were expected to contribute" to President Park's election campaign. He added that the political pressures in Korea were even more intense than those to which many American corporations were subjected during the traumatic and scarring 1972 American presidential election.

Foreign companies are particularly vulnerable to political intimidation from the ruling party, as most of them operate in joint ventures with Korean nationals. Many such ventures were begun with extensive government support and continue to obtain much of their business from the government. Moreover, many of the more important and larger enterprises are headed by Koreans who are close friends of President Park and who owe their positions —and affluence—to his patronage. Thus, Park Won-Suk, who heads Gulf's 50-percent-owned Korean Oil Company, is a former deputy director of the Korean central intelligence agency and a former Air Force chief of staff. The late S. K. Kim also owed his good fortune to President Park. Kim headed a group of companies, which included South Korea's largest cement manufacturer, a profitable trading company, and an influential news service, Orient Press. He also was president of the Korea Chamber of Commerce and Industry.

It is said that, when Kim was a businessman on the political "giving end," he himself balked when requested to make an especially heavy contribution.

Another Korean businessman tells of the treatment meted out to Kim for his recalcitrance. One of the president's intimate aides took him to the top of Namsan Mountain, the peak that overlooks Seoul, and in that rarified atmosphere, pulled every hair from Kim's greatly prized moustache. Kim and the other members of the Seoul business community got the message.

The ruling Democratic Republican Party used the Korean nationals to exert leverage on the foreign partners in the joint ventures. The Koreans were threatened with economic reprisals, such as tax audits, difficulties in clearing goods into customs, refusal of permits or the repatriation of dividends by the foreign partners, and other enumerated harassments, not excluding nationalization.

The Koreans transmitted their fears to their foreign associates. Some of the local foreign managers, exercising their own discretion, refused to comply. They were usually with smaller companies. In some instances, where the Korean partner had control over the purse, the foreign partners learned of the contribution after it had been made. (Thus, the Korean partners of General Motors Korea paid $250,000 to officials of the party, for which General Motors seeks reimbursement on the grounds that it had not authorized the payment.)

Most of the foreign partners, however, concluded that compliance was the better part of valor. Political intimidation produced the cash "donations," "gifts," "contributions" (to one of President Park's favorite projects, a technical high school in his home town), and the "half-compulsory" contributions (in the phrase used by the incumbent party chairman, Park Joon Kyu) for the "national defense fund" used to strengthen the fortifications at the 39th parallel and around Seoul. Over a period of six months, from the end of December 1973 to May 1974, about $40 million was bled from the business community for the national defense fund, according to the defense minister.

Some critics question whether the late Kim wasn't bluffing on the fate awaiting Gulf if its chairman had refused to submit to the political shakedown. Fortified by the judgment of hindsight, they contend that Gulf's shareholders did not receive full value for Dorsey's payoff in view of the Korean company's deteriorated financial position (it lost more than $6 million on its integrated petroleum operations in 1974 and is endeavoring to dispose of its interest in a naphtha cracking plant).

There is a short answer to the self-appointed keepers of the corporate conscience. Unlike Gulf's chairman, they weren't subjected to the late Kim's orchestration of pressures. And, if Kim had made good his threats, it would not have been their responsibility to face a questioning board of directors and a skeptical shareholders' meeting to explain how a $300 million investment was lost because of a loss of nerve.

Unlike the moralists in the media and among dissident church activists, Sister Jane Scully, president of Carlow College in Pittsburgh and a member of Gulf's board of directors, was able to visualize the complexities and dilemmas of applying ethical precepts in an amoral political environment. She aptly observed: "It troubles me that there are no easy answers."

The intermediary: the case of Northrup Corporation. Northrup utilized a battalion of political and commercial agents to promote procurement of its military aircraft by foreign governments. In the service of the company were such luminaries as a retired former chief of staff of the French Air Force and vice president of the French National Assembly, a World War II German Luftwaffe combat ace, a former German ambassador to Iran and member of the *bundestag,* a celebrated former CIA station chief with access to the royal monarchs of the Persian Gulf and Arabian Peninsula, and ubiquitous Swiss lawyers who roamed the European corridors of power. In all, according to a report prepared for the board of directors by the intenational accounting firm of Ernst & Ernst, Northrup employed during the period 1971 to 1973 between 400 and 500 consultants and agents, including a shadowy Swiss-based corporate sales agency.

In an apt and striking phrase, Northrup's president, Thomas V. Jones, described the agent as "the stethoscope on the workings of government." He is able to consummate government sales by promoting, again in Jones's words, "broad and high-level support at political levels that are important to the selection of any major government procurement."

Though the agent is used to influence sales, the concern of the investigators was Northrup's use of payoffs to overseas government officials to obtain its sales. A case in point is Northrup's Saudi Arabian agent, Adnan Khashoggi, who also provides marketing and consulting services for Lockheed, Chrysler, and Raytheon. Northrup documents show that it paid $450,000 to Khashoggi, who claimed that the money was demanded by two Saudi generals during negotiations for a multimillion dollar sales of fighter aircraft. Khashoggi has denied funneling the money to the Saudi officers.

The SEC's investigation into Northrup's domestic political contributions had disclosed that some $30 million in fees had been paid to overseas agents and consultants. The SEC contends that the company did not keep adequate records to "insure that such transfers and disbursements were actually made for the purposes indicated." In other words, Northrup had not identified on its corporate books the receipts of under-the-table payments.

It is blinking at reality to suppose that sophisticated aerospace managements are not aware that some portion of the fees paid to agents is used for payoffs to government officials to secure favorable decisions on government procurement of aircraft and military hardware. Northrup's payment to the two Saudi generals was in the form of non-interest-bearing advances on commissions due Khashoggi. And in a parallel investigation of the use of commissions for payoffs, Lockheed Aircraft Corporation conceded that "of the total commissions and other payments made during the period 1970 through June 29, 1975, at least 15 percent is known or thought to have flowed to foreign officials in a number of countries abroad." In all, Lockheed disbursed nearly $30 million to foreign officials and political parties for help in winning orders valued at more than $2 billion.

Yet for a principal to monitor how his agent uses his commissions—as the SEC believes is necessary—presents both legal and practical difficulties. The courts, for one thing, may be reluctant to require accountability from an agent on the expenditure of his fees because it would be a departure from the settled rule of common law that a principal is not responsible for the acts of his agent.

The other difficulty is probably more critical. Asking a successful agent to make a detailed accounting of his disbursements is apt to be rebuffed as none of the principal's business. A shrewd guess can be made of the direction of Adnan Khashoggi's commissions. He has built his Triad Group of companies into a $400 million multinational network of financial interests, with land, banking, and other holdings in the United States alone valued at roughly $100 million. But seeking similar information from other agents is a guaranteed way to lose their services. This contingency is immediately relevant for the Middle East market, probably the fastest growing and potentially the most lucrative in the world.

The go-between. The SEC is a domestically oriented institution. Its preoccupation since its inception forty years ago has been with the U.S. securities markets. Staff members are not expected to be international business experts. Yet the investigation into overseas payoffs requires a broader angle of vision of other cultures and customs than the training and experience of the lawyers of the enforcement division allow. The projection of American cultural or moral standards into other environments is intellectually confusing. And a perception of Middle East business as if it were an extension of American business is bound to lead to distortions in judgment. This is especially true when the role of the go-between is misconceived.

Islamic scholar Raphael Patai describes the compelling need for the services of the intermediary in the Moslem world, still gripped by the constraints of a traditional society, in order:

> not to be cheated in the marketplace, in locating and acquiring a job, in resolving conflict and litigation, in winning a court decision, in speeding government action, and in establishing and maintaining political influence and bureaucratic procedures, in finding a bride and, in fact, for the social scientist to locate and convince respondents to give an interview. [9]

Culture bridge. Although many Middle East rulers—and their Western-trained young technocrats—have superficially adapted their thinking to the concepts of the West, they are still suspicious of and uneasy with financial and business transactions undertaken with foreigners. The heads of the emergent Arab conglomerate family enterprises, particularly those with Western affiliations, and the older Maronite Christian Lebanese families, with their network of international banking and commercial connections, play an important role in providing a sense of confidence for the traditional oil-rich sheiks.

In addition, the commercial and banking families are the repositories of economic, financial, and political intelligence with respect to the individual countries, their rulers, and governing political factions. In this respect, the heads of the great Arab clans are equivalent to the West's international banks, local chambers of commerce and trade associations, and the professional groups (lawyers, accountants, and consultants) as information networks.

If the Middle East's intermediaries didn't exist, they would have to be invented. For the Western business executive, the intermediaries:

- Overcome the formidable language barrier.
- Penetrate the orbit of Moslem power. "Foreign firms entering the market," explains Robert E. Bernard, executive vice president of Kaiser Engineers in charge of international operations, "have difficulty getting to the handful of key people who make the decisions." [10] The intermediary, however, knows who among the palace courtiers has the ruler's ear and which ministers truly hold the levers of decision. (It was Adnan Khoshoggi who arranged Lockheed's first sale of C-130 Hercules transport aircraft to the Saudi air force in 1965. Since then Lockheed has been awarded multimillion-dollar contracts for the sale of radar and communications systems, Jetstar private aircraft, and most recently four Tristars to the Saudi airline.)
- Sandpaper the typical American business abrasiveness into acceptable Arab diplomatic verbiage—an important consideration in a culture that places a high value on the "spoken" word.
- Provide "thinking time" for the parties to consider all the implications involved in the proposed transaction. By the same token, if, upon reflection, it seems desirable for one of the parties to withdraw from the negotiations the presence of the intermediary allows this to be accomplished without incurring a loss of face.
- Short-circuit the Arab passion for verbosity and lyrical hyperbole.
- Perform the contract haggling—a ritualized form of "horse trading" in the Middle East (and other world regions) with which most U.S. executives are not psychologically attuned.
- Bear the brunt of attending the interminable talk sessions, which are at odds with the Western structured time frame.
- Obtain from each side the concessions that enable the parties to strike a bargain.
- Play down the U.S. businessman's obsession with a written contract, which to the traditional Arab mind is an affront to the honor of a commitment conveyed by the spoken word and sealed with a handclasp. (The typical voluminous contract, drafted by lawyers schooled in the American legal tradition of anticipating every conceivable breach or default and bristling with covenants invoking the right to litigation, is an anomaly in virtually

every legal environment save the Soviet Union, which, ironically, shares the American *idee fixe* of a prolix legal instrument.)

In sum, in dealing with Western businessmen, the traditional centers of Arab power and wealth are more comfortable with an intermediary of the same culture, who practices the same religion and shares a mutual pride in the renaissance of Moslem world influence. Where the intermediary has himself been exposed to Western education and influence and is involved in joint business undertaking with foreigners, he serves to unite the West's pyschological attitudes and cultural preconceptions with his own appreciation of local customs, negotiating habits, and sociological and political constraints.

Servant of the ruler. Consider Mehdi al-Tajir, one of the Middle East's leading middlemen. [11] A Bahraini-born Arab of an old and wealthy trading family, al-Tajir, like other well-to-do Bahrainis, was educated in England. His personal wealth is reputed to eclipse Khashoggi's. Al-Tajir is not only a capitalist-entrepreneur in his own right, but he is also an official of Dubai and the United Arab Emirates (a cluster of seven desert sheikdoms on the Persian Gulf-Arabian Peninsula, formerly known as the Trucial States). Al-Tajir acts as financial advisor to his ruler, Rashid bin Said al-Maktoum; he is head of the Office of the Ruler, the administrative office of the government, and is Director of Petroleum Affairs of Dubai. He also acts as the financial advisor to Sheik Zayed, ruler of Abu Dhabi, who is president of the emirates and the real power of the U.A.E. Al-Tajir is the U.A.E.'s ambassador to London—the emirates have had close financial ties with the City and political relations with Whitehall for nearly a century—and he is Ambassador-at-Large to the European Economic Community.

In sum, not only does Mehdi al-Tajir have personal entree to the centers of political and financial power in the Middle East and the West, but he is the link between the oil-rich emirates and the outside world. Al-Tajir is obviously "the man to see" for access to the Middle East's enormous pool of self-generating petrodollars, currently estimated at between $85 and $100 billion.

In the listening posts at the trade and entrepot centers as well as in Beirut, the financial capital of the Middle East (until the Christian-Moslem civil war made a shambles of the city), it is widely believed that al-Tajir was the man Boeing saw for effectuating its recent sales of 747's to Syria and Egypt. The company denies any such connection. Curiously, other U.S. firms that have retained al-Tajir to assist them in establishing a foothold in the area likewise swear they never heard of him. Yet by a strange coincidence, Syria bought over $100 million worth of Boeing's jets, the sale was financed by Dubai, and al-Tajir handled the negotiations. A similar procedure was followed in the May 1975 sale of $60 million in Boeing aircraft to Egyptair.

"I don't know what Mehdi al-Tajir got out of it," says a State Department

Foreign Service officer, "but I'd be willing to bet he got something." The word is that he received $22 million, 15 percent of the contract price.

Corporate baksheesh. The Mehdi al-Tajirs, Adnan Khashoggis, and other major Middle East intermediaries furnish their Western principals with vital supportive services. But they do something more to earn their handsome fees: they supply the magic elixir that makes certain any deal they handle will materialize.

It should be borne in mind that hundreds of years of Ottoman rule have stamped the contemporary Arab world with the dry rot of corruption. The go-between facilitates his—and his principal's—work by the judicious dispensation of *baksheesh*—a fact of cultural life without any of the West's overtones of impropriety.

The funds used for such payments are frequently paid by the customer to the seller's agent and are included in the purchase price. Or they are paid (as was done by Northrup and Lockheed) to the agent and transferred by him to the recipient of the payoff. In other situations, the local agent inflates the bid price and skims off the difference between the original price and his markup to cover the payment of bribes. In Mexico, for example, the "coyotes" —the sobriquet applied to the lawyer-politicians and other middlemen with government connections—utilize this technique for the payment of *mordida*.

Unlike the officials of the SEC's enforcement division, the ranking civilian officials of the Department of Defense are attuned to diverse overseas environments. It is not surprising, therefore, that in the spring of 1974 an official of the Defense Security Assistance Agency—the arms sales organization of the Pentagon—should address the Electronics Industry Association on the topic, "Agents' Fees in the Middle East." With a realism born of experience the speaker described how obtaining aircraft contracts involved the use of *baksheesh*—from the payment of substantial amounts of cash to the rent-free use of a villa on the French Riviera to occupancy of a fashionable London flat complete with car, chauffeur, and servants.

Such is the way French and British orders are obtained. The French and British aerospace industries are "masters in dealing through agents," the speaker observed. "They have no compunctions in agreeing to excessive fees, if, in the final analysis the sale is consummated," he said.

Though prominently featured in the headlines, Northrup is in reality only a minor player in the high stakes being played in the Middle East. Arms sales to the area—$8.4 billion for 1974–75—are probably Secretary of State Kissinger's most useful diplomatic currency for the attainment of this nation's strategic objectives in this critical world region. Not only are military sales important in redressing the balance of trade and for paying the cost of imported oil, but they enable the Department of Defense to maintain a technologically advanced arms industry with a minimum of subsidy.

The Northrup case underscores the difficulties involved in coming to grips with overseas payoffs, Not only are they deeply embedded in the Middle East's business and cultural environments, but they are inextricably tied to military sales now used as a legitimate means for the furtherance of competing foreign policies of the Soviet Union, Mainland China, France, Britan, Sweden, and the United States.

POLICY CONSIDERATIONS

Out of the welter of charges, innuendoes, headlines, congressional moral indignation, self-righteous media sermons, and corporate *mea culpa* breast-beating, a number of policy proposals have emerged to deal with overseas payoffs.

Corporate action. There are, to be sure, companies whose managements have successfully resisted whitemail solicitations by government officials and politicians. Such companies have recognized that payoffs, though temporarily relieving political pressures, may create even bigger problems later. The big payoff is not likely to be a one-time transaction; it is part of a way of life. And the ante is apt to be raised by another ruling group or political party upon discovering the sums paid to its predecessors, as with Gulf Oil and the Democratic Republican Party of South Korea.

A high-technology company with a commanding position in the market—IBM is an example—can turn down a venal official and make its "no" stick. But other, less fortunate firms, which have sought to follow the book of Scriptures, have lost out to competitors—U.S. and foreign—whose punctilio of conduct was not above that of the marketplace.

Companies whose superior technology or engineering capabilities place them in a privileged position to resist extortionate demands for payoffs can let it be known that at home and abroad they compete on product quality, price, delivery, and financing—not in the purchase of politicians. In the business world, as elsewhere, the crowd follows a leader.

But what of the companies—numbered in the thousands—whose size and market position prevent them from adopting a bold moral stance? These companies are impaled on the horns of a dilemma. If they adhere to ethical precepts and decline to pay off or buy their way into a contract, competitors from countries more tolerant of the practice will eliminate them from important markets. The ultimate victims of righteous conduct will be the workers who are laid off and stockholders whose dividends are reduced or eliminated. If these companies pay off in order to remain in an overseas market, they face exposure by the SEC or a congressional committee, or both. The resultant publicity may trigger retaliatory legal action—or even expropriation of an overseas investment.

A resolution of the dilemma might be for managements whose firms risk the loss of markets to tell their stockholders how much of their money is spent on payoffs each year to remain competitive. To be sure, the practice of making under-the-table payments is not thereby eliminated, but neither is it concealed. Guidelines for the partial disclosure of overseas payments now in preparation by the SEC (but not released at this writing) may facilitate such voluntary disclosures to stockholders.

A logical extension of such an approach by management would be for the stockholders, and the company's employees, to express their views on whether the practice of making payoffs should be continued or discontinued. If the practice is to be curtailed, the parties directly affected will have determined that they are willing to suffer the consequences of reduced earnings.

State Department action. The U.S. international corporation should not have to serve as a milk cow to overseas politicians—augmenting personal incomes, financing election campaigns, and setting up "escape funds," deposited in Swiss banks, for use in the event of a political disaster. The Department of State can play a decisive role in the eradiction of overseas payoffs by making it known that the diplomatic shield of the U.S. government will protect U.S.-based firms that are the targets of extortionate demands.

Even a government riddled with corruption has its *amour propre* touched when an American ambassador can point to a specific official—or officials—who are on the take. For the honest official who needs personal financial assistance or funds to arrange a "safe haven"—examples include Third World chiefs of state, prime ministers, and dictators—U.S. ambassadors rarely decline to help a supplicant. [12]

Legislative action. Some members of Congress have proposed the enactment of legislation making it a crime for a U.S. corporation to make payoffs to foreign officials or to contribute to overseas political parties. The proponents believe that such legislation will, among other things, help U.S. managers ward off extortion and deter them from initiating bribes.

Restrictive legislation, to be sure, can provide ersatz morality. But the baneful effects of such a law, if enacted, far outweigh its benefits—if any. A law that puts a brake on permissible business conduct abroad can be just as mischievous as a foreign policy that presupposes that it has a monopoly on morality. Each contains the ingredients for becoming quixotic or obnoxious. And for this reason, the Department of State opposes enactment of the proposed legislation.

Enforcement of extraterritorial legislation—and that is precisely what a congressional ban against overseas payoffs would be—has in the recent past involved the United States, and the U.S. overseas subsidiaries and their directors, in unpleasant controversies. The extraterritorial application of American antitrust concepts is not everywhere accepted as sound economic policy or a moral blessing.

A British court refused to enforce an order issued by a U.S. District Court that a British company grant exclusive patent licenses to another British company. Swiss officials objected to an attempt by a U.S. District Court to extend the reach of the Sherman Act to the Swiss watch industry. And a decree issued by a U.S. District Court aroused Canadian resentment because it had ordered the dissolution of a Canadian patent pool, whose participants included General Electric, Westinghouse, and Phillips, while directing the licensing of others.

Enforcement of the Trading with the Enemy Act—directed mainly against trade with Mainland China prior to the Nixon policy of *rapprochement*—brought U.S. overseas subsidiaries into conflict during the 1950s and 1960s with the governments of Britain, Belgium, Canada, and France. More recently, the Argentine government let it be known that, if the Argentine subsidiaries of General Motors, Ford, and Chrysler were prevented from exporting cars and trucks to Cuba under the U.S. embargo against trade with the Castro regime, they would be nationalized.

In December 1974, Litton Industries directed its Canadian subsidiary to cancel a contract for the sales of office furniture to the Cuban government, after learning that the proposed transaction was in violation of the United States' embargo policy. Litton's action was denounced by Alistair Gillespie, Canadian Minister of Trade, who said, "I consider this action an intolerable interference and a form of corporate colonialism."

In sum, a restrictive law against overseas payoffs by U.S. companies is not only difficult to enforce, but it is also self-defeating. U.S. companies would be displaced from lucrative markets because foreign competitors were not similarly restrained; the law would be resented as an interference with companies domiciled in host countries and subject to their—not U.S.—national laws; and finally, such extraterritorial legislation would be regarded as a shining example of hypocrisy by the United States, whose own household is scarcely a paragon of moral rectitude.

Agreement with other industrialized nations. A more fruitful approach than unilateral action by the United States is for the State Department to enlist the other industrialized nations to enter into an informal understanding to restrain *all* firms from making payoffs to the officials of foreign governments. A small beginning might be made in the area of military sales.

A precedent for such informal international action (which obviates the impractical treaty or convention approach) exists in the international alignment of export credits granted to the Soviet Union and the Eastern European Communist bloc countries. The *Union D'Assureurs des Credits Internationaux,* headquartered in Berne, consists of some twenty-three governments and private credit insurance organizations from eighteen countries. The rules of the association amount to no more than a loosely drawn gentlemen's agreement, without binding legal force. Yet the "Berne Union," since its establishment in 1934, has provided a reasonably effective forum for the coordination of international credit insurance.

Code of Conduct for Multinational Corporations and Third World Countries. UN Ambassador Daniel Moynihan (who essays the role of a Socratic gadfly to the Third World) might remind his ambassadorial colleagues at the United Nations that just as it takes two to tango, it also takes two to bribe.

As the Third World is the heartland of "grease," he could inquire if the governments of Africa, Asia, and Latin America are agreeable to have included in a UN Code of Conduct for Multinational Corporations a provision that foreign investors should neither make nor be pressured into making payoffs to government officials, or to politicians and their parties.

Though Ambassador Moynihan's masters at the State Department are not likely to permit him to lay such a suggestion—even though made with tongue in cheek—before his UN colleagues, the articulation of the idea would have a salutory effect. It would strip away the rhetorical pretentiousness of Third World diplomats, whose oratical self-righteousness disguises the blatant corruption of so many of their leaders and elite peers at home.

REFERENCES

[1] Louis D. Brandeis, *Other People's Money* (New York: Frederick A. Stokes, 1914), p. 92.
[2] See William O. Douglas, *Go East Young Man* (New York: Random House, 1974), p. 272. Mr. Justice Douglas served as an SEC commissioner and chairman from 1936 to 1939.
[3] Ray Garrett, speech before the American Society of Corporate Secretaries, June 27, 1975.
[4] See, for example, Ronald Wraith and Edgar Simpkins, *Corruption in Developing Countries* (New York: W. W. Norton, 1964).
[5] Luigi Barzini, *The Italians* (New York: Grosset & Dunlap, 1964), pp. 108–109.
[6] The facts relating to the bribery of the Honduran officials are based on the complaint (Civil Action No. 75-0509) filed by the SEC in the United States District Court for the District of Columbia, April 9, 1975.
[7] Norman Kogan, *The Government of Italy* (New York: Thomas Y. Crowell, 1962), p. 66.
[8] Peter Drucker, *Management: Tasks, Responsibilities, Practices* (New York: Harper & Row, 1974), p. 360.
[9] Raphael Patai, *The Arab Mind* (New York: Charles Scribner's Sons, 1973), p. 232. See also, Roy Jastram, "The Nakado Negotiator," *California Management Review* (Winter 1974), pp. 88–90. (Professor Jastram describes the importance of the intermediary to the American businessman whose experience in international business is restricted to markets governed by the Anglo-American common law or the civil law system.)
[10] *Business Week* (28 May 1975), p. 52.

[11] For a vivid account of Mehdi al-Tajir, from which the writer has borrowed, see *Forbes* (15 June 1975); and also Ray Vicker, *The Kingdom of Oil: The Middle East, Its People and Its Power* (New York: Charles Scribner's Sons, 1974).

[12] Miles Copeland, *Without Cloak or Dagger* (New York: Simon & Schuster, 1974), p. 217.

READING 13

The Social Audit*

George A. Steiner

INTRODUCTION

The notion that a business should make a social audit of its activities was first proposed twenty years ago by Bowen [1953:155–156]. The idea lay dormant for almost as long. It has been only during the past two to three years that American corporations have thought seriously about social audits. It is a concept, however, which is evolving rapidly and the basic thrust today is for a requirement in the future that all corporations, especially the larger ones, prepare a social audit for public distribution.

WHAT IS A SOCIAL AUDIT?

There is probably agreement, at a high level of abstraction, that the business social audit is a report of social performance in contrast to the financial report which is concerned with economic performance. There consensus ends.

There are fundamentally two different types of social audits. One is an audit required by the government. A large corporation must account to the government for many different programs. For example, the FDA and the FTC require companies to report on the characteristics of products (e.g. tests of flammable textiles and drugs). The EPA has set air pollution standards against which corporations must report their experience. The Equal Employment Opportunity Commission requires submission of data on employment of members of minority groups. The Department of Labor, the Securities and Exchange Commission, and many other federal, state, and local agencies require reports. Many concern economic programs and many relate to social programs. The reporting is piecemeal, that is, one report is made at a time, covering only one subject.

The second type of social audit is that for programs voluntarily undertaken by a company. This is the type of audit which will be discussed here.

There are at least five different concepts of and approaches to making a business social audit [Corson and Steiner, 1974]. First is that which identifies expenditures which have been made for social programs and/or describes in qualitative terms what has been done. This approach is concerned only with cost inputs and not benefits or accomplishments. A second concept is the

* From *Business and Society*, 2nd ed. New York, Random House, 1971, Chapter 12.

valuation of human assets. This audit is concerned with valuations of the productive capability of the company's human organization, the valuation of shareholder loyalty and banker or community good will, customer loyalty, and so on [Likert, in Baumol, et al., 1970]. The Barry Corporation of Columbus, Ohio, is one of the very few companies that combines such valuations with traditional financial reports in its annual report to stockholders. A third concept is a "program management approach." Used by the Bank of America, this concept seeks to measure costs and effectiveness of those activities the company is engaged in voluntarily for social reasons [Butcher, 1972]. A fourth concept, which might be called "the inventory approach," involves the cataloguing of what the company is doing in each major social program or not doing in social areas where there is a social expectation that it should be active. For each identified area this approach calls for data and/or a narrative description of what is or is not being done. A final concept may be called the "balance sheet approach." This approach, which will be discussed later, tries to quantify values contributed to society (assets) and detriments to society for actions taken or not taken (liabilities) [Abt, 1972(A); Linowes, 1972].

The great majority of social audits which have been made and distributed currently are of the first or fourth types. A good illustration is the pamphlet published by General Motors Corporation in 1972 and 1973 called *Report on Progress in Areas of Public Concern.* A few cost/benefit type audits have been made but not widely publicized. The second and fifth types are more proposals than practice, although Abt Associates, Inc., made a fifth type audit [Abt, 1972(B)].

It is worth adding that while the name "social audit" is likely to stick, many businessmen prefer other terms, such as "social statement" or "social report" or "business response to social priorities" or "report on corporate societal policies and actions." The social audit carries with it a connotation of quantification which, as will be shown later, is not achievable today. The other terms imply a more descriptive or qualitative definition, which is more in line with today's state of the art.

WHY COMPANIES HAVE MADE SOCIAL AUDITS

In the social audit survey noted earlier [Steiner, 1973] the question was asked: "Has your company attempted within the period since January 1, 1972, to inventory or to assess what has been done in any of a series of 'activity fields'?" A surprising 76 percent of the respondents answered yes to the question. Of the companies responding affirmatively, 89 percent said they had examined more than one activity field. It should be noted that the words "social audit" were not used, although respondents knew that was what was meant. Also, the questionnaire contained the CED list of possible areas of business social action (see Exhibit 1) to which respondents could refer.

EXHIBIT 1

Spectrum of Current Corporate Activities

Economic Growth and Efficiency
- Increasing productivity in the private sector of the economy
- Improving the innovativeness and performance of business management
- Enhancing competition
- Cooperating with the government in developing more effective measures to control inflation and achieve high levels of employment
- Supporting fiscal and monetary policies for steady economic growth
- Helping with the post-Vietnam conversion of the economy

Education
- Direct financial aid to schools, including scholarships, grants, and tuition refunds
- Support for increases in school budgets
- Donation of equipment and skilled personnel
- Assistance in curriculum development
- Aid in counseling and remedial education
- Establishment of new schools, running schools and school systems
- Assistance in the management and financing of colleges

Employment and Training
- Active recruitment of the disadvantaged
- Special functional training, remedial education, and counseling
- Provision of day-care centers for children of working mothers
- Improvement of work/career opportunities
- Retraining of workers affected by automation or other causes of joblessness
- Establishment of company programs to remove the hazards of old age and sickness
- Supporting where needed and appropriate the extension of government accident, unemployment, health and retirement systems

Civil Rights and Equal Opportunity
- Ensuring employment and advancement opportunities for minorities
- Facilitating equality of results by continued training and other special programs

EXHIBIT 1 (continued)

Spectrum of Current Corporate Activities

- Supporting and aiding the improvement of black educational facilities, and special programs for blacks and other minorities in integrated institutions
- Encouraging adoption of open-housing ordinances
- Building plants and sales offices in the ghettos
- Providing financing and managerial assistance to minority enterprises and participating with minorities in joint ventures

Urban Renewal and Development

- Leadership and financial support for city and regional planning and development
- Building or improving low-income housing
- Building shopping centers, new communities, new cities
- Improving transportation systems

Pollution Abatement

- Installation of modern equipment
- Engineering new facilities for minimum environmental effects
- Research and technological development
- Cooperating with municipalities in joint treatment facilities
- Cooperating with local, state, regional, and federal agencies in developing improved systems of environmental management
- Developing more effective programs for recycling and reusing disposable materials

Conservation and Recreation

- Augmenting the supply of replenishable resources, such as trees, with more productive species
- Preserving animal life and the ecology of forests and comparable areas
- Providing recreational and aesthetic facilities for public use
- Restoring esthetically depleted properties such as strip mines
- Improving the yield of scarce materials and recycling to conserve the supply

Culture and the Arts

- Direct financial support to art institutions and the performing arts
- Development of indirect support as a business expense through gifts in kind, sponsoring artistic talent, and advertising

EXHIBIT 1 (continued)

Spectrum of Current Corporate Activities

Participation on boards to give advice on legal, labor, and financial management problems
Helping secure government financial support for local or state arts councils and the National Endowment for the Arts

Medical Care

Helping plan community health activities
Designing and operating low-cost medical-care programs
Designing and running new hospitals, clinics, and extended-care facilities
Improving the administration and effectiveness of medical care
Developing better systems for medical education nurses' training
Developing and supporting a better national system of health care

Government

Helping improve management performance at all levels of government
Supporting adequate compensation and development programs for government executives and employees
Working for the modernization of the nation's governmental structure
Facilitating the reorganization of government to improve its responsiveness and performance
Advocating and supporting reforms in the election system and the legislative process
Designing programs to enhance the effectiveness of the civil services
Promoting reforms in the public welfare system, law enforcement, and other major governmental operations

Source: CED, 1971: 31-40.

Each corporation was also asked why it had undertaken to assess and in some cases to report on its social performance. A list of possible purposes was provided and respondents were asked to check the purposes which best explained their making a social audit. The answers are shown in Table 12-1. It is noteworthy that the most significant reasons were to examine what the company was doing and to appraise performance. It is also noteworthy that the social audits were not undertaken to offset audits of self-appointed outside groups or to increase profits. Respondents were asked what other motives

TABLE 12-1
Purposes Which Led Companies to Make a Social Audit

	NUMBER	PERCENTAGE	RANK
1. To identify those social pressures which the company feels pressured to undertake	55	5	9
2. To identify those social programs which the company feels it ought to be pursuing	157	14	3
3. To examine what the company is actually doing in selected areas	194	17	1
4. To appraise or evaluate performance in selected areas	162	14	2
5. To determine areas where our company may be vulnerable to attack	101	9	5
6. To inject into the general thinking of managers a social point of view	122	11	4
7. To ensure that specific decision-making processes incorporate a social point of view.	95	8	6
8. To inform the public of what the company is doing	70	6	8
9. To offset irresponsible audits made by outside self-appointed groups	41	4	10
10. To meet public demands for corporate accountability in the social area	78	7	7
11. To increase profits	37	3	11
12. Other	17	2	12

NOTE: 196 companies checked one or more purposes.

prompted their making a social audit, and a wide variety of answers were received, including: "as a guide to internal management," "part of marketing strategy," "part of long-range planning," "to balance commitment to social activity against job activity," and "to make sure the company is fulfilling its promises and commitments."

THE SPECTRUM OF SOCIAL ACTIVITIES REPORTED

The survey showed that some companies were involved in every one of the CED social programs listed in Exhibit 1. In addition, respondents listed 46 additional programs which they said they were pursuing. Some of these were subsets of CED programs but there were also many new ones [Corson and Steiner, 1974].

Respondents were asked to identify those programs which involved significant commitments of money and/or personnel time. Those which ranked highest are shown in Table 12-2.

TABLE 12-2
Rank Order Listing of Activities Which Were Noted Most Frequently to Involve Significant Commitments of Money and/or Personnel Time

RANK *	NUMBER OF RESPONSES
1. Ensuring employment and advancement opportunities for minorities	244
2. Direct financial aid to schools, including scholarships, grants, and tuition refunds	238
3. Active recruitment of the disadvantaged	199
4. Improvement of work/career opportunities	191
5. Installation of modern pollution abatement equipment	189
6. Increasing productivity in the private sector of the economy	180
7. Direct financial support to art institutions and the performing arts	177
8. Facilitating equality of results by continued training and other special programs (civil rights and equal opportunity)	176
9. Improving the innovative and performance of business management	174
10. Engineering new facilities for minimum environmental effects	169

* Rank: (1) indicates highest commitment.

THRUST TOWARD THE ACCOUNTABILITY SOCIAL AUDIT

As noted in Table 12-2, a social audit can be designed to achieve a wide variety of purposes. Space does not permit an examination of what audits might include for different purposes or how they should be made. From a social point of view the most significant social audit is an accounting of social performance made to the constituents of the company. While most social audits up to the present time have not been directed at giving a comprehensive accounting to a wide audience, the pressures are in that direction. It is quite likely, if such pressures grow, that the major purpose of social audits in the future will be to make an accounting to various legitimate interests concerned with corporate social activities [Corson and Steiner, 1974].

By accountability is meant reporting on or explanation of the discharge of responsibilities. In the case of the social audit the accountability, of course, concerns social responsibilities.

There is little question that here is an escalation of demand that all institutions, especially the larger and more important ones, be accountable to society for the discharge of their responsibilities. This fundamental idea is not new. Financial reports of corporations, for instance, represent long-established statements of accountability. Reporting by corporations, however, is not keeping pace with responsibilities they have accepted let alone those which various groups think they may have. As a result demands for an accounting are outracing practice.

There is a thrust today to get corporations to report activities in the social area on a systematic and audited basis comparable to the annual financial report. I do not think this is likely to happen soon. This does not mean, however, that corporations cannot make an accounting to the public which will be generally accepted as fulfilling reporting requirements. Take philanthropy, for instance. I think the public will accept a simple statement by a company that it gave away so many dollars for different categories of activity. Acceptability of such an accounting will not depend upon sophisticated cost/benefit analyses.

My guess is that we shall have a great deal of experimentation with various reporting methods before corporations settle on any general patterns of response. The mere fact that corporations are making social audits, however, reflects an acceptance of the idea of social responsibilities. The fact that many corporations are making social audits public is a reflection of the acceptance of the idea of accountability. Neither one of these ideas has a crystal-clear concensus about meaning. The ideas and standard practice will evolve. In the meantime, there are a great many different ways a corporation can discharge its conceived obligations [Bauer and Fenn, 1972].

WHAT SHOULD THE ACCOUNTABILITY SOCIAL AUDIT ENCOMPASS?

It has been demonstrated sufficiently in preceding chapters, and it will be further documented in later chapters, that society's expectations have grown to include a wide range of amenities, products, services, and information for the government, employees, consumers, investors, and the community. If a social audit is to include all such activities, it embraces everything a corporation is doing or not doing. If the social audit is to verify the various costs entailed and the benefits produced, it becomes an impossible task and the information which might be produced, were a large company to try to make it available, would most likely be indigestible.

On the other hand, if a social audit includes only a cataloging of activities which top managers are interested in pursuing and/or those activities which might improve the public image of the company if publicized, the principal function of the social audit will not be performed. The corporation really would not be making an accounting of the extent to which its social performance met expectations of its constituencies.

The social audit should, like the financial audit, satisfy the informational needs of those it is designed to serve—employees, consumers, shareholders, the general public, opinion makers, reformers, and others. The needs, of course, will change from time to time. Basically they will include: (a) activities required by legislation (e.g., equal opportunities for minority group members), (b) activities performed to meet contractual arrangements with labor unions (e.g., employee rights in layoffs), (c) activities voluntarily undertaken by the company (e.g., philanthropic undertakings), and (d) socially useful programs designed to make a profit (e.g., contracts to train hardcore unemployed for useful jobs).

Of strategic importance in defining the scope of the audit is the identification of those activities of such concern to the constituencies of the company at a particular time as to merit inclusion in the social audit. This is a difficult task but must be performed if the accountability social audit is to become reality.

IDENTIFYING AND RESPONDING TO CONSTITUENT EXPECTATIONS

Today the scope of few if any social audits are accountings of acceptable expectations of constituents. There are many reasons for this but three seem to stand out: (a) the whole idea of public accountable reporting is new; (b) the methodology for identifying social expectations and determining appropriate corporate response is in its infancy; (c) very little has been done to develop creditable measures of social performance. Enough has been said about (a) but more needs to be said about the other two.

Society has a number of ways to send messages to business about its expectations. One of the clearest, of course, is to put pressures upon the legislative process to enact laws. But there are other ways. Among them are crusading reformers; opinion makers in all walks of life, including business; various organized groups, such as unions, environmentalists, and trade associations; stockholders; government agencies; and public opinion pools.

Larger companies are now surveying these sources to identify expectations. The process is done by staff analysis of various message channels. There is no accurate and unchallenged method, however, to identify those constituent expectations of importance to a company nor the degree of obligation of the company to respond. The evolution of the accountability social audit will be restrained until an acceptable methodology to do this is perfected. Table 12-3 is a matrix, developed by General Electric, which could be used to spell out systematically constituent expectations. Notice that the list of activities is somewhat different from the CED list.

Once constituent expectations are identified, a major problem for a company arises in appraising the strength and direction of the expectations. There are really no accurate and tested ways to do this. Assuming that some conclusions can be reached about thrusts of expectations, the problem then becomes one of determining to what extent, if any, a company should respond. If it chooses not to respond, is it obliged to mention it in the social audit? We do not have satisfactory answers to these questions.

TABLE 12-3
Matrix Table for Recording Expectations of Major Company Constituents by Selected Social Program

SOCIAL AUDIT MATRIX

	Customers	Investors	Employees	Dealers Distributors	Suppliers	Competitors	Communities	Public	Government
Product and technical performance									
Economic performance									
Employment performance									
Environment and natural resources									
Community welfare and development									
Government-Business relations									
International trade and development									

THE MEASUREMENT PROBLEM IN EVALUATING BUSINESS SOCIAL PROGRAMS

The art and science of the social audit will not get very far without acceptable measures of business social performance. Such measures do not now exist and the problems involved in getting them are severe.

The nature of social performance measures depends upon who is looking at the programs and why. This suggests at least four different types of measures, as follows:

Contributions to Constituents

This approach focuses attention on "consumers" of social activities—society as a whole, a community, or groups and individuals, etc.—with respect to either their broad needs or specific demands. Measurement may be in terms of values received or benefits related to costs incurred.

If the evaluation is in terms of the extent to which a business social program helps society achieve the goals it sets for itself there is a deep problem of measurement. To begin with, this society has no well-formulated goals, let alone measures for determining how well we are achieving them.

Attempts have been made to develop cost/benefit evaluations of a company's social programs and to arrive at a sort of aggregate measure of net contribution to society. Probably the most ambitious one is that of Clark Abt [1972(A)]. He lists, in financial terms, in a sort of modified and combined balance sheet and income statement, social assets of a company; social commitments, obligations and equity; and social benefits and costs to staff, to the community, and to the general public, and comes to a net social income to clients. This method would be prohibitively expensive for a company of even moderate size. Linowes proposes a "Socio-Economic Operating Statement" which calculates, in dollars, for specific major programs, the "social improvements" and "detriments" that are involved. He winds up, like Abt, with an aggregate plus or minus for society [1972]. While simpler than Abt's, Linowes' Method is still too complex for practical application.

Subjective pools of opinion can also be used in evaluation. Some activist groups periodically poll their readers and publish the results in the form of ranked standings of companies with respect to how socially responsible they are deemed to be. Opinions of individuals about how they perceive the impact of social programs on themselves can be useful measures. An example is Blum's poll made to determine the extent to which a company was satisfying the basic human needs of its employees [1958].

Traditional Business Measures

A company may wish to evaluate its social programs in terms of benefits to itself. The standard may be in the form of the traditional return on investment. This is, of course, a cost/benefit equation from the company's point of view. In every instance brought to my attention the cost/benefit analyses have been extremely rough and far from complete in the sense of considering all the major costs and benefits. The reason for this will be clear shortly.

In response to criticism about its activities in South Africa the Mobil Oil Corporation published an "audit" of its employment policies in South Africa. It was a comparison of nonwhite and white employees in various jobs in terms of percentage of total employees, wages, and benefits. These are, of course, traditional business measures of performance.

Efficient Conduct of Programs

One might ask: How efficiently has the company conducted its programs? For most programs this evaluation must be subjective. In some instances, however, evaluation can be quantitative. For instance, we have had for some time mathematical models to improve company efficiency and these are now being directed to social programs. To illustrate, one input-output matrix has been developed to show how a firm can minimize wasteful use of resources [Elliott-Jones, 1972].

Survey Research

This approach uses whatever disciplines and measures are available and can be employed appropriately in evaluation. The Council on Economic Priorities, for instance, has been making rather detailed examinations of programs of different industries [Council on Economic Priorities, 1973; American Institute of Certified Public Accountants, 1972: 39–40, 72–74].

THE MEASUREMENT PROBLEM IS CRITICAL

The above illustrates the range of approaches to measurement that exists today. The literature on the subject is rather bleak at the present time. It is a fact that there are today no creditable generally accepted standards for measuring business social performance in general or with respect to most if not all of the social programs undertaken by business. There are understandable reasons why this is so.

For a standard to be generally accepted it must be understood; it must be measurable, preferably quantitatively; it should be comparatively simple; and two independent researchers should be able to derive the same or very close answers. This set of criteria is hard to satisfy in the social area in making a cost/benefit analysis which is central in the preparation of a sophisticated social audit.

For example, on the benefit side, trouble arises immediately. There will be for most programs no consensus about which benefits ought to be evaluated nor how much weight should be given to each one. Of great concern is the fact that benefits stretch over a long period of time which will make any quantification extremely difficult. Benefits will also depend upon things that a company cannot control.

Equally difficult questions arise on the cost side. Direct costs are easy to measure, but measuring indirect costs becomes more difficult. Opportunity costs, or opportunities foregone, become even more difficult to measure. Then there is the difficult economic question of joint costs.

Each social program must be considered individually and standards must be developed for it. The approach will range from essentially a quantitative measure, such as percentage of minority employees to total employees, modified as appropriate by qualitative considerations such as subtle racial or other injusticies. For some programs, such as antipollution programs, cost/benefit analyses may be the best approach. But here, as noted above, it is a long way from deciding upon a cost/benefit analysis to developing acceptable cost and benefit measures.

For many programs there is no way to go but to prepare description scenarios of what constitutes acceptable performance. For instance, suppose a utility says that one of its major social programs is to help local governments (where it is doing business) to improve their regional physical plans. One approach to evaluating performance will be to ask what constitutes reasonable, acceptable action. To answer this question further questions such as the following will have to be answered: Has the utility assigned a man full-time to the work? What does the local government think about the help it is getting? Are there tangible benefits which are discernible? By building a scenario such as this, one can begin to determine whether performance has been acceptable. Acceptable to whom? To reasonable people like you and me! If this approach is pursued with care I do think a model can be built for many important social programs, with both qualitative and quantitative elements, which will make it possible to decide upon magnitudes of performance along a spectrum from "extremely poor" to "exceptionally satisfactory."

It will be a long time, however, before such measures are developed and receive wide acceptance in and out of business.

In developing measures it must be widely understood that a measure suitable for evaluating one purpose of a company's social program may be completely inadequate to measure a different objective. Furthermore, it will be impossible to satisfy all dimensions of the problem of measurement and evaluation. There are certain dimensions that defy quantification and sometimes they may be the most important ones to evaluate.

It is in point to observe that at the present time efficient economic operation of a company is a major social responsibility and we do have rather clear and generally acceptable measures to evaluate such performance. They are not perfect but better than those in existence for social programs. This is fortunate because in terms of total social contribution that the typical corporation can make today the greatest benefit will come from its economic function.

Until better measures of social performance are available much of what passes for social audits will be in descriptive terms.

SHOULD MAKING A SOCIAL AUDIT BE MANDATORY?

There is logic in making a social audit mandatory. The present-day annual financial reporting of corporations is mandatory. It reflects an accounting of performance which society in decades past has expected from corporations. Today, as amply described in preceding chapters, society is expecting much more from its corporations. Why should corporate performance in meeting these new demands not be the subject of mandatory reporting? Actually, as noted previously, reporting is mandatory for many of the government's dictated social programs. It is not for voluntarily undertaken programs or for societal expectations not registered in law or contract. Once the problem of identifying expectations which corporations properly should meet has been reasonably well resolved, and once the measurement issue is reasonably resolved, the logic of mandatory reporting seems apparent.

Respondents of the CED social survey were asked: "In general, do you think that business firms will be required to make a social audit in the future?" A surprising 46 per cent of the respondents answered this question affirmatively. The larger the corporation the higher the proportion of "yes" responses. Respondents were asked whether they felt this prospect was acceptable to business. The great bulk of those who said they thought reporting would be required also said they thought the requirement would be acceptable to business. A large number took the time to explain their positions [Corson and Steiner, 1974, Appendix B]. Some typical responses are as follows:

"Yes. It's a matter of being responsive to a changing climate of public attitudes and demands. . . ."
"Yes, it places a healthy discipline on management to perform."
"The prospect is not only acceptable but I deem it to be necessary."

Respondents were asked what major obstacles they felt stood in the way of developing the social audit. The results are shown in Table 12-4.

Given a resolution of the scope and measurement issues executives obviously do not see a major problem in preparing a comprehensive social audit. This probably is due to the fact that companies now make many reports to the public and government agencies and it is considered not a monumental leap to add other items and prepare a comprehensive report.

TABLE 12-4
Important Obstacles to the Development of the Social Audit

	Order of Importance *					
	1	2	3	4	5	Rank
1. Inability to develop consensus on ways to organize information	15	29	43	41	22	4
2. Inability to develop consensus as to what activities shall be covered	38	35	50	34	8	3
3. Danger to the company in publishing the results of social audits	8	18	15	14	66	5
4. Inability to develop measures of performance which everyone will accept	98	57	29	8	4	1
5. General decline in pressures on business to undertake social programs	9	7	5	7	73	6
6. Inability to make creditable cost/benefit analysis to guide company actions	58	63	25	32	8	2

* Companies identified 1, 2, 3, 4, 5, in order of importance.

A MODEL FOR SOCIAL ACCOUNTABILITY AUDITING/REPORTING

If the respondents to the CED survey are correct and reporting is mandatory how will corporations be likely to meet the requirement? Until some format is developed by consensus or legislated by government, corporations will continue on a trial-and-error basis to develop ways to assess and report on the performance of social programs. To provoke thought about a uniform format the following model is suggested:

TABLE 12-5
A Model for Social Auditing/Reporting

1. An enumeration of social expectations and the corporation's response	A summary and candid enumeration, by program areas (e.g., consumer affairs, employee relations, physical environment, local community development), of what is expected and the corporation's reasoning as to why it has undertaken certain activities and not others.
2. A statement of the corporate social objectives and the priorities attached to specific activities	For each program area the corporation would report what it will strive to accomplish and what priority it places on various activities.
3. A description of the corporation's goals in each program area and of the activities it will carry on	For each priority activity, the corporation will state a specific goal (in quantitative terms when possible) and describe how it is striving to reach that goal (e.g., to better educational facilities in the community, it will make available qualified teachers from among members of its staff).
4. Statement indicating the resources committed to achieve objectives and goals	A summary report, in quantitative terms, by program area and activity of the costs, direct and indirect, assumed by the corporation.
5. A statement of the accomplishments and/or progress made in achieving each objective and each goal	A summary, describing in quantitative measures when feasible and through objective, narrative statement when quantification is impracticable, the extent of achievement of each objective and each goal.

SOURCE: Corson and Steiner, 1974.

The report, of course, should provide enough information to permit the reader—internal managers as well as the public—to compare the company's activities with those of other companies acting in the same social area.

So long as corporations can choose on a voluntary basis which social programs to pursue, the creditability of the social report may rest on the comprehensiveness and candor with which it is prepared. Creditability also can be increased if an "independent" analyst examines the corporate report and certifies to its accuracy. The social report might also be more readily accepted if the board of directors of the company reviews and approves it.

CONCLUDING OBSERVATION

"Business functions by public consent," the CED statement on *Social Responsibilities of Business Corporations* said ". . . its basic purpose is to serve constructively the needs of society—to the satisfaction of society" [p. 11]. Demands are growing and are not likely to diminish that corporations, especially the larger ones, continue to expand their efforts to appraise and inform about how well they are serving the needs of society. The social audit is a tool to do this. It is my judgment that it is not a current fad which will soon disappear. It is a new managerial requirement. How it will evolve, however, is not as clear.

REFERENCES

Abt, Clark: "Managing to Save Money While Doing Good." *Innovation,* January 1972a.

Abt, Clark: "Social Audits—The State of the Art." Presented at Conference on Corporate Social Responsibility. New York, October 1972b.

American Institute of Certified Public Accountants: *Social Measurement.* New York, American Institute of Certified Public Accountants, Inc., 1972.

Bauer, Raymond A., and Dan H. Fenn, Jr.: *The Corporate Social Audit.* New York, Social Science Frontiers Series, Russell Sage Foundation, 1972.

Baumol, William J., Rensis Likert, Henry C. Wallich, and John J. McGowan: *A New Rationale for Corporate Social Policy.* New York, Committee for Economic Development, 1970.

Blum, Fred H.: "Social Audit of the Enterprise." *Harvard Business Review,* March-April, 1958.

Bowen, Howard R.: *Social Responsibilities of the Businessman.* New York, Harper & Brothers, 1953.

Butcher, Bernard: "The Program Management Approach to the Corporate Social Audit." Paper presented at Conference on "Corporate Social Policy in a Dynamic Society." University of California, Berkeley, November 9–11, 1972.

Committee for Economic Development: *Social Responsibilities of Business Corporations.* New York, CED, 1971.

Corson, John J., and George A. Steiner: *Measuring Business Social Performance: The Corporate Social Audit.* New York, Committee for Economic Development, 1974.

Council on Economic Priorities: *Economic Priorities Report, Environmental Steel.* New York, Council on Economic Priorities, 1973.

Eliott-Jones, M. F.: "Matrix Methods in Corporate Social Accounting. Some Extensions of Input-Output Economics." Presented at Seminar on Corporate Social Accounts, Battelle Seattle Research Center, November 10–11, 1972.

General Motors Corporation: *Report on Progress in Areas of Public Concern.* Warren, Michigan, GM Technical Center, 1972 and 1973.

Linowes, David F.: "Measuring Social Programs in Business." *Social Audit Seminar—Selected Proceedings.* Washington, D.C., Public Affairs Council, July 1972.

Steiner, George A.: *Summary Results of Survey of Development Efforts to Measure the Social Performance of Business.* New York, Committee for Economic Development, 1973.

READING 14

Toward a Contingency Theory of Business Strategy*

Charles W. Hofer

Although there has been much emphasis on the processes by which strategies are developed, several recent studies have focused on the content of strategies. Propositions about strategy suggested by these studies are summarized as are several propositions from the normative literature. A conceptual framework for interrelating these propositions is described.

In the past two decades the concept of organizational strategy has emerged as one of the cornerstones of both management theory and practice. During this period, numerous papers, articles, and books have explored this concept and its myriad characteristics and nuances. Nevertheless, some aspects of the subject have received far more attention than others. For example, much greater emphasis has been placed on the organizational processes by which strategies are developed than on the content of the strategies themselves. Also, more attention has been focused on strategy formulation at the corporate level than at the business level. (The term business level refers to that level in an organization at which responsibility for the formulation of a multifunctional strategy for a single industry or product-market arena is determined; the term corporate level refers to the top level of the organization regardless of the number of industries in which it competes. Thus, for a multi-industry company, the business level normally would correspond to the divisional level. In a single product line company, however, the business and corporate levels would be the same.) Likewise, more emphasis has been placed on the analytical and informational aspects of the strategic planning process than on its behavioral and political dimensions. Finally, nearly all of the research studies and many of the papers and articles have been descriptive in their orientation, especially with respect to the content of the strategies involved.

Most of these biases reflect either the state of development of the field or the backgrounds and experiences of the early pioneers in the area. For example, one of the major reasons for the early emphasis on process rather than content was that far fewer variables were needed to describe the

* From *Academy of Management Journal,* December 1975, pp. 784–810. Reprinted by permission.

strategy formulation process than were needed to specify strategy content. By contrast, the greater focus on the corporate level reflected the greater relative importance ascribed to studies at this level, and the high proportion of descriptive effort was indicative of the general level of development of the field as a whole.

In the last decade, and particularly in the last five years, much more effort has been focused on normative models, theories, and research, especially with respect to the strategy formulation process. Thus, in 1965 Learned *et al.* [24] described several broad classes of variables which should be analyzed during the strategy formulation process. In the same year, Ansoff [5] proposed a more detailed procedure for analyzing the economic dimensions of the strategy formulation process. The next year, Warren [37] described more fully several ways in which behavioral and political variables should be incorporated in the process. Between 1967 and 1969, Aguilar [2], Athreya [8], Henry [19], Keegan [21], Ackerman [1], Collins [12], Ewing [13], Steiner [32], and Stevenson [34] extended understanding of the ways in which both behavioral and economic factors affect the strategic planning process. Ansoff [6] captured and integrated most of these findings in the set of descriptive and normative propositions on the strategy formulation process which he developed in 1969. Although many of his propositions remain untested, Bower [9], Carter [10], Allison [4], Steiner [33], Shank *et al.* [31], and Akel [3] have corroborated several of them in their recent studies of the strategic decision making and long-range planning processes. In sum, significant progress has been made toward the development of a theory of the strategic planning process even though much work remains to be done.

Much less progress has been made toward the development of theories of corporate and business strategy, however. One of the major reasons for this lack of progress has been the assumption that such strategies were situational, i.e., that they depended on so many factors unique to a given situation that no general propositions could be developed. Two other major factors which have limited progress in this area have been the lack of research tools powerful enough to deal with the large number of variables involved and the reluctance of many companies to provide the detailed data needed for studies of corporate and business strategy.

PURPOSE AND SCOPE

In spite of the limited attention given to conceptual analysis and empirical research on the content of business and corporate strategies, sufficient work has now been completed to permit the development of contingency theories of business and corporate strategy. [Unless one is willing to admit the possibility that there exists some strategy or set of strategies which are optimal for all businesses (corporations) no matter what their resources and no matter what environmental circumstances they face—an assumption that is inconsistent with all research studies on business (corporate) strategy conducted to date —any theory of business (corporate) strategy must be a contingency theory. Consequently, when the phrase "theory of business (corporate) strategy" is used in this paper, it is understood to mean a contingency theory of business (corporate) strategy.]

The purpose here is to take the first steps in the contingency theory direction. In doing so, the principal focus will be on the development of a theory of business strategy. The decision to concentrate on the business level rests on two assumptions. First, it was felt that the development of a theory of business strategy would require a smaller, less complex set of variables than would the development of a theory of corporate strategy. Second, and equally important, it was believed that over the long run a firm could not achieve success at a corporate level until it knew how to achieve success at a business level. Even with this restriction, however, a fully developed theory is not possible at this time. Instead, after a review of the literature dealing with the content of business and corporate strategies, the environmental variables and organizational characteristics and resources which can form the basis for a theory of business strategy are summarized, and some of the relationships among these variables are explored. Based on this classification of variables and the conceptual developments and research findings to date, a number of propositions about appropriate business strategies are then proposed. The article concludes with an assessment of the potential significance of contingency theories of business and corporate strategy and of the next steps involved in the development of such theories.

PREVIOUS THEORY AND RESEARCH

To date, both theory and research on the content of business and corporate strategy have developed in a piecemeal fashion. Moreover, much of this work has failed to differentiate between business and corporate strategies. As a consequence, this survey will cover the development of concepts about the content of strategy at both the business and corporate levels.

In general, few theoretical investigations of this type were conducted prior to the early 1960s, and most of those focused on the unique characteristics of the situation involved. One of the first exceptions to this was Ansoff's *Corporate Strategy* [5]. Although primarily process oriented, Ansoff did put forward in this work several propositions about the content of corporate strategy. For example, he argued that synergy should be a major factor in strategic choice, i.e., that:

1. Internal development is indicated when the start-up synergy is strong, even if operating synergy is weak.

2. Conglomerate diversification and absence of synergy usually call for acquisition.

In a similar vein, Levitt [25] argued that the stage of the product life cycle must be carefully considered in strategic decision making. For example, he proposed:

1. In the growth stage, instead of seeking ways of getting consumers to try the product, the originator should try to get them to prefer his brand.
2. Typically, the market maturity stage forces the producer to concentrate on holding his distribution outlets. In the case of branded products in particular, the originator must now, more than ever, communicate directly with the consumer.

Michael [26] added to Levitt's analysis by suggesting that products decline in two different ways and that the marketing strategies appropriate for these two types of decline are different. Wasson [38] and Fox [14] further extended Levitt's analysis of the influence of the product life cycle on business strategy by expanding their focus to cover all marketing policies and all functional areas respectively (see Tables 1 and 2). Ansoff and Stewart [7] provided a complementary view in their hypotheses about the ways in which variations in the rate and nature of technological change should affect the types of business strategies which a firm employs. For example, they argued that:

1. When the rate of change in the "state of the art" is rapid, firms should focus their R&D efforts on new product designs and product improvements. When it is slow, they should focus on process improvements.
2. There are four broad R&D strategies which a firm might successfully pursue. These are: "first to market," "follow the leader," "application engineering," and "me too."

In his analysis, Tilles [35] suggested several propositions on business and corporate strategy that applied to a wide variety of environmental and organization circumstances. Among them were the following:

1. In industries with high rates of technological change in product design, one shot, short term commitments of funds will not be profitable.
2. In mature industries, firms should seek to innovate in marketing, distribution, or credit rather than in product or process design.
3. In a single product line company, the allocation of funds to different functions in order to enhance or maintain its distinctive competences is of equal, if not greater, importance than investments in product development.
4. In oligopolistic industries, firms should disguise their intentions when their competitive position is weak and reveal them when it is strong.

Katz [20] and Glueck [17] have developed the most explicit and complete sets of propositions on business and corporate strategy to date. Specifically,

TABLE 1
Wasson's Hypotheses about Appropriate Strategies over the Product Cycle

DYNAMIC COMPETITIVE STRATEGY & THE MARKET LIFE CYCLE

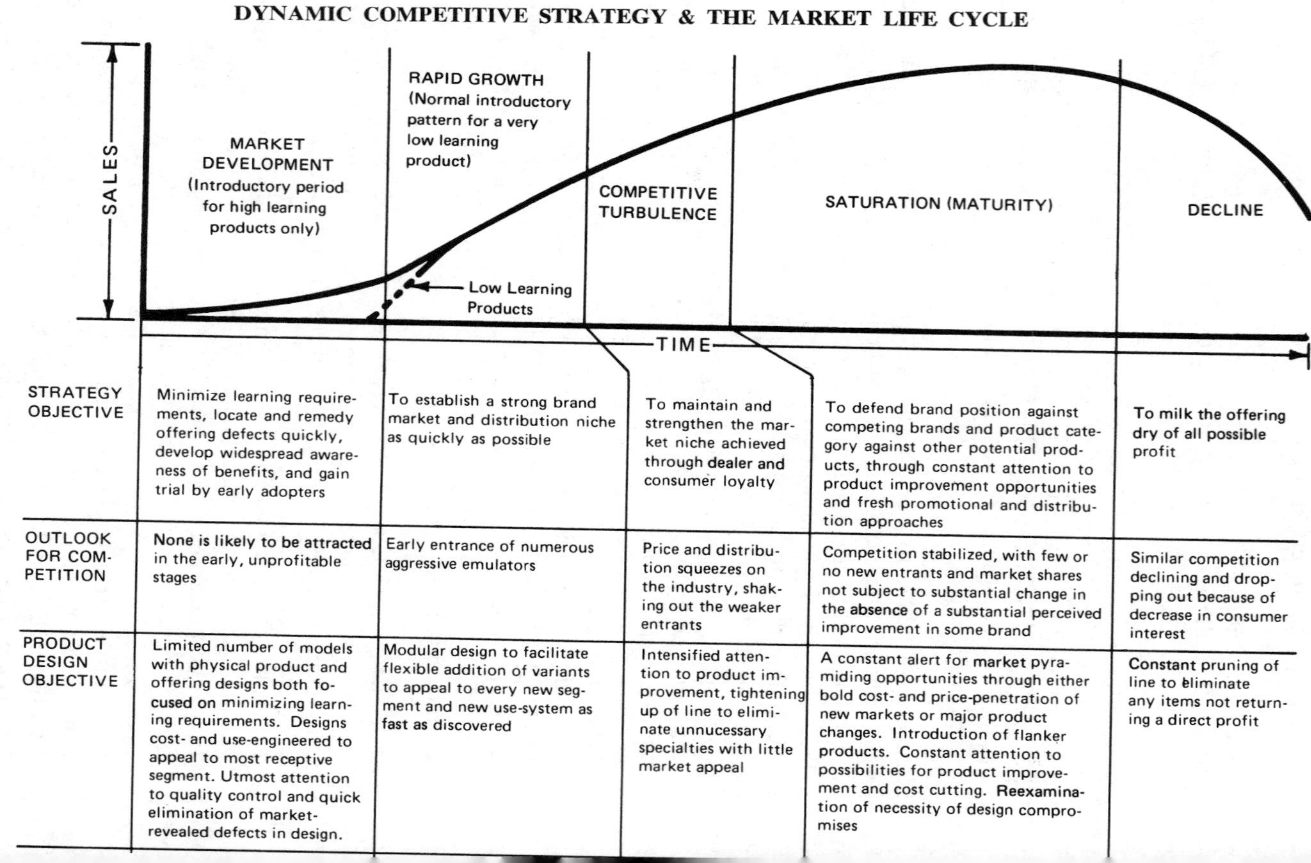

	MARKET DEVELOPMENT (Introductory period for high learning products only)	RAPID GROWTH (Normal introductory pattern for a very low learning product)	COMPETITIVE TURBULENCE	SATURATION (MATURITY)	DECLINE
STRATEGY OBJECTIVE	Minimize learning requirements, locate and remedy offering defects quickly, develop widespread awareness of benefits, and gain trial by early adopters	To establish a strong brand market and distribution niche as quickly as possible	To maintain and strengthen the market niche achieved through dealer and consumer loyalty	To defend brand position against competing brands and product category against other potential products, through constant attention to product improvement opportunities and fresh promotional and distribution approaches	To milk the offering dry of all possible profit
OUTLOOK FOR COMPETITION	None is likely to be attracted in the early, unprofitable stages	Early entrance of numerous aggressive emulators	Price and distribution squeezes on the industry, shaking out the weaker entrants	Competition stabilized, with few or no new entrants and market shares not subject to substantial change in the absence of a substantial perceived improvement in some brand	Similar competition declining and dropping out because of decrease in consumer interest
PRODUCT DESIGN OBJECTIVE	Limited number of models with physical product and offering designs both focused on minimizing learning requirements. Designs cost- and use-engineered to appeal to most receptive segment. Utmost attention to quality control and quick elimination of market-revealed defects in design.	Modular design to facilitate flexible addition of variants to appeal to every new segment and new use-system as fast as discovered	Intensified attention to product improvement, tightening up of line to eliminate unnucessary specialties with little market appeal	A constant alert for market pyramiding opportunities through either bold cost- and price-penetration of new markets or major product changes. Introduction of flanker products. Constant attention to possibilities for product improvement and cost cutting. Reexamination of necessity of design compromises	Constant pruning of line to eliminate any items not returning a direct profit

PRICING OBJECTIVE	To impose the minimum of value perception learning and to match the value reference perception of the most receptive segments. High trade discounts and sampling advisable	A price line for every taste, from low-end to premium models. Customary trade discounts. Aggressive promotional pricing, with prices cut as fast as costs decline due to accumulated production experience. Intensification of sampling	Increased attention to market-broadening and promotional pricing opportunities	Defensive pricing to preserve product category franchise. Search for incremental pricing opportunities, including private label contracts, to boost volume and gain an experience advantage	Maintenance of profit level pricing with complete disregard of any effect on market share
PROMOTIONAL GUIDELINES *Communications Objectives*	a) Create widespread awareness and understanding of offering benefits b) Gain trial by early adopters	Create and strengthen brand preference among trade and final users. Stimulate general trial	Maintain consumer franchise and strengthen dealer ties	Maintain consumer and trade loyalty, with strong emphasis on dealers and distributors. Promotion of greater use frequency	Phase out, keeping just enough to maintain profitable distribution
Most valuable media mix	In order of value: Publicity, Personal Sales, Mass communications	Mass media. Personal sales. Sales promotions, including sampling. Publicity	Mass media. Dealer promotions. Personal selling to dealers. Sales promotions. Publicity	Mass media. Dealer-oriented promotions	Cut down all media to the bone—use no sales promotions of any kind
DISTRIBUTION POLICY	Exclusive or selective, with distributor margins high enough to justify heavy promotional spending	Intensive and extensive, with dealer margins just high enough to keep them interested. Close attention to rapid resupply of distributor stocks and heavy inventories at all levels	Intensive and extensive, and a strong emphasis on keeping dealer well supplied, but with minimum inventory cost to him	Intensive and extensive, with strong emphasis on keeping dealer well supplied, but at minimum inventory cost to him	Phase out outlets as they become marginal
INTELLIGENCE FOCUS	To identify actual developing use-systems and to uncover any product weaknesses	Detailed attention to brand position, to gaps in model and market coverage, and to opportunities for market segmentation	Close attention to product improvement needs, to market-broadening chances, and to possible fresh promotion themes	Intensified attention to possible product improvements. Sharp alert for potential new inter-product competition and for signs of beginning product decline	Information helping to identify the point at which the product should be phased out

Source: Chester R. Wasson (38, pp. 247, 248). Used with permission.

Note: Strictly speaking, this is the cycle of the category market, and only a high learning introduction passes through all phases indicated above. The term, *product life cycle,* is sometimes applied indiscriminately to both brand cycles and category cycles. Most new brands are only emulative of other products already on the market, have a much shorter life cycle than the product category, and must follow a strategy similar to any low-learning product.

	FUNCTIONAL FOCUS	R&D	PRODUCTION	MARKETING	PHYSICAL DISTRIBUTION
Precommercialization	Coordination of R&D and other functions	Reliability tests Release blueprints	Production design Process planning Purchasing dept. lines up vendors & subcontractors	Test marketing Detailed marketing plan	Plan shipping schedules, mixed carloads Rent warehouse space, trucks
Introduction	Engineering: debugging in R&D production, and field	Technical corrections (Engineering changes)	Subcontracting Centralize pilot plants; test various processes; develop standards	Induce trial; fill pipelines; sales agents or commissioned salesmen; publicity	Plan a logistics system
Growth	Production	Start successor product	Centralize production Phase out subcontractors Expedite vendors output; long runs	Channel commitment Brand emphasis Salaried sales force Reduce price if necessary	Expedite deliveries Shift to owned facilities
Maturity	Marketing and logistics	Develop minor variants Reduce costs true value analysis Originate major adaptations to start new cycle	Many short runs Decentralize Import parts, low-priced models Routinization Cost reduction	Short-term promotions Salaried salesmen Cooperative advertising Forward integration Routine marketing research: panels, audits	Reduce costs and raise customer service level Control finished goods inventory
Decline	Finance	Withdraw all R&D from initial version	Revert to subcontracting; simplify production line Careful inventory control; buy foreign or competitive goods; stock spare parts	Revert to commission basis; withdraw most promotional support Raise price Selective distribution Careful phase-out, considering entire channel	Reduce inventory and services

SOURCE: Harold W. Fox [14:10–11].

Katz proposed four universal propositions about business and corporate strategy and eight others that were conditional only on the size of the organization involved (see Table 3) while Glueck identified 17 such hypotheses that were conditional on a variety of variables both external and internal to the firm (see Table 4). (Glueck's 17 hypotheses on business and corporate strategy were part of a larger set of 71 hypotheses about organizational strategy in general. Most of his other hypotheses dealt with the strategy formulation process.)

Since the concept of strategy was not developed extensively in the business literature until the late 1950s, almost no empirical research related to it was done until the early 1960s. There had been, of course, numerous studies in the field of industrial organization that had explored various aspects of competi-

TABLE 2

Fox's Hypotheses About Appropriate Business Strategies over the Product Life Cycle

Personnel	Finance	Management Accounting	Other	Customers	Competition
Recruit for new activities Negotiate operational changes with unions	LC plan for cash flows, profits, investments, subsidiaries	Payout planning: full costs/ revenues Determine optimum lengths of LC stages thru present-value method	Final legal clearances (regulatory hurdles, patents) Appoint LC coordinator	Panels & other test respondents	Neglects opportunity or is working on similar idea
Staff and train middle management Stock options for executives	Accounting deficit; high net cash outflow Authorize large production facilities	Help develop production & distribution standards Prepare sales aids like sales management portfolio		Innovators and some early adopters	(Monopoly) Disparagement of innovation Legal & extralegal interference
Add suitable personnel for plant Many grievances Heavy overtime	Very high profits, net cash outflow still rising Sell equities	Short-term analyses based on return per scarce resource		Early adopters & early majority	(Oligopoly) A few imitate, improve, or cut prices
Transfers, advancements; incentives for efficiency, safety, and so on Suggestion system	Declining profit rate but increasing net cash inflow	Analyze differential costs/ revenue Spearhead cost reduction, value analysis, and efficiency drives	Pressure for resale price maintenance Price cuts bring price wars; possible price collusion	Early adopters, early & late majority, some laggards; first discontinued by late majority	(Monopoly competition) First shakeout; yet many rivals
Find new slots Encourage early retirement	Administer system, retrenchment Sell unneeded equipment Export the machinery	Analyze escapable costs Pinpoint remaining outlays	Accurate sales forecast very important	Mainly laggards	(Oligopoly) After 2nd shakeout, only few rivals

tive behavior at an industry level. The focus of such studies was on how to improve the economic efficiency of the industry involved, however, not on the content of individual business or corporate strategies. Research on the content of strategy increased in the mid-1960s, but almost without exception it concentrated on the unique circumstances of the firms chosen for investigation. Most of these efforts also failed to differentiate between business and corporate strategy, and many discussed strategy content only as it related to the strategy formulation process. Since the late 1960s, however, a number of studies have emphasized the generic content of the organization's strategy. Moreover, although a few of these studies did not differentiate between business and corporate strategy, most did. In particular, the research of Chevalier [11], Fruhan [15, 16], the Boston Consulting Group [27], Udell [36], Khand-

TABLE 3
Katz's Propositions on Business and Corporate Strategy

Universal Propositions
1. Always lead from strength.
2. Concentrate resources where the company has (or could develop readily) a meaningful competitive advantage.
3. The narrowest possible product/market scope should be selected for each unit consistent with unit resources and market requirements.
4. A unit whose future earning power (discounted at the company's current cost of capital) is less than its liquidation value should be sold as quickly as possible.

Propositions for Large Companies
1. Planning is critical.
2. Give up the crumbs.
3. Preserve company strength and stability.

Propositions for Small Companies
1. Attack when the enemy retreats.
2. Do take full advantage of opportunities.
3. Be as inconspicuous as possible.
4. Respond quickly.
5. Retreat when the enemy attacks.

SOURCE: Robert L. Katz [20:349–364].

walla [22], and Schoeffler *et al.* [30] focused primarily on the content of business strategy; the work of Gutmann [18], Rumelt [28], and indirectly that of Kitching [23] concentrated on the content of corporate strategy. Table 5 provides a summary description of each of these studies, and Tables 6 and 7 present synopses of the hypotheses on appropriate business and corporate strategies derived from them.[1]

Together, these hypotheses and propositions represent a substantial body of knowledge about the types of business and corporate strategies most appropriate for different types of environmental circumstances. However, they often lack precision with regard to the circumstances to which they apply. Because of such imprecision, they seem contradictory in several instances. There are, in addition, numerous sets of environmental and organizational circumstances for which no propositions on business or corporate strategy have yet been developed. In sum, these findings provide a base, albeit a limited and, in places, a weak one, for the development of contingency theories of both business and corporate strategy. The next steps are to identify and classify the variables that will form the bases for these theories and to explore the relationships among them.

[1] A more detailed description of all the studies mentioned in this section is given in two papers available from the author: Hofer, Charles W., "Research on Strategic Planning: A Summary of Past Studies and Suggestions for Future Efforts," and Hofer, Charles W., "Research on a Contingency Theory of Strategic Behavior: Issues and Methods," presented to the Midwest Meetings of the Academy of Management, 1974.

TABLE 4
Glueck's Hypotheses on Business and Corporate Strategy

H18:	The most important factors in developing a strategy are relative dependence on the environment, complexity of product/service line, relative size of the firm, and volatility of the relevant marketplace. Less important factors are current technology and relative propositions of employees in education/training categories.
H21B:	The more dependent the firm is on its competitors, the less offensive it is likely to be in its strategy.
H23A:	The more volatile the market sector the firm chooses to operate in, the more flexible the strategic response needs to be in effective organizations.
H28:	Firms which operate with an offensive strategy will be more effective than those with a reactive or defensive strategy. (Modified Military Doctrine: The best defense is an offense.)
H29:	Small firms which create a strategy that stakes out specific market segments will be more effective than those who define themselves more broadly. (Opposite of Levitt's "Marketing Myopia.")
H30:	For dominant firms in an industry, the best strategies (in order) are innovation, intense marketing (fortification); the least are persecution and confrontation. [sic]
H30A:	For the small firm, the best strategies are innovation and segmentation; the least are improved promotion and distribution improvements.
H36:	Firms which are in mature industries with low volatility can be minimally effective by adopting a stability [incremental adjustments to the present] strategy.
H48:	Firms with long linked technologies will be more effective if they grow through vertical integration (Modified Thompson).
H49:	Firms with mediating technologies will be more effective if they grow by increasing the geographic area served (Modified Thompson).
H50:	Firms with intensive technologies will be more effective if they grow by incorporating the object worked on (Modified Thompson).
H53:	Companies with a large share of market will be more effective if they choose conglomerate growth strategy (Modified Kotler).
H54:	Companies with a small share of market will be more effective if they choose an intensive growth strategy (Modified Kotler).
H55:	If a company is in a high growth market, it will be more effective if it chooses intensive growth/integrative growth strategies (Modified Kotler).
H56:	If a company is in a mature product life cycle market, it will be more effective if it chooses intensive growth/conglomerate growth strategies (Modified Kotler).
H57A:	The most effective entry strategy is joint development (Kotler).
H57B:	Acquisition strategy is best when the company has little knowledge of the product, when speed is vital, or when other companies own key patents or control key resources (Kotler).

SOURCE: William F. Glueck [17:108–111].

					CHARACTERISTICS
TYPES OF RESEARCH	STUDIES DONE BY	TYPES OF ORGANIZATIONS STUDIED		NATURE OF STUDY	SAMPLE SIZE
1. Business strategy studies	Chevalier	large U.S. manufacturing firms	D and N[a]	CS[b] CS CS and L	4 6 4
	Fruhan	large U.S. manufacturing firms	D and N	L and CS CS CS and L	9 3 11
	Boston Consulting Group	medium to high technology industries	D and N	L	24
	Udell	medium to large U.S. businesses	D and N	CS	485 products
	Khandwalla	medium sized nondiversified U.S. manufacturing firms	D and N	CS	79 firms
	Schoeffler et al.	large U.S. businesses	D and N	CS	57 firms 620 businesses
2. Corporate strategy studies	Gutmann	medium to large U.S. manufacturing firms	D	CS	53
	Rumelt	large U.S. businesses (*Fortune* 500)	D and N	L and CS	236 500
	Kitching	large U.S. companies: $25 million to $2 billion	D and N	CS	22 firms 181 mergers

[a] D = Descriptive, N = Normative, H = Hypothesis Testing.
[b] CS = Cross-Sectional, L = Longitudinal.

KEY VARIABLES THAT INFLUENCE BUSINESS STRATEGY

As indicated previously, the primary interest of this article is in the development of a contingency theory of business strategy. Table 8 lists the environmental variables and organizational characteristics and resources that policy and economic theorists and the previously cited research studies have indicated are of major importance in determining the content of specific business strategies. (The lack of variables describing management or owner values or the firm's social responsibilities does not imply that such variables are not important in the final selection of a strategy. Such variables usually have little or no impact on the economic feasibility of a particular strategy, however. Thus, they are not relevant to a contingency theory of business strategy as defined in this paper and have, as a consequence, been excluded here.)

TABLE 5

Past Research on the Content of Business and Corporate Strategies

OF RESEARCH			
TIME SPAN OF STUDY	TYPES OF DATA ANALYSIS	FOCUS OF RESEARCH	SCOPE AND/OR LIMITATIONS OF FINDINGS
1 yr. 1 yr. 6 yrs.	Graphs	Effect of market share on profitability	Limited to industries in the saturation phase of the life cycle with low technological transfer
6 yrs. 4 yrs. 5 yrs.	Graphs	Effect of market share on profitability	Limited to industries in the saturation phase of the life cycle
2 yrs. to 37 yrs.	Graphs	Effect of experience on cost levels	Covers all phases of the life cycle. May not apply to industries with low manufacturing value added
1 yr.	Graphs	Nonprice aspects of marketing strategy	Findings based primarily on managerial opinion rather than real world actions and results
1 yr.	Product moment and interaction correlations	Importance of different functional tasks to profitability under different environmental conditions	Findings are based on the opinions of the managers surveyed, not on real world actions and results
3 yrs.	Multiple regression	Identify major strategic factors which influence profitability	Applicable primarily to manufacturing firms in the saturation phase of the life cycle
1954-58	Cross tabulation tables	Determine product/market strategies of high growth firms	No control groups
1949-69	Multiple regression	Determine the relative success of different types of strategies	May not apply to small firms
1960-65	Cross tabulation tables	Characteristics of successful mergers	No control groups. Applicable to most mergers

The list provided in Table 8 must be reduced if one is to develop an effective theory of business strategy, however, since the theory would have little explanatory power without such reductions. More specifically, if the list were not reduced, there would be a minimum of $2^{54} \approx 18{,}000{,}000{,}000{,}000{,}000$ different circumstances to be considered. (This calculation assumes that each variable can assume only two strategically significant values, that all variables are of relatively equal significance, and that none overlap with other variables on the list.) Under such conditions, any theory of business strategy would be, in essence, a situational one.

Fortunately both theoretical analysis and numerous research studies have shown that many of the variables in Table 8 are either interrelated or have a negligible impact on total organizational performance compared to other variables on the list. For example, in the introductory stage of the life cycle, the degree of seller concentration is usually irrelevant since, almost by definition, it is nearly always high. Also during this period, typically there is little

TABLE 6
A Summary of Hypotheses on Business Strategy Suggested by Various Research Studies

A. *Chevalier's Findings*

In industries with little or no technological transfer and in which the market share distribution among competitors can be affected by the actions of a single firm, companies should:

1. Dominate the market segments in which they operate.
2. Divest in market segments when market share is small and there is no hope of future growth.
3. Seek to be dominant in a small market rather than a follower in a large market.

B. *Fruhan's Findings*

In industries in the maturity and saturation phases of the life cycle, it is not economically worthwhile for a firm to seek to increase its market share through internal expansion if:

1. Extremely heavy financial resources are required.
2. An expansion strategy might be (have to be) cut off abruptly before the firm reaches its market share target.
3. Regulatory agencies continuously place new restrictions on the types of competitive behavior which firms can follow.

C. *The Boston Consulting Group's Findings*

1. Firms should try to gain a high share of market very early in the product life cycle since the total per unit costs of the value added decrease by 20 per cent to 30 per cent on a constant dollar basis every time total product experience doubles for the industry as a whole.
2. The producer who fails to reduce costs along the characteristic cost/volume slope will eventually become noncompetitive.
3. The producer with the largest cumulative market share (for the given product) should always be able to maintain the lowest cost.
4. New products must nearly always be sold at prices below costs until volume builds up.
5. Price must eventually go down as fast as costs, if there is any competition at all in the industry.
6. Market share is unstable until one producer clearly dominates the market and his prices are low enough to inhibit growth in the relative market share of any significant competitor, or until growth stops.

D. *Udell's Findings*

1. For all types of producers—industrial, consumer durable, and consumer nondurable—product and selling activities were perceived to be more important than pricing strategy.
2. The relative importance of a firm's product effort should vary directly with the strength of operational buying motives, the purchasing efforts and knowledge of the buyer, and the technical nature of the product.
3. The relative importance of a firm's sales effort should vary directly with the strength of sociopsychological buying motives, while varying inversely with the purchasing efforts and knowledge of the buyer and the technical nature of the product.

E. *Khandwalla's Findings*

1. The general effect of a dynamic, complex, uncertain environment is to raise the importance of a large number of strategic type activities, i.e., a complex environ-

TABLE 6 (Cont.)

ment apparently begets a complex and comprehensive corporate strategy; a simple environment seems to beget a simple corporate strategy.

2. In general, competition in products and distribution and product related technological change have a greater importance for corporate strategy than does process related technological change or price competition.

F. *Schoeffler et al.'s Findings*

1. A strong market position is profitable in the sense of increasing the expected ROI. This is especially true where purchase frequency is low, the production cycle is long, and the manufacturing intensity is low.
2. If a business has a strong market position, it can further enhance profitability by increasing its product differentiation, maintaining a high debt/equity ratio, and maintaining a stable capacity/market ratio.
3. Comparative quality is profitable especially when the purchase frequency is low, market growth is medium to high, the production cycle is long, and capital intensity and vertical integration are low.
4. High relative prices are only slightly more profitable than average prices, but low relative prices are significantly less profitable than are either medium or high prices.

or no segmentation of the market; buyer loyalty often is not very high, especially when the purchase frequency is low; and there usually is a low price elasticity of demand, few economies of scale, little automation or integration, and, consequently, few effects of experience curves. In addition, since process technology has not matured, the concepts of marginal and optimal plant size usually are not very important, although the degree of capacity utilization may be. Similar analyses can be made for other stages in the life cycle and for other variables. Doing so yields a substantially reduced list of variables which need to be considered in the development of a theory of business strategy. This list can be reduced even more by noting that some variables such as major changes in conditions of trade or environmental protection laws affect all firms in an industry in the same way. Thus, while such variables might affect overall industry profitability, they often can be neglected when formulating business strategies for competing within an industry. Stated differently, it is quite possible that some variables might affect a firm's corporate strategy, i.e., the question of whether the firm should compete in a given industry, without affecting the business strategies of those firms entering or remaining in the industry.

A further reduction in the number of strategically different circumstances which must be considered is made possible by noting that some values of some variables have little strategic significance. Using the life cycle example again, one notes that only the introductory, the maturity, and the decline stages appear to be strategically significant, i.e., very few if any changes in competitive position occur during the growth and saturation stages. This does not mean that firms do not have to change any of their activities during

TABLE 7
A Summary of Hypotheses on Corporate Strategy Suggested by Various Research Studies

A. *Gutmann's Findings*
1. The high growth manufacturing firms studied concentrated their efforts on a few segments of the industries in which they competed rather than trying to cover all segments.
2. Most of these firms (80 per cent) developed new products for their existing customers and a significant minority ($\approx$ 40 per cent) also developed new products for new customers. Very few, however, ($<$ 7 per cent) attempted to sell old products to new customers even though most were in the early stages of the product cycle. Almost none ($<$ 2 per cent) withdrew from their existing businesses.
3. Many ($>$ 50 per cent) made acquisitions, but the sales growth of those making acquisitions was not significantly different from the sales growth of those which did not. Few made divestitures.

B. *Rumelt's Findings*
1. Vertically integrated firms and firms engaged in unrelated businesses (but not having policies of rapid growth by acquisition) were the poorest performers, and firms that were somewhat diversified but related all of their activities to some central skill or strength were the highest performers.
2. The vertically integrated firms appeared to suffer from stagnant industries, but their long term commitments to a single industry and heavy investment in fixed plant made it extremely difficult for them to diversify into more dynamic sections of the economy. The poor performing unrelated firms were found to be characterized by organizational structures and administrative systems more suitable to companies engaged in activities that are related to one another.

C. *Kitching's Findings*
1. In general, vertical and horizontal acquisitions were the least likely to fail, concentric marketing and technology acquisition were the most likely to fail, and conglomerate acquisitions were in the middle.
2. Financial synergy produces the biggest dollar payment after acquisition, marketing synergy the second largest payment, and production and technological synergy the least dollar payment. At the same time, the effort required to achieve these synergistic potentials is inversely proportional to the size of the payout to be gained.

these latter periods, but rather that the changes which are needed appear to be mostly tactical in nature. Thus, for many industries, the growth and saturation stages could be dropped from the analysis. Again, similar reductions are possible with other variables.

With such reductions, it becomes reasonable to think about trying to develop a contingency theory of business strategy. Two major steps are involved. The first is to classify those variables and sets of variables that will significantly influence the content of business strategies and to specify the values of each of these variables which are strategically important. The second is to identify the types of strategies which are economically feasible for each different set of strategically significant environmental conditions. Table 9 lists for each stage of the product life cycle those variables that, based on prior

TABLE 8
Some Strategically Significant Environmental and Organizational Variables

BROADER ENVIRONMENTAL VARIABLES	INDUSTRY STRUCTURE VARIABLES	MARKET AND CONSUMER BEHAVIOR VARIABLES
Economic Conditions GNP trend interest rates money supply energy availability *Demographic Trends* growth rate of population age distribution of population regional shifts in population *Sociocultural Trends* life style changes consumer activism career expectations *Political/Legal Factors* antitrust regulations environmental protection laws	type of product degree of product differentiation # equal products price/cost structure economies of scale degree of automation degree of integration experience curves marginal plant size optimal plant size rate of product technological change rates of process technological change transportation and distribution costs barriers to entry critical mass for entry	stage of the life cycle market size seasonality cyclicality market segmentation buyer concentration buyer needs buyer loyalty elasticity of demand purchase frequency
SUPPLIER VARIABLES	COMPETITOR VARIABLES	ORGANIZATIONAL CHARACTERISTICS AND RESOURCES
degree of supplier concentration major changes in availability of raw materials major changes in conditions of trade	degree of seller concentration aggressiveness of competition degree of specialization in the industry degree of capacity utilization	market share degree of customer concentration quality of products value added length of the production cycle newness of plant and equipment labor intensity relative wage rate marketing intensity discretionary cash flow/gross capital investment

research and numerous case studies, appear to be of greatest significance in the determination of business strategy.

SOME PROPOSITIONS ON BUSINESS STRATEGY

The observations made in the preceding section can be summarized in the following descriptive (D) propositions:

D1. The most fundamental variable in determining an appropriate business strategy is the stage of the product life cycle.

TABLE 9

Environmental Variables and Organizational Characteristics and Resources That Are Strategically Significant at Different Stages of the Product Life Cycle

Types of Variables	Life Cycle Stages				
	Introduction	Growth	Maturity	Saturation	Decline
Market and consumer behavior variables	Buyer needs Purchase frequency	Buyer needs Buyer concentration Purchase frequency	Market segmentation Buyer needs Purchase frequency Buyer concentration	Market size Market segmentation Elasticity of demand Buyer loyalty Seasonality Cyclicality	Market size Buyer loyalty Elasticity of demand
Industry structure variables	Uniqueness of the product Rate of technological change in product design	Type of product Rate of technological change in product design Number of equal product Barriers to entry	Type of product Rate of technological change in process design Degree of product differentiation Number of equal products Transportation and distribution costs Barriers to entry	Degree of product differentiation Price/cost structure Experience curves Degree of integration Economics of scale	Degree of product differentiation Price/cost structure Marginal plant size Transportation and distribution costs
Competitor variables		Degree of specialization within the industry	Degree of specialization within the industry Degree of capacity utilization	Degree of seller concentration Aggressiveness of competition Degree of specialization in the industry	Degree of specialization within the industry Degree of capacity utilization

Supplier variables			Degree of supplier concentration	Degree of supplier concentration Major changes in availability of raw materials	Major changes in availability of raw materials
Broader environmental variables	Interest rates Money supply	GNP trend Money supply	GNP trend Antitrust regulations	Growth of population Age distribution of population Regional shifts of population Life style changes	Interest rates Age distribution of population
Organizational characteristics and resources	Quality of products	Market share Quality of products Marketing intensity	Market share Quality of products Value added Degree of customer concentration Marketing intensity Discretionary cash flow/gross capital investment	Market share Quality of products Length of production cycle Newness of plant and equipment Relative wage rate Marketing intensity	Market share Quality of products Length of the production cycle Relative wage rate Degree of customer concentration

NOTE: Within each category, the specific variables have been ranked in terms of their degree of significance for formulating viable business strategies. For example, in the maturity stage of the life cycle, only two competitor variables are considered to be significant for the formulation of a business strategy; namely, the degree of specialization in the industry and the degree of capacity utilization. Of these, the degree of specialization is thought to be more important.

D2. Major changes in business strategy are usually required during three stages of the life cycle: introduction, maturity, and decline.

D3. In the introductory stage of the life cycle, the major determinants of business strategy are the newness of the product, the rate of technological change in product design, the needs of the buyer, and the frequency with which the product is purchased.

D4. In the maturity stage of the life cycle, the major determinants of business strategy are the nature of buyer needs, the degree of product differentiation, the rate of technological change in process design, the degree of market segmentation, the ratio of distribution costs to manufacturing value added, and the frequency with which the product is purchased.

D5. In the decline stage of the life cycle, the major determinants of business strategy are buyer loyalty, the degree of product differentiation, the price elasticity of demand, the company's share of market, product quality, and marginal plant size.

Although these propositions repeat much of the information contained in Table 9, they also add to it by indicating the relative importance of the variables listed in this table. However, in some instances, even these propositions are not sufficiently precise. Thus, proposition D4 should really be broken into two parts:

D4A. In the maturity stage of the life cycle, the two major determinants of business strategy are the degree of product differentiation and the nature of the buyer's needs.

D4B. The secondary determinants of business strategy during the maturity phase of the product life cycle vary depending on the degree of product differentiation and the nature of the buyer's needs as indicated in the matrix shown in Figure 1.

Similar breakdowns could be made for each of the other stages of the life cycle and, in some instances, it would be desirable to have breakdowns within the breakdowns. Once these classification systems are established, it then is necessary to develop a series of normative propositions about appropriate types of business strategies for each of the cells of each matrix.

Although space limitations prevent the presentation of a comprehensive set of normative (N) propositions here, several are suggested for the maturity stage of the life cycle. (The decision was made to focus on the maturity stage of the life cycle because long term market share patterns for most industries are established during this stage and because there is substantial evidence to suggest that market share is highly and positively correlated with profitability, i.e., it is usually during the maturity stage of the life cycle that the competitive structure is developed which prevails throughout the saturation stage.)

		Degree of Product Differentiation	
		high	**low**
Nature of Buyer Needs	primarily economic	purchase frequency absolute price level rate of technological change in product design buyer concentration	rate of technological change in process design ratio of distribution costs to manufacturing value added purchase frequency buyer concentration degree of capacity utilization
	primarily noneconomic	market segmentation product complexity purchase frequency nature of barriers to entry	market segmentation degree of specialization within the industry marketing intensity manufacturing economies of scale ratio of distribution costs to manufacturing value added

Figure 1 Matrix: Nature of Buyer Needs and Degree of Product Differentiation

N1. When the degree of product differentiation is low, the nature of buyer needs primarily economic, the rate of technological change in process design high, the ratio of distribution costs to manufacturing value added high, the purchase frequency high, buyer concentration high, and the degree of capacity utilization low, businesses should:

(a) Allocate most of their R&D funds to improvements in process design rather than to new product development.

(b) Allocate most of their plant and equipment expenditures to new equipment purchases.

(c) Seek to integrate forward or backward in order to increase the value they add to the product.

(d) Attempt to improve their production scheduling and inventory control procedures in order to increase their capacity utilization.

(e) Attempt to segment the market.

(f) Attempt to reduce their raw material unit costs by standardizing their product design and using interchangeable components throughout their product line in order to qualify for volume discounts.

Hypothesis N1 is strongly supported by the experiences of ATI and Barr-Stalfort in the aerosol packaging field.[2] In 1965, this industry was on the threshold of the maturity stage of its life cycle. The rate of growth of demand had slowed substantially, even though it was still high; a number of firms had recently been forced into bankruptcy by strong price competition; there was moderate overcapacity; and yet the rate of technological change in process design remained high. ATI and Barr-Stalfort were the leaders of the industry in both size and profitability, although ATI was more than twice the size of Barr-Stalfort. Up through 1964, both companies had followed similar strategies of developing new products and improved versions of old products and of giving extensive customer service. ATI had achieved its size advantage primarily through the acquisition and subsequent turnaround of two other aerosol filling companies. In 1964, however, Barr-Stalfort changed its strategy after George Barr sold the company to the Pitway Corporation and a new general manager took charge. More specifically, Barr-Stalfort refocused most of its R&D efforts on process design, hired several industrial engineers to improve its plant layout and production scheduling, concentrated its sales effort on a few product types to help achieve economies of scale in purchasing, reinforced these purchasing economies by encouraging its customers to adopt standard size cans, caps and valves, and propellants, and began extensive private label filling operations so that it could share with its private label customers the markup normally taken by national marketers. ATI, by contrast, continued its old strategy because of the strong feelings of its president that innovation in product design was the only truly worthwhile business activity and because its divisional (plant) managers, all of whom had been former entrepreneurs, valued the autonomy which this strategy gave them.

In the decade since 1965, ATI's sales have increased less than 10 per cent; Barr-Stalfort's have more than doubled. During the same period, ATI's net profit has been essentially zero. Barr-Stalfort's, on the other hand, while lower as a percentage of sales than the profit which the company enjoyed during the growth phase of the life cycle, has been the highest in the industry and has provided the company with a return on its equity in excess of 10 per cent after taxes.

N2. When the degree of product differentiation is low, the nature of buyer needs primarily noneconomic, the degree of market segmentation slight, the degree of specialization within the industry low, the marketing intensity high, the manufacturing economies of scale medium, and the ratio of distribution costs to manufacturing value added high, businesses should:
  (a) Use universal rather than specialized marketing appeals.
  (b) Reduce their geographic scope or increase their marketing expenditures sufficiently so that their per capita marketing expenditures

* For more details, see *Aerosol Techniques, Inc.* (ICH 13G155).

within their geographic service area are in excess of the industry average.

(c) Attempt to keep their degree of capacity utilization high and their fixed assets relatively modern.

(d) Withdraw from the industry if their market share falls to less than 20 per cent of that held by the industry leader within their geographic service area. (PIMS data indicate that for nonsegmented markets, ROI falls off sharply for firms whose market share is less than 30–40 per cent of that of the industry leader; see Schoeffler *et al.* [30].)

Hypothesis N2 is supported by the experience of Heublein, Inc.[3] in the acquisition of the Theo. Hamm Brewing Company. Heublein had been quite successful in its major business—the manufacture and marketing of Smirnoff vodka—so much so that by the early 1960s it had a large cash flow which it wished to invest in other businesses that it felt might profit from its marketing skills. Initially, it purchased a wine company and a manufacturer/marketer of cordials and other liquors. The principal purpose of both acquisitions was to strengthen Heublein's distribution system in the "control" states, i.e., in states in which the distribution and sale of hard liquor was done by state agencies. After digesting these acquisitions, Heublein turned its attention to a proposal that it acquire Hamm's. Although Hamm's was a larger company than Heublein would have liked, Heublein decided to make the acquisition anyway because it felt that Hamm's presented a unique opportunity to get into the beer industry. At the time, Heublein realized that there was little product differentiation in the beer industry, that the marketing intensity was high, that there was little market segmentation, and that the rate of market growth was low. Nevertheless, it felt that by using its strong advertising and promotion skills it should be able to improve Hamm's competitive position. To accomplish this, immediately after the acquisition was consummated Hamm's advertising expenditures were significantly increased and its advertising theme was changed, as was its ad agency. In addition, a substantial effort was made to expand Hamm's geographic coverage. On the other hand, no changes were made in the operations of Hamm's three plants, all of which were relatively old.

In 1974, when Heublein sold Hamm's to a group of Hamm's distributors, it reported a capital loss of over $20 million. Moreover, Hamm's net profit for the entire decade of Heublein's ownership was negative. It also should be noted that four of Heublein's more promising managers had their careers cut short in "the land of sky blue waters." As is indicated in part (b) of proposition N2, Heublein's major mistake was its attempt to expand Hamm's geographic scope. At the time of the acquisition, Hamm's was a seminational

[3] For more details, see *Heublein, Inc. (B)* (ICH 13G126).

beer company with per capita marketing expenditures that were only about half those of the industry leaders. Survival dictated that the per capita level be increased, but Heublein did not do it since the expansion of Hamm's geographic scope effectively negated the increase in advertising. The correct strategy would have been to shrink Hamm's to a regional scope while increasing its marketing expenditures—a move which Hamm's distributors took within six months of buying the company.

N3. When the degree of product differentiation is high, the nature of the buyer's needs primarily noneconomic, the degree of market segmentation moderate to high, the product complexity high, the purchase frequency low, and there are barriers to entry in the distribution of technological areas, businesses should:
(a) Focus their R&D funds first on modifying and upgrading their existing product line, second on developing new products, and last on process innovations.
(b) Allocate substantial funds to the maintenance and enhancement of their distinctive competences, especially those in the marketing area.
(c) Develop a strong service capability in their distribution systems.
(d) Seek to expand the geographic scope of their operations if possible.

The light aircraft industry illustrates proposition N3 quite well.[4] Specifically, during the late 1960s Piper altered its traditional strategy of concentrating all of its energies on the flight training and personal flying segments of the market by developing two new twin engine models for the business and commuter airline market segments. Although the entire light aircraft industry suffered from the recession of 1969–70, Piper was hurt most. Not only did it fail to achieve significant penetration of the business and commuter markets with its new models, it also lost share in its traditional markets because of its lack of product development efforts there. By contrast, Cessna continued to improve its product line offerings in the latter segments and thereby increased its share in them. Cessna also utilized this period of reduced demand in the U.S. to strengthen its distribution systems in various overseas markets. As a consequence, it displaced Piper as the leading marketer of light aircraft outside the U.S., especially in Latin America.

N3A. When the degree of product differentiation is high, the nature of the buyer's needs primarily noneconomic, the degree of market segmentation medium to high, the product complexity low, the purchase frequency high, and the primary barriers to entry in the areas of distribution or technology, businesses should:

[4] For more details, see *A Note on the Light Aircraft Industry* (ICH 9-370-036), *Piper Aircraft Corporation* (ICH 9-369-007), and *Beech Aircraft Corporation* (ICH 9-369-008).

(a) Allocate substantial funds to the maintenance and enhancement of their distinctive competences, especially those in the marketing area.
(b) Focus their R&D funds first on process improvements and on developing new products and second on improving existing products.
(c) Develop a strong service capability in their distribution systems.
(d) Seek to expand the geographic scope of their operations if possible.

This proposition is similar to proposition N3. It differs with respect to the relative emphasis to be placed on different functional areas and on the focus of the firm's R&D efforts. These changes stem from the differences in product complexity (high versus low) and in purchase frequency (low versus high): Examples of products falling into this category are some types of hard liquor and paperback books. (Proposition N3A also holds for many of the segments of the liquor industry that are in the saturation phase of their life cycles in the U.S. The only difference is that since these segments have lower growth rates than the segments in the maturity phase, they require lower levels of reinvestment.)

A comprehensive theory of business strategy would require the development of similar propositions for all other sets of environmental conditions during the maturity stage of the life cycle and for all such sets of conditions during each of the other strategically significant stages of the life cycle. Such an exposition is impossible here, but several observations about the general contingency theory approach are appropriate. First, this approach supports most of the propositions previously suggested in the literature, although in many instances the degree of generality attached to such propositions is strongly circumscribed. For example, Tilles' proposition that single product line firms should spend as much, if not more, money to enhance their distinctive competences as they do to develop new products is shown to be much more appropriate for situations in which the degree of product differentiation is low than for those in which it is high. The contingency approach also highlights those periods of time when business strategies must be carefully reassessed, i.e., during changes in the life cycle, or when any of the other basic environmental characteristics of the industry change, or when a firm diversifies into product/market areas that have economic characteristics substantially different from those of its base businesses. In addition, the contingency approach reasserts the importance of the basic economic and technological forces in business strategy. Nearly all managers realize the significance of these factors. Nonetheless, since most are strong-willed people who are used to getting their own way, they often twist the truism that "there is always more than one viable strategy" out of shape in order to support the strategy they would like to follow, even though in some cases, e.g., ATI, this strategy may be totally inconsistent with the economic realities of the marketplace.

At the same time, one must be cautious about going overboard with the contingency approach. There is the danger, for example, that one may add more variables to the contingency matrix than are needed. Thus, there is some question as to whether purchase frequency is an extraneous variable in propositions N3 and N3A. Additionally, one should not overlook the fact that many useful insights can be gained by analyzing the effects which single variables may have no strategy, *ceteris paribus.* Consider the following single variable propositions, for example:

N4. Demographics affect the demand curves of businesses serving specialized groups of consumers more than those of businesses whose products have universal appeal.

N5. Broad economic trends affect the demand for luxury products more (either positively or negatively) than the demand for staple products.

N6. A company's distinctive competences are relatively more important in developing a viable business strategy for markets which are substantially segmented than for markets which are not segmented.

Proposition N4 would suggest that it might make sense to invest in Piper or Cessna stock in the early 1980s. This conclusion is based on two simple facts: (a) Most persons who purchase light aircraft do so between the ages of 35 and 45, and (b) those persons born during the post-World War II baby boom will reach this age category between 1980 and 1995. Similarily, Heublein's top managers might have inferred from proposition N6 that Heublein's distinctive competence in advertising and promotion might not prove to be as great a value to Hamm's as it had been in the marketing of vodka.

One must also avoid substituting these propositions for hard, creative thinking when formulating a business strategy. They cannot be used this way because there always are factors unique to each situation that will have an important bearing on the success of the strategy which is chosen. The proper way to use such propositions is as an additional check on the viability of the proposed strategy. Thus, if the strategy is consistent with most of the propositions, one can feel more confident of its workability. If it violates a significant number of them, it still may be valid, as there are always exceptions to any rule. Such a conflict is a clear signal for the company involved to reexamine its assumptions to see whether they are indeed valid, however.

SIGNIFICANCE OF THE CONTINGENCY THEORY APPROACH

If contingency theories of business and corporate strategy can be successfully developed, their implications are both obvious and important. At a minimum, they should help improve the productivity of corporations, large and small, by improving the strategy choices made by such organizations. This, of course, would lead directly to improvements in the overall productivity of society as a whole.

Such theories might also have a strong impact on the entire set of antitrust regulations. For example, if it is shown that under certain circumstances high profitability correlates strongly and positively with high market share because of experience curve effects, it then would be possible to calculate with reasonable precision the economic costs that would be incurred if antitrust provisions were used to prevent or even retard the concentration of such industries. On the other hand, it is likely that such theories would reveal other sets of circumstances in which economic costs would be lowered if the industries involved were fragmented to an even greater degree than called for by current antitrust standards. Over the long term, such knowledge should help reduce the amount of economic resources the nation wastes.

THE NEXT STEPS

This article has summarized the propositions on business and corporate strategy which have been developed to date. The environmental variables and organizational characteristics and resources that seem to be of greatest significance for the formulation of viable business strategies were then identified, as were the stages of the life cycle during which each was most important. Using this system of classifying variables as a base, a number of new propositions for business strategy were developed and, at the same time, a number of old ones were reaffirmed.

Nevertheless, much work remains to be done before such theories of business and corporate strategy are fully developed. Among the more important steps are the following:

1. Studies need to be conducted to identify exactly which environmental variables are most significant for each stage of the life cycle.
2. Using the framework suggested in this article and the information generated by studies described in step one, propositions about business strategy should be developed for all major sets of environmentally significant circumstances.
3. Additional studies should be conducted to test the propositions on business strategy developed in step two.

4. The theory development process described in this paper should be repeated with respect to strategy at the corporate level.

Efforts such as these will take a number of years to complete. However, the degree of success achieved in this task will determine the quality of the resource allocation decisions of the economy—an objective second to none in this period of scarce national and international resources.

REFERENCES

[1] Ackerman, Robert W.: *Organization and the Investment Process: A Comparative Study*. Doctoral dissertation, Harvard Business School, 1968.
[2] Aguilar, Francis J.: *Scanning the Business Environment*. New York, Macmillan, 1967.
[3] Akel, Anthony M.: *A Conceptual Framework for Viewing Industrial Research and Development Activities*. Doctoral dissertation, Northwestern University, Graduate School of Management, 1974.
[4] Allison, Graham T.: *Essence of Decision: Explaining the Cuban Missile Crisis*. Boston, Little, Brown, 1971.
[5] Ansoff, H. Igor: *Corporate Strategy*. New York, McGraw-Hill, 1965.
[6] Ansoff, H. Igor: "Toward a Strategic Theory of the Firm." In H. Igor Ansoff (ed.): *Business Strategy*. Baltimore, Penguin, 1969.
[7] Ansoff, H. Igor, and John Stewart: "Strategies for a Technology-Based Business." *Harvard Business Review*, Vol. 45, No. 6 (1967), 71–83.
[8] Athreya, Mrityunjay: *Guidelines for the Effectiveness of the Long-Range Planning Process*. Doctoral dissertation, Harvard Business School, 1967.
[9] Bower, Joseph L.: *Managing the Resource Allocation Process: A Study of Corporate Planning and Investment*. Boston, Division of Research, Harvard Business School, 1970.
[10] Carter, E. Eugene: *A Behavioral Theory Approach to Firm Investment and Acquisition Decisions*. Doctoral dissertation, Graduate School of Industrial Administration, Carnegie-Mellon University, 1969.
[11] Chevalier, Michel: "The Strategy Spectre Behind Your Market Share." *European Business*, No. 34, (1972), pp. 63–72.
[12] Collings, Robert L.: *Scanning the Environment for Strategic Information*. Doctoral dissertation, Harvard Business School, 1968.
[13] Ewing, David W.: *The Human Side of Planning*. New York, Macmillan, 1969.
[14] Fox, Harold W.: "A Framework for Functional Coordination." *Atlanta Economic Review*, Vol. 23, No. 6 (1973), 8–11.
[15] Fruhan, William E., Jr.: *The Fight for Competitive Advantage: A Study of U.S. Domestic Trunk Air Carriers*. Boston, Division of Research, Harvard Business School, 1972.
[16] Fruhan, William E. Jr.: "Pyrrhic Victories in Fights for Market Share." *Harvard Business Review*, Vol. 50, No. 5 (1972), 100–107.

[17] Glueck, William F.: "Business Policy: Reality and Promise." *Proceedings of the National Meetings of the Academy of Management,* 1972, pp. 108–111.

[18] Gutmann, Peter M.: "Strategies for Growth." *California Management Review,* Vol. 6, No. 4 (1964), 81–86.

[19] Henry, Harold W.: *Long Range Planning Practices in 45 Industrial Companies.* Englewood Cliffs, N.J., Prentice-Hall, 1967.

[20] Katz, Robert L.: *Cases and Concepts in Corporate Strategy.* Englewood Cliffs, N.J., Prentice-Hall, 1970.

[21] Keegan, Warren J.: *Scanning the International Business Environment: A Study of the Information Acquisition Process.* Doctoral dissertation, Harvard Business School, 1967.

[22] Khandwalla, Pradip: "The Techno-Economic Ecology of Corporate Strategy." Paper presented at the National Meetings of the Academy of Management, Business Policy and Planning Division sessions, 1974.

[23] Kitching, John: "Why Do Mergers Miscarry?" *Harvard Business Review,* Vol. 45, No. 6 (1967), 84–101.

[24] Learned, Edmund P., C. Roland Christensen, Kenneth R. Andrews, and William D. Guth: *Business Policy: Text and Cases.* Homewood, Ill., Irwin, 1965.

[25] Levitt, Theodore: "Exploit the Product Life Cycle." *Harvard Business Review,* Vol. 43, No. 6 (1965), 81–94.

[26] Michael, George: "Product Petrification: A New Stage in the Life Cycle." *California Management Review,* Vol. 14, No. 1 (1971), pp. 88–91.

[27] *Perspectives on Experience.* Boston, The Boston Consulting Group, 1970.

[28] Rumelt, Richard P.: *Strategy, Structure, and Economic Performance in Large American Industrial Corporations.* Boston, Harvard University Press, 1974.

[29] Schoeffler, Sidney: "Profit Impact on Marketing Strategy." Marketing Research Institute internal memorandum, November 1972.

[30] Schoeffler, Sidney, Robert D. Buzzell, and Donald F. Heany: "The Impact of Strategic Planning on Profit Performance." *Harvard Business Review,* Vol. 52, No. 2 (1974), 137–145.

[31] Shank, John K., Edward G. Niblock, and William T. Sandalls, Jr.: "Balance 'Creativity' and 'Practicality' in Formal Planning." *Harvard Business Review,* Vol. 53, No. 1 (1973), 81–90.

[32] Steiner, George A.: *Strategic Factors in Business Success.* New York, Financial Executives Research Foundation, 1969.

[33] Steiner, George A.: *Pitfalls in Comprehensive Long-Range Planning.* Oxford, Ohio, Planning Executives Institute, 1972.

[34] Stevenson, Howard H.: *Defining Corporate Strengths and Weaknesses: An Exploratory Study.* Doctoral dissertation, Harvard Business School, 1969.

[35] Tilles, Seymour: "Strategies for Allocating Funds." *Harvard Business Review,* Vol. 44 No. 1 (1966), 72–80.

[36] Udell, Jon G.: *Successful Marketing Strategies.* Madison, Wis., Mimir, 1972.

[37] Warren, E. Kirby: *Long-Range Planning: The Executive Viewpoint.* Englewood Cliffs, N.J., Prentice-Hall, 1966.

[38] Wasson, Chester R.: *Dynamic Competitive Strategy and Product Life Cycles.* St. Charles, Ill., Challenge Books, 1974.

CASE 23

Campaign GM

George A. Steiner

In 1970 the Project on Corporate Responsibility was created by Ralph Nader in Washington, D. C., and leaped into prominence with its "Campaign GM." The broad aims of the Project on Corporate Responsibility concerned such goals as making "corporate decision-makers more responsive to legitimate social demands, such as the need to end employment discrimination and develop the resources of economically disadvantaged communities." The main strategy of the Project was to get proxies from nonprofit institutions to vote proposals prepared by the Project. (See, "A Proposal on Corporate Responsibility," prepared by the Center for Law and Social Policy, and the Washington Research Project, Washington, D.C., October 20, 1969.)

Campaign GM was the first significant move of the Project. Two basic demands were made on the General Motors Corporation at its annual stockholders meeting in May 1970, as follows: first, set up a committee on corporate responsibility to study GM's performance in dealing with social and environmental issues and recommend changes "to make GM responsible," and, second, place three "public interest" directors on the Board.

The details of these two proposals as submitted to the stockholders of record, together with management's reasons why stockholders should reject them, were as shown in the accompanying facsimiles.

The Project requested large holders of GM stock to give it proxies to be used at the annual stockholders meeting to enforce its demands. Various university boards of trustees—Harvard, California, Michigan, and Texas, for instance—were requested to give The Project their proxies. Other large holders such as the charitable foundations also were solicited. No large holder gave The Project its proxies. Some, however, sympathized with the views of The Project.

The Rockefeller Foundation, for instance while casting its vote with management, criticized the corporation in explaining its position, some excerpts of which follow:

"There are constituents other than stockholders to whom corporations are also obligated. There are battles to be waged against racism, poverty, pollution, and urban blight which the Government alone cannot win; they can be won only if the status and power of American corporate industry are fully and effectively committed to the struggle.

What is needed from business today is leadership which is courageous, wise and compassionate, which is enlightened in its own and the public's interest, and

PROPOSAL

The Committee for Corporate Responsibility

Whereas the shareholders of General Motors are concerned that the present policies and priorities pursued by the management have failed to take into account the possible adverse social impact of the Corporation's activities, it is

Resolved that:

1. There be established the General Motors Shareholders Committee for Corporate Responsibility.

2. The Committee for Corporate Responsibility shall consist of no less than fifteen and no more than twenty-five persons, to be appointed by a representative of the Board of Directors, a representative of the Campaign to Make General Motors Responsible, and a representative of United Auto Workers, acting by majority vote. The members of the Committee for Corporate Responsibility shall be chosen to represent the following: General Motors Management, the United Auto Workers, environmental and conservation groups, consumers, the academic community, civil rights organizations, labor, the scientific community, religious and social service organizations, and small shareholders.

3. The Committee for Corporate Responsibility shall prepare a report and make recommendations to the shareholders with respect to the role of the corporation in modern society and how to achieve a proper balance between the rights and interests of shareholders, employees, consumers, and the general public. The Committee shall specifically examine, among other things:

   A. The Corporation's past and present efforts to produce an automobile which:

      (1) is nonpolluting
      (2) reduces the potentiality for accidents
      (3) reduces personal injury resulting from accidents
      (4) reduces property damage resulting from accidents
      (5) reduces the costs of repair and maintenance whether from accidents or extended use.

   B. The extent to which the Corporation's policies towards suppliers, employees, consumers and dealers are contributing to the goals of providing safe and reliable products.

   C. The extent to which the Corporation's past and present efforts have contributed to a sound national transportation policy and an effective low cost mass transportation system.

   D. The manner in which the Corporation has used its vast economic power to contribute to the social welfare of the nation.

   E. The manner by which the participation of diverse sectors of society in corporate decision-making can be increased including nomination and election of directors and selection of members of the committees of the Board of Directors.

4. The Committee's report shall be distributed to the shareholders and to the public no later than March 31, 1971. The Committee shall be authorized to employ staff members in the performance of its duties. The Board of Directors shall allocate to the Committee those funds the Board of Directors determines reasonably necessary for the Committee to accomplish its tasks. The Committee may obtain any information from the Corporation and its employees reasonably deemed relevant by the Committee, provided, however, that the Board of Directors may restrict the information to be made available to the Committee to information which the Board of Directors reasonably determines to be not privileged for buisness or competitive reasons.

PROPOSAL (continued)

The Stockholder has submitted the following statement in support of such resolution:

Reasons: "The purpose of this resolution is to enable shareholders to assess the public impact of the Corporation's decisions, and to determine the proper role of the Corporation in society. Past efforts by men such as Ralph Nader to raise these issues have been frustrated by the refusal of management to make its files and records available either to the shareholders or to the public. Only a committee representing a broad segment of the public with adequate resources and access to information can prepare a report which will accomplish these objectives."

The Board of Directors favors a vote AGAINST this resolution for the following reasons:

This resolution and the Proposal for Directors to Represent Special Interests by the same sponsor are parts of an attack on the General Motors Board of Directors and management on and on what General Motors has achieved on behalf of its stockholders and the public. In the opinion of the Board of Directors and management the attack is based on false conceptions and assumptions. It was launched by a stockholder (the Project), composed of seven members, which purchased 12 shares of General Motors stock in January 1970 for the express purpose of this attack. The Project has announced that while General Motors is its first target, similar attacks will be made on other large corporations.

The Project is a nonprofit corporation organized this year under the laws of the District of Columbia. Its formation was announced by Ralph Nader. Although he has stated that he is "not a formal participant in the Project" and the the "program" affecting General Motors is one "undertaken by a number of other young attorneys in Washington," he has promoted the Project and the Campaign to Make General Motors Responsible ("Campaign GM") by press interview, television appearance, and otherwise. For many years he has been identified with various campaigns against General Motors and was a prominent participant in a demonstration against the Corporation at the General Motors Building in New York in December 1969.

The names "Committee for Corporate Responsibility" and "Campaign to Make General Motors Responsible" together with this resolution which would establish a Committee for Corporate Responsibility and the statements in support of the resolution suggest that management's decisions "have failed to take into account the possible adverse social impact of the Corporation's activities. . ." This simply is not true. The true facts in regards to the concern and responsibility with which General Motors has pursued goals of social and public policy are set forth in the enclosed booklet, "GM's Record of Progress." We are proud of this record and all stockholders are urged to read the booklet. [Ed. note: for a more recent report see General Motors Corporation, ***1972 Report on Progress in Areas of Public Concern,*** (Warren, Michigan, GM Technical Center, 1972.)]

The objective of the resolution is to interpose a body unknown to corporate law or practice (the Committee for Corporate Responsibility)—purportedly investigatory in nature but structured for harassment and publicity—between the stockholders and the Board of Directors. The establishment of such a Committee would seriously hamper the Board of Directors in representing the stockholders and in carrying out its responsibilities to manage the business and affairs of the Corporation.

The proposed Committee, far from achieving "a proper balance between the rights and interest of shareholders, employees, consumers and the general public," is proposed to be appointed "by majority vote" of (i) a representative of "Campaign GM," which is a creature of the proponent of the resolution, (ii) a representative of the United Auto Workers, and (iii) a representative of the Board of Directors. This permits the crucial "majority vote," with power to elect the entire Committee, to be supplied by a representative of "Campaign GM" (which itself owns no General Motors stock) and by a

PROPOSAL (continued)

representative of the United Auto Workers. Members of the Committee would not be required to be stockholders of General Motors and would be chosen to represent General Motors management, the U.A.W., environmental and conservation groups, consumers, the academic community, civil rights organizations, labor, the scientific community, religious and social service organizations and small stockholders. It is obvious that the proponent of the resolution seeks this Committee to pursue its special interests.

The proposed method of appointing the proposed Committee makes it clear that its purpose is to harass the Corporation and its management and to promote the particular economic and social views espoused by the proponent of the resolution. The Board of Directors believes that this resolution, if adopted, would do serious damage to General Motors and to its stockholders and, in fact, to the general public.

The Board of Directors favors a vote AGAINST this Proposal for the Committee for Corporate Responsibility. Proxies solicited by the Board of Directors will be so voted unless stockholders specify in their proxies a contrary choice.

PROPOSAL

Directors to Represent Special Interests

Resolved: That Number 15 of the By-Laws of the Corporation be amended to read as follows:

15. The business of the Corporation shall be managed by a board of twenty-six members (an addition of three).

The Stockholder has submitted the following statement in support of such resolution:

Reasons: This amendment will expand the number of directors to enable representatives of the public to sit on the Board of Directors without replacing any of the current nominees of management. The proponents of this amendment believe that adding representatives of the public to the Board is one method to insure that the Corporation will consider the impact of its decisions on important public issues, including auto safety, pollution, repairs, mass transportation and equal employment opportunities.

The Board of Directors favors a vote AGAINST this resolution for the following reasons:

The Board of Directors finds no valid reason why the number of directors should be increased at the present time. Any suggestion that General Motors Corporation has been deficient in considering the interest of the public in such matters as auto safety, pollution, mass transportation and the like is entirely contrary to fact; the Company's record in this regard is set forth in the enclosed booklet.

The Board of Directors believes that each director, in addition to his responsibility to represent all the stockholders, has a very important responsibility to customers, employees, the public and society generally. This is in accord with the development of the modern American corporation and corporate theory to which General Motors wholeheartedly subscribes and in accordance with which it operates. But that is very different from having as members of the Board individuals, no matter how worthy, who would be elected to represent special interests and who would feel obliged to concentrate attention on those special interests whether or not the effect would be to disrupt the proper and effective functioning of the Board.

Moreover, the Board of Directors continues to believe that for a Board of Directors to be effective each member must feel a responsibility to represent all the stockholders. In fact, representation of special groups introduces the possibility of partisanship among board members which would impair the ability to work together, a requirement essential to the efficient functioning of a board of directors.

Stockholders should recognize that the resolution to amend the By-Laws to increase the number of Directors is not a simple, innocuous proposal. The real issue posed by this proposal is whether an opportunity should be created to inject into the Corporation's Board of Directors three additional directors who are selected not on the basis of their interest in the success of the Corporation but rather on the basis of their sympathy with the special interests of the proponent of the resolution. This is proposed under the guise that as "representatives of the public" they would insure that the Corporation "will consider the impact of its decisions on important public issues." The proposal is a reflection upon the service rendered to the Corporation and its stockholders by the present members of the Board of Directors who were elected because of their integrity and broad experience in many fields including public service. The suggestion that they have not taken into account the impact of their decisions upon the public has no basis in fact. The objective of this proposal is substantially the same as that of the proposal for the Committee for Corporate Responsibility.

If the proponent should be successful in increasing the number of directors and thereafter electing its nominees, the Board of Directors believes there would be similar internal harassment to the detriment of General Motors, its stockholders and the public.

The Board of Directors favors a vote AGAINST this Proposal for Directors to Represent Special Interests. Proxies solicited by the Board of Directors will be so voted unless stockholders specify in their proxies a contrary choice.

which greets change with an open mind. In our judgment, the management of General Motors did not display this spirit in its response to the two proposals offered by Campaign GM (a subgroup of the Committee on Corporate Responsibility).

We recognize that these proposals are, from management's viewpoint, unwieldy and impractical; Campaign GM itself conceded the difficulty it encountered in trying to determine a method of selecting members of a Committee for Corporate Responsibility. Because of these inadequacies we are prepared, this time, to sign our proxy as requested by management. But we are not prepared to let the matter rest there.

We do not share the view which was expressed by management that the Campaign GM proposals represent an 'attack' on the corporation. . . . We believe the language of the Campaign GM proposals is more reasonable and temperate than the response of management. We also believe the goals of the proposals have been designed to serve the public good by increasing the corporation's awareness of the major impact of its decisions and policies on society at large [*The Wall Street Journal,* September 1, 1970].

The demands of Campaign GM were not met because the overwhelming majority of stockholders gave their proxies to GM's management. Reactions in 1970, however, seemed to portend trouble for General Motors' management in 1971.

In September 1970 the General Motors Corporation announced that it was responding to criticism that the company's decisions sometimes did not take the public welfare into consideration, by forming a Public Policy Committee of five GM directors. Mr. Roche said that matters associated with community action and corporate citizenship will, therefore, have "a permanent place on the highest level of management." He said that he anticipates that the work of the committee "will demonstrate their understanding of General Motors and its industry, their awareness of the expanding role of business in society, and their comprehension of the responsibilities of the board of directors, who are charged with the successful operation of the business." The committee "will inquire into all phases of General Motors' operations that relate to matters of public policy and recommend actions to the full board." None of the members of the committee were officers of GM.

In January 1971 General Motors invited the Reverend Leon H. Sullivan to become the first black member of its board of directors. Reverend Sullivan, in commenting on his appointment said, "I told Mr. Roche he should have no illusions about what I am. He knows I'm a man who expresses his opinions, and that I will not be tied to the traditions of the board. I'm more interested in human returns than capital returns. My main concern is helping to improve the position of black people in America. I want to be a voice from the outside on the inside" [*Business Week,* April 10, 1971, p. 100].

At the May 1971 stockholders meeting, Campaign GM advanced new proposals to make GM "accountable to the people their decisions affect." These included a requirement for GM to list in the proxy it sends to shareholders the names of suggested directors made by nonmanagement shareholders; a proposal to require GM to disclose in its annual report information about such matters as minority hiring, air pollution, and automobile safety policies so that shareholders "may accurately evaluate the performance of management in meeting public responsibilities in these areas;" and a proposal to permit GM's key constituencies—employees, consumers, and dealers—to participate in the election of three of the directors of the company.

These proposals were overwhelmingly defeated. The Project on Corporate Responsibility held 12 of GM's 286 million shares of stock and were able to gather together less than 3 per cent of the shares voted. This was less than in 1970.

In 1972 The Project on Corporate Responsibility made two new proposals. One would require the directors of General Motors to appoint a committee to study the desirability of dividing the company into several independent corporations. The proposal suggested that the corporation should be broken up because its fear of antitrust action by the Government has prevented GM from competing for a larger share of the market. The function of the committee, therefore, would be to determine whether breaking up the company would not be in the best interests of the public as well as maximizing profits of the separated companies. The second proposal called for regular progress reports from GM's Public Policy Committee. These proposals received less than 2 per cent of the votes cast.

In three annual meetings, the overwhelming number of stockholders gave GM's management their vote of confidence and flatly rejected the proposals of "The Project." By the size of the vote it is obvious that even the foundations and nonprofit institutions holding GM stock voted with the management.

QUESTIONS

1. Identify the *fundamental issues* raised in this case about the business-society relationship and the way corporations are influenced and managed? Which of these issues raise major policy/strategy questions for GM?
2. Argue the *pros and cons* of The Project's proposal for the Committee for Social Responsibility. (For a sharp criticism of The Project on Corporate Responsibility see Henry G. Mann: "Who's Responsible?" *Barrons,* May 17, 1971.)
3. Argue the *pros and cons of placing special interest* representatives on boards of directors of American Corporations. (See Harold Koontz: "The Corporate Board and Special Interests." *Business Horizons,* October 1971, pp. 75–93; "Arthur Goldberg on Public Directors." *Business and Society Review/Innovation,* Spring 1973, pp. 35–39; and "responses to the Goldberg Proposal on Public Directors." *Business and Society Review,* Summer 1973, pp. 37–43.
4. *If you were a shareholder of* the company would you give your proxy to management or The Project? Explain.
5. Who is to determine what the social responsibilities are of a company like General Motors?
6. Do *you approve* the several *GM actions* which were taken to be more responsive to social interests?

CASE 24

South African Apartheid and Polaroid

On January 13, 1971, the Polaroid Corporation ran a full page statement in the Los Angeles Times (Part 1, p. 8) responding to critics who condemned the company for selling its products in South Africa. It was asserted that so long as Polaroid sold in South Africa its very presence there supported the South African government and its policies of racial separation and subjugation of the blacks. A number of other American companies doing business in South Africa have been similarly condemned.

Polaroid's South African sales amount to less than ½ per cent of its worldwide business. It formed a committee, with both black and white employees of the company, to study the question: "Is it right or wrong to do business in South Africa?" The newspaper statement said the first conclusion was arrived at quickly and unanimously, namely, "We abhor *apartheid,* the national policy of South Africa." The committee visited South Africa and, after talking with many people, came to the conclusion that Polaroid should stay in South Africa but undertake an experimental program with the following attributes. First, the company will take steps with its distributors and suppliers to improve "dramatically" salaries and benefits of nonwhite employees. Second, Polaroid's business associates will be obliged "to initiate a well-defined program to train nonwhite employees for important jobs within their companies." Third, the company will commit some of its profits earned in South Africa to encourage black education. Fourth, although Polaroid does not have investments in South Africa and does not at present intend to change that policy, it will investigate "the possibilities of creating a black-managed company in one or more of the free black African nations." The statement concluded:

"How can we presume to concern ourselves with the problems of another country? Whatever the practices elsewhere, South Africa alone articulates a policy exactly contrary to everything we feel our company stands for. We cannot participate passively in such a political system. Nor can we ignore it. That is why we have undertaken this experimental program."

QUESTIONS

1. Argue the case for and against Polaroid's decision to stay in South Africa. (See John Blashill: "The Proper Role of U.S. Corporations in South

Africa." *Fortune,* July 1972, pp. 49–52, 89–92; and Tim Smith: "South Africa: The Churches vs. The Corporations." *Business and Society Review,* Fall 1975, pp. 54–64.

2. Can you suggest any guidelines for American companies, doing business in a foreign company, in attempting to change major policies of foreign governments?

CASE 25

World Mining and Chemicals, Inc.

John F. Steiner

Victor White, Chairman of World Mining and Chemicals (WMC) was worried. He had just finished reading a report, which he had requested, concerning "payoffs" made by his executives around the world. The totals, when examined in relation to the company's earnings, staggered him. It was clear to White that he faced both a policy problem and a moral quandry.

As he paced his office, White reflected on the history of WMC. Founded in 1873 as American Mines by a tough financier named Matthew Baker, the company grew spectacularly from an independent coal mining outfit on the east coast of the United States to a worldwide operation. After World War I, Baker had the foresight to pursue overseas investments in mining and smelting operations. Upon his death in 1931, the company came into the hands of a group of New York investors which installed a professional management team and expanded operations into the ex-colonial states of the Third World. The name of the company was changed from American Mines to the less parochial WMC to avoid offending nationalistic foreign interests and to reflect the increasing diversification of the companies' activities.

In 1976 WMC had total sales of $2.5 billion. Approximately half the sales came from coal, nickel, bauxite, and copper operations and half from chemical activities, which included petrochemical, coal derivative, and desalinization plants. Worldwide economic conditions in 1975 were not favorable to WMC, and net profits had declined to $75 million. The chemicals operations registered a much higher rate of return on assets employed than the mining activities. White calculated that his company's return on equity and capital employed was considerably under the industry average.

Despite the relatively poor performance of 1975, WMC was being competently managed. Had it not been for severe labor problems in its mines in Angola and a disastrous fire in its New Jersey petrochemical facility, net profits would probably have been 50 per cent higher in 1975. In addition, WMC's top management prided itself on the way in which it was able to train and move up foreign nationals in its management levels. Indeed, it was White's policy to head each foreign activity with a foreign national whenever a suitable person could be found and, where one could not be found, the local managers were supposed to seek nationals and train them for top management positions.

Partly because of the presence of these foreign nationals in WMC's management the company had always been a pragmatically run operation. Its managers—including Victor White—had always been aware of the need for making various kinds of minor payments to businessmen and government officials overseas. Without these payments construction permits were unaccountably delayed by minor bureaucrats, supplies from foreign companies were often held up, and labor union officials found grievances where none had existed before.

Although some moralists called these payments "bribes," such views were largely ignored by the majority of WMC's executives. Little was said one way or the other about them. When they discussed this matter—which was seldom—WMC's managers argued that such payments facilitated business dealings and should be permitted where indigenous to other cultures. They were considered to be "tips" for services rendered.

Then in 1974 the Securities and Exchange Commission began an investigation into the illegal contributions made to President Nixon's 1972 campaign by American businessmen. During the course of this investigation the SEC made the unexpected discovery that a number of prominent American corporations engaged in overseas payoffs of one kind or another and that they juggled their books to hide the payments since such payments were not tax deductible. Following the SEC revelation, a Senate subcommittee began to hold hearings to investigate the allegations and the SEC began to move toward regulations that would require disclosure of such payments.

This march of events alarmed White, and he ordered an investigation of WMC's foreign subsidiaries to determine the extent of the company's involvement in payoff dealings overseas. A thorough report was compiled by Wayne Osgood, a senior vice president, which revealed that the volume and size of WMC's overseas payoffs was significant. In brief, the report showed that WMC's managers were making several types of payments to facilitate commercial dealings. These payments totalled $9.5 million for 1975, and White knew that the estimate in the report was probably low since Osgood found it difficult to get the cooperation of managers in compiling the report.

First, the report indicated that "lubrication" payments for small favors were commonly made by WMC's subsidiaries in Latin America, Asia, Africa, and the Middle East. Since these payments were made at many levels within the management hierarchy and were mostly smaller sums, they were difficult to trace. It was estimated, nevertheless, that they amounted to about $2 million.

Second, the report showed that WMC's top managers in several foreign countries were making payments which could not be considered as simple "facilitation" expenditures; they were too large and too regular. For example, the head of WMC's Southern European Regional office was making payments of several hundred thousand dollars per year to leaders of the Italian Christian Democratic party. This was necessary, he said, to safeguard the interests of WMC in matters that came before the Italian Parliament. It was estimated in the report that worldwide payments in this category amounted to close to $3 million.

Third, the managers of WMC's operations in Arab lands were making substantial payments to so-called "middlemen" who, by virtue of their contacts and familiarity with Middle East business customs, were able to demand large fees from their clients. The contract to build large desalinization plants in Saudi Arabia in 1975 had necessitated the payment of $2 million as a "commission" to such a middleman. Some of this money was used by the intermediaries to "bribe" Saudi Arabian government officials, a fact not previously known for sure but suspected by WMC managers. Without this "commission payment" WMC would never have been awarded the contract since the Saudi Arabian government refused to engage in direct dealings with WMC. The 1975 total for all "commission payments" to middlemen around the world was $4.5 million.

Compounding White's problems was a request for a "campaign contribution" for President Taron Chee of Malakor, a small Asian country. In his appeal President Chee had mentioned that if the contribution was not forthcoming WMC's $400 million investment in two copper mines and a copper smelter would surface as an issue in the forthcoming presidential and parliamentary elections. He threatened to raise the issue of expropriation and exploit the nationalist sentiment among right-wing political factions in Malakor. Chee requested a contribution of $10 million—enough, White knew, to insure election in the small country of 15 million people. White suspected that this amount could be "negotiated" down to $2 or $3 million, but that was still a large sum.

The payoff situation had become an agenda item at regularly scheduled board meetings, and discussions had revealed disagreement among the members. Several outside members, along with Wayne Osgood, were indignant and argued for the dismissal of managers of foreign operations who had made questionable payments. They rejected any argument that moral pragmatism might be an appropriate approach to payoff questions and argued that the risk of damaging disclosures which might tarnish WMC's image and drive stock prices down should be avoided. They pointed to the sad tale of the bribe United Brands had paid to officials of the Honduran government in 1974 and the subsequent suicide of United's chief executive officer Eli Black, the 40 per cent drop in United Brand's stock prices, and the expropriation of the company's holdings in Panama. These directors argued that it was morally repugnant and ultimately unprofitable to be less virtuous overseas than in the United States.

Others argued vehemently for moral pragmatism. They pointed to the fact that such payments were expected and often even legal in foreign lands. If WMC did not make them, competitors probably would and business would be lost. They observed that in the wake of the SEC hearings Lockheed had agreed to pass no bribes in its overseas dealings and had subsequently lost a jumbo-jet deal in India to a French company which allegedly made a $1.5 million contribution to the Congress Party. There was, these directors argued, no valid argument for the company becoming an instrument of global moral uplift. WMC was in business to return a profit for its stockholders.

Another viewpoint came from Hamilton Baker, the young grandson of WMC's founder Matthew Baker and a captious critic of the company's affairs. A drop-out divinity student, Baker was basically antiestablishment in his thought and delighted in ridiculing what he saw as the "narrow-minded and pompous thinking of greedy businessmen." Baker had disdained consideration of the overseas payoff question as a serious policy issue. He asserted that such payoffs were made routinely to police, politicians, government officials, and businessmen here in the United States. This being the case, it was sheer hypocrisy to proclaim that overseas business standards were less moral than American ones. The differences were, he argued, superficial, and he indicated that WMC should probably clean up its domestic operations before it could become a credible vehicle for spreading virtue overseas.

White felt there were serious financial and philosophical issues involved in a policy decision on this issue and decided to obtain more information. He got a copy of a study on overseas bribery by a group of distinguished professors. In part, it read as follows:

"Bribery is an accepted fact of international business life and, with the exception of some of the advanced industrial nations, is everywhere prevalent. Indeed, many foreign businessmen cannot understand the concern of sacrosanct American executives who condemn what to foreigners are harmless payments which facilitate commerce. Such payments may, in fact, perform positive functions within the overall social, political, and economic mileu within which they are made. For example:

- Small bribes to bureaucrats, a tradition in many Asian countries, compensate for low government salaries and enable lesser officials to make a comfortable living which they otherwise could not make on their salaries.
- Where political instability is high, government officials often can expect short tenure and money extorted from various sources—including foreign businesses—is considered an appropriate type of retirement pay.
- Payoffs and bribes are one way of making overly bureaucratic and codified governmental and legal systems function. In countries such as India and Italy where businesses must operate within a labyrinthine maze of laws and bureaus, small payments often serve to overcome potential obstructions and make an unwieldy system work.
- In modernizing countries corruption may help assimilate new groups into the political and economic life of a country, just as poor immigrants into the United States sold their votes to political machines in exchange for a role in the new order.
- Sometimes systems of corruption may make it possible for old and displaced

elites in a developing country to buy their way back into a new government. This may be preferrable to having a disgruntled group frozen out of power by formal electoral mechanisms or revolutionary propaganda."

As White read these and other passages in the study he began to doubt that an uncompromising stand against all overseas payments was appropriate. Yet he did not feel that all types of payments were justified. Although this study enlightened the chairman it failed to provide him with the answers he was seeking. He continued to contemplate his stance on the matter.

QUESTIONS

1. Does WMC need a policy on overseas payments? If so, what should such a policy say? If not, why not?
2. Should a distinction be made between types of money transactions commonly classified as "payoffs"?
3. Should American companies operating in foreign cultures continue to adhere to American standards of business morality or should they adapt to different moral climates?
4. If you were White, what actions would you take (other than simply writing a policy statement) to straighten out the affairs of WMC?

REFERENCES

Mary Bralove: "United Brands." *Wall Street Journal,* May 7, 1975.

Milton S. Gwirtzman and Alan R. Novak: "Reform of Bribery Abroad Involves U. S. Policy." *Los Angeles Times,* October 5, 1975.

John B. Schnapp: "The Case of the Crisis in Caribia." *Harvard Business Review,* November–December 1968.

Joseph Waldman: "Overseas Corruption of Business—A Philosophical Perspective." *Business and Society,* Fall 1974.

CASE 26

Atlantic Manufacturing Company

Michael Goodman is the general manager of the Metal Stamping Division of the Atlantic Manufacturing Company. His division is the largest in the company and is responsible for 65 per cent of the corporate net profits. He is sitting at his desk—angry, frustrated, and puzzled. A delegation of employees has just left his office threatening a strike if his production line is not slowed down. Yesterday, he became embroiled in a losing battle with the government's pollution supervisor because his air emissions were above allowable levels. Over the past six months, he has watched the productivity of his plant decline because central headquarters has forced him to employ increasing numbers of hard-core unemployed who, without requisite skills for their jobs, cannot meet productivity standards.

What bothers Goodman most is, on the one hand, being forced to take action that will reduce productivity and profits, while, on the other, being judged strictly on the returns on investment of his division. To make matters worse, he cannot seem to impress the president of the company with the fact that his speeches about all the great things the company should do to meet its social obligations are putting great pressure on Goodman to do things that will reduce his ability to achieve his profit goals. For instance, in a speech to the Local League of Women Voters last week, the president said: "Our company is and will continue to be on the forefront of those that stand as good citizens in the community. We recognize our obligations to help those with whom we are associated, inside as well as outside our company, to lead the good life." Goodman thinks there is a direct connection between such rhetoric and the increasing demands made upon him to do things which reduce his profits. The president disagrees with Goodman and points out that if the environment of a business, internally and externally, is vibrant and healthy the profits of the company will expand.

QUESTIONS

1. Identify some of the basic policy problems in this case. How do you account for the dichotomy between presidential rhetoric and Goodman's problems in implementing social programs? (See Philip T. Drotning: "Why Nobody takes Corporate Social Responsibility Seriously." *Business and Society Review,* Autumn 1972, pp. 68–72.)

2. You are hired as a consultant by this company to make recommendations for specific policies and plans to put the president's fundamental social aims into operation. What do you recommend? (See Terry McAdam: "How to Put Corporate Responsibility into Practice." *Business and Society Review/Innovation,* Summer 1973, pp. 8–20; and Robert W. Ackerman: *The Social Challenge to Business.* Cambridge, Mass.: Harvard University Press, 1975.)

CASE 27

Force Reduction At Machinery Systems

George A. Steiner

Bill Paust, Manager of the Engineering Department of Machinery Systems, was responsible for three sections. They were Design Engineering, Production Engineering, and Drafting. His department did all of the engineering for Machinery Systems (MS). MS was a division of International Business Systems (IBS), a large company having a worldwide business.

Business within the division had been good but, recently, things were slowing down because of the economic recession. Paust knew it was only a matter of time before adjustments in expense and products would be necessary. So, when Paust and the other department heads of MS were informed that IBS wanted a 10 per cent cutback in costs, he was not totally surprised.

When Paul Stevens, MS's president, read the directive to his managers, he included an additional 5 per cent cutback. Paust, being one of the senior managers within the division, objected to the addition but Stevens was determined to exceed the demands of the parent and held his ground. Now, it was up to Paust and the others to find ways and means to implement the reduction. The following morning Paust informed his section heads of the cutback and requested each of them to submit to him a proposal for the reduction of expenses.

Paust now sat at his desk reviewing the three proposals. It was rather routine and impersonal, for each manager had worked out an operating schedule and a budget. Each had indicated which projects he was cutting back and how many people were to be layed off. A footnote on the proposal from Design Engineering caught Paust's eye. It read: "Of the seven engineers I have to lay off, one of them is Terry Moore, the only black engineer I have in the design section."

This troubled Paust for two reasons. First, he had long been an advocate of civil rights and had strongly supported the IBS program of minority hiring. Second, his Division had major government contracts and was subject to periodic review to ensure that equal employment policies were followed. Paust's Department currently employed 7 per cent black nonprofessionals and 2.8 per cent black professionals. The laying off of Moore would cause a significant drop that would be noticed. Paust wanted to find a way of keeping Moore.

He had previously requested the personnel records of those employees to be laid off. He thumbed through the folders, selected Moore's, and read all of the personal data sheet. "Two years with company, thirty-three years old, married with two children, B.S. in electrical engineering, grades average, previous work experience satisfactory." He turned to the comments made when Moore was hired. "Attitude seemed good, and has potential of doing work within standards of this division." He then turned to the supervisors' quarterly assessment, and selected various comments. "Moore is well liked in the department, he is a pleasant fellow and gets along well with his co-workers. He is learning the procedure, and at present there seem to be no problems." Another comment read: "Having complaints from manufacturing on Moore's work. He is catching his mistakes too late and has had to put through a number of modification notices. Spoke to Moore and gave him suggestion to improve." Another read: "Still too many modification notices on Moore's work. Is now attending a refresher course in New York. Plan on assigning him to Mason on the advanced program circuit project when he returns. Should give him some help." These comments indicated to Paust that Moore was able to adjust and willing to work to improve his performance. But the notes, together with what he knew about other engineers in his Department, including those who were to be laid off, left no doubt in his mind that Moore was not as capable as the others.

Paust thought of some alternatives for keeping Moore. He could go to Stevens and explain the situation; but, he quickly rejected this because he knew that Stevens would not yield on a decision. Paust would have to find another way of solving the problem.

He considered not cutting back on the advanced program circuit project; again, he rejected this because a cutback here would not affect the present schedule nor create future problems.

Could he have Gene Howell, the design section head, lay off someone else? He reached for the phone and dialed Howell's extension. "Hi, Gene," said Paust, "I'm reviewing your proposal for the cutback and wanted to discuss the possibility of moving Moore to a current project in place of another man."

"I considered that possibility, Bill, but right now I'm behind schedule and will be short seven men. If I moved Moore in place of a more experienced man I'm afraid he won't be able to cut it. And, with the present situation that is something I can't afford to do," replied Howell.

"Why couldn't he cut it," questioned Paust.

"It would take any man a few months to know the project as well as a man who was working on it for nine months. Furthermore, consider the backlash I would encounter, if I replaced a white fellow with Moore; there would be talk of preferential treatment. To be perfectly honest, I need all of the morale I can muster to meet my schedule with a reduced staff."

"Do you see any alternatives?" asked Paust.

"No, not really," answered Howell.

"I understand," said Paust before saying good-bye and hanging up.

Paust knew he could not move Moore to Production Engineering, because he has asked that section head to cutback too. Moving Moore around within the Department was not feasible because he had no experience with the other engineering programs.

Paust removed a booklet from his desk which contained the IBS minority employment requirements. He turned to the last page and read the concluding paragraph: "A manager should recognize that he is expected to fulfill the above equal employment requirements within his Department, while achieving his profit goals. It is not an either/or situation, and one does not give relief to the other."

Paust knew his decision would have to satisfy both rules and that he would have to make it before tomorrow when he was to meet with Stevens.

QUESTIONS

1. What realistic alternatives are open to Paust? (This case was suggested by Theodore V. Purcell: "Case of the Borderline Black." *Harvard Business Review,* November–December 1971, in which alternative recommendations for the decision are discussed especially pp. 143–150. For further analysis of this case see Timothy B. Blodgett: " 'Borderline Black' Revisited." *Harvard Business Review,* March–April 1972, pp. 132–140; and a letter from Colin Barrett: *Harvard Business Review,* January–February 1972, pp. 161–163.)
2. If you were Paust what decision would you make? What justification would you give for your decision?
3. What policies would you suggest to prevent future problems of this nature?

REFERENCE

For a good short and operational statement of what one company is doing about equal opportunity and minority relations see *General Electric's Commitment to Progress in Equal Opportunity and Minority Relations,* Corporate Business Environment, Equal Opportunity/Minority Relations Operation (General Electric, New York, undated). For some of the wrong things managers have done see Elmer H. Burack, F. James Staszak and Gopal C. Pati: "An Organizational Analysis of Manpower Issues in Employing the Disadvantaged." *Journal of the Academy of Management,* September 1972, pp. 255–271. For a thorough and superb analysis see Theodore V. Purcell and Gerald F. Cavanagh: *Blacks in the Industrial World* (New York, The Free Press, 1972.)

CASE 28

Smokey Cigarette Company

You are the President of the Smokey Cigarette Company. A delegation of community leaders has just left your office after expressing in the strongest language that you have a deep social responsibility to stop advertising your products because advertising does, in fact, induce young people to start smoking and does also maintain demand among those who are now smoking. You feel that the Surgeon General's Report on the relationship between cigarette smoking and cancer does present convincing evidence of the connection. Yet, you still have some doubts. You know there is a close correlation between cigarette advertising and sales by brand. If you stopped advertising, sales would drop and there would be a serious impact on earnings and stock prices. Furthermore, many farmers and your own employees are dependent upon your company. What do you think your social responsibilities are in this case?

CASE 29

DuPont's Refusal to Supply Certain Information*

February 11, 1972

TO: Subcommittee on Monopoly of the Senate Select Committee on Small Business

FROM: Ralph Nader

Re refusal by the DuPont Company to provide certain information.

Jim Phelan, director of the student task force that produced the report, "DuPont in Delaware: The Company State," had the following experiences in seeking information from the company as a stockholder and a citizen:

1. DuPont refused to provide any data on air emissions and water effluent either in the aggregate or on a plant-by-plant basis, on the grounds that the former was confidential; the latter not collected. Note that in order to complete a permit application under the 1899 Refuse Act, plant-by-plant data on water effluents must be filed and must be public.

2. DuPont refused to provide any data on minority employment even though aggregate data is supplied to the Equal Employment Opportunity Commission. Company spokesmen maintained that they do not keep the data on a plant-by-plant basis. Two plant managers, apparently unaware that they did not keep those figures, provided them to the task force.

3. DuPont refused to supply the company telephone directory.

4. DuPont refued to reveal the total of company deposits in state banks.

5. DuPont refused to give a list of major stockholders and foundations with company stock, even though virtually all corporations with more than 500 stockholders are required to file at least a partial list of major stockholders with the Securities and Exchange Commission.

6. DuPont refused to disclose its membership in trade associations on the grounds that it would be too burdensome to compile the data.

7. DuPont reported aggregate figures on frequency of work accidents, but refused to report it on a plant-by-plant basis.

8. DuPont refused to reveal the number of employees in each plant, but did so in two cases. Company spokesmen indicated that this could enable competitors to discover secret manufacturing processes (e.g., by learning the number of engineers at work on a given project).

9. DuPont refused to disclose the value added per plant on the double

* Reprinted from U.S. Senate Select Committee on Small Business, *Role of Giant Corporations: Hearings Before the Subcommittee on Monopoly,* 92nd Cong., 1st Sess., Part 2A, 9&12 November 1971, pp. 1218–1219.

grounds that it was a trade secret and that, in any case, the information was not kept.

10. DuPont refused to provide any information on the employment of women other than to say that their promotion policies with respect to women were the same as for all other employees.

11. DuPont would not disclose the company's policy statement containing guidelines for employee political participation.

12. DuPont refused to provide a list of company investments in Delaware on the grounds that the information was not maintained on a state basis. When asked the capitalized or book value of their lands and buildings in Delaware, company spokesmen said these figures are confidential.

QUESTIONS

1. Should DuPont be forced to supply this type of information to anyone wanting it? Argue the issue pro and con.
2. What specific information should United States companies be obliged to make public that they are not now required by law to disclose publicly? (For some details, see Hearings.)
3. Through library research, support this assertion: American businesses disclose to the public far greater and more detailed operational information than businesses located in any other country of the world.

Appendix Readings

READING A

How to Evaluate a Firm*

Robert B. Buchele

The sharp drops in earnings and even losses recently suffered by many so-called "growth" companies, whose stocks had been bid so high, have cast doubts upon the adequacy of the established methods which are used by investment specialists to evaluate companies.

Equally dramatic but less evident have been the serious declines of numerous companies shortly after having been rated as "excellently managed" by the best known of the evaluation systems using a list of factors covering numerous aspects of corporate management.

What has happened to render these evaluation systems so inadequate? What lessons can be learned by persons whose work requires them to do over-all evaluations of companies—investors, acquisition specialists, consultants, long-range planners, and chief executives? Finally, what are the requirements for a system for evaluating firms that will function reliably under today's conditions?

After all, the decline of even blue chip companies is not a new phenomenon. To quote from an unpublished paper recently presented by Ora C. Roehl before a management conference at UCLA:

> The Brookings Institution sometime ago made a study of the 100 top businesses in the USA in the early 1900's, and they found that after 40 years only 36 were still among the leaders.
>
> "We all look at the Dow-Jones Industrial Average practically every day and we know the companies that are a part of the Average today—from Allied Chemical, Aluminum Company of America, and American Can to U. S. Steel, Westinghouse, and Woolworth. But, as we go back in time a bit, we find names that once were

 Reprinted from *California Management Review,* Vol. V, No. 1, pp. 5–16 by permission of The Regents.

important enough to be a part of the Average and which we have heard of, such as Hudson Motors, Famous Players-Lasky, and Baldwin Locomotive. It is not long, however, before we run into one-time business leaders whose names are strange to us, such as Central Leather, U. S. Cordage Company, Pacific Mail, American Cotton Oil Company, and one with a nostalgic sort of name, The Distilling and Cattle Feeding Company" [1].

What is new, however, is the current pace of such events. Stemming in part from the rise of industrial research expenditures from less than $200 million in 1930 to an estimated $12.4 billion in 1960 [2], the pace of industrial change has been accelerating for many years. It is now so rapid that firms can rise or fall more quickly than ever before.

Sophisticated technologies are spreading to many industries; in addition, as we shall see in this article, various management techniques contribute to the quickening pace of change. In consequence, the rapid rate of change now affects a great many American firms rather than just that minority known as "growth" companies.

PRESENT EVALUATION METHODS

Financial Analysis

This method typically consists of studying a "spread" of profit and loss figures, operating statements and balance sheet ratios for the past five or ten years. The underlying assumption is that the future performance of a company can be reliably projected from trends in these data. The reasoning is that these data represent the "proof of the pudding." If they're sound, the company as a whole, particularly its top management, must be sound, for a competent top management will keep a firm healthy.

Through the years this method has worked well because the basic assumption has been reasonably valid. Despite the fact that some blue chip companies have failed, it is still reasonably valid for the large firms who are thoroughly entrenched in their markets and who make substantial investments in executive development, in market development, and in any technology that promises to threaten one of their market positions.

However, the assumption is becoming less safe, especially in connection with medium-sized and small firms, as the pace of industrial change steadily accelerates. Thus, a firm whose financial record is unimpressive may be on the verge of a technological breakthrough that will send its profits rocketing ahead; conversely, a company that looks good in financial analyses may be doomed because it is being bypassed technologically or marketing-wise or because rigor mortis has taken over the executive offices.

In practice the financial analysis method is often supplemented by market research in the form of interviews with leading customers, by interviews with the firm's top executives, and by consultation with scientists capable of evaluating technological capabilities and trends. While these supplementary activities help, financial analysis still is neither adequately comprehensive nor adequately oriented to the future.

Thus, this type of market research can yield some insights into the effectiveness of past and present performance but is too superficial to tell much about the future. The interviews with top executives can be more misleading than informative simply because they are conducted by financial people inexperienced in management, marketing, or technology [3]. The use of scientists is a commendable step forward. However, it provides help in only one and possibly two of the many areas essential to a thorough education.

Key Factor Ratings

Systems more comprehensive than the financial analysis method have been developed, mainly by consultants seeking to understand firms' overall strengths and weaknesses in order to be able to prescribe for them. Such systems typically involve ratings based on a series of key factors underlying the financial factors themselves. Little has been published about these systems because the consulting firms regard them as proprietary secrets. One system that has been published and, therefore, is well known is that developed by the American Institute of Management [4]. That this system is not adequately future-oriented is clearly proved by the fact that numerous companies have encountered deep trouble shortly after being rated "excellently managed" by the AIM [5].

Professor Erwin Schell a decade ago set forth a comprehensive system with some future-oriented elements; however, he recently stated that his system should be revised to give greater emphasis to the future via more attention to the R&D function [6].

As indicated in the Outline for Evaluation of a Firm on pages 896–898, as it is at present and as it will be in the future, can be organized around a series of penetrating questions. Thorough study of the areas covered by these questions will yield a picture, oriented to the future, of the strengths and weaknesses of the firm under consideration and a reliable indication of its chances for success in the future.

There are, as the outline shows, four vital areas in a firm about which you should ask questions. They are its product lines and basic competitive position; its R&D and operating departments; its financial position as revealed by analysis of the traditional financial data plus an estimate of the quality of its financial management; its top management with emphasis not only upon its past record, but also on its adequacy to cope with the future.

When these data have been assembled and summarized, you are in a position to evaluate both the present situation and potential of the firm under study as an investment possibility or as a management problem.

The rest of this article will be devoted to a discussion of these factors one by one. First we shall pose the questions contained in the outline; then we shall discuss the techniques professional analysts use for obtaining such data and determining what it means.

OUTLINE FOR EVALUATION OF A FIRM

I. PRODUCT LINES AND BASIC COMPETITIVE POSITION

A A. Past

What strengths and weakness in products (or services) have been dominant in this firm's history—design features, quality-reliability, prices, patents, proprietary position?

B. Present

What share of its market(s) does the firm now hold, and how firmly? Is this share diversified or concentrated as to number of customers? In what phases of their life cycles are the present chief products and what is happening to prices and margins? How do customers and potential customers regard this firm's products? Are the various product lines compatible marketing-wise, engineering-wise, manufacturing-wise? If not, is each product line substantial enough to stand on its own feet?

C. Future

Is the market(s) as a whole expanding or contracting, and at what rate? What is the trend in this firm's share of the market(s)? What competitive trends are developing in numbers of competitors, technology, marketing pricing? What is its vulnerability to business cycle (or defense spending) changes? Is management capable of effectively integrating market research, R & D, and market development program for a new product or products?

II. R & D AND OPERATING DEPARTMENTS

A. R & D and Engineering

What is the nature and the depth of its R & D capability? Of engineering capability? What are engineering's main strengths and weaknesses re creativity, quality-reliability, simplicity? Is the R & D effort based on needs defined by market research, and is it an integral part of an effective new product development program? Are R & D efforts well planned, directed, and controlled? What return have R & D dollars paid in profitable new products? Have enough new products been produced? Have schedules been met?

B. Marketing

Nature of the Marketing Capability—What channels of distribution are used? How much of the total marketing job (research, sales, service, advertising and promotion) is covered? Is this capability correctly tailored to match the nature and diversity of the firm's product lines? Is there a capability for exploiting new products and developing new markets? Quality of the marketing capability—is market

OUTLINE FOR EVALUATION OF A FIRM (continued)

research capable of providing the factual basis that will keep the firm, especially its new product development and R & D programs, truly customer-oriented? Is there a capability for doing broad economic studies and studies of particular industries that will help management set sound growth and/or deversification strategies?

C. Manufacturing

What is the nature of the manufacturing processes, the facilities and the skills—are they appropriate to today's competition? How flexible are they—will they be, or can they be made, appropriate to tomorrow's competition? What is the quality of the manufacturing management in terms of planning and controlling work schedule-wise, cost-wise, and quality-wise? Is there evidence of an industrial engineering capability that steadily improves products and methods? Does manufacturing management effectively perform its part of the process of achieving new products?

D. Summary on R & D and Operating Departments

Is this a complete, integrated, balanced operation; or have certain strong personalities emphasized some functions and neglected others? What is the quality of performance of key R & D and operating executives; do they understand the fundamental processes of management, namely planning, controlling organizing, staffing and directing? Are plans and controls in each department inadequate, adequate or overdeveloped into a "paperwork mill?" Is there throughout the departments a habit of steady progress in reducing overhead, lowering breakeven points and improving quality? Are all departments future-minded? Do they cooperate effectively in developing worthy new products geared to meet the customer's future needs?

III. FINANCIAL ANALYSIS AND FINANCIAL MANAGEMENT

A. Financial Analysis

What main strengths and weaknesses of the firm emerge from analysis of the trends in the traditional financial data: earnings ratios (to sales, to tangible net worth, to working capital) and earnings-per-share; debt ratios (current and acid tests, to tangible net worth, to working capital, to inventory); inventory turnover; cash flow; and the capitalization structure? What do the trends in the basic financial facts indicate as to the firm's prospects for growth in sales volume and rate of earnings? Does "quality of earnings" warrant compounding of the earnings rate?

OUTLINE FOR EVALUATION OF A FIRM (continued)

B. Financial Management

What is the quality of financial management? Is there a sound program for steadily increasing return on investment? Do the long-range financial plans indicate that management understands the cost of capital and how to make money work hard? Have balance sheets and operating statements been realistically projected for a number of years into the future? Is there careful cash planning and strong controls that help the operating departments lower breakeven points? Are capital expenditures inadequate or exessive with respect to insuring future operating efficiently? Are capital investiment decisions based on thorough calculations? Does management have the respect of the financial community? Is the firm knowledgeable and aggressive in tax administration?

IV. TOP MANAGEMENT

A. Identification of Top Management and its Record

What person or group constitutes top management? Has present top management been responsible for profit-and-loss results of the past few years?

B. Top Management and the Future

What are top management's chief characteristics? How adequate or inadequate is this type of management for coping with the challenges of the future? Will the present type and quality of top management continue? Will it deteriorate, will it improve, or will it change its basic character?

C. Board of Directors

What influence and/or control does the Board of Directors exercise? What are the capabilities of its members? What are their motivations?

V. SUMMARY AND EVALUATION STRATEGY

What other factors can assume major importance in this particular situation? (Use a check list.) Of all the factors studied, which if any, is overriding in this particular situation? Which factors are of major importance by virtue of of the fact that they govern other factors? What are the basic facts-of-life about the economics and competition of of this industry now and over the next decade? In view of this firm's particular strengths and weaknesses, what are level of success, in this industry? What are the prospects of its succeeding by diversifying out of its industry?

PRODUCT LINES AND COMPETITION

The first things to investigate are a firm's product lines and its basic competitive position. This involves a study of its past, present, and future. Here are the lines your inquiry should take:

Past . . . What strengths and weaknesses in products (or services) have been dominant in this firm's history—design features, quality-reliability, prices, patents, proprietary position?

Present . . . What share of its market(s) does the firm now hold, and how firmly? Is this share diversified or concentrated as to number of customers? In what phases of their life cycles are the present chief products and what is happening to prices and margins? How do customers and potential customers regard this firm's products? Are the various product lines compatible marketing-wise, engineering-wise, manufacturing-wise? If not, is each product line substantial enough to stand on its own feet?

Future . . . Is the market(s) as a whole expanding or contracting, and at what rate? What is the trend in this firm's share of the market(s)? What competitive trends are developing in numbers of competitors, technology, marketing, pricing?

What is the vulnerability to business cycle (or defense spending) changes?

Is there the capability effectively to integrate market research, R & D and market development into a new products development program?

The past-present-future structure furnishes the material needed to determine whether the firm has presently or in-the-pipeline the type of products needed for success in the future.

A key technique here is to determine how much quantitative information the company executives have and, then, to spot-check the quality of that information by the evaluator's own research. The firm that has sound, pertinent market data usually has achieved the first step to success—a clear definition of the job to be done. Conversely, the firm that has only sparse, out-of-date, out-of-focus data and relies heavily on executives' opinions is usually a poor bet for the future. Unsupported opinions, no matter how strongly held or ably stated, can be misleading. Although top management often must rely on such opinions, failure to secure the data that are available is a serious weakness.

LIFE CYCLE CURVES FOR PRODUCTS MADE

Another device for focusing on the basic facts of life about a product line is the building of S, or life cycle curves. These curves plot sales and/or margins for a product against time. For a given firm such plots picture clearly the life expectancy of products. Composite plots can show the trends in life expectancies. Also, they can indicate developing gaps. When past data are joined to carefully projected estimates of the future, dangerous situations can be revealed. Thus, the firm that is currently highly profitable but has not provided for the future will show virtually all of its products at or near the period of peak profitability [7].

The question of compatibility of product lines may seem too elementary for mention; however, major mistakes are made in this area, especially by firms headed by scientists. Seeing their own skill as the key one in business, scientists tend to underestimate the importance and difficulty of other management activities. In consequence, they often develop or acquire products that present marketing problems far beyond the financial or managerial capability of the firm.

One science-based and scientist-led company, after an acquisition binge, was attempting to market ten distinct product lines through one centralized marketing organization, all with a total of less than $18 million annual volume. None of the products could individually support a top-flight marketing organization; yet no two of them could be effectively marketed through the same people. The result was disaster.

Integration of marked research, R&D, and market development into an effective new product development program is one of the newer and more difficult arts of management. Such integration, which is the heart of profit planning, apparently accounted for much of the success of the Bell and Howell Company during the decade of the '50s [8].

In vivid contrast to the coordinated profit planning of Bell and Howell, is the case of the small glamor firm that "went public" in early 1961 for $1,000,000 and has since seen the price of its stock triple. The scientist-president and his associates have developed a dazzling array of technically ingenious new products; however, they have little data on the market for the products and have not yet started to build an organization for distributing and selling them.

R&D AND OPERATING DEPARTMENTS

Having probed a firm's product lines and competitive position, the second vital area for investigation is its R&D, marketing, and operating divisions. Good questions to guide your analysis are

R&D and Engineering . . . What is the nature and the depth of the R&D capability? Of the engineering capability? What are the main strengths and weaknesses re creativity, quality-reliability, simplicity?

Is the R&D effort based on needs defined by market research, and is it an integral part of an effective new product development program? Are R&D efforts well planned, directed, and controlled? What return have R&D dollars paid in profitable new products? Have enough new products been produced, and have schedules been met?

A truly basic change in American industry since the start of World War II has been that thousands of companies have R&D programs, whereas earlier only a handful of firms did so. The figures cited earlier concerning the growth of R&D expenditures indicate that sophisticated technologies and rapidly changing products and markets characterize not only electronics and defense industries but also such diverse fields as food processing, photography, communications, pharmaceuticals, metallurgy, plastics, and equipments used in industrial automation processes. The consequence is that most firms beyond the "small business" category must have R&D programs; increasingly a firm must take on the characteristics of a "growth" firm in order to survive.

HOW TO EVALUATE A FIRM'S R&D

One of the newest of management activities, R&D management, is one of the hardest to evaluate. For lack of better technique, the vogue has been to assume that the volume of dollars spent on R&D is commensurate with results achieved. However, we now know that there has been great waste; also, there has been deception by firms "padding" their reported R&D expenditures to give the impression of being more R&D oriented than they really are.

A growing literature reports useful techniques for conceiving, planning, controlling, and directing R&D programs and for evaluating R&D output [9]. The truth is being established that R&D management is a capability different from and much rarer than the capability of performing straight engineering or scientific work.

The first task of the evaluator is to determine whether the selection of R&D programs is integrated with a sound overall long-range plan and is based on market research findings. The next task is to compare the nature and depth of the R&D capability with the job to be done. Can it cope with the firm's future needs in regard to maintaining and improving market position by an integrated new products program? The third job is to compare cost and output. Techniques for evaluating output include assessing the quantity and quality of patents produced, measurement of the contribution of R&D to increased (or maintained) sales volume and profit margins, and measurement of the contribution to lowered break-even points via improved materials and methods.

ARE ITS INNOVATIONS WELL-TIMED?

An evaluator needs to understand the time cycle required for research, development, and introduction to application; also, he must be able to relate this understanding to the basic facts about the market being served. Such an evaluator can tell when a firm is proceeding in the vanguard of the competition or when it is jumping on a bandwagon too late—as so many electronics firms did with respect to the transistor bandwagon.

MARKETING

Closely allied with R&D and product innovation are the marketing skills of the firm under analysis. Strengths and weaknesses in this area can be uncovered by digging into the following topics.

Nature of the Marketing Capability . . . What channels of distribution are used? How much of the total marketing job (research, sales, service, advertising, and promotion) is covered? Is this capability correctly tailored to match the nature and diversity of the firm's product lines?

Is there a capability for exploiting new products and for developing new markets?

Quality of the Marketing Capability . . . Is market research capable of providing the factual basis that will keep the firm, especially its new product development and R&D programs, truly customer-oriented? Is there a capability for doing broad economic studies and studies of particular industries that will help management set sound growth and/or diversification strategies?

The evaluator will already have learned much about market research capability in answering the product line questions posed earlier in this article. There it was indicated that the firm that knows the facts about trends in its market and technologies is well on the way to success in the future. This clearly places great responsibility on market research, a field still neglected or abused by many science-based firms, especially those in defense work.

To cope adequately with the challenges of the future requires more than market research in the old narrow concept; rather, it requires an ability at economic analysis of entire industries. Survival and growth in a rapidly changing economy sometimes demands more than a stream of new products; often it requires diversification into substantially different fields that offer greater growth and better profits for a given time period.

Diversification strategy is another subject that is currently being developed [10]. The aircraft industry today presents a case study in which certain firms are prospering because ten years ago they started to diversify while other firms are suffering badly because they failed to do so.

The accelerating rate of change in industry is a process that feeds on itself. Thus, sophisticated methods of market research and planning not only help a firm cope with rapid change but also foster more rapid change.

The evaluator must know enough about quantitative methods of research to be able to distinguish between valid use and abuse of market research. If not so equipped, he is at the mercy of the supersalesman with a smattering of scientific lore who can spin great tales about how a given firm has made a technological breakthrough that soon will have tremendous impact upon the market.

The evaluator must also be able to distinguish between creative market research and pedestrian fact-gathering that plods along a year too late to help management conquer the future. Only when market research secures fresh quantitative data on future markets can management integrate market development with product development.

MANUFACTURING

Next area to be studied is production. Questions to be asked include:

Manufacturing . . . What is the nature of the manufacturing processes, the facilities and the skills—are they appropriate to today's competition? How flexible are they—will they be or can they be made appropriate to tomorrow's competition?

What is the quality of the manufacturing management in terms of planning and controlling work schedule-wise, cost-wise, and quality-wise? Is there evidence of an industrial engineering capability that steadily improves products and methods? Does manufacturing management effectively perform its part of the process of achieving new products?

The answers to these questions call mainly for conventional type analysis which need not be commented upon here. This is not to say that there are not now, as always, new and better techniques being developed in the manufacturing field. Certainly an alert manufacturing management will use such progressive techniques as "value engineering" to simplify product designs and, thus, reduce costs; and it will use electronic data processing and other modern industrial engineering methods of controlling the work pace and other cost elements.

But, basically, manufacturing management still is, and long has been, evaluated on the basis of performance schedule-wise, cost- and quality-wise, and techniques for such evaluations are among the oldest and best-developed tools of management consultants and others concerned with industrial engineering.

The quickening pace of technological change does, however, require special attention to the ability of the engineering and manufacturing departments to cooperate effectively in bringing new products into production and in utilizing new processes. Also, it requires special caution with respect to firms with heavy investments in inflexible capital equipment because such investments might be susceptible to almost sudden obsolesence.

SUMMARY ON R&D AND OPERATIONS

To make the most of information acquired about a firm's operating departments and R&D, it is well at this point to pull all this sometimes diffuse information together into a sight summary that pulls the whole picture of operations into focus. Questions running along lines such as these help clarify it.

The Overall Picture . . . Is this a complete, integrated, balanced operation; or have certain strong personalities emphasized some functions and neglected others?

What is the quality of performance of the key R&D and operating executives; do they understand the fundamental processes of management, namely planning, controlling, organizing, staffing, and directing? Are plans and controls in each department inadequate, adequate, or overdeveloped into a "paperwork mill"?

Is there throughout the departments a habit of steady progress in reducing overhead, lowering breakeven points, and improving quality?

Are all departments future-minded; do they cooperate effectively in developing worthy new products geared to meet the customer's future needs?

Finance is the third area of a corporation which should be analyzed carefully in appraising its present and future development. In this connection, both the men handling a company's finances and the figures on the balance sheet should be studied. Beginning inquiries could be

Financial Analysis . . . What main strength and weaknesses of the firm emerge from analysis of the trends in the traditional financial data: earnings ratios (to sales, to tangible net worth, to working capital) and earnings-per-share; debt ratios (current and acid tests, to tangible net worth, to working capital, to inventory); inventory turnover; cash flow; and the capitalization structure?

What do the trends in the basic financial facts indicate as to the firm's prospects for growth in sales volume and rate of earnings? Does "quality of earnings" warrant compounding of the earnings rate?

Although this article has already pointed out limitations of financial analysis standing alone as a method of evaluating firms, its importance as one of the key elements of an evaluation should never be overlooked. Because financial analysis has been so important for so long, its techniques have been well developed. Therefore, it is not necessary to discuss them here.

One concept concerning "growth" companies, however, does require comment. The technique of evaluating a growth firm on the basis of an assumption that it will "plow back" its earnings and thereby achieve a compounded rate of increase in earnings per share is of questionable validity. By compounding earnings on a straight-line (or uninterrupted) basis, financial analysts arrive at estimates of future earnings that justify stock prices from 40 to 100 times present earnings per share.

NO FIRM PROGRESSES EVENLY

The concept of straight-line progress just doesn't square with the facts of life as observed by students of management. Especially in small and medium-sized companies, progress typically occurs in a sawtooth, rather than a straight-line pattern. This phenomenon is based partly on the existence of business cycles and partly on the fact the firms are affected by the strengths and limitations of humans in key positions. There are stages in which the typical growing firm requires managerial talents greater than—or, possibly, only different from—those talents essential to its start.

At these critical periods the earnings per share may slow down or even turn into losses. Such events devastate the compounding process; if one compounds a more realistic 5–10 per cent rate of growth per year, the result is far less sensational than is secured by compounding a 20–25 per cent. It is exceedingly rare that a firm achieves the higher percentages for any sustained period; Litton Industries and IBM appear to be the exceptions that prove the rule. The reference to quality of earnings is meant to shed light on the sustainability of the rate of improvements in earnings. Here the evaluator must distinguish between continuous, sustainable improvement and isolated events (such as a single acquisition or securing an especially favorable contract) or cyclical events (a period of high profitability certain to be followed by a corresponding low).

THE MONEY MEN

Figures alone don't tell the complete financial story of a firm. Its money management must be rated and this involves an evaluation of both policies and men, not only those in the financial division but also the men in charge of planning and top management. You need to know their attitudes about . . .

Financial Management . . . Is there a sound program for steadily increasing return or investment? Do the long-range financial plans indicate that management understands the costs of capital and how to make money work hard? Have balance sheets and operating statements been realistically projected for a number of years into the future?

Is there careful cash planning and strong controls that help the operating departments lower breakeven points? Are capital expenditures inadequate, adequate, or excessive with respect to insuring future operating efficiency? Are capital investment decisions based on thorough calculations?

Does management have the respect of the financial community?

Is the firm knowledgeable and aggressive in tax administration?

While many financial departments function only as record-keepers and rules-enforcers, some play a truly creative role. Financial management can today contribute as much or more to improvement in earnings per share as can any other part of management [11]. In fact, in recent years bold use of the newer forms of financing have in many cases contributed as much to the rapid rise of companies as have technological innovations. And, alas, bold but unwise financing has ruined many a promising young company.

The questions here are designed to help the evaluator discover whether or not the financial people are vigorously contributing in a number of ways to the steady improvement of earnings currently and in the long run.

RATING TOP MANAGEMENT

All study of management invariably and understandably leads to a searching examination of the top management men. Here there are pitfalls for the unwary. The analyst must first identify the true top management before he can examine their performance record. Things, in terms of who actually runs the show, are not always what they seem on the organization chart. So key topics are

Top Management and Its Record . . . What person or group constitutes top management? Has present top management been responsible for profit-and-loss results of the past few years?

The problem is to determine the individual or group of individuals who contribute directly and regularly to those decisions that shape the basic nature of this business and significantly affect profit and loss results. This usually cannot be determined reliably by direct questions to persons in key positions; few men are objective about themselves on these matters.

WATCH THEM WORK

Rare is the top executive who will admit that he is a one-man rule type; rare is the vice president or department head who will admit that he is a highly paid errand boy. Accordingly, direct observation of management at work is needed. Some additional information can also be gained through examination of minutes of meetings and files of memos.

After top management has been identified, the evaluator must ask whether this management has had time to prove itself one way or the other. The criterion is whether or not major decisions and programs put forth by this top management have come to fruition. It is not simply a matter of looking at profit and loss figures for a few years. We all know that in certain situations factors other than top management capability (for example, an inherited product line that is unusually strong) can produce good profits for a number of years.

Next comes consideration of

Top Management and the Future . . . What are top management's chief characteristics? How adequate or inadequate is this type of management for coping with the challenges of the future?

Will the present type and quality of top management continue, or will it deteriorate, will it improve, or will it change its basic character?

We must ask how and why top management has achieved the results that it has achieved so that we can judge how adequate it will be for meeting tomorrow's challenges. Exploring the how and why gets the evaluator into the subject of types of management and their effects on profitability—the thorniest area of contemporary management theory. Over the past twenty years a tremendous literature has accumulated on such subjects as participative leadership, autocratic versus bureaucratic versus democratic types of management and related subjects.

Some writers have claimed or implied great virtues for participative-democratic methods; others have attacked such methods as wasteful and ineffective, wholly inappropriate in industrial life and have advocated "benevolent autocracy." The confusion recently reached a zenith with the almost simultaneous publication of conflicting views by eminent professors from the same university [12].

Industrial psychologists and sociologists have provided valuable insights into management practices and their effects upon profitability. While a skilled social scientist could contribute importantly to the evaluation of a firm's top management, there is a more direct way of evaluating top management's capability for coping with future challenges.

The direct method is to determine how top management has in the past coped with the future. This technique is based on the idea that management is essentially the process of planning to achieve certain goals and, then, controlling activities so that the goals are actually attained. It is in the processes of planning and controlling that top management does its major decision making. Since planning and controlling are the heart of the managerial process, it is in these activities that top management most fully reveals its vital characteristics.

The evaluator can probe deeply into the content of the firm's past and current long-range and short-range plans, into the methods by which the plans are formulated, and into the controls used to bring those plans to fruition. This technique gets away, to a considerable extent, from subjective judgments; it deals with such facts as what was planned, how it was planned, and what actually happened.

Fortunately these activities can be studied without great difficulty and by persons who do not have formal training in the behavioral sciences. A simple yet highly informative procedure is to compare succeeding sets of old long-range plans with one another, with present plans and with actual events.

DO THEIR PLANS WORK?

First, a firm that is effectively tomorrow-minded will have long-range plans. These may not be neatly bound in a cover labeled "long-range plans"; however, they will exist either in minutes of meetings, in memos, in reports to stockholders, or in other places. Second, the old plans will contain evidence as to whether top management truly has studied the future to determine and anticipate the nature of the opportunities and threats that will inevitably arise.

Third, the old plans will contain evidence of the nature and quality of the solutions developed for meeting the challenges of the future—how creative, aggressive, and realistic management has been in initiative matters such as selecting R&D programs, establishing diversification strategy and program, developing new markets, planning the organizational changes needed to keep fit for new tasks, and effectively utilizing advanced techniques (e.g., operations research, automation, etc.) when feasible.

Special attention to initiative matters will indicate whether or not top management is creative and aggressive enough to keep up with an accelerating rate of change.

Fourth, comparison of succeeding sets of plans will indicate whether consistent progress has been made or top management is recklessly aggressive in that it undertakes unrealistic, ill-conceived, unachievable plans.

The same technique can be applied to short-range plans such as annual budgets, sales forecasts, and special developmental programs of many types. This study will indicate whether or not forecasts are typically accurate, whether or not plans typically are successfully completed, whether or not new products are developed on schedule, and whether or not they are supported by marketing, finance, and management programs ready to go at the right time. Again, as in the case of long-range plans, the inquiry will reveal whether decision-making is mature or immature. Has management made profitability a habit, or just a subject of wishful thinking?

A management that knows how to bring plans to fruition builds into every plan a set of controls designed to give early warning of problems and an indication that corrective action is needed. Examination of the controls and the ways in which they are used will indicate whether or not top management is on top of its problems or vice versa.

WHO MAKES THE PLANS?

Investigation of the methods by which plans are formulated and control is exercised will reveal a great deal about whether top management is autocratic, bureaucratic, or democratic. This inquiry holds more than academic interest; the extent to which lower levels of management contribute to the formulation of plans and the extent to which they are held accountable for results will tell much about the firm's down-the-line strength.

EXECUTIVE TURNOVER

Also, these factors are particularly important indicators of whether top management will retain its vigor, will improve, or will deteriorate. Thus, they indicate whether or not top management is making sincere efforts to recruit and develop middle management that will become a new and better generation of top management. Other insights into whether management is bringing in too little or too much new blood can be gained by examining age patterns and statistics on turnover in executive ranks, by reviewing formal executive development efforts and by interviews with some of the men.

YARDSTICK TO GAUGE GROWTH FACTORS

In summary, the technique of probing deeply into the firm's actual plans and controls and methods of planning and control can yield abundant evidence to indicate whether or not top management has the characteristics of a growth firm. These characteristics have been set forth in a major study by Stanford Research Institute of the factors that usually distinguish growth from nongrowth firms. They are

- Affinity for growth fields.
- Organized programs to seek and promote new opportunities.
- Proven competitive abilities in present lines of business.
- Courageous and energetic managements, willing to make carefully calculated risks.
- Luck.

Incidentally, this study found that high growth companies had twice the earning power of low growth companies, while maintaining four times the growth rate [13].

THE BOARD OF DIRECTORS

Rounding out the top management of every corporation is an enigmatic, unpublicized group of men about whom a competent analyst should be most curious. They are the Board of Directors. Questions such as these should be asked about them: What influence and/or control does the Board of Directors exercise? What are the capabilities of its members? What are their motivations?

In the author's experience one of the most frequent and serious errors of small and medium-sized firms is failure to have and use effectively a strong Board of Directors. Too often the entrepreneurial types who start firms disdain help until they are in deep trouble.

Especially in firms headed by a scientist or a super-salesman, a strong and active Board can be invaluable in helping make up for the top executives' lack of rounded managerial training and experience. Except in a few unusual situations, a Board must be an "outside," or nonemployee, Board to be strong.

DUMMIES OR POLICY MAKERS

To be active and helpful, an "outside" Board must have some motivation, either financial or the psychic motivation involved in being confronted with real problems and being able to contribute to their solution. Examination of files and minutes of Board meetings will reveal whether or not there is a good flow of information to the outside directors and a contribution by them to the solution of significant problems.

ADDING UP THE FACTS

With all the data in about the four vital areas of a firm, products and competition, operations and R&D, finance, and top management, the analyst ends his task by posing one more set of questions which might be called Summary and Evaluation Strategy. They should run something like this:

What other factors (use a checklist) [14] can assume major importance in this particular situation?

Of all the factors studied, which, if any, is overriding in this particular situation? Which factors are of major importance by virtue of the fact that they govern other factors?

What are the basic facts of life about the economics and competition of this industry now and over the next decade? In view of this firm's particular strengths and weaknesses, what are the odds that it will succeed and at what level of success, in this industry? What are the prospects of its succeeding by diversifying out of its industry?

DETERMINING OTHER VITAL FACTORS

There is a purpose behind every evaluation study. That purpose or the particular nature of the firm and its industry might place importance upon any of an almost infinite number of factors. Accordingly, the evaluator must thoughtfully run through a checklist containing such considerations as: personnel management practices (e.g., labor relations, profit-sharing, compensation levels), valuation questions (e.g., valuation of fixed or real assets or inventory or unique assets), geographical location as related to labor markets, taxes, cost of distribution, seasonality factors, in-process or impending litigation, or any matter footnoted in the financial reports so that the auditing firm is, in effect, warning of an unusual circumstance.

The purpose of a particular evaluation study often will determine which factor, if any, is overriding. Logically, the quality of top management should usually be the overriding factor. By definition a highly competent top management group can solve the other problems such as securing competent scientists and other personnel, developing new products, getting financing, etc. However, there may be an investment or acquisition situation in which the product line, for example, is the overriding factor because it is so obsolete that even the finest management could not effect a recovery within existing time and financial parameters.

MATCHING BUYER AND ACQUISITION

If the evaluation is being done to help decide the advisability of an acquisition, many additional considerations come into play. The problem is one of matching the acquiring and acquired firms; many firms have acquired grief rather than growth because they have neglected this point. At one extreme, acquisition of one healthy company by another may be unwise because the two are so different that the acquirer may mismanage the acquired company. At the other extreme, it may be wise for one unhealthy company to acquire another unhealthy one if the strengths of one remedy the weaknesses of the other, and vice versa.

THE CHARACTER OF THE COMPANY

The acquirer must precisely define his objectives in acquiring. Also, he must carefully consider the "character," or "climate," of the other firm in relation to his own. The subject of "company character" has not been well developed in management practice or literature [15]. Nevertheless, a consideration of the "character" of the two companies is highly relevant, and the outline presented in this article will help the evaluator consider some of the more obvious elements of "company character" such as the nature of its engineering and manufacturing skills, the type of distribution channels and marketing skills required, the type of managerial leadership practiced and top management's aggressiveness and the quality of its decisions in initiative matters.

In sum, the evaluation of a firm requires a clinical judgment of the highest order. The purposes of the evaluation study set the criteria for the judgment. Except in a few instances in which conditions are highly stable, the day is rapidly passing when simple financial analyses, or even financial analyses supplemented by a few interviews and judgments of scientists will suffice for evaluation of a firm.

REFERENCES

(The author, while retaining full responsibility for the content of this article, wishes to express thanks to Drs. Harold D. Koontz, William B. Wolf, J. F. Weston, and Mr. Ora B. Roehl for suggestions that have been most helpful. R. B. B.)

[1] "Evaluating Your Company's Future," an unpublished paper presented at the Fourth Annual Management Conference, UCLA Executive Program Association, Los Angeles, October 20, 1960, p. 2.

[2] Data from the National Science Foundation, cited in: *Research Management,* Autumn, 1960, Volume III, No. 3, p. 129.

[3] Lee Dake explains in detail a case in which a financial analyst and a management consultant arrived at opposite conclusions about a firm's prospects in "Are Analysts' Techniques Adequate for Growth Stocks?" *The Financial Analysts Journal,* Volume 16, No. 6, Nov.–Dec., 1960, pp. 45–49. Dake's thesis can be confirmed many times over in the present author's experience. Particularly distressing was the case where a persuasive but incompetent chief executive persuaded three investment firms to recommend his stock less than six months before declaration of losses exceeding the firm's tangible net worth!

[4] The factors are: (a) Economic Function; (b) Corporate Structure; (c) Health of Earnings; (d) Services to Stockholders; (e) Research and Development; (f) Directorate Analysis; (g) Fiscal Policies; (h) Production Efficiency; (i) Sales Vigor; (j) Executive Evaluation. The factors and their use are explained in detail in a series of ten reports: *The Management Audit Series.* New York, The American Institute of Management, starting in 1953.

[5] Most dramatic was the case of the Douglas Aircraft Company whose "excellently managed" rating for 1957–8–9 was followed by staggering losses in late '59 and '60. Among numerous other examples that can be cited are the 1957 ratings of Olin Mathiesen Chemical Co. and Allis-Chalmers Manufacturing Company, both of whom, soon after receiving "excellently managed" ratings, suffered serious declines that have been openly discussed in business magazines. For the ratings, see: *Manual of Excellent Managements.* New York, The American Institute of Management, 1957. For accounts of the travails of these firms see *Business Week,* April 15, 1961, pp. 147–149 and April 9, 1960, p. 79.

[6] "Industrial Administration Through the Eyes of an Investment Company." *Appraising Managerial Assets—Policies, Practices and Organization,"* General Management Series #151 (New York: American Management Association, 1950). The new emphasis is suggested in a postscript to a reprint

published in 1960 by the Keystone Custodian Funds, Inc., Boston, Mass., 1960, p. 13. Professor Schell suggested increased emphasis on tax administration, too. The original factors were: (a) Breadth and variety of viewpoint in administration; (b) Vigor and versatility in operating management; (c) Clarity and definiteness of long-term objectives; (d) Vigilance in matters of organization; (e) Dependence upon far-reaching plans; (f) Maintenance of integrated controls; (g) Upkeep in harmony with an advancing art; (h) Improvement as a normal expectancy; (i) Creativeness through high morale; (j) Effectiveness of managerial attitudes; (k) Resources for consistently distinguished leadership in a specific industry.

[7] For an illustration and discussion of use of life-cycle curves, see C. Wilson Randle: "Selecting the Research Program. A Top Management Function." *California Management Review,* Volume II, No. 2 (Winter, 1960), pp. 10–11.

[8] The Bell and Howell methods are described in two articles: "How to Coordinate Executives." *Business Week,* September 12, 1953, p. 130 ff., and "How to Plan Profits Five Years Ahead." *Nation's Business,* October 1955, p. 38.

[9] An invaluable review of this literature up to early 1957 is given in: Albert H. Rubenstein, "Looking Around: Guide to R&D," *Harvard Business Review,* Volume 35, No. 3, May–June, 1957, p. 133 ff. Among the most pertinent articles since Rubenstein's review are: Ora C. Roehl: "The Investment Analyst's Evaluation of Industrial Research Capabilities." *Research Management,* Volume III, No. 3, Autumn, 1960, p. 127 ff.; Maurice Nelles: "Changing the World Changers." Paper presented at the Ninth Annual Management Conference, The Graduate School of Business Administration, University of Chicago, March 1, 1961; C. Wilson Randle: "Problems of R&D Management." *Harvard Business Review,* Volume 37, No. 1, January–February 1959, p. 128 ff.; James B. Quinn: "How to Evaluate Research Output." *Harvard Business Review,* Volume 38, No. 2, March–April 1960, pp. 69 ff.; and "Long-Range Planning of Industrial Research." *Harvard Business Review,* Volume 39, No. 4, July–August 1961, pp. 88 ff.

[10] H. Igor Ansoff: "Strategies for Diversification." *Harvard Business Review,* September–October, 1957.

[11] For an exposition of this thought as applied to large firms, see: "The New Power of the Financial Executive." *Fortune,* Volume LXV, No. 1, January 1962, p. 81 ff. See also the new text by J. Fred Weston: *Managerial Finance.* New York, Holt, Rhinehart & Winston, 1962.

[12] Rensis Likert, reporting on a decade of social science research into patterns of management makes a case for participative management in *New Patterns of Management.* New York, McGraw-Hill Publishing Company, 1961. George Odiorne, reporting on studies of successful managements, warns strongly against the views of social scientists and makes a case for the more traditional, somewhat autocratic, business leader in *How Managers Make Things Happen.* New York: Prentice-Hall, Inc., 1961. Both authors are professors at the University of Michigan.

[13] *Environmental Change and Corporate Strategy.* Menlo Park, California, Stanford Research Institute, 1960, p. 8. A more recent report on this continuing research project is given by Robert B. Young, "Keys to Corporate Growth," *Harvard Business Review,* Volume 39, No. 6, Nov.–Dec., 1961,

pp. 51–62. Young concludes: "In short, the odds for corporate growth are highest when the top executives of a firm treat their future planning as a practical decision making challenge requiring personal participation, and direct their planning efforts toward the origins of opportunity itself. Such an approach can make the difference between having constantly to adapt to day to day crises and enjoying profitable future growth."

[14] For one such checklist, see: Robert G. Sproul, Jr.: "Sizing Up New Acquisitions." *Management Review,* XLIX, No. 1, Feb. 1960, pp. 80–82.

[15] A new textbook brings together for the first time the few and scattered writings on the subject of "company character." See William B. Wolf's *The Management of Personnel.* San Francisco, Wadsworth Publishing Company, Inc., 1961, pp. 8–43.

How to Read a Financial Report*

Merrill Lynch, Pierce, Fenner & Smith

If you are a certified public accountant you should skip this book. You don't need a basic course to hack through the jungle of corporate annual reports. If you aren't an accountant, however, please read on. This little book can lead you out of the wilderness with simple concepts and facts.

Since we men and women of Merrill Lynch, Pierce, Fenner & Smith are investment brokers, we want to take you as far as possible out of the jungle toward the trading posts where you buy securities more intelligently, and we hope with greater success. We also think this little book can help all readers cultivate more knowledge about the firms that employ them or sell them goods and services, as well as those in which they someday may own stock.

Where will your journey out of the jungle lead? From the all-but-trackless thicket of annual report prose to an often unrecognized oasis full of food for thought: the financial sheets.

All annual reports bring their readers written messages whose rhetoric ranges from stodgy to mod, from murky to magnificently clear. Usually these messages flaunt the signatures of corporate presidents or chairmen of the board, often both. The purpose of these messages, signed, or unsigned, is to put the best face possible on whatever has happened to the corporation during the year. There is nothing wrong in this, for optimism is no less a virtue in corporate executives than in generals.

Most annual reports will delight you with exquisite pictures of plants and products, people and places. Chances are you will see a great deal of the chief executive officers and corporate directors, too. More and more, annual reports are becoming lavish exercises in printing and publishing. This, too, is fine, so long as costs don't deprive stockholders of too much of their dividends. Since large corporations as a general rule must publish annual reports, then why not make those annual reports as pretty as possible as well as kind to the corporate managements which put them out?

So read the prose, enjoy the pictures, then turn to the balance sheet. You cannot miss it, for the balance sheet is the formidable section of numbers that somehow wind up all even—as though the whole corporation balanced

* Reprinted by permission of Merrill Lynch, Pierce, Fenner & Smith, Inc., New York.

TYPICAL MANUFACTURING COMPANY, INC

BALANCE SHEET—DECEMBER 31, 1973

ASSETS	1973	1972
Current Assets		
Cash	$ 450,000	$ 300,000
Marketable securities at cost (market value: 1973, $890,000; 1972, $480,000)	850,000	460,000
Accounts receivable *Less:* allowance for bad debt: 1973, $100,000; 1972, $95,000	2,000,000	1,900,000
Inventories	2,700,000	3,000,000
Total current assets	$6,000,000	$5,660,000
Fixed Assets (property, plant, and equipment)		
Land	$ 450,000	$ 450,000
Building	3,800,000	3,600,000
Machinery	950,000	850,000
Office equipment	100,000	95,000
	$5,300,000	$4,995,000
Less: accumulated depreciation	1,800,000	1,500,000
Net fixed assets	$3,500,000	$3,495,000
Prepayments and deferred charges	100,000	90,000
Intangibles (goodwill, patent, trademarks)	100,000	100,000
Total assets	$9,700,000	$9,345,000

LIABILITIES	1973	1972
Current liabilities		
Accounts payable	$1,000,000	940,000
Notes payable	850,000	1,000,000
Accrued expenses payable	330,000	300,000
Federal income taxes payable	320,000	290,000
Total current liabilities	$2,500,000	$2,530,000
Long-term liabilities First mortgage bonds; 5% interest, due 1985	2,700,000	2,700,000
Total liabilities	$5,200,000	$5,230,000
STOCKHOLDERS' EQUITY		
Capital stock		
Preferred stock, 5% cumulative, $100 par value each; authorized, issued, and outstanding 6,000 shares	600,000	600,000
Common stock, $5 par value each; authorized, issued, and outstanding 300,000 shares	1,500,000	1,500,000
Capital surplus	700,000	700,000
Accumulated retained earnings	1,700,000	1,315,000
Total stockholders' equity	$4,500,000	$4,115,000
Total liabilities and stockholders' equity	$9,700,000	$9,345,000

CONSOLIDATED INCOME STATEMENT	1973	1972
Net Sales	$11,000,000	$10,200,000
Cost of sales and operating expenses		
Cost of goods sold	8,200,000	7,684,000
Depreciation	300,000	275,000
Selling and administrating expenses	1,400,000	1,325,000
Operating profit	$ 1,100,000	$ 916,000
Other income		
Dividends and interest	50,000	27,000
Total income	$ 1,150,000	$ 943,000
Less: interest on bonds	135,000	135,000
Income before provision for federal income tax	$ 1,015,000	$ 808,000
Provision for federal income tax	480,000	365,000
Net profit for year	$ 535,000	$ 443,000
Common shares outstanding	300,000	300,000
Net earnings per share	$1.68	$1.38

ACCUMULATED RETAINED EARNINGS STATEMENT	1973	1972
Balance January 1	$ 1,315,000	$ 1,022,000
Net profit for year	535,000	443,000
Total	$ 1,850,000	$ 1,465,000
Less: dividends paid on preferred stock	30,000	30,000
common stock	120,000	120,000
Balance December 31	$ 1,700,000	$ 1,315,000

STATEMENT OF SOURCE AND APPLICATION OF FUNDS—1973

Funds were provided by			
Net income		$535,000	
Depreciation		300,000	
Total			$835,000
Funds were used for			
Dividends on preferred stock	$ 3	$ 30,000	
Dividends on common stock		120,000	
Plant and equipment		305,000	
Sundry assets		10,000	
Total			465,000
INCREASE IN WORKING CAPITAL			$370,000

Analysis of changes in working capital—1973

Changes in current assets		
Cash	$150,000	
Marketable securities	390,000	
Accounts receivable	100,000	
Inventories	(300,000)	
Total		$340,000
Changes in current liabilities		
Accounts payable	$ 60,000	
Notes payable	(150,000)	
Accrued expenses payable	30,000	
Federal income tax payable	30,000	
Total		$(30,000)

precariously in some sort of mathematical scales. Its language may be thorny and its rows of figures seem as impenetrable as anything else in your annual report, but the balance sheet holds the key to your journey out of the jungle and into the cultivated country of facts.

THE BALANCE SHEET

Accountants, like all other professional men, have developed a specialized vocabulary. This book will bring you a score or so of these technical terms that you will have to get straight in your mind. After that is done the whole tangled business will begin to clear up.

First you will find a sample balance sheet. Let's have a look at how it is put together. There is also, on the following page, an income and accumulated earnings statement, which we'll discuss at length later in this book. Following that is the section on sources and application of funds, and we'll go over that, too, in time. These sections make up Typical Manufacturing's total, official annual statement. This particular report is neither the simplest that could be issued nor the most complicated. It is a good sample of the kind of report issued by an up-to-date company such as Typical Manufacturing.

The balance sheet represents the financial picture as it stood on one particular day, December 31, 1973, as though the wheels of the company were momentarily at a standstill. Typical Manufacturing's balance sheet not only includes this year, but also the previous year. This is to let you compare how the company fared in its two latest years. We'll talk more about this later, too.

The balance sheet is divided into two sides: on the left are shown *assets;* on the right are shown *liabilities* and *stockholders' equity*. Both sides are always in balance. In the assets column, we list all the goods and property owned as well as claims against others yet to be collected. Under liabilities we list all debts due. Under stockholders' equity we list the amount the stockholders would split up if Typical were liquidated at its balance sheet value.

Assume that the corporation goes out of business on the date of the balance sheet. Assume also (what is probably never so) that the assets bring exactly what is shown in the balance sheet. If that occurs, the first little illustration shows you what Typical Manufacturing's stockholders might expect to receive as their portion of the business.

Total assets (*Less:* intangibles)	$9,600,000
Amount required to pay liabilities	5,200,000
Amount remaining for the stockholders	$4,400,000

Now that we have introduced you to the whole sheet, we are going to give you a guided tour of its parts. We'll take entries out of the sheet, one by one, and discuss how they are produced. Then we'll go on, item by item, to explain for you what they mean and how they work.

Assets

CURRENT ASSETS. In general, current assets include cash and those assets which in the normal course of business will be turned into cash in the reasonably near future, within a year from the date of the balance sheet.

Cash. This is just what you would expect—bills and silver in the till (petty cash fund) and money on deposit in the bank.

1	Cash	$450,000

Marketable securities. This asset represents temporary investment of excess or idle cash which is not needed immediately. It is usually invested in commercial paper and government securities. Because these funds may be needed on short notice, it is essential that the securities be readily marketable and subject to a minimum of price fluctuation. The general practice is to show marketable securities at cost, with the market value listed parenthetically.

2	Marketable securities at cost (Market value $89,000)	$850,000

Accounts receivable. Here we find the amount not yet collected from customers to whom goods were shipped prior to payment. Customers are usually given 30, 60, or 90 days in which to pay. The amount due from customers as shown in the balance sheet is $2,000,000. However, experience shows that some customers fail to pay their bills either because of financial difficulties or by reason of some catastrophic event (such as a tornado, a hurricane, or a flood) befalling their business. Therefore, in order to show the accounts receivable item at a figure representing reality, the total we see is after a provision for bad debts. This year that debt reserve was $100,000.

4	Accounts receivable *Less:* allowance for bad debt: 1973, $100,000	$2,000,000

Inventories. The inventory of a manufacturer is composed of three groups: raw materials to be used in the product, partially finished goods in process of manufacture, and finished goods ready for shipment to customers. The generally accepted method of valuation of the inventory is *cost* or *market, whichever is lower*. This gives a conservative figure. Where this method is used, the value for balance sheet purposes will be cost or perhaps less than cost if, as a result of deterioration, obsolescence, decline in prices, or other factors, less than cost can be realized on the inventory. Cost for purposes of inventory

BALANCE SHEET—DECEMBER 31, 1973

	ASSETS	1973	1972
	Current Assets		
1	Cash	$ 450,000	$ 300,000
2	Marketable securities at cost (market value: 1973, $890,000; 1972, $480,000)	850,000	460,000
4	Accounts receivable *Less:* allowance for bad debt: 1973, $100,000; 1972, $95,000	2,000,000	1,900,000
5	Inventories	2,700,000	3,000,000
6	**Total current assets**	$6,000,000	$5,660,000
7	Fixed assets (property, plant, and equipment)		
	Land	$ 450,000	$ 450,000
	Building	3,800,000	3,600,000
	Machinery	950,000	850,000
	Office equipment	100,000	95,000
		$5,300,000	$4,995,000
	Less: accumulated depreciation	1,800,000	$1,500,000
	Net fixed assets	$3,500,000	$3,495,000
	Prepayments and deferred charges	100,000	90,000
	Intangibles (goodwill, patent, trademarks)	100,000	100,000
	Total assets	$9,700,000	$9,345,000

valuation includes an allocation of production and other expenses as well as the cost of materials.

5	Inventories	$2,700,000

To summarize, the *total current assets* item includes primarily: cash, marketable securities, accounts receivable, and inventories.

6	Total current assets	$6,000,000

You will observe that these assets are *working assets* in the sense that they are in a constant cycle of being converted into cash. Inventories when sold become accounts receivable; receivables upon collection become cash; cash is used to pay debts and running expenses. We will discover later on in the book how to make current assets tell a story.

FIXED ASSETS. The next item, *fixed assets,* is sometimes referred to as *property, plant* and *equipment.* It represents those assets not intended for sale which are used over and over again in order to manufacture the product, display it, warehouse it, transport it. Accordingly, this category will include land, buildings, machinery, equipment, furniture, automobiles and trucks. The generally accepted and approved method for valuation is *cost minus the depreciation accumulated* by the date of the balance sheet. Depreciation is discussed in the next section.

7 Fixed assets (property, plant, and equipment)	
Land	$ 450,000
Buildings	3,800,000
Machinery	950,000
Office equipment	100,000
	$5,300,000

The figure thus displayed is not intended to reflect market value at present or replacement cost in the future. While it is recognized that the cost to replace plant and equipment at some future date may be higher, that possible cost is obviously variable. For this reason, up to now, most companies have followed a general rule: *acquisition cost less accumulated depreciation based on that cost.*

Depreciation. This has been defined for accounting purposes as the decline in useful value of a fixed asset due to wear and tear from use and passage of time, or even when not in use by reason of action of the elements. Fixed assets may also suffer a decline in useful value from obsolescence because new inventions and more advanced techniques come to light which make the present equipment out of date.

The cost incurred to acquire the property, plant, and equipment must be spread over its expected useful life, taking into consideration the factors discussed in the preceding paragraph. For example: If a delivery truck costs $10,000 and is expected to last five years, then, using a "straight-line" method of depreciation, it will decline at the rate of $2,000 each year. The balance sheet at the end of the first year would show:

Truck (cost)	$10,000
Less: accumulated depreciation	2,000
Net depreciated value	$ 8,000

The balance sheet at the end of the second year would show:

Truck (cost)	$10,000
Less: accumulated depreciation	4,000
Net depreciated value	$ 6,000

In our sample balance sheet, there is shown a figure for accumulated depreciation. This amount is the total of accumulated depreciation for buildings, machinery, and office furniture. Land is not subject to depreciation, and its listed value remains unchanged from year to year.

8	*Less:* accumulated depreciation	$1,800,000

The item *net fixed assets,* therefore, is the valuation for balance sheet purposes of the investment in property, plant, and equipment. As explained before, it generally consists of the cost of the various assets in this classification, diminished by the depreciation accumulated to the date of the financial statement.

9	Net fixed assets	$3,500,000

(*Depletion* is a term used primarily by mining and oil companies or any of the so-called extractive industries. Since Typical Manufacturing is not in the mining business, we do not show depletion on the balance sheet. Deplete, of course, means exhaust or use up. As the oil or other natural resources is used up, a depletion reserve is set up to compensate for the natural wealth the company no longer owns.)

Prepayments and deferred charges. *Prepayments* may arise from a situation such as this: During the year the company paid fire insurance premiums covering a three-year period, and the company leased certain computing machines and by contract paid rental for two years in advance. At the balance sheet date, there exists an unexpended item which will be used up in future years. In our example, two years' insurance premiums are still unused and one year's rental value of the computing machines is still unused at the end of the first year. If the advance payments had not been made, the company would have more cash in the bank. Therefore, payments made in advance from which the company has not yet received the benefits but for which it will receive benefits in the next accounting years are listed as prepayments among the assets.

Deferred charges represent a type of asset similar to prepayments. For example, our manufacturer may have spent a large sum of money for introducing a new product to the market, or for moving the plant to a new location, or for research and development. The benefits from this expenditure will be reaped over several years to come. Therefore, management does not think it reasonable to charge off the full expenditure in the year when payment was made. Instead, the cost incurred will be gradually written off over the next several years. This is in accordance with approved accounting principles.

BALANCE SHEET—DECEMBER 31, 1973

	ASSETS	1973	1972
	Current Assets		
	Cash	$ 450,000	$ 360,000
	Marketable securities at cost (market value: 1973, $890,000; 1972, $480,000)	850,000	460,000
	Accounts receivable *Less:* allowance for bad debt: 1973, $100,000; 1972, $95,000	2,000,000	1,900,000
	Inventories	2,700,000	3,000,000
	Total current assets	$6,000,000	$5,660,000
	Fixed assets (property, plant, and equipment)		
	Land	$ 450,000	$ 450,000
	Building	3,800,000	3,600,000
	Machinery	950,000	850,000
	Office equipment	100,000	95,000
		$5,300,000	$4,995,000
8	*Less:* accumulated depreciation	1,800,000	1,500,000
9	**Net fixed assets**	$3,500,000	$3,495,000
10	Prepayments and deferred charges	100,000	90,000
11	Intangibles (goodwill, patent, trademarks)	100,000	100,000
12	**Total assets**	$9,700,000	$9,345,000

10	Prepayments and deferred charges	$100,000

Intangibles. These may be defined as assets having no physical existence, yet having substantial value to the company. Examples? A franchise granted by a city to a cable TV company, allowing exclusive service in certain areas, or a patent granted by law for exclusive manufacture of a specific article.

Another intangible asset sometimes found in corporate balance sheets is *goodwill.* Company practices vary considerably in assigning value to this asset. Accounting rules now require one firm that buys another to write off this goodwill over a 40 year period.

11	Intangibles (goodwill, patents, trademarks)	$100,000

Some companies have reduced the asset value of the intangible assets to a nominal $1. This indicates that these assets do exist, but the company has no way of quantifying them. (How much is *your* goodwill worth?)

All of these items added together give the figure that is listed on the balance sheet as *total assets.*

12	Total assets	$9,700,000

Liabilities

CURRENT LIABILITIES. This item generally includes all debts that fall due within the coming year. It can be said that the *current assets* item is a companion to *current liabilities* because current assets are the source from which payments are made on current debts. The relationship between these two classifications is one of the most revealing things to be learned from the balance sheet, and we will go into that quite thoroughly later on. For now we need to define the sub-groups within the current liabilities item.

Accounts payable. The *accounts payable* item represents the amounts that the company owes to its regular business creditors from whom it has bought goods on open account. The company usually has 30, 60, or 90 days in which to pay. Sometimes, as an inducement to pay promptly, the suppliers give a cash discount of, say 2%. Therefore, if an account payable is $1,000 with terms of "2% in 10 days, net in 30 days," payment of the debt within 10 days earns $20 (2% of $1,000), and $980 will settle the invoice for $1,000.

13	Accounts payable	$1,000,000

Notes payable. If the money is owed to a bank or other lender, it appears on the balance sheet under *notes payable,* as evidence of the fact that a written promissory note has been given by the borrower.

14	Notes payable	$850,000

Accrued expenses payable. Now we have defined accounts payable as the money owed by the company to its regular business creditors. The company also owes, on any given day, salaries and wages to its employees, interest

LIABILITIES	1973	1972
Current liabilities		
13 Accounts payable	$1,000,000	940,000
Notes payable	850,000	1,000,000
Accrued expenses payable	330,000	300,000
Federal income taxes payable	320,000	290,000
Total current liabilities	$2,500,000	$2,530,000
Long-term liabilities		
First mortgage bonds; 5% interest, due 1985	2,700,000	2,700,000
Total liabilities	$5,200,000	$5,230,000
STOCKHOLDERS' EQUITY		
Capital stock		
Preferred stock, 5% cumulative, $100 par value each; authorized, issued, and outstanding 6,000 shares	600,000	600,000
Common stock, $5 par value each; authorized, issued, and outstanding 300,000 shares	1,500,000	1,500,000
Capital surplus	700,000	700,000
Accumulated retained earnings	1,700,000	1,315,000
Total stockholders' equity	$4,500,000	$4,115,000
Total liabilities and stockholders' equity	$9,700,000	$9,345,000

on funds borrowed from banks and from bondholders, fees to attorneys, insurance premiums, pensions, and similar items. To the extent that the amounts accrued are unpaid at the date of the balance sheet, these expenses are grouped as a total under *accrued expenses payable.*

15	Accrued expenses payable	$330,000

Federal income tax payable. The debt due to the Internal Revenue Service is the same type of liability as any other item under accrued expenses payable. However, by reason of the amount and the importance of the tax factor, it is generally stated separately as *federal income tax payable.*

16	Federal income tax payable	$320,000

Total current liabilities. Finally, the *total current liabilities* item sums up all of the items listed under this classification.

17	Total current liabilities	$2,500,000

LONG-TERM LIABILITIES. In discussing current liabilities, you will recall that we included debts due within one year from the balance sheet date. Here under the heading of *long-term liabilities* are listed debts due after one year from the date of the financial report. In our sample balance sheet, the only long-term liability is the 5% first mortgage bond item due in 1985. The money was received by the company as a loan from the bondholders, who in turn were given a certificate called a bond as evidence of the loan. The bond is really a formal promissory note issued by the company, which in this case agreed to repay the debt at maturity in 1985 and agreed also to pay interest at the rate of 5% per year. Bond interest is usually payable semi-annually. Furthermore, in addition to the written promise of the company to repay the loan at maturity, the bondholders have an added safeguard indicated by the words *first mortgage.* This means that if the company is unable to pay off the bonds in cash when they are due, bondholders have a claim or lien before other creditors on the mortgaged assets which may be sold and the proceeds used to satisfy the debt.

First mortgage bonds, 5% interest, due 1985	$2,700,000

Finally, all liabilities, current and long-term, are added up and listed under the heading *total liabilities.*

Total liabilities	$5,200,000

Stockholders' Equity

As we pointed out earlier, this item is the total equity interest that all stockholders have in this corporation. In other words, the corporation's net worth after subtracting all liabilities. This is separated for legal and accounting reasons into three categories: *capital stock, capital surplus,* and *accumulated retained earnings.*

	LIABILITIES	1973	1972
	Current liabilities		
	Accounts payable	$1,000,000	940,000
14	Notes payable	850,000	1,000,000
15	Accrued expenses payable	330,000	300,000
16	Federal income taxes payable	320,000	290,000
17	**Total current liabilities**	$2,500,000	$2,530,000
	Long-term liabilities		
18	First mortgage bonds; 5% interest, due 1985	2,700,000	2,700,000
19	**Total liabilities**	$5,200,000	$5,230,000
	STOCKHOLDERS' EQUITY		
	Capital stock		
20	Preferred stock, 5% comulative, $100 par value each; authorized, issued, and outstanding 6,000 shares	600,000	600,000
21	Common stock, $5 par value each; authorized, issued, and outstanding 300,000 shares	1,500,000	1,500,000
22	Capital surplus	700,000	700,000
	Accumulated retained earnings	1,700,000	1,315,000
	Total stockholders' equity	$4,500,000	$4,115,000
	Total liabilities and stockholders' equity	$9,700,000	$9,345,000

CAPITAL STOCK. In the broadest sense this represents shares in the proprietary interest in the company. These shares are represented by the stock certificates issued by the corporation to its shareholders. There may be several different types or classes of shares issued by a corporation, each class having attributes slightly different from those of another class.

Preferred stock. This means that these shares have some preference over other shares as regards dividends or in distribution of assets in case of liquidation or both. The specific provisions with respect to any issues of preferred stock can be obtained from the corporation's charter. The fact that in Typical Manufacturing, the preferred stock is designated *5% cumulative,* $100 *par value each,* means that each share is entitled to $5 dividends a year when declared by the Board of Directors before any dividends are paid to the common stockholders. The word cumulative means that if in any year the dividend is not paid, it accumulates in favor of the preferred shareholders and must be paid to them when available and declared before any dividends are distributed on the common stock. Sometimes preferred stockholders do not have a voice in company affairs unless the company fails to pay them dividends at the promised rate.

20	Preferred stock, 5% cumulative, $100 par value each; authorized, issued, and outstanding 6,000 shares	$600,000

Common stock. As we pointed out in our section on preferred stock, owners of the preferred are entitled to a dividend of $5 per share each year before owners of common stock receive anything. But $5 per share will be all the holders of this preferred stock will receive each year. Common stock, on the other hand, has no such limit on dividends payable each year. Therefore, in prosperous times when company earnings are high, dividends may also be high. And when earnings drop, so may dividends.

21	Common stock, $5 par value each; authorized, issued, and outstanding 300,000 shares	$1,500,000

CAPITAL SURPLUS. This is the amount paid in by shareholders over the par or legal value of each share. For example: say that the common stock has a $5 par value for each share. Assume that Typical Manufacturing sold 300,000 shares of stock for a total of $2,200,000. There will then be $2,200,-000 in stockholders' equity, allocated on the balance sheet between capital stock and capital surplus:

21	Common stock, $5 par value each; authorized issued and outstanding 300,000 shares	$1,500,000
22	Capital surplus	700,000
	Total of capital stock (common) and capital surplus	$2,200,000

ACCUMULATED RETAINED EARNINGS. Perhaps a good way to explain this item, which is sometimes called earned surplus, is to say that when a company first starts in business, it has no accumulated retained earnings. At the end of its first year, if its profits are $80,000 and dividends are paid on the preferred stock of $30,000 but no dividends are declared on the common stock, then the balance sheet will show accumulated retained earnings of $50,000. Let us go forward to the second year. Assume the profits are now $140,000 and that dividends paid are $30,000 on the preferred stock and $40,000 on the common stock. The accumulated retained earnings will be $120,000:

Balance at the end of first year	$ 50,000
Net profit for second year	140,000
Total	190,000
Less: all dividends	70,000
Accumulated retained earnings	$120,000

The balance sheet for Typical Manufacturing shows that the company has accumulated $1,700,000 in retained earnings:

23	Accumulated retained earnings	$1,700,000

Just What Does the Balance Sheet Show?

Before we undertake to analyze the balance sheet figures, a word on just what an investor can expect to learn is in order. A generation or more ago, before present accounting standards and principles had gained wide acceptance, considered imagination went into the preparation of balance sheets. This naturally made the public skeptical of financial reports. As time passes, however, more and more effort is being spent to make the figures in financial statements more reliable.

The investor, however, is still faced with a task of determining the significance of the figures. As we have already seen, a number of items are based to a large degree upon estimates, while others are necessarily somewhat arbitrary.

One more generalization is in order here. Since we all hope that Typical Manufacturing is a growing company, we can compare its last two years to see if certain items in the balance sheet show us growth, or shrinkage. Obviously, since the balance sheet balances, assets will be equalled by liabilities and stockholders' equity. But although the two totals always match, the preliminary lines can tell us a lot about the health of our company. We'll point out these special areas as we go along.

NET WORKING CAPITAL. There is one very important thing that we can find from carefully checking the balance sheet. That is *net working capital* or *net current assets,* sometimes simply called *working capital.* It is the difference between total current assets and total current liabilities. You will recall that current liabilities are debts due within one year from the date of the balance sheet. The source from which to pay those debts is current assets. Therefore, the working capital represents the amount that is left free and clear if all current debts are paid off. For Typical, this is:

6	Current assets	$6,000,000
17	*Less:* current liabilities	2,500,000
	Working capital	$3,500,000

If you consider yourself a conservative investor, you should insist that any company in which you invest maintains a comfortable amount of working capital. The ability of a company to meet its obligations, expand its volume, and take advantage of opportunities is often determined by its working capital. Moreover, since you want your company to grow, this year's working capital should be larger than last year's.

CURRENT RATIO. Probably the question in your mind is "Just what is a comfortable amount of working capital?" Well, there are several methods used by analysts to judge whether a particular company has a sound working capital position. To help you interpret the current position of a company in which you are considering investing, the *current ratio* is more helpful than the dollar total of working capital. The first rough test for an industrial company is to compare the current assets figure with the total current liabilities. While there are many exceptions, analysts generally say that minimum safety requires current assets to be at least twice as large as current liabilities. This means that for each $1 of current liabilities, there should be $2 in current assets.

To find the current ratio, divide current assets by current liabilities. In the Typical Manufacturing balance sheet, the figures are:

$$\frac{6 \quad \$6{,}000{,}000 \text{ current assets}}{17 \quad \$2{,}500{,}000 \text{ current liabilities}} = \frac{2.4}{1} \text{ or 2.4 to 1}$$

Therefore, for each $1 of current liabilities, there is $2.40 in current assets to back it up.

There are so many different kinds of companies, however, that this test requires a great deal of modification if it is to be really helpful in analyzing companies in different industries. Generally, companies that have a small inventory and easily collectible accounts receivable can operate safely with a lower current ratio than those companies having a greater proportion of their current assets in inventory and selling their products on credit.

HOW QUICK IS QUICK? In addition to net working capital and current ratio, there are other ways of testing the adequacy of the current position. What are *quick assets?* They're the assets you have to cover a sudden emer-

BALANCE SHEET—DECEMBER 31, 1973

	ASSETS	1973	1972
	Current Assets		
	Cash	$ 450,000	$ 300,000
	Marketable securities at cost (market value: 1973, $890,000; 1972, $480,000)	850,000	460,000
	Accounts receivable *Less:* allowance for bad debt: 1973, $100,000; 1972, 95,000	2,000,000	1,900,000
5	Inventories	2,700,000	3,000,000
6	**Total current assets**	$6,000,000	$5,660,000
	Fixed assets (property, plant, and equipment)		
	Land	$ 450,000	$ 450,000
	Building	3,800,000	3,600,000
	Machinery	950,000	850,000
	Office equipment	100,000	95,000
		$5,300,000	$4,995,000
	Less: accumulated depreciation	1,800,000	1,500,000
	Net fixed assets	$3,500,000	$3,495,000
	Prepayments and deferred charges	100,000	90,000
	Intangibles (goodwill, patent, trademarks)	100,000	100,000
	Total assets	$9,700,000	$9,345,000

gency, assets you could take right away to the bank, if you had to. They are those current assets which are quickly convertible into cash. This leaves out merchandise inventories, because such inventories have yet to be sold. Accordingly, quick assets are current assets minus inventories.

6	Current assets	$6,000,000
5	*Less:* inventories	2,700,000
	Quick assets	$3,300,000

LIABILITIES	1973	1972
Current liabilities		
Accounts payable	$1,000,000	940,000
Notes payable	850,000	1,000,000
Accrued expenses payable	330,000	300,000
Federal income taxes payable	320,000	290,000
17 **Total current liabilities**	$2,500,000	$2,530,000
Long-term liabilities First mortgage bonds; 5% interest, due 1985	2,700,000	2,700,000
Total liabilities	$5,200,000	$5,230,000
STOCKHOLDERS' EQUITY		
Capital stock		
Preferred stock, 5% cumulative, $100 par value each; authorized, issued, and outstanding 6,000 shares	600,000	600,000
Common stock, $5 par value each; authorized, issued, and outstanding 300,000 shares	1,500,000	1,500,000
Capital surplus	700,000	700,000
23 Accumulated retained earnings	1,700,000	1,315,000
Total stockholders' equity	$4,500,000	$4,115,000
Total liabilities and stockholders' equity	$9,700,000	$9,345,000

Net quick assets are found by taking the quick assets and subtracting the total current liabilities. A well-fixed industrial company should show a reasonable excess of quick assets over current liabilities. This provides a rigorous and important test of a company's ability to meet its obligations.

	Quick assets	$3,300,000
17	*Less:* current liabilities	2,500,000
	Net quick assets	$ 800,000

The *quick assets ratio* is found by dividing the quick assets by the current liabilities.

$$17 \quad \frac{\$3{,}300{,}000 \text{ quick assets}}{\$2{,}500{,}000 \text{ current liabilities}} = \frac{1.3}{1} \text{ or } 1.3 \text{ to } 1$$

As you can see, for each $1 of current liabilities, there is $1.30 in quick assets available.

INVENTORY TURNOVER. How big an inventory should a company have? That depends on a combination of many factors. An inventory is large or small depending upon the type of business and the time of the year. An automobile dealer, for example, with a large stock of autos at the height of the season is in a strong inventory position; yet that same inventory at the end of the season is a weakness in his financial condition.

How can we measure adequacy and balance of inventory? One way is to compare it with sales for the year to arrive at *Inventory Turnover.* Typical Manufacturing's sales for the year are $11,000,000, and the inventory at the balance sheet date is $2,700,000. Thus the turnover is 4.1 times, meaning that the goods are bought and sold out more than four times per year on the average. (Strict accounting requires computation of inventory turnover by comparing annual *cost of goods sold* with *average inventory.* This information is not readily available in the published statements, so many analysts look instead for *sales* related to inventory.)

Inventory as a percentage of current assets is another comparison that may be made between inventory and total current assets. In Typical Manufacturing the inventory of $2,700,000 represents 45% of the total current assets, which amount to $6,000,000. But there is considerable variation between different types of companies, and thus the relationship is significant only when comparisons are made among companies in a similar industry.

BOOK VALUE OF SECURITIES. There is another very important thing that can be learned from the balance sheet, and that is the *net book value* (the value at which something is carried on the books of the company) or *net asset value* of the company's securities. For a bond or a share of preferred stock, or for a share of common stock, this value represents the amount of corporate assets backing or protecting these securities. We can calculate these values for each of the three types of securities that our company has outstanding by a bit of simple arithmetic.

Net asset value per bond. In order to state this figure conservatively, the intangible assets are subtracted as though they have no value upon liquidation. Then the current liabilities of $2,500,000 are considered to have been paid off. This leaves $7,100,000 in assets available to pay off the bondholders. For Typical Manufacturing, we find there is $2,629 in net asset value protecting each $1,000 bond, calculated as follows:

12	Total assets	$9,700,000
11	*Less:* intangibles	100,000
	Total tangible assets	$9,600,000
17	*Less:* current liabilities	2,500,000
	Net tangible assets available to meet bondholders' claims	$7,100,000

$$\frac{\$7{,}100{,}000}{\underset{\text{bonds outstanding}}{2{,}700}} = \$2{,}629 \text{ net asset value per } \$1{,}000 \text{ bond}$$

Net asset value per share of preferred stock. To calculate the net asset value of a share of preferred stock, we determine first the total assets, conservatively stated at $9,600,000 (after eliminating $100,000 of intangible assets). Then the current liabilities of $2,500,000 and the long-term liabilities are considered to have been paid off. This leaves $4,400,000 of resulting assets protecting the preferred stock outstanding. Accordingly, $733 is the net asset value backing each share of preferred stock, calculated in this way:

12	Total assets		$9,700,000
11	*Less:* intangibles		100,000
	Total tangible assets		$9,600,000
17	*Less:* current liabilities	$2,500,000	
	long-term liabilities	2,700,000	
			$5,200,000
	Net assets backing the preferred stock		$4,400,000

$$\frac{\$4{,}400{,}000}{\underset{\text{shares of preferred stock outstandnig}}{6{,}000}} = \$733 \text{ net asset value per share of preferred stock}$$

BALANCE SHEET—DECEMBER 31, 1973

ASSETS	1973	1972
Current Assets		
Cash	$ 450,000	$ 300,000
Marketable securities at cost (market value: 1973, $890,000; 1972, $480,000)	850,000	460,000
Accounts receivable *Less:* allowance for bad debt: 1973, $100,000; 1972, $95,000	2,000,000	1,900,000
Inventories	2,700,000	3,000,000
Total current assets	$6,000,000	$5,660,000
Fixed assets (property, plant, and equipment)		
Land	$ 450,000	$ 450,000
Building	3,800,000	3,600,000
Machinery	950,000	850,000
Office equipment	100,000	95,000
	$5,300,000	$4,995,000
Less: accumulated depreciation	1,800,000	1,500,000
Net fixed assets	$3,500,000	$3,495,000
Prepayments and deferred charges	100,000	90,000
11 Intangibles (goodwill, patent, trademarks)	100,000	100,000
12 **Total assets**	$9,700,000	$9,345,000

Net book value per share of common stock. The net book value per share of common stock can be looked upon as meaning the amount of money each share would receive if the company were liquidated, based on balance-sheet values. Of course, the preferential liquidation rights of bondholders and preferred stockholders would first have to be satisfied. The answer, $12.67 net book value per share of common stock, is arrived at as follows:

12	Total assets		$9,700,000
11	*Less:* intangibles		100,000
	Total tangible assets		$9,600,000
17	*Less:* current liabilities	$2,500,000	
18	long-term liabilities	2,700,000	
20	preferred stock	600,000	
			5,800,000
	Net assets available for the common stock		$3,800,000

$\frac{\$3,800,000}{300,000 \text{ shares of common stock outstandnig}} = \$12.67$ net book value per share of common stock

An alternative method of arriving at the common stockholders' equity—conservatively stated at $3,800,000—is:

21	Common stock	$1,500,000
22	Capital surplus	700,000
23	Accumulated retained earnings	1,700,000
		$3,900,000
11	*Less:* intangible assets	100,000
	Total common stockholders' equity	$3,800,000

$\frac{\$3,800,000}{300,000 \text{ shares of common stock outstandnig}} = \$12.67$ net book value per share of common stock

Do not be misled by book value figures, particularly of common stocks. Profitable companies often show a very low net book value and very substantial earnings. Railroads, on the other hand, may show a high book value for their common stock but have such low or irregular earnings that the market price of the stock is much less than its apparent book value. Insurance companies, banks, and investment companies make exceptions to what we have said about net book value of common stock. Since their assets are largely liquid (cash, accounts receivable, and marketable securities), the book value of their common stock is sometimes a fair indication of market value.

CAPITALIZATION RATIOS. Before investing, you will want to know the proportion of each kind of security issued by the company you are considering. These proportions are sometimes referred to as *capitalization ratios*. A high proportion of bonds sometimes reduces the attractiveness of both the

	LIABILITIES	1973	1972
	Current liabilities		
	Accounts payable	$1,000,000	940,000
	Notes payable	850,000	1,000,000
	Accrued expenses payable	330,000	300,000
	Federal income taxes payable	320,000	290,000
17	**Total current liabilities**	$2,500,000	$2,530,000
	Long-term liabilities		
18	First mortgage bonds; 5% interest, due 1985	2,700,000	2,700,000
	Total liabilities	$5,200,000	$5,230,000
	STOCKHOLDERS' EQUITY		
	Capital stock		
20	Preferred stock, 5% cumulative, $100 par value each; authorized, issued, and outstanding 6,000 shares	600,000	600,000
21	Common stock, $5 par value each; authorized, issued, and outstanding 300,000 shares	1,500,000	1,500,000
22	Capital surplus	700,000	700,000
23	Accumulated retained earnings	1,700,000	1,315,000
	Total stockholders' equity	$4,500,000	$4,115,000
	Total liabilities and stockholders' equity	$9,700,000	$9,345,000

preferred and common stock, while too large an amount of preferred can detract from the value of the common. The principal reason is that bond interest must be paid before preferred stock dividends, and preferred stock dividends before common stock dividends.

The bond ratio is found by dividing the face value of the bonds, $2,700,000 for Typical Manufacturing, by the total value of the bonds, preferred stock, common stock, capital surplus, and accumulated retained earnings, amounting to $7,100,000. This shows that bonds amount to 38% of the total capitalization, that the company has outstanding. The capitalization of Typical Manufacturing therefore consists of the following:

18	Bonds	$2,700,000
20	Preferred stock	600,000
21	Common stock	1,500,000
22	Capital surplus	700,000
23	Accumulated retained earnings	1,700,000
	Less: intangibles	100,000
	Total capitalization	$7,100,000

The *preferred stock ratio* is found in the same way: divide the preferred stock of $600,000 by the entire capitalization of $7,100,000. The result is 8½%.

Naturally, the common stock ratio will be the difference between 100% and the total of the bond and preferred stock ratios—53½% in our example. The same result is reached by combining the common stock, capital surplus, and accumulated earnings and dividing by the total capitalization. Both capital surplus and accumulated earnings represent additional backing for the common stock. The capital surplus usually indicates the amount paid by stockholders in excess of the par value of the common stock; the accumulated retained earnings are undistributed profits plowed back to help the corporation grow. For Typical Manufacturing we add to the common stock of $1,500,000 the capital surplus of $700,000 and the accumulated retained earnings (minus $100,000 in intangibles) of $1,600,000 for a total of $3,800,000. This figure divided by $7,100,000 total capitalization gives 53½% as the common stock ratio. So, the proportion of bonds, preferred, and common stock for Typical Manufacturing is shown in the box on the right.

Since you have two-year figures in Typical's report, you can do the same calculation for the previous year and see if Typical's capitalization has grown or shrunk.

		Ratio	Amount
18	Bonds	$2,700,000	38 %
20	Preferred stock	600,000	8½
21	Common stock (Including capital surplus and retained earnings)	3,800,000	53½
	Total	$7,100,000	100 %

	LIABILITIES	1973	1972
	Current liabilities		
	Accounts payable	$1,000,000	940,000
	Notes payable	850,000	1,000,000
	Accrued expenses payable	330,000	300,000
	Federal income taxes payable	320,000	290,000
	Total current liabilities	$2,500,000	$2,530,000
	Long-term liabilities		
18	First mortgage bonds; 5% interest, due 1985	2,700,000	2,700,000
	Total liabilities	$5,200,000	$5,230,000
	STOCKHOLDERS' EQUITY		
	Capital stock		
20	Preferred stock, 5% cumulative, $100 par value each; authorized, issued, and outstanding 6,000 shares	600,000	600,000
21	Common stock, $5 par value each; authorized, issued, and outstanding 300,000 shares	1,500,000	1,500,000
22	Capital surplus	700,000	700,000
23	Accumulated retained earnings	1,700,000	1,315,000
	Total stockholders' equity	$4,500,000	$4,115,000
	Total liabilities and stockholders' equity	$9,700,000	$9,345,000

THE INCOME STATEMENT

Now we come to the payoff for many potential investors, the income statement. It shows how much the corporation makes or loses during the year. Some companies refer to this statement as *the earnings report* or *the statement of profit and loss*. We have called it the *the income statement*.

While the balance sheet shows the fundamental soundness of a company by reflecting its financial position at a given date, the income statement may be of greater interest to investors because it shows the record of its operating activities for the whole year. It serves as a valuable guide in anticipating how the company may do in the future. The figure given for a single year is not nearly the whole story. The historical record for a series of years is more important than the figure of any single year. Luckily for us, Typical includes two years in its statement.

An income statement matches the amounts received from selling the goods and other items of income against all the costs and outlays incurred in order to operate the company. The result is a *net profit* or a *net loss* for the year. The costs incurred usually consist of cost of the goods sold; overhead expenses such as wages and salaries; rent, supplies, depreciation; interest on money borrowed; and taxes.

NET SALES. The most important source of revenue always makes up the first item on the income statement. In Typical Manufacturing, it is *net sales*. If it were a railroad or a utility instead of a manufacturer, this item would be called *operating revenues*. In any case, it represents the primary source of money received by the company from its customers for goods sold or services rendered. The *net sales* item covers the amount received after taking into consideration returned goods and allowances for reduction of prices. By comparing this year and last, we can see if Typical had a better year, or a worse one.

26	Net sales	$11,000,000	$10,200,000

COST OF SALES AND OPERATING EXPENSES. In a manufacturing establishment, this represents all the costs incurred in the factory (including depreciation, which we have stated separately for Typical Manufacturing) in order to convert raw materials into finished products. These costs include the raw materials, the labor, and such factory overhead items as supervision, rent, electricity, supplies, maintenance, and repairs.

Cost of goods sold. The first, and largest, item which Typical Manufacturing lists under the heading of cost of sales and operating expenses is the *cost of goods sold:*

27	Cost of goods sold	$8,200,000	$7,684,000

Depreciation. As we already know, this is the decline in useful value of an asset due to wear and tear. Each year's decline in value of a machine used in the manufacturing process is a cost to be borne as an expense chargeable against production as an additional outlay.

28	Depreciation	$300,000	$275,000

	CONSOLIDATED INCOME STATEMENT	1973	1972
26	Net Sales	$11,000,000	$10,200,000
	Cost of sales and operating expenses		
27	Cost of goods sold	8,200,000	7,684,000
28	Depreciation	300,000	275,000
	Selling and administrating expenses	1,400,000	1,325,000
	Operating profit	$ 1,100,000	$ 916,000
	Other income Dividends and interest	50,000	27,000
	Total income	$ 1,150,000	$ 943,000
	Less: interest on bonds	135,000	135,000
	Income before provision for federal income tax	$ 1,015,000	$ 808,000
	Provisions for federal income tax	480,000	365,000
	Net profit for year	$ 535,000	$ 443,000

Comm shares outstanding	300,000	300,000
Net earnings per share	$1.68	$1.38

ACCUMULATED RETAINED EARNINGS STATEMENT	1973	1972
Balance January 1	$ 1,315,000	$ 1,022,000
Net profit for year	535,000	443,000
Total	$ 1,850,000	$ 1,465,000
Less: dividends paid on preferred stock	30,000	30,000
common stock	120,000	120,000
Balance December 31	$ 1,700,000	$ 1,315,000

Selling and administrative expenses. These expenses are generally grouped separately from cost of sales so that the reader of an income statement may see the extent of selling costs and administrative costs. Salesmen's salaries and commissions, advertising and promotion, travel, and entertainment are usually the significant items of *selling expenses*. Executives' salaries, office payroll, office expenses, and the like are the usual items included as *administrative expenses.*

29	Selling and administrative expenses	$1,400,000

Subtracting all operating costs from the net sales figure gives us the *operating profit.*

30	Operating profit	$1,100,000

An additional source of revenue comes from dividends and interest received by the company from its investment in stocks and bonds. This is listed separately under an item called, logically enough, *other income* (or *miscellaneous income*).

31	Other income Dividends and interest	$50,000

When operating profit and other income are combined, we get the company's *total income.*

32	Total income	$1,150,000

INTEREST EXPENSE. The interest paid to bondholders for the use of their money is sometimes referred to as a *fixed charge* for the reason that the interest must be paid year after year whether the company is making money or losing money. Interest differs from dividends on stocks, which are payable only if the board of directors declares them.

Interest paid is another cost of doing business and is deductible from earnings in order to arrive at a base for the payment of income taxes.

Typical Manufacturing's first mortgage bonds, carried on the balance sheet as a long-term liability, bear 5% interest on $2,700,000. Thus the interest expense in the income statement is equal to $135,000 per year.

33	*Less:* interest on bonds	$135,000

FEDERAL INCOME TAX. Assume tax rates of 22% on the first $25,000 of income and 48% on the income in excess of $25,000. Typical Manufacturing's income before taxes is $1,015,000; the tax comes to $480,000 (rounded off).

34	Income before provision for federal income tax	$1,015,000

35	Provision for federal income tax	480,000

NET PROFIT. After we have taken into consideration all income (the plus factors) and deducted all costs and expenses (the minus factors), we arrive at *net profit* for the year. While sometimes this item is also called *net income* we think that would be confusing in this booklet. So we use the term *net profit,* instead.

36	Net profit for the year	$ 535,000

Condensed, the income statement looks like this:

	Plus factors:		
26	Net sales	$11,000,000	
31	Other income	50,000	
	Total		$11,050,000
	Minus factors:		
27-29	Cost of sales and operating expenses	$9,900,000	
33	Interest on bonds	135,000	
35	Provision for federal income tax	480,000	
	Total		10,515,000
36	Net profit		$ 535,000

Analyzing the Income Statement

The income statement, like the balance sheet, will tell us a lot more if we make a few detailed comparisons. Before you select a company for investment, you will want to know something of its *operating margin of profit* and how this figure has changed over the years. Typical Manufacturing had sales for the year of $11,000,000 and showed $1,100,000 as the operating profit.

$$\frac{30 \quad \$\ 1{,}100{,}000 \text{ operating profit}}{26 \quad \$11{,}000{,}000 \text{ sales}} = 10\%$$

This means that for each dollar of sales there remained 10¢ as a gross profit from operations. By itself this figure is interesting, but it can be more significant in two ways.

In the first place, we can compare it with the margin of profit in the previous year.

$$\frac{30 \quad \$\ \ 916{,}000 \text{ operating profit}}{26 \quad \$10{,}200{,}000 \text{ sales}} = 9\%$$

Since Typical went from 9% to 10% profit margin, we can see that our firm really became more profitable, instead of merely growing.

	CONSOLIDATED INCOME STATEMENT	1973	1972
26	Net Sales	$11,000,000	$10,200,000
	Cost of sales and operating expenses		
27	Cost of goods sold	8,200,000	7,684,000
28	Depreciation	300,000	275,000
29	Selling and administrating expenses	1,400,000	1,925,000
30	Operating profit	$ 1,100,000	$ 916,000
31	Other income Dividends and interest	50,000	27,000
32	**Total income**	$ 1,150,000	$ 943,000
33	*Less:* interest on bonds	135,000	135,000
34	Income before provision for federal income tax	$ 1,015,000	$ 808,000
35	Provision for federal income tax	480,000	365,000
36	**Net profit for year**	$ 535,000	$ 443,000

Common shares outstanding	300,000	300,000
Net earnings per share	$1.68	$1.38

ACCUMULATED RETAINED EARNINGS STATEMENT	1973	1972
Balance January 1	$ 1,315,000	$ 1,022,000
Net profit for year	535,000	443,000
Total	$ 1,850,000	$ 1,465,000
Less: dividends paid on preferred stock	30,000	30,000
common stock	120,000	120,000
Balance December 31	$ 1,700,000	$ 1,315,000

Changes in profit margin can reflect changes in efficiency as well as changes in products manufactured or in types of customers served.

Second, we can also compare our company with other companies that do a similar type of business. If the margin of profit of our company is very low in comparison with other companies in the same field, it is an unhealthy sign. Naturally, if it is high, there are grounds for optimism.

Analysts also frequently use the *operating cost ratio* for the same purpose. The operating ratio is the complement of the margin of profit. The margin of profit in Typical Manufacturing is 10%. The operating cost ratio is 90%. The ratios may be summarized as follows:

		Amount	Ratio
26	Net sales	$11,000,000	100.0%
27-29	Operating costs	9,900,000	90.0
	Operating profit	$ 1,100,000	10.0%

Net profit ratio is still another guide to indicate how satisfactory the year's activities have been. In Typical Manufacturing, the year's net profit was $535,000. The net sales for the year amounted to $11,000,000. Therefore, Typical Manufacturing's profit was $535,000 on $11,000,000 of sales or:

$$\frac{36 \quad \$\ \ 535{,}000 \text{ net profit}}{26 \quad \$11{,}000{,}000 \text{ sales}} = 4.9\%$$

Last year, Typical's net profit was $443,000 on $10,200,000 in sales:

$$\frac{36 \quad \$\ \ 443{,}000 \text{ net profit}}{26 \quad \$10{,}200{,}000 \text{ sales}} = 4.3\%$$

This means that this year for every $1 of goods sold, 4.9¢ in profit ultimately went to the company. By comparing the operating margin and the net profit ratio from year to year for the same company and with other companies, we can best judge profit progress. For example, we can compare Typical to the average of all manufacturing corporations (these figures are supplied by the U.S. Federal Trade Commission):

	Operating Margin (after depreciation)		Profit Margin (after tax)	
Year	Average percentage	Typical's percentage	Average percentage	Typical's percentage
1968	8.8	9.5	5.0	5.3
1969	8.5	9.3	4.8	4.8
1970	7.0	8.4	4.0	4.6
1971	7.5	9.0	4.2	4.3
1972	7.7	10.0	4.2	4.9

The margin of profit ratio, the operating cost ratio, and the net profit ratio, like all those we examined in connection with the balance sheet, give us general information about the company and help us judge its prospects for the future. All these comparisons have significance for the long term, since they tell us about the fundamental economic condition of the company. But there remains one question: are the securities good investments for you now? To get an answer, we must look for some additional factors.

INTEREST COVERAGE. The bonds of Typical Manufacturing represent a very substantial debt, but they are due many years hence. The yearly interest, however is a fixed charge, and one of the first things we would like to know is how readily the company can pay the interest. More specifically, we would like to know whether the borrowed funds have been put to good use so that the earnings are ample and therefore available to meet the interest cost.

The available income representing the source for payment of the bond interest is $1,150,000 (total income before interest on bonds and provisions for income tax). The annual bond interest amounts to $135,000. This means the annual interest expense is covered 8.5 times.

$$\frac{32\quad \$1{,}150{,}000\ \text{total income}}{33\quad \$\ \ 135{,}000\ \text{interest on bonds}} = 8.5$$

Before an industrial bond can be considered a safe investment most analysts say that the company should earn its bond interest requirement three to four times over. By these standards, Typical Manufacturing has a fair margin of safety.

PREFERRED DIVIDEND COVERAGE. To calculate the *preferred dividend coverage* (the number of times preferred dividends were earned), we must use net profit as our base, since federal income taxes and all interest charges must be paid before anything is available for stockholders. Since we have 6,000 shares of $100 par value of preferred stock that pays a dividend of 5%, the total dividend requirement for the preferred stock is $30,000. Dividing the net income of $535,000 by this figure, we arrive at approximately 17.8 which means that the dividend requirement of the preferred stock has been earned more than seventeen times over, a very safe ratio, according to many analysts.

EARNINGS PER COMMON SHARE. The buyer of common stocks is often more concerned with the earnings per share of his stock than he is with the dividend. Usually earnings per share (or rather, prospective earnings per share) influence stock market prices. Our income statement shows the earning available for the common stock:

38	Net earnings per share	$1.68

	CONSOLIDATED INCOME STATEMENT	1973	1972
	Net sales	$11,000,000	$10,200,000
	Cost of sales and operating expenses		
	Cost of goods sold	8,200,000	7,684,000
	Depreciation	300,000	275,000
	Selling and administrating expenses	1,400,000	1,325,000
	Operating profit	$ 1,100,000	$ 916,000
	Other income Dividends and interest	50,000	27,000
32	**Total income**	$ 1,150,000	$ 943,000
33	*Less:* interest on bonds	135,000	135,000
	Income before provision for federal income tax	$ 1,015,000	$ 808,000
	Provision for federal income tax	480,000	365,000
36	**Net profit for year**	$ 535,000	$ 443,000

	Common shares outstanding	300,000	300,000
38	**Net earnings per share**	$1.68	$1.38

ACCUMULATED RETAINED EARNINGS STATEMENT	1973	1972
Balance January 1	$ 1,315,000	$ 1,022,000
Net profit for year	535,000	443,000
Total	$ 1,850,000	$ 1,465,000
Less: dividends paid on preferred stock	30,000	30,000
common stock	120,000	120,000
Balance December 31	$ 1,700,000	$ 1,315,000

But if it did not we could calculate it ourselves:

36	Net profit for the year	$535,000
	Less: dividend requirements on preferred stock	30,000
	Earnings available for the common stock	$505,000

$$\frac{\$505{,}000 \text{ earnings available}}{300{,}000 \text{ number of outstanding shares}} = \$1.68 \text{ earnings per share of common}$$

Because of the ever-increasing significance placed on the results of the year's operating activities, it is now required practice for earnings per share of common to be shown on the face of the income statement. Furthermore, where the capital structure of a firm includes securities which are convertible into common stock, the new rules of accounting call for more sensible reporting of earnings per share.

WHAT ABOUT LEVERAGE? A stock is said to have high leverage if the company that issued it has a large proportion of bonds and preferred stock outstanding in relation to the amount of common stock. A simple illustration will show why. Let us take, for example, a company with $10,000,000 of 4% bonds outstanding. If the company is earning $440,000 before bond interest, there will be only $40,000 left for the common stock after payment of $400,000 bond interest ($10,000,000 at 4% equals $400,000). However, an increase of only 10% in earnings (to $484,000) will leave $84,000 for common stock dividends, or an increase of more than 100%. If there is only a small common stock issue, the increase in earnings per share will appear very impressive.

You have probably realized that a decline of 10% in earnings would not only wipe out everything available for the common stock, but also result in the company's being unable to cover its full interest on its bonds without dipping into accumulated earnings. This is the great danger of so-called high-leverage stocks and also illustrates the fundamental weakness of companies that have a disproportionate amount of debt or preferred stock. Conservative investors usually steer clear of them, although these stocks do appeal to people who are willing to assume the risk.

Typical Manufacturing, on the other hand, is not a highly leveraged company. Last year, Typical paid $135,000 in bond interest and its net profit—plus this payment—came to $578,000. This left $443,000 for the common stock and retained earnings. Now look what happened this year. Net profit before subtracting bond interest rose $92,000, or about 16%. Since the bond interest stayed the same, net income after paying this interest also rose $92,000. But that is about 21% of $443,000. While this is certainly not a spectacular example of leverage, 21% is better than 16%.

EXTRAORDINARY! Events or transactions during one year which are significantly different from customary activities are now separated from recurring items and called extraordinary items.

What is an extraordinary item? An erupting volcano, for one. Other examples include selling a plant and dropping its product line, expropriation of properties by a foreign government, the sales of marketable securities resulting in a substantial capital gain or capital loss, or other sale of capital assets.

Here are two illustrations, from two other companies besides our Typical Manufacturing, of how these factors would be presented at the bottom of the earnings statement. Each shows the earnings per share of common stock.

Earnings before extraordinary items	$1.85	
Extraordinary items (net of tax)	(.53)	loss
Net earnings	$1.32	

Note: during 1973 the company sold one of its plants at loss and discontinued operations of a product line.

Earnings before extraordinary items	$2.10
Extraordinary items (net of tax)	1.20
Net earnings	$3.30

Note: during 1973 the company sold an investment in marketable securities at a profit of $2,300,000 (after consideration of applicable income tax).

You can see why it is essential for the extraordinary items to be separately identified, so investors may know the recurring earnings per share, allowing a comparison with other years.

PRIMARY EARNINGS PER SHARE. Now we come to the most nagging problem in the earnings report: deciding how much a share of common stock really earns. A new tool to help us is the use of the term *primary earnings per share.* This is determined by dividing the earnings for the year not only by the number of shares of common stock outstanding but by the common stock plus *common stock equivalents.*

Common stock equivalents are securities, such as convertible preferred stock, convertible bonds, stock options, warrants and the like, which enable the owner to become a common stockholder by exchanging or converting his security. These are deemed to be but one step short of common stock—their value stems in large part from the value of the common to which they relate.

As to convertible preferred stock and convertible bonds, they offer the holder a specified dividend rate or interest return coupled with the advantage of being able to participate in the increased potential earnings of common stock. They don't have to have been converted to common stock for these securities to be called a common stock equivalent. This is because they are in substance equivalent to common shares, enabling the holder at his discretion to cause an increase in the number of common shares by exchanging, or converting, and this dilutes the earnings per share. How do accountants determine a common stock equivalent? A convertible security is considered a common stock equivalent if, based on its market price when it is issued, its rate of return is less than two-thirds of the prime interest rate banks charge at that time. Now let's put our new terms to work in an example, remembering that it has nothing to do with our own company, Typical Manufacturing. We start with the facts we have available. We'll say we have 100,000 shares of common stock outstanding plus another 100,000 shares of preferred stock, convertible into common on a share-for-share basis. (That makes them common stock equivalents.) We add the two and get 200,000 shares altogether. Now let's say our earnings figure is $500,000 for the year. With these facts, our primary computation is easy:

$$\frac{\$500{,}000 \text{ earnings for the year}}{200{,}000 \text{ adjusted shares outstanding}} = \$2.50 \text{ primary earnings per share}$$

If the preferred stock paid $1 a share in dividends and were not convertible into common stock, the earnings would be $4 per share. Why? Because we would subtract the preferred stock dividend—$100,000—from our total earnings, leaving $400,000. But we would also divide that $400,000 figure into only 100,000 shares of common stock. Like this:

$$\frac{\$400{,}000 \text{ earnings left for common}}{100{,}000 \text{ outstanding shares}} = \$4 \text{ per share}$$

FULLY DILUTED EARNINGS PER SHARE. The primary earnings per share item, as we have just seen in the preceding section, takes into consideration common stock and common stock equivalents. The purpose of *fully diluted earnings per share* is to reflect dilution in earnings that would result if all contingent issuances of common stock had taken place at the beginning of the year.

This computation is the result of dividing the earnings for the year by: *common stock* and *common stock equivalents* and *all other securities which are convertible (even though for valid reasons not considered common stock equivalents).*

How would it work? First, remember that we have 100,000 shares of convertible preferred outstanding, as well as our 100,000 in common. Now let's say we also have convertible bonds with a par value of $10,000,000 outstanding. These bonds pay 6% interest and have a conversion ratio of 20 shares of common for every $1,000 bond. These bonds aren't common stock equivalents, but we have to count them in. If the 10,000 bonds were converted, we'd have another 200,000 shares of stock, so adding everything up gives us 400,000 shares. But by converting the bonds, we could skip the 6% interest payment, and that gains us another $600,000 gross earnings. So our final calculations look like this:

Earnings for the year		$500,000
Interest on the bonds	$600,000	
Less: the income tax applicable to deduction	300,000	
		300,000
Adjusted earnings		$800,000

$$\frac{\$800{,}000 \text{ adjusted earnings}}{400{,}000 \text{ adjusted shares outstanding}} = \$2 \text{ fully diluted earnings per share}$$

Now let's drive home the point you should always keep in mind when reading annual reports: be sure to remember what kind of earnings per share you are reading. Based on our examples here, earnings of $500,000 for the year can mean several different things to each share of common:

Before allowing for conversion: $4
Primary earnings: $2.50
Fully diluted earnings: $2

PRICE-EARNINGS RATIO. Both the price and the return on common stock vary with a multitude of factors. One such factor is the relationship that exists between the earnings per share and the market price. It is called the price-earnings ratio, and this is how it is calculated: If a stock is selling at 25 and earning $2 per share, its price-earnings ratio is 12½ to 1, usually shortened to 12½ and the stock is said to be selling at 12½ times earnings. If the stock should rise to 40, the price-earnings ratio would be 20. Or if the stock drops to 12, the price-earnings ratio would be a ridiculous 6.

In Typical Manufacturing which has no convertible common stock equivalents, the earnings per share were calculated at $1.68. If the stock were selling at 25, the price-earnings ratio would be about 15. This is the basic figure that you should use in viewing the record of this stock over a period of years and in comparing the common stock of this company with other similar stocks.

$$\frac{25 \text{ market price}}{\$1.68 \text{ earnings per share}} = 15$$

This means that Typical Manufacturing common stock is selling at approximately 15 times earnings.

Last year, Typical earned $1.38 per share. Let's say that its stock sold at the same price-earnings ratio then. This means that a share of Typical was selling for $20.75 or so, and anyone who bought Typical then would be pretty happy now. Just remember, in the real world, investors can never be certain that any stock will keep its same price-earnings ratio from year to year. The historical P/E multiple is a guide, not a guarantee.

THE ACCUMULATED RETAINED EARNINGS STATEMENT

If the income statement is the payoff for shareholders trying to discover how successful their company truly is for them, the accumulated retained earnings statement is the payoff for the company itself. It shows how much money the company has plowed back into itself—for new growth. Actually, accumulated retained earnings is a simple concept. Just as the stockholder sees more value when the price of the stock rises, the company has more value to itself when its accumulated retained earnings rise.

Naturally, the key element in this section of any financial statement is the size of the retained earnings as of the day the company closes its books for the year. To reach that figure, the company has to begin at the start of the year.

39	Balance January 1	$1,315,000

Then add in the year's net profit:

40	Net profit for year	535,000

And subtract the dividends paid to stockholders:

42	*Less:* dividends paid on	
	preferred stock	30,000
	common	120,000

The result of this adding and subtracting is the total at the end of the year.

45	Balance December 31	$1,700,000

What Does the Accumulated Retained Earnings Statement Show?

The most obvious thing the retained earnings section of Typical Manufacturing's statement can tell us is that common stockholders were paid $120,000 in dividends this year. Since we know from the balance sheet that Typical has 300,000 shares outstanding, the first thing we can learn here is what may be—after all—the most important point to some potential investors:

$$44 \quad \frac{\$120{,}000 \text{ dividends}}{300{,}000 \text{ shares}} = 40¢ \text{ a share}$$

Now when we look at the dividends-paid columns for both years, we can see that Typical not only paid 40¢ a share this year, but also the previous year.

Once we know the amount of dividend per share, we can easily discover the dividend *payout ratio*. This is simply the percentage of net earnings per share that is paid to stockholders.

$$38 \quad \frac{\$\ .40 \text{ dividend}}{\$1.68 \text{ earnings}} = 24\%$$

Typical is low, by the way. The average of all U.S. corporations is about 60%. What does this mean? Typical is plowing much of its income back into itself.

Of course the dividends on the 5% preferred stock will not change from year to year. That word *cumulative* in the balance statement description tells us that if Typical's management someday didn't pay a dividend on its preferred stock (and that could only happen if the company did not make enough profit to pay it), then the 5% payment for that year would accumulate. It would have to be paid to preferred stockholders before any dividends could ever be declared again on the common stock.

That's why preferred stock is called preferred. It gets first crack at any dividend money. We've already talked about convertible bonds and convertible preferred stock. Right now we're not interested in that aspect, because Typical Manufacturing doesn't have any convertible securities outstanding. Chances are those 6,000 shares of preferred stock, with their par value of $100 each, were issued to family members of Mr. Isaiah Typical, who founded the company back in 1923. When he took Typical public, he didn't keep any of the common stock. In those days, the guaranteed 5% dividend was more important to Isaiah. He was not interested in taking any more chances on Typical.

For us today, the important thing to be seen from the accumulated retained earnings statement is the bottom line—what's there at the end of the period.

45	Balance December 31	$1,700,000	$1,315,000

This tells us that Typical during the year has added $385,000 to its retained earnings. This means that if Typical should have some lean years in the future, it has plenty of retained earnings from which to keep on declaring those $5 dividends on the preferred stock and 40¢ dividends on the common.

	CONSOLIDATED INCOME STATEMENT	1973	1972
	Net sales	$11,000,000	$10,200,000
	Cost of sales and operating expenses		
	Cost of goods sold	8,200,000	7,684,000
	Depreciation	300,000	275,000
	Selling and administrating expenses	1,400,000	1,325,000
	Operating profit	$ 1,100,000	$ 916,000
	Other income		
	Dividends and interest	50,000	27,000
	Total income	$ 1,150,000	$ 943,000
	Less: interest on bonds	135,000	135,000
	Income before provision for federal income tax	$ 1,015,000	$ 808,000
	Provision for federal income tax	480,000	365,000
		$ 535,000	$ 443,000
	Common shares outstanding	300,000	300,000
38	**Net earnings per share**	$1.68	$1.38

	ACCUMULATED RETAINED EARNINGS STATEMENT	1973	1972
39	Balance January 1	$ 1,315,000	$ 1,022,000
40	Net profit for year	535,000	443,000
41	**Total**	$ 1,850,000	$ 1,465,000
42	*Less:* dividends paid on preferred stock	30,000	30,000
44	common stock	120,000	120,000
45	**Balance December 31**	$ 1,700,000	$ 1,315,000

There is one danger, however, in having a lot of retained earnings. If some other company—Shark Fast Foods & Electronics, for instance—decided to buy up Typical's common stock, it might gain enough control to vote out the current management. Then Shark might merge Typical into itself. Where would Shark get the money to buy Typical stock? By issuing new shares of its own stock, perhaps. And where would Shark get the money to pay the dividends on all that new stock of its own? From Typical's retained earnings. So Typical's management has the obligation to its stockholders to make sure that its retained earnings are put to work to increase the total earnings per share of the stockholders. Or else the stockholders might cooperate with Shark when it makes its raid.

THE STATEMENT OF SOURCE AND APPLICATION OF FUNDS

In the income and earnings statements, we've seen how much total money passed through Typical Manufacturing's hands last year, how much was made in profits, how much of that profit was apportioned out to shareholders, and how much was retained. Now we're going to learn more about how Typical works. We get this information from the section in the financial statement called *Source and Application of Funds.*

CASH FLOW. While we know that net profits came to $535,000 this year, if you look back at the income statement, you can see that total sales came to $11,000,000 and total operating costs came to $9,900,000. Now look at the breakdown of those costs and you see the item covering depreciation. It shows up again in the statement of source and application of funds.

46	Funds were provided by	
	Net Income	$535,000
	Depreciation	300,000
	Total	$835,000

Why is something that was first listed as a cost now listed as a source of funds? Because, if you'll remember the balance sheet definition of depreciation, it is the decline in useful value of a fixed asset due to wear and tear from time to time. You place this depreciation figure in your books as a cost of doing business during the year. But who do you pay this money to? You've already paid for whatever it is that's being depreciated. So this is money which you deduct, and you pay it to yourself. (Not really, of course. It's simply a bookkeeping entry. But it does free up this money to be included on the asset side of the books. It isn't new money, but it is "found" money.) You can either put it in the bank and add to it, against the day when you've got to actually replace that plant or truck. Or you can use it elsewhere in your business. So depreciation is another source of funds for your company during the year. And the combination of net profit and depreciation is known as *cash flow.*

48	Total	$835,000

WHERE THE CASH FLOW GOES. Once your company has told you where this cash flow came from during the year, it will tell you how it was used. Some of these uses have already been listed elsewhere, but the good financial statement goes through them again here.

49 Funds were used for	
Dividends on preferred stock	$ 30,000
Dividends on common stock	120,000
Plant and equipment	305,000
Sundry assets	10,000
	$465,000

Now comes the payoff on this section. By subtracting total funds used from total cash flow, we can see whether the company has increased its working capital during the year, or decreased it. From our analysis of Typical Manufacturing's balance sheet, you already know that working capital is important. And we know how to find out how much working capital Typical Manufacturing has. This particular section here, on the other hand, shows us quickly whether Typical's working capital is growing or shrinking. And it tells us what Typical spent its cash flow to do during the year: First of all, dividends; then, under *plant and equipment,* we'll tell you that Typical bought a new heavy-duty widget machine; and under *sundry assets,* a new company limousine for Board Chairman Patience Typical, old Isaiah Typical's daughter.

Analyzing the Statement of Source and Application of Funds

This part is rather easy in the case of Typical Manufacturing, because its statement includes a built-in analysis. (See items 55 to 63 on the small statement reproduced opposite.) This breakdown leads us to see how the working capital changes show up in the year-end balance sheet which began this book. By comparing this year with last, we can get the same figures:

Current assets		Changes:
Cash	$450,000 — $300,000 =	$150,000
Marketable securities	850,000 — 460,000 =	390,000
Accounts receivable	2,000,000 — 1,900,000 =	100,000
Inventories	2,700,000 — 3,000,000 =	(300,000)
		$340,000

Current liabilities		Changes:
Accounts payable	$1,000,000 — $940,000 =	$ 60,000
Notes payable	850,000 — 1,000,000 =	(150,000)

Accrued expenses payable		
330,000 — 300,000 =	30,000	
Federal income tax payable		
320,000 — 290,000 =	30,000	
	$(30,000)	

STATEMENT OF SOURCE AND APPLICATION OF FUNDS—1973

46	Funds were provided by		
	Net income	$535,000	
	Depreciation	300,000	
48	**Total**		$835,000
49	Funds were used for		
	Dividends on preferred stock	$ 30,000	
	Dividends on common stock	120,000	
	Plant and equipment	350,000	
	Sundry assets	10,000	
	Total		$465,000
	INCREASE IN WORKING CAPITAL		$370,000

Analysis of changes in working capital—1973

	Changes in current assets		
55	Cash	$150,000	
56	Marketable securities	390,000	
57	Accounts receivable	100,000	
58	Inventories	(300,000)	
	Total		$340,000
	Changes in current liabilities		
59	Accounts payable	$ 60,000	
60	Notes payable	(150,000)	
61	Accrued expenses payable	30,000	
62	Federal income tax payable	30,000	
63	**Total**		$ (30,000)

We can see from the source and application of funds section that depreciation gave Typical some of the funds which were translated into working capital. We can also see that this working capital shows up on our balance sheet books in the form of extra cash, more value in the marketable securities owned by Typical Manufacturing, more accounts receivable from its customers, and a lower amount of outstanding short-term notes it must repay.

Largely because of Typical's greater sales volume, we presume, Typical owes more accounts payable to its own suppliers. The company also has more accrued expenses and more income tax due. But Typical's inventories of unsold goods have dropped $300,000 during the year. That means the company is turning over its existing inventory faster, and making its capital work harder for the stockholders during the year.

RETURN ON EQUITY. Seeing how hard money works, of course, is one of the most popular ways investors use to come up with individual judgments on how much they think a certain stock ought to be worth. The market itself —the sum of all buyers and sellers—makes the real decision. But investors often try to make their own, in order to decide in turn if they want to invest at the market's price or wait. Most investors look for Typical's *return on equity,* which shows how hard their investment in Typical is working. In order to find Typical's current return on equity, look at the balance sheet and take the common stockholders' equity for *last* year—*not the current year* —and then we see how much Typical made this year on it. We use only the amount of net profit after the dividends have been paid on the preferred stock. For Typical Manufacturing, that means $535,000 net profit minus $30,000. Here is what we get:

$$\frac{\$505{,}000 \text{ this year's profit for common}}{\$3{,}415{,}000 \text{ last year's stockholders' equity}} = 14.8\% \text{ return on equity}$$

For every dollar of stockholders' equity, therefore, Typical made more than 14¢. Is that Good? Well, 14¢ on the dollar is better than Typical could have done by going out of business, taking its stockholders' equity and putting that $3,415,000 in the bank. So Typical obviously is better off in its own line of work. When we consider putting our money to work with Typical in its stock, we should compare Typical's 14¢. Not only to whatever Typical's business competitors make, but to Typical's investment competitors for our money. For instance, the average rate for all U.S. industry, according to the U.S. Federal Trade Commission, was 10.4¢ for the first half of 1972.

Just remember, that 14¢ is what Typical itself makes on the dollar. By no means is it what you will make in dividends on Typical's stock. What that return on equity tells you is whether Typical Manufacturing is relatively attractive as an enterprise. You can only hope that this attractiveness might be translated into demand for Typical stock, and its price.

Many analysts also like to see a company's annual return on the total capital available to the company. To get this figure, we use all the equity, plus all available borrowed funds. This becomes the total capital available. And for the total return on this figure, we use net income before income taxes and interest charges. A bigger capital base, and a larger income figure. For us stockholders, however, what we're most interested in is how hard our own share of the company is working. And that's why return on equity is preferred by us.

QUALIFYING AND CERTIFYING

WATCH THOSE FOOTNOTES. The annual reports of many companies contain this statement: "The accompanying footnotes are an integral part of the financial statements." The reason is that the financial reports themselves are kept concise and condensed. Therefore, any explanatory matter which cannot readily be abbreviated is set out in greater detail in footnotes.

Some examples of appropriate footnotes are:

- Changes in the company's method of depreciating fixed assets.
- Changes in the value of stock outstanding due to stock dividends and splits.
- Details of stock options granted to officers and employees.
- Employment contracts, profit sharing, pension and retirement plans.
- Contingent liabilities representing claims or lawsuits pending.

Most people do not like to read footnotes because they may be complicated and they are almost always hard to read. That's too bad, because footnotes sometimes can be dynamite. And even if they don't reveal that the corporation has been forced into bankruptcy, footnotes can still tell you many fascinating sidelights on the financial story. And those footnotes must be done in type that is as large as the numbers in the financial statement. So if Typical were to tell you in a footnote that it had gone broke, this couldn't be told in type so small you'd need a magnifying glass to read it.

INDEPENDENT AUDITS. The certificate from the independent accountants which is printed in the report says, first, that the auditing steps taken in the process of verification of the account meet the accounting world's approved standards of practice, and second, that the financial statements in the report have been prepared in conformity with generally accepted accounting principles.

As a result, when the annual report contains financial statements that have the stamp of approval from independent public accountants, you have an assurance that the figures can be relied upon as having been fairly presented.

THE LONG VIEW

We cannot emphasize too strongly that company records, in order to be very useful, must be compared. We can compare them to other company records, to industry averages or even to broader economic factors, if we want. But most of all, we can compare one company's annual activities to the same firm's results from other years.

This used to be done by keeping a file of old annual reports. Now many corporations include a ten-year summary in their financial highlights each year. This provides information to the investing public concerning a decade of long-term performance. That is why Typical Manufacturing, being a good company, has included a ten-year summary in its annual report. It's not a part of the statements vouched for by the auditors, but it is there for you to see.

Among the more important things a ten-year summary can show you are:

- The trend and consistency of sales fluctuations,
- The trend of earnings, particularly in relation to sales and the economy,
- The trend of net earnings as a percentage of sales,
- The trend of return on capital,
- Net earnings per share of common,
- Dividends, and dividend policy.

Other information from many companies for the decade may include changes in net worth, book value per share, capital expenditures for plant and machinery, long-term debt, capital stock changes by way of stock dividends and splits, number of employees, number of stockholders, number of outlets, and where appropriate, information on foreign subsidiaries and the extent to which many foreign operations have been embodied in the financial report.

Let us once more emphasize: financial statements are only half-valuable in a vacuum. To be truly useful they must be compared—to competitors and from year to year. This is why ten-year summaries are growing in popularity. They tell you more. And all of this is really important because of one central point: you are not only trying to find out how Typical is doing *now*. You want to predict how Typical *will* do—and how its stock will perform.

TEN YEAR FINANCIAL SUMMARY	1973	1972	1971	1970	1969	1968	1967	1966	1965	1964
Net Sales	$11,000,000	$10,200,000	$9,115,000	$9,550,000	$8,875,000	$7,870,000	$8,625,000	$7,575,000	$6,485,000	$5,365,000
Income before provision for income tax	1,015,000	808,000	802,000	855,000	790,000	716,000	755,000	674,000	590,000	488,000
Net profit for year	535,000	443,000	417,000	462,000	474,000	444,000	468,000	438,000	384,000	342,000
Earnings per share	1.68	1.38	1.29	1.44	1.48	1.38	1.46	1.36	1.18	1.04
Dividend per share	0.40	0.40	0.40	0.40	0.40	0.40	0.20	0.20	0.10	0.10
Net working capital	3,500,000	3,130,000	3,038,000	2,200,000	1,930,000	2,250,000	2,156,000	2,100,000	1,620,000	1,530,000
Net plant & equipment	3,500,000	2,495,000	3,315,000	3,185,000	2,730,000	2,625,000	2,465,000	2,165,000	2,090,000	1,820,000
Long-term debt	2,700,000	2,700,000	2,700,000	–	–	–	–	–	– –	–
Preferred stock	600,000	600,000	600,000	600,000	600,000	600,000	600,000	600,000	–	–
Common stock & surplus	3,900,000	3,515,000	3,251,000	3,014,000	2,852,000	2,558,000	2,294,000	1,946,000	1,628,000	1,346,000
Book value per share	12.67	11.38	10.57	9.81	9.31	8.53	7.65	6.49	5.43	4.49

References

Ackerman, Robert W.: "How Companies Respond to Social Demands." *Harvard Business Review,* July–August 1973.

Ackerman, Robert W.: *Managing Corporate Responsibility.* Boston, Harvard University Press, 1975.

Ackoff, Russell L.: *A Concept of Corporate Planning.* New York, Wiley, 1970.

Adizes, Ichak, and J. Fred Weston: "Comparative Models of Social Responsibility." *Academy of Management Journal,* March 1973.

Aguilar, Francis Joseph: *Scanning the Business Environment.* New York, Macmillan, 1967.

Aguilar, Francis J., Robert A. Howell, and Richard F. Vancil: *Formal Planning Systems—1970.* Graduate School of Business Administration, Harvard University, 1970.

Alchian, Armen A.: "Uncertainty, Evolution, and Economic Theory." *Journal of Political Economy,* June 1950.

Allison, Graham T.: *Essence of Decision: Explaining the Cuban Missile Crisis.* Boston, Little, Brown, 1971.

Altman, Edward J.: "Financial Ratios, Discriminant Analysis and the Prediction of Corporate Bankruptcy." *Journal of Finance,* September 1968.

Alutto, Joseph A., and Franklin Acito: "Decisional Participation and Sources of Job Satisfaction: A Study of Manufacturing Personnel." *Academy of Management Journal,* March 1974.

Ammer, Dean S.: "Has Big Business Lost the Entrepreneurial Touch?" *Business Horizons,* December 1970.

Anderson, Carl R., and Frank T. Paine: "Managerial Perceptions and Strategic Behavior." *Academy of Management Journal,* December 1975.

Andrews, Kenneth R.: *The Concept of Corporate Strategy.* Homewood, Ill., Dow Jones-Irwin, 1971.

Anshen, Melvin: "Changing the Social Contract: A Role for Business." *Columbia Journal of World Business,* November–December 1970.

Anshen, Melvin (ed.): *Managing the Socially Responsible Corporation.* New York, Macmillan, 1974.

Anshen, Melvin, and William D. Guth: "Strategies for Research in Policy Formulation." *Journal of Business,* October 1973.

Ansoff, H. Igor: *Corporate Strategy: An Analytic Approach to Business Policy for Growth and Expansion.* New York, McGraw-Hill, 1965.

Ansoff, H. Igor (ed.): *Business Strategy.* Baltimore, Md., Penguin, 1969.

Ansoff, H. Igor: "The Concept of Strategic Management." *Journal of Business Policy,* Summer 1972.

Ansoff, H. Igor, T. A. Anderson, F. Norton, and J. Fred Weston: "Planning for

Diversification Through Merger." *California Management Review,* Summer 1959.

Ansoff, H. Igor, *et al.*: "Does Planning Pay? The Effect of Planning on Success of Acquisitions in American Firms." *Long Range Planning,* December 1970.

Ansoff, H. Igor, and John Stewart: "Strategies for a Technology-Based Business." *Harvard Business Review,* November–December 1967.

Anthony, Robert N.: "The Trouble with Profit Maximization." *Harvard Business Review,* November–December 1960.

Anthony, Robert N.: "Framework for Analysis in Management Planning." *Management Services,* March–April 1964.

Anthony, Robert N.: *Planning and Control Systems: A Framework for Analysis.* Boston, Graduate School of Business Administration, Harvard University, 1965.

Anyon, G. Jay: *Entrepreneurial Dimensions of Management.* Wynnewood, Pa., Livingston, 1973.

Appleby, Paul H.: *Big Democracy.* New York, Alfred A. Knopf, 1945.

Appleby, Paul H.: *Policy and Administration.* University, Ala., University of Alabama Press, 1949.

Argyris, Chris: *The Impact of Budgets on People.* New York, Controllership Foundation, 1952.

Argyris, Chris: *Personality and Organization.* New York, Harper, 1957.

Argyris, Chris: *Integrating the Individual and the Organization.* New York, Wiley, 1964.

Argyris, Chris: *Intervention Theory and Method.* Reading, Mass., Addison-Wesley, 1970.

Argyris, Chris: *Management and Organizational Development: The Path from XA to YB.* New York, McGraw-Hill, 1971.

Argyris, Chris: "The CEO's Behavior: Key to Organizational Development." *Harvard Business Review,* March–April 1973a.

Argyris, Chris: "Personality and Organization Theory Revisited." *Administrative Science Quarterly,* June 1973b.

Asimov, Isaac: Letter to Editor. *Time,* January 20, 1973.

ASPA-BNA Survey: "Equal Employment Opportunity and Affirmative Action Programs." *Bulletin to Management,* December 13, 1973.

Ayres, Robert U.: *Technological Forecasting and Long-Range Planning.* New York, McGraw-Hill, 1969.

Bagley, Edward R.: "How to Avoid Glitches in Planning." *Management Review,* March 1972.

Bagley, Edward R.: *Beyond the Conglomerates.* New York, AMACOM, 1975.

Baier, Kurt, and Nicholas Rescher (eds.): *Values and the Future.* New York, Free Press, 1969.

Bailey, Stephen K.: *Congress Makes a Law.* New York, Columbia University Press, 1950.

Barkley, Paul W., and David W. Seckler: *Economic Growth and the Environmental Decay.* New York, Harcourt, 1972.

Barnard, Chester I.: *The Functions of the Executive.* Cambridge, Mass., Harvard University Press, 1954.

Barron, Frank: *Creative Person and Creative Process.* New York, Holt, Rinehart and Winston, 1969.

Bass, Bernard M., and Harold J. Leavitt: "Some Experiments in Planning and Operation." *Management Science,* 1963.

Bassett, Glenn A.: "The Qualifications of a Manager." *California Management Review,* Winter 1969.

Battalia, Lotz, and Associates. *A Decade of Change in Top Management Organization and Executive Job Titles.* New York, The Firm, 1969.

Bauer, Raymond A.: "The Study of Policy Formation: An Introduction." In Raymond A. Bauer and Kenneth J. Gergen (eds.), *The Study of Policy Formation.* New York, Free Press, 1968.

Bauer, Raymond A., and Dan H. Fenn, Jr.: *The Corporate Social Audit.* New York, Russell Sage Foundation, 1972.

Bauer, Raymond A., and Kenneth J. Gergen (eds.): *The Study of Policy Formation.* New York, Free Press, 1968.

Baumhart, Raymond: *Ethics in Business.* New York, Holt, Rinehart and Winston, 1968.

Baumol, William J.: *Business Behavior, Values and Growth.* New York, Harcourt, Brace and World, 1967.

Baumol, William J., Rensis Likert, Henry C. Wallich, and John J. McGowan: *A New Rational for Corporate Social Policy.* New York, Committee for Economic Development, 1970.

Beatty, Richard W.: "Blacks as Supervisors: A Study of Training, Job Performance, and Employers' Expectations." *Academy of Management Journal,* June 1973.

Beaver, William H.: "Financial Ratios as Predictors of Failure." *Journal of Accounting Research,* 1966.

Bell, Daniel: "The Corporation and Society in the 1970s." *The Public Interest,* Summer 1971.

Bell, Daniel: *The Coming of Post-Industrial Society.* New York, Basic Books, 1973.

Bell, E. C.: "Practical Long-Range Planning." *Business Horizons,* November 1968.

Berenson, Conrad: "The Product Liability Revolution." *Business Horizons,* October 1972.

Berkwitt, George J.: "How Good Are the Management Sciences?" *Dun's Review,* July 1968.

Bernstein, Marver H.: *The Job of the Federal Executive.* Washington, D. C., Brookings Institution, 1958.

Bettauer, Arthur: "Strategy for Divestments." *Harvard Business Review,* April–May 1967.

Bierman, Harold, Jr., and Allan R. Drebin: *Managerial Accounting: An Introduction.* New York, Macmillan, 1968.

Bither, Stewart W.: *Personality as a Factor in Management Team Decision Making.* University Park, Pa., Center for Research of the College of Business Administration, Pennsylvania State University, 1971.

Bleichan, Gerhard D.: "The Social Equation in Corporate Responsibility." Speech made at the Boston University Law School Centennial, 1972.

Boettinger, Henry M.: "The Management Challenge." In Edward C. Bursk (ed.): *Challenge to Leadership.* New York, Free Press, 1973.

Boise, William B.: "City Manager—Administrator or Political?" *Journal of General Management,* Winter 1975.

Bonge, John W., and Bruce P. Coleman: *Concepts for Corporate Strategy: Readings in Business Policy.* New York, Macmillan, 1972.

Bons, Paul M., Alan R. Bass, and S. S. Komorita: "Changes in Leadership Style as a Function of Military Experience and Type of Command." *Personnel Psychology,* Winter 1970.

Boston Consulting Group: *Perspectives in Experience.* Boston, The Boston Consulting Group, 1970.

Bouchard, Thomas J.: "Personality, Problem-Solving Procedure, and Performance in Small Groups." *Journal of Applied Psychology Monograph,* February 1969.

Bouchard, Thomas J., Jean Barsaloux, and Gail Drauden: "Brainstorming Procedure, Group Size, and Sex as Determinants of the Problem—Solving Effectiveness of Groups and Individuals." *Journal of Applied Psychology,* April 1974.

Bouchard, Thomas J., Gail Drauden, and Jean Barsaloux: "A Comparison of Individual, Subgroup, and Total Group Methods of Problem Solving." *Journal of Applied Psychology,* April 1974.

Boulden, James B.: "Merger Negotiations: A Decision Model." *Business Horizons,* February 1969.

Boulden, James B.: *Computer-Assisted Planning Systems.* New York, McGraw-Hill Book Company, 1976.

Boulden, James B., and Elwood S. Buffa: "Corporate Models: On-Line, Real-Time Systems." *Harvard Business Review,* July–August 1970.

Bowen, Howard R.: *Social Responsibilities of the Businessman.* New York, Harper, 1953.

Bower, Joseph L.: *Managing the Resource Allocation Process: A Study of Corporate Planning and Investment.* Boston, Graduate School of Business Administration, Harvard University, 1970.

Bower, Marvin: *The Will to Manage.* New York, McGraw-Hill, 1966.

Bowers, David G., and Stanley E. Seashore: "Predicting Organizational Effectiveness with a Four-Factor Theory of Leadership." *Administrative Science Quarterly,* September 1966.

Bradish, Richard D.: "Accountants in Top Management." *Journal of Accountancy,* June 1970.

Brady, Rodney H.: "MBO Goes to Work in the Public Sector." *Harvard Business Review,* March–April 1973.

Braybrooke, David, and Charles E. Lindblom: *A Strategy of Decision.* New York, Free Press, 1963.

Brenner, Marshall H.: "Management Development for Women." *Personnel Journal,* March 1972.

Brewer, Garry D.: *The Policy Sciences Emerge: To Nurture and Structure a Discipline.* Santa Monica, Cal., Rand Corporation, 1974.

Bright, James R.: *Technological Forecasting for Industry and Government.* Englewood Cliffs, N. J., Prentice-Hall, 1968.

Brightman, Harvey J., and Thomas F. Urban: "The Influence of the Dogmatic Personality upon Information Processing: A Comparison with a Bayesian Information Processor." *Organizational Behavior and Human Performance,* April 1974.

Broom, H. N.: *Business Policy and Strategic Action: Text, Cases and Management Game*. Englewood Cliffs, N. J., Prentice-Hall, 1969.

Brown, James K., and Rochelle O'Connor: *Planning and the Corporate Planning Director*. New York, National Industrial Conference Board, 1974.

Brown, Julius S.: "Risk Propensity in Decision Making: A Comparison of Business and Public School Administrators." *Administrative Science Quarterly*, December 1970.

Bryan, Judith F., and Edwin A. Locke. "Goal Setting as a Means of Increasing Motivation." *Journal of Applied Psychology*, June 1967.

Bryan, Stanley E.: "TFX—A Case in Policy Level Decision Making." *Academy of Management Journal*, March 1964.

Buchanan, Bruce: "Building Organizational Commitment: The Socialization of Managers in Work Organizations." *Administrative Science Quarterly*, December 1974.

Buchanan, Bruce: "To Walk an Extra Mile—The Whats, Whens, and Whys of Organizational Commitment." *Organizational Dynamics*, Spring 1975.

Buchele, Robert B.: "How to Evaluate a Firm." *California Management Review*, Fall 1962.

Buchele, Robert B.: *Business Policy in Growing Firms*, San Francisco, Chandler, 1967.

Buckley, Adrian: "Competitive Strategies for Investment." *Journal of General Management*, Spring 1975.

Buckley, John W.: "Goal-Process-System Integration in Management." *Business Horizons*, December 1971.

Burack, Elmer: *Organization Analysis: Theory and Applications*. Hinsdale, Ill., Dryden Press, 1975.

The Bureau of National Affairs, Inc.: "ASPA-BNA Survey: Use of Consultants." *Bulletin to Management*, March 4, 1971.

The Bureau of National Affairs, Inc.: "Women and Minorities in Management and in Personnel Management." *Personnel Policies Forum*, December 1971.

Burns, Tom, and G. M. Stalker: *The Management of Innovation*. London, Tavistock Publications, 1961.

Business Week: "Honeywell Tries to Make Its Merger Work." September 26, 1970.

Butler, William F., and Robert A. Kavesh: *Techniques of Business Forecasting*. Englewood Cliffs, N. J., Prentice-Hall, 1974.

Buzzell, Robert D., Bradley T. Gale, and Ralph G. M. Sultan: "Market Share—Key to Profitability." *Harvard Business Review*, January–February 1975.

Cameron, D. A.: "Risk Analysis and Investment Appraisal in Marketing," *Long Range Planning*, December 1972.

Cammillus, J. C.: "Evaluating the Benefits of Formal Planning Systems." *Long Range Planning*, June 1975.

Campbell, Hannah: *Why Did They Name It . . .?* New York, ACE Books, 1964.

Campbell, John P., Marvin D. Dunnette, Edward E. Lawler, and Karl E. Weick: *Managerial Behavior, Performance, and Effectiveness*. New York, McGraw-Hill, 1970.

Cannon, J. Thomas: *Business Strategy and Policy*. New York, Harcourt, Brace and World, 1968.

Cannon, Warren M.: "Organization Design: Shaping Structure to Strategy." *McKinsey Quarterly,* Summer 1972.

Caplan, Edwin H.: *Management Accounting and Behavioral Science.* Reading, Mass., Addison-Wesley, 1971.

Carroll, Archie B.: "An Organizational Need: Forecasting and Planning for the Social Environment." *Managerial Planning,* May–June 1973.

Carroll, Archie B., and George W. Beiler: "Landmarks in the Evolution of the Social Audit." *Academy of Management Journal,* September 1975.

Carroll, Stephen J., Jr., and Henry L. Tosi, Jr.: *Management by Objective: Applications and Research.* New York, Macmillan, 1973.

Carruth, Eleanore: "The 'Legal Explosion' Has Left Business Shell-Shocked." *Fortune,* April 1973.

Carter, E. Eugene: "The Behavioral Theory of the Firm and Top Level Corporate Decisions." *Administrative Science Quarterly,* December 1971.

Carter, E. Eugene: "What Are the Risks in Risk Analysis?" *Harvard Business Review,* July–August 1972.

Cartwright, John: "Corporate Planning in Local Government—Implications for the Elected Member." *Long Range Planning,* April 1975.

Cecil, Earl A., Larry L. Cummings, and Jerome M. Chertkoff: "Group Composition and Choice Shift: Implications for Administration." *Academy of Management Journal,* September 1973.

Cecil, Earl A., and Earl F. Lundgren: "An Analysis of Individual Decision Making Behavior Using a Laboratory Setting." *Academy of Management Journal,* September 1975.

Cetron, Marvin J.: *Industrial Applications of Technological Forecasting.* New York, Wiley, 1971.

Chamber of Commerce of the United States: *Business and the Consumer—A Program for the Seventies.* Washington, D. C., Chamber of Commerce of the United States, 1970.

Chamber of Commerce of the United States: *The Corporation in Transition.* Washington, D. C., Chamber of Commerce of the United States, 1973.

Chambers, John C., Satinder K. Mullick, and Donald D. Smith: "How to Choose the Right Forecasting Technique." *Harvard Business Review,* July–August 1971.

Chandler, Alfred D.: *Strategy and Structure: Chapters in the History of the American Industrial Enterprise.* Cambridge, Mass., MIT Press, 1962.

Chandra, Gyan, and Surendra Singhvi: *Budgeting for Profit.* Oxford, Ohio, Planning Executives Institute, 1975.

Channon, Derek F.: *The Strategy and Structure of British Enterprise.* Boston, Graduate School of Business Administration, Harvard University, 1973.

Charan, Ram: "Classroom Techniques in Teaching by the Case Method." *Academy of Management Proceedings,* August 1975.

Charnock, John: "Can Hospitals Be Managed by Objectives?" *Journal of General Management,* Winter 1975.

Chase Manhattan Corporation: *Annual Meeting of Stockholders.* New York, 1971.

Chevalier, Michel: "The Strategy Spectre Behind Your Market Share." *European Business,* Summer 1972.

Child, John: "Organizational Structure, Environment and Performance—The Role of Strategic Choice." *Sociology,* January 1972.

Christensen, C. Roland, Kenneth R. Andrews, and Joseph L. Bower: *Business Policy: Text and Cases*. Homewood, Ill., Irwin, 1973.

Churchman, C. W.: "Managerial Acceptance of Scientific Recommendations." *California Management Review*, Fall 1964.

Churchman, C. W., and A. H. Schainblatt: "The Researcher and the Manager: A Dialectic of Implementation." *Management Science*, February 1965a.

Churchman, C. W., and A. H. Schainblatt: "Commentary on the Researcher and the Manager." *Management Science*, October 1965b.

Clapp, Norton: "Corporate Responsibility to the Community." *University of Washington Business Review*, Spring 1968.

Clark, John M.: *Competition as a Dynamic Process*. Washington, D. C., The Brookings Institution, 1961.

Clark, Russell D.: "Group-induced Shift Toward Risk: A Critical Appraisal." *Psychological Bulletin*, August 1971.

Cleveland, Harlan: "The Decision Makers." *The Center Magazine*, September–October 1973.

Clifford, Donald K., Jr.: "Leverage in the Product Life Cycle." *Dun's Review of Modern Industry*, May 1965.

Clifford, Donald K., Jr.: *Managing the Threshold Company*. New York, McKinsey & Company, Inc., 1973a.

Clifford, Donald K., Jr.: "Growth Pains of the Threshold Company." *Harvard Business Review*, September–October 1973b.

Cohen, Kalman J., and Richard M. Cyert: "Strategy: Formulation, Implementation, and Monitoring." *Journal of Business*, July 1973.

Cohn, Theodore, and Roy A. Lindberg: *Survival & Growth: Management Strategies for the Small Firm*. New York, AMACOM, 1974.

Cole, Edward: "Management Priorities for the 1970's." *Michigan Business Review*, July 1970.

Collaros, Panayiota A., and Lynn R. Anderson: "Effect of Perceived Expertness upon Creativity of Members of Brainstorming Groups." *Journal of Applied Psychology*, April 1969.

Collins, Orvis F., and David G. Moore: *The Enterprising Man*. East Lansing, Mich., Graduate School of Business Administration, Michigan State University, 1964.

Committee for Economic Development: *Social Responsibilities of Business Corporations*. New York, Committee for Economic Development, 1971.

Cook, Curtis W.: "Corporate Strategy Change Contingencies." *Academy of Management Proceedings*, August 1975.

Cooper, Arnold, Edward Demuzzio, Kenneth Hatten, Elijah Hicks, and Donald Tock: "Strategic Responses to Technological Threat." *Academy of Management Proceedings*, August 1973.

Cooper, A. C., and D. E. Schendel: "Strategy Determination in Manufacturing Firms: Concepts and Research Findings." *Proceedings of the American Marketing Association Fall Conference*, August–September 1971.

Coppinger, Richard J., and E. Stewart Epley: "The Non-Use of Advanced Mathematical Techniques." *Managerial Planning*, May–June 1972.

Coppock, R., M. Dierkes, H. Snowball, and J. Thomas: "Social Pressure and

Business Actions." Paper presented at the Seminar on Corporate Social Accounts, Battelle Seattle Research Center, November 10–11, 1972.

Corey, E. Raymond, and Steven H. Star: *Organization Strategy: A Marketing Approach.* Boston, Graduate School of Business Administration, Harvard University, 1971.

Corke, D. K.: "Long Range Planning for Production." *Long Range Planning,* December 1970.

Corson, John J.: *Business in the Humane Society.* New York, McGraw-Hill, 1971.

Corson, John J., and George A. Steiner: *Measuring Business Social Performance: The Corporate Social Audit.* New York, Committee for Economic Development, 1974.

Cross, Hershner: "New Directions in Corporate Planning." Address to Operations Research Society of America, Milwaukee, Wisconsin, May 10, 1973.

Cross, Theodore L.: *Black Capitalism: Strategy for Business in the Ghetto.* New York, Atheneum, 1969.

Cummings, L. L., George P. Huber, and Eugene Arendt: "Effects of Size and Spatial Arrangements on Group Decision Making." *Academy of Management Journal,* September 1974.

Cyert, Richard M., and James G. March: *A Behavioral Theory of the Firm.* Englewood Cliffs, N. J., Prentice-Hall, 1963.

Dale, Ernest: *Planning and Developing the Company Organization Structure.* New York, American Management Association, 1952.

Dalton, Francis E., and John B. Miner: "The Role of Accounting Training in Top Management Decision Making." *Accounting Review,* January 1970.

Dalton, Gene W., Louis B. Barnes, and Abraham Zaleznik: *The Distribution of Authority in Formal Organizations.* Boston, Graduate School of Business Administration, Harvard University, 1968.

Davis, Gary A.: *Psychology of Problem Solving: Theory and Practice.* New York, Basic Books, 1973.

Davis, James V.: "The Strategic Divestment Decision." *Long Range Planning,* February 1974.

Davis, Keith: "Can Business Afford to Ignore Social Responsibilities?" *California Management Review,* Spring 1960.

Davis, Keith, and Robert L. Blomstrom: *Business, Society, and Environment.* New York, McGraw-Hill, 1971.

Day, George S.: "A Strategic Perspective on Product Planning." *Journal of Contemporary Business,* Winter 1975.

Dean, Joel: "Pricing Policies for New Products." *Harvard Business Review,* November–December, 1950.

Dearden, John: "Limits on Decentralized Profit Responsibility." *Harvard Business Review,* July–August 1962a.

Dearden, John: "Mirage of Profit Decentralization." *Harvard Business Review,* November–December 1962b.

Dearden, John: "The Case Against ROI Control." *Harvard Business Review,* May–June 1969.

Dearden, John: "MIS Is a Mirage." *Harvard Business Review,* January–February 1972.

Dearden, John, and V. L. Mote: "Operations Research at the Crossroads." *European Business,* October 1968.

de Carbonnel, Francois E., and Roy G. Dorrance: "Information Sources for Planning Decisions." *California Management Review,* Summer 1973.

Deets, M. King, and George C. Hoyt: "Variance Preferences and Variance Shifts in Group Investment Decisions." *Organizational Behavior and Human Performance,* July 1970.

Denhardt, Robert B.: "Alienation and the Challenge of Participation." *Personnel Administration,* September 1971.

Derthick, Martha: "Defeat at Fort Lincoln: A Case Study of a Housing Fiasco." *Public Interest,* Summer 1970.

Downey, H. Kirk, and John W. Slocum: "Uncertainty: Measures, Research, and Sources of Variation." *Academy of Management Journal,* September 1975.

Drucker, Peter F.: *The Practice of Management.* New York, Harper and Row, 1954.

Drucker, Peter F.: *Managing for Results.* New York, Harper and Row, 1964.

Drucker, Peter F.: *The Age of Discontinuity: Guidelines to our Changing Society.* New York, Harper and Row, 1969a.

Drucker, Peter F.: *Preparing Tomorrow's Business Leaders Today.* Englewood Cliffs, N. J., Prentice-Hall, 1969b.

Drucker, Peter F.: "The Performance Gap in Management Science: Reasons and Remedies." *Organizational Dynamics,* Autumn 1973a.

Drucker, Peter F.: "On Managing the Public Service Institution." *The Public Interest,* Fall 1973b.

Drucker, Peter F.: *Management: Tasks, Responsibilities, Practices.* New York, Harper and Row, 1974.

Dubin, Robert: "Business Behavior Behaviorally Viewed." In George B. Strother (ed.): *Social Science Approaches to Business Behavior.* Homewood, Ill., Irwin, 1962.

Dunbar, R. L. M.: "Budgeting for Control." *Administrative Science Quarterly,* March 1971.

Dymsza, William A.: *Multinational Business Strategy.* New York, McGraw-Hill, 1972.

Edelman, Murray: *The Symbolic Use of Politics.* Urbana, Ill., University of Illinois Press, 1964.

Editors of *Forbes:* "Management" and "Corporate Morality, Corporate Vitality." *Forbes,* September 15, 1967.

Eells, Richard: "Business for Sale: The Case for Corporate Support of the Arts." In Ivar Berg (ed.): *The Business of America.* New York, Harcourt, 1968.

Elsner, David M.: "Recession Spurs Sears to Cut Prices, Return to Past Sales Strategy." *Wall Street Journal,* February 10, 1975.

Emery, F. E., and E. L. Trist: "The Causal Texture of Organizational Environments." *Human Relations,* February 1965.

Emery, F. E., and E. L. Trist: *Towards A Social Ecology.* London and New York, Plenum Press, 1973.

Emory, C. William, and Powell Niland. *Making Management Decisions.* Boston, Houghton Mifflin, 1968.

England, George W.: "Personal Value Systems of American Managers." *Academy of Management Journal,* 1967.

England, George W.: "Personal Value Systems of Managers and Administrators." *Academy of Management Proceedings,* August 1973.

Enrick, Norbert Lloyd: *Marketing and Sales Forecasting: A Quantitative Approach.* San Francisco, Chandler, 1969.

Enthoven, Alain C.: "Analysis, Judgment, and Computers: Their Use in Complex Problems." *Business Horizons,* August 1969.

Epstein, Edwin M.: *The Corporation in American Politics.* Englewood Cliffs, N. J., Prentice-Hall, 1969.

Epstein, Edwin M.: "Dimensions of Corporate Power, Pt. 1." *California Management Review,* Winter 1973.

Epstein, Edwin M.: "Dimensions of Corporate Power, Pt. 2." *California Management Review,* Summer 1974.

Etzioni, Amitai: "Mixed Scanning: A Third Approach to Decision Making." *Public Administration Review,* December 1967.

Etzioni, Amitai: *A Comparative Analysis of Complex Organizations.* New York, Free Press, 1975.

Evans, Martin G.: "Failures in OD Programs—What Went Wrong?" *Business Horizons,* April 1974.

Ewing, David W.: *The Human Side of Planning.* New York, Macmillan, 1960.

Ewing, David W.: "Who Wants Corporate Democracy?" *Harvard Business Review,* September–October 1971.

Ewing, David W. (ed.): *Long Range Planning for Management.* New York, Harper and Row, 1972.

Farmer, Richard N., and W. Dickerson Hogue: *Corporate Social Responsibility.* Chicago, Science Research Associates, Inc., 1973.

Farmer, Richard N., and Barry M. Richman: "A Model for Research in Comparative Management." *California Management Review,* Winter 1964.

Farmer, Richard N., and Barry M. Richman: *Comparative Management and Economic Progress.* Homewood, Ill., Irwin, 1965.

Ferguson, Charles R.: *Measuring Corporate Strategy.* Homewood, Ill., Dow Jones-Irwin, 1974.

Fernandez, John P.: *Black Managers in White Corporations.* New York, Wiley, 1975.

Ferrell, Robert W.: *Managing Opportunity.* New York, American Management Association, 1972.

Fiedler, Fred E.: *A Theory of Leadership Effectiveness.* New York, McGraw-Hill, 1967.

Filley, Alan C.: "Committee Management: Guidelines from Social Science Research." *California Management Review,* Fall 1970.

Filley, Alan C., and Robert J. House: *Managerial Process and Organizational Behavior.* Glenview, Ill., Scott, Foresman and Company, 1969.

Fisher, G. H.: *Rand Policy Analysis Course: Tools and Techniques of Analysis for Public Policy Decisions.* Santa Monica, Cal., Rand Corporation, 1974.

Fleishman, Edwin A., and James G. Hunt (eds.): *Current Developments in the Study of Leadership.* Carbondale, Ill., Southern Illinois University Press, 1973.

Fleming, John E.: "Study of a Business Decision." *California Management Review,* Winter 1966.

Folsom, Marion B.: *Executive Decision Making.* New York, McGraw-Hill, 1962.

Forbes, A. M.: "Long Range Planning for the Small Firm." *Long Range Planning,* April 1974.

Forrester, Jay W.: "Advertising: A Problem in Industrial Dynamics." *Harvard Business Review,* March–April 1959.

Forrester, Jay W.: "The Structure Underlying Management Processes." *Academy of Management Proceedings,* December 1964.

Forsgren, Roderick A.: "The Academy of Management Member—Revisited." *Academy of Management Journal,* September 1974.

Foster, D. W.: "Developing a Product Market Strategy." *Long Range Planning,* March 1970.

Fouraker, Lawrence E., and J. M. Stopford: "Organizational Structure and Multinational Strategy." *Administrative Science Quarterly,* June 1968.

Fox, Harold: "A Framework for Functional Coordination." *Atlanta Economic Review,* November–December 1973.

Frankenhoff, William P., and Charles H. Granger: "Strategic Management: A New Managerial Concept for an Era of Rapid Change." *Long Range Planning,* April 1971.

French, Wendell L., and Cecil H. Bell: *Organization Development: Behavioral Science Interventions for Organizational Improvement.* Englewood Cliffs, N. J., Prentice-Hall, 1973.

Freud, Sigmund: *Group Psychology and the Analysis of the Ego.* New York, Bantam Books, 1960 (original German publication, 1921).

Fri, Robert W.: "How to Manage the Government for Results: The Rise of MBO." *Organization Dynamics,* Spring 1974.

Friedlander, Frank, and Stuart Greenberg: "Effect of Job Attitudes, Training, and Organization Climate on Performance of the Hard-Core Unemployed." *Journal of Applied Psychology,* August 1971.

Friedman, Milton: *Capitalism and Freedom.* Chicago, University of Chicago Press, 1962.

Froissart, Daniel: "The Day Our President and MBO Collided." *European Business,* Autumn 1971.

Fruhan, William E., Jr.: "Pyrrhic Victories in Fights for Market Share." *Harvard Business Review,* September–October 1972.

Fulmer, Robert M., and Leslie W. Rue: *The Practice and Profitability of Long Range Planning.* Oxford, Ohio, Planning Executives Institute, 1973.

Gallagher, Charles A.: "Perceptions of the Value of a Management Information System." *Academy of Management Journal,* March 1974.

Ganesh, S. R.: "Choosing an OD Consultant." *Business Horizons,* October 1971.

Gershefski, George W.: *The Development and Application of a Corporate Financial Model.* Oxford, Ohio, Planning Executives Institute, 1968.

Gerstenfeld, Arthur: "Technological Forecasting." *Journal of Business,* January 1971.

Gerstner, Louis V.: "Can Strategic Planning Pay Off?" *Business Horizons,* December 1972.

Gestetner, David: "Strategy in Managing International Sales." *Harvard Business Review,* September–October 1974.

Ghiselli, Edwin E.: *The Validity of Occupational Aptitude Tests.* New York, Wiley, 1966.

Gibson, James L., John M. Ivancevich, and James H. Donnelly, Jr.: *Organizations: Structure, Processes, Behavior.* Dallas, Texas, Business Publications, 1973.

Gibson, R. E.: "The Strategy of Corporate Research and Development." *California Management Review,* Fall 1966.

Gilmore, Frank F.: *Formulation and Advocacy of Business Policy.* Ithaca, N. Y., Cornell University, 1970.

Gilmore, Frank F.: "Overcoming the Perils of Advocacy in Corporate Planning." *California Management Review,* Spring 1973a.

Gilmore, Frank F.: "Formulating Strategy in Smaller Companies." *Harvard Business Review,* May–June 1973b.

Gilmore, Frank F., and R. G. Brandenberg: "Anatomy of Corporate Planning." *Harvard Business Review,* November–December 1962.

Ginzberg, Eli, Dale L. Hiestand, and Beatrice G. Reubens: *The Pluralistic Economy.* New York, McGraw-Hill, 1965.

Glueck, William F.: "Business Policy: Reality and Promise." *Academy of Management Proceedings,* August 1972a.

Glueck, William F.: *Business Policy: Strategy Formation and Management Action.* New York, McGraw-Hill, 1972b.

Glueck, William F.: "Decision Making: Organization Choice." *Personnel Psychology,* Spring 1974.

Glueck, William F., and Douglas C. Mankin: "Strategic Planning in the Hospital Setting." *Academy of Management Proceedings,* August 1975.

Goetz, Billy E.: *Management Planning and Control.* New York, McGraw-Hill, 1949.

Goetz, Billy E.: "Two Approaches to Managerial Planning: Part One." *The Engineering Economist,* Winter 1963.

Goetz, Billy E.: *Quantitative Methods: A Survey and Guide for Managers.* New York, McGraw-Hill, 1965.

Golembiewski, Robert T.: *Renewing Organizations: The Laboratory Approach to Planned Change.* Itasca, Ill., Peacock, 1972.

Goodman, Paul S., Paul Salipante, and Harold Paransky: "Hiring, Training, and Retaining the Hard-Core Unemployed: A Selected Review." *Journal of Applied Psychology,* August 1973.

Gordon, Paul J.: "Letters to Professors A. Svenson and U. Mazzucoto." *Academy of Management Journal,* December 1966.

Gordon, Robert A., and James E. Howell: *Higher Education for Business.* New York, Columbia University Press, 1959.

Gray, Edmund R. (ed.): *Readings in Business Policy.* New York, Appleton-Century-Crofts, 1968.

Grayson, C. Jackson, Jr.: "Management Science and Business Practice." *Harvard Business Review,* July–August 1973.

Green, Thad B.: "An Empirical Analysis of Nominal and Interacting Groups." *Academy of Management Journal,* March 1975.

Greenberg, Philip, Steve M. Panser, and Gary Silverman: *The Expectations of*

Today's MBAs and the Potential Impact on Business Management. Special Report, Graduate School of Business Administration, UCLA, 1969.

Greenwood, William T.: "A Doctoral Field in Business Policy-Strategy." The University of Georgia, undated.

Gregory, Carl E.: *The Management of Intelligence: Scientific Problem Solving and Creativity.* New York, McGraw-Hill, 1967.

Greiner, Larry E.: "Evolution and Revolution as Organizations Grow." *Harvard Business Review,* July–August 1972.

Greiner, Larry E., D. Paul Leitch, and Louis B. Barnes: "Putting Judgment Back Into Decisions." *Harvard Business Review,* March–April 1970.

Grieco, V. A.: *Management of Small Business.* Columbus, Ohio, Merrill, 1975.

Grinyer, Peter H.: "Some Dangerous Axioms of Corporate Planning." *Journal of Business Policy,* No. 1, 1973.

Grinyer, Peter H., and David Norburn: "Strategic Planning in 21 U. K. Companies." *Long Range Planning,* August 1974.

Gross, Bertram M.: *The Managing of Organizations.* New York, Free Press, 1964.

Guest, Robert H.: *Organizational Change: The Effect of Successful Leadership.* Homewood, Ill., Irwin-Dorsey, 1962.

Gulick, Luther, and L. Urwick (eds.): *Papers on the Science of Administration.* New York, Institute of Public Administration, 1937.

Gustafson, David H., Ramesh K. Shukla, André Delbecq, and G. William Walster: "A Comparative Study of Differences in Subjective Likelihood Estimates Made by Individuals, Interacting Groups, Delphi Groups, and Nominal Groups." *Organizational Behavior and Human Performance,* April 1973.

Gustafson, David P., and Nicholas J. DiMarco: "The Management Consultant Selection Process." *Academy of Management Proceedings,* August 1973.

Guth, William D.: "U. S. Perspectives on the Teaching of Business Policy." In *Some Selected Working Papers from the International Seminar for Teachers of Business at the Irish Management Institute.* Division of Business Policy and Planning, Academy of Management, 1971.

Guth, William D.: "The Growth and Profitability of the Firm: A Managerial Explanation." *Journal of Business Policy,* Spring 1972.

Guth, William D.: "A Research Strategy for the Division of Business Policy and Planning." Memorandum to the Members of Division of Business Policy and Planning, Academy of Management, February 1973.

Guth, William D., and Renato Tagiuri: "Personal Values and Corporate Strategies." *Harvard Business Review,* September–October 1965.

Gutman, Peter M.: "Strategies for Growth." *California Management Review,* Summer 1964.

Haas, John A., Avner M. Porat, and James A. Vaughn: "Actual vs. Ideal Time Allocations Reported by Managers: A Study of Managerial Behavior." *Personnel Psychology,* Spring 1969.

Haddad, W. F., and G. D. Pugh: *Black Economic Development.* Englewood Cliffs, N. J., Prentice-Hall, 1969.

Haire, Mason: *Psychology in Management.* New York, McGraw-Hill, 1964.

Haire, Mason, Edwin E. Ghiselli, and Lyman W. Porter: *Managerial Thinking: An International Study.* New York, Wiley, 1966.

Haitovsky, Yoel, George Treyz, and Vincent Su: *Forecasts with Quarterly Macroeconometric Models.* New York, Columbia University Press, 1974.

Hall, Jay, Vincent O'Leary, and Martha Williams: "The Decision-Making Grid: A Model of Decision-Making Styles." *California Management Review,* Winter 1964.

Hall, William K.: "Strategic Planning Models: Are Top Managers Really Finding Them Useful?" *Journal of Business Policy,* Winter 1973.

Hamilton, William F., and Michael A. Moses: "A Computer-Based Corporate Planning System." *Management Science,* October 1974.

Hammond, John S.: "Do's and Don'ts of Computer Models for Planning." *Harvard Business Review,* March–April 1974.

Hardy, James M.: *Corporate Planning for Non-Profit Organizations.* New York, Association Press, 1973.

Harrison, E. Frank: *The Managerial Decision-Making Process.* Boston, Houghton Mifflin, 1975.

Harrison, Roger: "Understanding Your Organization's Character." *Harvard Business Review,* May 1972.

Harvey, Allan: "Factors Making for Implementation Success and Failure." *Management Science,* February 1970.

Hayek, Friedrich A.: *The Road to Serfdom.* Chicago, University of Chicago Press, 1944.

Heald, Morrell: *The Social Responsibilities of Business: Company and Community, 1900–1960.* Cleveland, Ohio, The Press of Case Western Reserve University, 1970.

Heckman, Nikolaus: "Planning in a German Engineering Business." *Long Range Planning,* June 1971.

Heidrick and Struggles, Inc.: *Profile of a President.* Boston, Heidrick and Struggles, Inc., 1972.

Heller, Frank A.: *Managerial Decision-Making: A Study of Leadership Styles and Power Sharing Among Senior Managers.* London, Tavistock Publications, 1971.

Henning, Dale A.: *Non-Financial Controls in Smaller Enterprises.* Seattle, Wash., Washington State Department of Commerce and Economic Development, 1964.

Herold, David M.: "Long Range Planning and Organizational Performance: A Cross Valuation Study." *Academy of Managerial Journal,* March 1972.

Hertz, David B.: *New Power for Management.* New York, McGraw-Hill, 1969.

Hertz, David B.: "An Interview with David Bendel Hertz." *Organizational Dynamics,* Spring 1973.

Heyne, Paul T.: *Private Keepers of the Public Interest.* New York, McGraw-Hill, 1968.

Heyne, Paul T.: "The Free-Market System is the Best Guide for Corporate Decisions." *Financial Analysts Journal,* September–October 1971.

Hidy, Ralph W., and Paul E. Cawein (eds.): *Individual Enterprise and National Growth.* Boston, D. C. Heath, 1967.

Higdon, Hal: *The Business Healers.* New York, Random House, 1969.

Hill, Walter A., and John A. Ruhe: "Attitudes and Behaviors of Black and White Supervisors in Problem Solving Groups." *Academy of Management Journal,* September 1974.

Hines, George H.: "Achievement Motivation, Occupations, and Labor Turnover in New Zealand." *Journal of Applied Psychology,* December 1973.
Hitch, Charles J.: *Decision-Making for Defense.* Berkeley and Los Angeles, University of California Press, 1966.
Hlavacek, James D., and Victor A. Thompson: "Bureaucracy and New Product Innovation." *Academy of Management Journal,* September 1973.
Hofer, Charles W.: "Some Preliminary Research on Patterns of Strategic Behavior." *Academy of Management Proceedings,* August 1973.
Hofer, Charles W.: "Policy as an Academic Discipline: Its Curricular Needs." *Academy of Management Proceedings,* August 1975a.
Hofer, Charles W.: "Toward a Contingency Theory of Business Strategy." *Academy of Management Journal,* December 1975b.
Holden, Paul E., Carlton A. Pederson, and Gayton E. Germane: *Top Management.* New York, McGraw-Hill, 1968.
Hollander, Stanley C.: *Management Consultants and Clients.* East Lansing, Mich., Graduate School of Business Administration, Michigan State University, 1972.
Holloman, Charles R., and Hal W. Hendrick: "Problem Solving in Different Sized Groups." *Personnel Psychology,* Autumn 1971.
Holmberg, Steven R.: "Monitoring Long-Range Plans." *Long Range Planning,* June 1974.
Holmberg, Steven R.: "Utility Strategic Planning: Functional or Corporate?" *Managerial Planning,* January–February 1975.
Holton, Richard H.: "Marketing Policies in Multinational Corporations." *California Management Review,* Summer 1971.
Hopkins, David S., and Earl L. Bailey: *The Chief Marketing Executive.* New York, National Industrial Conference Board, 1971.
Hornaday, John A., and John Aboud: "Characteristics of Successful Entrepreneurs." *Personnel Psychology,* Summer 1971.
Hornaday, John A., and Charles S. Bunker: "The Nature of the Entrepreneur." *Personnel Psychology,* Spring 1970.
House, Robert J., and John B. Miner: "Merging Management and Behavioral Theory: The Interaction Between Span of Control and Group Size." *Administrative Science Quarterly,* September 1969.
Howell, Robert A.: "Managing by Objectives—A Three Stage System." *Business Horizon,* February 1970a.
Howell, Robert A.: "Plan to Integrate Your Acquisitions." *Harvard Business Review,* November–December 1970b.
Hrebiniak, Lawrence G.: "Effects of Job Level and Participation on Employee Attitudes and Perceptions of Influence." *Academy of Management Journal,* December 1974.
Humble, John W.: "Corporate Planning and Management by Objectives." *Long Range Planning,* June 1969.
Humble, John W.: "Avoiding the Pitfalls of the MBO Trap." *European Business,* Autumn 1970.
Humphrey, George M., with James C. Derieux: "It Looked Easier on the Outside." *Collier's,* April 2, 1954.
Hundal, P. S.: "A Study of Entrepreneurial Motivation: Comparison of Fast- and

Slow-Progressing Small-Scale Industrial Entrepreneurs in Punjab, India." *Journal of Applied Psychology,* August 1971.

Hunt, James G., and Lars L. Larson (eds.): *Contingency Approaches to Leadership.* Carbondale, Ill., Southern Illinois University Press, 1974.

Hussey, David E.: "Corporate Planning for a Church," *Long Range Planning,* April 1974a.

Hussey, David E.: *Corporate Planning: Theory and Practice.* New York, Pergamon Press, 1974b.

Hutchins, Robert: "A Center Conversation, 'Get Ready for Anything.'" *Center Report,* June 1975.

Inkson, J. H. K., D. S. Pugh, and D. J. Hickson: "Organizational Context and Structure: An Abbreviated Replication." *Administrative Science Quarterly,* September 1970.

Irwin, Patrick H.: "Why Aren't Companies Doing a Better Job of Planning?" *Management Review,* November 1971.

Irwin, Patrick H.: "Towards Better Strategic Management." *Long Range Planning,* December 1974.

Jacobs, T. O.: *Leadership and Exchange in Formal Organizations.* Alexandria, Va., Human Resources Research Organization, 1971.

Jacoby, Neil H.: *Corporate Power and Social Responsibility: A Blueprint for the Future.* New York, Macmillan, 1973.

James, Barrie G.: "The Theory of the Corporate Life Cycle." *Long Range Planning,* June 1973.

Janis, Irving L.: *Victims of Groupthink.* Boston, Houghton Mifflin, 1972.

Jantsch, Erich: *Technological Forecasting in Perspective.* Paris, Organization for Economic Cooperation and Development, 1967.

Jerome, William Travers, III: *Executive Control: The Catalyst.* New York, Wiley, 1961.

Johnson, Harold L.: *Business in Contemporary Society: Framework and Issues.* Belmont, Cal., Wadsworth, 1971.

Johnson, Thomas E., and David J. Werner: "Management Education: An Interdisciplinary Problem Solving Approach." *Academy of Management Journal,* June 1975.

Jones, Charles O.: *An Introduction to the Study of Public Policy.* Belmont, Cal., Wadsworth, 1970.

Jones, Reginald H.: "What Is the Future of the Corporation." Address to the Detroit Economic Club, Detroit, Michigan, November 25, 1974.

Kahn, Herman, and B. Bruce-Briggs: *Things to Come.* New York, Macmillan, 1972.

Kahn, Herman, and Anthony J. Wiener: *The Year 2000.* New York, Macmillan, 1967.

Kakar, Sudhir: *Frederick Taylor: A Study in Personality and Innovation.* Cambridge, Mass., MIT Press, 1970.

Karmel, Barbara: "Group Decision-Making: Effects of Attitude, Sample and Leader Variables." *Academy of Management Proceedings,* August 1972.

Kast, Fremont E.: "Management Concepts and Practices: European Style." *Business Horizons,* Winter 1964.

Kast, Fremont E., and James E. Rosenzweig: *Organization and Management: A Systems Approach.* New York, McGraw-Hill, 1970.

Kast, Fremont E., and James E. Rosenzweig: *Contingency Views of Organization and Management.* Chicago, Science Research Associates, 1973.

Kastens, Merritt L.: "Who Does the Planning?" *Managerial Planning,* January–February 1972.

Katcher, David A.: "Consulting from Within." *California Management Review,* Summer 1972.

Katz, Daniel, and Robert L. Kahn: *The Social Psychology of Organizations.* New York, Wiley, 1966.

Katz, Robert L.: *Cases and Concepts in Corporate Strategy.* Englewood Cliffs, N. J., Prentice-Hall, 1970.

Kegan, Daniel L.: "Organizational Development: Description, Issues, and Some Research Results." *Academy of Management Journal,* December 1971.

Kelley, Lane, and Clayton Reeser: "The Persistance of Culture as a Determinant of Differentiated Attitudes on the Part of American Managers of Japanese Ancestry." *Academy of Management Journal,* March 1973.

Kepner, Charles H., and Benjamin B. Tregoe: *The Rational Manager: A Systematic Approach to Problem Solving and Decision Making.* New York, McGraw-Hill, 1965.

Kerr, Steven: "On the Folly of Rewarding A, While Hoping for B." *Academy of Management Journal,* December 1975.

Khandwalla, Pradip N.: "The Techno-Economic Ecology of Corporate Strategy." *Journal of Management Studies,* October 1973.

Kipnis, David, Arnold Silverman, and Charles Copeland: "Effects of Emotional Arousal on the Use of Supervised Coercion with Black and Union Employees." *Journal of Applied Psychology,* February 1973.

Kitching, John: "Why Do Mergers Miscarry?" *Harvard Business Review,* November–December 1967.

Klein, Walter H., and David C. Murphy (eds.): *Policy: Concepts in Organizational Guidance.* Boston, Little, Brown, 1973.

Kono, Toyohiro: "An Analysis of Corporate Growth in Japan." *Management Japan,* No. 4, 1970.

Koontz, Harold: "The Corporate Board and Special Interest." *Business Horizons,* October 1971.

Koontz, Harold, and Cyril O'Donnell: *Principles of Management.* New York, McGraw-Hill, 1955, 1964, 1972.

Korman, Abraham K.: "Organizational Achievement, Aggression and Creativity: Some Suggestions Toward an Integrated Theory." *Organizational Behavior and Human Performance,* September 1971.

Kotler, Philip: "Corporate Models: Better Marketing Plans." *Harvard Business Review,* July–August 1970.

Kraber, Richard W.: "Acquisition Analysis: New Help From Your Computer." *Financial Executive,* March 1970.

Kraut, Allen I.: "The Entrance of Black Employees Into Traditionally White Jobs." *Academy of Management Journal,* September 1975.

Krishnan, Rama: "Business Philosophy and Executive Responsibility." *Academy of Management Journal,* December 1973.

Lawler, Edward E.: *Pay and Organizational Effectiveness: A Psychological View.* New York, McGraw-Hill, 1971.

Lawrence, Paul R., and Jay W. Lorsch: "Differentiation and Integration in Complex Organizations." *Administrative Science Quarterly,* June 1967a.

Lawrence, Paul R., and Jay W. Lorsch: *Organization and Environment: Managing Differentiation and Integration.* Boston, Graduate School of Business, Harvard University, 1967b.

Leavitt, Harold J.: "It's a Valuable Management Tool, But . . . Motivation is Not Enough." *Stanford Graduate School of Business Bulletin,* Autumn 1966.

Leavitt, Harold J., William R. Dill, and Henry B. Eyring: *The Organizational World.* New York, Harcourt, Brace, Jovanovich, 1973.

Lebestky, D. A., and F. D. Tuggle: "Manager-Consultant Conflict: An Experiential Approach." *Academy of Management Journal,* June 1975.

Levinson, Harry: *Organizational Diagnosis.* Cambridge, Mass., Harvard University Press, 1972.

Levitt, Theodore: "Exploit the Product Life Cycle." *Harvard Business Review,* November–December 1965.

Levitt, Theodore: "The Dangers of Social Responsibility." *Harvard Business Review,* September–October 1968.

Life Office Management Association: "Creating a Corporate Plan for a Life Insurance Company: A Case Study." *Financial Planning and Control Report No. 17.* New York, Life Office Management Association, 1970.

Likert, Rensis: *New Patterns of Management.* New York, McGraw-Hill, 1961.

Likert, Rensis: *The Human Organization: Its Management and Value.* New York, McGraw-Hill, 1967.

Lindblom, Charles E.: *Bargaining: The Hidden Hand in Government.* Santa Monica, Cal., Rand Corporation, 1955.

Lindblom, Charles E.: "The Science of 'Muddling Through'." *Public Administration Review,* Spring 1959.

Lindblom, Charles E.: *The Intelligence of Democracy: Decision Making Through Mutual Adjustment.* New York, Free Press, 1965.

Lindblom, Charles E.: *The Policy Making Process.* Englewood Cliffs, N. J., Prentice-Hall, 1968.

Litwin, George H., and Adrienne Siebrecht: "Integrators and Entrepreneurs: Their Motivation and Effect on Management." In *Hospital Progress.* St. Louis, Mo., Catholic Hospital Association, 1967.

Litzinger, William D.: "The Motel Entrepreneur and the Motel Manager." *Academy of Management Journal,* December 1965.

Livingston, J. Sterling: "Myth of the Well-Educated Manager." *Harvard Business Review,* January–February 1971.

Locke, Edwin A.: "The Relationship of Intentions to Level of Performance." *Journal of Applied Psychology,* February 1966.

Lorsch, Jay W.: *Product Innovation and Organization.* New York, Macmillan, 1965.

Lorsch, Jay W., and Stephen A. Allen, III: *Managing Diversity and Interdependence: An Organizational Study of Multidivisional Firms.* Boston, Graduate School of Business Administration, Harvard University, 1973.

Lorsch, Jay W., and John J. Morse: *Organizations and Their Members: A Contingency Approach.* New York, Harper and Row, 1974.

Los Angeles Times. "An Interview With Justin Dart," May 5, 1974.

Louden, J. Keith: *The Effective Direction in Action.* New York, AMACOM, 1975.

Louis, Arthur M.: "The View from the Pinnacle: What Business Thinks." *Fortune,* September 1969.

Lowin, A.: "Participative Decision Making: A Model, Literature Critique, and Prescriptions for Research." *Organizational Behavior and Human Performance,* January 1968.

Luck, David J., and Arthur E. Prell: *Market Strategy.* New York, Appleton-Century-Crofts, 1968.

Lundberg, Olof, and Max D. Richards: "A Relationship Between Cognitive Style and Complex Decision Making: Implications for Business Policy." *Academy of Management Proceedings,* August 1972.

Lundstedt, Sven: "A Note on Asking Questions." *Journal of General Psychology,* 1968.

Lusk, Edward J., and Bruce L. Oliver: "American Managers' Personal Value Systems—Revisited." *Academy of Management Journal,* September 1974.

McAdam, Terry: "How to Put Corporate Responsibility Into Practice." *Business and Society Review/Innovation,* Summer 1973.

McCarthy, Daniel J., Robert J. Minichiello, and Joseph R. Curran (eds.): *Business Policy and Strategy: Concepts and Readings.* Homewood, Ill., Irwin, 1975.

McCarthy, E. Jerome: *Basic Marketing: A Managerial Approach,* rev. ed. Homewood, Ill., Richard D. Irwin, Inc., 1964.

McClelland, David C., and David G. Winter: *Motivating Economic Achievement.* New York, Free Press, 1969.

McConkey, Dale D.: "Implementation: The Guts of MBO." *Advanced Management Journal,* July 1972.

McConkey, Dale D.: "MBO—Twenty Years Later, Where Do We Stand?" *Business Horizons,* August 1973.

MacCrimmon, Kenneth R.: "Managerial Decision-Making." In Joseph W. McGuire (ed.): *Contemporary Management: Issues and Viewpoints.* Englewood Cliffs, N.J., Prentice-Hall, 1974.

McDonald, Alonzo: "Conflict at the Summit: A Deadly Game." *Harvard Business Review,* March 1972.

McDonald, John: "Sears Makes It Look Easy." *Fortune,* May 1964.

McDonald, Philip R., and Joseph O. Eastlack, Jr.: "Top Management Involvement with New Products." *Business Horizons,* December 1971.

McFarland, Dalton E.: *Management: Principles and Practices.* New York, Macmillan, 1967.

McGregor, Douglas: "An Uneasy Look at Performance Appraisal." *Harvard Business Review,* May 1957.

McGregor, Douglas: *The Human Side of Enterprise.* New York, McGraw-Hill, 1960.

McGregor, Douglas: *The Professional Manager.* New York, McGraw-Hill, 1967.

McKay, Charles W., and Guy D. Cutting: "A Model for Long Range Planning in Higher Education." *Long Range Planning,* October 1974.

McKenney, James L., and Peter G. W. Keen: "How Managers' Minds Work." *Harvard Business Review,* May–June 1974.

McManus, Michael L.: "Precepts and Caveats for Professor-Consultants." *Academy of Management Proceedings,* August 1973.

McNair, Malcolm P.: *The Case Method at the Harvard Business School.* New York, McGraw-Hill, 1954.

McNichols, Thomas J.: *Policy Making and Executive Action: Cases on Business Policy.* New York, McGraw-Hill, 1972.

Mace, Myles L., and George G. Montgomery: *Management Problems of Corporate Acquisition.* Boston, Graduate School of Business Administration, Harvard University, 1962.

Mahoney, Thomas A., Thomas H. Jerdee, and Stephen J. Carroll: *Development of Managerial Performance . . . A Research Approach.* Cincinnati, Ohio, South-Western, 1963.

Mahoney, Thomas A., Thomas H. Jerdee, and Stephen J. Carroll. "The Job(s) of Management." *Industrial Relations,* February 1965.

Maier, Norman R. F.: *Problem Solving and Creativity in Individuals and Groups.* Belmont, Cal., Brooks/Cole, 1970.

Mann, Roland (ed.): *The Arts of Top Management.* New York, McGraw-Hill, 1971.

Manne, Henry G.: "Shareholder Social Proposals Viewed by an Opponent." *Stanford Law Review,* February 1972.

Manners, George E.: "Another Look at Group Size, Group Problem Solving, and Member Consensus." *Academy of Management Journal,* December 1975.

March, James G., and Herbert A. Simon: *Organizations.* New York, Wiley, 1958.

Margulies, Newton, and John Wallace: *Organizational Change: Techniques and Applications.* Glenview, Ill., Scott, Foresman, 1973.

Marrow, Alfred J., and John R. P. French: "Changing a Stereotype in Industry." *Journal of Social Issues,* May 1945.

Marshak, Jacob: "Economics of Inquiring, Communicating, Deciding." *American Economic Review,* No. 2, 1968.

Mason, Edward S.: "The Apologetics of 'Managerialism.'" *Journal of Business,* January 1958.

Mason, R. Hal, Jerome Harris, and John McLoughlin: "Corporate Strategy: A Point of View." *California Management Review,* Spring 1971.

Matarazzo, Joseph D.: *Wechsler's Measurement and Appraisal of Adult Intelligence.* 5th Ed. Baltimore, Md., Williams and Wilkins, 1972.

Meadows, Dennis, *et al.: The Limits to Growth.* New York, Universe Books, 1972.

Michael, Donald N.: *On Learning to Plan—and Planning to Learn.* San Francisco, Jossey-Bass, 1973.

Michael, George.: "Product Petrification: A New Stage in the Life Cycle." *California Management Review,* Fall 1971.

Mihalasky, John: "Questions: What Do Some Executives Have More Of? Answer: Intuition. Maybe." *Think,* November–December 1969.

Miles, Raymond E.: *Theories of Management: Implications for Organizational Behavior and Development.* New York, McGraw-Hill, 1975.

Miles, Raymond E., Charles C. Snow, and Jeffrey Pfeffer: "Organization-Environment: Concepts and Issues." *Industrial Relations,* October 1974.
Miller, Arjay: "New Roles for the Campus and the Corporation." *Michigan Business Review,* November 1966.
Miller, Danny: "Towards a Contingency Theory of Strategy Formulation." *Academy of Management Proceedings,* August 1975.
Miller, Ernest C.: *Advanced Techniques for Strategic Planning.* New York, American Management Association, 1971.
Milliken, J. Gordon, and Edward J. Morrison: *Aerospace Management Techniques: Commercial and Governmental Applications.* Denver, Colo., Denver Research Institute, University of Denver, 1971.
Miner, John B.: *Studies in Management Education.* New York, Springer, 1965.
Miner, John B.: *The School Administrator and Organizational Character.* Eugene, Ore., University of Oregon Press, 1967.
Miner, John B.: "Bridging the Gulf in Organizational Performance." *Harvard Business Review,* July 1968a.
Miner, John B.: "The Managerial Motivation of School Administrators." *Educational Administration Quarterly,* Winter 1968b.
Miner, John B.: "Psychological Evaluations as Predictors of Consulting Success." *Personnel Psychology,* Autumn 1970a.
Miner, John B.: "Executive and Personnel Interviews as Predictors of Consulting Success." *Personnel Psychology,* Winter 1970b.
Miner, John B.: "Personality Tests as Predictors of Consulting Success." *Personnel Psychology,* Summer 1971a.
Miner, John B.: "Changes in Student Attitudes Toward Bureaucratic Role Prescriptions During the 1960s." *Administrative Science Quarterly,* September 1971b.
Miner, John B.: "Success in Management Consulting and the Concept of Eliteness Motivation." *Academy of Management Journal,* September 1971c.
Miner, John B.: *Management Theory.* New York, Macmillan, 1971d.
Miner, John B.: *The Management Process: Theory, Research, and Practice.* New York, Macmillan, 1973a.
Miner, John B.: *Intelligence in the United States.* Westport, Conn., Greenwood, 1973b.
Miner, John B.: "The Management Consulting Firm as a Source of High-Level Managerial Talent." *Academy of Management Journal,* June 1973c.
Miner, John B.: "Personnel Strategies in the Small Business Organization." *Journal of Small Business Management,* July 1973d.
Miner, John B.: "The OD- Management Development Conflict." *Business Horizons,* December 1973e.
Miner, John B.: *The Human Constraint: The Coming Shortage of Managerial Talent.* Washington, D. C., BNA Books, 1974a.
Miner, John B.: "Student Attitudes Toward Bureaucratic Role Prescriptions and the Prospects for Managerial Talent Shortages." *Personnel Psychology,* Winter 1974b.
Miner, John B.: *The Challenge of Managing.* Philadelphia, Saunders, 1975.
Miner, John B.: "The Uncertain Future of the Leadership Concept: An Over-

view." In J. G. Hunt and L. L. Larson (eds.): *Leadership Frontiers.* Kent, Ohio, Kent State University Press, 1976.

Miner, John B., and Mary Green Miner: *Personnel and Industrial Relations: A Managerial Approach.* New York, Macmillan, 1973.

Mintzberg, Henry: *The Nature of Managerial Work.* New York, Harper and Row, 1973a.

Mintzberg, Henry: "Policy as a Field of Management Theory." *Journal of Business Policy,* No. 4, 1973b.

Mintzberg, Henry: "The Manager's Job: Folklore and Fact." *Harvard Business Review,* July–August 1975a.

Mintzberg, Henry: "Policy as a Field of Management Theory." *Academy of Management Proceedings,* August 1975b.

Mishan, Ezra J.: "On Making the Future Safe for Mankind." *The Public Interest,* Summer 1971.

Mitchell, Terence R.: "Motivation and Participation: An Integration." *Academy of Management Journal,* December 1973.

Moberg, Dennis J., and James L. Koch: "A Critical Appraisal of Integrated Treatments of Contingency Findings." *Academy of Management Journal,* March 1975.

Mockler, Robert J.: "Theory and Practice of Planning." *Harvard Business Review,* March–April 1970.

Mockler, Robert J.: *The Management Control Process.* New York, Appleton-Century-Crofts, 1972.

Moose, Sandra O., and Alan J. Zakon: "Divestment—Cleaning Up Your Corporate Portfolio." *European Business,* Autumn 1971.

Moose, Sandra O., and Alan J. Zakon: "Frontier Curve Analysis: As a Resource Allocation Guide." *Journal of Business Policy,* Spring 1972.

Moranian, Thomas, Donald Grunewald, and Richard Reidenbach (eds.): *Business Policy and Its Environment.* New York, Holt, Rinehart and Winston, 1965.

Morse, Nancy, and E. Reimer: "The Experimental Change of a Major Organizational Variable." *Journal of Abnormal and Social Psychology,* January 1956.

Moskowitz, Herbert: "Managers as Partners in Business Decision Research." *Academy of Management Journal,* September 1971.

Mulder, Mauk: "Power Equalization through Participation?" *Administrative Science Quarterly,* March 1971.

Mulder, Mauk, and Henk Wilke: "Participation and Power Equalization." *Organizational Behavior and Human Performance,* September 1970.

Murdick, Robert G., Richard H. Eckhouse, R. Carl Moor, and Thomas W. Zimmerer: *Business Policy: A Framework for Analysis.* Columbus, Ohio, Grid, 1972.

Nagashima, Yukinori: "Response of Japanese Companies to Environmental Changes." *Long Range Planning,* January 1976.

Negandhi, Anant R. (ed.): *Environmental Settings In Organizational Functioning.* Kent, Ohio, College of Business Administration, Kent State University, 1970.

Negandhi, Anant R.: "Comparative Management and Organization Theory: A Marriage Needed." *Academy of Management Journal,* June 1975.

Negandhi, Anant R., and Bernard C. Reimann: "A Contingency Theory of Organization Reexamined in the Context of a Developing Country." *Academy of Management Journal,* June 1972.

Nesheim, John L.: "Strategies and Tactics for Fighting Take-Over." *Business Horizons,* October 1970.

Neuschel, Robert P.: "Presidential Style: Updated Versions." *Business Horizons,* June 1969.

Newell, Allen, and Herbert A. Simon: *Human Problem Solving.* Englewood Cliffs, N. J., Prentice-Hall, 1972.

Newman, William H.: "Strategy and Management Structure." *Academy of Management Proceedings,* August 1971.

Newman, William H.: *Constructive Control.* Englewood Cliffs, N.J., Prentice-Hall, 1975.

Newman, William H., and James P. Logan: *Strategy, Policy, and Central Management.* Cincinnati, Ohio, South-Western, 1971.

Newman, William H., Charles E. Summer, and E. Kirby Warren: *The Process of Management: Concepts, Behavior, and Practice.* Englewood Cliffs, N. J., Prentice-Hall, 1972.

Norman, Richard A.: "Business Decision Making: A Phenomenological Approach." *California Management Review,* Winter 1967.

Novick, David (ed.): *Program Budgeting.* Cambridge, Mass., Harvard University Press, 1965.

Novick, David (ed.): *Current Practice in Program Budgeting: Analysis and Case Studies Covering Government and Business.* New York, Crane, Russak, 1973.

O'Connell, Jeremiah J.: *Managing Organizational Innovation.* Homewood, Ill., Irwin, 1968.

O'Connor, Rochelle: *Corporate Guides To Long-Range Planning.* New York, The Conference Board, Inc., 1976.

Organ, Dennis W.: "Linking Pins Between Organizations and Environment." *Business Horizons,* December 1971.

Osborn, Richard N., and James G. Hunt: "Environment and Organizational Effectiveness." *Administrative Science Quarterly,* June 1974.

Osmond, Neville: "Top Management: Its Tasks, Roles and Skills." *Journal of Business Policy,* Winter 1971.

O'Toole, James O., *et al.*: *Work in America. Report of a Special Task Force to the Secretary of Health, Education, and Welfare.* Cambridge, Mass., MIT Press, 1973.

Oxenfeldt, Alfred R.: *Pricing Strategies.* New York, AMACOM, 1975.

Paine, Frank T., and William Naumes: *Strategy and Policy Formation: An Integrative Approach.* Philadelphia, Saunders, 1974.

Palmer, Michael: "The Application of Psychological Testing to Entrepreneurial Potential." *California Management Review,* Spring 1971.

Palmore, Erdman B.: "The Introduction of Negroes into White Organizations." *Human Organization,* January 1955.

Parker, Treadway C.: *The Formation and Management of New Business Ventures.* New York, The Presidents Association of the American Management Association, 1973.

Patchen, Martin: "The Locus and Basis of Influence on Organizational Decisions." *Organizational Behavior and Human Performance,* April 1974.

Patton, Arch: "Top Management's Stake in the Product Life Cycle." *Management Review,* June 1959.

Patz, Alan L.: "Notes: Business Policy and the Scientific Method." *California Management Review,* Spring 1975.

Pelz, Donald C., and Frank M. Andrews: *Scientists in Organizations: Productive Climates for Research and Development.* New York, Wiley, 1966.

Pennington, Malcolm W.: "Why Has Planning Failed?" *Long Range Planning,* March 1972.

Perrow, Charles: "The Short and Glorious History of Organizational Theory." *Organizational Dynamics,* Summer 1973.

Peters, Joseph P.: *Concept Commitment Action.* New York, United Hospital Fund of New York and the Health and Hospital Planning Council of Southern New York, Inc., 1974.

Peterson, Richard B.: "A Cross-Cultural Perspective of Supervisory Values." *Academy of Management Journal,* March 1972.

Pfeffer, Jeffrey: "Size and Composition of Corporate Boards of Directors: The Organization and Its Environment." *Administrative Science Quarterly,* June 1972.

Pfeffer, Jeffrey, and Gerald R. Salancik: "Organizational Decision Making as a Political Process: The Case of a University Budget." *Administrative Science Quarterly,* June 1974.

Pierson, Frank C., *et al.: The Education of American Businessmen.* New York, McGraw-Hill, 1959.

Pohl, Herman H.: "The Coming Era of the Financial Executive." *Business Horizons,* June 1973.

Polli, Rolando, and Victor Cook: "Validity of the Product Life Cycle." *Journal of Business.* October 1969.

Pondy, L. R., and J. G. Birnberg: "An Experimental Study of the Allocation of Financial Resources within Small, Hierarchical Task Groups." *Administrative Science Quarterly,* June 1969.

Popp, Gary E., and Herbert G. Hicks: "Teaching Business Policy and Entrepreneurship: An Experiential Approach Revisited." *Academy of Management Proceedings,* August 1973.

Powell, Reed M., and J. L. Schlacter: "Participative Management—A Panacea?" *Academy of Management Journal,* June 1971.

President's Commission on National Goals: *Report of the President's Commission on National Goals.* Washington, D. C., U. S. Government Printing Office, 1960.

Preston, Lee E., and James E. Post: *Private Management and Public Policy.* Englewood Cliffs, N. J., Prentice-Hall, 1975.

Price, James L. *Organizational Effectiveness: An Inventory of Propositions.* Homewood, Ill., Irwin, 1968.

Pugh, D. S., D. J. Hickson, C. R. Hinings, and C. Turner: "The Context of Organizational Structures." *Administrative Science Quarterly,* March 1969.

Purcell, Theodore V.: "How GE Measures Managers in Fair Employment," *Harvard Business Review,* November 1974.

Raia, Anthony P.: "A Second Look at Goals and Controls." *California Management Review,* Summer 1966.

Raia, Anthony P.: *Managing by Objectives.* Glenview, Ill., Scott, Foresman and Company, 1974.
Rapoport, Leo A., and William P. Drews: "Mathematical Approach to Long-Range Planning." *Harvard Business Review,* May–June 1962.
Rawls, James R., Robert A. Ullrich, and Oscar Tivis Nelson, Jr.: "A Comparison of Managers Entering or Reentering the Profit and Nonprofit Sectors." *Academy of Management Journal,* September 1975.
Reeser, Clayton: "The Use of Sophisticated Analytical Methods for Decision Making in the Aerospace Industry." *MSU Business Topics,* Autumn 1971.
Reimann, Bernard C.: "The Public Philosophy of Organizations." *Academy of Management Journal,* September 1974.
Reynolds, William H.: "The Edsel Ten Years Later." *Business Horizons,* Fall 1967.
Rhenman, Eric: *Organization Theory for Long Range Planning.* New York, Wiley, 1973.
Richards, Max D.: "An Exploratory Study of Strategic Failure." *Academy of Management Proceedings,* August 1973.
Richards, Steven A., and Cabot L. Jaffee: "Blacks Supervising Whites: A Study of Interracial Difficulties in Working Together in a Simulated Organization." *Journal of Applied Psychology,* June 1972.
Richman, Barry M.: "Achieving Corporate Objectives: Significance of Cultural Variables." *Academy of Management Proceedings,* December 1964.
Richman, Barry M.: "The Corporation and the Quality of Life: Part I: Typologies." *Management International,* 1973.
Ringbakk, K. A.: "Why Planning Fails." *European Business,* Spring 1971.
Ringbakk, K. A.: "The Corporate Planning Life Cycle—An International Point of View." *Long Range Planning,* September 1972.
Ringbakk, K. A.: "New Concepts for Strategic Planning." *Planning Review,* March 1975.
Roberts, John C., and Carl H. Castore: "The Effects of Conformity, Information, and Confidence Upon Subjects' Willingness to Take Risk Following a Group Discussion." *Organizational Behavior and Human Performance,* December 1972.
Rockefeller, David: Address to the Advertising Council, reported in the *Los Angeles Times,* January 3, 1971.
Rockefeller, John D., III: *The Second American Revolution.* New York, Harper and Row, 1973.
Roe, C. William: "The Academic Institution's Policies Toward Management Consulting—A Model for Uniform Guidelines." *Academy of Management Proceedings,* August 1973.
Roethlisberger, F. J., and William J. Dickson: *Management and the Worker.* Cambridge, Mass., Harvard University Press, 1939.
Rogers, Rolf E.: *Organizational Theory.* Boston, Allyn and Bacon, 1975.
Rokeach, Milton: *The Nature of Human Values.* New York, Free Press, 1973.
Roper Report: "What Should a Corporation Do?" No. 2, New York, October 1971.
Rosen, Stephen: "The Future from the Top: Presidential Perspectives on Planning." *Long Range Planning,* August 1974.
Ross, Joel E., and Michael J. Kami: *Corporate Management in Crisis: Why the Mighty Fall.* Englewood Cliffs, N. J., Prentice-Hall, 1973.

Rourke, Francis E.: *Bureaucracy, Politics and Public Policy*. Boston, Little, Brown, 1968.

Rue, Leslie W.: "Tools and Techniques of Long Range Planners." *Long Range Planning,* October 1974.

Rue, Leslie W., and Robert M. Fulmer: "Is Long Range Planning Profitable?" *Academy of Management Proceedings,* August 1973.

Rumelt, Richard P.: *Strategy, Structure, and Economic Performance*. Boston, Graduate School of Business Administration, Harvard University, 1974.

Salveson, Melvin E.: "The Management of Strategy." *Long Range Planning,* February 1974.

Saunders, Charles B.: "What Should We Know About Strategy Formulation?" *Academy of Management Proceedings,* August 1973.

Sayles, Leonard R.: *Managerial Behavior*. New York, McGraw-Hill, 1964.

Schattschneider, E. E.: *Two Hundred Million Americans in Search of Government*. New York, Holt, Rinehart, and Winston, 1969.

Schein, Virginia E.: "The Relationship Between Sex Role Stereotypes and Requisite Management Characteristics." *Journal of Applied Psychology,* February 1973.

Schein, Virginia E.: "Relationships Between Sex Role Stereotypes and Requisite Management Characteristics Among Female Managers." *Journal of Applied Psychology,* June 1975.

Schendel, Dan E.: "Needs and Developments in Policy Curricula at the Ph.D. Level." Unpublished paper, Krannert Graduate School of Industrial Administration, Purdue University, 1975.

Schendel, Dan E., and Kenneth J. Hatten: "Business Policy or Strategic Management: A Broader View for an Emerging Discipline." *Academy of Management Proceedings,* August 1972.

Schendel, Dan E., Richard Patton, and James Riggs: "Corporate Turnaround Strategies." Working Paper, Purdue University, August 1974.

Schlaifer, Robert: *Probability and Statistics for Business Decisions*. New York, McGraw-Hill, 1959.

Schmookler, Jacob: *Invention and Economic Growth*. Cambridge, Mass., Harvard University Press, 1966.

Schoeffler, Sidney, Robert D. Buzzell, and Donald F. Heany: "Impact of Strategic Planning on Profit Performance." *Harvard Business Review,* March–April 1974.

Schollhammer, Hans: "The Comparative Management Theory Jungle." *Academy of Management Journal,* March 1969.

Schollhammer, Hans: *Locational Strategies of Multinational Firms*. Los Angeles, Center for International Business, Pepperdine University, 1974.

Schoner, Bertram, Gerald L. Rose, and G. C. Hoyt: "Quality of Decisions: Individual Versus Real and Synthetic Groups." *Journal of Applied Psychology,* August 1974.

Schrieber, Albert N. (ed.): *Corporate Simulation Models*. Seattle, Wash., Graduate School of Business Administration, University of Washington, 1970.

Schroder, Harold M., Michael J. Driver, and Siegfried Streufert: *Human Information Processing*. New York, Holt, Rinehart, and Winston, 1967.

Scott, Bruce R.: "The Industrial State: Old Myths and New Realities." *Harvard Business Review,* March–April 1973.

Scurrah, Martin J., Moshe Shani, and Carl Zipfel: "Influence of Internal and External Change Agents in a Simulated Educational Organization." *Administrative Science Quarterly,* March 1971.

Searfoss, D. Gerald, and Robert M. Monczka: "Perceived Participation in the Budget Process and the Motivation to Achieve the Budget." *Academy of Management Journal,* December 1973.

Sethi, S. Prakash: *Up Against the Corporate Wall.* Englewood Cliffs, N. J., Prentice-Hall, 1974.

Shames, William H.: *Venture Management.* New York, Free Press, 1974.

Shank, John K., and A. Michael Burnell: "Smooth Your Earnings Growth Rate." *Harvard Business Review,* January–February 1974.

Shell, Richard L., and David F. Stelzer: "Systems Analysis: Aid to Decision Making." *Business Horizons,* December 1971.

Shocker, Allan D., and S. Prakash Sethi: "An Approach to Incorporating Societal Preferences in Developing Corporate Action Strategies." *California Management Review,* Summer 1973.

Shuckett, Donald H., and Edward J. Mock: *Decision Strategies in Financial Management.* New York, AMACOM, 1973.

Shull, Fremont A., André L. Delbecq, and L. L. Cummings: *Organizational Decision Making.* New York, McGraw-Hill, 1970.

Simon, Herbert A.: *Administrative Behavior.* New York, Macmillan, 1957a.

Simon, Herbert A.: *Models of Man.* New York, Wiley, 1957b.

Simonetti, Jack L.: "The Effect of Management Policy on Organization Structure and the Management Effectiveness of Firms Operating in Italy." Unpublished paper, undated, circa 1973–74.

Skibbins, Gerald J.: *Organizational Evolution: A Program for Managing Racial Change.* New York, AMACOM, 1974.

Sloan, Alfred P., Jr.: *My Years with General Motors.* New York, Doubleday and Company, 1964.

Smith, Gene: "RCA Profits Topple, Kodak Sets Mark." *The New York Times,* October 15, 1970.

Smith, Norman R.: *The Entrepreneur and His Firm: The Relationship Between Type of Man and Type of Company.* East Lansing, Mich., Graduate School of Business Administration, Michigan State University, 1967.

Soden, John V.: "Planning for the Computer Services Spin-out." *Harvard Business Review,* September–October 1972.

Soelberg, Peer: "Unprogrammed Decision Making." *Academy of Management Proceedings,* December 1966.

Solomons, David: *Divisional Performance: Measurement and Control.* New York, Financial Executives Research Foundation, 1965.

Sord, Burnard H., and Glenn A. Welsch: *Business Budgeting: A Survey of Management Planning and Control Practices.* New York, Controllership Foundation, 1958.

Sord, Bernard H., and Glenn A. Welsch: *Managerial Planning and Control.* Austin, Texas, University of Texas Printing Division, 1964.

Stagner, Ross: "Corporate Decision Making: An Empirical Study." *Journal of Applied Psychology,* February 1969.

Starbuck, William H.: "On Teaching Business Policy." *Academy of Management Journal,* December 1966.

Starr, Martin K.: *Management: A Modern Approach.* New York, Harcourt, Brace, Jovanovich, 1971.

Stedman, Murray S., Jr.: "Liberalism is Dying." *Temple University Alumni Review,* Spring 1975.

Stedry, A. C.: *Budget Control and Cost Behavior.* Chicago, Markham, 1967.

Steele, John E., and Lewis B. Ward: "MBAs: Mobile, Well Situated, Well Paid." *Harvard Business Review,* January–February 1974.

Steiner, George A.: "Why and How to Diversify." *California Management Review,* Summer 1964.

Steiner, George A.: "Program Budgeting, Business Contribution to Government Management." *Business Horizons,* Spring 1965.

Steiner, George A.: "The Critical Role of Top Management in Long Range Planning." *Arizona Review,* April 1966.

Steiner, George A.: "Approaches to Long Range Planning for Small Business." *California Management Review,* Fall 1967.

Steiner, George A.: *Strategic Factors in Business Success.* New York, Financial Executives Research Foundation, 1969a.

Steiner, George A.: *Top Management Planning.* New York, Macmillan, 1969b.

Steiner, George A.: "Rise of the Corporate Planner." *Harvard Business Review,* September–October 1970.

Steiner, George A.: *Comprehensive Managerial Planning.* Oxford, Ohio, Planning Executives Institute, 1971.

Steiner, George A.: "Social Policies for Business." *California Management Review,* Winter 1972a.

Steiner, George A.: "The Redefinition of Capitalism and Its Impact on Management Practice and Theory." *Academy of Management Proceedings,* August 1972b.

Steiner, George A.: *Pitfalls in Comprehensive Long Range Planning.* Oxford, Ohio, Planning Executives Institute, 1972c.

Steiner, George A. (ed.): *Selected Major Issues in Business' Role in Modern Society.* Los Angeles, Graduate School of Management, UCLA, 1973.

Steiner, George A.: "Comprehensive Managerial Planning." In Joseph W. McGuire (ed.): *Contemporary Management: Issues and Viewpoints.* Englewood Cliffs, N. J., Prentice-Hall, 1974.

Steiner, George A. (ed.): *Changing Business Society Interrelationships.* Los Angeles, Graduate School of Management, UCLA, 1975a.

Steiner, George A.: *Business and Society,* Second Edition. New York, Random House, 1975b.

Steiner, George A.: "National Policy Assessment and Action Program." *Planning Review,* 1975c.

Steiner, George A., and Warren M. Cannon (eds.): *Multinational Corporate Planning.* New York, Crowell-Collier and Macmillan Company, 1966.

Steiner, George A., and William G. Ryan: *Industrial Project Management.* New York, Macmillan, 1968.

Steiner, George A., and Hans Schollhammer: "Pitfalls in Multi-National Long Range Planning." *Long Range Planning,* April 1975.

Steiner, Ivan D.: *Group Process and Productivity.* New York, Academic Press, 1972.

Steinmetz, Lawrence L.: "Critical Stages of Small Business Growth." *Business Horizons,* February 1969.

Steinmetz, Lawrence L., and Charles D. Greenidge: "Realities that Shape Managerial Style." *Business Horizons,* October 1970.

Stewart, Robert F.: *A Framework for Business Planning.* Report No. 162, Long Range Planning Service. Menlo Park, Cal., Stanford Research Institute, February 1963.

Stieglitz, Harold: *The Chief Executive—And His Job.* Personnel Policy Study No. 214. New York, National Industrial Conference Board, 1969.

Stogdill, Ralph M.: *Handbook of Leadership.* New York, Free Press, 1974.

Strauch, Ralph E.: *A Critical Assessment of Quantitative Methodology as a Policy Analysis Tool.* Santa Monica, Cal., Rand Corporation, 1974.

Strauss, George, Raymond E. Miles, Charles C. Snow, and Arnold S. Tannenbaum: *Organizational Behavior: Research and Issues.* Madison, Wis., Industrial Relations Research Association, 1974.

Streufert, Siegfried, and Susan C. Streufert: "Effects of Increasing Failure and Success on Military and Economic Risk Taking." *Journal of Applied Psychology,* October 1970.

Sturdivant, Frederick D., and James L. Ginter: "Assessing Social Performance: A Preliminary Model." Division of Research Working Paper, College of Administrative Science, The Ohio State University, 1974.

Summer, Charles E., Jr., and Jeremiah J. O'Connell: *The Managerial Mind.* Homewood, Ill., Irwin, 1964.

Sylvester, Richard R.: *The Effects of Management Techniques on Commercial Diversification Project Success.* Doctoral Dissertation, Graduate School of Business, UCLA, 1970.

Tannenbaum, Arnold S., Bogdon Kavcic, Menachem Rosner, Mino Vianello, and Georg Wieser: *Hierarchy in Organizations: An International Comparison.* San Francisco, Jossey-Bass, 1974.

Tannenbaum, Robert, and Warren H. Schmidt: "How to Choose a Leadership Pattern." *Harvard Business Review,* March 1958.

Tarnowieski, Dale: *The Changing Success Ethic.* New York, American Management Association, 1973.

Taylor, Calvin W.: *Climate for Creativity.* Elmsford, N. Y., Pergamon Press, 1972.

Taylor, Ronald N.: "Age and Experience as Determinants of Managerial Information-Processing and Decision-Making Performance." *Academy of Management Journal,* March 1975.

Taylor, Ronald N., and Marvin D. Dunnette: "Influence of Dogmatism, Risk-taking Propensity, and Intelligence on Decision-Making Strategies for a Sample of Industrial Managers." *Journal of Applied Psychology,* August 1974.

Terleckyj, Nestor E.: "Measuring Progress Toward Social Goals: Some Possibilities at National and Local Levels." *Management Science,* August 1970.

Terreberry, Shirley: "The Evolution of Organizational Environments." *Administrative Science Quarterly,* March 1968.

TFX Contract Investigation. Hearings Before the Permanent Subcommittee on

Investigations of the Committee on Government Operations, U. S. Senate, 88th Congress. Washington, D. C., U. S. Government Printing Office, 1963.

Thain, Donald H.: "Stages of Corporate Development." *Business Quarterly,* Winter 1969.

Thompson, James D.: *Organizations in Action.* New York, McGraw-Hill, 1967.

Thompson, Stewart: *Management Creeds and Philosophies.* New York, American Management Association, 1958.

Thune, Stanley S., and Robert J. House: "Where Long Range Planning Pays Off." *Business Horizons,* August 1970.

Tilles, Seymour: "How to Evaluate Corporate Strategy." *Harvard Business Review,* July–August 1963.

Tilles, Seymour: "Strategies for Allocating Funds." *Harvard Business Review,* January–February 1966.

Timmons, Jeffry A.: "Black is Beautiful—Is It Bountiful?" *Harvard Business Review,* November 1971.

Tipgos, Manuel A.: "Structuring a Management Information System for Strategic Planning." *Managerial Planning,* January–February 1975.

Toffler, Alvin: *Future Shock.* New York, Random House, 1970.

Tomkins, Silvan S.: *Affect Imagery Consciousness: Volume I, The Positive Affects.* New York, Springer Publishing, 1962.

Tosi, Henry L.: "A Reexamination of Personality as a Determinant of the Effects of Participation." *Personnel Psychology,* Spring 1970.

Tosi, Henry L., Robert J. House, and Marvin D. Dunnette: *Managerial Motivation and Compensation.* East Lansing, Mich., Graduate School of Business Administration, Michigan State University, 1972.

Towl, Andrew L.: *To Study Administration by Cases.* Boston, Graduate School of Business Administration, Harvard University, 1969.

Truman, David B.: *The Governmental Process.* New York, Alfred Knopf, 1951.

Tuason, Roman V.: "Corporate Life Cycle and the Evolution of Corporate Strategy." *Academy of Management Proceedings,* August 1973.

Twiss, B. C.: "Strategy for Research and Development." *Long Range Planning,* September 1970.

U. S. Department of Health, Education, and Welfare: *Work in America.* Washington, D. C., U. S. Government Printing Office, 1973.

U. S. 90th Congress, 1st Session, House of Representatives, Research and Technical Programs Subcommittee of the Committee on Government Operations: *The Use of Social Research in Federal Domestic Programs, Part I,* 1967.

Vance, Stanley C.: *Managers in the Conglomerate Era.* New York, Wiley-Interscience, 1971.

Vance, Stanley C.: "Toward a Collegial Office of the President." *California Management Review,* Fall 1972.

Vancil, Richard F.: ". . . So You're Going to Have a Planning Department!" *Harvard Business Review,* May–June 1967.

Vancil, Richard F.: *Formal Planning Systems: A Brief Description of the Data Bank Constructed for Research.* Boston, Harvard Business School, Spring 1970a.

Vancil, Richard F.: "The Accuracy of Long Range Planning." *Harvard Business Review,* September–October 1970b.

Vancil, Richard F. (ed.): *Formal Planning Systems—1971.* Boston, Harvard Business School, Harvard University, 1971.

Vancil, Richard F.: "Better Management of Corporate Development." *Harvard Business Review,* September–October 1972a.

Vancil, Richard F. (ed.): *Formal Planning Systems.* Boston, Harvard Business School, 1972b (mimeographed).

Vancil, Richard F.: "What Kind of Management Control Do You Need?" *Harvard Business Review,* March–April 1973.

Vancil, Richard F., Francis J. Aguilar, and Robert A. Howell: *Formal Planning Systems—1968.* Boston, Graduate School of Business Administration, Harvard University, 1968.

Vancil, Richard F., Francis J. Aguilar, and Robert A. Howell (eds.): *Formal Planning Systems—1969.* Boston, Harvard School of Business, 1969 (mimeographed).

Van de Ven, Andrew H., and André L. Delbecq: "Nominal Versus Interacting Group Processes for Committee Decision-Making Effectiveness." *Academy of Management Journal,* June 1971.

Van de Ven, Andrew H., and André L. Delbecq: "The Effectiveness of Nominal, Delphi, and Interacting Group Decision Making Processes." *Academy of Management Journal,* December 1974.

Vesper, Karl H., and John Schlendorf: "Views on College Courses in Venture Initiation." *Academy of Management Journal,* September 1973.

Vroom, Victor H.: *Some Personality Determinants of the Effects of Participation.* Englewood Cliffs, N. J., Prentice-Hall, 1960.

Vroom, Victor H., and Arthur J. Jago: "Decision Making as a Social Process: Normative and Descriptive Models of Leader Behavior." *Decision Sciences,* December 1974.

Vroom, Victor H., and Bernd Pahl: "Relationship Between Age and Risk Taking Among Managers." *Journal of Applied Psychology,* October 1971.

Vroom, Victor H., and Philip W. Yetton: *Leadership and Decision-Making.* Pittsburgh, Pa., University of Pittsburgh Press, 1973.

Wainer, Herbert A., and Irwin M. Rubin: "Motivation of Research and Development Entrepreneurs: Determinants of Company Success." *Journal of Applied Psychology,* June 1969.

Walker, Charles R.: *Technology, Industry, and Man: The Age of Acceleration.* New York, McGraw-Hill, 1968.

Wallace, M. E.: "Behavioral Considerations in Budgeting." *Management Accounting,* December 1966.

Walton, Clarence C.: *Ethos and the Executive.* Englewood Cliffs, N. J., Prentice-Hall, 1969.

Warren, Kirby E.: *Long Range Planning: The Executive Viewpoint.* Englewood Cliffs, N. J., Prentice-Hall, 1966.

Wasson, Chester: *Product Management: Product Life Cycles and Competitive Marketing Strategy.* St. Charles, Ill., Challenge Books, 1971.

Webber, James B., and Martha A. Dula: "Effective Planning Committees for Hospitals." *Harvard Business Review,* May–June 1974.

Webber, Ross A.: "The Relationship of Group Performance to the Age of

Members in Homogeneous Groups." *Academy of Management Journal,* September 1974.

Weber, Max: *Essays in Sociology* (translated by H. H. Gerth and C. W. Mills). New York, Oxford University Press, 1946.

Webster, Frederick A.: "A Model of Vertical Integration Strategy." *California Management Review,* Winter 1967.

Welsch, Glenn A.: *Budgeting: Profit Planning and Control.* Englewood Cliffs, N. J., Prentice-Hall, 1957.

Weston, J. Fred: "ROI Planning and Control." *Business Horizons,* August 1972.

Weston, J. Fred, and Eugene F. Brigham: *Essentials of Managerial Finance,* 2nd ed. New York, Holt, Rinehart and Winston, 1971.

Wheelwright, Steven C., and Sypros Makridakis: *Forecasting Methods for Management.* New York, Wiley, 1973.

Whybark, D. Clay: "Comparing an Adaptive Decision Model and Human Decisions." *Academy of Management Journal,* December 1973.

Whyte, William F.: *Money and Motivation.* New York, Harper, 1955.

Wilemon, David L., and Gary R. Gemmill: "The Venture Manager as a Corporate Innovator." *California Management Review,* Fall 1973.

Wilson, Ian H.: "Socio-Political Forecasting: A New Dimension to Strategic Planning." *Michigan Business Review,* July 1974a.

Wilson, Ian H.: "Reforming the Strategic Planning Process: Integration of Social and Business Needs." *Long Range Planning,* October 1974b.

Woodward, Joan: *Management and Technology.* London, Her Majesty's Printing Office, 1958.

Woodward, Joan: *Industrial Organization: Theory and Practice.* London, Oxford University Press, 1965.

Wright, Robert: "Are You Wasting Your Consultants?" *Business Horizons,* October 1969.

Wrigley, Leonard: *Divisional Autonomy and Diversification.* Unpublished Doctoral Dissertation, Harvard Business School, 1970.

Zand, Dale E.: "Trust and Managerial Problem Solving." *Administrative Science Quarterly,* June 1972.

Author Index

A

Aboud, John, 744, 747, 756, 979
Abt, Clark, 840
Acito, Franklin, 644
Ackerman, Robert W., 47, 66, 607, 868, 885, 965
Ackoff, Russell L., 260, 965
Adizes, Ichak, 58, 965
Aerosol Age, 130
Aguilar, Francis Joseph, 53, 189, 219, 619, 632, 868, 965, 995
Akel, Anthony M., 868
Alchian, Armen A., 215, 965
Allen, Stephen A. III, 52, 609, 616, 617, 618, 619, 625, 626, 982
Allison, Graham T., 204, 211, 215, 607, 685, 763, 868, 965
Altman, Edward J., 203, 965
Alutto, Joseph A., 644, 965
American Institute of Certified Public Accountants, 840
Ammer, Dean S., 753, 965
Anderson, Carl R., 778, 965
Anderson, Lynn R., 268, 971
Anderson, T. A., 172, 203, 965
Andrews, Frank M., 236, 988
Andrews, Kenneth R., 9, 19, 20, 30, 34, 59, 61, 607, 609, 869, 965, 971
Anshen, Melvin, 8, 58, 61, 965
Ansoff, H. Igor, 7, 19, 33, 172, 191, 202, 203, 209, 219, 260, 868, 913, 965, 966
Anthony, Robert N., 7, 22, 152, 215, 633, 640, 966
Anyon, G. Jay, 743, 750, 966
Appleby, Paul H., 27, 760, 768, 770, 966
Arendt, Eugene, 252, 972
Argyris, Chris, 77, 279, 634, 642, 646, 966
Asimov, Isaac, 174, 966
ASPA-BNA Survey, 649, 649*t*, 966
Athos, Anthony G., 302
Athreya, Mrityunjay, 868
Auto Week, 499
Automotive News, 498, 499
Ayers, Robert U., 154, 966

B

Bagley, Edward R., 83, 172, 966
Baier, Kurt, 155, 966
Bailey, Earl L., 979
Bailey, Stephen K., 211, 966
Barkley, Paul W., 59, 966
Barnard, Chester I., 213, 647, 966
Barnes, Louis B., 212, 647, 972, 977
Barrett, Colin, 888
Barron, Frank, 236, 966
Barsaloux, Jean, 244, 968
Barzini, Luigi, 823
Bass, Alan R., 642, 968
Bass, Bernard M., 642, 967
Bassett, Glenn A., 79*f*
Battalia, Lotz and Associates, 253, 967
Bauer, Raymond A., 8, 68, 225, 685, 763, 840, 967
Baumhart, Raymond, 59, 967
Baumol, William J., 62, 215, 840, 967
Beatty, Richard W., 651, 967
Beaver, William H., 203, 967
Beiler, George, 68, 970
Bell, Cecil H., 163, 975
Bell, Daniel, 50, 59, 967
Bell, E. C., 643, 967
Benham, Thomas W., 47
Berenson, Conrad, 45, 967
Berg, T. L., 343
Berkwitt, George J., 967
Berlew, David G., 302
Bernstein, Marver H., 767, 967
Bettauer, Arthur, 203, 967
Bierman, Harold, Jr., 967
Birnberg, J. G., 633, 988
Bither, Stewart W., 251, 252, 967
Bladgett, Timothy B., 888

Blashill, John, 878
Bleichan, Gerhard D., 61, 967
Blomstrom, Robert L., 53, 972
Blum, Fred H., 840
Boettinger, Henry M., 7, 967
Boise, William B., 767, 968
Bonge, John W., 8, 968
Bons, Paul H., 642, 968
Boston Consulting Group, The, 202, 968
Bouchard, Thomas J., 244, 252, 968
Boulden, James B., 165, 209, 218, 968
Bowen, Howard R., 59, 840, 968
Bower, Joseph L., 9, 19, 34, 607, 609, 633, 868, 968, 971
Bower, Marvin, 78, 302, 646, 968
Bowers, David G., 75, 968
Bradish, Richard D., 227, 968
Brady, Rodney H., 636, 767, 968
Bralove, Mary, 883
Brandeis, Louis D., 823
Brandenberg, R. G., 152, 343, 976
Braybrooke, David, 968
Brenner, Marshall H., 651, 968
Brewer, Garry D., 764, 968
Brigham, Eugene F., 203, 996
Bright, James R., 154, 968
Brightman, Harvey J., 236, 968
Broom, H. N., 9, 969
Brown, James K., 19, 188*t*, 969
Brown, Julius S., 235, 969
Bruce-Briggs, B., 50, 685, 970
Bryan, Judith F., 635, 638, 969
Bryan, Stanley E., 211, 969
Buchanan, Bruce, 644, 645*t*, 646, 969
Buchele, Robert B., 969
Buckley, Adrian, 198, 969
Buckley, John W., 609, 969
Buffa, Elwood S., 165, 968
Bunker, Charles S., 744, 979
Burack, Elmer, 759, 888, 969
Bureau of National Affairs, Inc., 273, 274, 649, 969
Burnell, A. Michael, 203, 991
Burns, Tom, 616, 969
Bursk, Edward C., 967
Burt, H. E., 302
Business Week, 142, 221, 498, 499, 823, 912, 913, 969
Butcher, Bernard, 840
Butler, William F., 154, 969
Buzzell, Robert D., 202, 203, 221, 869, 969, 990
Byrom, Fletcher L., 61

C

Cameron, D. A., 219, 969
Cammillus, J. C., 171, 969
Campbell, Hannah, 201, 969
Campbell, John P., 72, 229, 969
Cannon, J. Thomas, 19, 183*t*, 202, 969
Cannon, Warren M., 22, 609, 610, 611, 970, 992
Caplan, Edwin H., 635, 970
Carroll, Archie B., 67, 68, 970
Carroll, Stephen J., Jr., 257, 636, 638, 668, 970, 984
Carruth, Eleanor, 45, 970
Carter, E. Eugene, 219, 265, 868, 970
Cartwright, John, 759, 970
Castore, Carl H., 248, 989
Cavanagh, Gerald F., 888
Cawein, Paul E., 35, 978
Cecil, Earl A., 248, 263, 970
Cetron, Marvin J., 172, 970
Chamber of Commerce of the United States, 63, 67, 970
Chambers, John C., 154, 219, 970
Chandler, Alfred D., 19, 30, 51, 83, 263, 610, 611, 614, 970
Chandra, Gyan, 636, 970
Channon, Derek F., 612, 614, 622, 970
Charan, Ram, 13, 970
Charnock, John, 761, 970
Chase Manhattan Corp., 65, 970
Chertkoff, Jerome M., 248, 970
Chevalier, Michel, 202, 868, 970
Child, John, 52, 970
Christensen, C. Roland, 9, 19, 34, 607, 608, 869, 971
Churchman, C. W., 218, 971
Clapp, Norton, 61, 971
Clark, John M., 215, 971
Clark, Russell D., 247, 971
Cleveland, Harlan, 55, 971
Clifford, Donald K., Jr., 21, 84, 196, 610, 611, 971
Cohen, Kalman J., 152, 971
Cohn, Theodore, 202, 971
Cole, Edward, 153, 971
Coleman, Bruce P., 8, 968
Collaros, Panayiota A., 268, 971
Collings, Robert L., 868

Collins, Orvis F., 746, 747, 752, 756, 971
Committee for Economic Development (CED), 53, 59, 61, 63, 68, 840, 971
Commonwealth of Pennsylvania, Program Budget, 325
Cook, Curtis W., 778, 780, 971
Cook, Victor, 196, 988
Cooper, A. C., 19, 971
Cooper, Arnold, 203, 971
Copeland, Charles, 4, 649, 981
Copeland, Miles, 824
Coppinger, Richard J., 217, 971
Coppock, R., 63, 971
Cordtz, Dan, 142
Corey, E. Raymond, 615, 972
Corke, D. K., 629, 972
Corson, John J., 47, 53, 64, 68, 840, 972
Council on Economic Priorities, 841
Cross, Hershner, 170, 972
Cross, Theodore L., 755, 972
Cummings, Larry L., 226, 242, 248, 252, 970, 972, 991
Curran, Joseph R., 8, 983
Cutting, Guy D., 759, 983
Cyert, Richard M., 152, 209, 214, 215, 971, 972

D

Dake, Lee, 912
Dale, Ernest, 619, 972
Dalton, Francis E., 228, 972
Dalton, Gene W., 647, 972
Davis, Gary A., 239, 972
Davis, James V., 209, 972
Davis, Keith, 53, 59, 66, 972
Day, George S., 198, 203, 972
Dean, Joel, 196, 972
Dearden, John, 219, 619, 639, 972
de Carbonnell, Francois E., 189, 973
Deets, M. King, 248, 973
Delbecq, André, 226, 242, 243, 244*t*, 245, 977, 991, 995
Demuzzio, Edward, 203, 971
Denhardt, Robert B., 643, 973
Derieux, James C., 979
Derthick, Martha, 760, 973
Dickson, William J., 646, 989
Dierkes, M., 63, 971
Dill, William R., 302, 759, 982
DiMarco, Nicholas, 273, 278
Donnelly, James H., Jr., 209, 759, 976
Dorrance, Roy G., 189, 973
Douglas, William O., 823
Downey, H. Kirk, 53, 973
Drauden, Gail, 244, 968
Drebin, Allan R., 967
Drews, William P., 201, 989
Driver, Michael J., 230, 990
Drotning, Philip T., 884
Drucker, Peter F., 29, 30, 47, 50, 53, 158, 182, 212, 218, 302, 629, 636, 638, 759, 760, 768, 823, 973
Dubin, Robert, 257, 973
Dula, Martha A., 177, 759, 995
Dunbar, R. L. M., 634, 973
Dunnette, Marvin D., 72, 229, 235, 647, 969, 993, 994
Dymsza, William A., 203, 973

E

Eastlack, Joseph O., Jr., 228, 632, 983
Eckhouse, Richard H., 986
Edelman, Murray, 767, 973
Editors of *Forbes,* 87, 973
Eells, Richard, 59, 973
Eliott-Jones, M. F., 841
Elsner, David M., 36, 973
Emery, F. E., 43, 52, 973
Emory, C. William, 212, 973
England, George W., 21, 232, 233, 974
Enrick, Norbert Lloyd, 154, 974
Enthoven, Alain C., 218, 974
Epley, E. Stewart, 217, 971
Epstein, Edwin M., 49, 974
Etzioni, Amitai, 263, 759, 974
Evans, Martin G., 282, 974
Ewing, David W., 63, 630, 868, 974
Eyring, Henry B., 759, 982

F

Farmer, Richard N., 51, 59, 609, 974
Fenn, Dan H., Jr., 68, 685, 840, 967
Ferguson, Charles R., 191, 974
Fernandez, John P., 651, 974
Ferrell, Robert W., 182, 974
Fiedler, Fred E., 774, 775, 965
Filley, Alan C., 214, 250, 252, 974
Fisher, G. H., 764, 974
Fleishman, Edwin A., 75, 302, 974

Fleming, John E., 182, 975
Folsom, Marion B., 211, 975
Forbes, 142, 174, 498, 499, 593, 824
Forbes, editors of, 87, 973
Forbes, A. M., 975
Forrester, Jay W., 5, 196, 975
Forsgren, Roderick A., 278, 975
Fortune, 142, 913
Foster, D. W., 196, 975
Fouraker, Lawrence E., 612, 975
Fox, Harold, 198, 868, 975
Frankenhoff, William P., 7, 30, 33, 975
French, John R. P., 651, 984
French, Wendell L., 279, 975
Freud, Sigmund, 247, 249, 975
Fri, Robert W., 975
Friedlander, Frank, 650, 975
Friedman, Milton, 60, 975
Friedrich, Alfred, 628*f*
Froissart, Daniel, 975
Fruhan, William E., Jr., 202, 221, 868, 975
Fulmer, Robert W., 172, 975, 990
Futurist, The, 50, 155

G

Gale, Bradley T., 203, 969
Gallagher, Charles A., 639, 975
Ganesh, S. R., 280, 975
Gardner, John W., 302
Garrett, Ray, 823
Geiger, Theodore, 763
Gemmill, Gary R., 754, 755*t,* 996
General Electric Co., 888
General Motors Corp., 841
Gergen, Kenneth J., 763, 967
Germane, Gayton E., 257, 979
Gershefski, George W., 201, 975
Gerstenfeld, Arthur, 219, 975
Gerstner, Louis V., 172, 208, 213, 975
Gestetner, David, 203, 976
Ghiselli, Edwin E., 229, 302, 646, 699, 976, 977
Gibson, James L., 209, 759, 976
Gibson, R. E., 203, 976
Gilmore, Frank F., 152, 284, 285*f*, 343, 976
Ginter, James L., 69, 993
Ginzberg, Eli, 976
Glueck, William F., 8, 9, 19, 202, 264*t,* 265, 759, 779, 869, 976
Goetz, Billy E., 7, 216, 640, 976
Goldberg, Arthur, 876
Golembiewski, Robert T., 279, 976
Goodman, Paul S., 650, 976
Gordon, M. E., 699
Gordon, Paul J., 8, 976
Gordon, Robert A., 3, 4, 976
Granger, Charles H., 7, 30, 33, 975
Gray, Edmund R., 8, 976
Grayson, C. Jackson, Jr., 218, 976
Green, Thad B., 245, 976
Greenberg, Philip, 976
Greenberg, Stuart, 650, 975
Greenidge, Charles D., 83, 993
Greenwood, William T., 8, 977
Gregory, Carl E., 204, 977
Greiner, Larry E., 86, 212, 619, 977
Grieco, V. A., 750, 977
Grinyer, Peter H., 172, 210, 211, 977
Gross, Bertram M., 20, 27, 977
Grunewald, Donald, 53, 986
Guest, Robert H., 647, 977
Gulick, Luther, 610, 977
Gustafson, David H., 245, 977
Gustafson, David P., 273, 278, 977
Guth, William D., 4, 8, 21, 22, 202, 232, 869, 965, 977
Gutman, Jonathan, 361
Gutman, Peter M., 21, 194, 869, 977
Gwirtzman, Milton S., 883

H

Haas, John A., 72, 977
Haddad, W. F., 755, 977
Haire, Mason, 646, 647, 699, 977
Haitovsky, Yoel, 219, 978
Hall, Douglas T., 302
Hall, Jay, 75, 978
Hall, William K., 217, 218, 639, 978
Hamilton, William F., 201, 978
Hammond, John S., 219, 639, 978
Hansen, Roger D., 763
Hardy, James M., 759, 978
Harris, E. F., 302
Harris, Jerome, 191, 984
Harris, Reuben P., 51
Harrison, E. Frank, 210*f*, 216, 263, 978

Harrison, Roger, 78, 79, 81*t*, 978
Harvey, Allan, 218, 978
Hatten, Kenneth J., 7, 8, 30, 33, 203, 780, 971, 990
Hayek, Friedrich A., 60, 978
Heald, Morrell, 53, 978
Heany, Donald F., 202, 221, 869, 990
Heckman, Nikolaus, 629, 978
Heidrich and Struggles, Inc., 257, 978
Heller, Frank A., 76, 266, 266*t*, 268, 642, 978
Hendrick, Hal W., 253, 979
Henning, Dale A., 633, 978
Henry, Harold W., 869
Herold, David M., 172, 978
Hertz, David B., 166, 218, 978
Heyne, Paul T., 60, 978
Hicks, Elijah, 203, 971
Hicks, Herbert G., 744, 988
Hickson, D. J., 52, 269, 980, 988
Hidy, Ralph W., 35, 978
Hiestand, Dale L., 976
Higdon, Hal, 274, 276, 283, 978
Hill, Walter A., 650, 978
Hilton, George, 592
Hines, George H., 744, 745*t*, 979
Hinings, C. R., 52, 988
Hitch, Charles J., 211, 764, 979
Hlavacek, James D., 754, 979
Hofer, Charles W., 8, 182, 190, 194, 196, 198, 776, 777, 778, 779, 782, 979
Hogue, W. Dickerson, 59, 974
Holden, Paul E., 257, 979
Hollander, Stanley C., 271, 279, 979
Holloman, Charles R., 253, 979
Holmberg, Steven R., 218, 633, 979
Holton, Richard H., 203, 979
Hopkins, David S., 979
Hornaday, John A., 744, 747, 756, 979
House, Robert J., 172, 214, 252, 647, 974, 979, 994
Howell, James E., 3, 4, 979
Howell, Robert A., 203, 219, 619, 629, 632, 638, 979, 995
Hoyt, George C., 245, 248, 973, 990
Hrebiniak, Lawrence G., 644, 979
Huber, George P., 252, 972
Huddleston, W., 592
Humble, John W., 152, 638, 979
Humphrey, George M., 765, 979
Hundal, P. S., 745, 979
Hunt, James G., 75, 616, 974, 980, 987
Hussey, David E., 149, 759, 980
Hutchins, Robert, 11, 980

I

Inkson, J. H. K., 269, 980
Irwin, Patrick H., 7, 172, 980
Ivancevich, John M., 209, 759, 976

J

Jacobs, T. O., 647, 980
Jacoby, Neil H., 58, 980
Jaffee, Cabot L., 651, 989
Jago, Arthur L., 76, 266, 267, 642, 995
James, Barrie G., 86, 980
Janis, Irving L., 249, 763, 980
Jantsch, Erich, 154, 980
Jastram, Roy, 823
Jennings, Eugene E., 302
Jerdee, Thomas H., 257, 984
Jerome, William Travers III, 630, 640, 980
Johnson, Harold L., 53, 980
Johnson, Thomas E., 230, 980
Jones, Charles O., 762, 768, 980
Jones, Reginald H., 47, 980
Journal of Commerce, 592

K

Kahn, Herman, 50, 685, 980
Kahn, Robert L., 87, 981
Kakar, Sudhir, 263, 980
Kami, Michael J., 38, 220, 627, 989
Karmel, Barbara, 252, 980
Karp, Richard, 142
Kast, Fremont E., 278, 759, 774, 981
Kastens, Merritt L., 172, 981
Katcher, David A., 282, 981
Katz, Daniel, 87, 981
Katz, Robert L., 183–84*t*, 869, 981
Kavcic, Bogdon, 643, 993
Kavesh, Robert A., 154, 969
Keegan, Warren J., 869
Keen, Peter G. W., 218, 231, 639, 984
Kegan, Daniel L., 282, 981
Kelley, Lane, 234, 981

Kepner, Charles H., 204, 981
Kerr, Steven, 647, 648*t*, 981
Khandwalla, Pradip N., 76, 202, 869, 981
Kipnis, David, 649, 981
Kitching, John, 203, 869, 981
Klein, Walter H., 8, 981
Koch, James L., 774, 986
Kogan, Norman, 823
Komorita, S. S., 642, 968
Kono, Toyohiro, 194, 981
Koontz, Harold, 19, 254, 758, 876, 981
Korman, Abraham K., 238, 981
Kotler, Philip, 203, 981
Kraber, Richard W., 201, 981
Kraut, Allen I., 650, 981
Krishnan, Rama, 63, 981
Krupp, Sherman, 699

L

Larson, Lars L., 75, 980
Lawler, Edward E., 72, 229, 647, 969, 982
Lawrence, Paul R., 51, 52, 269, 609, 610, 616, 629, 687, 982
Learned, Edmund P., 869
Leavitt, Harold J., 274, 642, 759, 967, 982
Lebestky, D. A., 274, 982
Leitch, D. Paul, 212, 977
Levinson, Harry, 303, 759, 982
Levitt, Theodore, 60, 196, 198, 343, 869, 982
Life Office Management Association, 982
Likert, Rensis, 62, 303, 610, 642, 643, 840, 913, 967, 982
Lindberg, Roy A., 202, 971
Lindblom, Charles E., 259, 260, 762, 764, 968, 982
Linowes, David F., 841
Litwin, George H., 745, 982
Litzinger, William D., 747, 982
Livingston, J. Sterling, 181, 228, 982
Locke, Edwin A., 634, 635, 638, 969, 982
Logan, James P., 19, 633, 987
Lorsch, Jay W., 51, 52, 269, 609, 610, 616, 617, 618, 619, 625, 626, 629, 687, 982, 983
Los Angeles Times, 211, 498, 983
Louden, J. Keith, 983
Louis, Arthur M., 63, 983
Loving, Rush, 593
Lowin, A., 258, 983
Luck, David J., 21, 195*t*, 196, 199*t*, 203, 983
Lundberg, Olof, 230, 983
Lundgren, Earl F., 264
Lundstedt, Sven, 205, 983
Lusk, Edward J., 21, 233, 983

M

McAdam, Terry, 59, 885, 983
McCarthy, Daniel J., 8, 983
McCarthy, E. Jerome, 629, 983
McClelland, David C., 303, 745, 755, 983
McConkey, Dale D., 638, 983
MacCrimmon, Kenneth R., 226, 983
McDonald, Alonzo, 83, 983
McDonald, John, 35, 983
McDonald, Philip R., 228, 632, 983
McFarland, Dalton E., 21, 983
McGowan, John J., 62, 840, 967
McGregor, Douglas, 610, 636, 642, 983
McGuire, Joseph W., 149, 992
McKay, Charles W., 759, 983
McKenney, James L., 218, 230, 281, 984
McLoughlin, John, 191, 984
McManus, Michael L., 278, 984
McNair, Malcolm P., 4, 984
McNichols, Thomas L., 20, 984
Mace, Myles L., 203, 984
Mackworth, Norman H., 303
Mahoney, Thomas A., 72, 257, 984
Maier, Norman R. F., 642, 984
Makridakis, Sypros, 219, 996
Manual of Excellent Managements, 912
Management Science, 639
Mankin, Douglas C., 759, 976
Mann, Roland, 194, 984
Manne, Henry G., 60, 876, 984
Manners, George E., 253, 984
Management Audit Series, 912
March, James G., 209, 214, 215, 668, 972, 984
Margulies, Newton, 279, 283, 984
Marrow, Alfred J., 651, 984

Marshak, Jacob, 639, 984
Marshall, Gordon L., 303
Mason, Edward S., 215, 984
Mason, R. Hal, 191, 984
Matarazzo, Joseph D., 231, 984
Mayo, Elton, 303
Meadows, Dennis, 45, 984
Meyers, James H., 361
Michael, Donald N., 263, 984
Michael, George, 198, 869, 984
Mihalasky, John, 204, 984
Miles, Raymond E., 51, 52, 759, 984, 985, 993
Miller, Arjay, 61, 985
Miller, Danny, 777, 778, 985
Miller, Ernest C., 165, 217, 218, 985
Milliken, J. Gordon, 639, 985
Miner, John B., 25, 48, 72, 75, 78, 82, 208, 228, 229, 252, 257, 276, 277, 277*t*, 281, 282, 609, 638, 639, 642, 646, 648, 652, 699, 752, 759, 769, 774, 781, 972, 979, 985, 986
Miner, Mary Green, 648, 986
Minichiello, Robert J., 8, 983
Mintzberg, Henry, 4, 8, 73, 74*t*, 257, 259, 743, 776, 986
Mishan, Ezra J., 45, 986
Mitchell, Terence R., 635, 986
Moberg, Dennis J., 774, 986
Mock, Edward J., 203, 991
Mockler, Robert J., 149, 640, 986
Monczka, Robert M., 635, 991
Montgomery, George G., 203, 984
Moody's Handbook of Common Stocks, 142
Moody's Industrial Manual, 142
Moor, R. Carl, 986
Moore, David G., 746, 747, 752, 756, 971
Moose, Sandra O., 198, 986
Moranian, Thomas, 53, 986
Morrison, Edward J., 194, 639, 985
Morse, John J., 52, 609, 610, 983
Morse, Nancy, 634, 986
Moses, Michael A., 201, 978
Moskowitz, Herbert, 229, 986
Mote, V. L., 973
Motor Trend, 498
Mulder, Mauk, 268, 986
Mullick, Satinder K., 154, 219, 970
Murdick, Robert G., 986
Murphy, David C., 8, 981

N

Nagashima, Yukinori, 52, 986
Nation's Business, 913
Naumes, William, 8, 280, 281, 770*t*, 987
Negandhi, Anant R., 51, 52, 610, 986
Nelles, Maurice, 913
Nelson, Oscar Tivis, Jr., 769, 989
Nesheim, John L., 203, 987
Neuschel, Robert P., 77, 77*t*, 987
New York Times, 592, 593
Newell, Allen, 259, 987
Newman, William H., 19, 20, 43, 52, 343, 609, 618, 620–21*t*, 633, 640, 987
Niblock, Edward G., 869
Niland, Powell, 212, 973
Norburn, David, 210, 211, 977
Norman, Richard A., 261, 987
Norton, F., 172, 203, 965
Novack, Alan R., 883
Novick, David, 177, 178, 758, 987

O

O'Connell, Jeremiah J., 11, 275, 647, 987, 993
O'Connor, Rochelle, 19, 159, 188*t*, 969, 985
Odiorne, George, 668, 913
O'Donnell, Cyril, 19, 759, 981
O'Leary, Vincent, 75, 978
Oliver, Bruce L., 21, 233, 983
Organ, Dennis W., 7, 987
Osborn, Richard N., 616, 987
Osmond, Neville, 72, 987
O'Toole, James O., 48, 155, 987
Ouchi, William G., 51
Oxenfeldt, Alfred R., 203, 987

P

Pahl, Bernd, 235, 995
Paine, Frank T., 8, 280, 281, 770*t*, 778, 965, 987
Palmer, Michael, 743, 987
Palmore, Erdman B., 650, 987
Panser, Steve M., 976
Paransky, Harold, 650, 976

Parker, Treadway C., 753, 754, 987
Patai, Raphael, 823
Patchen, Martin, 268, 987
Pati, Gopal C., 888
Patton, Arch, 196, 988
Patton, Edwin P., 592
Patton, Richard, 202, 203, 990
Patz, Alan L., 11, 174, 988
Paul, Norman L., 303
Pederson, Carlton A., 257, 979
Pelz, Donald C., 236, 987
Pennington, Malcolm M., 172, 988
Perrow, Charles, 52, 611, 988
Peters, Joseph P., 759, 988
Peterson, Richard B., 234, 988
Pfeffer, Jeffrey, 51, 253, 633, 985, 988
Pierson, Frank C., 4, 988
Pinckney, Jacqueline, 650
Pohl, Herman H., 228, 988
Polli, Rolando, 196, 988
Pondy, L. R., 633, 988
Popp, Gary E., 744, 988
Porat, Avner M., 72, 977
Porter, Lyman W., 646, 977
Post, James E., 67, 988
Powell, Reed M., 634, 988
Prell, Arthur E., 21, 195*t*, 196, 199*t*, 203, 983
President's Commission on National Goals, 988
Preston, Lee E., 67, 988
Price, James L., 229, 988
Pugh, D. S., 52, 269, 980, 988
Pugh, G. D., 755, 977
Purcell, Theodore V., 650, 888, 988

Q

Quinn, James B., 913

R

Raia, Anthony P., 634, 636, 637*f*, 638, 988, 989
Railway Age, 592, 593
Randle, C. Wilson, 913
Rapoport, Leo A., 201, 989
Rawls, James R., 769, 989
Reeser, Clayton, 217, 234, 981, 989
Reidenbach, Richard, 53, 986
Reilley, E. W., 343
Reimann, Bernard C., 81, 610, 986, 989
Reimer, E., 634, 986
Reissman, Leonard, 361
Rescher, Nicholas, 155, 966
Research Management, 912
Reubens, Beatrice G., 976
Reynolds, William H., 220, 989
Rhenman, Eric, 43, 52, 53, 87, 989
Richards, Max D., 87, 230, 983, 989
Richards, Steven A., 651, 989
Richman, Barry M., 51, 58, 609, 974, 989
Riggs, James, 202, 203, 990
Ringbakk, K. A., 88, 152, 172, 175, 176*t*, 989
Roberts, John C., 248, 989
Rockefeller, David, 69, 989
Rockefeller, John D. III, 46, 63, 203, 989
Roe, C. William, 278, 989
Roehl, Ora C., 913
Roethlisberger, F. J., 646, 989
Rogers, Rolf E., 759, 989
Rokeach, Milton, 232, 989
Roper Report, 67, 989
Rose, Gerald L., 245, 990
Rosen, Stephen, 198, 989
Rosenzweig, James E., 759, 774, 981
Rosen, Menachem, 643, 993
Ross, Joel E., 38, 220, 627, 989
Rourke, Francis E., 768, 990
Rubenstein, Albert H., 913
Rubin, Irwin M., 745, 995
Rue, Leslie W., 172, 217, 975, 990
Ruhe, John A., 650, 978
Rumelt, Richard P., 612, 613, 614, 685, 869, 990
Ryan, William G., 618, 992

S

Salancik, Gerald R., 633, 988
Salipante, Paul, 650, 976
Salveson, Melvin E., 170, 208, 990
Sandalls, William T., Jr., 869
Saunders, Charles B., 8, 990
Sayles, Leonard R., 257, 990
Schainblatt, A. H., 218, 971
Schattschneider, E. E., 762, 990
Schein, Edgar, 303, 699
Schein, Virginia E., 651, 990

Schendel, D. E., 7, 8, 19, 30, 33, 202, 203, 780, 971, 990
Schick, Allen, 325
Schlacter, J. L., 634, 988
Schlaifer, Robert, 216, 990
Schlendorf, John, 744, 995
Schmidt, Warren H., 75, 76, 993
Schmookler, Jacob, 46, 990
Schnapp, John B., 883
Schoeffler, Sidney, 202, 221, 869, 990
Schollhammer, Hans, 51, 173, 203, 990, 992
Schoner, Bertram, 243, 990
Schrieber, Albert N., 201, 990
Schroder, Harold M., 230, 990
Scott, Bruce R., 52, 84, 85*t*, 609, 612, 614, 685, 990
Scurrah, Martin J., 283, 991
Searfoss, D. Gerald, 635, 991
Seashore, Stanley E., 75, 968
Seckler, David W., 59, 966
Sethi, S. Prakash, 43, 67, 991
Shames, William H., 750, 753, 754, 991
Shani, Moshe, 283, 991
Shank, John K., 203, 869, 991
Shell, Richard L., 991
Shepherd, H. R., 130
Shocker, Allan D., 67, 991
Shuckett, Donald H., 203, 991
Shukla, Ramesh K., 245, 977
Shull, Fremont A., 226, 242, 991
Siebrecht, Adrienne, 747, 982
Siegel, M., 592
Siekman, Philip, 142
Silverman, Arnold, 649, 981
Silverman, Gary, 976
Simon, Herbert A., 214, 215, 259, 263, 647, 668, 987, 991
Simonetti, Jack L., 622, 991
Simpkins, Edgar, 823
Singhvi, Surendra, 636, 970
Skibbins, Gerald J., 215, 991
Sloan, Alfred P., Jr., 37, 216, 223, 263, 619, 991
Slocum, John W., 53, 973
Smith, Donald D., 154, 219, 970
Smith, Gene, 221, 991
Smith, Norman R., 269, 745, 748, 749*f*, 991
Smith, Tim, 878
Snow, Charles C., 51, 985, 993
Snowball, H., 63, 971
Soden, John V., 619, 991
Soelberg, Peer, 264, 991
Solomons, David, 619, 634, 991
Sord, Burnard H., 630, 634, 991
Special Analyses, Budget of the U. S. Government, 325
Sproul, Robert G., Jr., 914
Stagner, Ross, 265, 265*t*, 991
Stalker, G. M., 616, 969
Standard & Poor's Industry Surveys, 142
Standard & Poor's Stock Reports, 142
Star, Steven H., 615, 972
Starbuck, William H., 4, 992
Starr, Martin, 216, 992
Staszak, F. James, 888
Stedman, Murray S., Jr., 761, 992
Stedry, A. C., 634, 992
Steele, John E., 228, 992
Steiner, George A., 20, 22, 27, 37, 44, 46, 47, 49, 54*t*, 57, 61, 63, 64, 66, 68, 149, 150, 155, 169, 173, 174, 202, 203, 209, 215, 217*t*, 222, 258, 262, 618, 630, 639, 750, 758, 759, 840, 841, 869, 972, 992
Steiner, Ivan D., 245, 250, 253, 993
Steinmetz, Lawrence L., 83, 85, 751, 993
Stelzer, David F., 991
Stevenson, Howard H., 869
Stewart, John, 202, 203, 966
Stewart, Robert F., 152, 993
Stieglitz, Harold, 257, 993
Stogdill, Ralph M., 644, 993
Stopford, J. M., 612, 975
Strauch, Ralph E., 764, 993
Strauss, George, 51, 993
Streufert, Siegfried, 248, 990, 993
Streufert, Susan C., 230, 248, 993
Sturdivant, Frederick D., 69, 993
Su, Vincent, 219, 978
Sultan, Ralph G. M., 203, 969
Summer, Charles E., 11, 609, 987, 993
Sylvester, Richard R., 632, 993

T

Tagiuri, Renato, 21, 22, 232, 977
Tannenbaum, Arnold S., 51, 643, 993
Tannenbaum, Robert, 75, 76, 993
Tarnowieski, Dale, 48, 993
Taylor, Calvin W., 237, 993
Taylor, Ronald N., 229, 231, 235, 993
Technological Forecasting, 154

Terleckyj, Nestor E., 155, 993
Terreberry, Shirley, 52, 993
TFX Contract Investigation, 212, 993
Thain, Donald H., 84, 85, 609, 994
Thomas, J., 63, 971
Thompson, James D., 609, 610, 626, 994
Thompson, Stewart, 27, 994
Thompson, Victor A., 754, 979
Thune, Stanley S., 172, 994
Tilles, Seymour, 198, 219, 869, 994
Time, 498, 499
Timmons, Jeffry A., 755, 994
Tipgos, Manuel A., 639, 994
Tock, Donald, 203, 971
Toffler, Alvin, 45, 994
Tomkins, Silvan S., 236, 994
Tosi, Henry L., 634, 635, 636, 638, 647, 668, 970, 994
Towl, Andrew L., 994
Trains, 592
Tregoe, Benjamin B., 204, 981
Treyz, George, 219, 978
Trist, E. L., 43, 52, 973
Truman, David B., 762, 994
Tuason, Roman V., 84, 85*t*, 994
Tuggle, F. D., 274, 982
Turner, C., 52, 988
Twiss, B. C., 203, 994

U

Udell, Jon G., 869
Ullrich, Robert A., 769, 989
U. S. Department of Health, Education, and Welfare, 994
U. S. Industrial Outlook, 142
U. S. News and World Report, 499
U. S. 90th Congress, 1st Session, House of Representatives, Research and Technical Programs Subcommittee of the Committee on Government Operations, 764, 994
Urban, Thomas F., 236, 968
Urwick, L., 610, 977

V

Vance, Stanley C., 83, 87, 225, 687, 747, 748, 994
Vancil, Richard F., 149, 169, 219, 619, 629, 632, 633, 994, 995
Van de Ven, Andrew H., 242, 243, 244*t*, 995
Van Doren, Mark, 303
Vaughn, James A., 72, 977
Vesper, Karl H., 744, 995
Vianello, Mino, 643, 993
Vicker, Ray, 824
Vroom, Victor H., 76, 235, 266, 267, 268, 634, 642, 995

W

Wainer, Herbert A., 745, 995
Waldman, Joseph, 883
Walker, Charles R., 46, 995
Wall Street Journal, 592, 593
Wallace, John, 279, 283, 984
Wallace, M. E., 634, 995
Wallich, Henry C., 62, 840, 967
Walster, G. William, 245, 977
Walton, Clarence C., 53, 995
Ward, A. Dudley, 800
Ward, Lewis B., 228, 302, 303, 992
Warren, Kirby E., 172, 609, 869, 987, 995
Wasson, Chester, 198, 869, 995
Webber, James B., 177, 759, 995
Webber, Ross A., 252, 995
Weber, Max, 52, 996
Webster, Frederick A., 203, 996
Weick, Karl E., 72, 229, 969
Wells, William, 361
Welsch, Glenn A., 630, 634, 991, 996
Werner, David J., 230, 980
Weston, J. Fred, 58, 172, 203, 219, 619, 913, 965, 996
Wheelwright, Steven C., 219, 995
Whitehead, Alfred North, 303, 800
Whybark, D. Clay, 228, 996
Whyte, William F., 646, 996
Wiener, Anthony J., 50, 980
Wieser, Georg, 643, 993
Wilemon, David L., 754, 755*t*, 996
Wilke, Henk, 268, 986
Williams, Martha, 75, 978
Wilson, Ian H., 47, 53, 67, 155, 361, 996
Winter, David G., 745, 755, 983
Wolf, William B., 914
Wolfle, Dael, 303

Woodward, Joan, 610, 616, 996
Wraith, Ronald, 823
Wright, Robert, 274, 996
Wrigley, Leonard, 612, 613, 996

Y

Yetton, Philip W., 76, 267, 268, 642, 995
Young, Robert B., 913

Z

Zakon, Alan J., 198, 986
Zalenznik, Abraham, 647, 972
Zand, Dale E., 254, 996
Zimmerer, Thomas W., 986
Zipfel, Carl, 283, 991

Subject Index

A

Academy of Management, 278
Achievement motivation, 754–55
  the entrepreneur and, 744–46
Ackerman, Robert W., reading by, 669–85
Adaptive approach to decision making, 260–61, 269–70
Administrative man, concept of, 262
Advocates, role of, 283–86
Aerosol Techniques, Inc. (Case 1), 105–130
Affirmative action policies, 648–51
Age, and decision making, 231–32
A. H. Robins Co. (Case 11), 500–505
American Assembly of Collegiate Schools of Business, 4
American Motors Corp., 205, 607
  (Case 10), 478–99
Amtrak (Case 17), 570–93
Analytical tools for decision making, 215–19
A. T. Kearney & Co., 274
Atlantic Manufacturing Co. (Case 26), 884–85
Authority, use of, 646–48

B

Baldwin Locomotive Works, 157
Barnard, Chester I., reading by, 784–800
Battelle Memorial Institute, 201
Bich, Baron Marcel, 200
Black managers, 650–51
Boards of directors, 253–54
Booz, Allen and Hamilton, 274
Boston Consulting Group, the, 198
Boulton, Karen, case by, 478–99
Bridges, Harry, 95–96
Brock, David A., case by, 570–93
Bryan, John H., Jr., 102–104
Buchele, Robert B., reading by, 893–912
Budgets, 253–60
Burroughs Corp., 362–72
Business policy courses, 3–15, 744, 781
Business schools, 781–82
Business success
  evaluation of (Reading), 893–912
  strategic factors in, 202–203

C

Cambria Steel, 87
Carley, William M., case by, 715–20
Carlson, Chester, 201
Carnegie Corp., 3–4
Carroll, Stephen J., reading by, 654–68
Case method, in policy courses, 4, 8, 12–14, 776–82
Case study in policy making, 221–22
Central Leather Co., 87
Chase Manhattan Corp., 65
Chief executive officers (CEOs), 5–7, 76–77, 175–77, 228
  planning role of, 169–70
  profiles of (Reading 1), 89–104
  values of, 233–34
Chile Copper Co., 87
Coca-Cola Co., 22, 201
Cognitive style, of decision making, 230–31
Communications systems, 639
Computer industry (Reading 7), 362–72
Computer models, 201–202
Connecticut General Insurance Corp., 92–93
Connelly, John F., 33
Consolidated Edison Co., 213
Consolidated Foods Corp., 102–104
Consultants, role of, 271–86
Contingencies, in decision approaches, 269–70
Contingency plans, 165

Contingency theory
  of leadership, 774–75
  of organizational design, 610–11
  of policy/strategy, 773–83
  (Reading 14), 842–69
Control Data Corp., 362–72
Control systems, 640
Corrigan, Wilfred J., 98–102
Creativity, in decision making, 236–39, 242–45
Cresap, McCormick and Paget, 274
Crown Cork and Seal Co., Inc., 33–34

D

Dart, Justin, 204
Data bases, 154–55
Decentralized structure, 618–22
Decision making, 207–55
  alternative approaches to, 257–70
  group aspects of, 241–55
  individuals, 225–40
  shared, 266–68
Delphi technique, 243–44
Discussion group technique, in decision making, 243–44
Dixie Cup Co., 201
Dogmatism in decision making, 235–36
Douglas Aircraft Co., 201, 204
Doutt, John, case by, 400–12
Drexler Technology Corp. (Case 15), 525–39
Dudick, Thomas S., case by, 521–24
DuPont Co., 201, 219, 612
  (Case 29), 890–91
Durant, Will, 146
Durard Plastics Co. (Case 14), 521–24

E

Eastman Kodak Co., 43
Ecological Monitoring Corp. (Case 5), 381–99
Econometric models, 201
Economic environment, 43–44
Economic man, concept of, 207, 262
Eddy, George G., case by, 729–40
Edsel automobile, 220
Eisenhower, President, 761, 765
Ela, Patrick H., case by, 143–46
Entrepreneurial approach to decision making, 259, 269
Entrepreneurship, 743–56
Environment, influence of, 41–55, 615–18
Equal employment opportunity, 648–51
Ethical standards, 9, 784–800
Evaluation of strategies, 207–24
Exxon Corp., 67

F

Fairchild Camera & Instrument Corp., 98–102
Feasibility testing, 164
Female managers, 650–51
Financial reports, how to read (Reading), 915–62
Fisk, George, reading by, 344–61
Forbes, 87
Ford Foundation, 3–4
Ford Motor Co., 36–37
  (Case 20), 715–720
Forecasts, 154–55
Formal structured approach to decision making, 258, 269
Fortune, 45, 780
Fry Consultants, 274

G

Gap analysis, 190–91
General Dynamics Co., 633
General Electric Co., 47, 67, 170, 221, 308–15, 362–72, 650
General Mills, Inc., 94–95
General Motors Corp., 36–37, 70, 153, 216, 618
  (Case 23), 870–76
Gerber Co., 191
Gerstenberg, Richard, 70
Goodman, Paul L., case by, 525–39
Gordon and Howell report, 3–4
Government, influence of, 44–45
Government organizations; *see* Not-for-profit organizations
Gray, Edmund R., case by, 594–604
Green, Steven M., case by, 478–99
Group cohesion, 242–50
Group size, input on decision making, 252–54

Groups, policy-making, 241–55
Groupthink, 249–50, 763

H

Hanna Co., 765
Harvard Business School, 4, 290–91, 295, 299
Hefner, Hugh, 201
Heublein, Inc. (Case 16), 540–69
Hewlett-Packard Co. (Case 9B), 473–77
Hickcox, Robert, case by, 570–93
Hill, Richard, case by, 444–66
Hofer, Charles W.
  cases by, 105–30, 540–69
  reading by, 842–69

I

IBM, 37–38, 201, 220, 362–72, 632
  (Case 19), 700–714
Incremental approach to decision making, 259–60, 262–63, 762
Identification of policies and strategies, 181–206
Illini Farm Equipment Co. (Case 4), 373–80
Individuals as decision makers, 225–40
Integration, in organizations, 615–22, 626–40
  (Reading 10), 686–99
Intelligence, role of in decision making, 229–30
Intuition, 204
Intuitive-anticipatory approach, in decision making, 258–59, 269
Intuitive-anticipatory approach, in planning, 149–50
Inventions, 201

J

John Hancock Mutual Life Insurance Co., 61
Johnson, President, 758, 760
Jones, Thomas V., 90–92
Journal of Industrial Engineering, 218

K

Kami, Michael J., reading by, 362–72
Kennedy, President, 607
Knowledge, role of in decision making, 226–29
Kramer Carton Co. (Case 8), 444–66

L

Latona, Joseph, case by, 400–12
Leadership, contingency theory of, 774–75
Leadership styles, 76, 266; *see also* Managerial styles
Legal environment, 45
Lehigh Coal and Navigation Co., 87
Lesikar, Raymon V., case by, 594–604
Life cycles, organizational, 83–88
Life cycles, product, 196–99, 845–68
Life Office Management Assoc., 201
Life styles, consumer, 344–61
Limited domain theory, 774–75
Linkage, in budgets, 631–32
Litton Industries (Case 6), 400–12
Livingston, J. Sterling, reading by, 287–303
Lockheed Co., 200–201, 220, 627
Long Range Planning, 218
Long-range planning objectives, 158–59

M

McColough, Peter C., 89–90
McDonnell-Douglas Co., 155, 204, 220
McFarland, James P., 94–95
McKinsey & Co., 201, 274, 609
McNamara, R., former Secretary of Defense, 212
Machinery Systems (Case 27), 886–88
Management By Objectives (MBO), 636–38, 758
  (Reading 8), 654–68
Management consulting, 274–78
Management information systems, 639
Management, operational, 7
Management process, 72–73
Management Science, 218
Management, strategic, 7–9, 32–33
Management teams, for decision making, 250–54

Managerial influence on plans, 632–33
Managerial jobs, 72–74
Managerial philosophies, 57–58, 622
Managerial planning systems, 149–79
Managerial styles, 71–96
Managerial values, 153–54, 769
Managers, changing attitudes of, 48–49
  education of (Reading 2), 287–303
Marcor Co., 34, 36
Market, niches of, 200–201, 327, 335–36
Matrix, product/market, 193–96
Matrix, product portfolio, 198–200
Mattell, Inc. (Case 9A), 467–72
MBA programs, 228
Merrill, Lynch, Pierce, Fenner & Smith, reading by, 915–62
Metropolis City Museum of Art (Case 3), 143–46
Michigan State University, 746
Midvale Steel & Ordinance Co., 87
Miner, John B., reading by, 686–99
Minnesota Mining & Manufacturing (3M), 201, 204
Minorities, employment of, 648–51
Minority entrepreneurship, 755–56
Missions, company, 157
Mississippi Test Facility (Case 18), 594–604
Models, corporate planning, 152
Models, decision, 209
Monsanto Chemical Co., 627
Montgomery Ward, 36
Morals, business (Reading 11), 784–800
Moyers, W., former White House Press Secretary, 211
"Muddling through" in decision making, 260, 262–63, 762

N

National Cash Register Co. (NCR), 224, 362–72
National priorities, 344–61
Negotiated decisions, 246
Nehemkis, Peter, reading by, 801–23
Newman, William H., reading by, 326–43
Nixon, President, 758, 760
Nominal group technique, 243–44
Northrop Corp., 90–92, 817
Not-for-profit (NFP) organizations, 8–9, 757–71
  planning in, 175–77
Novick, David, reading by, 314–25

O

Oil Producing and Exporting Countries (OPEC), 44
Operational Research Quarterly, 218
Organization-development (OD), 279–82
Organization structure, 51–52, 607–23
Organization theory, 778–79
Organizational change, environment and, 41–43
Organizational commitment, 643–46
Organizational life cycles, 83–88
Organizational styles, 71–88

P

Participation in the budget process, 634–36
Participation, policy implementation and, 641–43
Payoffs, in business abroad (Reading 12), 801–23
Pederson, Carlton A., case by, 525–39
People, role of in implementation of policy, 641–53
Philadelphia National Corp., 97–98
PIMS Project Team (Profit Impact of Market Strategies), 202
Planning-Programming-Budgeting System (PPBS), 177–78, 758
  (Reading 4), 314–25
Planning, strategic, 7–8, 149–79
Planning systems, and policy implementation, 625–40
Playboy, 201
Polaroid Corp. (Case 2), 131–42
  (Case 24), 877–78
Policies, nature of, 24–28
President, office of, 82–83
Product life cycles, 196–99, 776–77
Product-market matrix, 193–96
Product portfolio approach to identifying strategies, 198–200
Product strategy, social sanctions and (Reading 6), 344–61

Program Evaluation and Review Technique (PERT), 638
Programmable decisions, 245–46
Public sector policy, 27–28, 757–71

R

Rationality, in decision making, 213–15
Ravenscroft, Richard S., 97–98
RCA Co., 37–38, 220–21, 362–72
Remington Rand Co., 201
Research in the policy area, 8, 14–15, 779–81
Riker Laboratories, 204
Risk-taking propensity in decision making, 234–35
Risky shift, in decision making, 246–49
Rizzo, John R., reading by, 654–68
Roberts, Henry R., 92–93
Rockefeller, John D. III, 70
Role theory, policy and, 25
Roles, managerial, 73–74
Rolls Royce Co., 220, 627
Romney, George, 607
Ross, Joel E., reading by, 362–72
Roy, J. Russell, case by, 570–93

S

Satisficing, 262–63
Scheduling models, 638
Schlender, William, case by, 507–20
School of business curriculums, 3–4
Schwartz, Eleanor Brantley, case by, 507–20
Sears, Richard Warren, 34
Sears, Roebuck & Co., 22, 30, 34–36, 50
Securities and Exchange Commission, 69, 801–23
Semantic difficulties, 19–20
Shell Oil Co., 95–96
Short-range planning, 161
Situation audits, 153, 185–89
Ski-Kit, Inc. (Case 7), 413–43
Sloan, Alfred, 36, 204
Small business, decision approaches in, 262
Small City B (Case 22), 729–40
Smith Brothers, 201
Smokey Cigarette Co. (Case 28), 889
Social audits, 67–69
(Reading 13), 825–40
Social environment, 46–49
Social indicators, 155
Social responsibilities of business, 9, 57–70
(Reading 3), 304–13
(Reading 9), 669–85
Social sanctions, product strategy and (Reading 6), 344–61
Social Security Administration, 759
Social skill in group decision making, 252
Social values, 155, 344–51, 784–800
Societe Bic, 200
Sord, Burnard H., case by, 729–40
Standard Oil Co., 67
Standard operating procedures (SOP), 25–26, 636
Steiner, George A.
cases by, 373–80, 721–28, 870–76, 877–78, 884–85, 886–89
reading by, 825–40
Steiner, John F., case by, 879–83
Stouffer Foods Services Group (Case 6), 400–12
Strategic business units (SBUs), 170
Strategic factors for success, 202–203
Strategic management, 7–9
Strategic planning, 7–9, 17–24, 30–32, 149–79
social responsibility and (Reading 3), 304–13
Strategy, development of, 182–85
evaluation of, 207–24
identification of, 181–206
implementation of, 607–53
profile of, 191–93
(Reading 5), 326–43
Sun Oil Co., 201
Synergy, 204–205

T

Tactics, strategy versus, 22–24
Tasty Food, Inc. (Case 12), 506
Technological change, 45–46
Timex Co., 22
Top managers, tasks of, 29–30; *see also* Chief executive officers
Tosi, Henry L., reading by, 654–68

U

U. S. Department of Defense, 177, 212
United Technology, Inc. (Case 21), 721–28
Univac Co., 362–72
University of Minnesota, 232
University professors, as consultants, 278–79

V

Value systems, of managers, 153–54
Values, influence of on decisions, 232–34
Venture management, 744, 752–55

W

Watson, H. Scott, case by, 381–99
White Motor Corp. (Case 13), 507–20
Williams, Robert, case by, 413–43
Wilson, Ian H., reading by, 304–13
Wise, T. A., case by, 700–14
Women, employment of, 648–51
Wong, H. Deane, case by, 131–42
Wood, Robert F., 30
Work in America, 48
Workers, changing attitudes of, 48
World Mining and Chemicals, Inc. (Case 25), 879–83
Worldwide forces, 49
WOTS-Up analysis, 189–90

X

Xerox Corp., 50, 89–90, 201

Y

Youth, attitudes of, 48

Z

Zonana, Victor F., case by, 500–505